NEULAND
--
THE FUTURE OF
GERMAN GRAPHIC DESIGN
--

EDITED & DESIGNED BY
TWOPOINTS.NET
--
PUBLISHED BY ACTAR
--

NEULAND
--
THE FUTURE OF
GERMAN GRAPHIC DESIGN
--

THIS BOOK ALLOWED US TO ENTER NEW TERRITORY
(<NEULAND>). WHEN ACTAR PUBLISHERS APPROACHED
US WITH THE SUGGESTION OF PRODUCING A BOOK
ABOUT GERMAN GRAPHIC DESIGN, WE WERE BOTH DE-
LIGHTED AND SKEPTICAL. ON THE ONE HAND WE HAD
LIVED, STUDIED AND WORKED IN GERMANY AND CON-
TINUE TO HAVE STRONG TIES TO THE COUNTRY, EVEN
THOUGH WE MOVED TO BARCELONA IN 2005. ON THE
OTHER HAND, WE WONDERED IF THIS PROJECT WAS
EVEN POSSIBLE IN LIGHT OF A NUMBER OF FUNDA-
MENTAL QUESTIONS.

THE INTERNATIONAL PUBLISHING COMMUNITY AL-
READY FEATURES NUMEROUS PUBLICATIONS ABOUT
SWISS, DUTCH, BRITISH OR SCANDINAVIAN GRAPHIC
DESIGN, WITH A SCANT FEW DEDICATED TO CONTEM-
PORARY GERMAN GRAPHIC DESIGN.

WAS THIS LACK OF PUBLICATIONS THE RESULT OF
THE INFERIOR QUALITY OF CONTEMPORARY GERMAN
GRAPHIC DESIGN? OR, ARE GERMAN DESIGN TALENTS
SIMPLY HARDER TO TRACK DOWN?

ANOTHER QUESTION WAS WHETHER WE COULD EVEN
DISCUSS <GERMAN> GRAPHIC DESIGN GIVEN OUR THE
WORK OF OUR CONTEMPORARIES: WHERE AN ITALIAN
DESIGNER ILLUSTRATES IN THE STYLE OF JAPA-
NESE MANGA (COMICS); WHEN AN ENGLISHMAN BASES
HIS WORK ON 1970S GERMAN DESIGN OR A DUTCHMAN
IS REINTERPRETING SWISS GRID-BASED TYPOGRA-
PHY; NOW, GERMAN GRAPHIC DESIGNERS ARE LIVING
ABROAD WHILE FOREIGN GRAPHIC DESIGNERS ARE
LIVING IN GERMANY.

IS IT POSSIBLE TO DEFINE <CONTEMPORARY GERMAN
GRAPHIC DESIGN>? FROM THE START, WE DECIDED TO
VIEW THIS PROJECT AS A FORUM FOR THE WORK OF
GERMAN DESIGNERS WORKING ABROAD AND OF FOR-
EIGNERS PRACTICING WITHIN GERMANY. WE LEAVE
IT UP TO READERS TO DECIDE WHETHER THIS COL-
LECTION OF WORK CONSTITUTES A <GERMAN STYLE>
OR NOT.

SELECTING THE GRAPHIC DESIGNERS WAS A LONG AND
INTENSIVE PROCESS. WE WANTED TO FIND AS MANY
YOUNG AND STILL UNKNOWN GRAPHIC DESIGNERS AS
POSSIBLE. OUR SOURCES WERE NUMEROUS BLOGS,

MAGAZINES, AND PERSONAL RECOMMENDATIONS. WE
ALSO RELIED ON THE KNOWLEDGE OF MANY IMPORTANT
FIGURES IN UNIVERSITY-LEVEL DESIGN INSTITU-
TIONS THROUGHOUT VARIOUS EUROPEAN COUNTRIES.
AFTER A THREE MONTH REVIEW PROCESS THAT SAW
OVER 700 PORTFOLIOS, WE DREW A FINAL SELECTION
OF FIFTY GRAPHIC DESIGNERS AND GRAPHIC DESIGN
OFFICES TO BE FEATURED IN <NEULAND>. WE WISH
TO REITERATE OUR DEEPEST APPRECIATION OF EV-
ERYONE WHO SUBMITTED MATERIAL FOR OUR REVIEW.

DURING THE SELECTION PROCESS WE OBSERVED A
MAJOR SHIFT IN GERMAN GRAPHIC DESIGN. NOT
ONLY HAVE THE PRACTICAL CAPABILITIES OF THE
DESIGNER REACHED A NEW LEVEL, BUT ALSO THE DE-
SIGNER'S INCREASING DESIGNATION AS AUTHOR SUG-
GESTS THE EXISTENCE OF AN INTERESTING FUTURE
FOR GERMAN GRAPHIC DESIGN. THIS UP-AND-COMING
GENERATION IS BREAKING FREE OF CULTURAL AND
GEOGRAPHICAL LIMITATIONS AND WORKING WITHIN AN
INTERNATIONAL CONTEXT.

NOTE ON THE DESIGN
--

IT IS UNCOMMON FOR THE DESIGNER TO HAVE THE
OPPORTUNITY TO SAY A FEW WORDS ABOUT THE DE-
SIGN. YET, IN THIS CIRCUMSTANCE, ONE WHERE
THIS BOOK'S CONTENT INVESTIGATES NOT ONLY DE-
SIGN, BUT ALSO THE DESIGNER, WE FELT IT WAS AN
OPPORTUNE MOMENT TO BREAK WITH TRADITION.

TYPE DESIGN: ALL THE FONTS USED IN THIS BOOK
ARE BASED ON A VERY SIMPLE GRID, COMPOSED A
PROPORTION OF FOUR UNITS HIGH BY TWO UNITS
WIDE. A SERIES OF OTHER LINKS BETWEEN THEM
MAKE IT POSSIBLE TO FORM A FONT FROM THIS
GRID. WE FELT IT WAS IMPORTANT TO CONSISTENT-
LY WORK WITHIN THESE LIMITATIONS SO THAT ANY
UNEXPECTED ASPERITIES WOULD HELP PROVIDE THE
FONT WITH ITS CHARACTER.

MAPS: AS PREVIOUSLY MENTIONED, THIS BOOK REP-
RESENTS OUR ENTRY INTO A NEW TERRITORY (<NEU-
LAND>). OUR INTRODUCTION SERVES AS A CHART FOR
THIS NEW AND UNKNOWN COUNTRY. IT DOCUMENTS THE
RESULTS OF OUR SEARCH, AS WELL AS ADDITIONAL
INFORMATION THAT MAY BE HELPFUL FOR DESIGNERS
WISHING TO GET ACQUAINTED WITH GERMANY. THE
MAPS PROVIDE AN OVERVIEW OF THE GERMAN DESIGN
SCENE AS EMBODIED IN OUR BOOK. IT SHOWS WHERE
OUR <NEULAND> DESIGNERS HAVE STUDIED AND WHERE
THEY CURRENTLY RESIDE. IT LOCATES GREAT BOOK-
SHOPS, CONFERENCES AND ORGANIZATIONS AND ABOVE
ALL, IT BEARS MARKS OF WHERE THE HISTORY OF
GERMAN DESIGN HAS LEFT ITS TRACES.

WE HOPE YOU ENJOY YOUR JOURNEY!
TWOPOINTS.NET

INDEX
--
P.204
P.034
P.196
P.184
P.230
P.202
P.302
P.212
P.172
P.370
P.254
P.312
P.328
P.380

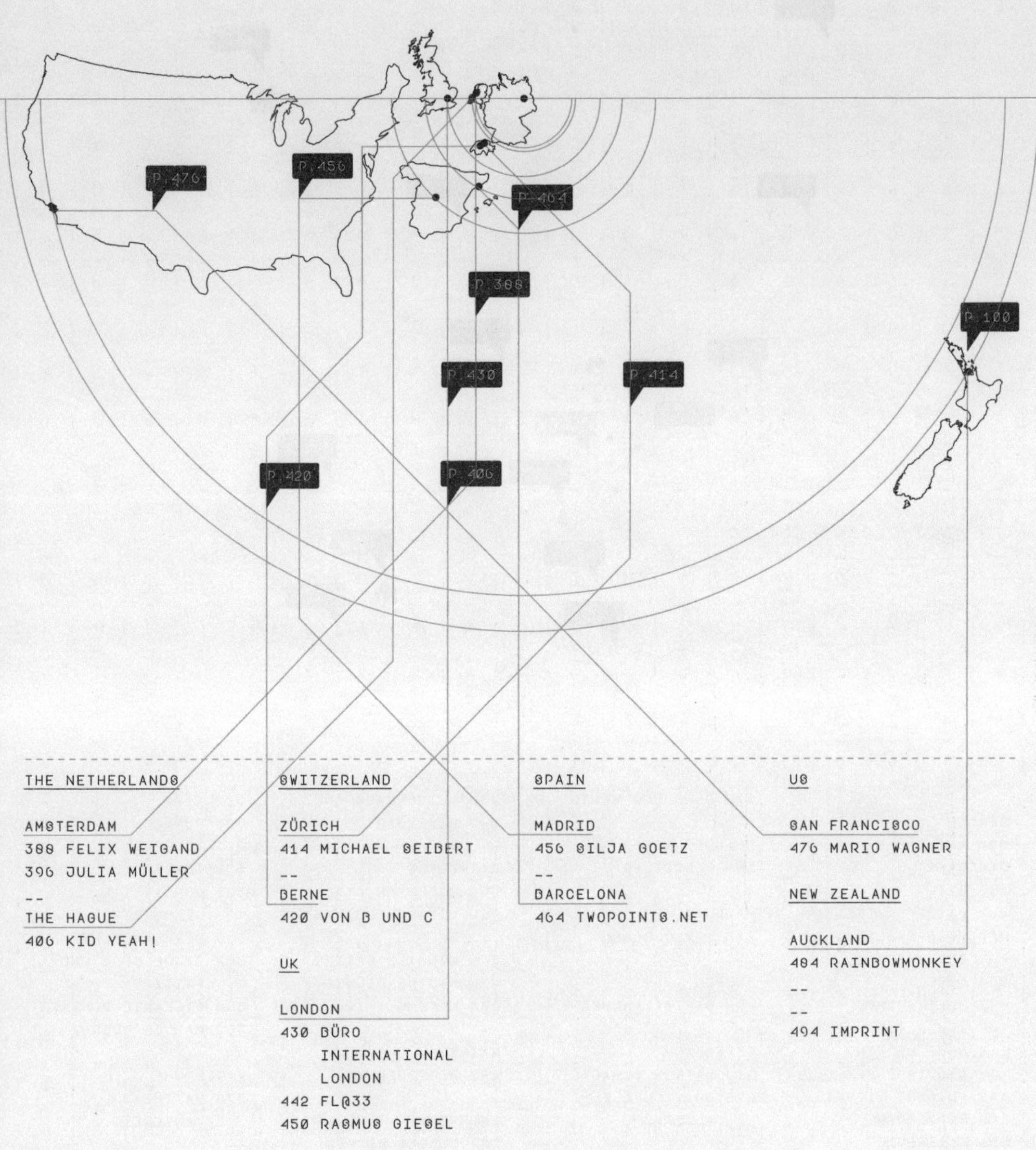

P. 476
P. 456
P. 464
P. 388
P. 100
P. 430
P. 414
P. 420
P. 406

TP_KURIER_SANS

A	B	C	D	E	F	G	H	I	J	K	L	M	N	O	P	Q	R	S
T	U	V	W	X	Y	Z	a	b	c	d	e	f	g	h	i	j	k	l
m	n	o	p	q	r	s	t	u	v	w	x	y	z
0	1	2	3	4	5	6	7	8	9
!	'	#	$	%	@	'	(	)	*	+	,	-	.	/	:	;	<	=
>	?	@	[	\	]	^	_	`	{	}	~	¡	¢	£	¥	¦	§	"
©	ª	«	¬		°	±	²	³	´	µ	¶	·	¸	¹	º	»	¼	½	¾
¿	À	Á	Â	Ã	Ä	Å	Æ	Ç	È	É	Ê	Ë	Ì	Í	Î	Ï	Ð	Ñ
Ò	Ó	Ô	Õ	Ö	×	Ø	Ù	Ú	Û	Ü	Ý	Þ	ß	à	á	â	ã	ä
å	æ	ç	è	é	ê	ë	ì	í	î	ï	ð	ñ	ò	ó	ô	õ	ö	÷
ø	ù	ú	û	ü	ý	þ	ÿ	ı	Œ	œ	Š	Ÿ	Ž	ž	ƒ	ˆ	ˇ	˘
˙	˚	˛	˜	˝	Ω	–	—	'	'	‚	"	"	„	†	‡	•	…	‰
‹	›	⁄	€	™	Ω	∂	∆	∏	∑	√	∞	∫	≈	≠	≤	≥	◊	fi
fl	˳	π

TP_KURIER_SANS_ITALIC

A	B	C	D	E	F	G	H	I	J	K	L	M	N	O	P	Q	R	S
T	U	V	W	X	Y	Z	a	b	c	d	e	f	g	h	i	j	k	l
m	n	o	p	q	r	s	t	u	v	w	x	y	z
0	1	2	3	4	5	6	7	8	9
!	'	#	$	%	@	'	(	)	*	+	,	-	.	/	:	;	<	=
>	?	@	[	\	]	^	_	`	{	}	~	¡	¢	£	¥	¦	§	"
©	ª	«	¬		°	±	²	³	´	µ	¶	·	¸	¹	º	»	¼	½	¾
¿	À	Á	Â	Ã	Ä	Å	Æ	Ç	È	É	Ê	Ë	Ì	Í	Î	Ï	Ð	Ñ
Ò	Ó	Ô	Õ	Ö	×	Ø	Ù	Ú	Û	Ü	Ý	Þ	ß	à	á	â	ã	ä
å	æ	ç	è	é	ê	ë	ì	í	î	ï	ð	ñ	ò	ó	ô	õ	ö	÷
ø	ù	ú	û	ü	ý	þ	ÿ	ı	Œ	œ	Š	Ÿ	Ž	ž	ƒ	ˆ	ˇ	˘
˙	˚	˛	˜	˝	Ω	–	—	'	'	‚	"	"	„	†	‡	•	…	‰
‹	›	⁄	€	™	Ω	∂	∆	∏	∑	√	∞	∫	≈	≠	≤	≥	◊	fi
fl	•	π

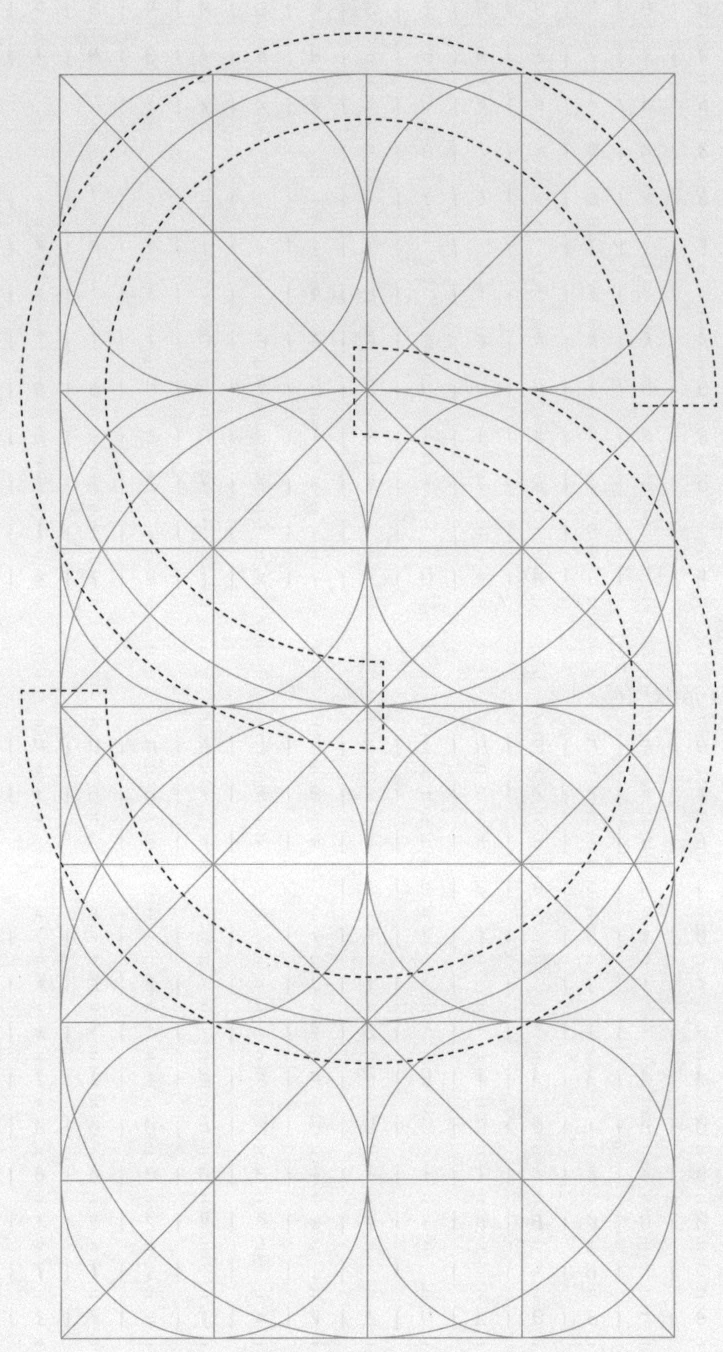

```
TP_KURIER_SERIF

| A | B | C | D | E | F | G | H | I | J | K | L | M | N | O | P | Q | R | S |
| T | U | V | W | X | Y | Z | a | b | c | d | e | f | g | h | i | j | k | l |
| m | n | o | p | q | r | s | t | u | v | w | x | y | z |
| 0 | 1 | 2 | 3 | 4 | 5 | 6 | 7 | 8 | 9 |
| ! | " | # | $ | % | & | ' | ( | ) | * | + | , | - | . | / | : | ; | < | = |
| > | ? | @ | [ | \ | ] | ^ | _ | ` | { | } | ~ | ¡ | ¢ | £ | ¥ | ¦ | § | " |
| © | ª | « | ¬ | ° | ± | ² | ³ | ´ | µ | ¶ | · | ¸ | ¹ | º | » | ¼ | ½ | ¾ |
| ¿ | À | Á | Â | Ã | Ä | Å | Æ | Ç | È | É | Ê | Ë | Ì | Í | Î | Ï | Ð | Ñ |
| Ò | Ó | Ô | Õ | Ö | + | Ø | Ù | Ú | Û | Ü | Ý | Þ | ß | à | á | â | ã | ä |
| å | æ | ç | è | é | ê | ë | ì | í | î | ï | ð | ñ | ò | ó | ô | õ | ö | ÷ |
| ø | ù | ú | û | ü | ý | þ | ÿ | ı | Œ | œ | š | Ÿ | Ž | ž | ƒ | ˆ | ˇ | ˘ |
| ˙ | ˚ | ˛ | ˜ | ˝ | Ω | - | — | ' | ' | , | " | " | „ | † | ‡ | • | … | ‰ |
| ‹ | › | ⁄ | € | ™ | Ω | ∂ | Δ | ∏ | ∑ | √ | ∞ | ∫ | ≈ | ≠ | ≤ | ≥ | ◊ | fi |
| fl | • | π |


TP_KURIER_SERIF_ITALIC

| A | B | C | D | E | F | G | H | I | J | K | L | M | N | O | P | Q | R | S |
| T | U | V | W | X | Y | Z | a | b | c | d | e | f | g | h | i | j | k | l |
| m | n | o | p | q | r | s | t | u | v | w | x | y | z |
| 0 | 1 | 2 | 3 | 4 | 5 | 6 | 7 | 8 | 9 |
| ! | " | # | $ | % | & | ' | ( | ) | * | + | , | - | . | / | : | ; | < | = |
| > | ? | @ | [ | \ | ] | ^ | _ | ` | { | } | ~ | ¡ | ¢ | £ | ¥ | ¦ | § | " |
| © | ª | « | ¬ | ° | ± | ² | ³ | ´ | µ | ¶ | · | ¸ | ¹ | º | » | ¼ | ½ | ¾ |
| ¿ | À | Á | Â | Ã | Ä | Å | Æ | Ç | È | É | Ê | Ë | Ì | Í | Î | Ï | Ð | Ñ |
| Ò | Ó | Ô | Õ | Ö | + | Ø | Ù | Ú | Û | Ü | Ý | Þ | ß | à | á | â | ã | ä |
| å | æ | ç | è | é | ê | ë | ì | í | î | ï | ð | ñ | ò | ó | ô | õ | ö | ÷ |
| ø | ù | ú | û | ü | ý | þ | ÿ | ı | Œ | œ | š | Ÿ | Ž | ž | ƒ | ˆ | ˇ | ˘ |
| ˙ | ˚ | ˛ | ˜ | ˝ | Ω | - | — | ' | ' | , | " | " | „ | † | ‡ | • | … | ‰ |
| ‹ | › | ⁄ | € | ™ | Ω | ∂ | Δ | ∏ | ∑ | √ | ∞ | ∫ | ≈ | ≠ | ≤ | ≥ | ◊ | fi |
| fl | • | π |
```

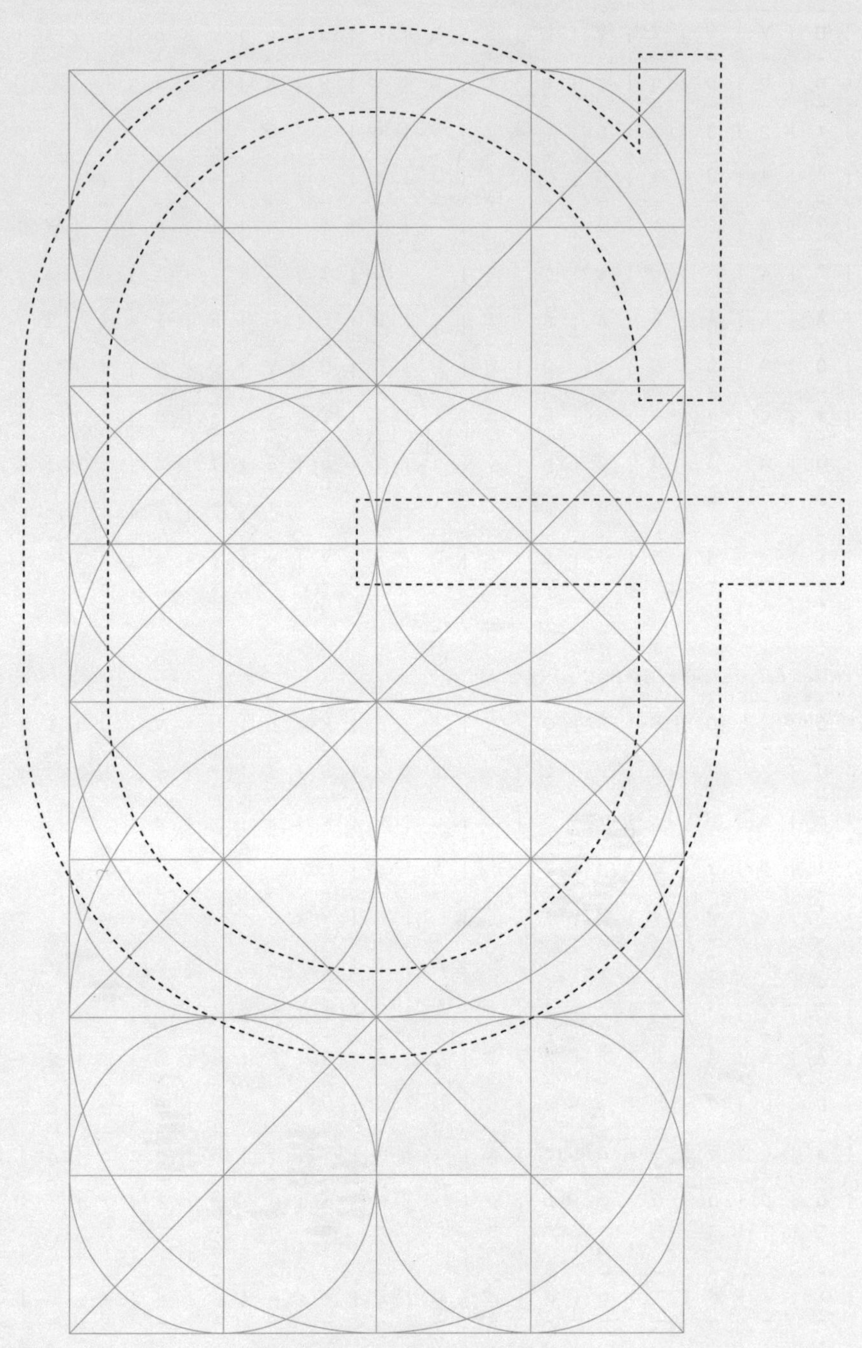

COMPARISON OF LOCATION AND STUDY PLACE
OF THE NEULAND DESIGNERS
--

NEULAND
DESIGNERS

DESIGN
SCHOOLS

4
2
1

OVERVIEW OF DETAIL MAPS
SHOWN ON THE FOLLOWING PAGES
--

NEULAND DESIGNERS
DESIGN SCHOOLS
BOOKSTORES
CONFERENCES
DESIGN HISTORY
TYPE FOUNDRIES
AIRPORTS

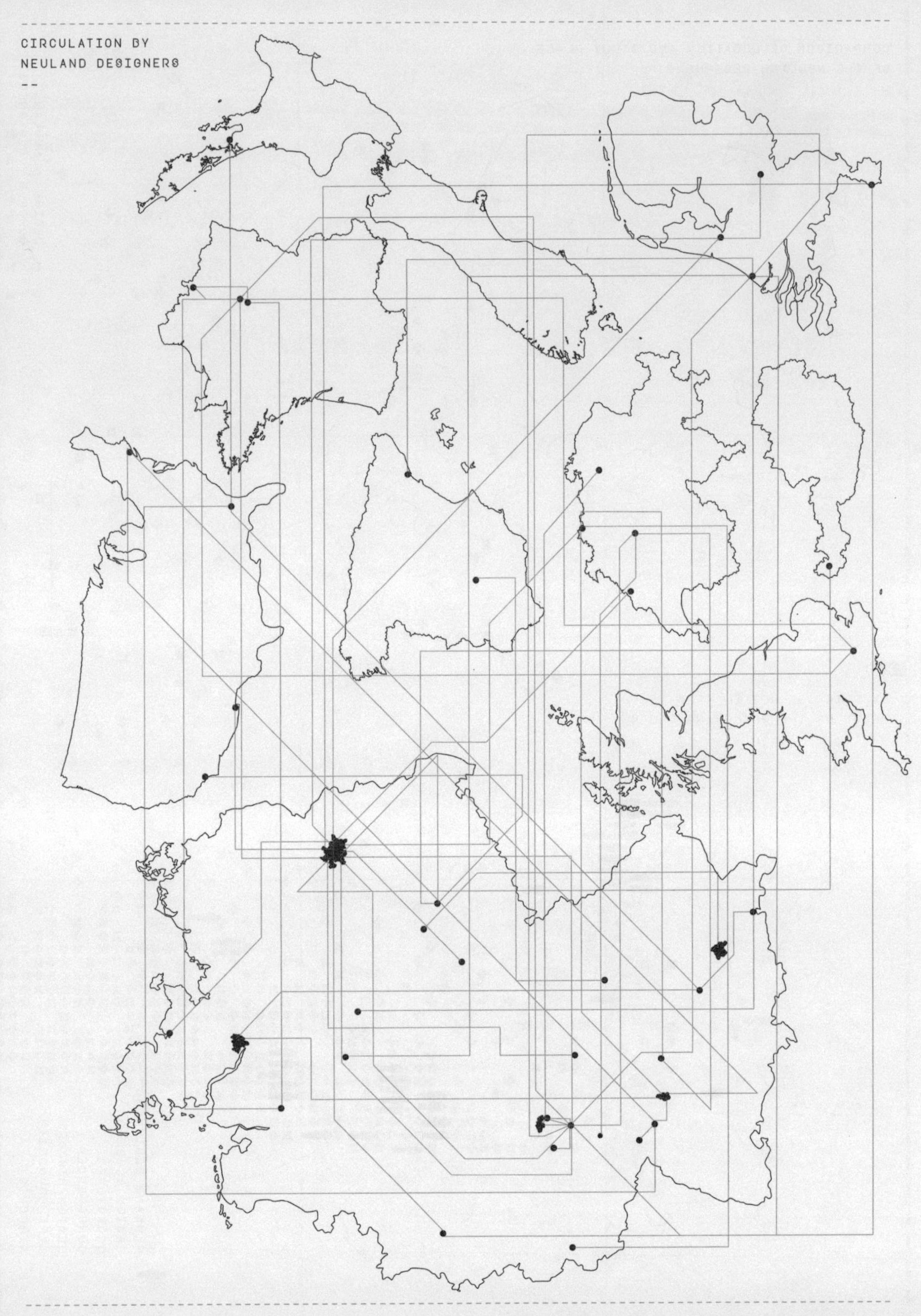

CIRCULATION BY
NEULAND DESIGNERS
--

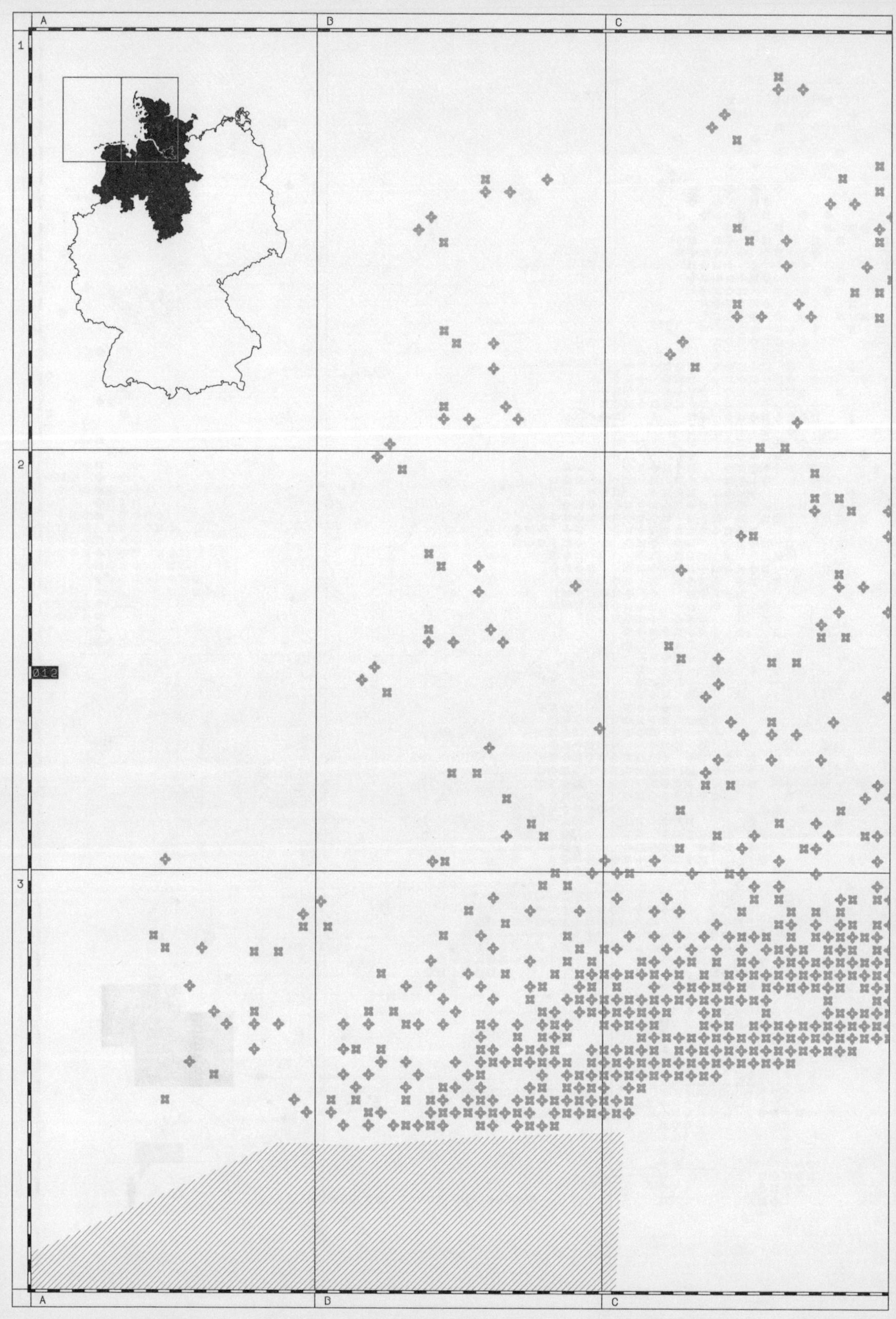
012

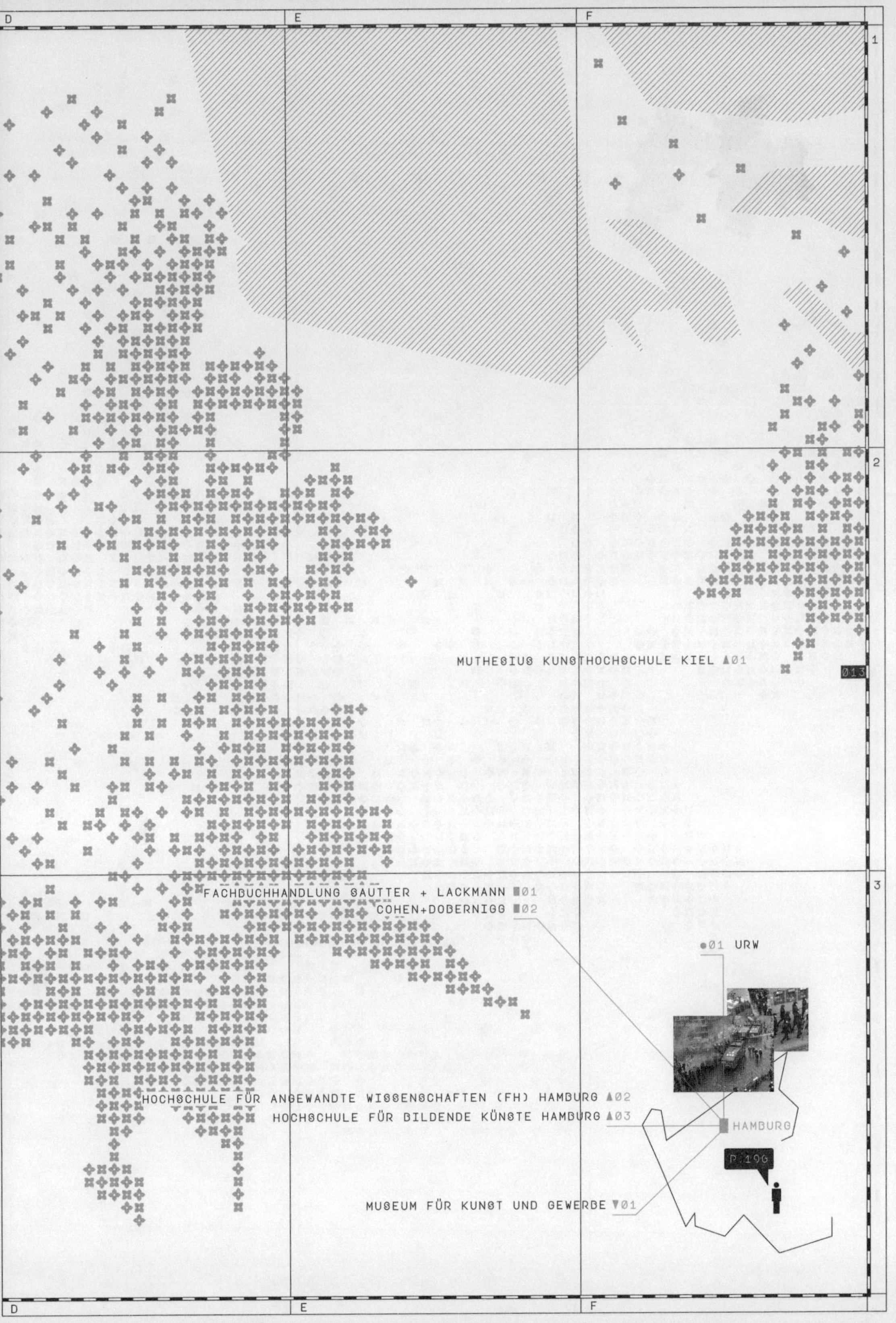
D
E
F
1
2
3
MUTHESIUS KUNSTHOCHSCHULE KIEL ▲Ø1
Ø13
FACHBUCHHANDLUNG SAUTTER + LACKMANN ■Ø1
COHEN+DOBERNIGG ■Ø2
●Ø1 URW
HOCHSCHULE FÜR ANGEWANDTE WISSENSCHAFTEN (FH) HAMBURG ▲Ø2
HOCHSCHULE FÜR BILDENDE KÜNSTE HAMBURG ▲Ø3
HAMBURG
P.196
MUSEUM FÜR KUNST UND GEWERBE ▼Ø1
D
E
F

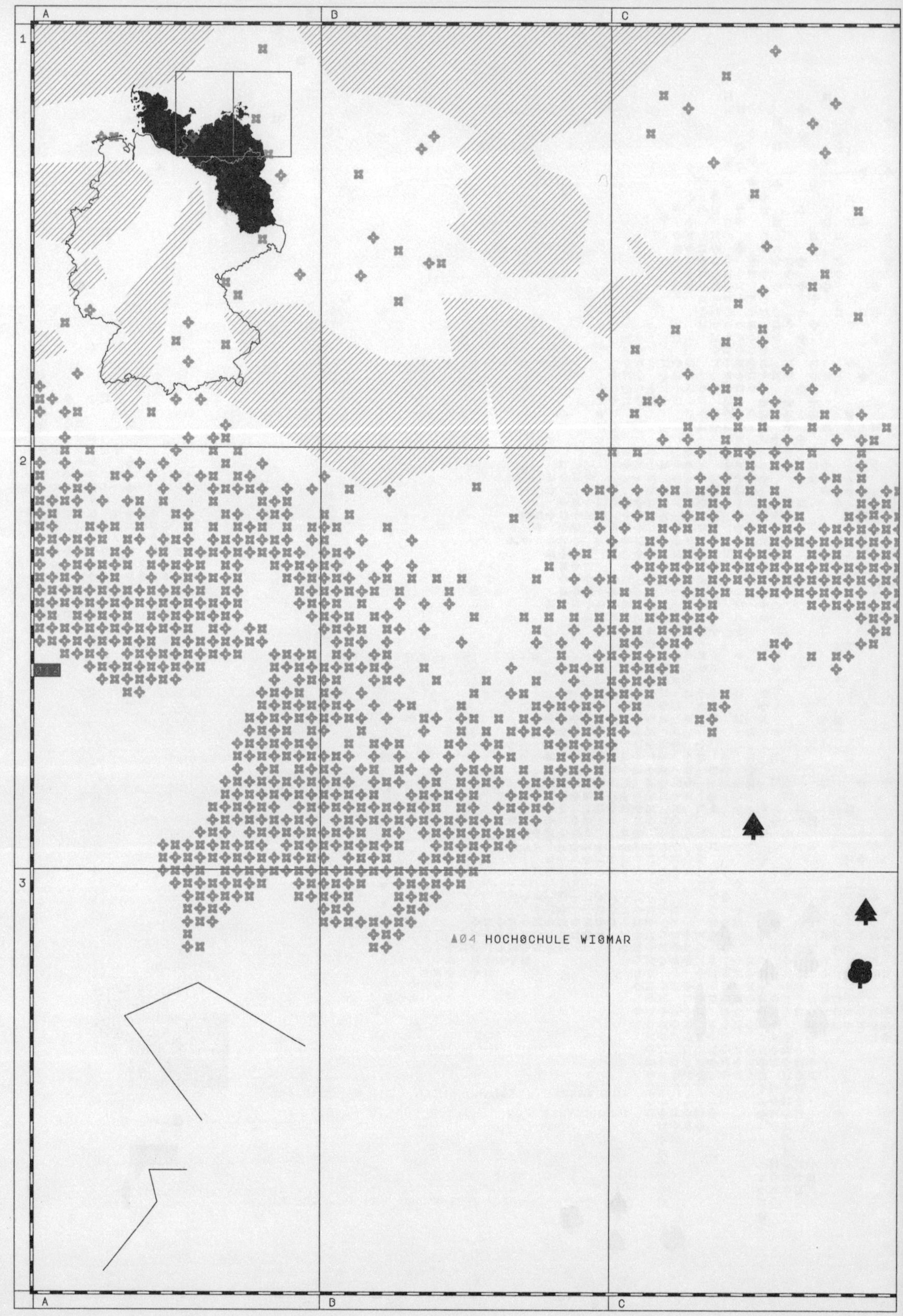

A	B	C
1
2
3
▲04 HOCHSCHULE WISMAR

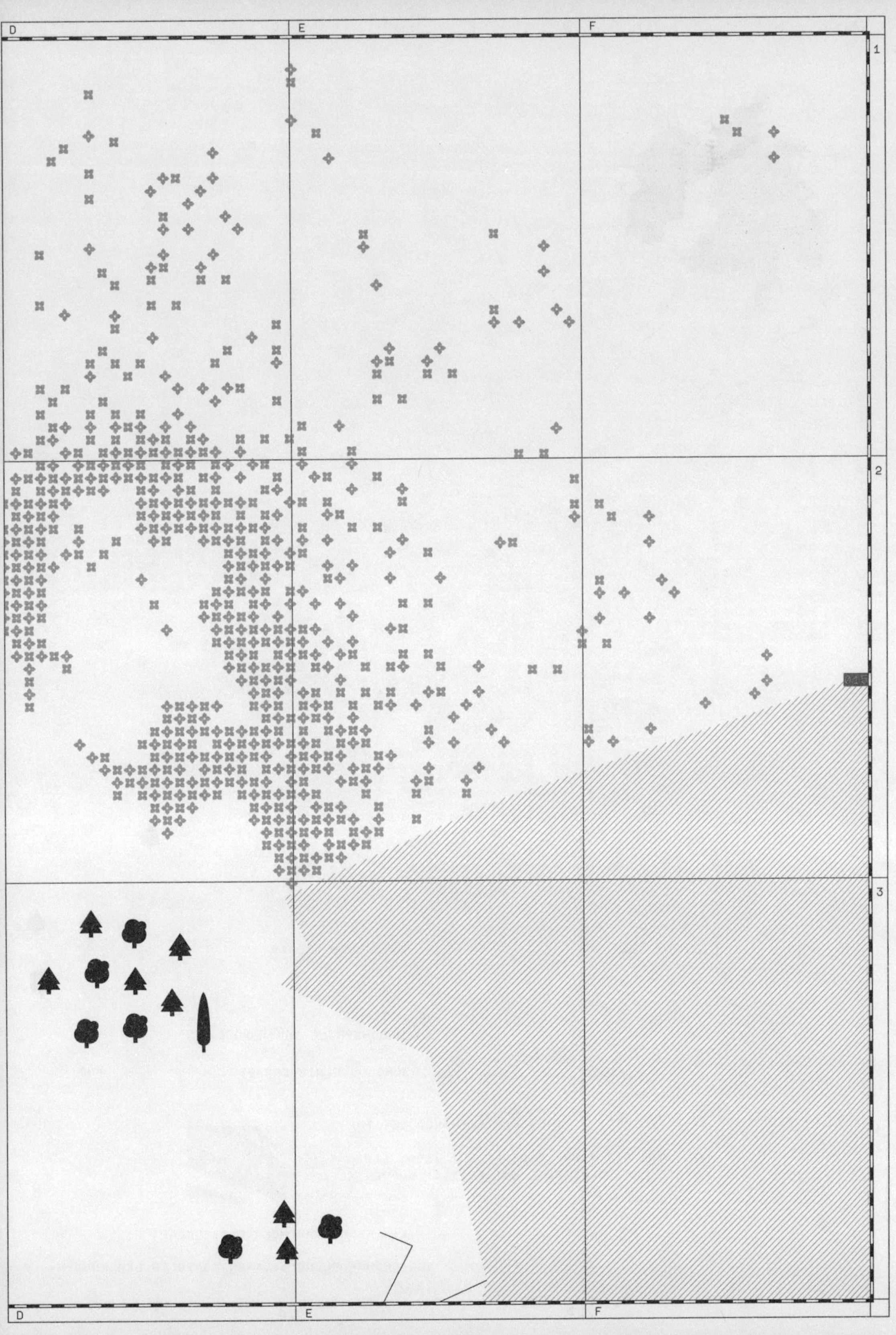

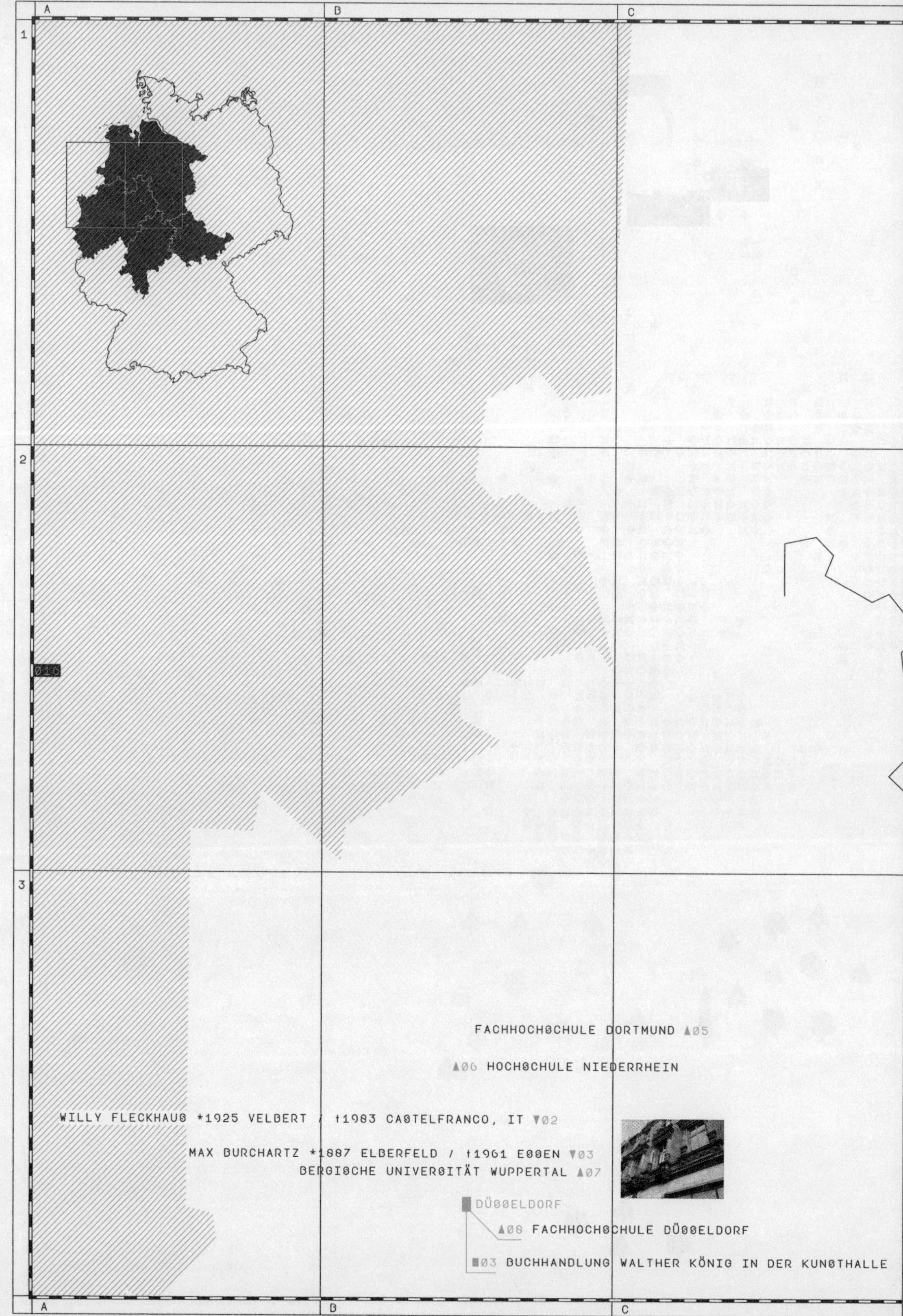
A
B
C
1
2
3
016
FACHHOCHSCHULE DORTMUND ▲05
▲06 HOCHSCHULE NIEDERRHEIN
WILLY FLECKHAUS *1925 VELBERT / †1983 CASTELFRANCO, IT ▼02
MAX BURCHARTZ *1887 ELBERFELD / †1961 ESSEN ▼03
BERGISCHE UNIVERSITÄT WUPPERTAL ▲07
DÜSSELDORF
▲08 FACHHOCHSCHULE DÜSSELDORF
■03 BUCHHANDLUNG WALTHER KÖNIG IN DER KUNSTHALLE

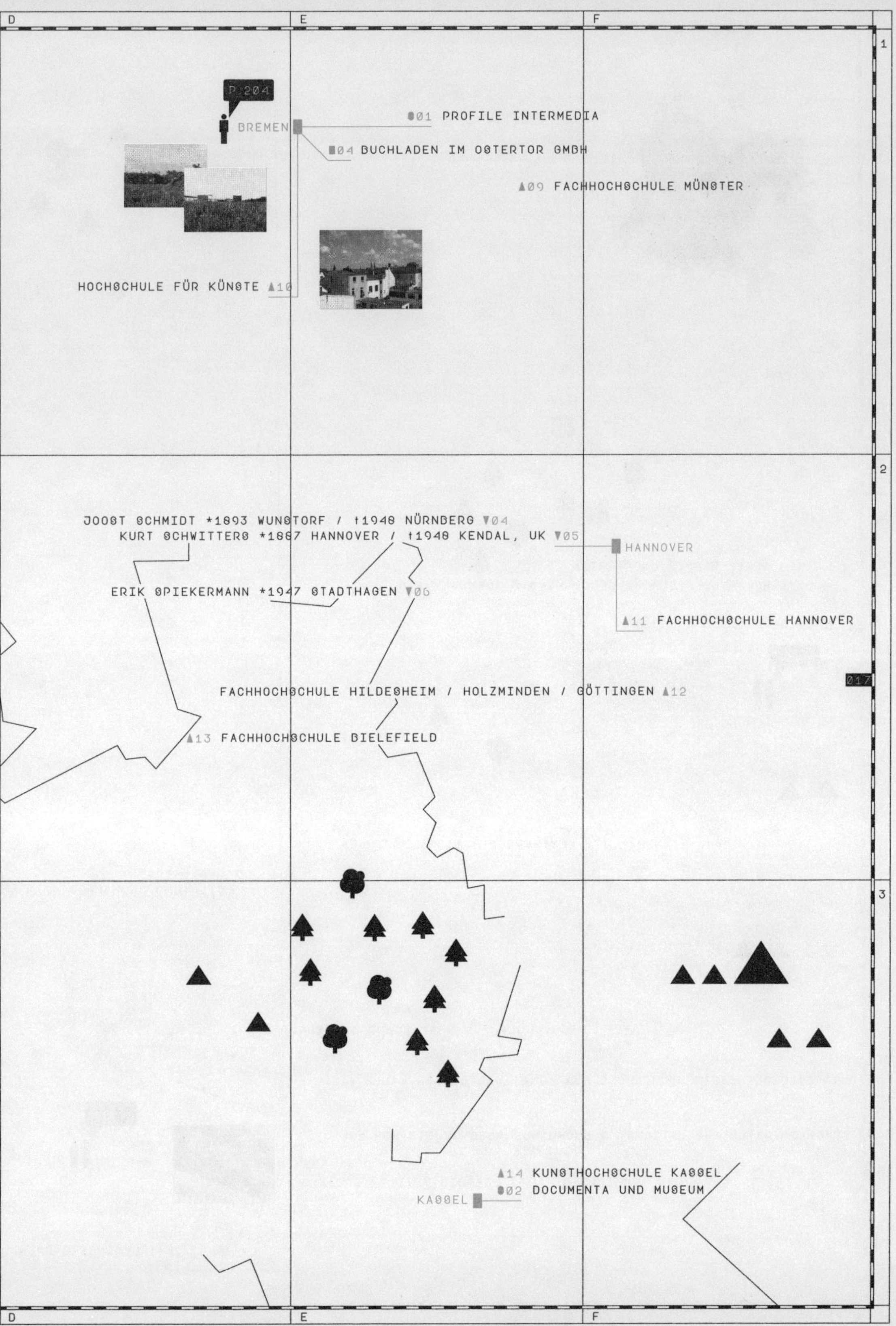

D
E
F
1
2
3
P 204
BREMEN
001 PROFILE INTERMEDIA
004 BUCHLADEN IM OSTERTOR GMBH
009 FACHHOCHSCHULE MÜNSTER
HOCHSCHULE FÜR KÜNSTE 10
JOOST SCHMIDT *1893 WUNSTORF / †1948 NÜRNBERG 04
KURT SCHWITTERS *1887 HANNOVER / †1948 KENDAL, UK 05
ERIK SPIEKERMANN *1947 STADTHAGEN 06
HANNOVER
11 FACHHOCHSCHULE HANNOVER
017
FACHHOCHSCHULE HILDESHEIM / HOLZMINDEN / GÖTTINGEN 12
13 FACHHOCHSCHULE BIELEFIELD
14 KUNSTHOCHSCHULE KASSEL
002 DOCUMENTA UND MUSEUM
KASSEL

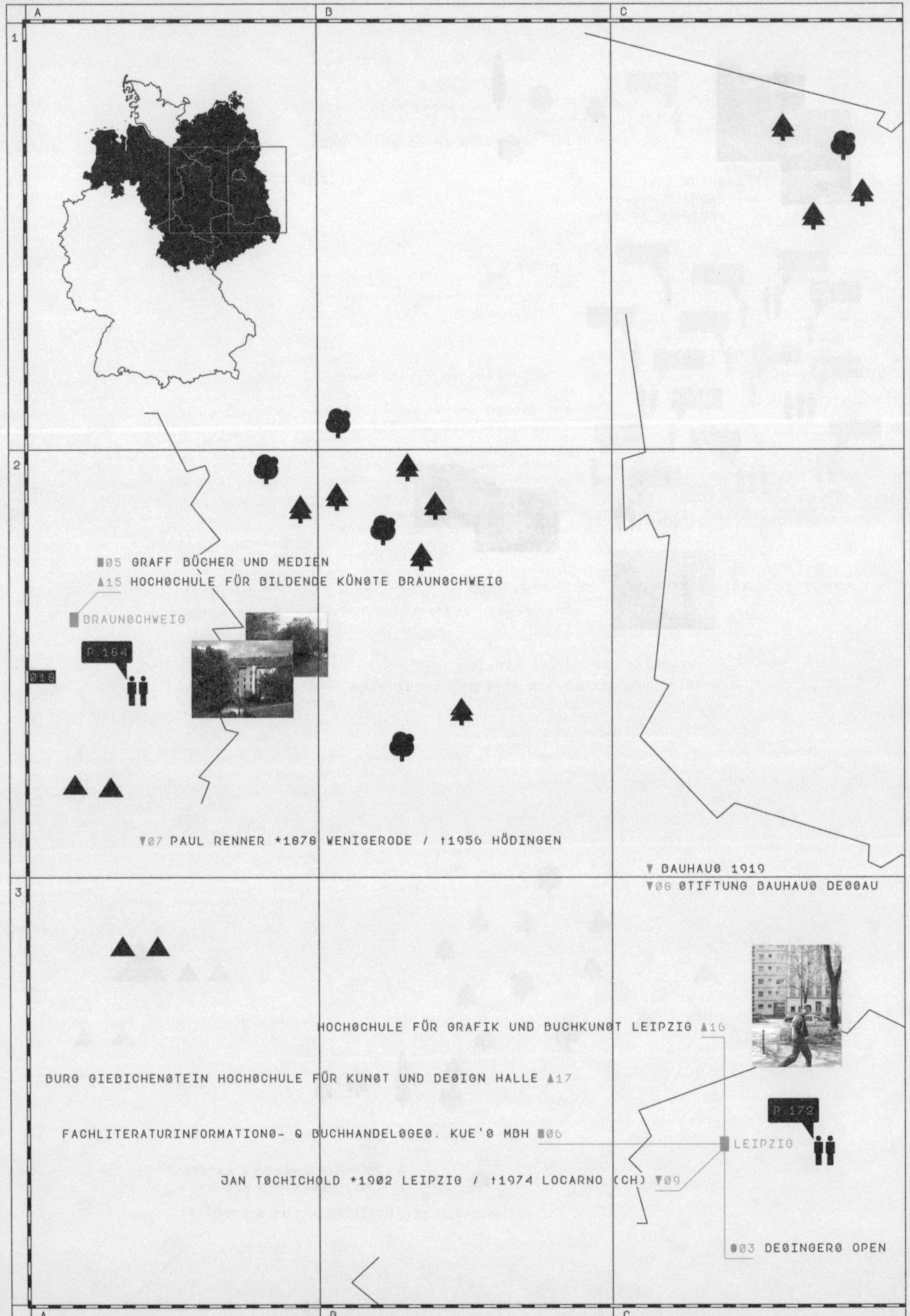

A B C
1
2
■05 GRAFF BÜCHER UND MEDIEN
▲15 HOCHSCHULE FÜR BILDENDE KÜNSTE BRAUNSCHWEIG
BRAUNSCHWEIG
P 184
018
▼07 PAUL RENNER *1878 WENIGERODE / †1956 HÖDINGEN
▼ BAUHAUS 1919
▼08 STIFTUNG BAUHAUS DESSAU
3
HOCHSCHULE FÜR GRAFIK UND BUCHKUNST LEIPZIG ▲16
BURG GIEBICHENSTEIN HOCHSCHULE FÜR KUNST UND DESIGN HALLE ▲17
FACHLITERATURINFORMATIONS- & BUCHHANDELSGES. KUE'S MBH ■06
JAN TSCHICHOLD *1902 LEIPZIG / †1974 LOCARNO (CH) ▼09
P 172
LEIPZIG
●03 DESINGERS OPEN
A B C

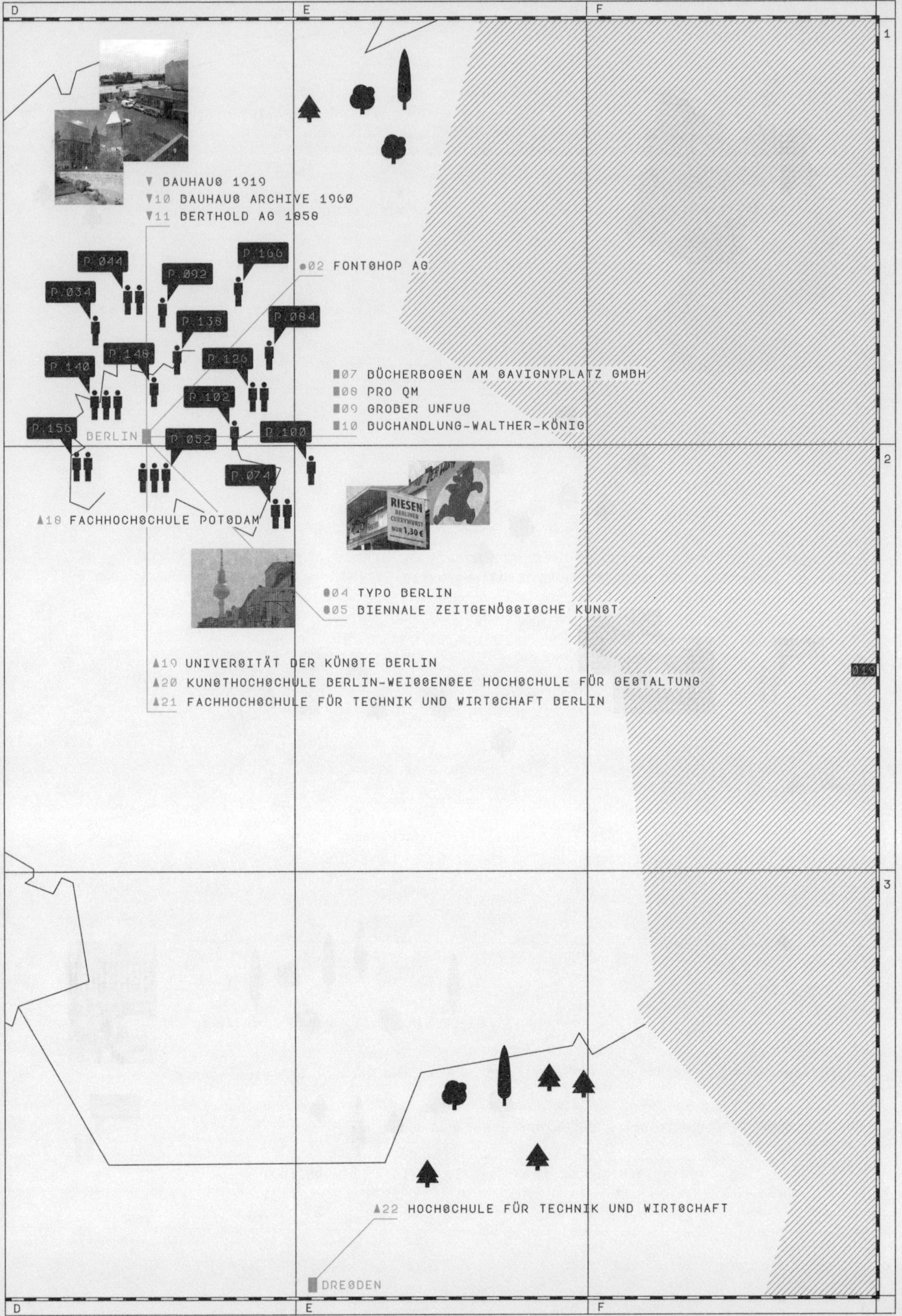

D
E
F
1
2
3
▼ BAUHAUS 1919
▼10 BAUHAUS ARCHIVE 1960
▼11 BERTHOLD AG 1858
P.044
P.166
P.092
P.034
●02 FONTSHOP AG
P.138
P.084
P.148
P.126
P.140
■07 BÜCHERBOGEN AM SAVIGNYPLATZ GMBH
■08 PRO QM
P.102
■09 GROBER UNFUG
■10 BUCHANDLUNG-WALTHER-KÖNIG
P.156
BERLIN
P.052
P.100
P.074
▲18 FACHHOCHSCHULE POTSDAM
RIESEN
BERLINER
CURRYWURST
NUR 1,30 €
DER HAUT
●04 TYPO BERLIN
●05 BIENNALE ZEITGENÖSSISCHE KUNST
▲19 UNIVERSITÄT DER KÜNSTE BERLIN
▲20 KUNSTHOCHSCHULE BERLIN-WEISSENSEE HOCHSCHULE FÜR GESTALTUNG
▲21 FACHHOCHSCHULE FÜR TECHNIK UND WIRTSCHAFT BERLIN
019
▲22 HOCHSCHULE FÜR TECHNIK UND WIRTSCHAFT
DRESDEN
D
E
F

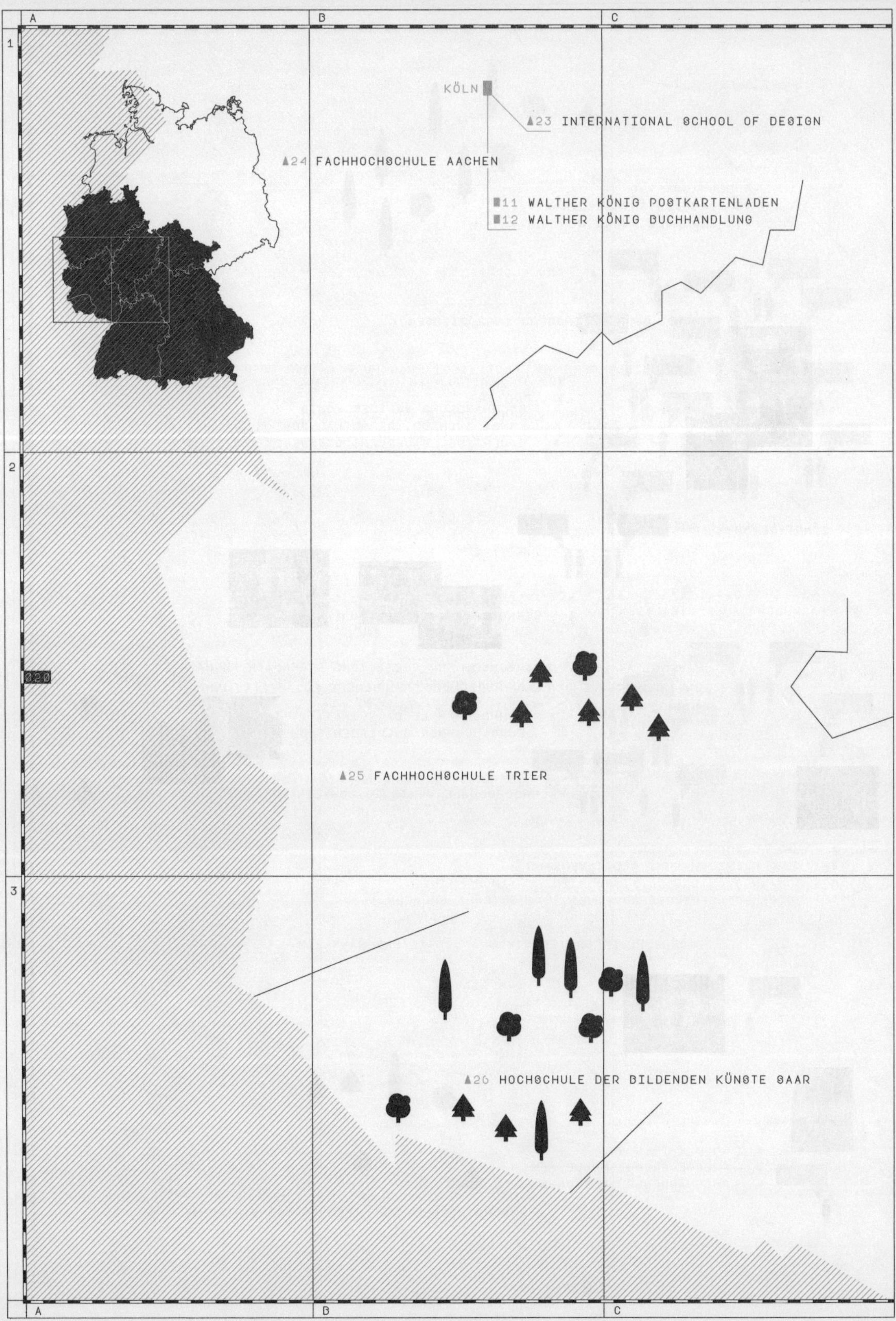
A
B
C
1
KÖLN
▲23 INTERNATIONAL SCHOOL OF DESIGN
▲24 FACHHOCHSCHULE AACHEN
■11 WALTHER KÖNIG POSTKARTENLADEN
■12 WALTHER KÖNIG BUCHHANDLUNG
2
020
▲25 FACHHOCHSCHULE TRIER
3
▲26 HOCHSCHULE DER BILDENDEN KÜNSTE SAAR
A
B
C

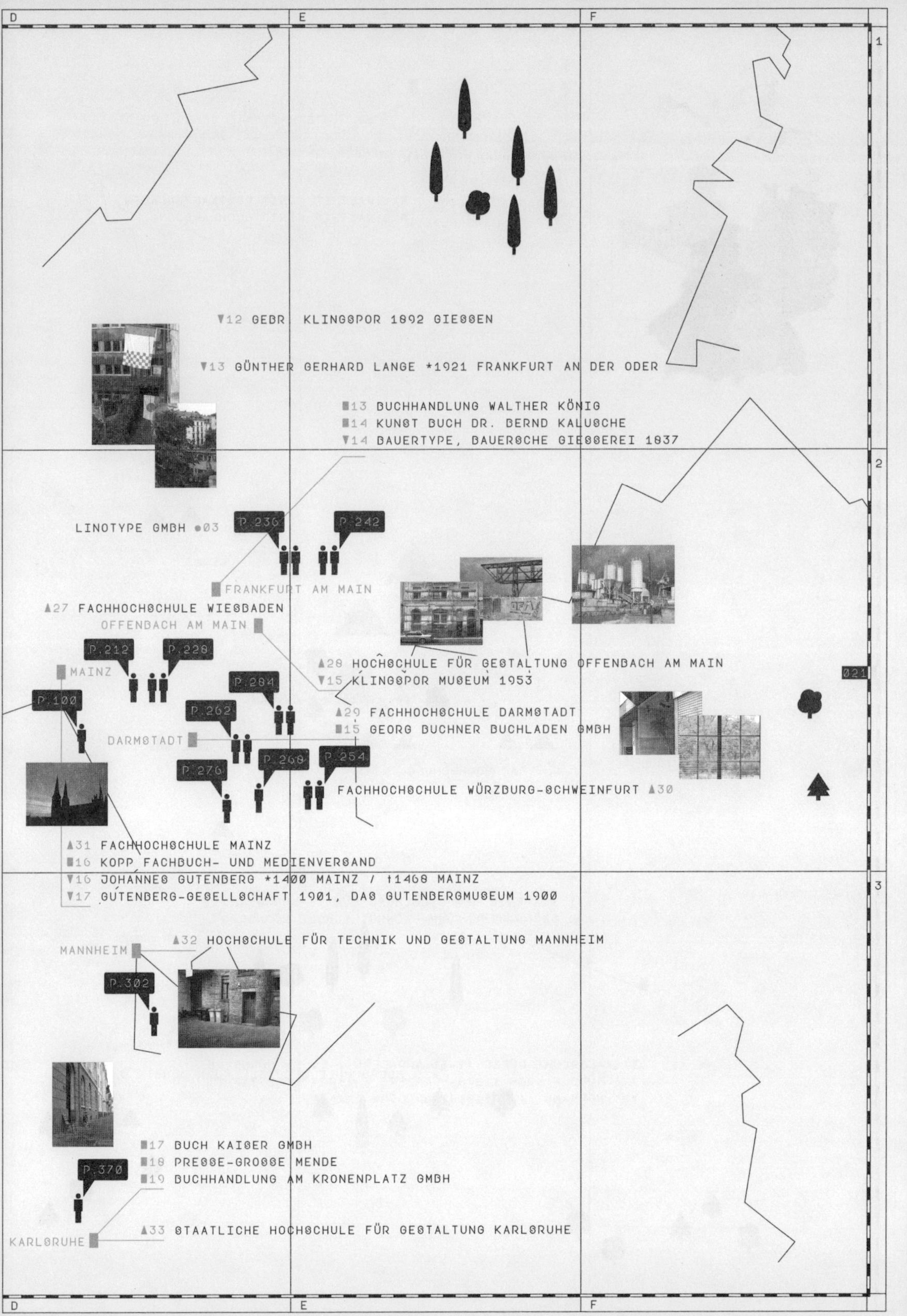
D
E
F
1
2
021
3
▼12 GEBR. KLINGSPOR 1892 GIESSEN
▼13 GÜNTHER GERHARD LANGE *1921 FRANKFURT AN DER ODER
▪13 BUCHHANDLUNG WALTHER KÖNIG
▪14 KUNST BUCH DR. BERND KALUSCHE
▼14 BAUERTYPE, BAUERSCHE GIESSEREI 1837
LINOTYPE GMBH ●03
P.236
P.242
▪FRANKFURT AM MAIN
▲27 FACHHOCHSCHULE WIESBADEN
OFFENBACH AM MAIN▪
P.212
P.220
▪MAINZ
P.100
▲28 HOCHSCHULE FÜR GESTALTUNG OFFENBACH AM MAIN
▼15 KLINGSPOR MUSEUM 1953
P.284
P.262
▲29 FACHHOCHSCHULE DARMSTADT
▪15 GEORG BUCHNER BUCHLADEN GMBH
DARMSTADT▪
P.276
P.268
P.254
FACHHOCHSCHULE WÜRZBURG-SCHWEINFURT ▲30
▲31 FACHHOCHSCHULE MAINZ
▪16 KOPP FACHBUCH- UND MEDIENVERSAND
▼16 JOHANNES GUTENBERG *1400 MAINZ / †1468 MAINZ
▼17 GUTENBERG-GESELLSCHAFT 1901, DAS GUTENBERGMUSEUM 1900
MANNHEIM▪
▲32 HOCHSCHULE FÜR TECHNIK UND GESTALTUNG MANNHEIM
P.302
▪17 BUCH KAISER GMBH
▪18 PRESSE-GROSSE MENDE
▪19 BUCHHANDLUNG AM KRONENPLATZ GMBH
P.370
▲33 STAATLICHE HOCHSCHULE FÜR GESTALTUNG KARLSRUHE
KARLSRUHE▪
D
E
F

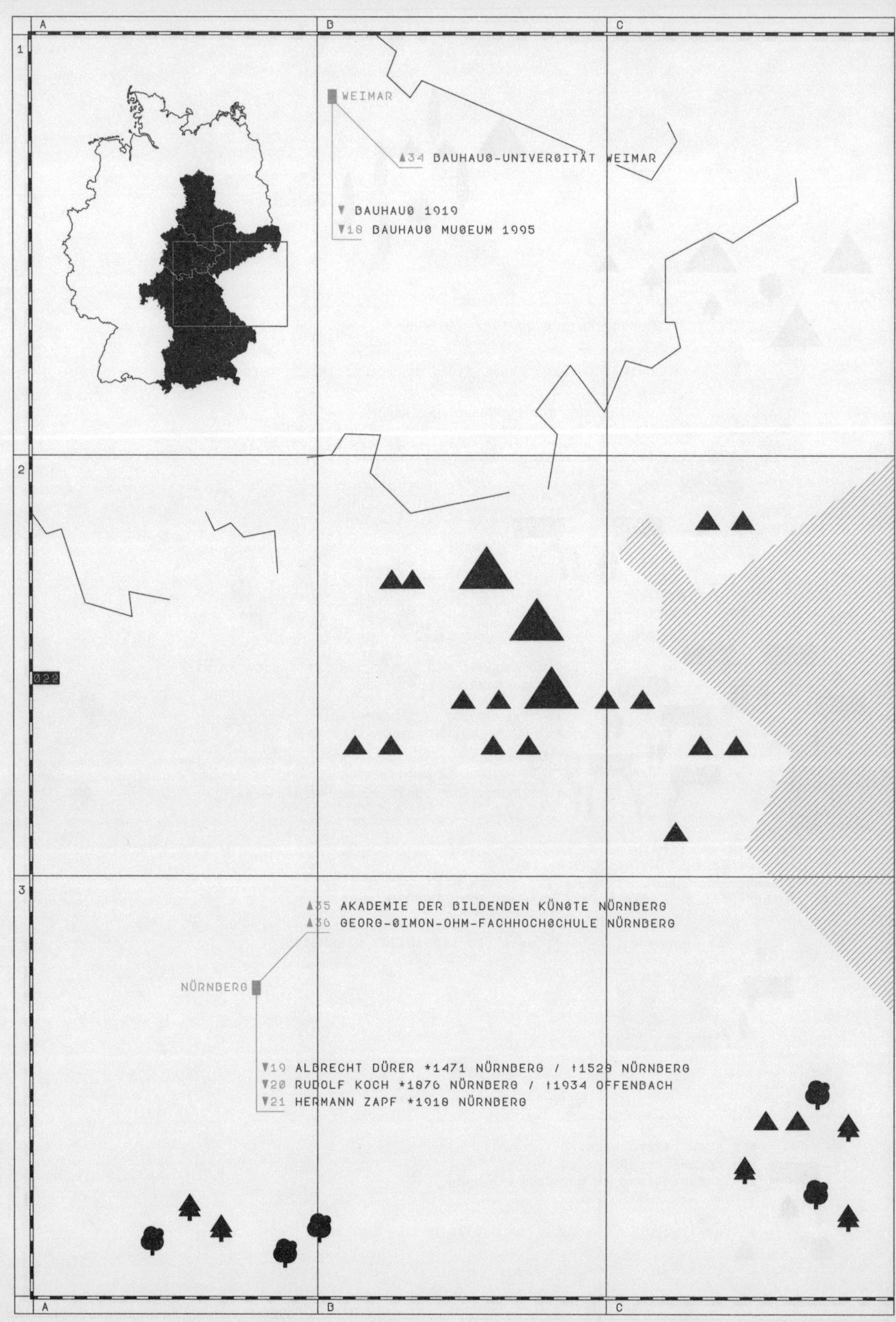
A
B
C
1
WEIMAR
▲34 BAUHAUS-UNIVERSITÄT WEIMAR
▼ BAUHAUS 1919
▼18 BAUHAUS MUSEUM 1995
2
022
3
▲35 AKADEMIE DER BILDENDEN KÜNSTE NÜRNBERG
▲36 GEORG-SIMON-OHM-FACHHOCHSCHULE NÜRNBERG
NÜRNBERG
▼19 ALBRECHT DÜRER *1471 NÜRNBERG / †1528 NÜRNBERG
▼20 RUDOLF KOCH *1876 NÜRNBERG / †1934 OFFENBACH
▼21 HERMANN ZAPF *1918 NÜRNBERG

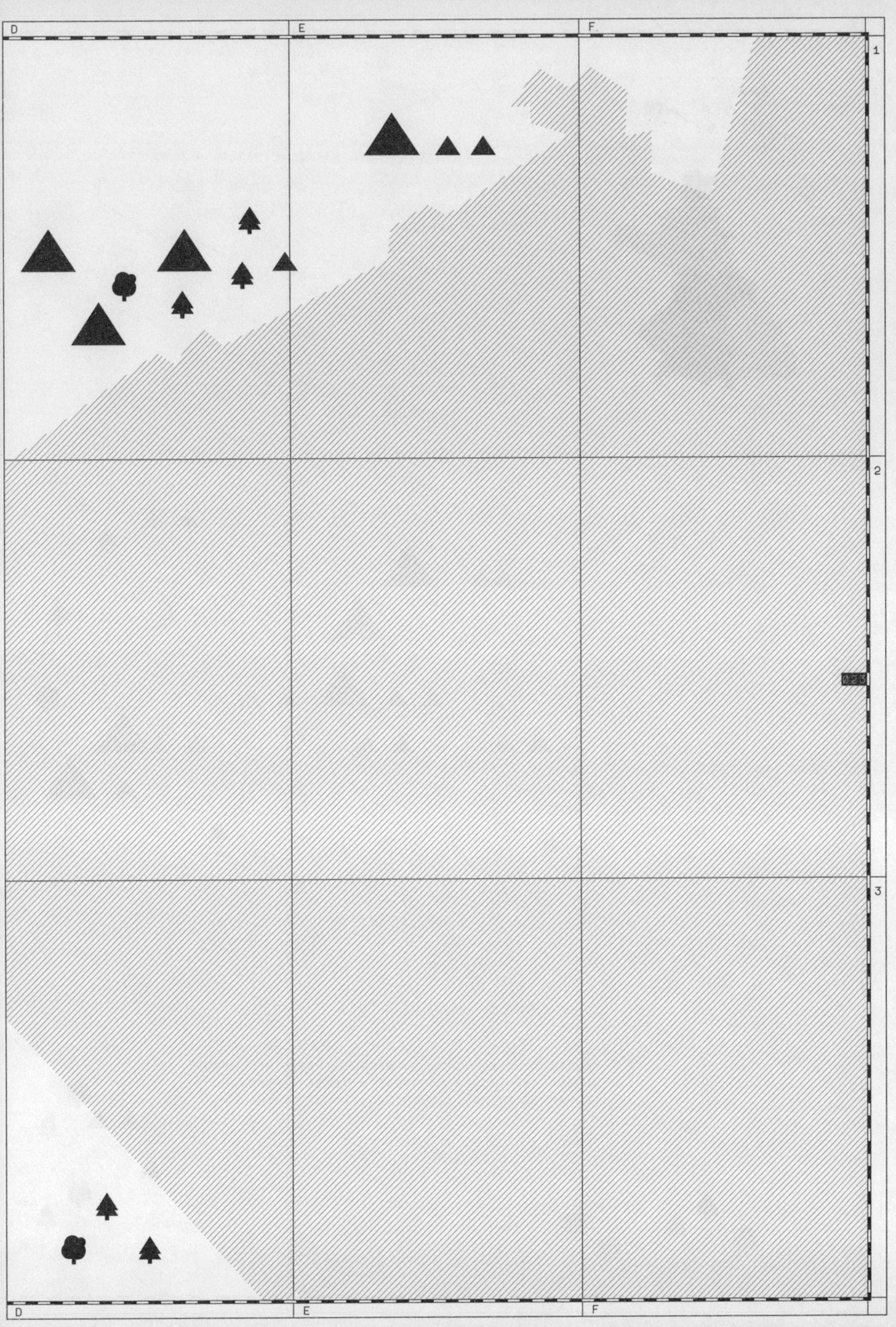

D
E
F
1
2
3
D
E
F
023

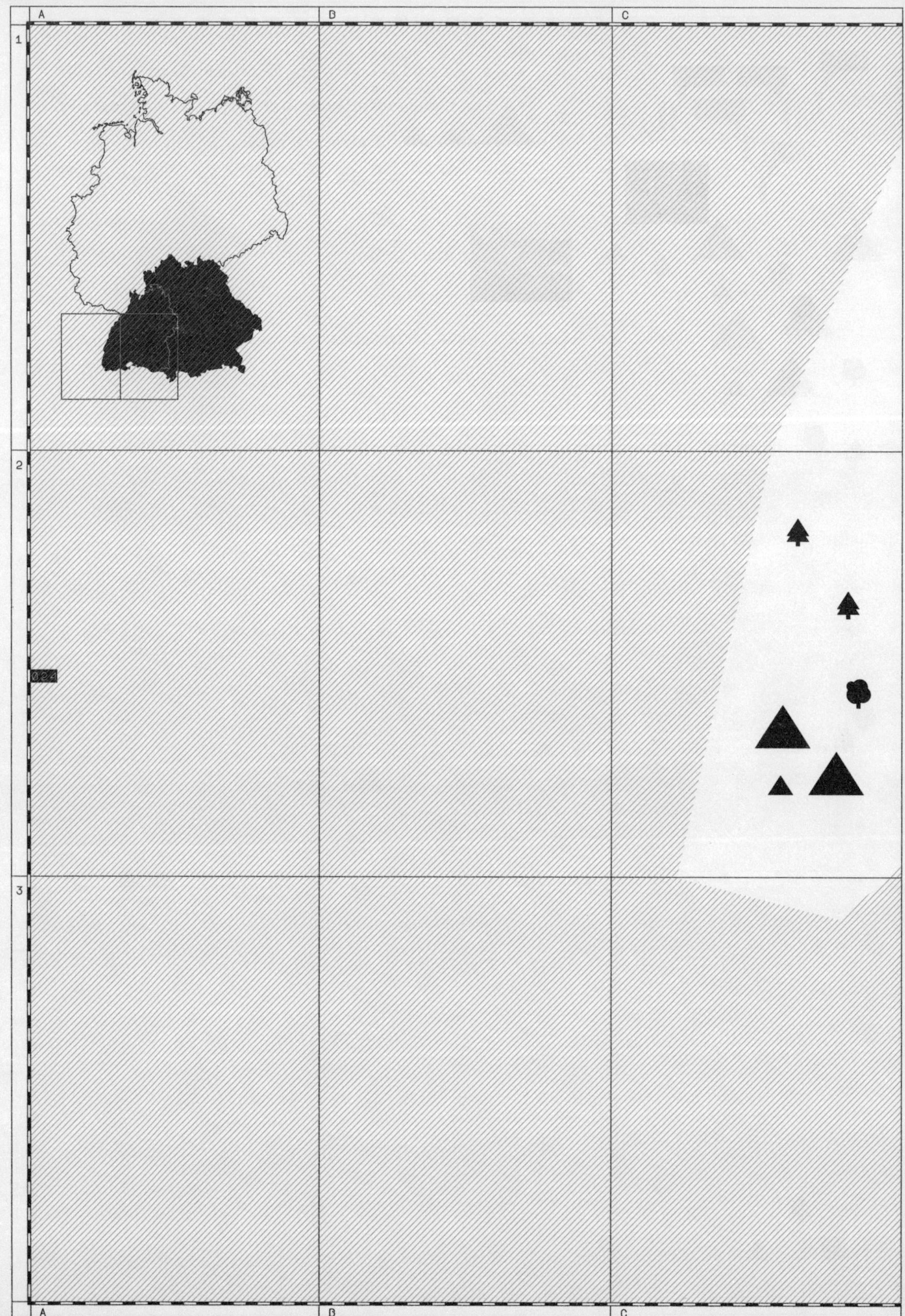

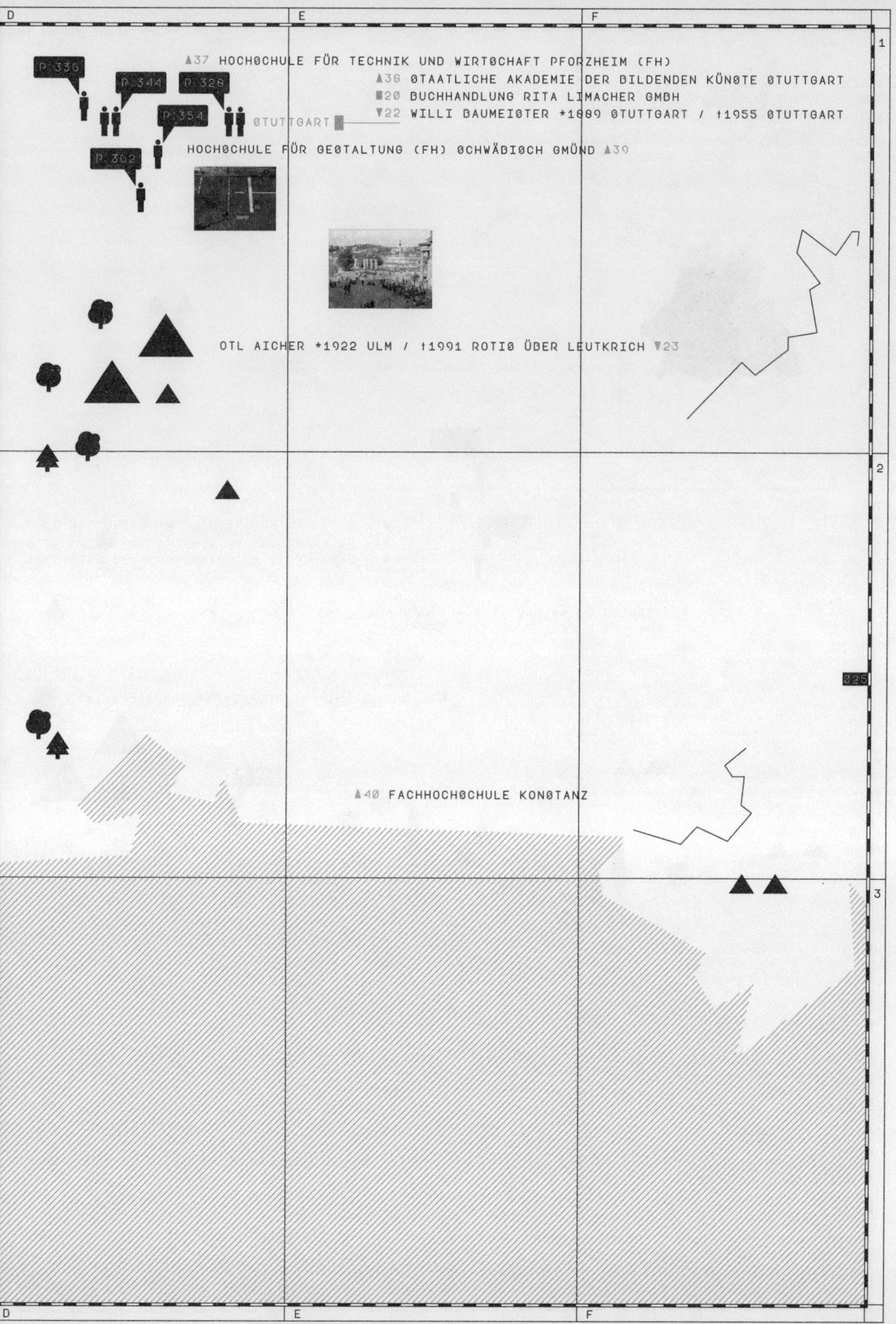

D
E
F
1
▲37 HOCHSCHULE FÜR TECHNIK UND WIRTSCHAFT PFORZHEIM (FH)
▲38 STAATLICHE AKADEMIE DER BILDENDEN KÜNSTE STUTTGART
■20 BUCHHANDLUNG RITA LIMACHER GMBH
▼22 WILLI BAUMEISTER *1889 STUTTGART / †1955 STUTTGART
P.336
P.344
P.328
P.354
STUTTGART
HOCHSCHULE FÜR GESTALTUNG (FH) SCHWÄBISCH GMÜND ▲39
P.362
OTL AICHER *1922 ULM / †1991 ROTIS ÜBER LEUTKRICH ▼23
2
▲40 FACHHOCHSCHULE KONSTANZ
025
3
D
E
F

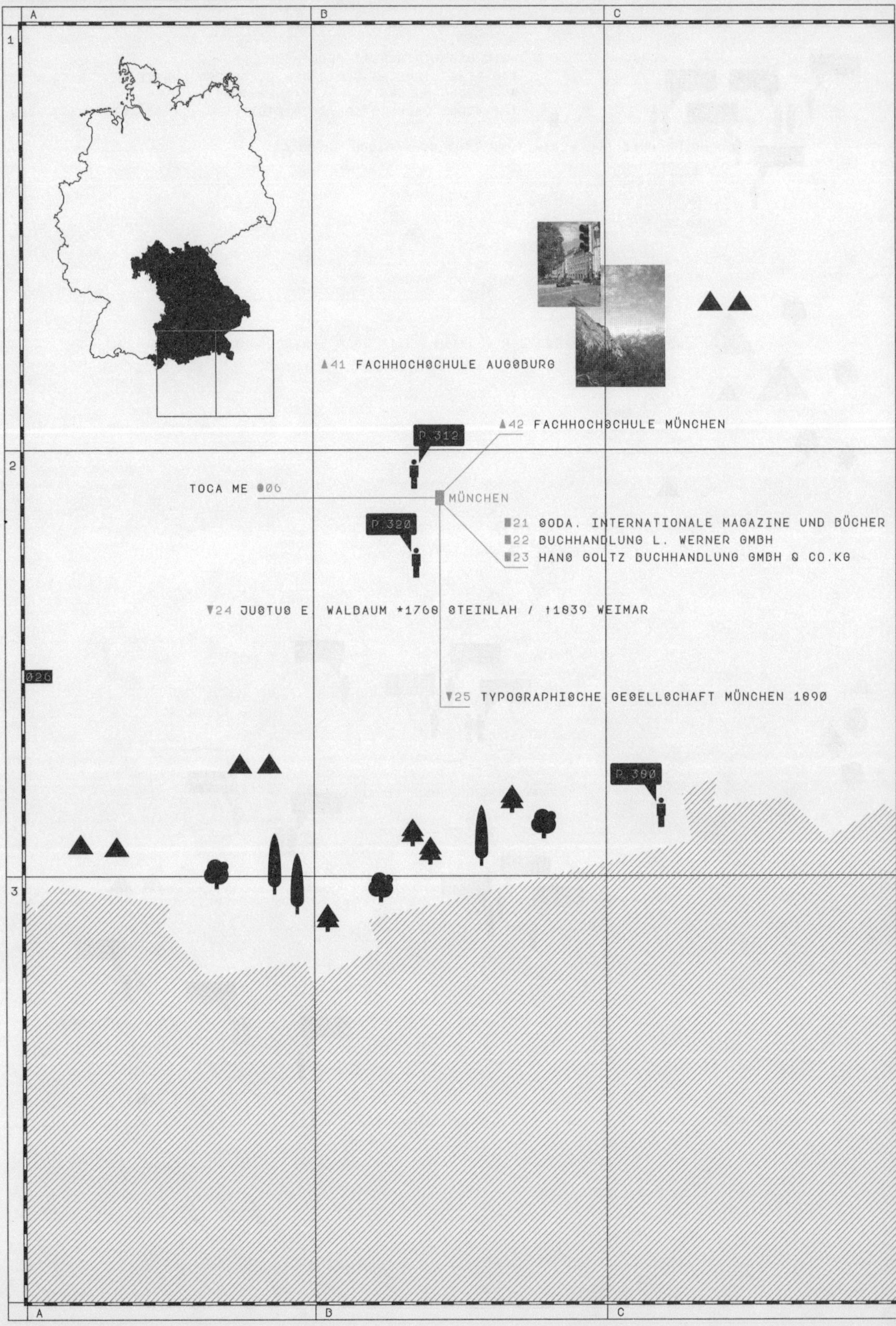
▲41 FACHHOCHSCHULE AUGSBURG
P.312
▲42 FACHHOCHSCHULE MÜNCHEN
TOCA ME 006
MÜNCHEN
■21 SODA. INTERNATIONALE MAGAZINE UND BÜCHER
■22 BUCHHANDLUNG L. WERNER GMBH
P.320
■23 HANS GOLTZ BUCHHANDLUNG GMBH & CO.KG
▼24 JUSTUS E. WALBAUM *1768 STEINLAH / †1839 WEIMAR
026
▼25 TYPOGRAPHISCHE GESELLSCHAFT MÜNCHEN 1890
P.300

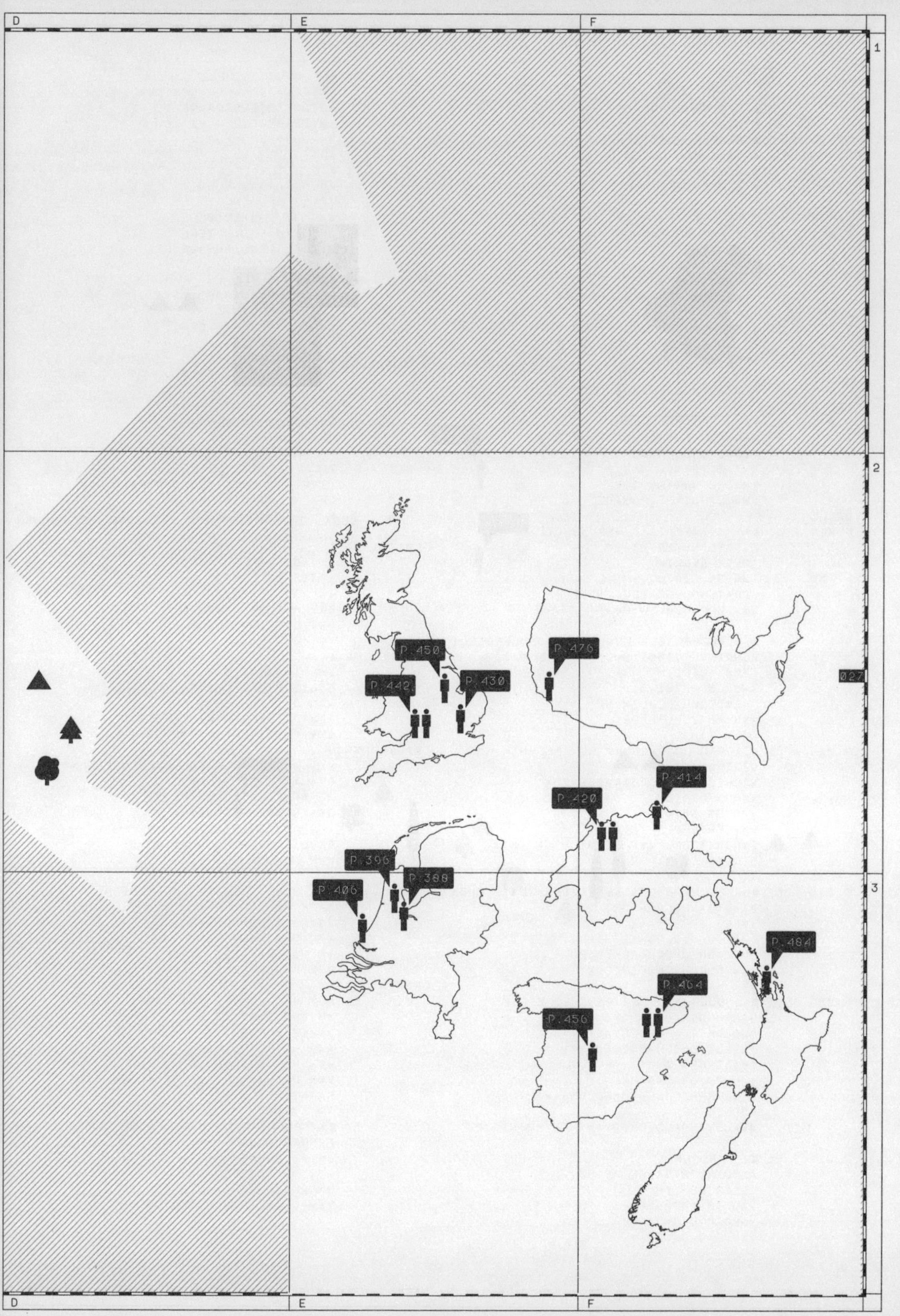

D
E
F
1
2
3
027
P. 450
P. 476
P. 442
P. 430
P. 414
P. 420
P. 396
P. 388
P. 406
P. 484
P. 464
P. 456

P.017 / E1 ●01 PROFILE INTERMEDIA
           AM SPEICHER XI NO. 8,
           28217 BREMEN
           +49 421 95951350
           WWW.PROFILE-INTERMEDIA.DE
DARMSTADT
P.021 / D2 ▲29 FACHHOCHSCHULE DARMSTADT
           OLBRICHWEG 10,
           64287 DARMSTADT
           WWW.FBG.H-DA.DE
           CONFERENCE: WWW.HALBFUENF.NET
           --
P.021 / D2 ■15 GEORG BÜCHNER BUCHLADEN GMBH
           LAUTESCHLÄGERSTRASSE 18,
           64289 DARMSTADT
           +49 6151 77424
           GEORG-BUECHNER.BUCHLADEN@T-ONLINE.DE
           WWW.GEORG-BUECHNER-BUCHLADEN.DE
DESSAU
P.018 / C3 ▼08 STIFTUNG BAUHAUS DESSAU
           GROPIUSALLEE 38,
           06846 DESSAU
           +49 340 6508-0
           SERVICE@BAUHAUS-DESSAU.DE
           WWW.BAUHAUS-DESSAU.DE
DORTMUND
P.016 / C3 ▲05 FACHHOCHSCHULE DORTMUND
           MAX-OPHÜLS-PLATZ 2,
           44139 DORTMUND
           +49 231 9112-426
           PRESSESTELLE@FH-DORTMUND.DE
           WWW.FH-DORTMUND.DE
           MAGAZINE: WWW.SEITEEINS.NET
DRESDEN
P.019 / E3 ▲22 HOCHSCHULE FÜR TECHNIK UND
           WIRTSCHAFT
           FRIEDRICH-LIST-PLATZ 1,
           01069 DRESDEN
           +49 351 462-0
           HAEUSSLE@VERWALTUNG.HTW-DRESDEN.DE
           WWW.HTW-DRESDEN.DE
           EXHIBITION: FORMSCHLUSS
DÜSSELDORF
P.016 / B3 ▲09 FACHHOCHSCHULE DÜSSELDORF
           GEORG-GLOCK-STR. 15,
           40474 DÜSSELDORF
           +49 0211 4351-201
           DESIGN@FH-DUESSELDORF.DE
           WWW.FH-DUESSELDORF.DE
           --
P.016 / B3 ■01 BUCHHANDLUNG WALTHER KÖNIG
           IN DER KUNSTHALLE
           GRABBEPLATZ 4,
           40213 DÜSSELDORF
           +49 211 136210
           DUESSELDORF@BUCHHANDLUNG-WALTHER-
           KOENIG.DE
           WWW.BUCHHANDLUNG-WALTHER-KOENIG.DE
ELBERFELD
P.016 / B3 ▼03 MAX BURCHARTZ
           (TYPOGRAPHER, GRAPHIC DESIGNER,
           ARTIST, TEACHER AND THEORETICIAN)
           ◆ <ALLEGORY OF THE HARMONY>
FRANKFURT
AM MAIN
P.021 / D2 ■13 BUCHHANDLUNG WALTHER KÖNIG
           IM STADEL
           SCHAUMAINKAI 63,
           60596 FRANKFURT AM MAIN
           +49 69 66370795
           FRANKFURTSTAEDEL@BUCHHANDLUNG-
           WALTHER-KOENIG.DE
           WWW.BUCHHANDLUNG-WALTHER-KOENIG.DE
           --

P.021 / D2 ■14 KUNST-BUCH DR. BERND KALUSCHE
           RÖMERBERG 7,
           60311 FRANKFURT AM MAIN
           +49 69 29988244
           KUNST-BUCH@ONLINEHOME.DE
           WWW.KUNST-BUCH-KALUSCHE.EU
           --
P.021 / D2 ▼14 BAUERTYPE, BAUERSCHE GIESSEREI
           HAMBURGER ALLEE 45,
           FRANKFURT AM MAIN W13
FRANKFURT
AN DER ODER
P.021 / D1 ▼13 GÜNTHER GERHARD LANGE
           (TYPE DESIGNER, TYPOGRAPHER
           AND TEACHER)
           ◆ AG BUCH
GIESSEN
P.021 / D1 ▼12 GEBR. KLINGSPOR
           ◆ TYPE FOUNDRY
HALLE
P.018 / B3 ▲17 BURG GIEBICHENSTEIN HOCHSCHULE
           FÜR KUNST UND DESIGN HALLE
           CAMPUS DESIGN NEUWERK 7,
           06108 HALLE (SAALE)
           +49 345 7751-508, -984
           BURGPOST@BURG-HALLE.DE
           WWW.BURG-HALLE.DE
HAMBURG
P.013 / F3 ▲02 HOCHSCHULE FÜR ANGEWANDTE
           WISSENSCHAFTEN (FH)
           ARMGARTSTRASSE 24,
           22087 HAMBURG
           WARTENAU 15, 22089 HAMBURG
           +49 40 428750
           WWW.DESIGN.HAW-HAMBURG.DE
           CONFERENCE: WWW.STILVORLAGEN.DE
           --
P.013 / F3 ▲03 HOCHSCHULE FÜR BILDENDE KÜNSTE
           LERCHENFELD 2,
           22081 HAMBURG
           +49 40 428990
           WWW.HFBK-HAMBURG.DE
           EXHIBITION: GALERIE.HFBK-HAMBURG.DE
           --
P.013 / F3 ■01 BUCHHANDLUNG SAUTTER + LACKMANN
           ADMIRALITÄTSTRASSE 71/72,
           20459 HAMBURG
           +49 40 373196
           INFO@SAUTTER-LACKMANN.DE
           WWW.SAUTTER-LACKMANN.DE
           --
P.013 / F3 ■02 COHEN + DOBERNIGG
           STERNSTRASSE 4,
           20357 HAMBURG
           +49 40 4018510
           BUCH@COFOBUCH.DE
           WWW.CODOBUCH.DE
           --
P.013 / F3 ●01 URW
           POPPENBÜTTELER BOGEN 36,
           22399 HAMBURG
           +49 40 606050
           INFO@URWPP.DE
           WWW.URWPP.DE/DEUTSCH/HOME.HTML
P.013 / F3 ▼01 MUSEUM FÜR KUNST UND GEWERBE
           STEINTORPLATZ,
           20099 HAMBURG
           +49 40 4281342732
           SERVICE@MKG-HAMBURG.DE
           WWW.MKG-HAMBURG.DE
           --

MANNHEIM
P.021 / D3 ▲32 HOCHSCHULE FÜR TECHNIK UND
           GESTALTUNG MANNHEIM
           PAUL-WITTSACK-STRASSE 10,
           68163 MANNHEIM
           +49 621 2926159
           WWW.GESTALTUNG.FH-MANNHEIM.DE
           MAGAZINE: WWW.KOMMA-MANNHEIM.DE
MUNICH
P.026 / B2 ▲42 FACHHOCHSCHULE MÜNCHEN
           INFANTERIESTRASSE 14,
           80797 MÜNCHEN
           +49 89 12654201
           DESIGN@HM.EDU
           WWW.FH-MUENCHEN.DE/HOME/FB/FB12
           --
P.026 / B2 ■21 SODA. INTERNATIONALE MAGAZINE
           UND BÜCHER
           RUMFORDSTRASSE 3,
           80469 MÜNCHEN
           +49 89 20245353
           INFO@SODABOOKS.COM
           WWW.SODABOOKS.COM
           --
P.026 / B2 ■22 BUCHHANDLUNG L. WERNER GMBH
           TÜRKENSTRASSE 30,
           80333 MÜNCHEN
           +49 89 2805448
           INFO@BUCHHANDLUNG-WERNER.DE
           WWW.BUCHHANDLUNG-WERNER.DE
           --
P.026 / B2 ■23 HANS GOLTZ BUCHHANDLUNG
           GMBH & CO.K
           TÜRKENSTRASSE 36,
           80799 MÜNCHEN
           +49 89 284906
           INFO@GOLTZ.DE
           WWW.GOLTZ.DE
           --
P.026 / B2 ●01 TOCA ME
           TOUCHME@TOCA-ME.COM
           WWW.TOCA-ME.COM
           --
P.026 / B2 ▼25 TYPOGRAPHISCHE GESELLSCHAFT
           MÜNCHEN
           WWW.TGM-ONLINE.DE
MÜNSTER
P.017 / E1 ▲09 FACHHOCHSCHULE MÜNSTER
           SENTMARINGER WEG 53,
           48151 MÜNSTER
           +49 251 8365301
           WWW.FH-MUENSTER.DE/DESIGN
           WWW.DREIRAUM.MS
NIEDERRHEIN
P.016 / B3 ▲06 HOCHSCHULE NIEDERRHEIN
           FRANKENRING 20,
           47798 KREFELD
           +49 2151 8224312
           MARITA.GEHNEN@HS-NIEDERRHEIN.DE
           WWW.HS-NIEDERRHEIN.DE
           WWW.DESIGNKREFELD.DE
           MAGAZINE: BOTENSTOFF
NÜRNBERG
P.021 / A3 ▲35 AKADEMIE DER BILDENDEN KÜNSTE
           NÜRNBERG
           BINGSTRASSE 60,
           90480 NÜRNBERG
           +49 911 94040
           WWW.ADBK-NUERNBERG.DE
           --
P.021 / A3 ▲36 GEORG-SIMON-OHM-HOCHSCHULE
           NÜRNBERG
           KESSLERPLATZ 12,
           90489 NÜRNBERG
           +49 911 58800
           WWW.G.FH-NUERNBERG.DE

P.021 / A3 ▼19 ALBRECHT DÜRER
           (PAINTER, WOODCARVER AND COPPER
           ENGRAVER)
           ♦ <THE FOUR BOOKS ON MEASUREMENT>
           --
P.021 / A3 ▼20 RUDOLF KOCH
           (TYPE DESIGNER, TYPOGRAPHER,
           CALLIGRAPHER AND TEACHER)
           ♦ KABEL
           --
P.021 / A3 ▼21 HERMANN ZAPF
           (TYPE DESIGNER, TYPOGRAPHER,
           CALLIGRAPHER, AUTHOR AND TEACHER)
           ♦ PALATINO, OPTIMA UND ZAPFINO
OFFENBACH
AM MAIN
P.021 / D2 ▲28 HOCHSCHULE FÜR GESTALTUNG
           OFFENBACH AM MAIN
           SCHLOSSSTRASSE 31,
           63065 OFFENBACH AM MAIN
           +49 69 800590
           PRESSE@HFG-OFFENBACH.DE
           WWW.HFG-OFFENBACH.DE
           --
P.021 / D2 ▼15 KLINGSPOR MUSEUM
           MUSEUM OF TYPE
           HERRNSTRASSE 80,
           63061 OFFENBACH AM MAIN
           +49 69 80652954
           KLINGSPORMUSEUM@OFFENBACH.DE
           WWW.KLINGSPOR-MUSEUM.DE
PFORZHEIM
P.025 / D1 ▲37 HOCHSCHULE FÜR TECHNIK UND
           WIRTSCHAFT (FH) PFORZHEIM
           HOLZGARTENSTRASSE 36,
           75175 PFORZHEIM
           +49 7231 286035
           WWW.GESTALTUNG.FH-PFORZHEIM.DE
           MAGAZINE: PUNZE
POTSDAM
P.019 / D2 ▲18 FACHHOCHSCHULE POTSDAM
           PAPPELALLEE 8-9,
           14469 POTSDAM
           +49 331 5801401
           WWW.DESIGN.FH-POTSDAM.DE
           EXHIBITION: WWW.APPLAUS-POTSDAM.DE
           MAGAZINE: WWW.ECHTZEIT.ORG
SAARBRÜCKEN
P.020 / B3 ▲26 HOCHSCHULE DER BILDENDEN KÜNSTE
           KEPLERSTRASSE 3-5,
           66117 SAARBRÜCKEN
           +49 681 92652101
           INFO@HBKS.UNI-SB.DE
           WWW.HBKSAAR.DE
SCHWÄBISCH
GMÜND
P.025 / F1 ▲39 HOCHSCHULE FÜR GESTALTUNG (FH)
           SCHWÄBISCH GMÜND
           REKTOR-KLAUS-STRASSE 100,
           73525 SCHWÄBISCH GMÜND
           +49 7171 602600
           INFO@HFG-GMUEND.DE
           WWW.HFG-GMUEND.DE
STADTHAGEN
P.017 / E2 ▼06 ERIK SPIEKERMANN
           (TYPE DESIGNER, TYPOGRAPHER
           AND AUTHOR)
           ♦ META
STEINLACH
P.026 / A2 ▼24 JUSTUS E. WALBAUM
           (TYPE FOUNDER, TYPE DESIGNER
           AND PUNCH CUTTER)
           ♦ WALBAUM

STUTTGART
P.025 / E1 ▲38 STAATLICHE AKADEMIE DER
           BILDENDEN KÜNSTE STUTTGART
           AM WEISSENHOF 1,
           70191 STUTTGART
           +49 711 284400
           WWW.ABK-STUTTGART.DE
           --
P.025 / E1 ■20 BUCHHANDLUNG RITA LIMACHER
           KÖNIGSTRASSE 28,
           70173 STUTTGART
           +49 711 292509
           MAIL@LIMACHER.DE
           WWW.LIMACHER.DE
           --
P.025 / E1 ▼22 WILLI BAUMEISTER
           (PAINTER, TYPOGRAPHER, COMMERCIAL
           ARTIST, STAGE DESIGNER AND TEACHER)
           ♦ <RING NEUE WERBEGESTALTER>
TRIER
P.020 / B2 ▲25 FACHHOCHSCHULE TRIER
           SCHNEIDERSHOF J/105,
           54293 TRIER
           +49 651 8103445
           N.THUL@FH-TRIER.DE
           WWW.FH-TRIER.DE
ULM
P.025 / F1 ▼23 OTL AICHER
           (TYPE DESIGNER, GRAPHIC DESIGNER,
           AUTHOR AND TEACHER)
           ♦ LUFTHANSA AIRLINES,
           1972 SUMMER OLYMPICS
VELBERT
P.016 / B3 ▼02 WILLY FLECKHAUS
           (GRAPHIC DESIGNER, TYPOGRAPHER,
           TEACHER AND ART DIRECTOR)
           ♦ TWEN, SUHRKAMP
WEIMAR
P.021 / B1 ▲34 BAUHAUS-UNIVERSITÄT WEIMAR
           GESCHWISTER-SCHOLL-STRASSE 8,
           99423 WEIMAR
           +49 36 43580
           INFO@UNI-WEIMAR.DE
           WWW.UNI-WEIMAR.DE
           EXHIBITION: WWW.UNI-WEIMAR.DE/RUND
           GANG
           CONFERENCE: PROJEKTIL
           --
P.021 / B1 ▼19 BAUHAUS MUSEUM WEIMAR
           THEATERPLATZ 1,
           99423 WEIMAR
           +49 3643 7450
           TOURIST-INFO@WEIMAR.DE
WERNIGERODE
P.018 / A2 ▼07 PAUL RENNER
           (GRAPHIC ARTIST, PAINTER,
           TYPE DESIGNER, AUTHOR AND TEACHER)
           ♦ FUTURA
WIESBADEN
P.021 / D2 ▲27 FACHHOCHSCHULE WIESBADEN
           KURT-SCHUMACHER-RING 18,
           65197 WIESBADEN
           + 49 611 9495100
           DEKANAT@DCSM.FH-WIESBADEN.DE
           WWW.GESTALTUNG.FH-WIESBADEN.DE
           MAGAZINE: QUER
WISMAR
P.014 / B3 ▲04 HOCHSCHULE WISMAR
           +49 3841 7530
           POSTMASTER@HS-WISMAR.DE
           WWW.HS-WISMAR.DE
           WWW.FH-WISMAR.DE
           --

WUNSTORF
P.017 / E2 ▼04 JOOST SCHMIDT
           (PAINTER, TYPOGRAPHER AND TEACHER)
           ♦ BAUHAUS
WÜRZBURG
P.021 / F2 ▲30 FACHHOCHSCHULE WÜRZBURG
           SCHWEINFURT
           MÜNZSTRASSE 12,
           97070 WÜRZBURG
           +49 0931 3511206
           DESIGN@FH-WUERZBURG.DE
           HTTP://RZWWWNEU.FH-WUERZBURG.DE/
           FH/FB/GESTALTUNG/INDEX1.HTML
WUPPERTAL
P.016 / B3 ▲07 BERGISCHE UNIVERSITÄT WUPPERTAL
           GAUSSSTRASSE 20,
           42119 WUPPERTAL
           +49 202 4390
           WEBMASTER@UNI-WUPPERTAL.DE
           WWW.FBF.UNI-WUPPERTAL.DE
NOT SHOWN
ON THE MAP

           ● ADC
           ADC BRANDS AND IDEAS CONGRESS 2008
           ADC AUSSTELLUNG
           WWW.ADC.DE
           --
           ● LEAD AWARD
           WWW.DEICHTORHALLEN.DE/479.HTML
           WWW.LEADACADEMY.DE
           --
           ● 100 BESTE PLAKATE
           WWW.100-BESTE-PLAKATE.DE
           --
           ● DIE SCHÖNSTEN BÜCHER DEUTSCHLANDS
           WWW.STIFTUNG-BUCHKUNST.DE
           --
           ● ILLUSTRATIVE E.V.
           GORMANNSTR. 23, 10119 BERLIN
           +49 30 48491929
           WWW.ILLUSTRATIVE.DE
           --

WELCOME TO
NEULAND
--
THE FUTURE OF
GERMAN GRAPHIC DESIGN
--

MY NAME IS ANTHONY SALVADOR AND
I'M ORIGINALLY FROM LOS ANGELES.
I PREMATURELY ENDED MY STUDIES
AT THE ART CENTER IN PASADENA TO
WORK IN BERLIN AND POSSIBLY PURSUE
FURTHER STUDIES IN EUROPE. I FOCUS
MOST OF MY ATTENTION ON PRINTED
MATTER WITHIN THE CULTURAL SECTOR
AND HAVE COME TO FIND JOY IN COL-
LABORATION… ESPECIALLY WHEN I GET
TO PAY THE HEATING BILL AFTER-
WARDS.

--

WHAT IS GERMAN?

A LANGUAGE I'M STILL TRYING TO
UNDERSTAND.

WHAT IS GERMAN DESIGN?

IT'S HARD TO SAY BECAUSE I FEEL
THAT THE WORLD IS SO INTERCON-
NECTED THAT REGIONAL AESTHETICS/
IDEAS HAVE BEEN INFLUENCED BY MANY
OTHER IDEAS NOT FROM THAT REGION.
THIS MIGHT BE MAINLY DUE TO THE
SHARING OF IDEAS/KNOWLEDGE MADE
RAPIDLY AVAILABLE BY MEANS OF THE
INTERNET. I FEEL THAT GERMAN DE-
SIGN COULD BE GENERALIZED AS BEING
STRICT AND RIGID, YET I FIND THAT
IF YOU LOOK, YOU CAN FIND WORK
THAT HAS ATTITUDE AND LIFE.

DESCRIBE YOUR WORKING PROCESS.

IT REALLY DEPENDS ON THE PROJ-
ECT. SOMETIMES I WORK JUST BY
TALKING TO THE CLIENT AND INTER-
CHANGING IDEAS ABOUT WHAT SHOULD
BE MADE AND GET TO WORK VISUAL-
IZING THOSE THOUGHTS. OTHER TIMES
I HAVE A CLIENT WHO HAS NO IDEA
WHAT THEY WANT, AND I JUST HAVE TO
GO BUILD SOMETHING OR THINK ABOUT
SOMETHING COMPLETELY DIFFERENT
AND IRRELEVANT TO DEVELOP SOME
SORT OF THOUGHT IN MY SUBCON-
SCIOUS. I DON'T THINK I'VE TACKLED
PROJECTS BY USING THE SAME PROCESS
TWICE.

WHAT DO YOU AIM TO ACHIEVE WITH
YOUR WORK?

I WOULD LIKE TO END WORLD HUN-
GER… OR AT LEAST DEVELOP SOME
BOOKLETS WITH TIPS ON HOW TO DO
THAT.

YOU'VE INVITED A FRIEND TO
GERMANY; NAME ONE PLACE THEY
REALLY MUST VISIT AND A QUINT-
ESSENTIAL EXPERIENCE YOU REC-
OMMEND.

TOUGH TO SAY, BECAUSE I PERSON-
ALLY HAVEN'T EXPLORED ENOUGH OF
GERMANY YET. BUT IF A FRIEND CAME
HERE, I WOULD SAY TO VISIT BERLIN.
IT'S MUCH TOO EASY TO FIND A BUNCH
OF THINGS TO DO HERE THAT START
EARLY IN THE MORNING AND END (OR
CONTINUE) WELL BEYOND THE SAME
TIME YOU STARTED THE DAY BEFORE.
I DO RECOMMEND THIS FUNKY BAR
CALLED PONG.

WHAT IS THE MOST IMPORTANT
LESSON YOU HAVE LEARNED IN YOUR
PROFESSION SO FAR?

I FEEL THAT SOME PEOPLE TAKE
THIS <PROFESSION> A BIT TOO SERI-
OUSLY. I HAVE LEARNED THAT IF YOU
DON'T HAVE FUN WITH YOUR WORK, IT
WILL BECOME A CHORE AND THE VOICE
IN YOUR WORK WILL REFLECT THAT. IF
THAT BECOMES THE CASE, IT CAN BE
HARD TO BUILD UP THE SPIRIT AGAIN
TO EXPLORE, SO SOMETIMES IT'S GOOD
TO IMPROVISE AND LET THINGS SLIDE.

--

ANTHONY SALVADOR

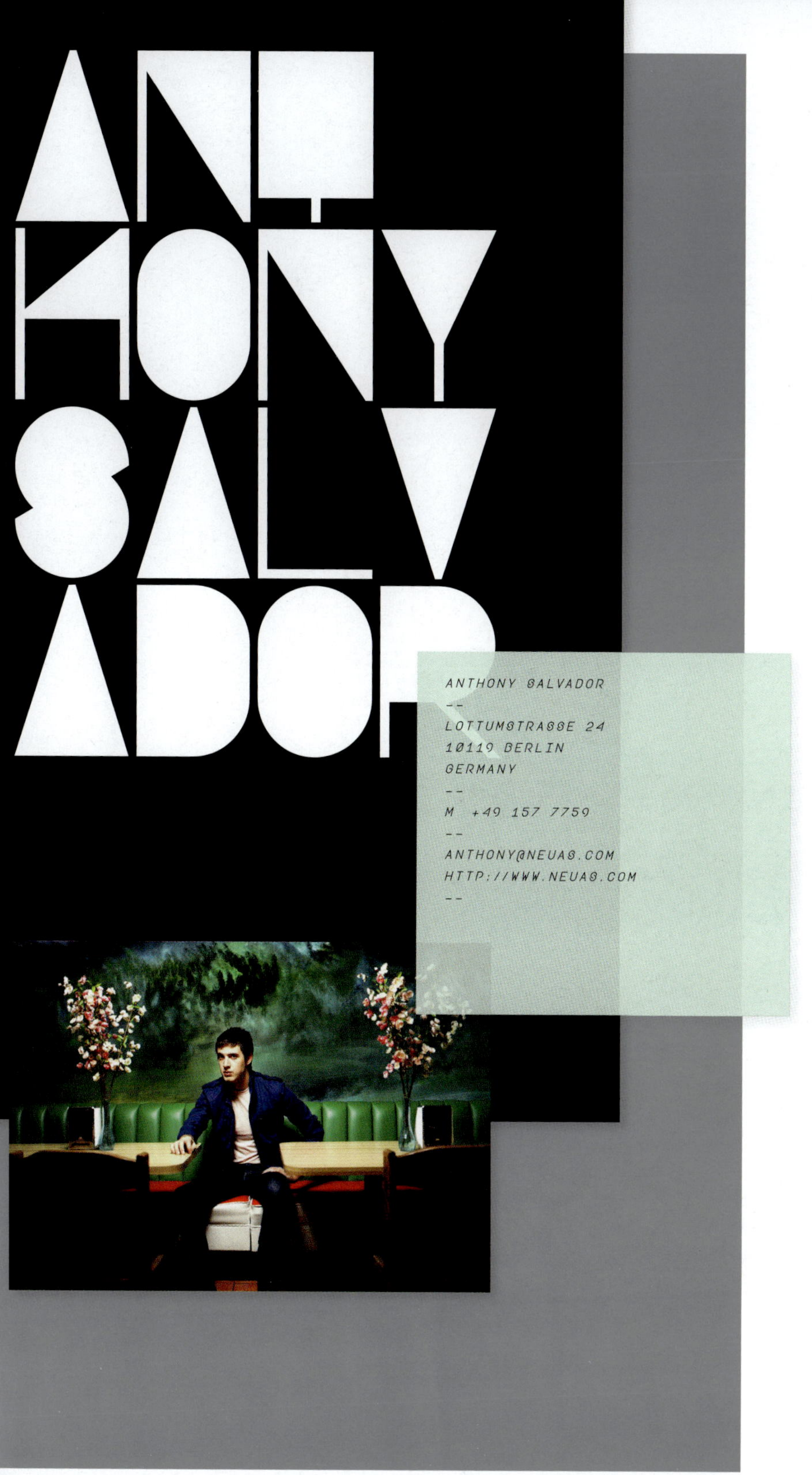

ANTHONY SALVADOR
- -
LOTTUMSTRASSE 24
10119 BERLIN
GERMANY
- -
M +49 157 7759
- -
ANTHONY@NEUA9.COM
HTTP://WWW.NEUA9.COM
- -

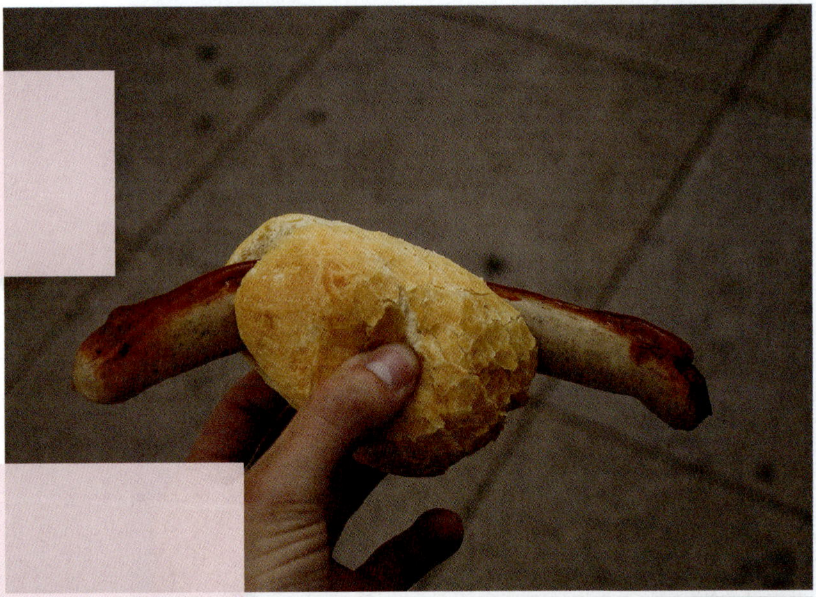

SOMETHING UTTERLY GERMAN
--

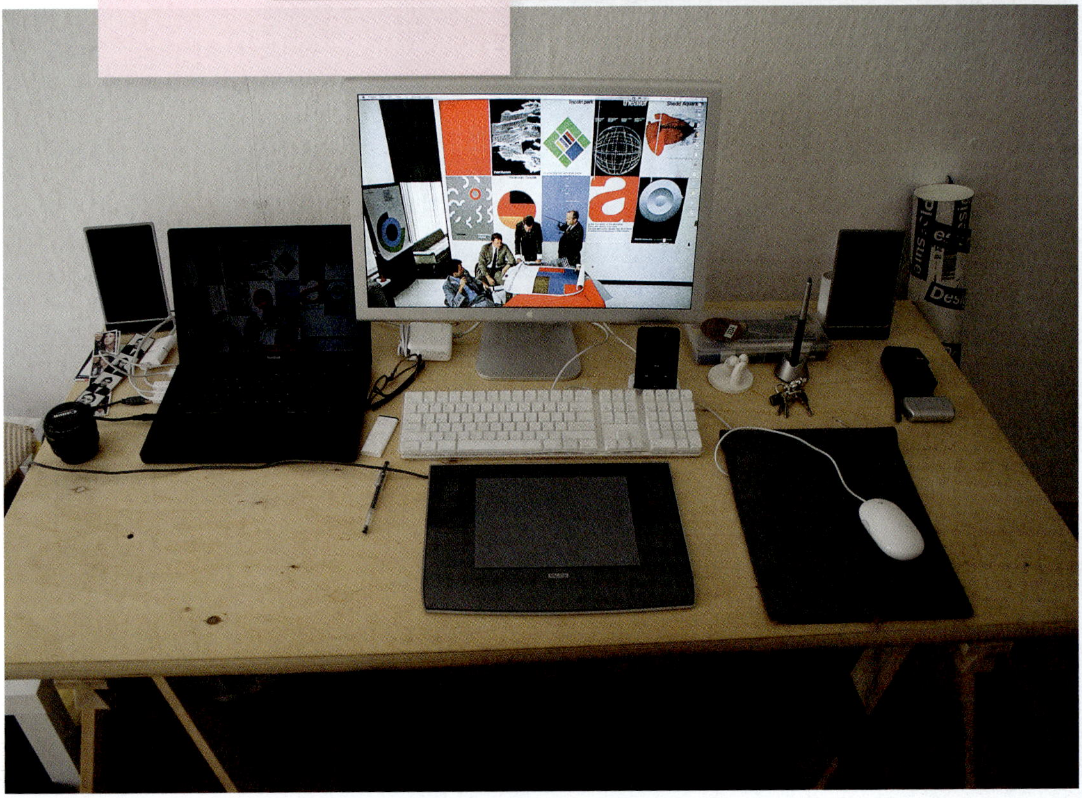

WORKPLACE
--

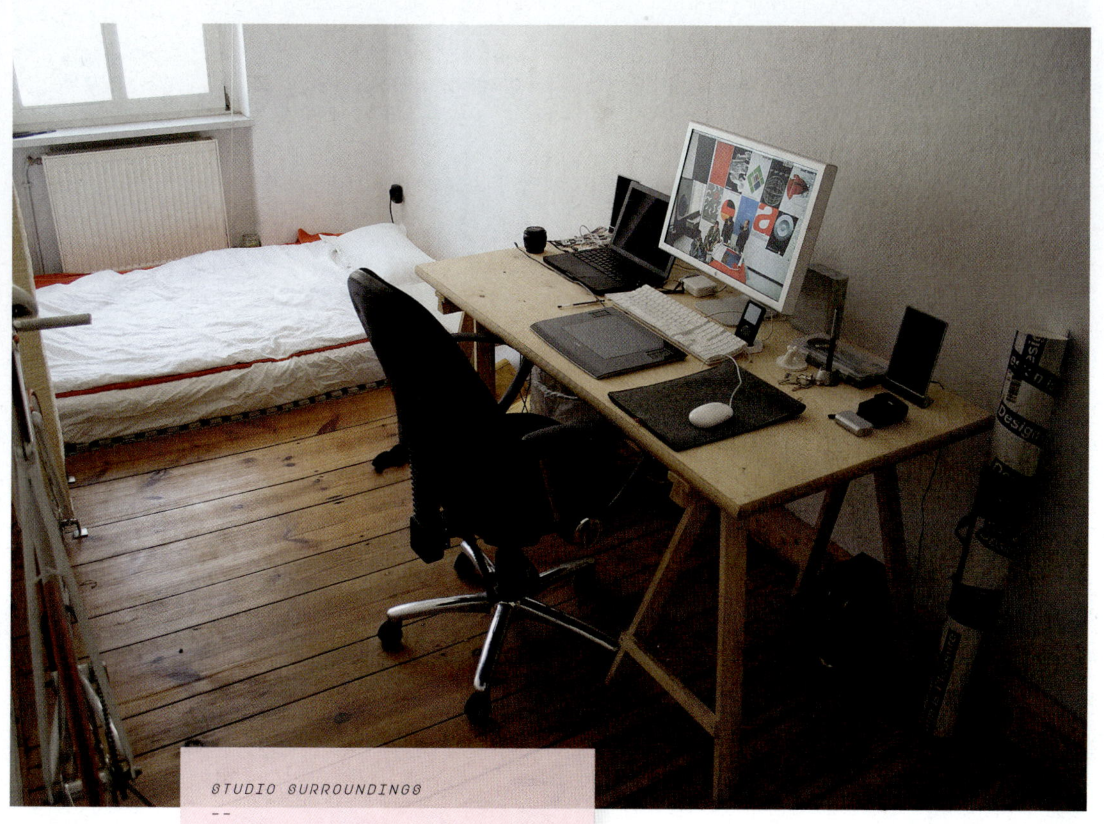
STUDIO SURROUNDINGS
--

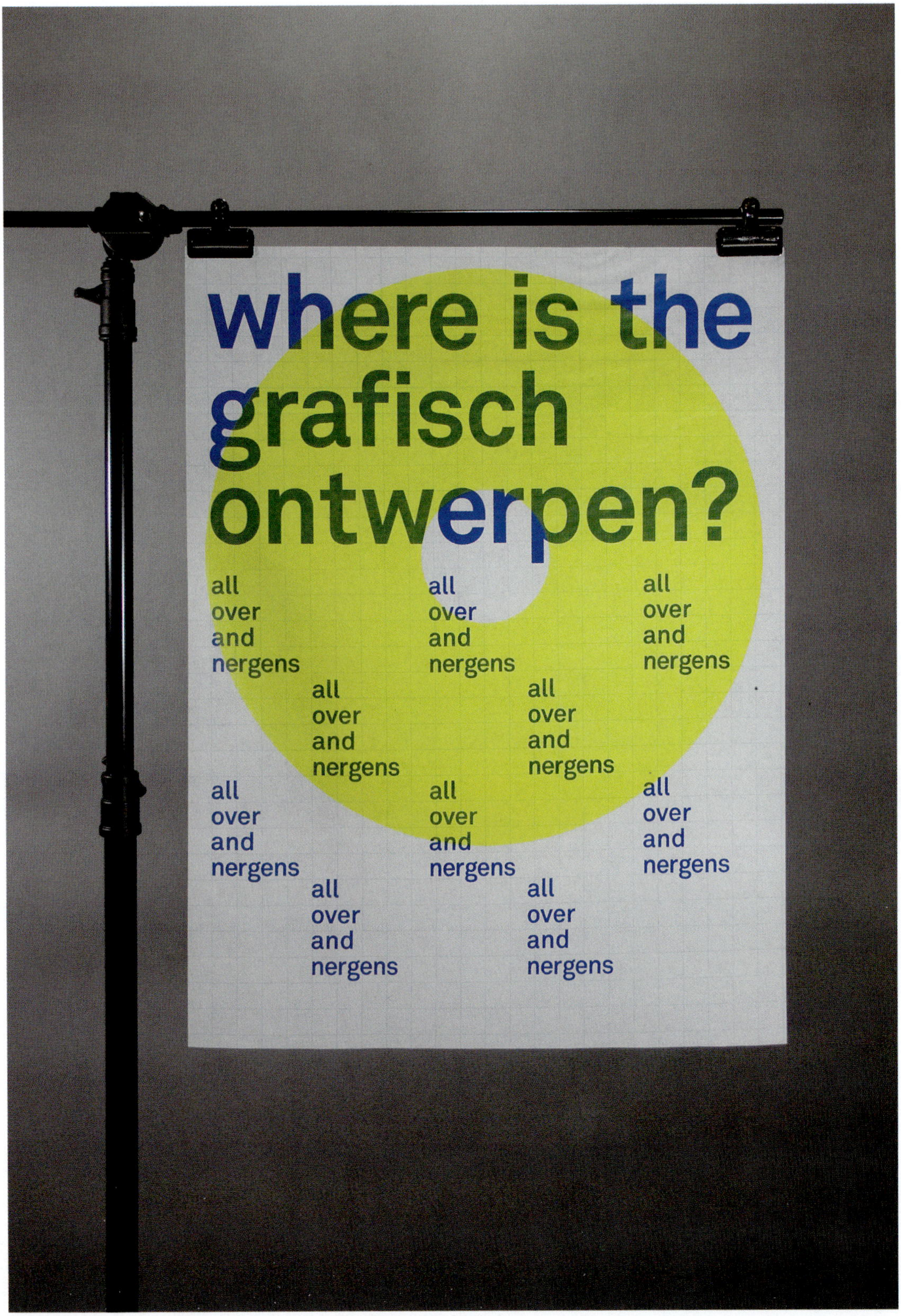

where is the grafisch ontwerpen?
all
over
and
nergens
all
over
and
nergens
all
over
and
nergens
all
over
and
nergens
all
over
and
nergens
all
over
and
nergens
all
over
and
nergens
all
over
and
nergens
all
over
and
nergens

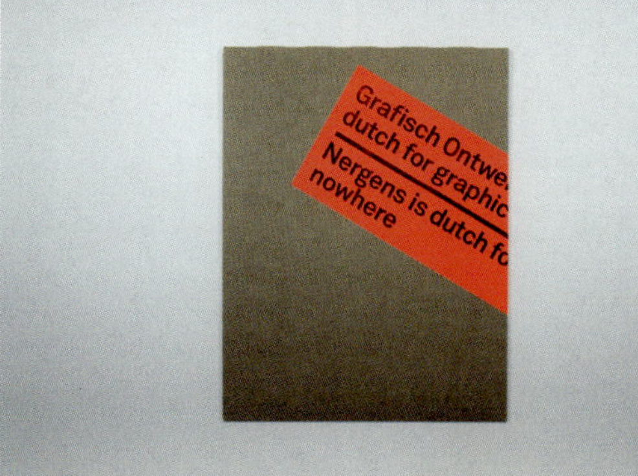

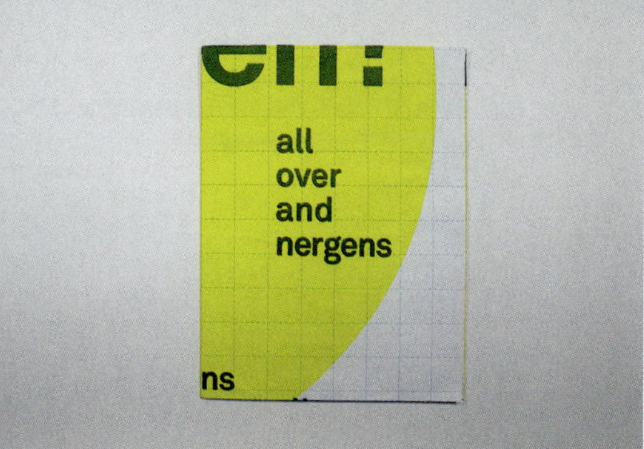

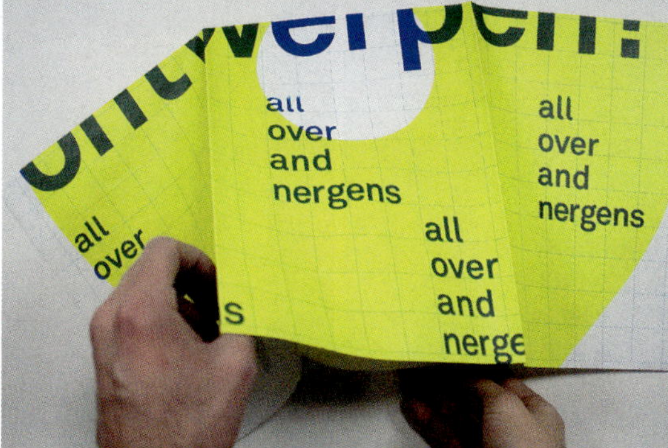

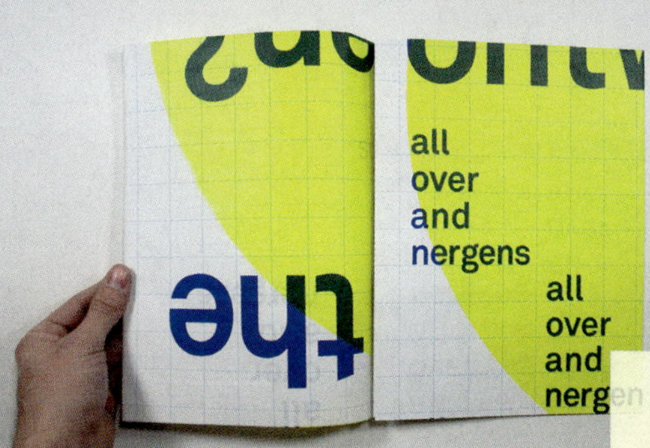

GRAFISCH ONTWERPEN
--
THE IDEA FOR THIS POSTER CAME
FROM A TRIP I TOOK WITH A FRIEND
TO THE NETHERLANDS. I CAME TO
REALIZE THAT GOOD DESIGN IS SEEM-
INGLY EVERYWHERE, YET NOWHERE
AT THE SAME TIME. THE POSTER WAS
SCREEN-PRINTED AS AN EDITION OF
50 WITH THE HELP OF TONY ZEPEDA.
--

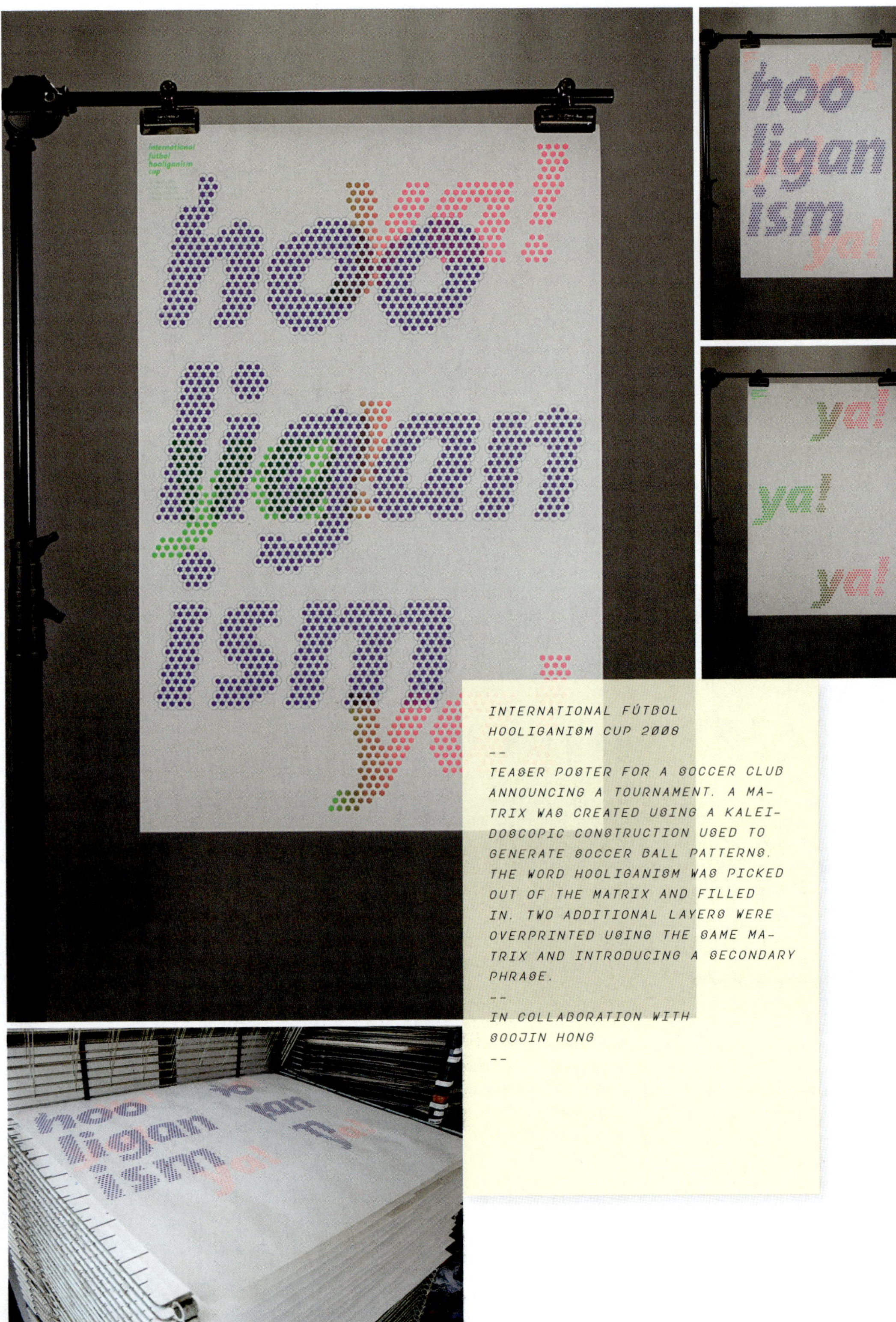

international
fútbol
hooliganism
cup

INTERNATIONAL FÚTBOL
HOOLIGANISM CUP 2008
--
TEASER POSTER FOR A SOCCER CLUB
ANNOUNCING A TOURNAMENT. A MA-
TRIX WAS CREATED USING A KALEI-
DOSCOPIC CONSTRUCTION USED TO
GENERATE SOCCER BALL PATTERNS.
THE WORD HOOLIGANISM WAS PICKED
OUT OF THE MATRIX AND FILLED
IN. TWO ADDITIONAL LAYERS WERE
OVERPRINTED USING THE SAME MA-
TRIX AND INTRODUCING A SECONDARY
PHRASE.
--
IN COLLABORATION WITH
SOOJIN HONG
--

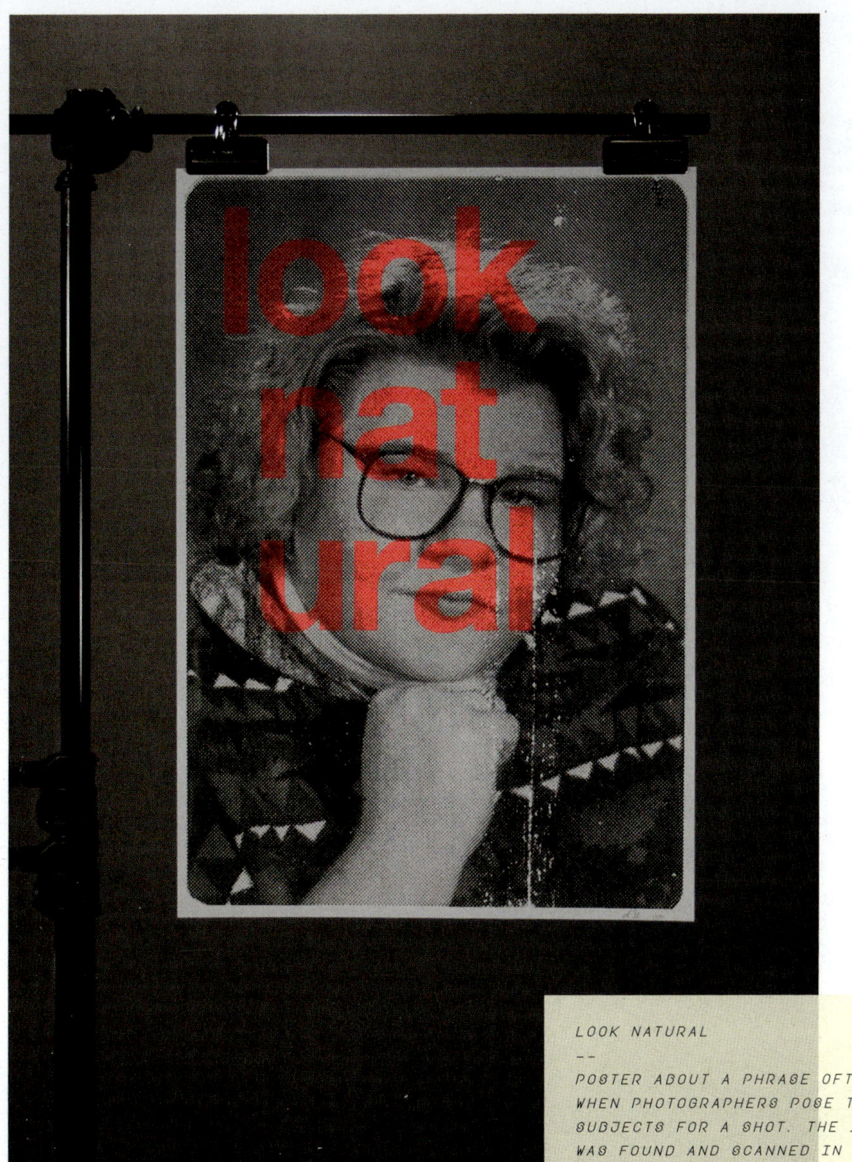

look
nat
ural

LOOK NATURAL
--
POSTER ABOUT A PHRASE OFTEN SAID
WHEN PHOTOGRAPHERS POSE THEIR
SUBJECTS FOR A SHOT. THE IMAGE
WAS FOUND AND SCANNED IN TO MAKE
FILM WORK FOR A SALT PRINT WHICH
WAS THEN BLOWN UP AND TURNED
INTO FILM WORK FOR A SILK SCREEN.
--

Foto de Hans Van der Meer

expo

EXPOSICIÓN DE LA
MODERNA SOCIEDAD DE BARCELONA
--
THE IDENTITY FOR THE EMSB WORKS
OFF EXISTING MATERIAL AND TEX-
TURES. THE MARK IS KEPT NEUTRAL
WHILE LETTING THE WORK IN THE
EXHIBITION CREATE THE TONE AND
VOICE. THE BOOKLET IS PRINTED
ON A CONTINUOUS ROLL TO DIMIN-
ISH PRODUCTION COSTS AND IS SELF
BOUND.
--
TUTOR: SIMON JOHNSTON
--

EMSB/ Exposición de la
Moderna Sociedad
de Barcelona

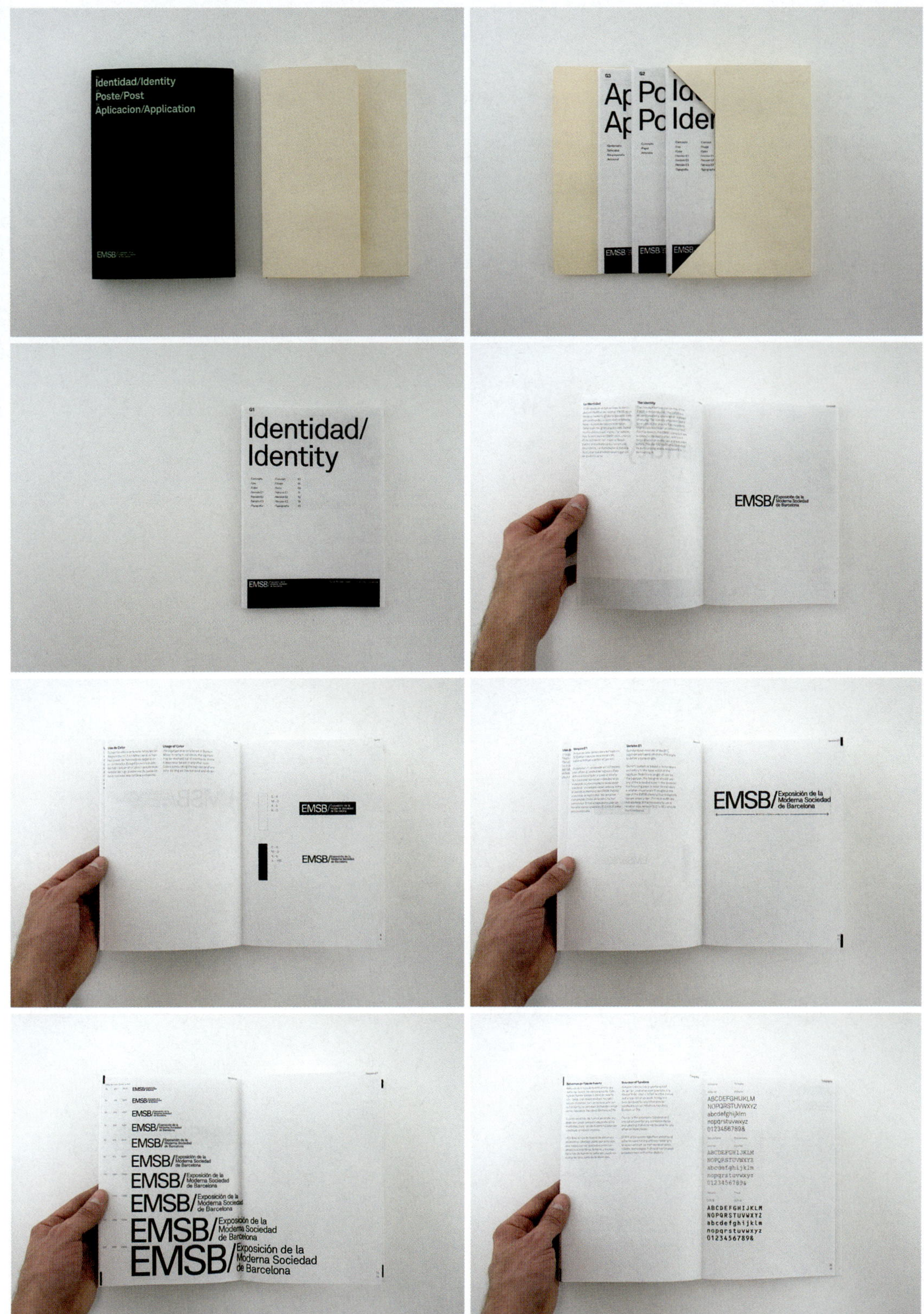

THERE ARE TWO OF US - A FRENCH/GERMAN COUPLE - PLUS ONE INTERN AND SOME ASSOCIATED DESIGNERS. AS THINKING DESIGNERS WITH A LENGTHY EXPERIENCE OF WORKING FOR CLIENTS AND AGENCIES AS FREELANCERS, WE FOUNDED BANK™ BECAUSE WE LIKE THE IDEA OF BEING IN CONTACT WITH OTHER POINTS OF VIEW AND OTHER OPINIONS WHILE WORKING ON SOMETHING. AS A WORKING GROUP WITH AN INTERNATIONAL NETWORK OF OTHER DESIGNERS/ARTISTS/MUSICIANS WE ARE ABLE TO CONNECT TALENTS FROM DIFFERENT FIELDS FOR CERTAIN NEEDS.

--

WHAT IS GERMAN?

SEBASTIAN BISSINGER: A REAL-LIFE EXAMPLE: MY PARTNER AND GIRLFRIEND LAURE BOER HAS A SPANISH GRANDMOTHER AND A FRENCH ONE, BUT SHE'S FRENCH. OUR LATEST INTERN HAS GRANDPARENTS WHO LIVED IN MEXICO AND IS HALF POLISH, BUT HE GREW UP IN GERMANY. THE MOTHER OF MY GERMAN/FRENCH SON WAS BORN IN FRANCE, HER FATHER IS AFRO-AMERICAN, HER MOTHER HALF FRENCH, HALF PERUVIAN. HER STEPFATHER IS GERMAN, BUT HIS FIRST WIFE WAS KOREAN. SO HER STEPSISTER IS HALF GERMAN AND HALF KOREAN AND MEANWHILE HAS MARRIED AN AMERICAN. MY FATHER WAS BORN IN AUSTRIA AND GREW UP IN MEXICO, AND HIS MOTHER WHO WAS OF GERMAN ORIGIN HAD ALREADY BEEN BORN THERE. MY SISTER HAS A SON WHOSE FATHER IS BRITISH. ONE OF MY BEST FRIENDS AND A BUSINESS PARTNER, NIKOLAI WOLFF, IS MARRIED TO AN ARGENTINEAN WOMAN AND HAS TWO CHILDREN, OUR NEIGHBORS AT THE OFFICE BOTH COME FROM THE STATES, OUR PREVIOUS INTERN WAS A SWEDE. MY OTHER BEST FRIENDS ARE BRITISH, HUNGARIAN AND HALF ITALIAN. THE BRITISH MAN IS LIVING WITH A GREEK WOMAN WHO WAS ACTUALLY BORN IN GERMANY, THE HUNGARIAN WAS IN FACT BORN IN GERMANY, HAS A CHILD WITH AN IRISH WOMAN AND TWO MORE WITH AN AUSTRIAN WOMAN. THE HALF ITALIAN - HE WAS BORN IN GERMANY TOO - IS LIVING WITH A BULGARIAN WOMAN. MY COUSIN HAS JUST MARRIED A CANADIAN GIRL, MY UNCLE IS LIVING WITH A RUMANIAN, AND MY AUNT HAS BEEN MARRIED TO HER HUSBAND, A VENEZUELAN OF GERMAN ORIGIN, FOR THIRTY YEARS.

P.S. ALL BUT THREE OF THOSE MENTIONED LIVE IN GERMANY.

WHAT IS GERMAN DESIGN?

VISUAL FORMS OF EXPRESSION SEEM INCREASINGLY TO BE ASSOCIATED WITH CERTAIN SCENES, TENDENCIES AND FASHIONS THAT ARE NOT CONFINED TO COUNTRIES. A MINGLING OF INFLUENCES IS TAKING PLACE IN DESIGN WHICH ON THE ONE HAND COME FROM EVERY PART OF THE WORLD AND ON THE OTHER FROM EVERY POSSIBLE DISCIPLINE. TODAY IT'S MUCH HARDER THAN IT WAS TEN OR FIFTEEN YEARS AGO TO DEMONSTRATE A <HERITAGE> SPECIFIC TO ONE COUNTRY.

PLEASE DESCRIBE YOUR WORKING PROCESS.

WE ALWAYS TRY TO FIGURE OUT WHAT THE REAL NEEDS OF THE CLIENT OR A CERTAIN PROJECT ARE AND THEN WE FIND AN APPROPRIATE FORM FOR IT. WE WORK PRETTY FREELY ON DIFFERENT APPROACHES, LOOKING OVER IT TOGETHER AND FIGURING OUT WHICH IS THE MOST INTERESTING WAY TO GO. WE ALL WORK IN PARALLEL ON DIFFERENT ASPECTS OF ONE JOB. TO REALIZE ONE'S OWN PROJECTS (FROM DESIGN TO EVENTS LIKE WWW.GOODANDPLENTY.DE OR THE ASSOCIATION OF FEMALE DESIGNERS 1/2 - HTTP://1DEMI.CANALBLOG.COM) IS A VERY IMPORTANT PART OF OUR WORK.

WHAT DO YOU AIM TO ACHIEVE WITH YOUR WORK?

WE TRY TO TAKE PART IN THE CONSTANT DEVELOPMENT OF VISUAL CULTURE BY DOING THINGS THAT ARE MORE INTERESTING, MORE PUZZLING AND MORE EFFECTIVE THAN MOST OF THE GRAPHIC DESIGN WE ALL SEE EVERY DAY. FOR US IT'S IMPORTANT TO HAVE SOCIAL AND POLITICAL RESPONSIBILITY INSTEAD OF SERVING AND NOT QUESTIONING OMNIPRESENT CAPITALISTIC STUPIDITY.

YOU'VE INVITED A FRIEND TO GERMANY; NAME ONE PLACE THEY REALLY MUST VISIT AND A QUINTESSENTIAL EXPERIENCE YOU RECOMMEND.

THE DEUTSCHES MUSEUM IN MUNICH.

BA NK

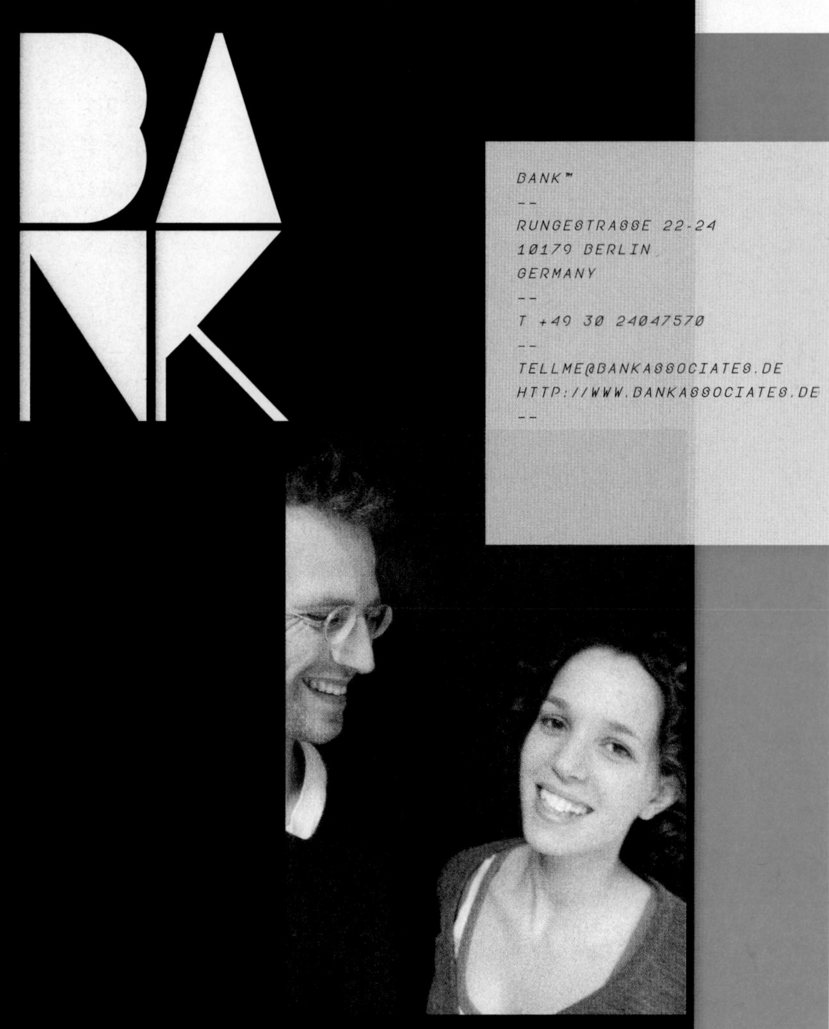

BANK™
--
RUNGESTRASSE 22-24
10179 BERLIN
GERMANY
--
T +49 30 24047570
--
TELLME@BANKASSOCIATES.DE
HTTP://WWW.BANKASSOCIATES.DE
--

WHAT IS THE MOST IMPORTANT
LESSON YOU HAVE LEARNED IN YOUR
PROFESSION SO FAR?

LINE SPACING. SO THAT YOU CAN
ALSO READ BETWEEN THE LINES.

--

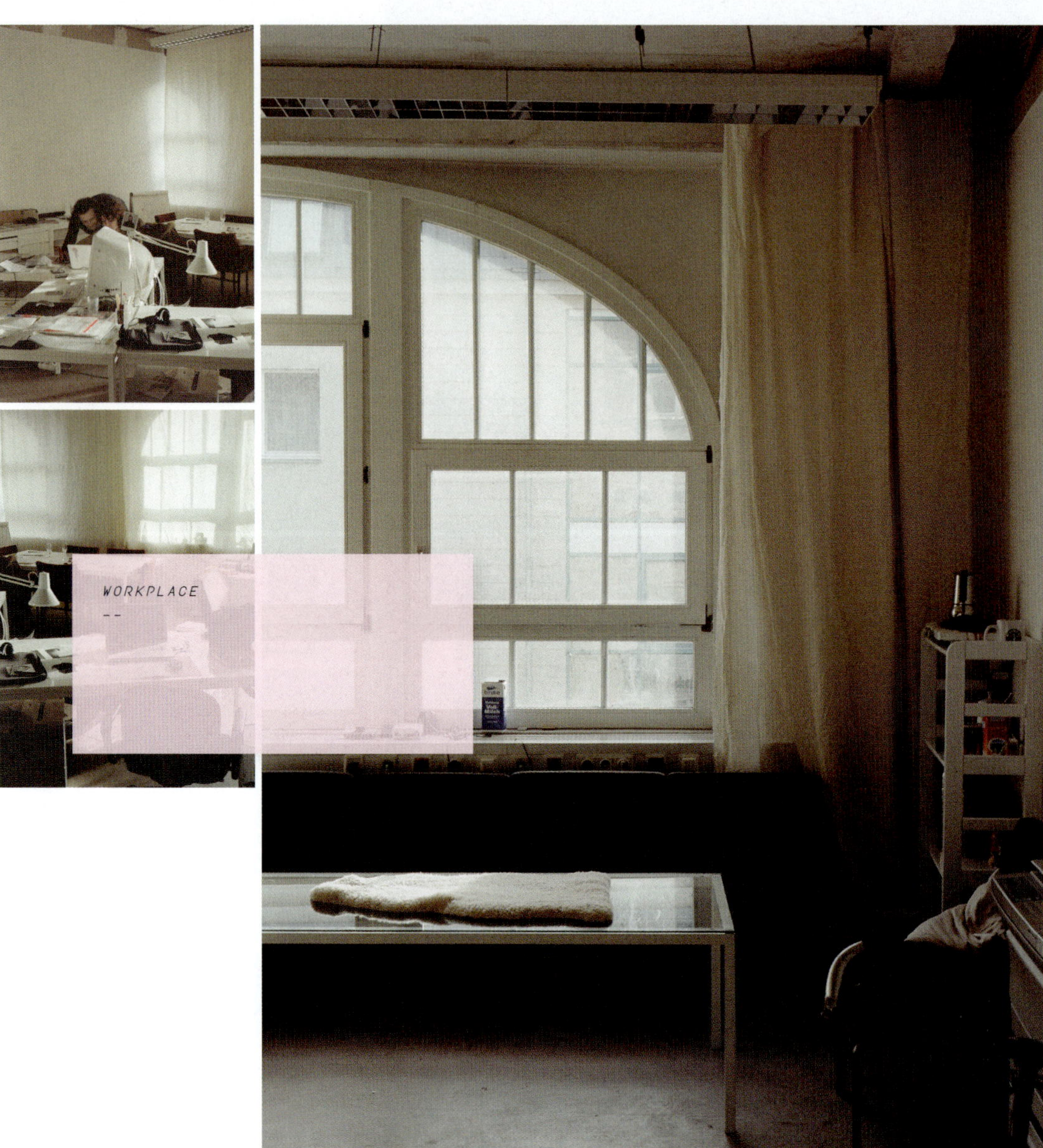
WORKPLACE
--
© ADAM SLOWIK

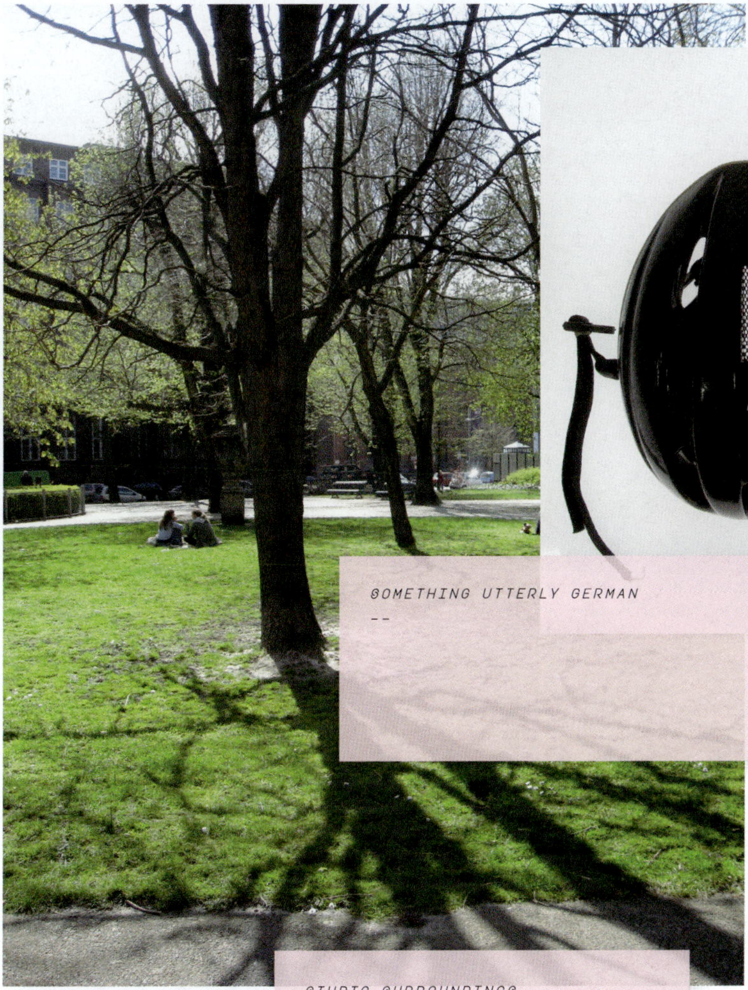

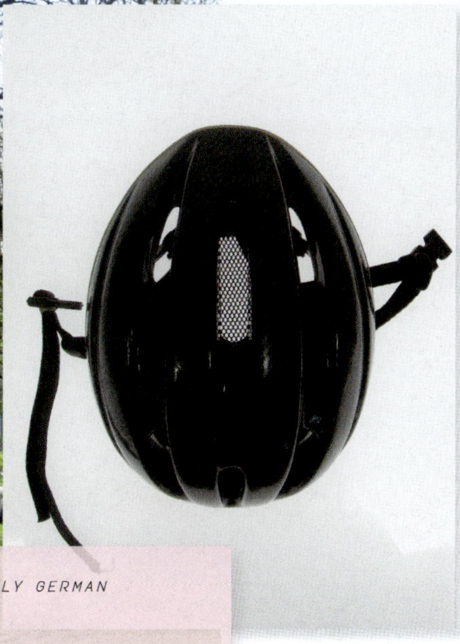

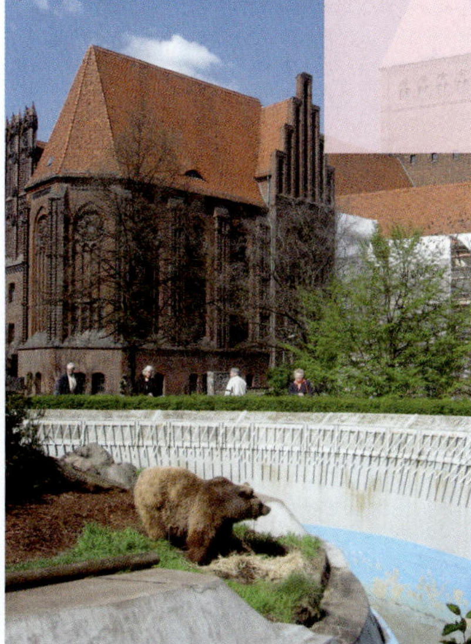

SOMETHING UTTERLY GERMAN
--

STUDIO SURROUNDINGS
--

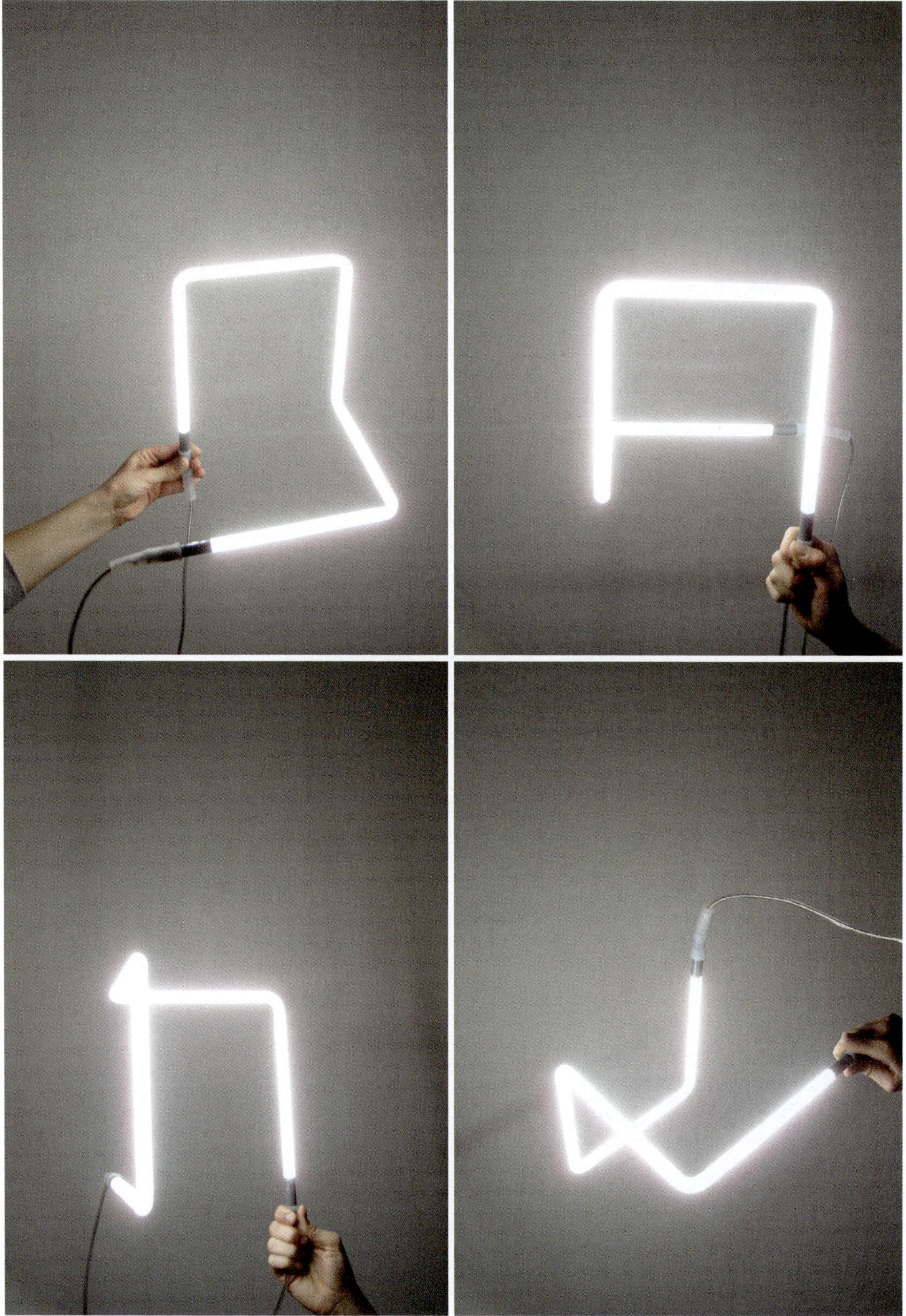

REWIND.
SEBASTIAN, MAIK AND ELISABETH MET
AT THE BAUHAUS UNIVERSITY IN WEI-
MAR. SOME YEARS LATER THEY WOULD
FORM CATK.

PAUSE.
THEY EXPLORED THEIR OWN PATHS.
THEY DEVELOPED THEIR SKILLS. THEY
ESTABLISHED A STYLE. THEY WORKED
WITH FABRICA, DIE GESTALTEN, HESSE
DESIGN, HORT AND MANY OTHER CLI-
ENTS. YET, THEIR PATHS CONVERGED
ON BERLIN, AND AFTER TRAVELING IN-
SIDE GERMANY AND ABROAD, THE PAUSE
FOR CATK WAS OVER.

PLAY.
CATK STARTS PLAYING TOGETHER IN
BERLIN. CATK'S FIELD OF WORK IS
DIRECTION, GRAPHIC DESIGN, MOTION
GRAPHICS, SOUND DESIGN, ILLUSTRA-
TION, EDITORIAL DESIGN AND VIDEO
FOR CULTURE, ART, FASHION AND
MUSIC. THEY CAN BE DESCRIBED AS A
DESIGN STUDIO, YET THEY ARE MUCH
MORE THAN THAT. ASK, AND A CRE-
ATIVE VISUAL RESPONSE IN ANY AREA
WILL BE PROVIDED.

FORWARD.
AT CATK THE FUTURE IS BRIGHT.
FRIENDS ARE WORKING TOGETHER
AND THEY'RE BUILDING A NETWORK
ENABLING THEM TO DEVELOP ANY
CREATIVE PROJECT. THEIR NETWORK
INCLUDES MUSICIANS, PHOTOGRAPHERS,
SOFTWARE DEVELOPERS AND WRITERS.
ANY CREATIVE PROSPECT IS POSSIBLE.
CATK IS WORLDWIDE AND ENJOYS ITS
CAPACITY FOR ORGANIC GROWTH. WITH
A DEFINED STYLISTIC APPROACH,
THEY RENEW THEIR STYLE WITH EVERY
PROJECT, CREATING SOMETHING FRESH
AND UNIQUE EVERY SINGLE TIME. CATK
CAN DANCE TO POP OR TO CLASSICAL.
THE CLIENT LIST WILL CONTINUE TO
GROW AS IT NOW INCLUDES UNIVER-
SAL MUSIC, WARNER MUSIC, BENETTON,
FABRICA, COLORS MAGAZINE, T-COM,
COMEDY CENTRAL, AND MANY SMALL,
INDEPENDENT CLIENTS.

COLOR MATTERS, MUSIC MATTERS AND
COMMUNICATION MATTERS AT CATK. AC-
TUALLY, EVERYTHING MATTERS.

--

WHAT IS GERMAN?

E. TAKING A LEISURELY BREAKFAST…
S. … WITH ROLLS, CHEESE, SAUSAGE,
HONEY, JAM, NUTELLA, PLUM PURÉE…
M. AND SCRAMBLED EGG.

WHAT IS GERMAN DESIGN?

S. THE SK4 BY DIETER RAMS AND HANS
GUGELOT
E. AND THE OPEL MANTA.
M. TURRICAN.

DESCRIBE YOUR WORKING PROCESS.

A. WE GENERALLY GET STARTED AND
THEN PLAN HOW WE'LL CONTINUE, IN
THE MIDST OF IT ALL WE QUARREL AND
RUN OUT OF THE PLACE SHOUTING.
AFTER EVERYONE'S CALMED DOWN WE
SORT OUT THE RESULTS AND REACH A
HARMONIOUS OUTCOME.

WHAT DO YOU AIM TO ACHIEVE WITH
YOUR WORK?

M. A MACHINE DRUM AND A PROFES-
SIONAL CAMERA AND A CHAIR AND A
TRIP TO BRAZIL.
S. A PORSCHE.
E. BEING ABLE TO BUY SEBASTIAN UND
MAIK EVERYTHING THEY WANT

YOU'VE INVITED A FRIEND TO
GERMANY; NAME ONE PLACE THEY
REALLY MUST VISIT AND A QUINT-
ESSENTIAL EXPERIENCE YOU REC-
OMMEND.

M. IN BERLIN SPEND A PROPER RAVE
NIGHT IN THE PANORAMABAR AND AT S
THE NEXT MORNING HAVE A NICE CON-
VERSATION WITH THE TAXI DRIVER.
E. GO TO THE ISLAND OF RÜGEN, FIND
THE LAST NON-TOURISTY CORNER AND
BUILD A <KLECKERBURG> (A SAND CAS-
TLE MADE FROM DRIPPING-WET SAND).
S. I HAVEN'T THE FAINTEST IDEA.

WHAT IS THE MOST IMPORTANT
LESSON YOU HAVE LEARNED IN YOUR
PROFESSION SO FAR?

A. NOT TO TAKE DESIGN AND YOURSELF
TOO SERIOUSLY.

--

E = ELISABETH
S = SEBASTIAAN
M = MAIK
A = ALL

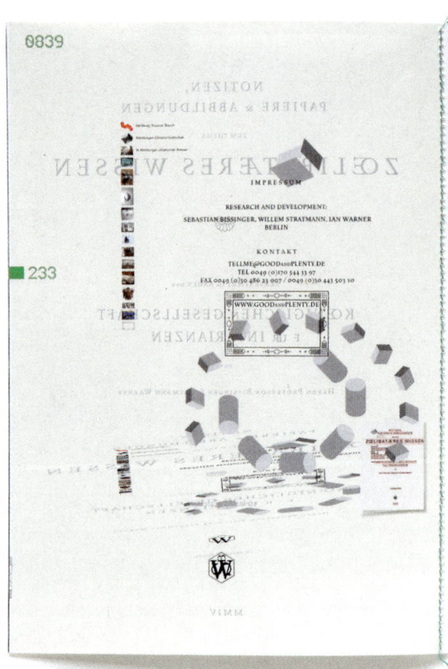
IMPRESSUM

RESEARCH AND DEVELOPMENT:
SEBASTIAN BISSINGER, WILLEM STRATMANN, IAN WARNER
BERLIN

KONTAKT

TELLME@GOODandPLENTY.DE
TEL 0049 (0)170 544 33 97
FAX 0049 (0)30 486 23 007 / 0049 (0)30 443 503 10

WWW.GOODandPLENTY.DE

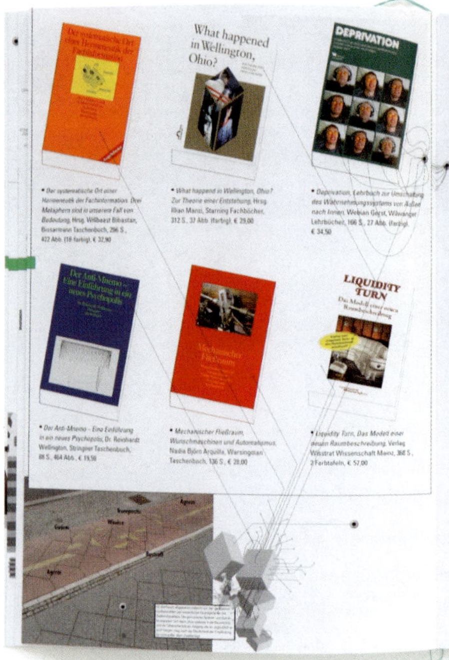
What happened in Wellington, Ohio?

DEPRIVATION

LIQUIDITY TURN

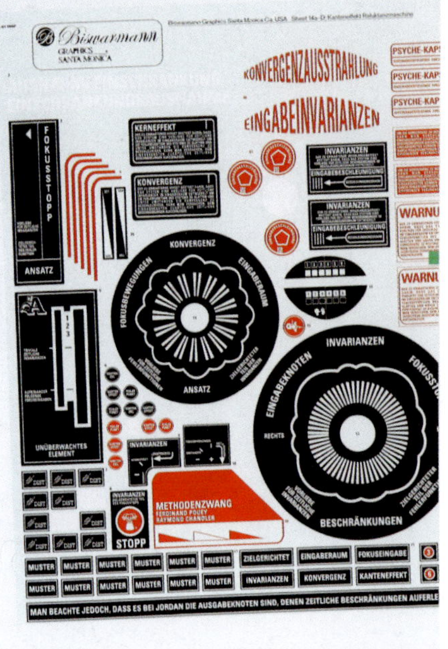
Bissarmann GRAPHICS SANTA MONICA

KONVERGENZAUSSTRAHLUNG
EINGABEINVARIANZEN

PSYCHE-KAP
PSYCHE-KAP
PSYCHE-KAP

FOKUSSTOPP
ANSATZ

KERNEFFEKT
KONVERGENZ

INVARIANZEN
EINGABEBESCHLEUNIGUNG

INVARIANZEN
EINGABEBESCHLEUNIGUNG

WARNU
WARNU

KONVERGENZ
FOKUSBEWEGUNGEN
EINGABERAUM
ANSATZ

INVARIANZEN
EINGABEKNOTEN
RECHTS
FOKUSST

UNÜBERWACHTES ELEMENT

INVARIANZEN
METHODENZWANG
FERDINAND POUEY
RAYMOND CHANDLER
STOPP

BESCHRÄNKUNGEN

MUSTER MUSTER MUSTER MUSTER MUSTER MUSTER   ZIELGERICHTET EINGABERAUM FOKUSEINGABE
MUSTER MUSTER MUSTER MUSTER MUSTER MUSTER   INVARIANZEN KONVERGENZ KANTENEFFEKT

MAN BEACHTE JEDOCH, DASS ES BEI JORDAN DIE AUSGABEKNOTEN SIND, DENEN ZEITLICHE BESCHRÄNKUNGEN AUFERLE

MUSEUM FÜR GESTALTUNG, ZURICH
--
CONTRIBUTION TO THE MAGAZINE DIE
KLASSE, NO. 2 / 16 PAGES. THE
CONTRIBUTION IS ALSO PUBLISHED
SEPARATELY WITH A STITCHED BIND-
ING.
--
CREATIVE DIRECTION, RESEARCH, ED-
ITING, TEXT, DESIGN, PHOTOGRAPHY:
BANK IN COLLABORATION WITH IAN
WARNER (BLOTTO)
--

NOTIZEN,
PAPIERE & ABBILDUNGEN
ZUM THEMA
ZŒLIBATÆRES WISSEN

PRÆSENTIERT IM NAMEN DER
KŒNIGLICHEN GESELLSCHAFT
FUER INVARIANZEN
VON
HERRN PROFESSOR BISSINGER STRATMANN WARNER

16 farbige Tafeln

MMIV

233

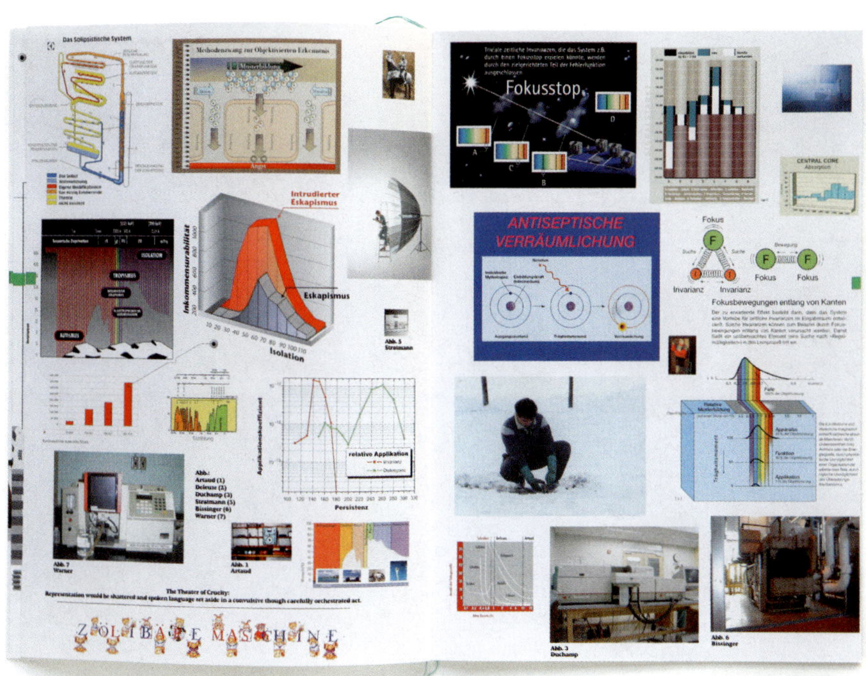

Das Solipsistische System
Methodenreizung zur Objektivierten Erkenntnis
Musterbildung
Angst
Intrudierter
Eskapismus
Inkommensurabilität
ISOLATION
TROPISMUS
AUFBAU
Eskapismus
10 20 30 40 50 60 70 80 90 100 110
Isolation
Abb. 5
Stratmann
relative Applikation
Applikationskoeffizient
Persistenz
Abb.
Artaud (1)
Deleuze (2)
Duchamp (3)
Stratmann (5)
Bissinger (6)
Warner (7)
Abb. 7
Warner
Abb. 1
Artaud
The Theater of Cruelty:
Representation would be shattered and spoken language set aside: in a convulsive though carefully orchestrated act.
ZŒLIBATÆRE MASCHINE
Triviale zeitliche Invarianzen, die das System z.B.
durch einen Fokusstop erzielen könnte, werden
durch den zielgerichteten Teil der Fehlerfunktion
ausgeschlagen.
Fokusstop
A B C D
CENTRAL CORE
Absorption
ANTISEPTISCHE
VERRÄUMLICHUNG
Fokus
Bewegung
Suche
F
Suche
F F
Invarianz Invarianz Fokus Fokus
Fokusbewegungen entlang von Kanten
Abb. 3
Duchamp
Abb. 6
Bissinger

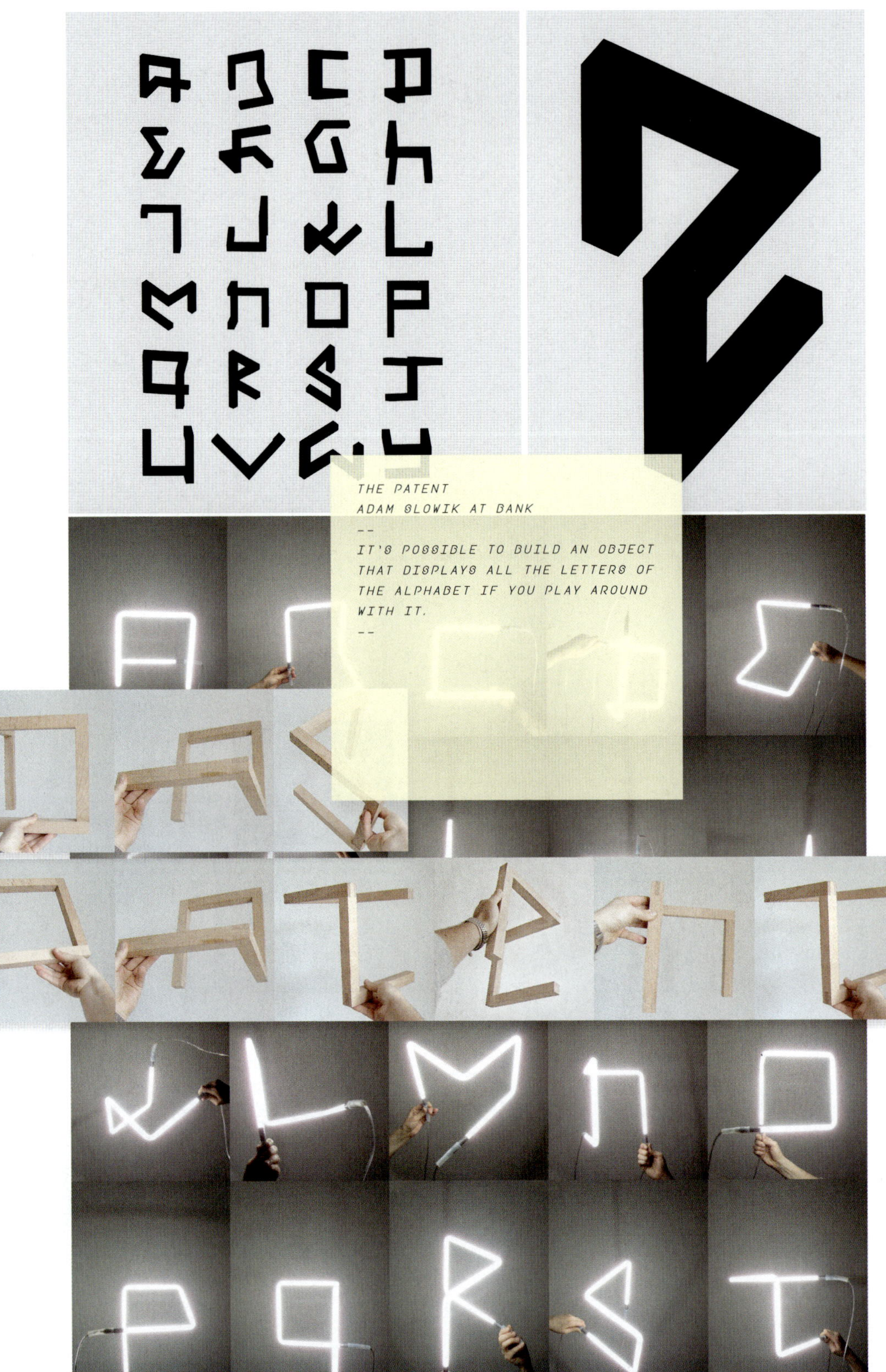
THE PATENT
ADAM SLOWIK AT BANK
--
IT'S POSSIBLE TO BUILD AN OBJECT
THAT DISPLAYS ALL THE LETTERS OF
THE ALPHABET IF YOU PLAY AROUND
WITH IT.
--

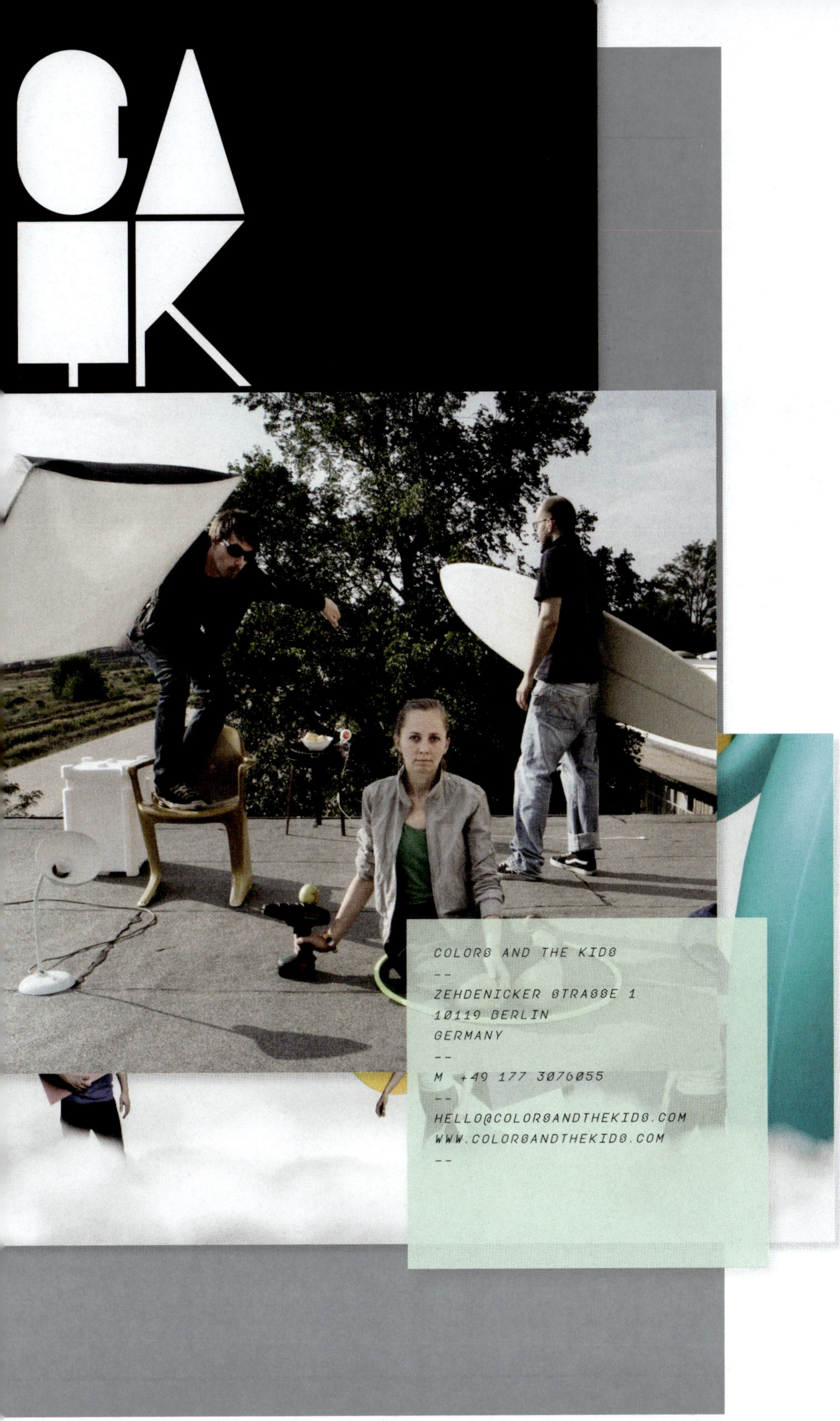

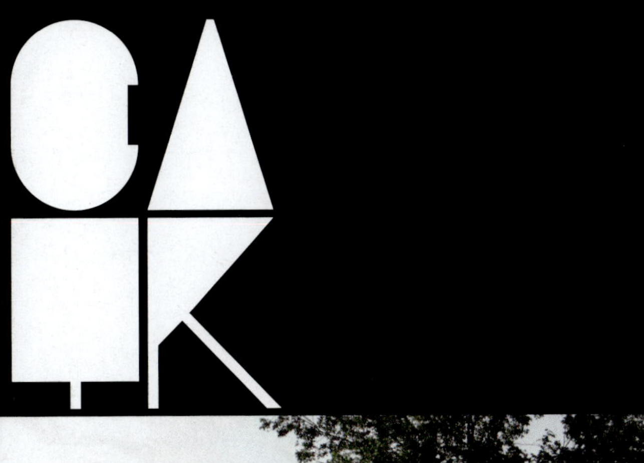

COLORS AND THE KIDS
--
ZEHDENICKER STRASSE 1
10119 BERLIN
GERMANY
--
M +49 177 3076055
--
HELLO@COLORSANDTHEKIDS.COM
WWW.COLORSANDTHEKIDS.COM
--

WORKPLACE
--

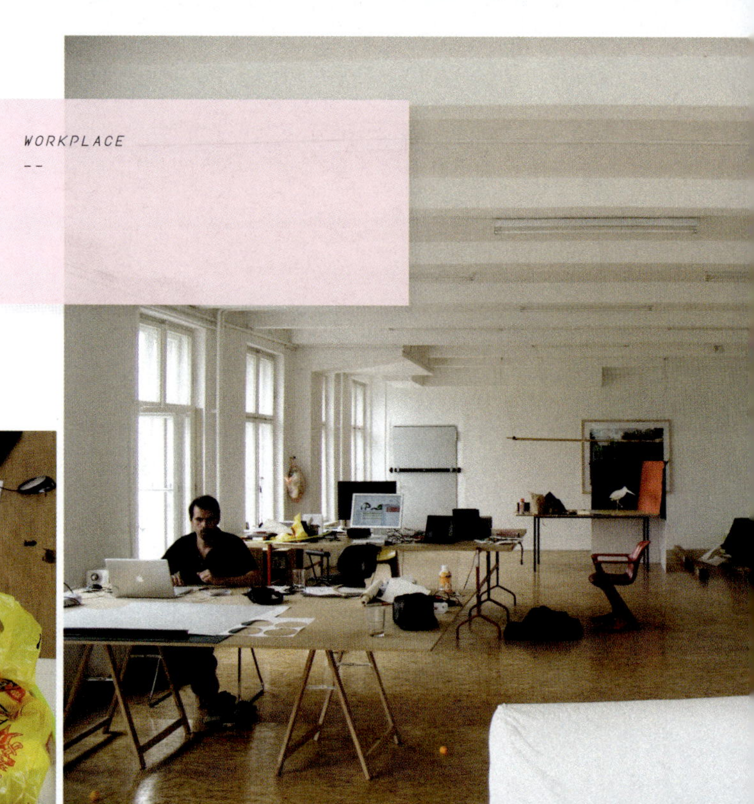

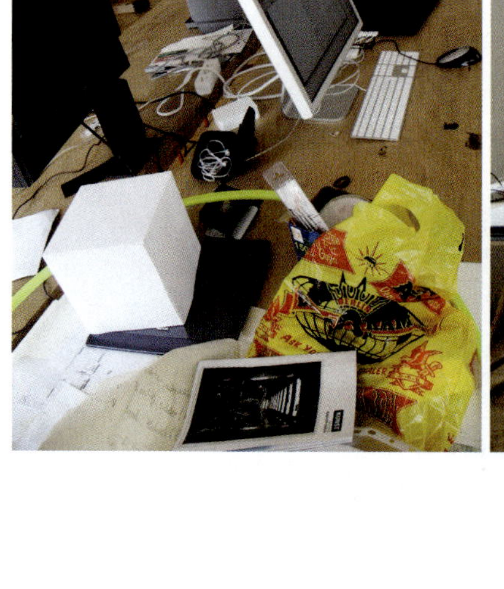

SOMETHING UTTERLY GERMAN
--

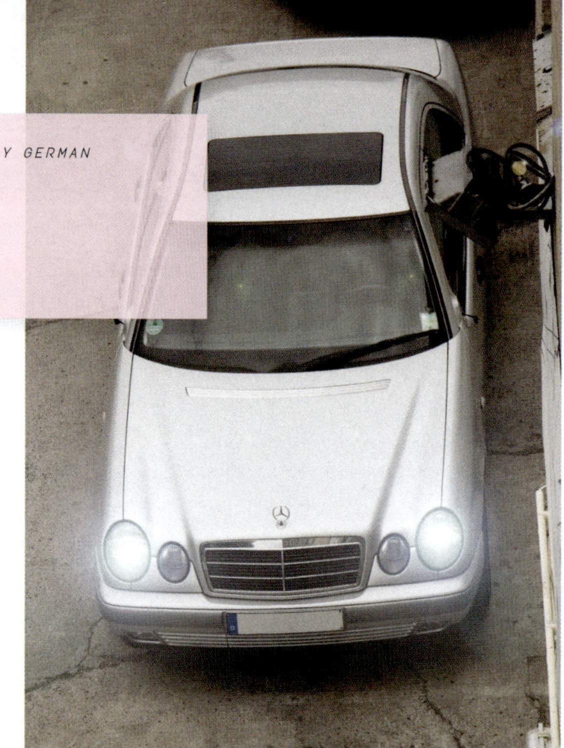

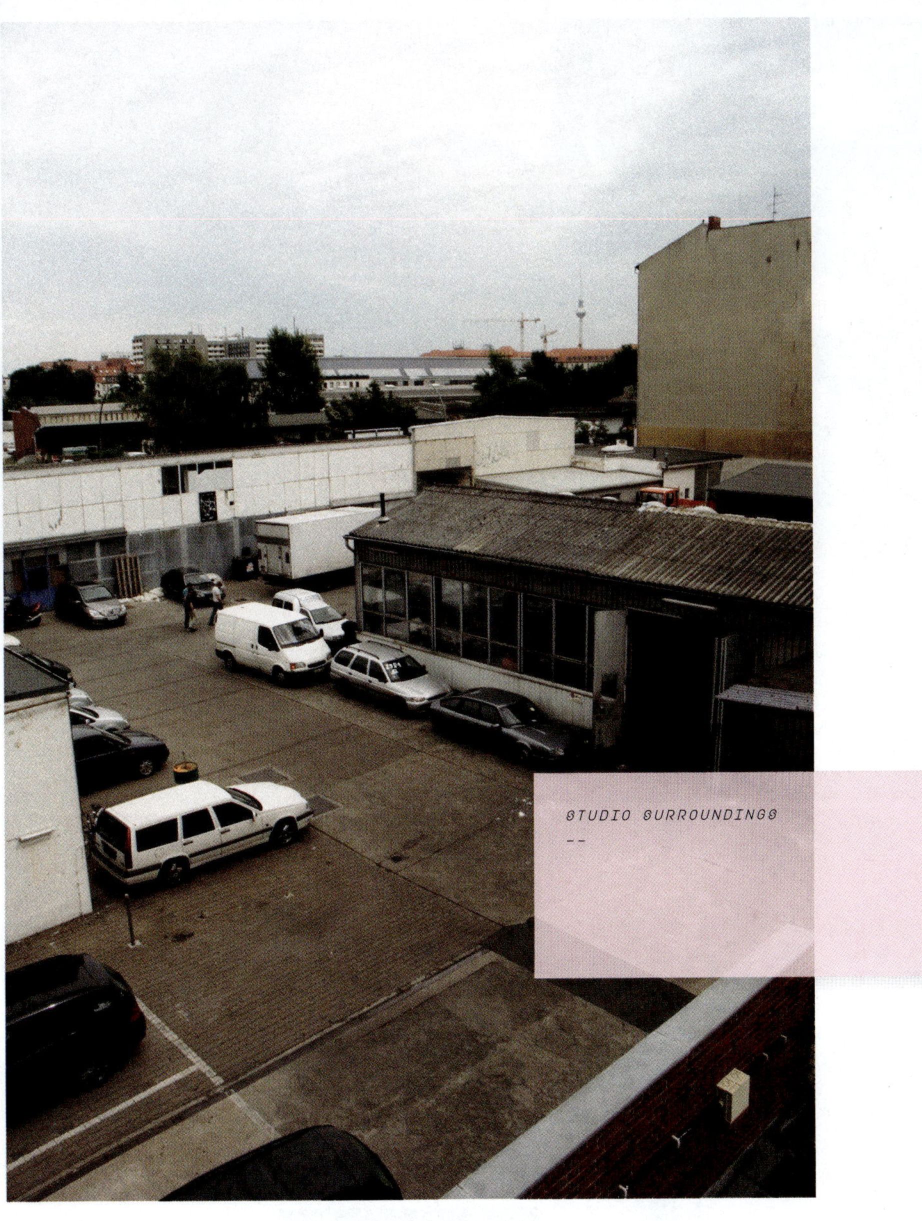
STUDIO SURROUNDINGS
--

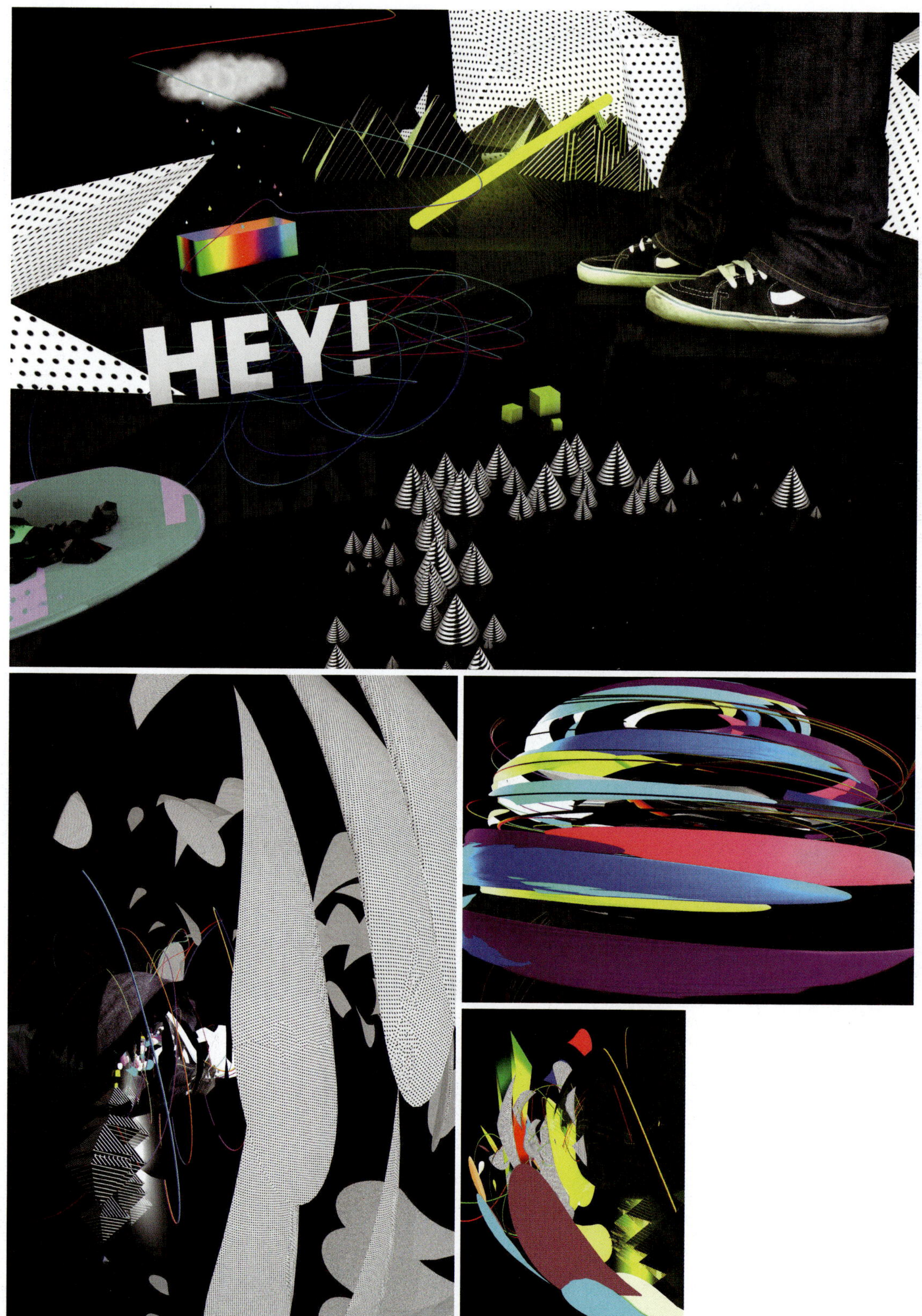
HEY!

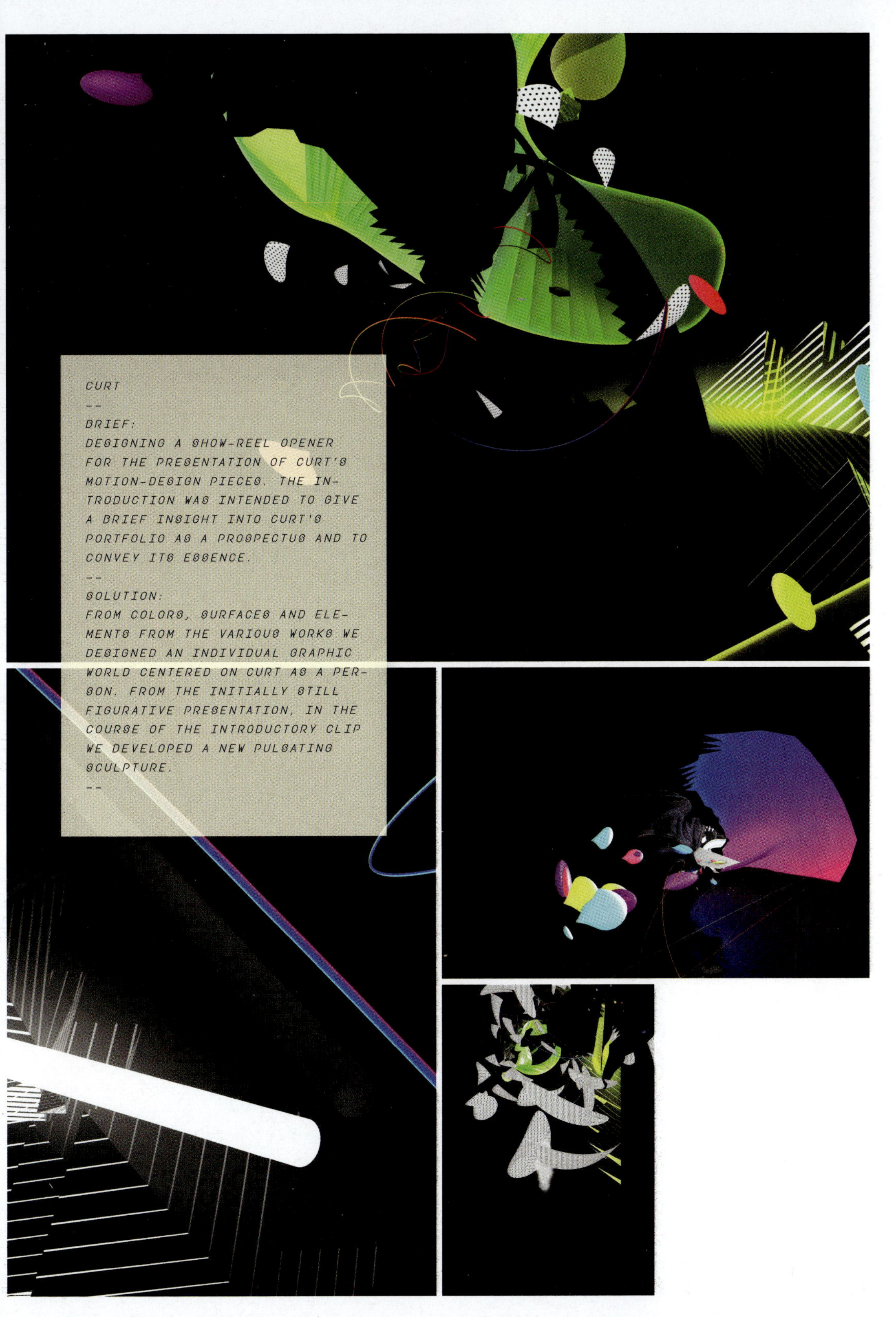

CURT
--
BRIEF:
DESIGNING A SHOW-REEL OPENER
FOR THE PRESENTATION OF CURT'S
MOTION-DESIGN PIECES. THE IN-
TRODUCTION WAS INTENDED TO GIVE
A BRIEF INSIGHT INTO CURT'S
PORTFOLIO AS A PROSPECTUS AND TO
CONVEY ITS ESSENCE.
--
SOLUTION:
FROM COLORS, SURFACES AND ELE-
MENTS FROM THE VARIOUS WORKS WE
DESIGNED AN INDIVIDUAL GRAPHIC
WORLD CENTERED ON CURT AS A PER-
SON. FROM THE INITIALLY STILL
FIGURATIVE PRESENTATION, IN THE
COURSE OF THE INTRODUCTORY CLIP
WE DEVELOPED A NEW PULSATING
SCULPTURE.
--

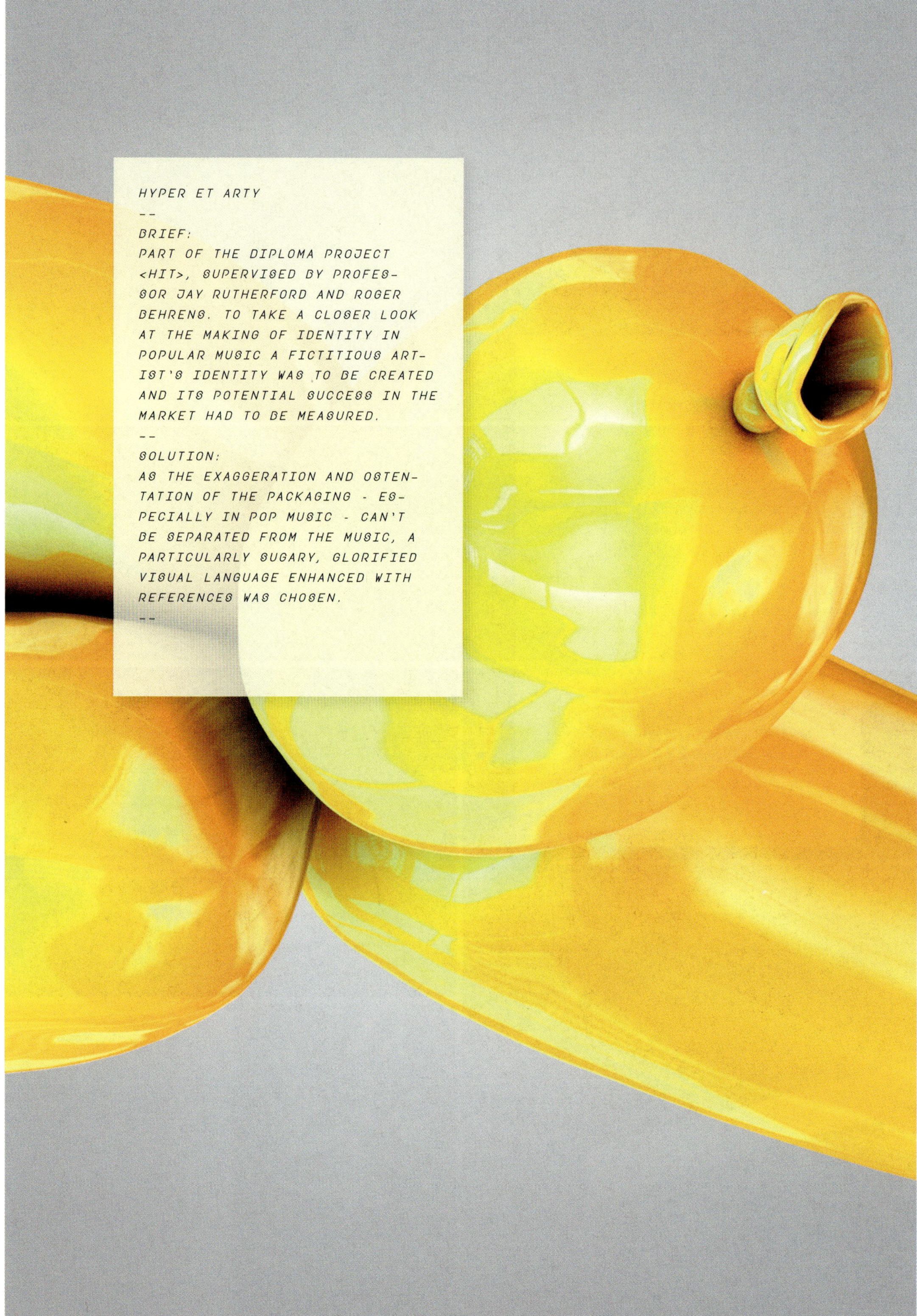

HYPER ET ARTY
--
BRIEF:
PART OF THE DIPLOMA PROJECT
<HIT>, SUPERVISED BY PROFES-
SOR JAY RUTHERFORD AND ROGER
BEHRENS. TO TAKE A CLOSER LOOK
AT THE MAKING OF IDENTITY IN
POPULAR MUSIC A FICTITIOUS ART-
IST'S IDENTITY WAS TO BE CREATED
AND ITS POTENTIAL SUCCESS IN THE
MARKET HAD TO BE MEASURED.
--
SOLUTION:
AS THE EXAGGERATION AND OSTEN-
TATION OF THE PACKAGING - ES-
PECIALLY IN POP MUSIC - CAN'T
BE SEPARATED FROM THE MUSIC, A
PARTICULARLY SUGARY, GLORIFIED
VISUAL LANGUAGE ENHANCED WITH
REFERENCES WAS CHOSEN.
--

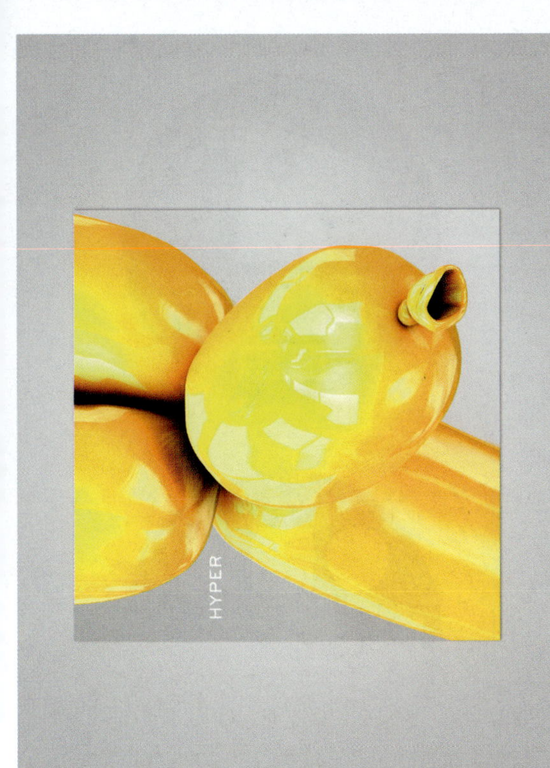

HYPER

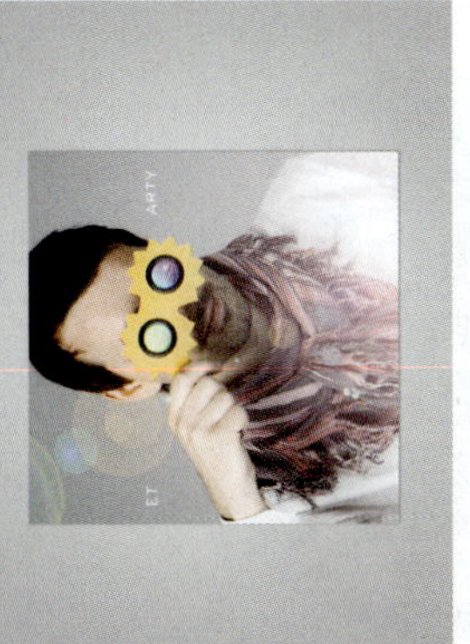

ARTY
ET

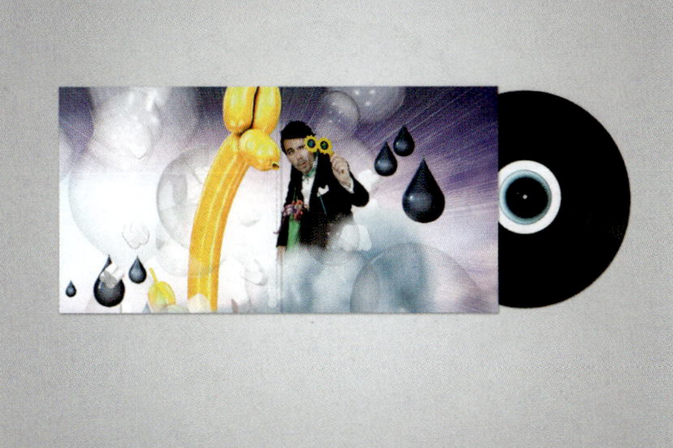

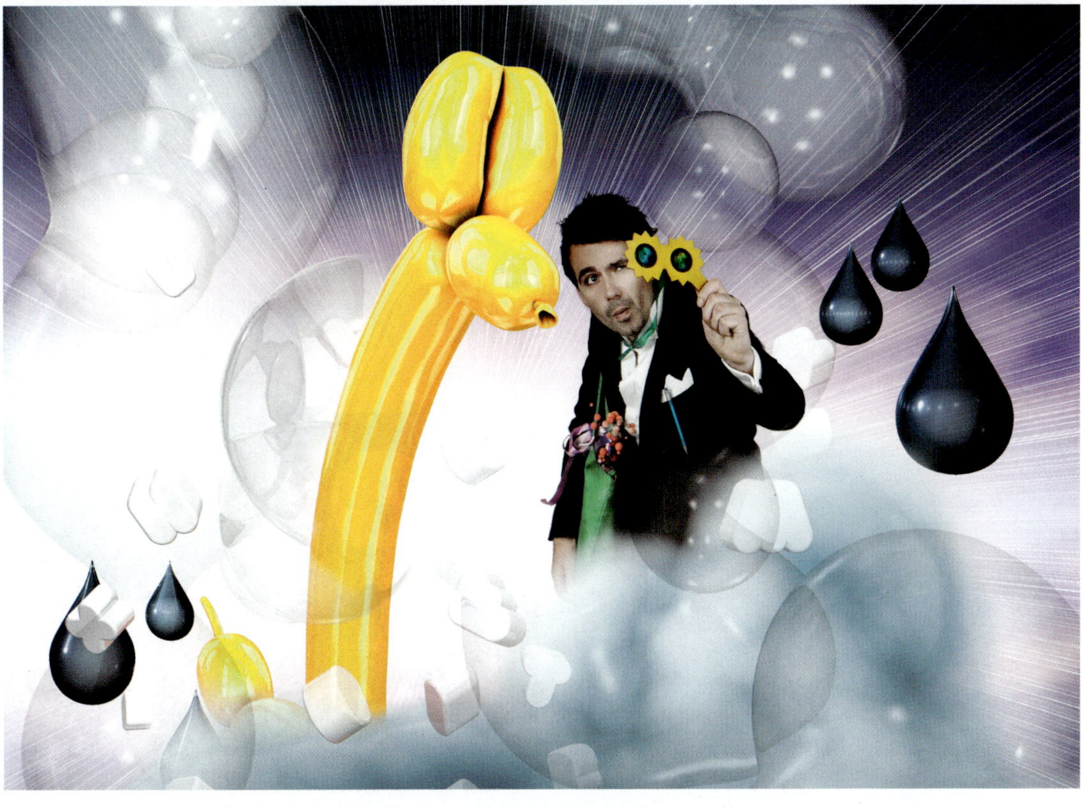

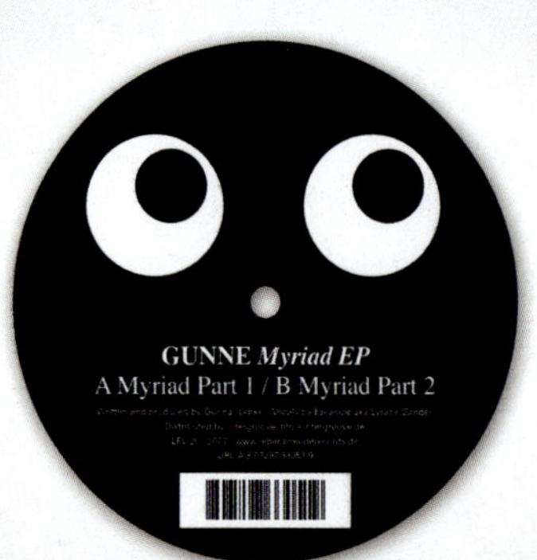

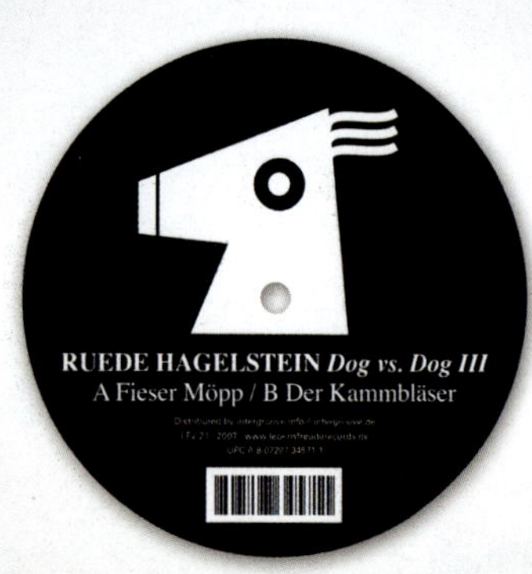

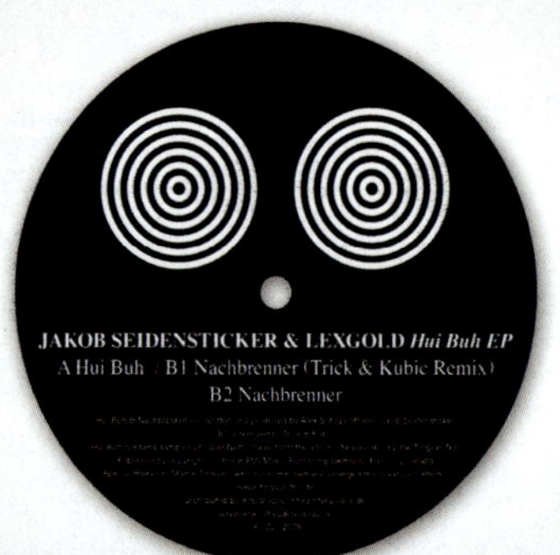

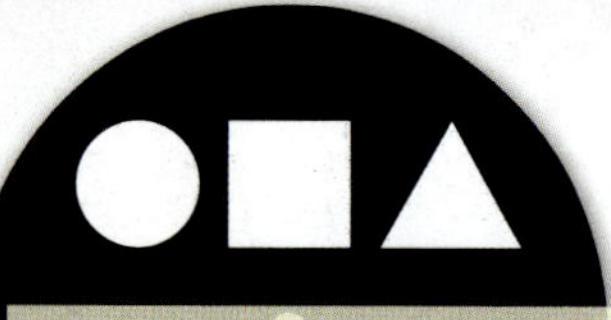

LEBENSFREUDE RECORDS
--
BRIEF:
DEVELOPMENT OF CONCEPT AND DE-
SIGN FOR THE RECORDS OF THE BER-
LIN LABEL LEBENSFREUDE RECORDS.
BECAUSE OF LOWER SALES FIGURES
ON THE VINYL MARKET, A LOW, FI-
NANCIAL OUTLAY WAS AN IMPORTANT
CONSIDERATION FOR THE LABEL.
--
SOLUTION:
IN DEVELOPING THE CONCEPT WE RE-
STRICTED OURSELVES TO USING ONE-
COLOR PRINTING AND A SIMPLE DE-
SIGN SYSTEM WHICH PRODUCES GOOD
RESULTS WITHOUT GREAT EXPENSE.
THE LABEL CONSISTS OF INFORMAL
TYPOGRAPHY AND IN EACH CASE AN
ILLUSTRATION THAT REFERS TO THE
TITLE.
--

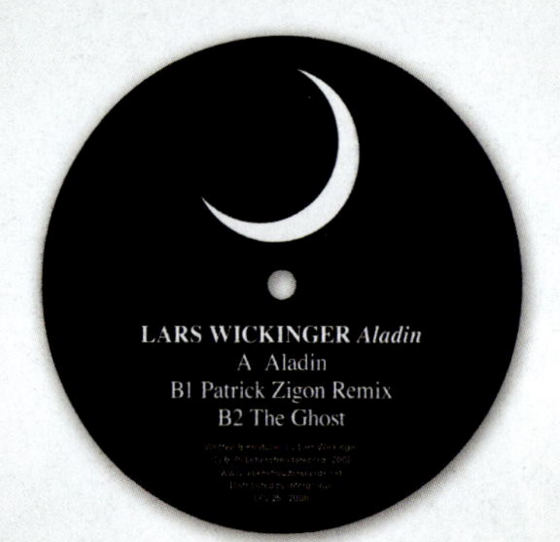

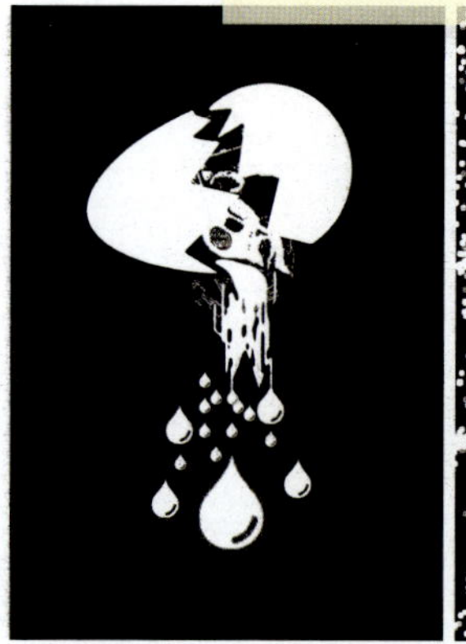

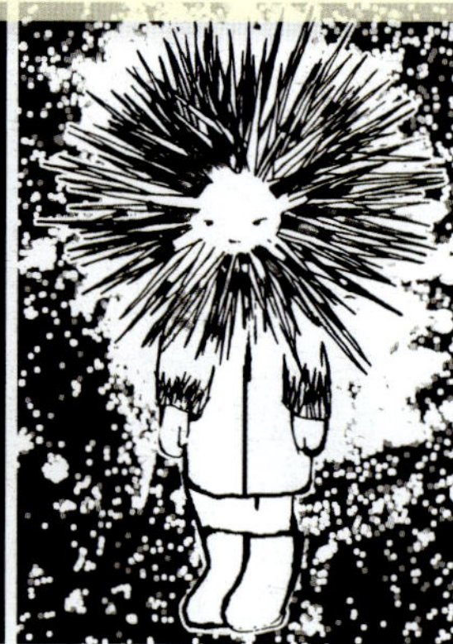

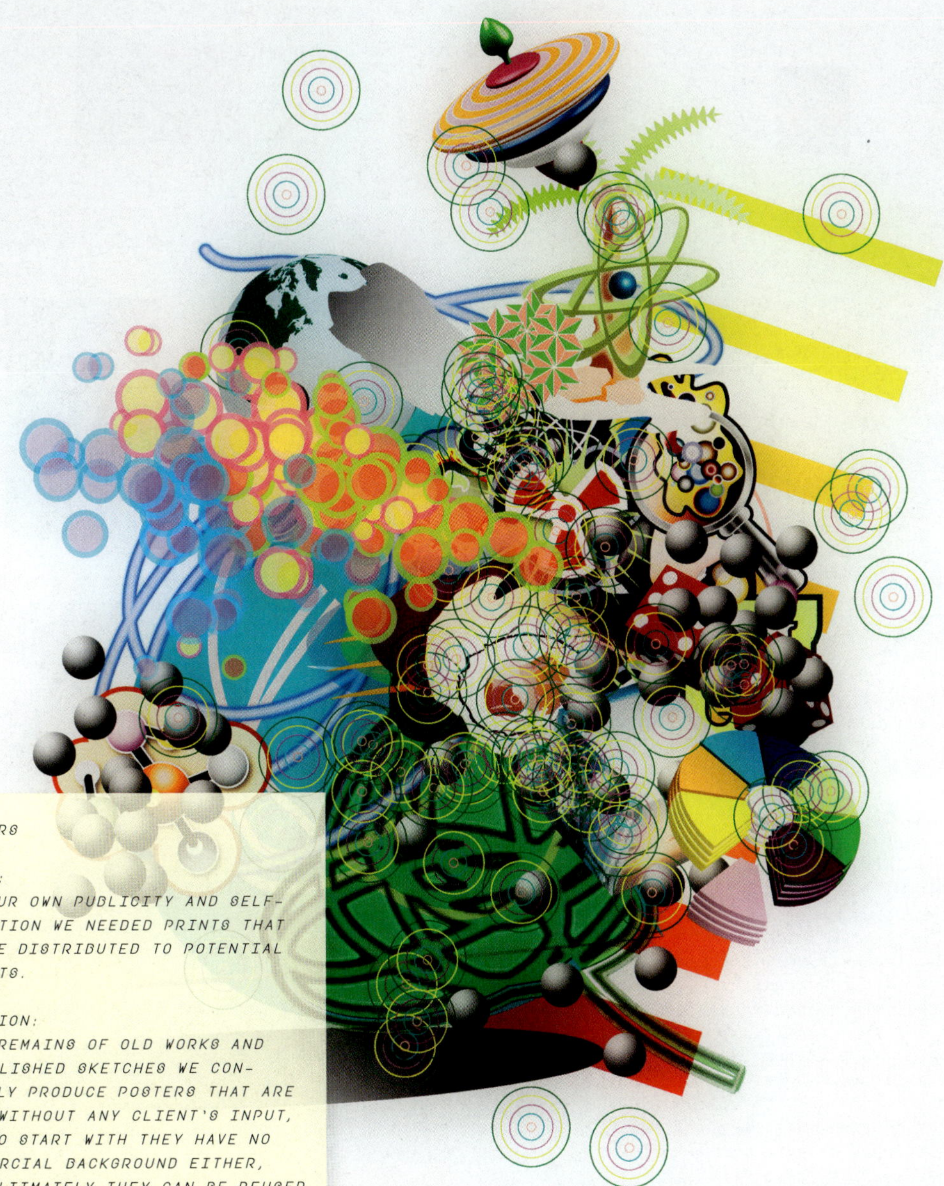

POSTERS
--
BRIEF:
FOR OUR OWN PUBLICITY AND SELF-
PROMOTION WE NEEDED PRINTS THAT
CAN BE DISTRIBUTED TO POTENTIAL
CLIENTS.
--
SOLUTION:
FROM REMAINS OF OLD WORKS AND
UNPUBLISHED SKETCHES WE CON-
STANTLY PRODUCE POSTERS THAT ARE
MADE WITHOUT ANY CLIENT'S INPUT,
AND TO START WITH THEY HAVE NO
COMMERCIAL BACKGROUND EITHER,
BUT ULTIMATELY THEY CAN BE REUSED
FOR THAT TOO.
--

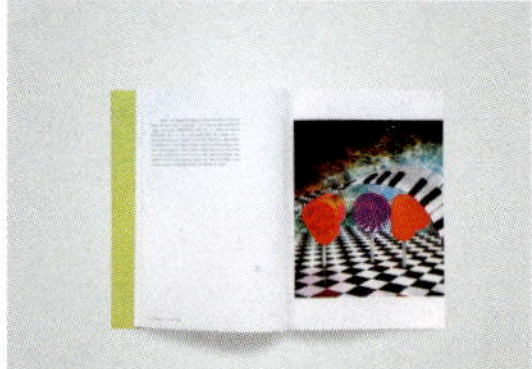

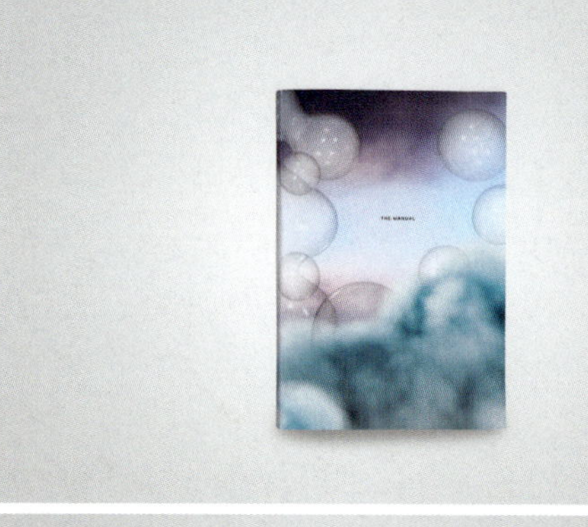

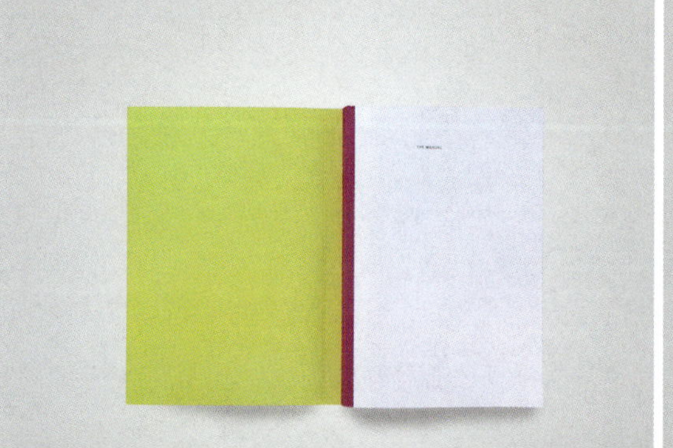

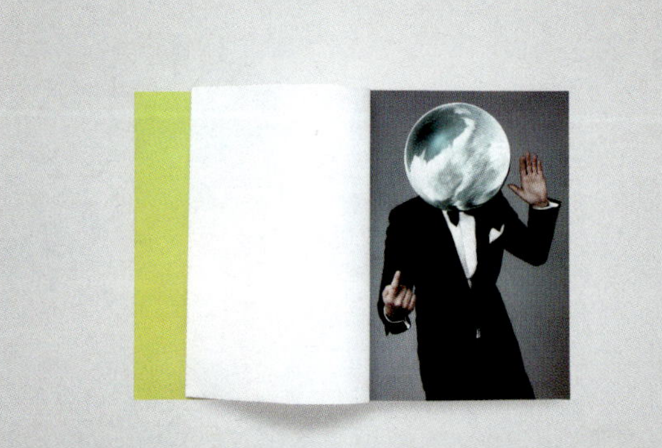

THE MANUAL
--
BRIEF:
PART OF THE DIPLOMA PROJECT <HIT>
CARRIED OUT AT THE BAUHAUS UNI-
VERSITY IN WEIMAR, SUPERVISED BY
PROFESSOR JAY RUTHERFORD. <THE
MANUAL> BY <THE KLF>, WHICH IS
CONCERNED WITH THE PRODUCTION OF
A NUMBER ONE HIT, WAS TO BE GIVEN
A NEW LAYOUT AND ILLUSTRATED.
--
SOLUTION:
AS THE TEXT OF <THE KLF> RELATES
TO A COMBINATION OF SAMPLES AND
NEWLY PRODUCED MUSIC MATERIAL,
A SIMILAR METHODOLOGY WAS USED
FOR THE ILLUSTRATIONS. PICTORIAL
COMPOSITIONS WERE CREATED FROM
PRE-EXISTING AND NEW MATERIAL.
THE SETTING OF THE TEXT AND THE
SWISS BROCHURE ARE DELIBERATELY
REMINISCENT OF CATALOG DESIGN TO
EMPHASIZE THE POETIC AND ARTIS-
TIC ACCOMPLISHMENT OF THE TEXT.
--

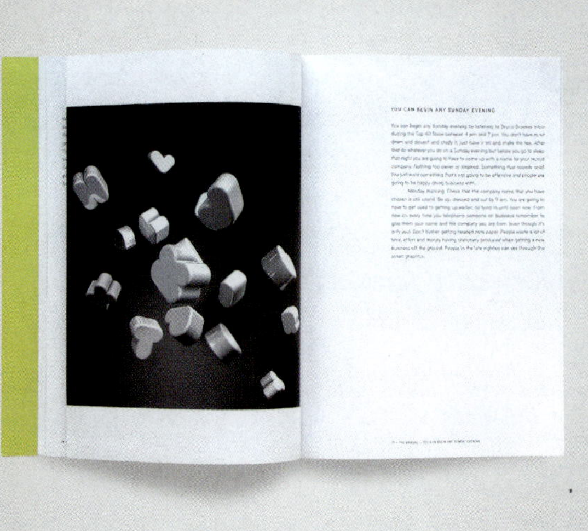

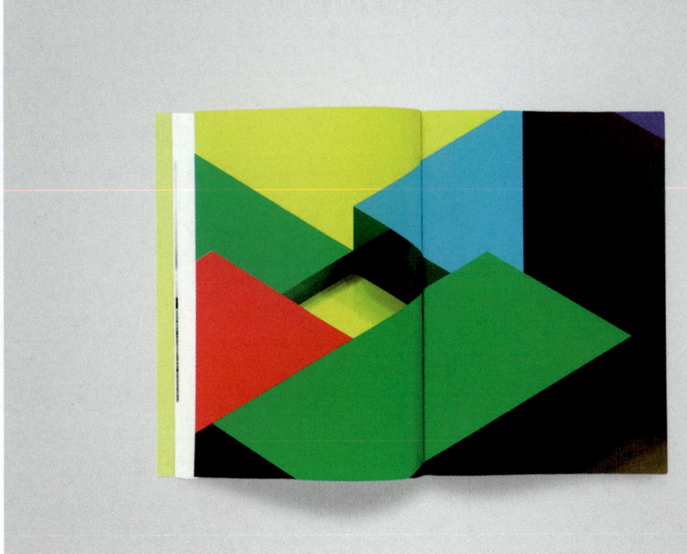
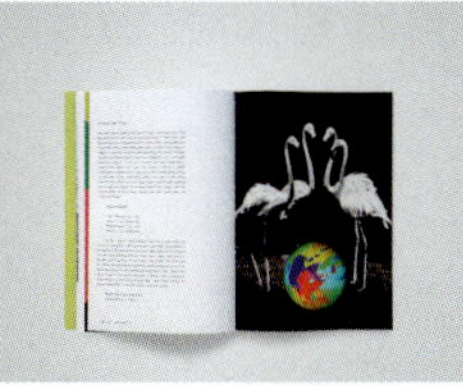
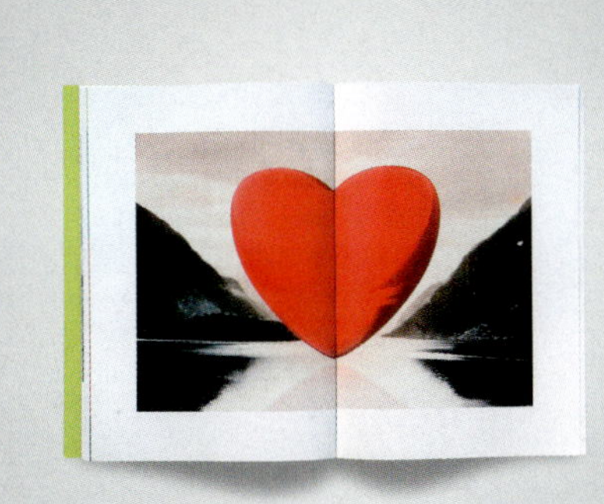
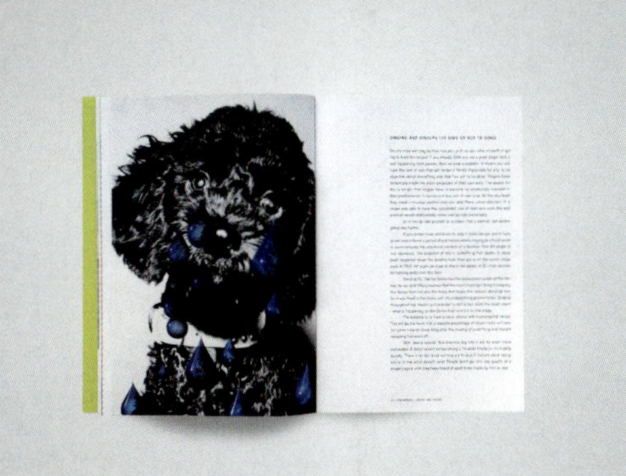
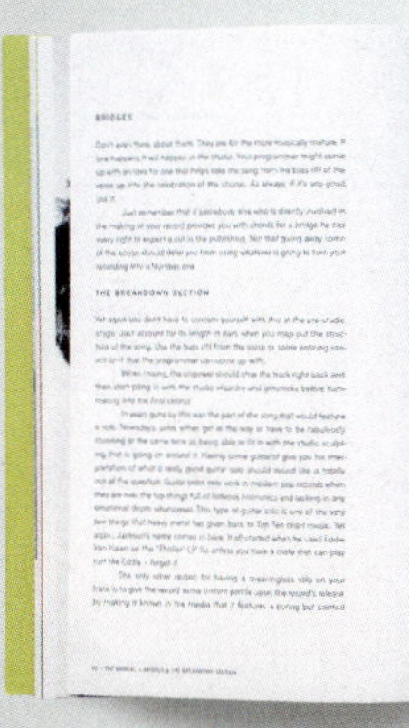
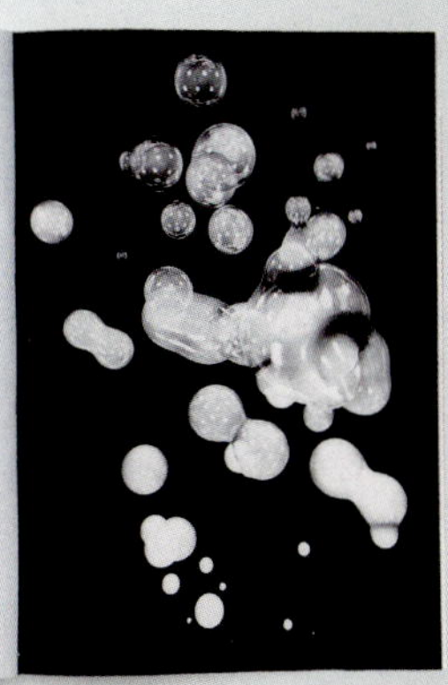
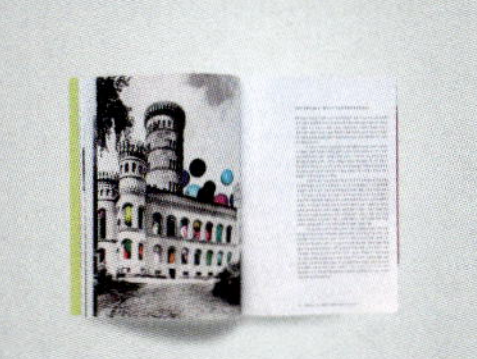

KATJA GRETZINGER IS A GRAPHIC
DESIGNER LIVING AND WORKING IN
BERLIN AND ZURICH. AS WELL AS COL-
LABORATING WITH THE SWISS GRAPHIC
ARTIST GREGOR HUBER SHE REGULARLY
WORKS TOGETHER WITH OTHER STUDIOS
AND DESIGNERS. DURING THE LAST TWO
YEARS SHE HAS BEEN A RESEARCHER AT
THE DESIGN DEPARTMENT OF THE JAN
VAN EYCK ACADEMIE IN MAASTRICHT.
SHE ENGAGES WITH QUESTIONS OF
POLITICS IN DESIGN AND QUESTIONS
ABOUT THE CONSEQUENCES OF KNOWL-
EDGE AND IGNORANCE FOR DESIGN.

--

WHAT IS GERMAN?

I THINK THAT THE CLICHÉS THAT
EXIST REGARDING GERMANY ARE EVER
WIDER OF THE MARK, BECAUSE ON THE
ONE HAND OUR CULTURE IS CHANG-
ING MORE AND MORE AS A RESULT OF
GLOBALIZATION, AND ON THE OTHER
THE INDIVIDUAL REGIONS OF GERMANY
ARE SO DIFFERENT THAT DEFINITIONS
OF WHAT'S GERMAN ARE NEVER REALLY
ACCURATE. BUT THAT'S JUST WHAT
MAKES THIS COUNTRY SO INTERESTING
- AT LEAST FOR ME; IT'S OPEN AND
DIVERSE.

WHAT IS GERMAN DESIGN?

I FIND IT JUST AS HARD TO REDUCE
GERMAN DESIGN TO A COMMON DE-
NOMINATOR, FOR THERE'S EVERYTHING
SOMEWHERE OUT THERE, AND A LOT OF
VERY GOOD STUFF, AND I REGARD IT
AS IMPOSSIBLE TO LUMP IT TOGETHER
UNDER A SINGLE HEADING. HOWEVER,
GERMAN GRAPHIC DESIGN AS A WHOLE
IS STILL CAPABLE OF DEVELOPMENT.
I OFTEN OBSERVE A TENDENCY TOWARDS
PRAGMATIC STANDARD SOLUTIONS.
ORIGINAL AND WELL-CONSIDERED DE-
SIGN HAS DIFFICULTY IN PREVAILING.
I THINK THE PROBLEM ON THE ONE
HAND IS A LACK OF TRUST IN THE DE-
SIGNER, AND ON THE OTHER ECONOMIES
ARE OFTEN MADE IN THE WRONG PLACE,
FOR OFTEN QUANTITY IS PUT BEFORE
QUALITY. BUT GOOD DESIGN NEEDS
TIME - TO RESEARCH INTO MATERIALS
OR EXPLORE NEW WAYS OF USING THEM.
IT'S NOT A QUESTION OF PRESSING A
BUTTON, IT'S AN INDIVIDUAL PROCESS
IN WHICH YOU AGAIN AND AGAIN HAVE
TO STRIKE OUT ON NEW PATHS. IN
MY EXPERIENCE IN SWITZERLAND AND
HOLLAND THEY'RE MORE COURAGEOUS
OR HAVE MORE CONFIDENCE IN DESIGN-
ERS' SKILL AND EXPERIENCE, THEY
GIVE THEM MORE LEEWAY. THEREFORE
GRAPHIC DESIGN IS MORE AVANT-GARDE
THERE. IN ADDITION OUR <QUANTITY
CULTURE> ALSO HAD AN IMPACT ON THE
PERCEPTION OF DESIGN. IN SWITZER-
LAND, FOR INSTANCE, GOOD TYPOG-
RAPHY IS PART OF THEIR CULTURE
- THEREFORE ALMOST EVERYONE ALSO
SEES WHEN SOMETHING ISN'T RIGHT.

DESCRIBE YOUR WORKING PROCESS.

WORKING PROCESSES ARE GUIDED
BY PROJECTS AND THEREFORE THEY'RE
ALWAYS DIFFERENT.

WHAT DO YOU AIM TO ACHIEVE WITH
YOUR WORK?

DOING GOOD, INTERESTING DESIGN,
BUT ALSO HAVING MORE DISCUSSION
ABOUT DESIGN, QUESTIONING CONVEN-
TIONS AND LOOKING CRITICALLY AT
WAYS OF ACTING AND THINKING.

YOU'VE INVITED A FRIEND TO
GERMANY; NAME ONE PLACE THEY
REALLY MUST VISIT AND A QUINT-
ESSENTIAL EXPERIENCE YOU REC-
OMMEND.

I'D NO DOUBT SUGGEST WHAT I'VE
UNDERTAKEN MYSELF: HE SHOULD GO TO
BRANDENBURG AND WALK IN THE FOR-
ESTS THERE.

WHAT IS THE MOST IMPORTANT LES-
SON YOU HAVE LEARNED IN YOUR
PROFESSION SO FAR?

OPEN-MINDEDNESS.

--

KATJA GRETZINGER

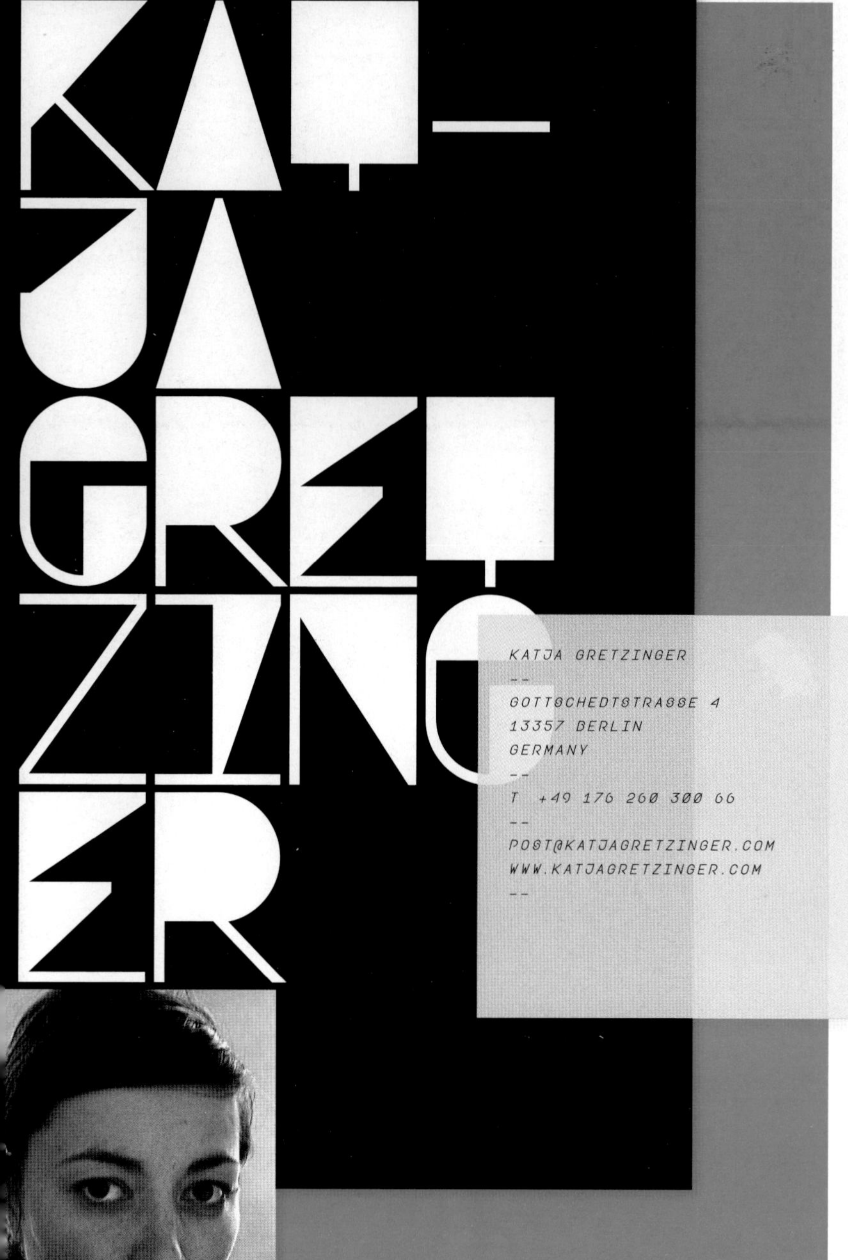

KATJA GRETZINGER
--
GOTTSCHEDTSTRASSE 4
13357 BERLIN
GERMANY
--
T +49 176 260 300 66
--
POST@KATJAGRETZINGER.COM
WWW.KATJAGRETZINGER.COM
--

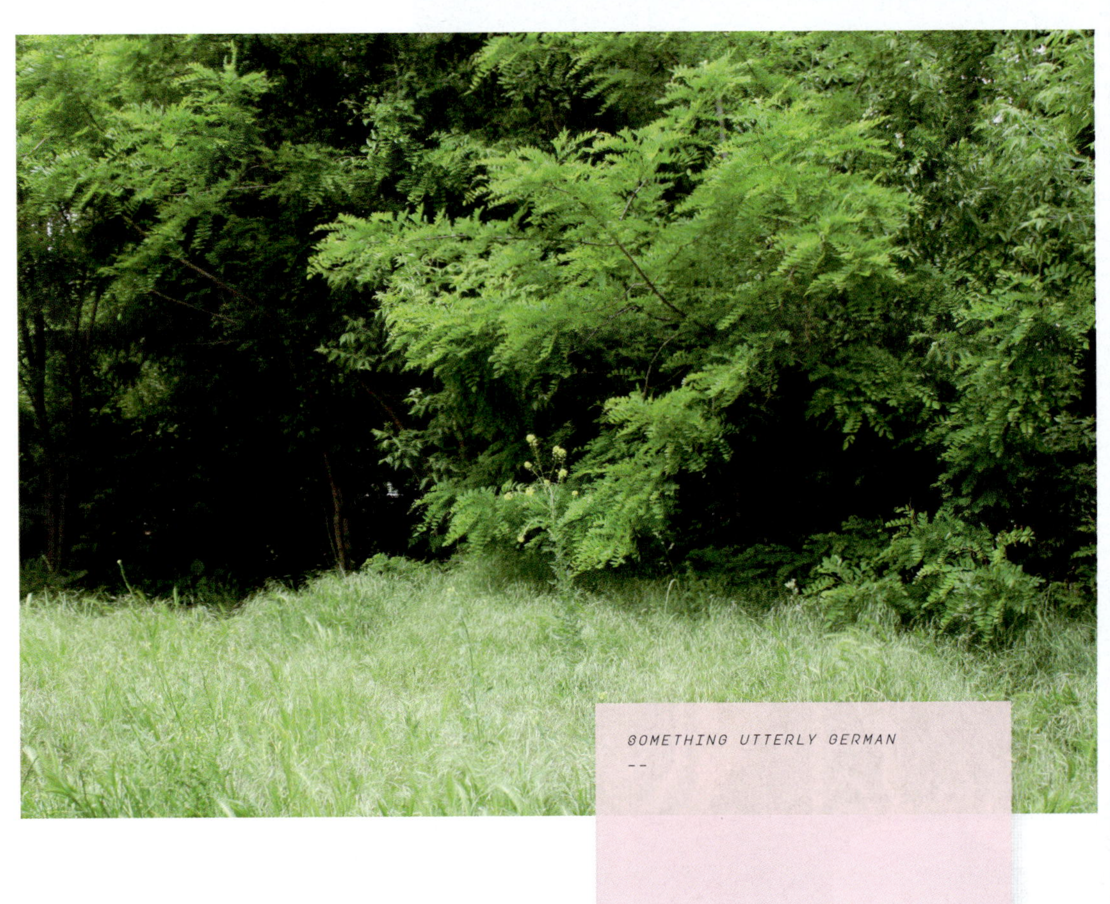
SOMETHING UTTERLY GERMAN
--

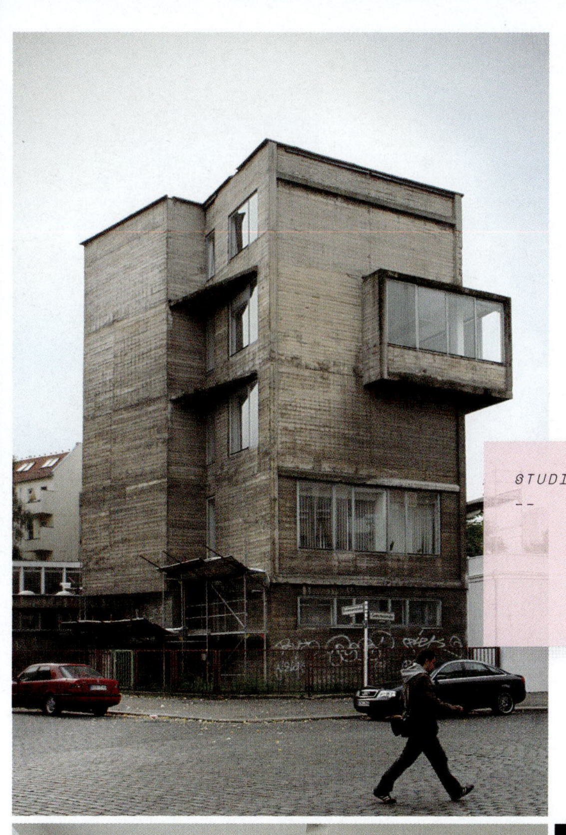

STUDIO SURROUNDINGS
--

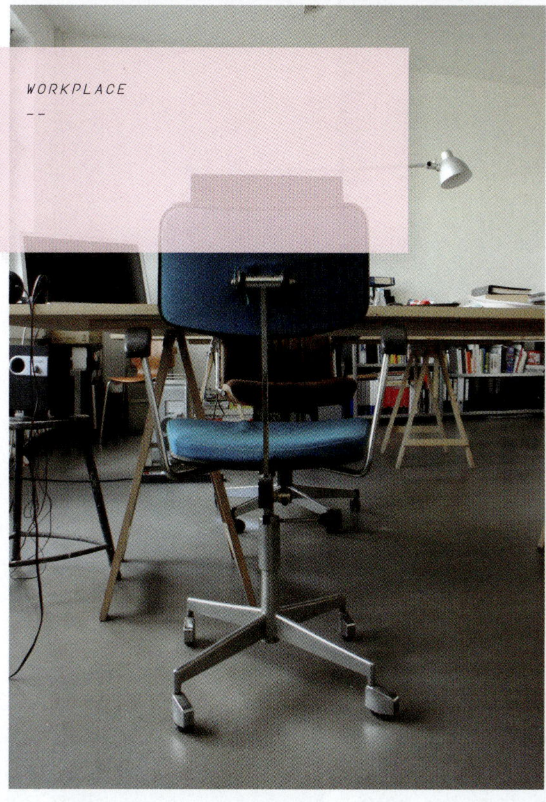

WORKPLACE
--

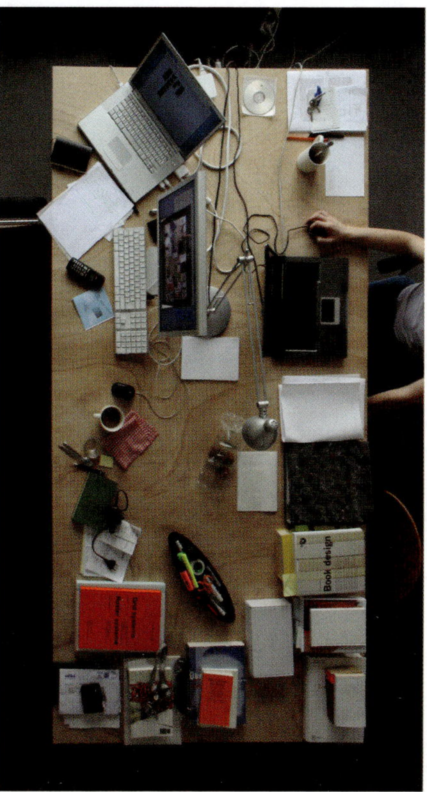

Book design

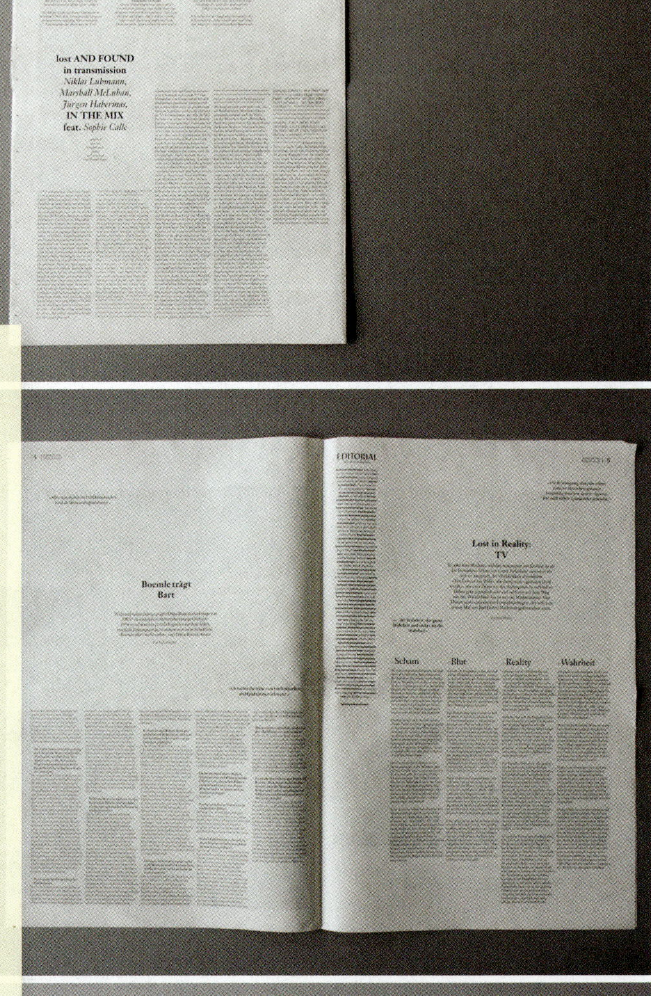

ROTE FABRIK ZEITUNG
LOST IN TRANSMISSION
--
THE ROTE FABRIK ZEITUNG IS A
NEWSPAPER PUBLISHED MONTHLY BY
THE ROTE FABRIK IN ZURICH. EACH
EDITION IS DEVOTED TO A NEW
CENTRAL THEME. THIS EDITION WAS
PUBLISHED UNDER THE TITLE LOST
IN TRANSMISSION. FOR GREGOR AND
ME THE QUESTION OF WHAT MODERN
FILTER SYSTEMS MEAN FOR OUR PER-
SONALITY AND OUR SELF-PERCEPTION
WAS IMPORTANT. TO WHAT EXTENT
ARE WE OURSELVES A PRODUCT OF
THOSE FILTER SYSTEMS, AND TO WHAT
EXTENT ARE IDENTITIES LIQUEFIED
AS A RESULT? THEREFORE WE WORKED
WITH GOOGLE AND PICTURE SEARCH
ENGINES, AND USED ORLAN'S QUOTA-
TION <THIS IS MY BODY, THIS IS MY
SOFTWARE> IN THE TITLE. THE DE-
SIGN OF THIS ISSUE IS NOT SUBJECT
TO ANY FIXED PAGE MATRIX. ONE
OF OUR AIMS IN OUR WORK FOR THE
ROTE FABRIK ZEITUNG IS TO MANAGE
WITH AS FEW CONSTANTS AS POS-
SIBLE, AND SEE THE NEWSPAPER AS A
WHOLE ENTITY.
--
IN COLLABORATION WITH
GREGOR HUBER
--

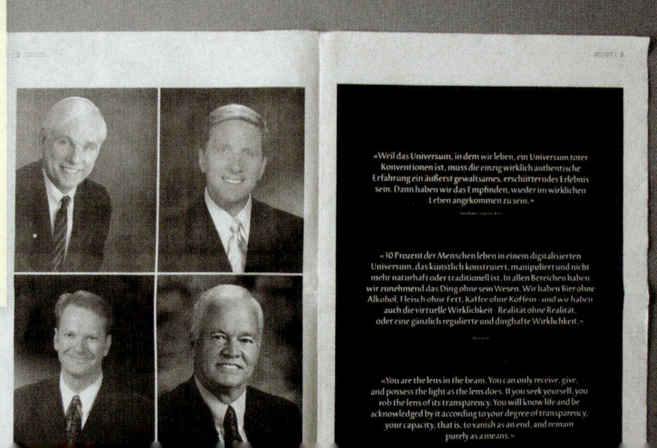

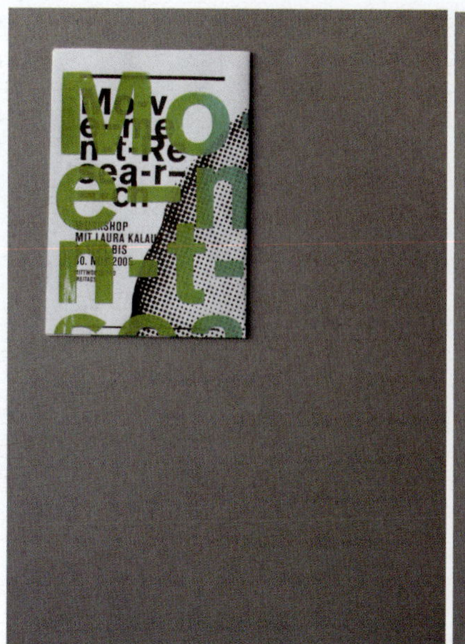

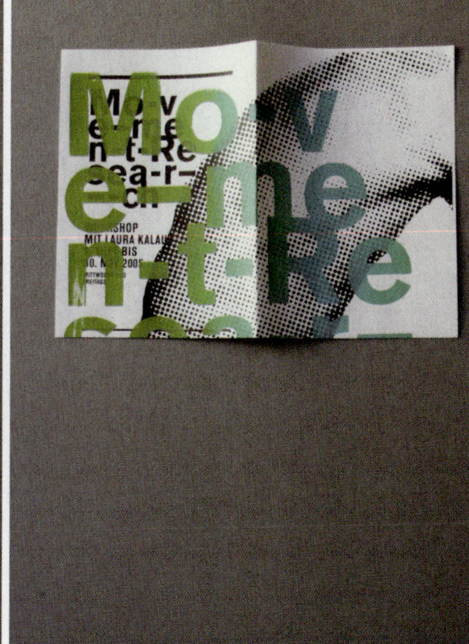

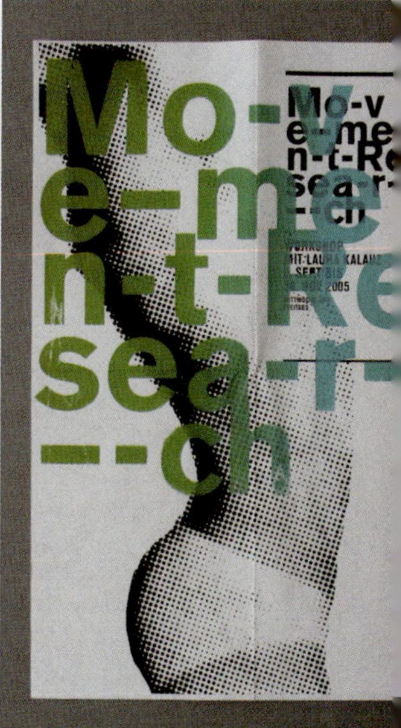

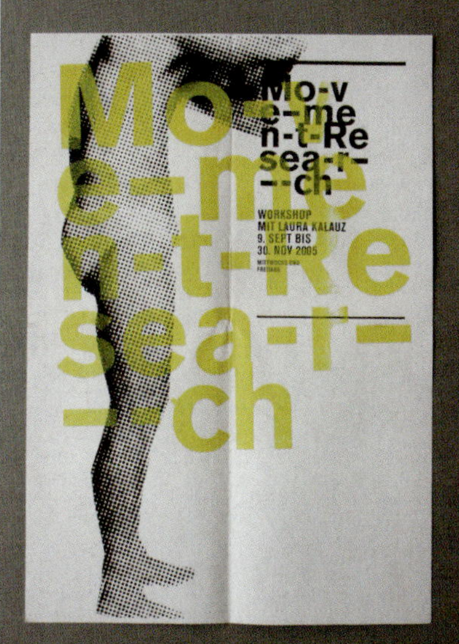

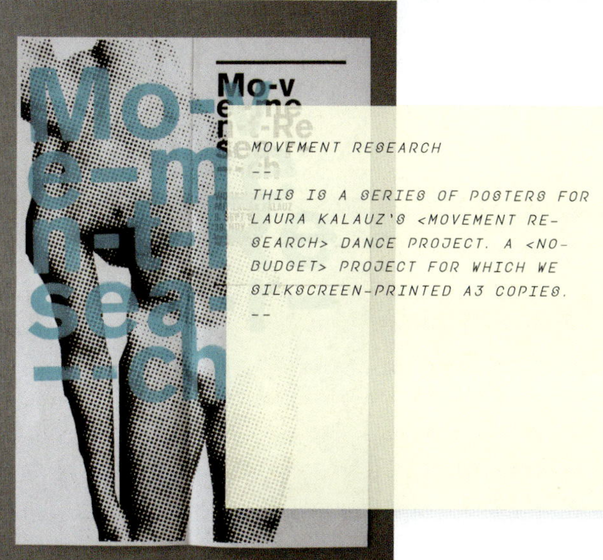

MOVEMENT RESEARCH
--
THIS IS A SERIES OF POSTERS FOR
LAURA KALAUZ'S <MOVEMENT RE-
SEARCH> DANCE PROJECT. A <NO-
BUDGET> PROJECT FOR WHICH WE
SILKSCREEN-PRINTED A3 COPIES.
--

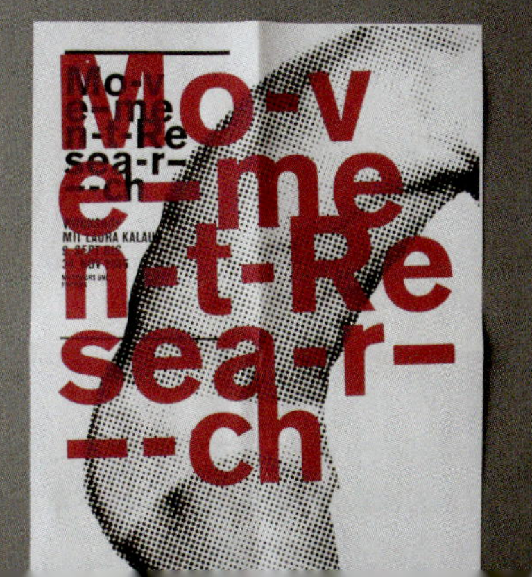

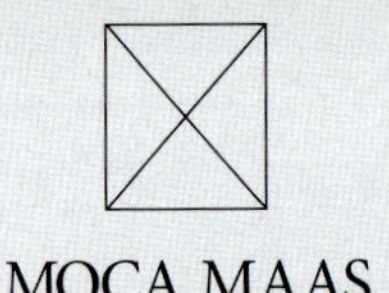

MOCA MAAS, MUSEUM OF CONTEM-
PORARY ART MAASTRICHT (ANT-
ONY HUDEK, ARTISTIC DIRECTOR &
FOUNDER, ELLA KLASCHKA, ARTISTIC
ADVISOR, KATJA GRETZINGER, DIREC-
TOR VISUAL IDENTITY), IS A MUSEUM
THAT DOESN'T HAVE ANY CURATORS
AND HAS NO PHILOSOPHY EXCEPT THE
FUNDAMENTAL IDEA OF REPRESENTING
ITSELF. IN MY ROLE AS <DIRECTOR
OF VISUAL IDENTITY> I DESIGNED
AN IMAGE FOR MOCA MAAS. THE AIM
WAS TO DESIGN AN IMAGE THAT IS
BASICALLY SELF-CONTRADICTORY. IT
WAS SUPPOSED TO FUNCTION AS A
KIND OF EMPTY SHELL OF THE IM-
PRESSION OF A MUSEUM, BUT TO DENY
ITSELF A PRECISELY DEFINED IDEN-
TITY. OF COURSE THAT'S COMPLETELY
IMPOSSIBLE. THEREFORE IT'S AN
ATTEMPT, SO TO SPEAK, THAT ILLUS-
TRATES THE ATTEMPT.
--

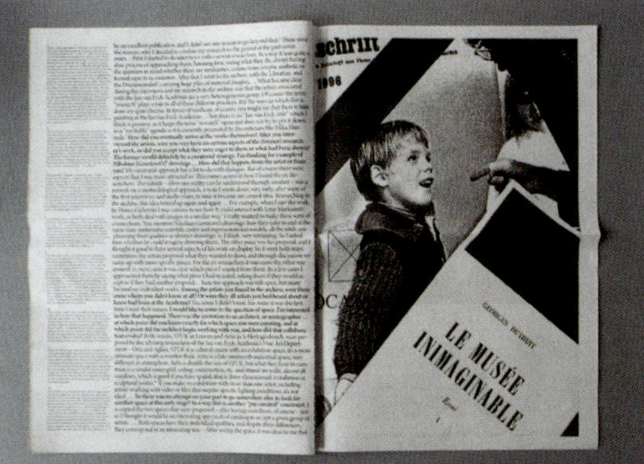

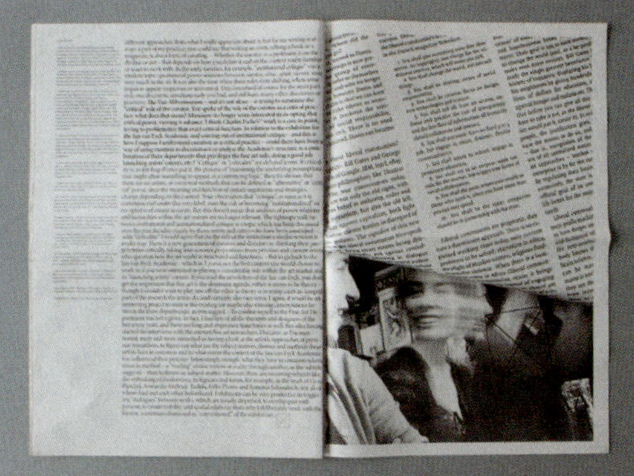

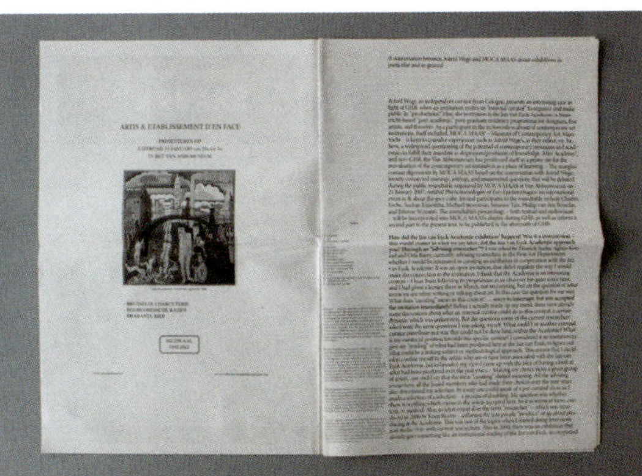

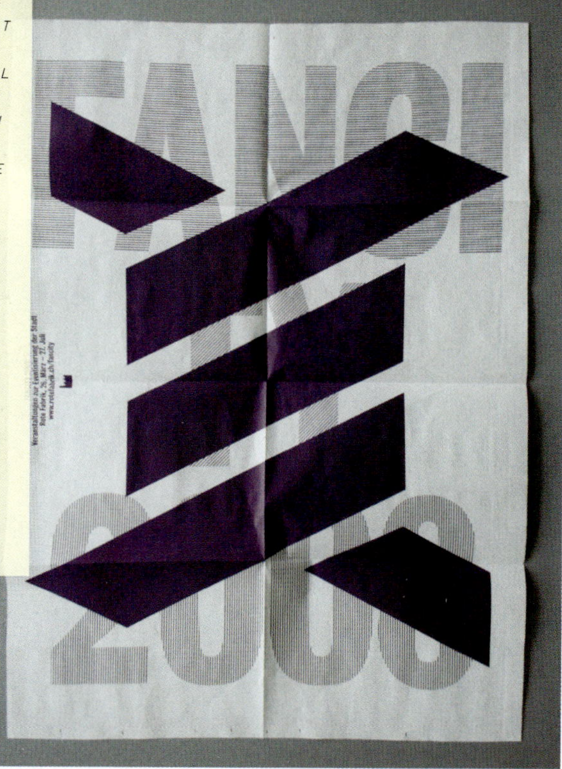

FANCITY

--

I DESIGNED THIS LOGO TOGETHER
WITH GREGOR HUBER FOR THE FAN-
CITY PROJECT BY ANKE HAGEMANN
WHICH WAS CONCERNED WITH CHANGES
TO THE PUBLIC SPACE IN THE CITY
OF ZURICH DURING THE EUROPEAN
FOOTBALL CHAMPIONSHIPS. IT ACTU-
ALLY AROSE FROM A SUGGESTION THAT
COME FROM SOMEONE OUTSIDE THE
TEAM: WE SHOULD DEPICT A FOOTBALL
WITH BARBED WIRE ROUND IT. INI-
TIALLY WE THOUGHT THE SUGGESTION
WAS IMPOSSIBLE, BUT IN THE END
THE ORDINARINESS AND POSTER-LIKE
NATURE INTERESTED US, AND WE OB-
SERVED THAT A SIMILARLY <AGGRES-
SIVE> LOGO WAS ALSO TO BE FOUND
ASSOCIATED WITH THE EUROPEAN
CHAMPIONSHIPS.

--

IN COLLABORATION WITH
GREGOR HUBER

--

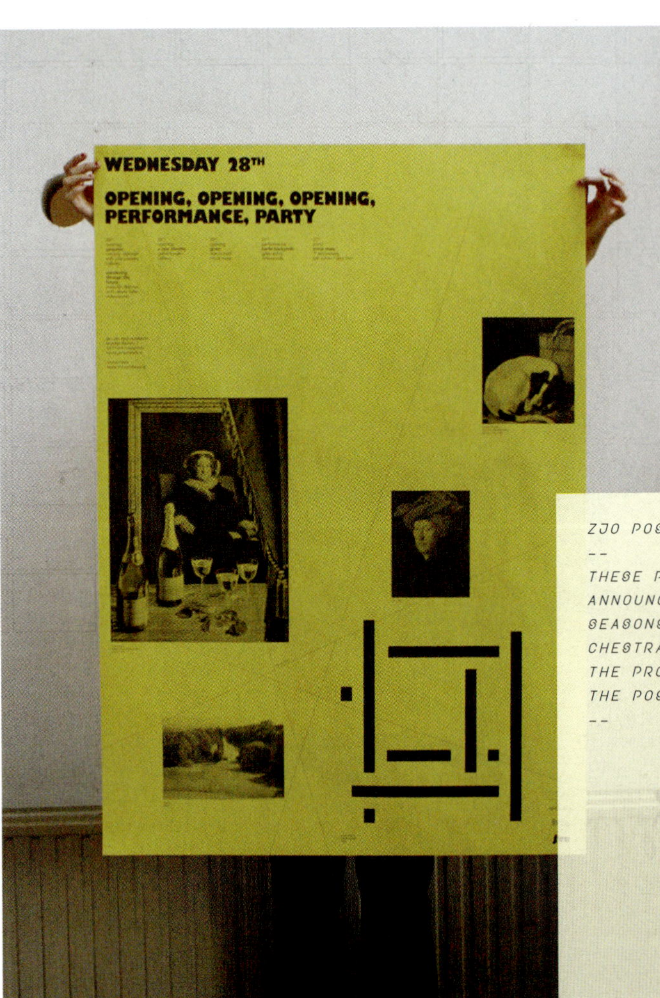

ZJO POSTERS
--
THESE PLACARDS ARE THE PROGRAM
ANNOUNCEMENTS OF THE LAST THREE
SEASONS OF THE ZURICH JAZZ OR-
CHESTRA. THE PLACARD COMPLEMENTS
THE PROGRAM THAT'S ON THE BACK OF
THE POSTER.
--

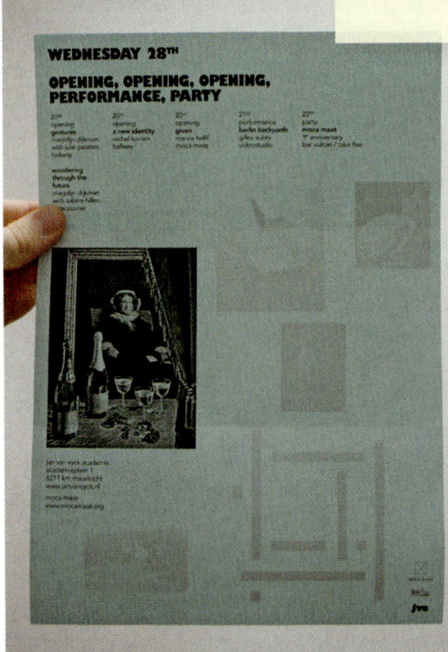

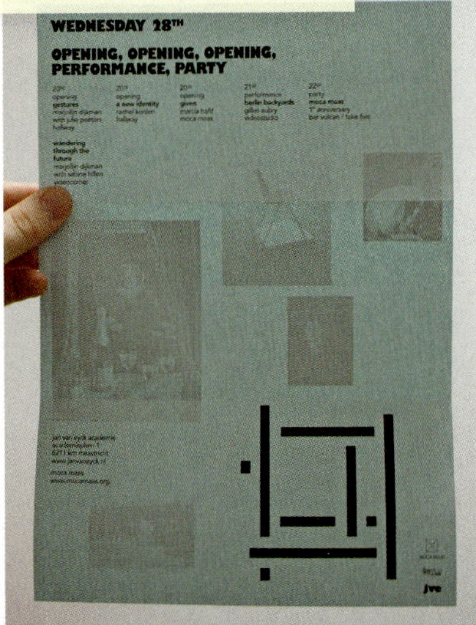

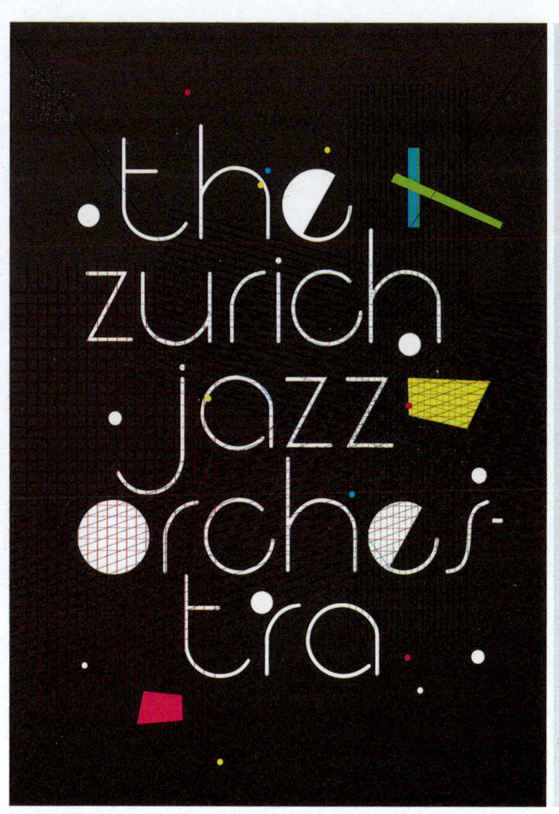
the
zurich
jazz
orches-
tra

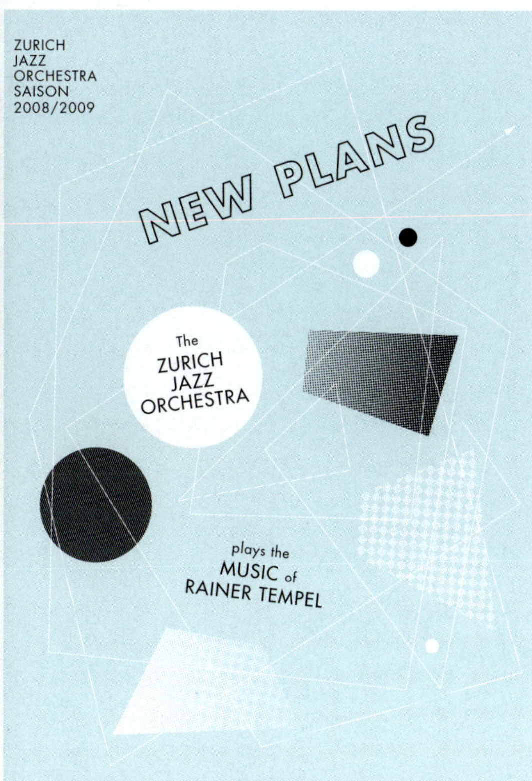
ZURICH
JAZZ
ORCHESTRA
SAISON
2008/2009
NEW PLANS
The
ZURICH
JAZZ
ORCHESTRA
plays the
MUSIC of
RAINER TEMPEL

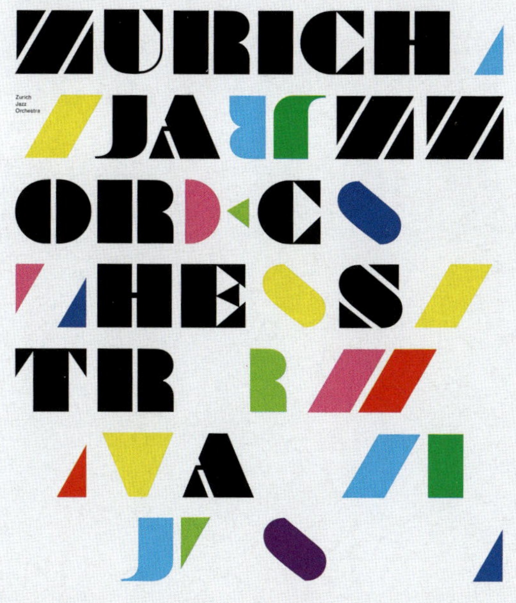
2006
2007
ZURICH
JAZZ
ORCHESTRA
Zurich
Jazz
Orchestra

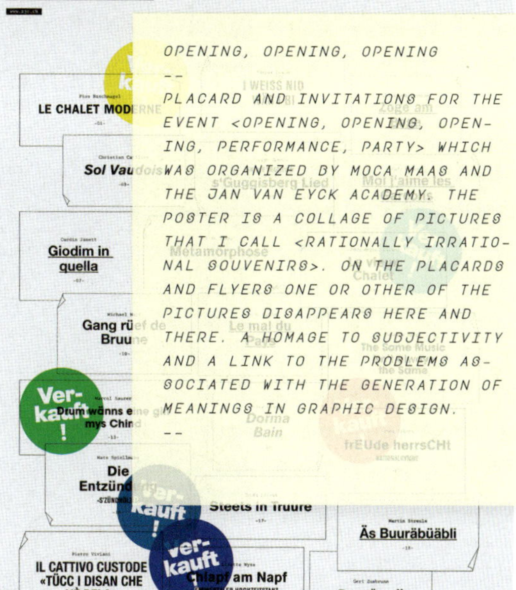
Zurich
Jazz
Orchestra
Swiss
Song Book
I WEISS NID
LE CHALET MODERNE
Zoge an
s'Guggisberg Lied
Moi l'aime les
Sol Vaudois
Metamorphose
Giodim in
quella
Chalet
Gang rüef de
Bruu
Le mal du
Pays
The Some Music
the Same
Ver-
kauft!
Dtum wänns eine g
mys Chind
Dorma
Bain
Die
Entzünd
frEUde herrsCHt
ver-
kauft!
Steets in truure
Äs Buuräbüäbli
IL CATTIVO CUSTODE
«TÜCC I DISAN CHE
L'È BELA»
ver-
kauft!
hlapf am Napf
Ruggüserli

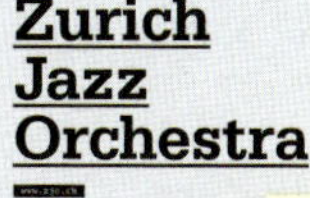
OPENING, OPENING, OPENING
--
PLACARD AND INVITATIONS FOR THE
EVENT <OPENING, OPENING, OPEN-
ING, PERFORMANCE, PARTY> WHICH
WAS ORGANIZED BY MOCA MAAS AND
THE JAN VAN EYCK ACADEMY. THE
POSTER IS A COLLAGE OF PICTURES
THAT I CALL <RATIONALLY IRRATIO-
NAL SOUVENIRS>. ON THE PLACARDS
AND FLYERS ONE OR OTHER OF THE
PICTURES DISAPPEARS HERE AND
THERE. A HOMAGE TO SUBJECTIVITY
AND A LINK TO THE PROBLEMS AS-
SOCIATED WITH THE GENERATION OF
MEANINGS IN GRAPHIC DESIGN.
--

MICHAEL HEIMANN AND HENDRIK
SCHWANTES FOUNDED THE BERLIN-
BASED DESIGN PRACTICE HEIMANN UND
SCHWANTES IN SUMMER 2007. AFTER
STUDYING AND WORKING IN BASEL AND
ZURICH TYPOGRAPHER MICHAEL HEI-
MANN WAS KNOWN FOR HIS PRECISELY
EXECUTED, COMPLEX BOOK PROJECTS
WITH HIS FORMER COMPANY GROENLAND.
BERLIN. HENDRIK SCHWANTES WORKED
FOR THE SWISS PUBLISHER AND DE-
SIGNER LARS MÜLLER BEFORE DESIGN-
ING ON A FREELANCE BASIS FOR CLI-
ENTS AND FRIENDS IN BERLIN, MAINLY
IN THE FIELDS OF ART AND ARCHITEC-
TURE. THE STARTING POINT FOR OUR
COOPERATION IS OUR COMMON INTEREST
IN AVOIDING EVERYDAY DESIGN BUSI-
NESS AND REQUESTIONING THE CON-
STELLATION OF A DESIGN PRACTICE IN
ITS SOCIAL AND ECONOMIC FUNCTION.

--

WHAT IS GERMAN?

- BEIGE
- ROUND
- INDETERMINATE

WHAT IS GERMAN DESIGN?

- GRASS GREEN TO TURQUOISE
- OVAL
- FULLY FUNCTIONAL

DESCRIBE YOUR WORKING PROCESS.

- WHITE AND BLACK
- CLUSTER-LIKE
- CONDENSED

WHAT DO YOU AIM TO ACHIEVE WITH
YOUR WORK?

- COLORFUL
- ANGULAR
- DENSE

YOU'VE INVITED A FRIEND TO
GERMANY; NAME ONE PLACE THEY
REALLY MUST VISIT AND A QUINT-
ESSENTIAL EXPERIENCE YOU REC-
OMMEND.

- DEPENDS ON THE FRIEND

WHAT IS THE MOST IMPORTANT
LESSON YOU HAVE LEARNED IN YOUR
PROFESSION SO FAR?

- TO MAKE GRAY BLACK AND WHITE
- TO MAKE OVAL ANGULAR
- TO CONDUCT DISCUSSIONS

--

HEIMANN UND SCHWANTES

HEIMANN UND SCHWANTES
--
KREUZBERGSTRASSE 30
10965 BERLIN
GERMANY
--
T.   +49 30 39746451
F.   +49 30 39746228
--
INFO@HEIMANNUNDSCHWANTES.DE
HTTP://WWW.HEIMANNUNDSCHWANTES.DE
--

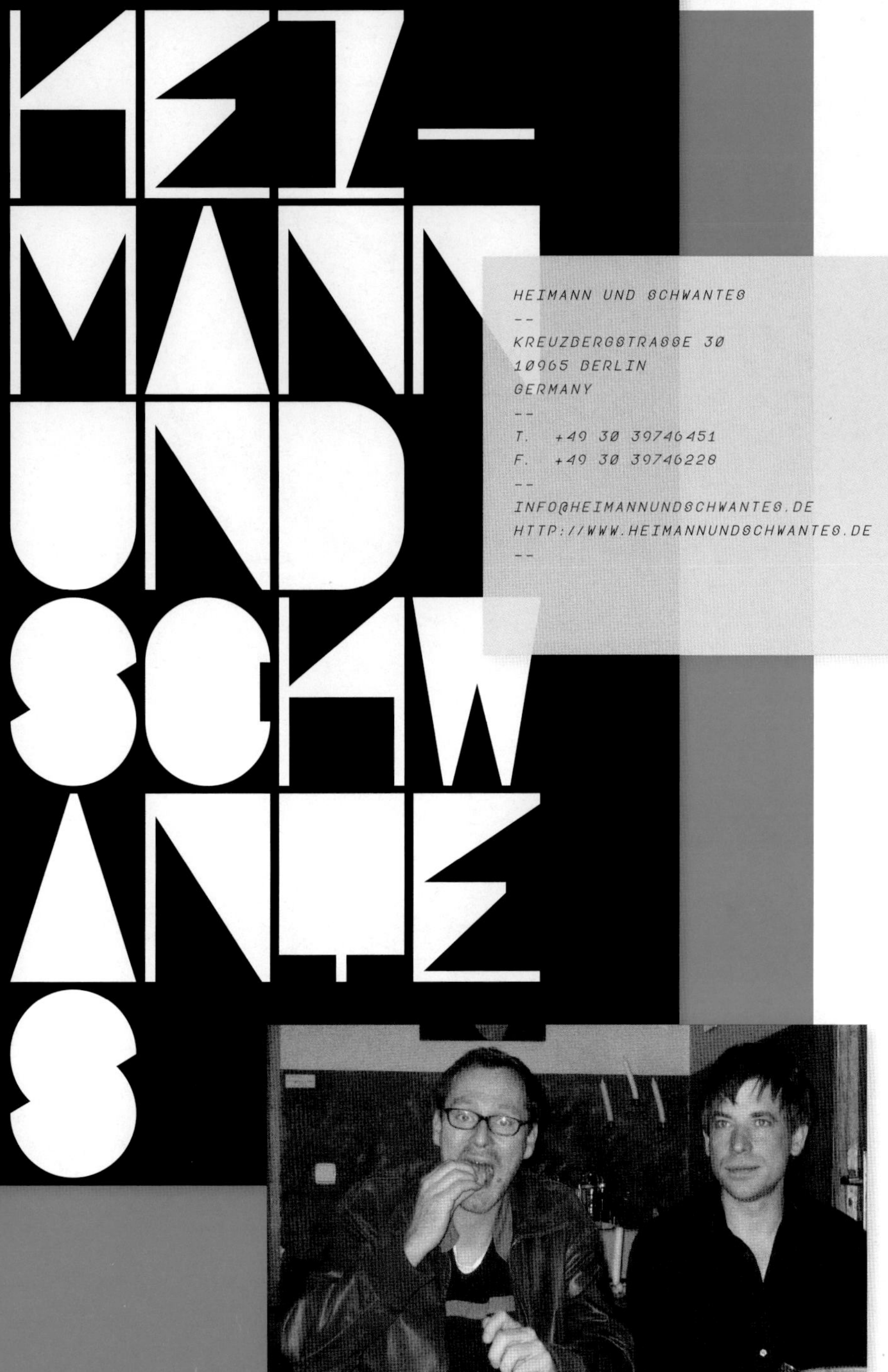

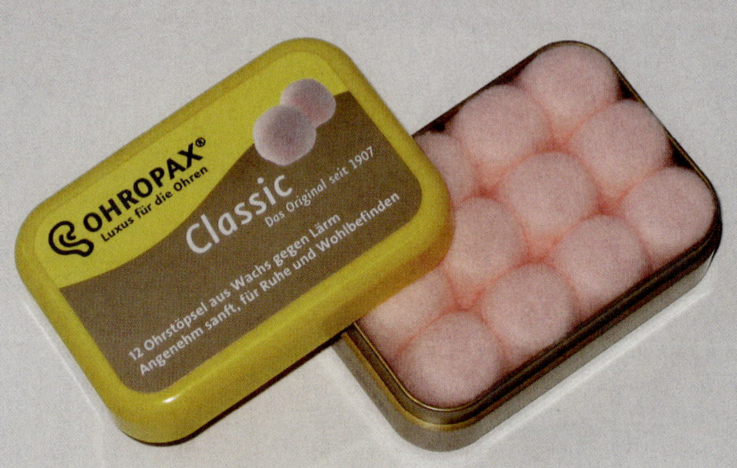

SOMETHING UTTERLY GERMAN
--

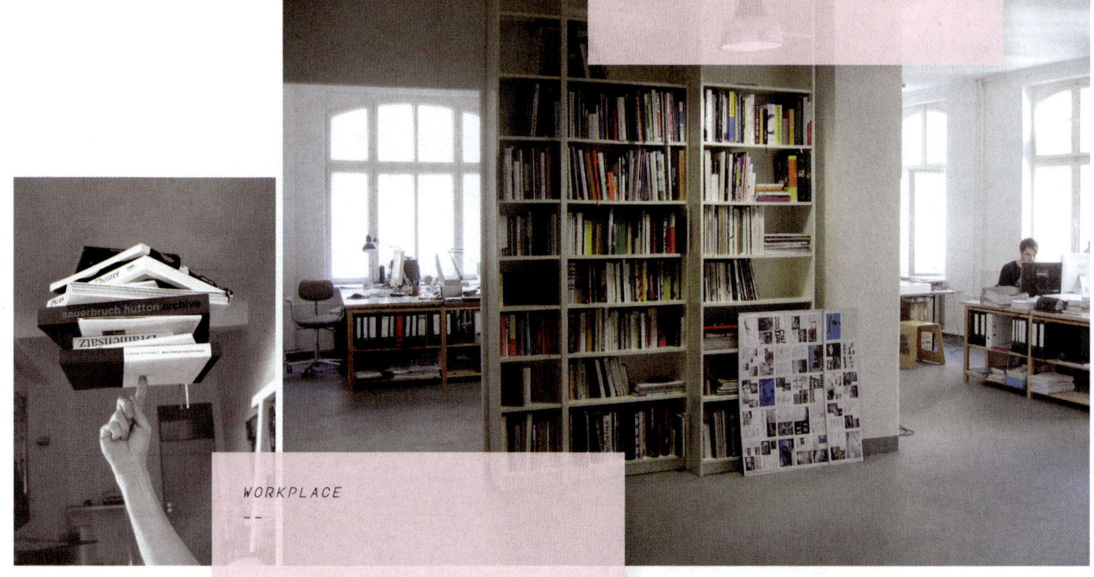

WORKPLACE
--

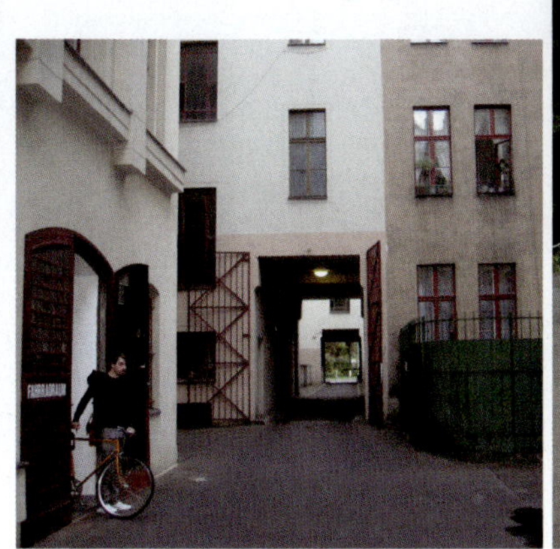

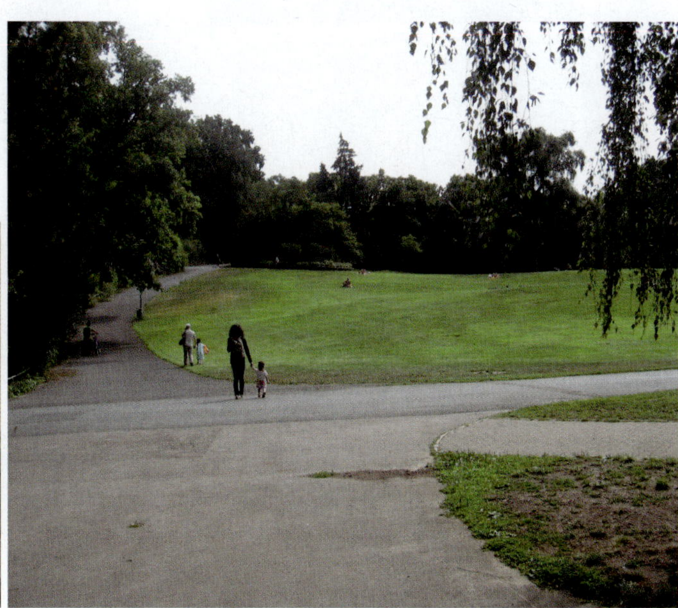

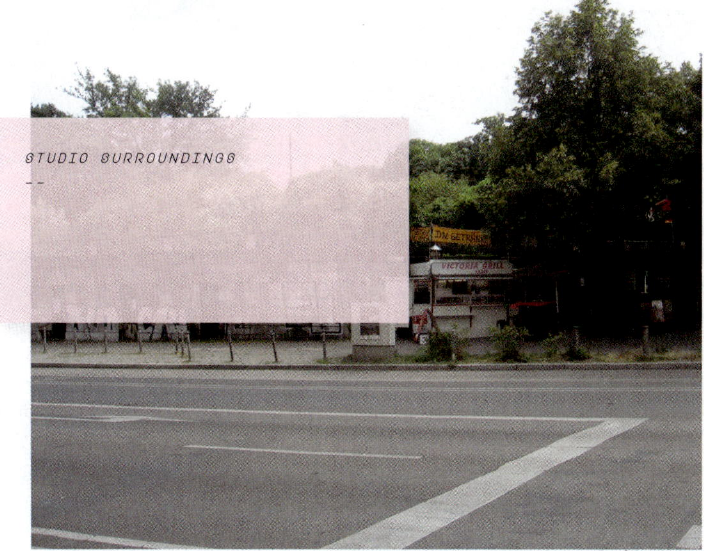
STUDIO SURROUNDINGS

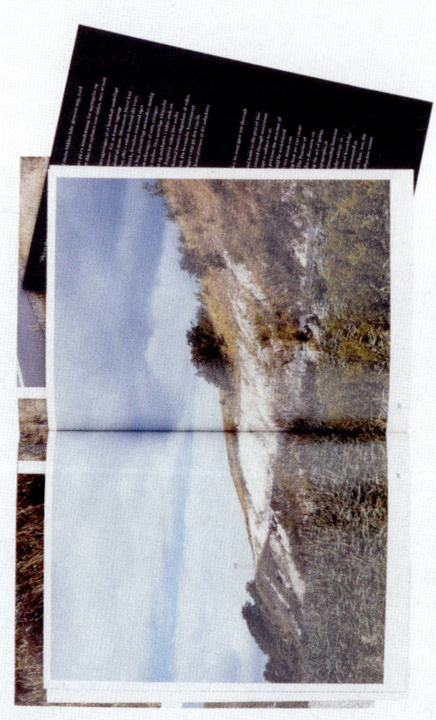

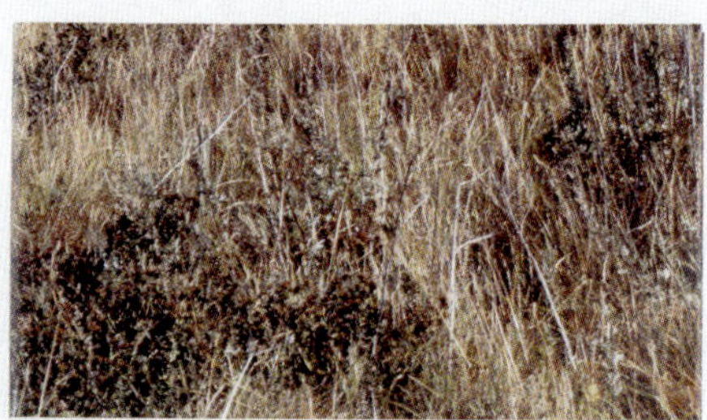

Olafur Eliasson, Movement Meter for Lernacken

MOVEMENT METER FOR LERNACKEN
OLAFUR ELIASSON
--
THE SPECTATOR EXPERIENCES OLAFUR
ELIASSON'S LIGHT INSTALLATION BY
MOVING TOWARDS THE ARTWORK. OUR
TASK WAS TO ILLUSTRATE THIS EXPE-
RIENCE THROUGH THE STATIC MEDIUM
OF A BOOK. A FOLDED POSTER COVER
CONTAINS TWO BROCHURES: THE
FIRST BROCHURE SHOWS THE INSTAL-
LATION IN THE ARTIST'S ENVI-
RONMENT WITH A NUMBER OF ATMO-
SPHERIC PHOTOGRAPHS. THE SECOND
BROCHURE VISUALIZES THE ARTIS-
TIC CONCEPT BASED ON SKETCHES
AND ARCHITECTURAL PLANS. OLAFUR
ELIASSON'S MOVEMENT METER FOR
LERNACKEN WAS ACCORDED A SPECIAL
AWARD BY THE SELECTION COMMITTEE
AT THE <DIE SCHÖNSTEN SCHWEIZER
BÜCHER 2002> (THE MOST BEAUTIFUL
SWISS BOOKS 2002) COMPETITION.
--

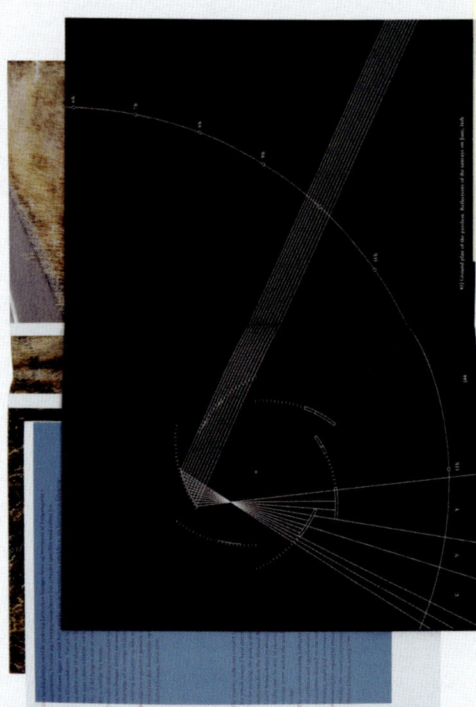

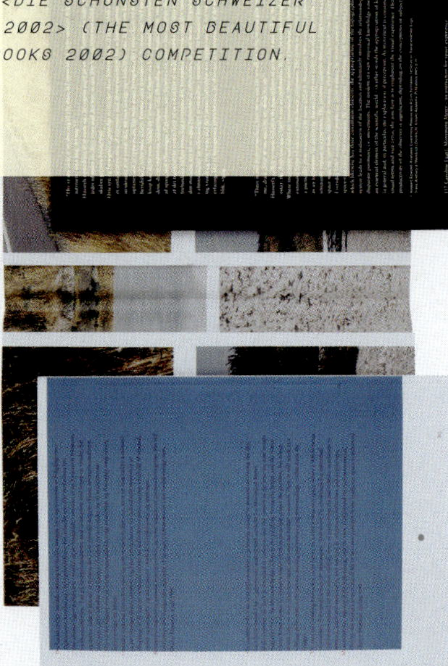

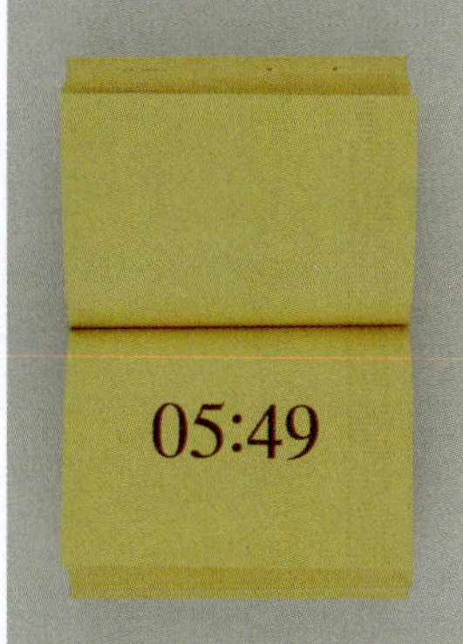

05:49

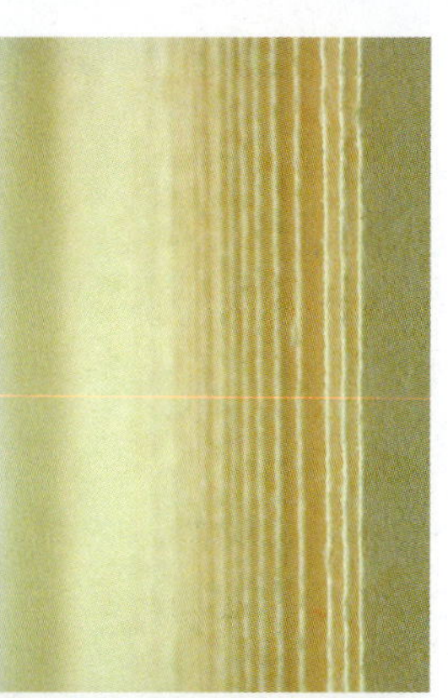

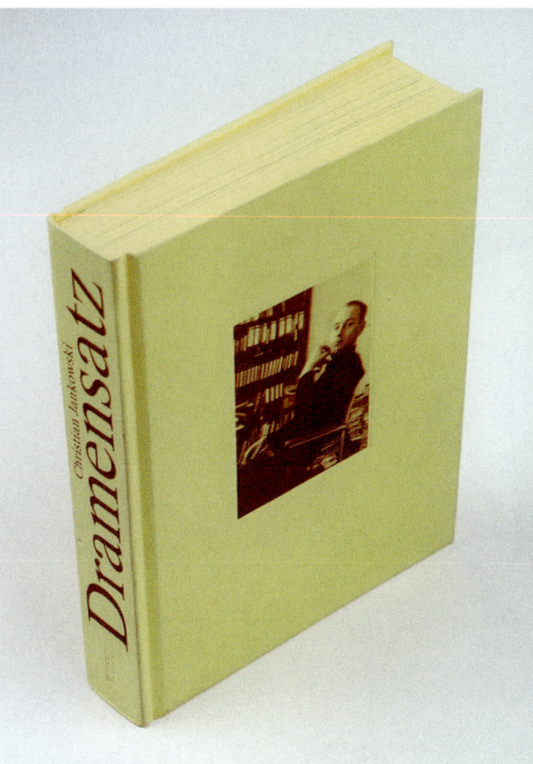

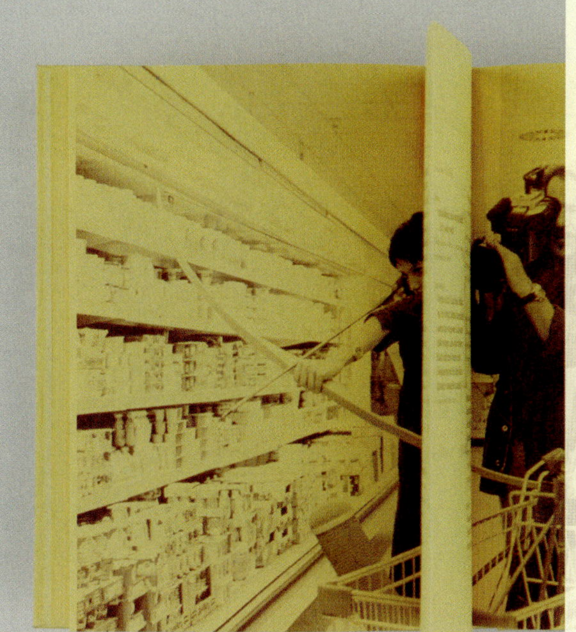

DRAMENSATZ
CHRISTIAN JANKOWSKI
--
VIDEO IS THE ARTIST CHRISTIAN
JANKOWSKI'S PREFERRED MEDIUM;
CULTURAL & ART ACTIVITIES ARE HIS
<PLAYING FIELD>. <DRAMENSATZ>
IS A COLLECTION OF 10 VIDEOS IL-
LUSTRATED AS TRANSCRIBED DIALOGS
PRESENTED AS TYPOGRAPHED DRAMA
FORMAT (DRAMENSATZ). THE VIDEO'S
LINEAR SEQUENCE IS PARALLEL TO
THE BOOK'S LINEARITY AND IS REP-
RESENTED BY CONSECUTIVE MINUTES
AND SECONDS CORRESPONDING TO THE
VIDEO'S REAL TIME. A BAND COM-
POSED OF ALL TITLES ACCOMPANIES
THE PAGES AND GUIDES THE READER
THROUGH THE BOOK AS VIDEO TRACK.
OUR CONCEPT DEVELOPED IN COLLAB-
ORATION WITH THE ARTIST AND CURA-
TOR PHILIPP KAISER IS UNDERLINED
BY THE COLOR AND FONT REFERENCE
TO THE RECLAM SERIES. THE BOOK
WAS ACCORDED AN AWARD AS ONE OF
<THE MOST BEAUTIFUL SWISS BOOKS
2003.>
--

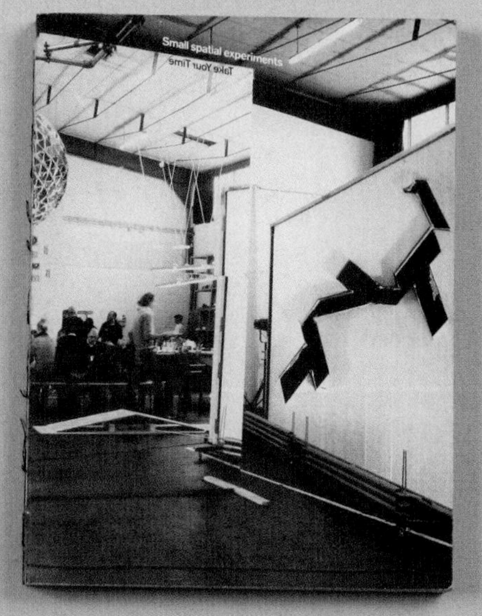

Small spatial experiments
Take Your Time

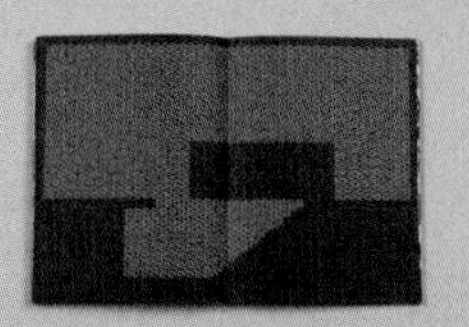

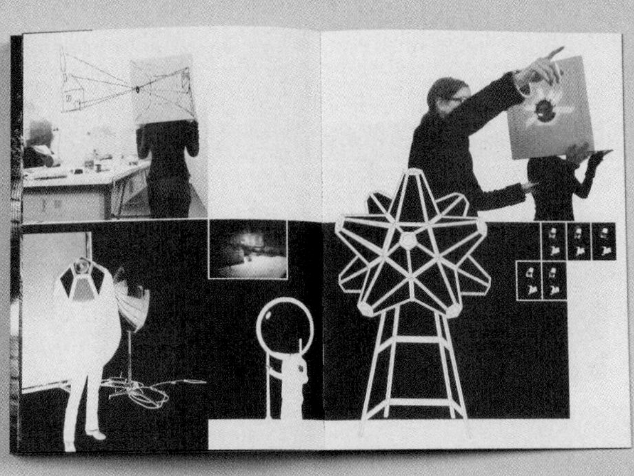

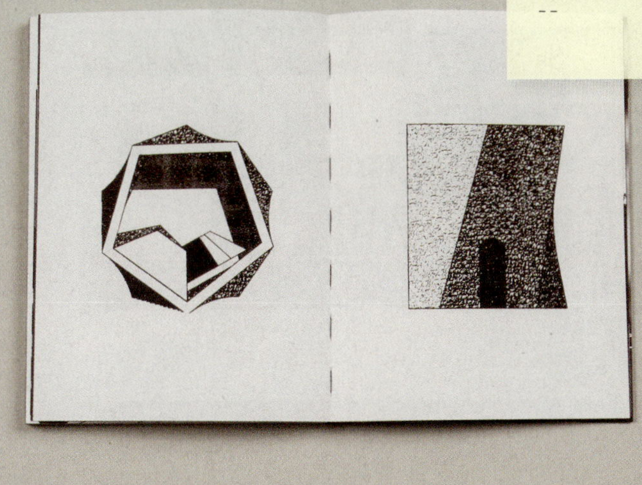

STUDIO OLAFUR ELIASSON
TAKE YOUR TIME
SMALL SPATIAL EXPERIMENTS
2008
--

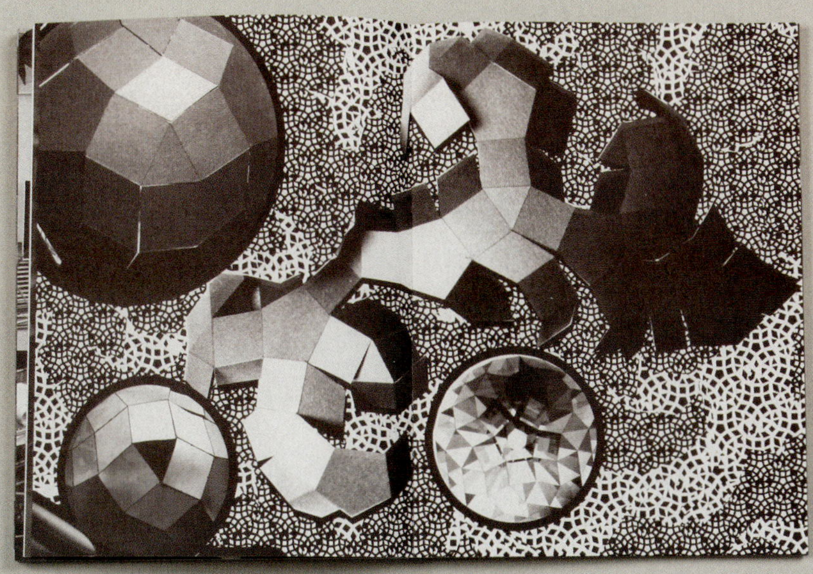

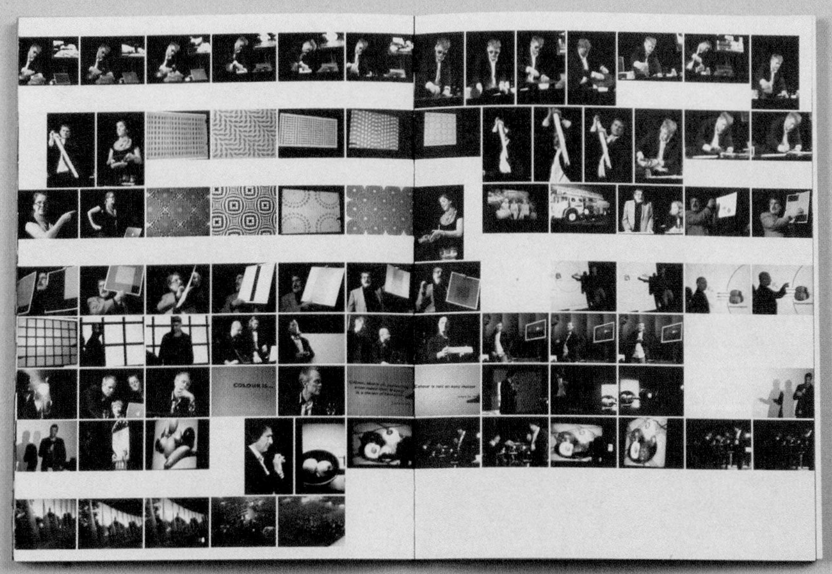

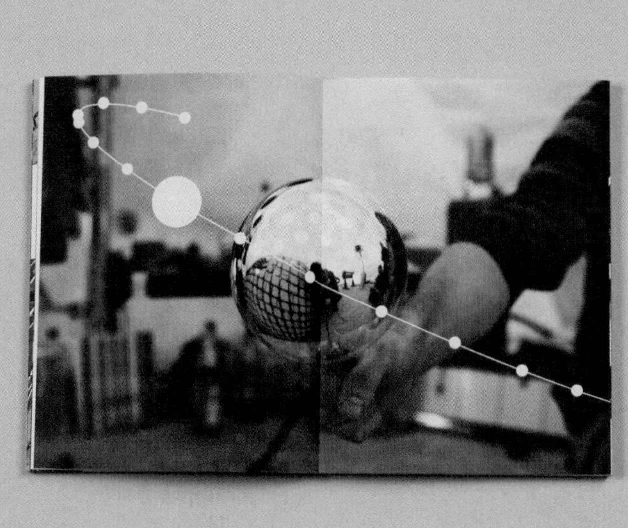

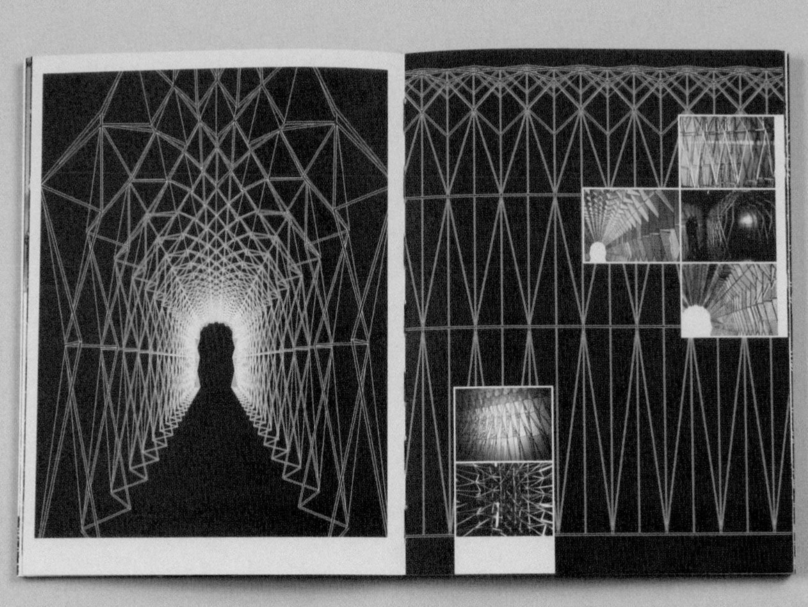

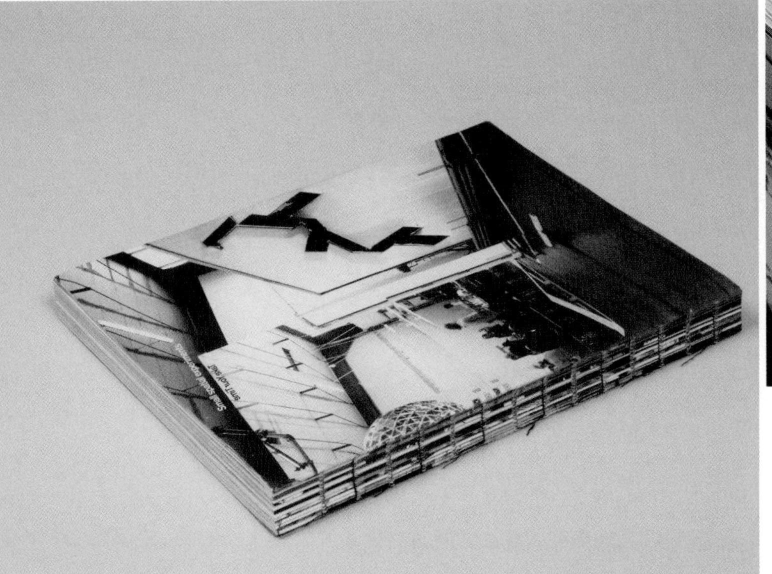

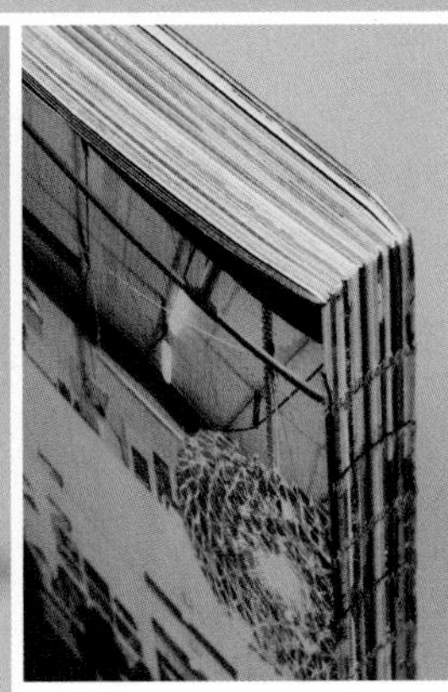

HE DID NOT DEMONSTRATE HIS TAL-
ENT FOR GRAPHIC DESIGN AT AN EARLY
AGE. WHEN HE WAS SIX HE TOOK PART
IN A GERMANY-WIDE DRAWING COMPE-
TITION INSPIRED BY <HARIBO GUM-
MIBÄRCHEN> (JELLY-BABY BEARS MADE
BY HARIBO). HE TOTALLY FAILED.
INSTEAD HIS SISTER WON THE MAIN
PRIZE: A GOLDEN JELLY-BABY BEAR
PENDANT ON A GOLDEN CHAIN. UNDE-
TERRED BY THIS CHILDHOOD EXPERI-
ENCE HE STUDIED COMMUNICATION DE-
SIGN IN BAVARIA, IN BETWEEN TIMES
GOING TO NEW YORK AND ACQUIRING
EXPERIENCE AND A LOT OF INSPIRA-
TION. THIS GAVE THE DETERMINING
IMPETUS FOR HIM TO GO TO BERLIN
AFTER COMPLETING HIS STUDIES WHERE
HE FOUNDED THE DESIGN STUDIO ICE
CREAM FOR FREE™ AT THE END OF
2005.

ICE CREAM FOR FREE™ IS A BERLIN
DESIGN STUDIO FOUNDED BY OLIVER
WIEGNER AT THE END OF 2005. AS IT
DEVELOPED OUT OF A COLLECTIVE,
ICFF™ HAS ACCESS TO A MULTIDIS-
CIPLINARY TEAM OF DESIGNERS. THE
FOCUS IS ON PRINTS. ITS STYLE RE-
SULTS FROM IMPRESSIONS OF CURRENT
STREET ART AND THE ART SCENE IN
BERLIN AND THROUGHOUT THE WORLD.

--

WHAT IS GERMAN?

TURNING UP PUNCTUALLY, EVERY-
THING WITH YOU, A CLEAR CONCEPT
AND FIRST OF ALL ARRESTING RISK,
LOCKING IT UP AND LETTING IT DIE
OF HUNGER.

WHAT IS GERMAN DESIGN?

GERMAN DESIGN IS STOLID AND
STIFF, BUT IT'S TO BE HOPED IT'S
ON THE PATH TO IMPROVEMENT WHERE
BERLIN'S CONCERNED.

DESCRIBE YOUR WORKING PROCESS.

SOMETIMES I MULL A PROJECT
OVER, HAVE ASSOCIATIONS, DEVELOP
A CONCEPT AND TRY TO ENVISAGE THE
RESULT. IT CAN BE A VERY UNCLEAR
IMAGE, BUT OCCASIONALLY IT'S SO
PALPABLE THAT I'D LIKE TO EXPRESS
IT DIRECTLY FROM MY MEMORY. BUT
THE FACT THAT'S NOT POSSIBLE ALSO
BRINGS THE ADVANTAGE THAT IN THE
SUBSEQUENT IMPLEMENTATION PROCESS
A LOT OF THINGS ARE CHANGED AGAIN,
FOR THE BETTER. SO THE OUTCOME OF-

TEN LOOKS DIFFERENT COMPARED WITH
THE FIRST MENTAL IMAGE, BUT THIS
METHOD IS HELPFUL FOR ARRIVING AT
A FIRST IDEA.

WHAT DO YOU AIM TO ACHIEVE WITH
YOUR WORK?

EACH TIME WHEN I START A PROJ-
ECT, I'D LIKE TO GO A STEP FUR-
THER. I TRY TO PROVOKE OR CHAL-
LENGE WITH EVER MORE STRANGENESS
OR AN INDIVIDUAL ESTHETIC. I LIKE
TO GENERATE MISUNDERSTANDING.
I FEEL IT'S MORE INTERESTING IF
THE VIEWER DOESN'T UNDERSTAND MY
WORK STRAIGHT AWAY AND IS THERE-
FORE FORCED TO COME TO TERMS WITH
IT. AND OF COURSE I LIKE CREATING
BEAUTIFUL THINGS.

YOU'VE INVITED A FRIEND TO
GERMANY; NAME ONE PLACE THEY
REALLY MUST VISIT AND A QUINT-
ESSENTIAL EXPERIENCE YOU REC-
OMMEND.

THAT FRIEND SHOULD GO TO BERLIN
AND DO WHATEVER HE WANTS. YOU CAN
DO THAT IN BERLIN.

WHAT IS THE MOST IMPORTANT
LESSON YOU HAVE LEARNED IN YOUR
PROFESSION SO FAR?

THAT YOU HAVE TO ASSERT YOUR-
SELF.

--

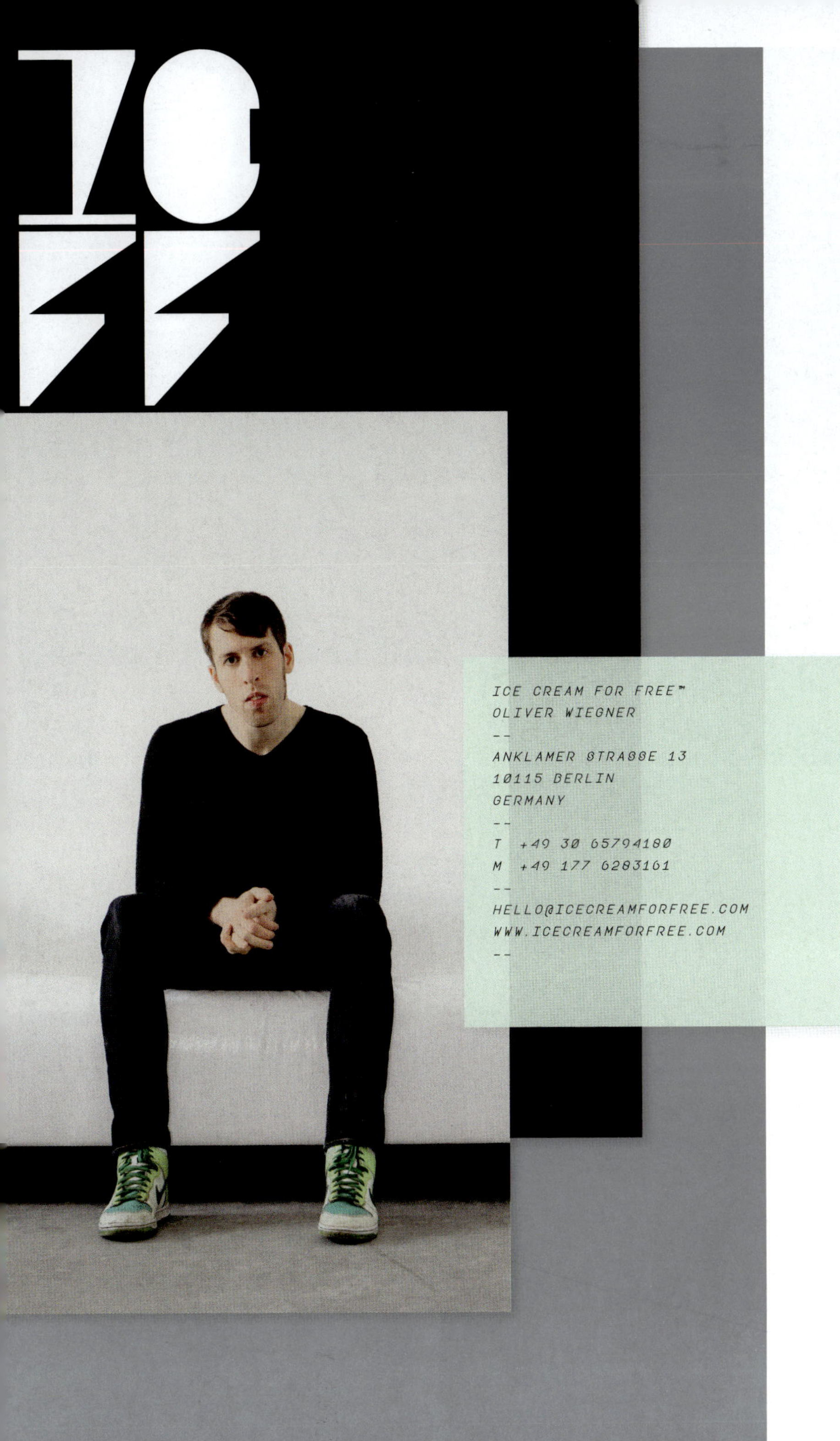

ICE CREAM FOR FREE™
OLIVER WIEGNER
--
ANKLAMER STRASSE 13
10115 BERLIN
GERMANY
--
T +49 30 65794180
M +49 177 6283161
--
HELLO@ICECREAMFORFREE.COM
WWW.ICECREAMFORFREE.COM
--

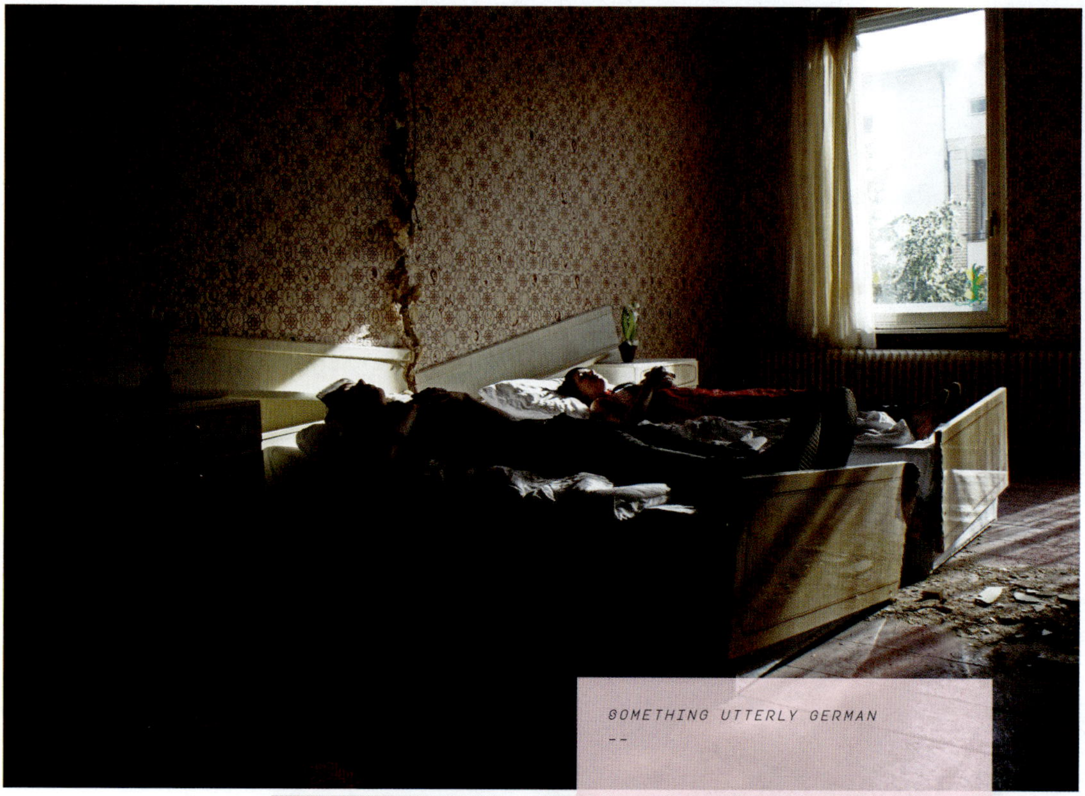

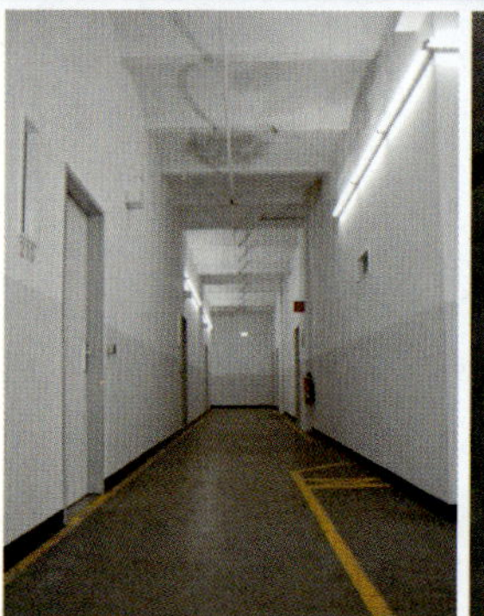

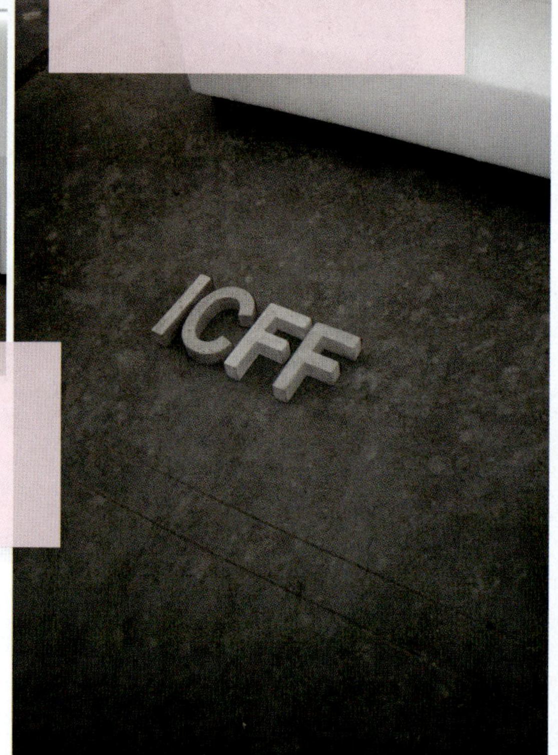

SOMETHING UTTERLY GERMAN
--

STUDIO SURROUNDINGS
--

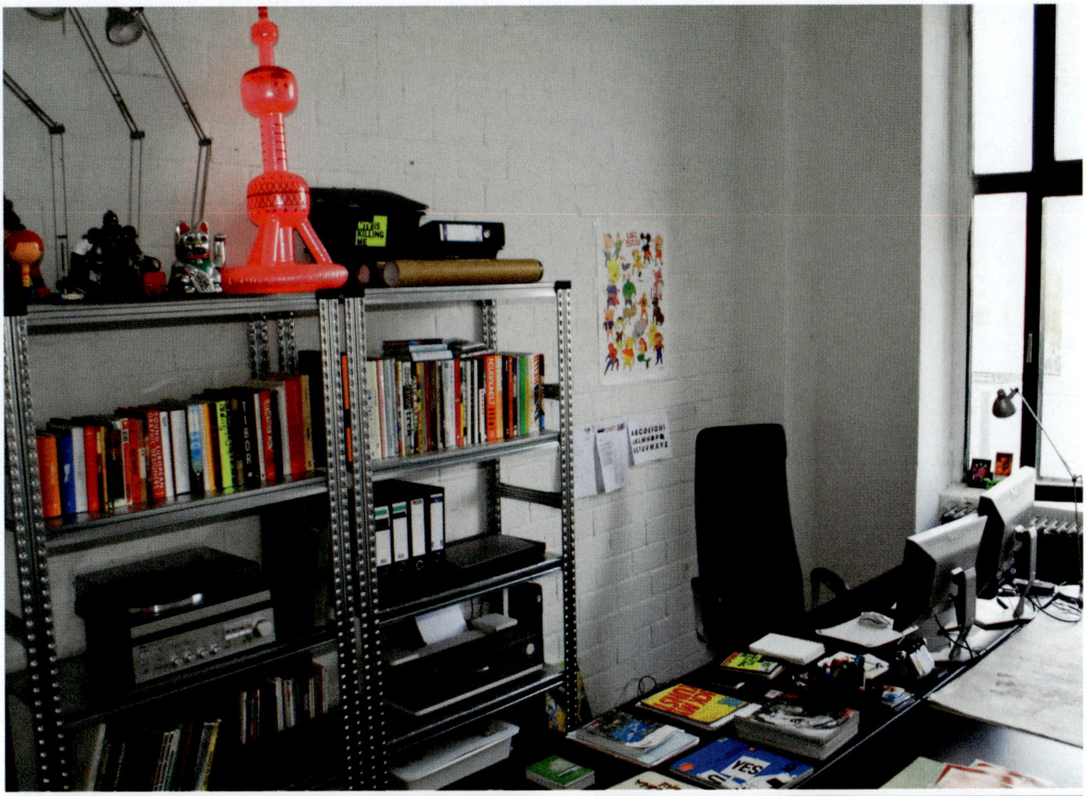

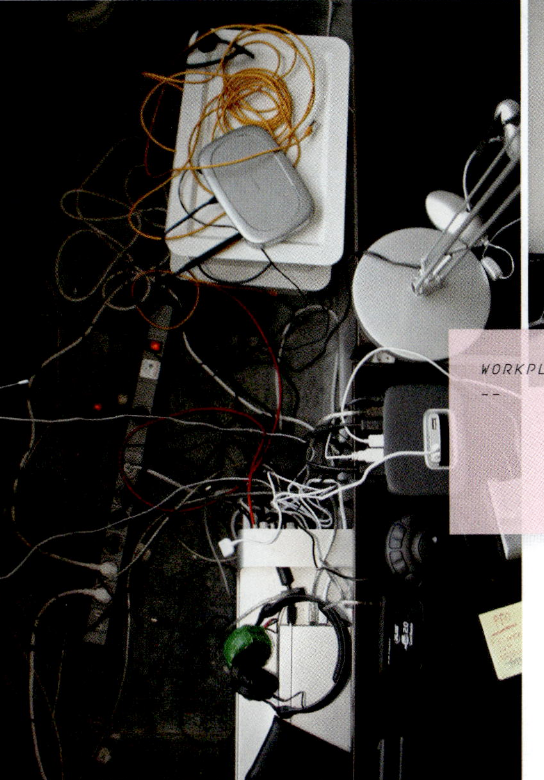
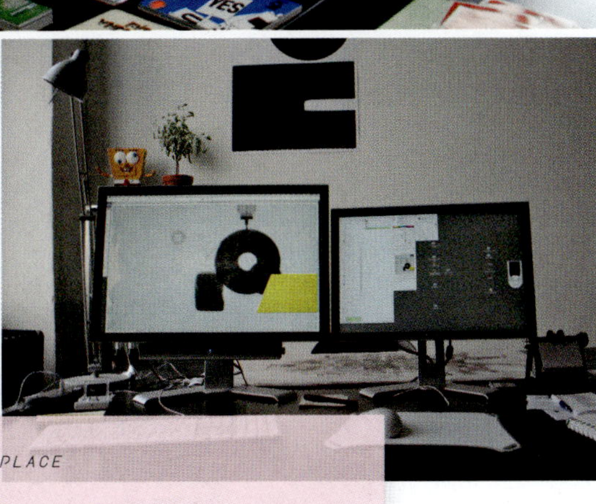

WORKPLACE
‒ ‒

DOG / HORSE
--
ILLUSTRATIONS ON SOME T-SHIRTS
FOR THE TOKYO-BASED FASHION LA-
BEL <AND A>. THEY ASKED ME TO
DO SOME ILLUSTRATIONS INSPIRED
BY SOME OTHER ILLUSTRATIONS I'D
DONE BEFORE.
--

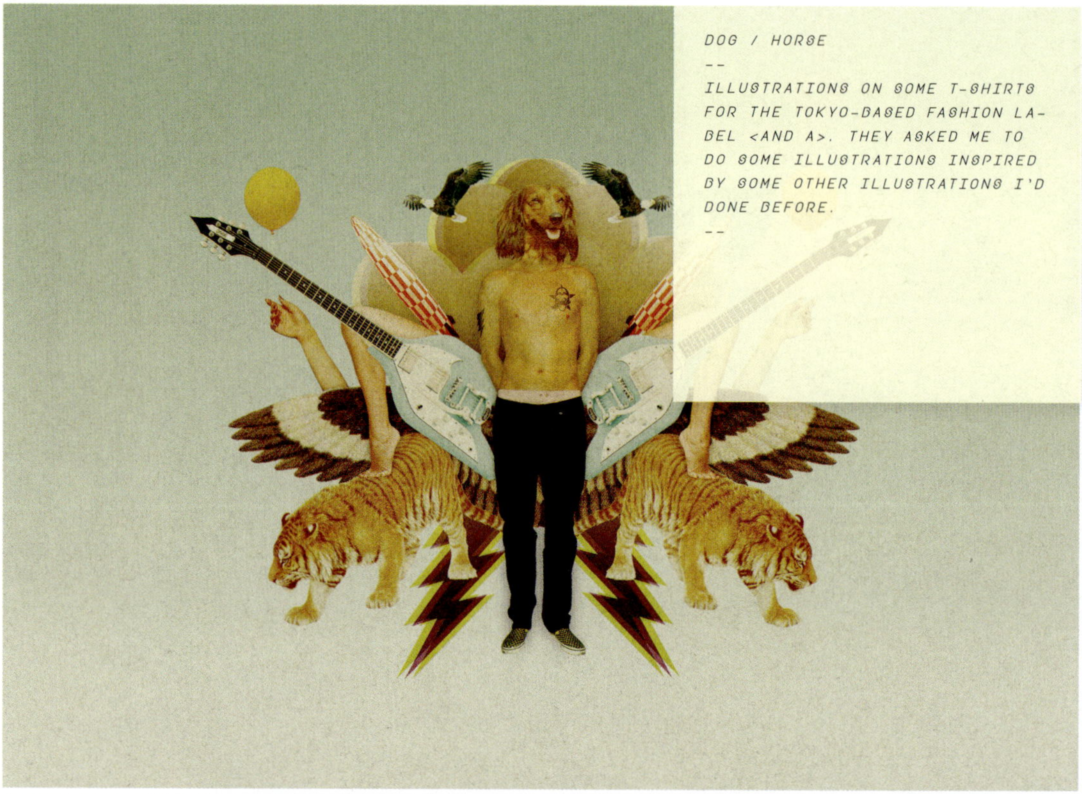

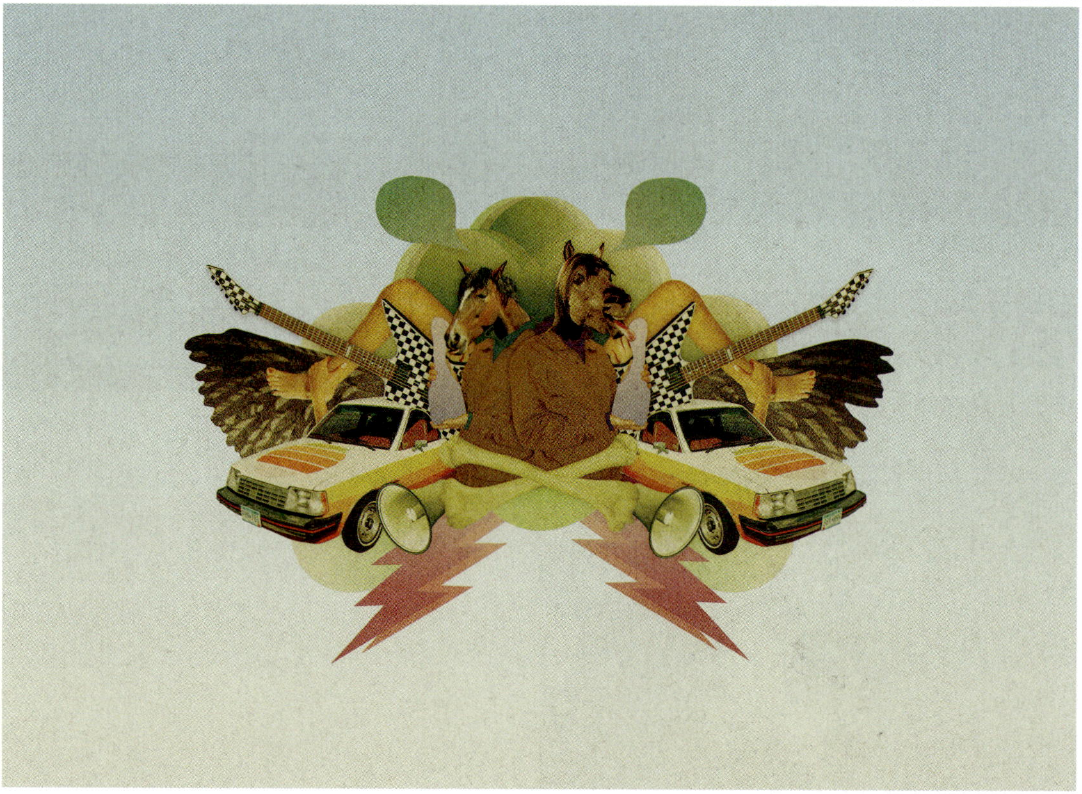

DOG / HORSE
--
ILLUSTRATIONS ON SOME T-SHIRTS
FOR THE TOKYO-BASED FASHION LA-
BEL <AND A>. THEY ASKED ME TO

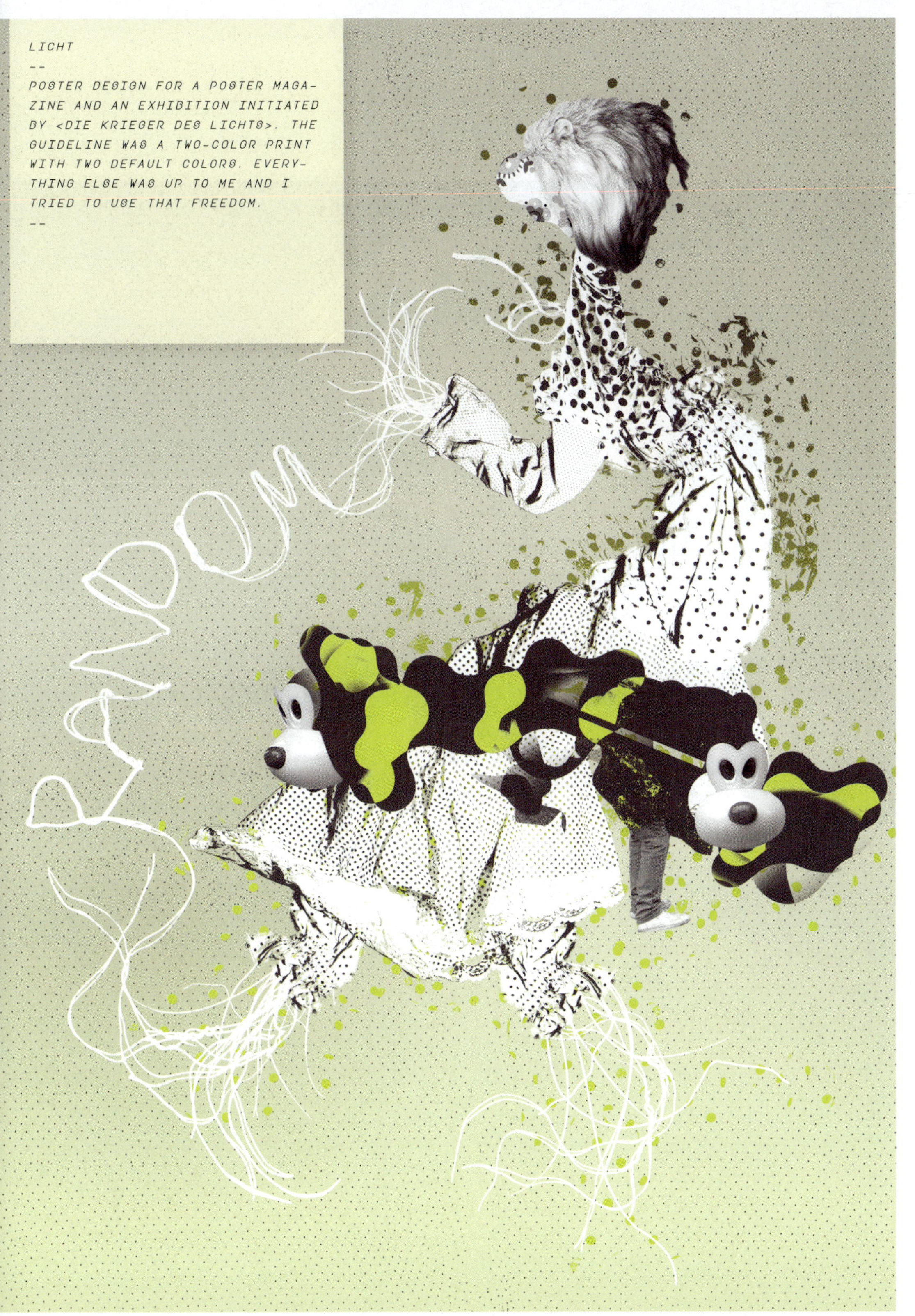
LICHT
--
POSTER DESIGN FOR A POSTER MAGA-
ZINE AND AN EXHIBITION INITIATED
BY <DIE KRIEGER DES LICHTS>. THE
GUIDELINE WAS A TWO-COLOR PRINT
WITH TWO DEFAULT COLORS. EVERY-
THING ELSE WAS UP TO ME AND I
TRIED TO USE THAT FREEDOM.
--

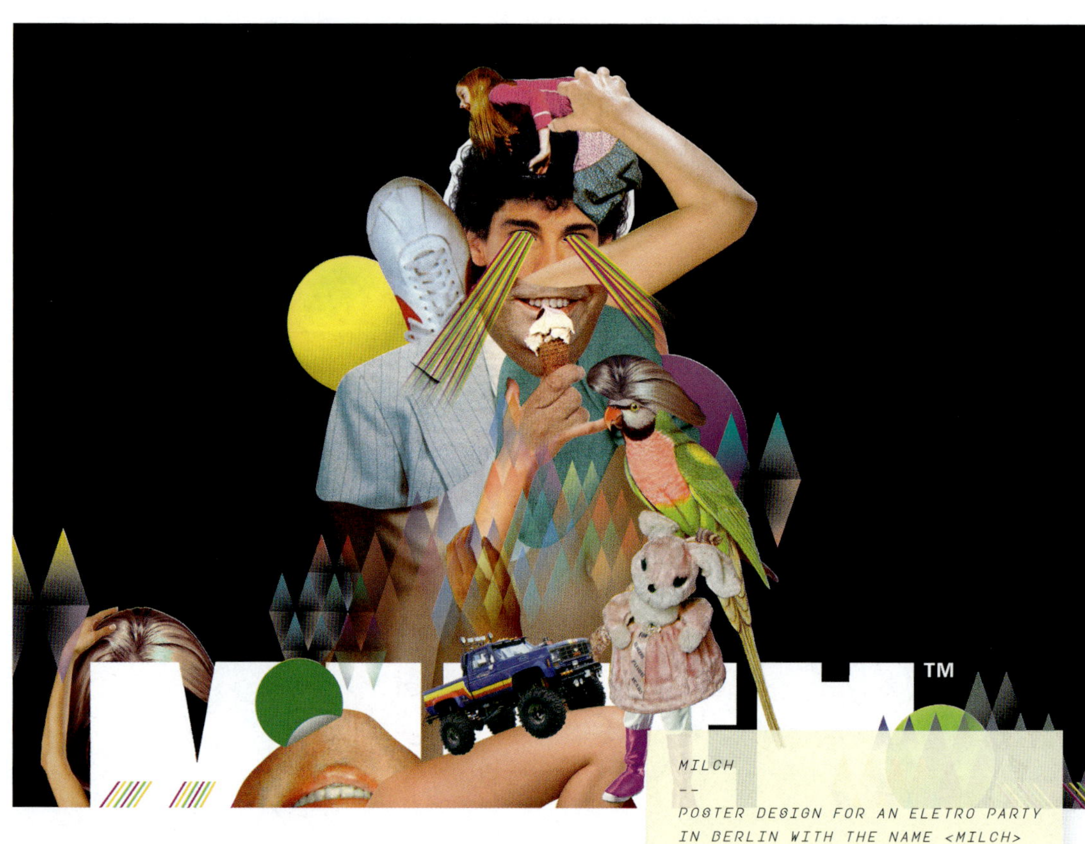

MILCH
--
POSTER DESIGN FOR AN ELETRO PARTY
IN BERLIN WITH THE NAME <MILCH>
WHICH IS THE GERMAN WORD FOR
MILK. SO I MIXED UP A LOT OF
WEIRD STUFF EXCEPT MILK.
--

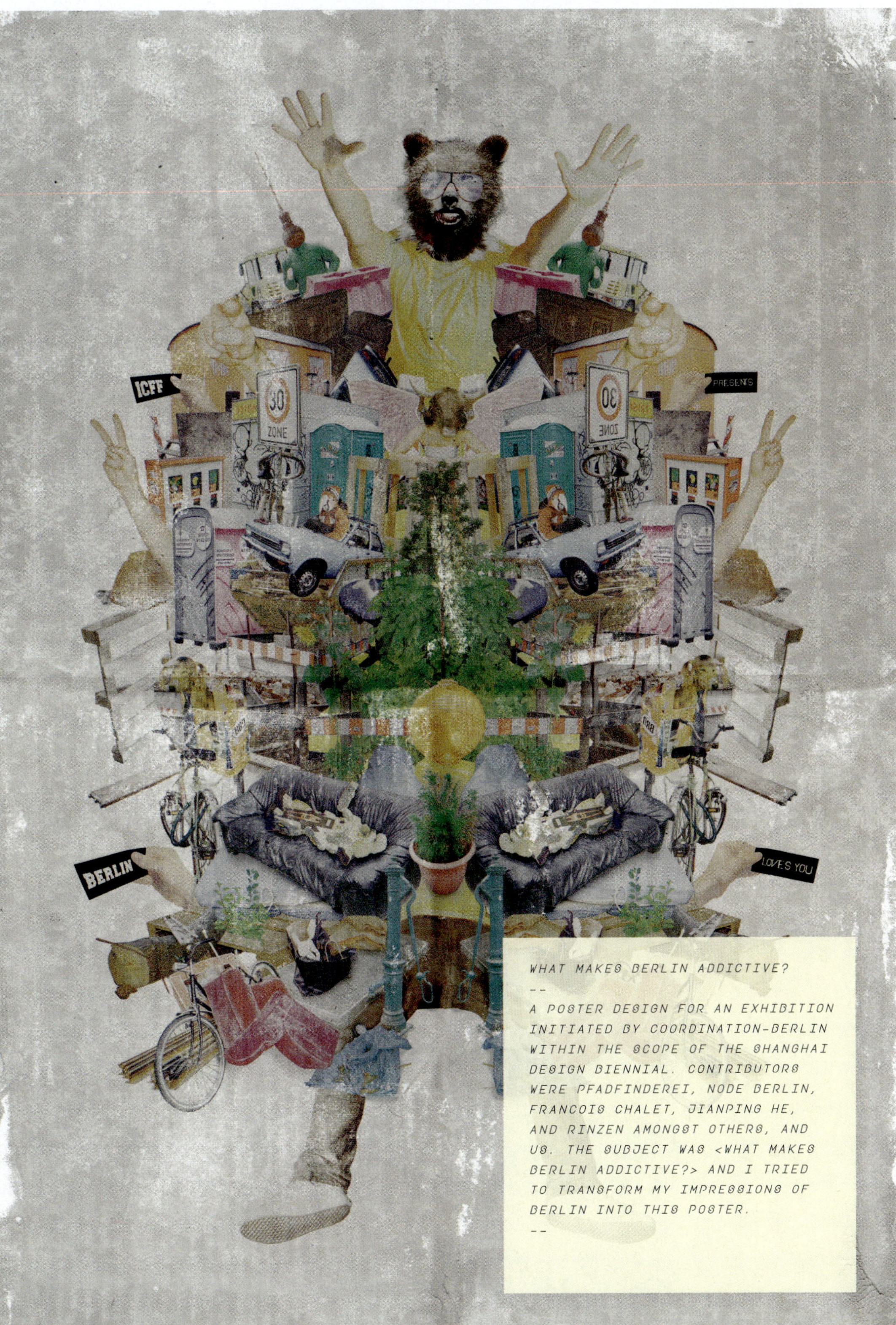

ICFF
PRESENTS
BERLIN
LOVES YOU
30 ZONE

WHAT MAKES BERLIN ADDICTIVE?
--
A POSTER DESIGN FOR AN EXHIBITION
INITIATED BY COORDINATION-BERLIN
WITHIN THE SCOPE OF THE SHANGHAI
DESIGN BIENNIAL. CONTRIBUTORS
WERE PFADFINDEREI, NODE BERLIN,
FRANCOIS CHALET, JIANPING HE,
AND RINZEN AMONGST OTHERS, AND
US. THE SUBJECT WAS <WHAT MAKES
BERLIN ADDICTIVE?> AND I TRIED
TO TRANSFORM MY IMPRESSIONS OF
BERLIN INTO THIS POSTER.
--

FORMING THE FORMLESS…
IS NOT ONLY THE TASK OF EVERY
GRAPHIC DESIGNER, BUT ALSO THE
TITLE OF MY BOOK PROJECT ABOUT
CLOUD-LOVERS AND EXPERIMENTAL
CLOUD SCIENTISTS. THE BOOK WAS
CREATED IN SUMMER 2007 IN THE CON-
TEXT OF MY DIPLOMA PROJECT AT THE
HOCHSCHULE DARMSTADT. AFTER GRADU-
ATING I WAS DRAWN TO OUR WONDERFUL
CAPITAL CITY BERLIN, WHERE I NOW
WORK FOR VARIOUS DESIGN AGENCIES
ON A FREELANCE BASIS. MY STRENGTHS
LIE IN THE FIELDS OF BOOK DESIGN,
EDITORIAL DESIGN, CORPORATE DESIGN
AND TYPOGRAPHY. MY GOAL IS A DE-
SIGN OFFICE OF MY OWN, BUT AS WE
KNOW THE PATH IS THE GOAL.

--

WHAT IS GERMAN?

NICE PEOPLE, PUNCTUALITY,
GOOD BEER!

WHAT IS GERMAN DESIGN?

FUNCTIONAL, SIMPLE, BUT AT THE
SAME TIME MODERN, PRECISE, LOVE
OF DETAIL.

DESCRIBE YOUR WORKING PROCESS.

DEFINITION OF THE PROBLEM AND
RESEARCH, ANALYSIS, COLLECTING
MATERIAL, CONCEPT FOR THE VISUAL
DESIGN, ELABORATION, IMPLEMENTA-
TION AND PRODUCTION.

WHAT DO YOU AIM TO ACHIEVE WITH
YOUR WORK?

DRAWING ATTENTION TO THINGS THAT
ARE LOST IN THE HECTIC EVERYDAY
ROUND. AND FOR OTHER PEOPLE TO DE-
RIVE ENJOYMENT FROM MY WORKS.

YOU'VE INVITED A FRIEND TO
GERMANY; NAME ONE PLACE THEY
REALLY MUST VISIT AND A QUINT-
ESSENTIAL EXPERIENCE YOU REC-
OMMEND.

HE SHOULD COME TO BERLIN AND ENJOY
LIFE. AND OF COURSE EAT A CURRIED
SAUSAGE.

WHAT IS THE MOST IMPORTANT
LESSON YOU HAVE LEARNED IN YOUR
PROFESSION SO FAR?

THAT YOU SHOULD NEVER UNDERSELL
YOURSELF. AND THAT IT'S EXACTLY
WHAT I'LL ALWAYS WANT TO DO.

--

JU–LIA ROMPEL

JULIA ROMPEL

--

JULIA.ROMPEL@WEB.DE
HTTP://WWW.JULIA-ROMPEL.DE

--

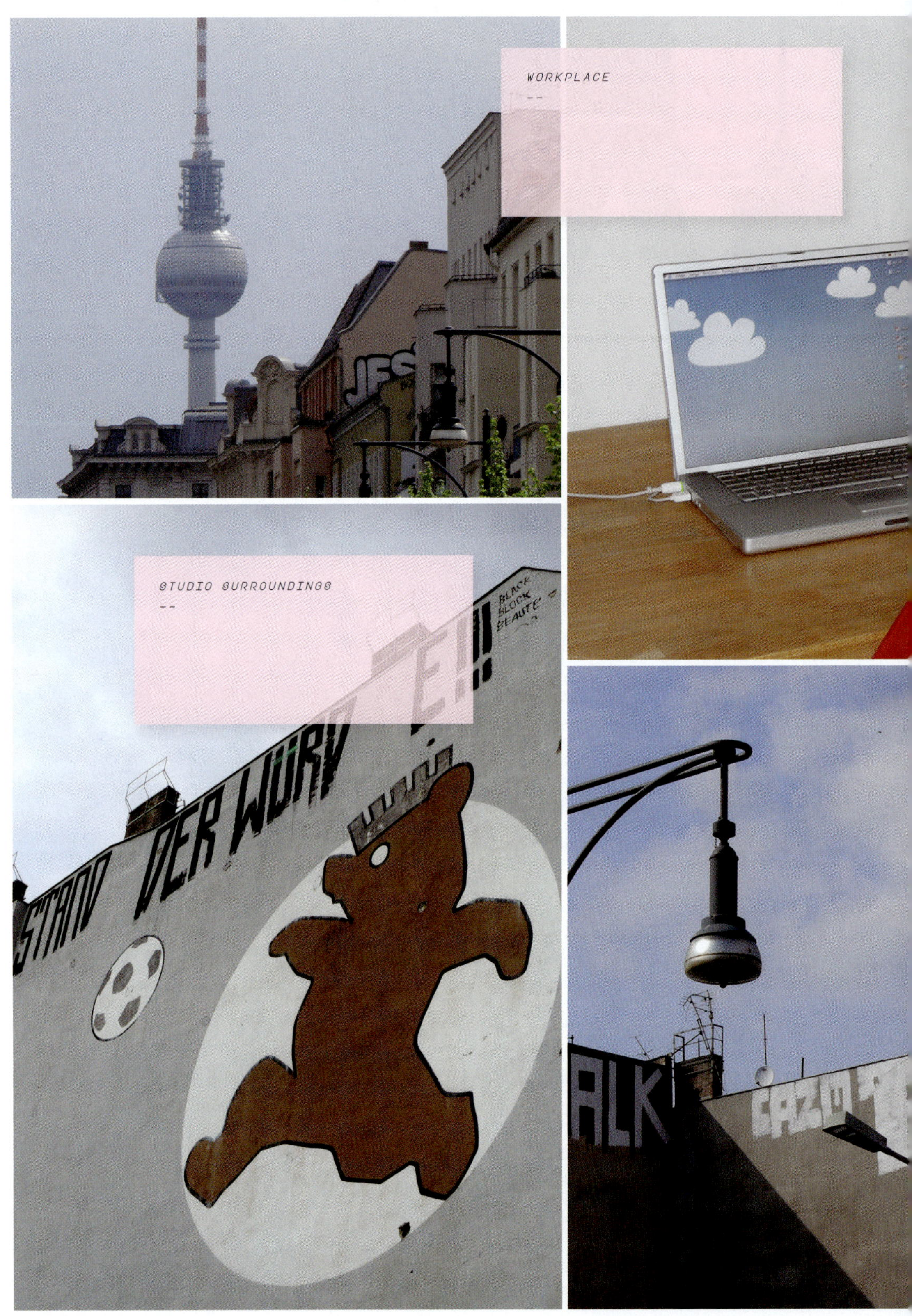
WORKPLACE
--
STUDIO SURROUNDINGS
--

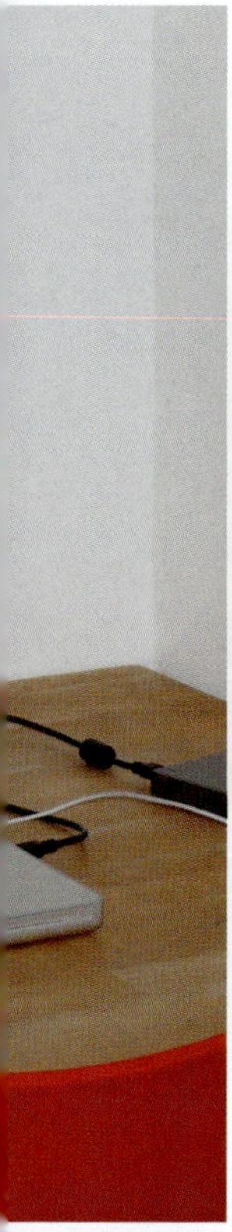

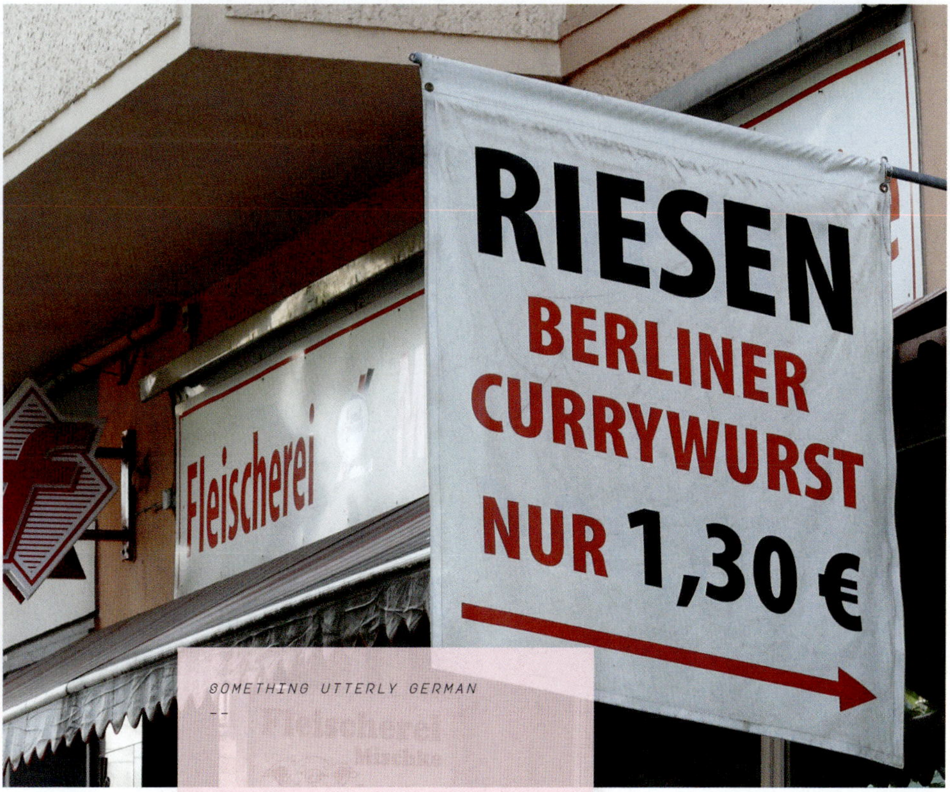

SOMETHING UTTERLY GERMAN
--

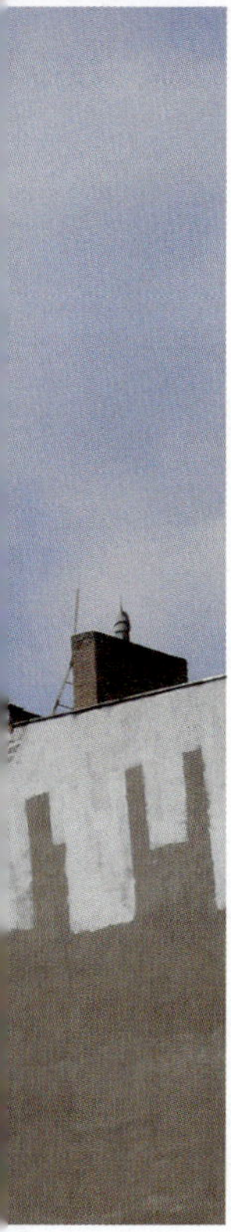

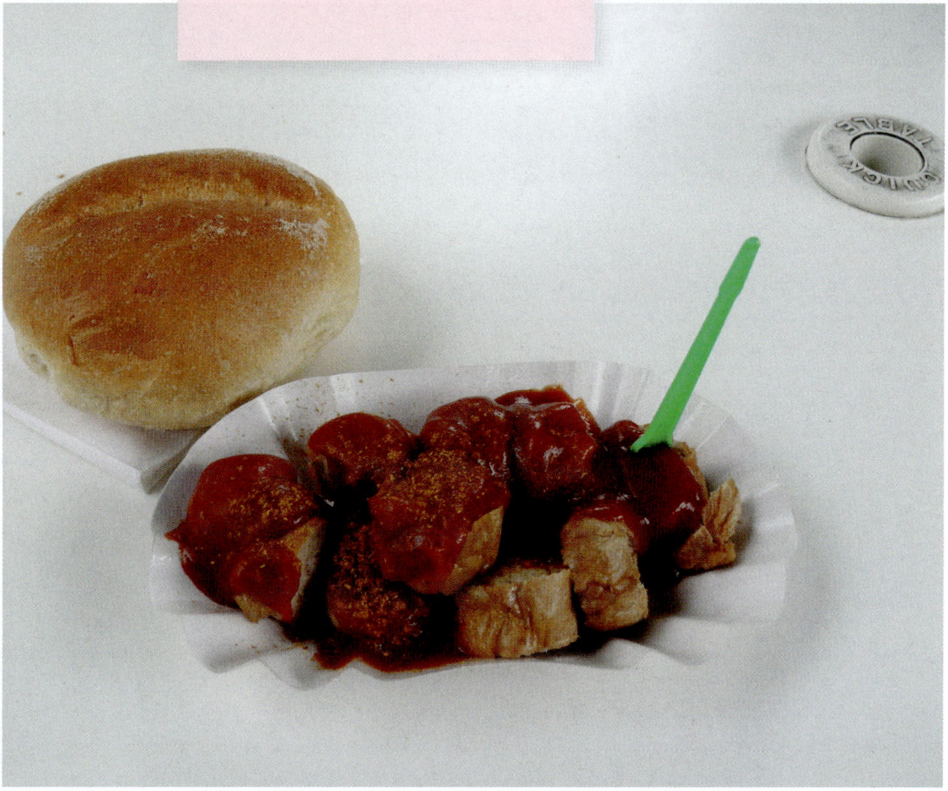

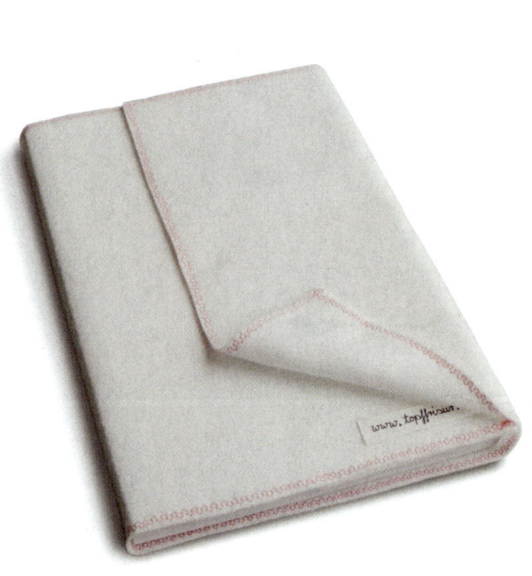

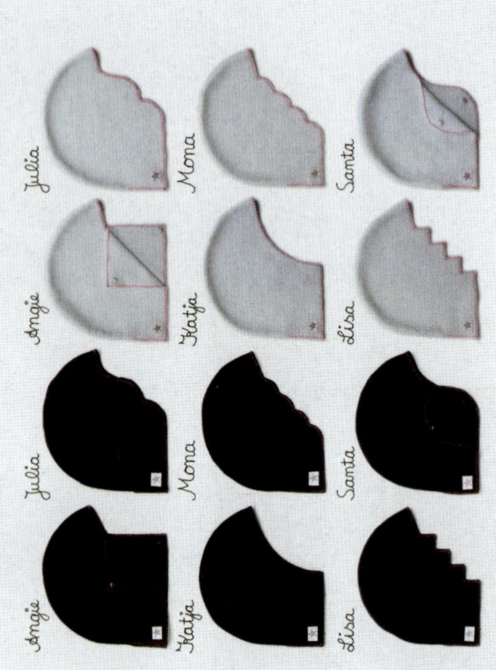

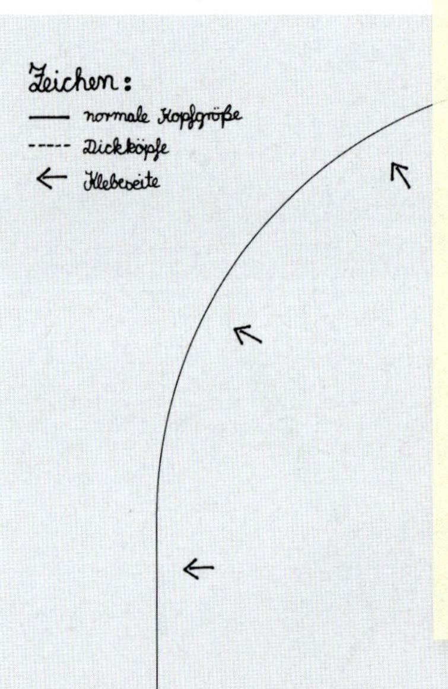

THE PERFECT PUDDING-BASIN
HAIRCUT
WWW.TOPFFRISUR.DE
--
THE WEBSITE AMUSINGLY INTRODUCES
A COMPLETELY NEW METHOD OF HAIR
DESIGN WITH THE HELP OF A PATTERN
SHEET. THIS CAN BE DOWNLOADED
FREE OF CHARGE IN SIX VERSIONS
FROM THE WEBSITE WWW.TOPFFRI-
SUR.DE, OR PURCHASED IN PRINTED
FORM. IN ADDITION FELT CAPS WERE
CREATED BASED ON THE CUTS OF THE
HAIRDOS. THE BOOK SHOWS THE DE-
VELOPMENT OF THE PUDDING-BASIN
HAIRCUT AND HOW TO DO IT.
--
TERM PROJECT AT
HOCHSCHULE DARMSTADT
TUTOR: PROF. MIKE RICHTER
--

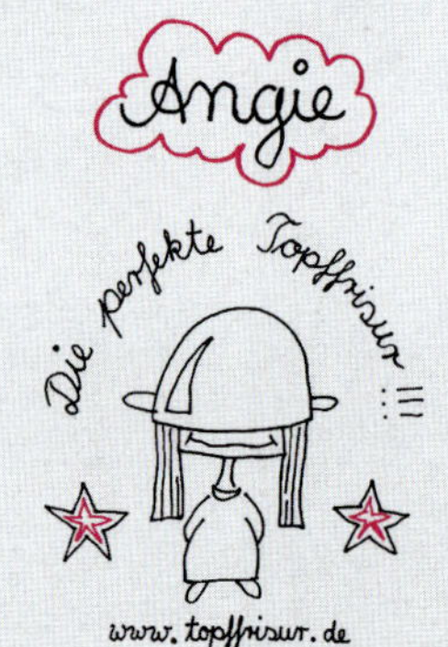

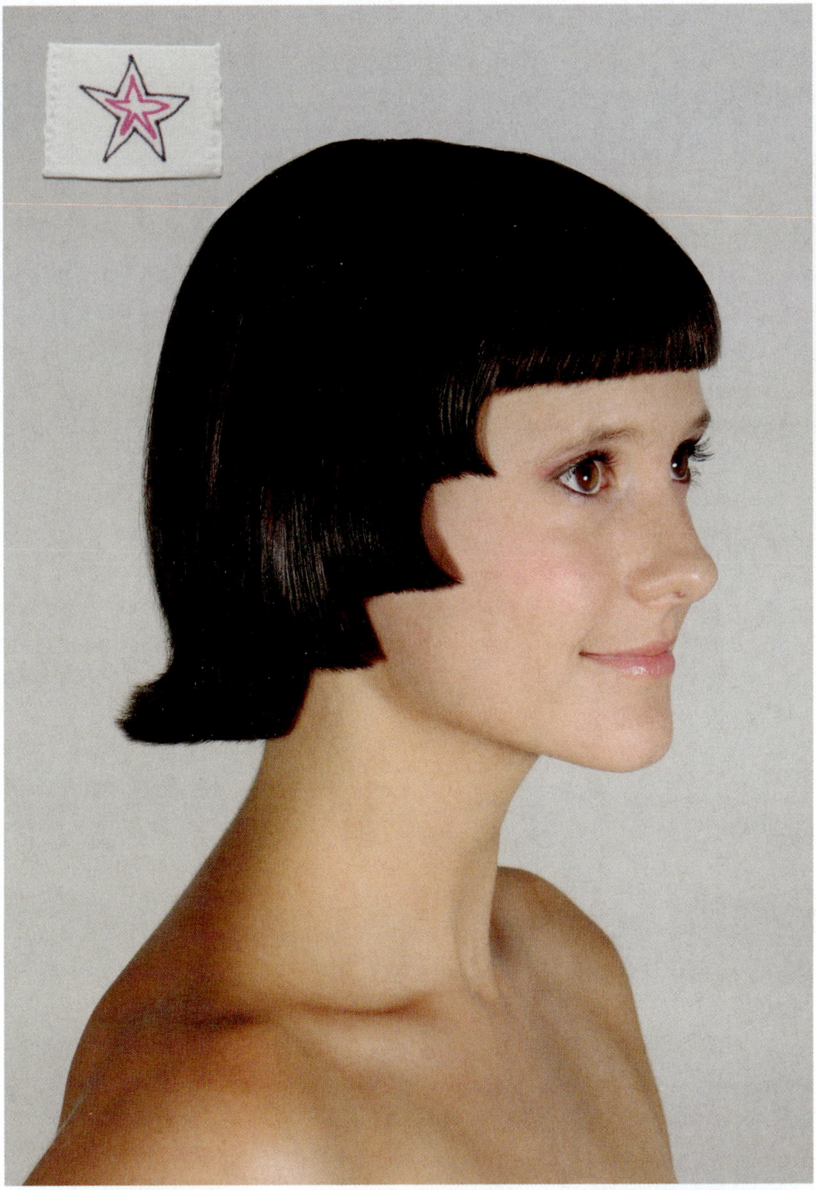

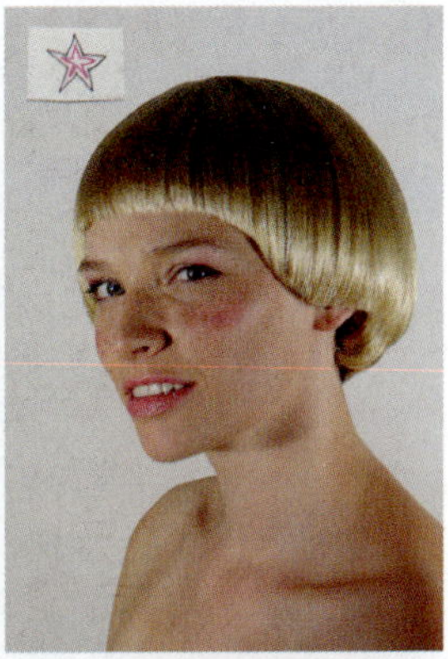

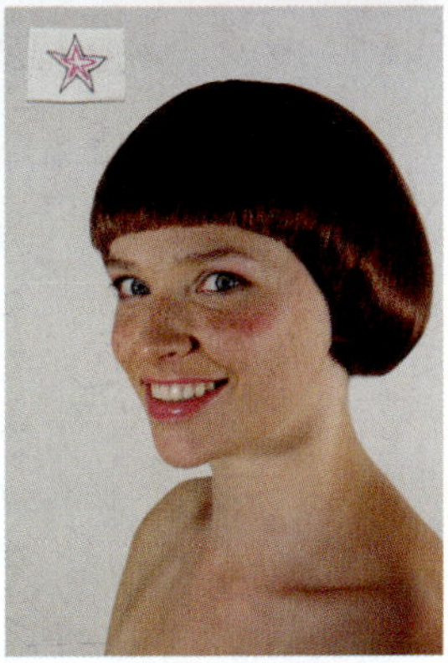

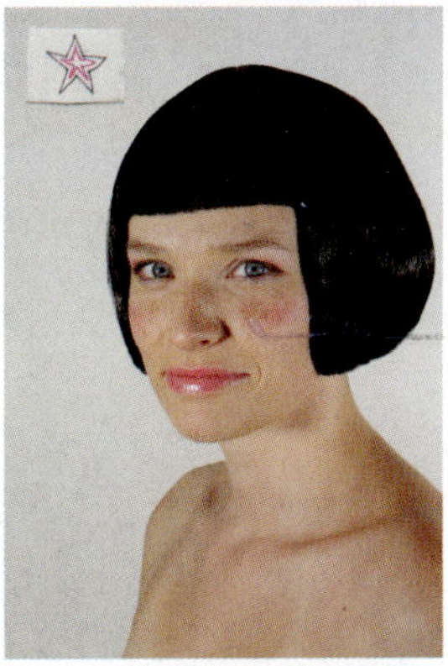

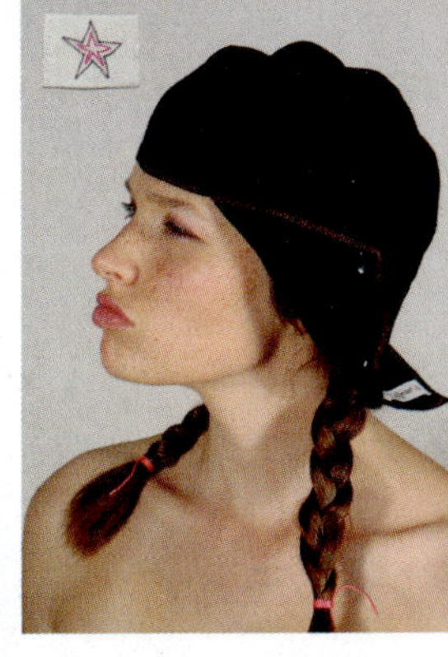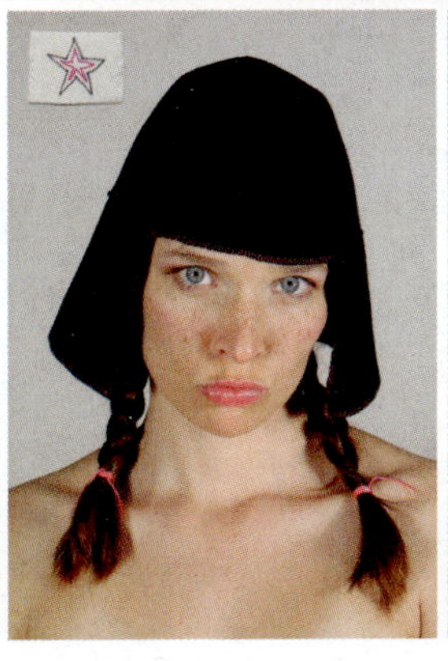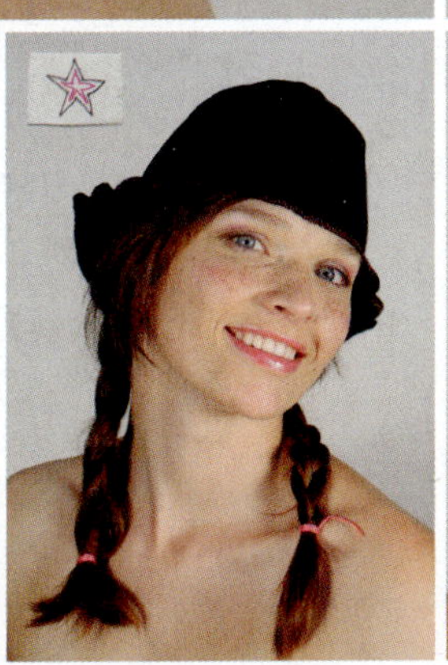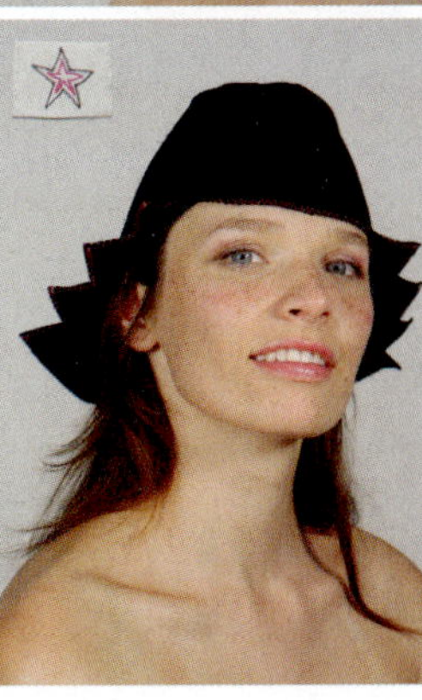

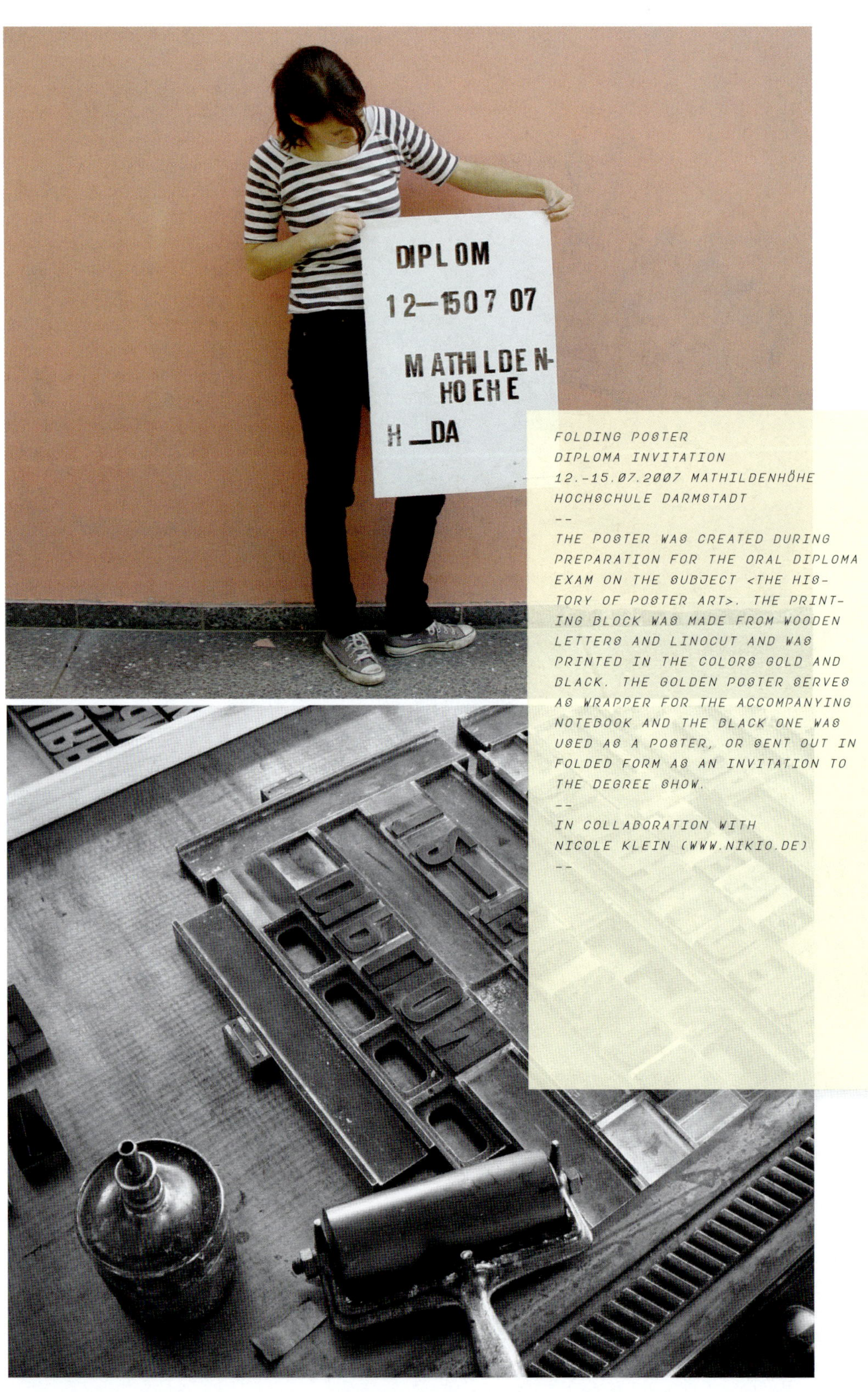

DIPLOM
12—15 07 07
MATHILDEN-
HOEHE
H _DA

FOLDING POSTER
DIPLOMA INVITATION
12.-15.07.2007 MATHILDENHÖHE
HOCHSCHULE DARMSTADT
--
THE POSTER WAS CREATED DURING
PREPARATION FOR THE ORAL DIPLOMA
EXAM ON THE SUBJECT <THE HIS-
TORY OF POSTER ART>. THE PRINT-
ING BLOCK WAS MADE FROM WOODEN
LETTERS AND LINOCUT AND WAS
PRINTED IN THE COLORS GOLD AND
BLACK. THE GOLDEN POSTER SERVES
AS WRAPPER FOR THE ACCOMPANYING
NOTEBOOK AND THE BLACK ONE WAS
USED AS A POSTER, OR SENT OUT IN
FOLDED FORM AS AN INVITATION TO
THE DEGREE SHOW.
--
IN COLLABORATION WITH
NICOLE KLEIN (WWW.NIKIO.DE)
--

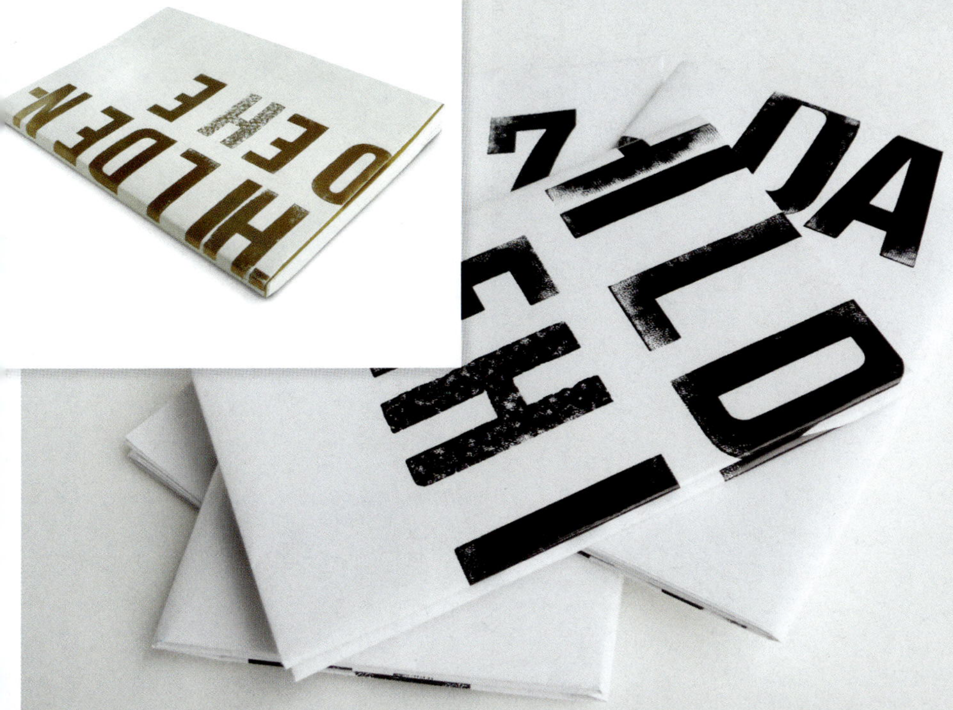

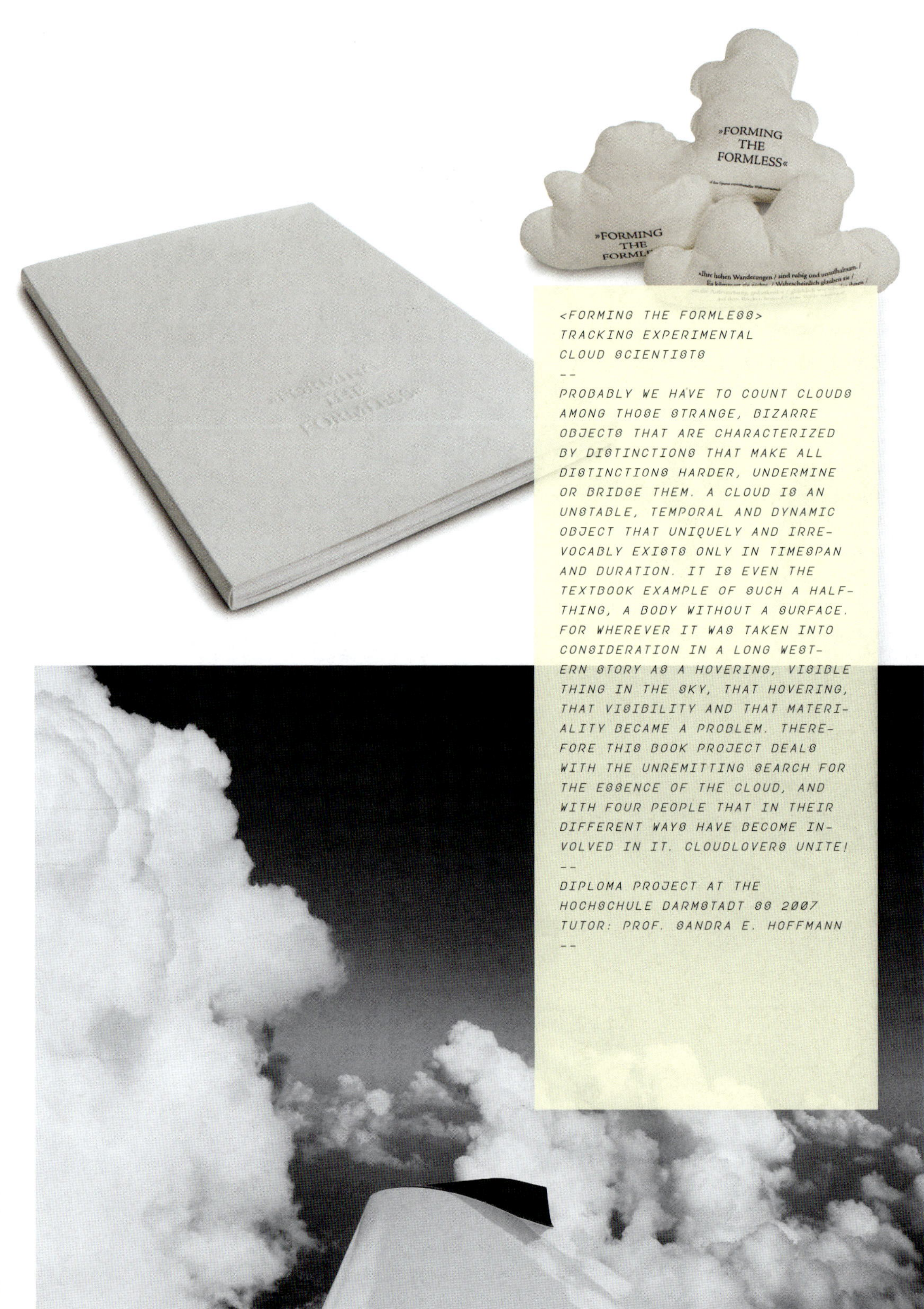

<FORMING THE FORMLESS>
TRACKING EXPERIMENTAL
CLOUD SCIENTISTS
--
PROBABLY WE HAVE TO COUNT CLOUDS
AMONG THOSE STRANGE, BIZARRE
OBJECTS THAT ARE CHARACTERIZED
BY DISTINCTIONS THAT MAKE ALL
DISTINCTIONS HARDER, UNDERMINE
OR BRIDGE THEM. A CLOUD IS AN
UNSTABLE, TEMPORAL AND DYNAMIC
OBJECT THAT UNIQUELY AND IRRE-
VOCABLY EXISTS ONLY IN TIMESPAN
AND DURATION. IT IS EVEN THE
TEXTBOOK EXAMPLE OF SUCH A HALF-
THING, A BODY WITHOUT A SURFACE.
FOR WHEREVER IT WAS TAKEN INTO
CONSIDERATION IN A LONG WEST-
ERN STORY AS A HOVERING, VISIBLE
THING IN THE SKY, THAT HOVERING,
THAT VISIBILITY AND THAT MATERI-
ALITY BECAME A PROBLEM. THERE-
FORE THIS BOOK PROJECT DEALS
WITH THE UNREMITTING SEARCH FOR
THE ESSENCE OF THE CLOUD, AND
WITH FOUR PEOPLE THAT IN THEIR
DIFFERENT WAYS HAVE BECOME IN-
VOLVED IN IT. CLOUDLOVERS UNITE!
--
DIPLOMA PROJECT AT THE
HOCHSCHULE DARMSTADT SS 2007
TUTOR: PROF. SANDRA E. HOFFMANN
--

»FORMING
THE
FORMLESS«

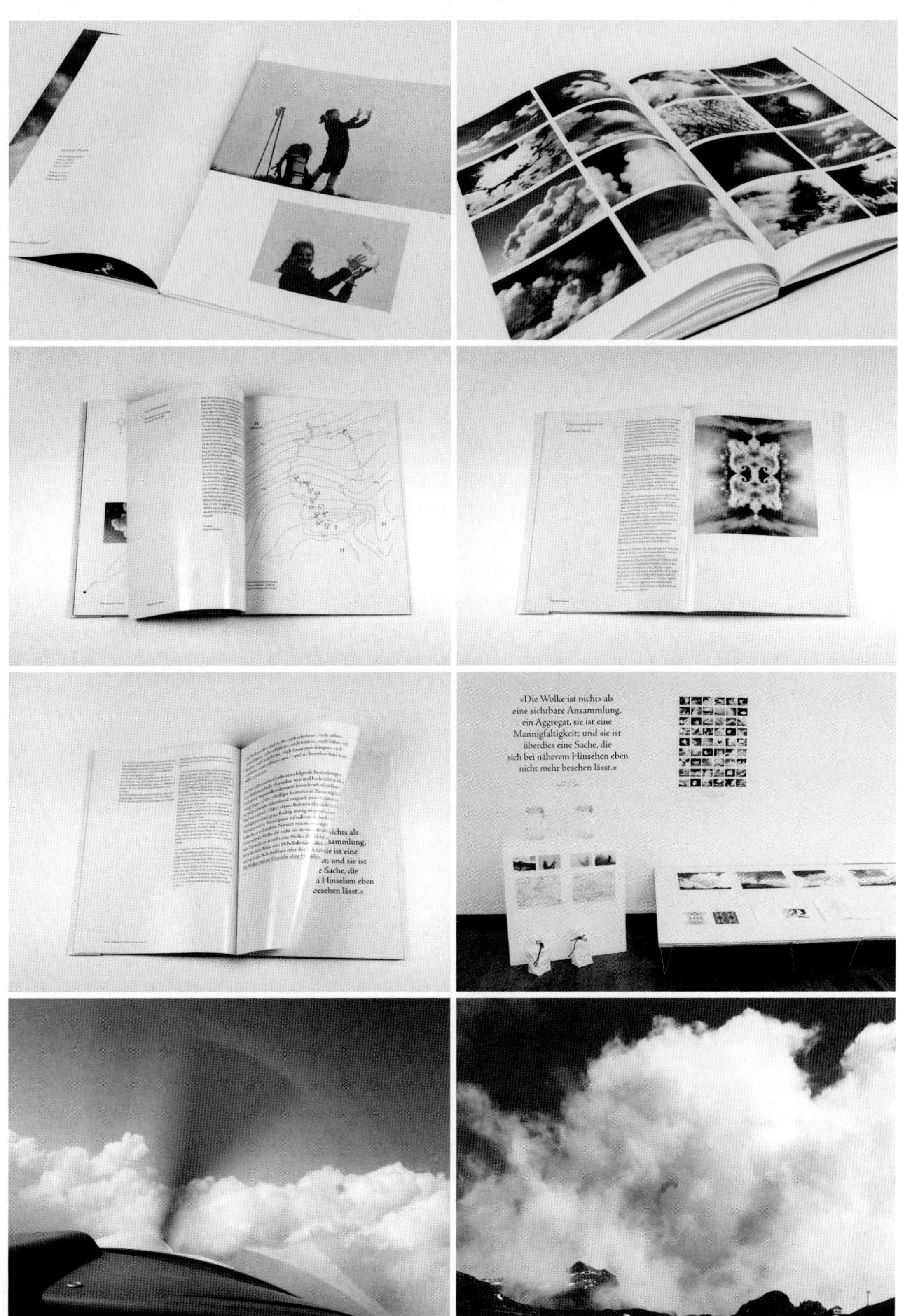
»Die Wolke ist nichts als
eine sichtbare Ansammlung,
ein Aggregat, sie ist eine
Mannigfaltigkeit; und sie ist
überdies eine Sache, die
sich bei näherem Hinsehen eben
nicht mehr besehen lässt.«

I WAS BORN IN 1979 IN OFFENBACH A.
M. NEAR FRANKFURT. AFTER FINISHING
SCHOOL IN 1999 I STARTED STUDYING
ARCHITECTURE IN DARMSTADT FOR 2
YEARS. IN SUMMER 2001 I CHANGED MY
MIND AND STUDIED GRAPHIC DESIGN.
KEKIRETTA.NET WAS FOUNDED IN 2005
WHILE I WAS STUDYING AT UNIVERSI-
TY OF APPLIED SCIENCES IN DARM-
STADT. AFTER STAYING IN ZURICH FOR
INTERNSHIPS AT ELEKTROSMOG AND
INSTITUTE DESIGN2CONTEXT OF HGKZ,
HEADED BY RUEDI BAUR, I STARTED
WORKING FOR SEVERAL OFFICES IN
DARMSTADT AND FRANKFURT. IN 2005
I PUBLISHED <TAPE - AN EXCURSION
THROUGH THE WORLD OF ADHESIVE
TAPES> AT DIE GESTALTEN VERLAG
BERLIN. AFTER GRADUATING IN 2006,
I MOVED TO BERLIN TO WORK FOR OF-
FICES LIKE FONS HICKMANN M23, SVEN
VÖLKER STUDIO, META DESIGN AND ASB
ONE AND TO DEVELOP SELF-INITIATED
PROJECTS. IN 2006 I RAN A WORKSHOP
FOR <TAPE-ENTHUSIASTIC> STUDENTS
IN MILAN ORGANIZED BY SIGNJAM
PROJECTS, WITH JERSEY SEYMOUR AND
FLORIAN BÖHM AS GUESTS. IN 2007 A
LECTURE FOLLOWED, TOGETHER WITH
DIANA DJEDDI AS A GUEST SPEAKER.
AT THE END OF 2007, I WAS PART OF
<YDMI - YOUNG DESIGNERS MEET THE
INDUSTRY> INITIATED BY THE GERMAN
DESIGN COUNCIL IN FRANKFURT. IN
2008 I GAVE ANOTHER LECTURE AT THE
HFG KARLSRUHE ABOUT THE PERIOD
FOLLOWING GRADUATION.

--

WHAT IS GERMAN?

MODESTY,
NOT BEING NATIONALISTIC.

WHAT IS GERMAN DESIGN?

BEING INNOVATIVE,
WITHOUT SHOCKING PEOPLE.

DESCRIBE YOUR WORKING PROCESS.

PRECEDING THE DESIGN PROCESS, A
COMPREHENSIVE RESEARCH INTO THE
COMPETITORS TAKES PLACE. IN ADDI-
TION I LIKE DERIVING INSPIRATION
FROM MY COLLECTION CONSISTING OF
SO-CALLED <READYMADES> (EVERY-
DAY OBJECTS DESIGNED IN AN UNCON-
SCIOUSLY INTERESTING WAY).

WHAT DO YOU AIM TO ACHIEVE WITH
YOUR WORK?

I'D LIKE TO USE PUBLICATIONS OF
VARIOUS KINDS TO DRAW ATTENTION TO
TRENDS IN DESIGN, AND TO COLLATE
THINGS IN ORDER TO INSPIRE OTHER
DESIGNERS IN THAT WAY. OF COURSE
I'D ALSO BE VERY HAPPY TO EXPAND
GERMAN'S DESIGN AWARENESS WITH
MY WORK SO THAT IN CONTACT WITH
THE CLIENT WE DIDN'T ALWAYS COME
UP AGAINST READY-MADE IMAGES AND
PATHS.

YOU'VE INVITED A FRIEND TO
GERMANY; NAME ONE PLACE THEY
REALLY MUST VISIT AND A QUINT-
ESSENTIAL EXPERIENCE YOU REC-
OMMEND.

THE VISITOR SHOULD HIRE A
BIKE, AND STARTING ON PRENZLAUER
ALLEE RIDE ALONG KARL-LIEBKNECHT
STRASSE TOWARDS ALEXANDERPLATZ,
FOLLOW UNTER DEN LINDEN TO THE
BRANDENBURG GATE AND PERHAPS CAR-
RY ON TOWARDS THE TIERGARTEN. ON
THE WAY BACK INCLUDE A DETOUR TO
THE KARL-MARX-ALLEE, WHICH IS ALSO
A QUITE UNIQUE EXPERIENCE. - WHAT
IMPRESSES ME THERE IS THE PALPABLE
LARGENESS OF THE HISTORIC BUILD-
INGS IN BERLIN, COMPARABLE TO THE
POWER OF THE WAVES OF THE ATLANTIC
IN FRANCE.

WHAT IS THE MOST IMPORTANT LES-
SON YOU HAVE LEARNED IN YOUR
PROFESSION SO FAR?

TO WORK VERY ACCURATELY, FOR
SOME MISTAKES SIMPLY CAN'T BE REC-
TIFIED, FOR EXAMPLE OFFSET PRINTED
MATERIAL. - BUT THAT ALSO APPLIES
TO OTHER FIELDS SUCH AS COMMUNICA-
TION, SAY.

--

KEKIRETTA

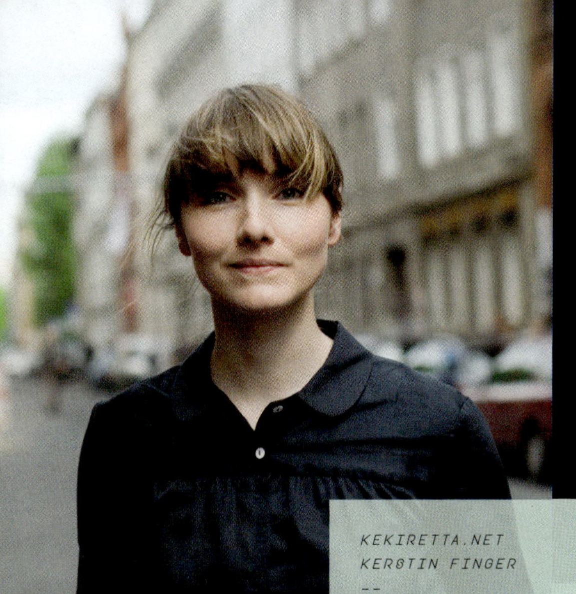

KEKIRETTA.NET
KERSTIN FINGER
--
HEINRICH-ROLLER-STRASSE 19
10405 BERLIN
GERMANY
--
T +49 30 41715563
M +49 177 7378220
--
HELLO@KEKIRETTA.NET
WWW.KEKIRETTA.NET
WWW.SOPHISTICATEDBUMMBUMM.NET
--

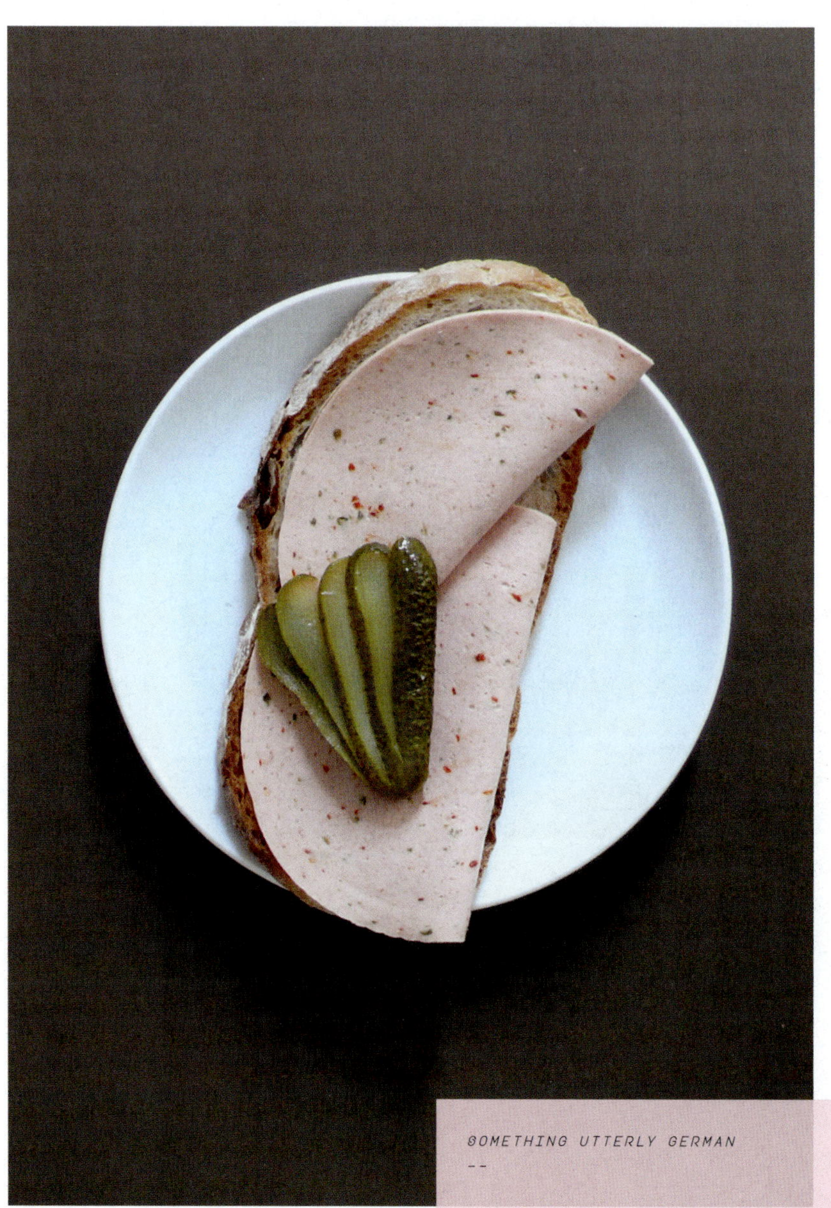

SOMETHING UTTERLY GERMAN
--

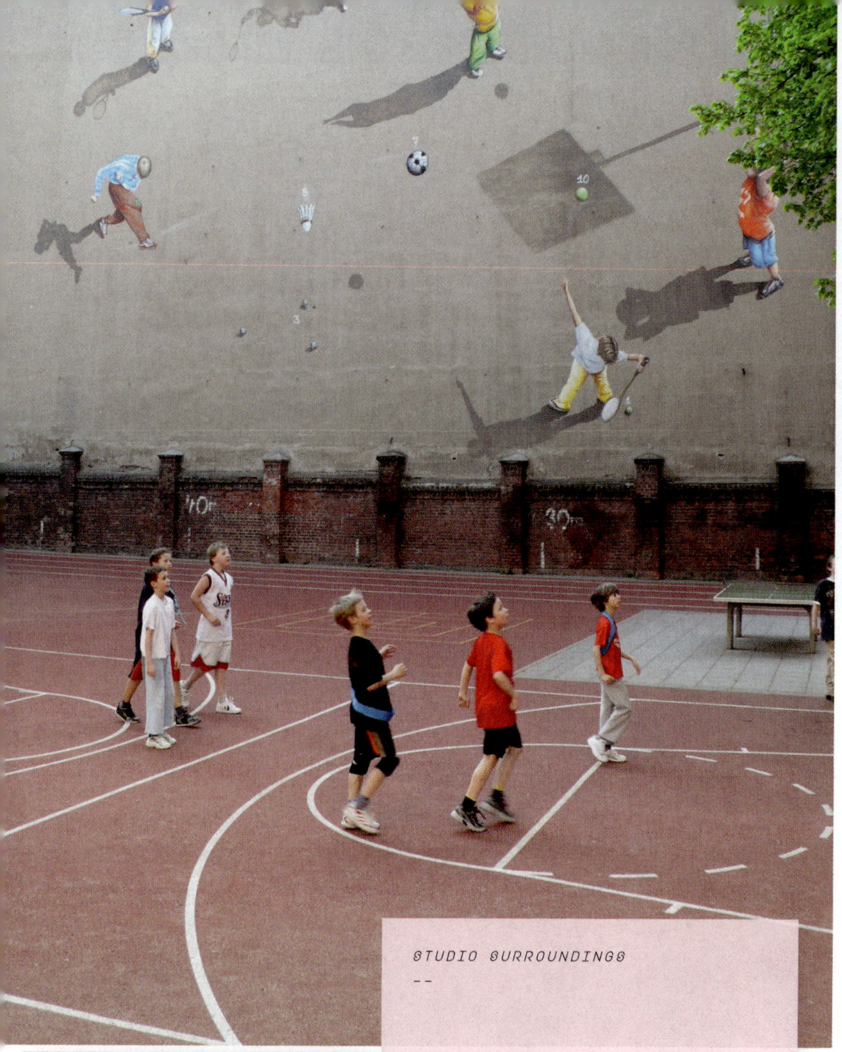

STUDIO SURROUNDINGS
--

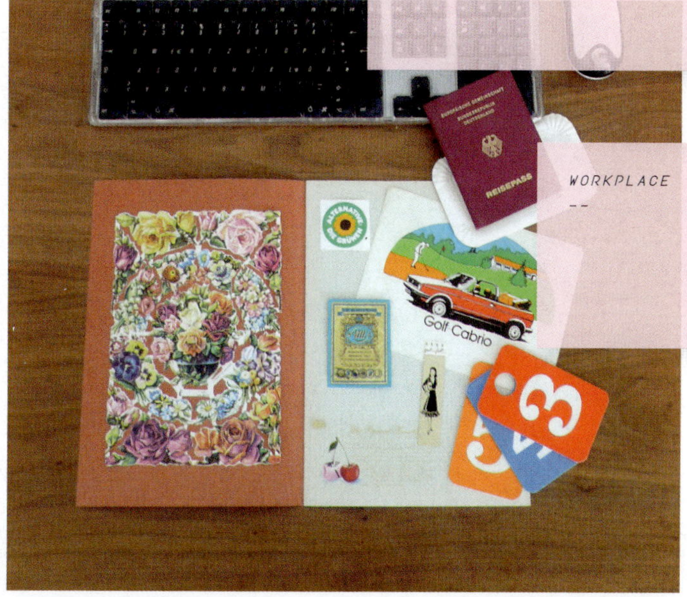
WORKPLACE
--

Zeitraum 1957–1977
Staatsform Demokratisch-Parlamentarischer Bundesstaat
Stand der Technik Synthesizer und Super 8

Radikal PENG!

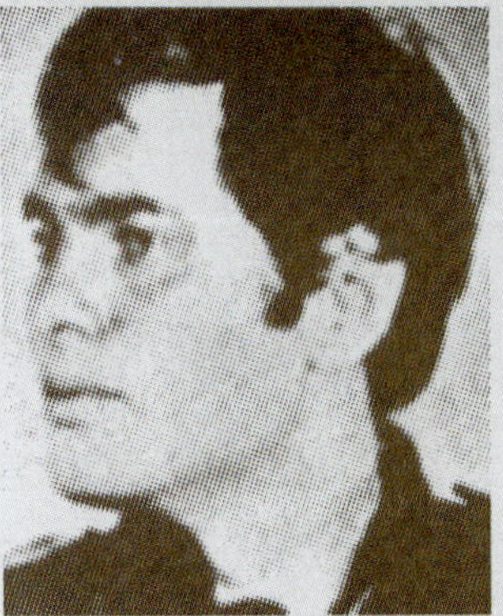

Baader, Andreas * 6. Mai 1943 in München

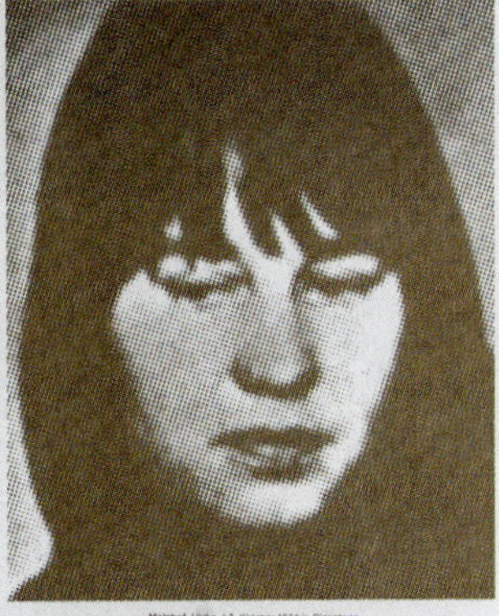

Meinhof, Ulrike * 7. Oktober 1934 in Oldenburg

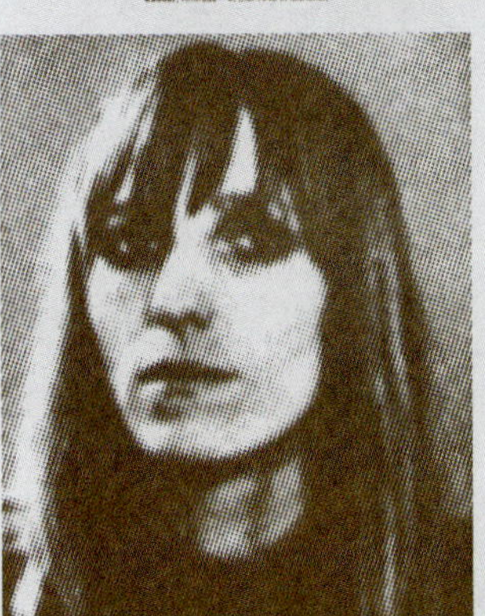

Ensslin, Gudrun * 15. August 1940 in Bartholomä

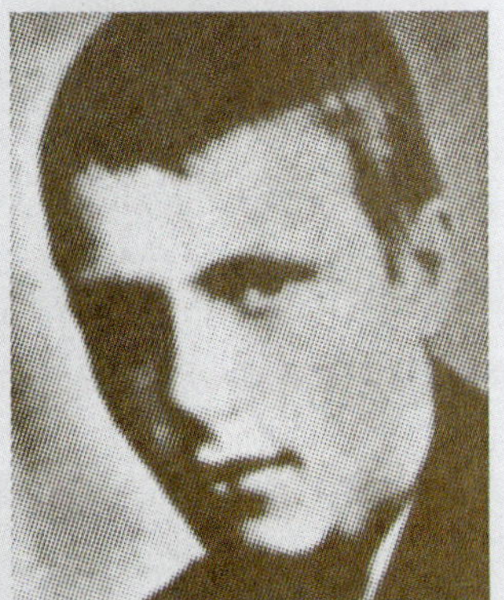

Raspe, Jan-Carl * 24. Juli 1944 in Berlin

Die Rote Armee Fraktion

Die Erschießung Benno Ohnesorgs am 2. Juni 1967 wird als ein unmissverständliches Zeichen der Gewaltbereitschaft staatlicher Behörden gedeutet. Sein Tod wird deshalb zum Signal für die Radikalisierung der Studentenbewegung (APO).

Am 2. April 1968 werden in Frankfurt am Main zwei Kaufhäuser in Brand gesteckt. Die Polizei nimmt vier Verdächtige fest, darunter die Studentin Gudrun Ensslin und ihren Freund Andreas Baader. Ensslin will damit gegen die Gleichgültigkeit protestieren, mit der die Menschen in der Bundesrepublik den Krieg in Vietnam hinnehmen. Während des Prozesses gegen die Brandstifter zeigt die Journalistin Ulrike Meinhof in ihren Beiträgen in der Hamburger Zeitschrift «Konkret» Verständnis für diesen Anschlag auf den «Konsumterror». Nach dem Prozeß tauchen Baader und Ensslin unter. Durch Zufall kann die Polizei Andreas Baader im April 1970 erneut verhaften.

Während eines Transports aus dem Gefängnis in Berlin-Tegel wird Baader jedoch am 14. Mai 1970 mit Waffengewalt befreit; ein Mensch wird dabei schwer verletzt. Maßgeblich beteiligt an der Aktion sind Ulrike Meinhof und der Baader-Anwalt Horst Mahler. Die gewaltsame Befreiung ist die Geburtsstunde der Roten Armee Fraktion (RAF), die häufig auch als Baader-Meinhof-Gruppe bezeichnet wird. Andreas Baader, Gudrun Ensslin, Horst Mahler und Ulrike Meinhof gehen nun in den Untergrund. Zusammen mit anderen lassen sie sich in einem militärischen Trainingscamp radikaler Palästinenser in Jordanien militärisch ausbilden. Nach ihrer Rückkehr in die Bundesrepublik erbeuten die RAF-Mitglieder bei Banküberfällen Geld und beschaffen sich damit Wohnungen, Autos, Waffen und gefälschte Papiere. Mit einer Serie von Brand- und Sprengstoffanschlägen gegen Einrichtungen der US-Armee und des Axel-Springer-Konzerns beginnt der «antimperialistische Kampf» der RAF. Über sechzig Personen werden dabei verletzt und vier getötet. Die intensive Fahndung der Polizei hat schließlich Erfolg: Im Juni 1972 können in verschiedenen Städten der Bundesrepublik mit Andreas Baader, Gudrun Ensslin, Ulrike Meinhof, Holger Meins und Jan-Carl Raspe die führenden Köpfe der ersten RAF-Generation festgenommen werden.

Im «Deutschen Herbst» 1977 erreicht die Terrorwelle ihren Höhepunkt mit der Entführung des Arbeitgeberpräsidenten Hanns-Martin Schleyer am 5. September. Die Terroristen fordern die Freilassung von elf inhaftierten Gesinnungsgenossen, darunter Andreas Baader und Gudrun Ensslin. Diesmal bleibt die Bundesregierung jedoch hart. Zur Unterstützung der Schleyer-Kidnapper entführen deshalb palästinensische Terroristen am 13. Oktober 1977 die Lufthansa-Maschine «Landshut» nach Mogadischu. Am 18. Oktober gelingt es jedoch einer Spezialeinheit des Bundesgrenzschutzes, der GSG 9, die Maschine zu stürmen und die Geiseln zu befreien. Daraufhin verüben Andreas Baader, Gudrun Ensslin und Jan-Carl Raspe in ihren Zellen Selbstmord. Einen Tag später wird im Elsaß im Kofferraum eines Autos die Leiche Hanns-Martin Schleyers gefunden.

Formierung der Frauenbewegung

Rede von Helke Sander auf der 23. Delegiertenkonferenz des
«Sozialistischen Deutschen Studentenbundes» 1968 in Frankfurt/Main

[...]

Die Trennung zwischen Privatleben und gesellschaftlichem Leben wirft die Frau immer zurück in den individuell auszutragenden Konflikt ihrer Isolation. Sie wird immer noch für das Privatleben, für die Familie, erzogen, die ihrerseits von Produktionsbedingungen abhängig ist, die wir bekämpfen. Die Rollenerziehung, das anerzogene Minderwertigkeitsgefühl, der Widerspruch zwischen ihren eigenen Erwartungen und den Ansprüchen der Gesellschaft erzeugen das ständige schlechte Gewissen, den an sie gestellten Forderungen nicht gerecht zu werden, bzw. zwischen Alternativen wählen zu müssen, die in jedem Fall einen Verzicht auf vitale Bedürfnisse bedeuten. [...]

In unserer selbstgewählten Isolation machten wir also folgendes: wir konzentrierten unsere Arbeit auf die Frauen mit Kindern, weil sie am schlechtesten dran sind. Frauen mit Kindern können über sich erst wieder nachdenken, wenn die Kinder sie nicht dauernd an die Versagungen der Gesellschaft erinnern. Da die politischen Frauen ein Interesse daran haben, ihre Kinder eben nicht mehr nach dem Leistungsprinzip zu erziehen, war die Konsequenz die, daß wir den Anspruch der Gesellschaft, daß die Frau die Kinder zu erziehen hat, zum ersten Mal ernst nehmen. Und zwar in dem Sinne, daß wir uns weigern, unsere Kinder weiterhin nach den Prinzipien des Konkurrenzkampfes und Leistungsprinzips zu erziehen, von denen wir wissen, daß auf ihrer Erhaltung die Voraussetzung zum Bestehen des kapitalistischen Systems überhaupt beruht.

Wir wollen versuchen, schon innerhalb der bestehenden Gesellschaft Modelle einer utopischen Gesellschaft zu entwickeln. In dieser Gegengesellschaft müssen aber unsere eigenen Bedürfnisse endlich einen Platz finden. So ist die Konzentration auf die Erziehung nicht ein Alibi für die verdrängte eigene Emanzipation, sondern die Voraussetzung dafür, die eigenen Konflikte produktiv zu lösen. Die Hauptaufgabe besteht darin, daß unsere Kinder nicht auf Inseln fernab jeglicher gesellschaftlichen Realität gedrängt werden, sondern darin, den Kindern durch Unterstützung ihrer eigenen emanzipatorischen Bemühungen die Kraft zum Widerstand zu geben, damit sie ihre eigenen Konflikte mit der Realität zugunsten einer zu verändernden Realität lösen können. [...]

Feminismus bezeichnet eine Richtung der Frauenbewegung, die von einem Dualismus der Geschlechter ausgeht und die die in der bisherigen Geschichte vorherrschende Dominanz der Männer beseitigen will. Feministinnen betonen die besondere weibliche Wesensart, die der männlichen völlig gleichwertig gegenübersteht. Ihre besondere Aufmerksamkeit gilt dem Abbau der Vernachlässigung und Benachteiligung weiblicher Eigenschaften, Denkweisen, Leistungen in allen Lebensbereichen.

Willy Brandt wird Bundeskanzler

Noch am Abend der Bundestagswahl vom 28. September 1969 meldet SPD-Kanzlerkandidat Willy Brandt seinen Anspruch auf die Führung einer Regierung aus SPD und F.D.P. an. Obwohl die Sozialdemokraten über drei Prozent Stimmen hinzugewinnen konnten, verfügen sie zusammen mit der F.D.P. im Bundestag nur über eine Mehrheit von 12 Sitzen. Trotzdem einigen sich die Parteivorsitzenden von SPD und F.D.P., Willy Brandt und Walter Scheel, auf die Bildung einer Regierungskoalition. Durch diesen «Machtwechsel» enden für die CDU/CSU 20 Jahre Regierungsverantwortung in Bonn. In den folgenden 13 Jahren bestimmen sozial-liberale Bundesregierungen die Politik. Mit der Wahl von Willy Brandt zum Bundeskanzler wird erstmals seit 1930 wieder ein Sozialdemokrat Kanzler.

Die «Ära Brandt» schlägt ein neues Kapitel in der Geschichte der Bundesrepublik Deutschland auf. Eine enorme Reform- und Aufbruchstimmung ergreift das ganze Land. Sie manifestiert sich auch in der ersten Regierungserklärung, die Willy Brandt am 28. Oktober 1969 vor dem Deutschen Bundestag abgibt. Brandts darin enthaltene Leitsätze wie «Wir wollen ein Volk der guten Nachbarn sein» und «Mehr Demokratie wagen» wurden berühmt. «Mein eigentlicher Erfolg war, mit dazu beigetragen zu haben, dass in der Welt, in der wir leben, der Name unseres Landes und der Begriff des Friedens wieder in einem Atemzug genannt werden können.»

Der Spion im Kanzleramt

Am 24. April 1974 platzt die Bombe: Günter Guillaume, persönlicher Referent von Bundeskanzler Willy Brandt, wird in Bonn verhaftet. Er gesteht DDR-Agent und Offizier der Nationalen Volksarmee der DDR zu sein. Fast zwei Jahre lang hatte Guillaume direkt neben dem Bundeskanzler gesessen, hatte Zugang zu geheimen Akten und den Gesprächsrunden im engsten Kreis um Brandt. Nach der Entlarvung stürzt die Bundesrepublik in eine schwere innenpolitische Krise. Brandt übernimmt die Verantwortung für die Agentenaffäre und erklärt seinen Rücktritt, tief enttäuscht von den Verantwortlichen in der DDR, mit denen er auf dem Weg der deutsch-deutschen Entspannungspolitik war, derart hintergangen zu werden.

Öl für uns alle

Die erste und bisher folgenreichste Ölkrise beginnt im Herbst 1973, als die Organisation der Erdöl exportierenden Länder (OPEC) bewusst die Fördermengen drosselt und sie bewusst als politische Waffe verwendet. Sie verhängt ein Embargo gegen die Niederlande und die USA wegen ihrer israelfreundlichen Haltung im israelisch-arabischen Jom-Kippur-Krieg und schränkt die Exporte ein.

Am 16. Oktober 1973 steigt der Ölpreis von rund drei Dollar pro Barrel auf über fünf Dollar. Dies entspricht einem Anstieg um ca. 70 Prozent. Im Verlauf des nächsten Jahres erhöht sich der Weltölpreis auf über zwölf Dollar.

Die Bundesrepublik wird von dem Boykott hart getroffen, da sie ihren Energiebedarf zu 55 Prozent mit importiertem Erdöl deckt. So wird als direkte Reaktion auf die Krise an vier Sonntagen im November und Dezember 1973 ein Fahrverbot verhängt («Sonntagsfahrverbot») sowie neue Geschwindigkeitsbegrenzungen eingeführt. Diese Politik hat zwar kaum einen wirtschaftlichen Effekt, gibt der Bevölkerung aber das Gefühl, aktiv etwas zur Bewältigung der Krise beitragen zu können. 1974 muss Deutschland für seine Ölimporte rund 17 Milliarden DM mehr bezahlen als im Jahr zuvor, was eine Konjunkturkrise einleitet («Ölpreisschock»). Die Ölkrise markiert damit das Ende des Wirtschaftswunders. In der Folge treten bisher weitgehend unbekannte Erscheinungen auf wie Kurzarbeit, Arbeitslosigkeit, steigende Sozialausgaben, verstärkte Inflation, Streiks, steigende Staatsverschuldung, Rationalisierung, Unternehmenspleiten. Die Arbeitslosenquote steigt zwischen 1973 und 1974 von 2,2 auf 4,2 Prozent.

Die Ölkrise von 1973 demonstriert die Störanfälligkeit moderner Industriestaaten gegenüber einer Vielzahl von Einflussfaktoren sowie deren Abhängigkeit fossiler Energieträger. Alternative Treibstoffe wie Pflanzenöl und Biodiesel rücken ins öffentliche Interesse; es wird vermehrt in Kernenergie, regenerative Energiequellen, die Wärmedämmung von Gebäuden und in die Effizienzsteigerung von Motoren und Heizgeräten investiert.

Die Wiedereinführung der Zeitumstellung im Jahr 1980 gilt ebenfalls als Nachwirkung der Ölkrise. Man ist der Überzeugung, dadurch das Tageslicht besser nutzen zu können, um Energie sparen.

Entstehung des Umweltschutzes

Mit Beginn der sozialliberalen Koalition 1969 wird das Thema der Umweltbelastungen als politisches Thema identifiziert und entsprechende Problemlösungen angestoßen. 1970 verabschiedet die Bundesregierung ein Sofortprogramm zum Umweltschutz und legt 1971 das erste Umweltprogramm vor; darin werden über 100 Gesetze und Verordnungen angekündigt. Dieses Umweltprogramm führt zu einem größeren Umweltbewusstsein in der Bevölkerung. Während im September 1970 laut einer INFAS-Umfrage nur 41% der Befragten den Begriff Umweltschutz kennen, ist dieser im November 1971 bereits 92% bekannt.

Die Zuständigkeit für den technischen Umweltschutz erhält 1969 das Bundesministerium des Innern, die Abteilung für Naturschutz bleibt jedoch beim Landwirtschaftsministerium. Aber erst durch die Ausdehnung der mit den Ländern konkurrierenden Gesetzgebung auf die Bereiche Abfallbeseitigung, Luftreinhaltung und Lärmbekämpfung wird 1972 die Umweltkompetenz des Bundes entscheidend gestärkt. Als erstes Umweltschutzgesetz tritt am 30. März 1971 das «Fluglärmgesetz» in Kraft. Am 18. Januar 1974 verabschiedet der Bundestag einstimmig das für die Luftreinhaltung maßgebliche «Bundesimmissionsschutzgesetz». Weitere Gesetze, wie 1975 das «Bundesnaturschutzgesetz». Angesichts der einsetzenden Wirtschaftskrise folgen, geraten die umweltpolitischen Reformbestrebungen zusehends unter Druck. Mit der Ölkrise von 1973/74 rückt der Umweltschutz nach der ersten erfolgreichen Etablierung ökologischer wirtschaftlicher Argumente ins Hintertreffen. Aus der Enttäuschung über diesen Rückgang und der daran verbundenen Unklagkeit der Regierung entstehen zahlreiche Umweltgruppen und Bürgerinitiativen im Bereich Umwelt. Der sogenannte «Umweltprotest» formiert sich.

Dieses neue Bewusstsein entwickelt sich, als man feststellt, dass sich industrielle Tätigkeiten nachteilig sehr negativ auf die Umwelt auswirken können. Maßgeblich zu diesem Wertewandel beigetragen haben öffentliche Massstäbe wie das Fischsterben im Rhein, die Übersäuerung von Gewässern oder die Chemiekatastrophen wie etwa in Seveso oder Bhopal.

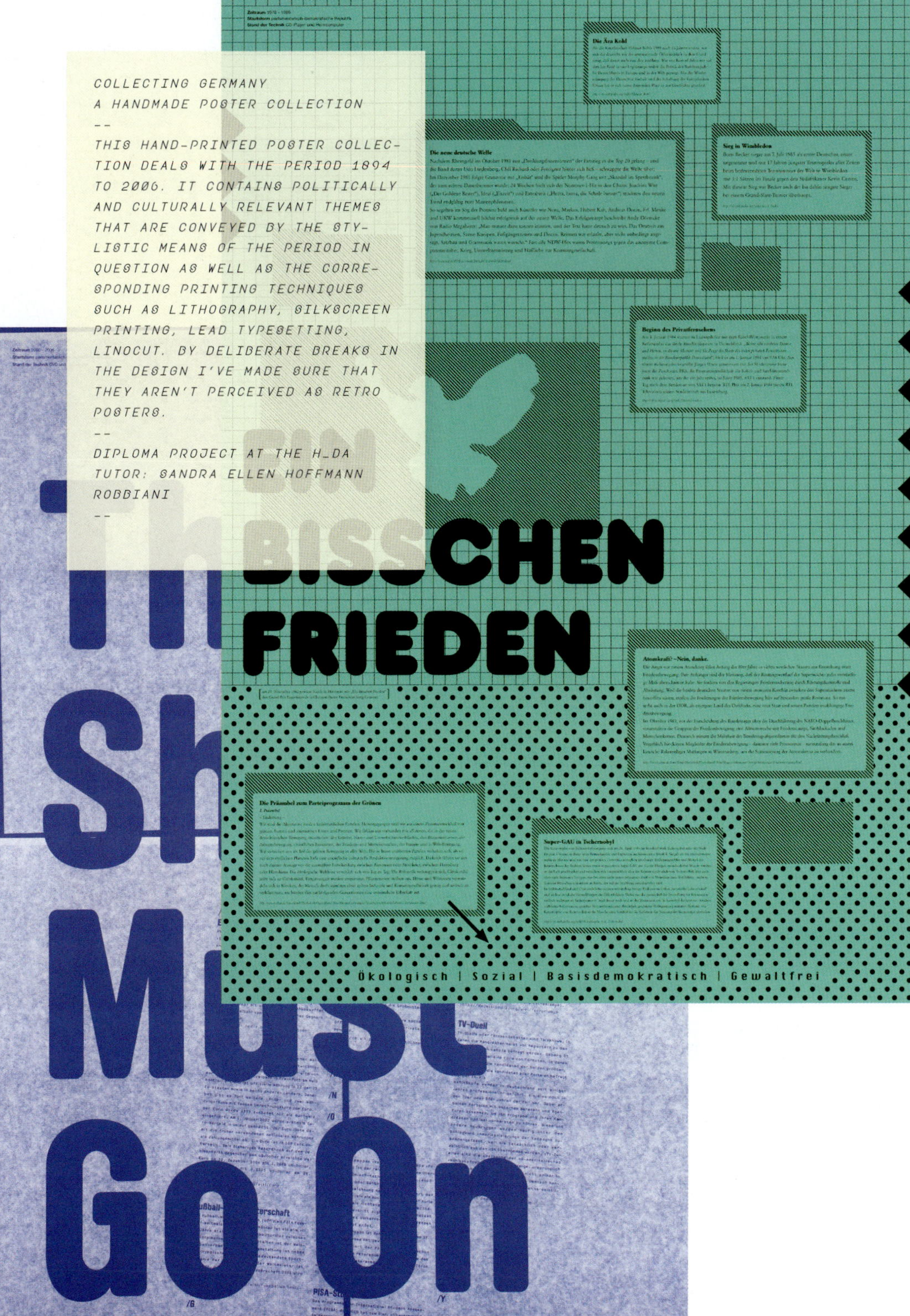

COLLECTING GERMANY
A HANDMADE POSTER COLLECTION
--
THIS HAND-PRINTED POSTER COLLEC-
TION DEALS WITH THE PERIOD 1894
TO 2006. IT CONTAINS POLITICALLY
AND CULTURALLY RELEVANT THEMES
THAT ARE CONVEYED BY THE STY-
LISTIC MEANS OF THE PERIOD IN
QUESTION AS WELL AS THE CORRE-
SPONDING PRINTING TECHNIQUES
SUCH AS LITHOGRAPHY, SILKSCREEN
PRINTING, LEAD TYPESETTING,
LINOCUT. BY DELIBERATE BREAKS IN
THE DESIGN I'VE MADE SURE THAT
THEY AREN'T PERCEIVED AS RETRO
POSTERS.
--
DIPLOMA PROJECT AT THE H_DA
TUTOR: SANDRA ELLEN HOFFMANN
ROBBIANI
--
EIN BISSCHEN FRIEDEN
The Show Must Go On
Ökologisch | Sozial | Basisdemokratisch | Gewaltfrei

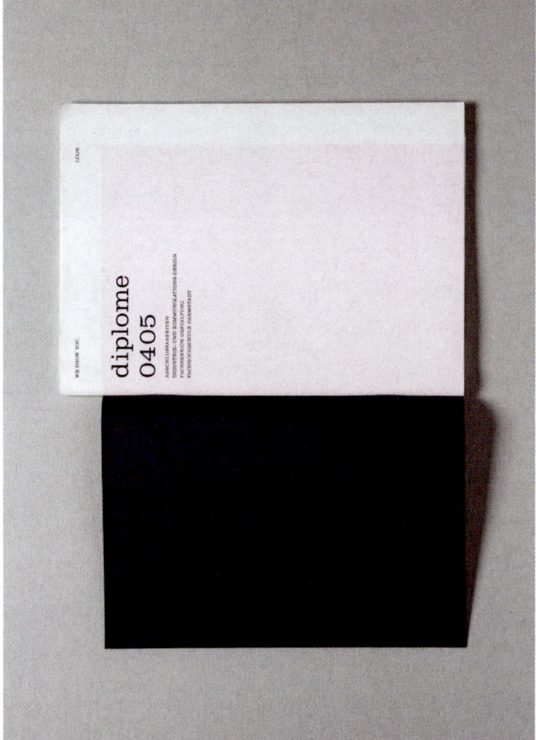
WE SHOW YOU.
LOOK.
diplome
0405
ABSCHLUSSARBEITEN
INDUSTRIE- UND KOMMUNIKATIONS-DESIGN
FACHBEREICH GESTALTUNG
FACHHOCHSCHULE DARMSTADT
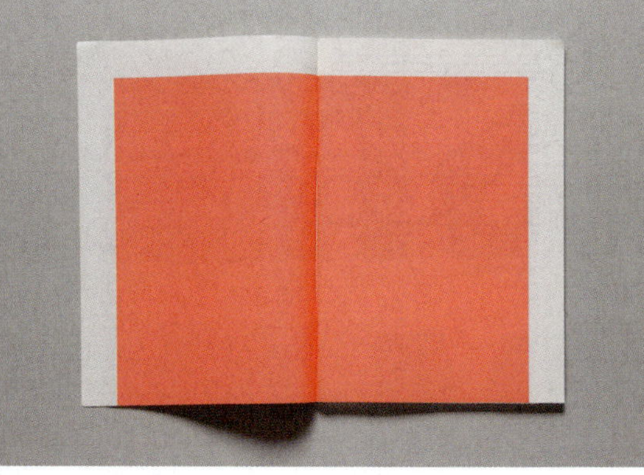

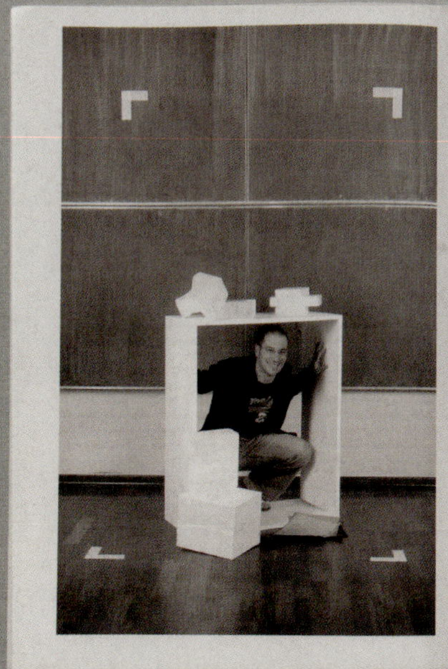
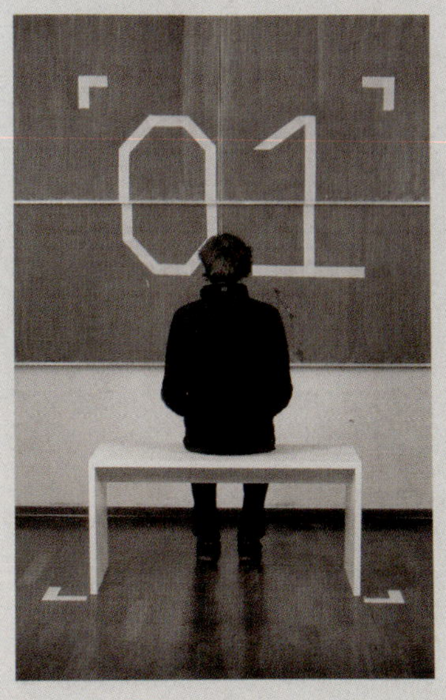

01

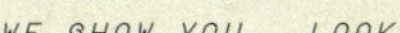

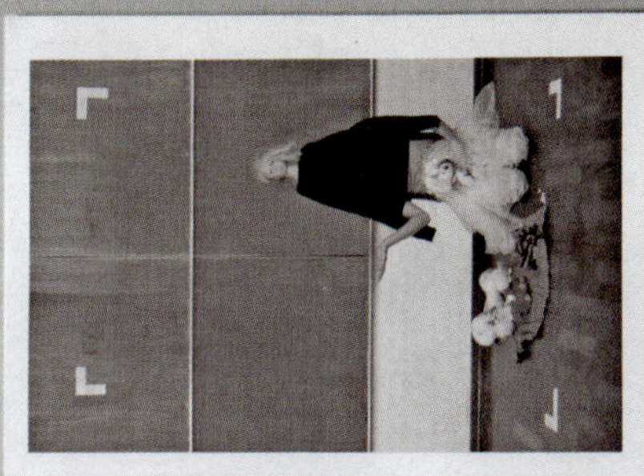

1

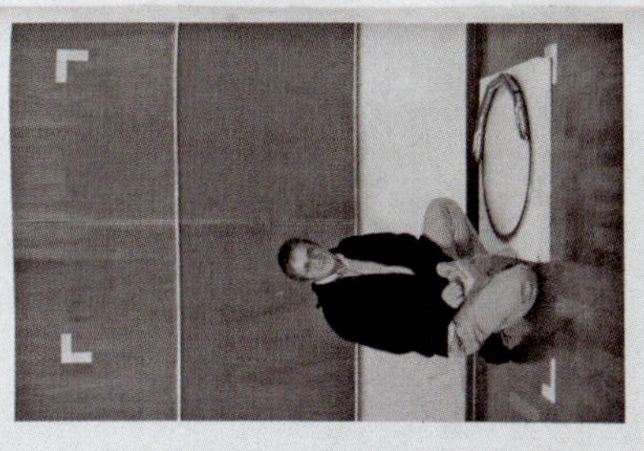

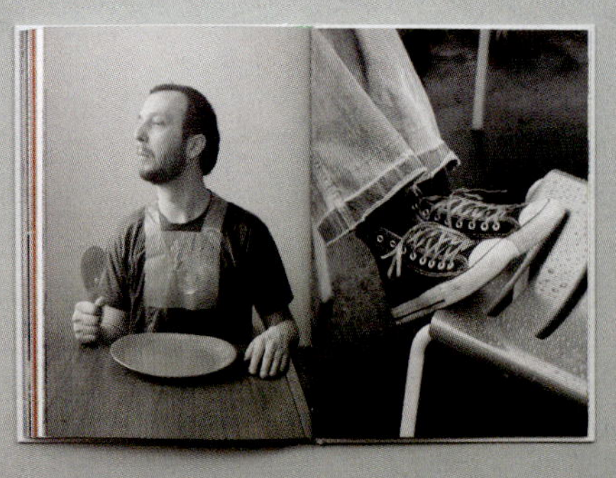

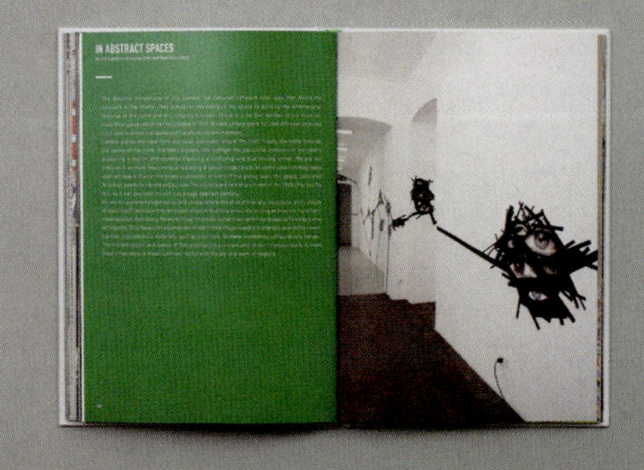

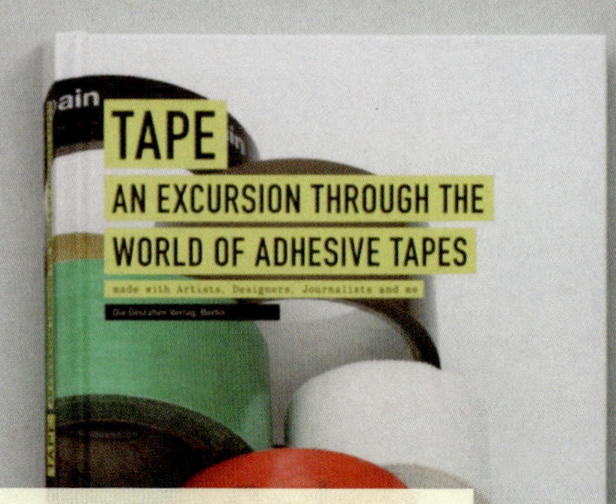

TAPE - AN EXCURSION THROUGH THE WORLD OF ADHESIVE TAPES
--
TAPE SHOWS THE VARIETY OF WORK BEING DONE WITH THIS MATERIAL AND TAKES READERS ON A DELIGHTFUL JOURNEY THROUGH THE WORLD OF STICKY CREATIVITY. THE BOOK FEATURES ARTWORK IN WHICH TAPE IS USED ILLUSTRATIVELY WITH EXAMPLES OF INTERIORS, FASHION, FURNITURE AND ARCHITECTURE.
--
THE PROJECT STARTED VERY EXPERIMENTALLY AS A BOOK PROJECT AT THE UNIVERSITY OF APPLIED SCIENCES DARMSTADT (H_DA). LATER, I WORKED ON IT AGAIN ON MY OWN, AND THEN IN COOPERATION WITH THE PUBLISHING HOUSE.
--

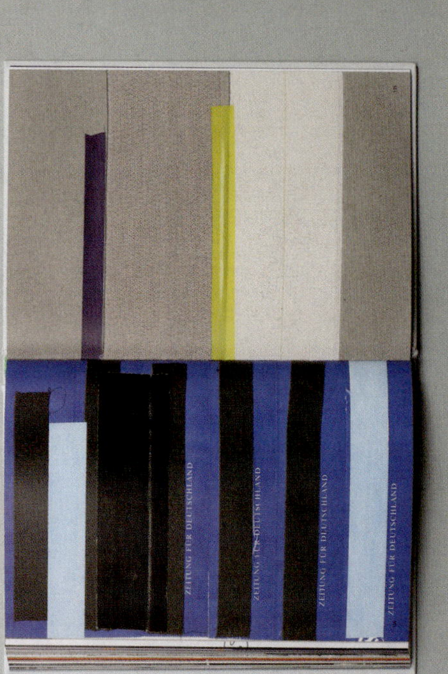

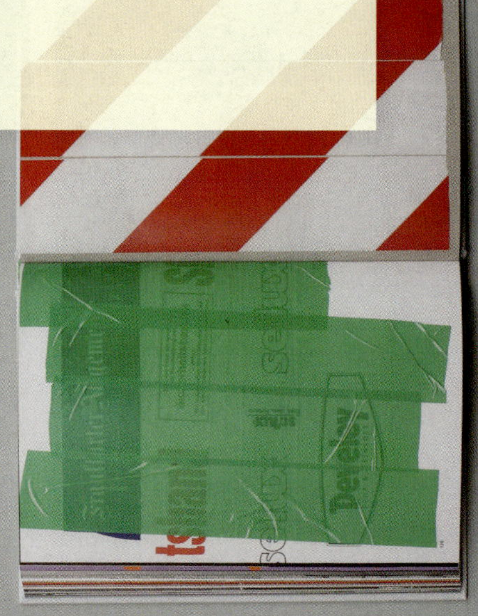

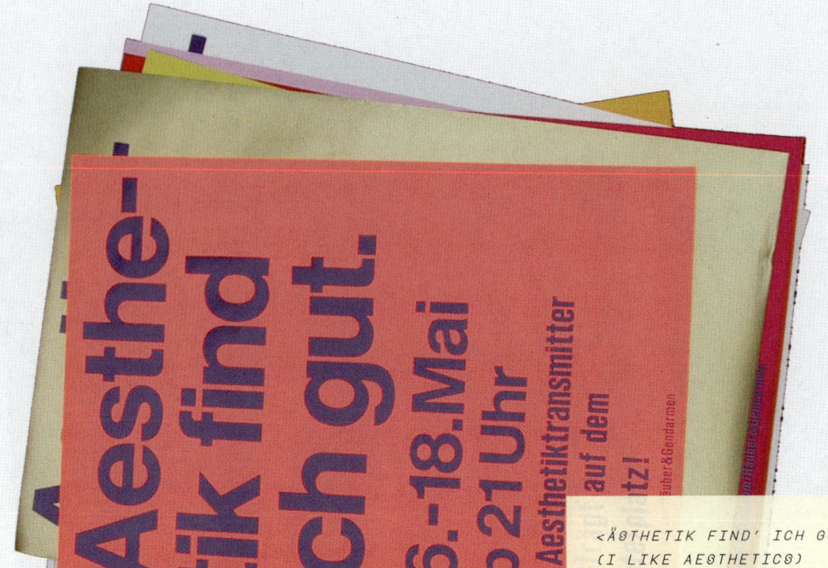

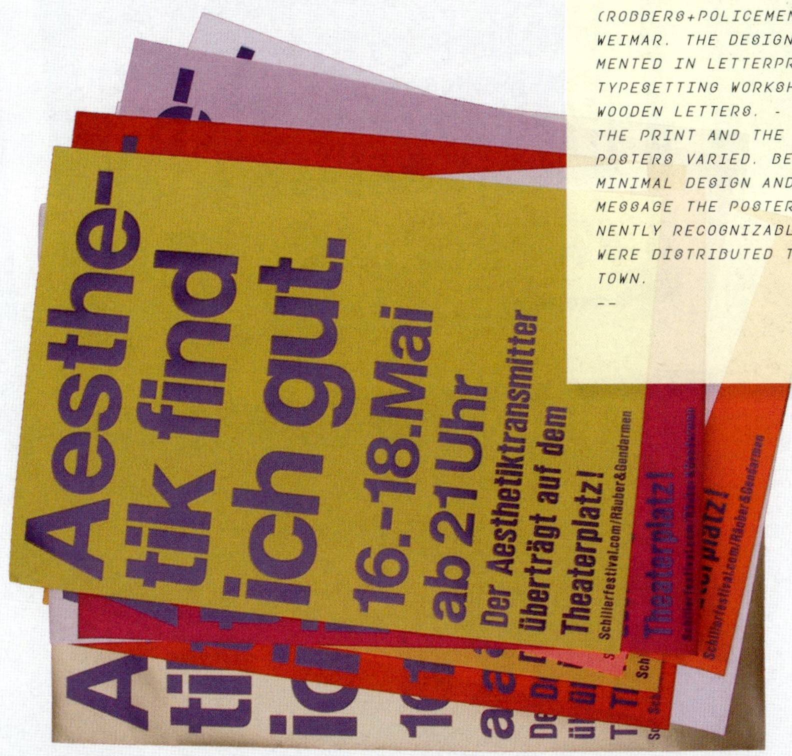

<ÄSTHETIK FIND' ICH GUT>
(I LIKE AESTHETICS)
--
THE SERIES OF POSTERS <ÄS-
THETIK FIND' ICH GUT> (I LIKE
AESTHETICS) WAS PRODUCED FOR
THE <RENNSALON> DESIGN COL-
LECTIVE FROM FRANKFURT ON THE
OCCASION OF THE 2005 SCHIL-
LER FESTIVAL <RÄUBER+GENDARMEN>
(ROBBERS+POLICEMEN), HELD IN
WEIMAR. THE DESIGN WAS IMPLE-
MENTED IN LETTERPRESS AT A LEAD
TYPESETTING WORKSHOP USING OLD
WOODEN LETTERS. - THE COLOUR OF
THE PRINT AND THE PAPER ON THE
POSTERS VARIED. BECAUSE OF THE
MINIMAL DESIGN AND THE SUCCINCT
MESSAGE THE POSTERS WERE EMI-
NENTLY RECOGNIZABLE WHEN THEY
WERE DISTRIBUTED THROUGH THE
TOWN.
--

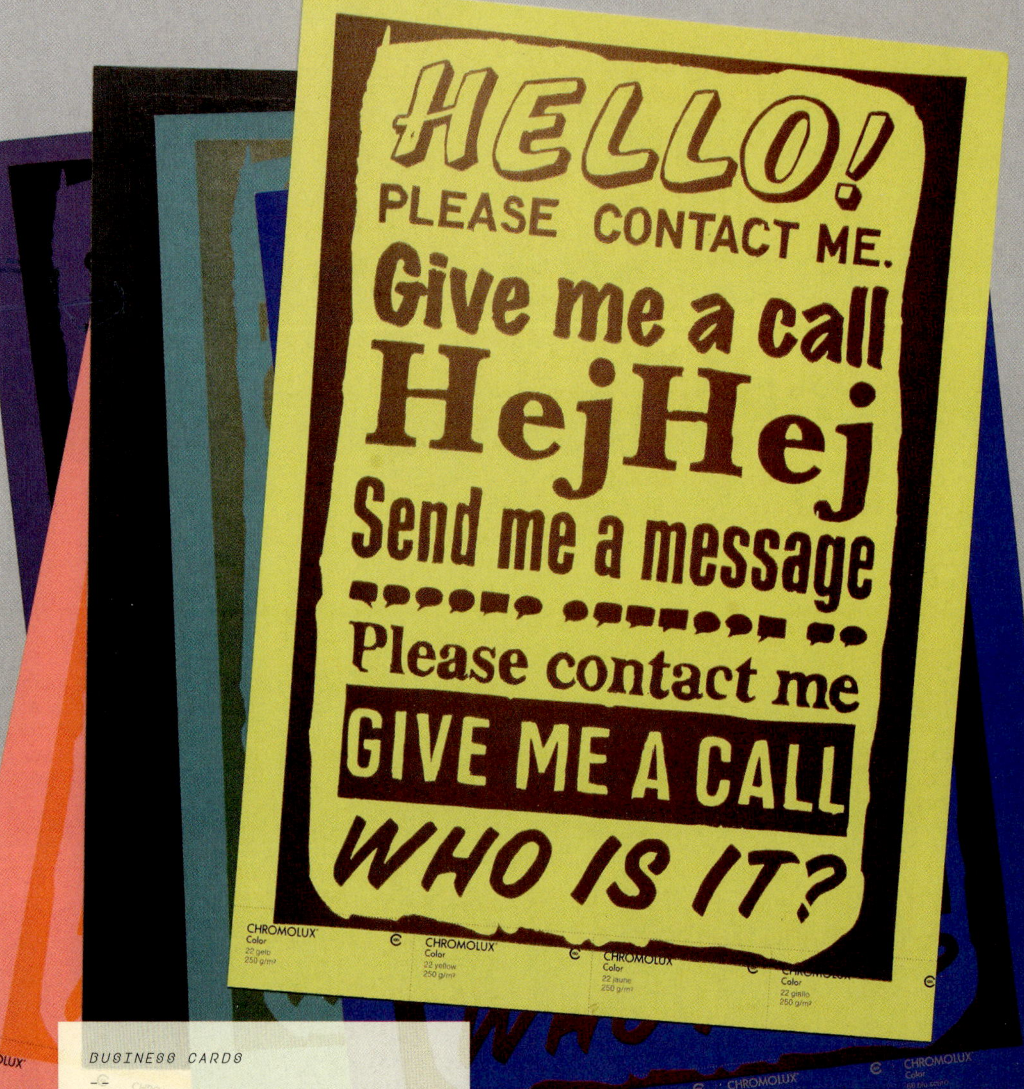

BUSINESS CARDS

INSPIRED BY WORDS OR PHRASES IN OUR DAILY COMMUNICATION, I PRINTED THESE LINOCUT BUSINESS CARDS IN DIFFERENT COLORS AND ON DIFFERENT PAPERS. AFTER PRINTING THEM IN A4 SIZE THEY WERE CUT INTO NORMAL BUSINESS CARD SIZES SO THAT ON EVERY CARD YOU CAN FIND A DIFFERENT PART OF THE PHRASES.
--

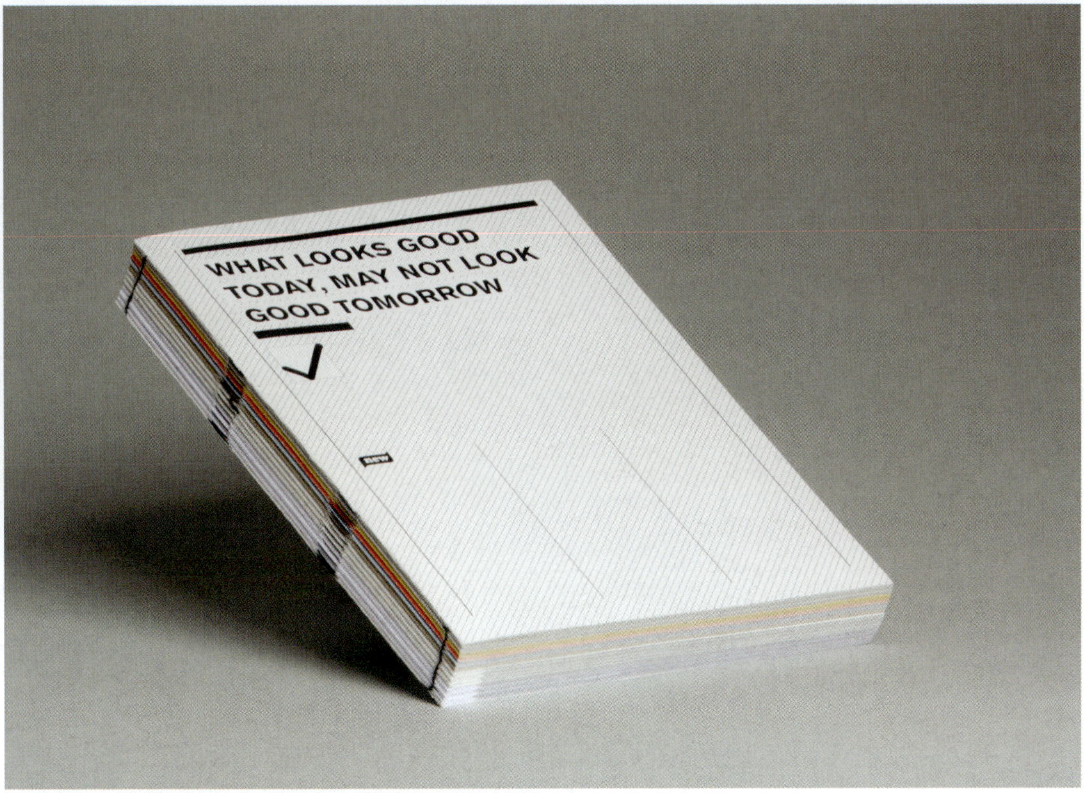

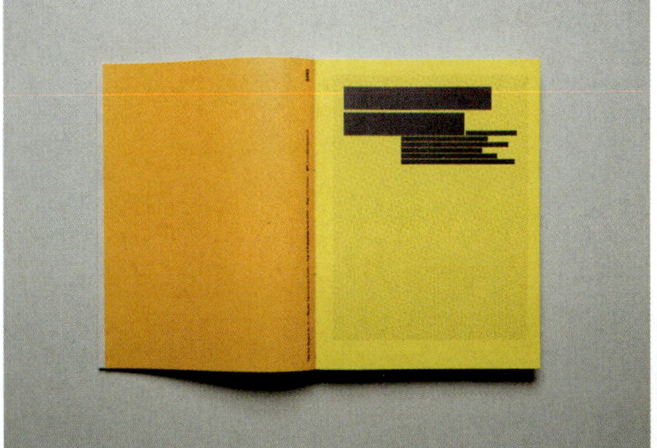
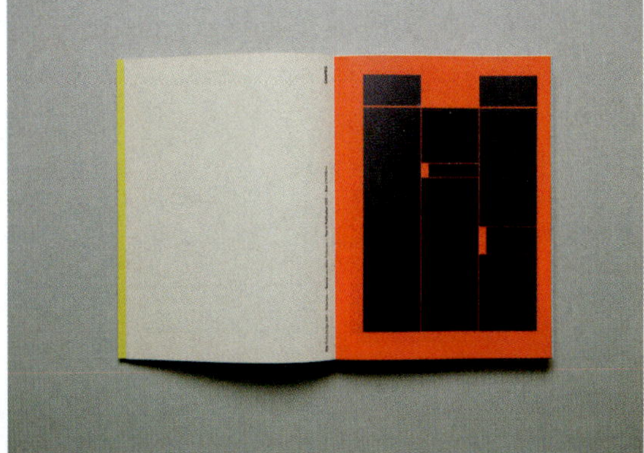

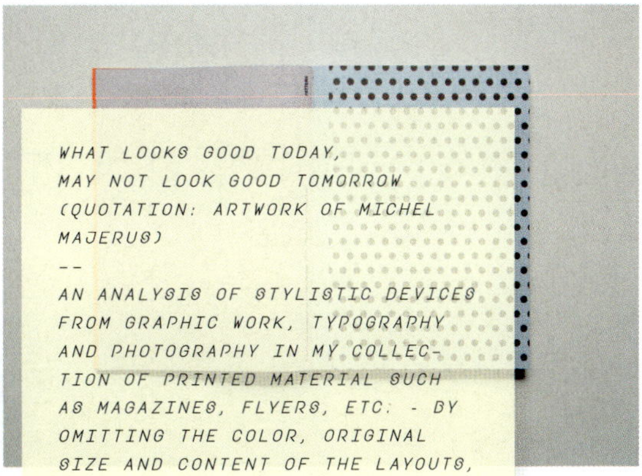

WHAT LOOKS GOOD TODAY,
MAY NOT LOOK GOOD TOMORROW
(QUOTATION: ARTWORK OF MICHEL
MAJERUS)
--
AN ANALYSIS OF STYLISTIC DEVICES
FROM GRAPHIC WORK, TYPOGRAPHY
AND PHOTOGRAPHY IN MY COLLEC-
TION OF PRINTED MATERIAL SUCH
AS MAGAZINES, FLYERS, ETC. - BY
OMITTING THE COLOR, ORIGINAL
SIZE AND CONTENT OF THE LAYOUTS,
THE BOOK CONTAINS VERY ABSTRACT
PRODUCTS THAT HAVE NEARLY LOST
THEIR IDENTITY. I SEE THE BOOK AS
AN INSPIRATION FOR OTHER DESIGN-
ERS DURING THE CREATIVE PROCESS.
--
H_DA (UNIVERSITY OF APPLIED SCI-
ENCES DARMSTADT)
TUTOR: SANDRA ELLEN HOFFMANN
ROBBIANI
--

NODE IS A BERLIN AND OSLO BASED GRAPHIC DESIGN STUDIO, FOUNDED IN 2003 BY ANDERS HOFGAARD (NORWEGIAN) AND SERGE ROMPZA (GERMAN). VLADIMIR LLOVET CASADEMONT (GERMAN/SPANISH) JOINED THE COLLABORATION IN 2006. ALL THREE STUDIED AT THE GERRIT RIETVELD ACADEMY, AMSTERDAM.

THE STUDIO WORKS FOR INTERNATIONAL CLIENTS AND ON SELF-INITIATED PROJECTS ACROSS A VARIETY OF MEDIA: BOOKS, MAGAZINES, POSTERS, TYPEFACES, IDENTITIES, EXHIBITION DESIGN, SIGNAGE AND WEBSITES. NODE COLLABORATES WITH FREELANCE DESIGNERS, ILLUSTRATORS, PHOTOGRAPHERS AND PROGRAMMERS.

--

WHAT IS GERMAN?

TO DEFINE WHAT IS GERMAN IS SUCH A VAST THEME THAT IT'S DIFFICULT TO GIVE A MEANINGFUL ANSWER. WE ALSO MIGHT NOT BE VERY WELL SUITED TO ANSWERING THAT QUESTION.

WHAT IS GERMAN DESIGN?

TO TRY TO COME UP WITH A GENERAL COMMENT ABOUT GERMAN DESIGN, WE COULD SAY THAT IS PRACTICALLY ORIENTED, PROFESSIONAL, NO-NONSENSE AND MAYBE A BIT DRY. HOWEVER, WE BELIEVE THAT THERE IS MUCH INTERESTING, EXPERIMENTAL DESIGN BEING DONE THAT MIGHT NOT BE PICKED UP BY THE ECONOMY, AND THEREFORE IS LESS VISIBLE. WE HOPE THAT THIS BOOK WILL HELP SHOW SOME OF THESE DEVELOPMENTS. OUR BACKGROUND IS SOMEWHAT MIXED, AS OUR STUDIO CONSISTS OF ONE GERMAN, ONE GERMAN-SPANISH AND ONE NORWEGIAN DESIGNER WHO HAVE ALL STUDIED (PARTLY) IN THE NETHERLANDS. WE FEEL OUR WORK IS MORE RELATED TO DUTCH (AND MAYBE SWISS) GRAPHIC DESIGN, BUT WE TRY TO PUT THIS INTO A GERMAN CONTEXT.

DESCRIBE YOUR WORKING PROCESS.

OUR WORKING PROCESS DEPENDS VERY MUCH ON THE PROJECT WE ARE DOING AND THE IDEAS THAT WE GET. WE FIND IT IMPORTANT ALWAYS TO HAVE AN IDEA AS A BASIS FOR OUR DESIGN. IT CAN TAKE ANYTHING FROM FIVE MINUTES TO SEVERAL DAYS TO COME UP WITH THIS IDEA. THE DESIGN MAY BE GIVEN BY THE IDEA, BUT DESIGNING, GIVING FORM, IS STILL THE MOST WORK-INTENSIVE PART OF A PROJECT.

WHAT DO YOU AIM TO ACHIEVE WITH YOUR WORK?

WE DO NOT HAVE AN EXPLICIT GOAL, BUT WE TRY TO MAKE SOME KIND OF DISCOVERY WITH EVERY PROJECT WE DO. DOING INTERESTING WORK AND BEING ABLE TO MAKE A LIVING FROM IT IS MAYBE WHAT IT BOILS DOWN TO.

YOU'VE INVITED A FRIEND TO GERMANY; NAME ONE PLACE THEY REALLY MUST VISIT AND A QUINTESSENTIAL EXPERIENCE YOU RECOMMEND.

BERLIN IS OUR BASE AND THE PLACE WE KNOW THE BEST. IT'S THE KIND OF CITY WHERE THERE'S ALWAYS SOMETHING NEW TO DISCOVER. A QUINTESSENTIAL WEEKEND IN BERLIN COULD INCLUDE A COUPLE OF MUSEUMS AND GALLERIES, A DINNER IN AN <UNOFFICIAL> RESTAURANT, AND A PARTY IN SOME ABANDONED HOUSE.

WHAT IS THE MOST IMPORTANT LESSON YOU HAVE LEARNED IN YOUR PROFESSION SO FAR?

WE LEARN THINGS ALL THE TIME, IT'S DIFFICULT TO PICK OUT ONE IMPORTANT THING. MAYBE TO USE GOOD PRINTERS?

--

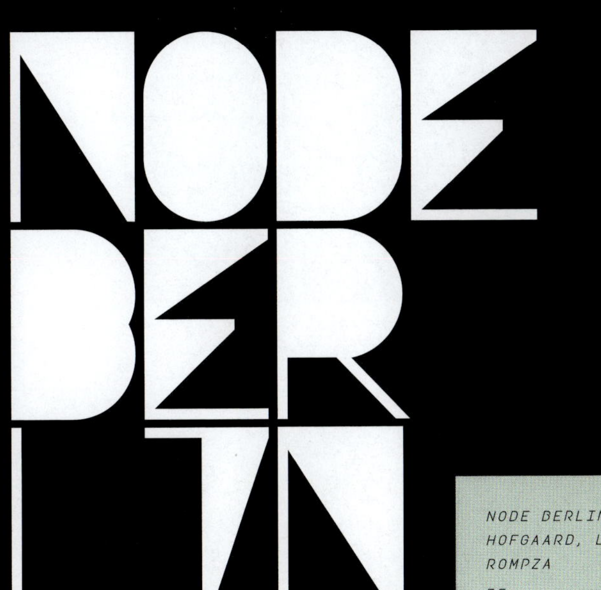

NODE BERLIN OSLO
HOFGAARD, LLOVET CASADEMONT &
ROMPZA
--
LOBECKSTRASSE 30-35,
AUFGANG D, STUDIO 413,
10969 BERLIN
GERMANY
--
T +49 30 69205144
--
MAIL@NODEBERLIN.COM
HTTP://WWW.NODEBERLIN.COM
--

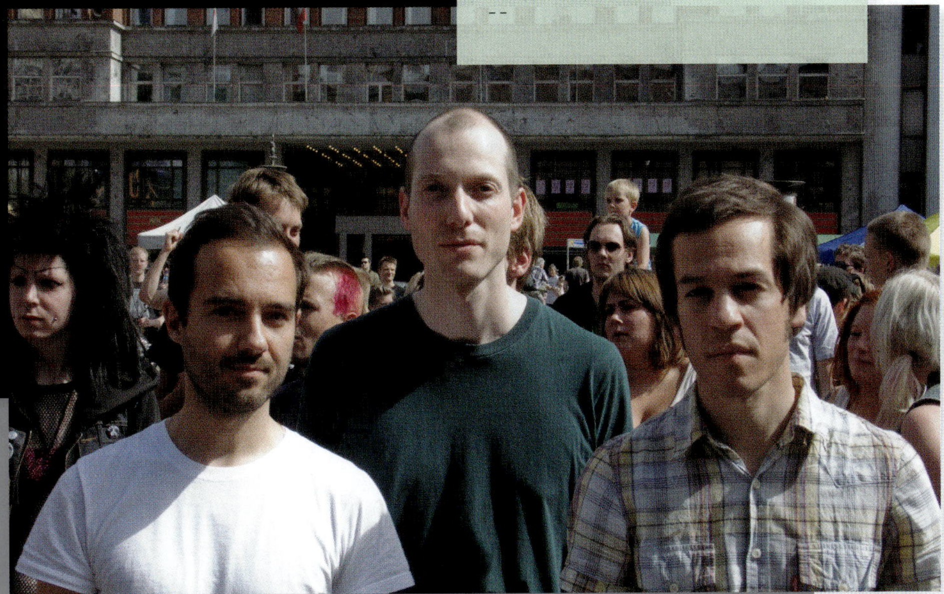

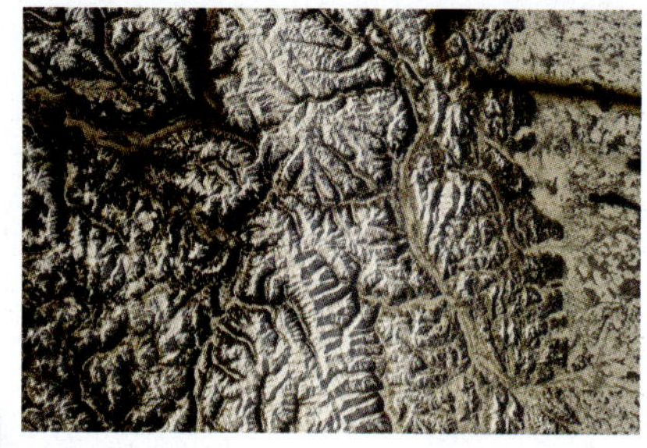

GERMANY/MUNICH AREA, GERMAN ALPS
NASA JOHNSON SPACE CENTER - EARTH
SCIENCES AND IMAGE ANALYSIS (NASA-
JSC-ESQIA)

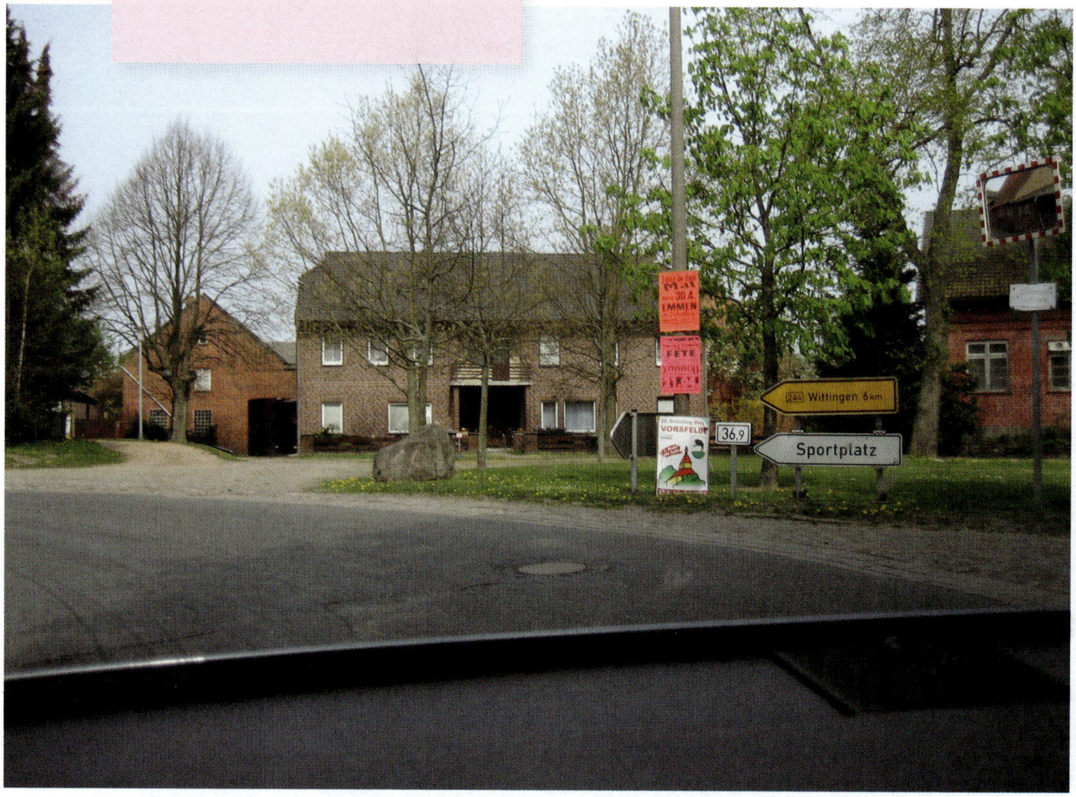

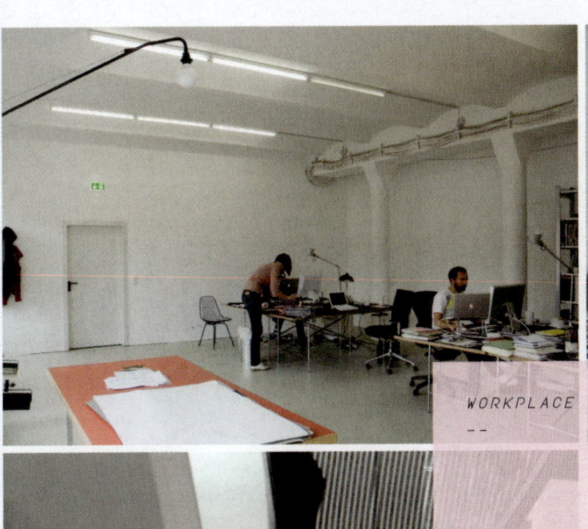
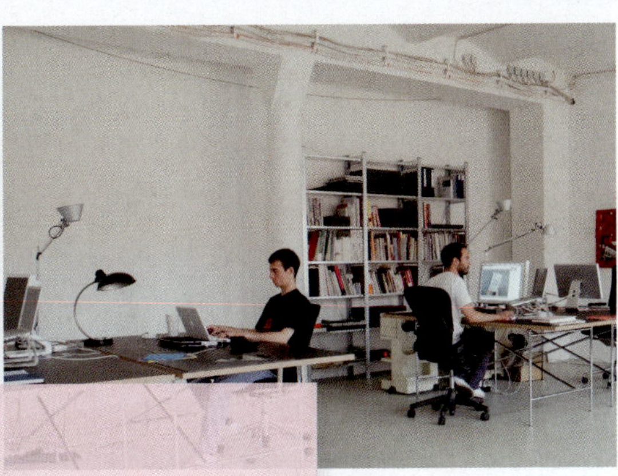
WORKPLACE
--
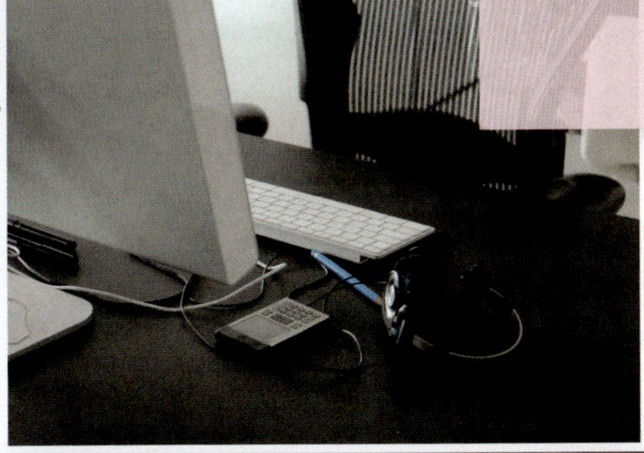
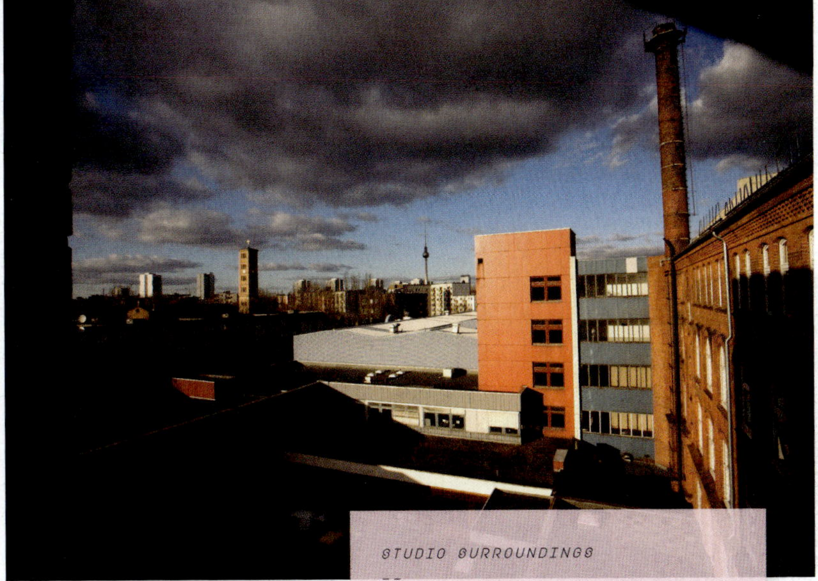
STUDIO SURROUNDINGS

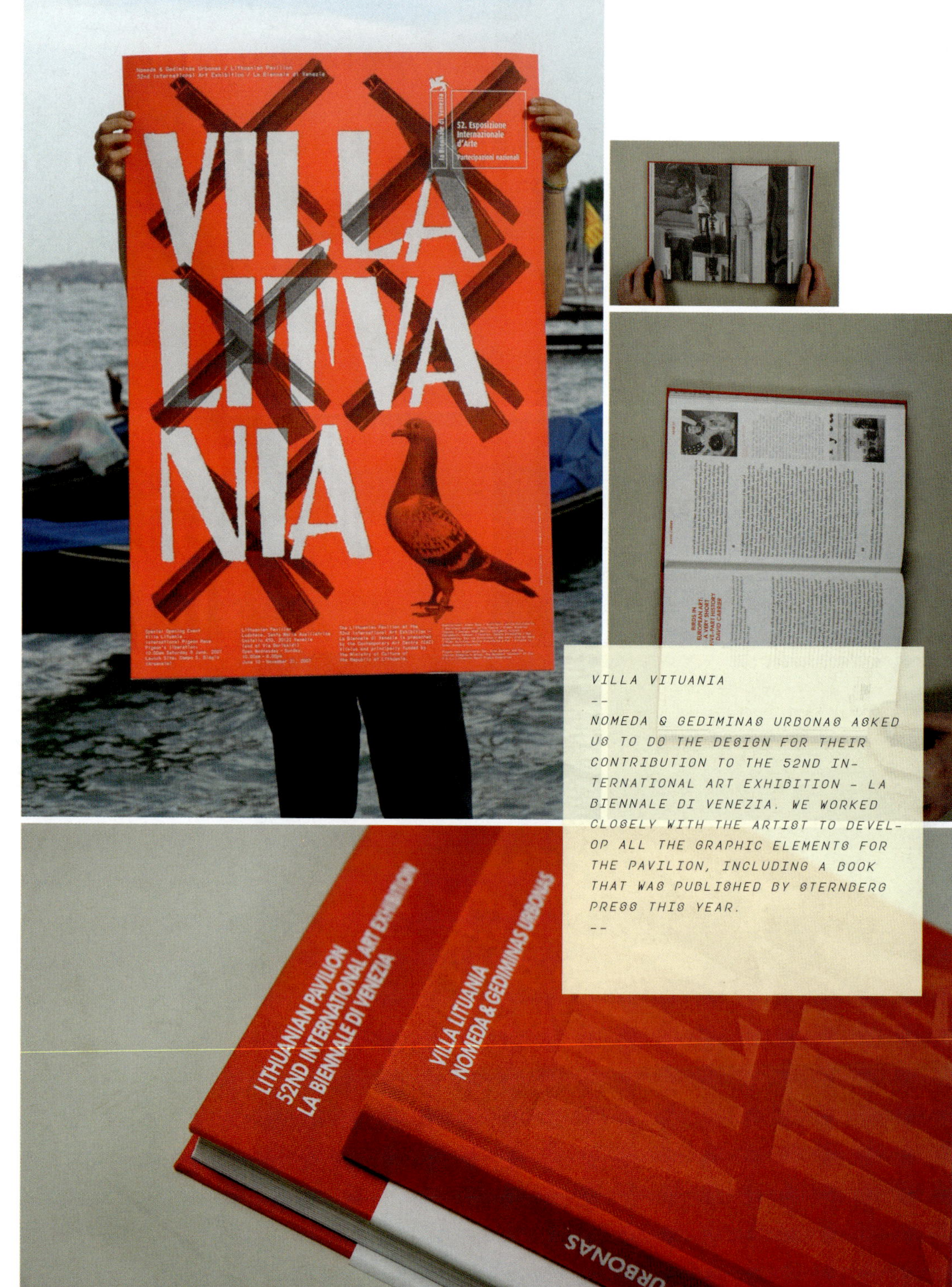

VILLA VITUANIA
--
NOMEDA & GEDIMINAS URBONAS ASKED
US TO DO THE DESIGN FOR THEIR
CONTRIBUTION TO THE 52ND IN-
TERNATIONAL ART EXHIBITION - LA
BIENNALE DI VENEZIA. WE WORKED
CLOSELY WITH THE ARTIST TO DEVEL-
OP ALL THE GRAPHIC ELEMENTS FOR
THE PAVILION, INCLUDING A BOOK
THAT WAS PUBLISHED BY STERNBERG
PRESS THIS YEAR.
--

VILLA LITVANIA
LITHUANIAN PAVILION
52ND INTERNATIONAL ART EXHIBITION
LA BIENNALE DI VENEZIA
VILLA LITUANIA
NOMEDA & GEDIMINAS URBONAS
NOMEDA & GEDIMINAS URBONAS

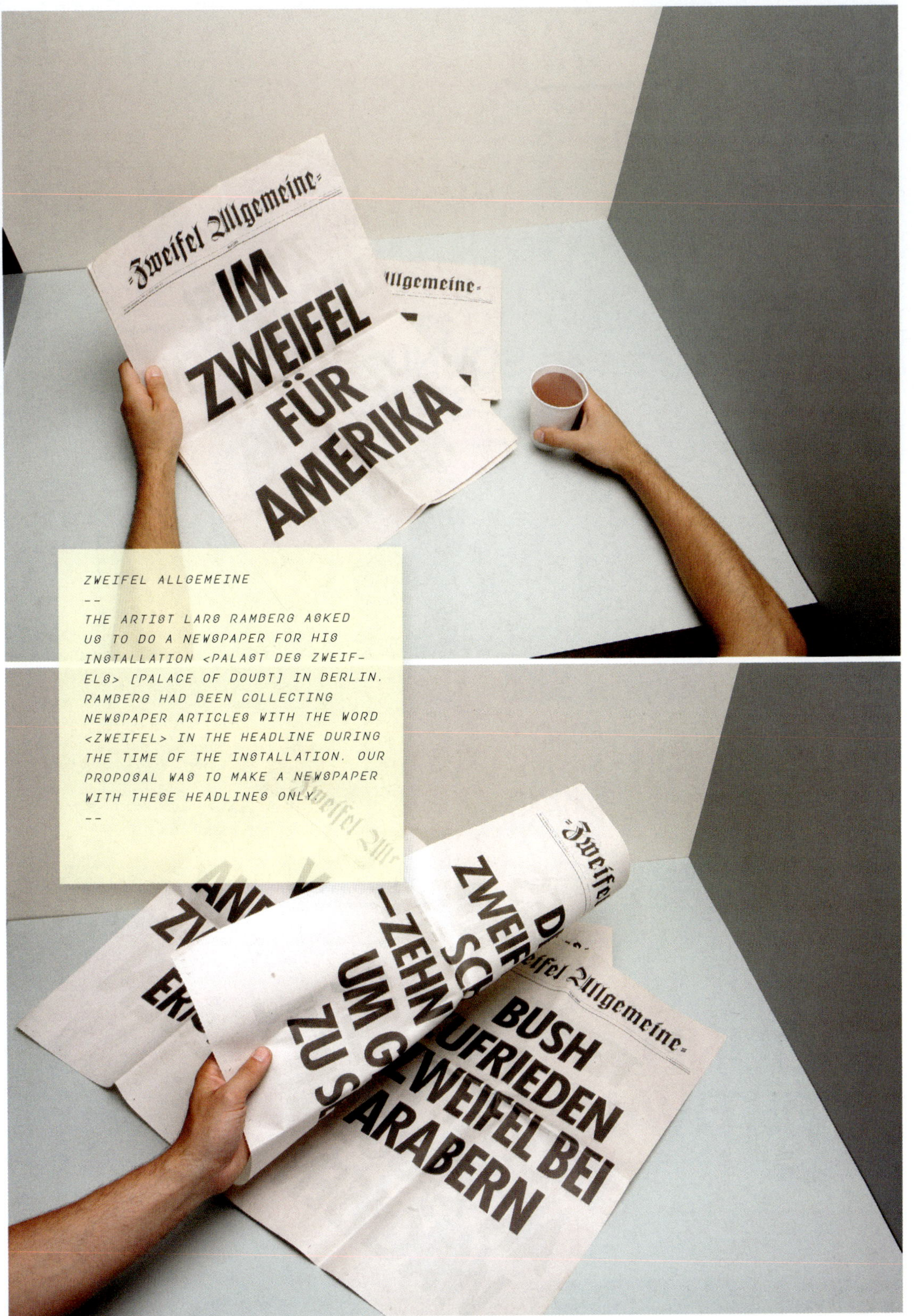
Zweifel Allgemeine
IM ZWEIFEL FÜR AMERIKA
Allgemeine
ZWEIFEL ALLGEMEINE
--
THE ARTIST LARS RAMBERG ASKED
US TO DO A NEWSPAPER FOR HIS
INSTALLATION <PALAST DES ZWEIF-
ELS> [PALACE OF DOUBT] IN BERLIN.
RAMBERG HAD BEEN COLLECTING
NEWSPAPER ARTICLES WITH THE WORD
<ZWEIFEL> IN THE HEADLINE DURING
THE TIME OF THE INSTALLATION. OUR
PROPOSAL WAS TO MAKE A NEWSPAPER
WITH THESE HEADLINES ONLY.
--
Zweifel Allgemeine
ZWEIFEL
BUSH
ZUFRIEDEN
ZEHN
UM GEZWEIFEL BEI
ZU ARABERN

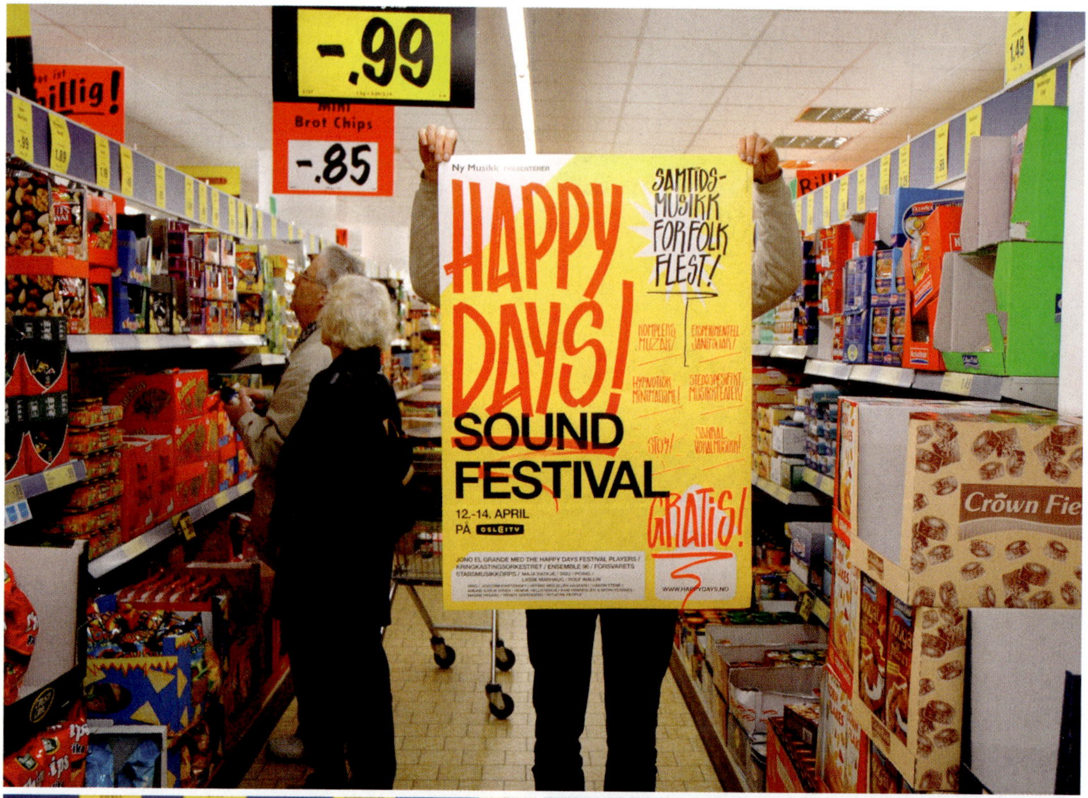

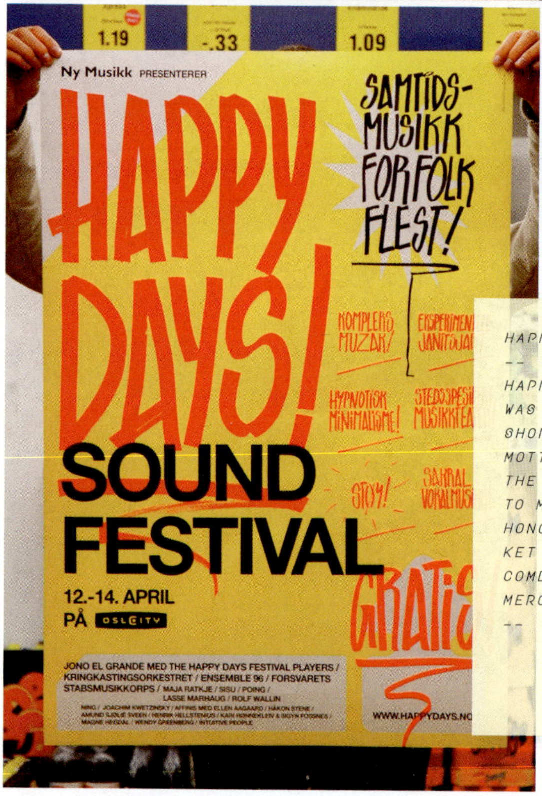

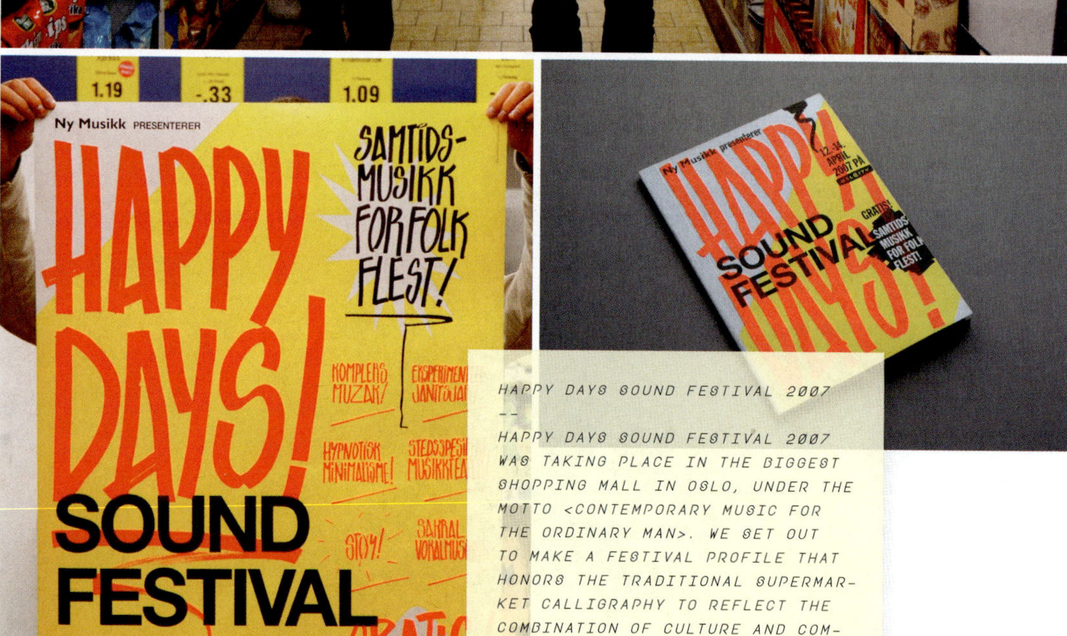
Ny Musikk PRESENTERER
HAPPY DAYS!
SOUND FESTIVAL
SAMTIDS-MUSIKK FOR FOLK FLEST!
KOMPLEKS MUZAK!
EKSPERIMENTELL JANITSJAR!
HYPNOTISK MINIMALISME!
STEDSSPESIFIKT MUSIKKTEATER!
STØY!
SAKRAL VOKALMUSIKK!
12.-14. APRIL
PÅ OSLO CITY
GRATIS!
JONO EL GRANDE MED THE HAPPY DAYS FESTIVAL PLAYERS /
KRINGKASTINGSORKESTRET / ENSEMBLE 96 / FORSVARETS
STABSMUSIKKORPS / MAJA RATKJE / SISU / POING /
LASSE MARHAUG / ROLF WALLIN
WWW.HAPPYDAYS.NO

HAPPY DAYS SOUND FESTIVAL 2007
--
HAPPY DAYS SOUND FESTIVAL 2007
WAS TAKING PLACE IN THE BIGGEST
SHOPPING MALL IN OSLO, UNDER THE
MOTTO <CONTEMPORARY MUSIC FOR
THE ORDINARY MAN>. WE SET OUT
TO MAKE A FESTIVAL PROFILE THAT
HONORS THE TRADITIONAL SUPERMAR-
KET CALLIGRAPHY TO REFLECT THE
COMBINATION OF CULTURE AND COM-
MERCE.
--

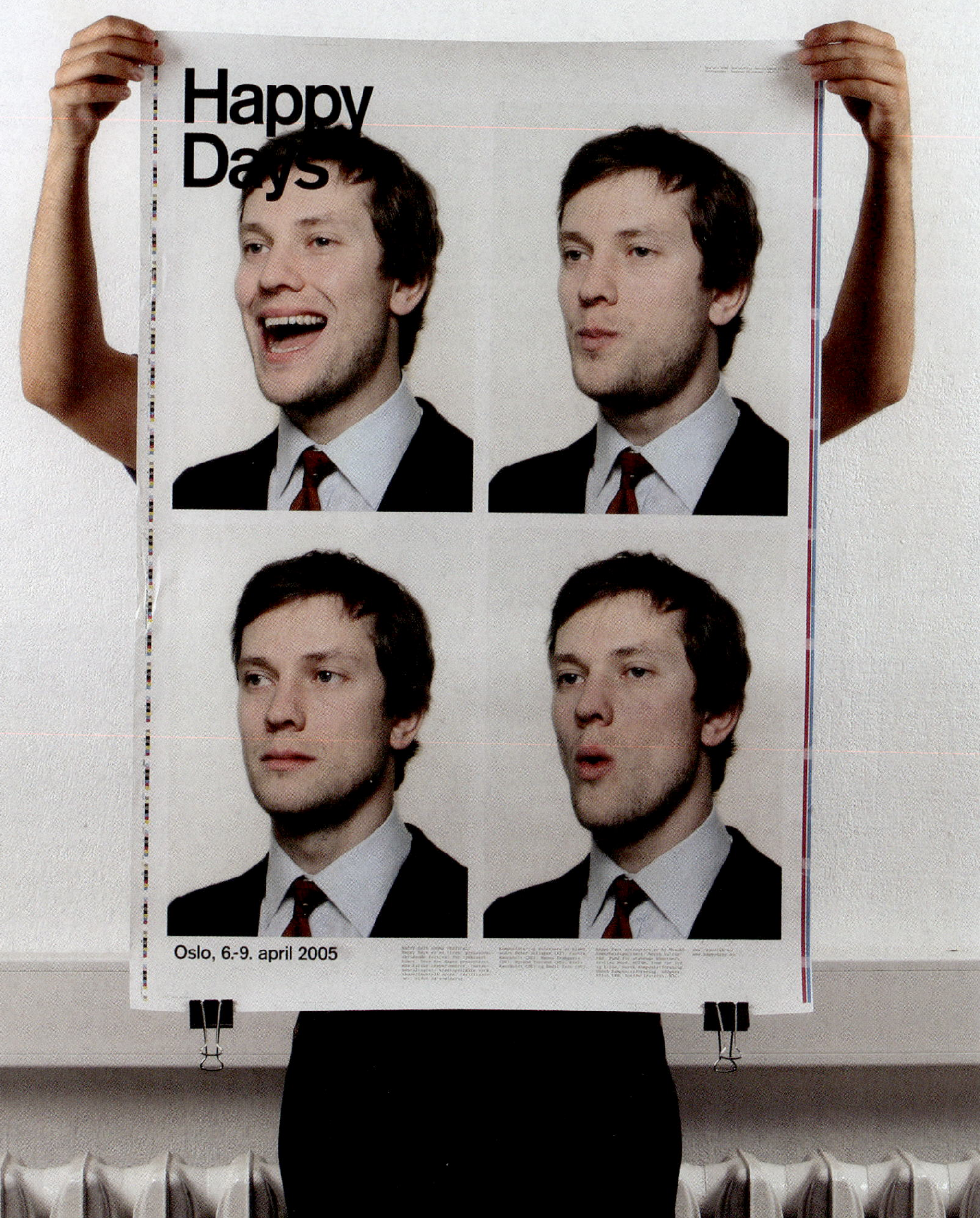

Happy Days
Oslo, 6.-9. april 2005

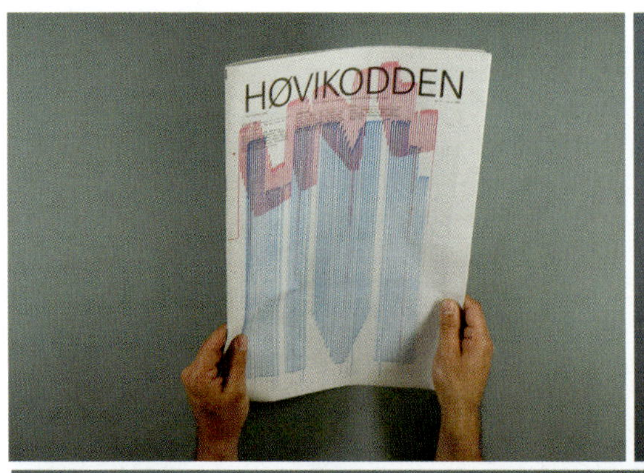

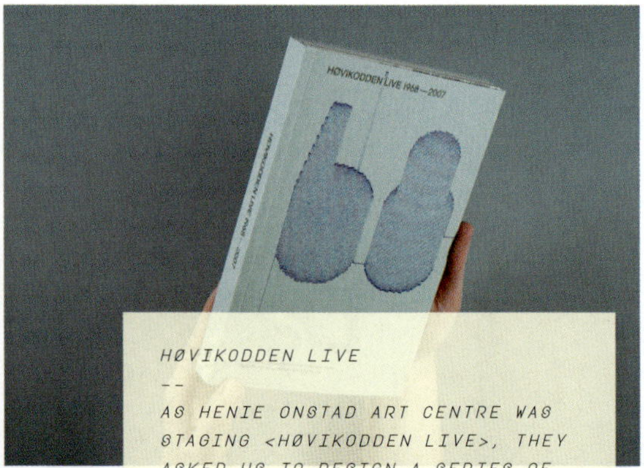

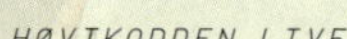

HØVIKODDEN LIVE
--
AS HENIE ONSTAD ART CENTRE WAS
STAGING <HØVIKODDEN LIVE>, THEY
ASKED US TO DESIGN A SERIES OF
ELEMENTS.
--
FOR THIS PROJECT, WE COOPERATED
WITH DANIEL MAARLEVELD, JAAN
EVART AND JULIAN HAGEN, CREATORS
OF THE PENJET - AN ORDINARY INK-
JET PRINTER WITH A PEN ATTACHED
TO ITS PRINT-HEAD, DRAWING ITS
MOVEMENTS.
--

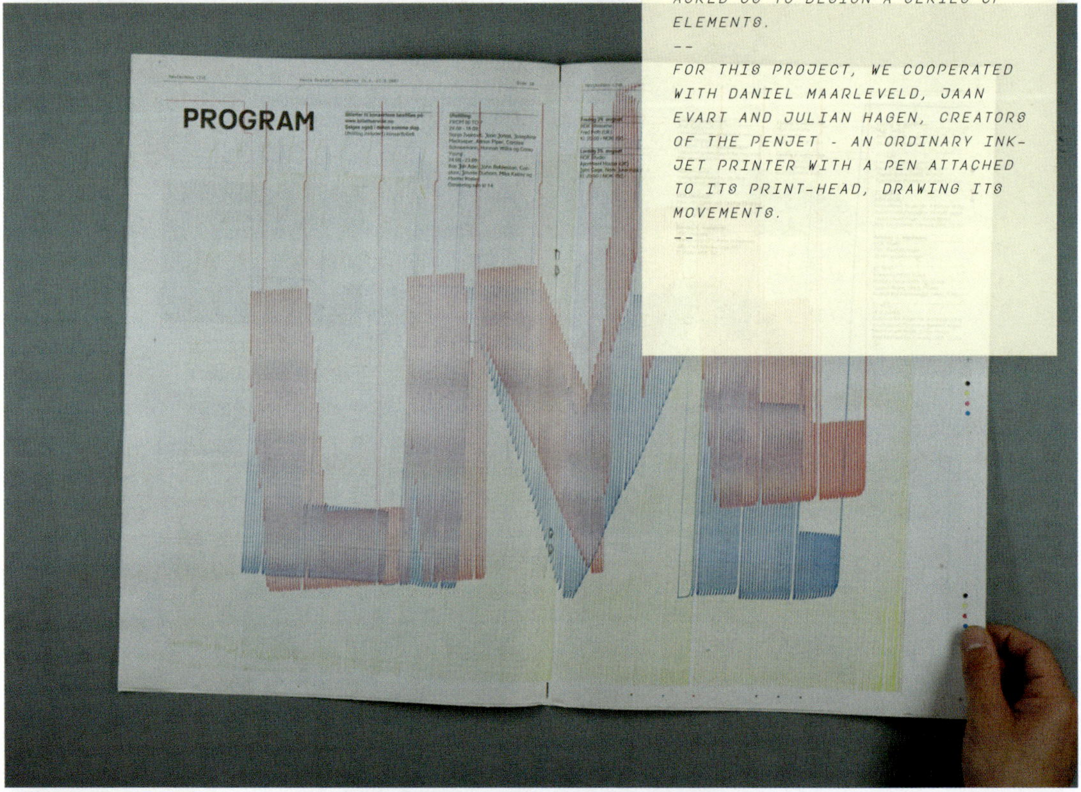

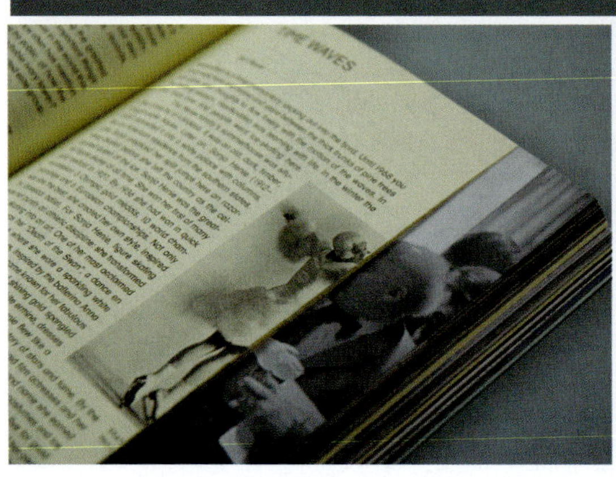

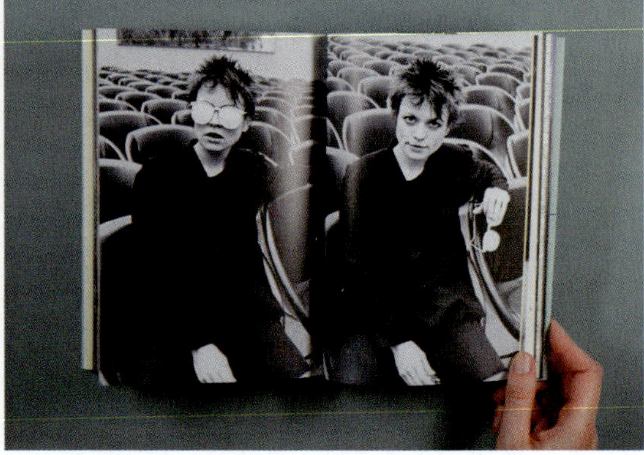

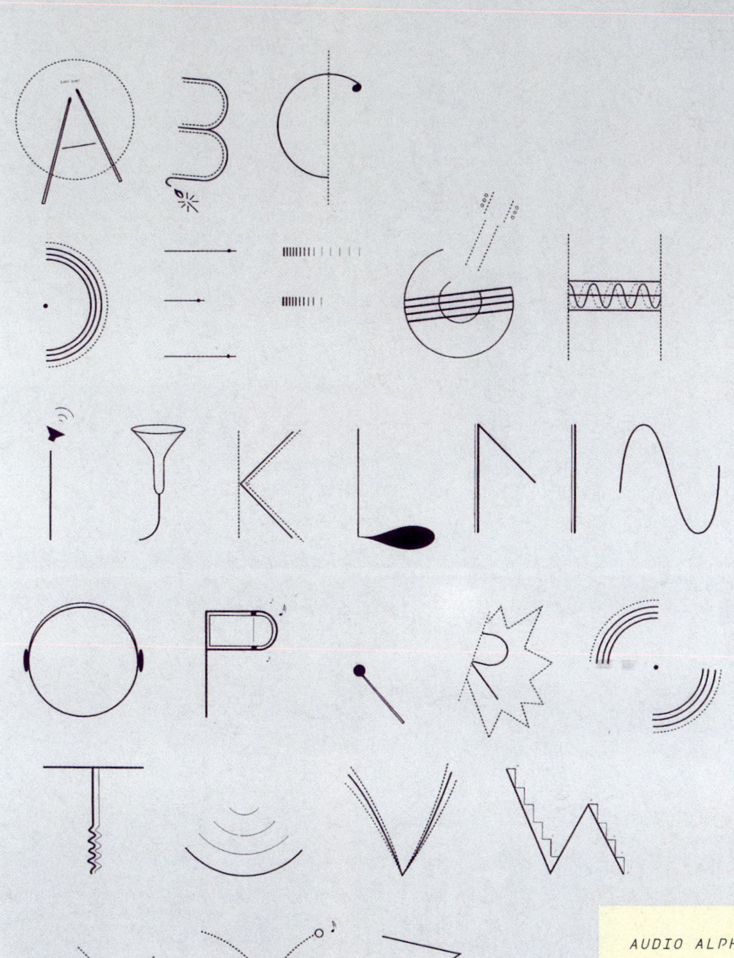

AUDIO ALPHABET
--
NY MUSIKK (NORWEGIAN SECTION OF
THE INTERNATIONAL SOCIETY FOR
CONTEMPORARY MUSIC) ASKED US TO
DO A PURELY VISUAL PROJECT ABOUT
SOUND IN PUBLIC SPACE.
--
FOR THIS PROJECT WE COOPERATED
WITH FELIX WEIGAND TO DEVELOP AN
ALPHABET THAT PLAYS WITH VISUAL
MUSICAL REFERENCES.
--

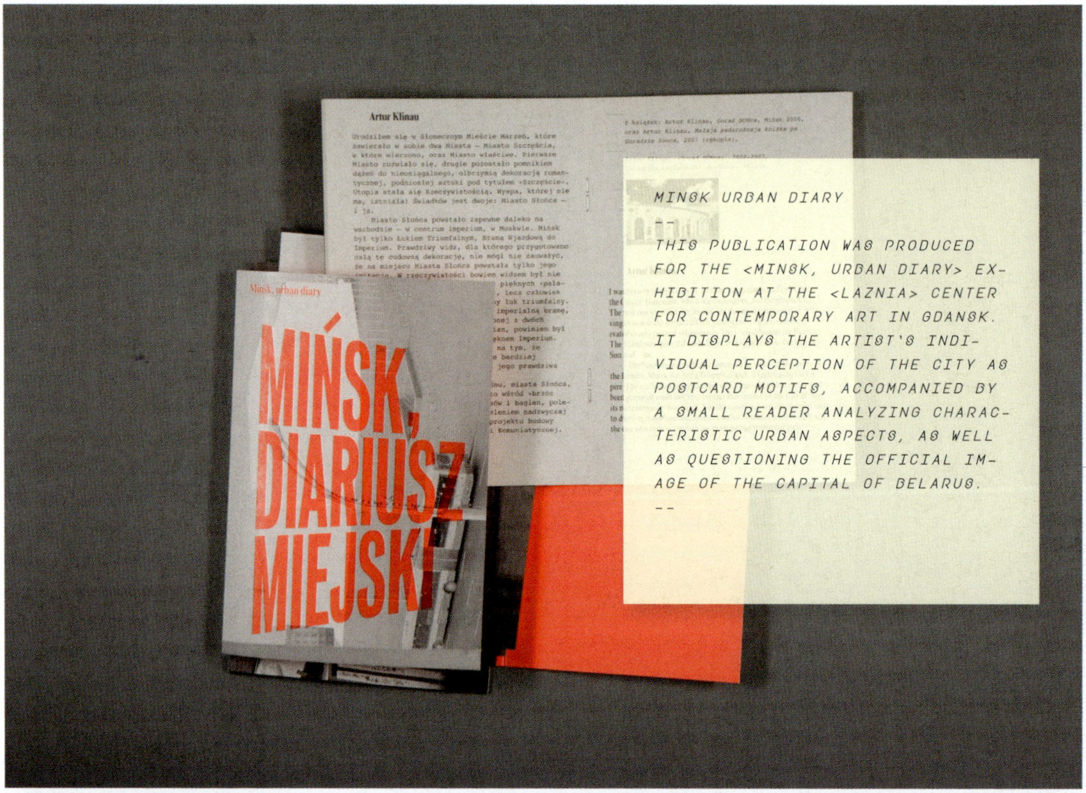

MINSK URBAN DIARY
--
THIS PUBLICATION WAS PRODUCED FOR THE <MINSK, URBAN DIARY> EXHIBITION AT THE <LAZNIA> CENTER FOR CONTEMPORARY ART IN GDANSK. IT DISPLAYS THE ARTIST'S INDIVIDUAL PERCEPTION OF THE CITY AS POSTCARD MOTIFS, ACCOMPANIED BY A SMALL READER ANALYZING CHARACTERISTIC URBAN ASPECTS, AS WELL AS QUESTIONING THE OFFICIAL IMAGE OF THE CAPITAL OF BELARUS.
--

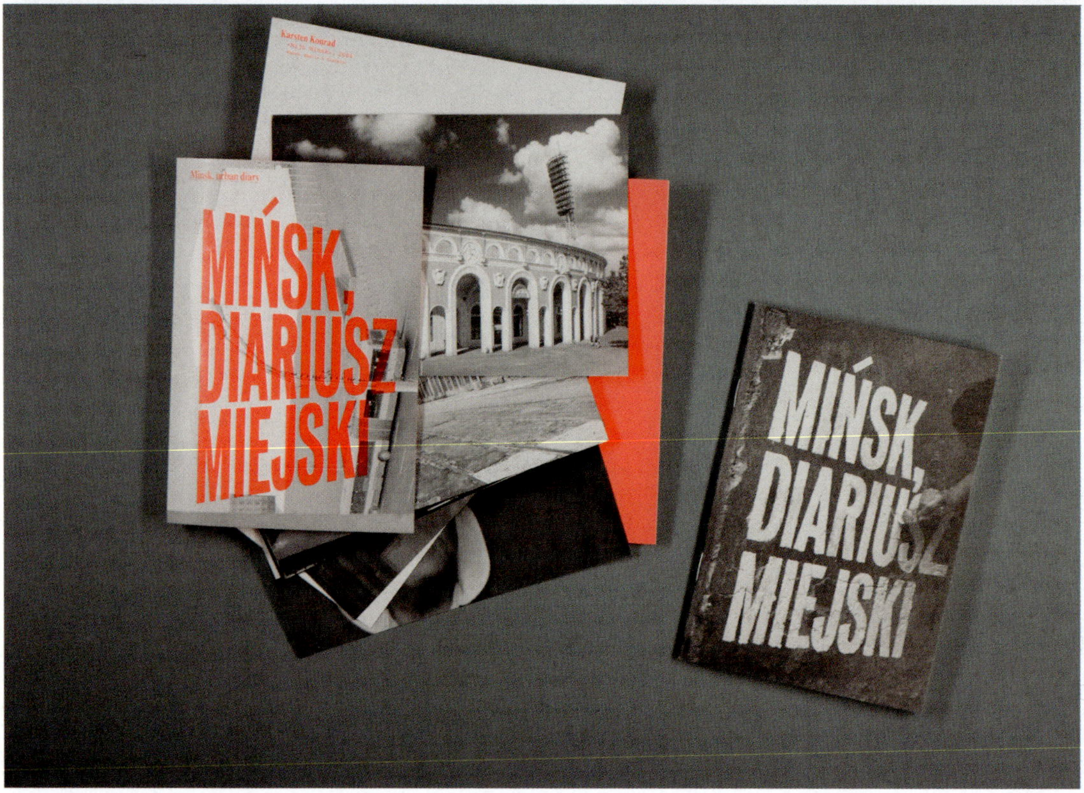

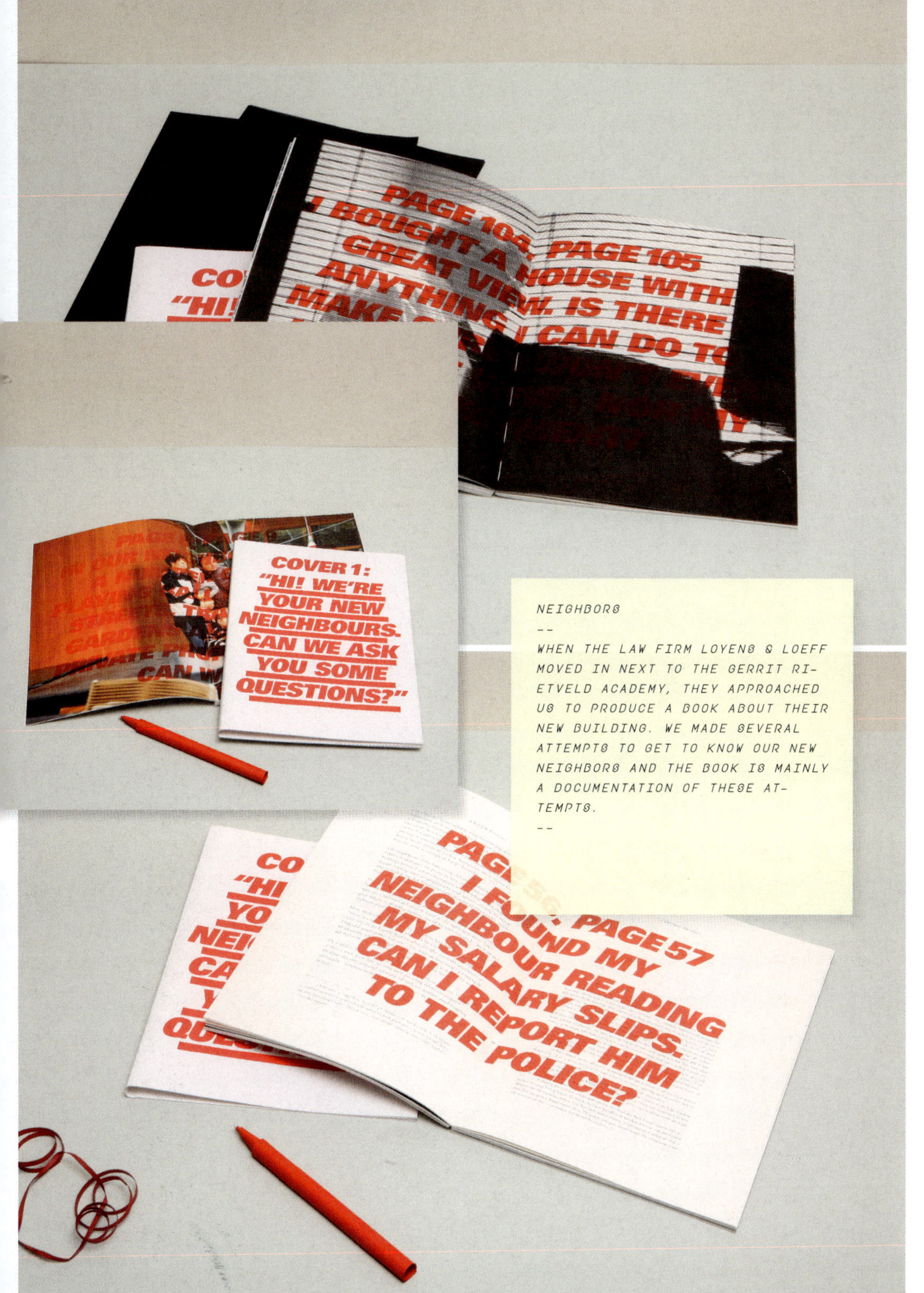

PAGE 104, PAGE 105
I BOUGHT A HOUSE WITH
A GREAT VIEW. IS THERE
ANYTHING I CAN DO TO
MAKE SURE
COVER
"HI!
COVER 1:
"HI! WE'RE
YOUR NEW
NEIGHBOURS.
CAN WE ASK
YOU SOME
QUESTIONS?"
PAGE 56
I FOUND MY
NEIGHBOUR READING
MY SALARY SLIPS.
CAN I REPORT HIM
TO THE POLICE?
PAGE 57
NEIGHBORS
--
WHEN THE LAW FIRM LOYENS & LOEFF
MOVED IN NEXT TO THE GERRIT RI-
ETVELD ACADEMY, THEY APPROACHED
US TO PRODUCE A BOOK ABOUT THEIR
NEW BUILDING. WE MADE SEVERAL
ATTEMPTS TO GET TO KNOW OUR NEW
NEIGHBORS AND THE BOOK IS MAINLY
A DOCUMENTATION OF THESE AT-
TEMPTS.
--

STUDIOHEYHEY CONSISTS OF GINA
MÖNCH AND JOHN RUSSO. WE GOT TO-
GETHER WHILE STUDYING AT THE HOCH-
SCHULE DARMSTADT/MATHILDENHÖHE.

--

WHAT IS GERMAN?

GOETHE
MEETS CLUB URLAUB
(HOLIDAY CLUB).

WHAT IS GERMAN DESIGN?

ULM SCHOOL
MEETS NEULAND.

DESCRIBE YOUR WORKING PROCESS.

TRIAL AND ERROR
MEETS HIT AND RUN.

WHAT DO YOU AIM TO ACHIEVE WITH
YOUR WORK?

DO IT
MEETS DIY.

YOU'VE INVITED A FRIEND TO
GERMANY; NAME ONE PLACE THEY
REALLY MUST VISIT AND A QUINT-
ESSENTIAL EXPERIENCE YOU REC-
OMMEND.

RAIN IN AUGUST
MEETS HOLIDAY ON ICE.

WHAT IS THE MOST IMPORTANT
LESSON YOU HAVE LEARNED IN YOUR
PROFESSION SO FAR?

STOMACH
MEETS HEAD.

--

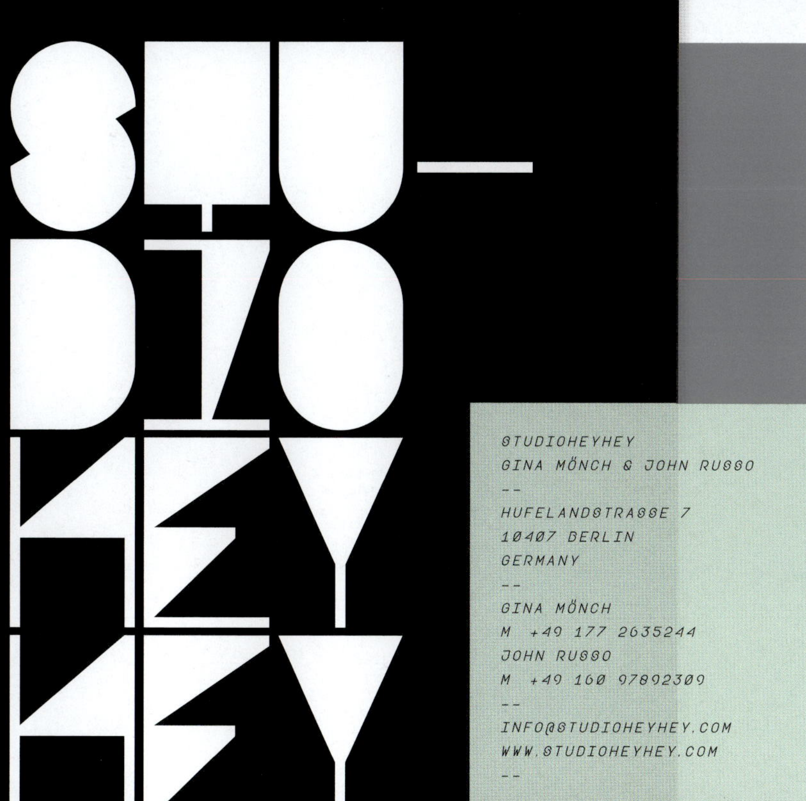

@STUDIOHEYHEY
GINA MÖNCH & JOHN RUSSO
--
HUFELANDSTRASSE 7
10407 BERLIN
GERMANY
--
GINA MÖNCH
M +49 177 2635244
JOHN RUSSO
M +49 160 97892309
--
INFO@STUDIOHEYHEY.COM
WWW.STUDIOHEYHEY.COM
--

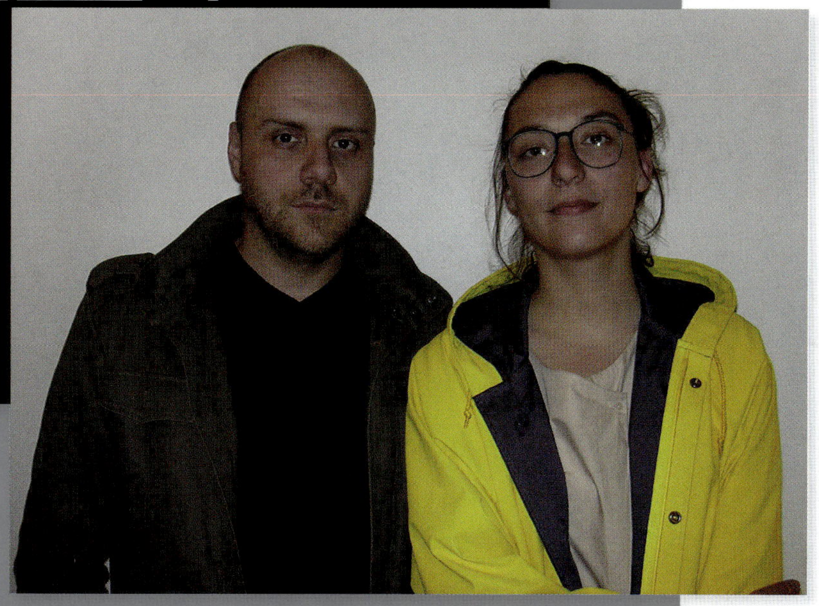

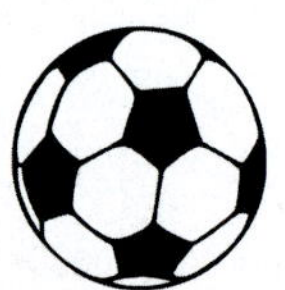

SOMETHING UTTERLY GERMAN
--

WORKPLACE
--

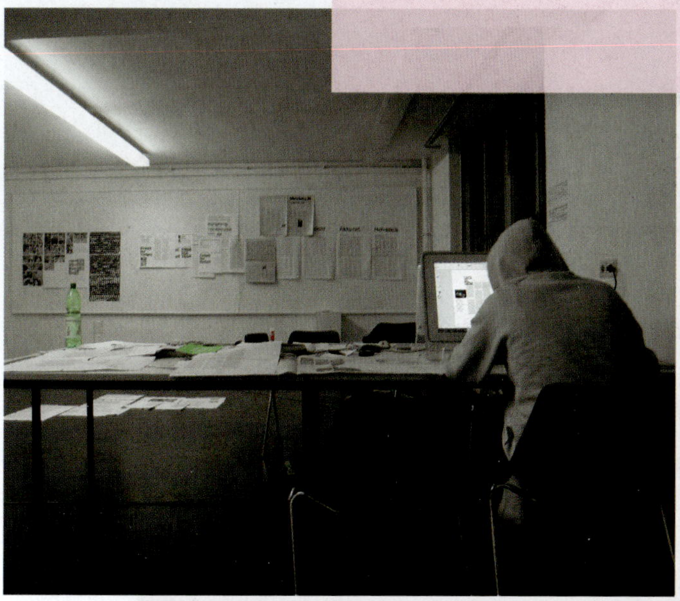

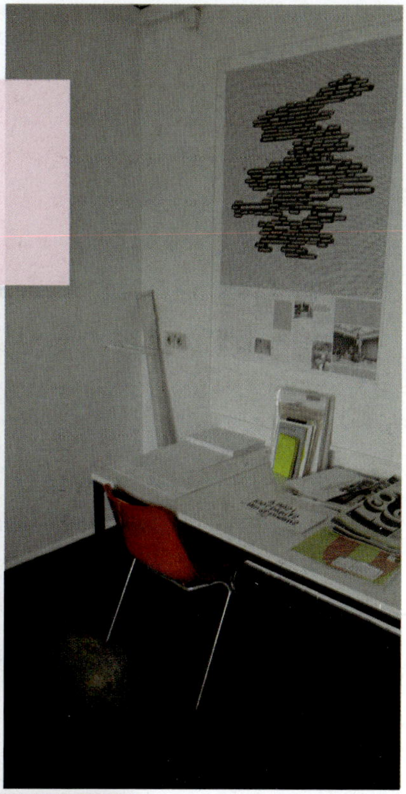

STUDIO SURROUNDINGS
--

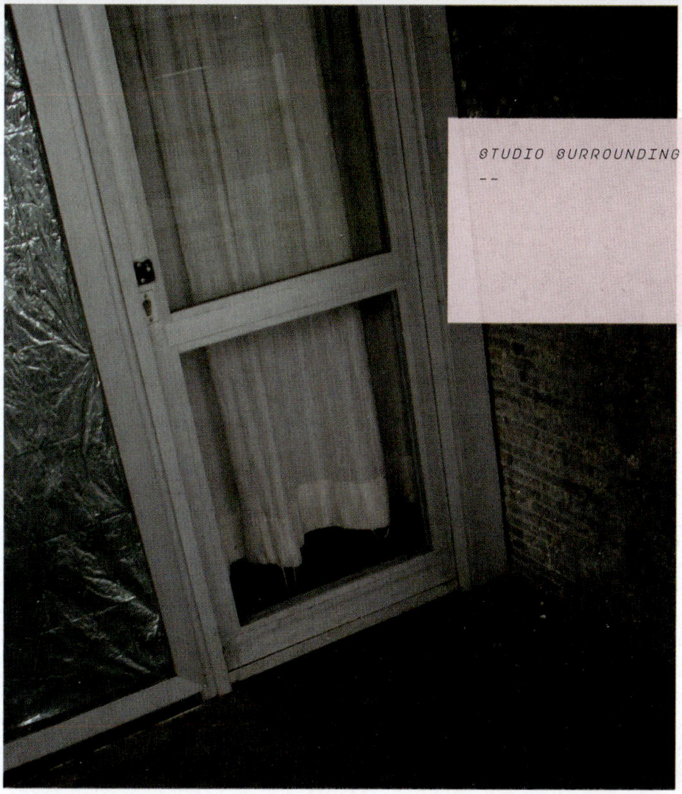

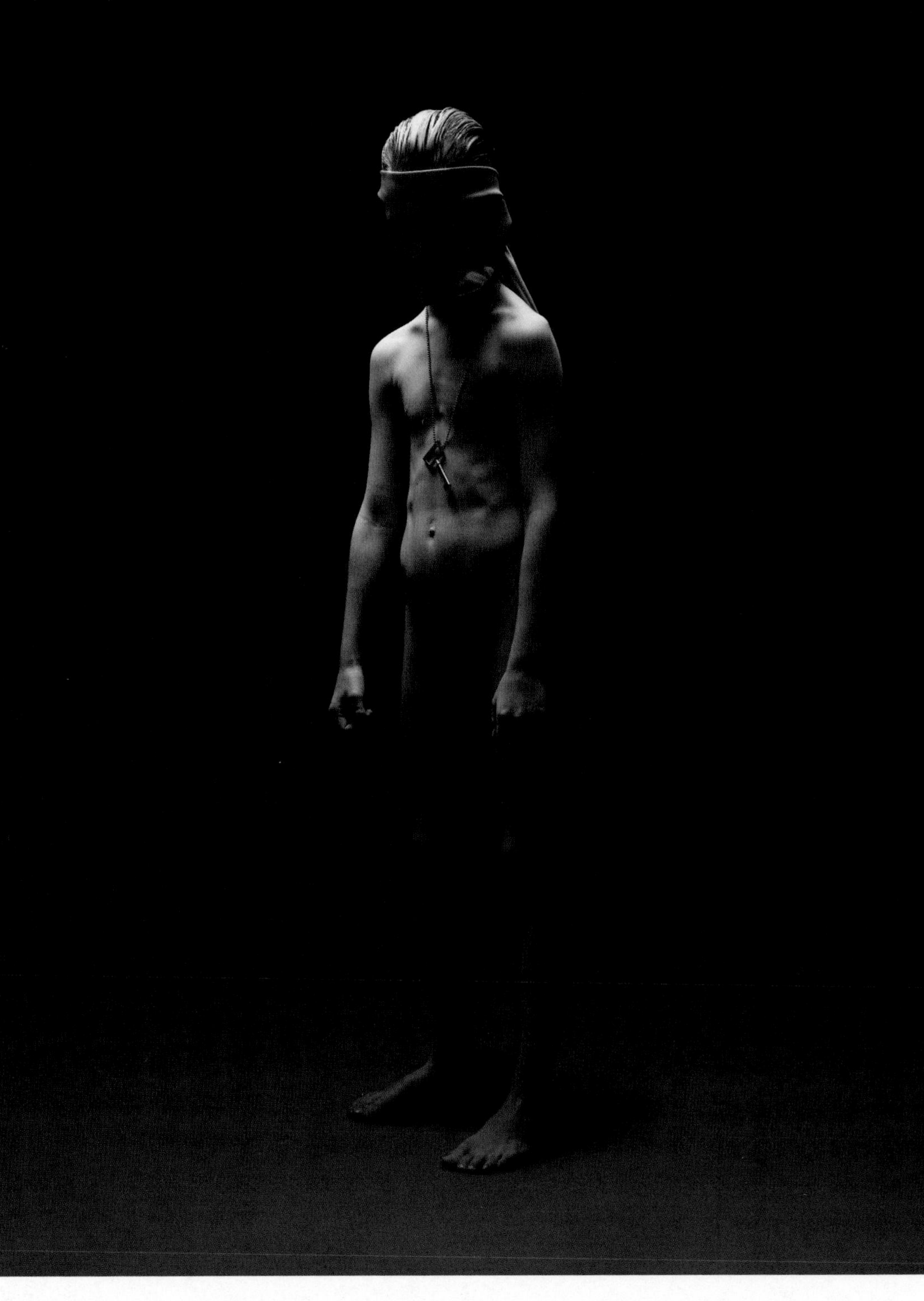

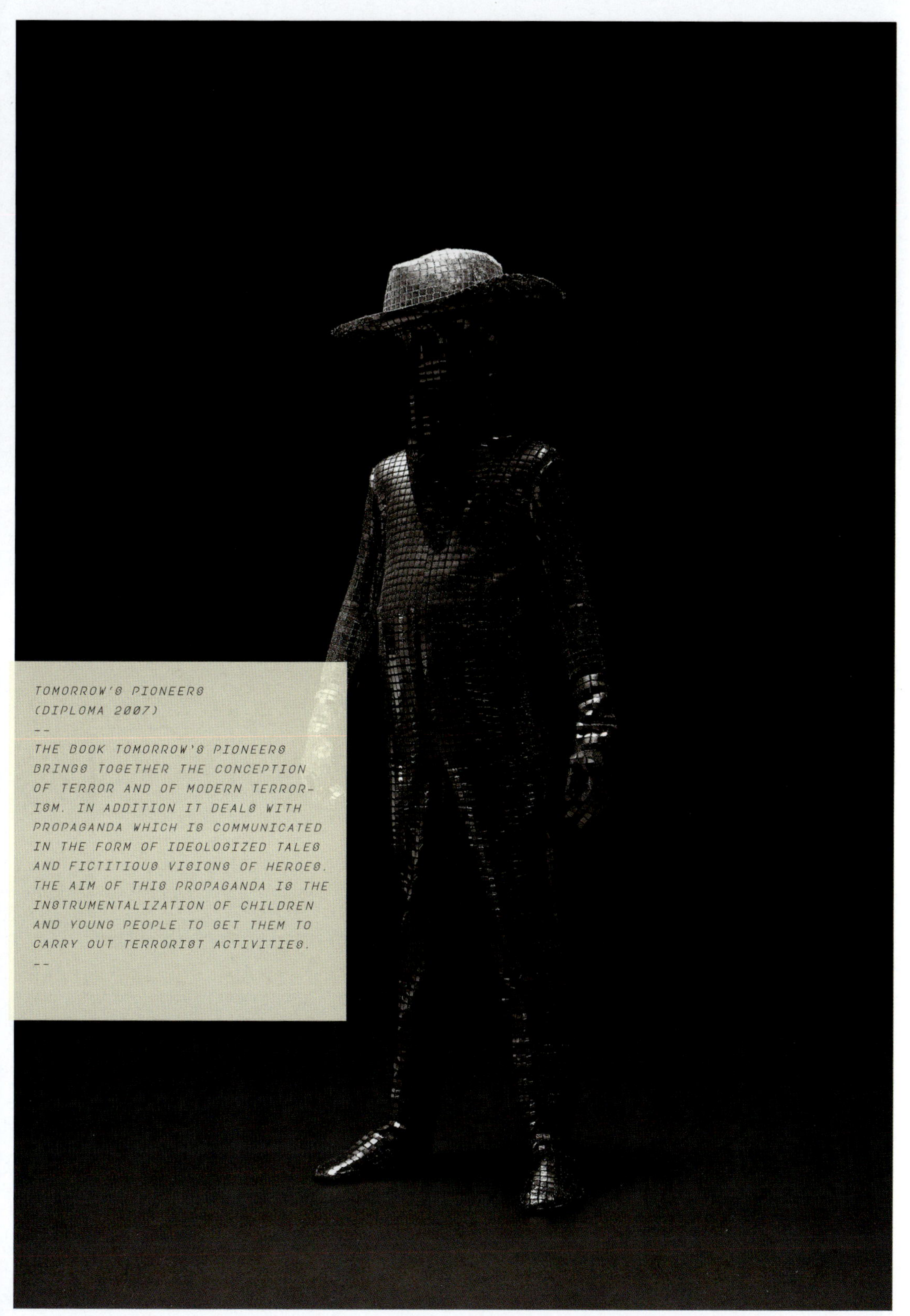

TOMORROW'S PIONEERS
(DIPLOMA 2007)
--
THE BOOK TOMORROW'S PIONEERS
BRINGS TOGETHER THE CONCEPTION
OF TERROR AND OF MODERN TERROR-
ISM. IN ADDITION IT DEALS WITH
PROPAGANDA WHICH IS COMMUNICATED
IN THE FORM OF IDEOLOGIZED TALES
AND FICTITIOUS VISIONS OF HEROES.
THE AIM OF THIS PROPAGANDA IS THE
INSTRUMENTALIZATION OF CHILDREN
AND YOUNG PEOPLE TO GET THEM TO
CARRY OUT TERRORIST ACTIVITIES.
--

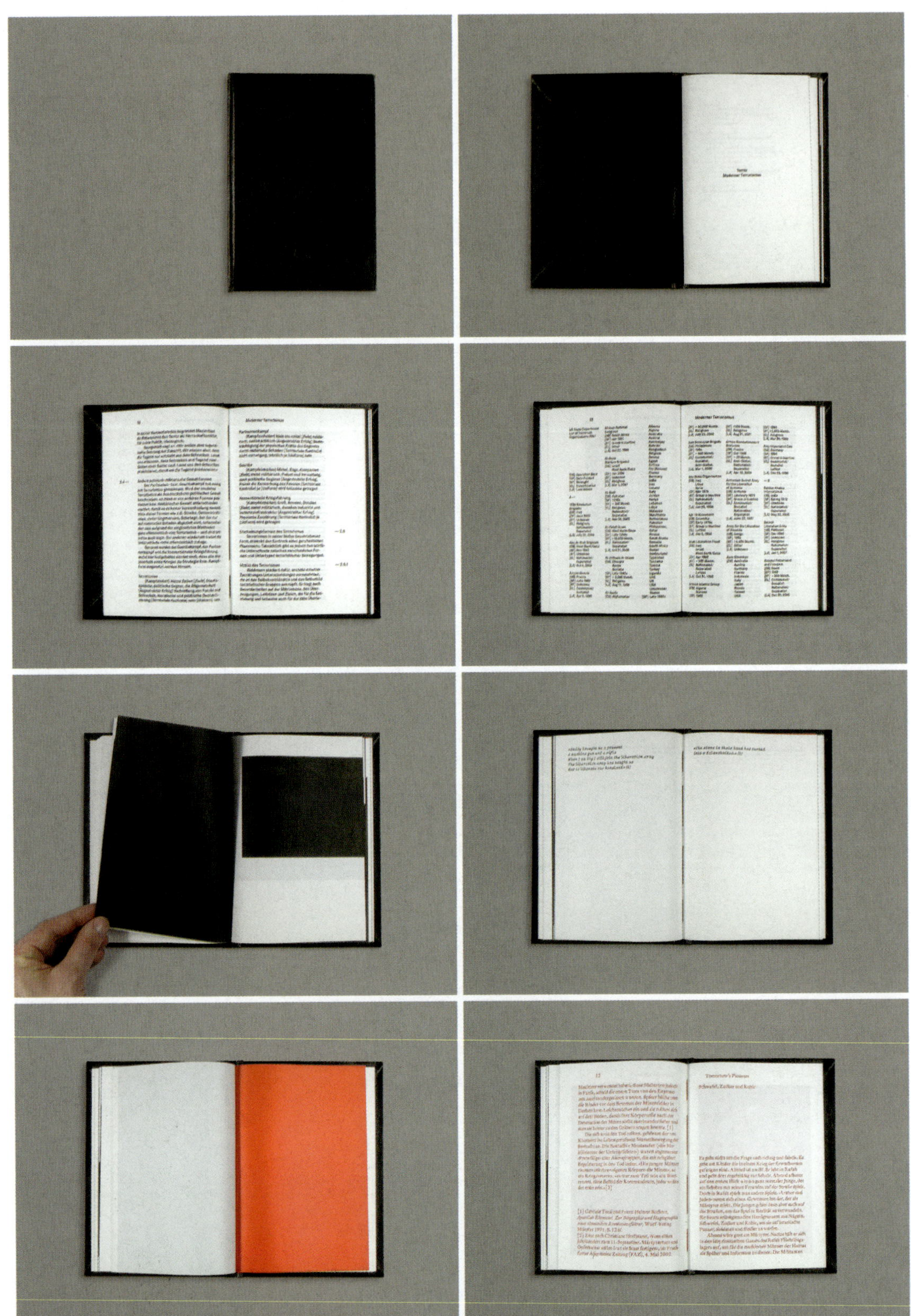

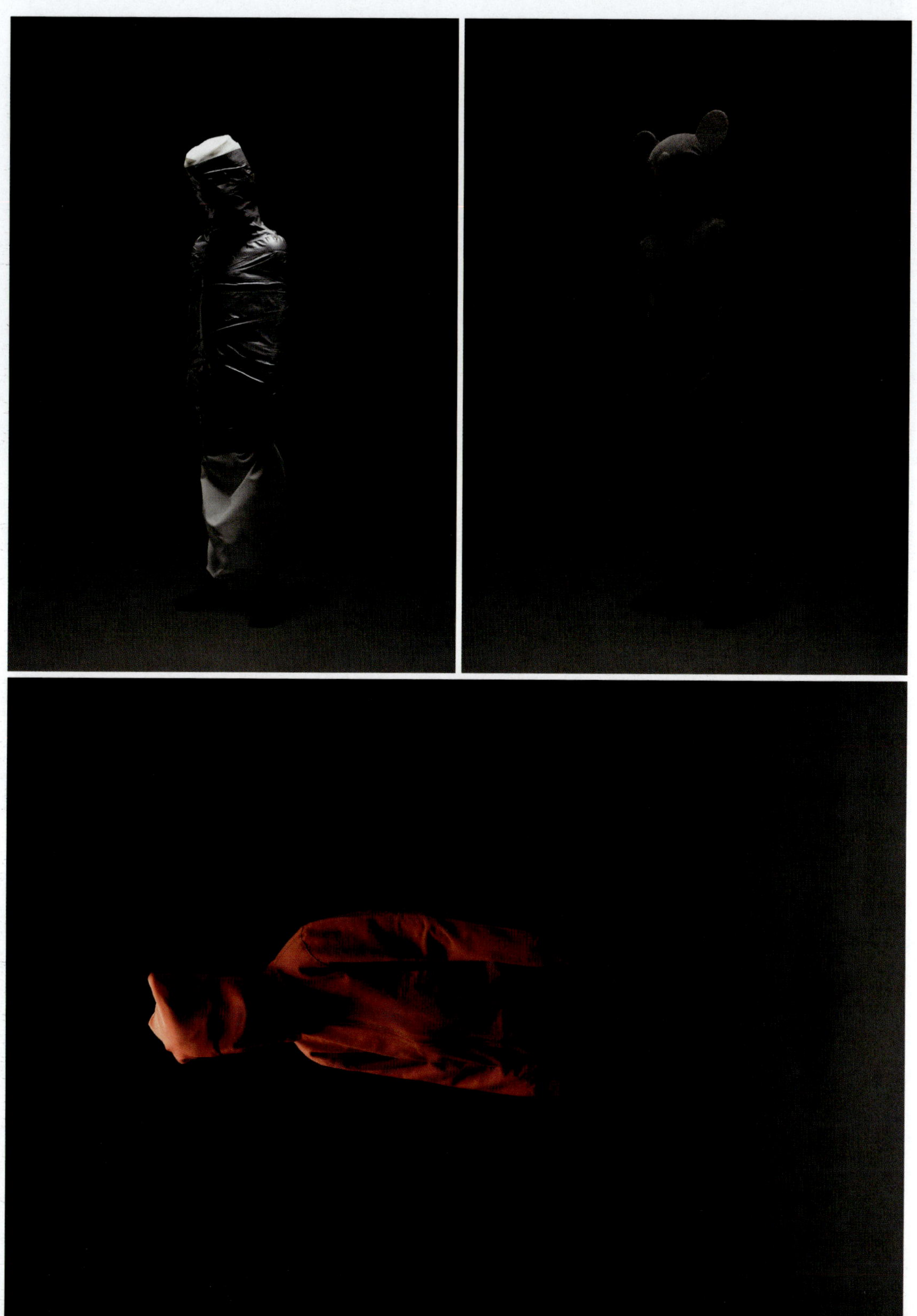

OLBRICHWEG 10/2
--
THE CENTRAL PROJECT
<OLBRICHWEG10/2> WAS AN INSTAL-
LATION IN THE FORM OF A ONE-
DAY SHOW OF WORK BY THE DESIGN
DEPARTMENT OF HOCHSCHULE DARM-
STADT. THE INSTALLATION SHOWS A
SELECTION OF WORKS, OBJECTS AND
FOUND ITEMS FROM THE PAST 36
YEARS (1971-2007). THE <DING DER
DINGE> AS IT WAS CALLED WAS ALSO
THE TRIGGER FOR DISCOURSE AND
DONORS OF MATERIALS FOR THE PIC-
TURES AND CONTRIBUTIONS TO THE
2ND EDITION OF THE OLBRICHWEG 10
NEWSPAPER. THE INSTALLATION WAS
DOCUMENTED IN THE 2ND EDITION
AND DESCRIBED IN TEXTS BY VARI-
OUS AUTHORS.
--
THE AIM OF THE 2ND EDITION OF
OLBRICHWEG 10 WAS TO COMMUNI-
CATE TO THE PUBLIC AN UP-TO-DATE
STATEMENT BY THE DESIGN DEPART-
MENT OF HOCHSCHULE DARMSTADT.
THE DARMSTÄDTER ECHO WAS IN-
VOLVED IN THIS, TAKING OVER THE
PRODUCTION AND DISTRIBUTION OF
OLBRICHWEG 10/2 IN AN EDITION OF
30,000 COPIES.
--
THE <DING DER DINGE> WAS A <ONE-
DAY FLYER> EXACTLY LIKE THE DAILY
PAPER OLBRICHWEG 10/2.
HERE TODAY, GONE TOMORROW.
--
NEWSPAPER:
GINA MÖNCH, JOHN RUSSO
--
INSTALLATION:
MATHIAS BIEGEL, LUKAS BREIT-
KREUTZ, MICHAELA DECHERT, SE-
BASTIAN ESCHE, GINA MÖNCH, JOHN
RUSSO, ROMERO STEINHAUSER
--
DESIGN DEPARTMENT OF HOCHSCHULE
DARMSTADT
TUTOR: PROFESSOR SANDRA HOFFMANN

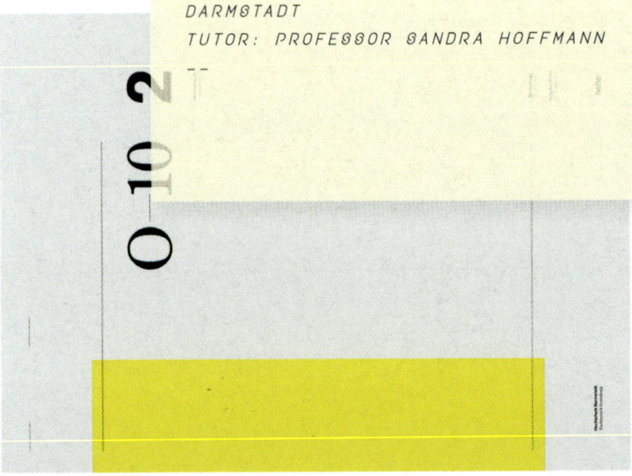

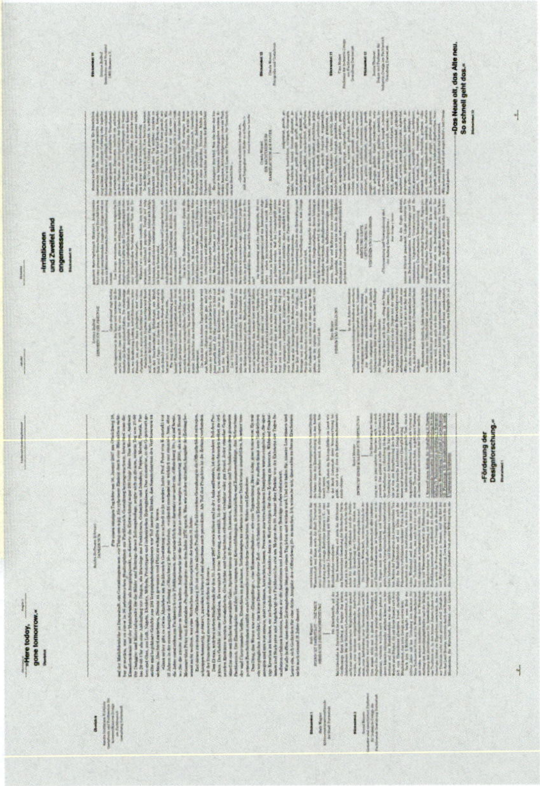

O-10 2

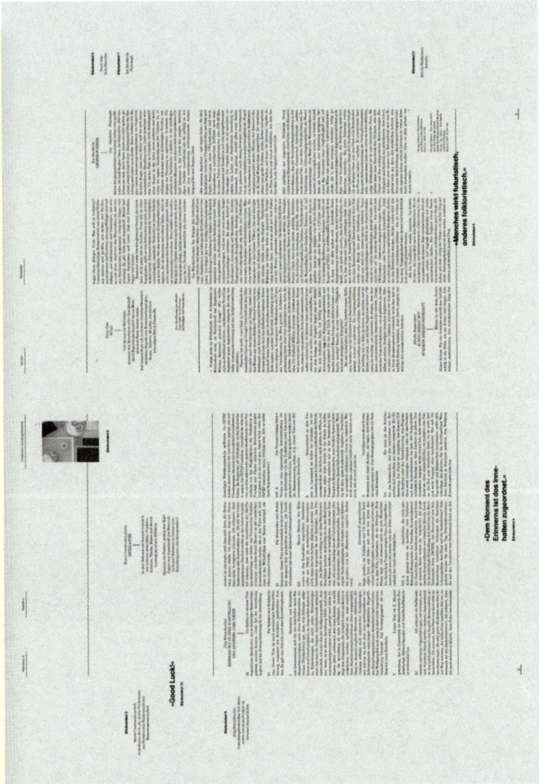

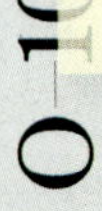

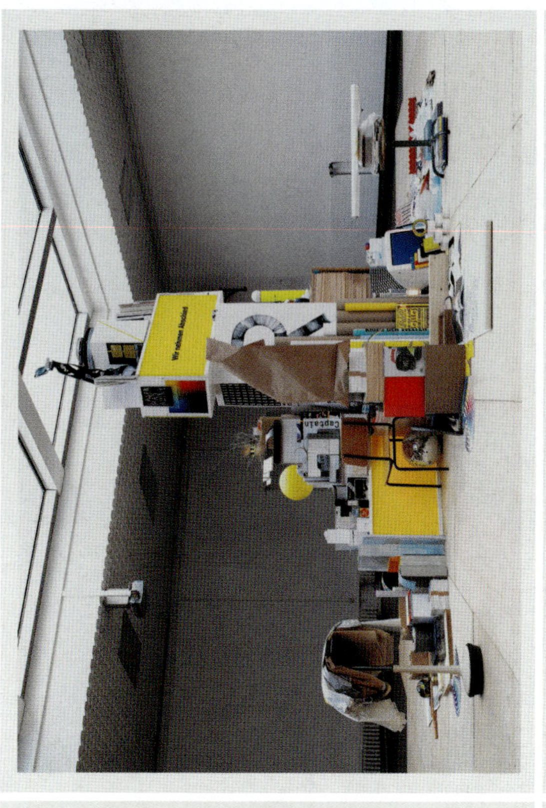
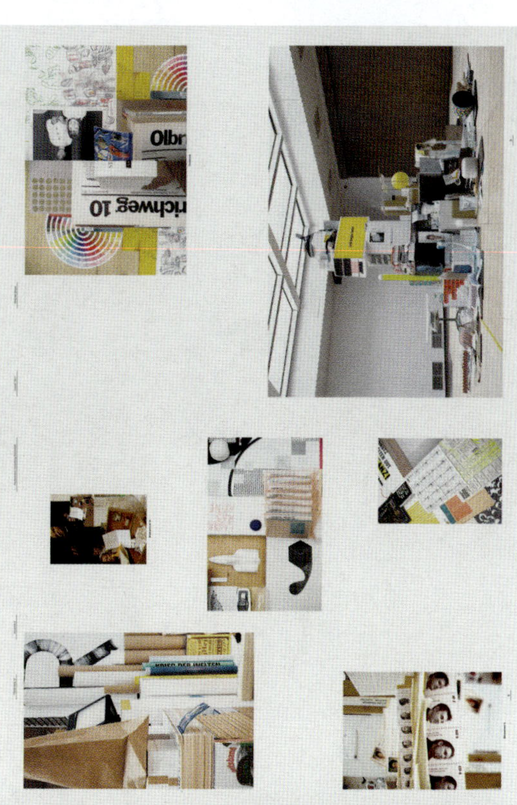
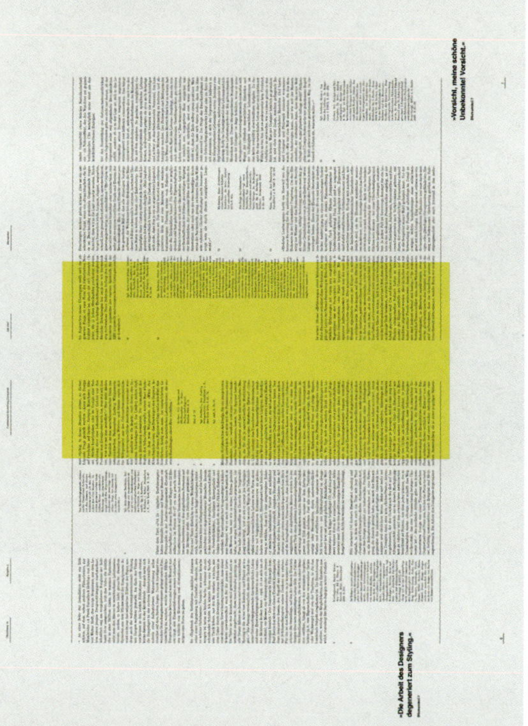
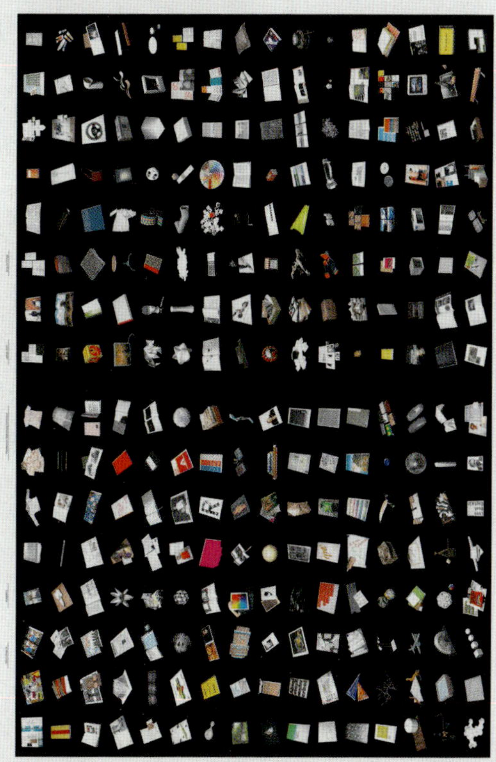

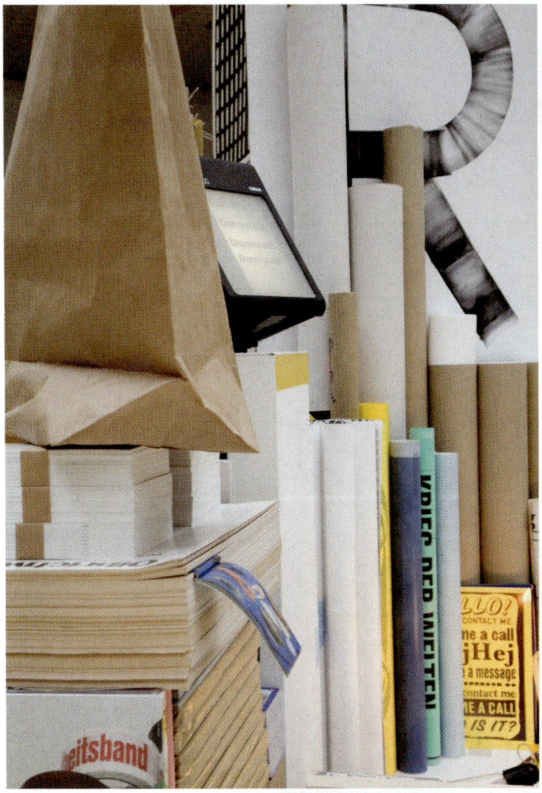

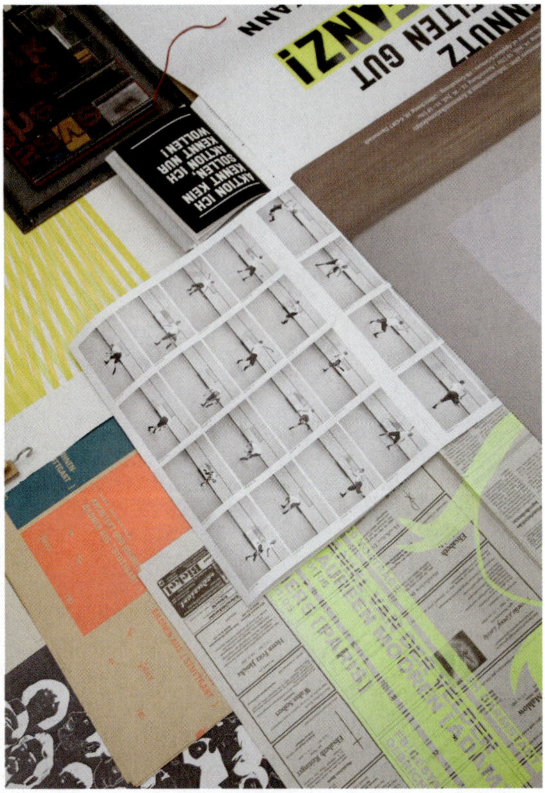

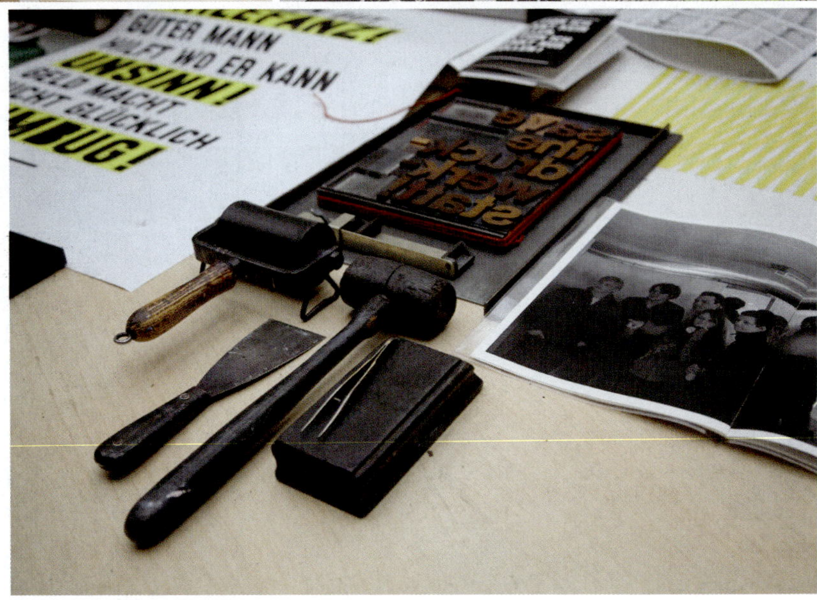

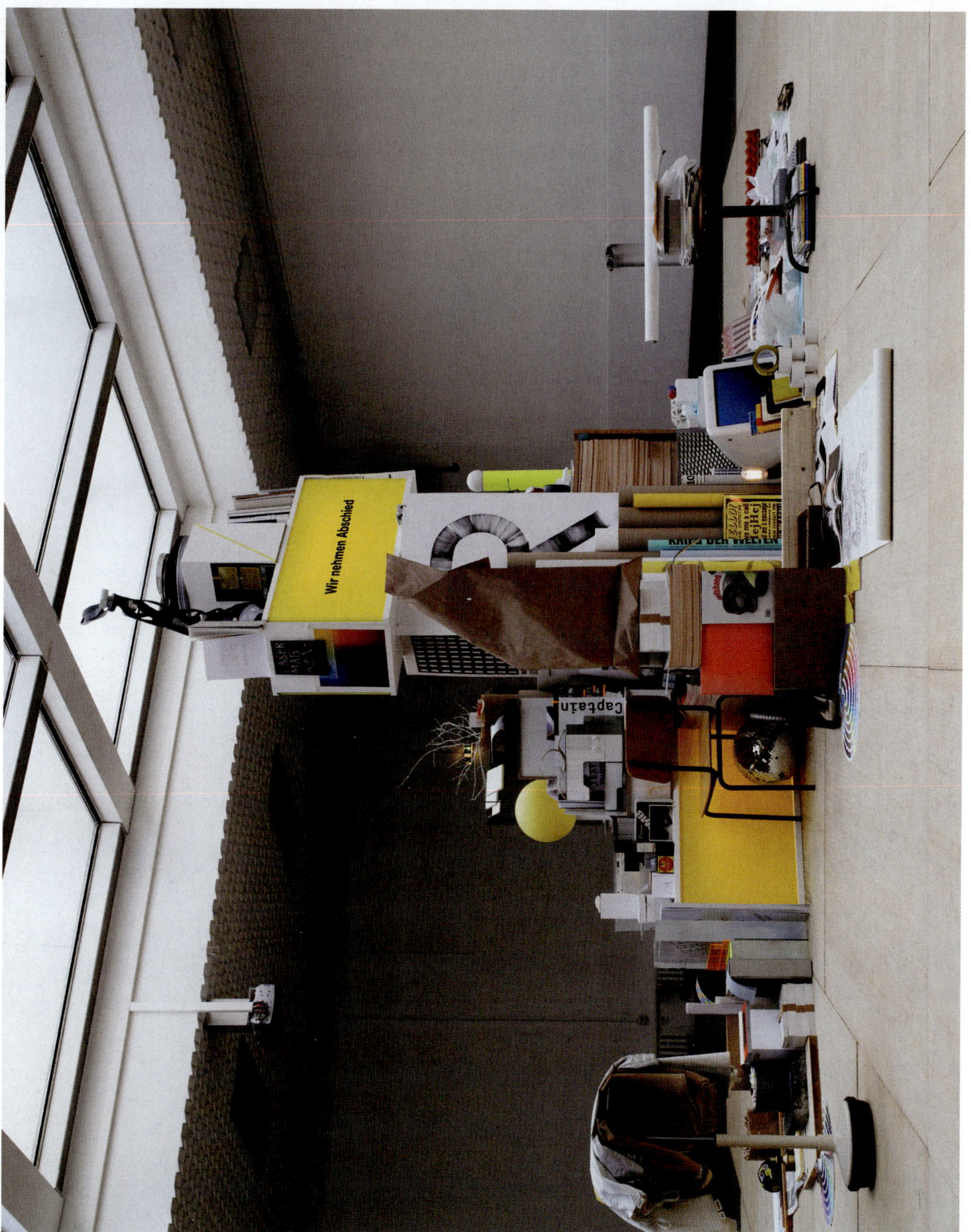

THIBAUD TISSOT WAS BORN AND STUD-
IED IN LA CHAUX-DE-FONDS (SWIT-
ZERLAND) WHERE WITH YASSIN BAGGAR
HE FOUNDED DYNAMO, A PARALLEL
STRUCTURE FOR SELF-COMMISSIONED
PROJECTS. HE NOW LIVES IN BERLIN
AND WORKS AS DESIGNER FOR ONLAB.

--

WHAT IS GERMAN?

GOOD QUESTION… A STRANGE MIX OF
WARMTH AND COLDNESS, SOMETIMES
SURPRISING.

WHAT IS GERMAN DESIGN?

SOMETHING UNDEFINED. I DON'T
REALLY KNOW THE WORK OF GERMAN
DESIGNERS, BUT I THINK THAT IT'S
QUITE DIFFICULT TO TALK OF A <GER-
MAN WAVE>.

DESCRIBE YOUR WORKING PROCESS.

I HAVE NO GENERAL RECIPE, BUT I
KNOW I'M OBSESSED…

WHAT DO YOU AIM TO ACHIEVE WITH
YOUR WORK?

TO TELL STORIES IN DISCOVERING
AND RELATING NEW TOPICS, DEVELOP-
ING SURPRISING VISUAL SYSTEMS AND
HAVING FUN.

YOU'VE INVITED A FRIEND TO
GERMANY; NAME ONE PLACE THEY
REALLY MUST VISIT AND A QUINT-
ESSENTIAL EXPERIENCE YOU REC-
OMMEND.

I WOULD INVITE HIM FOR A <FRÜH-
STÜCK> [GERMAN BREAKFAST] ON SUN-
DAY HERE IN PRENZLAUER BERG, ROUND
THE CORNER ON A SIDEWALK CAFÉ.

WHAT IS THE MOST IMPORTANT
LESSON YOU HAVE LEARNED IN YOUR
PROFESSION SO FAR?

DESIGN IS NOT A QUICK PROCESS…

--

TIS—SOT

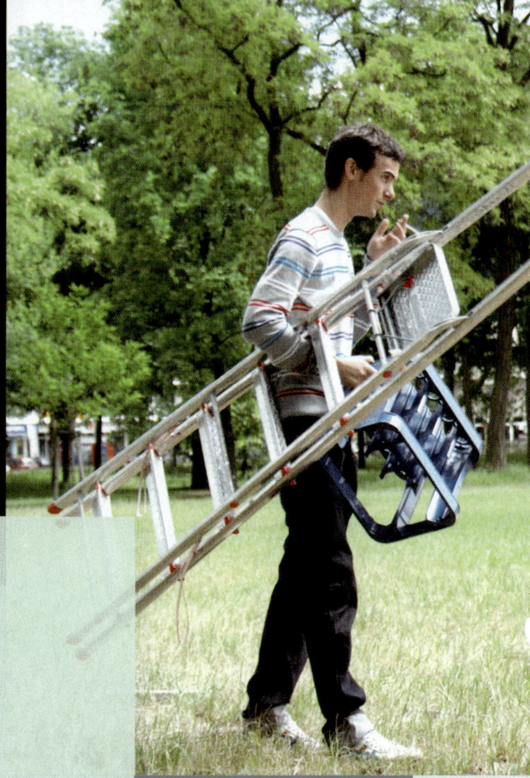

THIBAUD TISSOT
--
SCHÖNHAUSER ALLEE 44
10435 BERLIN
GERMANY
--
M +49 176 75554666
--
THIBAUD@DYNAMO.LI
WWW.DYNAMO.LI
--

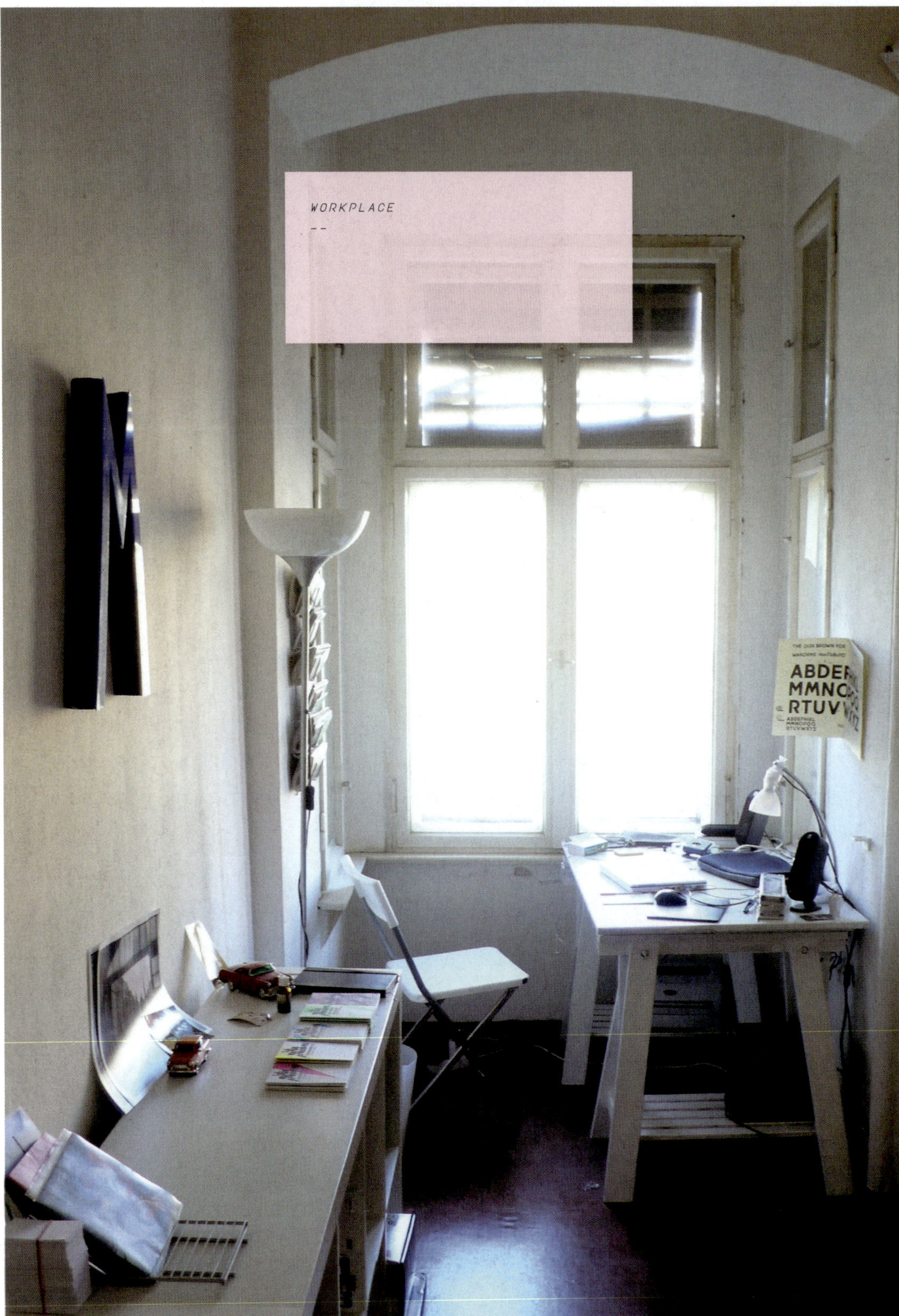

WORKPLACE

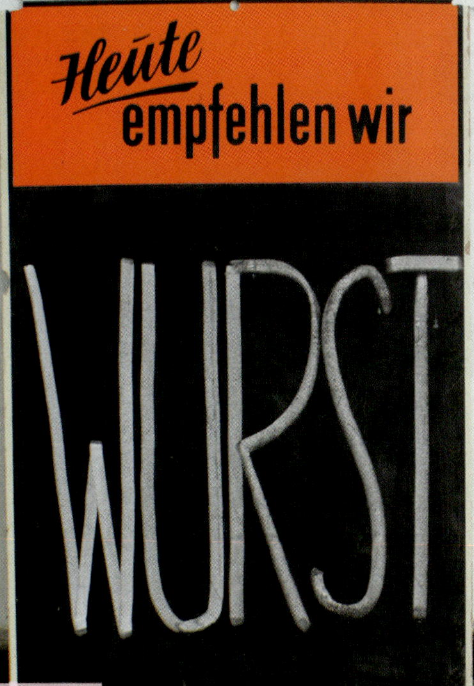

SOMETHING UTTERLY GERMAN
--

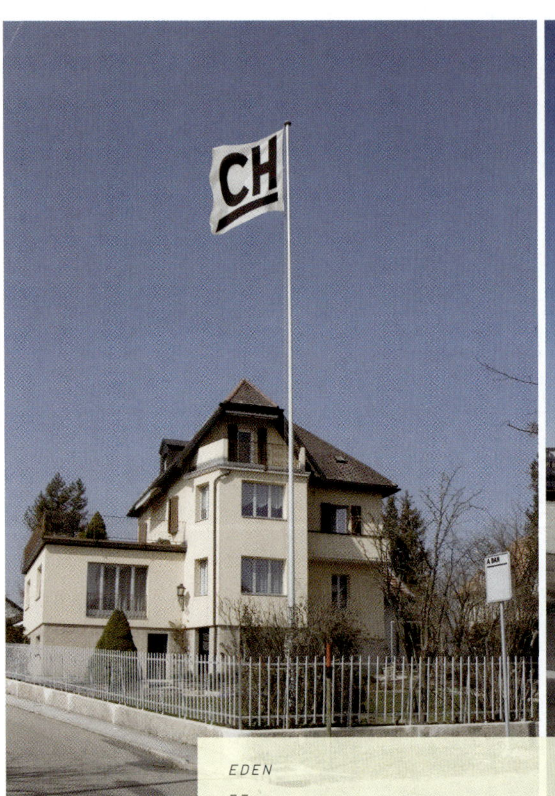

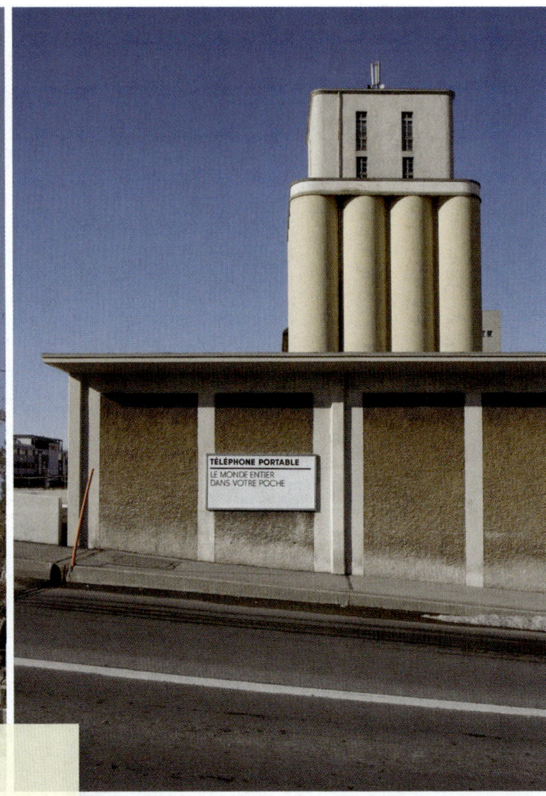

EDEN
--
DIPLOMA PROJECT ON THE THEME OF
UNIFORMITY AND STANDARDIZATION.
REFLECTION ON THE DESIGNER'S
ROLE AND THE PLACE OF IMAGES IN
TODAY'S SOCIETY, ITS POWER OVER
SOCIAL CONSCIOUSNESS. TO SOLVE
THE PROBLEM OF THE EXCESS OF
PICTURES AND SIGNS IN DAY-TO-DAY
LIFE, WHY NOT SIMPLY UPROOT AND
FORBID THEM? WHAT HAPPENS? WHAT
ARE THE CONSEQUENCES OF A RADI-
CAL CORPORATE DESIGN PROCESS FOR
OUR SOCIETY FROM A GLOBAL POINT
OF VIEW? THIS RESEARCH TRIES
TO PROJECT AND ILLUSTRATE THESE
QUESTIONS.
--
EAA LA CHAUX-DE-FONDS (CH)
TUTORS: LAURENT COCCHI AND LAU-
RENT COTTARD
--

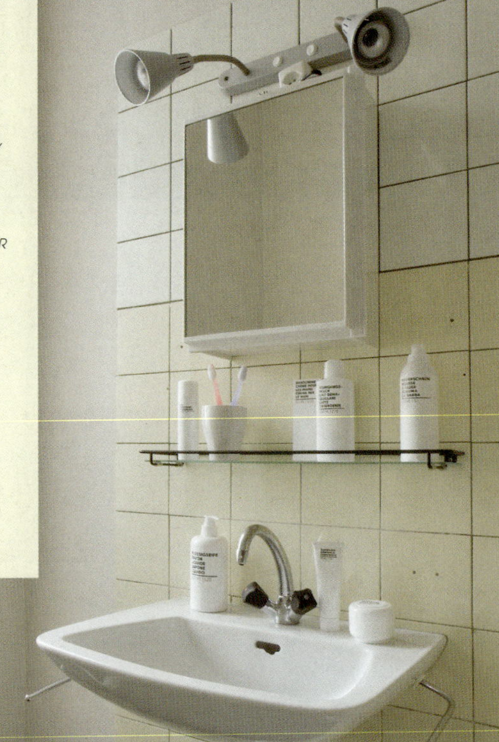

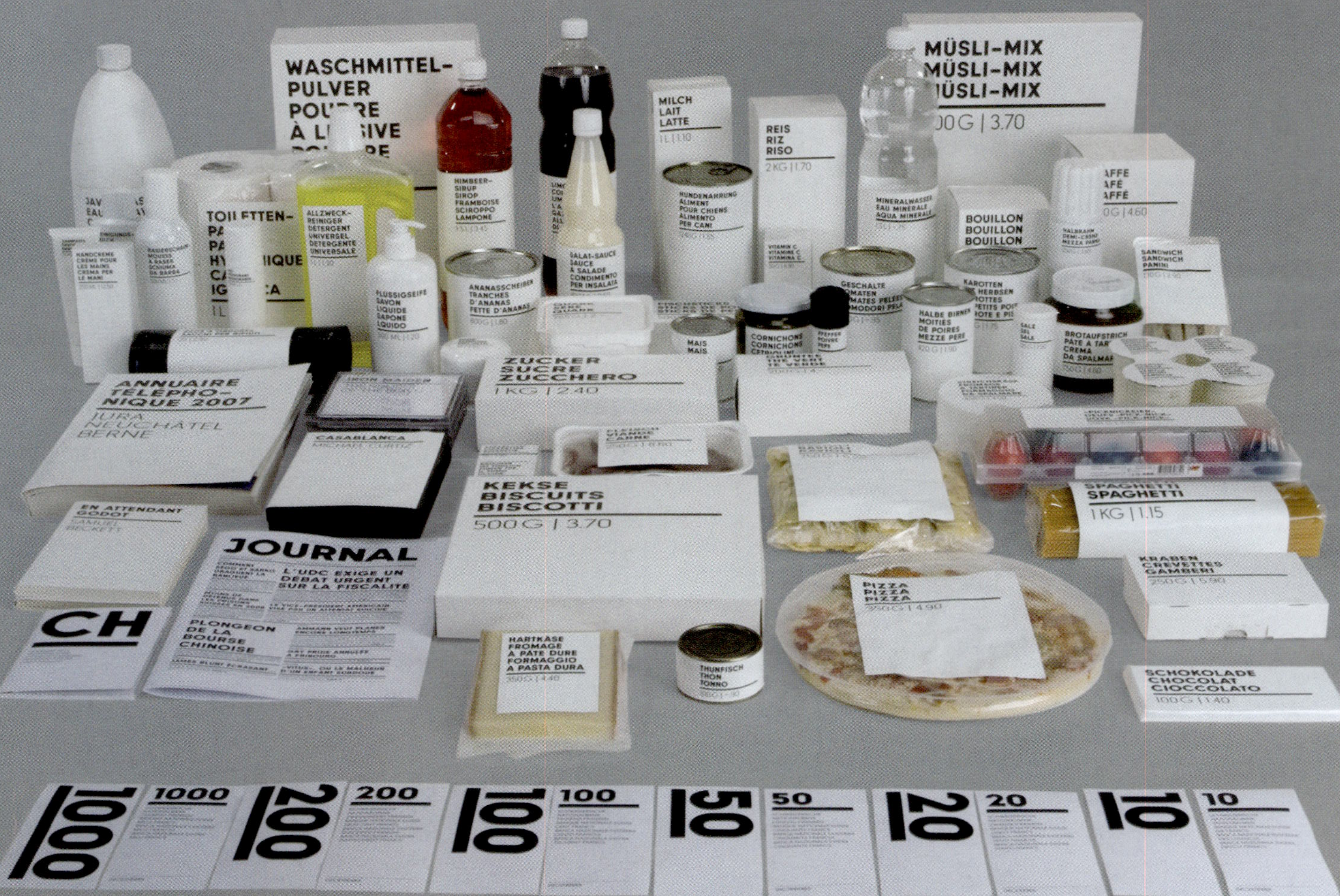
WASCHMITTEL-
PULVER
POUDRE
À LESSIVE
MÜSLI-MIX
MÜSLI-MIX
MÜSLI-MIX
300 G | 3.70
MILCH
LAIT
LATTE
1 L | 1.10
REIS
RIZ
RISO
2 KG | 1.70
TOILETTEN-
PA
PA
HY
CA
IG
1 L
ALLZWECK-
REINIGER
DETERGENT
UNIVERSEL
DETERGENTE
UNIVERSALE
1 L | 1.30
HIMBEER-
SIRUP
SIROP
FRAMBOISE
SCIROPPO
LAMPONE
1.5 L | 3.45
MINERALWASSER
EAU MINÉRALE
AQUA MINERALE
1.5 L | .75
BOUILLON
BOUILLON
BOUILLON
FLÜSSIGSEIFE
SAVON
LIQUIDE
SAPONE
LIQUIDO
500 ML | 1.20
HANDCREME
CRÈME POUR
LES MAINS
CREMA PER
LE MANI
RASIERSCHAUM
MOUSSE
À RASER
SCHIUMA
DA BARBA
HUNDENAHRUNG
ALIMENT
POUR CHIENS
ALIMENTO
PER CANI
VITAMIN C
VITAMINE C
VITAMINA C
SALAT-SAUCE
SAUCE
À SALADE
CONDIMENTO
PER INSALATA
ANANASSCHEIBEN
TRANCHES
D'ANANAS
FETTE D'ANANAS
800 G | 1.80
GESCHÄLTE
TOMATEN
TOMATES PELÉES
POMODORI PELATI
KAROTTEN
HERBSEN
POIS
MEZZE
HALBE BIRNEN
MOITIÉS
DE POIRES
MEZZE PERE
420 G | 1.95
CORNICHONS
CORNICHONS
CETRIOLINI
MAIS
MAIS
PFEFFER
POIVRE
PEPE
SALZ
SEL
SALE
BROTAUFSTRICH
PÂTE À TARTINER
CREMA
DA SPALMARE
SANDWICH
SANDWICH
PANINI
KAFFE
AFÉ
AFFÉ
G | 4.60
ZUCKER
SUCRE
ZUCCHERO
1 KG | 2.40
KEKSE
BISCUITS
BISCOTTI
500 G | 3.70
ANNUAIRE
TÉLÉPHO-
NIQUE 2007
JURA
NEUCHÂTEL
BERNE
CASABLANCA
MICHAEL CURTIZ
EN ATTENDANT
GODOT
SAMUEL
BECKETT
JOURNAL
L'UDC EXIGE UN
DÉBAT URGENT
SUR LA FISCALITÉ
PLONGEON
DE LA
BOURSE
CHINOISE
CH
FLEISCH
VIANDE
CARNE
SPAGHETTI
SPAGHETTI
1 KG | 1.15
KRABEN
CREVETTES
GAMBERI
250 G | 5.90
HARTKÄSE
FROMAGE
À PÂTE DURE
FORMAGGIO
A PASTA DURA
350 G | 4.40
THUNFISCH
THON
TONNO
PIZZA
PIZZA
PIZZA
350 G | 4.90
SCHOKOLADE
CHOCOLAT
CIOCCOLATO
100 G | 1.40
1000
200
100
50
20
10

KIEV
--
PERSONAL PROJECT CARRIED OUT
AFTER A TRIP TO KIEV. REFLECTION
ON THE POLITICAL STATUS AND SO-
CIAL SITUATION OF UKRAINE, ON THE
DESTINY OF THIS COUNTRY THROUGH-
OUT TIME BY MEANS AN INTERACTION
OF PHOTOGRAPHY, STATISTICAL DATA,
NEWSPAPER ARTICLES AND LITERARY
TEXTS.
--

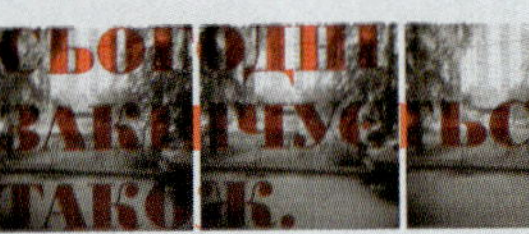

УЧОРА
ЗАКІНЧЕНО.
СЬОГОДНІ
ЗАКІНЧУЄТЬСЯ
ТАКОЖ.
СТРИБАТИ
ЙДЕ.

УЧОРА ЗАКІНЧЕНО.
СЬОГОДНІ ЗАКІНЧУЄТЬСЯ ТАКОЖ.
СТРИБАТИ ЙДЕ.

Vchera zakinzheno.
S'ohodni zakinchajutsya takozh.
Skakaty jde.

HIER A PRIS FIN.
AUJOURD'HUI PREND FIN AUSSI.
LE PRINTEMPS S'EN VA.

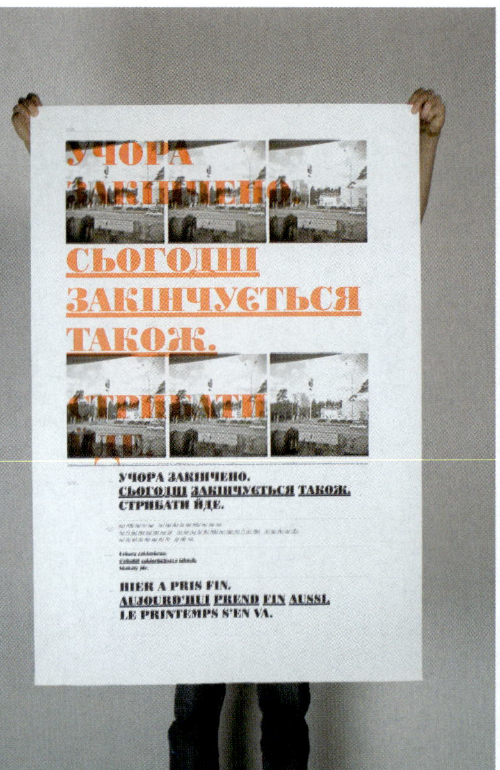

УЧОРА
ЗАКІНЧЕНО.
СЬОГОДНІ
ЗАКІНЧУЄТЬСЯ
ТАКОЖ.
СТРИБАТИ
ЙДЕ.

УЧОРА ЗАКІНЧЕНО.
СЬОГОДНІ ЗАКІНЧУЄТЬСЯ ТАКОЖ.
СТРИБАТИ ЙДЕ.

Vchera zakinzheno.
S'ohodni zakinchajutsya takozh.
Skakaty jde.

HIER A PRIS FIN.
AUJOURD'HUI PREND FIN AUSSI.
LE PRINTEMPS S'EN VA.

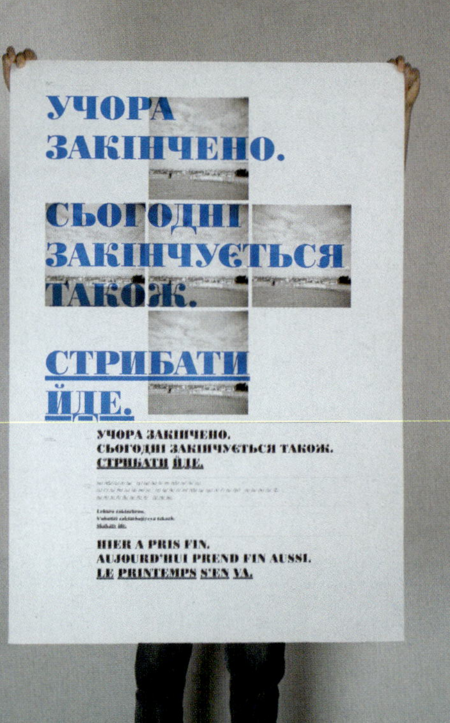

УЧОРА
ЗАКІНЧЕНО.
СЬОГОДНІ
ЗАКІНЧУЄТЬСЯ
ТАКОЖ.
СТРИБАТИ
ЙДЕ.

УЧОРА ЗАКІНЧЕНО.
СЬОГОДНІ ЗАКІНЧУЄТЬСЯ ТАКОЖ.
СТРИБАТИ ЙДЕ.

Vchera zakinzheno.
S'ohodni zakinchajutsya takozh.
Skakaty jde.

HIER A PRIS FIN.
AUJOURD'HUI PREND FIN AUSSI.
LE PRINTEMPS S'EN VA.

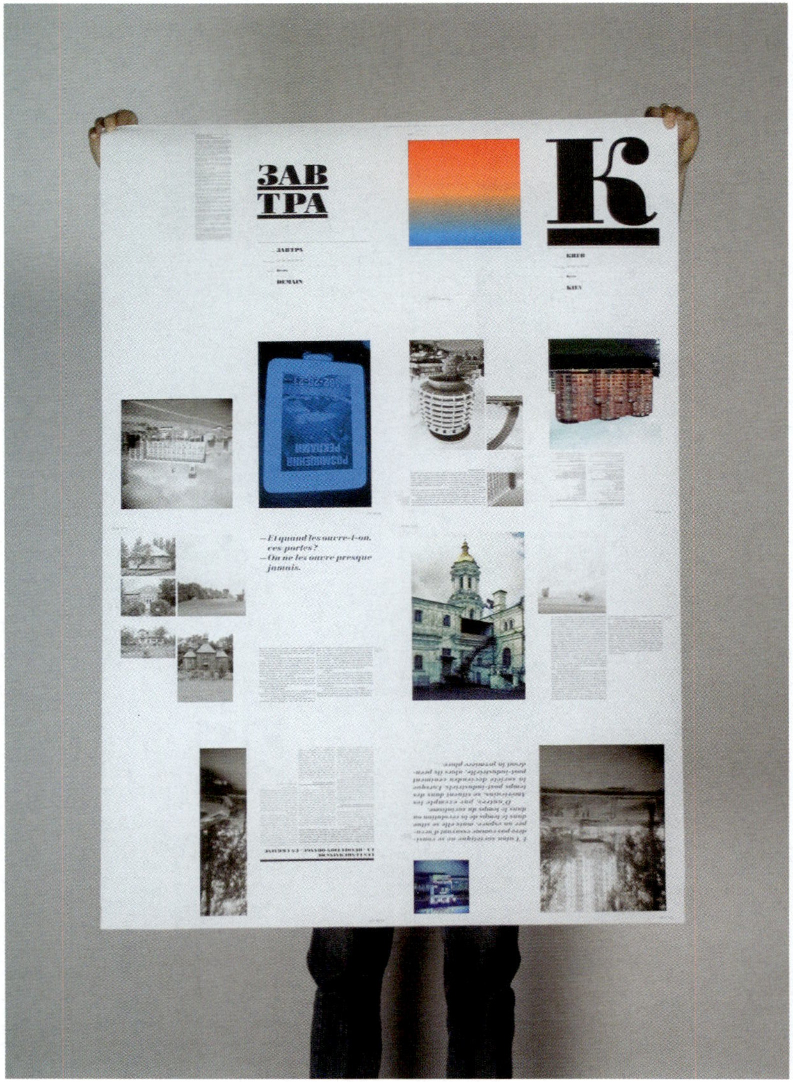

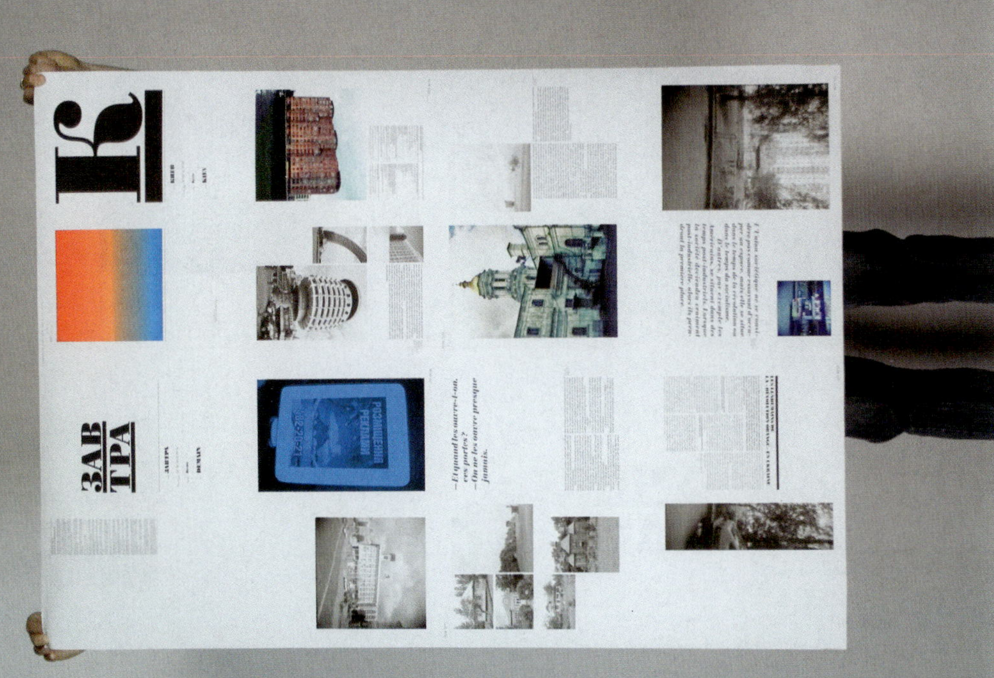

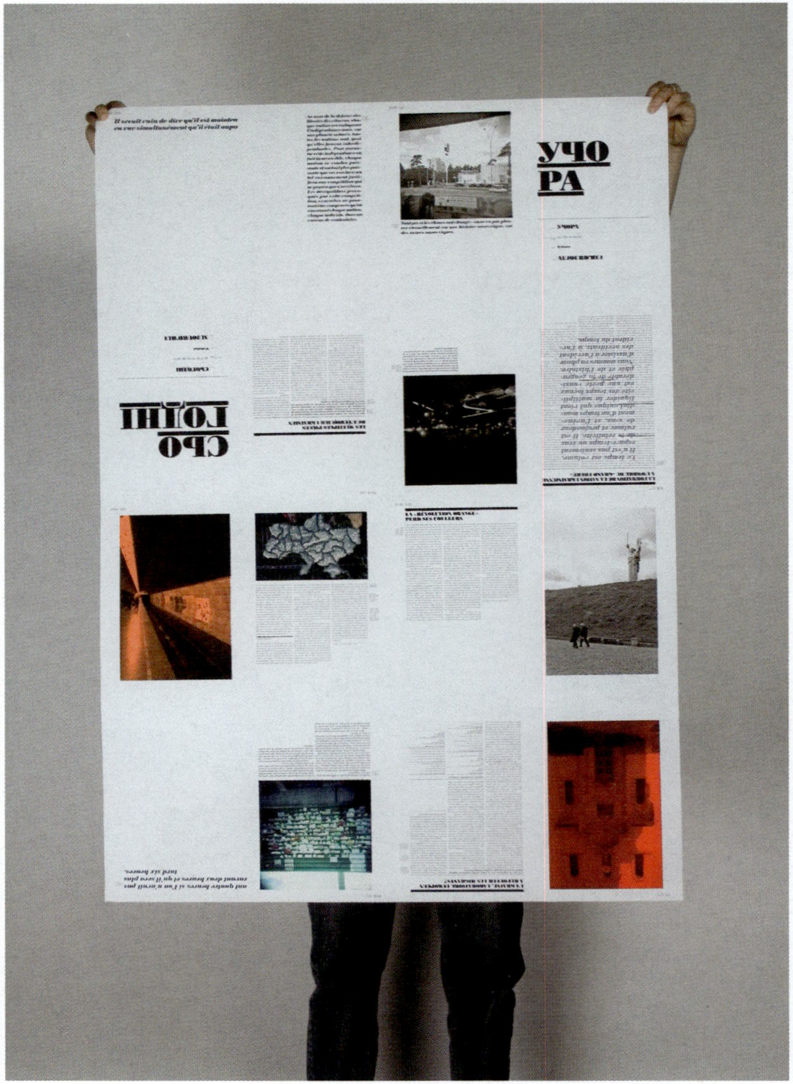

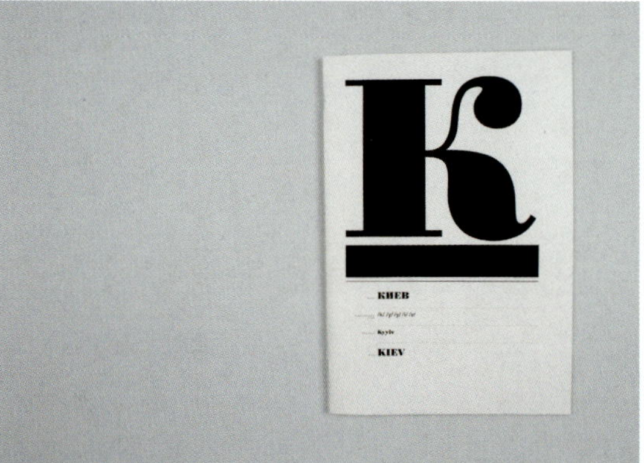

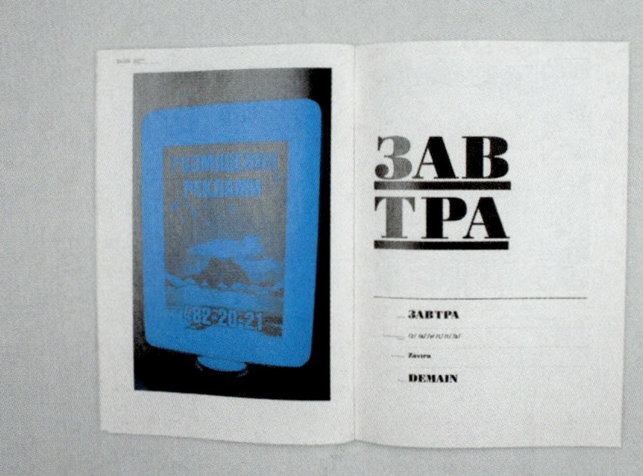

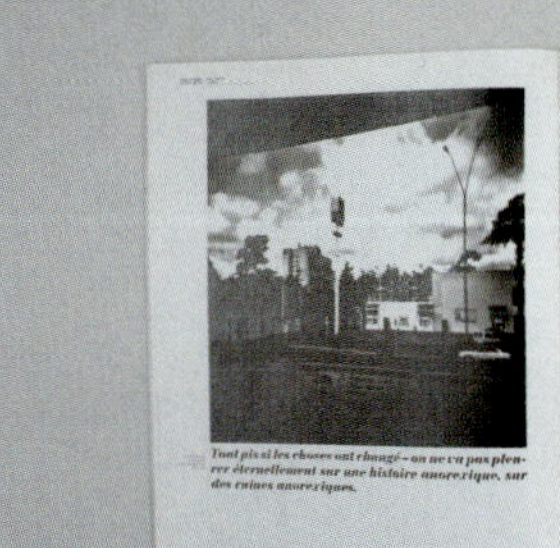

L'UKRAINE, LABORATOIRE EUROPÉEN
À REFOULER LES MIGRANTS?

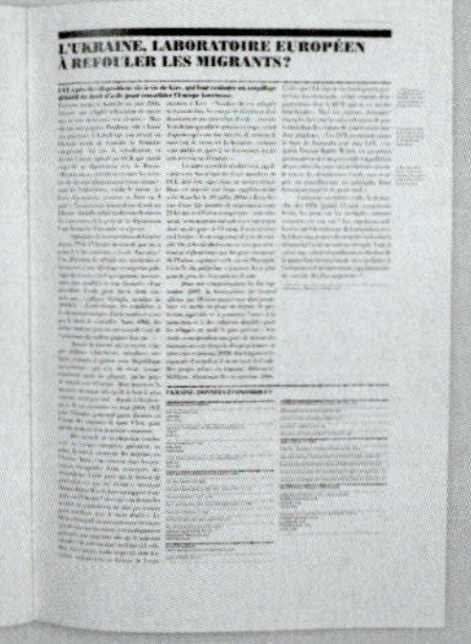

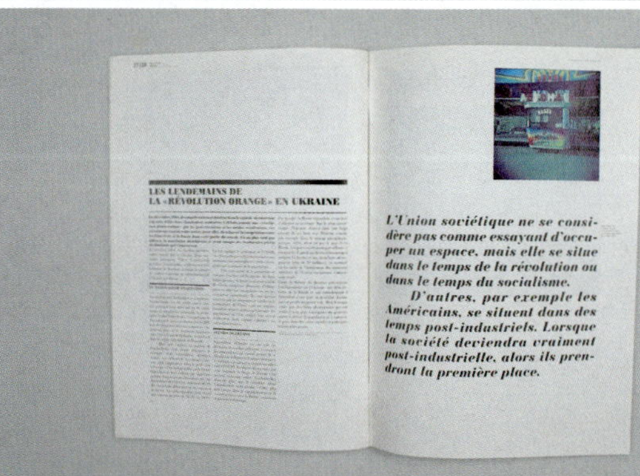

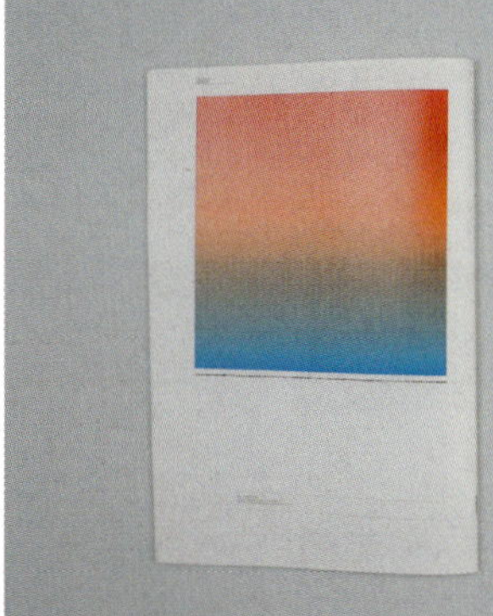

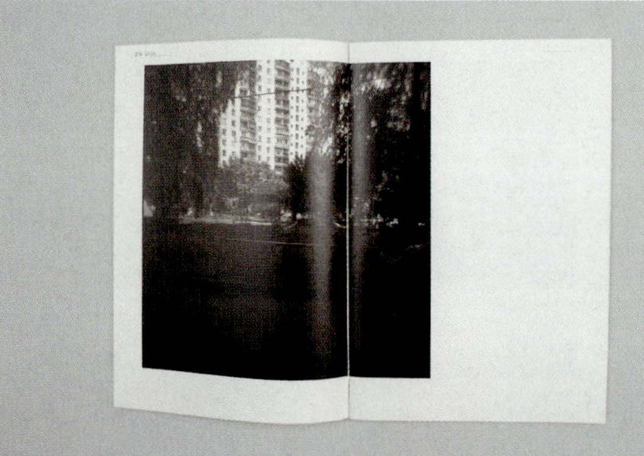

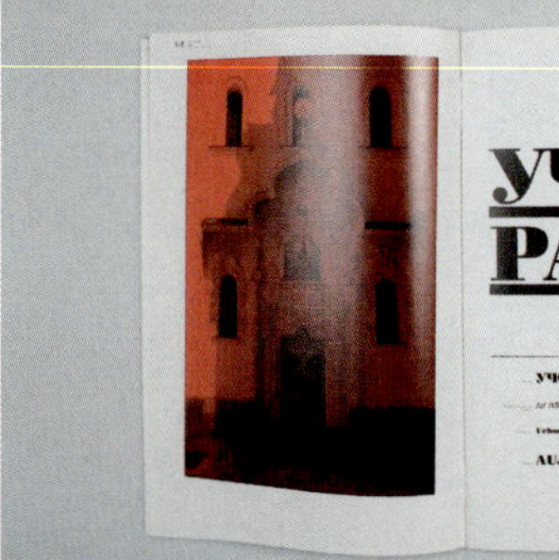

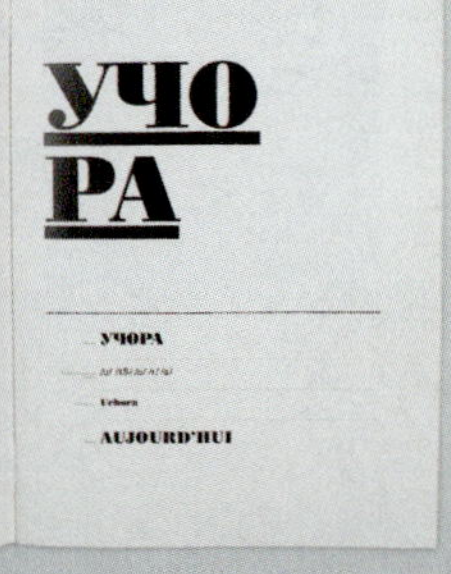

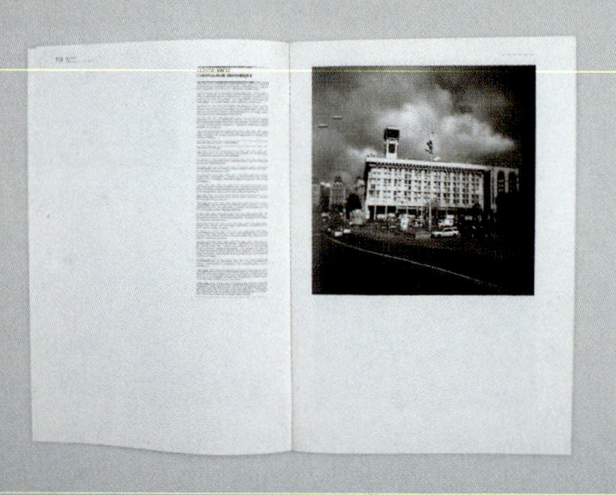

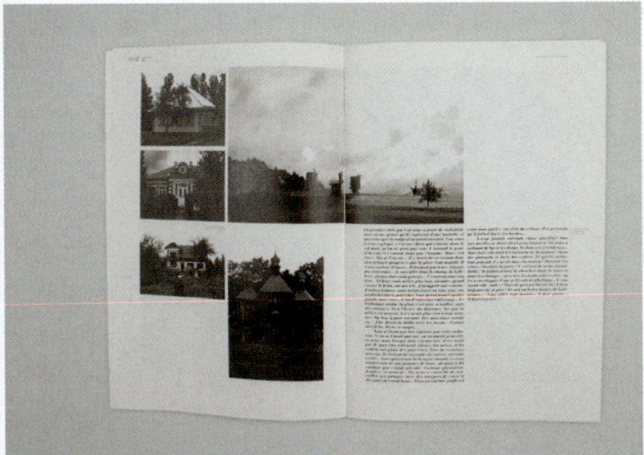

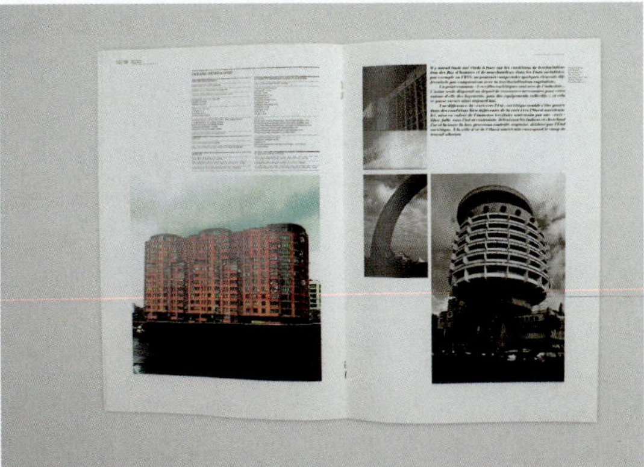

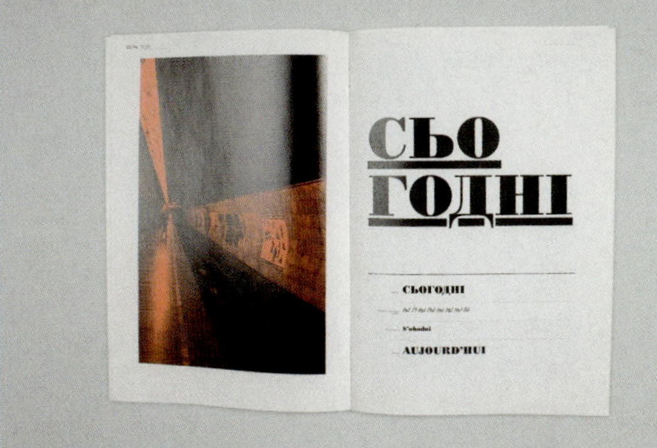

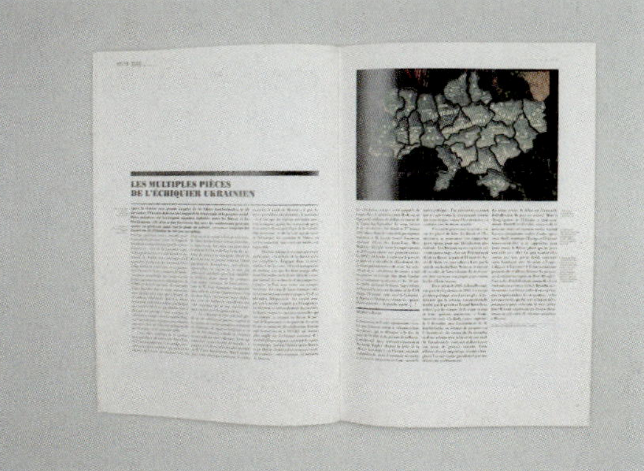

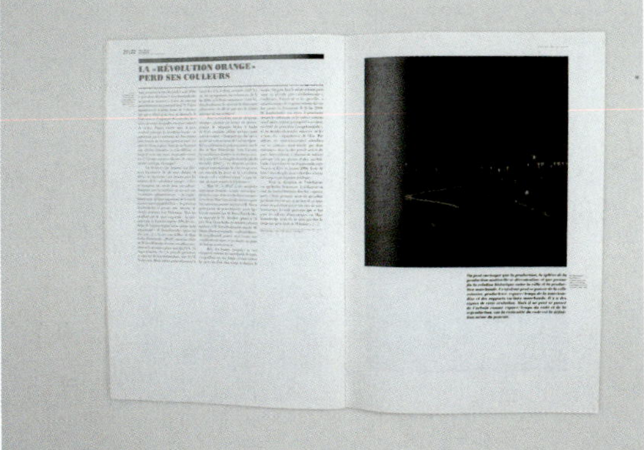

I'M 32 / STUDIED AT THE SCHWÄBISCH
GMÜND HOCHSCHULE FÜR GESTALTUNG
/ AM LIVING HAPPILY IN BERLIN /
PREFER WORKING ON BOOKS / AM CUR-
RENTLY WORKING FOR SCROLLAN / I
KNIT IN SECRET

--

WHAT IS GERMAN?

EARLY MORNING, WHOLE-MEAL BREAD
AND DEPOSITS ON BOTTLES.

WHAT IS GERMAN DESIGN?

FUNCTIONAL, CONCEPTUAL AND OFTEN
CONVENTIONAL TOO.

DESCRIBE YOUR WORKING PROCESS.

SCALING MOUNTAINS OF BOOKS /
RUNNING A RESEARCH MARATHON /
STRUCTURING CONTENT, WORKING OUT
CONCEPTS / DREAMING UP DESIGNS,
SWALLOWING WHITE CHOCOLATE, SCRAP-
PING DRAWINGS / MAKING DECISIONS
/ LOVING DETAILS / INVESTING MY
LIFE'S BLOOD.

WHAT DO YOU AIM TO ACHIEVE WITH
YOUR WORK?

TO SMOOTH THE VIEWER'S ACCESS TO
THE CONTENTS BY MEANS OF DESIGN.

YOU'VE INVITED A FRIEND TO
GERMANY; NAME ONE PLACE THEY
REALLY MUST VISIT AND A QUINT-
ESSENTIAL EXPERIENCE YOU REC-
OMMEND.

GO TO ALBUCH / ON FRESH SUM-
MER DAYS WALK THROUGH THE FOREST /
SCRAMBLE OVER RUINED CASTLES / GO
TO HOFCAFE RADLER AND ENJOY ONION
PANCAKES.

WHAT IS THE MOST IMPORTANT
LESSON YOU HAVE LEARNED IN YOUR
PROFESSION SO FAR?

TO GO ALONG WITH THE CLIENT'S
WISHES WITHOUT ABANDONING ONE'S
OWN IDEALISM.

--

TYPO LABOR

TYPOLABOR
NICOLE SCHWARZ
--
HEIDENFELDSTRASSE 12
10249 BERLIN
GERMANY
--
T +49 30.27496990
--
NICOLE@TYPOLABOR.DE
WWW.TYPOLABOR.DE
--

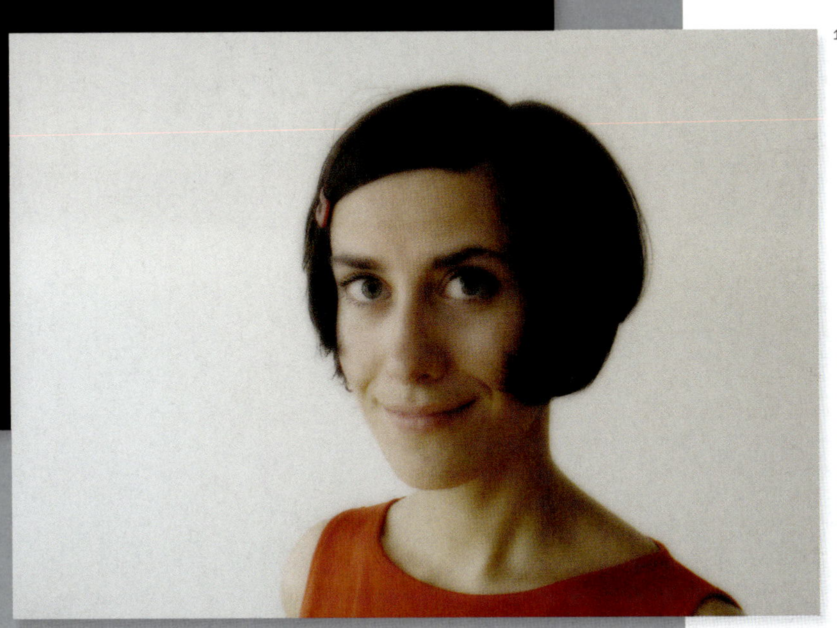

SOMETHING UTTERLY GERMAN
--

Wir
müssen
draussen
bleiben !

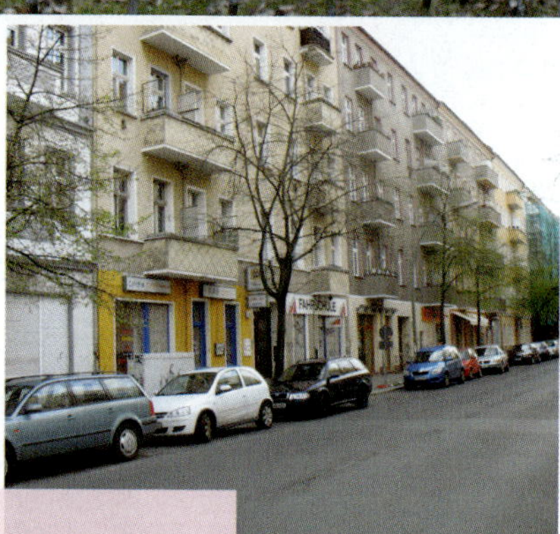

STUDIO SURROUNDINGS
--

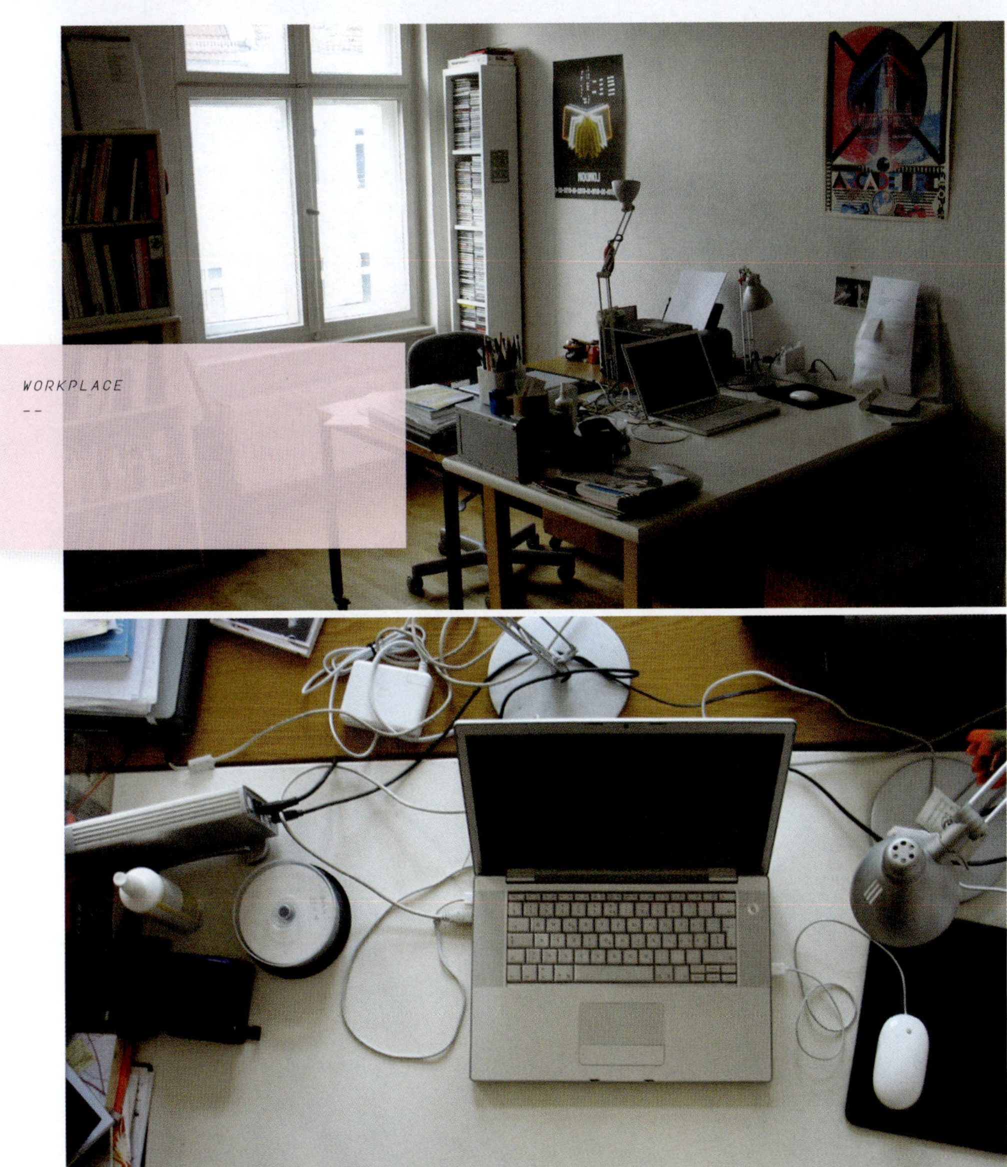

WORKPLACE
--

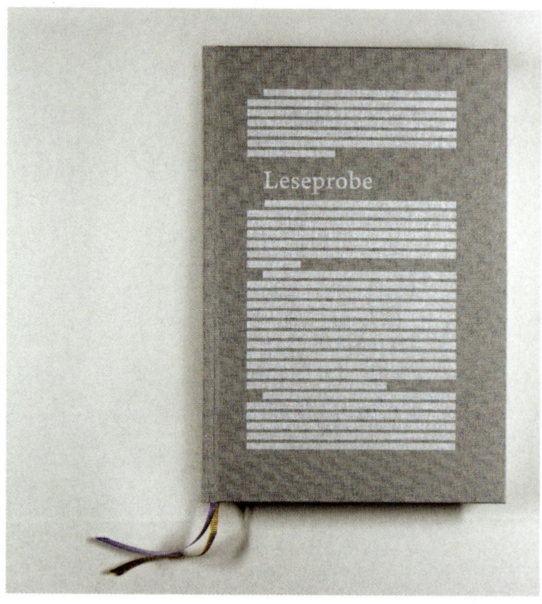

LESEPROBE (READING TEST)
TYPOGRAFISCHE UNTERSUCHUNGEN DES
LESENS (TYPOGRAPHICAL STUDIES OF
READING)
DIPLOMA PROJECT, 07.2007
--
A BOOK ABOUT READING RAISING
TYPOGRAPHICAL QUESTIONS ABOUT
POOR READING SKILLS AS WELL AS
SUGGESTING SOLUTIONS FOR FUR-
THER THEORETICAL AND EXPERIMEN-
TAL THINKING. HOW DO WE LEARN TO
READ, HOW DOES READING OPER-
ATE AND WHY DO MANY PEOPLE HAVE
PROBLEMS WITH READING? READING
LEARNING PROCESSES, READING PRO-
CESSES AND POOR READING SKILLS
FORM THE FIRST PART OF THE BOOK,
AND IN THE SECOND PART SERVE AS
A MODEL FOR READING EXPERIMENTS
TO IMPROVE LEGIBILITY FOR POOR
READERS. LETTERS AND PUNCTUATION
MARKS ARE ANALYZED AND RETHOUGHT
AS A TYPOGRAPHICAL EXPERIMENT.
IT OFFERS APPROACHES TO FURTHER
THINKING, SUCH AS THE DESIGNING
OF A SCRIPT FOR DYSLEXICS, AND
PROVIDES NEW INSIGHTS FOR TEACH-
ERS AND SCHOOLBOOK DESIGNERS.
--

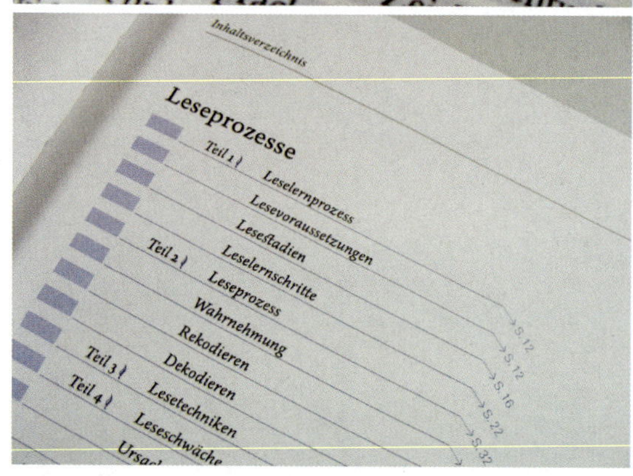

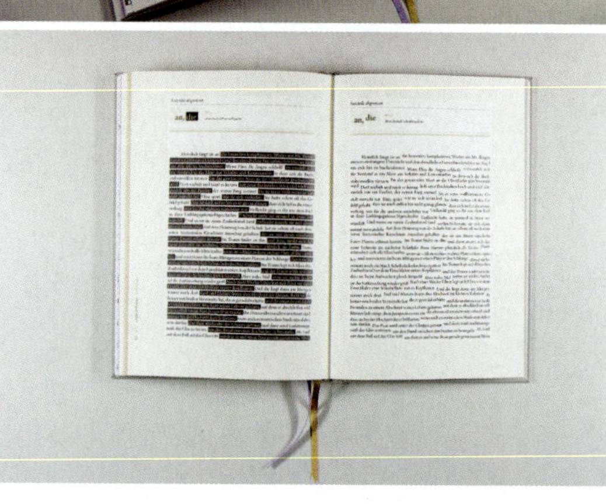

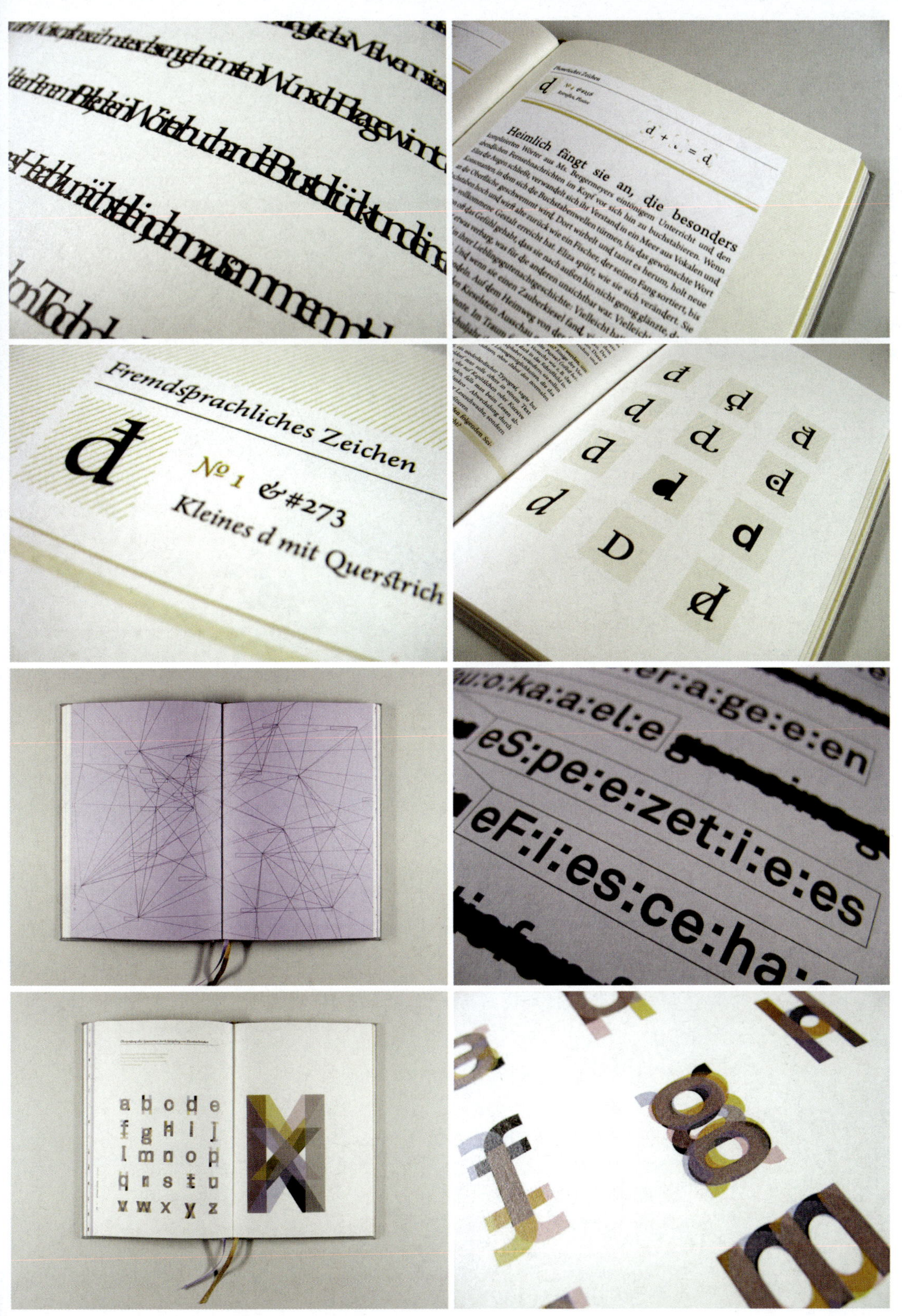

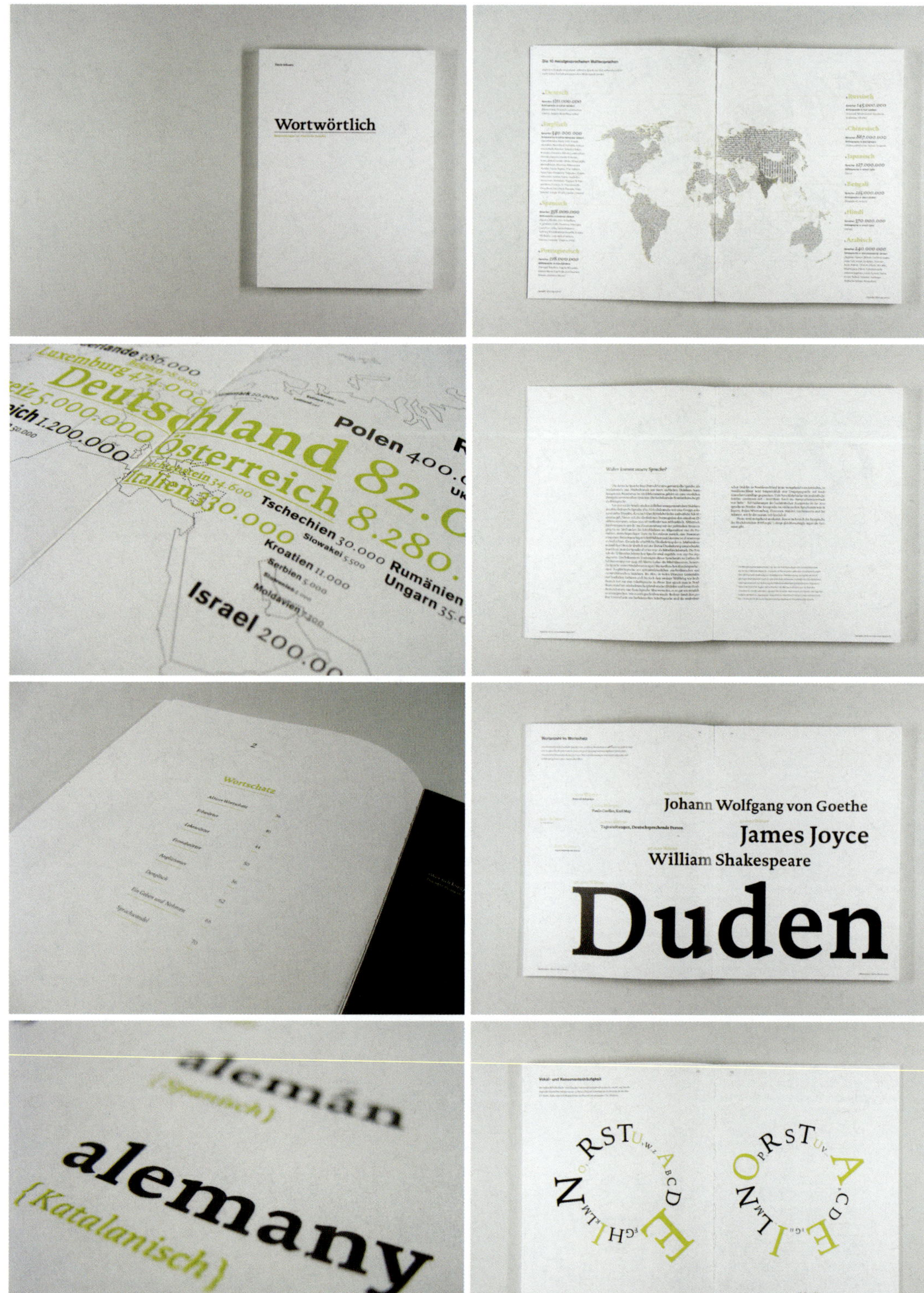
Wortwörtlich
Deutsch
Österreich 82.0
Tschechien 8.280.
Polen 400.0
Deutschland 5.000.000
Luxemburg 474.0
Italien 30.000
Kroatien 11.000
Serbien 5.000
Moldavien 7.500
Israel 200.00
Slowakei 5.500
Rumänien
Ungarn 35.0
Wortschatz
Woher kommt unsere Sprache?
Wortschatz im Menschen
Johann Wolfgang von Goethe
James Joyce
William Shakespeare
Duden
alemán
(Spanisch)
alemany
(Katalanisch)
Vokal- und Konsonantenhäufigkeit
[Deutsch]
[Italienisch]

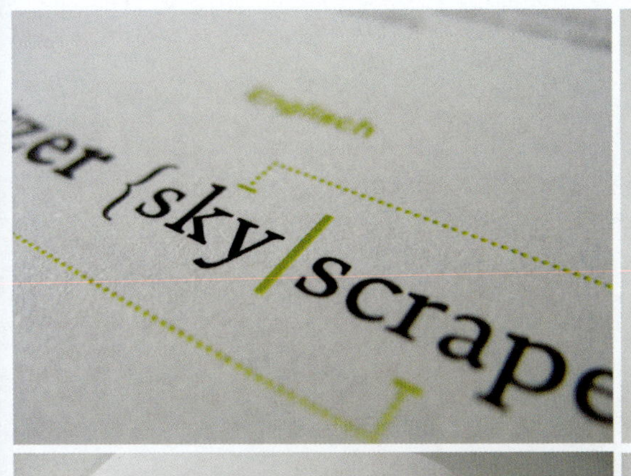

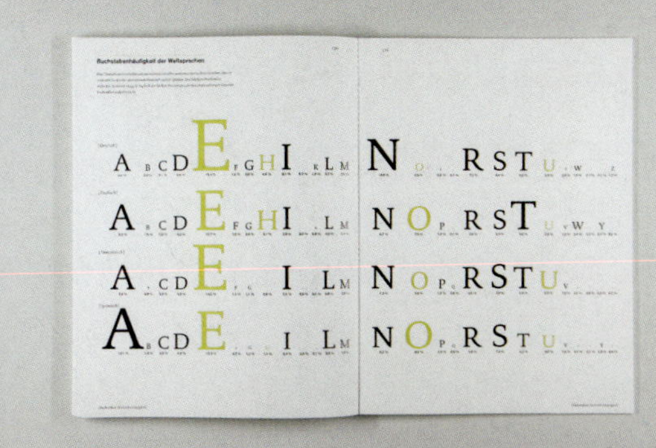

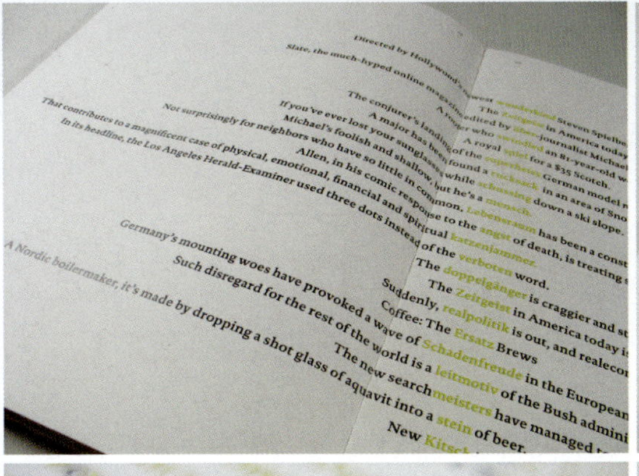

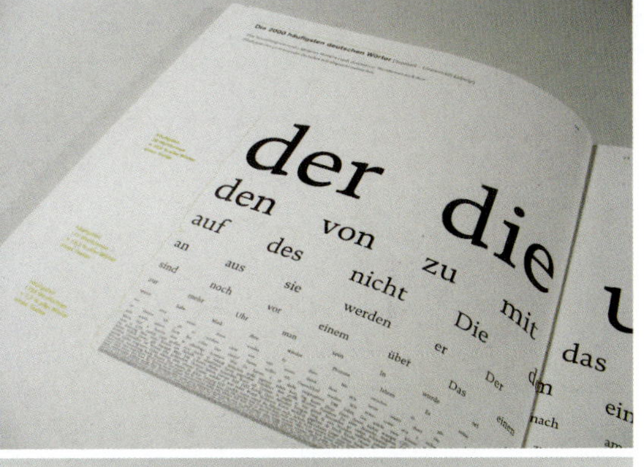

WORTWÖRTLICH (WORD FOR WORD)
BEOBACHTUNGEN ZUR DEUTSCHEN
SPRACHE (OBSERVATIONS ON THE
GERMAN LANGUAGE) 02.2007
--
THE BOOK WORTWÖRTLICH DEALS WITH
OBSERVATIONS OF THE GERMAN LAN-
GUAGE. IT IS NOT GRAMMATICAL OR
SPELLING CONCERNS THAT DETERMINE
THE CONTENTS, BUT A ZOOM START-
ING FROM THE LANGUAGE BY WAY OF
VOCABULARY AND WORDS DOWN TO THE
LETTER. A PURELY TYPOGRAPHICAL
IMPLEMENTATION WITH MAPS, DIA-
GRAMS AND LISTS SHOWS THE WORLD
OF FALSE FRIENDS, DENGLISH, LOST
WORDS, MOST FREQUENT WORDS,
LETTER PROFILES AND ANGLICISMS
THOUGHT TO BE UNNECESSARY.
--
HFG SCHWÄBISCH GMÜND
TUTORS: PROF. GÜNTHER BISTE AND
TANJA HUBER
--

DIE FLIEGENDEN TEILCHEN IS A DE-
SIGN OFFICE IN BERLIN CONCENTRAT-
ING ON TYPOGRAPHY AND BOOK DESIGN
AND WORKING MAINLY FOR THE FIELDS
OF CULTURE, THE ENVIRONMENT AND
RESEARCH. FOUNDED AFTER STUD-
IES AT THE MUTHESIUS-HOCHSCHULE
IN KIEL, DIE FLIEGENDEN TEILCHEN
WENT TO THE NETHERLANDS FOR TWO
YEARS, ANDRÉ HEERS TO THE HAGUE TO
DO HIS MASTER'S DEGREE IN TYPE AND
MEDIA AT THE KÖNIGLICHE AKADEMIE,
ANNETTE STAHMER TO MAASTRICHT TO
WORK ON A RESEARCH PROJECT REGARD-
ING THE RELATIONSHIP BETWEEN VOICE
AND SCRIPT AT THE JAN VAN EYCK
ACADEMIE. AFTER THAT THEY MOVED
TO PORTUGAL AND BELGIUM. AFTER
SPENDING FIVE YEARS ABROAD, DIE
FLIEGENDEN TEILCHEN CAME BACK TO
GERMANY AND WORKED FOR VARIOUS
PUBLISHERS AND CULTURAL AND SCI-
ENTIFIC INSTITUTIONS. THEY EXPERI-
MENT, EXPLORE PERIPHERAL FIELDS
OF DESIGN, INTERNATIONALLY AND ON
A CROSS-DISCIPLINARY BASIS, GIVE
LECTURES AND HOLD WORKSHOPS.

--

WHAT IS GERMAN?

GERMAN IS HOW YOU FEEL WHEN YOU
LIVE AND WORK ABROAD.

WHAT IS GERMAN DESIGN?

AT ITS BEST GERMAN DESIGN WAS
AND IS RADICALLY SIMPLE AND VERY
WELL THOUGHT THROUGH (THINK OF
DESIGN NOTABILITIES LIKE JAN TSCH-
ICHOLD OR DIETER RAMS). UNFOR-
TUNATELY ON AN EVERYDAY BASIS IT
OFTEN LACKS COURAGE, HUMOR AND
LIGHTNESS. ONE REASON FOR THIS
COULD BE THAT IN GERMANY DESIGN IS
NOT SEEN AS AN IMPORTANT CULTUR-
AL CONTRIBUTION (AS IT IS IN THE
NETHERLANDS, FOR INSTANCE), BUT
AS PROVIDING A SERVICE. MOREOVER
PERHAPS IT'S ALSO PART OF THE GER-
MAN MENTALITY TO TAKE THINGS VERY
SERIOUSLY AND BE FRIGHTENED OF
MAKING MISTAKES.

DESCRIBE YOUR WORKING PROCESS.

GENERALLY WE BEGIN WITH A VI-
SION, WE TRY TO REJECT THE <ANGEL
OF IMAGINATION> AS FAR AS POS-
SIBLE (FOR INSTANCE, WHAT KIND OF
THINGS CAN A POSTER BE?). FOR THIS
WE NEED SOME FREE SPACE TO THINK,
OFTEN IT'S HELPFUL TO LEAVE THE

OFFICE, GO FOR A WALK OR GO AND
SIT IN A CAFÉ. WE DEVELOP VARIOUS
IDEAS, GIVE ONE ANOTHER RECIPROCAL
INSPIRATION, COLLECT MATERIAL, DO
RESEARCH, MAKE SKETCHES ON PAPER
AND ON THE SCREEN, AND SLOWLY WORK
FORWARD DOWN TO THE TYPOGRAPHICAL
DETAIL. IN THIS THE <DISRUPTIVE>
INTERVENTION OF THE OTHER PERSON
IS ALWAYS AN IMPORTANT STIMULATING
AND REGULATING FACTOR.

WHAT DO YOU AIM TO ACHIEVE WITH
YOUR WORK?

ON THE ONE HAND WE'D LIKE TO
GO ON DEVELOPING OUR DESIGN, I.E.
FIND NEW IDEAS FOR THE VARIOUS
DESIGN COMMISSIONS, ELABORATE OUR
OWN FORMS AND COMBINE THEM IN AN
UNUSUAL WAY. IN ADDITION IT'S IM-
PORTANT TO US TO REFLECT VARIOUS
DESIGN-RELEVANT THEMES, SUCH AS
THE RELATIONSHIP BETWEEN VOICE AND
SCRIPT OR TEXT AND IMAGE, QUES-
TIONS OF PERCEPTION AND TASTE, IN
INDEPENDENT PROJECTS. IN DOING
THIS WE WORK PARTLY IN A CROSS-
DISCIPLINARY WAY WITH PEOPLE FROM
DIFFERENT SPECIALISMS.

YOU'VE INVITED A FRIEND TO
GERMANY; NAME ONE PLACE THEY
REALLY MUST VISIT AND A QUINT-
ESSENTIAL EXPERIENCE YOU REC-
OMMEND.

COME TO BERLIN AND DRINK TEA
WITH US!

WHAT IS THE MOST IMPORTANT
LESSON YOU HAVE LEARNED IN YOUR
PROFESSION SO FAR?

IT WAS AN IMPORTANT LEARNING
PROCESS ON THE ONE HAND TO DEVELOP
IDEAS FREELY AND UNENCUMBERED, AND
ON THE OTHER TO IMPLEMENT THOSE
IDEAS REALISTICALLY, IN THE GIVEN
TIME FRAME AND FINANCIAL CONTEXT.

--

FLIEGENDE TEILCHEN

FLIEGENDE TEILCHEN
ANNETTE STAHMER & ANDRÉ HEERS
--
CHORINER STRASSE 81
10119 BERLIN
GERMANY
--
T +49 30 81016186
--
POST@FLIEGENDETEILCHEN.COM
WWW.FLIEGENDETEILCHEN.COM
--

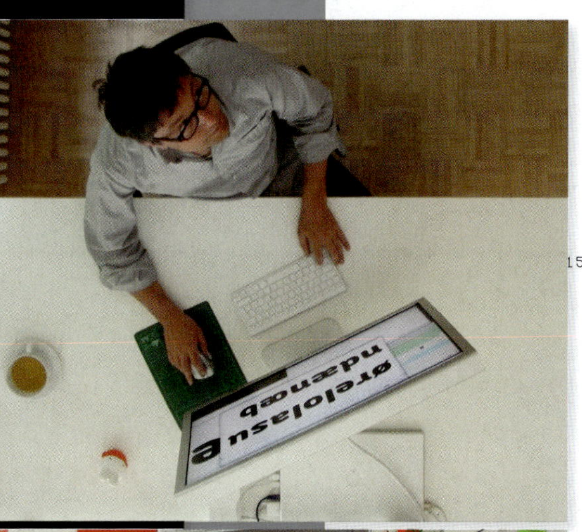

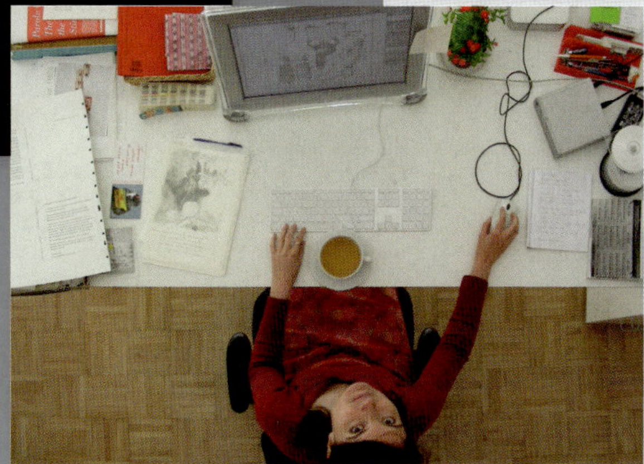

SOMETHING UTTERLY GERMAN

--

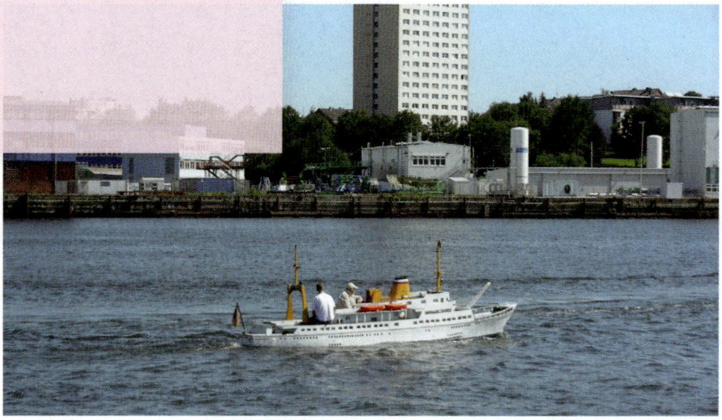

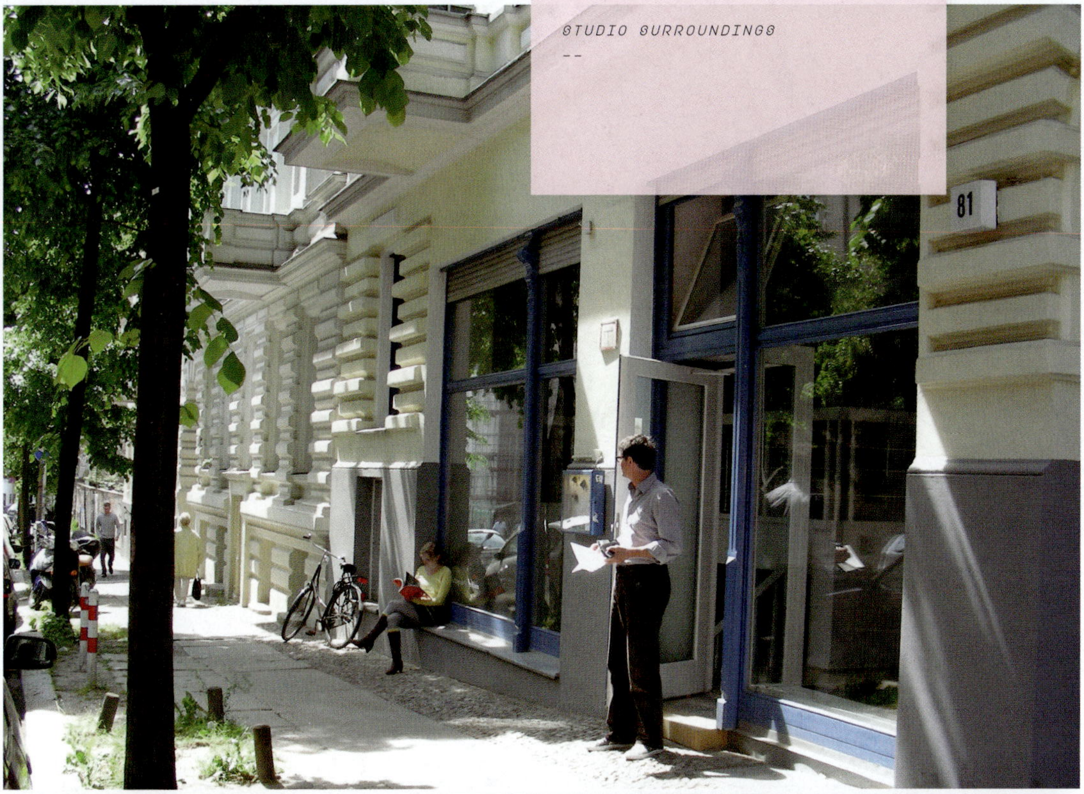

STUDIO SURROUNDINGS
--

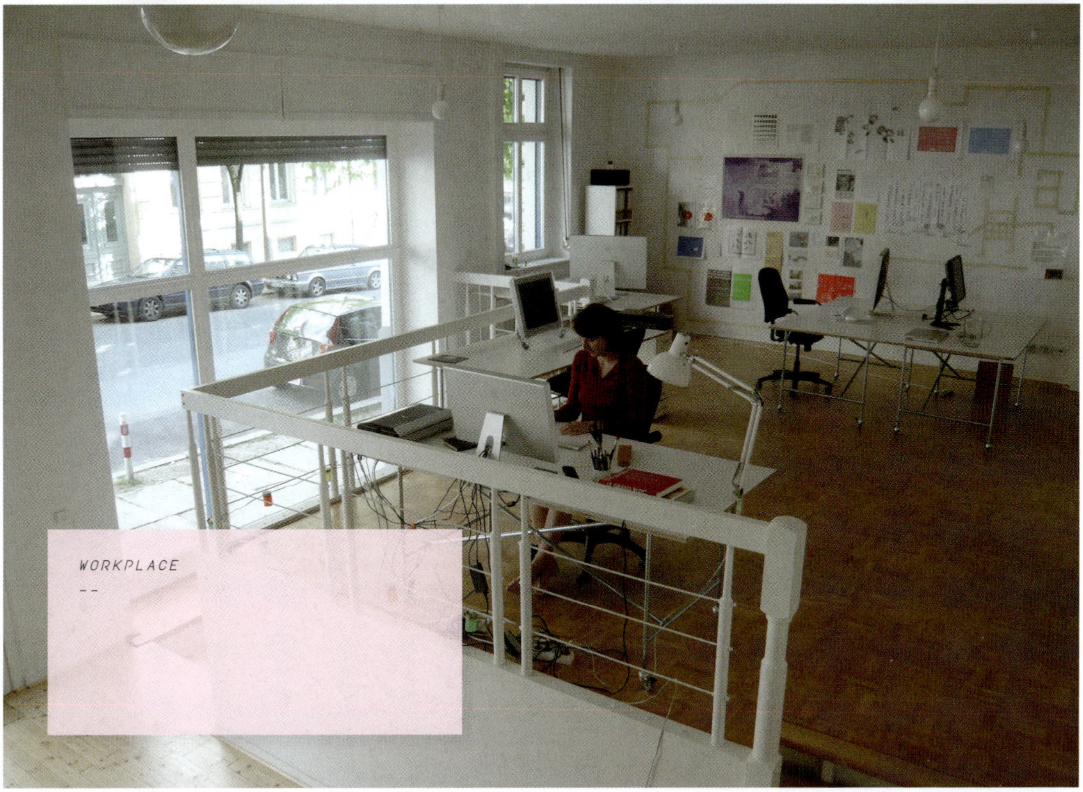

WORKPLACE
--

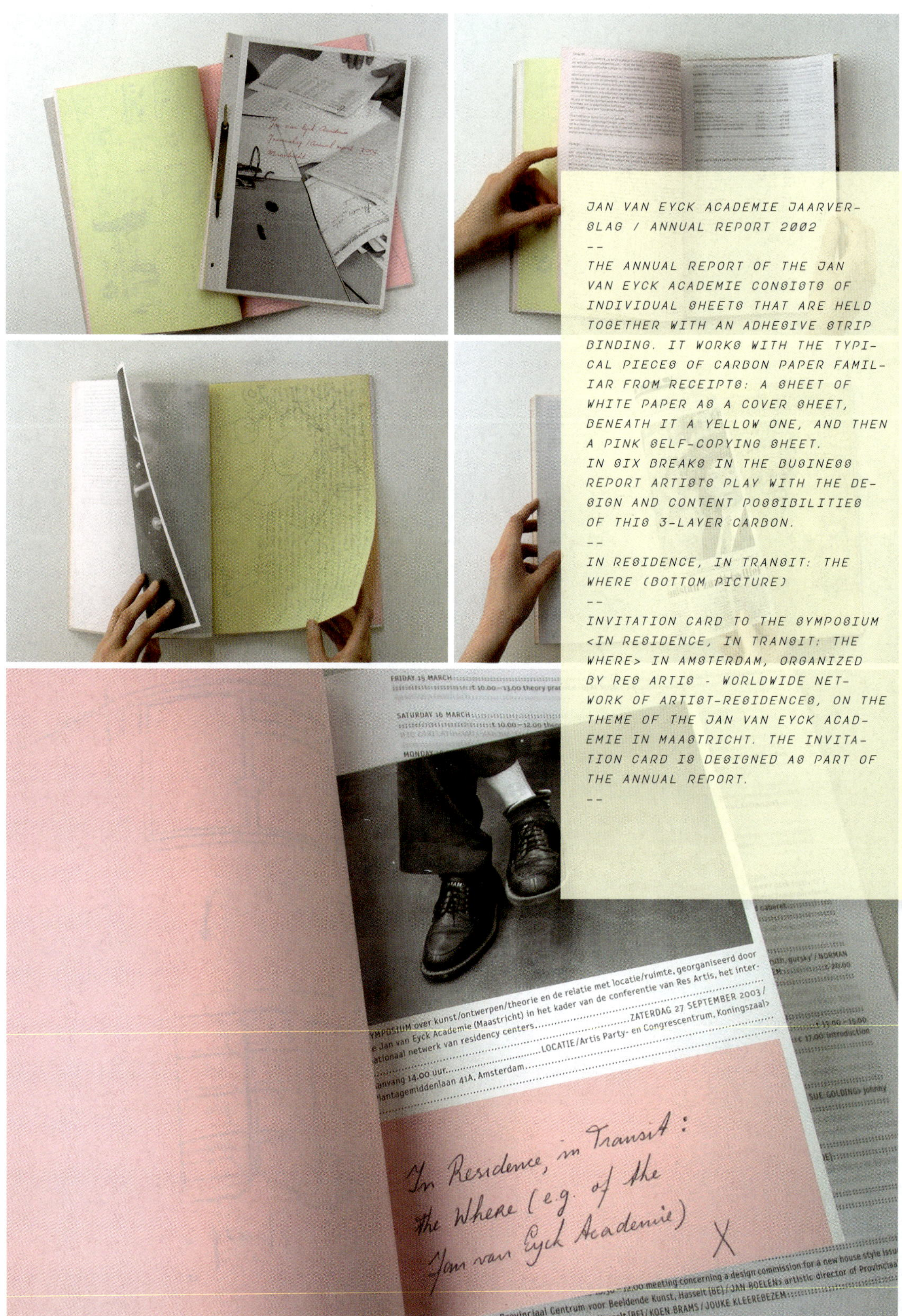

JAN VAN EYCK ACADEMIE JAARVER-
SLAG / ANNUAL REPORT 2002
--
THE ANNUAL REPORT OF THE JAN
VAN EYCK ACADEMIE CONSISTS OF
INDIVIDUAL SHEETS THAT ARE HELD
TOGETHER WITH AN ADHESIVE STRIP
BINDING. IT WORKS WITH THE TYPI-
CAL PIECES OF CARBON PAPER FAMIL-
IAR FROM RECEIPTS: A SHEET OF
WHITE PAPER AS A COVER SHEET,
BENEATH IT A YELLOW ONE, AND THEN
A PINK SELF-COPYING SHEET.
IN SIX BREAKS IN THE BUSINESS
REPORT ARTISTS PLAY WITH THE DE-
SIGN AND CONTENT POSSIBILITIES
OF THIS 3-LAYER CARBON.
--
IN RESIDENCE, IN TRANSIT: THE
WHERE (BOTTOM PICTURE)
--
INVITATION CARD TO THE SYMPOSIUM
<IN RESIDENCE, IN TRANSIT: THE
WHERE> IN AMSTERDAM, ORGANIZED
BY RES ARTIS - WORLDWIDE NET-
WORK OF ARTIST-RESIDENCES, ON THE
THEME OF THE JAN VAN EYCK ACAD-
EMIE IN MAASTRICHT. THE INVITA-
TION CARD IS DESIGNED AS PART OF
THE ANNUAL REPORT.
--

FRIDAY 15 MARCH
SATURDAY 16 MARCH
MONDAY
SYMPOSIUM over kunst/ontwerpen/theorie en de relatie met locatie/ruimte, georganiseerd door
e Jan van Eyck Academie (Maastricht) in het kader van de conferentie van Res Artis, het inter-
ationaal netwerk van residency centers...........LOCATIE/Artis Party- en Congrescentrum, Koningszaal>
...ZATERDAG 27 SEPTEMBER 2003 /
anvang 14.00 uur.
Plantagemiddenlaan 41A, Amsterdam.
In Residence, in Transit:
the Where (e.g. of the
Jan van Eyck Academie)
X
Provinciaal Centrum voor Beeldende Kunst, Hasselt [BE] / JAN BOELEN> artistic director of Provinciaal

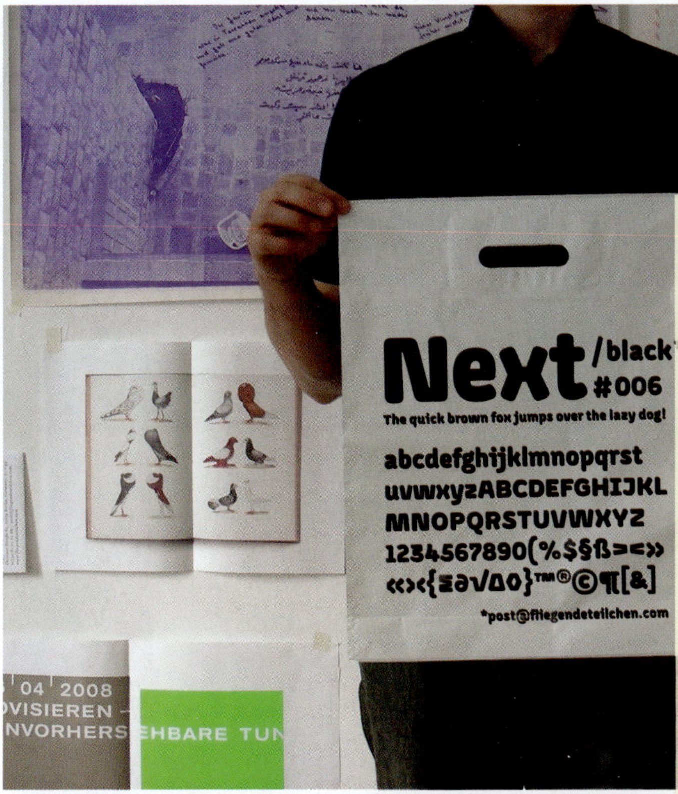

NEXT
--
<NEXT> IS A TYPE FONT THAT WAS DESIGNED TO REACT TO THE SPECIFIC PARTICULARITIES OF FLEXOGRAPH-IC PRINTING (SQUEEZED MARGINS, DISTORTION WHEN QUICK ROTATION IS USED). THE SHAPES CREATED IN RESEARCH AND EXPERIMENTS CAN BE READ VERY WELL EVEN IN LONG TEXTS, AND AT THE SAME TIME ARE ALSO SUITABLE AS A HEADLINE FONT BECAUSE OF THEIR ORIGINAL DETAILS. SUPPLEMENTED BY THREE OTHER FACES, <NEXT> SHOULD AP-PEAR IN LATE 2008 / EARLY 2009 AT OURTYPE / FONTSHOP BENELUX.
--

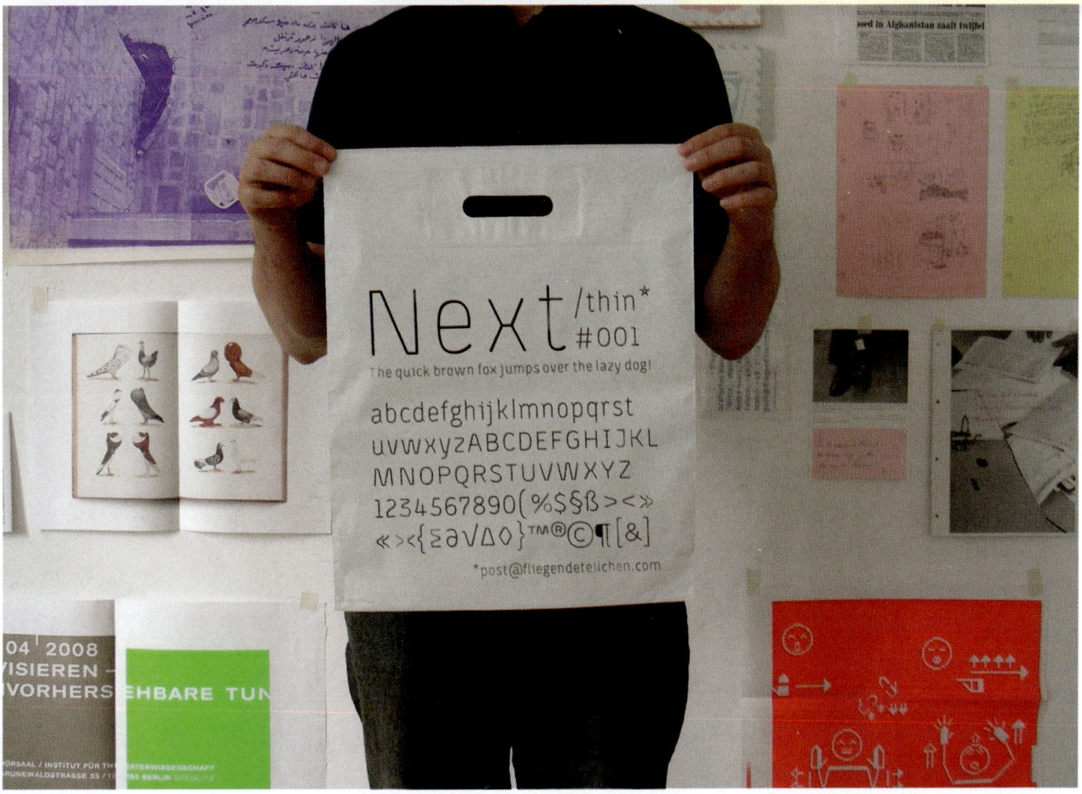

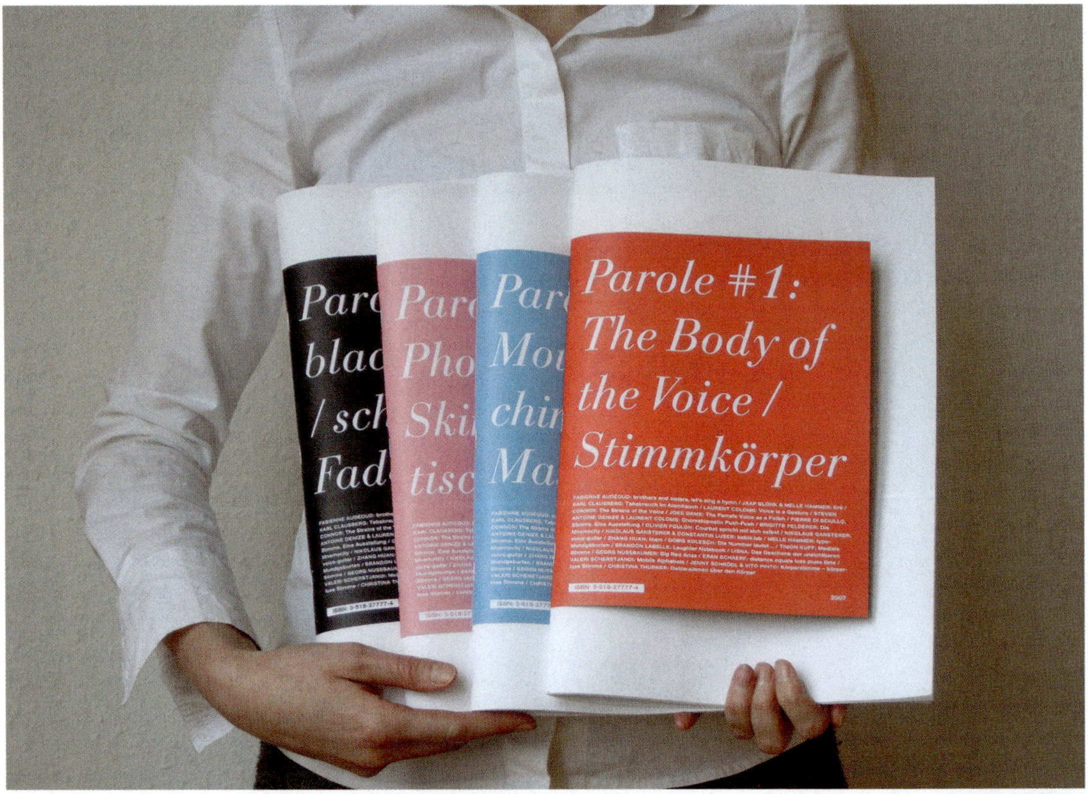

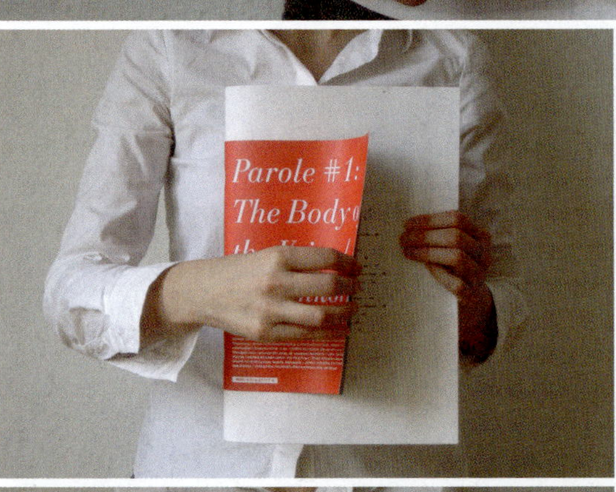
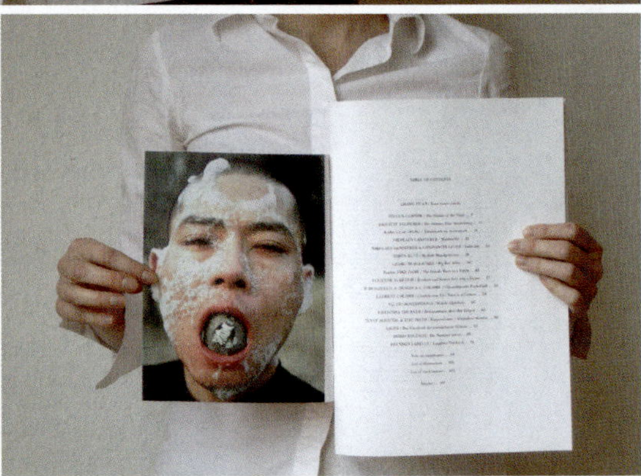
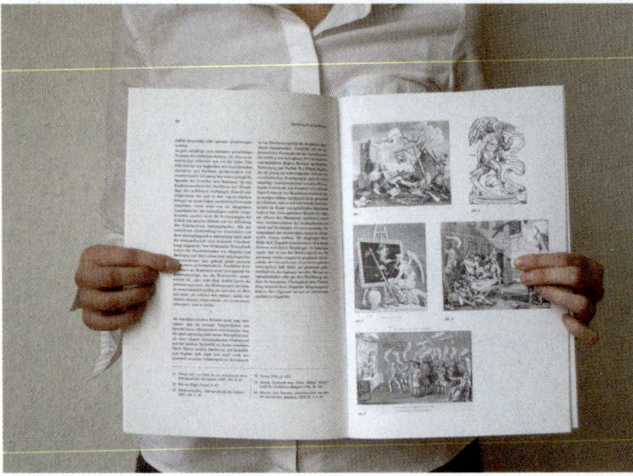
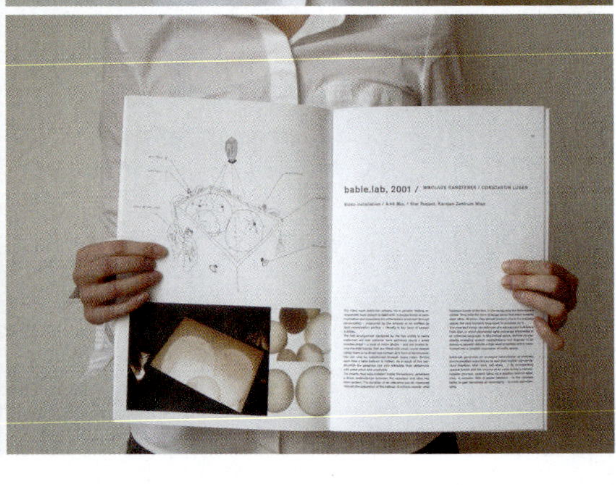

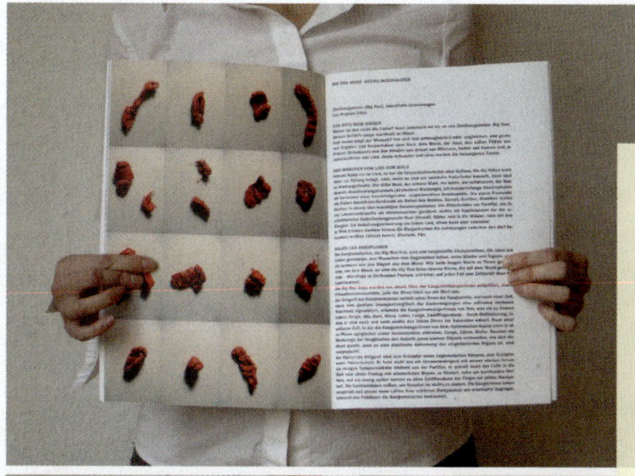

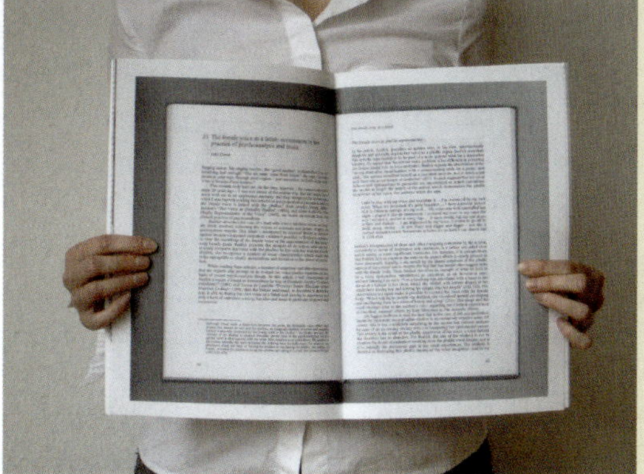

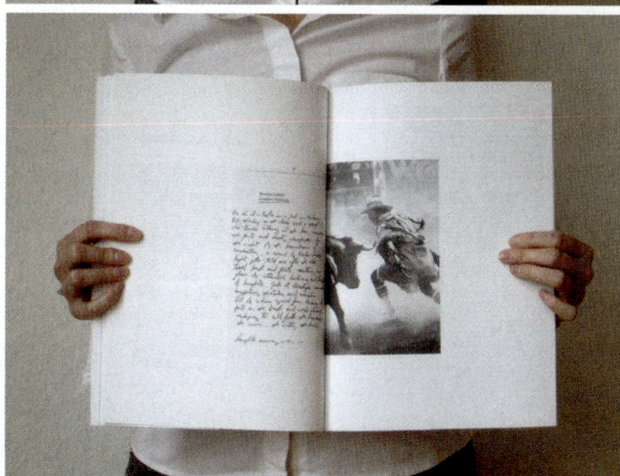

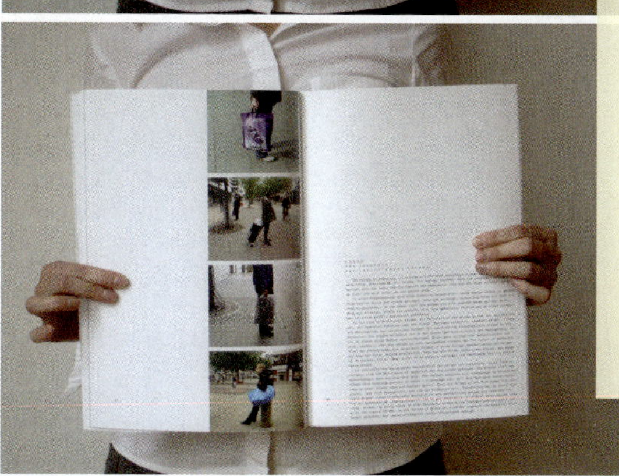

PAROLE #1:
THE BODY OF THE VOICE / STIMMKÖRPER
--
THE PUBLICATION <THE BODY OF THE VOICE/STIM-
MKÖRPER>, EDITED BY ANNETTE STAHMER (SALON
VERLAG COLOGNE, 2008) COMPRISES 24 CONTRI-
BUTIONS BY INTERNATIONALLY FAMOUS ARTISTS,
DESIGNERS AND SCIENTISTS WHO ARE CONCERNED
WITH THE <FLEETING MATERIAL> OF SPEECH AND
THE ATTEMPTS TO GRASP IT, MAKE IT VISIBLE AND
GIVE IT A BODY.
THE SPECTRUM OF THE CONTRIBUTIONS RANGES
FROM THE HISTORY OF SPEECH BUBBLES AND THE
<ORAL BIRTH PANGS> OF A MEDIUM AT THE BE-
GINNING OF THE 20TH CENTURY, BY WAY OF THE
<KRÉ> VOICE AND SCRIPT PERFORMANCE BY JAAP
BLONK AND MELLE HAMMER AND THE WORKS OF THE
AUSTRIAN COMPOSER GEORG NUSSBAUMER, INCLUD-
ING A CHOIR OF FEMALE OPERA SINGERS PRODUC-
ING ORAL SCULPTURES BY CHEWING, BY WAY OF
THE <PHONORAMA> EXHIBITION AT THE ZKM IN
KARLSRUHE, THE NEWLY DEVELOPED INTERACTIVE
COMPUTER GAME <POUSSE-POUSSE À ONOMATOPÉE>
BY THE FRENCH DESIGNER/FONT DESIGNER PIERRE
DI SCIULLO, DOWN TO WILLIAM FORSYTHE'S LATEST
INSTALLATION-PERFORMANCE <HUMAN WRITES> AT
THE ZURICH SCHAUSPIELHAUS.
THE THEME IS ILLUMINATED FROM VARIOUS PER-
SPECTIVES, RESULTING IN A NEW, STIMULATING
LOOK AT THE MOST IMPORTANT MEANS OF COMMU-
NICATION, SPEECH, AND ITS VISUALIZATION AND
<MATERIALIZATION>.
<THE BODY OF THE VOICE / STIMMKÖRPER> HAS A
PARTICULAR DESIGN CONCEPT THAT WORKS WITH
THE THEME. THUS EVERY ARTICLE IS DESIGNED
DIFFERENTLY, AND IN FACT IN THE LAYOUT OF AN
ALREADY EXISTING BOOK THAT HAS AN INTEREST-
ING CONTENTUAL OR EVEN FORMAL CONNECTION TO
THE ARTICLE IN QUESTION. THE BOOKS QUOTED AND
THEIR DESIGNERS ARE INDICATED IN A LIST OF
SOURCES.
IN THIS APPROACH THE BOOK IS UNDERSTOOD AS A
BODY OF TEXT, WITH ITS OWN FORM AND HISTORY.
THE IDEA IS TO SEPARATE THE FORM OF THIS BODY
FROM ITS CONTENT AND FILL IT WITH A NEW MEAN-
ING THAT STANDS IN AN INTERESTING RELATION-
SHIP OF TENSION WITH THE ORIGINAL WORK. THUS
17 BOOKS ARE CONTAINED IN DESIGN TERMS IN
<THE BODY OF THE VOICE / STIMMKÖRPER>.
<PAROLE> IS PLANNED AS A SERIES OF WRITINGS
THAT EXPLORE THE QUESTION OF A MATERIALITY OF
SPEECH.
--

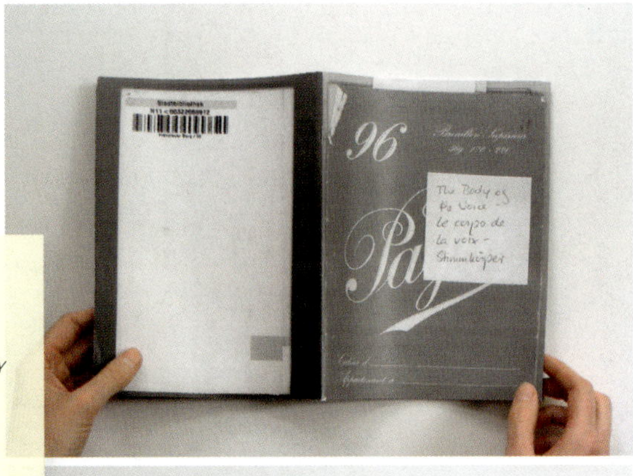

THE BODY OF THE VOICE / READER
--
THE NARRATIVE READER <THE BODY
OF THE VOICE> RECOUNTS THE STORY
OF A BODY AND ITS VOICE TRANS-
VERSALLY THROUGH SOME 60 DIF-
FERENT BOOKS AND SOURCES. BY
MEANS OF MARKING PLACES IN THE
TEXT AND DIVIDING IT INTO FOUR-
TEEN CHAPTERS THE READER IS LED
THROUGH TEXTS THAT ARE REVEALED
IN ALL THEIR MATERIALITY.
--

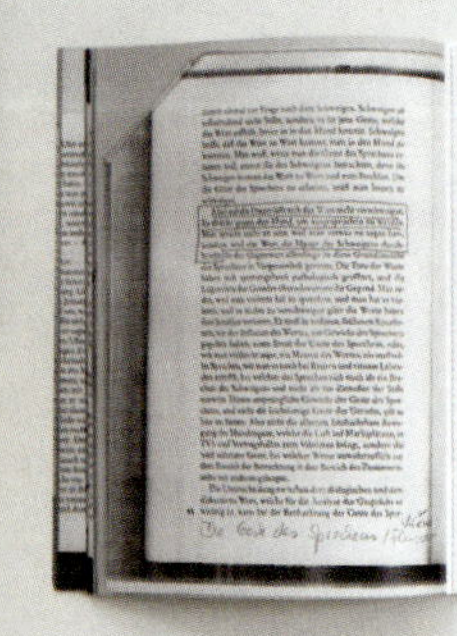
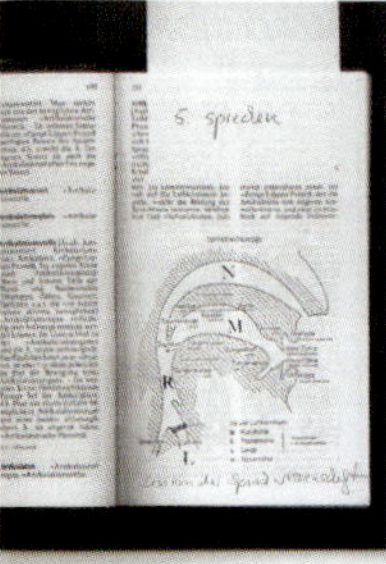
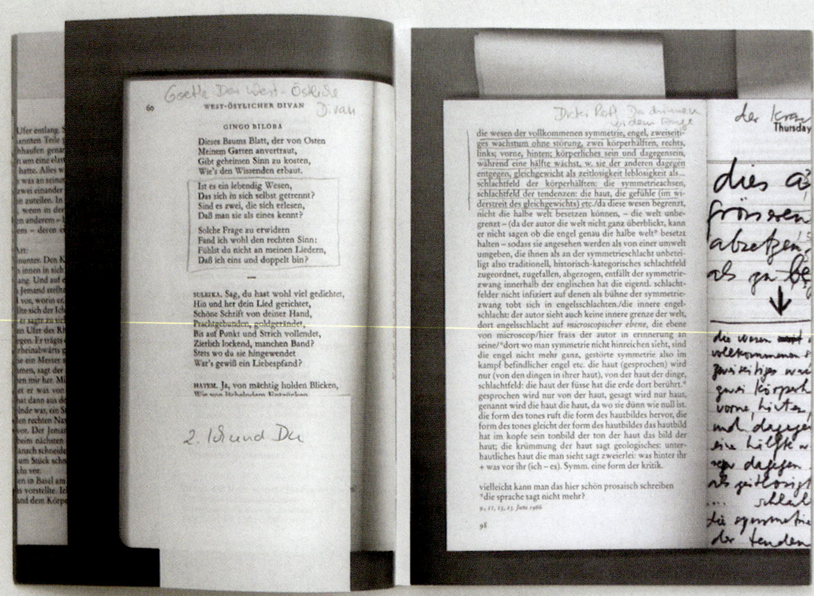

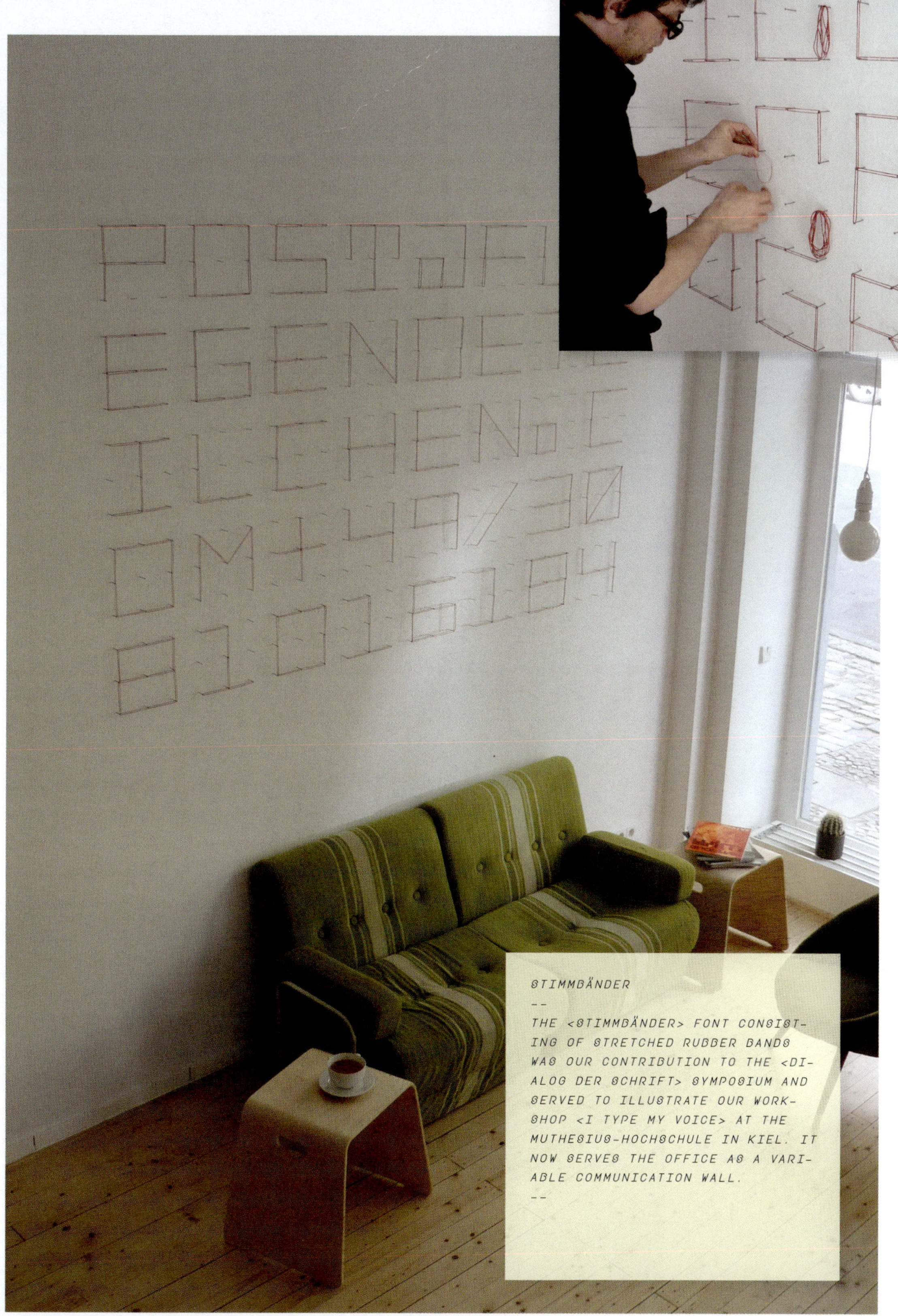
STIMMBÄNDER
--
THE <STIMMBÄNDER> FONT CONSIST-
ING OF STRETCHED RUBBER BANDS
WAS OUR CONTRIBUTION TO THE <DI-
ALOG DER SCHRIFT> SYMPOSIUM AND
SERVED TO ILLUSTRATE OUR WORK-
SHOP <I TYPE MY VOICE> AT THE
MUTHESIUS-HOCHSCHULE IN KIEL. IT
NOW SERVES THE OFFICE AS A VARI-
ABLE COMMUNICATION WALL.
--

ANDREAS WESLE (1976) IS A DESIGNER
AND ART DIRECTOR. HIS DESIGN HAS
WON SEVERAL NATIONAL AND INTERNA-
TIONAL DISTINCTIONS. HE LIVES AND
WORKS IN BERLIN, VIENNA AND ISNY.

--

WHAT IS GERMAN?

I AM GERMAN

WHAT IS GERMAN DESIGN?

FOR INSTANCE THE SPIRIT AND
FORMAL PRINCIPLE THAT THE WORK OF
SOMEONE LIKE DIETER RAMS OBEYS;
BUT SO DOES THE WORK OF SOMEONE
LIKE A G FRONZONI - FOR WHAT IS
ENDURING IS NOT GERMAN DESIGN, BUT
GOOD DESIGN.

DESCRIBE YOUR WORKING PROCESS.

DOING, THINKING, GOING FOR A
WALK (VARIABLE)

WHAT DO YOU AIM TO ACHIEVE WITH
YOUR WORK?

TOO MUCH?

YOU'VE INVITED A FRIEND TO
GERMANY; NAME ONE PLACE THEY
REALLY MUST VISIT AND A QUINT-
ESSENTIAL EXPERIENCE YOU REC-
OMMEND.

I'D TAKE HIM HOME AND COOK CABBAGE
FRITTERS FOR HIM.

WHAT IS THE MOST IMPORTANT
LESSON YOU HAVE LEARNED IN YOUR
PROFESSION SO FAR?

DESIGN IS ATTITUDE (HELMUT
SCHMIDT).

--

WESLE

ANDREAS WESLE
--
KASTANIENALLEE 52
10119 BERLIN
GERMANY
--
F +49 30 55950363
M +49 176 20844567
--
POST@ANDREASWESLE.DE
WWW.ANDREASWESLE.DE
--

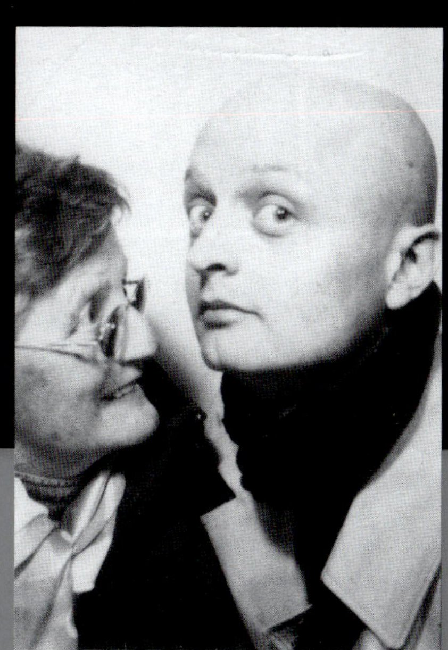

WORKPLACE
--

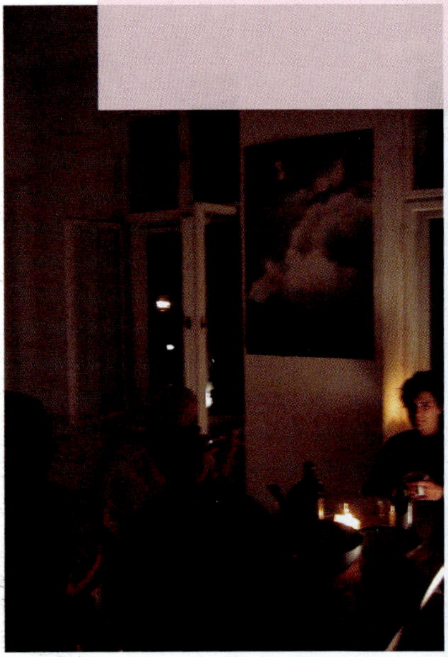

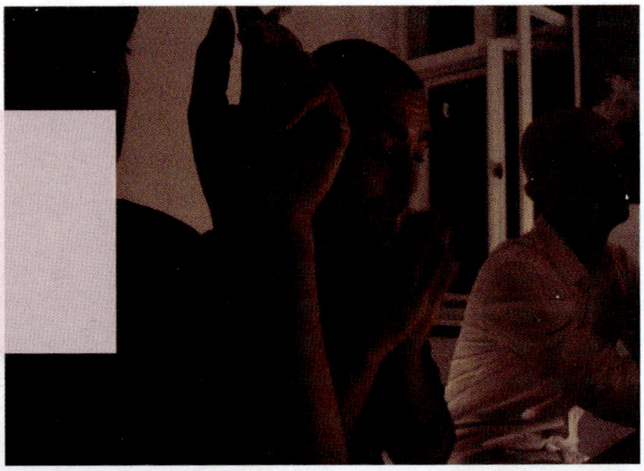

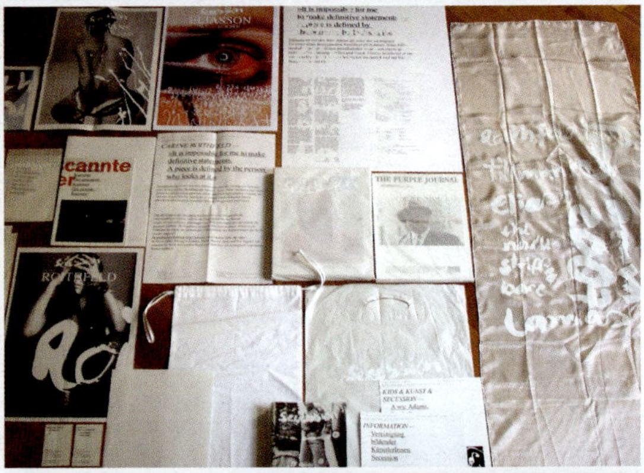

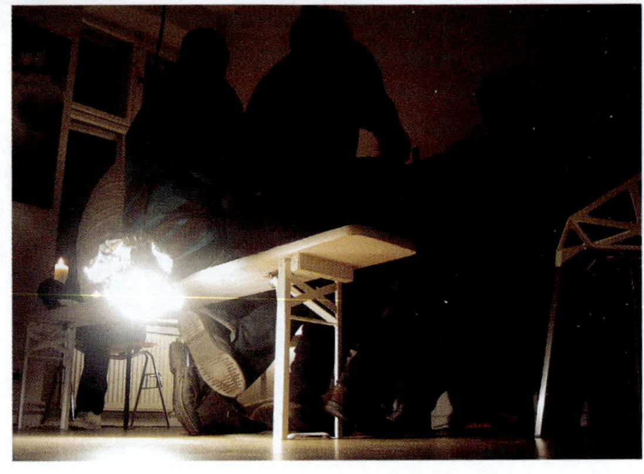

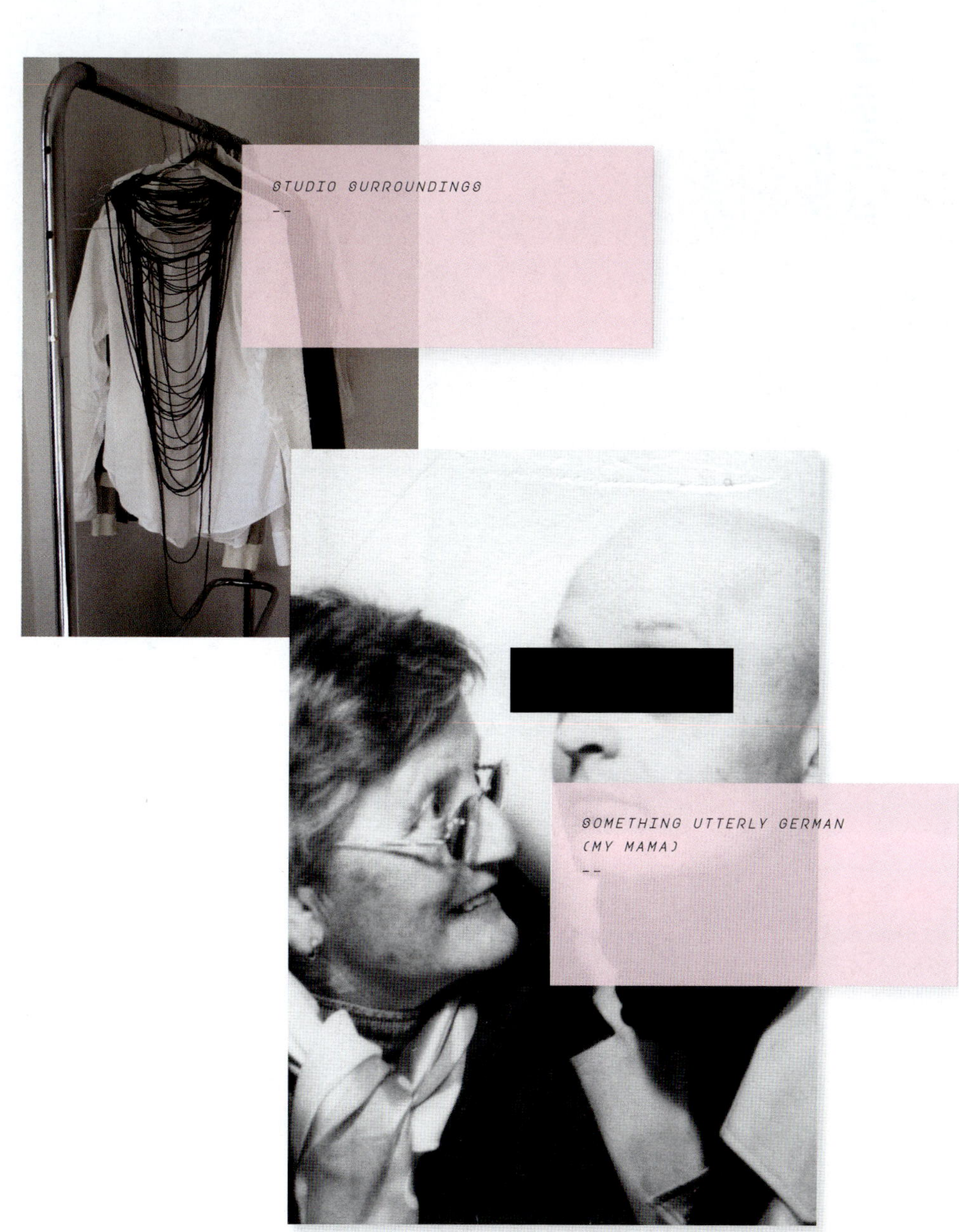
STUDIO SURROUNDINGS
--
SOMETHING UTTERLY GERMAN
(MY MAMA)
--

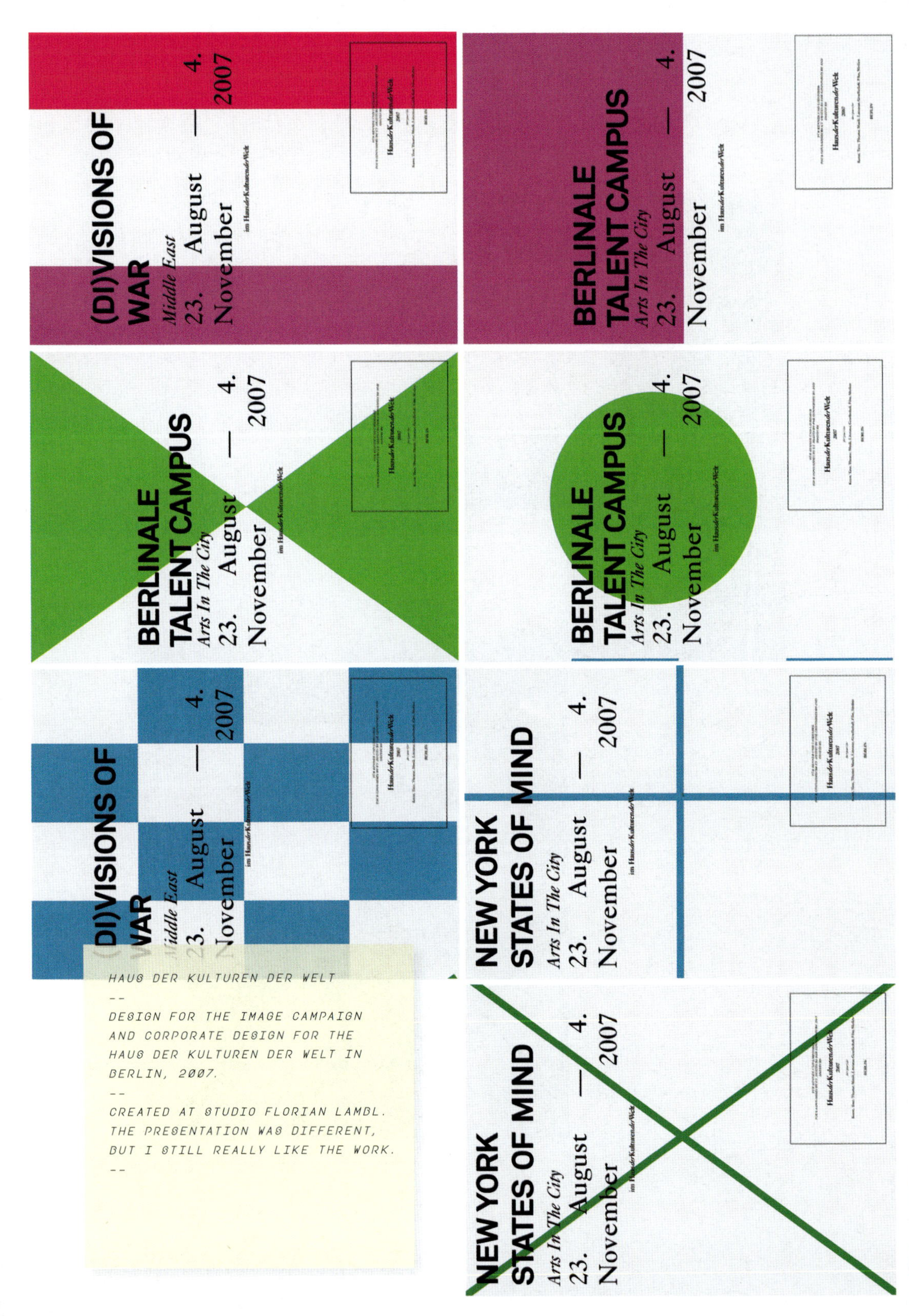

(DI)VISIONS OF WAR
Middle East
23. August — 4. 2007
November
im Haus der Kulturen der Welt

BERLINALE TALENT CAMPUS
Arts In The City
23. August — 4. 2007
November
im Haus der Kulturen der Welt

BERLINALE TALENT CAMPUS
Arts In The City
23. August — 4. 2007
November
im Haus der Kulturen der Welt

BERLINALE TALENT CAMPUS
Arts In The City
23. August — 4. 2007
November
im Haus der Kulturen der Welt

(DI)VISIONS OF WAR
Middle East
23. August — 4. 2007
November
im Haus der Kulturen der Welt

NEW YORK STATES OF MIND
Arts In The City
23. August — 4. 2007
November
im Haus der Kulturen der Welt

NEW YORK STATES OF MIND
Arts In The City
23. August — 4. 2007
November
im Haus der Kulturen der Welt

HAUS DER KULTUREN DER WELT
--
DESIGN FOR THE IMAGE CAMPAIGN
AND CORPORATE DESIGN FOR THE
HAUS DER KULTUREN DER WELT IN
BERLIN, 2007.
--
CREATED AT STUDIO FLORIAN LAMBL.
THE PRESENTATION WAS DIFFERENT,
BUT I STILL REALLY LIKE THE WORK.
--

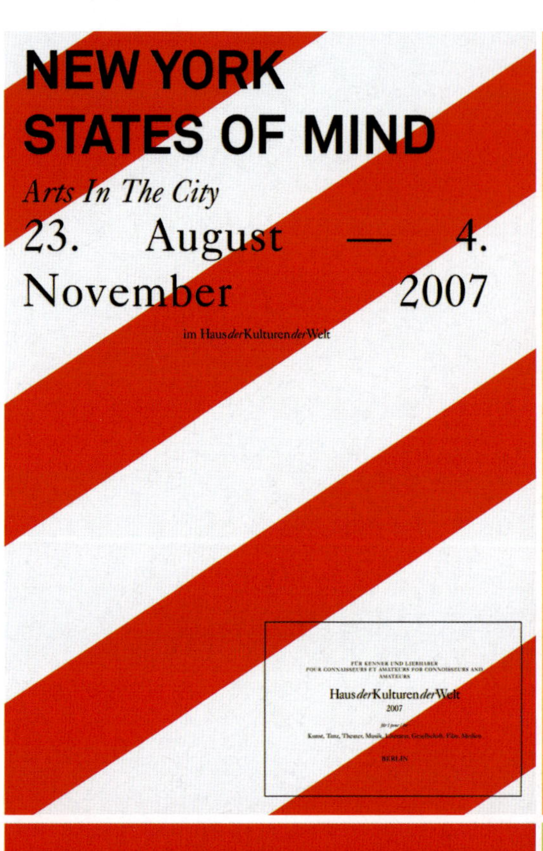

NEW YORK
STATES OF MIND
Arts In The City
23. August — 4.
November 2007
im Haus der Kulturen der Welt
FÜR KENNER UND LIEBHABER
POUR CONNAISSEURS ET AMATEURS FOR CONNOISSEURS AND AMATEURS
Haus der Kulturen der Welt
2007
für / pour / for
Kunst, Tanz, Theater, Musik, Literatur, Gesellschaft, Film, Medien
BERLIN

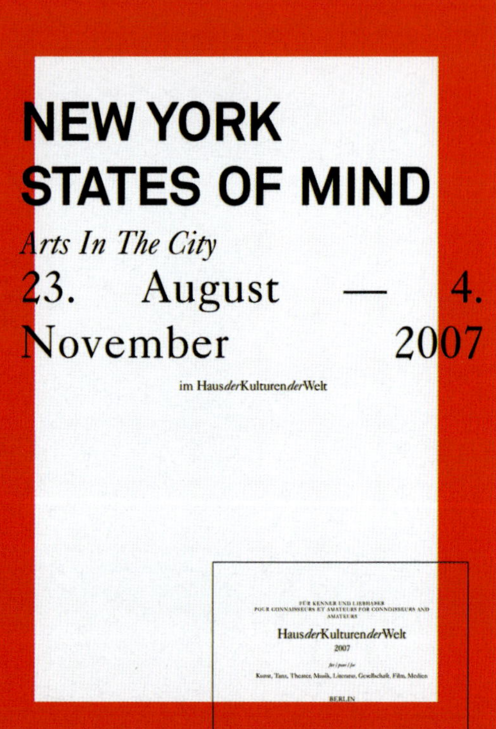

NEW YORK
STATES OF MIND
Arts In The City
23. August — 4.
November 2007
im Haus der Kulturen der Welt
FÜR KENNER UND LIEBHABER
POUR CONNAISSEURS ET AMATEURS FOR CONNOISSEURS AND AMATEURS
Haus der Kulturen der Welt
2007
für / pour / for
Kunst, Tanz, Theater, Musik, Literatur, Gesellschaft, Film, Medien
BERLIN

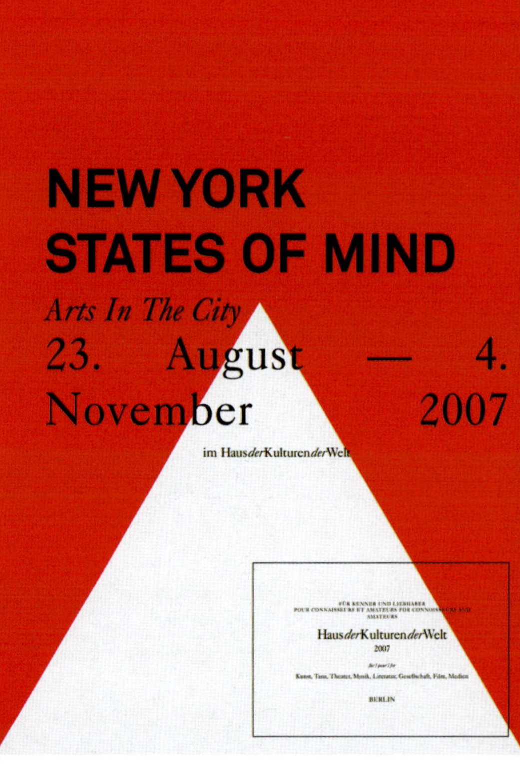

NEW YORK
STATES OF MIND
Arts In The City
23. August — 4.
November 2007
im Haus der Kulturen der Welt
FÜR KENNER UND LIEBHABER
POUR CONNAISSEURS ET AMATEURS FOR CONNOISSEURS AND AMATEURS
Haus der Kulturen der Welt
2007
für / pour / for
Kunst, Tanz, Theater, Musik, Literatur, Gesellschaft, Film, Medien
BERLIN

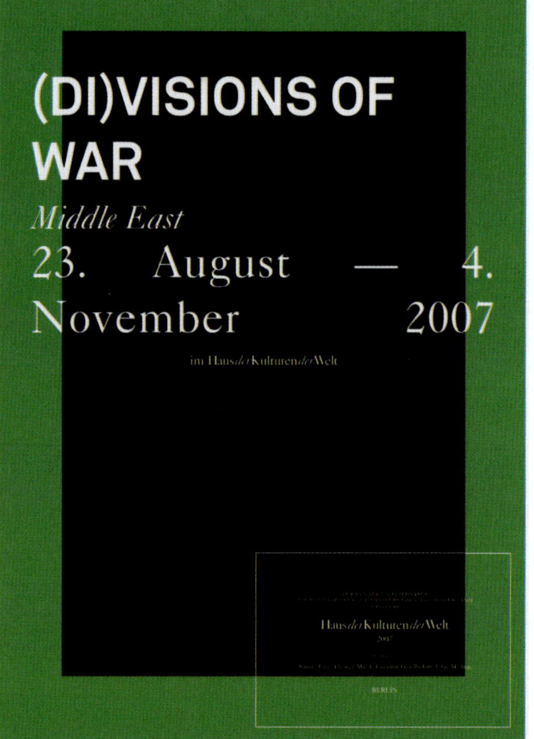

(DI)VISIONS OF
WAR
Middle East
23. August — 4.
November 2007
im Haus der Kulturen der Welt
Haus der Kulturen der Welt
2007
BERLIN

WE [CHRISTOPHER JUNG AND TO-
BIAS WENIG] MET IN LEIPZIG AT
THE 1999 ADMISSION TEST FOR THE
HOCHSCHULE FÜR GRAFIK UND BUCH-
KUNST [HGB - ACADEMY OF VISUAL
ARTS, LEIPZIG]. IN 2000 WE STARTED
STUDYING AT THE HGB. OUR PROFES-
SORS WERE CYAN [DANIELA HAUFE,
DETLEF FIEDLER; SYSTEM DESIGN AND
FOUNDATION STUDIES], GÜNTER KARL
BOSE [TYPOGRAPHY], TO MENTION ONLY
TWO OUTSTANDING TEACHERS FROM
OUR ACADEMY. SINCE THEN WE HAVE
WORKED TOGETHER ON ALMOST ALL OUR
PROJECTS. IN 2004 WE STARTED DOING
JUNGUNDWENIG [JUNG = YOUNG, UND =
AND, WENIG = LITTLE]. OUR WORK IN-
CLUDES BOOKS, MAGAZINES, CD-COV-
ERS, FILM AND MULTIMEDIA WORKS FOR
CLIENTS IN THE CULTURAL SECTOR.

WE WORK IN THE BOONDOCKS OF
LEIPZIG. IT'S THE OLD HORSE STABLE
THAT BELONGED TO A SOAP FACTORY.
WE ARE LUCKY TO HAVE SO MUCH SPACE
WHERE WE CAN HANG UP OUR POST-
ERS, SPREAD OUT ALL OUR LAYOUTS,
READ SOME BOOKS OR PLAY BOWLS… AND
BERLIN IS JUST AROUND THE CORNER
- THE CITY WHERE WE'VE STARTED OUR
NEW OFFICE - YUCHEE.

WE WANT OUR DESIGN TO FIT THE
PROJECT; AND AT THE END IT SHOULD
LOOK GOOD AND MAKE THE CLIENT,
OTHERS AND US HAPPIER. ALTHOUGH
WE CAN'T DENY THAT THE ENVIRONMENT
AROUND THE HGB INFLUENCED THE WAY
OUR DESIGN LOOKS NOW. PEOPLE LIKE
CYAN, GÜNTER KARL BOSE, MARKUS
DRESSEN AND OF COURSE THE FAMOUS
LEIPZIG TYPOGRAPHERS JAN TSCHICH-
OLD AND WALTER TIEMANN HAVE LEFT
THEIR MARK… IT'S IMPORTANT NOT TO
FORGET THE ROOTS OF EVERYTHING.
SO MANY PEOPLE MAKE FANCY AND
SOMETIMES EVEN GOOD-LOOKING STUFF,
BUT HOW LONG WILL IT LAST? FORM
BECOMES MORE AND MORE A QUESTION
OF PUBLIC INTEREST. UNFORTUNATELY,
CONTENT AND THE OBJECTIVE VIEW
OF WHETHER SOMETHING IS GOOD OR
BAD ARE NOT DEBATED TO THE SAME
DEGREE.

MOST OF THE TIME WE GET THE GREAT-
EST SATISFACTION OUT OF VERY SMALL
THINGS WHILE WE WORK. A LETTER
THAT LOOKS LIKE AN ANIMAL, AN AL-
MOST EMPTY PAGE WITH TWO OR THREE
WELL PLACED BASIC ELEMENTS ON IT,
A NICE COLOR OR SURFACE… IT CAN BE
ANYTHING.

APART FROM GRAPHIC DESIGN, WE
BOTH LIKE MUSIC VERY MUCH, BUT IN
THE END IT DOESN'T REALLY MATTER
IF IT'S LITERATURE, ARCHITECTURE
OR INDUSTRIAL DESIGN, IT'S ABOUT
LIGHT AND DARK, LOUD AND QUIET…
WE ARE ALL MORE OR LESS DOING THE
SAME THINGS, TRYING TO PUT SOME
LOVE INTO IT; AND IF YOU CAN SEE
THAT THERE IS SOME, IT DOESN'T
MATTER WHAT GENRE IT IS - IT CAN
BE SHOE-MAKING OR EXCAVATOR-DRIV-
ING.

--

WHAT IS GERMAN?

BOCKWURST.

WHAT IS GERMAN DESIGN?

STRIPS OF PORK.

PLEASE DESCRIBE YOUR WORKING
PROCESS.

FRESH, DEVOUT, HAPPY, FREE.

WHAT DO YOU AIM TO ACHIEVE WITH
YOUR WORK?

TOBI WANTS TO BUY
AN OLED SOME DAY.

YOU'VE INVITED A FRIEND TO
GERMANY; NAME ONE PLACE THEY
REALLY MUST VISIT AND A QUINT-
ESSENTIAL EXPERIENCE YOU REC-
OMMEND.

-

WHAT IS THE MOST IMPORTANT LES-
SON YOU HAVE LEARNED IN YOUR
PROFESSION SO FAR?

-

--

JUNG UND WENIG

JUNG UND WENIG
--
REICHENBERGER STRASSE 136
10999 BERLIN
GERMANY
--
T +49 30 55105623
--
INFO@JUNGUNDWENIG.COM
WWW.JUNGUNDWENIG.COM
--

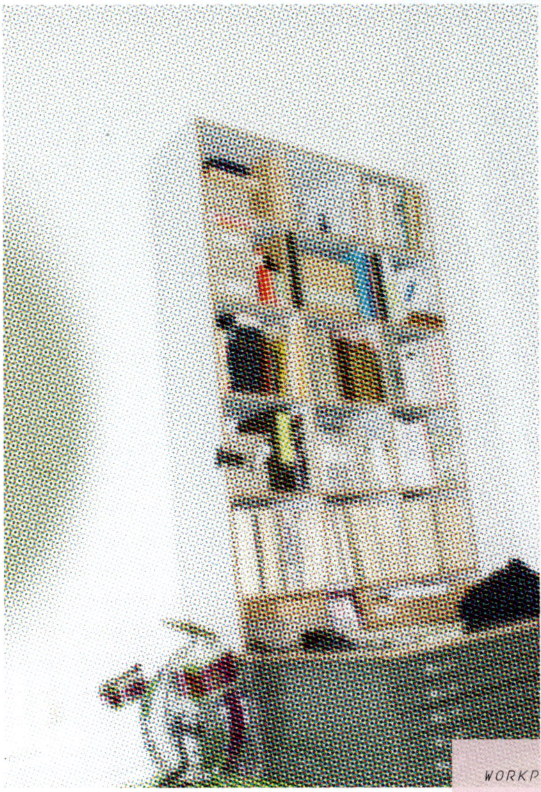

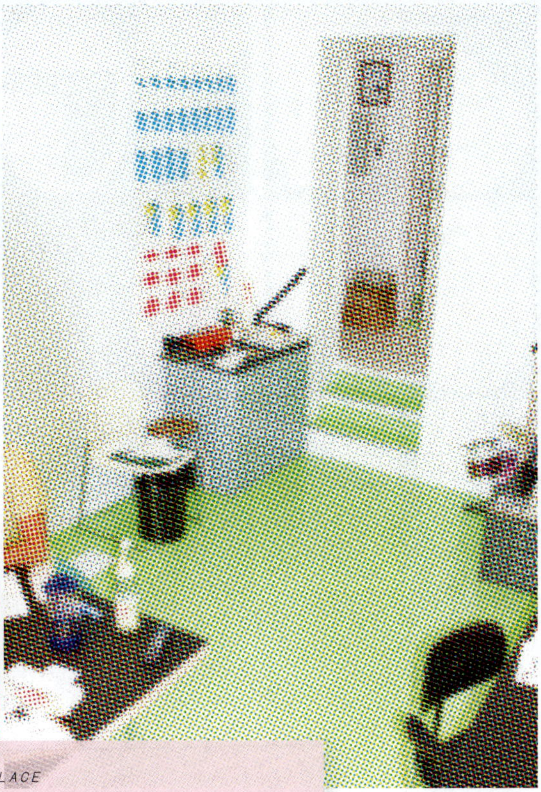

WORKPLACE
--

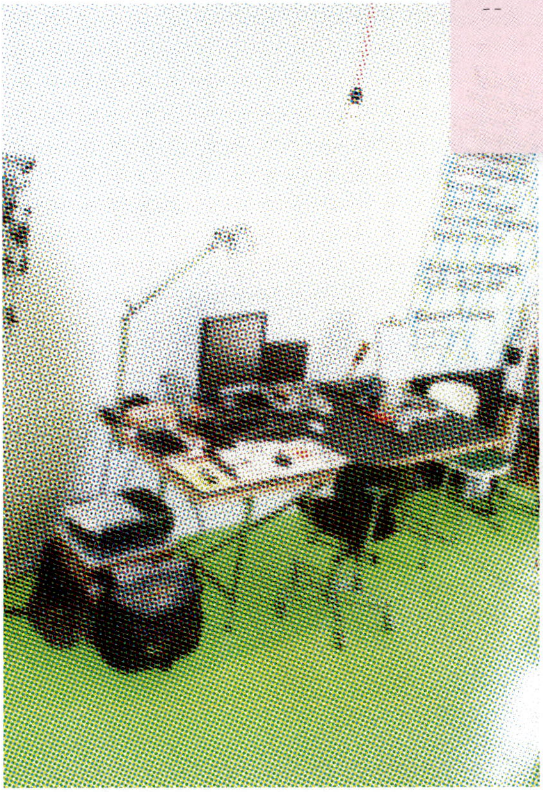

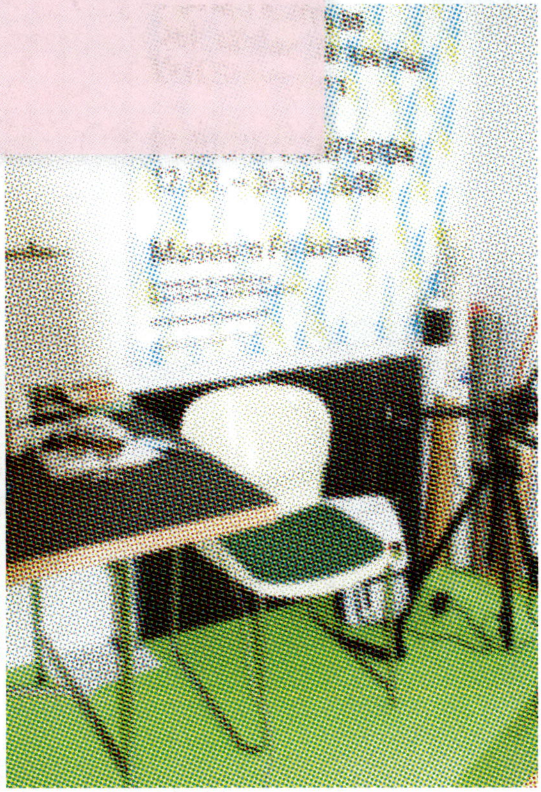

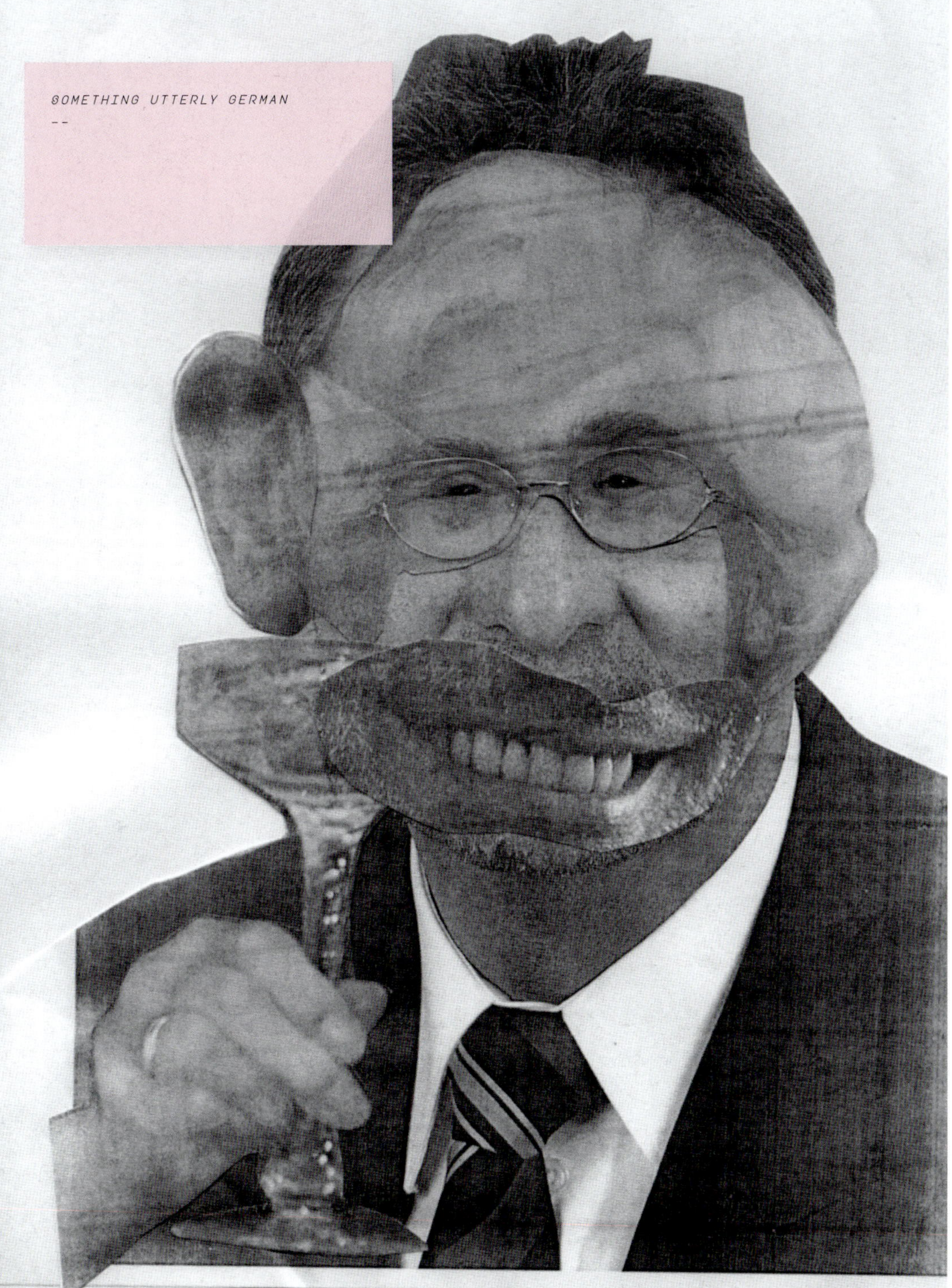

SOMETHING UTTERLY GERMAN
--

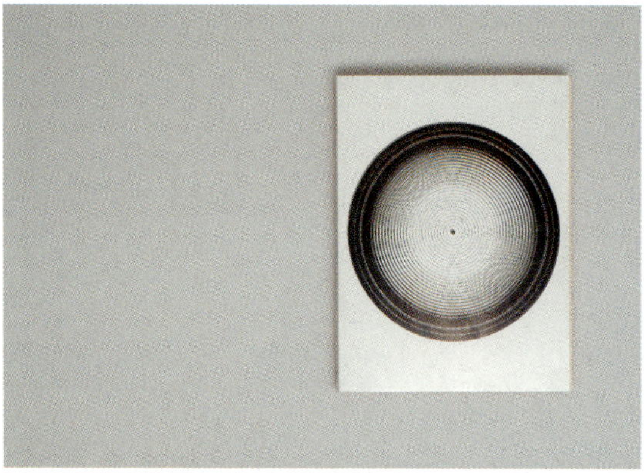

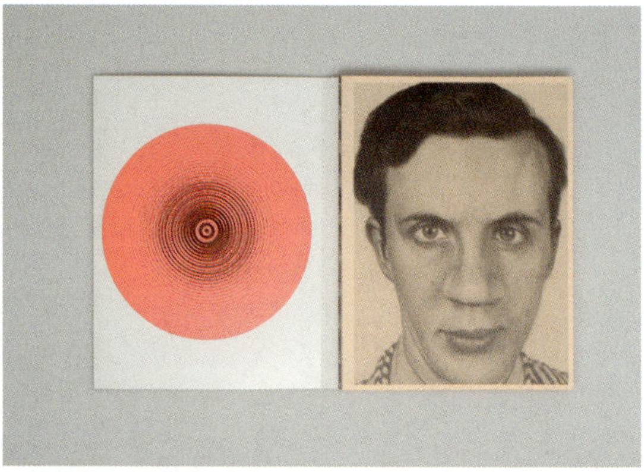

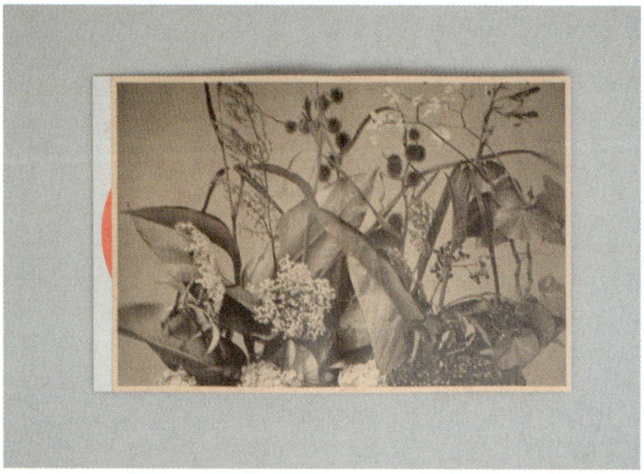

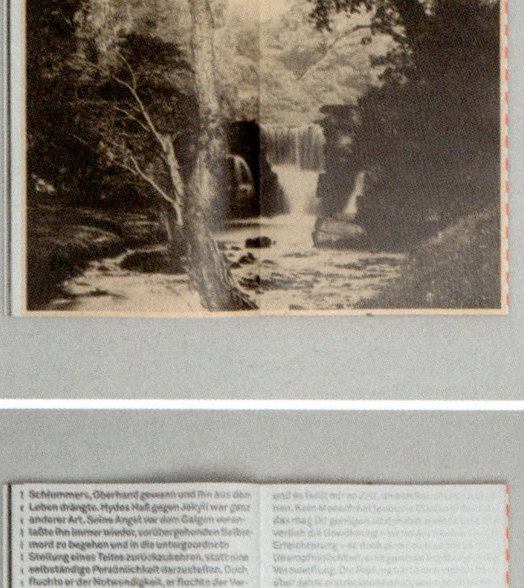
Schlummers, Oberhand gewann und ihn aus dem
Leben drängte. Hydes Haß gegen Jekyll war ganz
anderer Art. Seine Angst vor dem Galgen veran-
laßte ihn immer wieder, vorübergehenden Selbstmord zu begehen und in die untergeordnete
Stellung eines Teiles zurückzukehren, statt eine
selbständige Persönlichkeit darzustellen. Doch
fürchte er der Notwendigkeit, er fürchte der Ver-
zagtheit, die Jekyll jetzt befallen hatte, und er
war beleidigt über die Abneigung, mit der er be-
trachtet wurde. Daher auch die unwürdigen Pos-
sen, die er mir spielte, indem er in meiner Hand-
schrift Gotteslästerungen an die Seiten meiner
Bücher schrieb, Briefe meines Vaters verbrannte
und sein Porträt vernichtete, und wenn er nicht
Angst vor dem Tode gehabt hätte, so hätte er sich
schon längst zugrunde gerichtet, um mich mitzu-
reißen. Aber seine Liebe zum Leben ist wunder-
bar; ich gehe sogar weiter: obgleich mich eine
Schwäche befällt und ich zu Eis erstarre beim
bloßen Gedanken an ihn, bringe ich es fertig, ihn
von Herzen zu bemitleiden, wenn ich mir die Ver-
worfenheit und Leidenschaft seines Hanges zum
Leben vergegenwärtige und wenn ich daran denke, wie er sich vor meiner Macht fürchtet, ihn
durch Selbstmord auszulöschen. Es ist sinnlos.

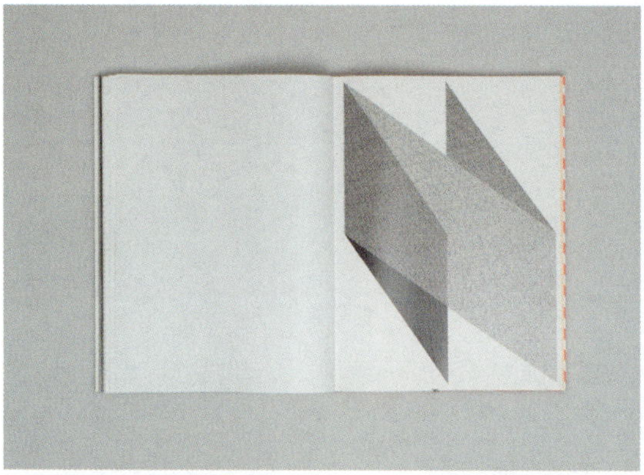

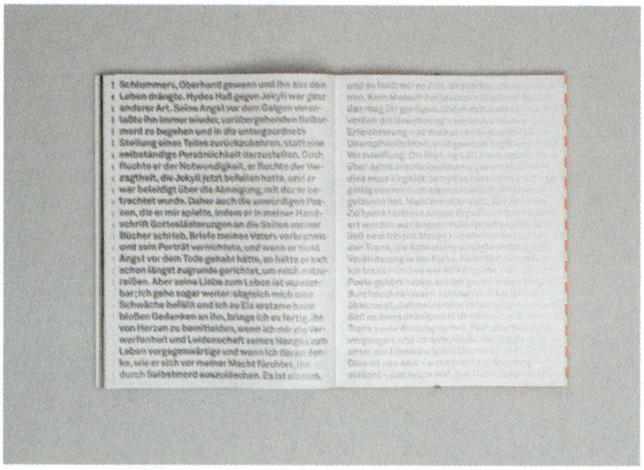

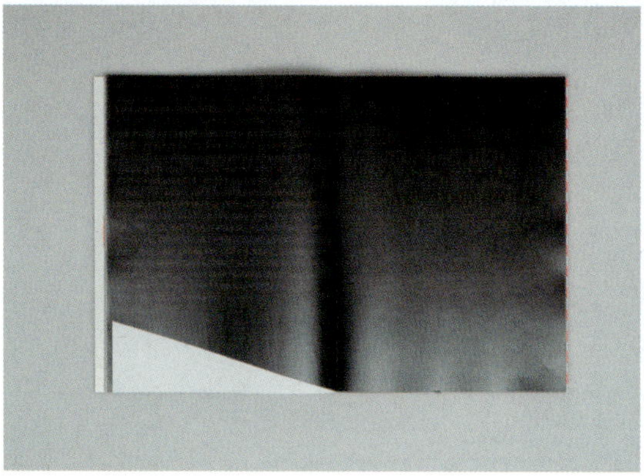

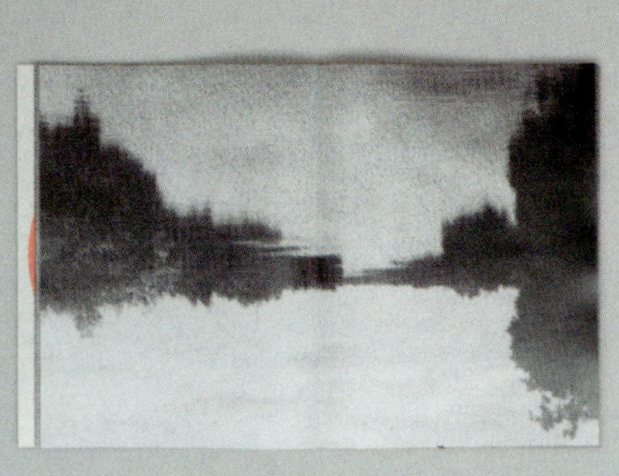

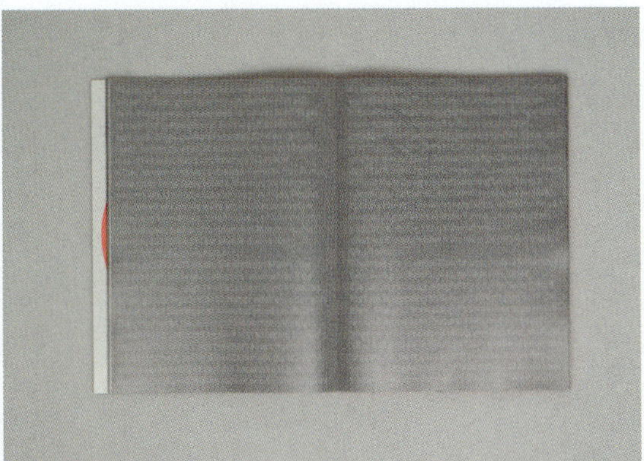

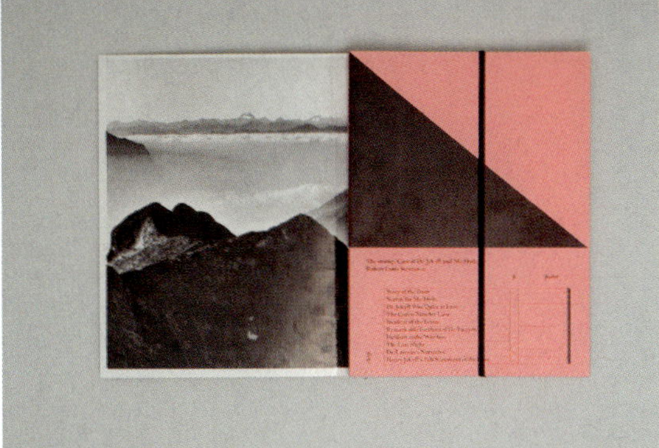

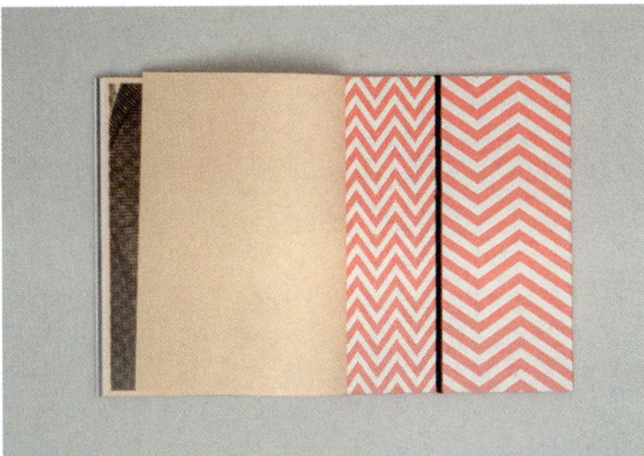

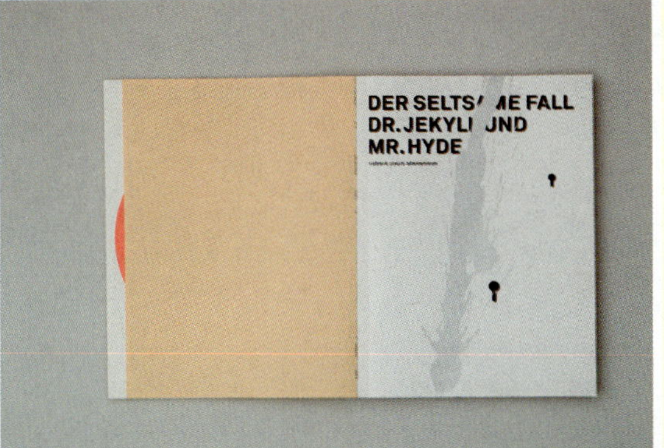

THE STRANGE CASE OF DR.JEKYLL AND MR.HYDE
--
WE ENDED OUR STUDIES AT THE HOCHSCHULE FÜR GRAFIK UND BUCHKUNST IN LEIPZIG WITH THE BOOK THE STRANGE CASE OF DR.JEKYLL AND MR.HYDE BY ROBERT LOUIS STEVENSON. FOR OUR DESIGN WE DECIDED ON A TWIN VOLUME THAT SHOWS BOTH THE GERMAN AND THE ORIGINAL ENGLISH TEXT. THE PICTURES SELECTED BY US DO NOT ILLUSTRATE THE STORY CHRONOLOGICALLY AS IT PROCEEDS, BUT ARE PUT WITH IT AS PURELY SUBJECTIVE IMPRESSIONS. THE PICTURES COME FROM VARIOUS SOURCES, SUCH AS MEDICAL SPECIALIST LITERATURE, MANUALS FOR THE MODERN HOUSEWIFE, OUR OWN FLEA-MARKET FINDS OR WELL-KNOWN PICTURES FROM THE EARLY DAYS OF PHOTOGRAPHY. THE FIRST CHAPTER IN THE GERMAN PART IS CONCEALED UNDER RUB-OFF INK. HIDING AND CONCEALING, WHICH IS IN HARMONY WITH THE NAME HYDE, IS A CONSTANT THEME IN OUR DESIGN. ON THE FOLLOWING PAGES WE PRINTED THE FONT AND THE BACKGROUND SURROUNDING IT IN HALF-TONE. IF YOU LOOK CLOSELY AT THE TEXT THE MATRIX DOTS MINGLE TO THE POINT OF ILLEG- IBILITY. IN THE PROCESS THE FONT AND SUBFONT BLUR INTO AN INDIVISIBLE ENTITY, JUST AS DR. JEKYLL IS INSEPARABLY TIED TO MR. HYDE. THE LEGIBILITY IS CONDITIONED BY BRIGHTNESS, THE INCIDENCE OF LIGHT, DISTANCE AND THE ANGLE TO THE BODY OF THE BOOK. AS THE STORY PROCEEDS THE MATRIX IS DARKENED DOWN TO BLACK. THE PROGRESSION WHICH LIKEWISE CONTINUES ON THE TRIMMED EDGES OF THE BOOK ALSO CARRIES THE DARKENING ACTION ON TO THE OUTSIDE. IN THE FINAL CHAPTER OF THE STORY [JEKYLL'S STATE- MENT] WE LAID A GRADUATION TO WHITE OVER THE FONT. ON LEAFING THROUGH, THE TEXT IS RE- LEASED TO ALL SIDES IN A KIND OF VORTEX, IN A CLOCKWISE DIRECTION. THE GERMAN PART ENDS, AS IT BEGAN, WITH A PICTURE SECTION ON COLORED PAPER. AFTER TURNING THE BOOK ROUND YOU NOW GET THE ENGLISH PART, THE STRANGE CASE OF DR.JEKYLL AND MR.HYDE. THE LIST OF CONTENTS FOLLOWS, MAKING IT POSSIBLE FOR THE READER TO FIND HIS WAY IN THE LOOSE COLLECTION OF SHEETS. THE FOLIOS ARE HELD TOGETHER WITH A RUBBER BAND THAT GOES ACROSS THE PAGES LYING UNDERNEATH. BY MEANS OF A CUT IN THE MIDDLE OF THE SHEET IT BECOMES POSSIBLE FOR THE READER TO FLICK THROUGH THE TEXT IN A SINGLE MOVEMENT. A VARIETY OF PRINTING TECHNIQUES ARE USED IN OUR INTERPRETATION OF THE TEXT: DIGITAL PRINTING, ARTISTIC OFFSET AND SILK SCREEN PRINTING.
--

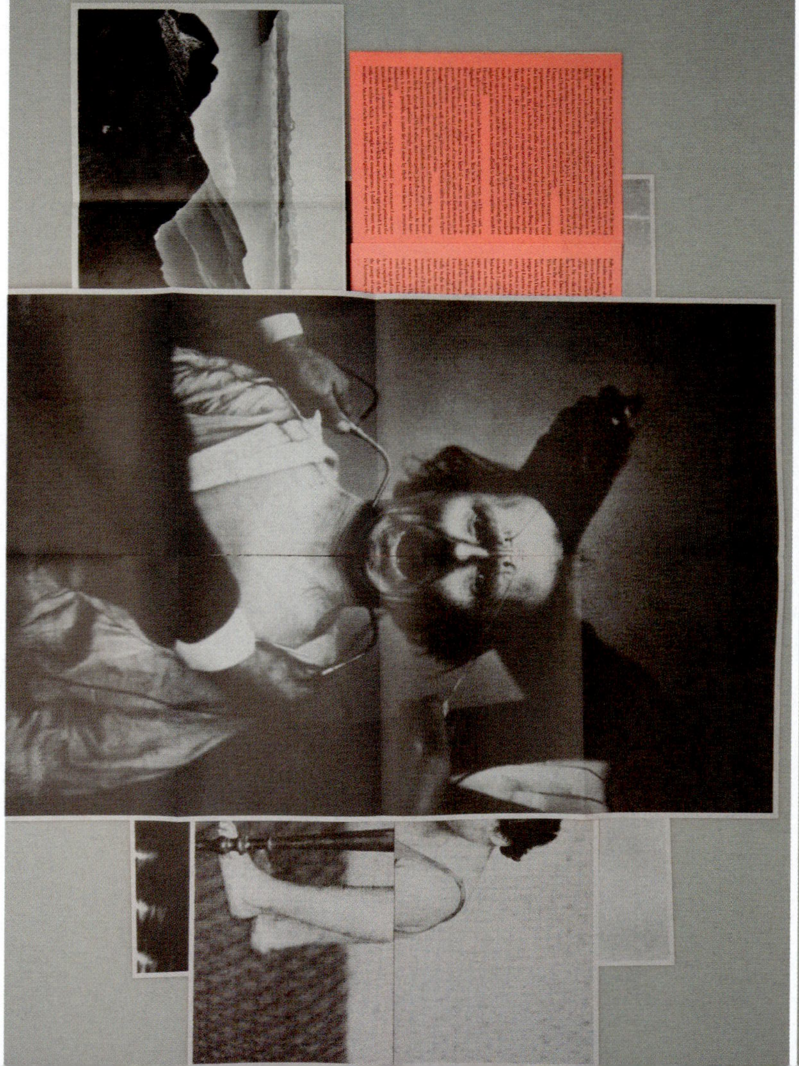

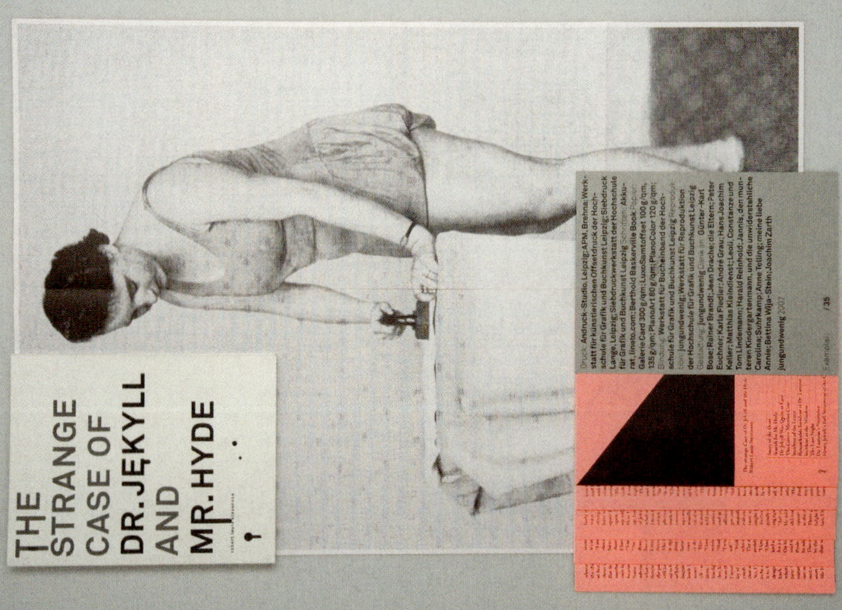

THE STRANGE CASE OF DR. JEKYLL AND MR. HYDE

Druck: Andruck-Studio, Leipzig; APM, Brehna; Werkstatt für künstlerischen Offsetdruck der Hochschule für Grafik und Buchkunst Leipzig; Siebdruck Lange, Leipzig; Siebdruckwerkstatt der Hochschule für Grafik und Buchkunst Leipzig. Schriften: Akkurat, lineto.com; Berthold Baskerville Book. Papier: Galerie Card 300 g/qm; LuxoSamtoffset 100 g/qm, 135 g/qm; PlanoArt 80 g/qm; PlanoColor 120 g/qm; Bindung: Werkstatt für Buchbindend der Hochschule für Grafik und Buchkunst Leipzig. Reproduktion jungundwenig; Werkstatt für Reproduktion der Hochschule für Grafik und Buchkunst Leipzig. Gestaltung: jungundwenig. Dank an: Günter-Karl Bose; Rainer Brandt; Jean Drache; die Eltern; Peter Euchner; Karla Fiedler; André Grau; Hans-Joachim Keller; Matthias Kleindienst; Leoli, Constanze und Tom Lindemann; Harald Reinhold-Jannis, den munteren Kindergartenmann, und die unwiderstehliche Carolina-Suhrkamp; Anne Telling; meine liebe Annie; Bettina Wija-Stein; Joachim Zarth

jungundwenig 2007

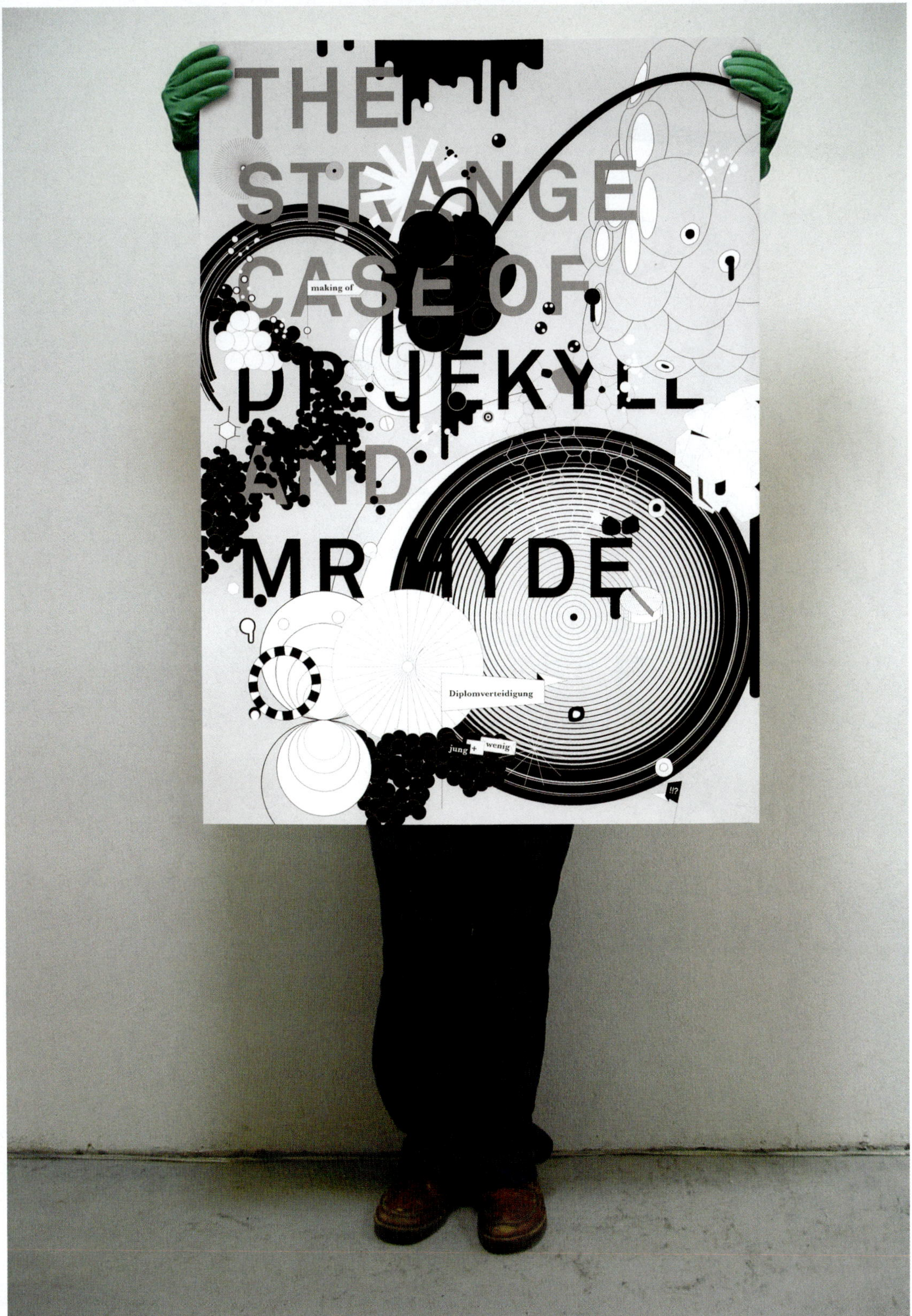

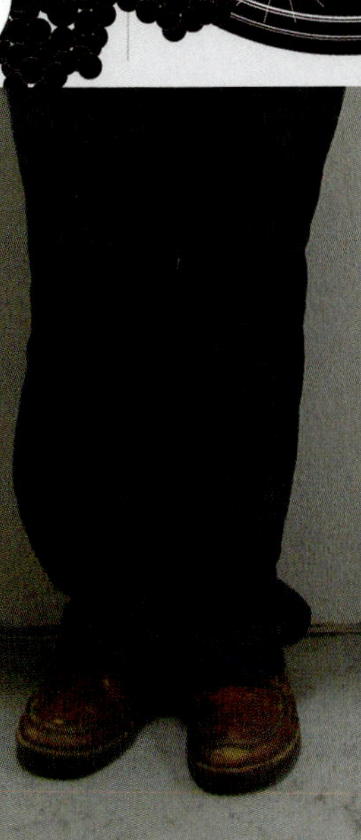

THE
STRANGE
CASE OF
DR. JEKYLL
AND
MR. HYDE
making of
Diplomverteidigung
jung + wenig
!!?

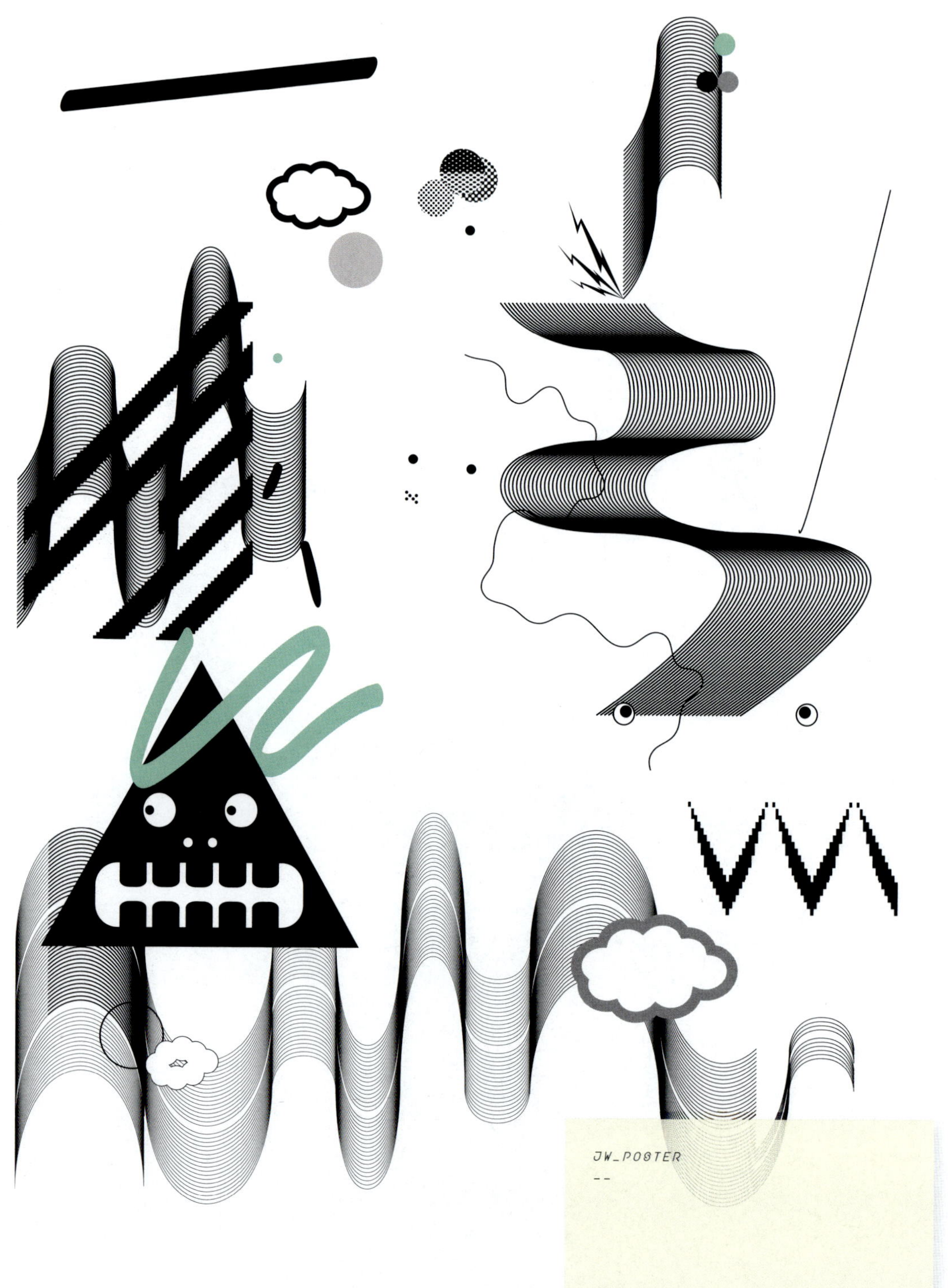
JW_POSTER
--

Zbyněk Baladrán
Michael Beutler
Luca Buvoli
Simon Dybbroe Møller
Cyprien Gaillard
Dionisio González
Konsortium
Ciprian Mureşan
Deimantas Narkevicius
Veit Stratmann

FUSION//CONFUSION
12.01. – 30.03.2008

Di bis So 10 bis 18 Uhr, Fr bis 21 Uhr

Museum Folkwang

Kahrstraße 16
45128 Essen

www.museum-folkwang.de

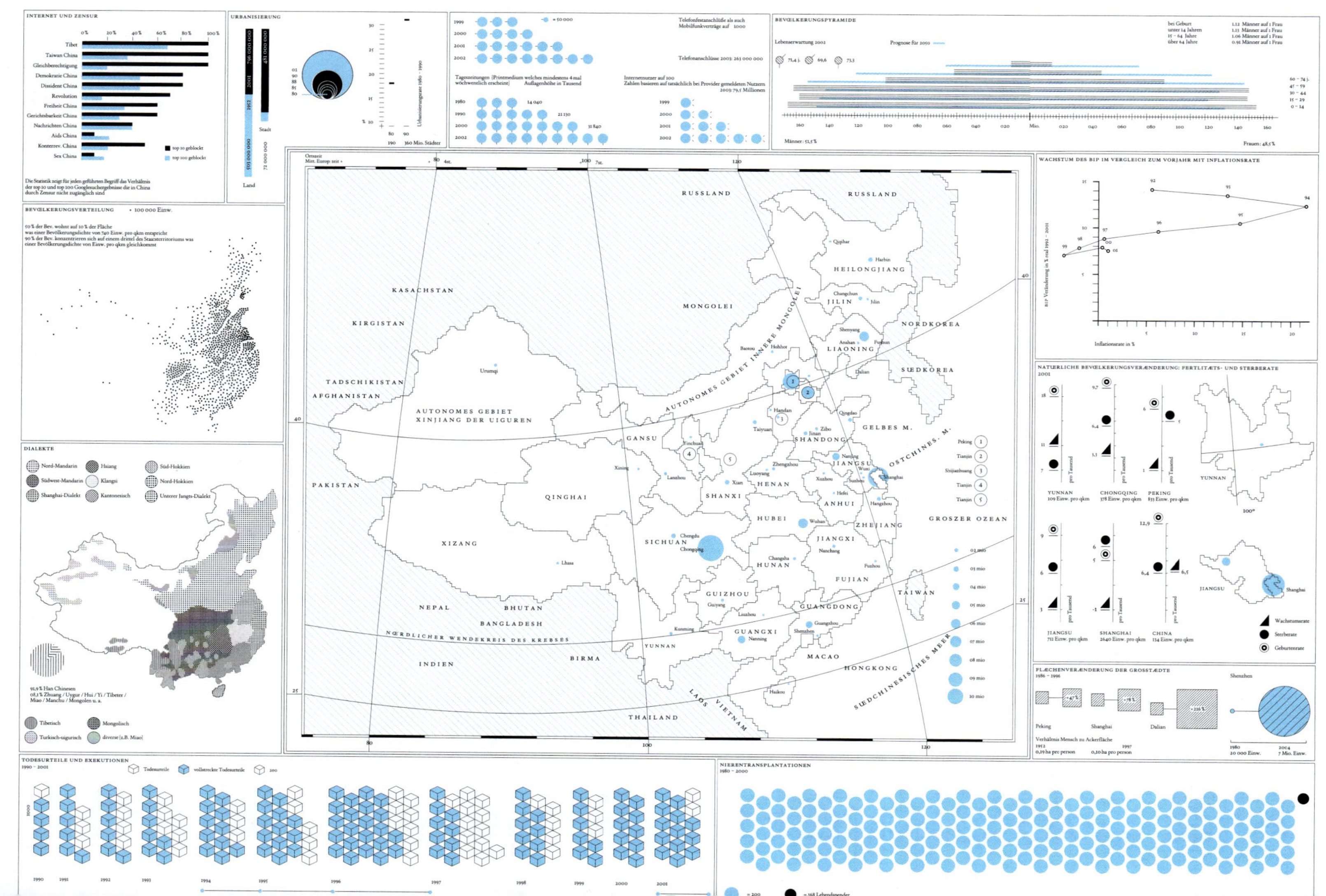

INTERNET UND ZENSUR
0% 20% 40% 60% 80% 100%
Tibet
Taiwan China
Gleichberechtigung
Demokratie China
Dissident China
Revolution
Freiheit China
Gerichtsbarkeit China
Nachrichten China
Aids China
Konterrev. China
Sex China
top 10 geblockt
top 100 geblockt
Die Statistik zeigt für jeden geführten Begriff das Verhältnis der top 10 und top 100 Googlesuchergebnisse die in China durch Zensur nicht zugänglich sind

BEVÖLKERUNGSVERTEILUNG   • 100 000 Einw.
50 % der Bev. wohnt auf 10 % der Fläche was einer Bevölkerungsdichte von 740 Einw. pro qkm entspricht
90 % der Bev. konzentrieren sich auf einem drittel des Staatsterritoriums was einer Bevölkerungsdichte von Einw. pro qkm gleichkommt

DIALEKTE
Nord-Mandarin
Südwest-Mandarin
Shanghai-Dialekt
Hsiang
Klangsi
Kantonesisch
Süd-Hokkien
Nord-Hokkien
Unterer Jangts-Dialekt
91,9 % Han Chinesen
08,1 % Zhuang / Uygur / Hui / Yi / Tibeter / Miao / Manchu / Mongolen u. a.
Tibetisch
Turkisch-uigurisch
Mongolisch
diverse (z.B. Miao)

URBANISIERUNG
181 000 000
796 000 000
493 000 000
1912
2001
Stadt
Land
72 000 000
503 000 000
Urbanisierungsrate 1980 - 1990
360 Mio. Städter

Telefonfestanschlüsse als auch Mobilfunkverträge auf 1000
= 50 000
Telefonanschlüsse 2003: 263 000 000
Tageszeitungen (Printmedium welches mindestens 4 mal wöchentlich erscheint) Auflagenhöhe in Tausend
14 040
21 130
31 840
1980 1990 2000 2002
Internetnutzer auf 100
Zahlen basieren auf tatsächlich bei Provider gemeldeten Nutzern 2003: 79,5 Millionen
1999 2000 2001 2002

BEVÖLKERUNGSPYRAMIDE
bei Geburt   1.12 Männer auf 1 Frau
unter 14 Jahren   1.13 Männer auf 1 Frau
15 - 64 Jahre   1.06 Männer auf 1 Frau
über 64 Jahre   0.91 Männer auf 1 Frau
Lebenserwartung 2002   Prognose für 2010
71,4 j.   69,6   73,3
60 - 74 j.
47 - 59
30 - 44
15 - 29
0 - 14
160 140 120 100 080 060 040 020 Mio. 020 040 060 080 100 120 140 160
Männer: 51,5 %   Frauen: 48,5 %

WACHSTUM DES BIP IM VERGLEICH ZUM VORJAHR MIT INFLATIONSRATE
BIP Veränderung in % real 1992 - 2001
Inflationsrate in %

NATÜRLICHE BEVÖLKERUNGSVERÄNDERUNG: FERTILITÆTS- UND STERBERATE
2001
YUNNAN   109 Einw. pro qkm
CHONGQING   178 Einw. pro qkm
PEKING   833 Einw. pro qkm
JIANGSU   711 Einw. pro qkm
SHANGHAI   2640 Einw. pro qkm
CHINA   134 Einw. pro qkm
pro Tausend
Wachstumsrate
Sterberate
Geburtenrate

FLÆCHENVERÆNDERUNG DER GROSSTÆDTE
1986 - 1996
Peking   Shanghai   Dalian   Shenzhen
Verhältnis Mensch zu Ackerfläche
1992 0,19 ha pro person
1997 0,10 ha pro person
1980 20 000 Einw.
2004 7 Mio. Einw.

TODESURTEILE UND EXEKUTIONEN
1990 - 2001
Todesurteile   vollstreckte Todesurteile   = 100
1990 1991 1992 1993 1994 1995 1996 1997 1998 1999 2000 2001

NIERENTRANSPLANTATIONEN
1980 - 2000
= 200   = 168 Lebendspender

RUSSLAND
KASACHSTAN
KIRGISTAN
TADSCHIKISTAN
AFGHANISTAN
PAKISTAN
INDIEN
NEPAL
BHUTAN
BANGLADESH
BIRMA
THAILAND
LAOS
VIETNAM
MONGOLEI
HEILONGJIANG
JILIN
LIAONING
NORDKOREA
SUEDKOREA
AUTONOMES GEBIET INNERE MONGOLEI
AUTONOMES GEBIET XINJIANG DER UIGUREN
GANSU
QINGHAI
XIZANG
SICHUAN
YUNNAN
GUIZHOU
GUANGXI
GUANGDONG
HUNAN
HUBEI
SHANXI
SHAANXI
HENAN
SHANDONG
JIANGSU
ANHUI
JIANGXI
FUJIAN
ZHEJIANG
TAIWAN
HONGKONG
MACAO
GELBES M.
OSTCHINES. M.
GROSZER OZEAN
SUEDCHINESISCHES MEER
NÖRDLICHER WENDEKREIS DES KREBSES
Urumqi
Qiqihar
Harbin
Changchun
Jilin
Shenyang
Fushun
Anshan
Dalian
Baotou
Hohhot
Handan
Taiyuan
Yinchuan
Xining
Lanzhou
Xian
Luoyang
Zhengzhou
Jinan
Zibo
Qingdao
Nanjing
Wuxi
Suzhou
Shanghai
Hangzhou
Hefei
Xuzhou
Wuhan
Chengdu
Chongqing
Lhasa
Changsha
Nanchang
Fuzhou
Guiyang
Liuzhou
Kunming
Nanning
Guangzhou
Shenzhen
Haikou
Peking   1
Tianjin   2
Shijiazhuang   3
Tianjin   4
Tianjin   5
03 mio
03 mio
04 mio
05 mio
06 mio
07 mio
08 mio
09 mio
10 mio

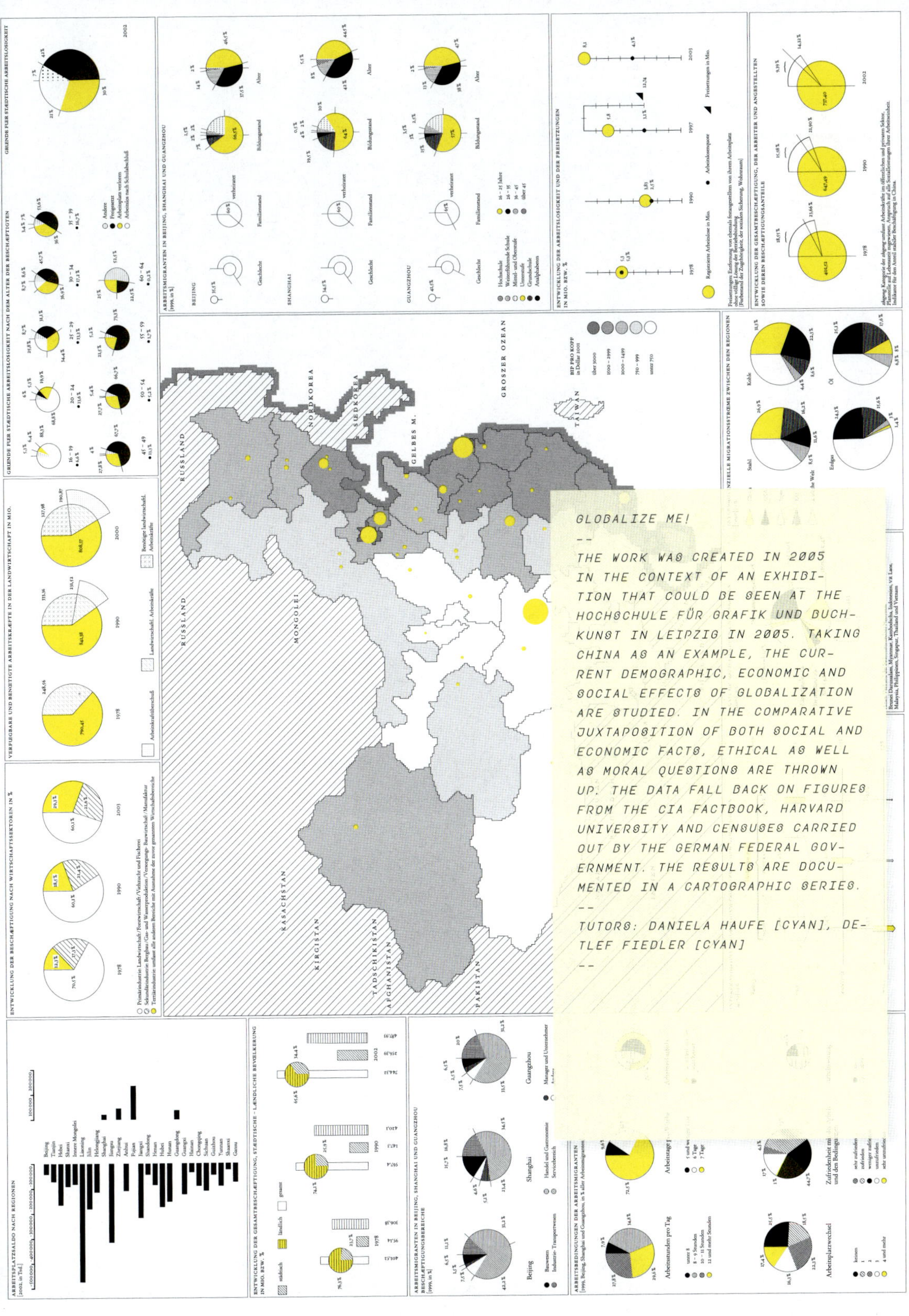
GLOBALIZE ME!
--
THE WORK WAS CREATED IN 2005
IN THE CONTEXT OF AN EXHIBI-
TION THAT COULD BE SEEN AT THE
HOCHSCHULE FÜR GRAFIK UND BUCH-
KUNST IN LEIPZIG IN 2005. TAKING
CHINA AS AN EXAMPLE, THE CUR-
RENT DEMOGRAPHIC, ECONOMIC AND
SOCIAL EFFECTS OF GLOBALIZATION
ARE STUDIED. IN THE COMPARATIVE
JUXTAPOSITION OF BOTH SOCIAL AND
ECONOMIC FACTS, ETHICAL AS WELL
AS MORAL QUESTIONS ARE THROWN
UP. THE DATA FALL BACK ON FIGURES
FROM THE CIA FACTBOOK, HARVARD
UNIVERSITY AND CENSUSES CARRIED
OUT BY THE GERMAN FEDERAL GOV-
ERNMENT. THE RESULTS ARE DOCU-
MENTED IN A CARTOGRAPHIC SERIES.
--
TUTORS: DANIELA HAUFE [CYAN], DE-
TLEF FIEDLER [CYAN]
--

TIM FAULWETTER AND PETER WERNER,
BOTH BORN IN 1976, SHARE AN INTER-
EST IN THE DYNAMICS AND REGEN-
ERATIVE POWER OF URBAN SUBCUL-
TURES. SINCE THEIR FIRST MEETING
IN 1998 THAT CURIOSITY HAS AGAIN
AND AGAIN SERVED AS A CATALYST
FOR THEIR COLLABORATION. IN 2001
TIM FAULWETTER AND PETER WERNER
FOUNDED REBOOTLAB.COM AND HAVE
BEEN WORKING TOGETHER EVER SINCE
ON INTERCULTURAL AND TANGIBLE
DESIGN PROJECTS. THE MAJORITY
OF THEIR PROJECTS DEVELOP DE-
SIGN FOR INTERACTIVE MEDIA OR PUT
THE EMPHASIS ON ILLUSTRATION AND
GRAPHIC DESIGN. JUST LIKE SUBCUL-
TURES, REBOOTLAB.COM IS CONSTANTLY
REINVENTING ITSELF AND IS BOTH A
REFUGE AND A DESIGN DEVELOPMENT
LABORATORY.

TIM FAULWETTER TODAY WORKS AS A
GRAPHIC DESIGNER IN HAMBURG, AFTER
COMPLETING HIS VISUAL COMMUNICA-
TION STUDIES IN JULY 2005. PETER
WERNER WAS AWARDED HIS DEGREE IN
VISUAL COMMUNICATION IN 2004, AND
WORKS IN BRAUNSCHWEIG AS A FREE-
LANCE DESIGNER.

--

WHAT IS GERMAN?

POWER STATION MUSIC, GERMAN EN-
GINEERING SKILLS, SEPARATING OUT
RUBBISH, BEER BREWED IN ACCOR-
DANCE WITH THE PURITY LAW, GARDEN
GNOMES, <GEMÜTLICHKEIT>

WHAT IS GERMAN DESIGN?

IT'S OUR IMPRESSION THAT IT'S
NO LONGER POSSIBLE TO TALK OF
DESIGNERS OF OUR GENERATION FROM
GERMANY PRODUCING TYPICALLY GER-
MAN DESIGN. DESIGN IS INTERNA-
TIONAL. WE OURSELVES TEND TO BE
GUIDED MORE BY INTERNATIONAL THAN
NATIONAL MODELS. IF YOU LOOK AT
GOOD CONTEMPORARY DESIGN TODAY,
YOU RECOGNIZE THE DESIGNER'S ATTI-
TUDE, HIS OR HER OWN STYLE AS WELL
AS HIS INFLUENCES, BUT ONLY RARELY
A SPECIFIC NATIONAL BACKGROUND.

PLEASE DESCRIBE YOUR WORKING
PROCESS.

ANALYZING, CONSIDERING, TALKING,
TRYING OUT, LOOKING, REFLECTING,
COMPARING NOTES, CRITICIZING, DIS-
CARDING, TRYING AGAIN

WHAT DO YOU AIM TO ACHIEVE WITH
YOUR WORK?

FOR US OUR WORK TOGETHER IS A
COUNTERBALANCE TO OUR DAY-TO-DAY
WORK AS DESIGNERS. AS REBOOTLAB.
COM WE ENJOY CREATIVE FREEDOM
AND SHARE OUR ENJOYMENT IN JOINT
PROJECTS THAT GO BEYOND OUR DAILY
BUSINESS AS DESIGNERS.

YOU'VE INVITED A FRIEND TO
GERMANY; NAME ONE PLACE THEY
REALLY MUST VISIT AND A QUINT-
ESSENTIAL EXPERIENCE YOU REC-
OMMEND.

HE SHOULD GO TO THE HARZ MOUN-
TAINS IN WINTER AND GO TOBOGGANING,
THEN GET BLIND DRUNK ON MALT BEER,
NEXT TRAVEL ON TO DESSAU AND VISIT
THE BAUHAUS - AND ONCE HE'S AL-
READY THERE, ALSO MAKE A SIDE-TRIP
TO DESSAU SÜD…

WHAT IS THE MOST IMPORTANT
LESSON YOU HAVE LEARNED IN YOUR
PROFESSION SO FAR?

TO SHARE YOUR IDEAS AND WHAT
YOU'VE LEARNT AND NOT KEEP THEM
TO YOURSELF. TO HOLD OPEN, CLEAR
CONVERSATIONS WITH CLIENTS AND
COLLEAGUES. TO INSPIRE ONE ANOTHER
RECIPROCALLY IN THE TEAM - FOR
IT'S OUR EXPERIENCE THAT WORKING
IN A TEAM IS ALWAYS MORE PRODUC-
TIVE AND ENRICHING THAN WORKING
ALONE.

--

REBOOTLAB

REBOOTLAB.COM
--
C/O STUDIO B12
METHFESSELSTRASSE 2
38106 BRAUNSCHWEIG
GERMANY
--
MAIL@REBOOTLAB.COM
WWW.REBOOTLAB.COM
--

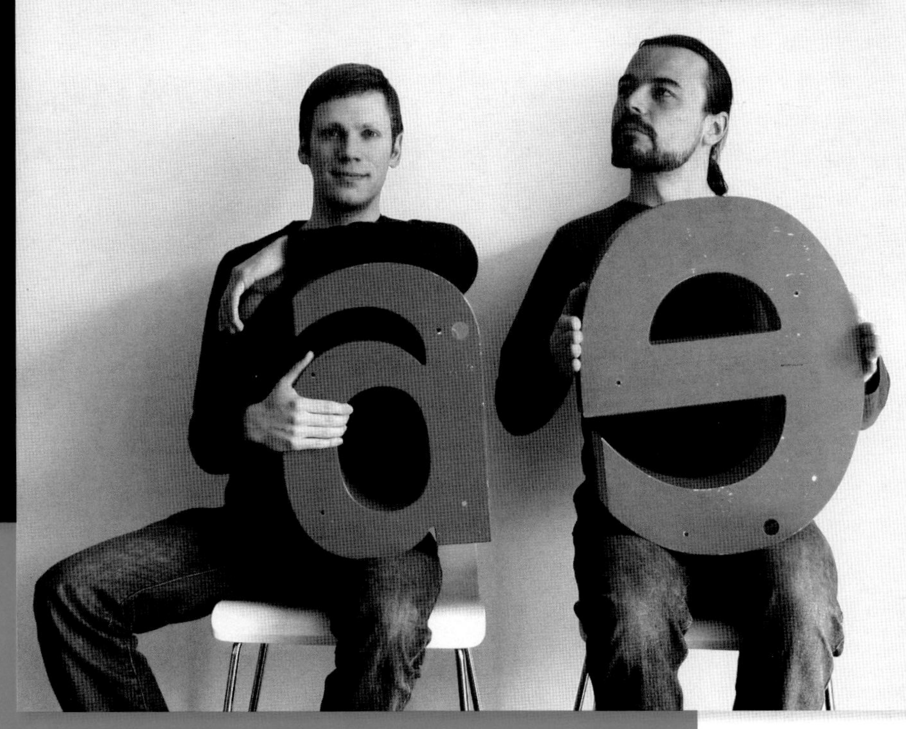

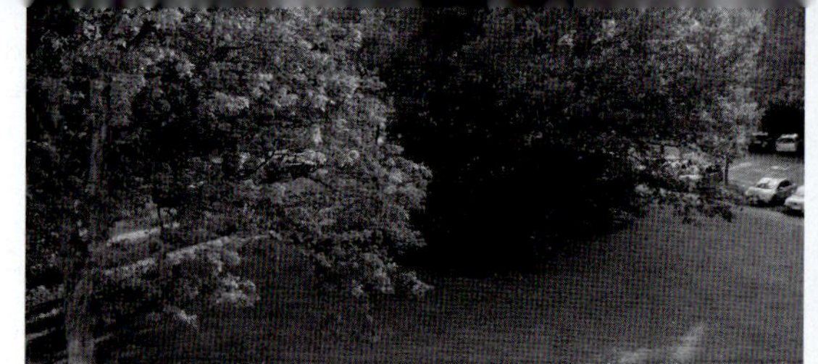

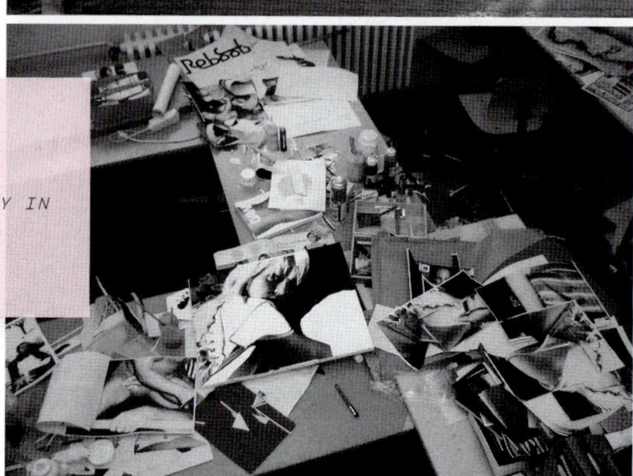

IMPRESSIONS OF OUR PLACE OF
WORK. REBOOTLAB.COM AT WORK.
WHEN WE'RE WORKING ON JOINT
PROJECTS, WE MEET ALTERNATELY IN
HAMBURG AND BRAUNSCHWEIG.
--

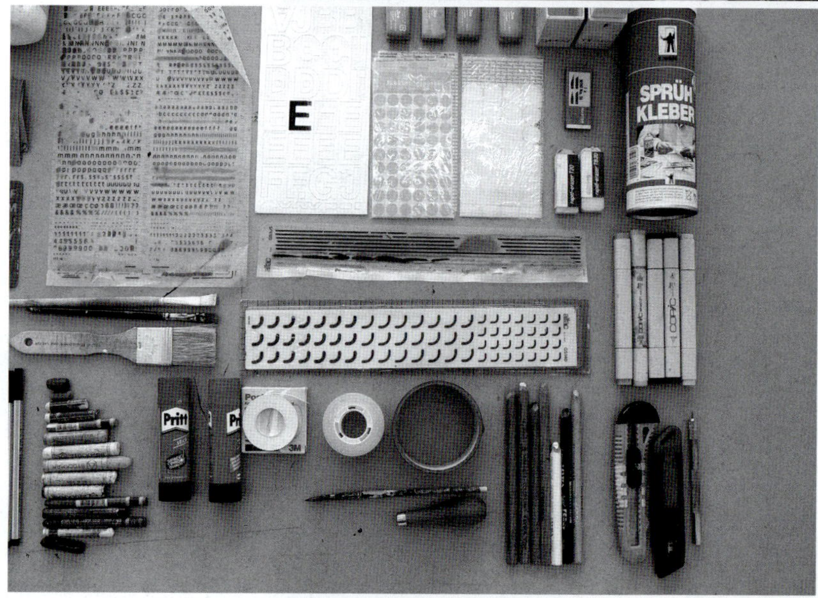

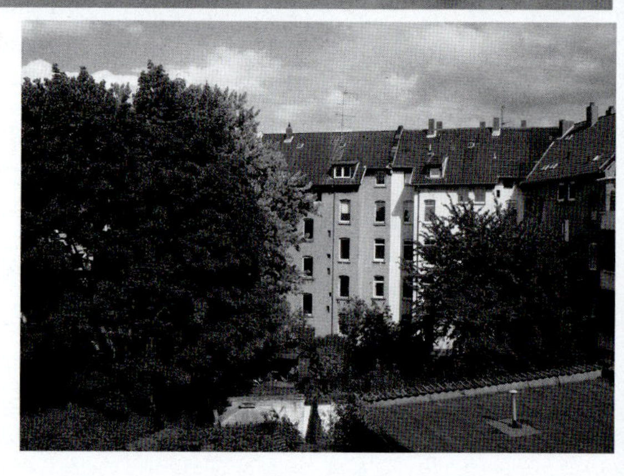

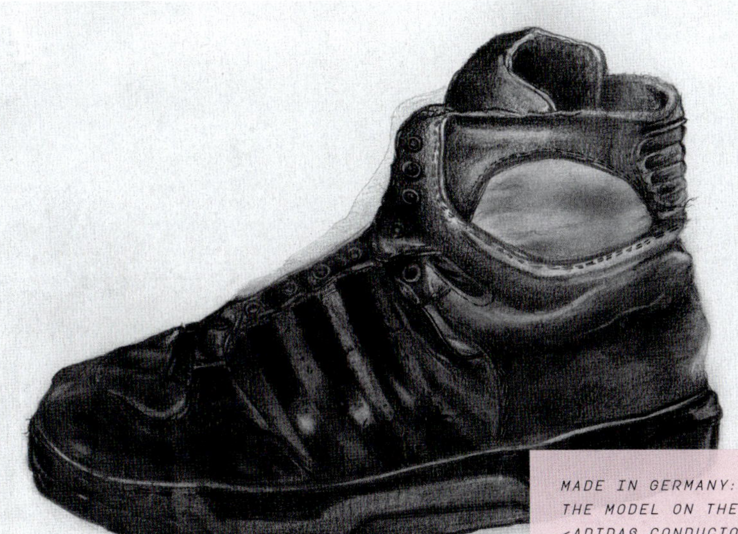

MADE IN GERMANY: SHOES BY ADIDAS.
THE MODEL ON THE PICTURE IS THE
<ADIDAS CONDUCTOR>, ONE OF OUR
FAVORITE SHOES FROM THE 80S.
--

FOR THE PICTURE WE'VE COLLECTED
THINGS THAT WE WORK WITH AND THAT
ARE IN OUR PLACE OF WORK.
--

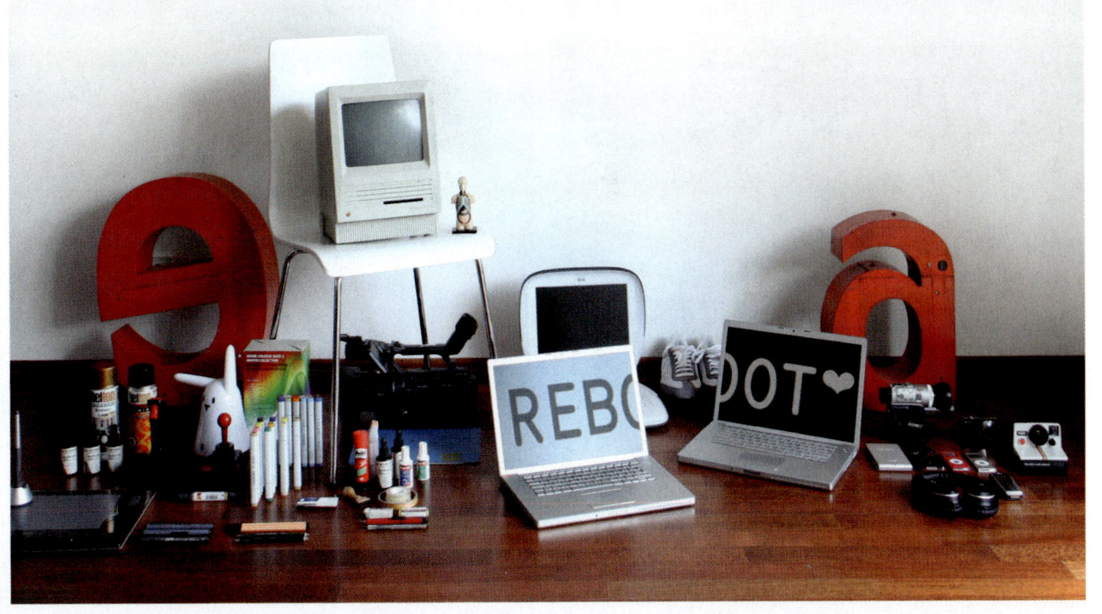

REBO
OT

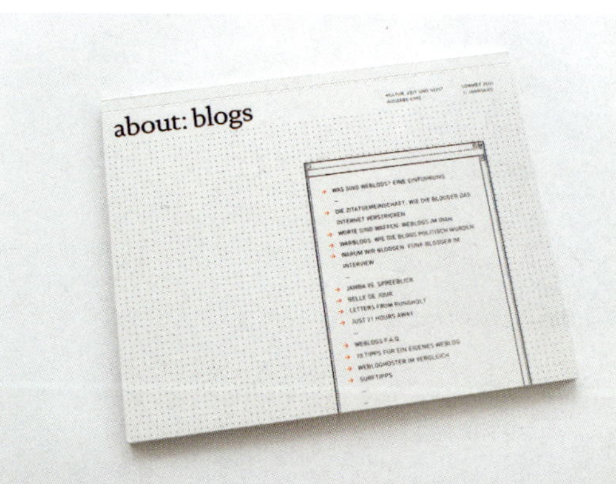

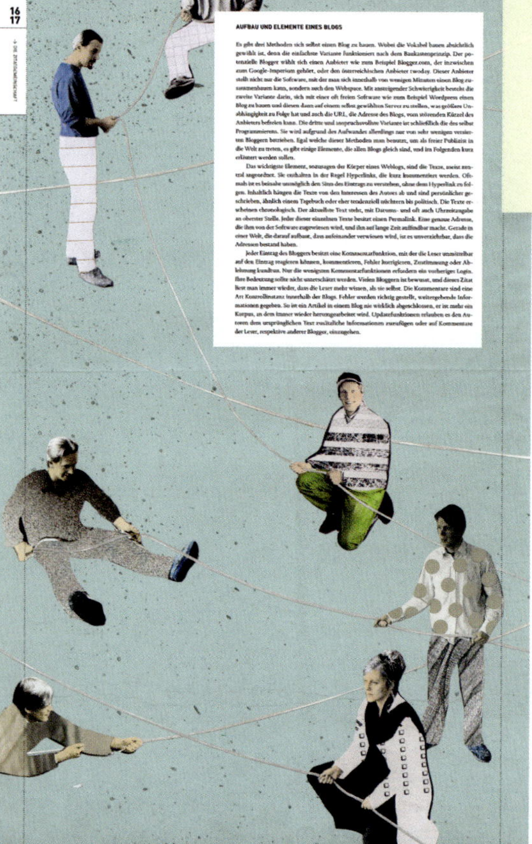

ABOUT:
--
THE SINGLE-TOPIC MAGAZINE ABOUT:
IS TIM FAULWETTER'S DIPLOMA PROJ-
ECT. IT IS A COUNTER-PROPOSAL TO
THE CURRENT MEDIA PRACTICE OF
TREATING TOPICS ONLY SUPERFI-
CIALLY. IN EACH ISSUE, IN TERMS
OF BOTH CONTENT AND DESIGN, THE
MAGAZINE CONCERNS ITSELF EX-
CLUSIVELY WITH ONE TOPIC FROM
CULTURE AND CURRENT AFFAIRS.
IN THE FIRST ISSUE ABOUT: BLOGS
THE READER LEARNS MORE ABOUT
THE PHENOMENON OF THE WEBLOG.
THE DIRECTNESS AND GENUINENESS
OF THIS NEW MEDIUM IS BROUGHT
VIVIDLY TO LIFE WITH THE HELP OF
ORIGINAL BLOG ENTRIES, AS WELL AS
STORIES AND INTERVIEWS IN WHICH
THE BLOGGERS SPEAK FOR THEM-
SELVES.
--
DIPLOMA PROJECT BY
TIM FAULWETTER, FH HANNOVER, DE-
SIGN AND MEDIA DEPARTMENT, 2005
--

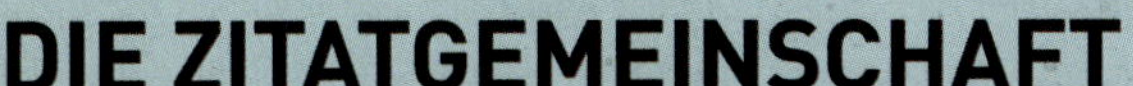

DIE ZITATGEMEINSCHAFT

Wie die Blogger das Internet verstricken

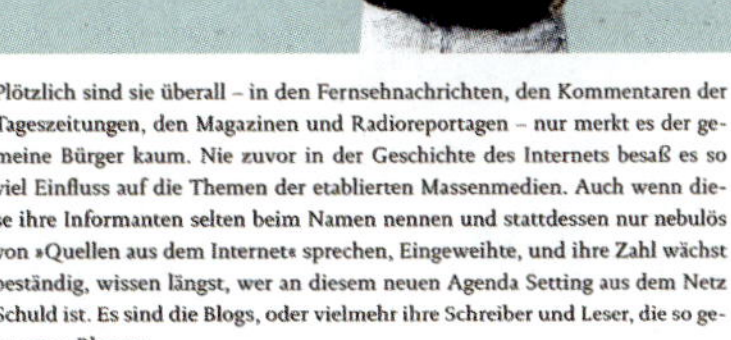

Plötzlich sind sie überall – in den Fernsehnachrichten, den Kommentaren der Tageszeitungen, den Magazinen und Radioreportagen – nur merkt es der gemeine Bürger kaum. Nie zuvor in der Geschichte des Internets besaß es so viel Einfluss auf die Themen der etablierten Massenmedien. Auch wenn diese ihre Informanten selten beim Namen nennen und stattdessen nur nebulös von »Quellen aus dem Internet« sprechen, Eingeweihte, und ihre Zahl wächst beständig, wissen längst, wer an diesem neuen Agenda Setting aus dem Netz Schuld ist. Es sind die Blogs, oder vielmehr ihre Schreiber und Leser, die so genannten Blogger.

Bei einem Zwischenfall im Irak am 04. März 2005, erschießen amerikanische Soldaten an einem Kontrollposten den italienischen Agenten Calipari und verletzen die Journalistin Sgrena durch ihre Kugeln. Der Vorfall sorgt für schwere Verstimmungen zwischen den beiden Verbündeten USA und Italien. Die italienische Regierung drängt auf eine schnelle Aufklärung. Als das US-Militär zwei Monate später den Untersuchungsbericht veröffentlicht, sind die sensiblen Stellen geschwärzt. Es ist ein italienischer Blogger, dem es mit einfachsten Mitteln gelingt, das Unlesbare lesbar zu machen. Der komplette Bericht gibt einen tiefen Einblick in die Psyche der von täglichen Anschlägen zutiefst verunsicherten US-Soldaten.

Seit Ende 2004 beschäftigt sich die Bundesregierung mit den zweifelhaften Geschäften der Klingeltonanbieter. Nach Angaben aus Regierungskreisen will man mit dem neuen Gesetzentwurf vor allem die Kostenkontrolle und Transparenz für die zumeist jugendlichen Kunden erhöhen. Die ersten Berichte, die zuvor auf die zweifelhaften Geschäftsgebaren der Anbieter, allen voran des Marktführers Jamba, im rechtlich Nebel mit Minderjährigen hinwiesen, wurden zwar von den Redakteuren der etablierten Onlinezeitungen, wie zum Beispiel Heise verfasst, eine größere Aufmerksamkeit wurde dem Thema allerdings erst zuteil, als sich der Unmut, auch Dank einer pointierteren Sicht- und Schreibweise, in den unzähligen Blogs potenzierte.

Blogger berichten aus Krisenregionen und isolierten Staaten, von Orten, an die kein westlicher Journalist gelangt. Salam Pax' blogt aus Bagdad während des dritten Irakkrieges und erreicht kurzzeitige Berühmtheit, als die britische Tagespresse seine täglichen Postings während des Feldzuges übernimmt. Es sind Blogger aus Indonesien, die als erstes von dem Tsunami berichteten. Und es sind Blogger, die über die Zustände in totalitären Regimes schreiben, in denen Pressefreiheit ein Fremdwort ist. In China gibt es zum Beispiel trotz aufwändigster staatlicher Kontrolle mehr als eine halbe Million Blogger.

Unser Planet wird zunehmend vernetzt, die technischen Hürden sinken, ehrfürchtig spricht man vom Informationszeitalter und beinahe überall wo Informationen entstehen kann man inzwischen mit einem Blogger rechnen, der diese dann in seinem Blog veröffentlicht.

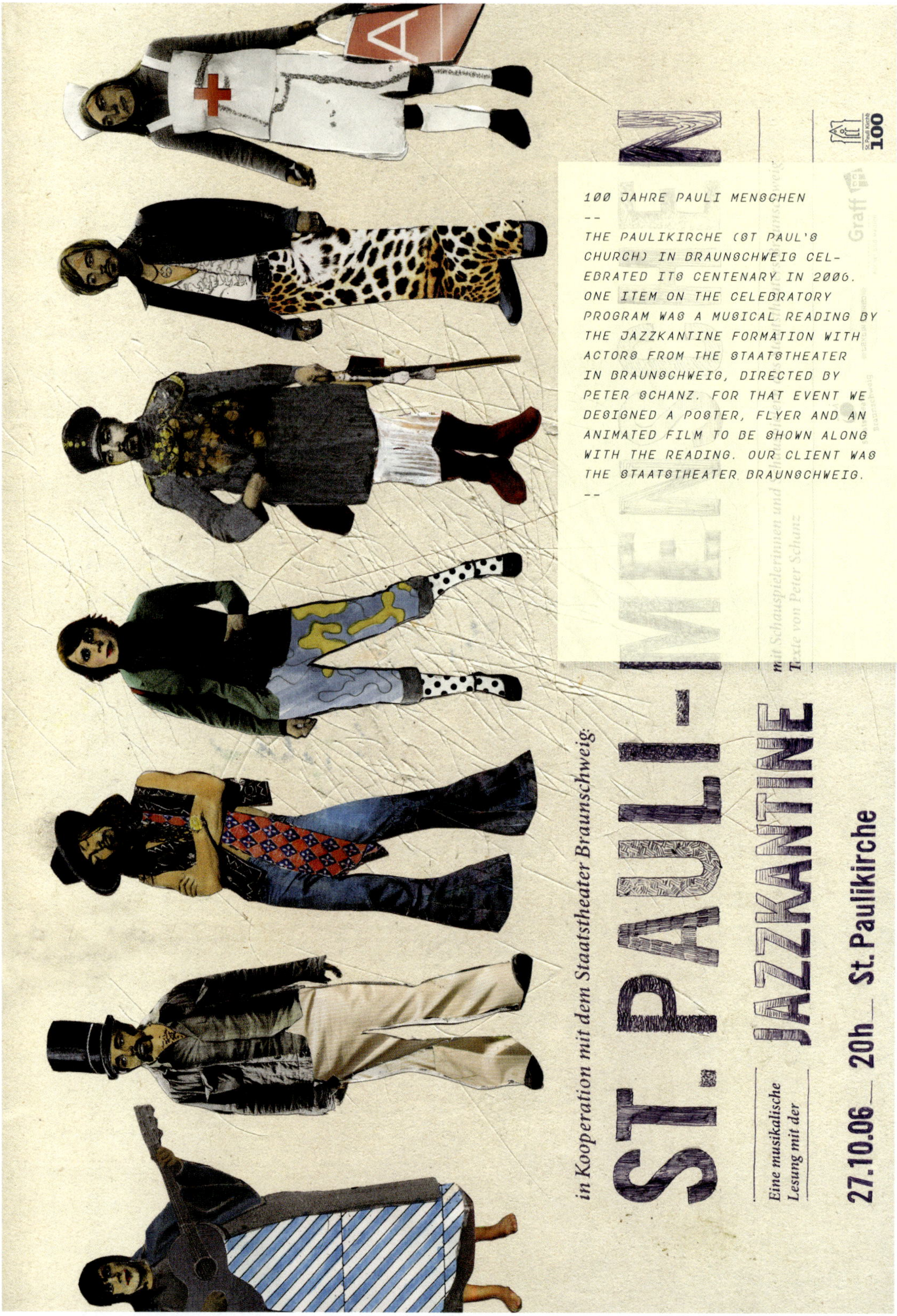

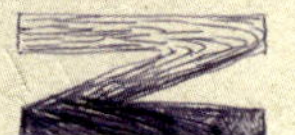

100 JAHRE PAULI MENSCHEN
--
THE PAULIKIRCHE (ST PAUL'S CHURCH) IN BRAUNSCHWEIG CELEBRATED ITS CENTENARY IN 2006. ONE ITEM ON THE CELEBRATORY PROGRAM WAS A MUSICAL READING BY THE JAZZKANTINE FORMATION WITH ACTORS FROM THE STAATSTHEATER IN BRAUNSCHWEIG, DIRECTED BY PETER SCHANZ. FOR THAT EVENT WE DESIGNED A POSTER, FLYER AND AN ANIMATED FILM TO BE SHOWN ALONG WITH THE READING. OUR CLIENT WAS THE STAATSTHEATER BRAUNSCHWEIG.
--

ST.PAULI-MENSCHEN
ST. JAZZKANTINE
in Kooperation mit dem Staatstheater Braunschweig:
Eine musikalische Lesung mit der
mit Schauspielerinnen und
Texte von Peter Schanz
27.10.06 _ 20h _ St. Paulikirche
Graff

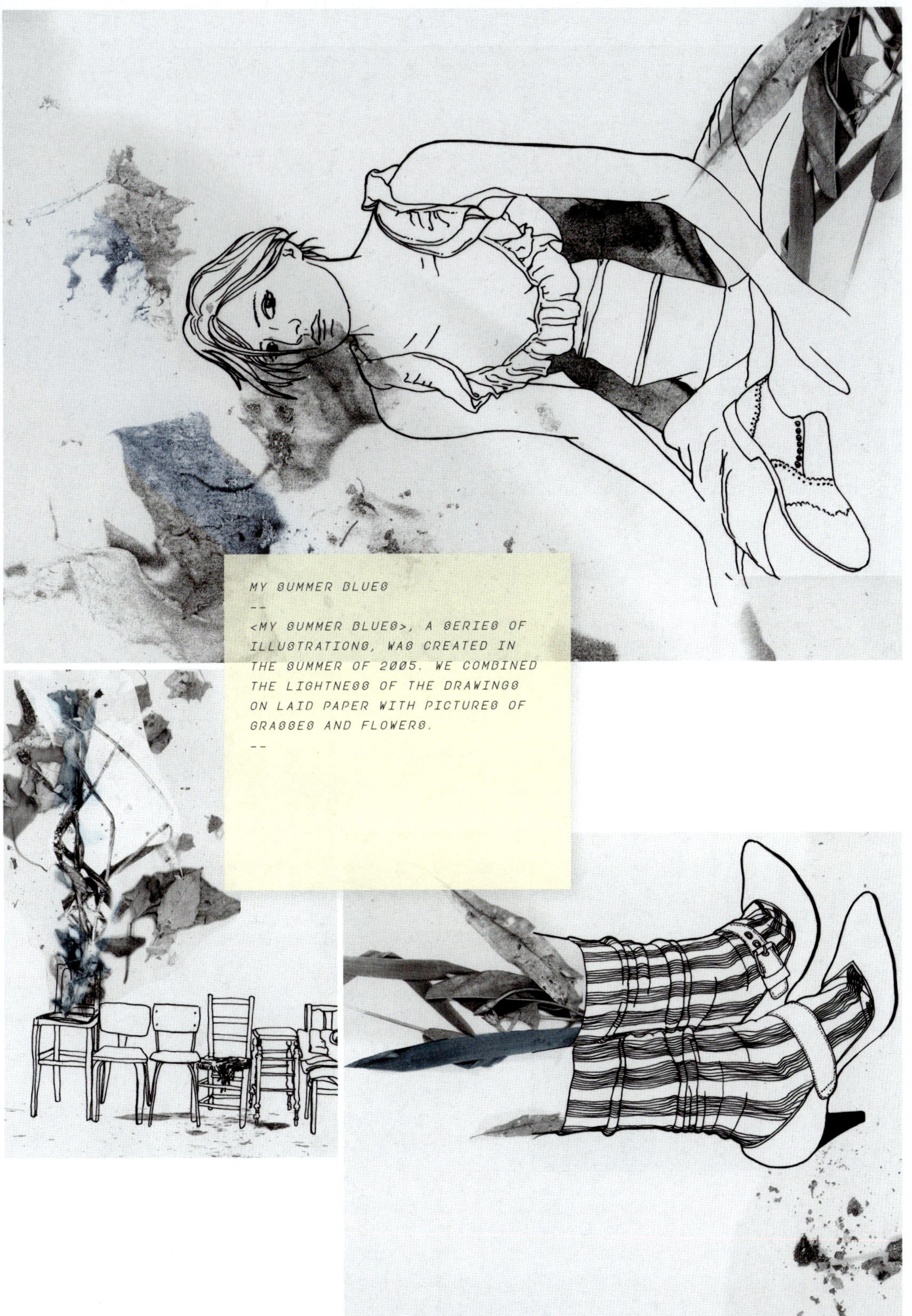
MY SUMMER BLUES
--
<MY SUMMER BLUES>, A SERIES OF
ILLUSTRATIONS, WAS CREATED IN
THE SUMMER OF 2005. WE COMBINED
THE LIGHTNESS OF THE DRAWINGS
ON LAID PAPER WITH PICTURES OF
GRASSES AND FLOWERS.
--

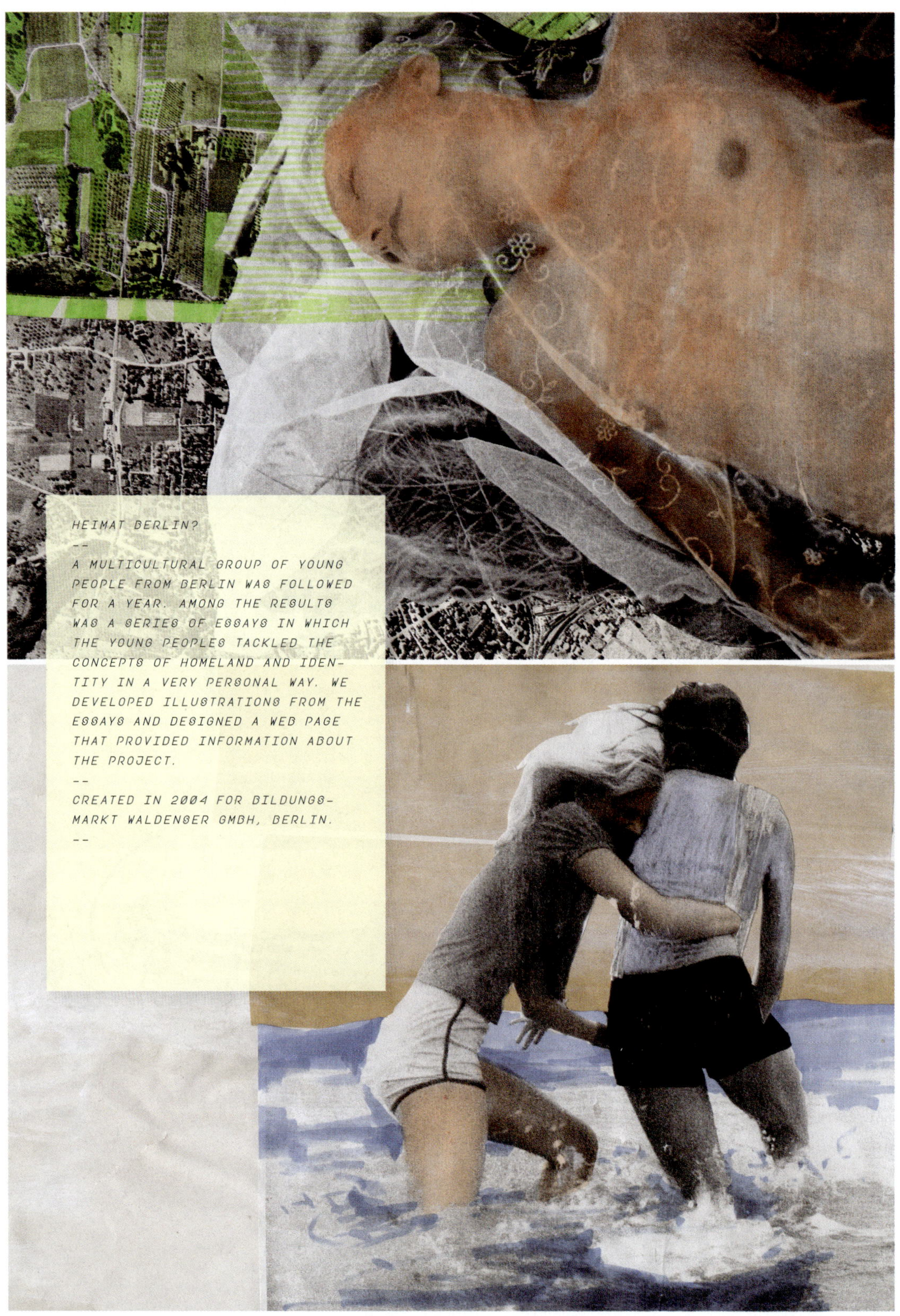

HEIMAT BERLIN?
--
A MULTICULTURAL GROUP OF YOUNG
PEOPLE FROM BERLIN WAS FOLLOWED
FOR A YEAR. AMONG THE RESULTS
WAS A SERIES OF ESSAYS IN WHICH
THE YOUNG PEOPLES TACKLED THE
CONCEPTS OF HOMELAND AND IDEN-
TITY IN A VERY PERSONAL WAY. WE
DEVELOPED ILLUSTRATIONS FROM THE
ESSAYS AND DESIGNED A WEB PAGE
THAT PROVIDED INFORMATION ABOUT
THE PROJECT.
--
CREATED IN 2004 FOR BILDUNGS-
MARKT WALDENSER GMBH, BERLIN.
--

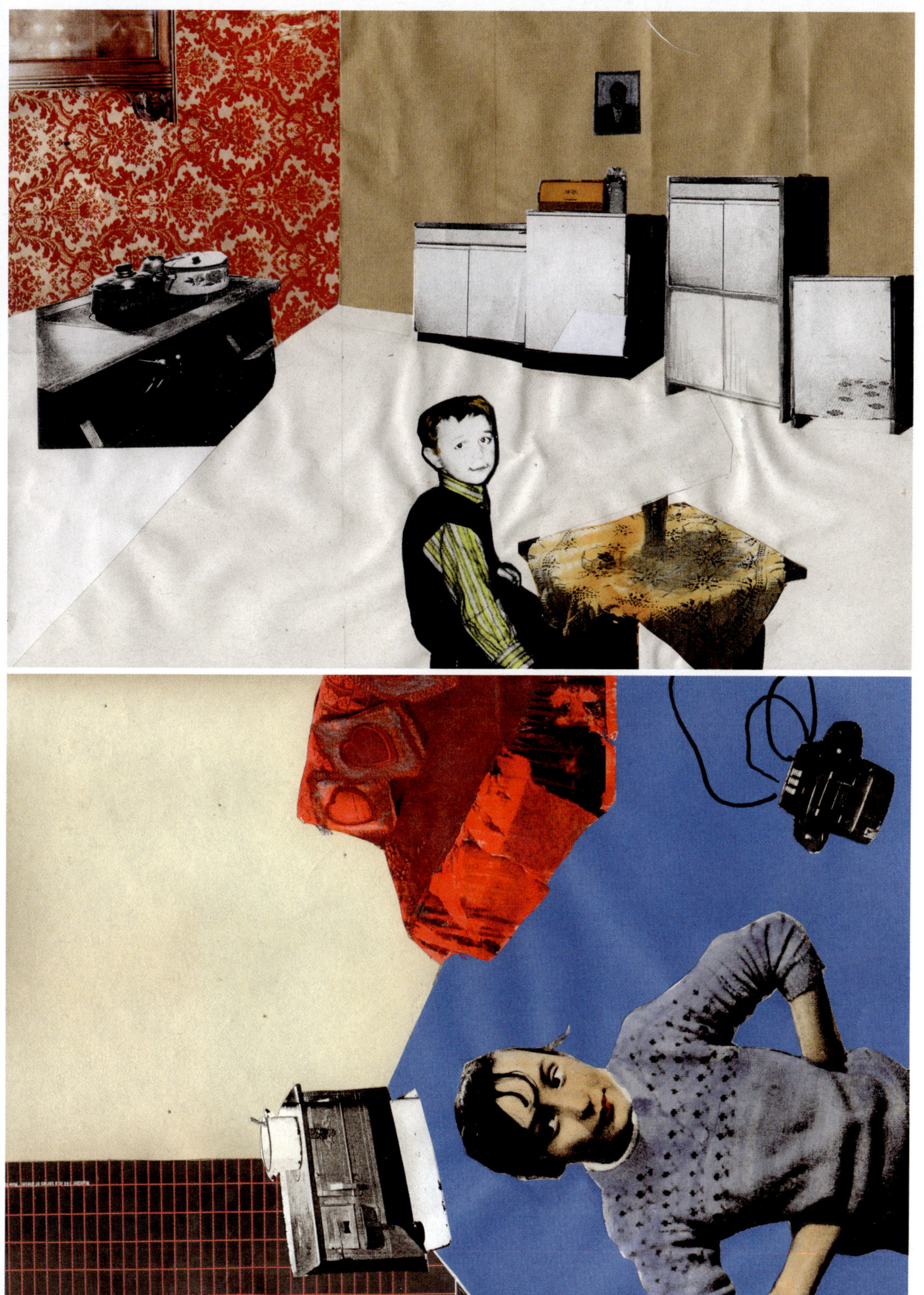

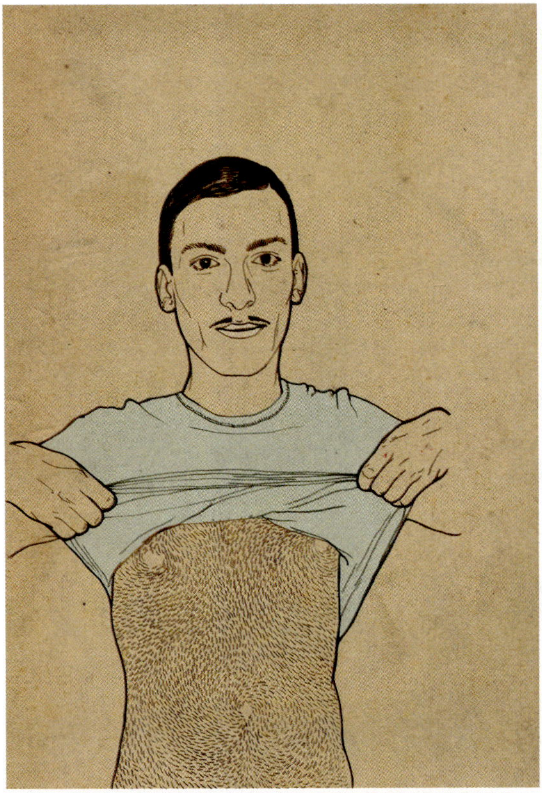

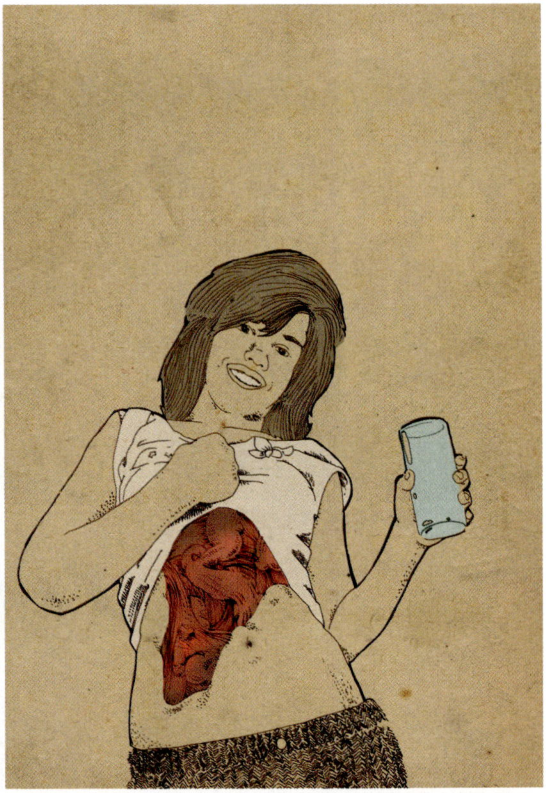

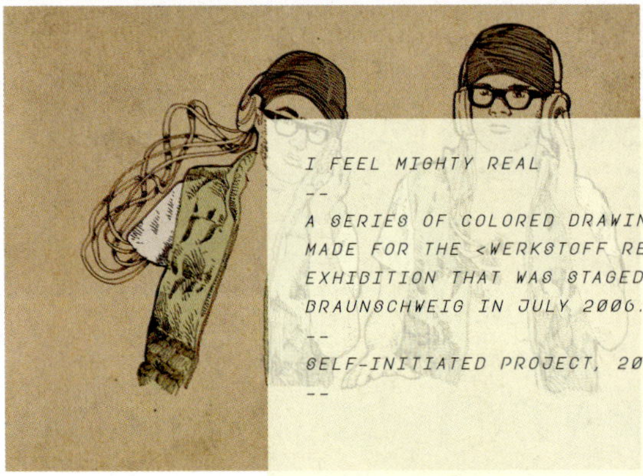

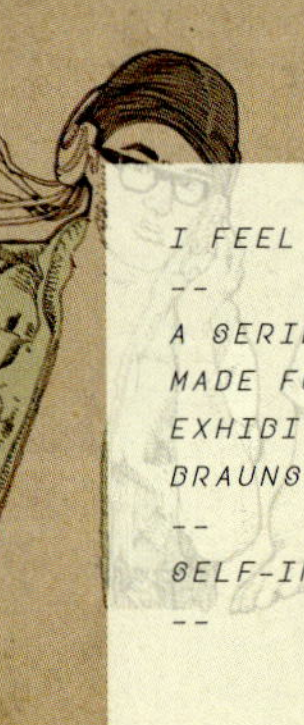

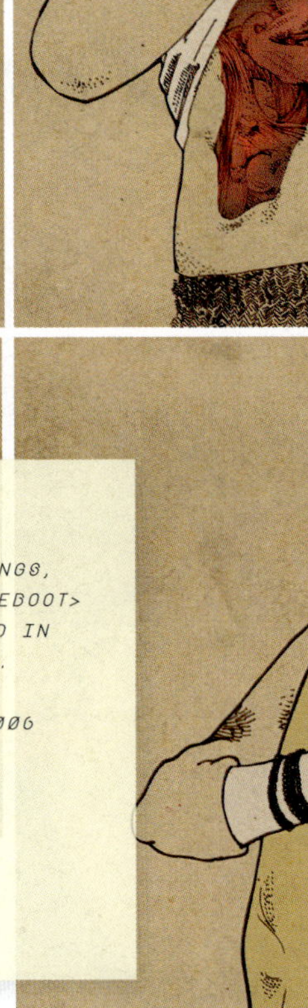

I FEEL MIGHTY REAL
--
A SERIES OF COLORED DRAWINGS,
MADE FOR THE <WERKSTOFF REBOOT>
EXHIBITION THAT WAS STAGED IN
BRAUNSCHWEIG IN JULY 2006.
--
SELF-INITIATED PROJECT, 2006
--

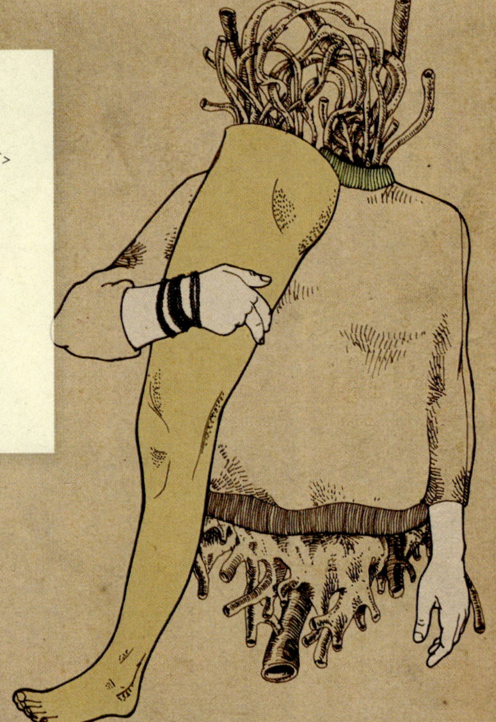

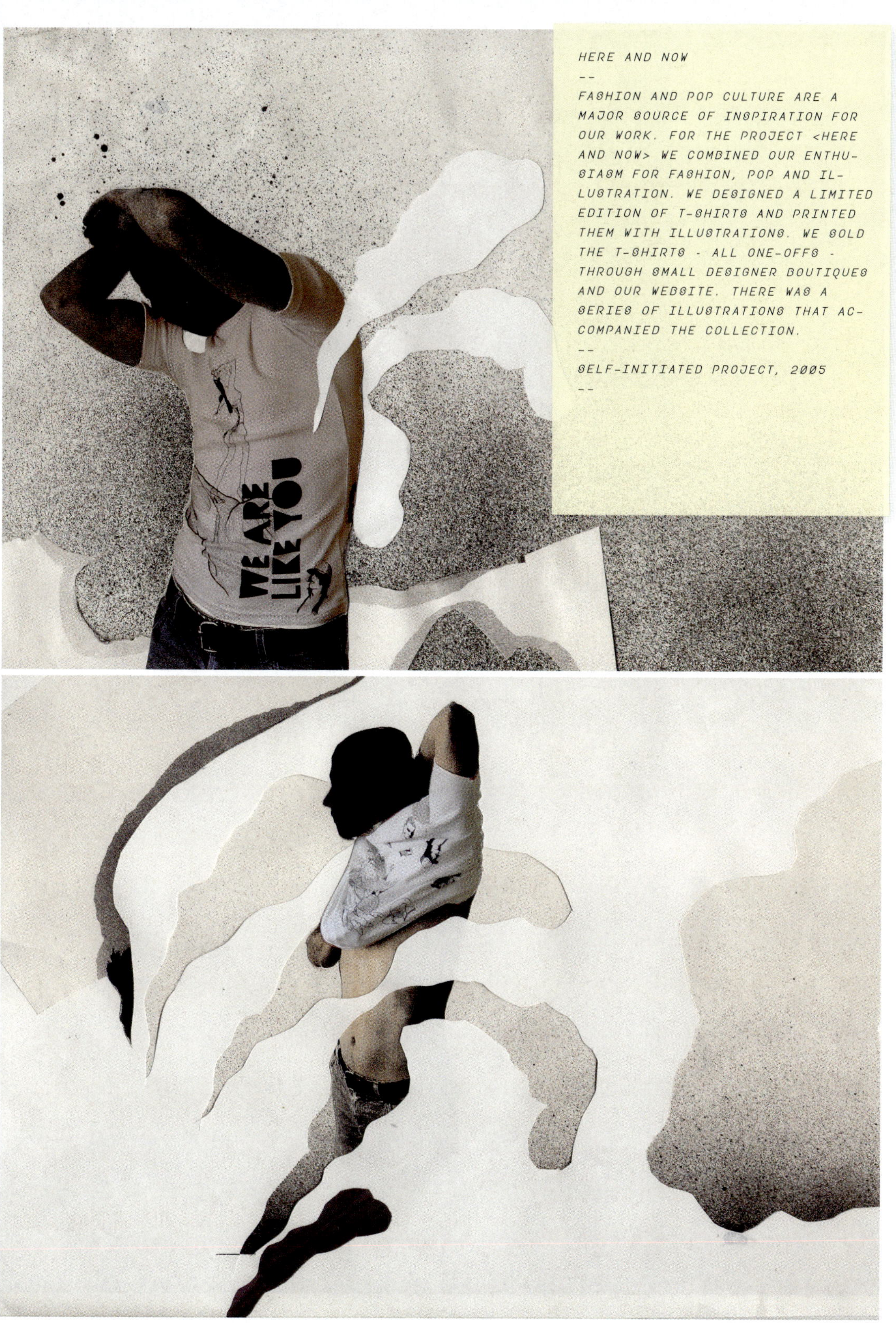

HERE AND NOW
--
FASHION AND POP CULTURE ARE A
MAJOR SOURCE OF INSPIRATION FOR
OUR WORK. FOR THE PROJECT <HERE
AND NOW> WE COMBINED OUR ENTHU-
SIASM FOR FASHION, POP AND IL-
LUSTRATION. WE DESIGNED A LIMITED
EDITION OF T-SHIRTS AND PRINTED
THEM WITH ILLUSTRATIONS. WE SOLD
THE T-SHIRTS - ALL ONE-OFFS -
THROUGH SMALL DESIGNER BOUTIQUES
AND OUR WEBSITE. THERE WAS A
SERIES OF ILLUSTRATIONS THAT AC-
COMPANIED THE COLLECTION.
--
SELF-INITIATED PROJECT, 2005
--
WE ARE LIKE YOU

TIMO BOESE IS A GERMAN DESIGNER
FOCUSING ON MOTION GRAPHICS AND
ILLUSTRATION. FROM A BACKGROUND
OF TRADITIONAL EDUCATION SUCH AS
DRAWING AND PAINTING HE BEGAN
WORKING AS A MOTION DESIGNER AND
ANIMATOR WHILE HE WAS STILL STUDY-
ING GRAPHIC DESIGN. HE RECEIVED
A UNIVERSITY DEGREE IN 2004. HE
HAS WORKED FOR NUMEROUS TOP BRAND
CLIENTS (E.G. BACARDI, DAIMLER
CHRYSLER JEEP, FIFA, JACK DANIELS,
LEXUS, L'OREAL, NIVEA, PANASONIC,
TOYOTA, TWENTIETH CENTURY FOX)
AND FOR AGENCIES WORLDWIDE; HIS
WORKS HAVE BEEN SHOWN AT FESTIVALS
AND EXHIBITIONS AROUND THE GLOBE.
STATIC WORKS HAVE BEEN FEATURED IN
INTERNATIONAL MAGAZINES AND DE-
SIGN BOOKS. RIGHT NOW HE IS BASED
IN HAMBURG, GERMANY, WHERE HE IS
WORKING AS AN ART DIRECTOR.

--

WHAT IS GERMAN?

PROFESSIONALISM, PERFECTIONISM,
PRAGMATISM, PRECESSION AND PATHO-
GENESIS.

WHAT IS GERMAN DESIGN?

GRAY.

PLEASE DESCRIBE YOUR WORKING
PROCESS.

GERMAN.

WHAT DO YOU AIM TO ACHIEVE WITH
YOUR WORK?

FREEDOM & DEVASTATION

YOU'VE INVITED A FRIEND TO
GERMANY; NAME ONE PLACE THEY
REALLY MUST VISIT AND A QUINT-
ESSENTIAL EXPERIENCE YOU REC-
OMMEND.

HE SHOULD SPEND SOME TIME GET-
TING DRUNK IN BERLIN AND GO SKIING
IN THE ALPS.

WHAT IS THE MOST IMPORTANT
LESSON YOU HAVE LEARNED IN YOUR
PROFESSION SO FAR?

SHORT CUTS

--

LOWERGROUND

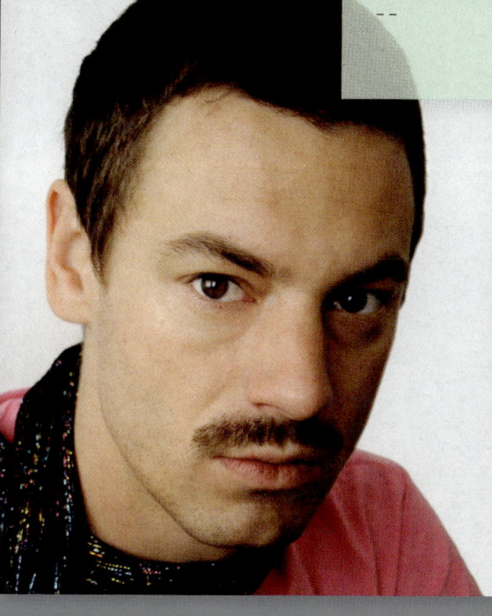

LOWERGROUND
TIMO BOESE

--

EIMSBÜTTELER STRASSE 47A
22769 HAMBURG
GERMANY

--

T +49 40 23558450
M +49 176 21527862

--

BOESE@LOWERGROUND.COM
WWW.LOWERGROUND.COM

--

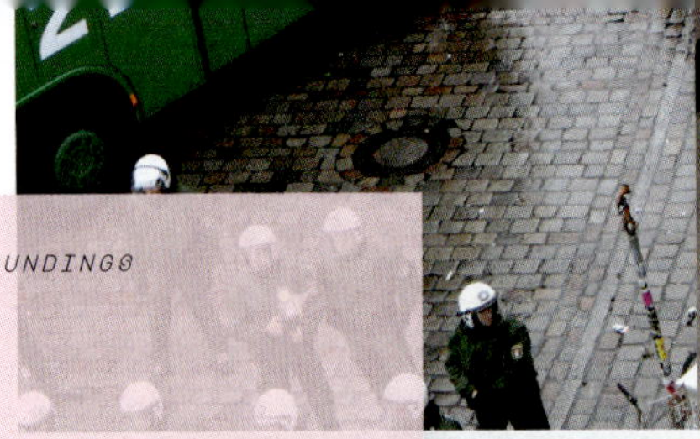

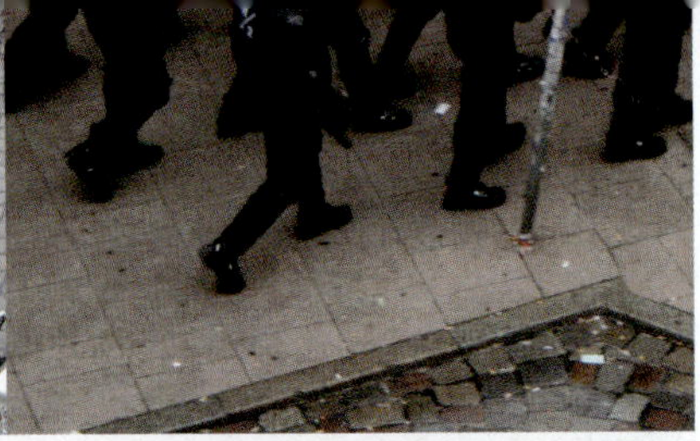

STUDIO SURROUNDINGS
--

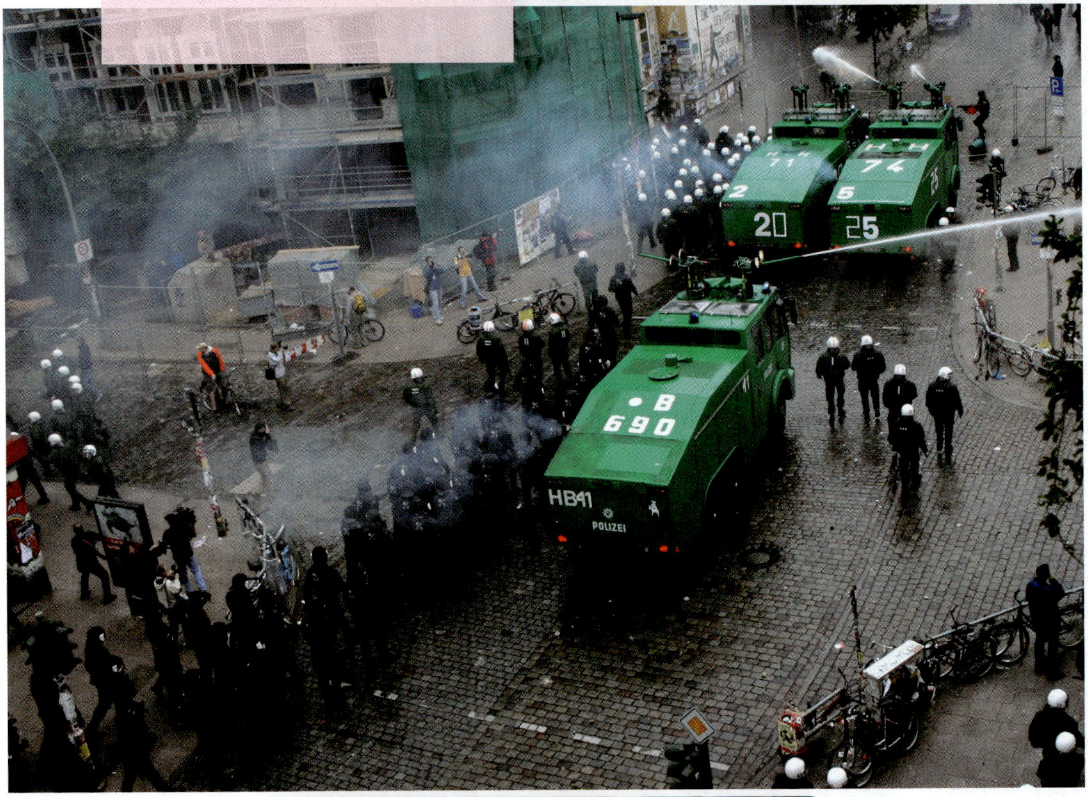

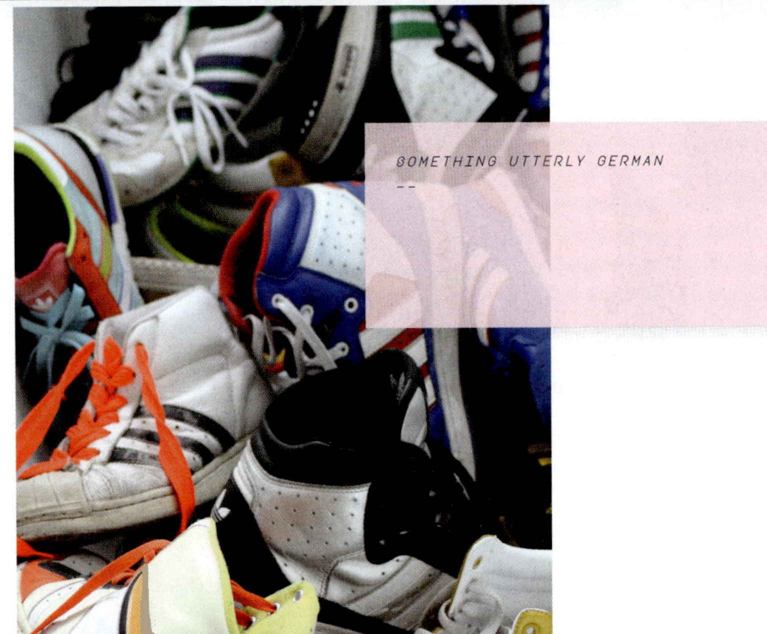

SOMETHING UTTERLY GERMAN
--

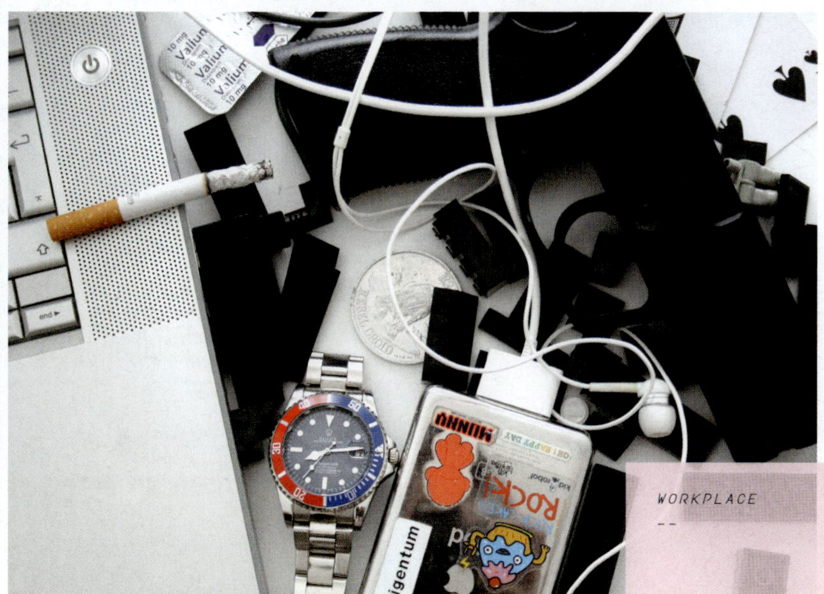

WORKPLACE
--

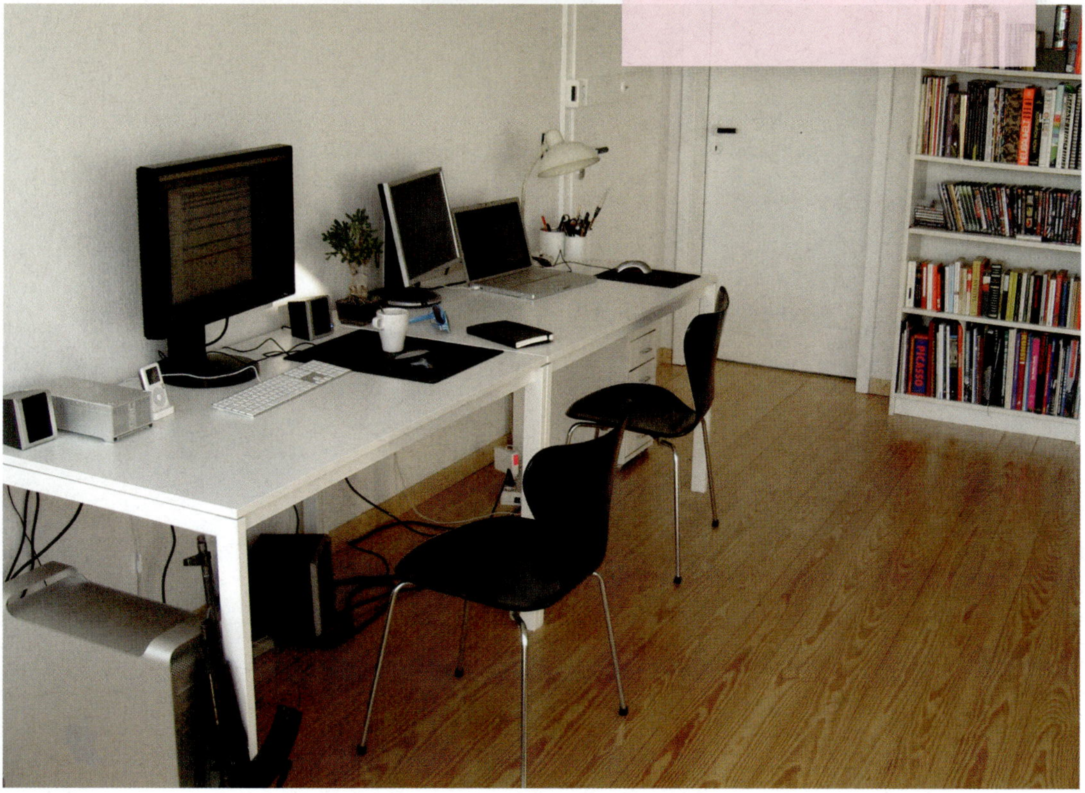

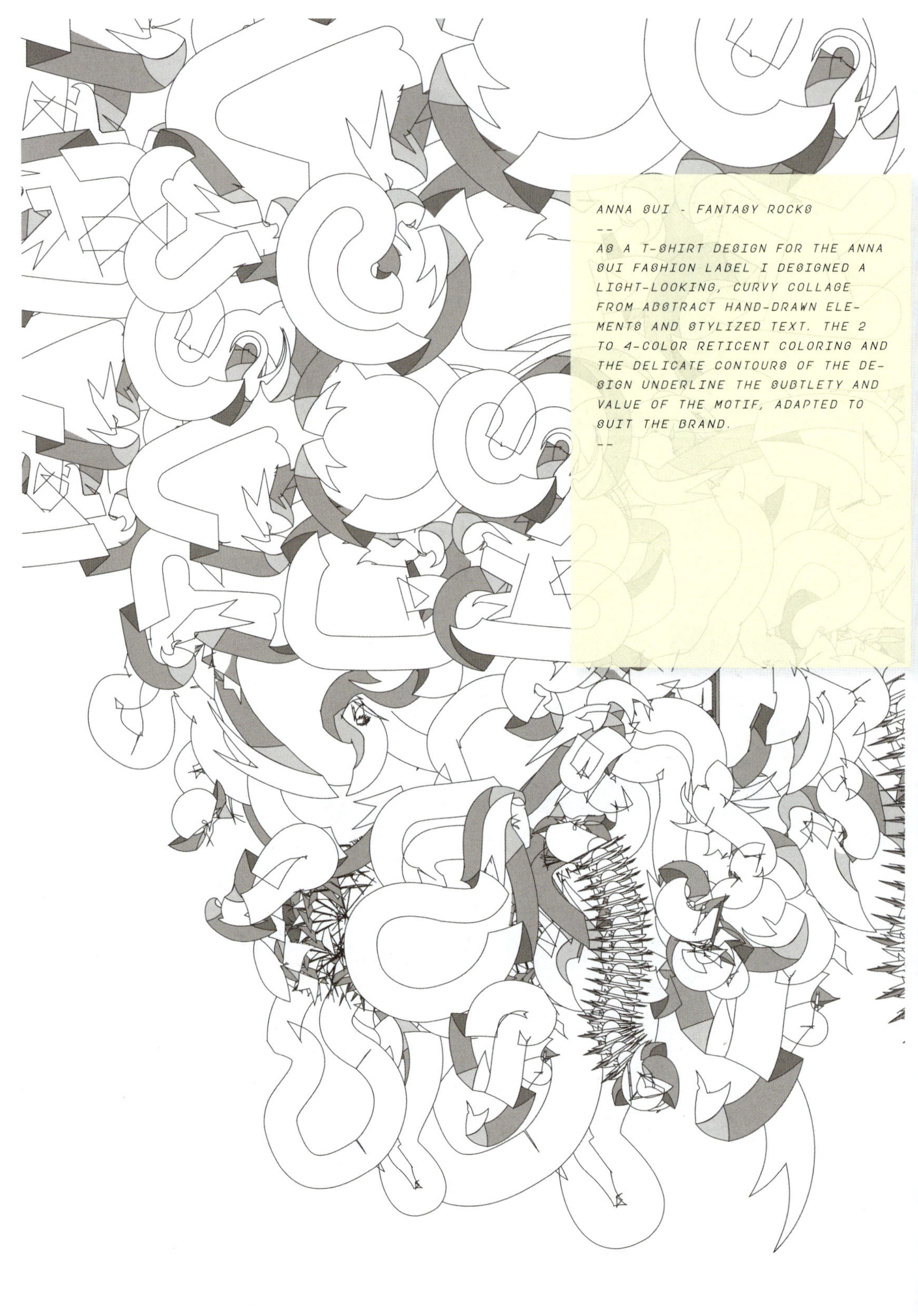
ANNA SUI - FANTASY ROCKS
--
AS A T-SHIRT DESIGN FOR THE ANNA
SUI FASHION LABEL I DESIGNED A
LIGHT-LOOKING, CURVY COLLAGE
FROM ABSTRACT HAND-DRAWN ELE-
MENTS AND STYLIZED TEXT. THE 2
TO 4-COLOR RETICENT COLORING AND
THE DELICATE CONTOURS OF THE DE-
SIGN UNDERLINE THE SUBTLETY AND
VALUE OF THE MOTIF, ADAPTED TO
SUIT THE BRAND.
--

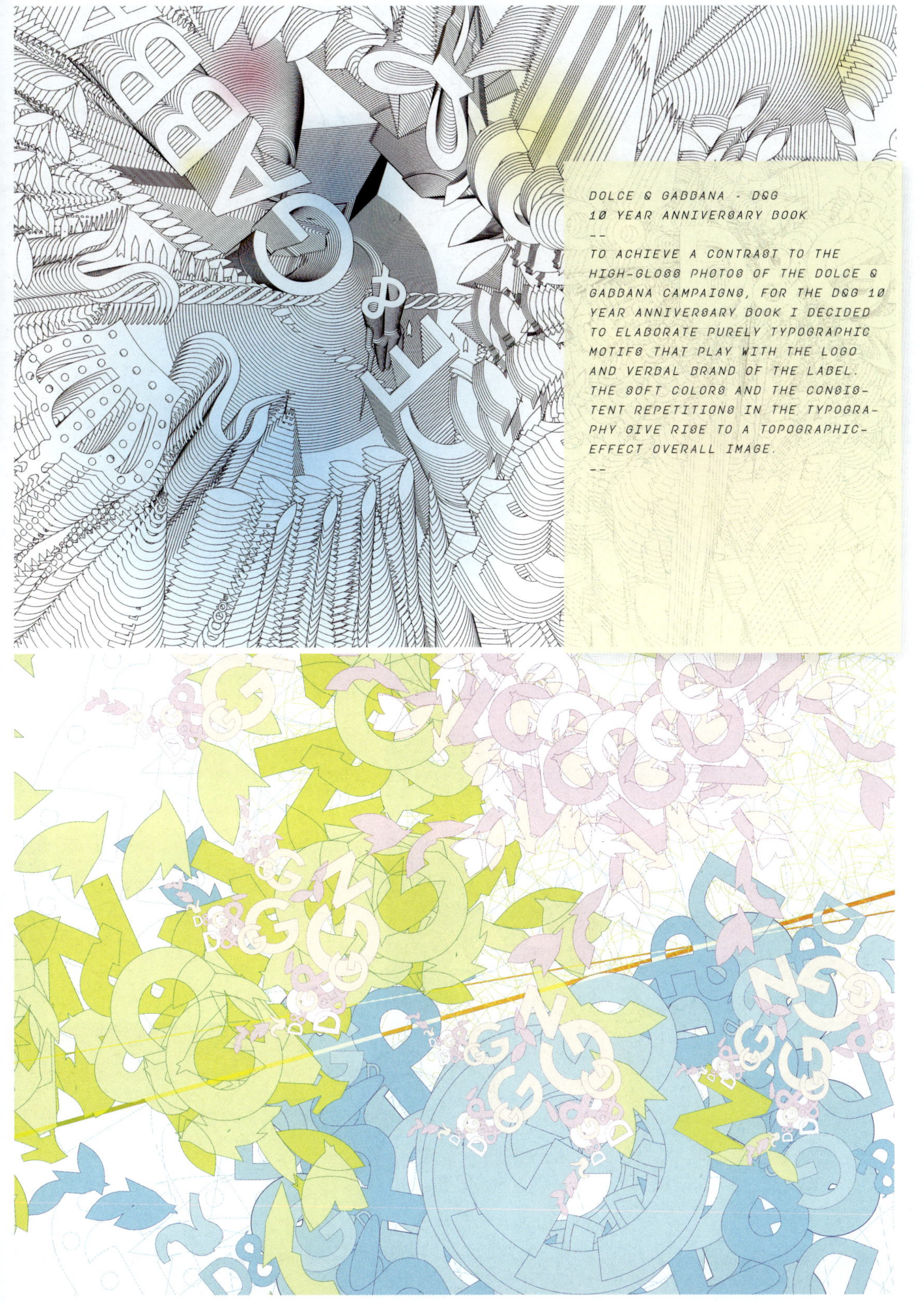

DOLCE & GABBANA - D&G
10 YEAR ANNIVERSARY BOOK
--
TO ACHIEVE A CONTRAST TO THE
HIGH-GLOSS PHOTOS OF THE DOLCE &
GABBANA CAMPAIGNS, FOR THE D&G 10
YEAR ANNIVERSARY BOOK I DECIDED
TO ELABORATE PURELY TYPOGRAPHIC
MOTIFS THAT PLAY WITH THE LOGO
AND VERBAL BRAND OF THE LABEL.
THE SOFT COLORS AND THE CONSIS-
TENT REPETITIONS IN THE TYPOGRA-
PHY GIVE RISE TO A TOPOGRAPHIC-
EFFECT OVERALL IMAGE.
--

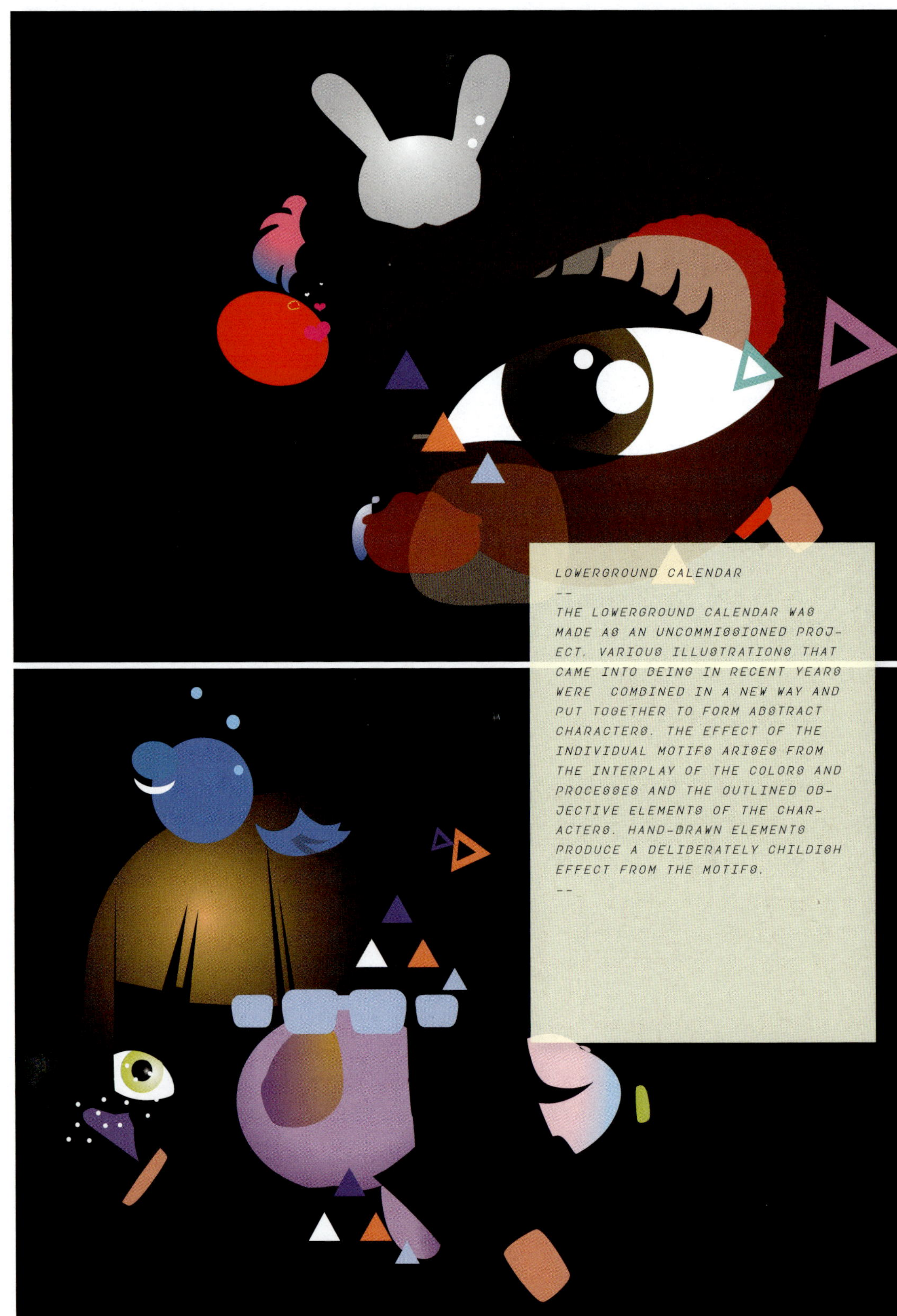

LOWERGROUND CALENDAR
--
THE LOWERGROUND CALENDAR WAS
MADE AS AN UNCOMMISSIONED PROJ-
ECT. VARIOUS ILLUSTRATIONS THAT
CAME INTO BEING IN RECENT YEARS
WERE COMBINED IN A NEW WAY AND
PUT TOGETHER TO FORM ABSTRACT
CHARACTERS. THE EFFECT OF THE
INDIVIDUAL MOTIFS ARISES FROM
THE INTERPLAY OF THE COLORS AND
PROCESSES AND THE OUTLINED OB-
JECTIVE ELEMENTS OF THE CHAR-
ACTERS. HAND-DRAWN ELEMENTS
PRODUCE A DELIBERATELY CHILDISH
EFFECT FROM THE MOTIFS.
--

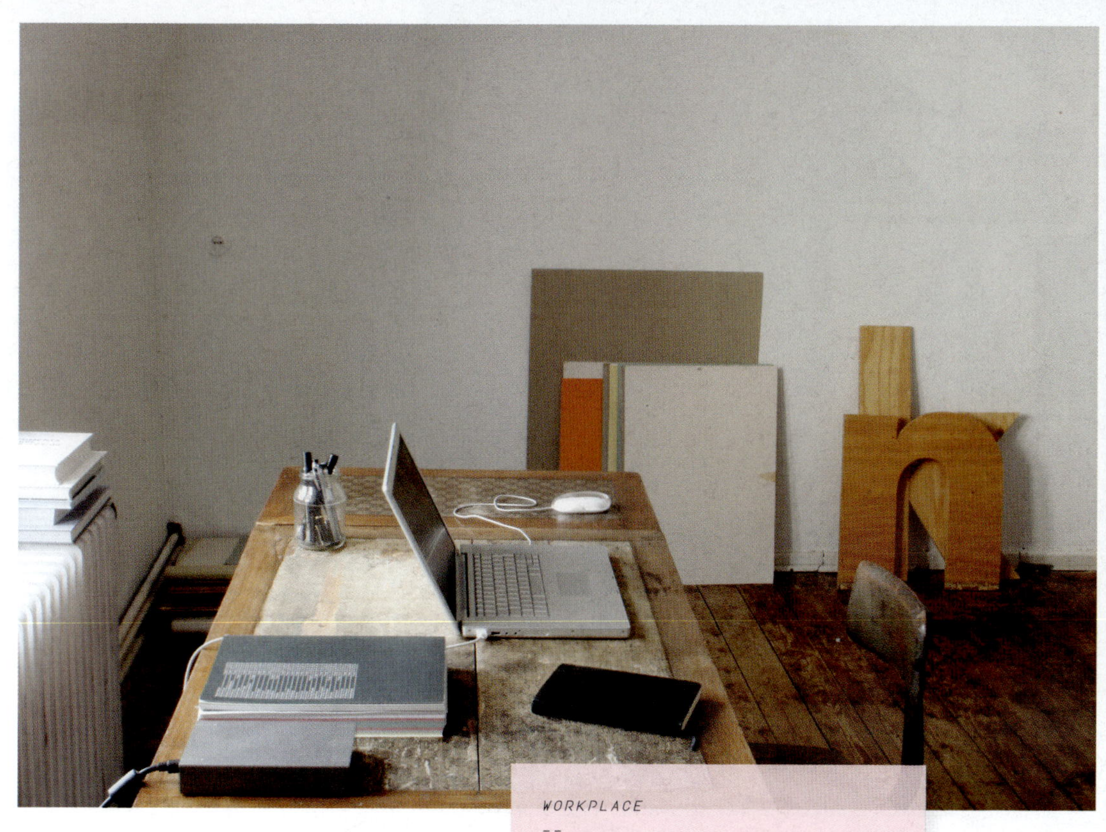
WORKPLACE
--

HEINZ

CHRISTIAN HEINZ
--
HOFFMANNSTRASSE 1
28201 BREMEN
GERMANY
--
T +49 421 53798924
M +49 177 6034723
--
C.HEINZ@HFK-BREMEN.DE
--

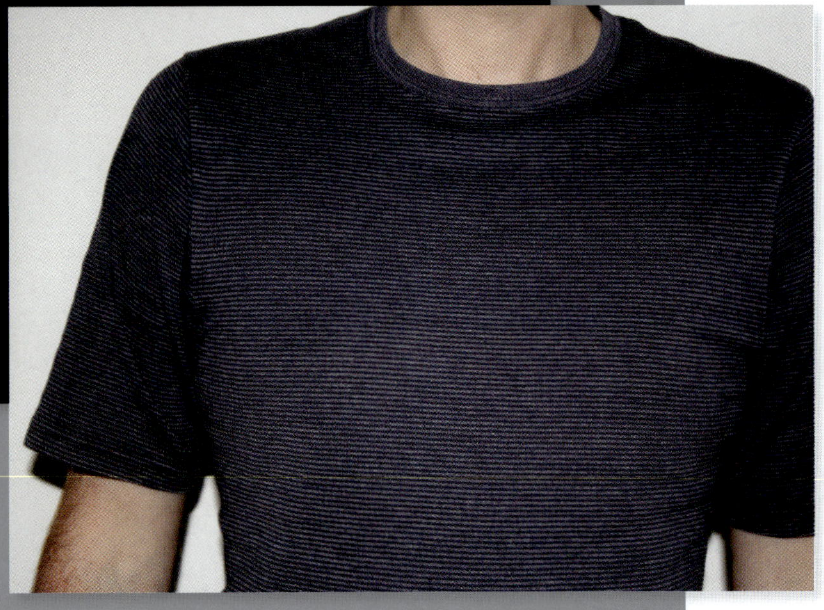

I'M FASCINATED BY CLASSIFICATION
SYSTEMS. THE HIERARCHIZATION OF
EVERYDAY OBJECTS. HOW THINGS STAND
IN SPACE IN RELATION TO ONE ANOTH-
ER. WHAT POSSIBILITIES THERE ARE
FOR LINKING THEM. THROUGH CLASSI-
FICATION NEW SPATIAL IMAGES ARISE
OVER AND OVER AGAIN. CLASSIFICA-
TION SHARPENS MY EYES, IT INFLU-
ENCES MY DESIGN.

--

WHAT IS GERMAN?

TO BE ABLE TO ANSWER THAT QUES-
TION YOU SHOULD LEAVE THE COUNTRY.
AFTER A 5-WEEK STAY IN CAIRO I'D
SAY: SILENCE, AIR, FOREST. OR WAIT-
ING AT 3 A.M. FOR THE PEDESTRIAN
CROSSING LIGHT TO TURN GREEN.

WHAT IS GERMAN DESIGN?

THE BAUHAUS AND THE ULM HOCH-
SCHULE WERE INSTITUTIONS THAT MADE
A LASTING IMPRESSION ON DESIGN IN
GERMANY. THEY GAVE GERMAN DESIGN
A PROFILE EVEN INTERNATIONALLY.
THEY'RE STILL REFERENCE POINTS FOR
US TODAY. HOWEVER, IF YOU LOOK BE-
YOND NATIONAL BOUNDARIES, THE DIF-
FERENT CONCEPTIONS OF DESIGN FROM
VARIOUS COUNTRIES INFLUENCE DESIGN
DEVELOPED IN GERMANY. FOR ME GER-
MAN DESIGN TODAY IS ABOVE ALL A
TANGLE OF REGIONAL, NATIONAL AND
INTERNATIONAL THOUGHT PROCESSES.

PLEASE DESCRIBE YOUR WORKING
PROCESS.

OPENING UP SPACES FOR IDEAS, EN-
TERING THEM AND THEN CLASSIFYING
AND DESIGNING. DON'T THROW AWAY
WHAT FALLS OFF AT THE MARGINS OF
THE WORKING PROCESS.

WHAT DO YOU AIM TO ACHIEVE WITH
YOUR WORK?

OPENING UP SPACES FOR THOUGHT.
SHOWING PERSPECTIVES. PROMOTING
DIALOGUE.

YOU'VE INVITED A FRIEND TO
GERMANY; NAME ONE PLACE THEY
REALLY MUST VISIT AND A QUINT-
ESSENTIAL EXPERIENCE YOU REC-
OMMEND.

THE TRANSOCEANIC CITY OF BREMEN
/ SCHWINDENDE ORTE / 53° 06'01.28'
N / 8° 45'48.24' E

WHAT IS THE MOST IMPORTANT
LESSON YOU HAVE LEARNED IN YOUR
PROFESSION SO FAR?

DESIGN PROCESSES ARE COMMUNICA-
TION PROCESSES. DESIGN INTERVENES
INTO OUR SOCIAL-CULTURAL STRUC-
TURE, SPECIFIES PATHS, MAPS OUT
SIGHT LINES, PRODUCES MEANINGS,
AND STRUCTURES AND SHAPES OUR EN-
VIRONMENT - AND US IN IT.

--

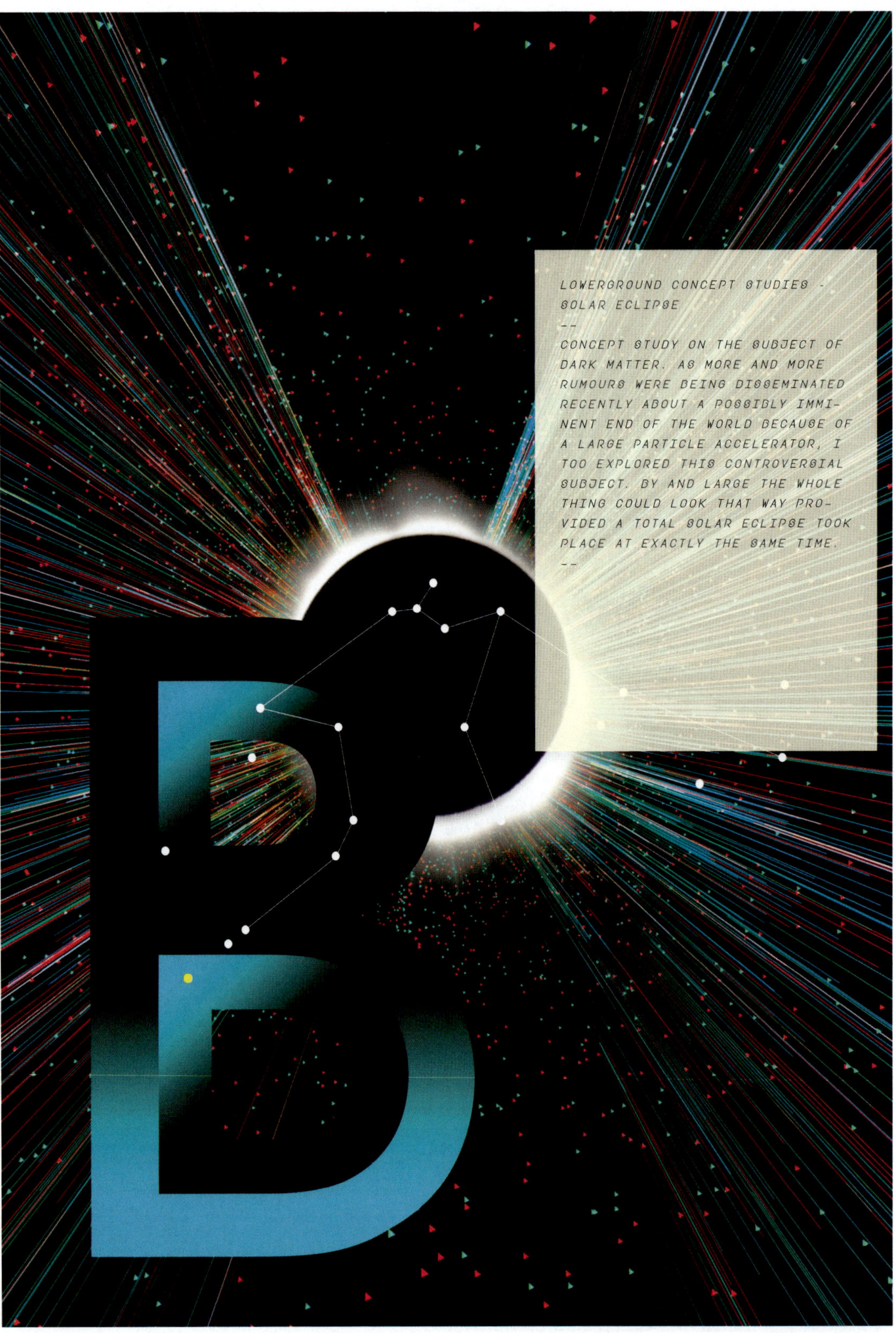

LOWERGROUND CONCEPT STUDIES -
SOLAR ECLIPSE
--
CONCEPT STUDY ON THE SUBJECT OF
DARK MATTER. AS MORE AND MORE
RUMOURS WERE BEING DISSEMINATED
RECENTLY ABOUT A POSSIBLY IMMI-
NENT END OF THE WORLD BECAUSE OF
A LARGE PARTICLE ACCELERATOR, I
TOO EXPLORED THIS CONTROVERSIAL
SUBJECT. BY AND LARGE THE WHOLE
THING COULD LOOK THAT WAY PRO-
VIDED A TOTAL SOLAR ECLIPSE TOOK
PLACE AT EXACTLY THE SAME TIME.
--

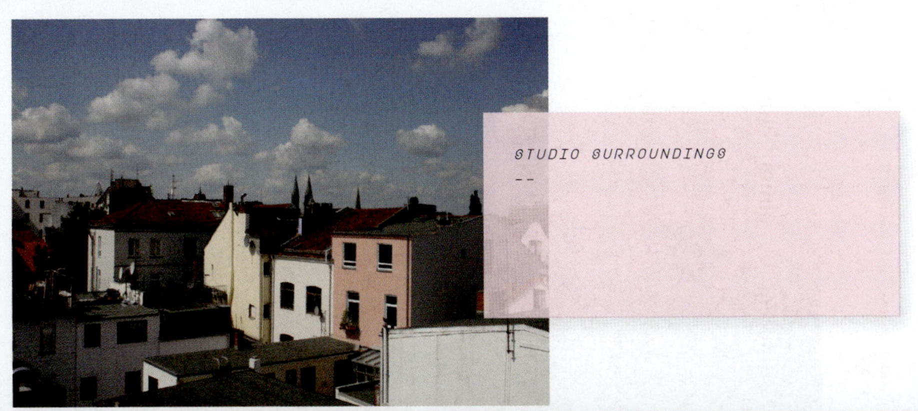

STUDIO SURROUNDINGS
--

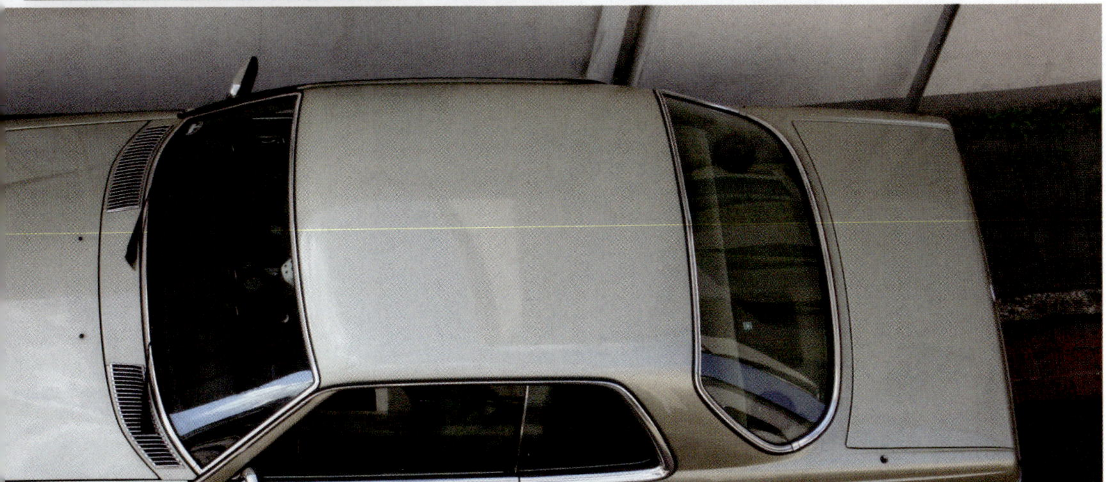

SOMETHING UTTERLY GERMAN
--

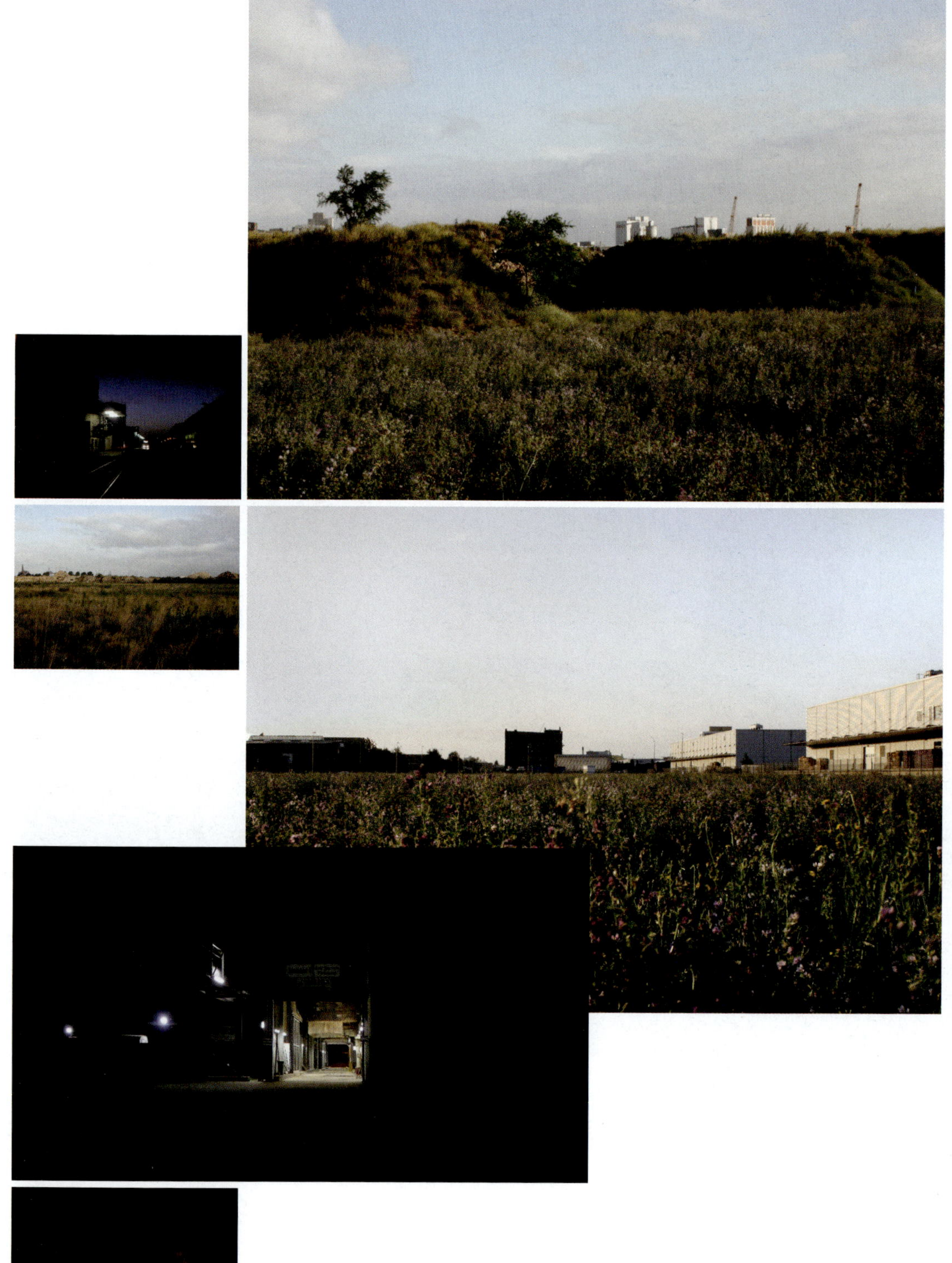

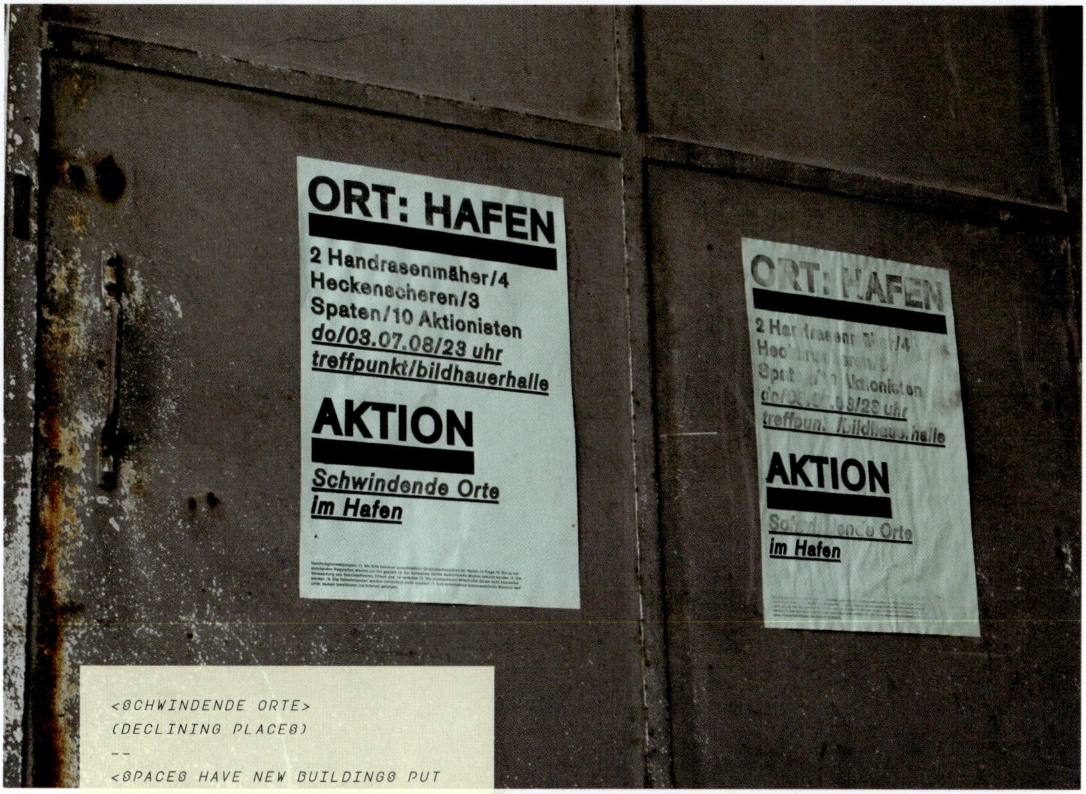

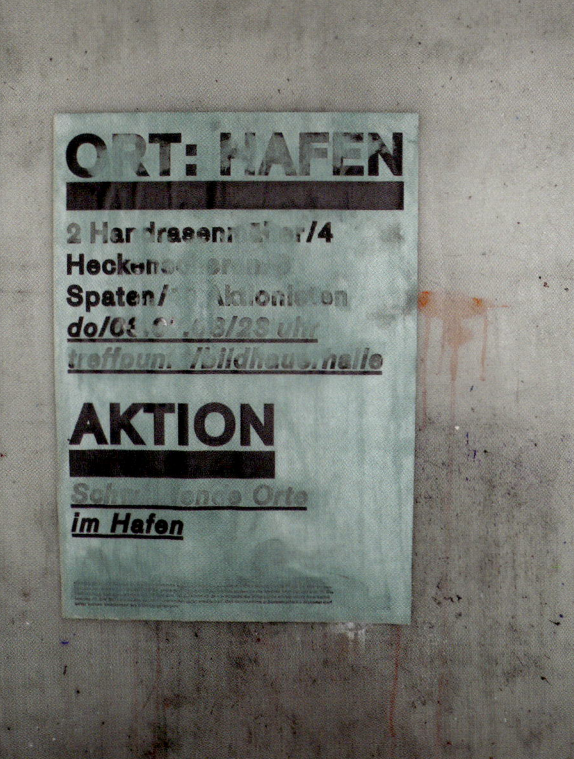

<SCHWINDENDE ORTE>
(DECLINING PLACES)
--
<SPACES HAVE NEW BUILDINGS PUT
ON THEM, THEY ARE PHANTASIZED,
TRODDEN ON, THEY COLLABORATE,
EXTEND, ARE SHIFTED, DESTROYED OR
REDEVELOPED […]> (I. NIERHAUS).
THE PROJECT <SCHWINDENDE ORTE>
CALLS FOR DERELICT OPEN SPACES IN
THE HARBOR TO BE USED AS SPACES
FOR CULTURAL ACTION. SEEMINGLY
FORGOTTEN MEANINGLESS PLACES ARE
DISCOVERED AND DESCRIBED ANEW.
THE FLEETING NATURE OF THE AC-
TION IS LINKED TO THE DISAPPEAR-
ING TEXT ON THE POSTERS AND THE
WRITING THAT IS BLURRED BY THE
RAIN. WHAT REMAINS IS THE AP-
PEAL FOR THE NEXT INTERVENTION:
<AKTION IM HAFEN> (ACTION IN THE
HARBOR).
--
UNIVERSITY OF ARTS BREMEN, 2008
TUTOR: MARTIN LORENZ
--

ORT: HAFEN

2 Handrasenmäher/4 Heckenscheren/3 Spaten/10 Aktionisten
do/03.07.08/23 uhr
treffpunkt/bildhauerhalle

AKTION

Schwindende Orte
im Hafen

Handlungsanweisungen: /1. Als Orte kommen ausschließlich Originalschauplätze im »Hafen« in Frage /2. Die zu verwendenden Requisiten werden vor Ort gestellt /3. Zur Aufnahme dürfen audiovisuelle Medien benutzt werden /4. Die Verwendung von Spezialeffekten, Filtern usw. ist verboten /5. Die entstandenen Mitschnitte dürfen nicht bearbeitet werden /6. Die Teilnehmenden werden namentlich nicht erwähnt /7. Das entstandene dokumentarische Material darf unter keinen Umständen ins Internet gelangen.

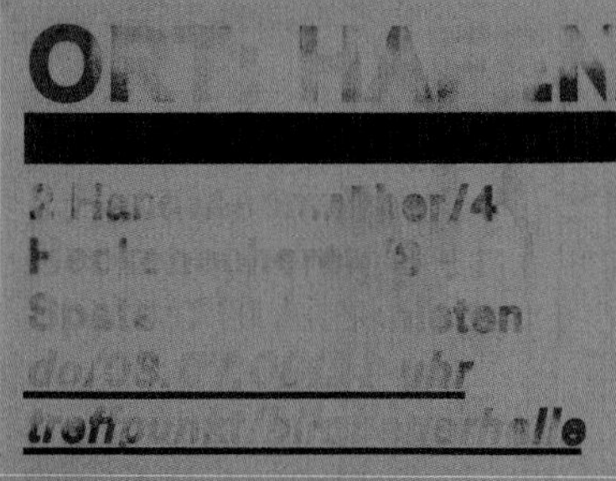

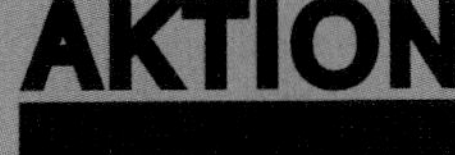

ORT: HAFEN

2 Handrasenmäher/4 Heckenscheren/3 Spaten/10 Aktionisten
do/03.07.08/23 uhr
treffpunkt/bildhauerhalle

AKTION

Schwindende Orte
im Hafen

Handlungsanweisungen: /1. Als Orte kommen ausschließlich Originalschauplätze im »Hafen« in Frage /2. Die zu verwendenden Requisiten werden vor Ort gestellt /3. Zur Aufnahme dürfen audiovisuelle Medien benutzt werden /4. Die Verwendung von Spezialeffekten, Filtern usw. ist verboten /5. Die entstandenen Mitschnitte dürfen nicht bearbeitet werden /6. Die Teilnehmenden werden namentlich nicht erwähnt /7. Das entstandene dokumentarische Material darf unter keinen Umständen ins Internet gelangen.

ORT: HAFEN

2 Handrasenmäher/4 Heckenscheren/3 Spaten/10 Aktionisten
do/03.07.08/23 uhr
treffpunkt/bildhauerhalle

AKTION

Schwindende Orte
im Hafen

Handlungsanweisungen: /1. Als Orte kommen ausschließlich Originalschauplätze im »Hafen« in Frage /2. Die zu verwendenden Requisiten werden vor Ort gestellt /3. Zur Aufnahme dürfen audiovisuelle Medien benutzt werden /4. Die Verwendung von Spezialeffekten, Filtern usw. ist verboten /5. Die entstandenen Mitschnitte dürfen nicht bearbeitet werden /6. Die Teilnehmenden werden namentlich nicht erwähnt /7. Das entstandene dokumentarische Material darf unter keinen Umständen ins Internet gelangen.

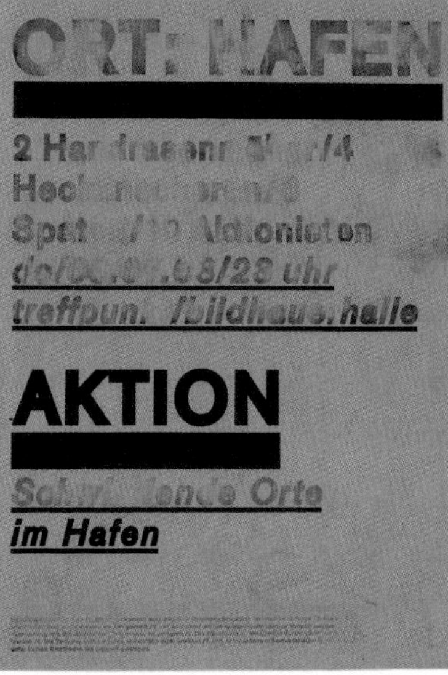

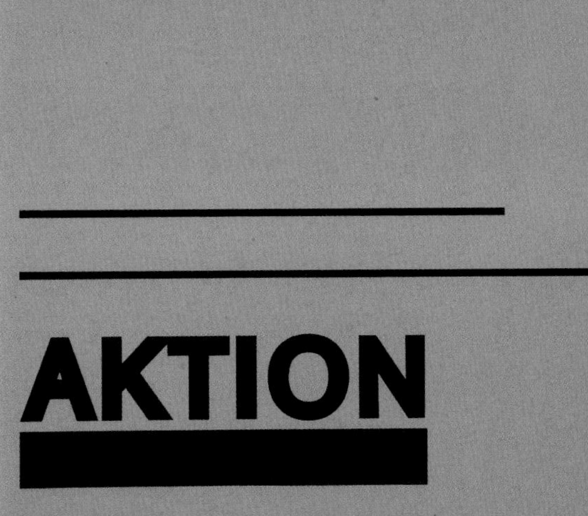

KATRIN SCHACKE, BORN IN ERFURT
IN 1982, STUDIED COMMUNICATION
DESIGN AT THE HOCHSCHULE FÜR
GESTALTUNG IN OFFENBACH AM MAIN
AND THE HOCHSCHULE FÜR KUNST UND
GESTALTUNG IN ZURICH. IN SPRING
2008 SHE TOOK HER DEGREE IN THE
FIELD OF VISUAL COMMUNICATION AT
THE HFG OFFENBACH. SHE WORKS IN
THE FIELDS OF EDITORIAL DESIGN AND
CORPORATE DESIGN, PHOTOGRAPHY AND
ILLUSTRATION FOR CLIENTS LIKE THE
ART DIRECTORS CLUB OF GERMANY, THE
CITY OF FRANKFURT AM MAIN OR THE
NIPPON CONNECTION FILM FESTIVAL.
HER WORKS HAVE ATTRACTED SEVERAL
AWARDS FROM NATIONAL AND INTERNA-
TIONAL DESIGN JURIES.

--

WHAT IS GERMAN?

FENCES.

WHAT IS GERMAN DESIGN?

VERNACULAR - SENSIBLE - SOME-
TIMES A BIT CHILLY.

PLEASE DESCRIBE YOUR WORKING
PROCESS.

1. DEFINING, ASSOCIATING,
   SEARCHING, ASKING
2. COLLECTING, CONNECTING,
   TALKING, TESTING
3. CHALLENGING, DOUBTING,
   REJECTING
4. REASSEMBLING, TRYING OUT,
   SEEING
5. IMPROVING, POSITIONING,
   FINE-TUNING, EXCHANGING
6. PHOTOGRAPHING, TYPESETTING,
   DOING CLEAN DRAWINGS

STEPS 1 TO 5 ARE REPEATED AS OF-
TEN AS WANTED (SEPARATELY FROM ONE
ANOTHER OR ALSO IN THIS SEQUENCE)
UNTIL THE DESIRED RESULT IS OB-
TAINED.

WHAT DO YOU AIM TO ACHIEVE WITH
YOUR WORK?

I'D LIKE TO CREATE ENTHUSIASM
FOR THEMES THAT APPEAR RATHER UN-
ATTRACTIVE BECAUSE OF LONG-WINDED
WORDING, CONFUSING COMPLEXITY OR
THE MATTER-OF-FACT PRESENTATION
OF FACTS. I TRY TO TEMPT PEOPLE
WITH PICTURES. FAMILIAR THINGS ARE
TAKEN OUT OF THEIR CONTEXT AND
PRESENTED FROM AN UNACCUSTOMED
ANGLE. FEELING PUZZLED MAKES PEO-
PLE CURIOUS AND HOPEFULLY ENCOUR-
AGES THEM TO LOOK MORE CLOSELY.
TO FACILITATE ACCESS TO COMPLEX
OR DRY FACTS AND CIRCUMSTANCES,
INFORMATION IS BEST PREPARED AS
VIVIDLY AND CLEARLY AS POSSIBLE.
IT'S IMPORTANT TO AVOID TEDIUM AND
GIVE GUIDANCE.

YOU'VE INVITED A FRIEND TO
GERMANY; NAME ONE PLACE THEY
REALLY MUST VISIT AND A QUINT-
ESSENTIAL EXPERIENCE YOU REC-
OMMEND.

CYCLE ALONG THE RIVER MAIN TO
THE FRANKFURT FLEA MARKET, POKE
AROUND THERE FOR SEVERAL HOURS
AND PURCHASE A PENDANT LIGHT,
RECORDS OR A FUR, AS YOU CHOOSE.
THEN GO TO THE KLEINMARKTHALLE
AND BUY GOODIES FROM FAR-OFF COUN-
TRIES AND EAT THEM AS YOU LIE LA-
ZILY IN THE SUNSHINE BY THE MAIN.
IN THE EVENING DRINK SWEETENED
ÄPPLER (TYPE OF CIDER), LISTEN TO
MUSIC AND ENJOY THE SUNSET AT THE
SCHWEDLER SEE. THEN GO DANCING.

WHAT IS THE MOST IMPORTANT
LESSON YOU HAVE LEARNED IN YOUR
PROFESSION SO FAR?

IT WON'T WORK IF YOU DON'T MAKE
DECISIONS.

--

SCH-ACKE

KATRIN SCHACKE
--
SENEFELDERSTRASSE 9
63069 OFFENBACH AM MAIN
GERMANY
--
T +49 69 83832755
M +49 1577 1827974

HALLO@KATRINSCHACKE.DE
WWW.KATRINSCHACKE.DE
--

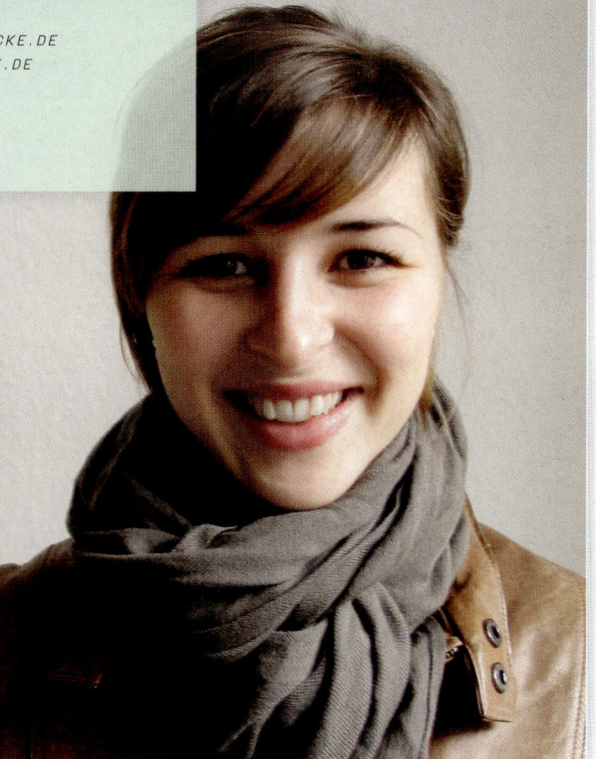

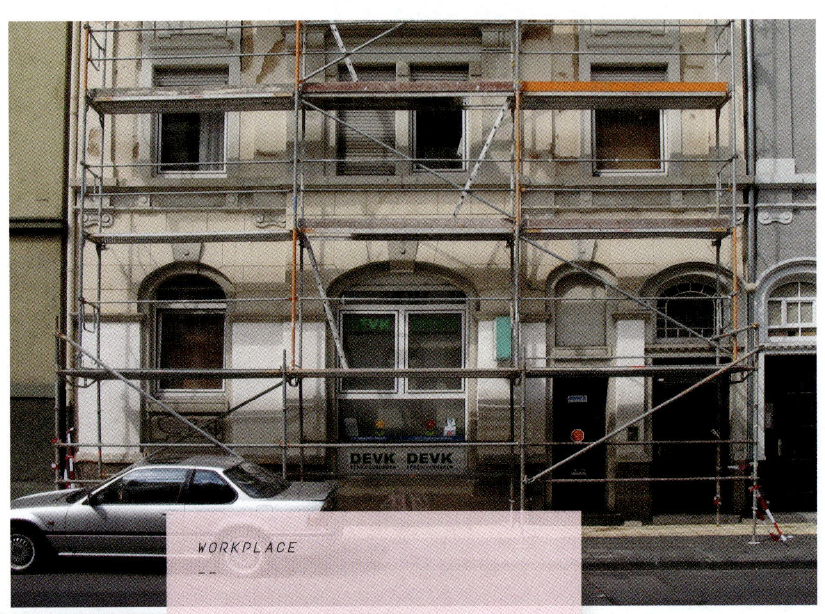

WORKPLACE
--

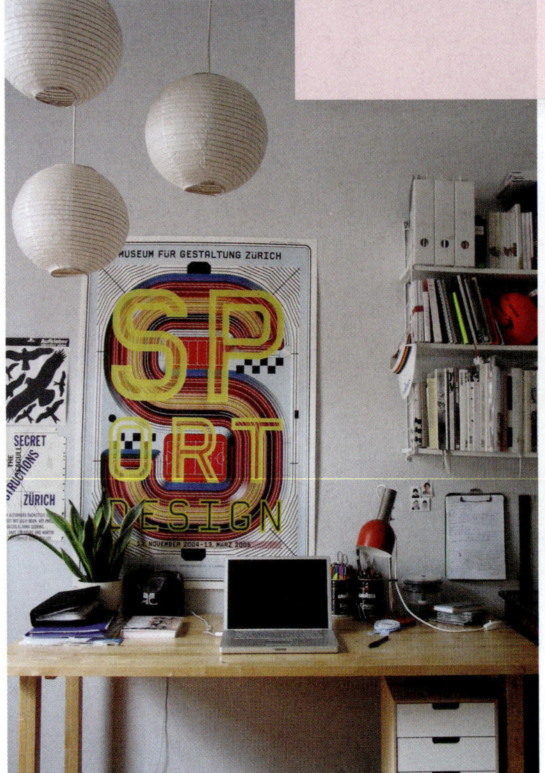

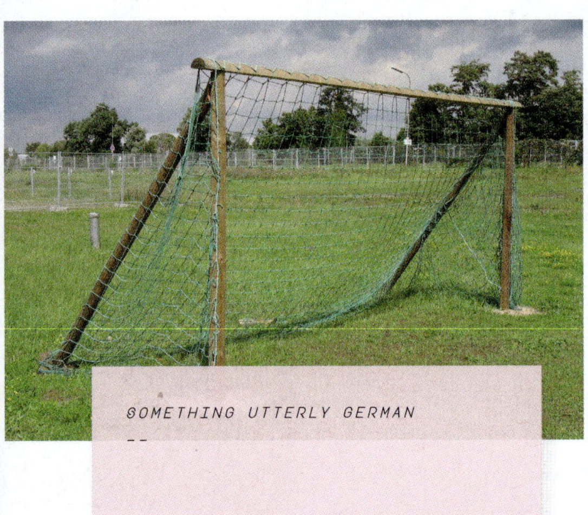

SOMETHING UTTERLY GERMAN
--

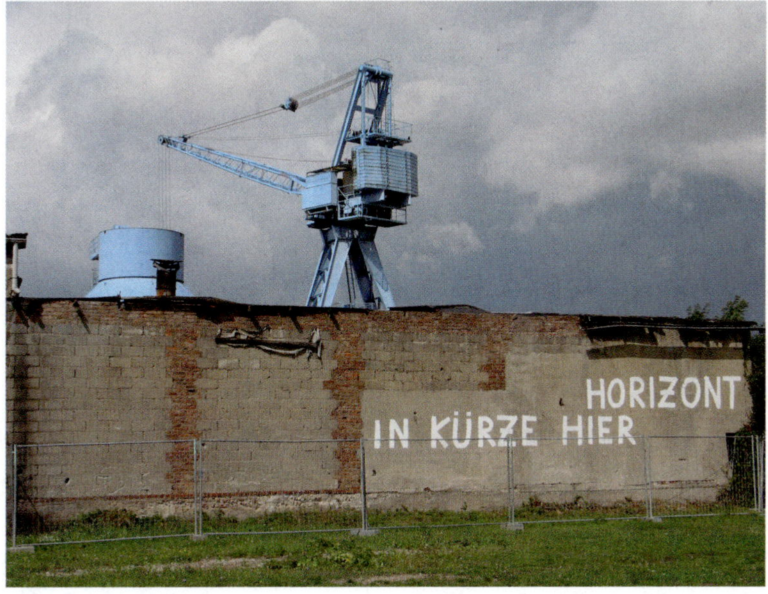
HORIZONT
IN KÜRZE HIER

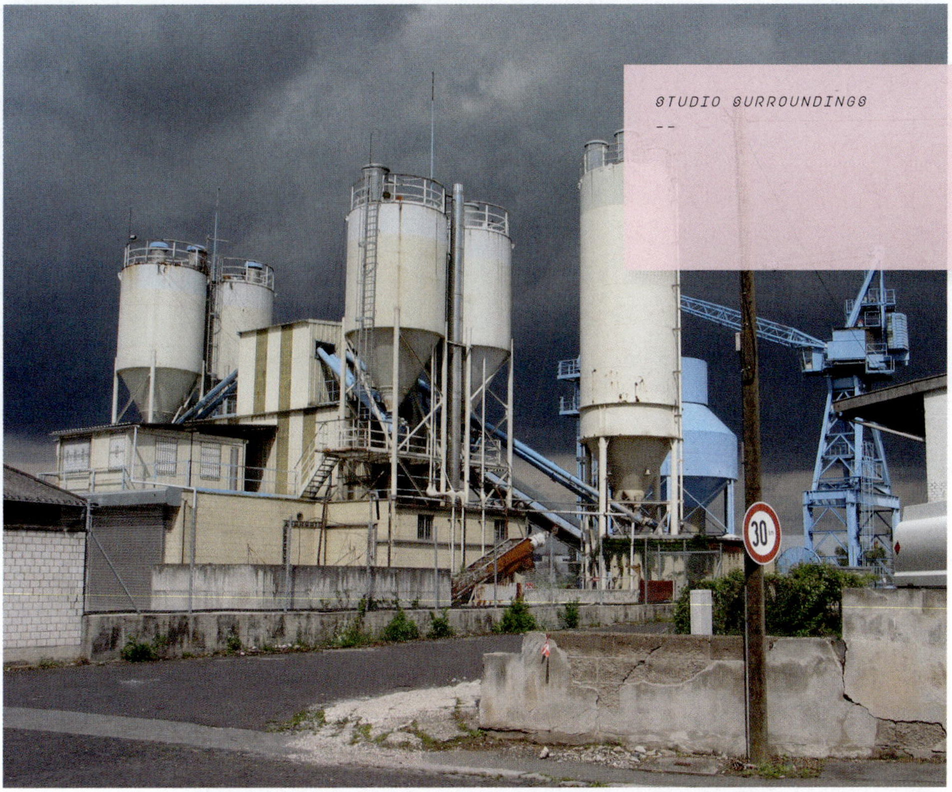

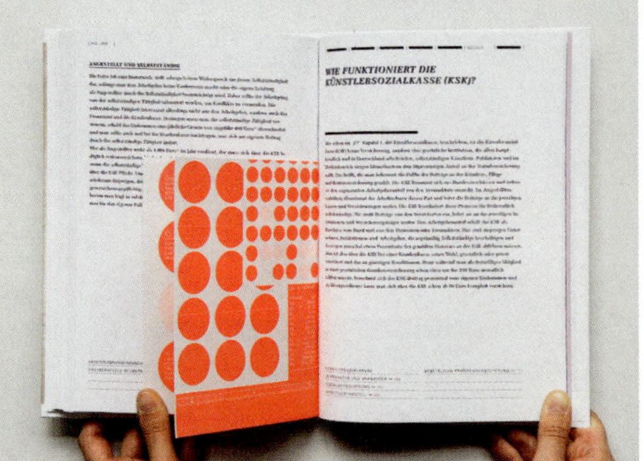
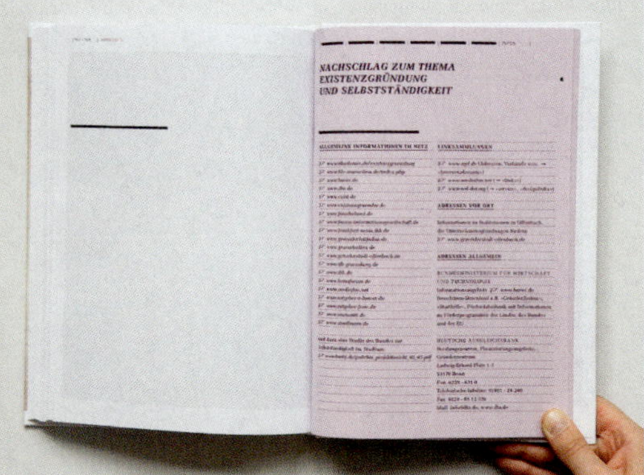
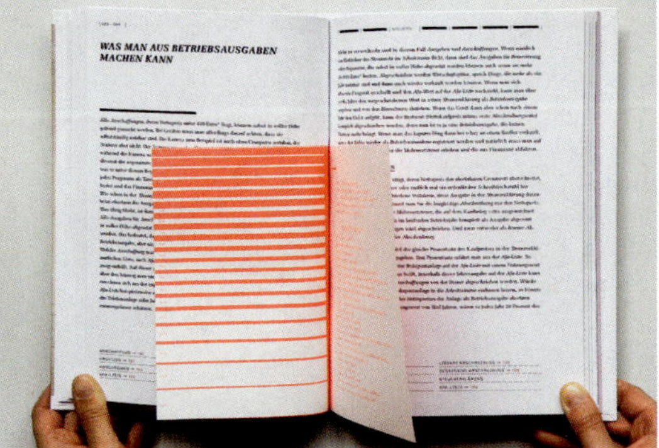
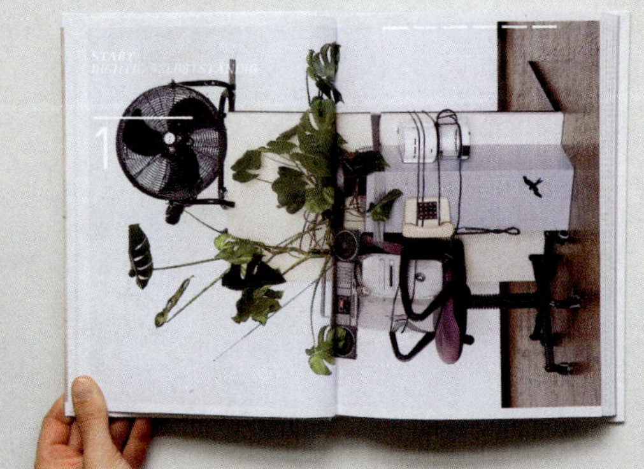
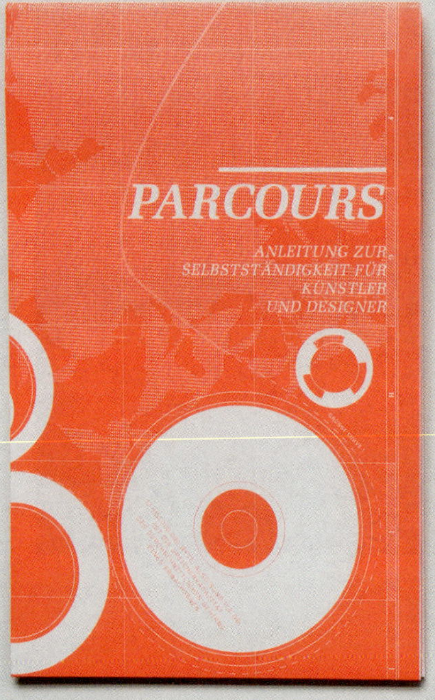
PARCOURS
ANLEITUNG ZUR
SELBSTSTÄNDIGKEIT FÜR
KÜNSTLER
UND DESIGNER
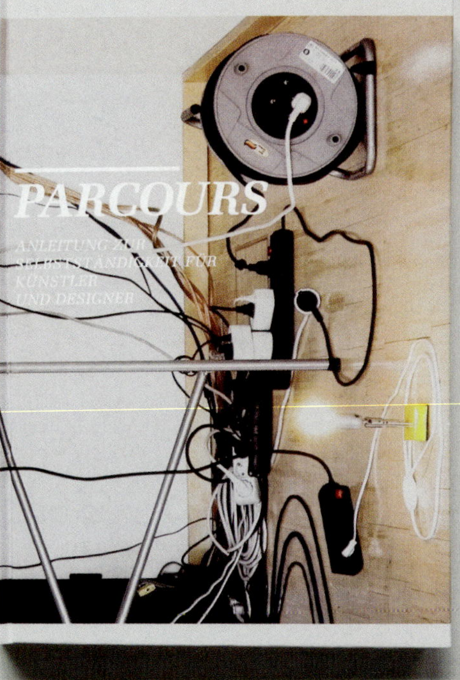
PARCOURS
ANLEITUNG ZUR
SELBSTSTÄNDIGKEIT FÜR
KÜNSTLER
UND DESIGNER

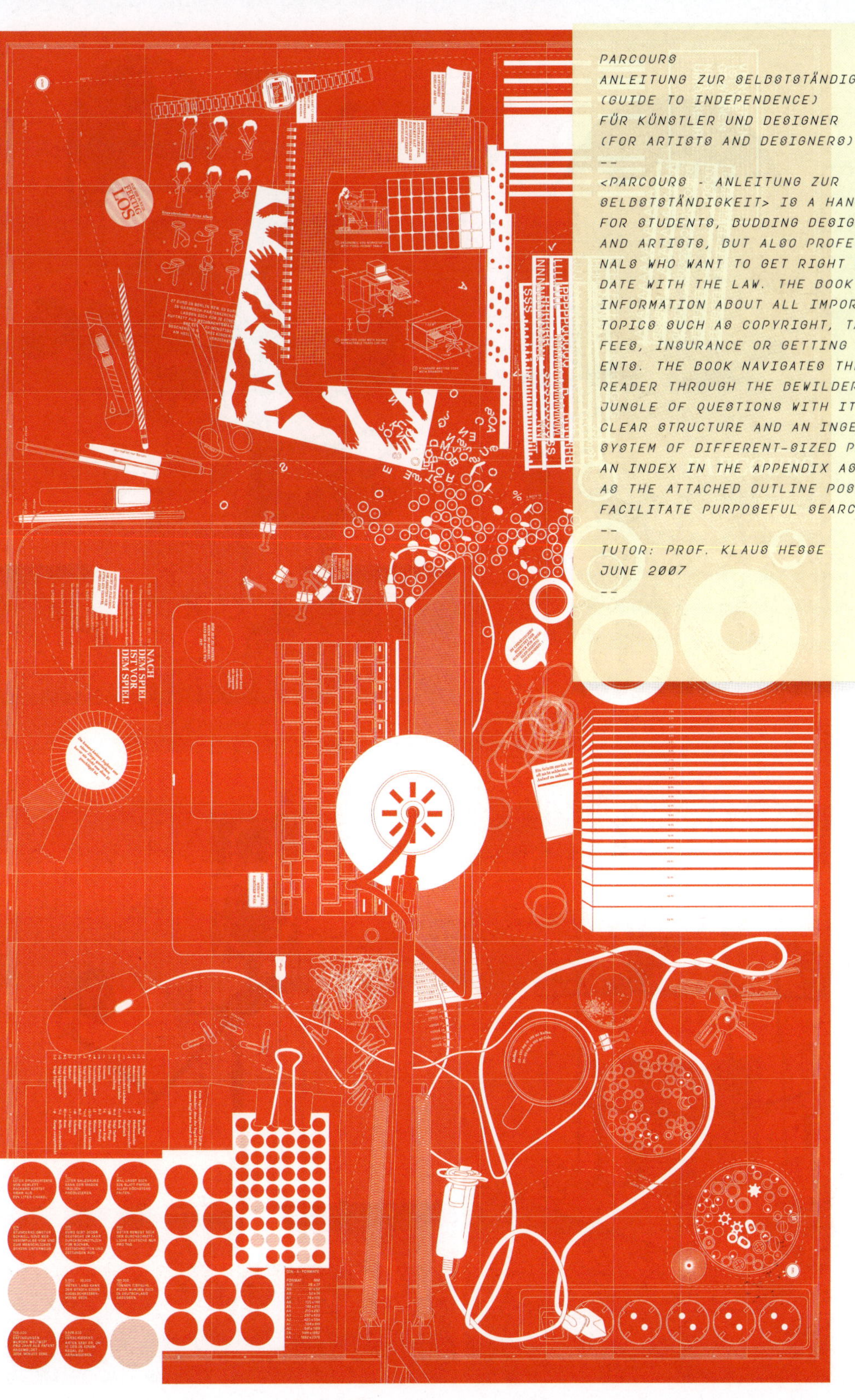

PARCOURS
ANLEITUNG ZUR SELBSTSTÄNDIGKEIT
(GUIDE TO INDEPENDENCE)
FÜR KÜNSTLER UND DESIGNER
(FOR ARTISTS AND DESIGNERS)
--
<PARCOURS - ANLEITUNG ZUR
SELBSTSTÄNDIGKEIT> IS A HANDBOOK
FOR STUDENTS, BUDDING DESIGNERS
AND ARTISTS, BUT ALSO PROFESSIO-
NALS WHO WANT TO GET RIGHT UP TO
DATE WITH THE LAW. THE BOOK GIVES
INFORMATION ABOUT ALL IMPORTANT
TOPICS SUCH AS COPYRIGHT, TAXES,
FEES, INSURANCE OR GETTING CLI-
ENTS. THE BOOK NAVIGATES THE
READER THROUGH THE BEWILDERING
JUNGLE OF QUESTIONS WITH ITS
CLEAR STRUCTURE AND AN INGENIOUS
SYSTEM OF DIFFERENT-SIZED PAGES.
AN INDEX IN THE APPENDIX AS WELL
AS THE ATTACHED OUTLINE POSTER
FACILITATE PURPOSEFUL SEARCHING.
--
TUTOR: PROF. KLAUS HESSE
JUNE 2007
--

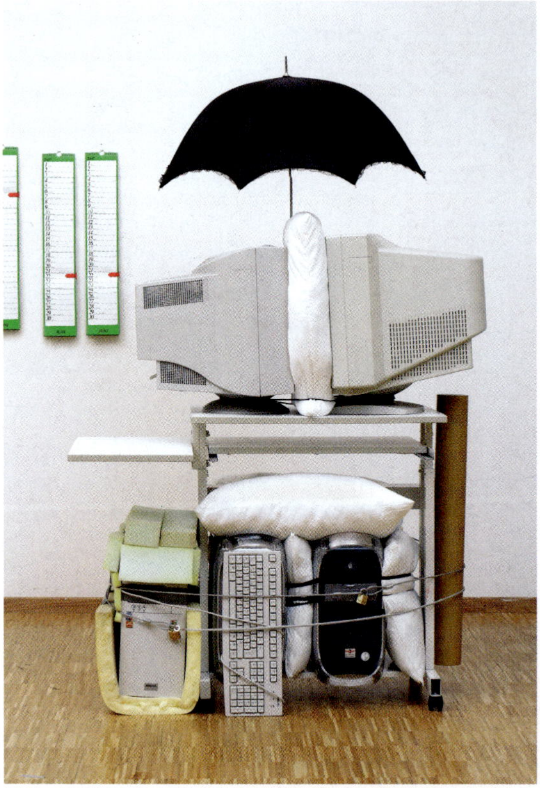

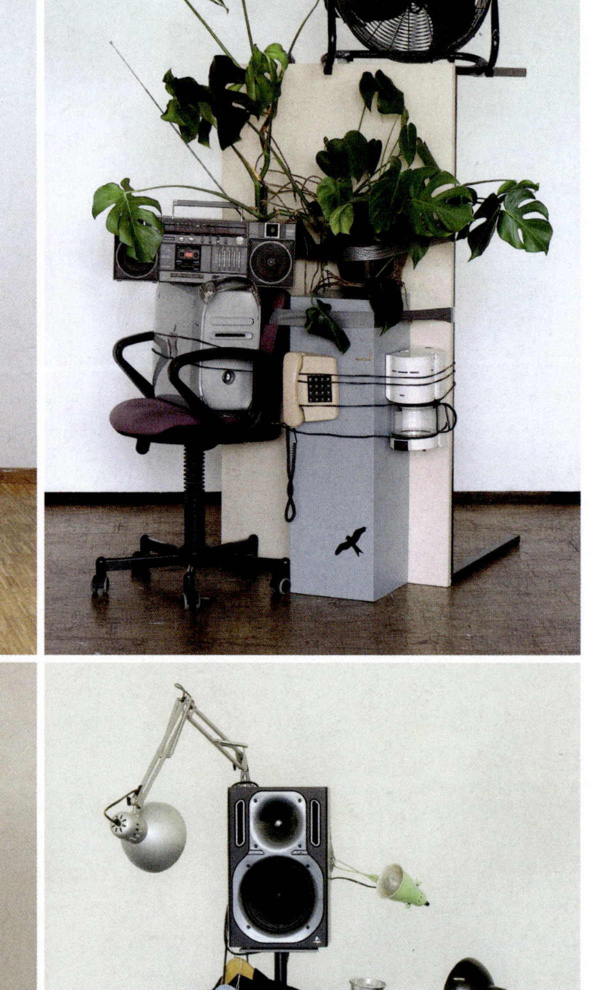

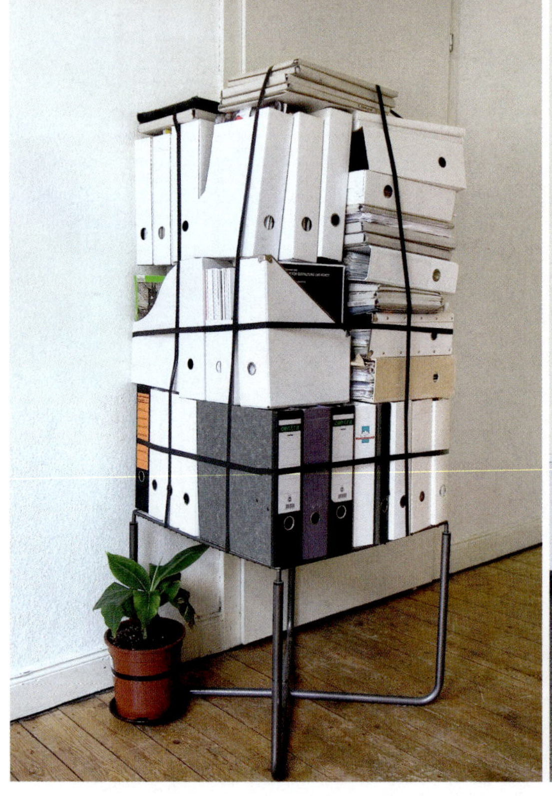

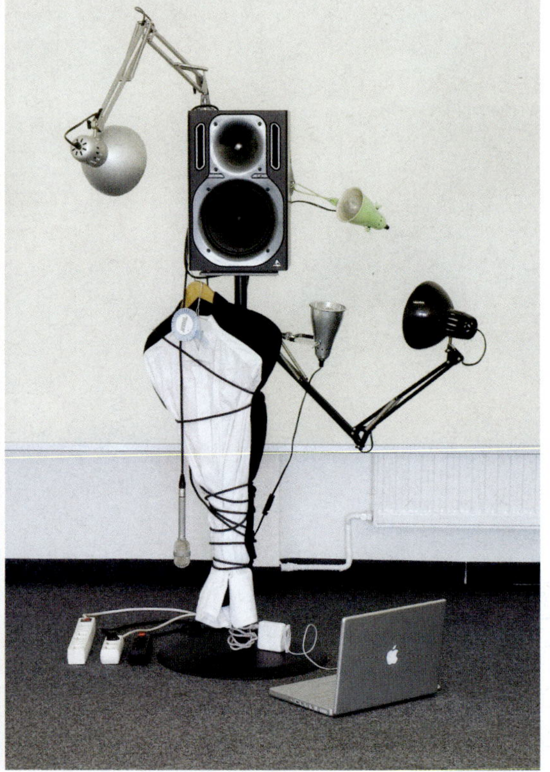

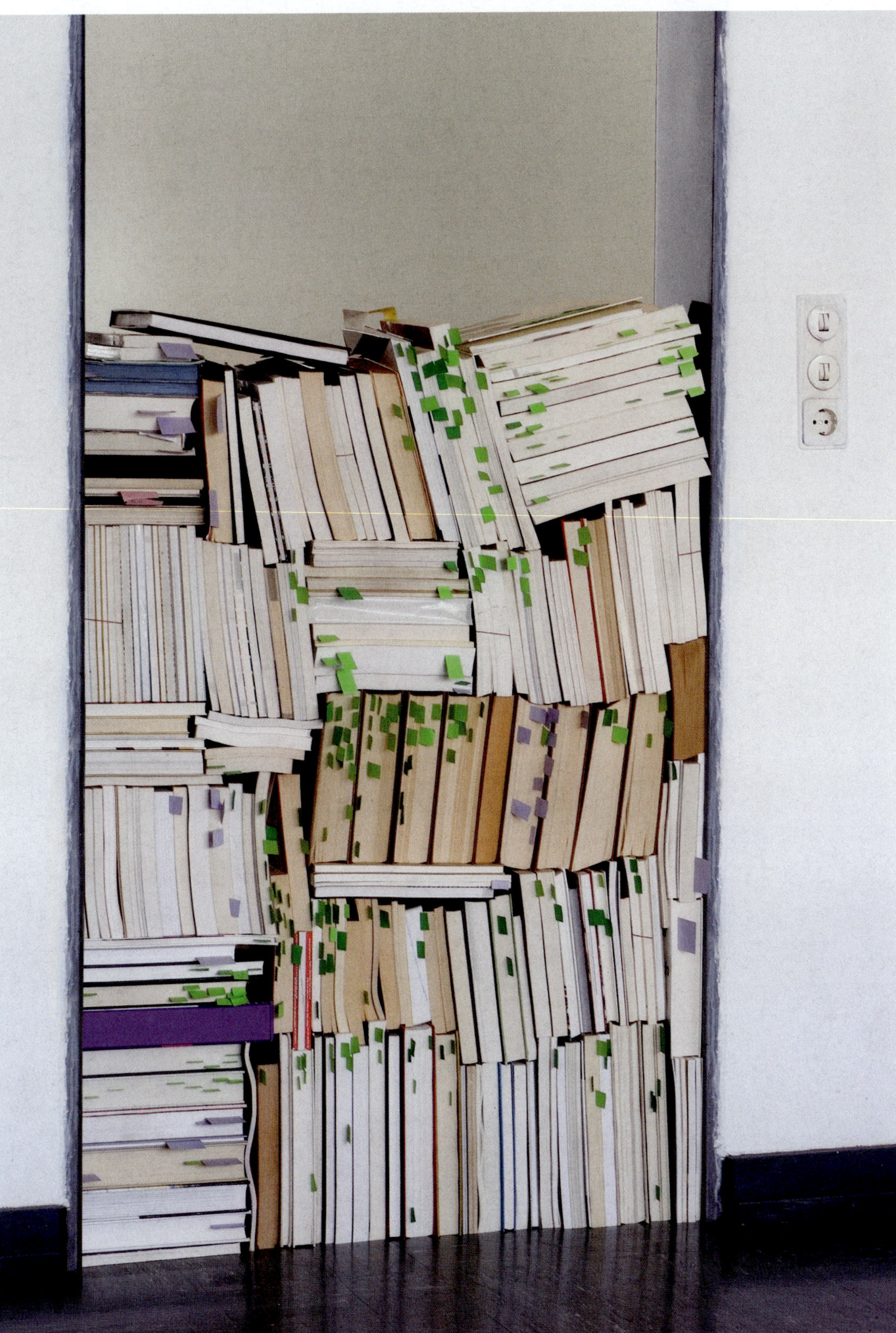

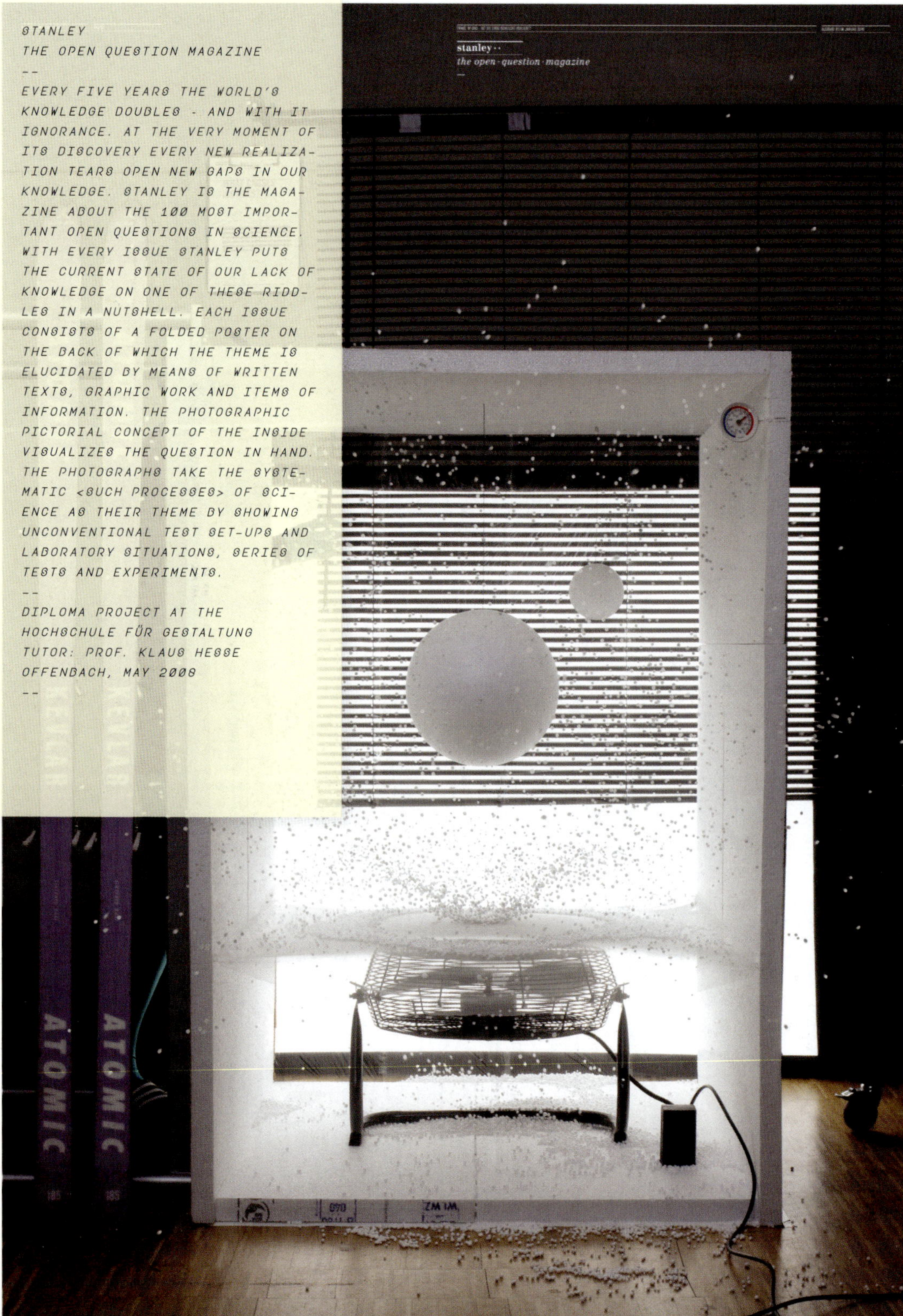

STANLEY
THE OPEN QUESTION MAGAZINE
--
EVERY FIVE YEARS THE WORLD'S
KNOWLEDGE DOUBLES - AND WITH IT
IGNORANCE. AT THE VERY MOMENT OF
ITS DISCOVERY EVERY NEW REALIZA-
TION TEARS OPEN NEW GAPS IN OUR
KNOWLEDGE. STANLEY IS THE MAGA-
ZINE ABOUT THE 100 MOST IMPOR-
TANT OPEN QUESTIONS IN SCIENCE.
WITH EVERY ISSUE STANLEY PUTS
THE CURRENT STATE OF OUR LACK OF
KNOWLEDGE ON ONE OF THESE RIDD-
LES IN A NUTSHELL. EACH ISSUE
CONSISTS OF A FOLDED POSTER ON
THE BACK OF WHICH THE THEME IS
ELUCIDATED BY MEANS OF WRITTEN
TEXTS, GRAPHIC WORK AND ITEMS OF
INFORMATION. THE PHOTOGRAPHIC
PICTORIAL CONCEPT OF THE INSIDE
VISUALIZES THE QUESTION IN HAND.
THE PHOTOGRAPHS TAKE THE SYSTE-
MATIC <SUCH PROCESSES> OF SCI-
ENCE AS THEIR THEME BY SHOWING
UNCONVENTIONAL TEST SET-UPS AND
LABORATORY SITUATIONS, SERIES OF
TESTS AND EXPERIMENTS.
--
DIPLOMA PROJECT AT THE
HOCHSCHULE FÜR GESTALTUNG
TUTOR: PROF. KLAUS HESSE
OFFENBACH, MAY 2008
--

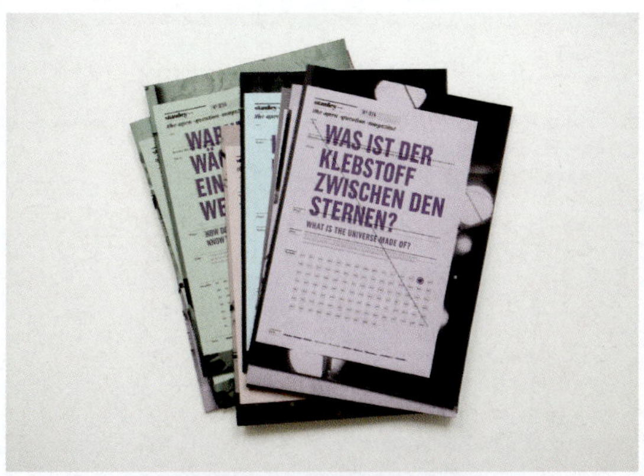
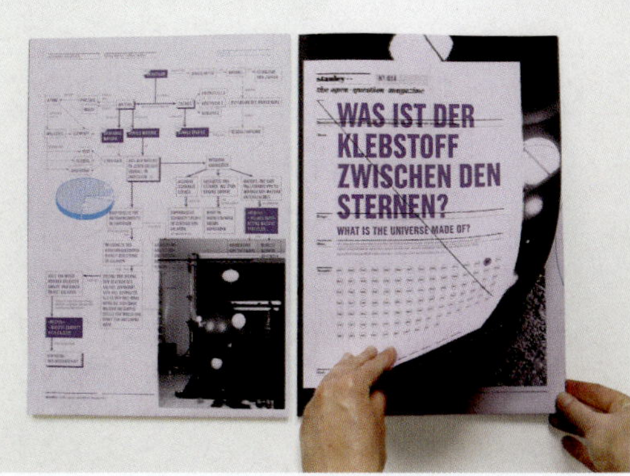

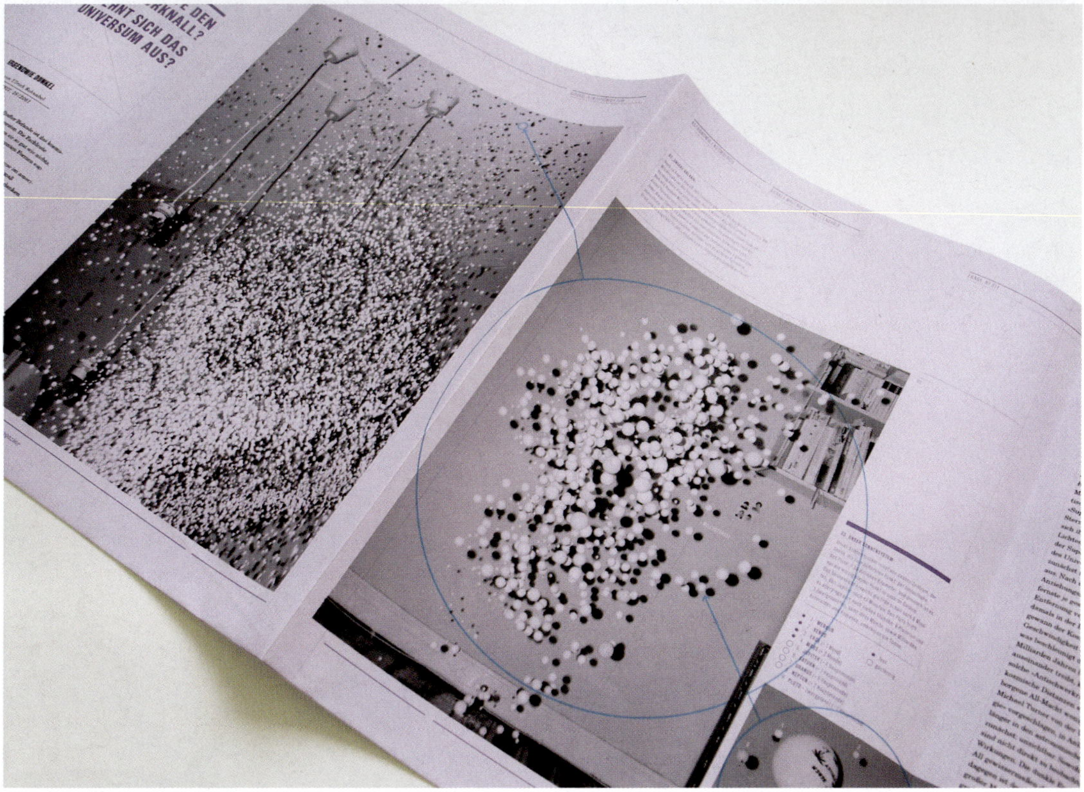

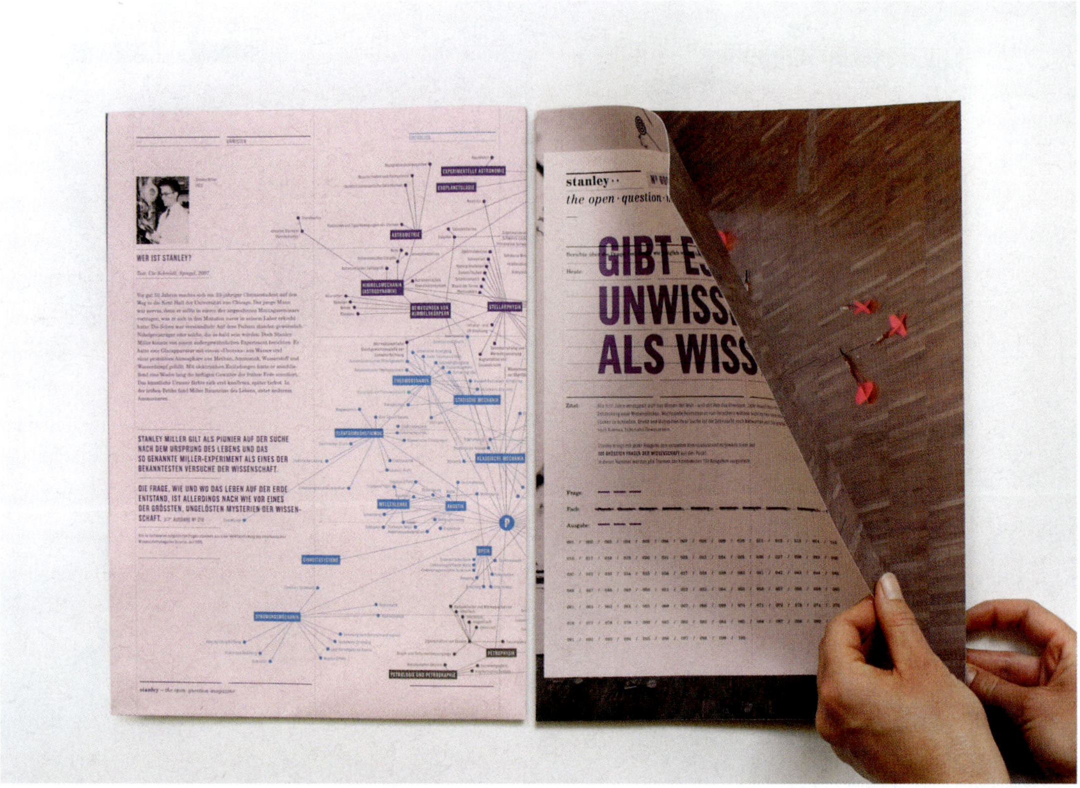

stanley
the open · question ·
N° 00
GIBT ES
UNWISS
ALS WISS
Bericht über
Heute:
Zitat:
Frage:
Fach:
Ausgabe:

stanley · · — the open question magazine
WER IST STANLEY?
STANLEY MILLER GILT ALS PIONIER AUF DER SUCHE NACH DEM URSPRUNG DES LEBENS UND DAS SO GENANNTE MILLER-EXPERIMENT ALS EINES DER BEKANNTESTEN VERSUCHE DER WISSENSCHAFT.
DIE FRAGE, WIE UND WO DAS LEBEN AUF DER ERDE ENTSTAND, IST ALLERDINGS NACH WIE VOR EINES DER GRÖSSTEN, UNGELÖSTEN MYSTERIEN DER WISSENSCHAFT.

THERE ARE KNOWN KNOWNS:
THERE ARE THINGS WE KNOW
THAT WE KNOW.
THERE ARE KNOWN UNKNOWN
THAT IS TO SAY THERE ARE TH
THAT WE NOW KNOW WE DO
BUT THERE ARE ALSO UNKNOWN
UNKNOWN THERE ARE THINGS WE DO NOT
WE DON'T KNOW.
AND EACH YEAR WE DISCOVER
OF THOSE UNKNOWN UNKNOWN

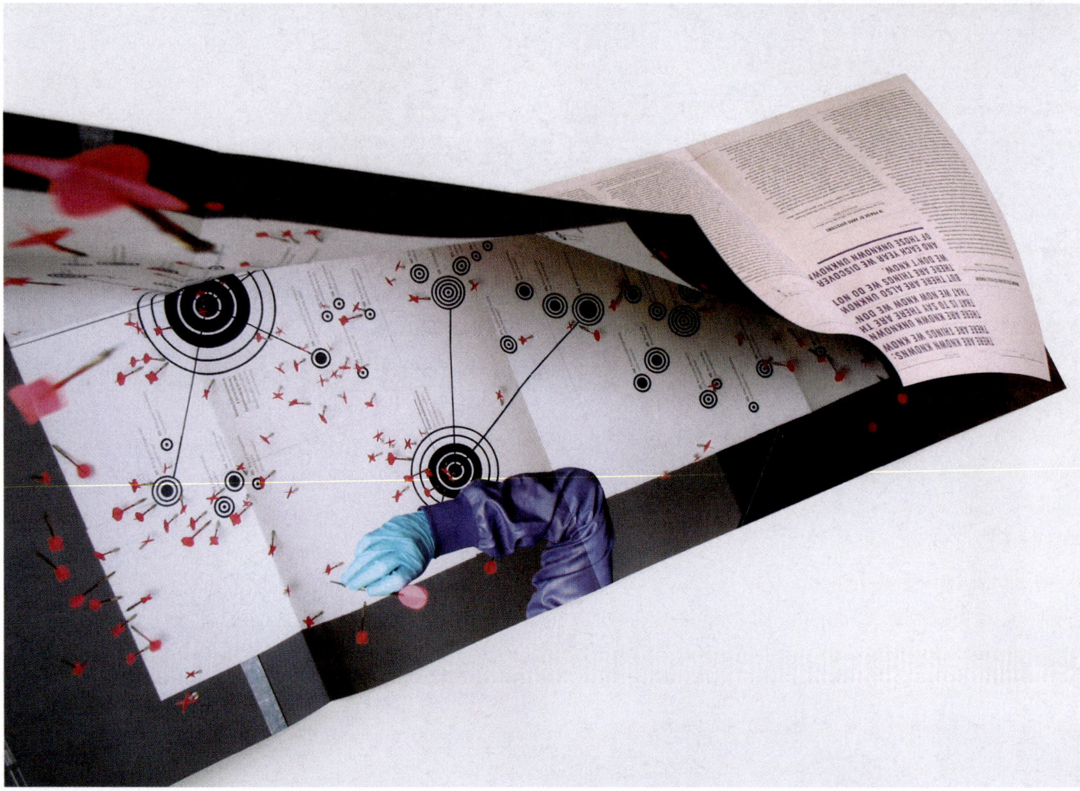

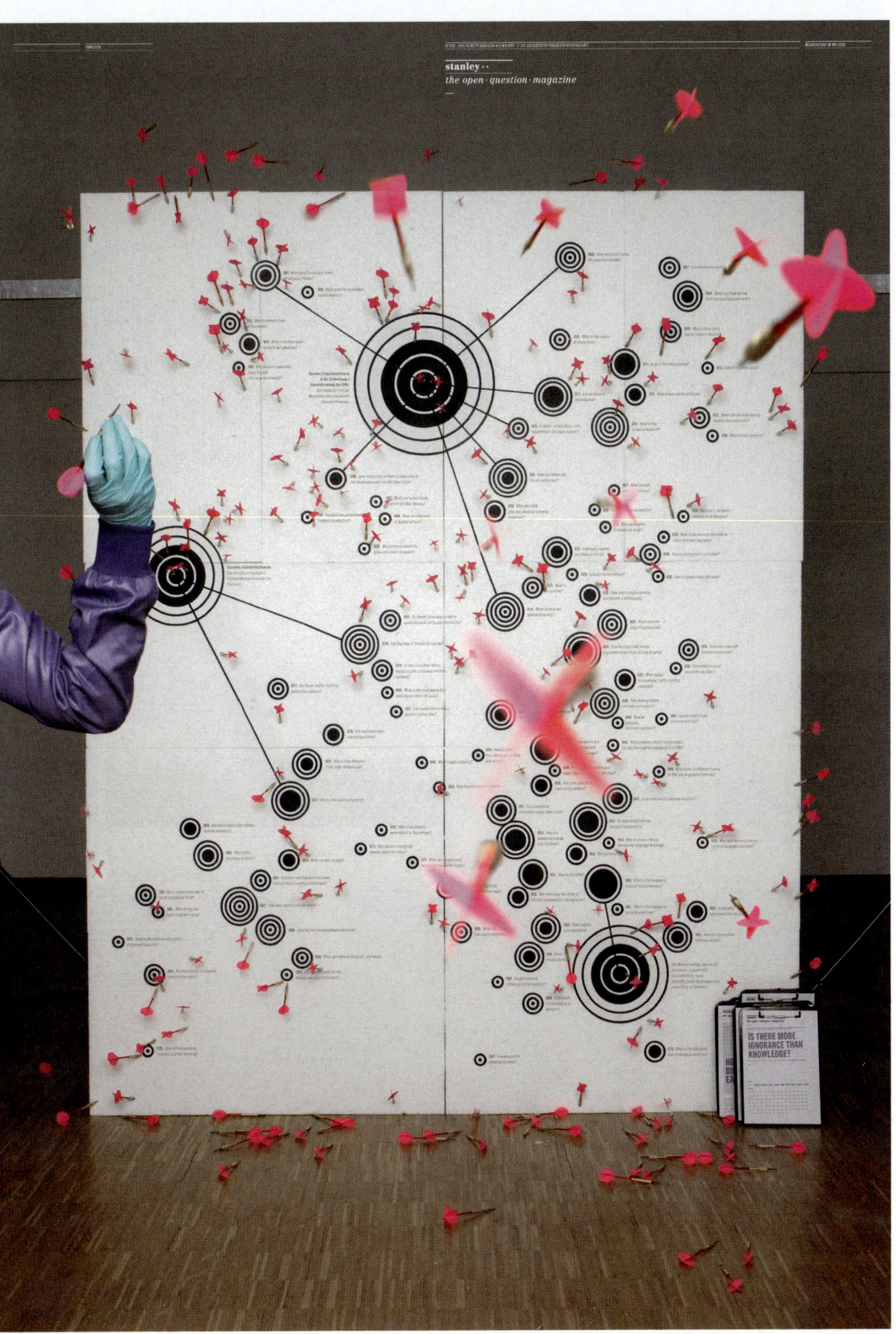

stanley ··
the open · question · magazine
IS THERE MORE
IGNORANCE THAN
KNOWLEDGE?

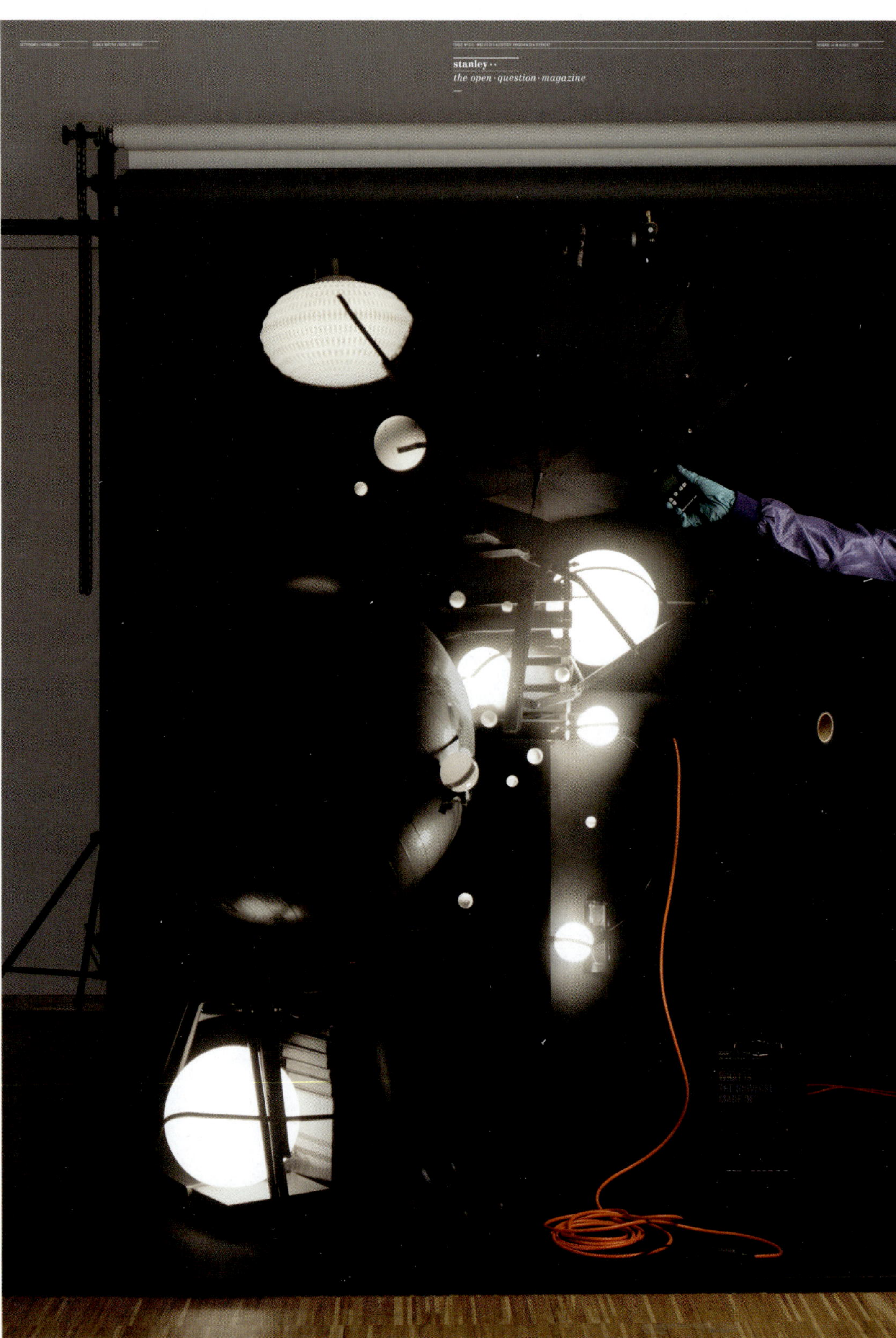

stanley ··
the open · question · magazine

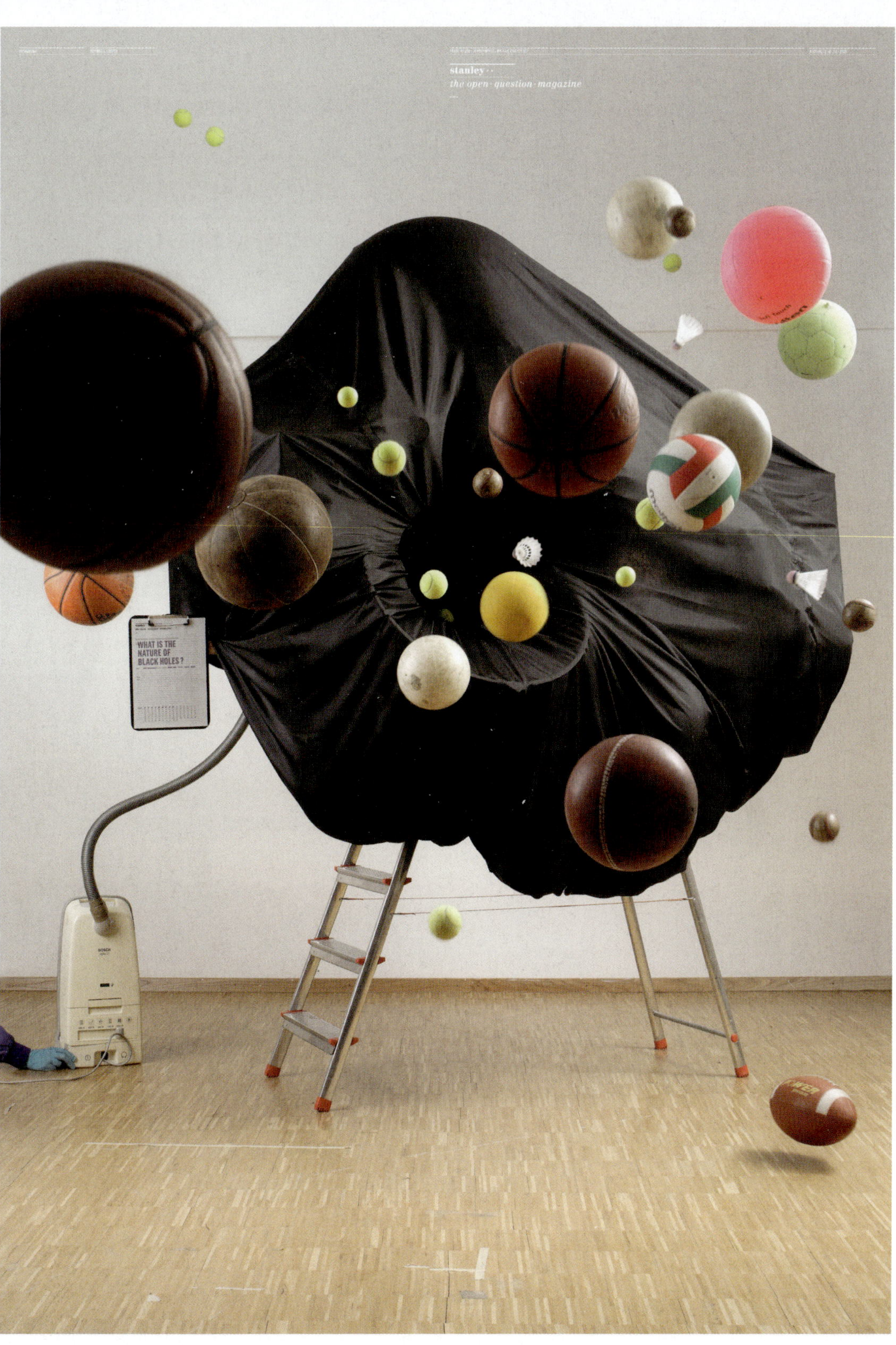
stanley
the open·question·magazine
WHAT IS THE
NATURE OF
BLACK HOLES ?

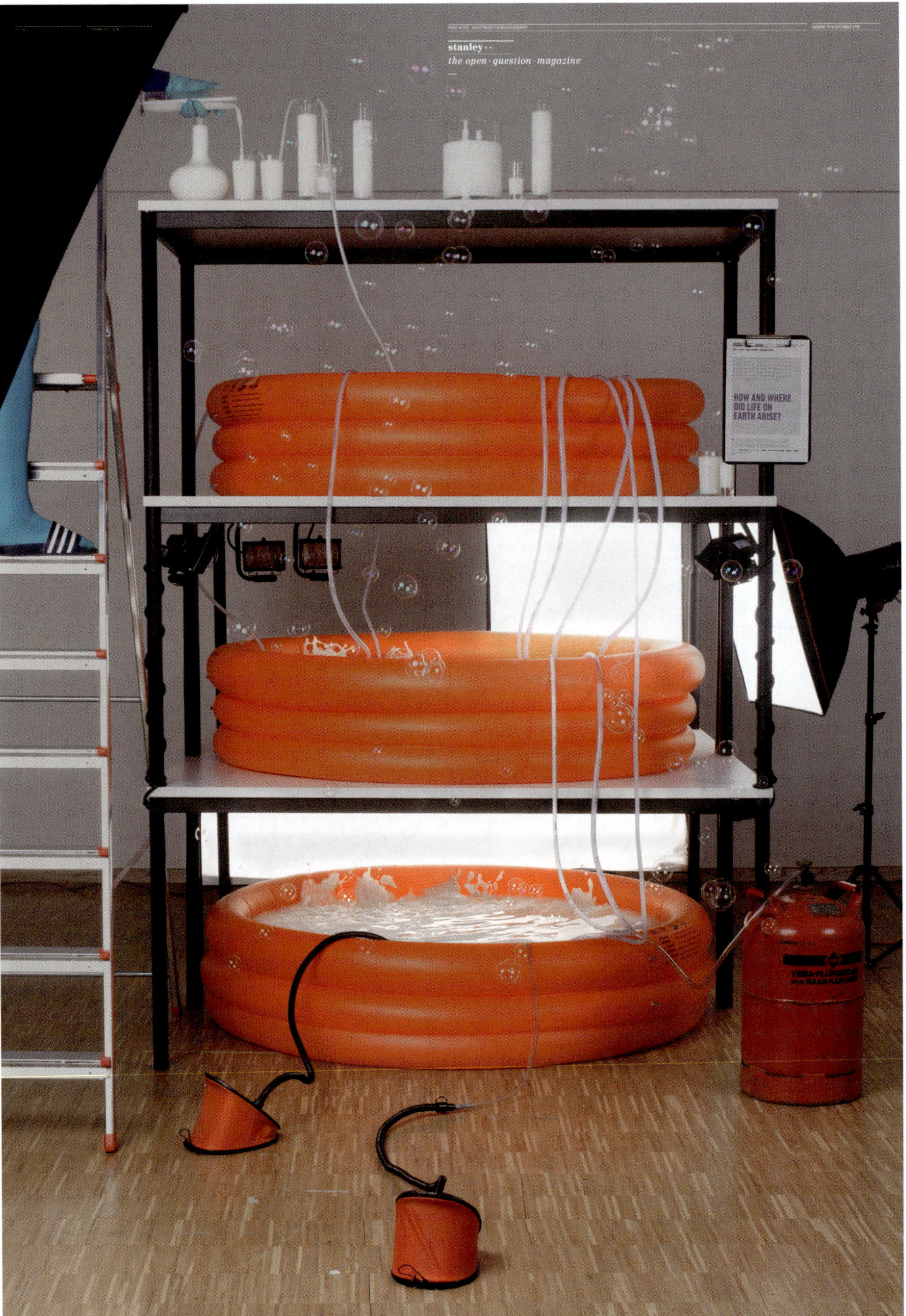
stanley ··
the open · question · magazine
HOW AND WHERE
DID LIFE ON
EARTH ARISE?

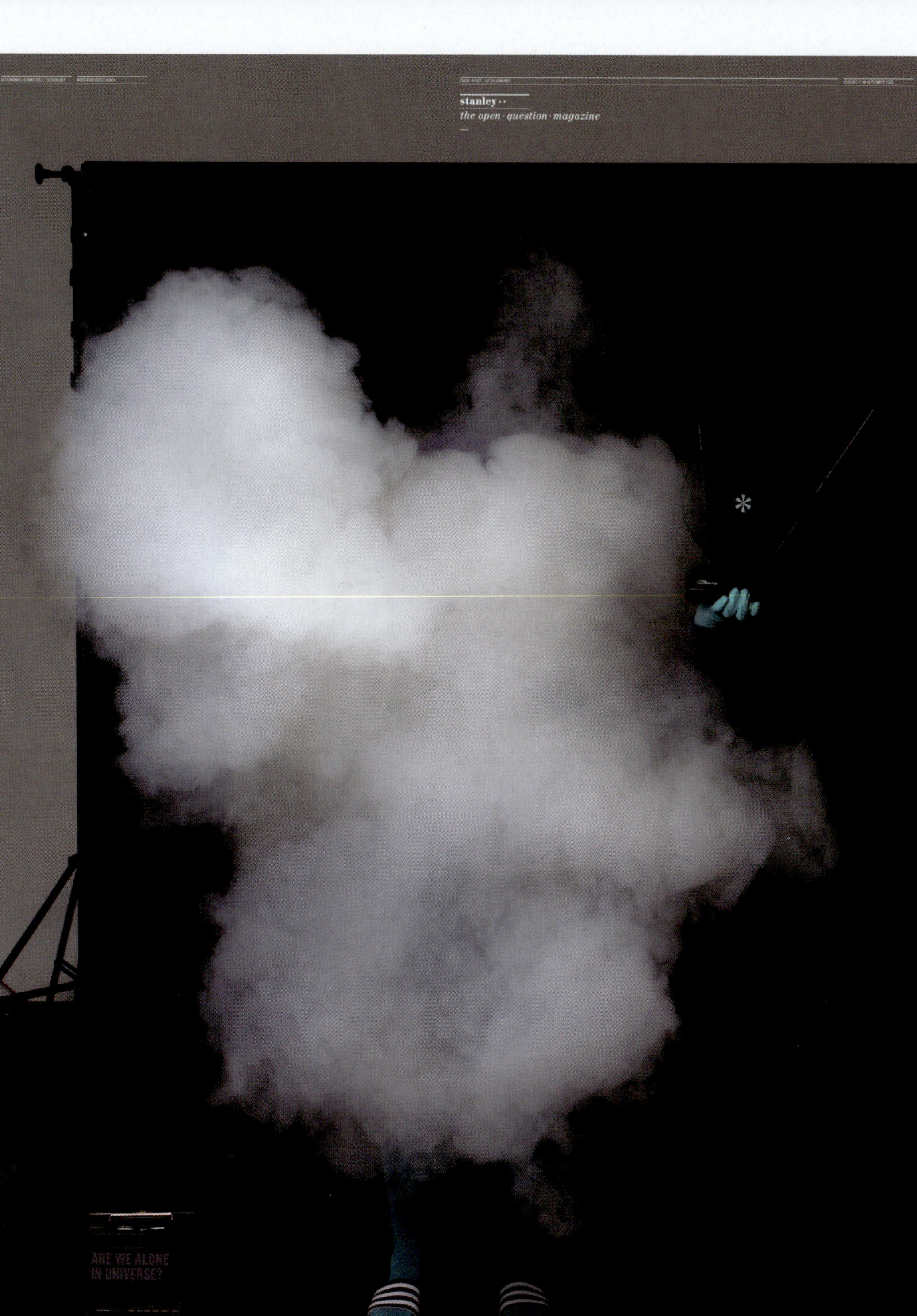
stanley··
the open · question · magazine
ARE WE ALONE
IN UNIVERSE?

U9 VISUELLE ALLIANZ STANDS FOR
DESIGNED COMMUNICATION. PRODUCING
INTERESTING ASSOCIATIONS BETWEEN
TEXT AND IMAGE AND BETWEEN FORM
AND TYPOGRAPHY IS CLOSE TO OUR
HEARTS. TO DO THIS IN THE MAJOR-
ITY OF CASES WE PREFER THE GENTLE
SOUND OF THE VISUAL KETTLEDRUM.

U9 VISUELLE ALLIANZ WAS FOUNDED AS
A LIMITED COMPANY (GMBH) BY BRITA
WIESBACH AND ANDREAS GNASS ON
1.1.2000.

--

WHAT IS GERMAN?

THE FOREST, IT'S THE FOREST.

WHAT IS GERMAN DESIGN?

THE CUCKOO CLOCK.

PLEASE DESCRIBE YOUR WORKING
PROCESS.

WHERE WAS THE BRIEF RIGHT NOW?
OH YES, THERE. OH NO, NOW WHAT'S
THAT SUPPOSED TO MEAN? HAVE A TEN-
TATIVE GO. LEAVE OFF. SKETCHBOOK.
SHOWER. ANY OLD HOW. YES. HMM. TRY
AGAIN. TALK. RACK MY BRAINS. SNIFF
A SCENT: HOT ON THE TRAIL. DO IT.
GO ON DOING IT. SHOW IT.

WHAT DO YOU AIM TO ACHIEVE WITH
YOUR WORK?

TARGET GROUP. RESPECT. SATISFAC-
TION.

YOU'VE INVITED A FRIEND TO
GERMANY; NAME ONE PLACE THEY
REALLY MUST VISIT AND A QUINT-
ESSENTIAL EXPERIENCE YOU REC-
OMMEND.

AFTER A SUMMER THUNDERSTORM
PENETRATE DEEP INTO A FOREST. RUN
QUITE FAST, RIGHT INTO THE UNDER-
GROWTH. THEN STAND STILL, LET YOUR
PULSE SLOW DOWN. CLOSE YOUR EYES -
BREATHE IN.

WHAT IS THE MOST IMPORTANT
LESSON YOU HAVE LEARNED IN YOUR
PROFESSION SO FAR?

OUR PROFESSION IS A PROFESSION
OF AFFLUENCE. THE COLLECTIVE FEAR
THAT CAN BE OBSERVED AT PRES-
ENT SHOWS HOW THIN THE ICE WE'RE
DESIGNING ON IS. WHAT COMES NEXT:
TERROR, EPIDEMICS OR ECONOMIC CRI-
SES? WHAT DO WE DO THEN: EXHIBI-
TION POSTERS, WEB PAGES, CORPORATE
IMAGES? HARDLY. IT WOULD TEND TO
BE SIGNPOSTING SYSTEMS FOR BUNKER
COMPLEXES, HOSPITALS OR CAVES.
PERHAPS ALSO PRETTY PICTURES
TO DISTRACT PEOPLE OR PAMPHLETS
AGAINST EVIL.

--

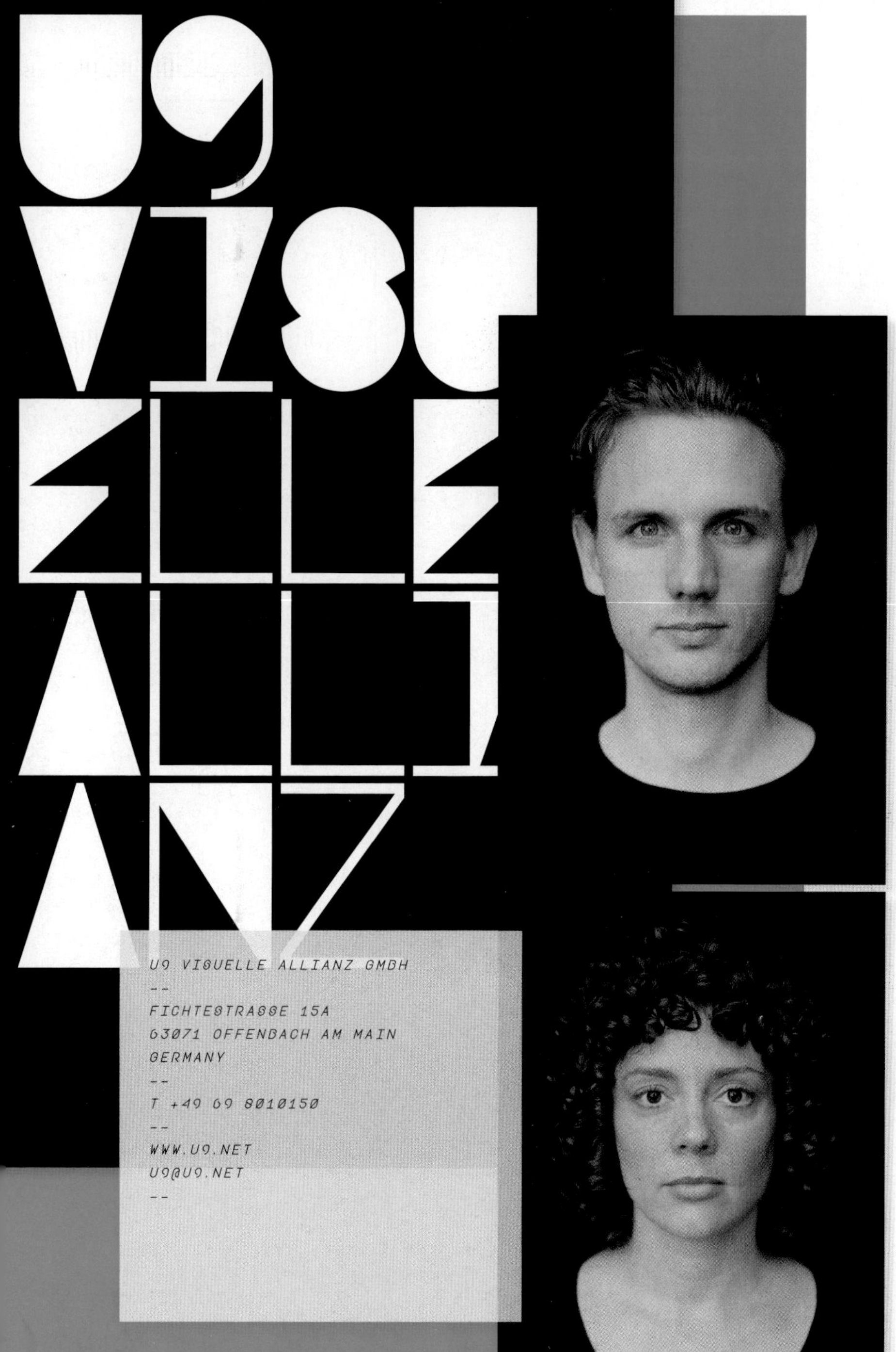

U9 VISUELLE ALLIANZ GMBH
--
FICHTESTRASSE 15A
63071 OFFENBACH AM MAIN
GERMANY
--
T +49 69 8010150
--
WWW.U9.NET
U9@U9.NET
--

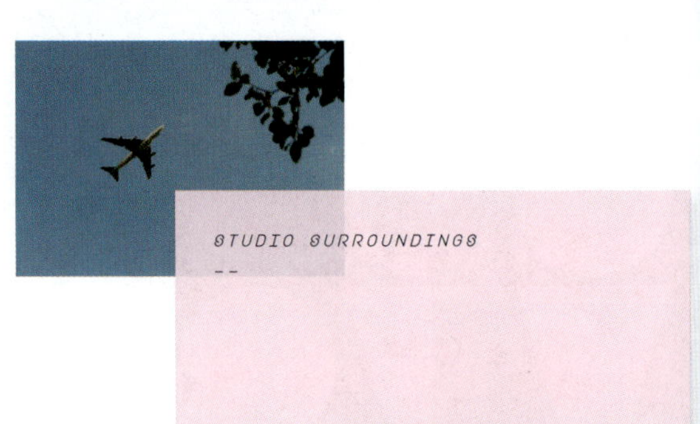

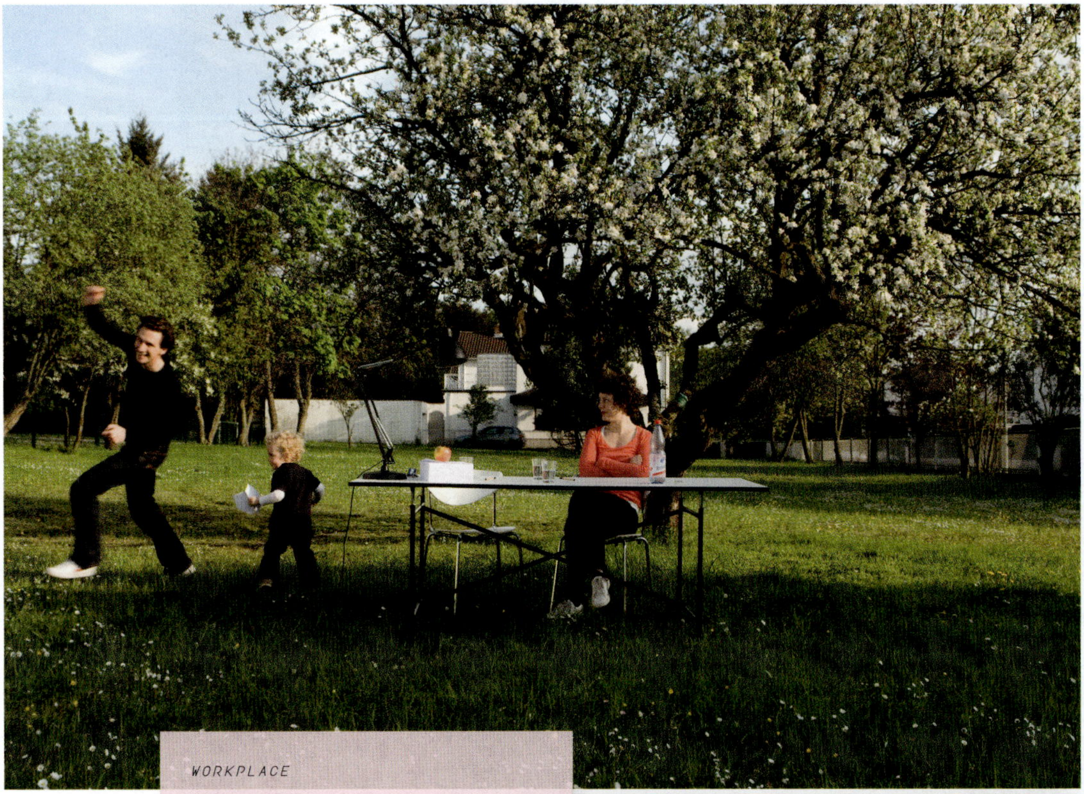

WORKPLACE
--

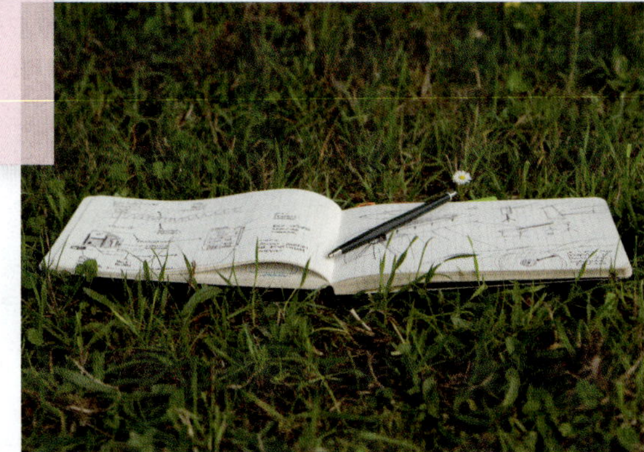

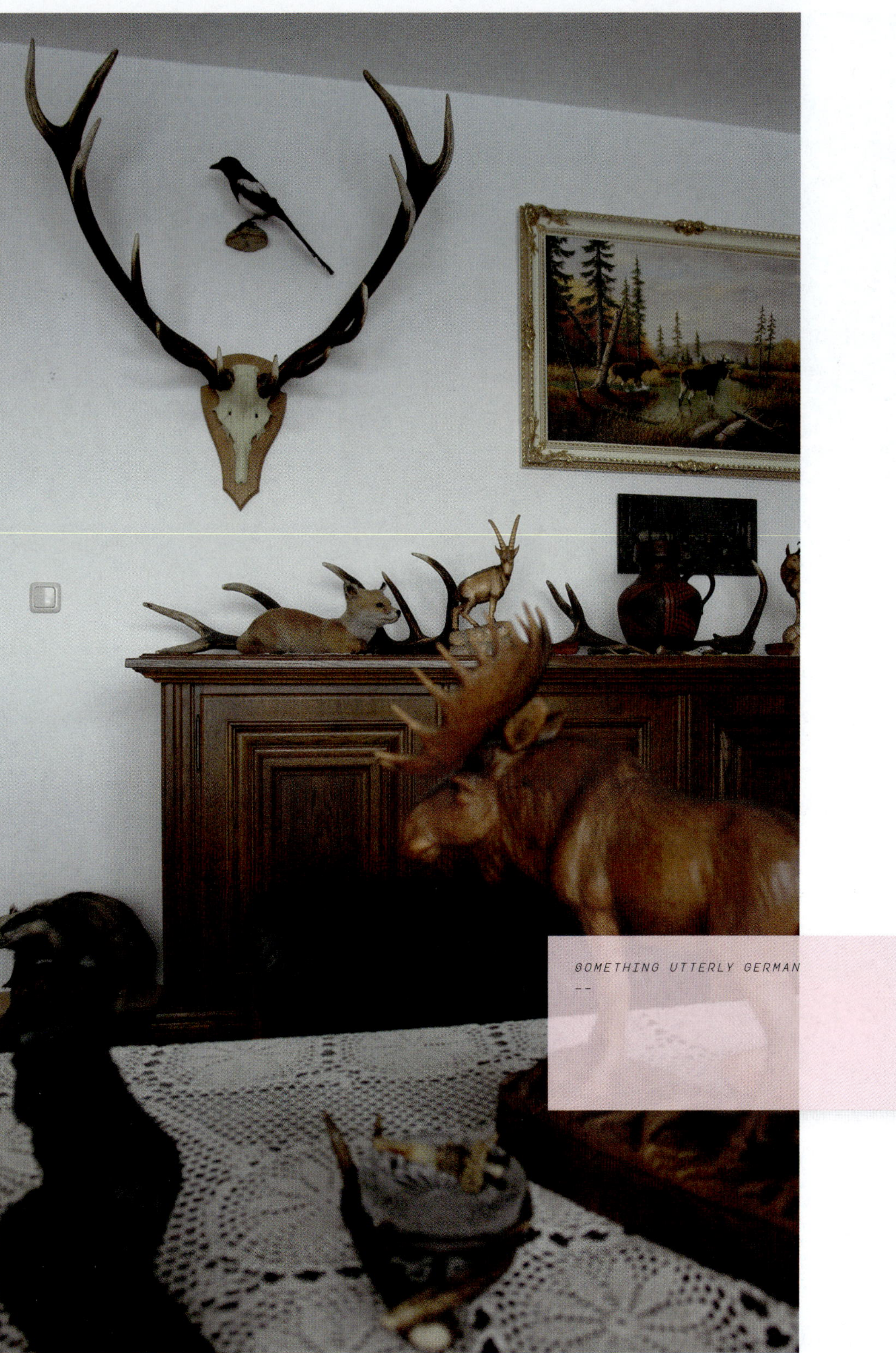
SOMETHING UTTERLY GERMAN
--

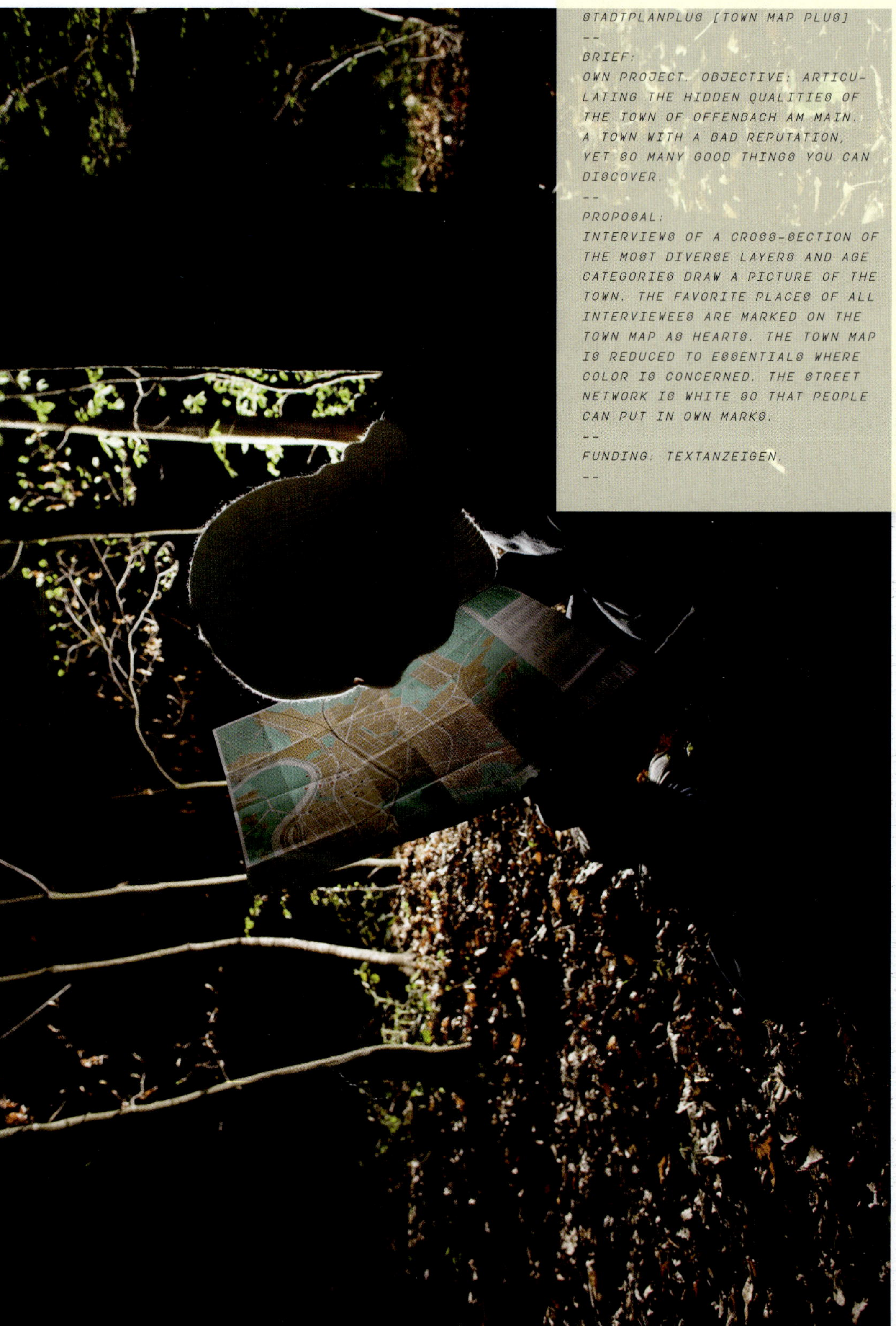

STADTPLANPLUS [TOWN MAP PLUS]
--
BRIEF:
OWN PROJECT. OBJECTIVE: ARTICU-
LATING THE HIDDEN QUALITIES OF
THE TOWN OF OFFENBACH AM MAIN.
A TOWN WITH A BAD REPUTATION,
YET SO MANY GOOD THINGS YOU CAN
DISCOVER.
--
PROPOSAL:
INTERVIEWS OF A CROSS-SECTION OF
THE MOST DIVERSE LAYERS AND AGE
CATEGORIES DRAW A PICTURE OF THE
TOWN. THE FAVORITE PLACES OF ALL
INTERVIEWEES ARE MARKED ON THE
TOWN MAP AS HEARTS. THE TOWN MAP
IS REDUCED TO ESSENTIALS WHERE
COLOR IS CONCERNED. THE STREET
NETWORK IS WHITE SO THAT PEOPLE
CAN PUT IN OWN MARKS.
--
FUNDING: TEXTANZEIGEN.
--

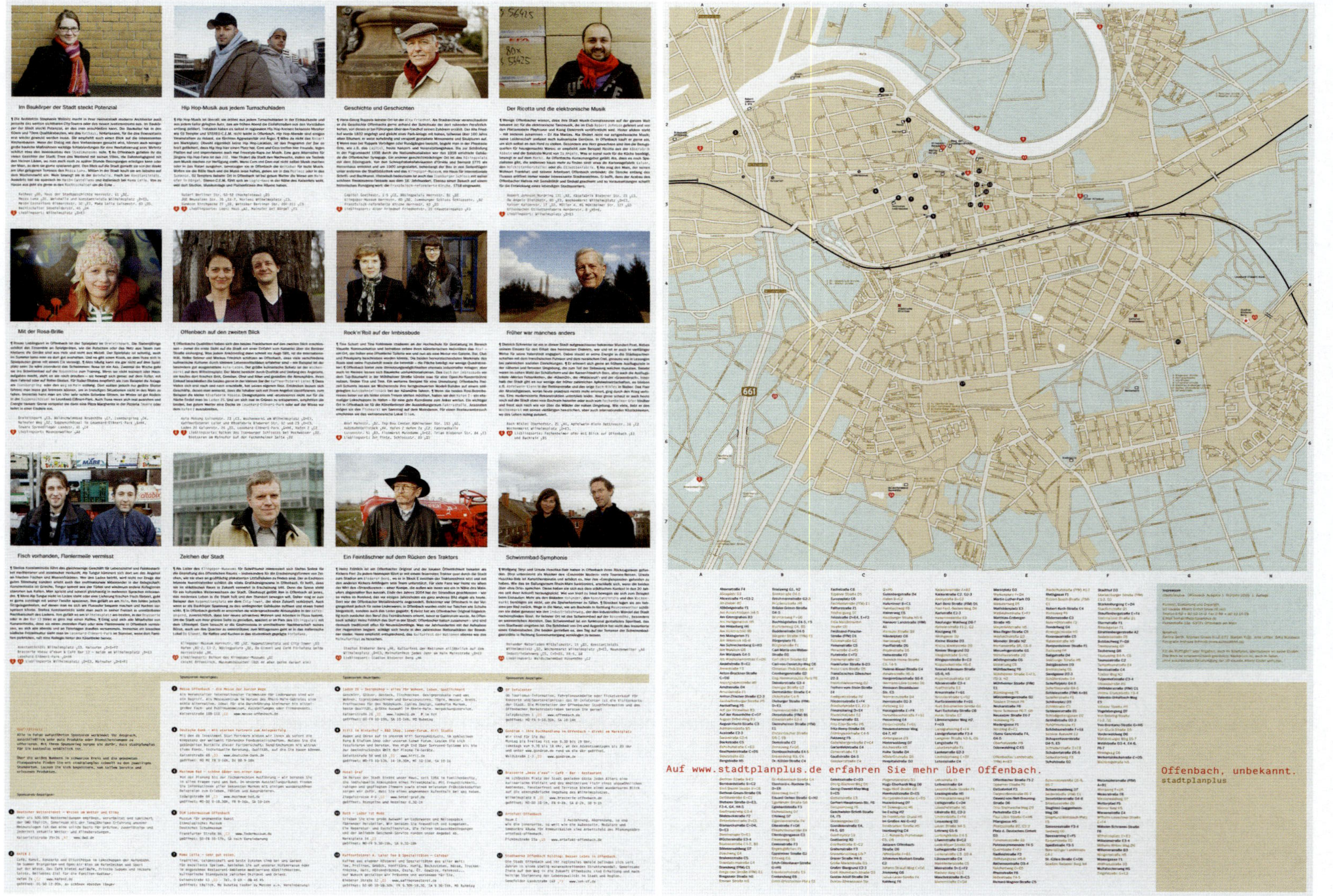

Im Baukörper der Stadt steckt Potenzial

Hip Hop-Musik aus jedem Turnschuhladen

Geschichte und Geschichten

Der Ricotta und die elektronische Musik

Mit der Rosa-Brille

Offenbach auf den zweiten Blick

Rock'n'Roll auf der Imbissbude

Früher war manches anders

Fisch vorhanden, Flaniermeile vermisst

Zeichen der Stadt

Ein Feintäschner auf dem Rücken des Traktors

Schwimmbad-Symphonie

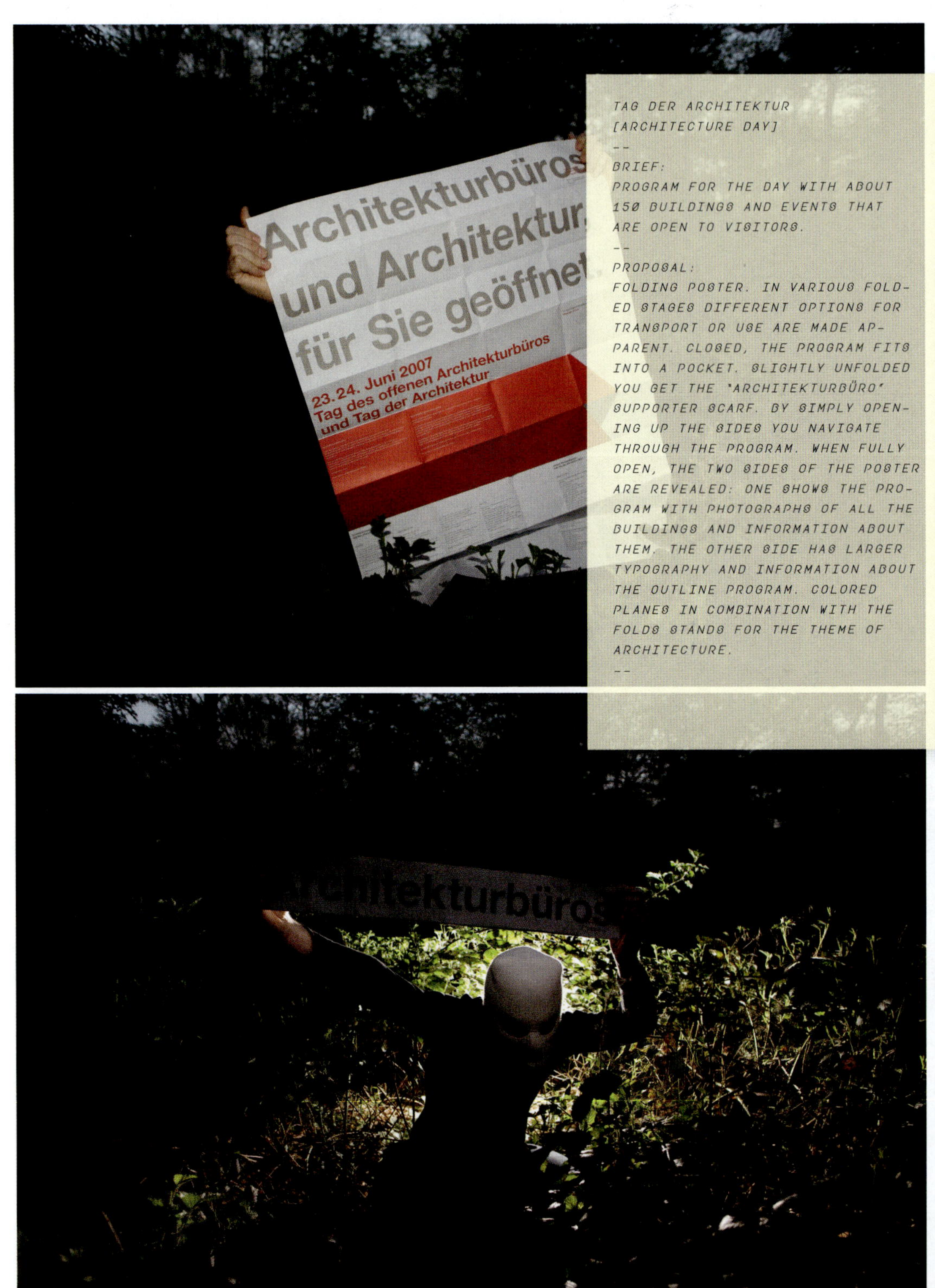
Architekturbüros
und Architektur
für Sie geöffnet
23. 24. Juni 2007
Tag des offenen Architekturbüros
und Tag der Architektur

TAG DER ARCHITEKTUR
[ARCHITECTURE DAY]
--
BRIEF:
PROGRAM FOR THE DAY WITH ABOUT
150 BUILDINGS AND EVENTS THAT
ARE OPEN TO VISITORS.
--
PROPOSAL:
FOLDING POSTER. IN VARIOUS FOLD-
ED STAGES DIFFERENT OPTIONS FOR
TRANSPORT OR USE ARE MADE AP-
PARENT. CLOSED, THE PROGRAM FITS
INTO A POCKET. SLIGHTLY UNFOLDED
YOU GET THE 'ARCHITEKTURBÜRO'
SUPPORTER SCARF. BY SIMPLY OPEN-
ING UP THE SIDES YOU NAVIGATE
THROUGH THE PROGRAM. WHEN FULLY
OPEN, THE TWO SIDES OF THE POSTER
ARE REVEALED: ONE SHOWS THE PRO-
GRAM WITH PHOTOGRAPHS OF ALL THE
BUILDINGS AND INFORMATION ABOUT
THEM. THE OTHER SIDE HAS LARGER
TYPOGRAPHY AND INFORMATION ABOUT
THE OUTLINE PROGRAM. COLORED
PLANES IN COMBINATION WITH THE
FOLDS STANDS FOR THE THEME OF
ARCHITECTURE.
--

Architekturbüros

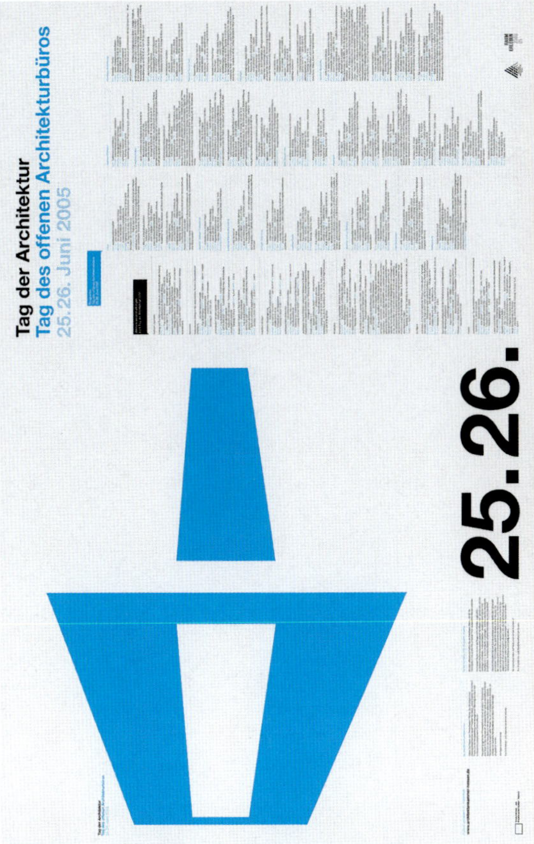

Architekturbüros
und Architektur,
für Sie geöffnet.
23.24. Juni 2007
Tag des offenen Architekturbüros
und Tag der Architektur

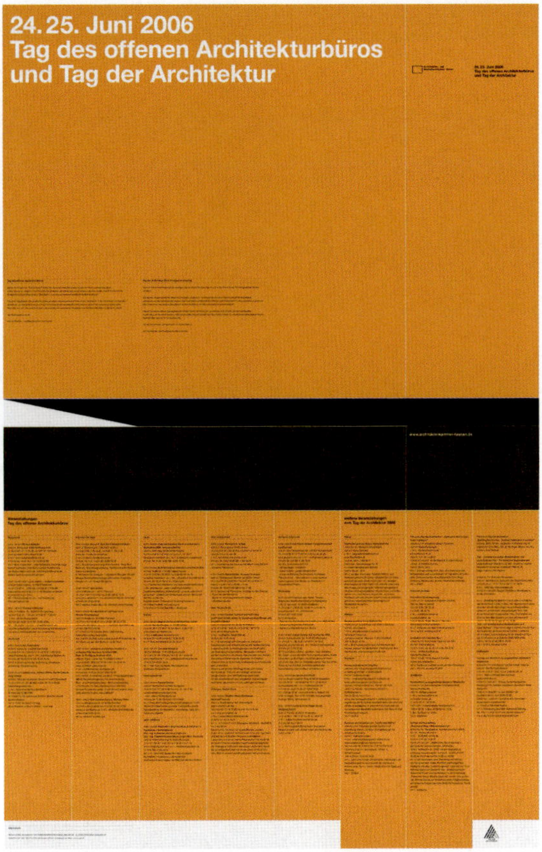

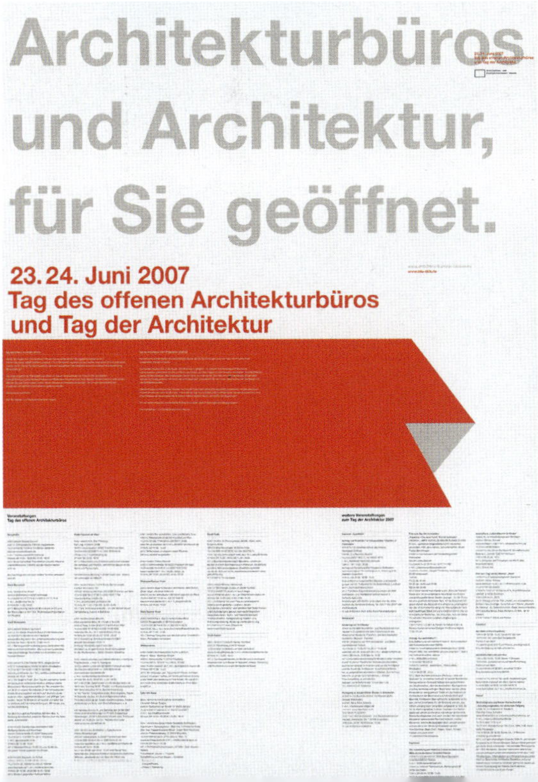

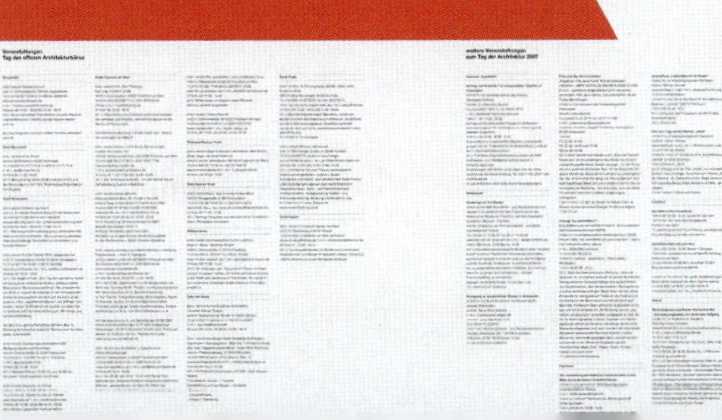

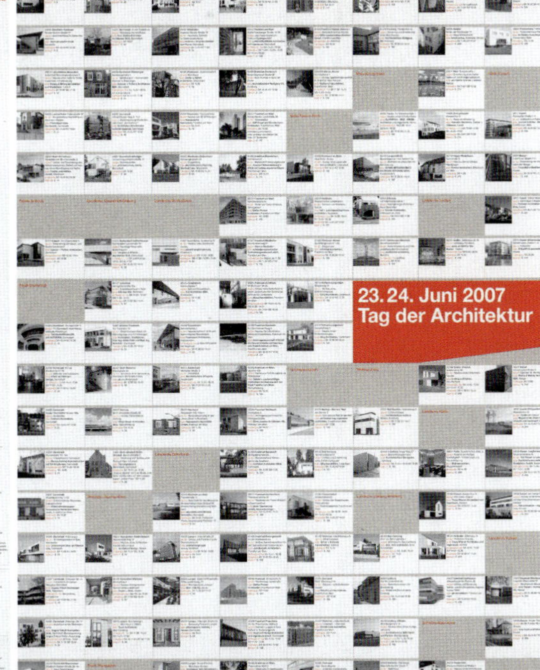
23.24. Juni 2007
Tag der Architektur

THE FEIGENBAUMPUNKT IS A VERY
INTERESTING PARAMETER. ON THE ONE
HAND NO REGULARITY OF ANY KIND CAN
BE DISCERNED IN THE BEHAVIOR OF
THE CRITICAL ORBIT. ON THE OTHER
THE SITUATION WITH NEIGHBORING PA-
RAMETERS IS ALSO VERY COMPLICATED:
A LOOK AT THE FEIGENBAUM DIAGRAM
AGAIN REVEALS, ON THE LEFT-HAND
SIDE, PERIODIC WINDOWS OF ARBI-
TRARY DENSITY WITH A WIDE VARIETY
OF PERIODS. SO IT COULD BE SAID
THAT WITH THE FEIGENBAUM POINT WE
HAD REACHED <CHAOS> IN THE LOGIS-
TIC FAMILY. ANOTHER IMPORTANT CON-
CEPT IS THAT OF <ENTROPY>; AS WE
WILL SEE, THE FEIGENBAUM DIAGRAM
CONSTITUTES THE TRANSITION POINT
TO SYSTEMS WITH POSITIVE ENTROPY.

--

WHAT IS GERMAN?

THIS QUESTION. AND: A CUP OF
REAL COFFEE, A LITTLE PACK OF
EVAPORATED MILK, A SPOON AND A TWO
WRAPPED SUGAR CUBES ON A SAUCER.

WHAT IS GERMAN DESIGN?

WE DON'T BELIEVE THAT THERE
IS ANY SUCH THING AS GERMAN
DESIGN YET.

PLEASE DESCRIBE YOUR WORKING
PROCESS.

FINDING SYSTEMS THAT FROM A
CERTAIN POINT DEVELOP A LIFE OF
THEIR OWN.

WHAT DO YOU AIM TO ACHIEVE WITH
YOUR WORK?

SATISFACTION.

YOU'VE INVITED A FRIEND TO
GERMANY; NAME ONE PLACE THEY
REALLY MUST VISIT AND A QUINT-
ESSENTIAL EXPERIENCE YOU REC-
OMMEND.

EAT A VEGETARIAN DONER KEBAB
AND DRINK A BEER WITH US HERE IN
FRANKFURT.

WHAT IS THE MOST IMPORTANT
LESSON YOU HAVE LEARNED IN YOUR
PROFESSION SO FAR?

APPLE-Z.

--

FEIGENBAUMPUNKT

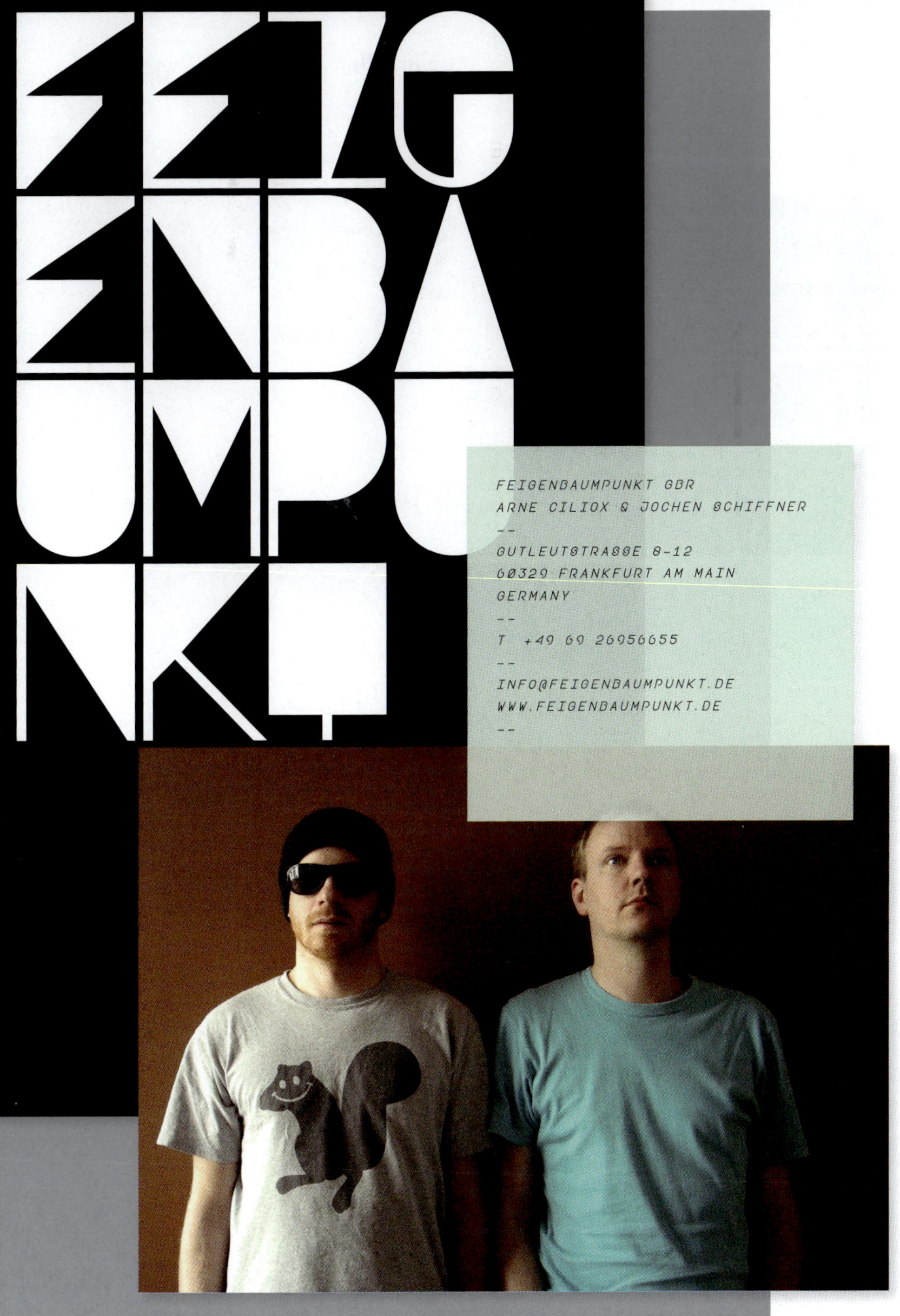

FEIGENBAUMPUNKT GBR
ARNE CILIOX & JOCHEN SCHIFFNER
--
GUTLEUTSTRASSE 8-12
60329 FRANKFURT AM MAIN
GERMANY
--
T +49 69 26956655
--
INFO@FEIGENBAUMPUNKT.DE
WWW.FEIGENBAUMPUNKT.DE
--

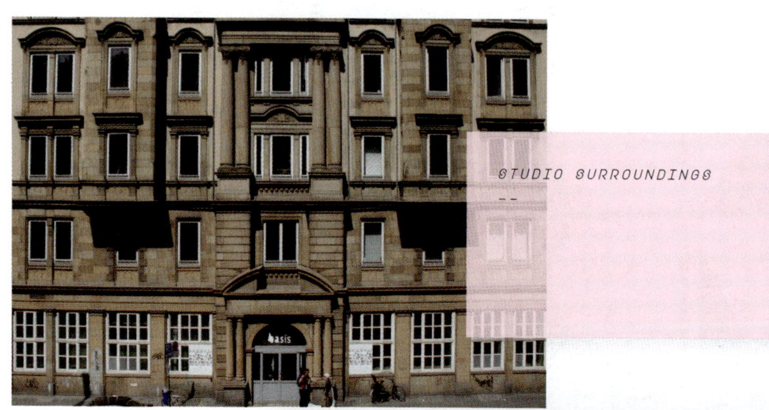

STUDIO SURROUNDINGS
--

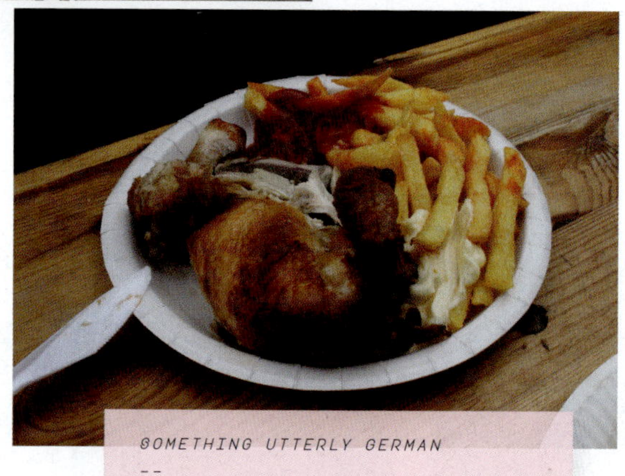

SOMETHING UTTERLY GERMAN
--

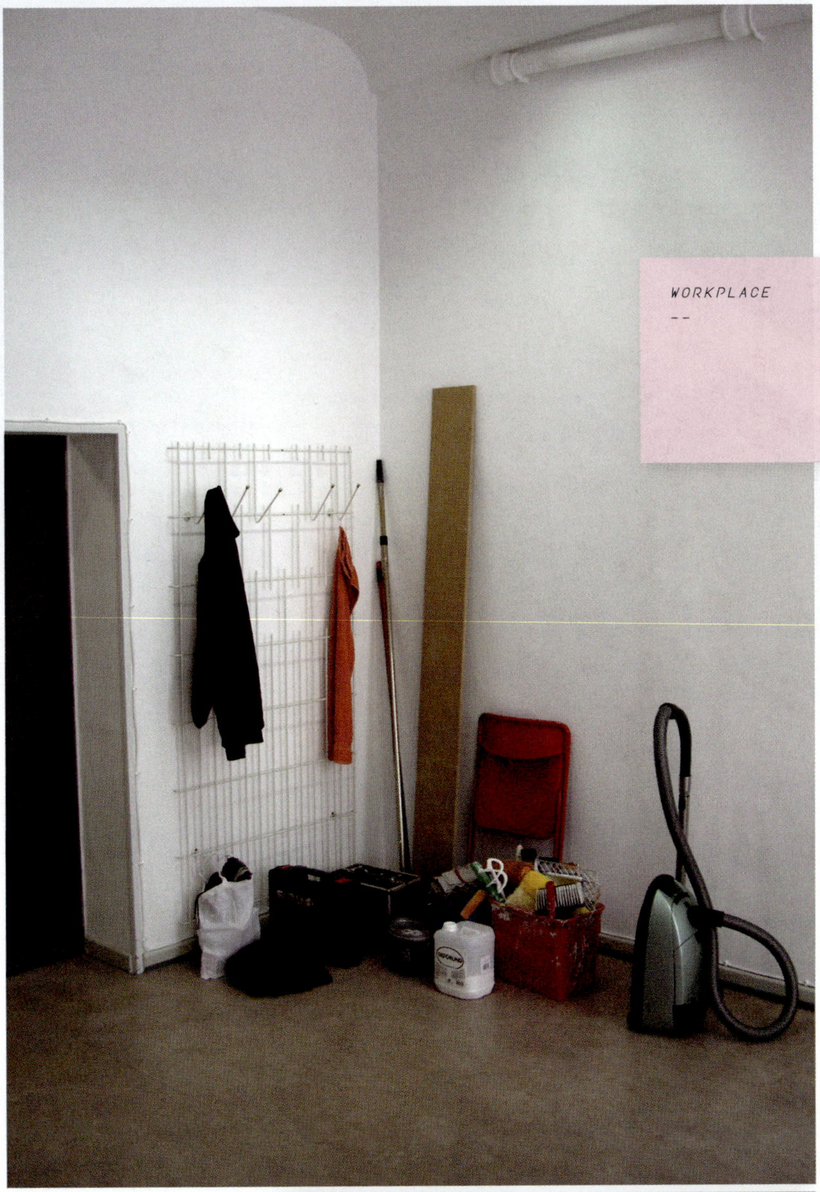

WORKPLACE
--

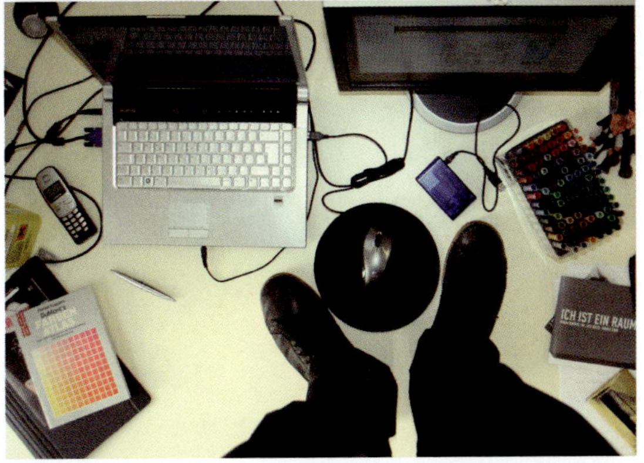

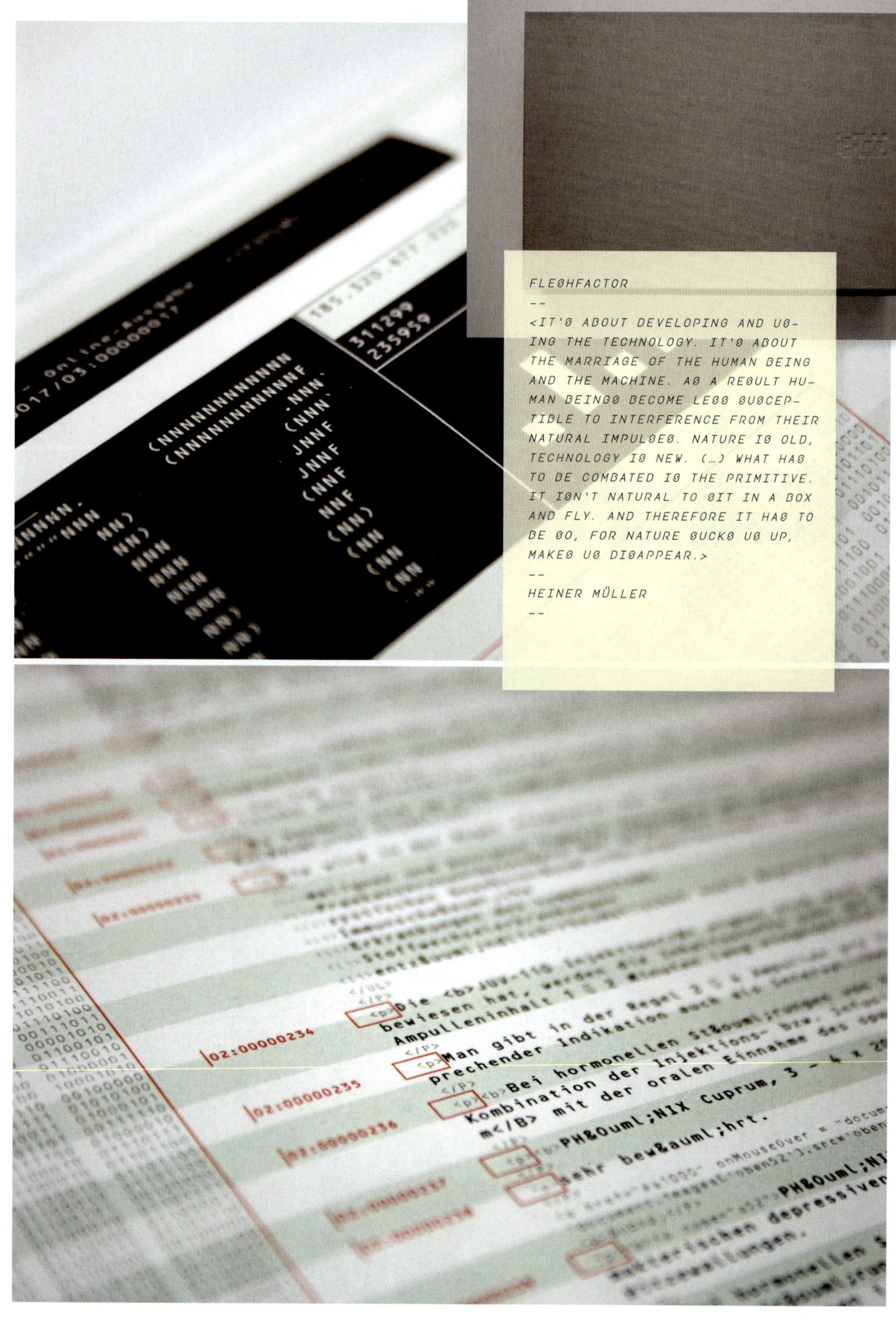

FLESHFACTOR
--
<IT'S ABOUT DEVELOPING AND US-
ING THE TECHNOLOGY. IT'S ABOUT
THE MARRIAGE OF THE HUMAN BEING
AND THE MACHINE. AS A RESULT HU-
MAN BEINGS BECOME LESS SUSCEP-
TIBLE TO INTERFERENCE FROM THEIR
NATURAL IMPULSES. NATURE IS OLD,
TECHNOLOGY IS NEW. (...) WHAT HAS
TO BE COMBATED IS THE PRIMITIVE.
IT ISN'T NATURAL TO SIT IN A BOX
AND FLY. AND THEREFORE IT HAS TO
BE SO, FOR NATURE SUCKS US UP,
MAKES US DISAPPEAR.>
--
HEINER MÜLLER
--

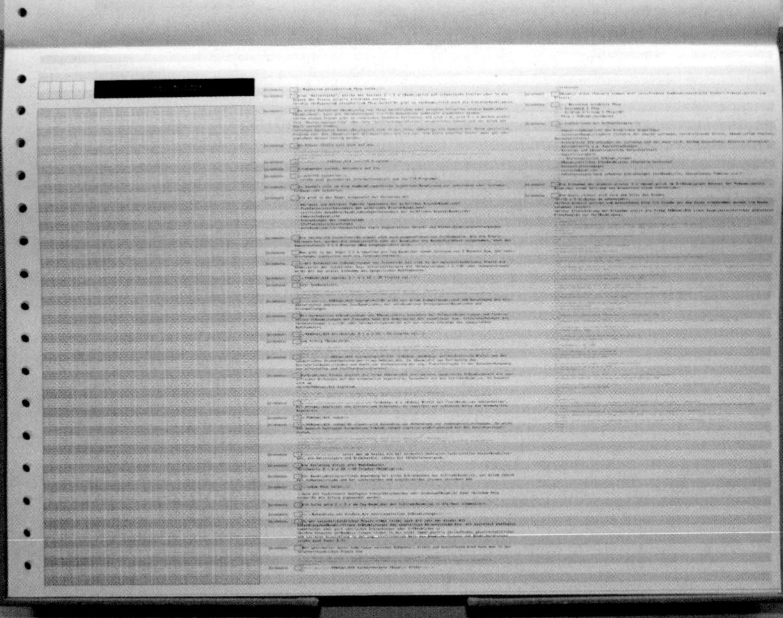

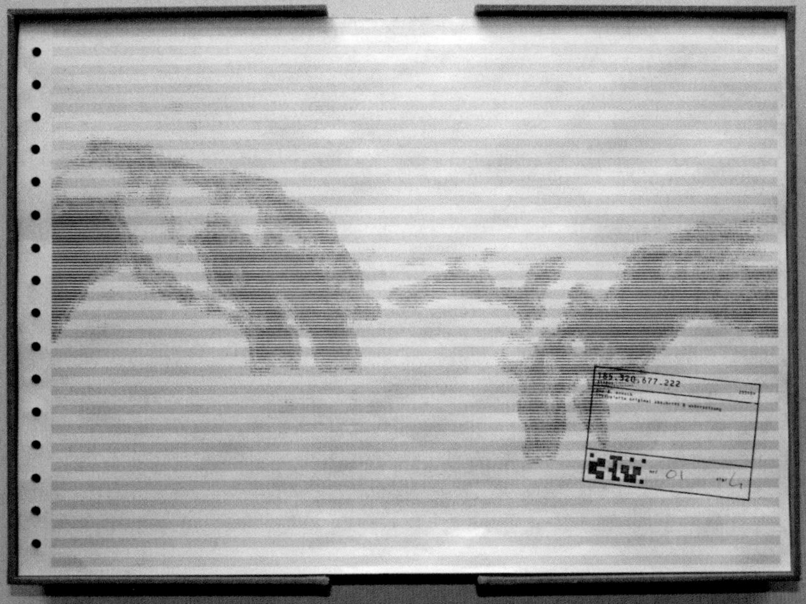
185.320.677.222

PIXELGARTEN IS A YOUNG DESIGN OF-
FICE. IT WAS FOUNDED IN 2004 BY
CATRIN ALTENBRANDT AND ADRIAN
NIESSLER. PIXELGARTEN DOES NOT SEE
ITSELF AS A TRADITIONAL GRAPHIC
DESIGN STUDIO, BUT WORKS OPENLY
AND INDEPENDENTLY OF ANY SPECIFIC
MEDIUM.

--

WHAT IS GERMAN?

GERMAN IS: PUNCTUAL, ORDERLY,
ACCURATE, RELIABLE… AND GERMANY
HAS THE BEST SAUSAGE - AS WE'VE
JUST BEEN TOLD BY SOME JAPANESE
PEOPLE! SO GERMAN = GOOD SAUSAGE!

WHAT IS GERMAN DESIGN?

…GERMAN DESIGN IS THAT TOO - BUT
NOT JUST THAT. GERMAN DESIGN IS…
NOT IN FACT TYPICALLY GERMAN! BUT
- AS WE SEE IT - OPEN TO THE WORLD
AND INNOVATIVE! …AND PERHAPS IT'S
ALSO OFTEN UNDERVALUED. AND GER-
MAN DESIGN IS ALSO VERY DIVERSE …
LIKE - IN FACT JUST LIKE GERMAN
SAUSAGE!

PLEASE DESCRIBE YOUR WORKING PROCESS.

IT VARIES A LOT - THERE ISN'T
ANY REGULAR WORKING PROCESS -
WITH US IT DEPENDS GREATLY ON THE
PROJECT. BUT OFTEN WE START WITH
RESEARCH AND FIRST SKETCHES (OF
IDEAS). YOU SEE, OUR PROJECTS ARE
OFTEN VERY DIFFERENT - THEY RANGE
FROM ART DIRECTION FOR MAGAZINES
TO PHOTO SHOOTS AND PURE INSTALLA-
TIONS.

WHAT DO YOU AIM TO ACHIEVE WITH YOUR WORK?

…WORLD PEACE! NO, JOKING ASIDE
- WE'RE SATISFIED IF OUR WORK IS
NOTICED AND PEOPLE LIKE IT, AND
SOMETIMES PERHAPS IT ALSO MAKES
THEM LAUGH.

YOU'VE INVITED A FRIEND TO GERMANY; NAME ONE PLACE THEY REALLY MUST VISIT AND A QUINT-ESSENTIAL EXPERIENCE YOU REC-OMMEND.

1. COME TO FRANKFURT OF COURSE!
2. TO SEE THAT IT'S NOT ONLY
   BERLIN THAT'S CREATIVE.

WHAT IS THE MOST IMPORTANT LESSON YOU HAVE LEARNED IN YOUR PROFESSION SO FAR?

TO REMAIN CALM NO MATTER HOW
TIGHT THE DEADLINE MAY BE! EVERY-
THING WILL TURN OUT OKAY! …IS OUR
MOTTO.

--

PIXELGARTEN

PIXELGARTEN

--

C/O BASIS FRANKFURT
ELBESTRASSE 10 HH
60329 FRANKFURT AM MAIN
GERMANY

--

T   +49 69 80087940
M   +49 160 7257997

--

HALLO@PIXELGARTEN.DE
WWW.PIXELGARTEN.DE

--

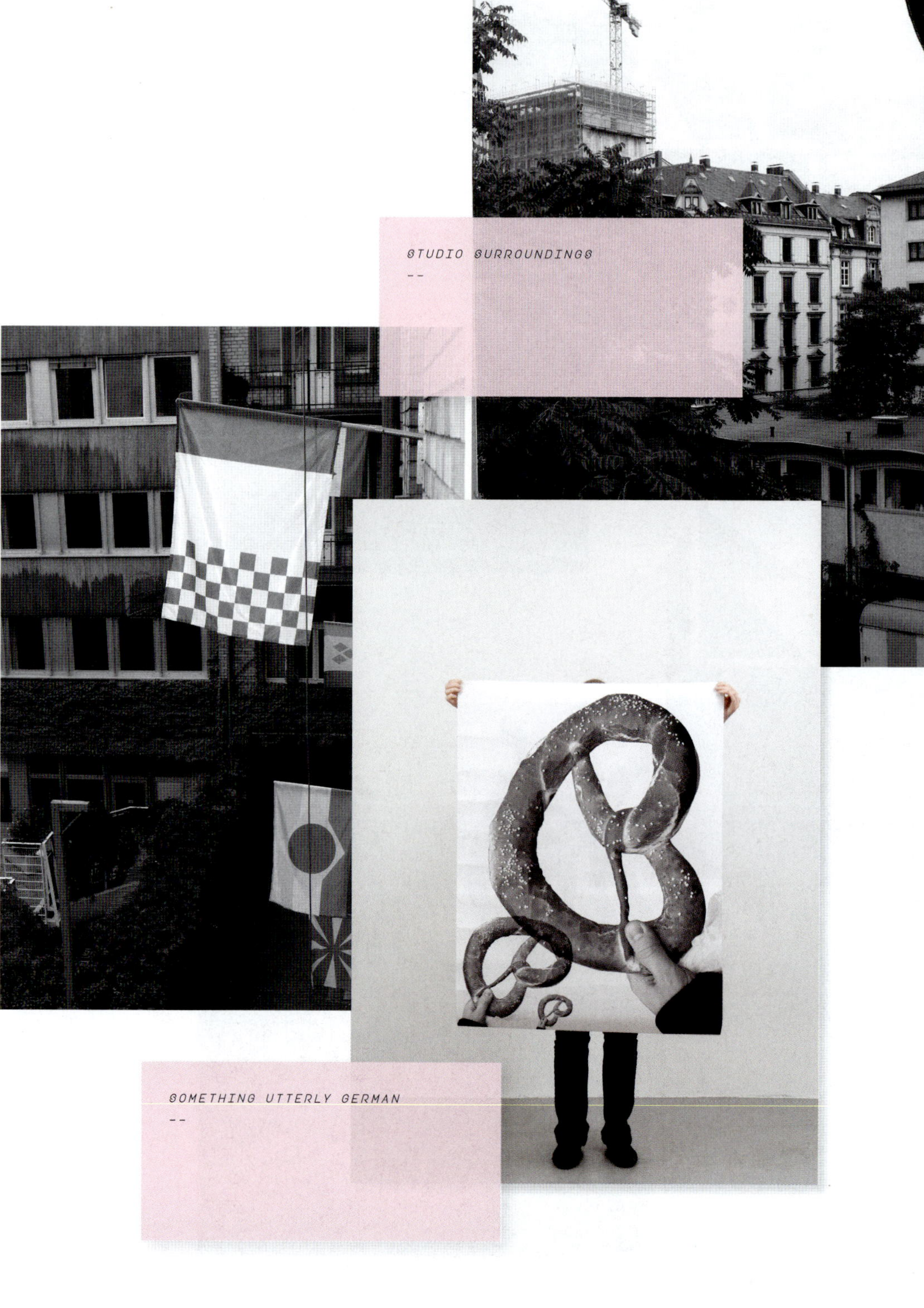
STUDIO SURROUNDINGS
--
SOMETHING UTTERLY GERMAN
--

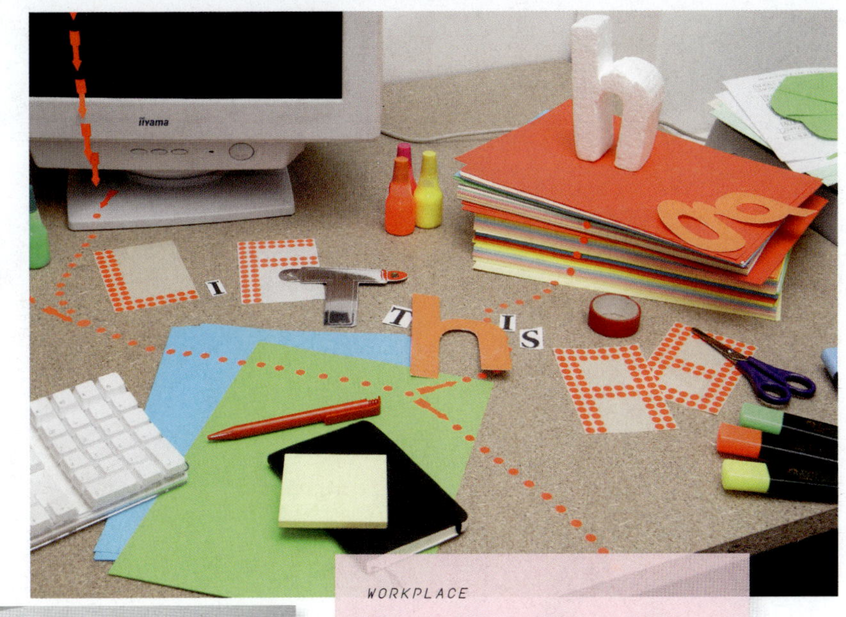

WORKPLACE
--

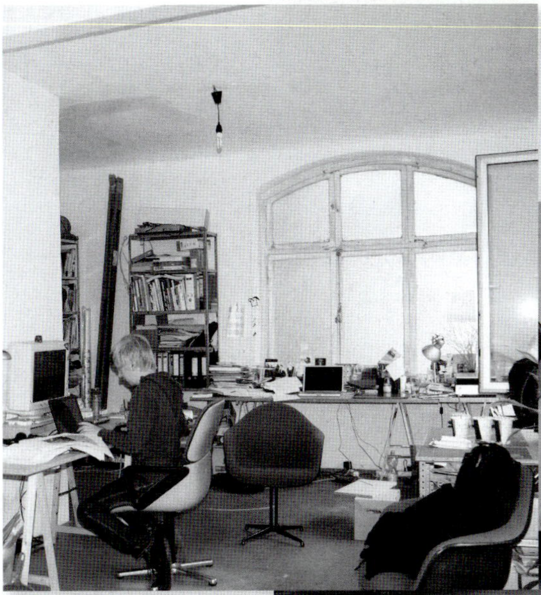

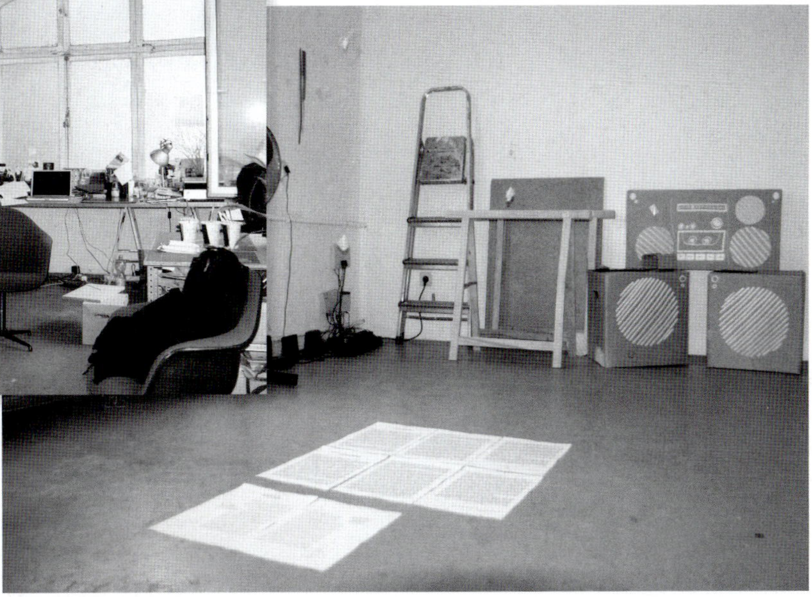

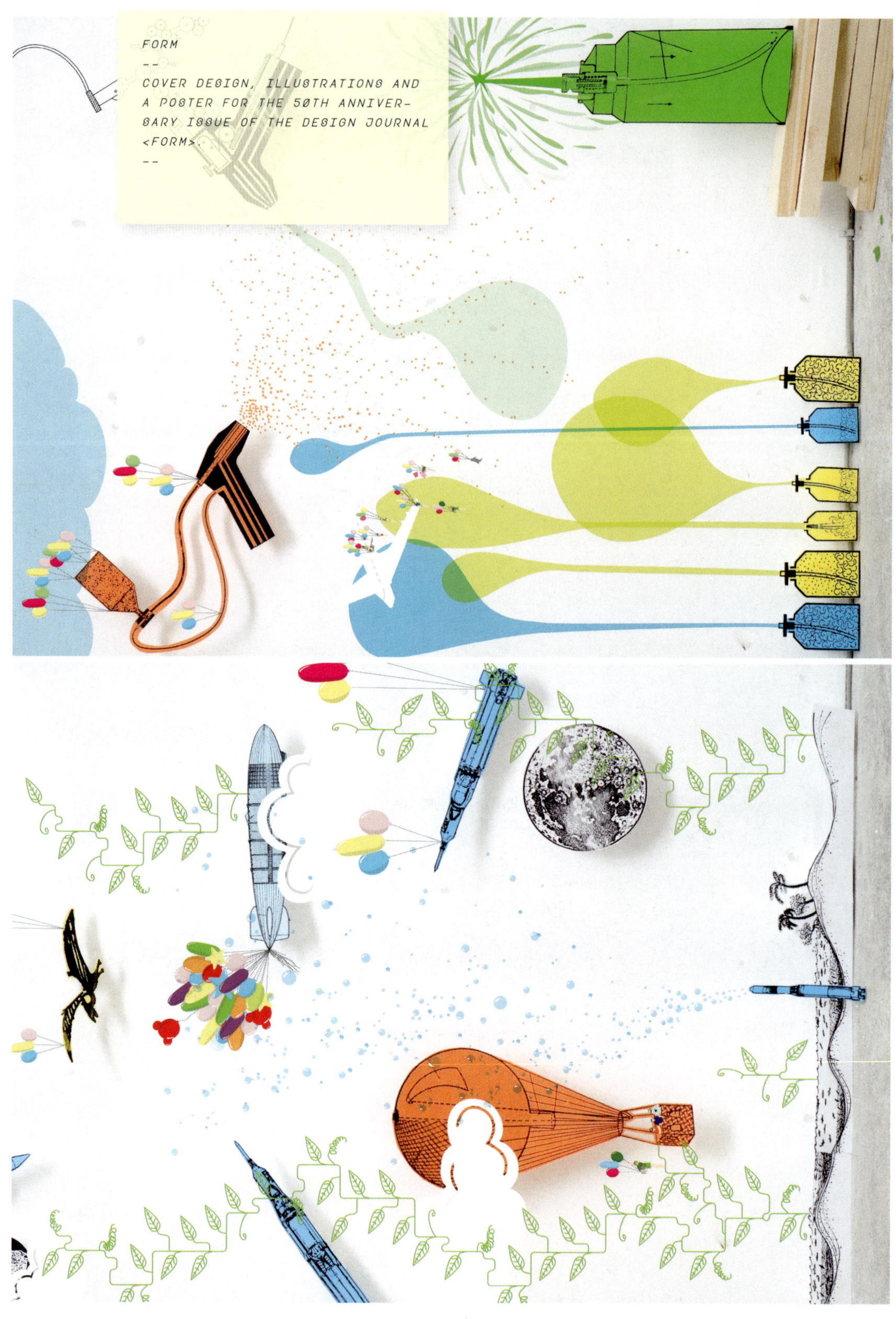

FORM
--
COVER DESIGN, ILLUSTRATIONS AND
A POSTER FOR THE 50TH ANNIVER-
SARY ISSUE OF THE DESIGN JOURNAL
<FORM>.
--

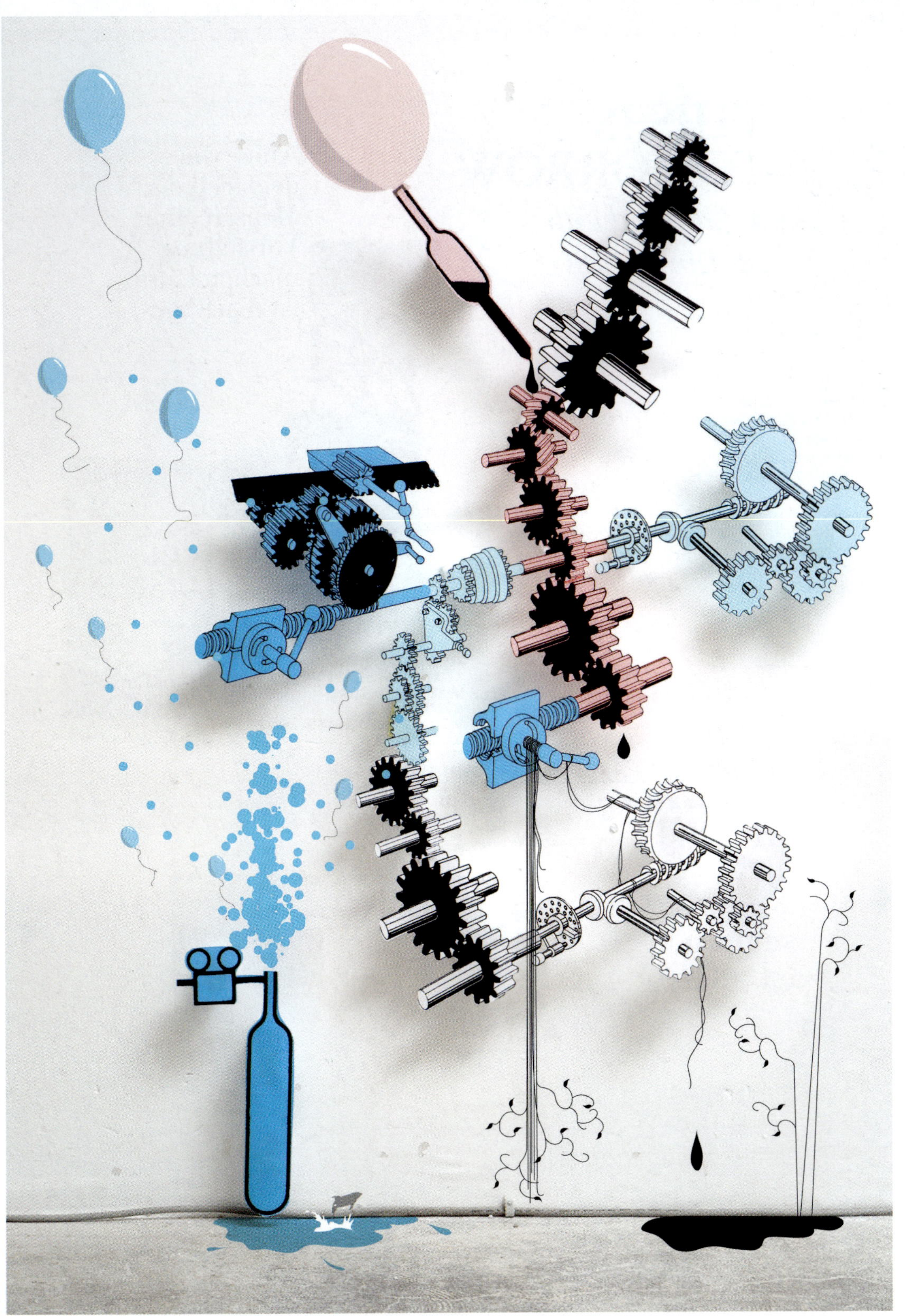

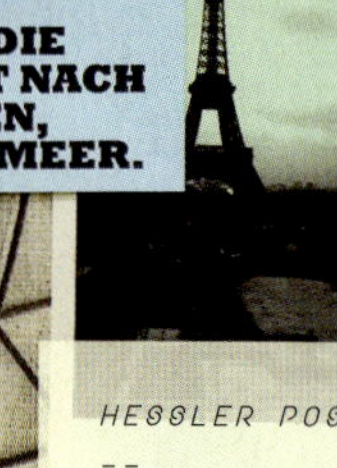
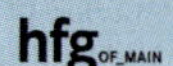

THIS IS TOMORROW
auf die Zukunft ist kein Verlass

Alles, von dem sich der Mensch eine Vorstellung machen kann, ist machbar.

Antrittsvorlesung
Prof. Dr. Martina Heßler
Kultur- und Technikgeschichte

Mittwoch, 15. November, 18.30 Uhr, Aula der Hochschule für Gestaltung, Schloßstraße 31, Offenbach am Main

Man kann sich heute einen Personal Computer vorstellen, der so klein ist, dass man ihn im Auto mitnehmen, ja sogar in die Tasche stecken kann. Er könnte an ein landesweites Computernetz angeschlossen sein und dem einzelnen auf Anfrage beinahe unbegrenzte Informationen bieten.

Die Vitalität selbst ist das Resultat einer Vision. Wenn es keine Vision mehr gibt von etwas Großem, Schönem, Wichtigem, dann reduziert sich die Vitalität, und der Mensch wird lebensschwächer.

DER EINZIG WAHRE REALIST IST DER VISIONÄR.

WENN DU EIN SCHIFF BAUEN WILLST, DANN TROMMLE NICHT MAENNER ZUSAMMEN, UM HOLZ ZU BESCHAFFEN, AUFGABEN ZU VERGEBEN UND DIE ARBEIT EINZUTEILEN, SONDERN LEHRE SIE DIE SEHNSUCHT NACH DEM WEITEN, ENDLOSEN MEER.

TO
THI
TOMORROW
THIS IS

Wir sind nichts. Was wir suchen, ist alles.

HESSLER POSTER
--
POSTER FOR THE LECTURE <THIS IS TOMORROW> BY PROFESSOR MARTINA HESSLER
--

hfg OF_MAIN

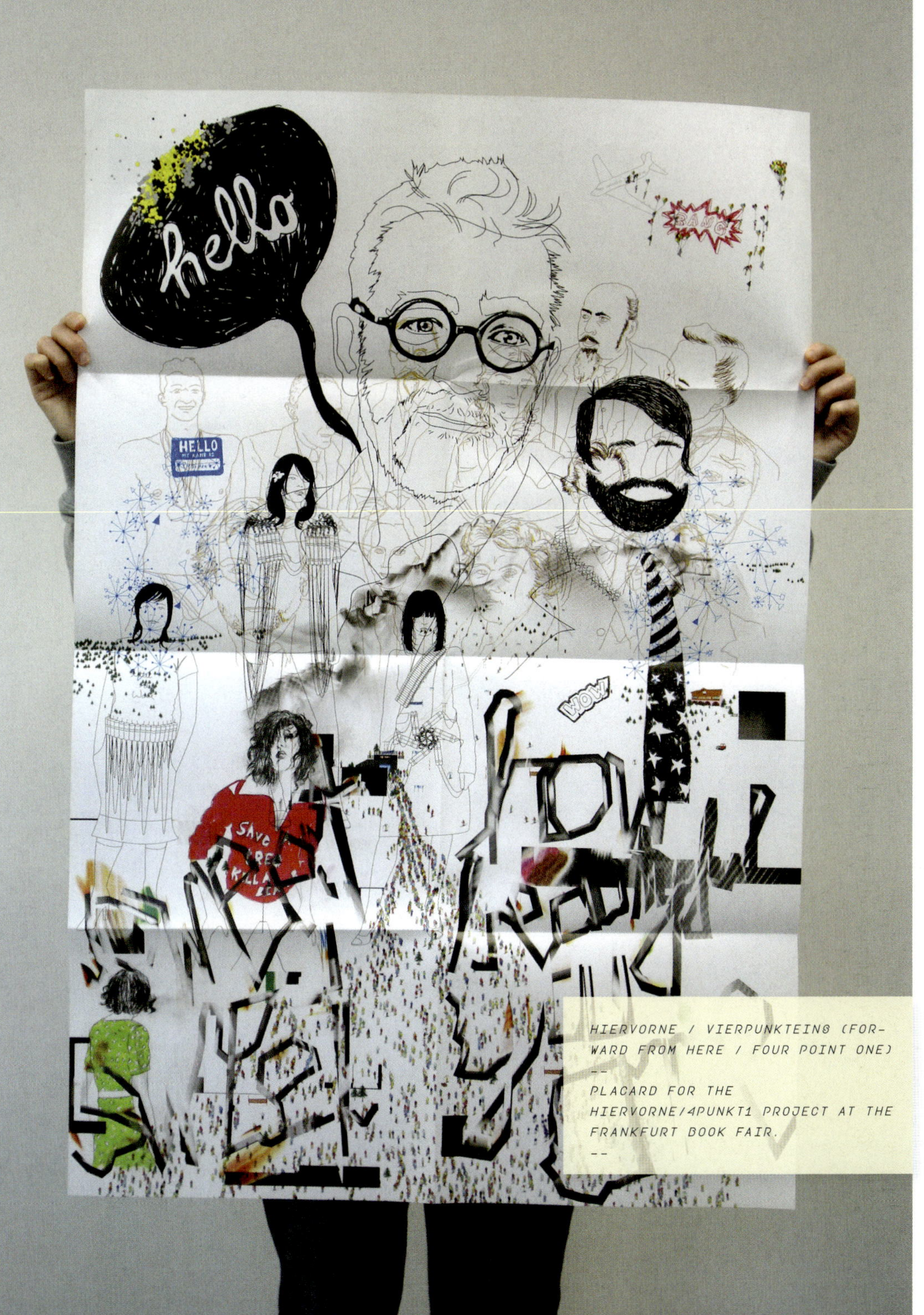

HIERVORNE / VIERPUNKTEINS (FOR-
WARD FROM HERE / FOUR POINT ONE)
--
PLACARD FOR THE
HIERVORNE/4PUNKT1 PROJECT AT THE
FRANKFURT BOOK FAIR.
--

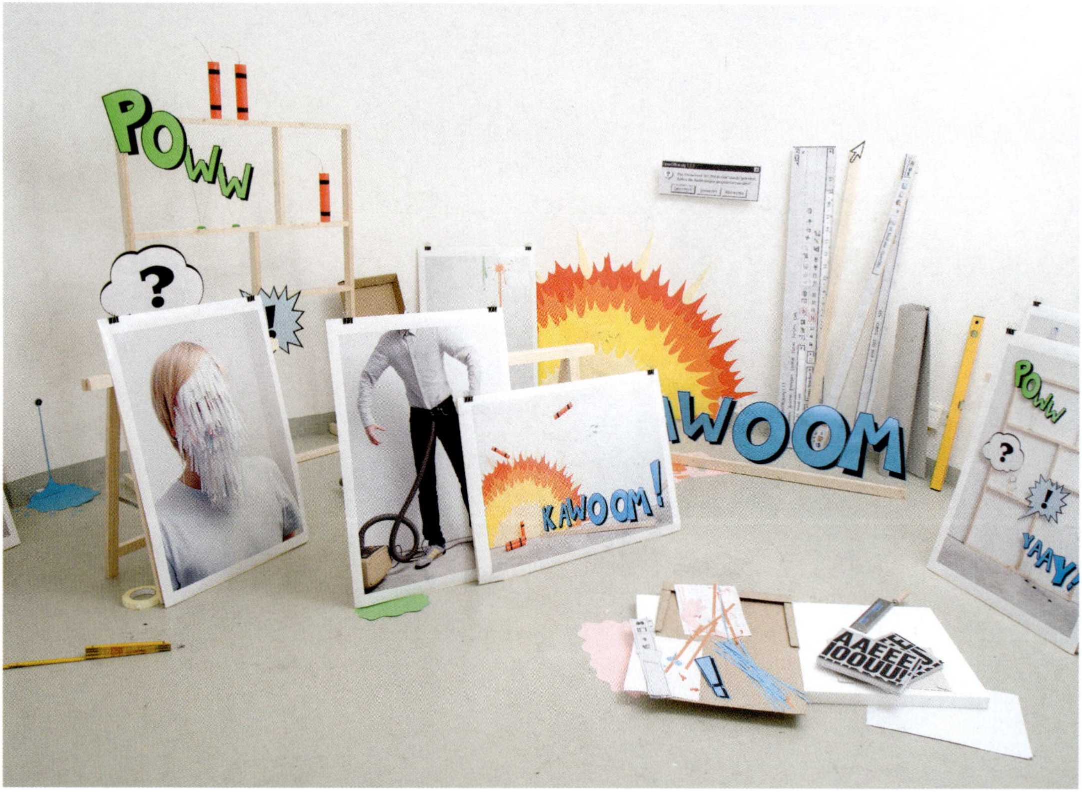

POWW
?
!
KAWOOM!
WOOM
AAEEE IOOUU!
POWW
?
!
YAAY!

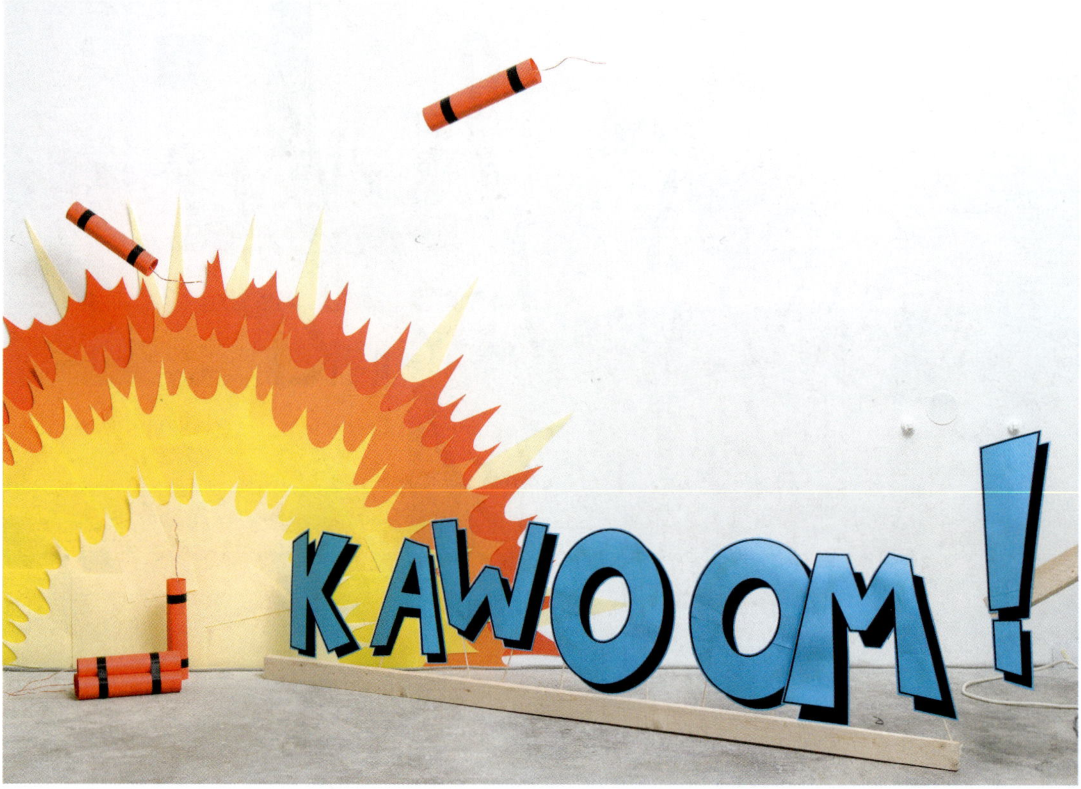

KAWOOM !

WE ARE TWO FEMALE COMMUNICATION
DESIGN STUDENTS. WE LIKE WORKING
TOGETHER AND LIKE WORKING ALONE.
OUR TEMPORARY OFFICE IS IN THE
DESIGN DEPARTMENT OF THE HOCH-
SCHULE DARMSTADT. CURRENTLY WE ARE
WORKING TOGETHER ON OUR DEGREE.
OUR MAIN FOCUS IS IN THE FIELD OF
PRINT; FIRST AND FOREMOST TYPOGRA-
PHY, GRAPHIC ART UND ILLUSTRATION.

--

WHAT IS GERMAN?

CAN DEPOSIT SCHEMES
AND RECYCLING
ORGANIC PRODUCE
AND BATTERY FARMS
DONER KEBABS
AND PICKLED EGGS
ENVY
AND TOLERANCE

WHAT IS GERMAN DESIGN?

RETICENT
AND STRIDENT
OLD
AND NEW
GROTESQUE
AND FRAKTUR [BLACK-LETTER TYPE]
CONSCIOUS OF TRADITION
AND ENJOYING EXPERIMENTATION

PLEASE DESCRIBE YOUR WORKING
PROCESS.

THINKING, READING, TALKING,
WORKING, DANCING

WHAT DO YOU AIM TO ACHIEVE WITH
YOUR WORK?

LOOKING, READING, THINKING,
TALKING, DANCING, WORKING.

YOU'VE INVITED A FRIEND TO
GERMANY; NAME ONE PLACE THEY
REALLY MUST VISIT AND A QUINT-
ESSENTIAL EXPERIENCE YOU REC-
OMMEND.

1. NO MATTER WHERE;
2. USE PUBLIC TRANSPORT!

WHAT IS THE MOST IMPORTANT
LESSON YOU HAVE LEARNED IN YOUR
PROFESSION SO FAR?

THE COMPUTER IS MY BEST FRIEND
AND GREATEST ENEMY, PROGRESS AND
REGRESSION IN ONE.

--

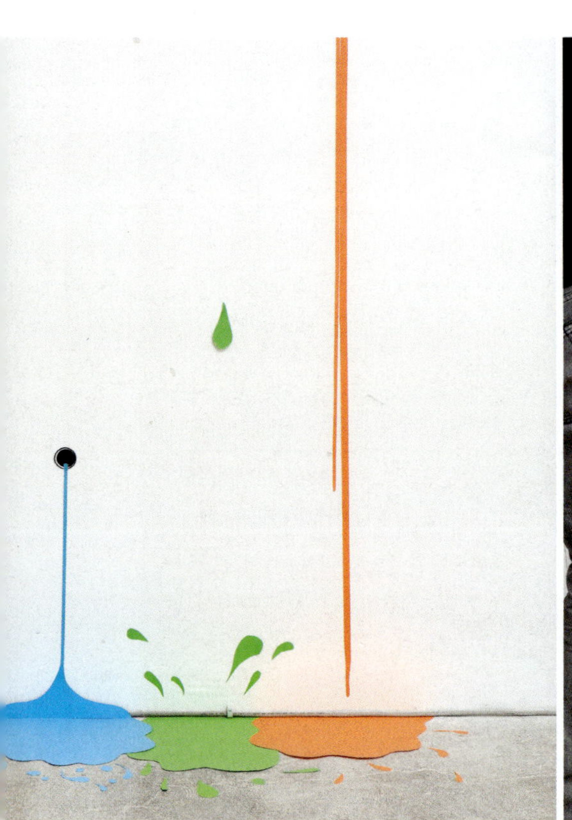
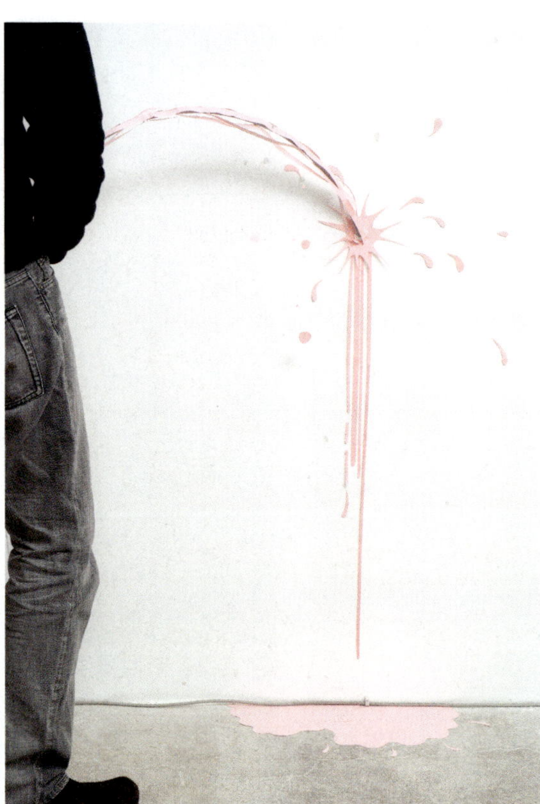
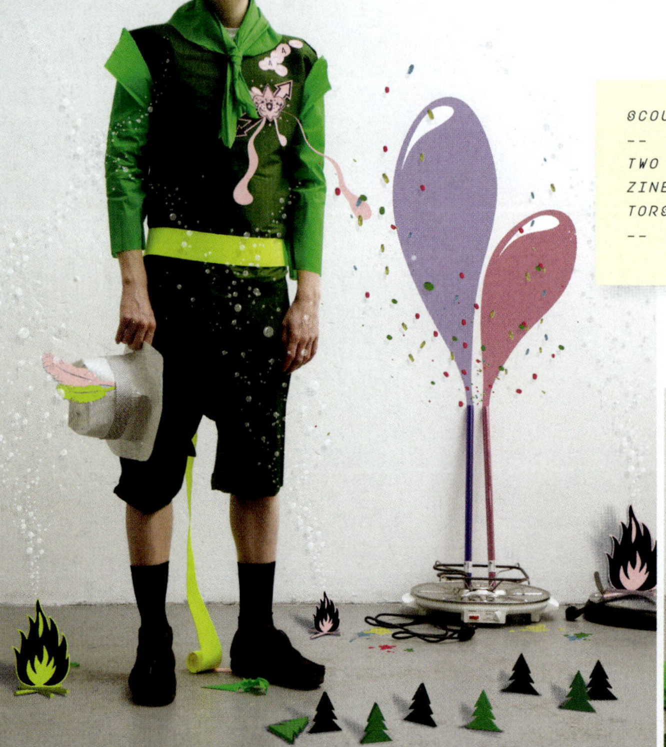

SCOUT UNIFORM
--
TWO ILLUSTRATIONS FOR THE MAGA-
ZINE SUSHI 10 OF THE ART DIREC-
TORS CLUB OF GERMANY
--

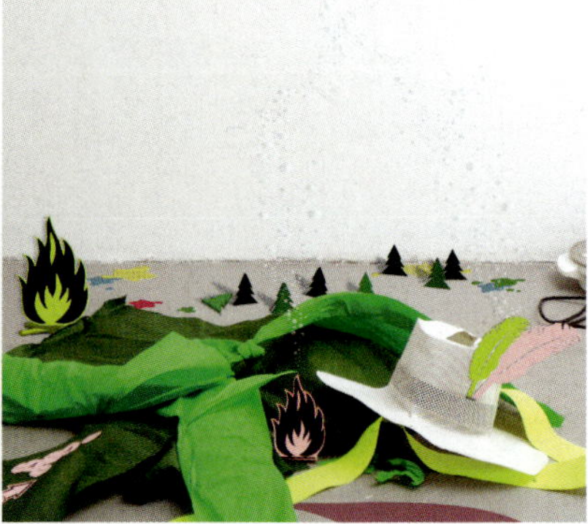

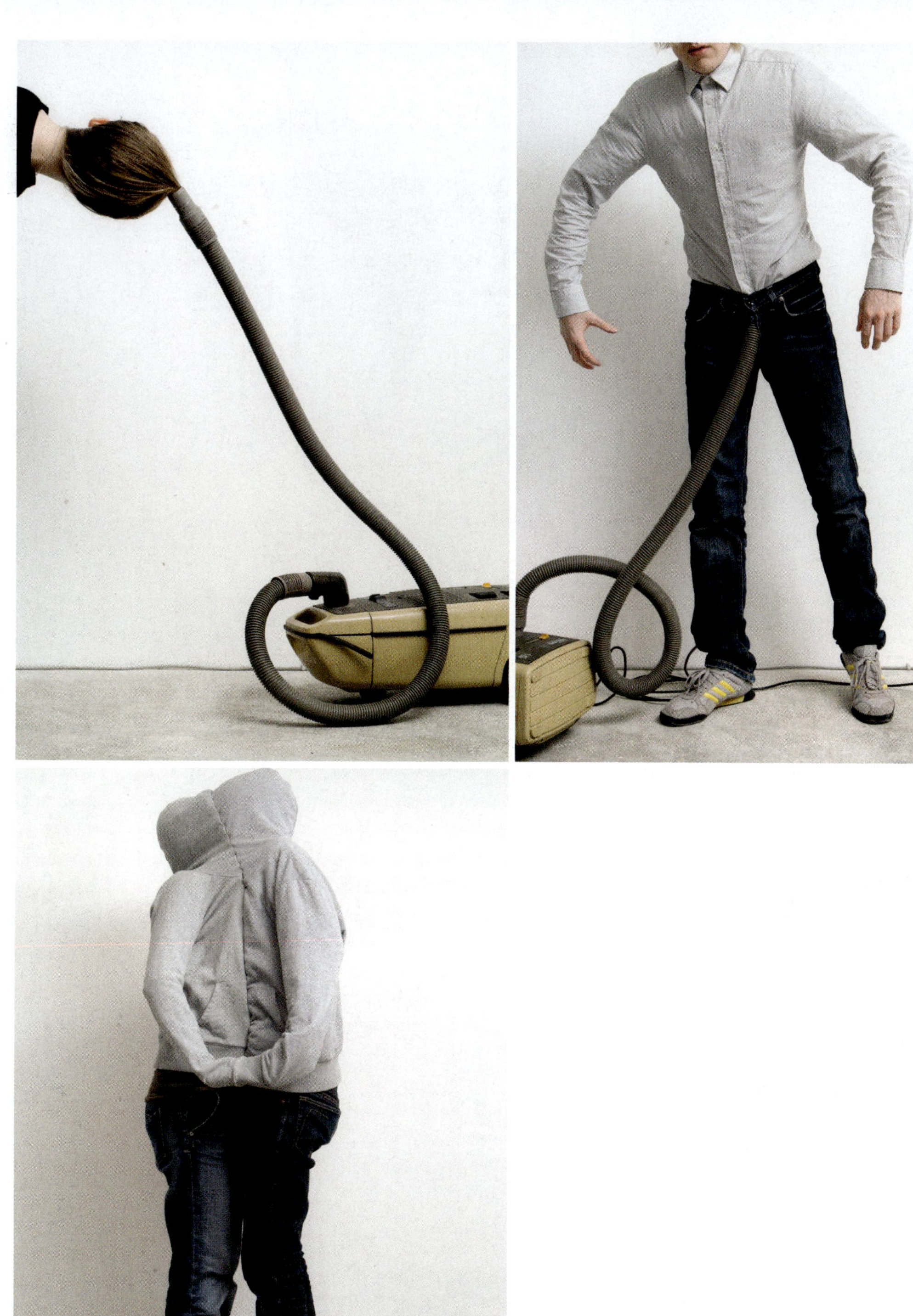

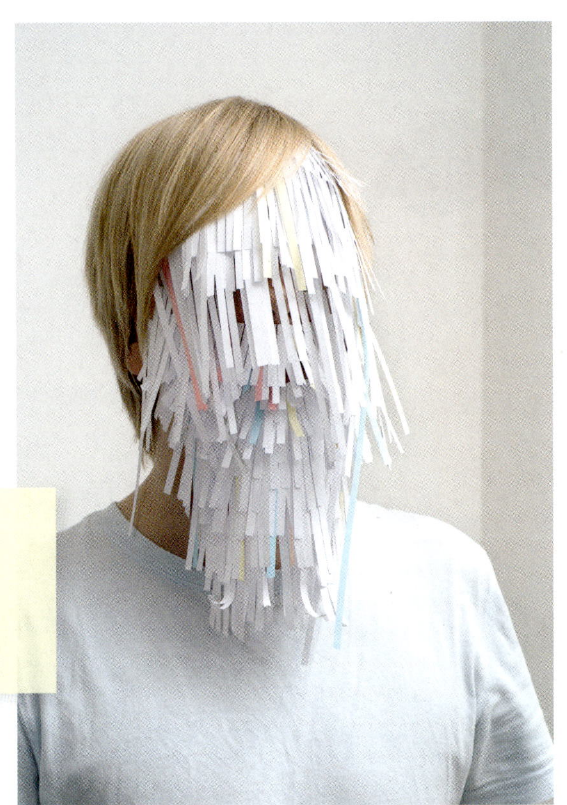

UM WAS ES NICHT GEHT
--

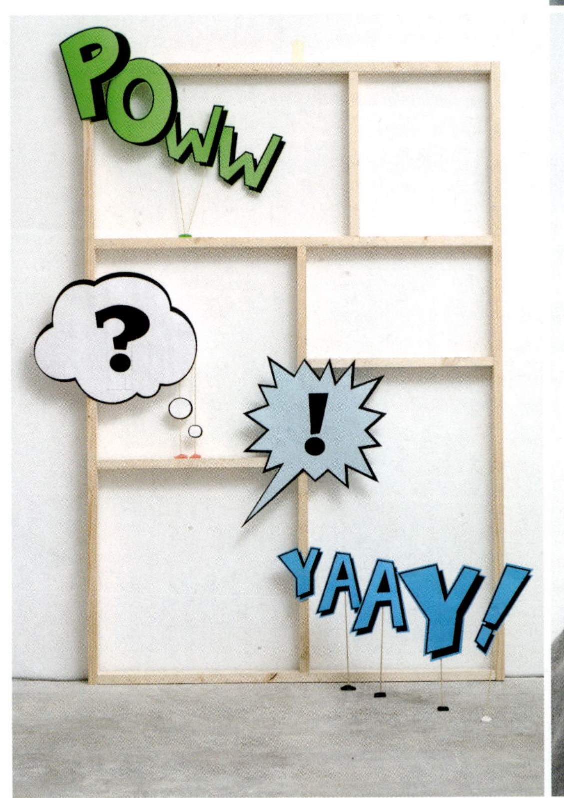

POww
?
!
YAAY!

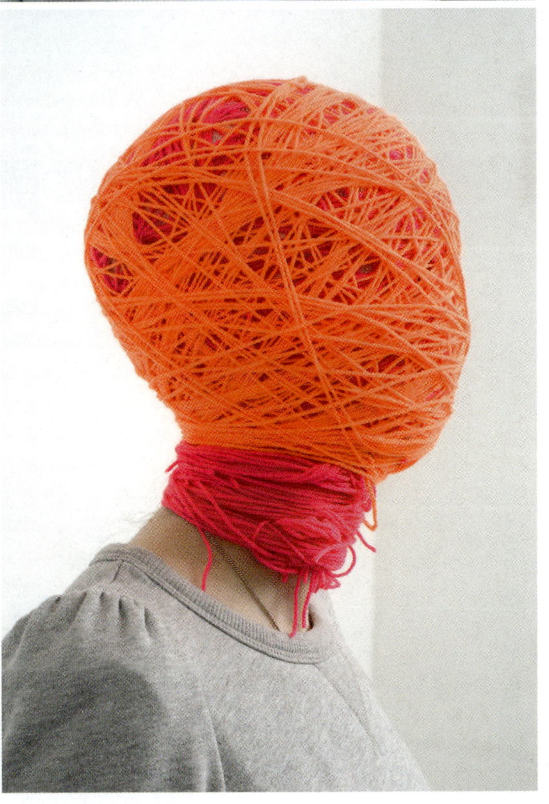

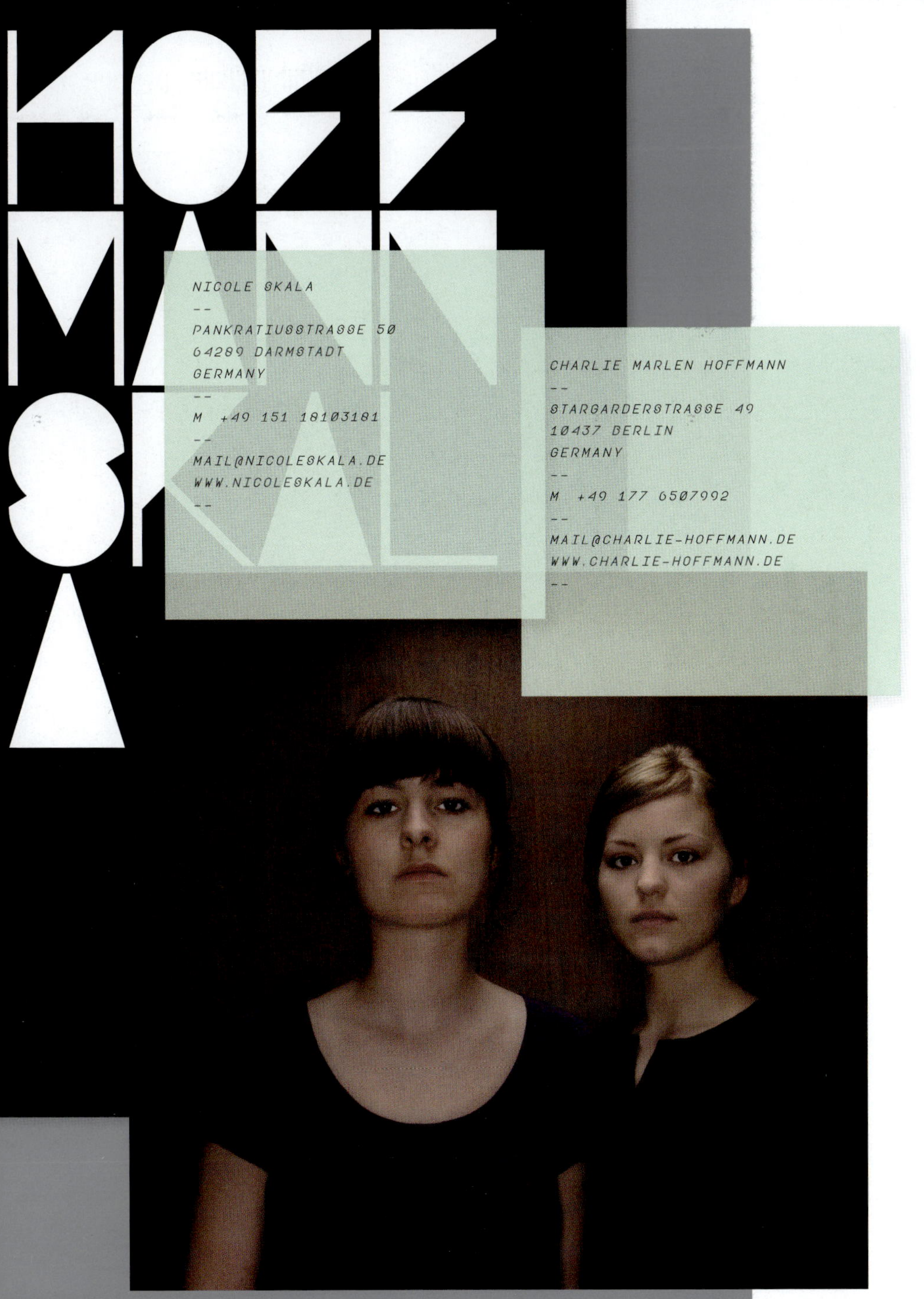

HOFF
MANN
SKALA

NICOLE SKALA
--
PANKRATIUSSTRASSE 50
64289 DARMSTADT
GERMANY
--
M +49 151 18103181
--
MAIL@NICOLESKALA.DE
WWW.NICOLESKALA.DE
--

CHARLIE MARLEN HOFFMANN
--
STARGARDERSTRASSE 49
10437 BERLIN
GERMANY
--
M +49 177 6507992
--
MAIL@CHARLIE-HOFFMANN.DE
WWW.CHARLIE-HOFFMANN.DE
--

SOMETHING UTTERLY GERMAN
--

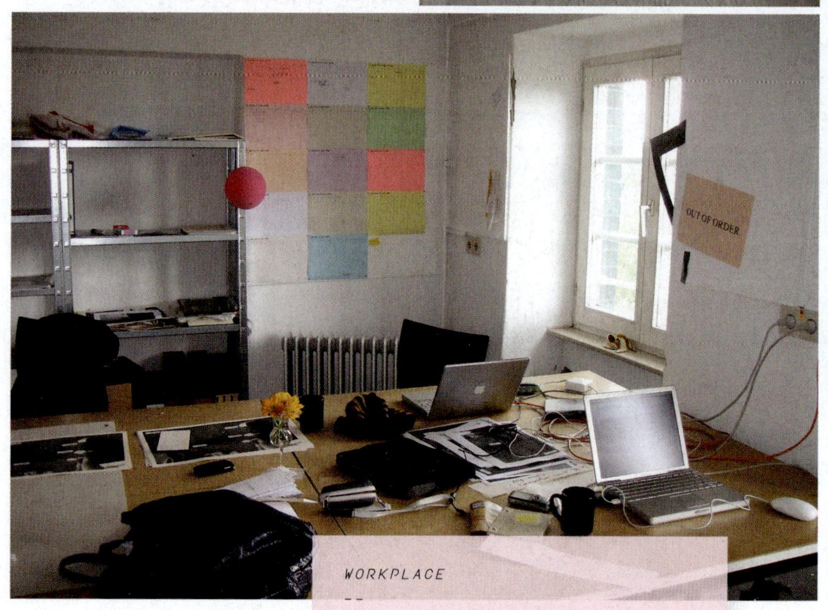

WORKPLACE
--

STUDIO SURROUNDINGS
--

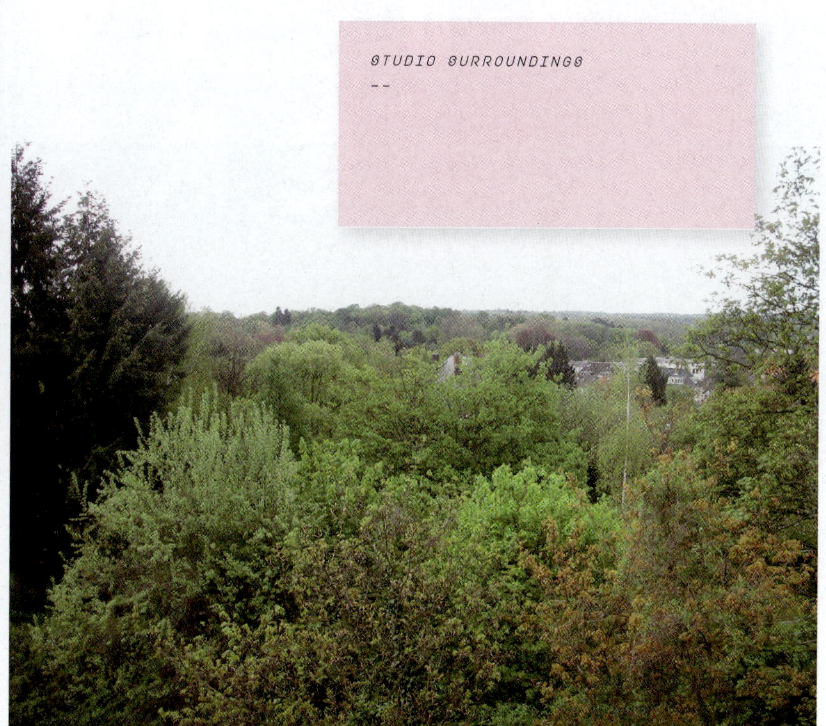

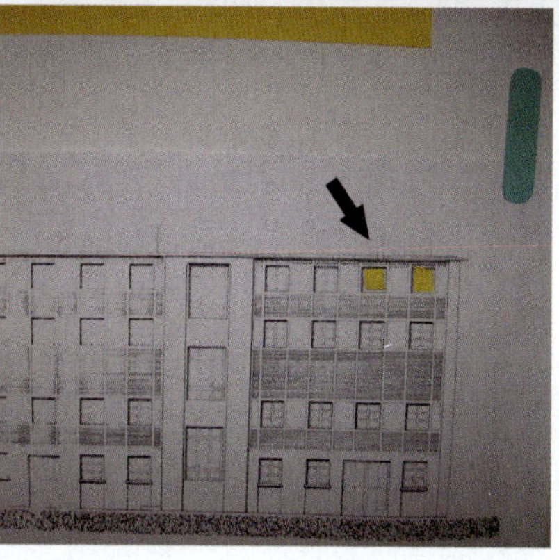

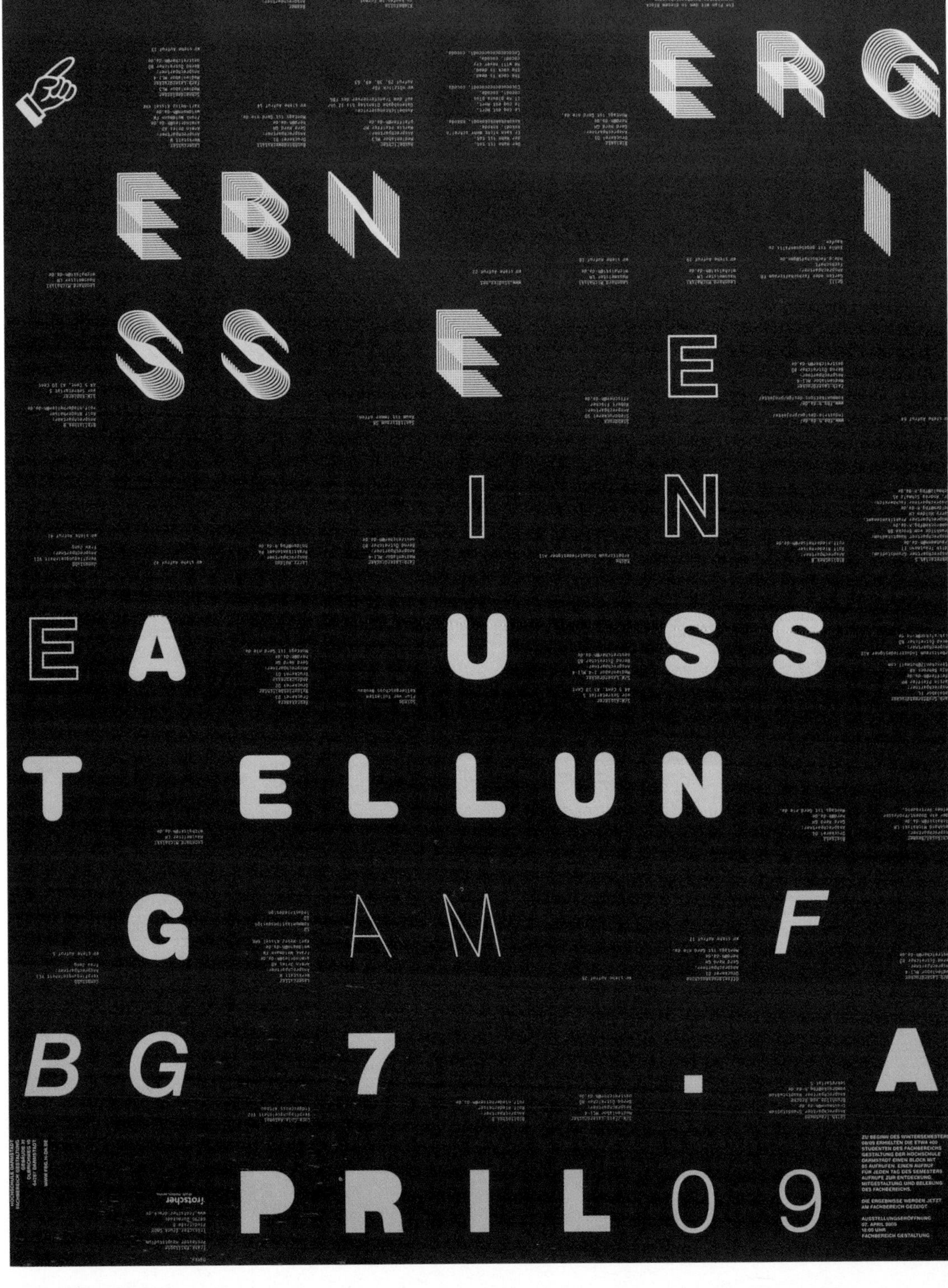

3 40.00
ERGEBNISSE EINER AUSSTELLUNG AM 7. APRIL 09
BG
ZU BEGINN DES WINTERSEMESTERS
09/09 ERHIELTEN DIE ETWA 450
STUDENTEN DES FACHBEREICHS
GESTALTUNG DER HOCHSCHULE
DARMSTADT EINEN BLOCK MIT
85 AUFRUFEN. EINEN AUFRUF
FÜR JEDEN TAG DES SEMESTERS
AUFRUFE ZUR ENTDECKUNG,
MITGESTALTUNG UND BELEBUNG
DES FACHBEREICHS.
DIE ERGEBNISSE WERDEN JETZT
AM FACHBEREICH GEZEIGT.
AUSSTELLUNGSERÖFFNUNG
07. APRIL 2009
12:00 UHR
FACHBEREICH GESTALTUNG

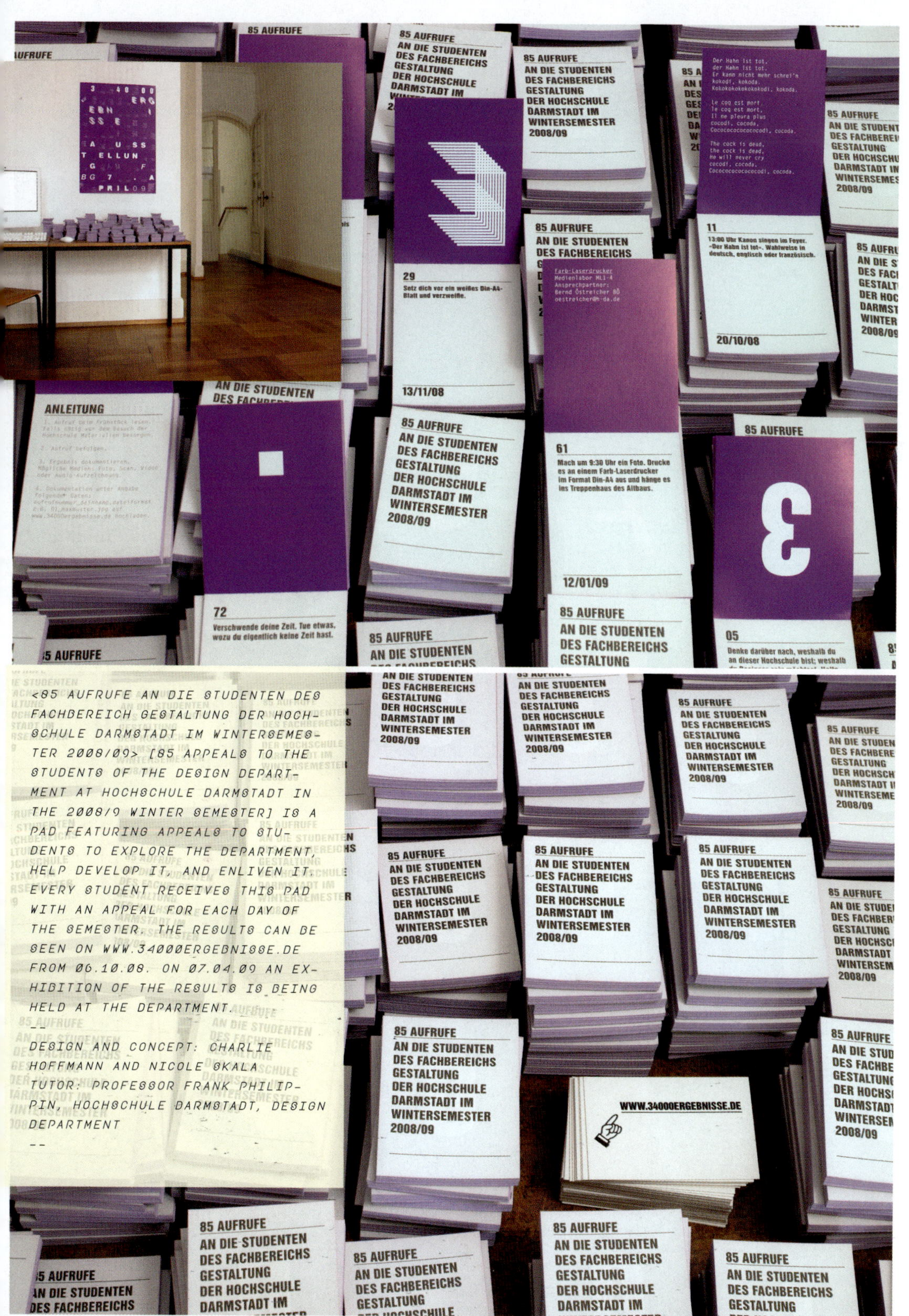

<85 AUFRUFE AN DIE STUDENTEN DES FACHBEREICH GESTALTUNG DER HOCH-SCHULE DARMSTADT IM WINTERSEMES-TER 2008/09> [85 APPEALS TO THE STUDENTS OF THE DESIGN DEPART-MENT AT HOCHSCHULE DARMSTADT IN THE 2008/9 WINTER SEMESTER] IS A PAD FEATURING APPEALS TO STU-DENTS TO EXPLORE THE DEPARTMENT, HELP DEVELOP IT, AND ENLIVEN IT. EVERY STUDENT RECEIVES THIS PAD WITH AN APPEAL FOR EACH DAY OF THE SEMESTER. THE RESULTS CAN BE SEEN ON WWW.34000ERGEBNISSE.DE FROM 06.10.08. ON 07.04.09 AN EX-HIBITION OF THE RESULTS IS BEING HELD AT THE DEPARTMENT.
__
DESIGN AND CONCEPT: CHARLIE HOFFMANN AND NICOLE SKALA
TUTOR: PROFESSOR FRANK PHILIP-PIN, HOCHSCHULE DARMSTADT, DESIGN DEPARTMENT
--
85 AUFRUFE
AN DIE STUDENTEN DES FACHBEREICHS GESTALTUNG DER HOCHSCHULE DARMSTADT IM WINTERSEMESTER 2008/09
WWW.34000ERGEBNISSE.DE
ANLEITUNG
29
Setz dich vor ein weißes Din-A4-Blatt und verzweifle.
11
13:00 Uhr Kanon singen im Foyer. ~Der Hahn ist tot~. Wahlweise in deutsch, englisch oder französisch.
Der Hahn ist tot, der Hahn ist tot. Er kann nicht mehr schrei'n kokodi, kokoda. Kokokokokokokodi, kokoda.
Le coq est mort, le coq est mort. Il ne pleura plus cocodi, cocoda, Cocococococococodi, cocoda.
The cock is dead, the cock is dead. He will never cry cocodi, cocoda, Cocococococococodi, cocoda.
Farb-Laserdrucker Medienlabor M11-4 Ansprechpartner: Bernd Österreicher bö oestreicher@m-da.de
20/10/08
61
Mach um 9:30 Uhr ein Foto. Drucke es an einem Farb-Laserdrucker im Format Din-A4 aus und hänge es ins Treppenhaus des Altbaus.
12/01/09
72
Verschwende deine Zeit. Tue etwas, wozu du eigentlich keine Zeit hast.
05
Denke darüber nach, weshalb du an dieser Hochschule bist; weshalb
13/11/08

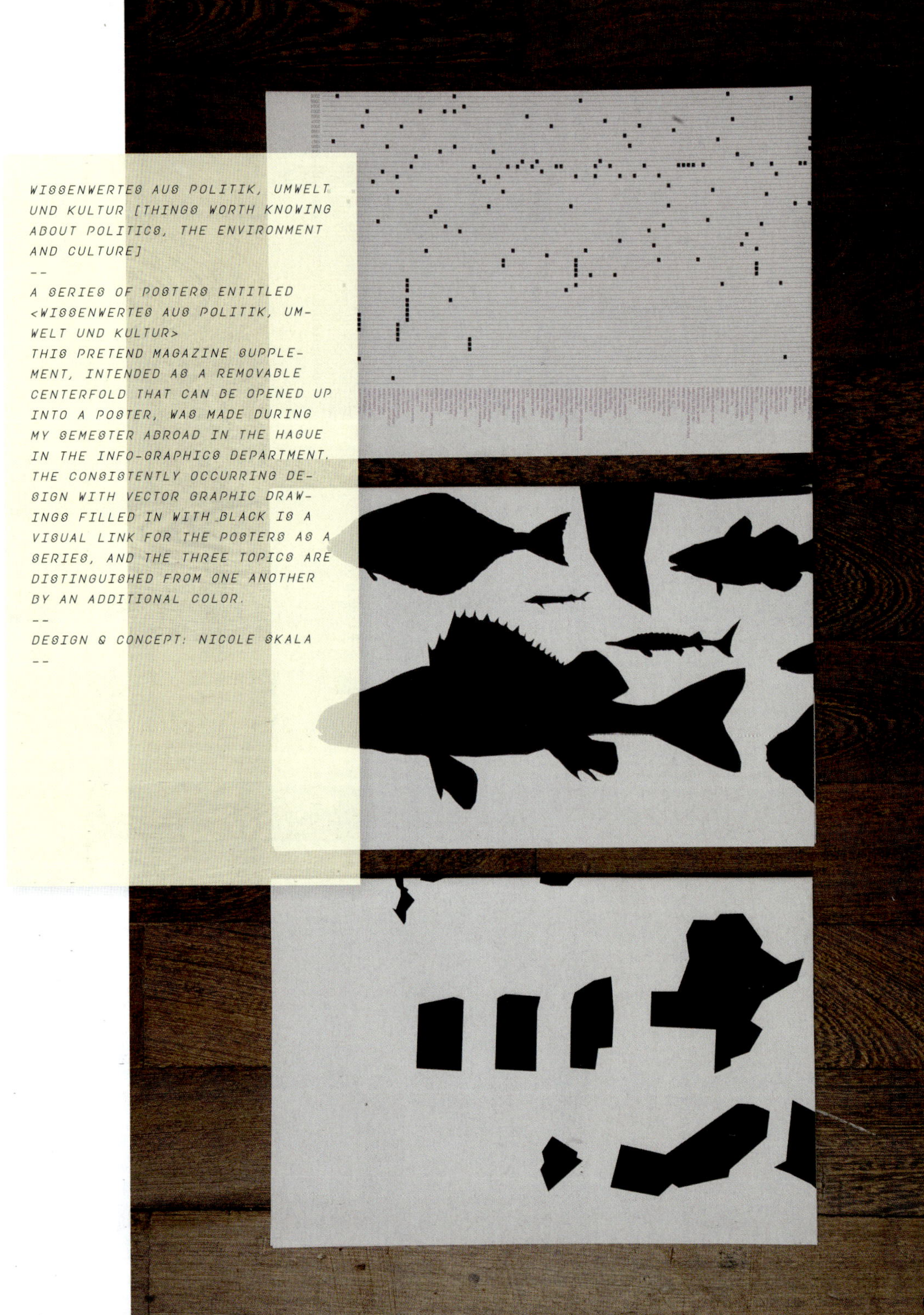

WISSENWERTES AUS POLITIK, UMWELT
UND KULTUR [THINGS WORTH KNOWING
ABOUT POLITICS, THE ENVIRONMENT
AND CULTURE]
--
A SERIES OF POSTERS ENTITLED
<WISSENWERTES AUS POLITIK, UM-
WELT UND KULTUR>
THIS PRETEND MAGAZINE SUPPLE-
MENT, INTENDED AS A REMOVABLE
CENTERFOLD THAT CAN BE OPENED UP
INTO A POSTER, WAS MADE DURING
MY SEMESTER ABROAD IN THE HAGUE
IN THE INFO-GRAPHICS DEPARTMENT.
THE CONSISTENTLY OCCURRING DE-
SIGN WITH VECTOR GRAPHIC DRAW-
INGS FILLED IN WITH BLACK IS A
VISUAL LINK FOR THE POSTERS AS A
SERIES, AND THE THREE TOPICS ARE
DISTINGUISHED FROM ONE ANOTHER
BY AN ADDITIONAL COLOR.
--
DESIGN & CONCEPT: NICOLE SKALA
--

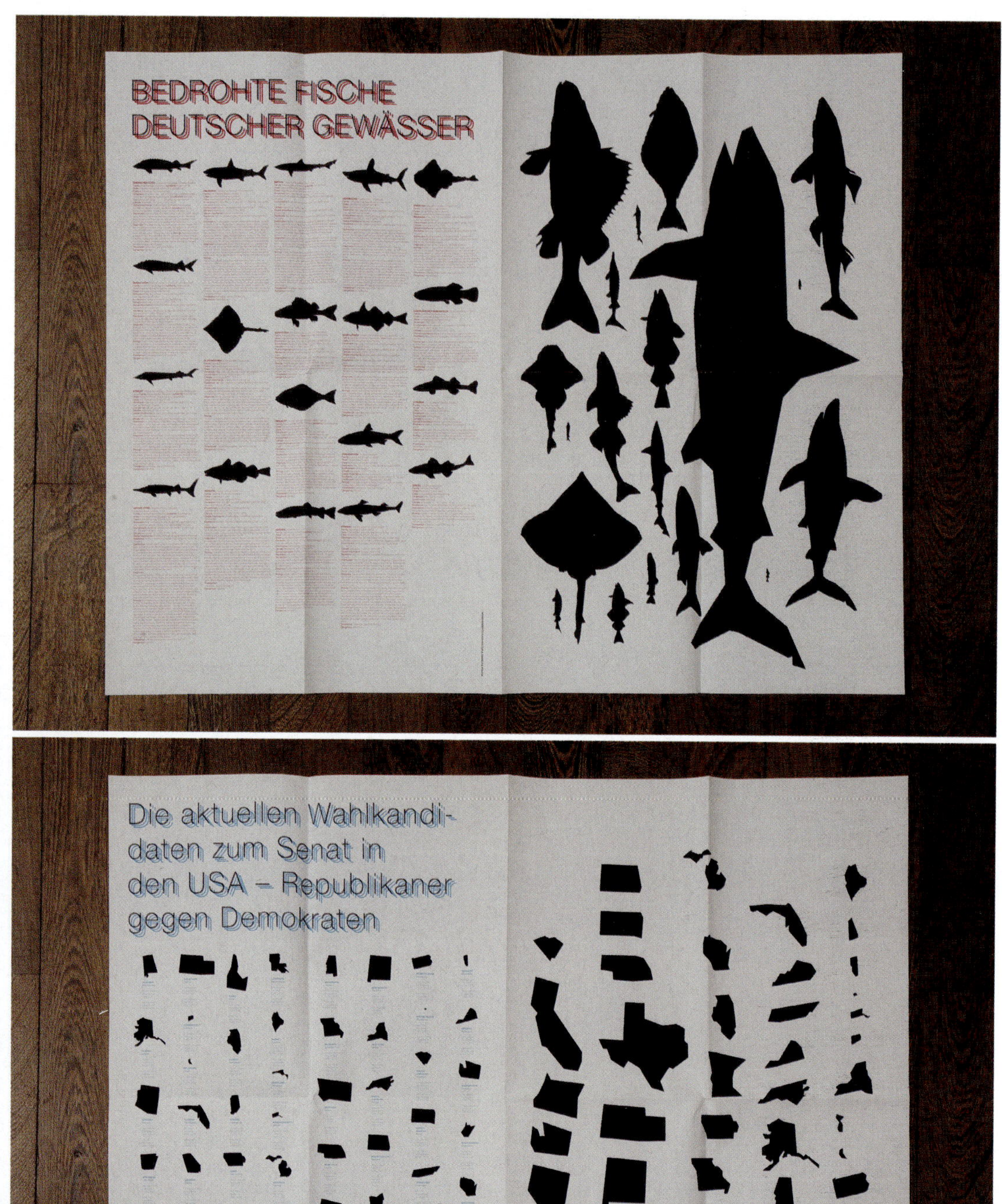
BEDROHTE FISCHE
DEUTSCHER GEWÄSSER
Die aktuellen Wahlkandi-
daten zum Senat in
den USA – Republikaner
gegen Demokraten

WE ARE STUDENTS AT THE HOCHSCHULE
DARMSTADT AND ARE IN THE PROCESS
OF TAKING OUR DEGREE. WE DON'T
HAVE AN OFFICE OF OUR OWN. THE
PROJECT SHOWN WAS DONE DURING OUR
SEMESTER ABROAD IN LISBON. THE
MAIN FOCUS OF OUR WORK CONCEN-
TRATES ON THE FIELDS OF TYPOGRAPHY
AND GRAPHIC ART, IN JAKOB'S CASE
ILLUSTRATION TOO.

--

WHAT IS GERMAN?

L ROMANTICISM, IDEALISM, UNFORTU-
NATELY ALSO INTELLECTUAL INFLEX-
IBILITY AND A TENDENCY TO BE KNOW-
ALLS.
R PUNCTUALITY. ORDERLINESS. BEER.
BREAD.

WHAT IS GERMAN DESIGN?

L UNPRETENTIOUS AND RICH IN CON-
TENT. STRICTLY TO THE POINT (IF
IT'S GOOD).
R GOOD. CLEAR. SUBTLE.

PLEASE DESCRIBE YOUR WORKING
PROCESS.

L IT KEEPS CHANGING. BUT MOSTLY IT
FLUCTUATES BACK AND FORTH BETWEEN
IDEAS AND IMPLEMENTATIONS.
R COLLECTING. READING. EXPERIMENT-
ING. DEVELOPING AN IDEA. SELECT-
ING. ELABORATING. DONE.

WHAT DO YOU AIM TO ACHIEVE WITH
YOUR WORK?

L TO APPEAL TO PEOPLE AND ENTER-
TAIN THEM, SOMETIMES ALSO TO EN-
RAGE THEM.
R LAUGHTER. CONTENT. FORM. INSPI-
RATION.

YOU'VE INVITED A FRIEND TO
GERMANY; NAME ONE PLACE THEY
REALLY MUST VISIT AND A QUINT-
ESSENTIAL EXPERIENCE YOU REC-
OMMEND.

L GO TO ANY TOWN CENTER AND MARVEL
AT THE ASTONISHING AMOUNT OF TIME
GERMANS SPEND DRINKING COFFEE AND
RELAXING.
R MATHILDENHÖHE DARMSTADT. PLAY
BOULES.

WHAT IS THE MOST IMPORTANT
LESSON YOU HAVE LEARNED IN YOUR
PROFESSION SO FAR?

L TO CHALLENGE THINGS. AND THAT
NOTHING'S SO BENEFICIAL FOR THE
DESIGN PROCESS AS RECIPROCAL CRIT-
ICISM.
R ONLY WHAT YOU THINK IS GOOD
TURNS OUT GOOD.

--

L JAKOB LIESENFELD
R VALERIE RAPP

--

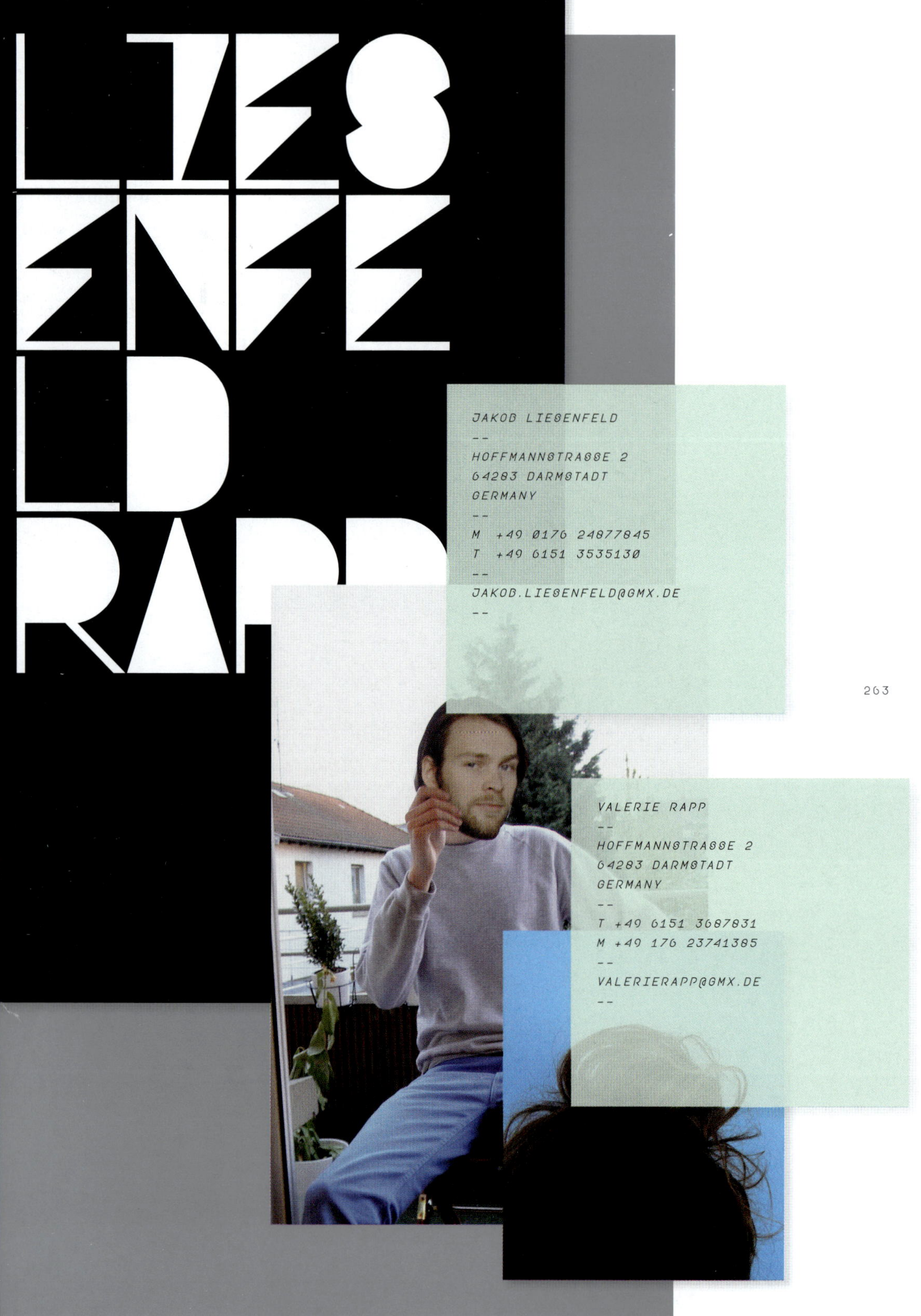

JAKOB LIESENFELD
--
HOFFMANNSTRASSE 2
64283 DARMSTADT
GERMANY
--
M +49 0176 24877845
T +49 6151 3535130
--
JAKOB.LIESENFELD@GMX.DE
--

VALERIE RAPP
--
HOFFMANNSTRASSE 2
64283 DARMSTADT
GERMANY
--
T +49 6151 3687831
M +49 176 23741385
--
VALERIERAPP@GMX.DE
--

263

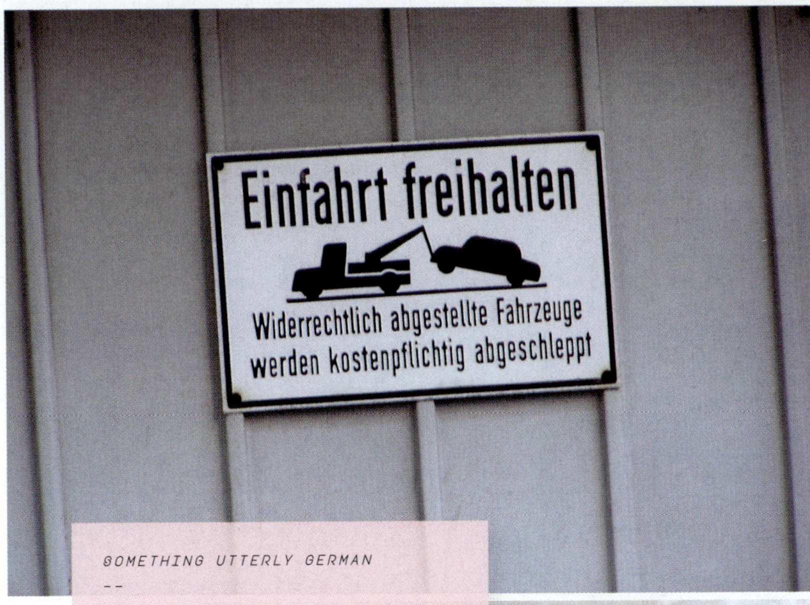

SOMETHING UTTERLY GERMAN
--

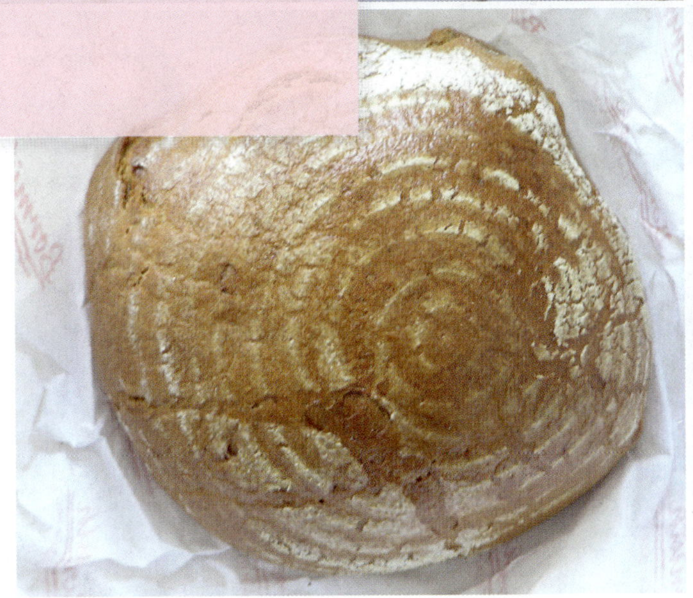

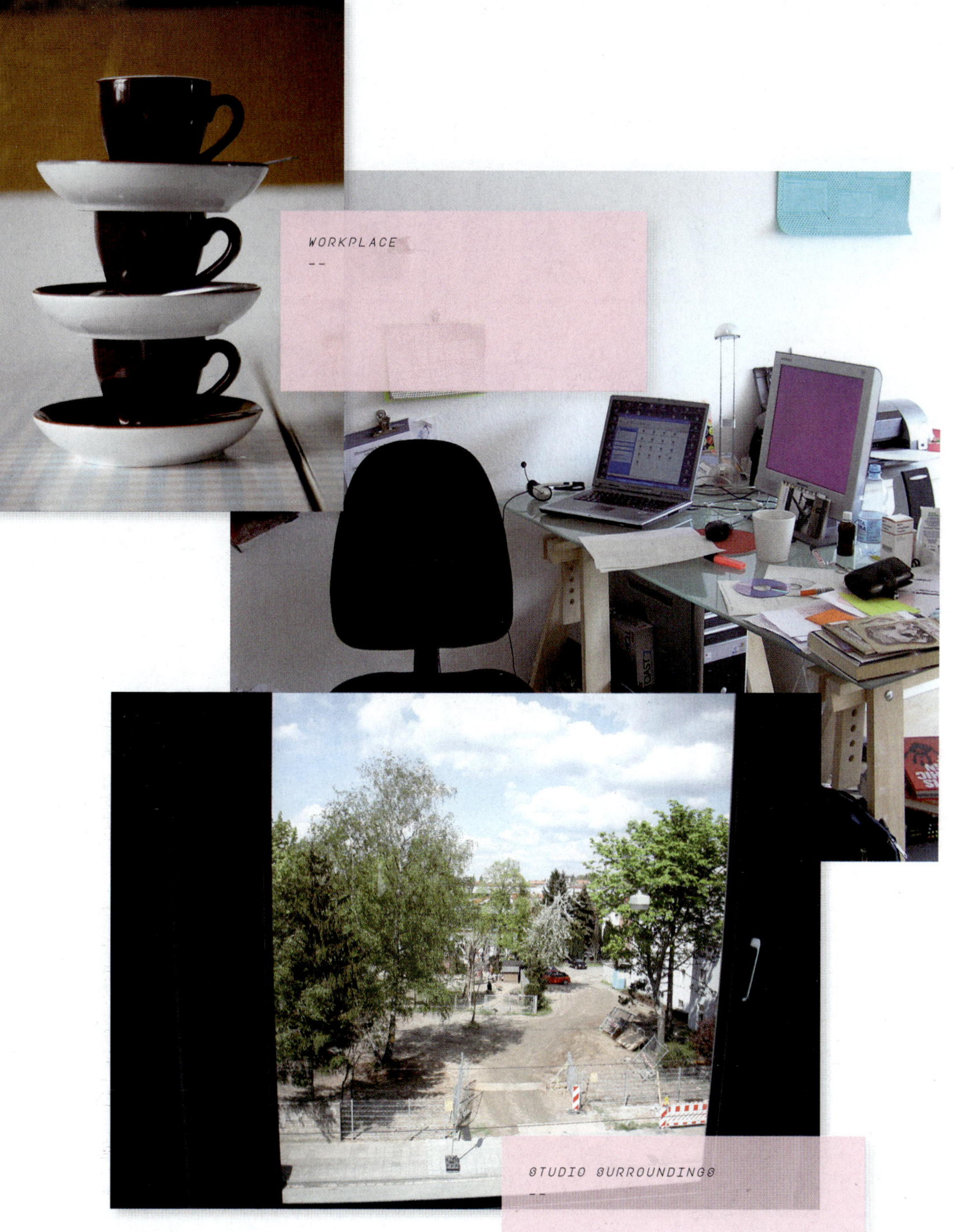
WORKPLACE
--

STUDIO SURROUNDINGS
--

AZULEJOS
SANTOS
LAPA
EXHIBITIONPATH THROUGH SANTOS AND LAPA
STARTING AT THE MUSEU NACIONAL DE ARTE ANTIGUA
28.02.07 - 06.04.07
SPONSORED BY THE MUSEU NACIONAL DO AZULEJOS

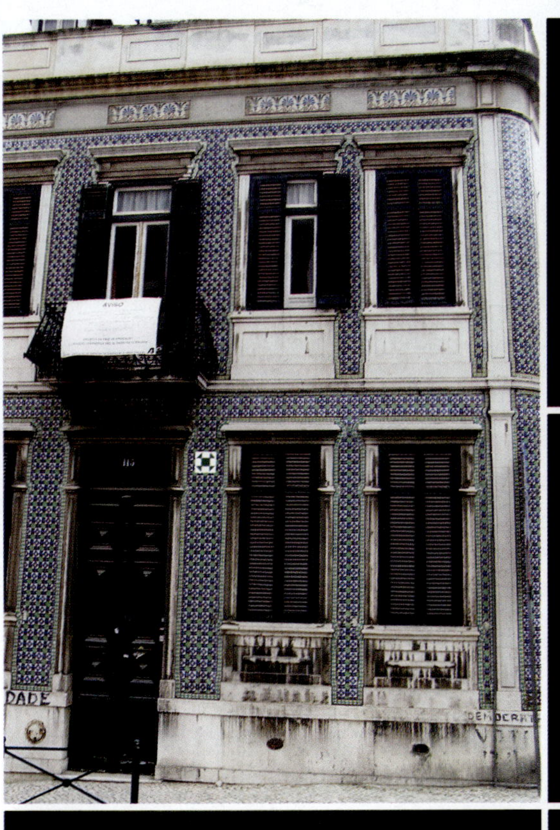

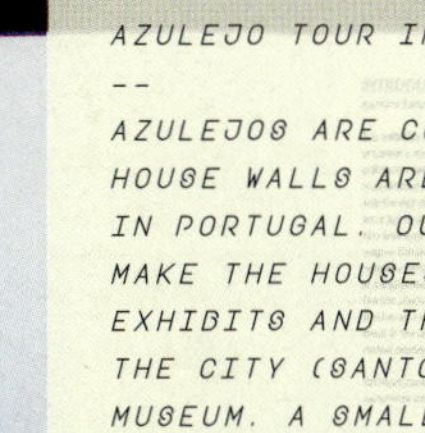

AZULEJO TOUR IN LISBON
--
AZULEJOS ARE COLORED TILES THAT
HOUSE WALLS ARE OFTEN CLAD WITH
IN PORTUGAL. OUR IDEA WAS TO
MAKE THE HOUSES THEMSELVES INTO
EXHIBITS AND THE DISTRICT OF
THE CITY (SANTOS / LAPA) INTO A
MUSEUM. A SMALL BROCHURE LEADS
VISITORS ROUND THE EXHIBITION
ROUTE AND THE HOUSES ARE MARKED
BY SMALL DRAWINGS.
--
TUTOR: ALEXANDRA BARRADAS
--

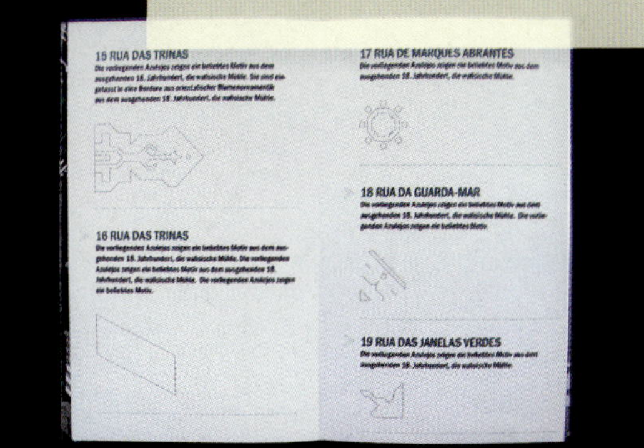

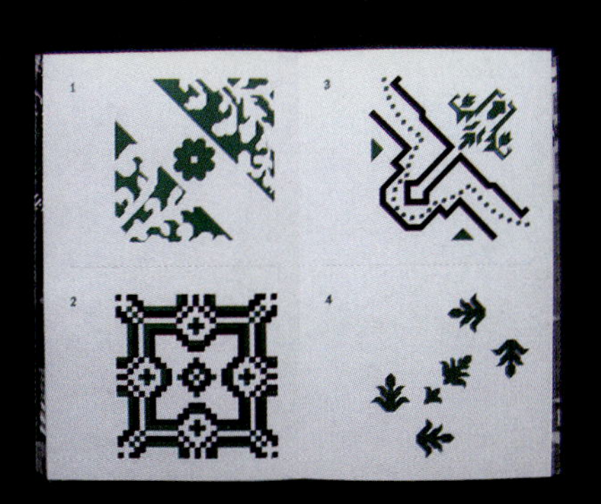

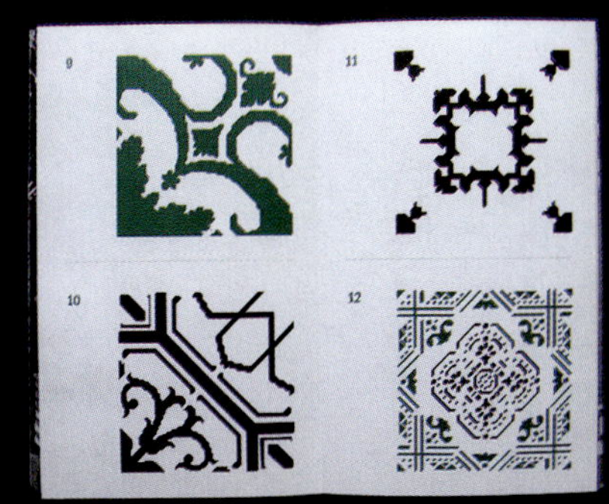

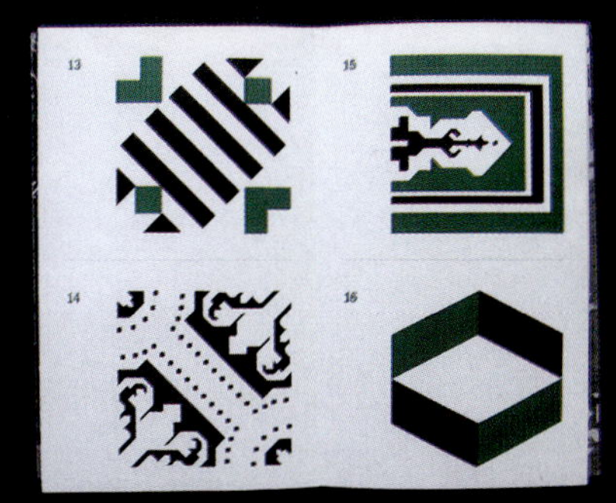

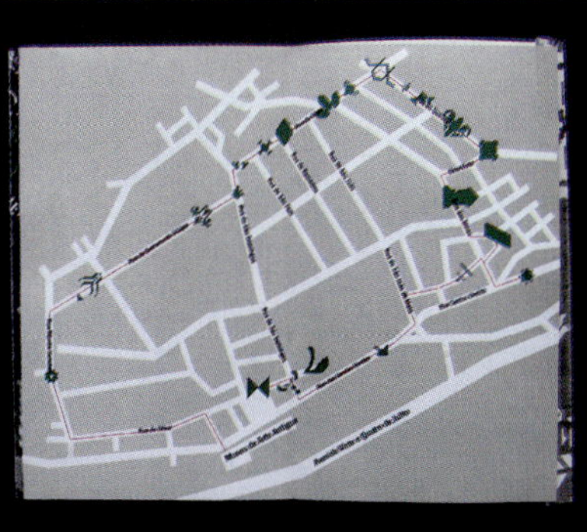

I'M A GRAPHIC DESIGNER AND STUDIED
AT THE HOCHSCHULE DARMSTADT. I
WORK PREDOMINANTLY FOR CULTURAL
INSTITUTIONS WITH AN EMPHASIS ON
BOOK/MAGAZINE DESIGN, POSTERS,
CORPORATE ID, ETC.

--

WHAT IS GERMAN?

PART OF THE WHOLE.

WHAT IS GERMAN DESIGN?

SOMETHING THAT'S FLOURISHING
RIGHT NOW.

PLEASE DESCRIBE YOUR WORKING
PROCESS.

THINK, SELECT, FIND, COLLECT,
FORWARD, BACKWARD, BACKWARD, FOR-
WARD.

WHAT DO YOU AIM TO ACHIEVE WITH
YOUR WORK?

FEELINGS.

YOU'VE INVITED A FRIEND TO
GERMANY; NAME ONE PLACE
THEY REALLY MUST VISIT AND A
QUINTESSENTIAL EXPERIENCE YOU
RECOMMEND.

GO TO FRANKFURT FOR A MEAL AT
<CLUB MICHEL> AND GO DANCING AT
<OSTBAHNHOF CLUB>. IF WE WERE
IN BERLIN, THEN GO TO THE PRO QM
BOOKSHOP AND THE PANORAMA BAR.

WHAT IS THE MOST IMPORTANT
LESSON YOU HAVE LEARNED IN YOUR
PROFESSION SO FAR?

EVERYTHING IS POSSIBLE.

--

SATTER

MICHAEL SATTER
--
NIEDER-RAMSTÄDTER-STRASSE 23
64283 DARMSTADT
GERMANY
--
M +49 160 91037156
T +49 6151 1595195
--
MICHAEL@LASERMAG.DE
WWW.LASERMAG.DE
WWW.MICHAELSATTER.DE
--

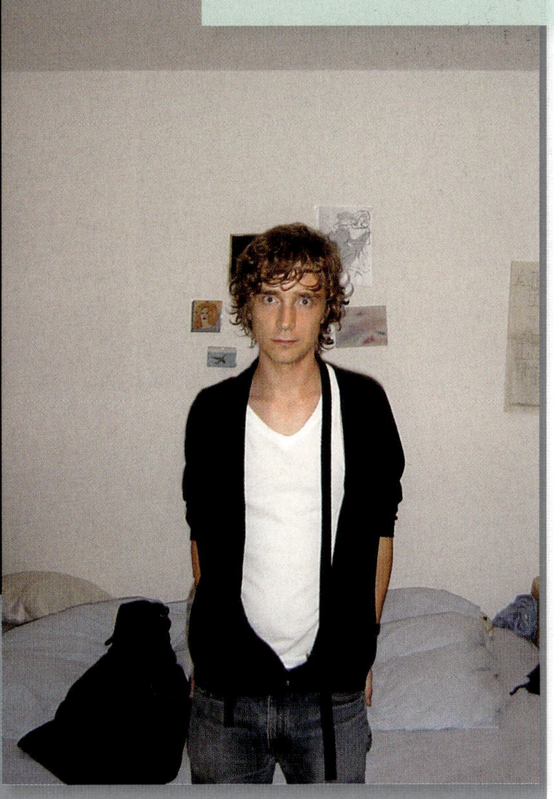

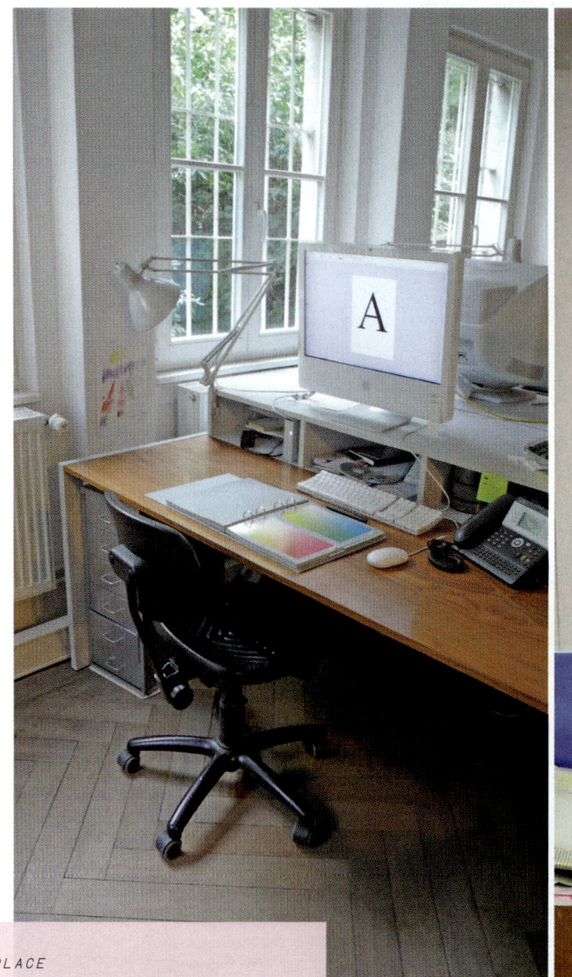

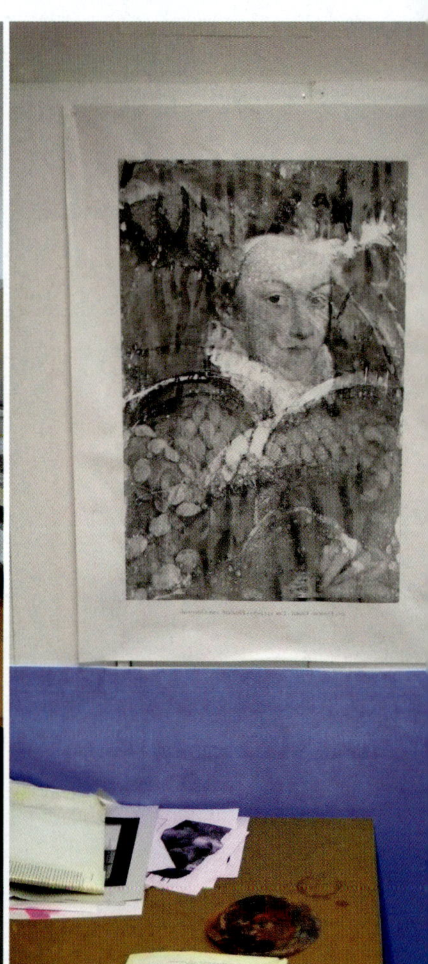

WORKPLACE
--

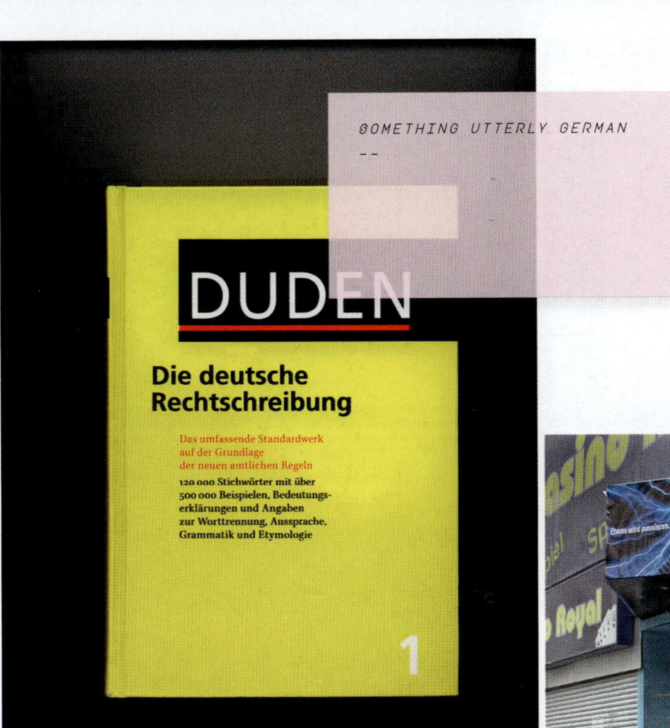
DUDEN
Die deutsche
Rechtschreibung
Das umfassende Standardwerk
auf der Grundlage
der neuen amtlichen Regeln
120 000 Stichwörter mit über
500 000 Beispielen, Bedeutungs-
erklärungen und Angaben
zur Worttrennung, Aussprache,
Grammatik und Etymologie
1

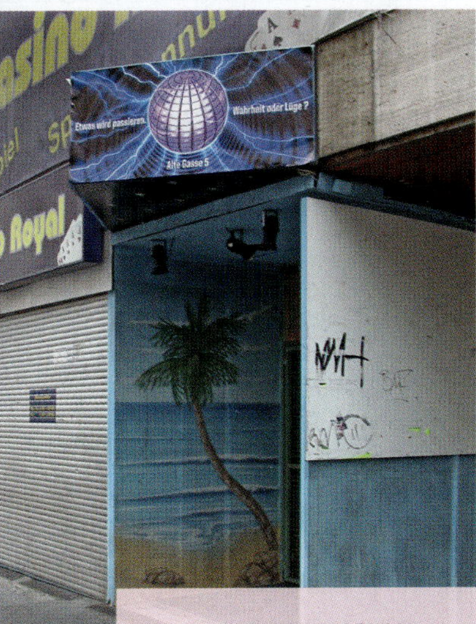
Etwas wird passieren
Wahrheit oder Lüge ?
Alte Gasse 5

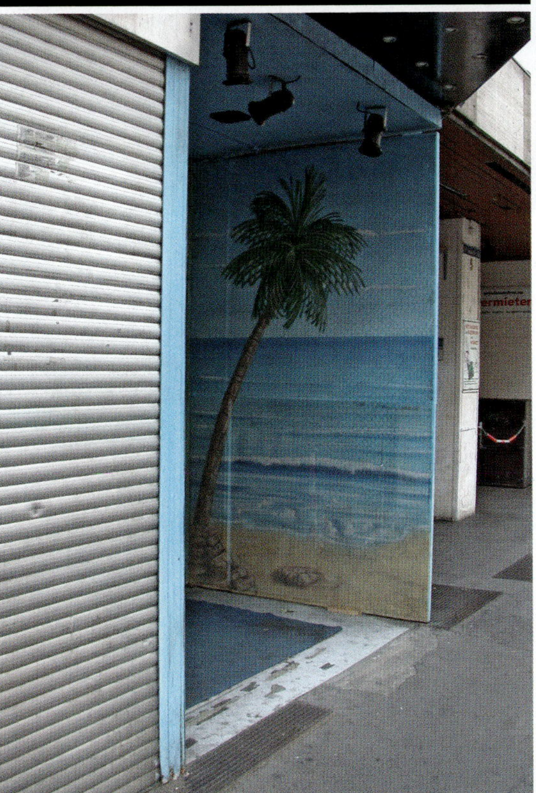

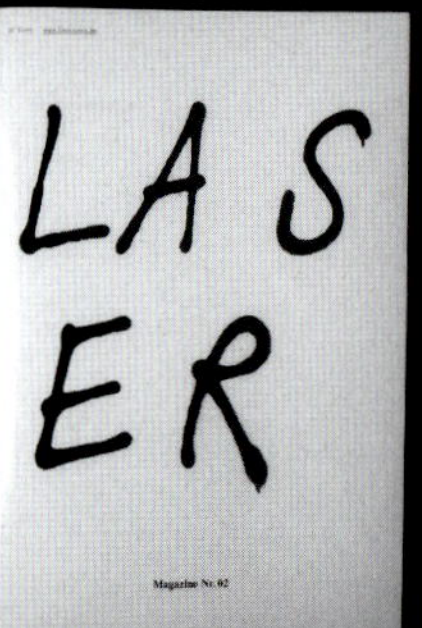

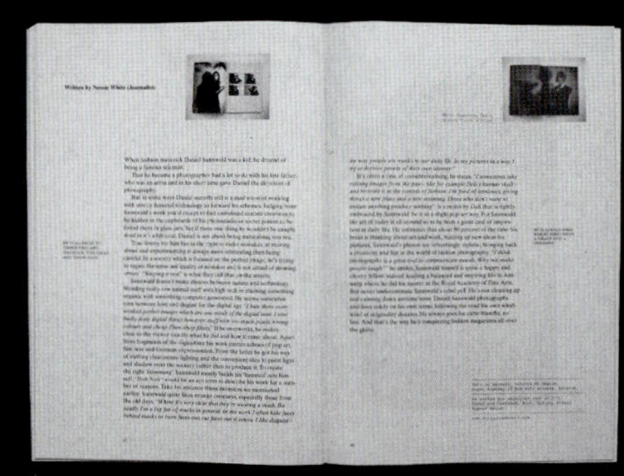

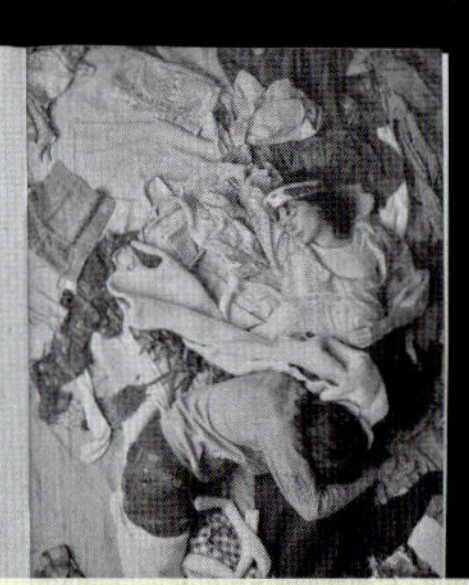

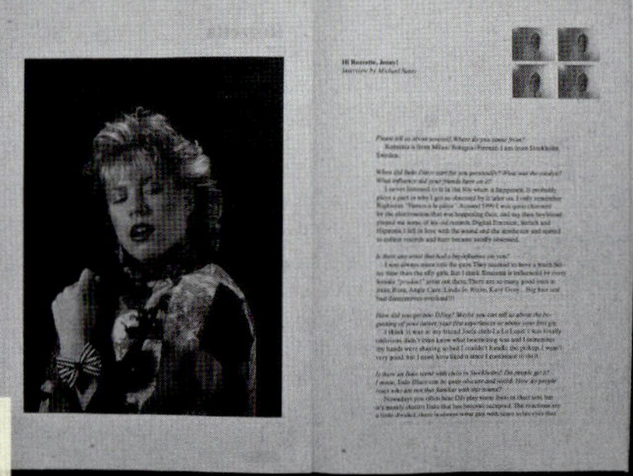

LASER MAGAZINE 1/2

--

IN 2005 I DECIDED TO PUBLISH A MAGAZINE MYSELF. THE LASER MAGAZINE OFFERS YOUNG TALENTS A PLATFORM ENABLING THEM TO SHOW THEIR WORKS. MY INTEREST HERE LIES IN WORKING IN THE MAGAZINE MEDIUM, TYPOGRAPHICAL EXPERIMENTATION AND COMMUNICATION WITH OTHER DESIGNERS OR ARTISTS. THE MAGAZINE ALWAYS CONSISTS PARTLY OF SELF-DESIGNED FONTS. THE FIRST ISSUE SHOWS THE WORKS OF ISABELLE FEIN, GINA MÖNCH, THOMAS BERGER AND MARIA TACKMAN. AS THE SECOND EDITION WAS TO BE MORE WIDE-RANGING IN TERMS OF CONTENT, I GOT TOGETHER WITH NICOLE KLEIN (WWW.NIKIO.DE), TINA KOHLMANN AND TINA SCHOTT (WWW.ROXI.ORG). THE SECOND ISSUE SHOWS THE WORKS OF HUI-HUI FASHION, JAN FAMILY, ANNA GIERTZ, CLAUS RICHTER, ROZZETTA, SZPILMAN AWARD, DANIEL SANNWALD, TINA SCHOTT AND VIER 5.

--

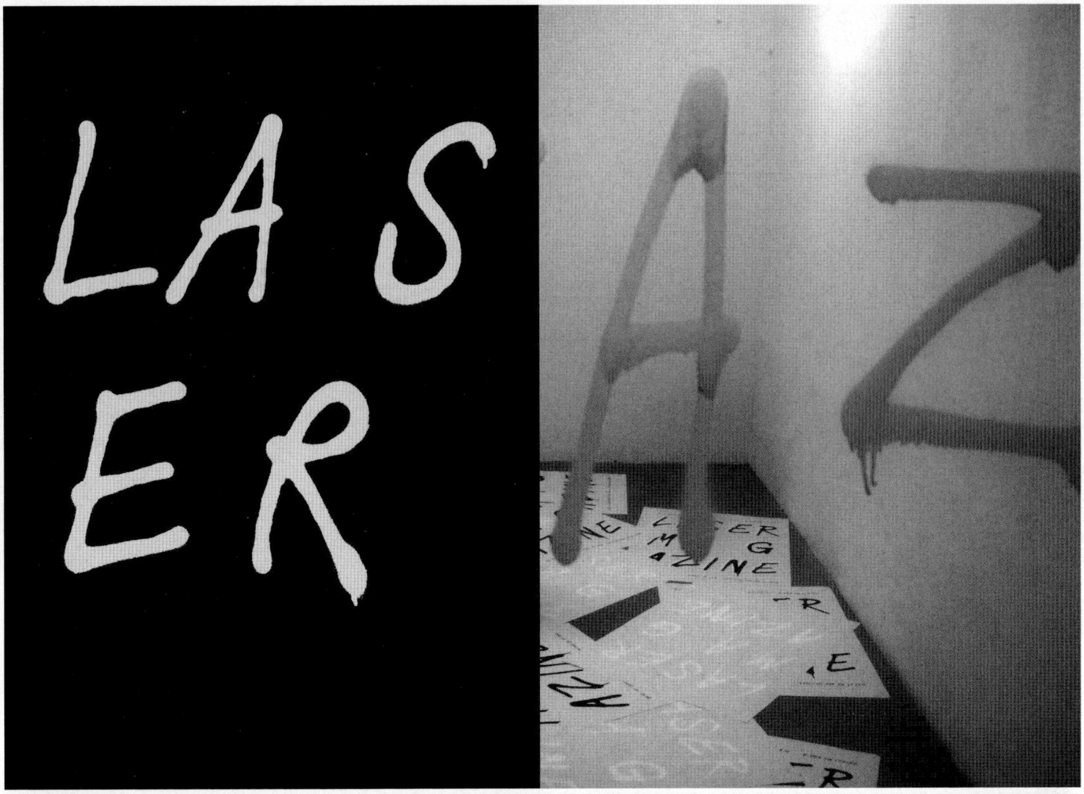

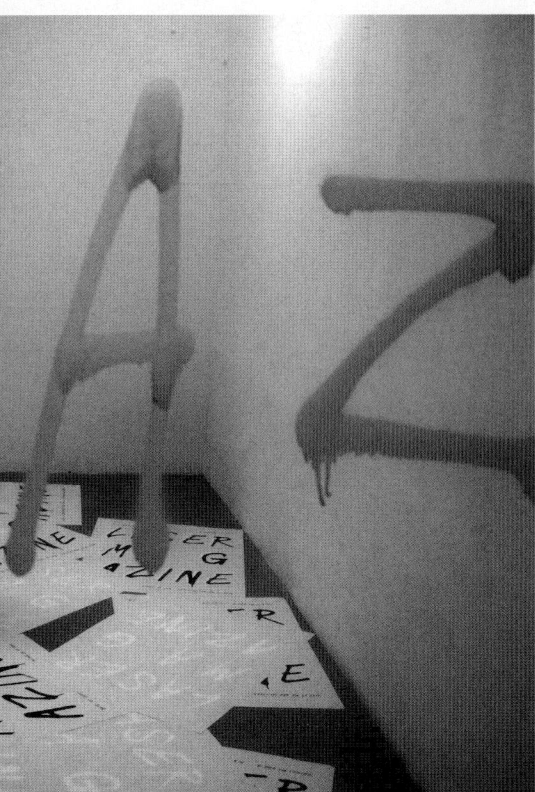

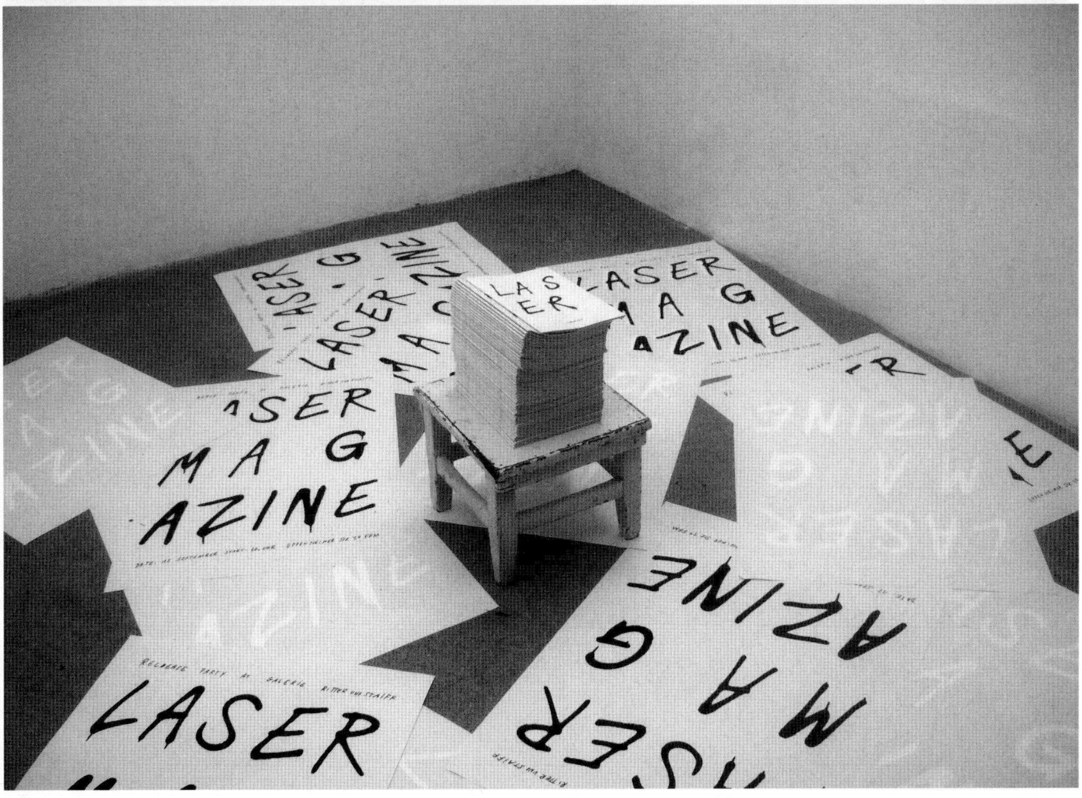

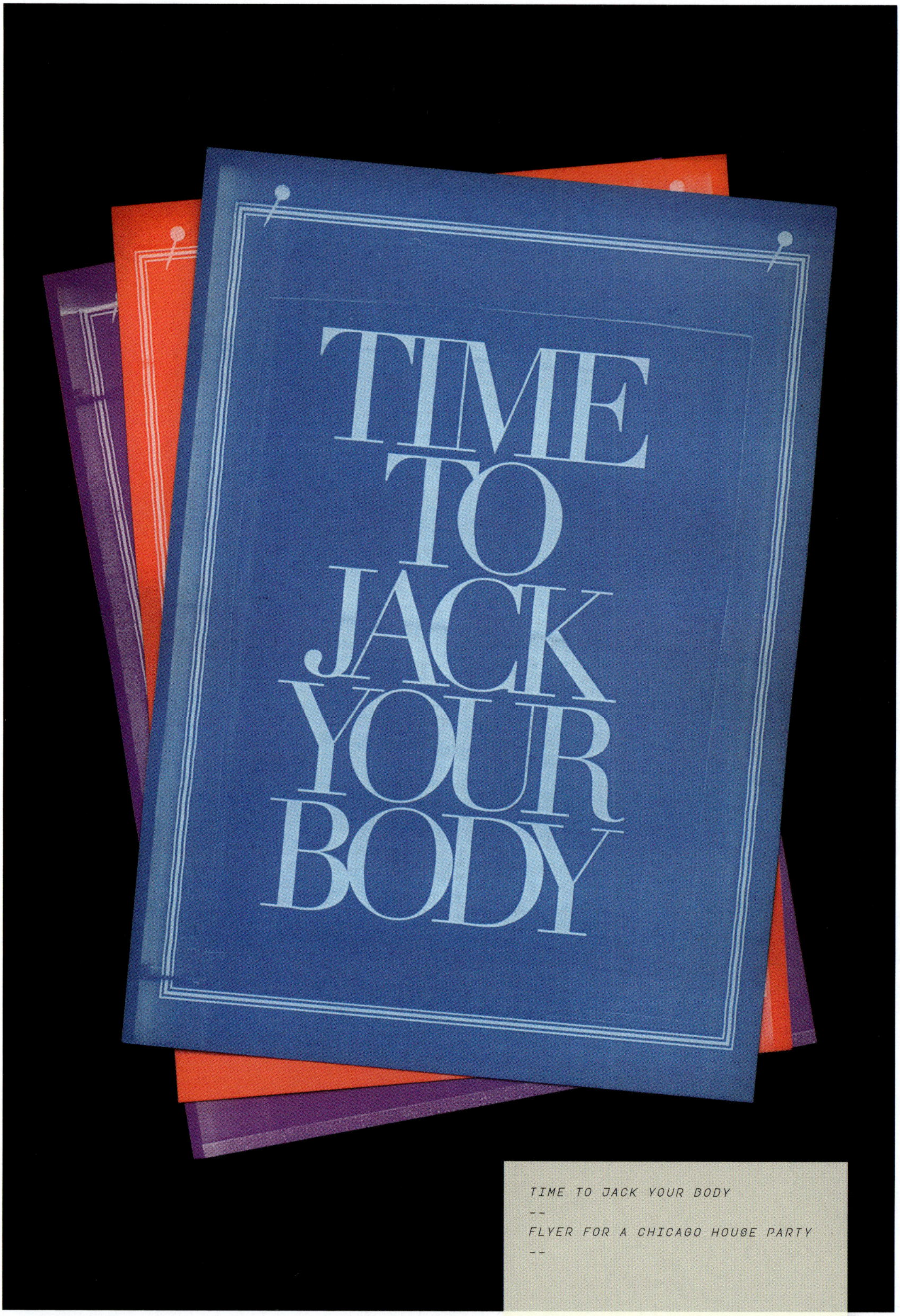

TIME
TO
JACK
YOUR
BODY

TIME TO JACK YOUR BODY
--
FLYER FOR A CHICAGO HOUSE PARTY
--

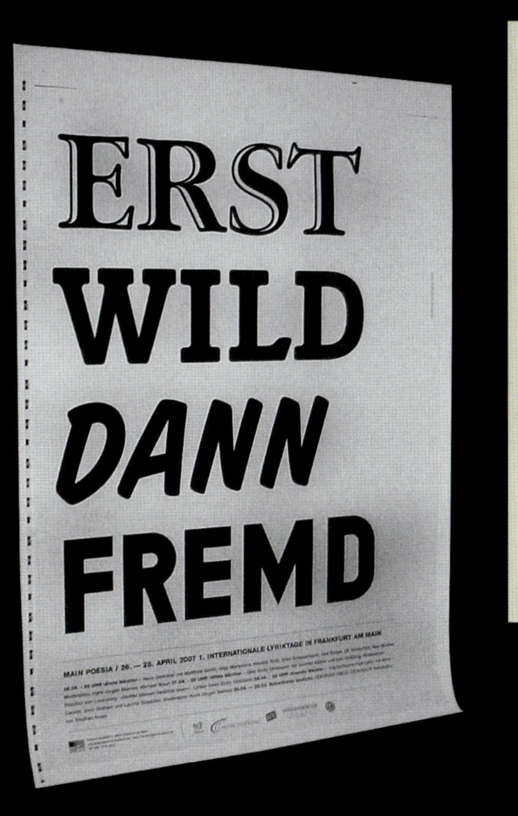

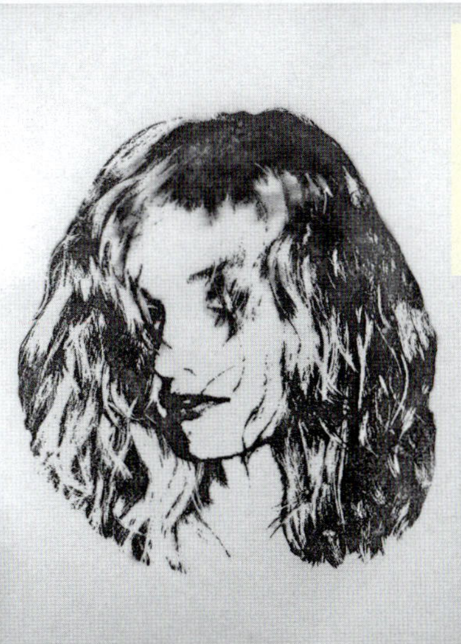

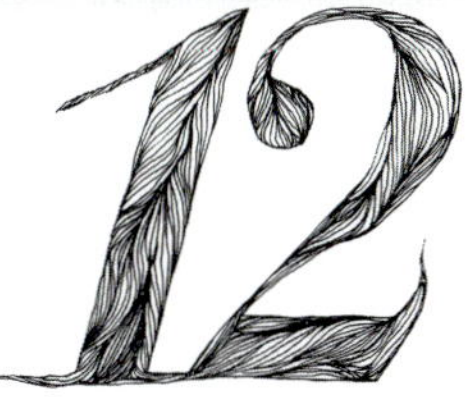
12

NADINE HILBIG WAS BORN ON
07.05.1979 IN LANGEN, GERMANY.
AFTER HER ABITUR (FINAL SCHOOL-
LEAVING EXAM) SHE WORKED FOR A
YEAR IN AN ADVERTISING AGENCY AND
THEN BEGAN TO STUDY COMMUNICA-
TION DESIGN AT THE FH DARMSTADT
(2000 TO 2004). IN 2003 SHE SPENT
SIX MONTHS AS AN INTERN WITH SODA
MAGAZINE IN ZURICH. AFTER TAKING
HER DEGREE SHE COMPLETED A ONE-
YEAR POSTGRADUATE COURSE AT THE
HOCHSCHULE FÜR GESTALTUNG IN OF-
FENBACH. AT THIS POINT SHE FOUNDED
THE SMALL LIEBFRAUEN FASHION LA-
BEL TOGETHER WITH YVONNE HÜTTIG.
DURING AND AFTER HER STUDIES SHE
WORKED FREELANCE FOR VARIOUS OF-
FICES. SINCE THE END OF 2006 SHE
HAS BEEN EMPLOYED WITH THE KRAENK
VISUELL AGENCY.

--

WHAT IS GERMAN?

ICH, DU, ER, SIE,
ES, WIR, IHR, SIE.

WHAT IS GERMAN DESIGN?

WHAT WE MAKE OF IT.

PLEASE DESCRIBE YOUR WORKING
PROCESS.

THINKING, THINKING, THINKING…
AND THEN IMPLEMENTING.

WHAT DO YOU AIM TO ACHIEVE WITH
YOUR WORK?

THE MOST BEAUTIFUL/BEST WORK IS
WHAT YOU'RE SATISFIED WITH YOUR-
SELF.

YOU'VE INVITED A FRIEND TO
GERMANY; NAME ONE PLACE THEY
REALLY MUST VISIT AND A QUINT-
ESSENTIAL EXPERIENCE YOU REC-
OMMEND.

DRINKING AN ORIGINAL FRANKFURT
ÄPPELWOI (APPLE WINE, A TYPE OF
DRY CIDER).

WHAT IS THE MOST IMPORTANT
LESSON YOU HAVE LEARNED IN YOUR
PROFESSION SO FAR?

NOT TO DESPAIR.

--

HIL BIG

NADINE HILBIG
--
SPESSARTRING 75
64287 DARMSTADT
GERMANY
--
M +49 177 6445244
--
NADINE_HILBIG@WEB.DE
--

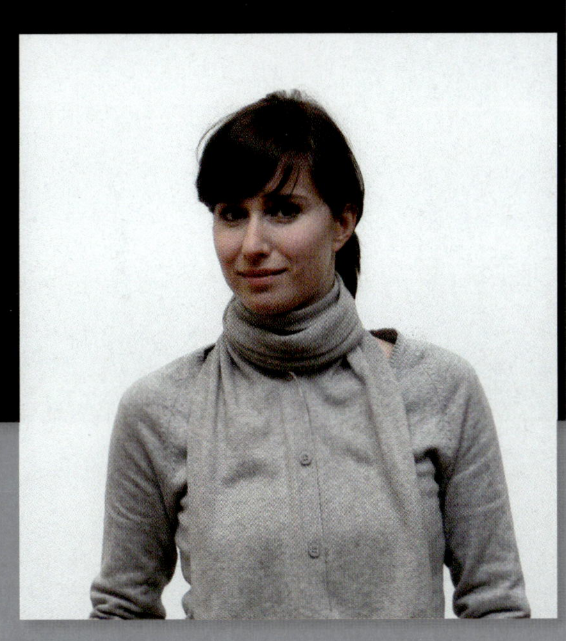

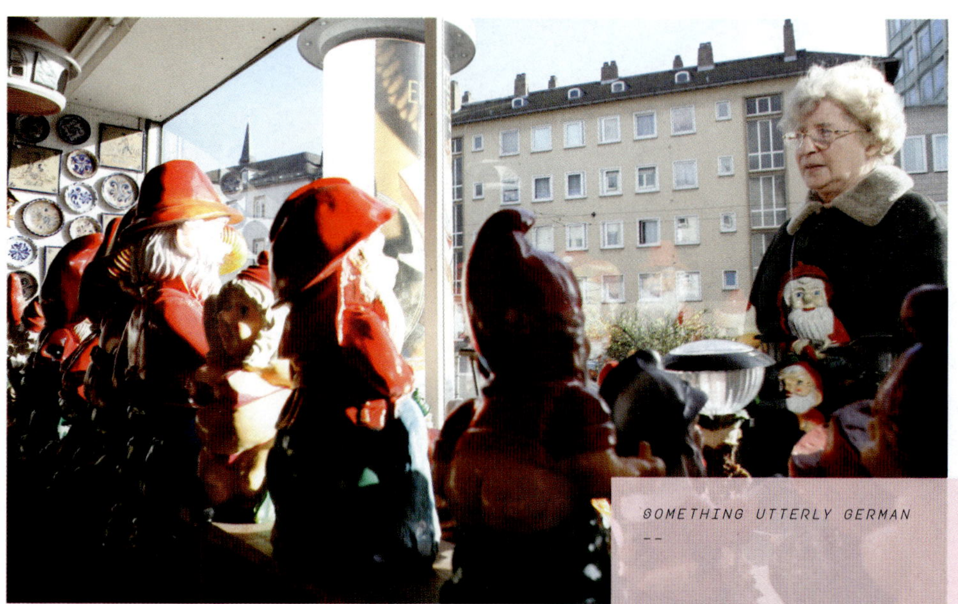
SOMETHING UTTERLY GERMAN
- -

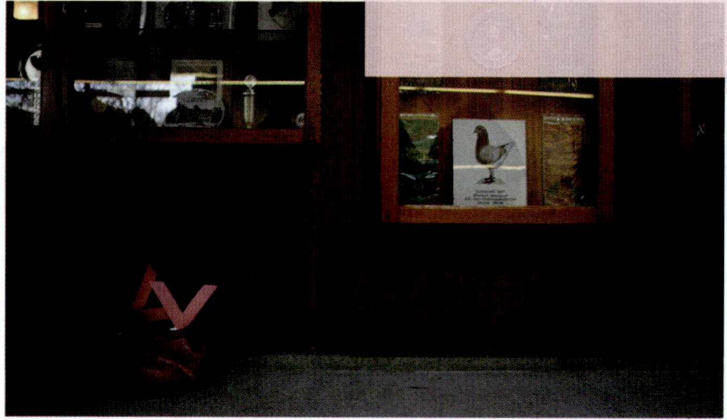

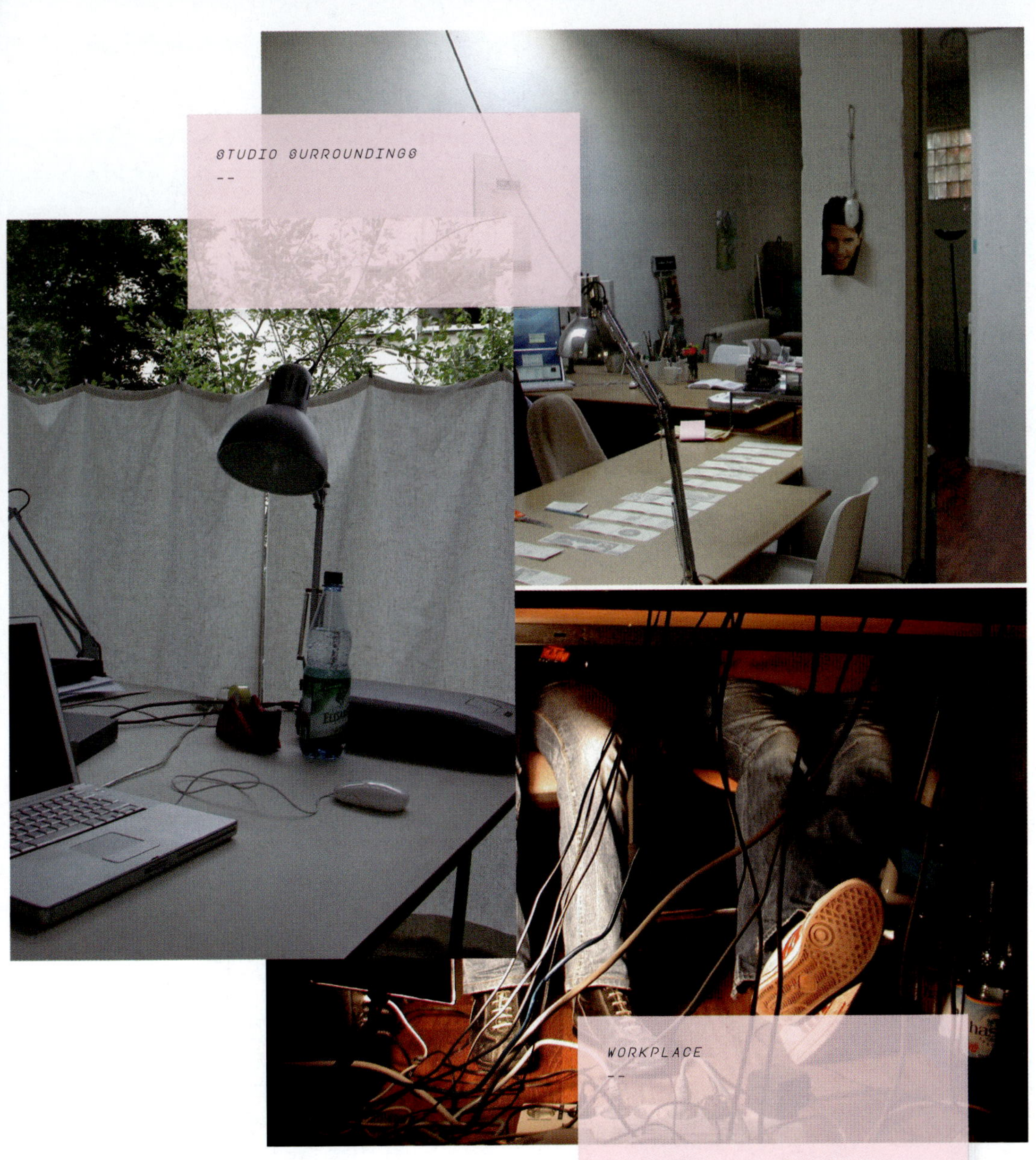
STUDIO SURROUNDINGS
--
WORKPLACE
--

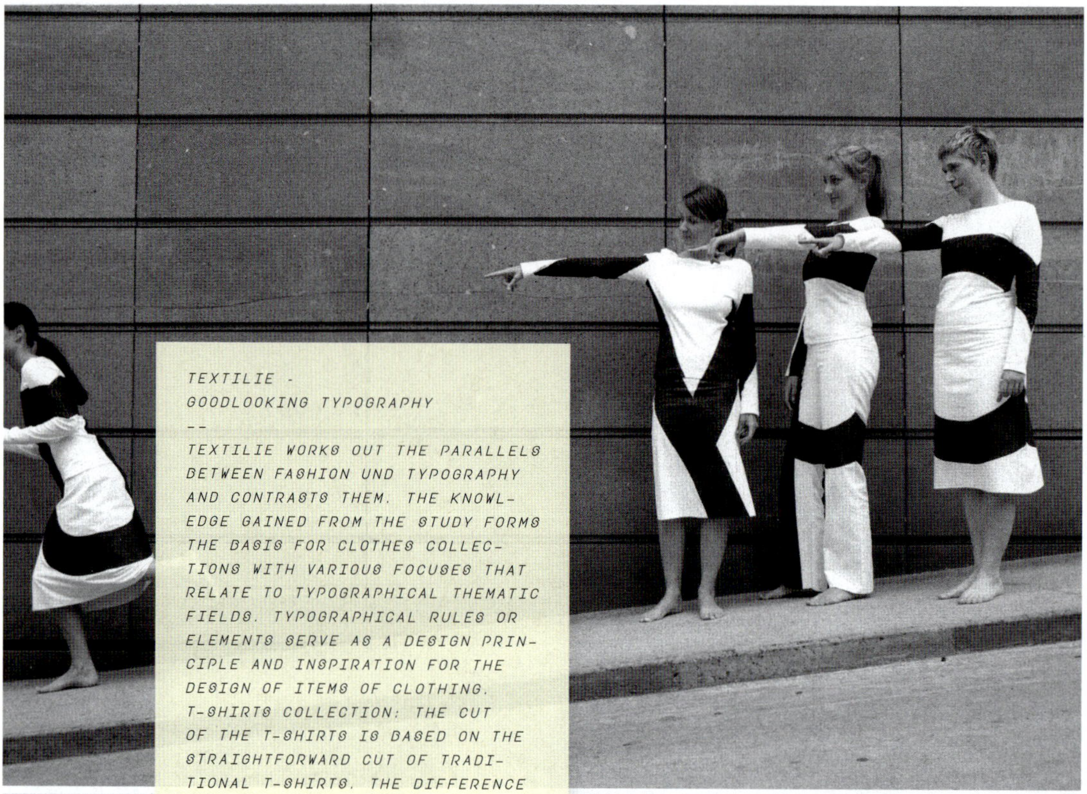

TEXTILIE -
GOODLOOKING TYPOGRAPHY
--
TEXTILIE WORKS OUT THE PARALLELS
BETWEEN FASHION UND TYPOGRAPHY
AND CONTRASTS THEM. THE KNOWL-
EDGE GAINED FROM THE STUDY FORMS
THE BASIS FOR CLOTHES COLLEC-
TIONS WITH VARIOUS FOCUSES THAT
RELATE TO TYPOGRAPHICAL THEMATIC
FIELDS. TYPOGRAPHICAL RULES OR
ELEMENTS SERVE AS A DESIGN PRIN-
CIPLE AND INSPIRATION FOR THE
DESIGN OF ITEMS OF CLOTHING.
T-SHIRTS COLLECTION: THE CUT
OF THE T-SHIRTS IS BASED ON THE
STRAIGHTFORWARD CUT OF TRADI-
TIONAL T-SHIRTS. THE DIFFERENCE
LIES IN THE FACT THAT IT IS NOT
THE CAPITAL LETTER T THAT IS
TAKEN AS A MODEL, BUT THE LOWER-
CASE T. THE INDIVIDUAL MODELS
SHOW THE DISTINGUISHING FEATURES
OF VARIOUS FONTS.
BASISLINIE COLLECTION: THE PRO-
PORTIONS OF THE HUMAN BEING AND
FONT ARE CONTRASTED. FROM THIS
IT CAN BE DEDUCED THAT THE AS-
CENDER CORRESPONDS TO THE HEAD
AND SHOULDER AREA, THE EXTENT OF
THE X-HEIGHT CONSEQUENTLY COR-
RESPONDS TO THE CHEST, STOMACH
AND UPPER THIGH AREA DOWN TO THE
KNEE LINE, AND THE DESCENDER TO
THE CALF AND FOOT AREA. BASED ON
THIS SYSTEM, THE LETTERS ARE AP-
PLIED TO CLOTHES.
--
TUTOR: PROF. SANDRA E. HOFFMANN,
FH DARMSTADT
--

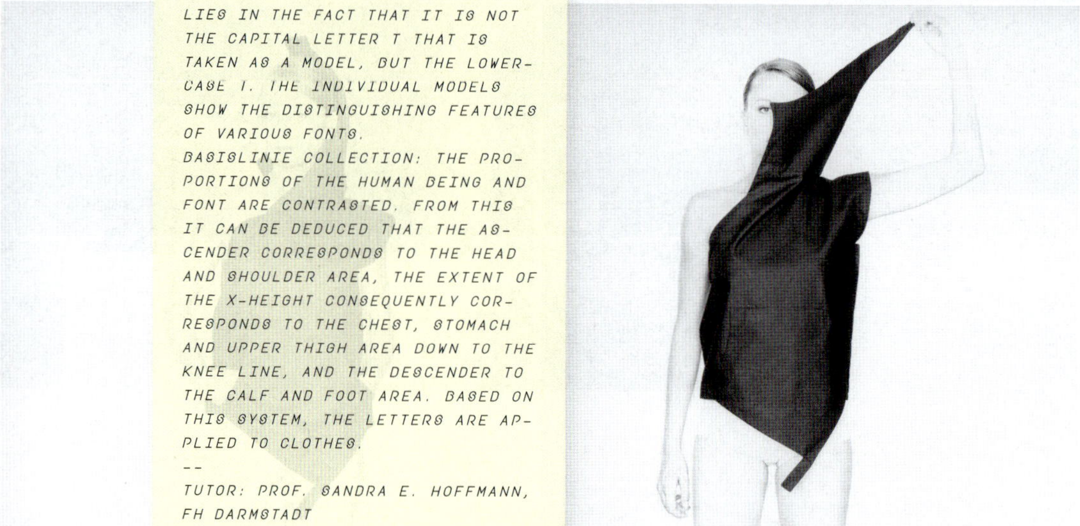

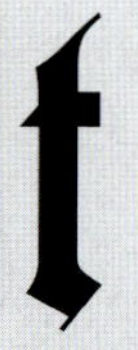

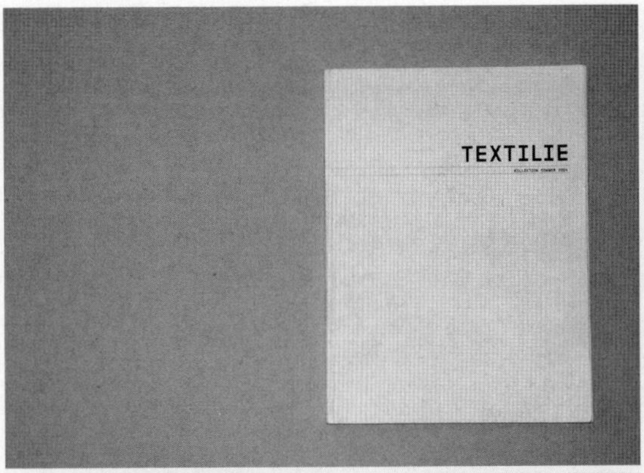

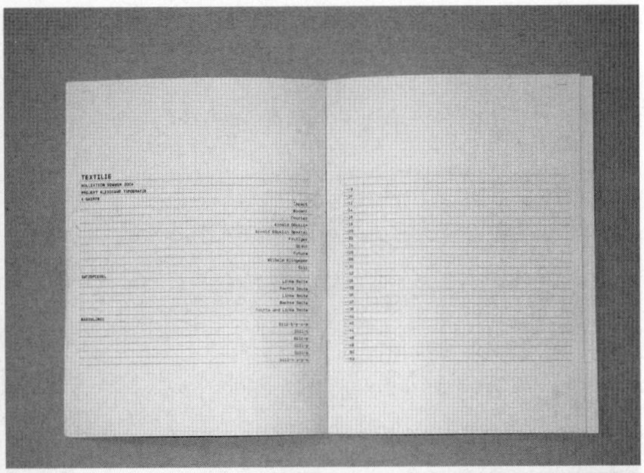

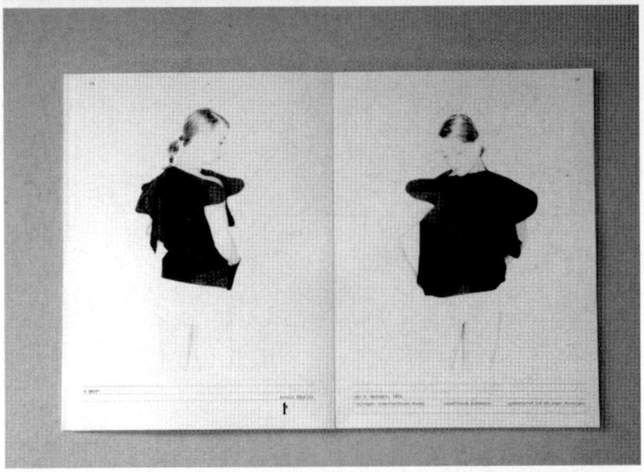

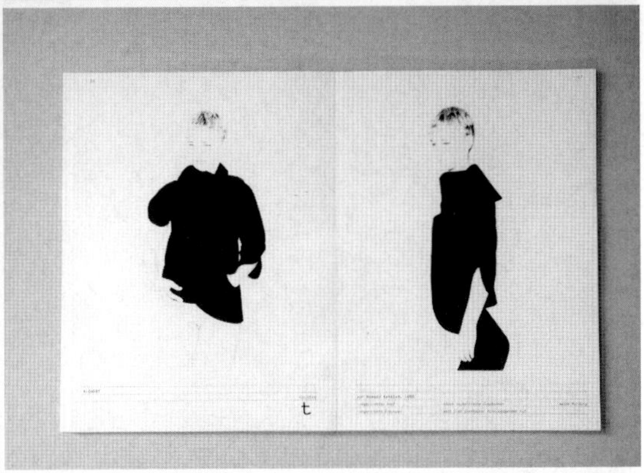

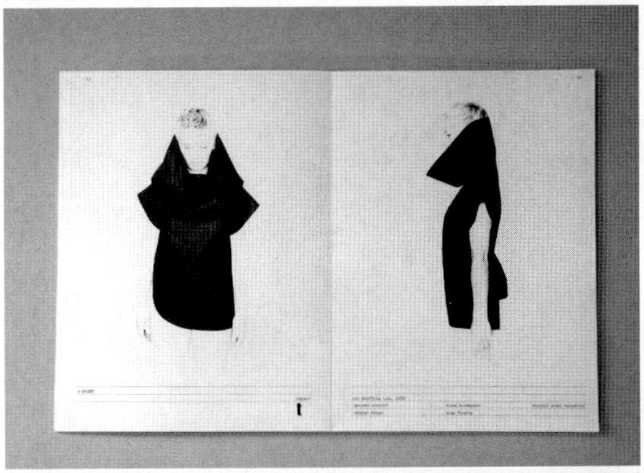

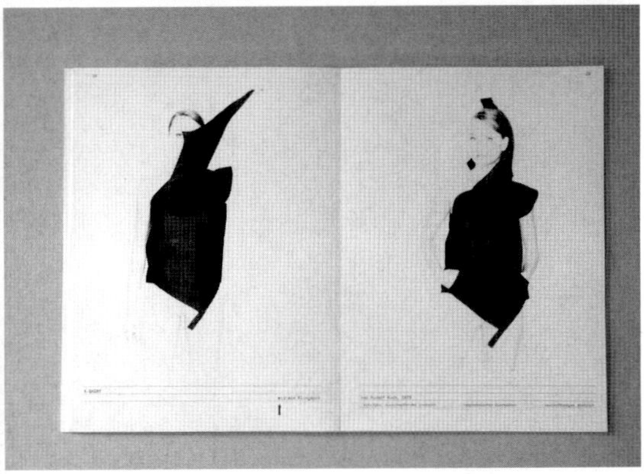

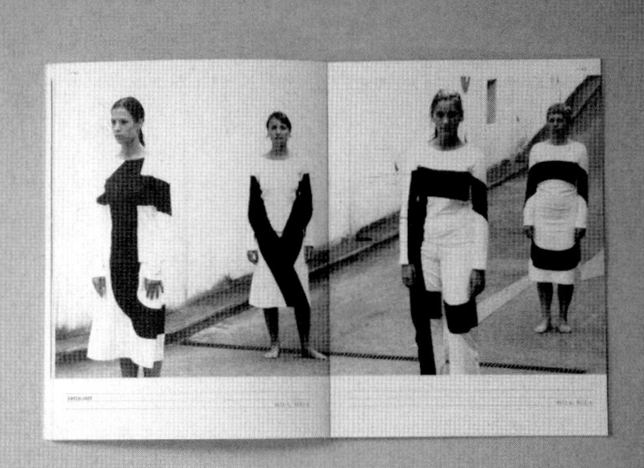

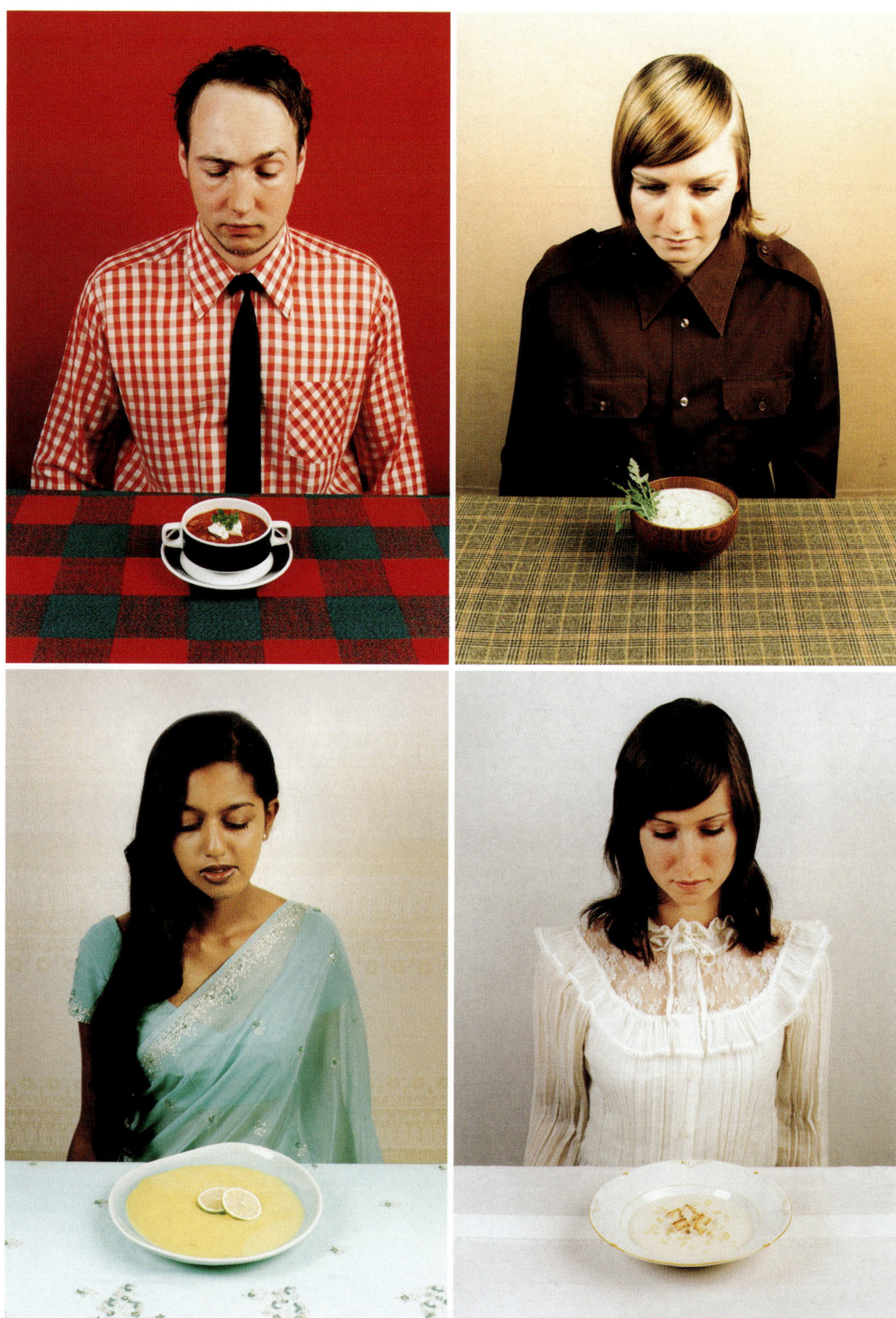

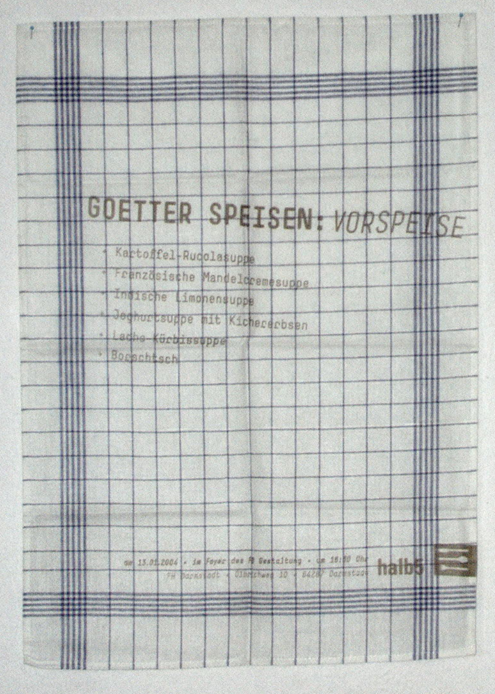

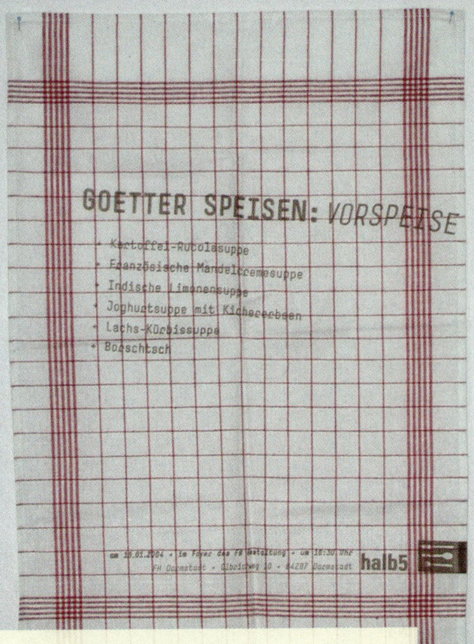

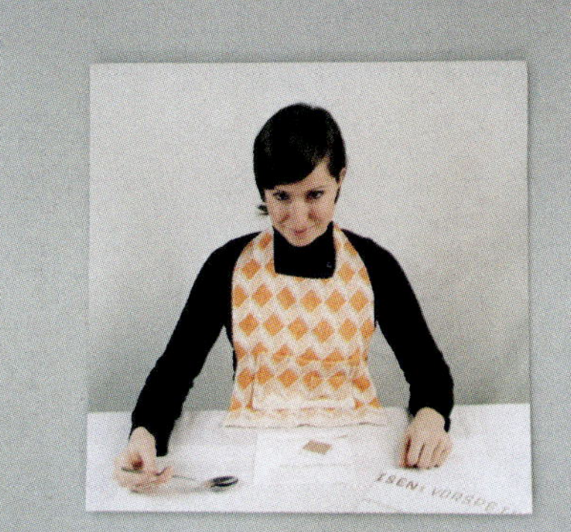

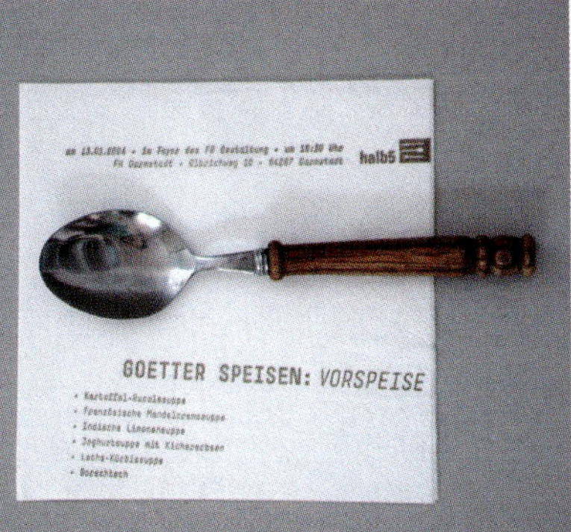

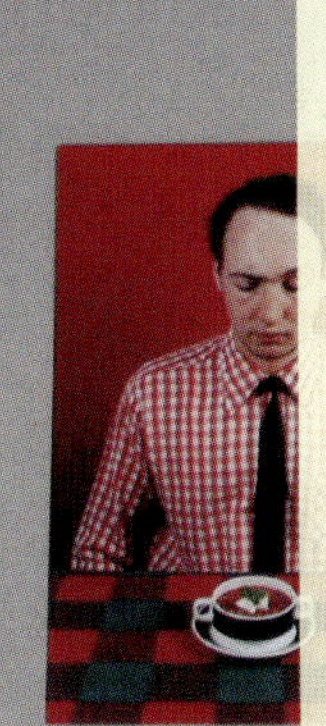

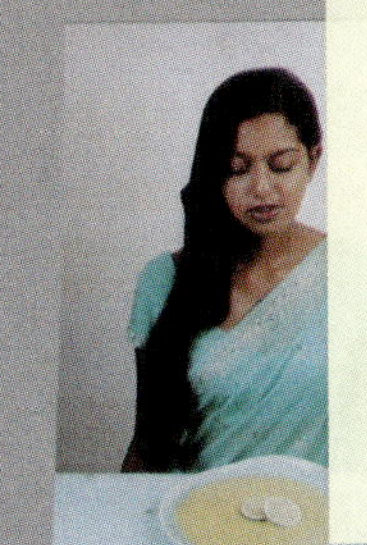

GÖTTER SPEISEN/VORSPEISE (FOODS
OF THE GODS, STARTERS)
--
IN THE CONTEXT OF THE HALB5 LEC-
TURES AT THE FH DARMSTADT THE
GÖTTER SPEISEN/VORSPEISE EVENT
INVITED MORE THAN 100 GUESTS AND
SERVED UP SIX SOUPS FROM VARI-
OUS COUNTRIES AT A LONG TABLE.
INSTEAD OF A CONVENTIONAL MENU
LARGE-FORMAT PRINTS SHOWED THE
SOUPS THAT WERE ON OFFER (SEE
POSTCARDS). TABLE NAPKINS AND
TOWELS DID NOT SERVE THEIR USUAL
PURPOSE EITHER, BUT WERE USED AS
POSTERS AND INVITATIONS. FOR THE
SOUP ENTHUSIAST THERE WAS ALSO
A SUPPENSET (SOUP SET) TO BUY
INCLUDING A HAND-TAILORED BIB, A
SOUP SPOON AND A BOUILLON CUBE
AS WELL AS A NAPKIN AND PRINTED
PAPER TABLECLOTH, ALONG WITH THE
COLLECTION OF RECIPES.
--
PHOTOGRAPHS BY DIANA DJEDDI AND
KATRIN ROTHE
--
TUTOR: PROF. SANDRA E. HOFFMANN,
FH DARMSTADT
--

TOBIAS BENDER AND STEPHAN
TRISCHLER GOT TO KNOW EACH OTHER
DURING THEIR STUDIES. AFTER WORK-
ING SUCCESSFULLY ON COMMON PROJ-
ECTS THEY FOUNDED KRAENK VISUELL
IN 2000. SINCE THEN THE DESIGN
BUREAU HAS WORKED FOR A GROWING
NUMBER OF COMPANIES AND CULTURAL
INSTITUTIONS.

KRAENK VISUELL WAS FOUNDED BY TO-
BIAS BENDER AND STEPHAN TRISCHLER
IN 2000 WHILE THEY WERE STILL
STUDENTS (OF VISUAL COMMUNICA-
TION AT THE FH DARMSTADT). SINCE
THEN THE AGENCY HAS BEEN WORKING
FOR A GROWING CLIENT BASE FROM THE
FIELDS OF BUSINESS, CULTURE AND
EDUCATION. THEIR CORE SKILL IS THE
REALIZATION OF INDIVIDUAL DESIGN
AND COMMUNICATION CONCEPTS FOR
PRINTING AND DIGITAL MEDIA.

--

WHAT IS GERMAN?

THE AUTOBAHN FROM COLOGNE TO
FRANKFURT.

WHAT IS GERMAN DESIGN?

GERMAN DESIGN IS LONG-LIVED, OR-
DERLY AND WELL THOUGHT THROUGH.

PLEASE DESCRIBE YOUR WORKING
PROCESS.

THINKING > SKETCHING > INSPIR-
ING/DISCUSSING > ELABORATING >
IMPROVING > IMPROVING > IMPROVING
> IMPROVING...

WHAT DO YOU AIM TO ACHIEVE WITH
YOUR WORK?

POSITIVE NOTICE.

YOU'VE INVITED A FRIEND TO
GERMANY; NAME ONE PLACE THEY
REALLY MUST VISIT AND A QUINT-
ESSENTIAL EXPERIENCE YOU REC-
OMMEND.

COME TO DARMSTADT AND DRINK A
SCHNAPPS WITH US.

WHAT IS THE MOST IMPORTANT
LESSON YOU HAVE LEARNED IN YOUR
PROFESSION SO FAR?

LEARNING.

--

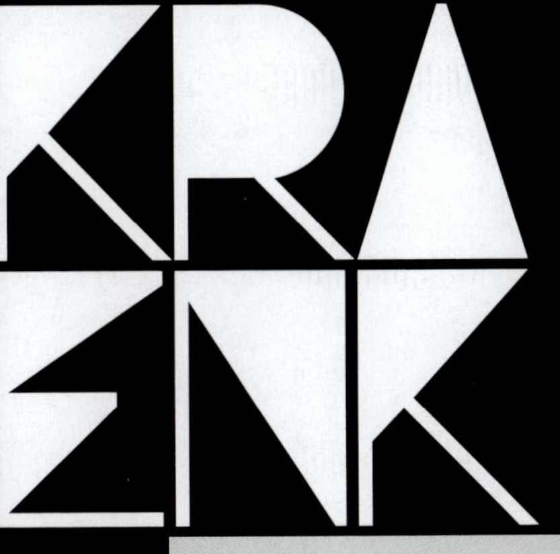

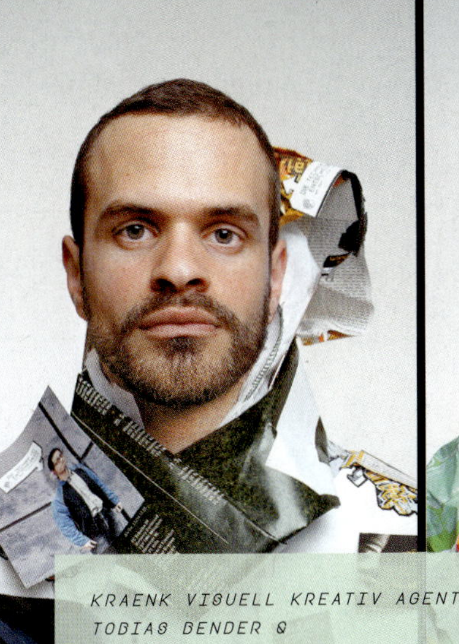

KRAENK VISUELL KREATIV AGENTUR
TOBIAS BENDER &
STEPHAN TRISCHLER
--
OBER-RAMSTÄDTER-STRASSE 96
WACKERFABRIK, HALLE G.1
64367 MÜHLTAL
GERMANY
--
T +49 6151 606336
--
INFO@KRAENK.DE
WWW.KRAENKVISUELL.DE
--

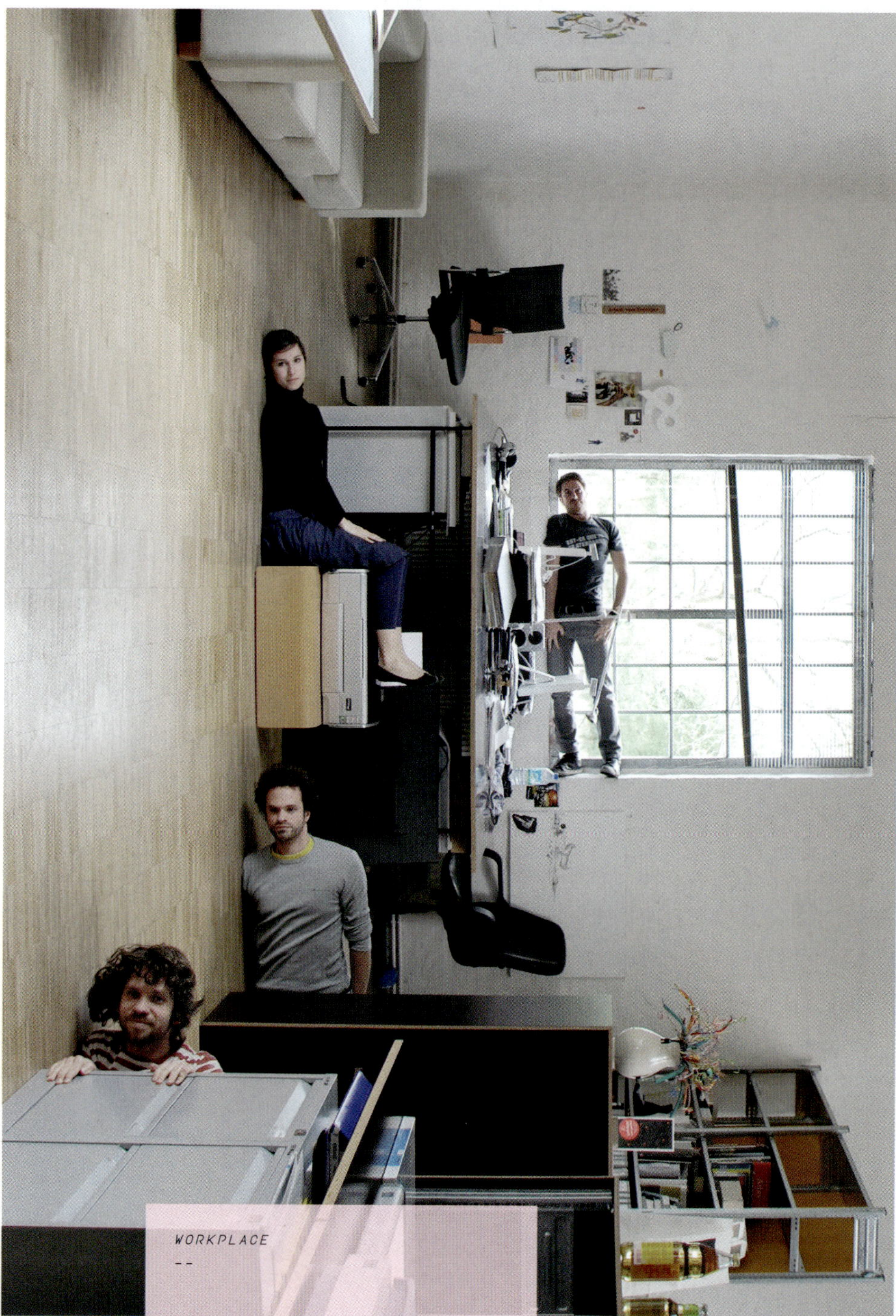
WORKPLACE
- -

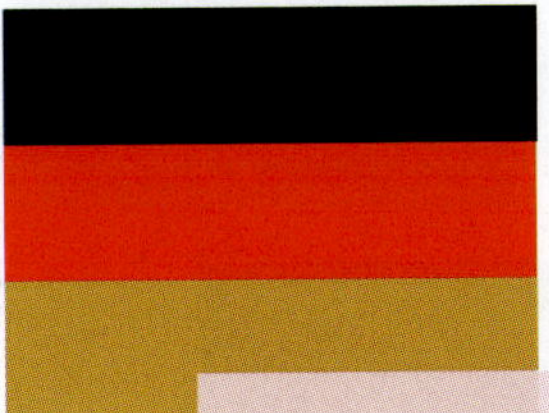

SOMETHING UTTERLY GERMAN
--

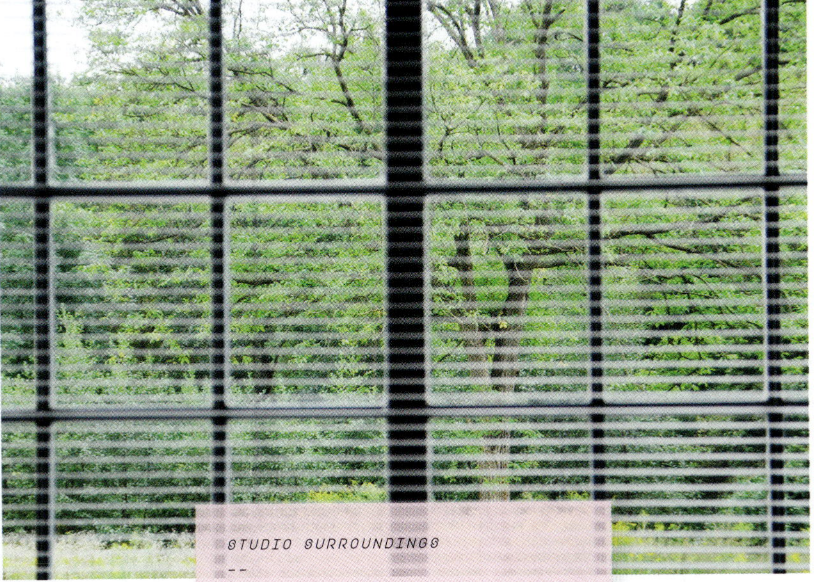

STUDIO SURROUNDINGS
--

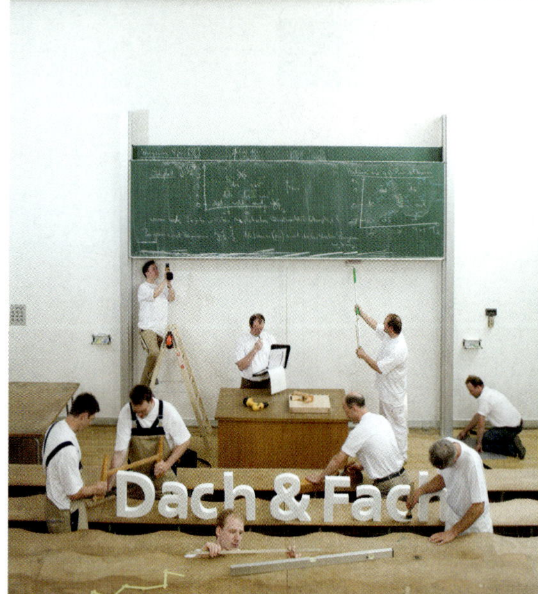

Dach & Fach

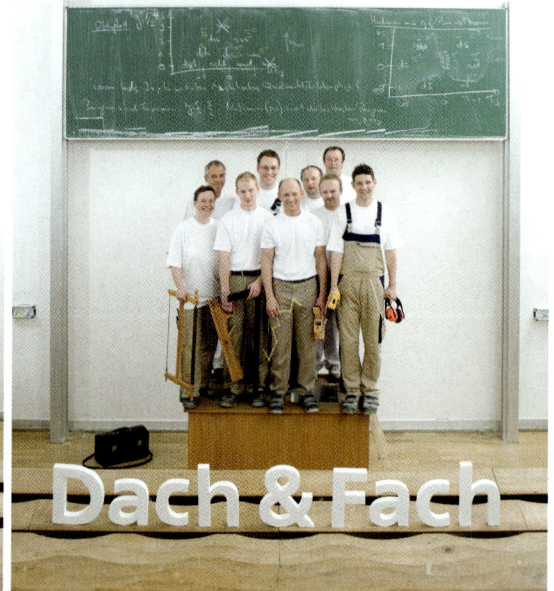

Dach & Fach

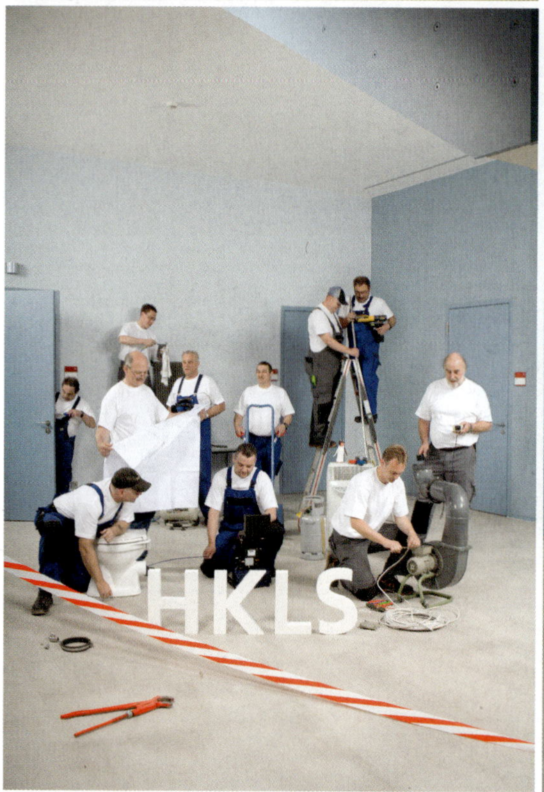

HKLS

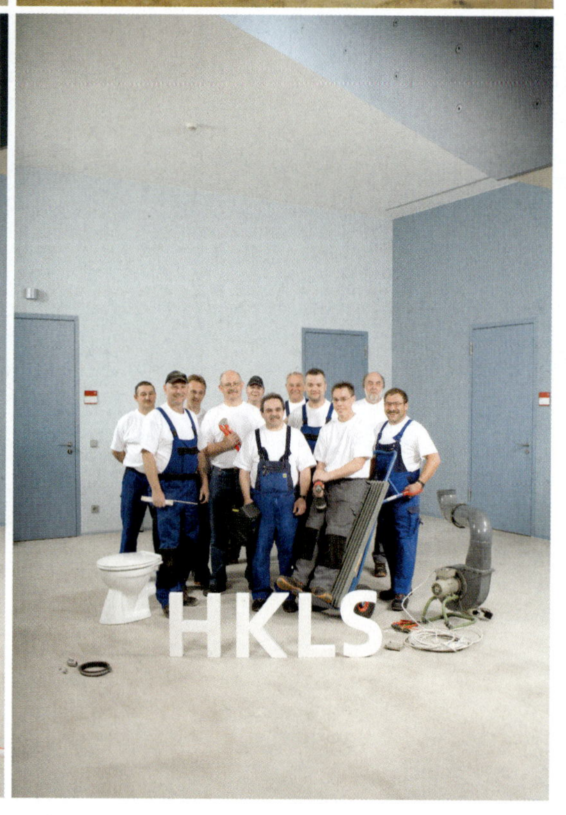

HKLS

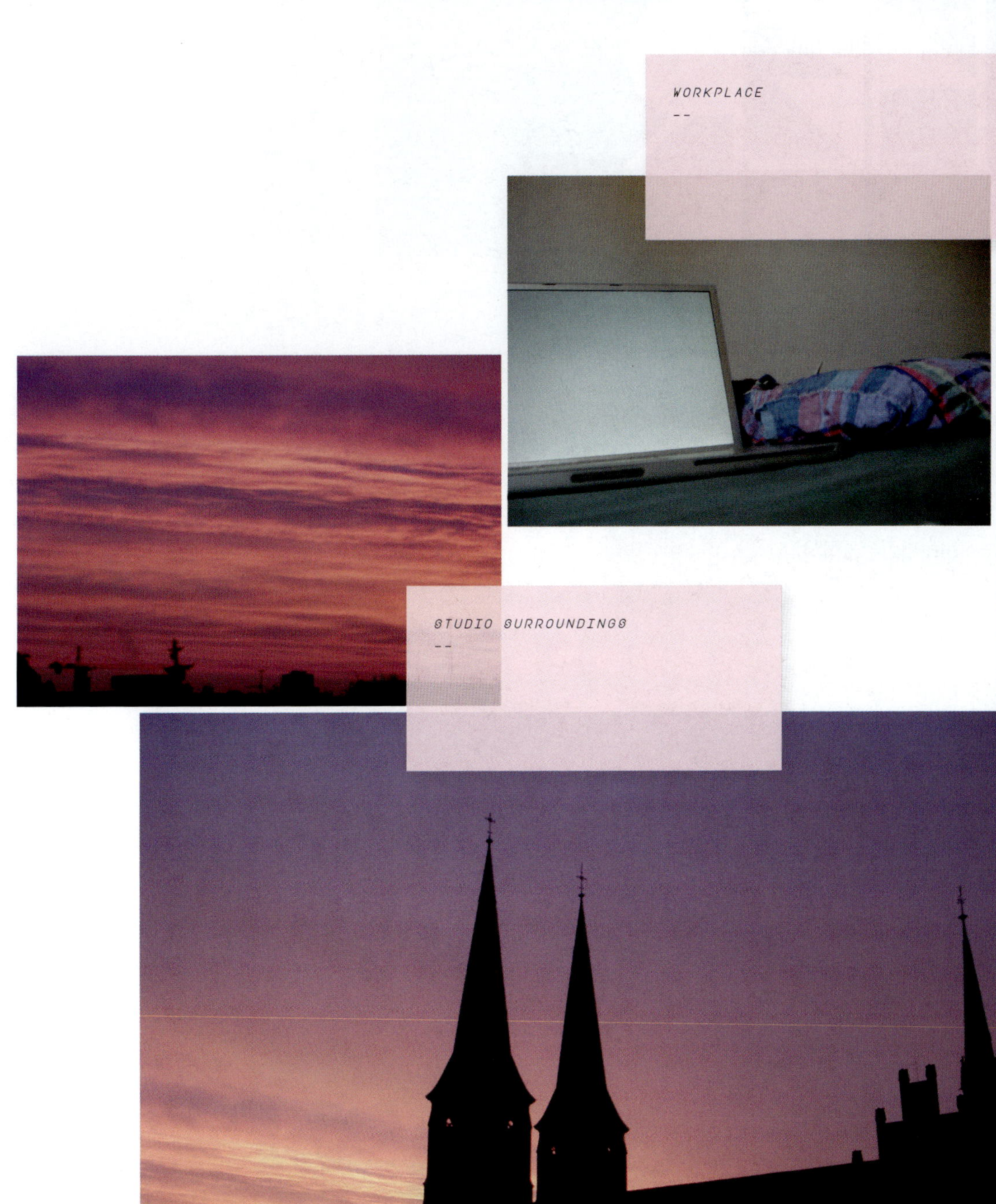

WORKPLACE
--

STUDIO SURROUNDINGS
--

HERRDELL

DONATUS DELL
--
GRABENSTRASSE 31
55124 MAINZ
GERMANY
--
T +49 6131 9725533
M +49 177 2822455
--
INFO@HERRDELL.DE
WWW.HERRDELL.DE
--

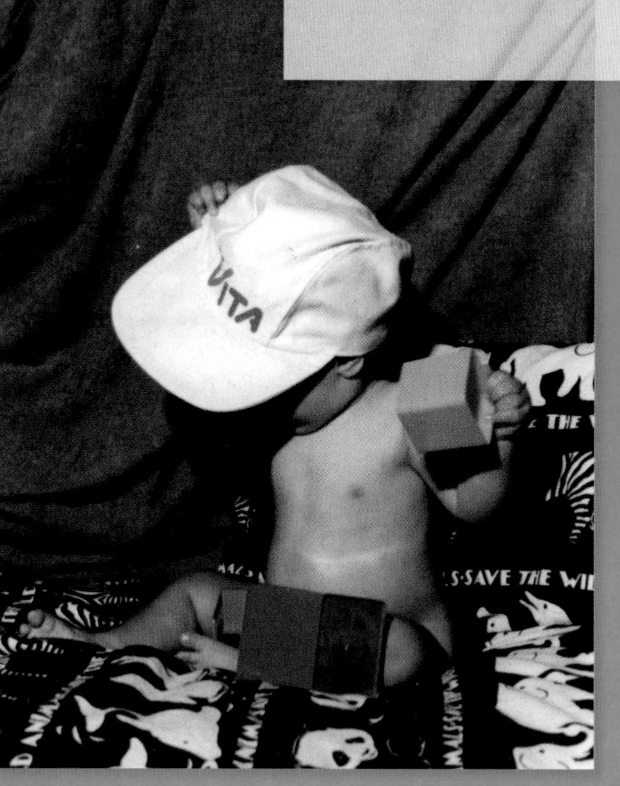

I'VE BEEN DESIGNING EVER SINCE I
COULD THINK. FIRST I TOOK PHOTO-
GRAPHS, THEN I DID TYPOGRAPHY AND
COLLAGES AND THOUGHT ABOUT THINGS.
THEN I WORKED IN A FEW AGENCIES
AND ALSO ALWAYS ON MY OWN PROJECTS
ON THE SIDE. SMALL SUBTLE PROJECTS
I PUT MY HEART INTO. SO SLOWLY
DURING THE COURSE OF MY STUD-
IES I SWITCHED FROM PHOTOGRAPHY
TO GRAPHIC DESIGN. AND NOW I WORK
MAINLY AT AN AGENCY FOR CORPORATE
COMMUNICATIONS IN MAINZ. IT'S GOOD
FUN. YEAH. REALLY THERE'S NOT MUCH
MORE TO BE SAID.

--

WHAT IS GERMAN?

LOUD AND PRAGMATIC.

WHAT IS GERMAN DESIGN?

COARSE.

PLEASE DESCRIBE YOUR WORKING
PROCESS.

THINKING AND THEN DOING.

WHAT DO YOU AIM TO ACHIEVE WITH
YOUR WORK?

GIVE PLEASURE TO PEOPLE'S EYES.

YOU'VE INVITED A FRIEND TO
GERMANY; NAME ONE PLACE THEY
REALLY MUST VISIT AND A QUINT-
ESSENTIAL EXPERIENCE YOU REC-
OMMEND.

VISIT SAARLAND AND EAT SCHWENK-
ER (LOCAL GRILLED MEAT SPECIALTY).

WHAT IS THE MOST IMPORTANT
LESSON YOU HAVE LEARNED IN YOUR
PROFESSION SO FAR?

GOOD CLIENTS AND BAD CLIENTS.

--

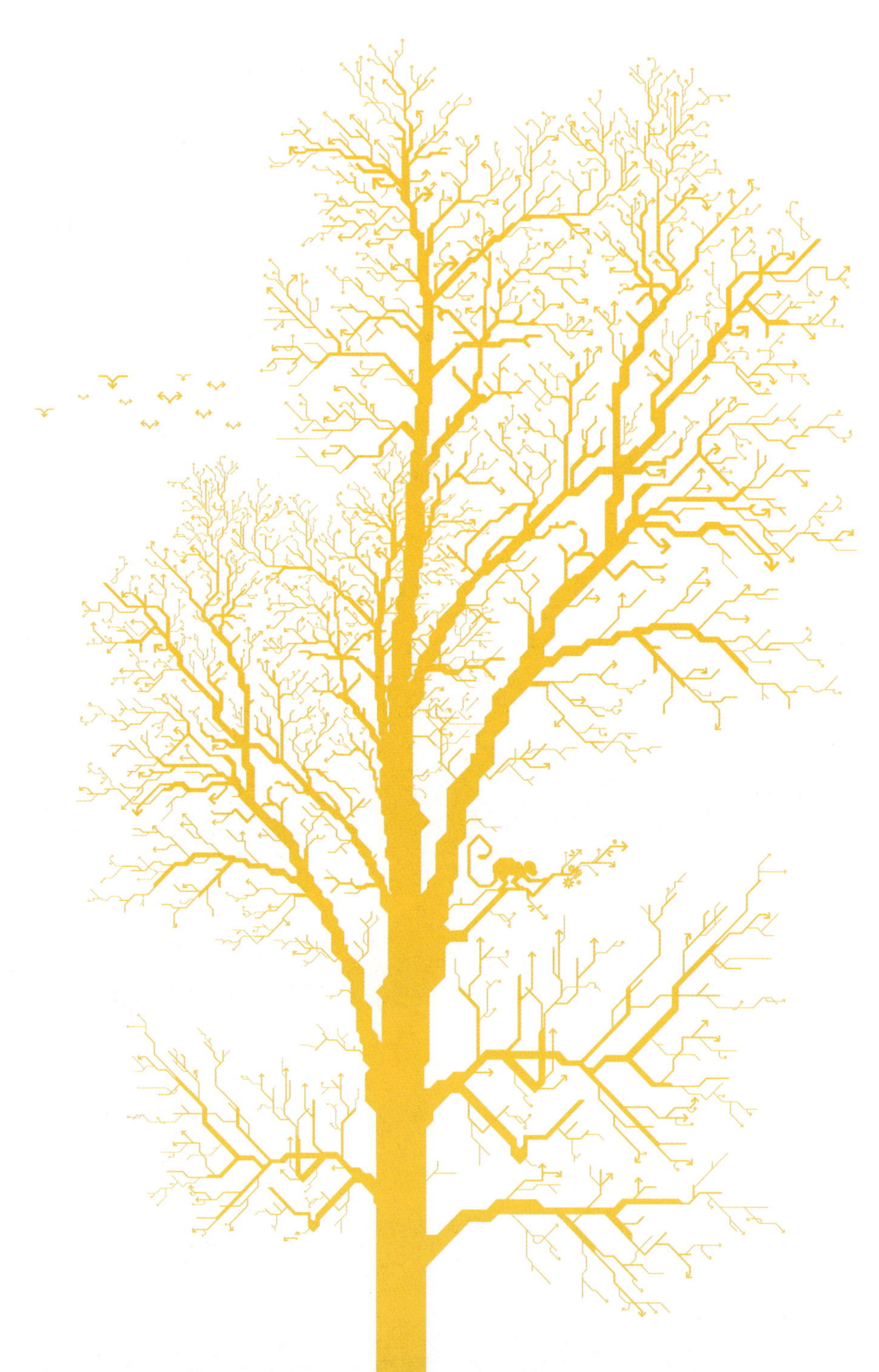

CORPORATE DESIGN 603QM
(CULTURAL EVENTS)
--
603QM HAS AN INSTANTLY RECOG-
NIZABLE LOOK BECAUSE OF THE
STOEFELER FONT THAT WAS DESIGNED
SPECIALLY FOR IT AND BECAUSE OF
THE HOUSE COLOR HK85 (YELLOW),
WHICH IS ALSO DOMINANT IN THE
ARCHITECTONIC CONCEPT AND THE
DECOR OF THE EVENT LOCATION. A
FURTHER DISTINGUISHING FEATURE
IS THE 45° AND 90° ANGLES THAT
ARE DERIVED FROM THE FORMS USED
IN THE FONT AND ARE PICKED UP IN
THE ILLUSTRATIONS, SO CHARACTER-
IZING A COMPLETELY INDIVIDUAL
PICTORIAL LANGUAGE THAT RUNS
THROUGH THE WHOLE APPEARANCE.
--

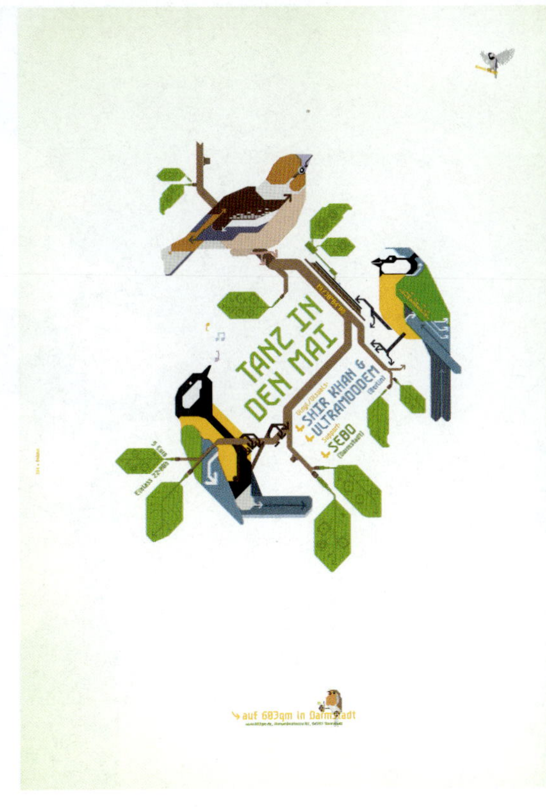

TANZ IN
DEN MAI
SHIR KHAN &
ULTRAMODDEM
(Berlin)
SEBO
(Darmstadt)
auf 603qm in Darmstadt

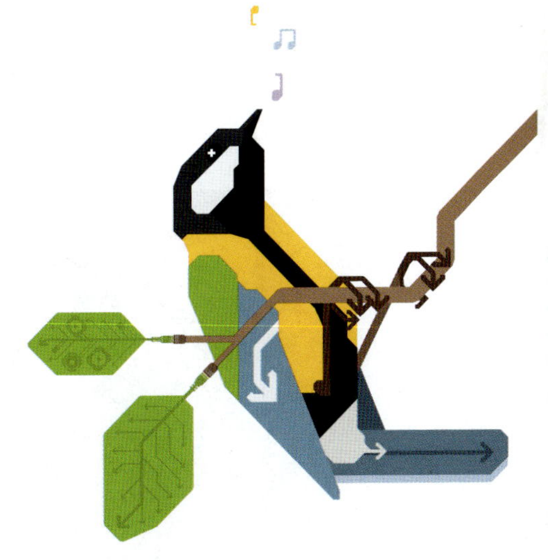

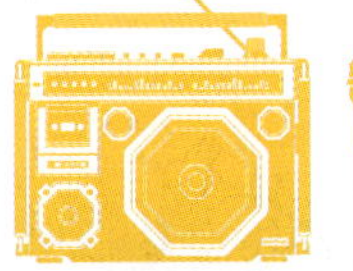

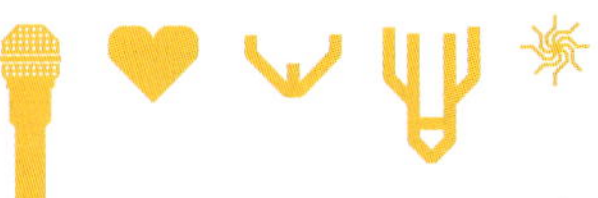

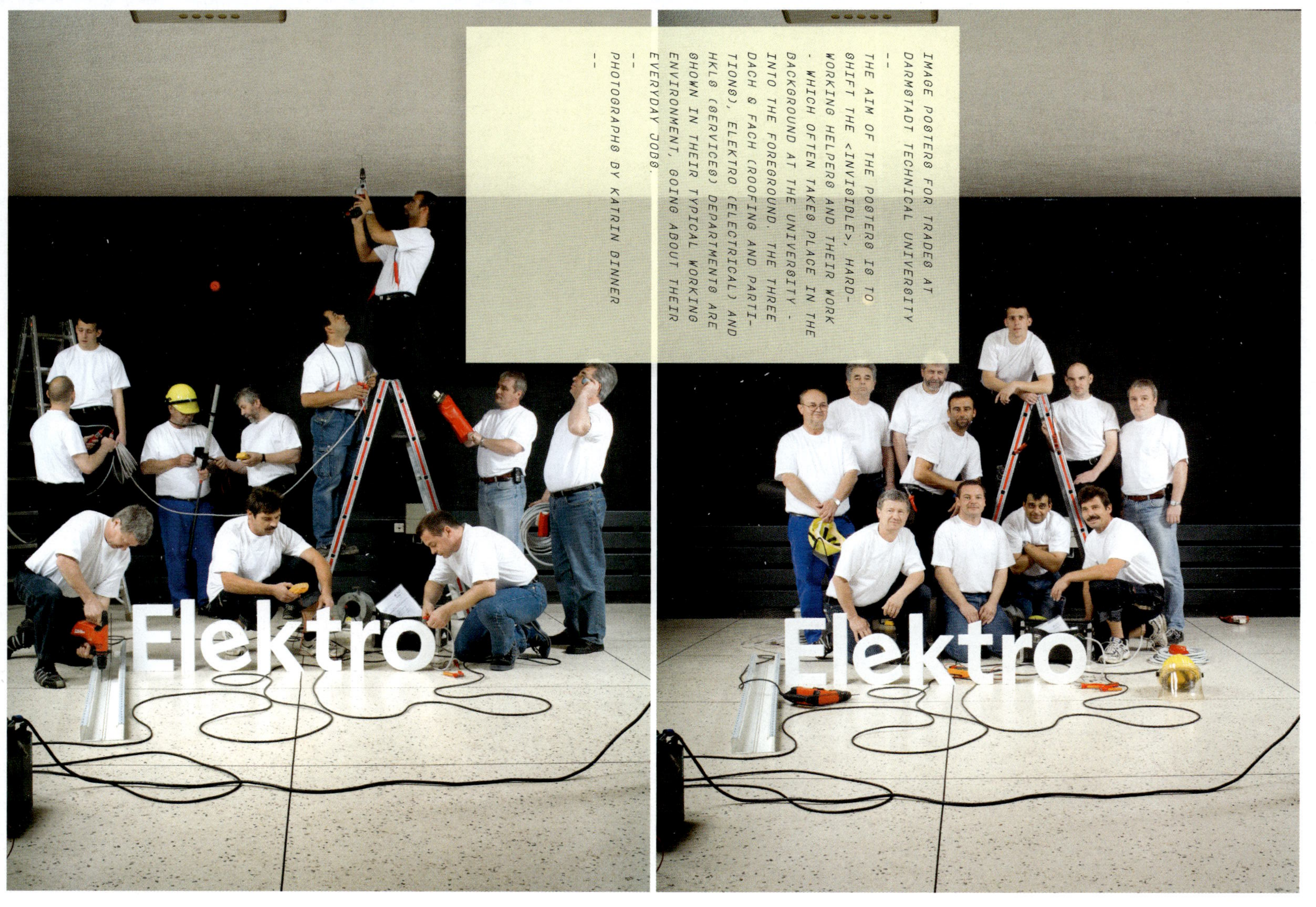

IMAGE POSTERS FOR TRADES AT
DARMSTADT TECHNICAL UNIVERSITY
--
THE AIM OF THE POSTERS IS TO
SHIFT THE <INVISIBLE>, HARD-
WORKING HELPERS AND THEIR WORK
- WHICH OFTEN TAKES PLACE IN THE
BACKGROUND AT THE UNIVERSITY -
INTO THE FOREGROUND. THE THREE
DACH & FACH (ROOFING AND PARTI-
TIONS), ELEKTRO (ELECTRICAL) AND
HKLS (SERVICES) DEPARTMENTS ARE
SHOWN IN THEIR TYPICAL WORKING
ENVIRONMENT, GOING ABOUT THEIR
EVERYDAY JOBS.
--
PHOTOGRAPHS BY KATRIN BINNER
--

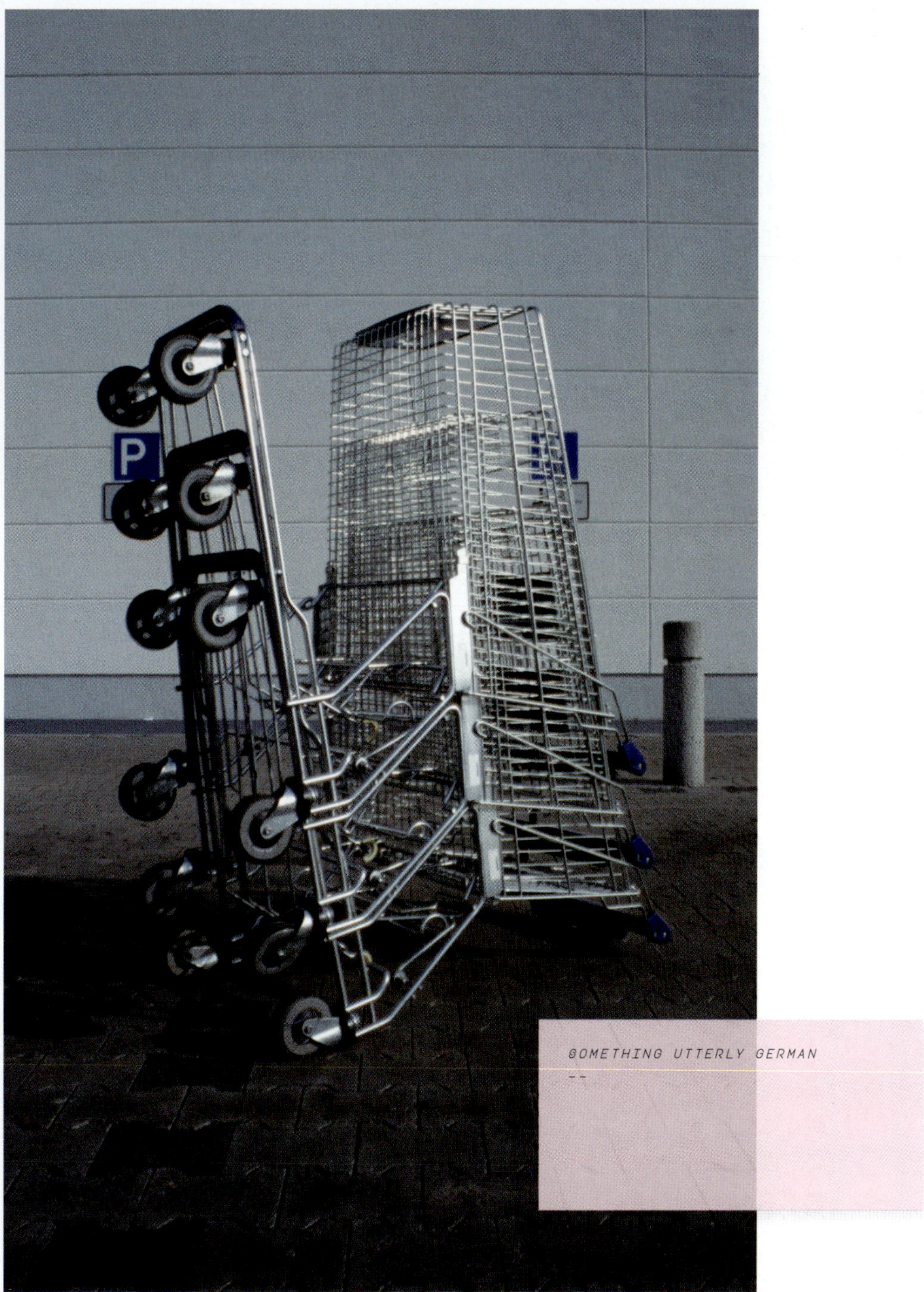

SOMETHING UTTERLY GERMAN
--

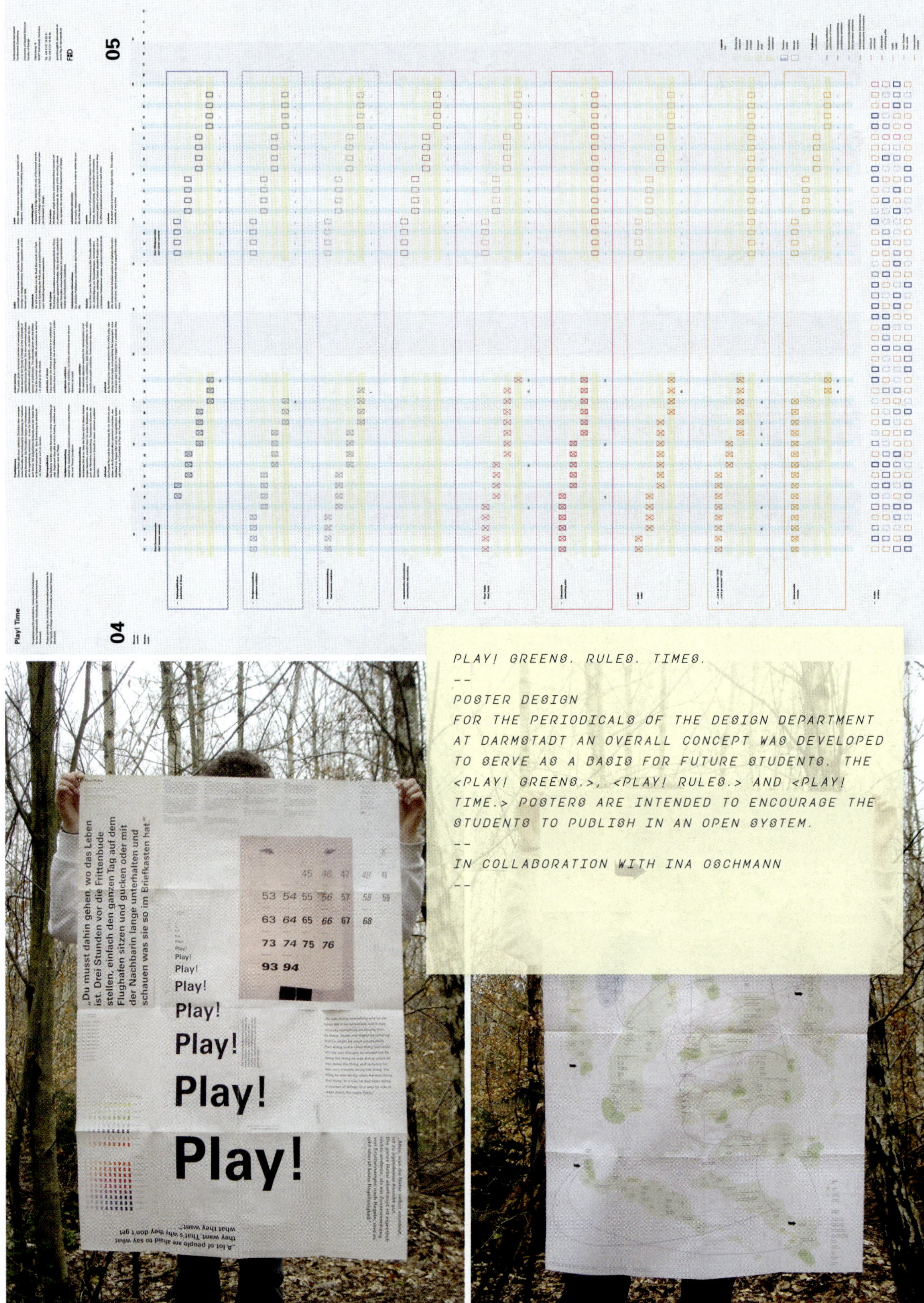
PLAY! GREENS. RULES. TIMES.
--
POSTER DESIGN
FOR THE PERIODICALS OF THE DESIGN DEPARTMENT
AT DARMSTADT AN OVERALL CONCEPT WAS DEVELOPED
TO SERVE AS A BASIS FOR FUTURE STUDENTS. THE
<PLAY! GREENS.>, <PLAY! RULES.> AND <PLAY!
TIME.> POSTERS ARE INTENDED TO ENCOURAGE THE
STUDENTS TO PUBLISH IN AN OPEN SYSTEM.
--
IN COLLABORATION WITH INA OSCHMANN
--
Play!
Play!
Play!
Play!
Play!
Play!
Play!

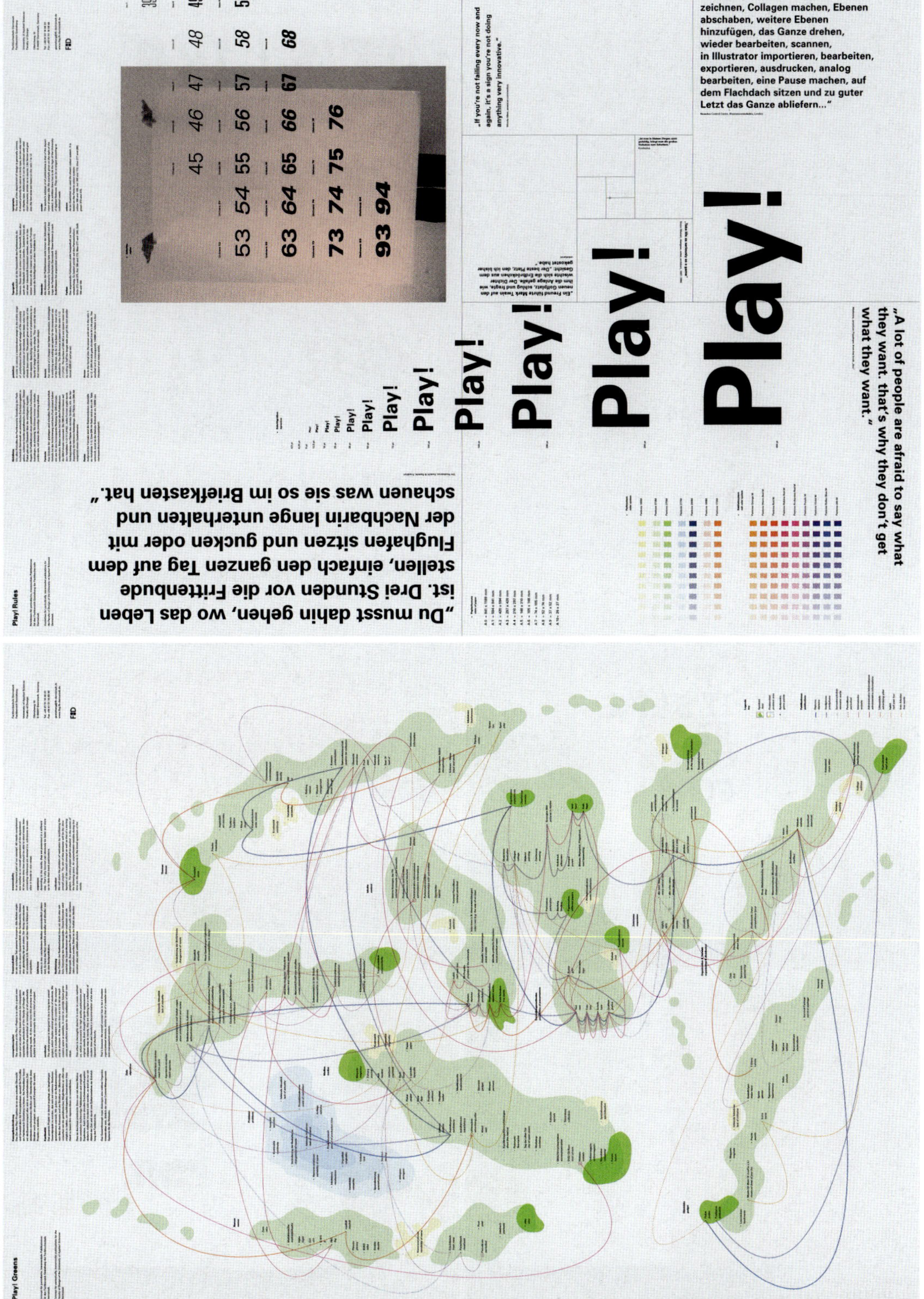

FID
Play! Rules
Play! Greens
„Zeichnen, eine Tasse Kaffee trinken, zeichnen, nachdenken, noch mehr zeichnen, Collagen machen, Ebenen abschaben, weitere Ebenen hinzufügen, das Ganze drehen, wieder bearbeiten, scannen, in Illustrator importieren, bearbeiten, exportieren, ausdrucken, analog bearbeiten, eine Pause machen, auf dem Flachdach sitzen und zu guter Letzt das Ganze abliefern…"
„If you're not failing every now and again, it's a sign you're not doing anything very innovative."
„A lot of people are afraid to say what they want. that's why they don't get what they want."
„Du musst dahin gehen, wo das Leben ist. Drei Stunden vor die Frittenbude stellen, einfach den ganzen Tag auf dem Flughafen sitzen und gucken oder mit der Nachbarin lange unterhalten und schauen was sie so im Briefkasten hat."
Play!
Play!
Play!
Play!
Play!
Play!
39 49 59
48 58 68
47 57 67
46 56 66 76
45 55 65 75
53 54 64 65
63 64 65 66 67
73 74 75 76
93 94

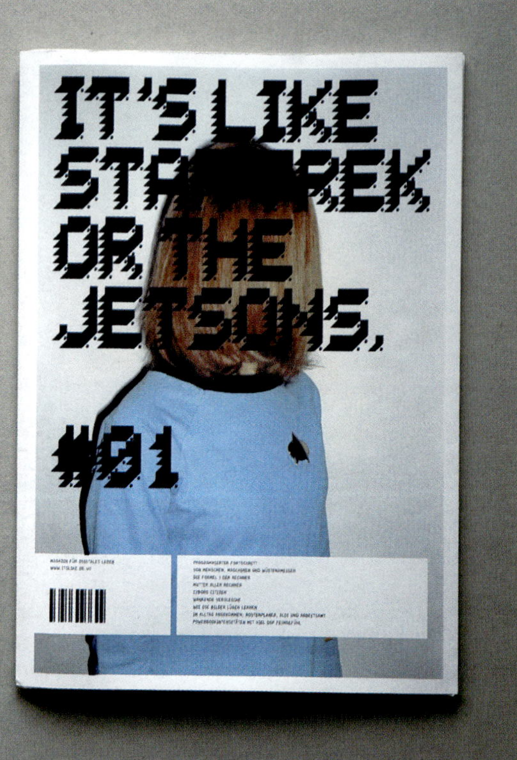
IT'S LIKE
STAR TREK
OR THE
JETSONS.
#01

IT'S LIKE
DD

FONT.

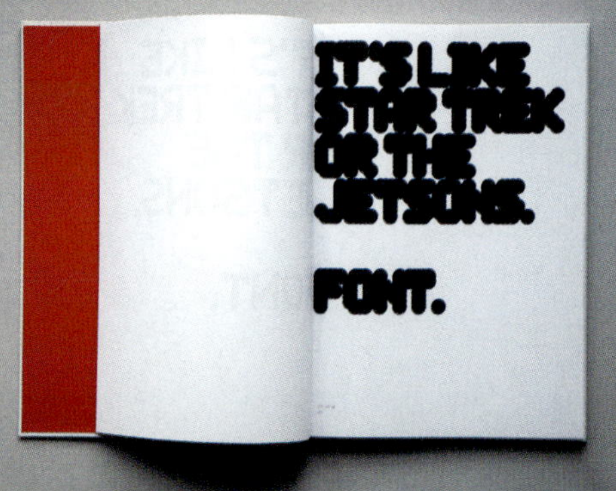
IT'S LIKE
STAR TREK
OR THE
JETSONS.

FONT.

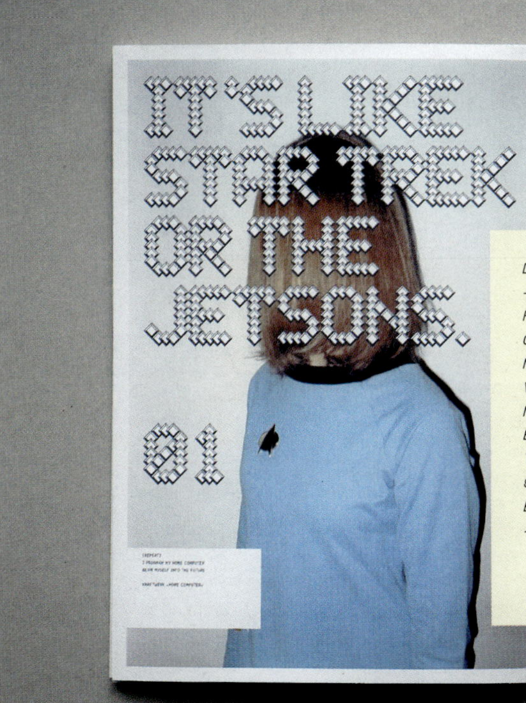

DD IT'S LIKE FONT.
--
FONT CATALOG WITH 101 <CUTS>
OF THE <DD IT'S LIKE FONT>. A
MATRIX-BASED FORM OF THE ENDLESS
VARIATIONS OF THE BASIC LETTER
MADE POSSIBLE BY MEANS OF THE
EXCHANGE OF INDIVIDUAL ELEMENTS.
THUS THE FONT CAN BE ADAPTED AT
SMALL EXPENSE AS A DISPLAY FOR
EVERY CONCEIVABLE USE.
--

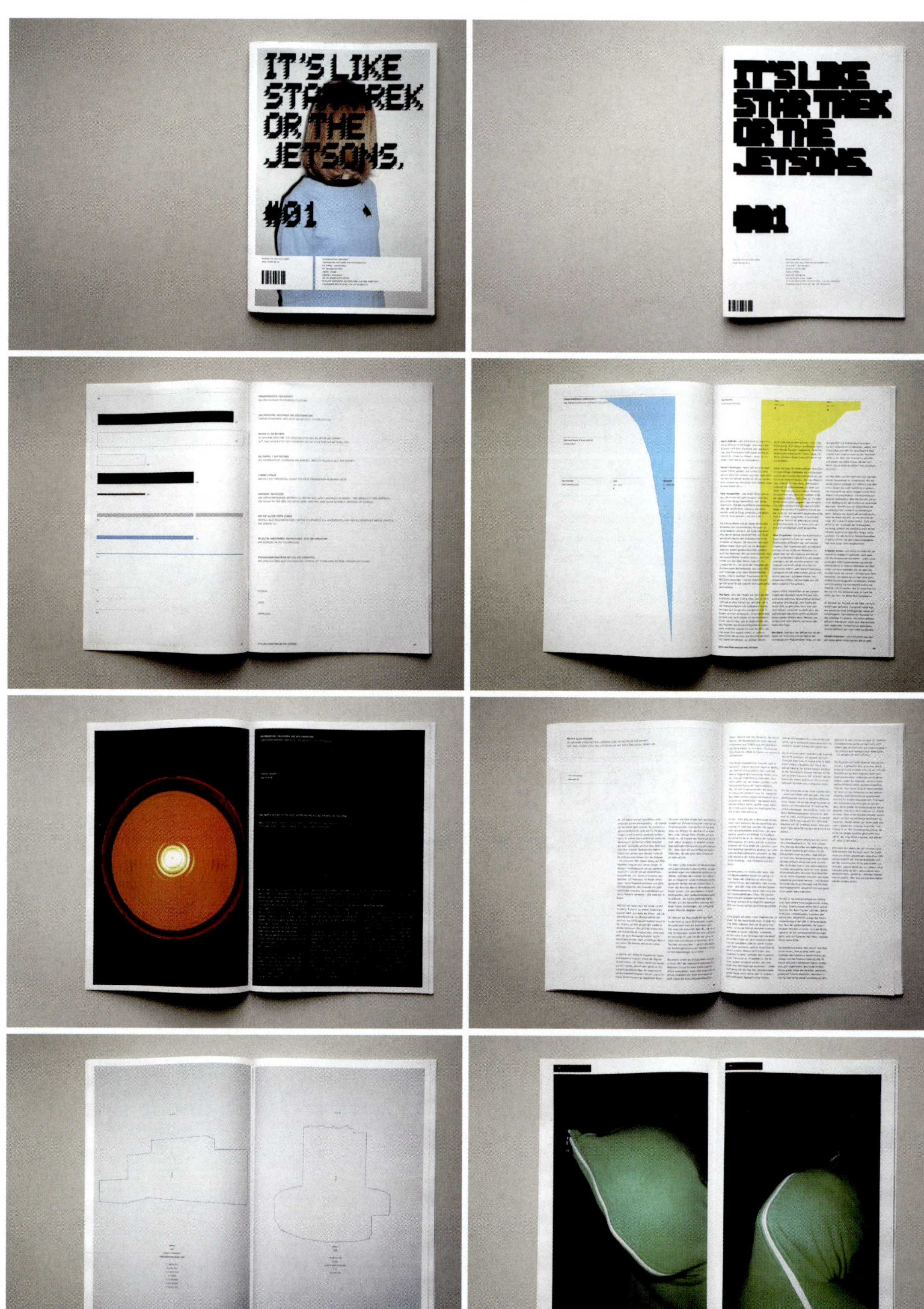

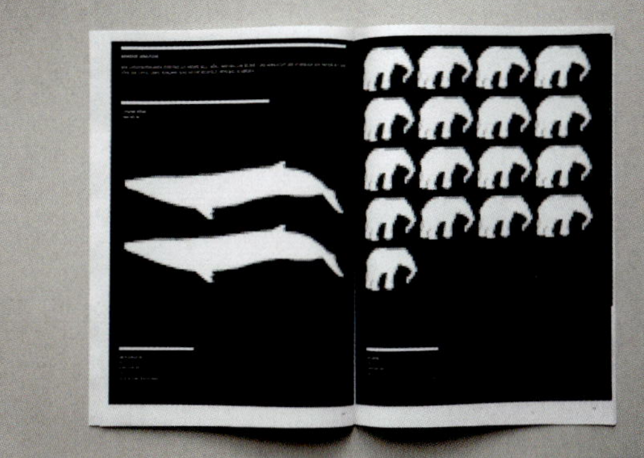

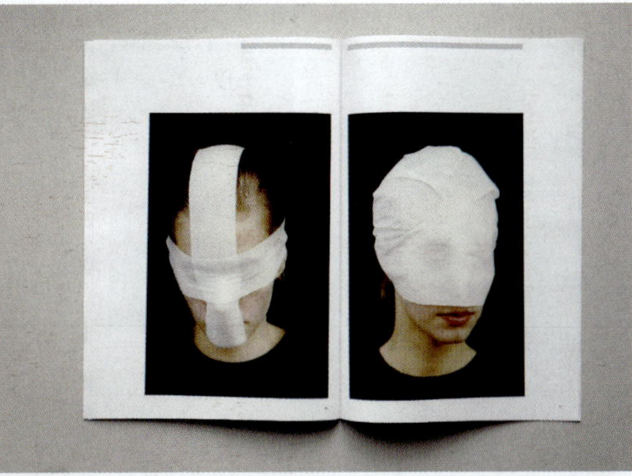

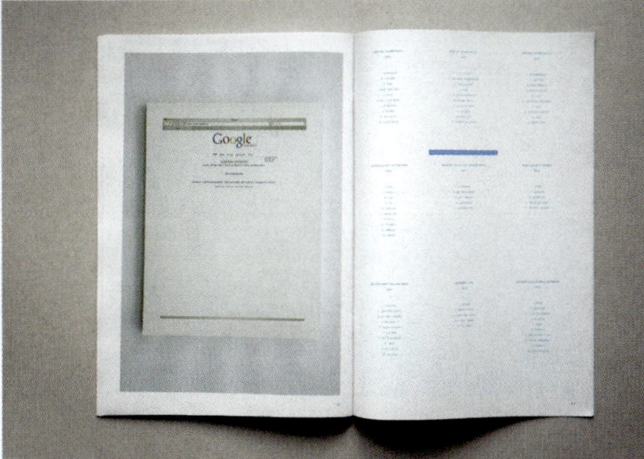

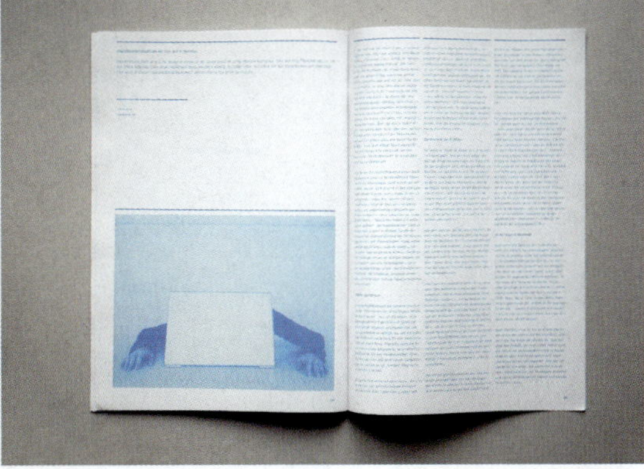

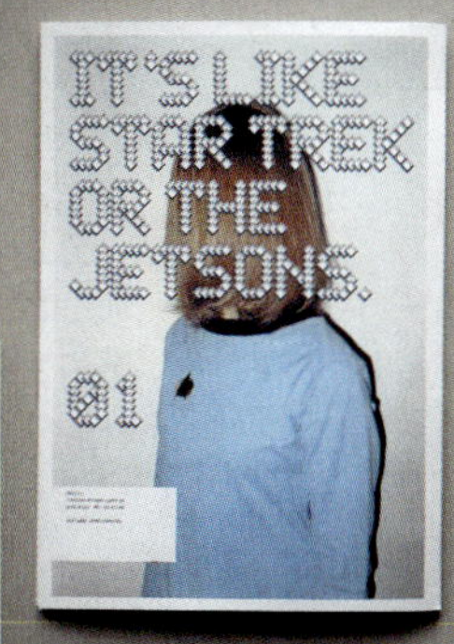

IT'S LIKE STAR TREK OR
THE JETSONS.
--
MY DIPLOMA PROJECT HAS TO DO WITH
A MAGAZINE ABOUT THE ASPECTS OF
DIGITAL LIVING. THEMES LIKE THE
EXTREMELY RAPID, EXPONENTIAL
DEVELOPMENT OF COMPUTER PER-
FORMANCE AND THE EFFECTS ON THE
HUMAN BEING AND SOCIETY ASSOCI-
ATED WITH IT REPRESENT THE MAIN
FOCUS.
--

I'M 25 YEARS OLD AND I LIVE IN
MANNHEIM (GERMANY). CURRENTLY I'M
STUDYING GRAPHIC DESIGN AT THE
HOCHSCHULE DARMSTADT.

IN 2006 I WORKED FOR FINEST / MAG-
MA IN KARLSRUHE WITH LARS HARMSEN
AND FLORIAN GAERTNER. IN 2007 –
2008 I STUDIED AT THE UNIVERSITY
OF ARTS IN BERN, SWITZERLAND.

--

WHAT IS GERMAN?

GERMAN IS THOROUGHNESS.

WHAT IS GERMAN DESIGN?

FOR ME GERMAN DESIGN IS ABOVE
ALL THE WORK OF STUDENTS AND
THE YOUNG GENERATION OF GRAPHIC
DESIGNERS. IN MY OPINION THAT'S
WHERE THE GREATEST MOMENTUM AND
THE MOST COURAGEOUS PROJECTS COME
FROM, APART FROM A FEW EXCEPTIONS
AMONG ESTABLISHED GRAPHIC DESIGN-
ERS. AS INFLUENCES NOW COME FROM
EVERYWHERE VIA THE INTERNET AND
BLOGS, IT'S HARD FOR ME TO TALK
ABOUT <GERMAN DESIGN> AS MEAN-
WHILE EVERYTHING IS INTERMINGLED.

PLEASE DESCRIBE YOUR WORKING
PROCESS.

1. DOING RESEARCH
   AND COLLECTING
2. EVALUATING AND DISCARDING
3. ARRANGING AND DESIGNING

WHAT DO YOU AIM TO ACHIEVE
WITH YOUR WORK?

OPENING UP WAYS OF LOOKING AT
THINGS THAT ARE PERHAPS NOT KNOWN
OTHERWISE.

YOU'VE INVITED A FRIEND TO
GERMANY; NAME ONE PLACE
THEY REALLY MUST VISIT AND A
QUINTESSENTIAL EXPERIENCE YOU
RECOMMEND.

LUISENPARK MANNHEIM, A TRIP ON A
GONDOLETTA.

WHAT IS THE MOST IMPORTANT
LESSON YOU HAVE LEARNED IN YOUR
PROFESSION SO FAR?

GOOD DESIGN MUST FIRST AND FORE-
MOST NOT BE ONE THING: IT'S AS YOU
LIKE IT.

--

BECKER

TOBIAS BECKER
--
WEIDENSTRASSE 3-5
68165 MANNHEIM
GERMANY
--
T +49 163 8306110
--
TOBIAS@8-W.CC
WWW.8-W.CC
--

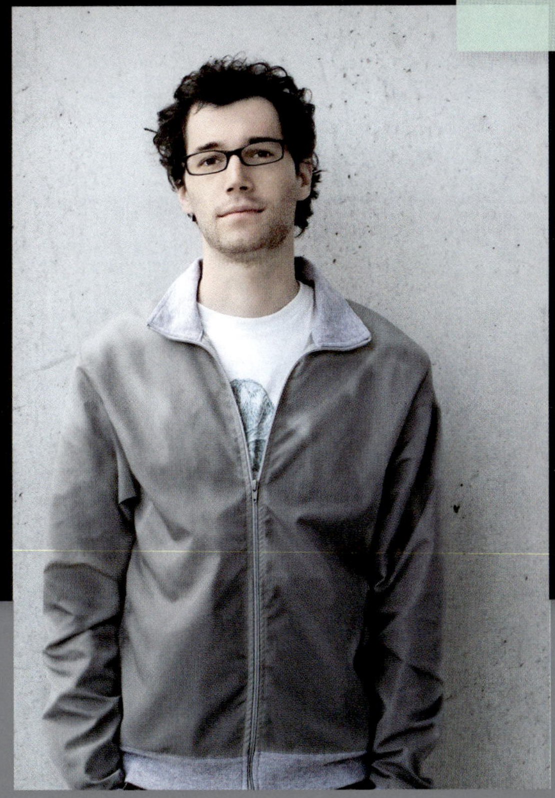

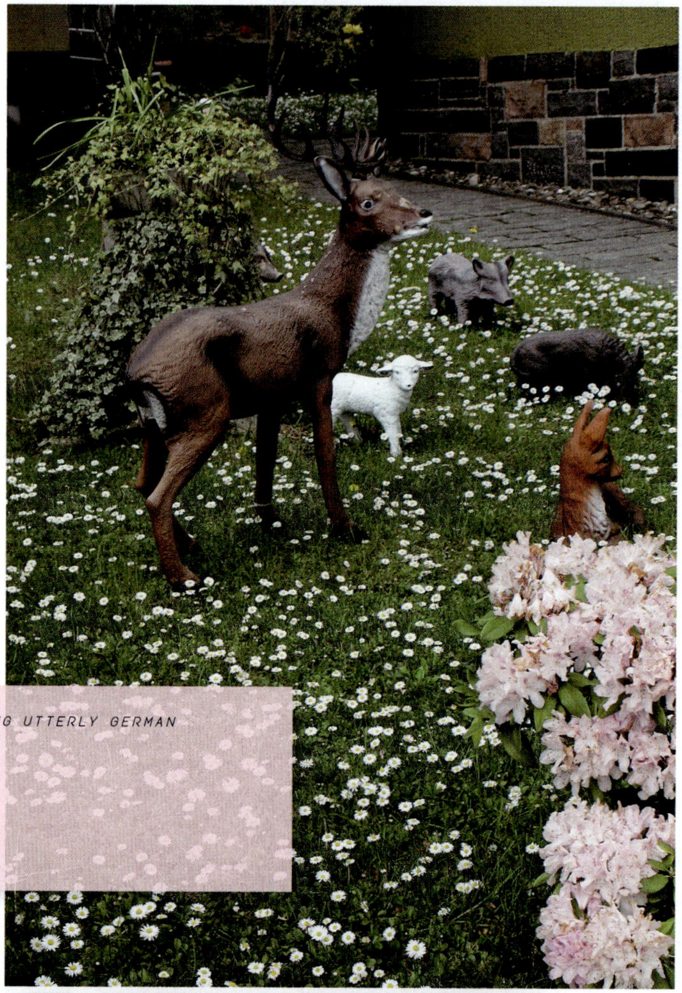

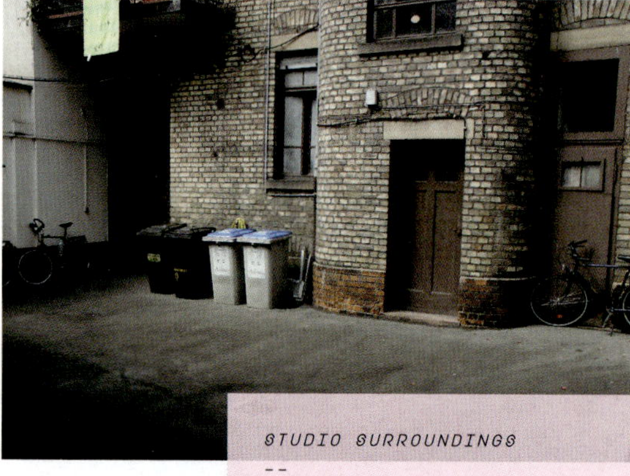

SOMETHING UTTERLY GERMAN
--

STUDIO SURROUNDINGS
--

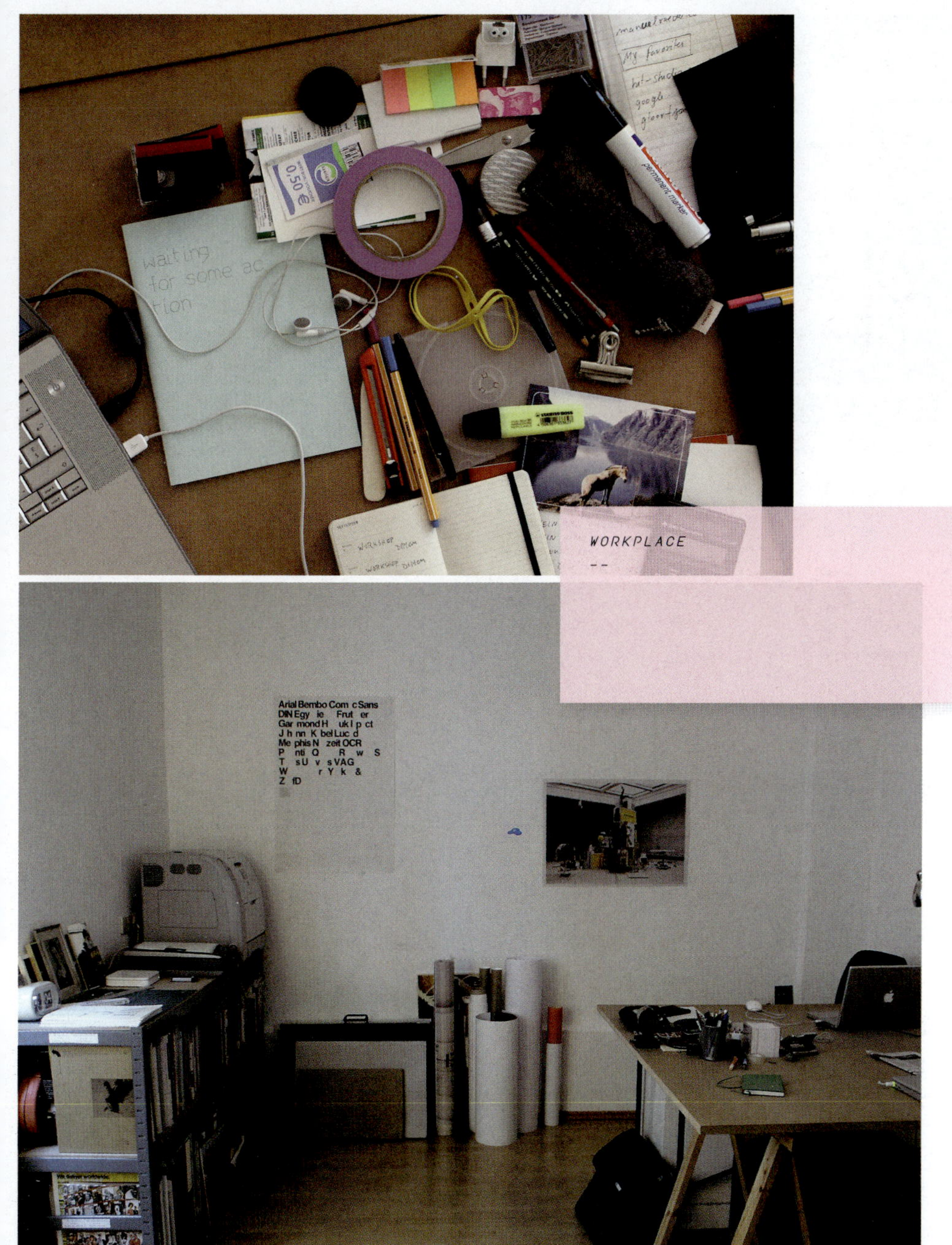

WORKPLACE

Anleitung
zum Lügen / zur Wahrheit

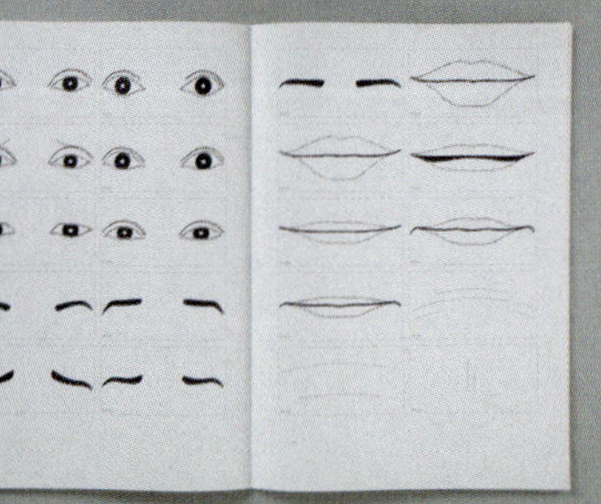

Ärger und Zorn

1 Ziehen Sie die Augenbrauen zusammen und nach unten, achten Sie darauf, dass sie an den Innenseiten zu Nase hinauf weisen.

2 Halten Sie sie in dieser Stellung und versuchen Sie gleichzeitig die Augen weit aufzureißen, sodass ihre Oberlider die gesenkten Brauen berühren und starren Sie unverwandt geradeaus.

3 Sobald Sie sicher sind, die Bewegungen von Augenbrauen und Augenlidern korrekt auszuführen zu können, entspannen Sie die obenliegenden Augenlider.

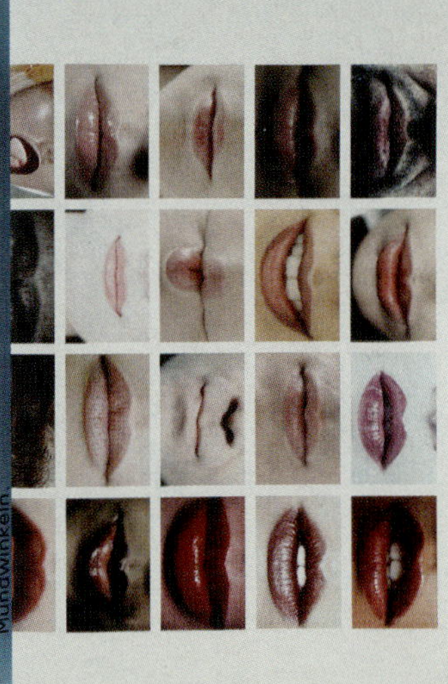

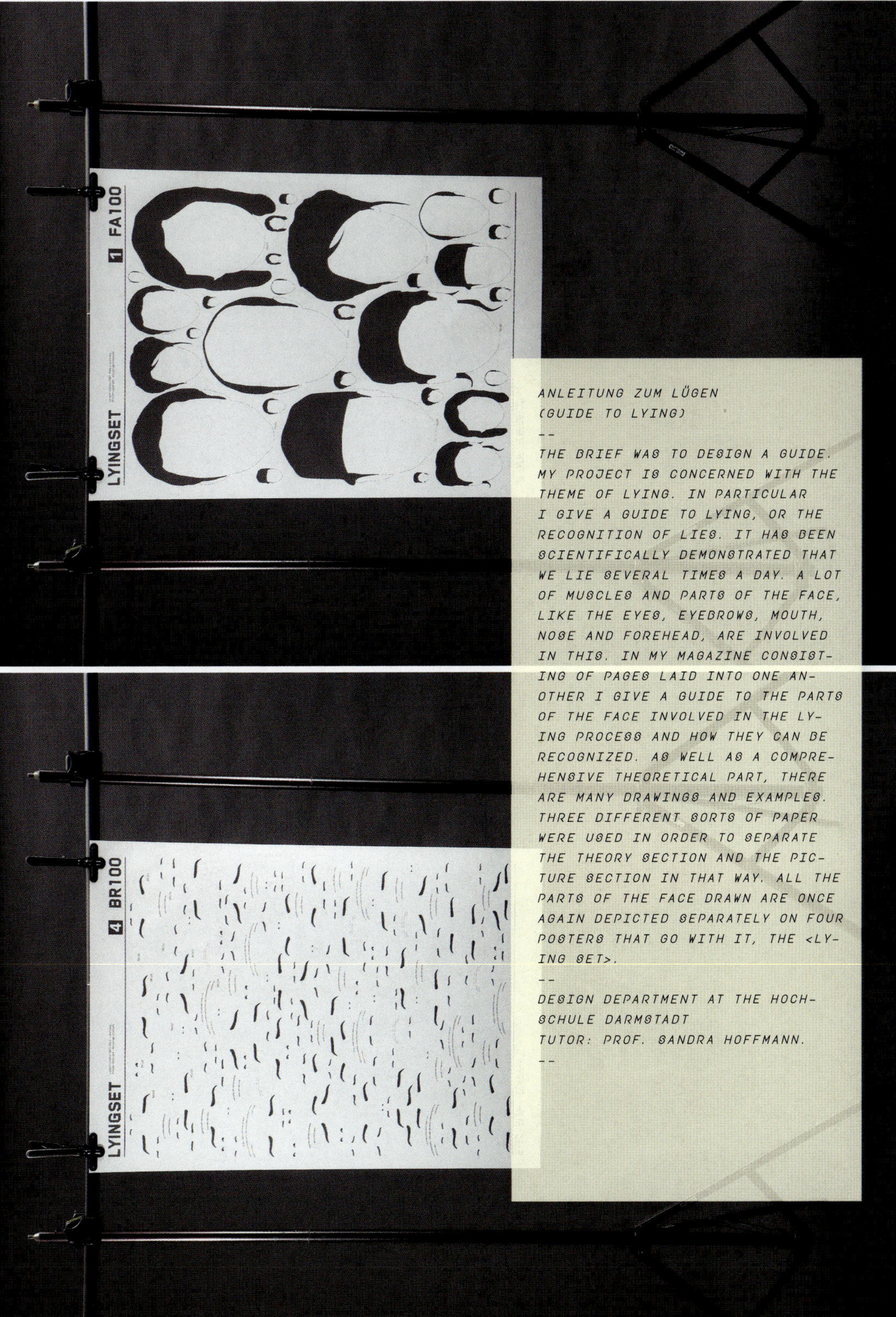

ANLEITUNG ZUM LÜGEN
(GUIDE TO LYING)
--
THE BRIEF WAS TO DESIGN A GUIDE.
MY PROJECT IS CONCERNED WITH THE
THEME OF LYING. IN PARTICULAR
I GIVE A GUIDE TO LYING, OR THE
RECOGNITION OF LIES. IT HAS BEEN
SCIENTIFICALLY DEMONSTRATED THAT
WE LIE SEVERAL TIMES A DAY. A LOT
OF MUSCLES AND PARTS OF THE FACE,
LIKE THE EYES, EYEBROWS, MOUTH,
NOSE AND FOREHEAD, ARE INVOLVED
IN THIS. IN MY MAGAZINE CONSIST-
ING OF PAGES LAID INTO ONE AN-
OTHER I GIVE A GUIDE TO THE PARTS
OF THE FACE INVOLVED IN THE LY-
ING PROCESS AND HOW THEY CAN BE
RECOGNIZED. AS WELL AS A COMPRE-
HENSIVE THEORETICAL PART, THERE
ARE MANY DRAWINGS AND EXAMPLES.
THREE DIFFERENT SORTS OF PAPER
WERE USED IN ORDER TO SEPARATE
THE THEORY SECTION AND THE PIC-
TURE SECTION IN THAT WAY. ALL THE
PARTS OF THE FACE DRAWN ARE ONCE
AGAIN DEPICTED SEPARATELY ON FOUR
POSTERS THAT GO WITH IT, THE <LY-
ING SET>.
--
DESIGN DEPARTMENT AT THE HOCH-
SCHULE DARMSTADT
TUTOR: PROF. SANDRA HOFFMANN.
--

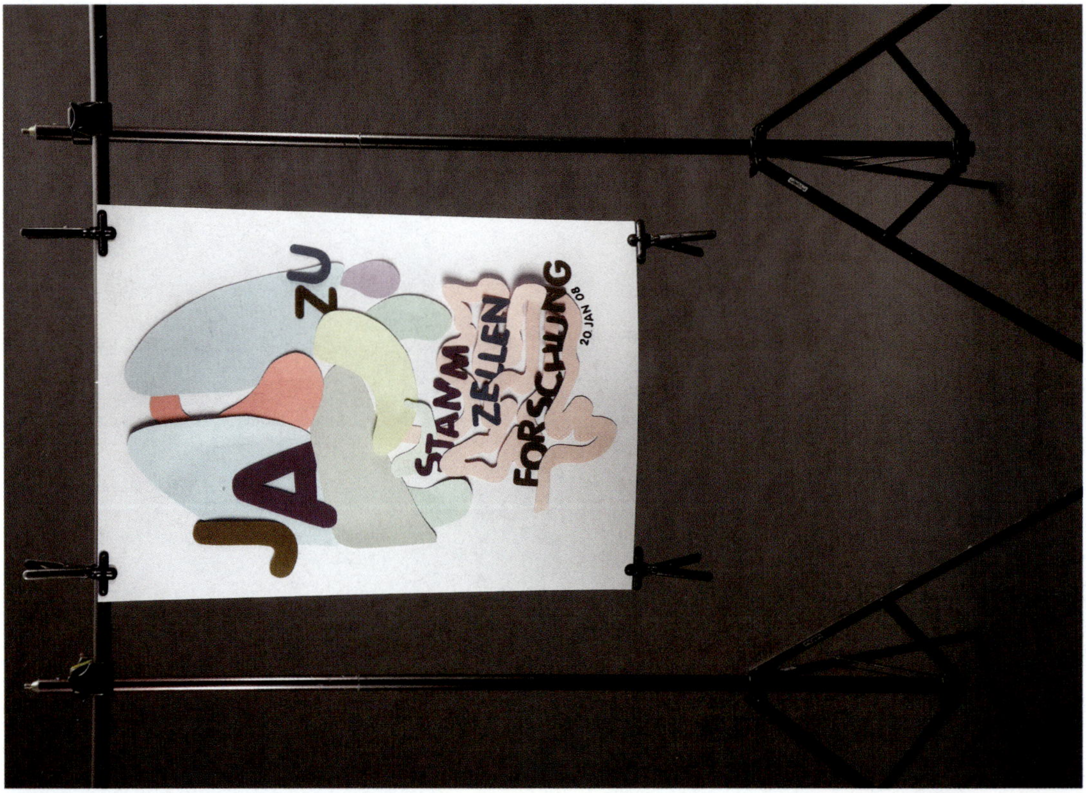

ZU
JA
STAMM
ZELLEN
FORSCHUNG
20 JAN 08

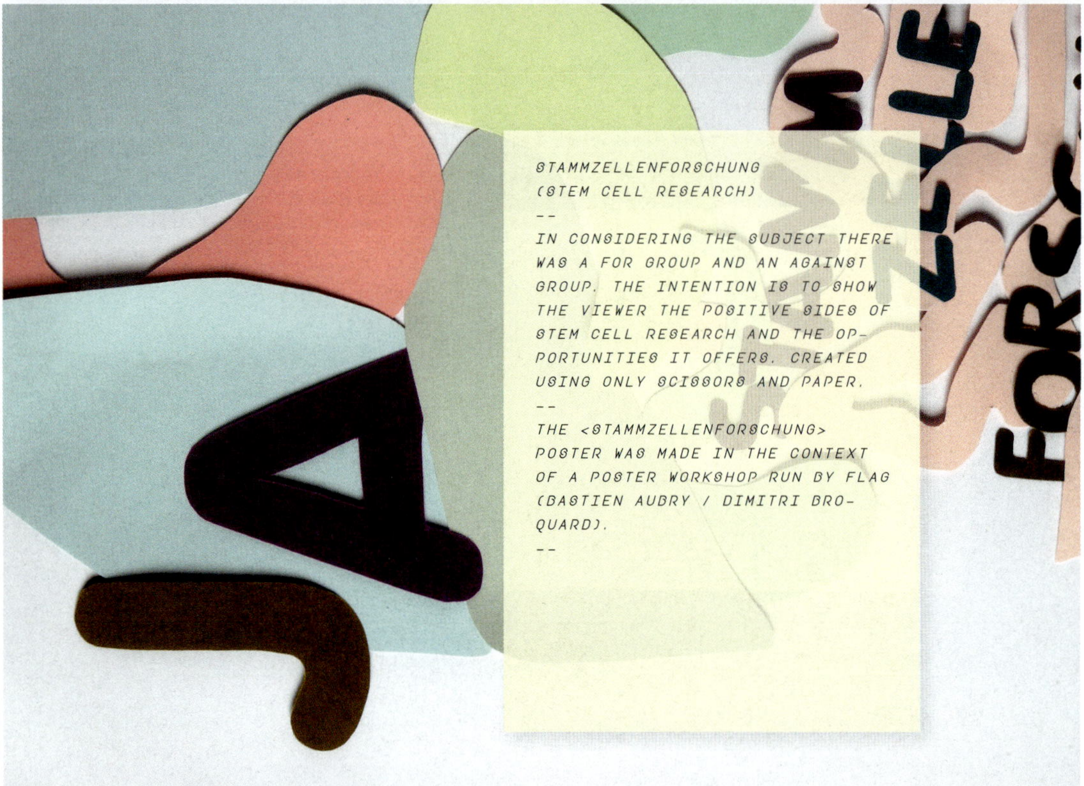

STAMMZELLENFORSCHUNG
(STEM CELL RESEARCH)
--
IN CONSIDERING THE SUBJECT THERE
WAS A FOR GROUP AND AN AGAINST
GROUP. THE INTENTION IS TO SHOW
THE VIEWER THE POSITIVE SIDES OF
STEM CELL RESEARCH AND THE OP-
PORTUNITIES IT OFFERS. CREATED
USING ONLY SCISSORS AND PAPER.
--
THE <STAMMZELLENFORSCHUNG>
POSTER WAS MADE IN THE CONTEXT
OF A POSTER WORKSHOP RUN BY FLAG
(BASTIEN AUBRY / DIMITRI BRO-
QUARD).
--

MASSTAB 1:1
(SCALE 1:1, OR FULL-SCALE)
ARCHITEKTUR IM SELBSTVERSUCH
(TRY YOUR OWN HAND AT ARCHITEC-
TURE)
--
<MASSTAB 1:1> WAS AN ARCHITEC-
TURE EXHIBITION WHERE ARCHI-
TECTS SHOWED <ARCHITEKTUR IM
SELBSTVERSUCH>. SOME OF THEM
WERE UNUSUAL PROJECTS THAT THEY
IMPLEMENTED FOR THEMSELVES, IN
WHICH BOUNDARIES IN DESIGN AND
BUILDING WERE SOUNDED OUT. THE
BRIEF WAS TO DESIGN AN EXHIBI-
TION CATALOG FOR THAT EXHIBITION.
THE CATALOG WAS TO BE DESIGNED AS
ECONOMICALLY AS POSSIBLE (MAXI-
MUM SIZE A3 FORMAT). MY IDEA
WAS TO DESIGN A SMALL A5-FORMAT
BROCHURE FOR EACH ARCHITECT /
ARCHITECTURAL PRACTICE. THUS
AN A3 SHEET WAS FOLDED DOWN AND
PROVIDED WITH A COVER. TWO DIF-
FERENT SORTS OF PAPER WERE USED
FOR THIS. AN INTERVIEW WITH EACH
ARCHITECT FORMED THE MAIN PART
THAT WAS PRESENTED ACROSS THE
FULL A3 FORMAT. FOR DIFFERENTIA-
TION A DIFFERENT COLOR OF PAPER
WAS USED FOR EACH ARCHITECT. THE
EXHIBITION CONCEPT WAS THAT VISI-
TORS WOULD COLLECT THE A5 BRO-
CHURES AND AT THE END KEEP THEM
IN A FOLDER.
--
PROJECT AT THE HKB BERN
TUTOR: URS LEHNI AND RAFAEL KOCH.
--

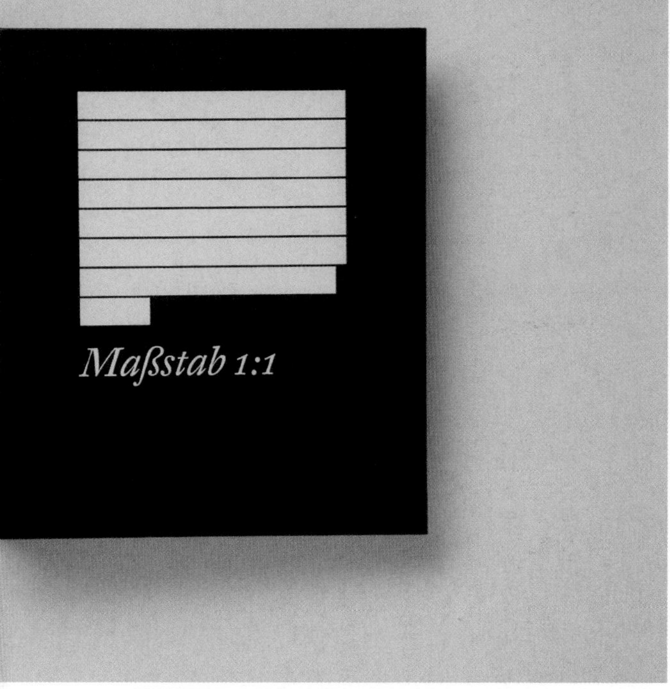

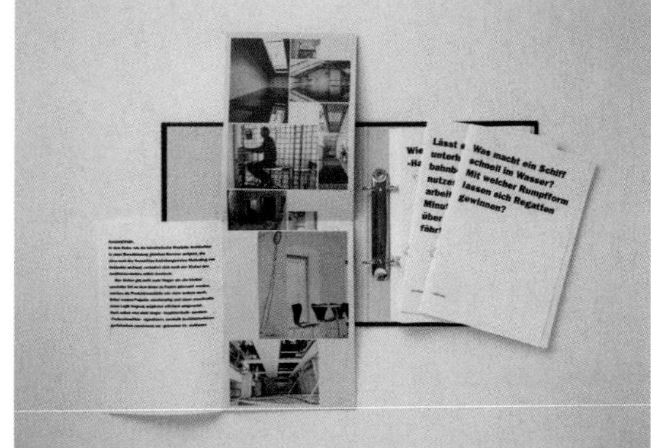

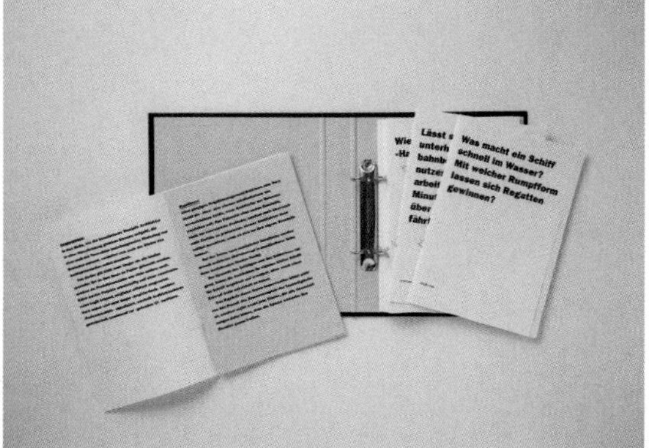

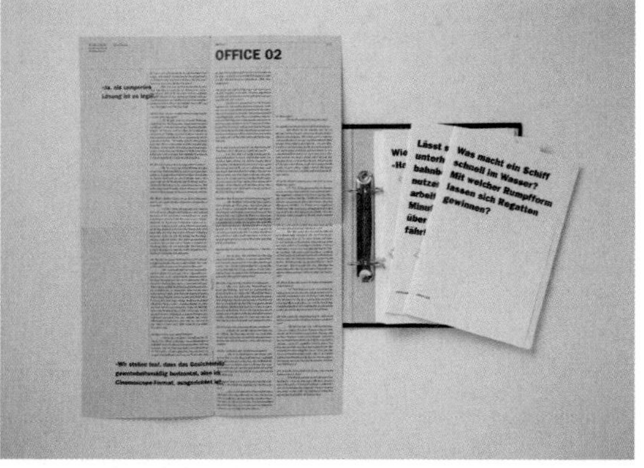

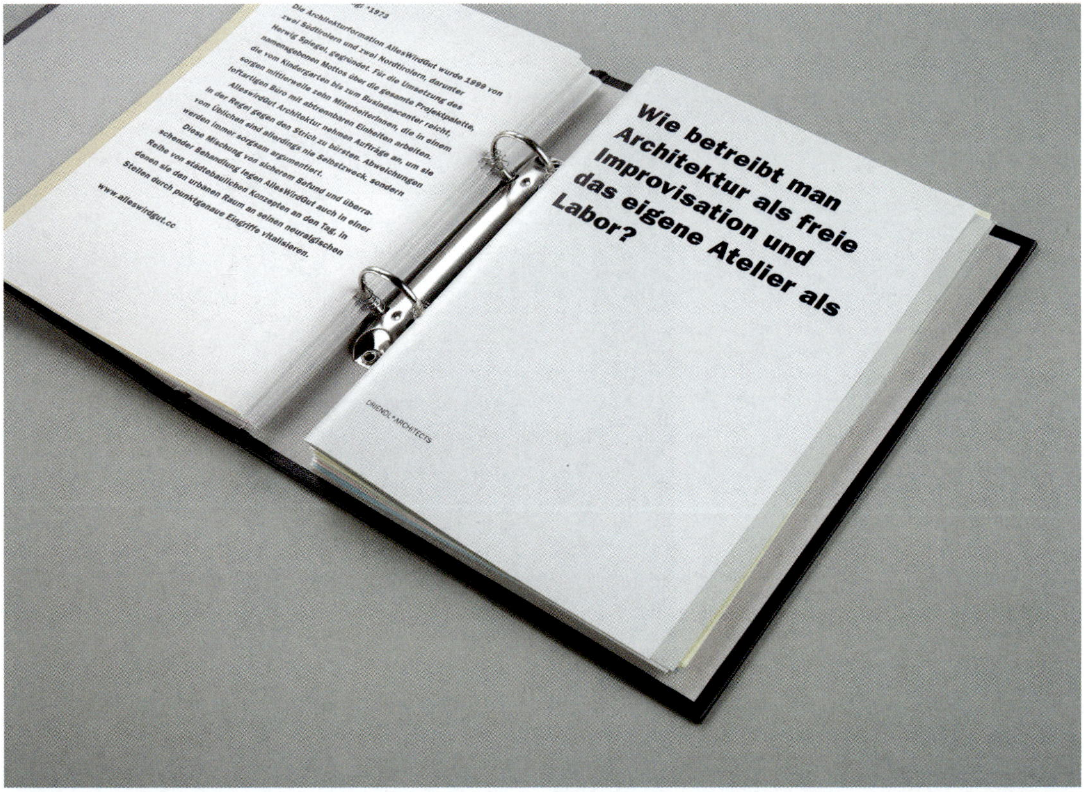

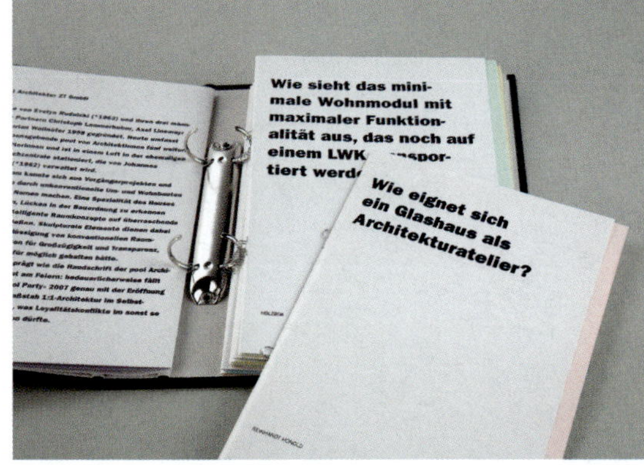

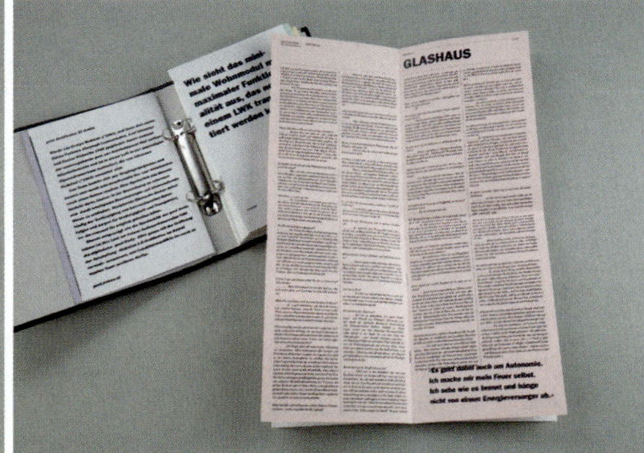

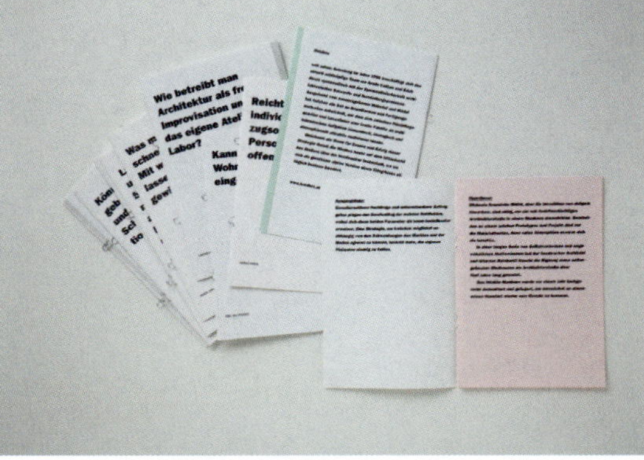

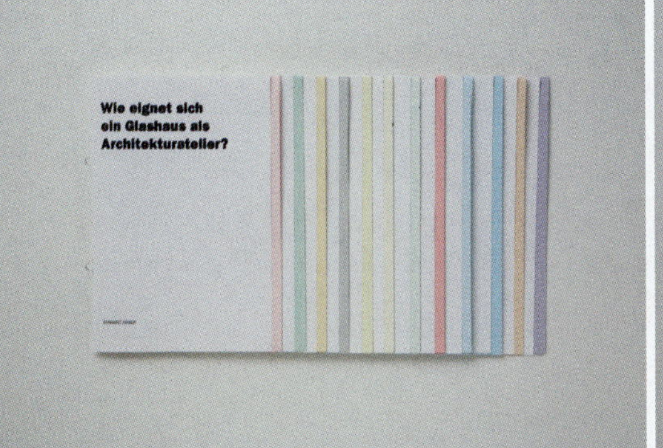
Wie eignet sich
ein Glashaus als
Architekturatelier?

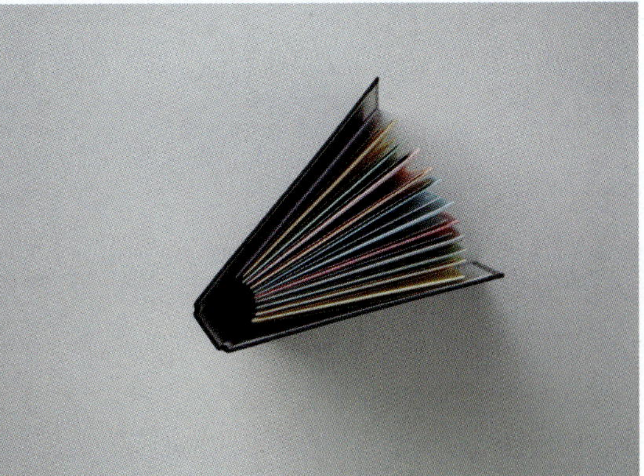

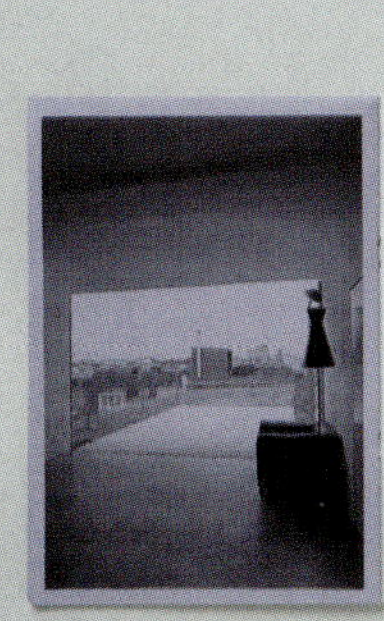

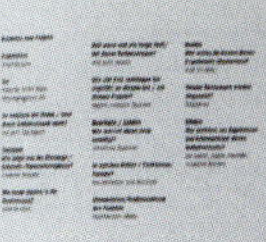

C100 STUDIO IS A MULTIDISCIPLINARY
DESIGN STUDIO WORKING ON VARIOUS
PROJECTS INCLUDING CONCEPTION,
CREATIVE DIRECTION, GRAPHIC DESIGN
AND ILLUSTRATION FOR A DIVERSE
RANGE OF CLIENTS. SPECIALIZING IN
DELIVERING INVENTIVE AND PRECISE
VISUAL SOLUTIONS, WE APPROACH EACH
PROJECT WITH ENTHUSIASM, DEDICA-
TION, AND AN INDIVIDUAL STYLE THAT
IS EVIDENT IN OUR WORKS.

--

WHAT IS GERMAN?

LET ME ANSWER THIS WITH THE CLI-
CHÉ OF HOW THE TYPICAL GERMAN USED
TO BE: HE WAS AN ACCURATE PEDANT,
WHO WAS AFRAID TO OFFEND ANYTHING
AND TENDED TO CRITICIZE RATHER
THAN COMMEND. MAYBE THIS WAS BE-
CAUSE OF HIS HISTORY (WW2), OR A
TYPICAL SIGN OF GERMAN <ANGST>.
NOWADAYS, LUCKILY, THIS PREJUDICE
IS PAST AS YOUNG GERMANS TEND TO
GO IN THE OPPOSITE DIRECTION. SAU-
ERKRAUT USED TO BE TYPICALLY GER-
MAN, THOUGH I DON'T LIKE IT.

WHAT IS GERMAN DESIGN?

MOST OF THE TIMES IT'S PRETTY
BORING BECAUSE GERMAN DESIGNERS
OFTEN DON'T DARE BREAK BARRIERS
AND PREFER TO REPEAT STUFF THEY'VE
SEEN SEVERAL TIMES BEFORE RATHER
THAN EXPERIMENT. NEVERTHELESS, IN
SOME CASES GERMAN DESIGN CAN ALSO
BE VERY EXCITING AND VERY GOOD!

PLEASE DESCRIBE YOUR WORKING
PROCESS.

THINK - CREATE - RETHINK - REC-
REATE.

WHAT DO YOU AIM TO ACHIEVE WITH
YOUR WORK?

IN MOST CASES WHAT I WANT TO
ACHIEVE IS FOR PEOPLE TO UN-
DERSTAND THE MESSAGE I TRIED TO
COMMUNICATE WITH MY WORK. THAT'S
ALSO THE MOST IMPORTANT PART WHEN
WORKING WITH CLIENTS, AS IT SHOWS
IF YOU'VE MANAGED TO TRANSFORM THE
INITIAL BRIEF INTO A GOOD DESIGN.
ALSO, IN A FEW CASES IT'S JUST FOR
THE VIEWERS' OPTICAL PLEASURE,
WITHOUT ANY SPECIAL MEANING. PURE
FUN!

YOU'VE INVITED A FRIEND TO
GERMANY; NAME ONE PLACE THEY
REALLY MUST VISIT AND A QUINT-
ESSENTIAL EXPERIENCE YOU REC-
OMMEND.

HE SHOULD GO THE ENGLISCHE
GARTEN IN MUNICH AND HANG OUT IN
A BIERGARTEN. IF HE/SHE SURFS HE
SHOULD ALSO CHECK OUT THE STANDING
WAVE AT EISBACH.

WHAT IS THE MOST IMPORTANT
LESSON YOU HAVE LEARNED IN YOUR
PROFESSION SO FAR?

IT'S ALL ABOUT AUTHENTICITY.

--

C1ØØ

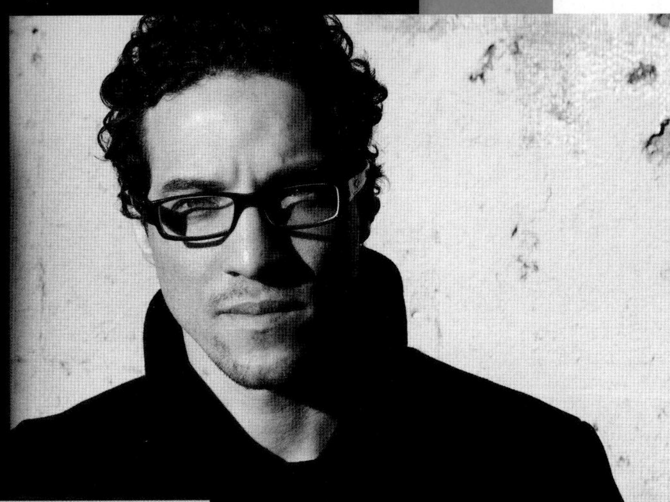

C1ØØ STUDIO
--
CLAUDE-LORRAIN-STRASSE 7
81543 MUNICH
GERMANY
--
T +49 89 37415083
--
HELLO@C1ØØSTUDIO.COM
WWW.C1ØØSTUDIO.COM
--

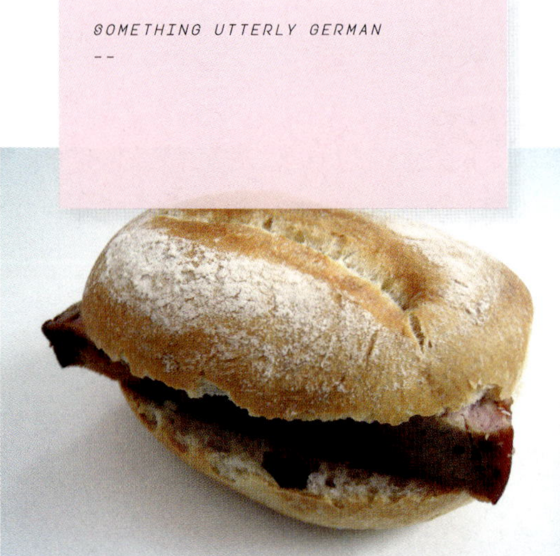

SOMETHING UTTERLY GERMAN
--

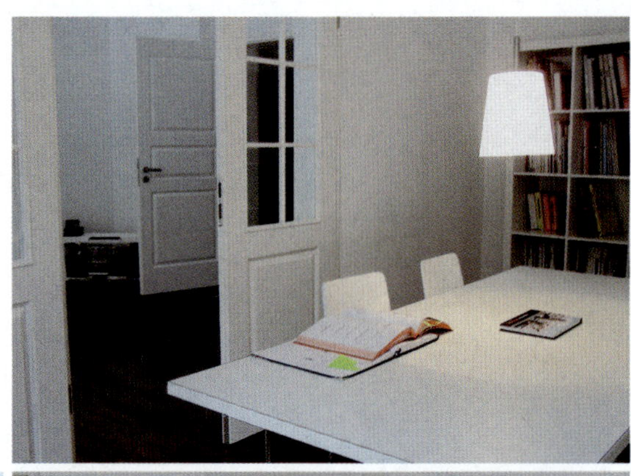

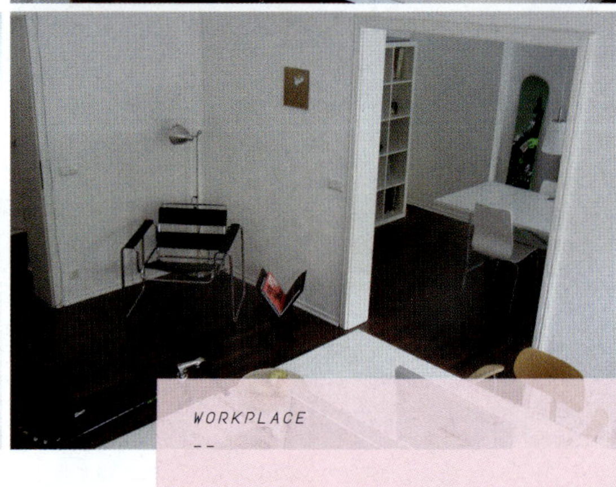

WORKPLACE
--

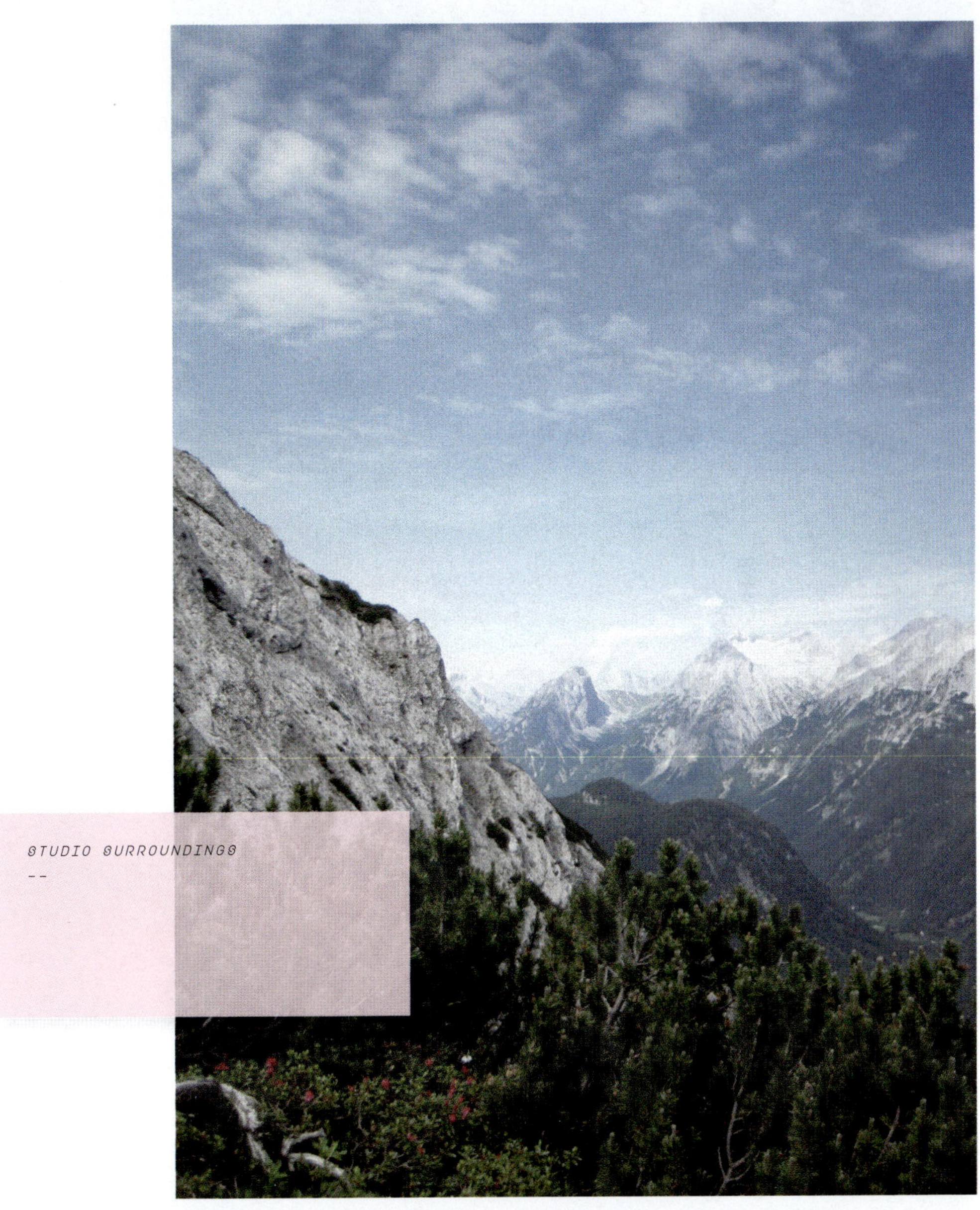
STUDIO SURROUNDINGS
--

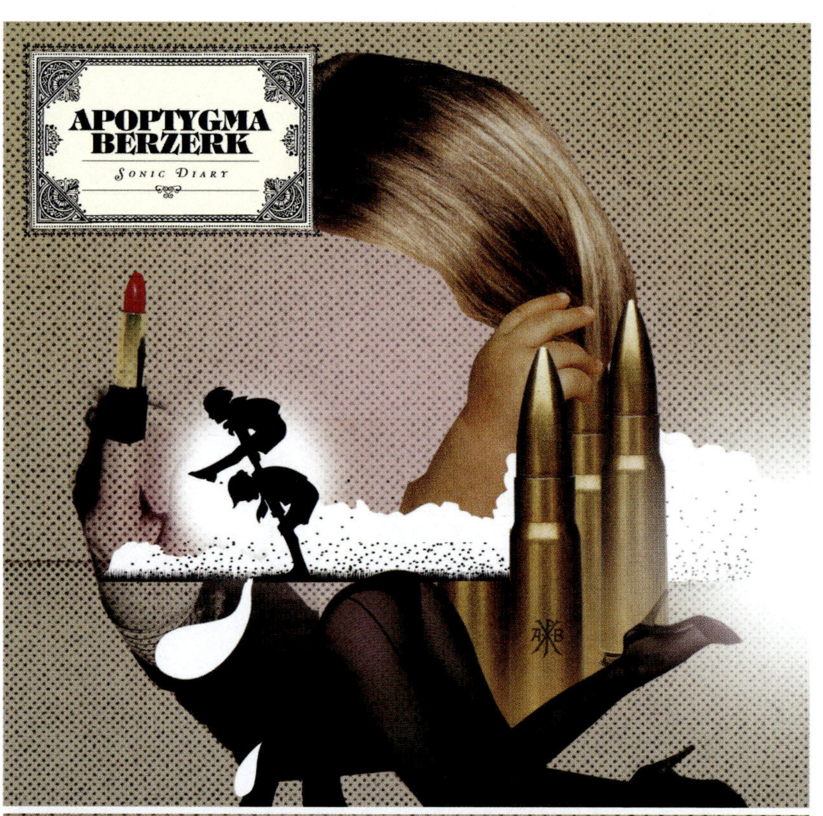

APOPTYGMA
BERZERK
SONIC DIARY

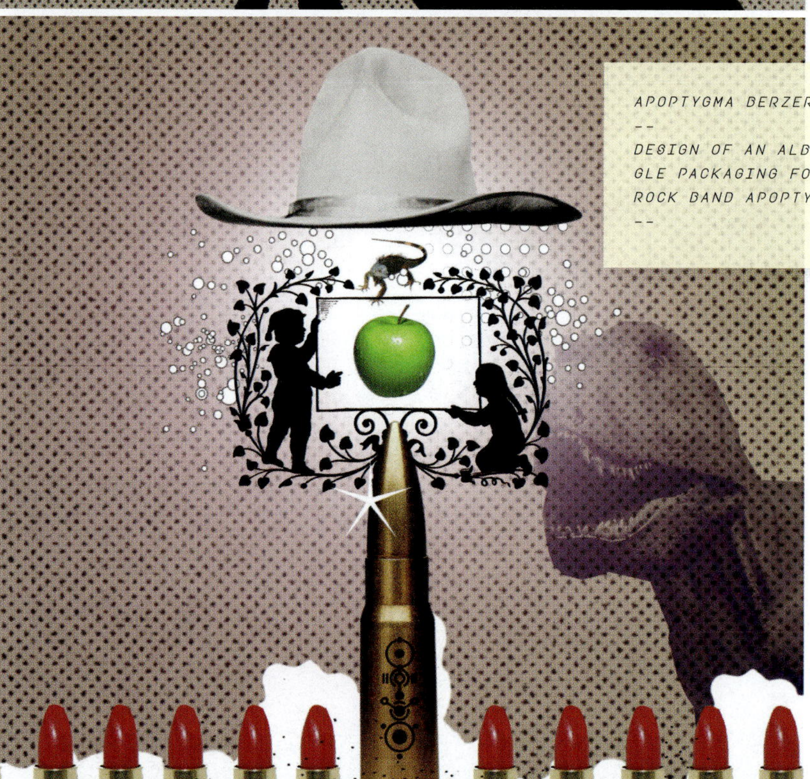

APOPTYGMA BERZERK
--
DESIGN OF AN ALBUM AND MAXI SIN-
GLE PACKAGING FOR THE NORWEGIAN
ROCK BAND APOPTYGMA BERZERK.
--

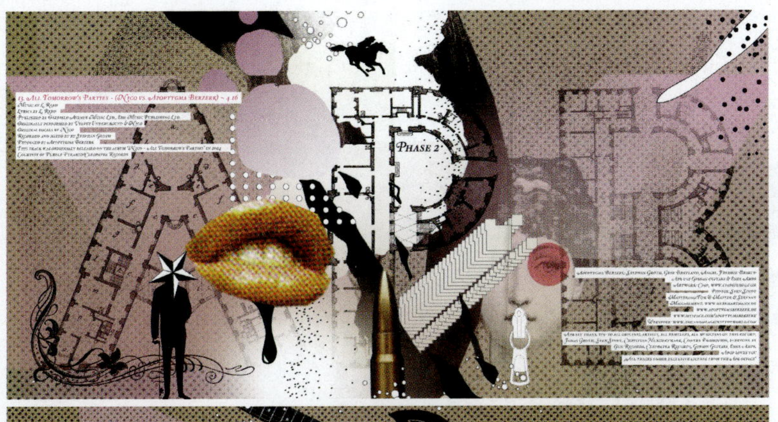
13. ALL TOMORROW'S PARTIES - (NICO VS. APOPTYGMA BERZERK) ~ 4.16
PHASE 2

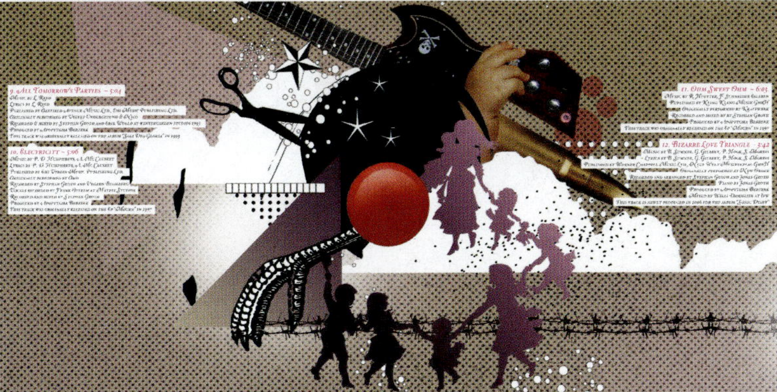
9. ALL TOMORROW'S PARTIES ~ 0.04

10. ELECTRICITY ~ 3.06

11. OHM SWEET OHM ~ 6.01

12. BIZARRE LOVE TRIANGLE ~ 3.42

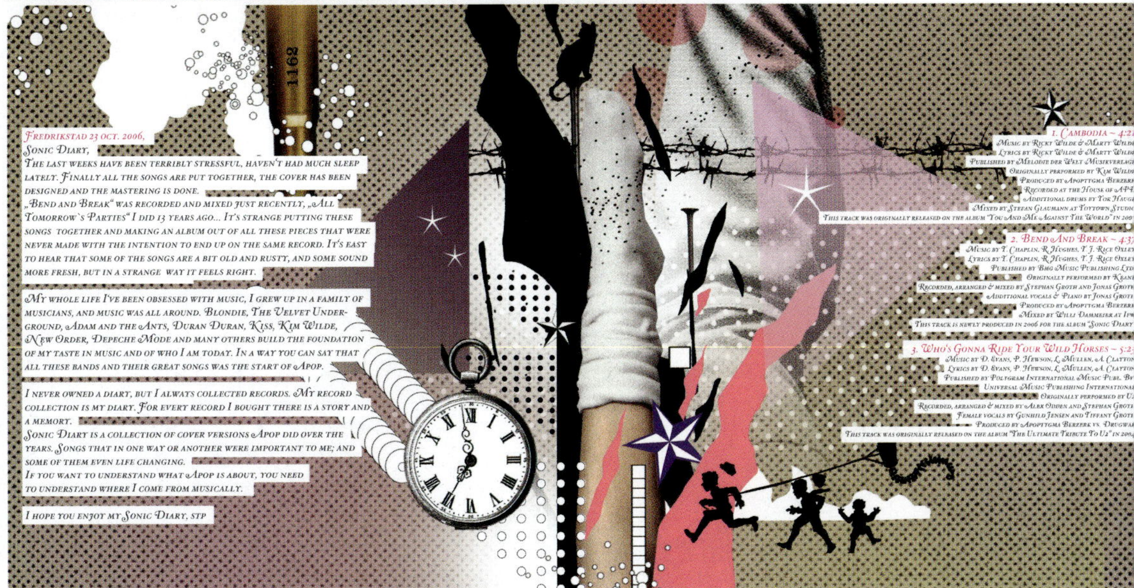
FREDRIKSTAD 23 OCT. 2006,
SONIC DIARY,
THE LAST WEEKS HAVE BEEN TERRIBLY STRESSFUL, HAVEN'T HAD MUCH SLEEP
LATELY. FINALLY ALL THE SONGS ARE PUT TOGETHER, THE COVER HAS BEEN
DESIGNED AND THE MASTERING IS DONE.
„BEND AND BREAK" WAS RECORDED AND MIXED JUST RECENTLY, „ALL
TOMORROW`S PARTIES" I DID 13 YEARS AGO... IT'S STRANGE PUTTING THESE
SONGS TOGETHER AND MAKING AN ALBUM OUT OF ALL THESE PIECES THAT WERE
NEVER MADE WITH THE INTENTION TO END UP ON THE SAME RECORD. IT'S EASY
TO HEAR THAT SOME OF THE SONGS ARE A BIT OLD AND RUSTY, AND SOME SOUND
MORE FRESH, BUT IN A STRANGE WAY IT FEELS RIGHT.

MY WHOLE LIFE I'VE BEEN OBSESSED WITH MUSIC, I GREW UP IN A FAMILY OF
MUSICIANS, AND MUSIC WAS ALL AROUND. BLONDIE, THE VELVET UNDER-
GROUND, ADAM AND THE ANTS, DURAN DURAN, KISS, KIM WILDE,
NEW ORDER, DEPECHE MODE AND MANY OTHERS BUILD THE FOUNDATION
OF MY TASTE IN MUSIC AND OF WHO I AM TODAY. IN A WAY YOU CAN SAY THAT
ALL THESE BANDS AND THEIR GREAT SONGS WAS THE START OF APOP.

I NEVER OWNED A DIARY, BUT I ALWAYS COLLECTED RECORDS. MY RECORD
COLLECTION IS MY DIARY. FOR EVERY RECORD I BOUGHT THERE IS A STORY AND
A MEMORY.
SONIC DIARY IS A COLLECTION OF COVER VERSIONS APOP DID OVER THE
YEARS. SONGS THAT IN ONE WAY OR ANOTHER WERE IMPORTANT TO ME; AND
SOME OF THEM EVEN LIFE CHANGING.
IF YOU WANT TO UNDERSTAND WHAT APOP IS ABOUT, YOU NEED
TO UNDERSTAND WHERE I COME FROM MUSICALLY.

I HOPE YOU ENJOY MY SONIC DIARY, STP

1. CAMBODIA ~ 4:21
MUSIC BY RICKY WILDE & MARTY WILDE
LYRICS BY RICKY WILDE & MARTY WILDE
PUBLISHED BY MELODIE DER WELT MUSIKVERLAG
ORIGINALLY PERFORMED BY KIM WILDE
PRODUCED BY APOPTYGMA BERZERK
RECORDED AT THE HOUSE OF APB
ADDITIONAL DRUMS BY TOR HAUGE
MIXED BY STEFAN GLAUMANN AT TOYTOWN STUDIO
THIS TRACK WAS ORIGINALLY RELEASED ON THE ALBUM "YOU AND ME AGAINST THE WORLD" IN 200

2. BEND AND BREAK ~ 4:37
MUSIC BY T. CHAPLIN, R. HUGHES, T. J. RICE OXLEY
LYRICS BY T. CHAPLIN, R. HUGHES, T. J. RICE OXLEY
PUBLISHED BY BMG MUSIC PUBLISHING LTD
ORIGINALLY PERFORMED BY KEANE
RECORDED, ARRANGED & MIXED BY STEPHAN GROTH AND JONAS GROTH
ADDITIONAL VOCALS & PIANO BY JONAS GROTH
PRODUCED BY APOPTYGMA BERZERK
MIXED BY WILLI DAMMEIER AT IPW
THIS TRACK IS NEWLY PRODUCED IN 2006 FOR THE ALBUM "SONIC DIARY

3. WHO'S GONNA RIDE YOUR WILD HORSES ~ 5:21
MUSIC BY D. EVANS, P. HEWSON, L. MULLEN, A. CLAYTON
LYRICS BY D. EVANS, P. HEWSON, L. MULLEN, A. CLAYTON
PUBLISHED BY POLYGRAM INTERNATIONAL MUSIC PUBL. BY
UNIVERSAL MUSIC PUBLISHING INTERNATIONAL
ORIGINALLY PERFORMED BY U2
RECORDED, ARRANGED & MIXED BY ALEX ODDEN AND STEPHAN GROTH
FEMALE VOCALS BY GUNHILD JENSEN AND TIFFANY GROTH
PRODUCED BY APOPTYGMA BERZERK VS. DRUGWAR
THIS TRACK WAS ORIGINALLY RELEASED ON THE ALBUM "THE ULTIMATE TRIBUTE TO U2" IN 2004

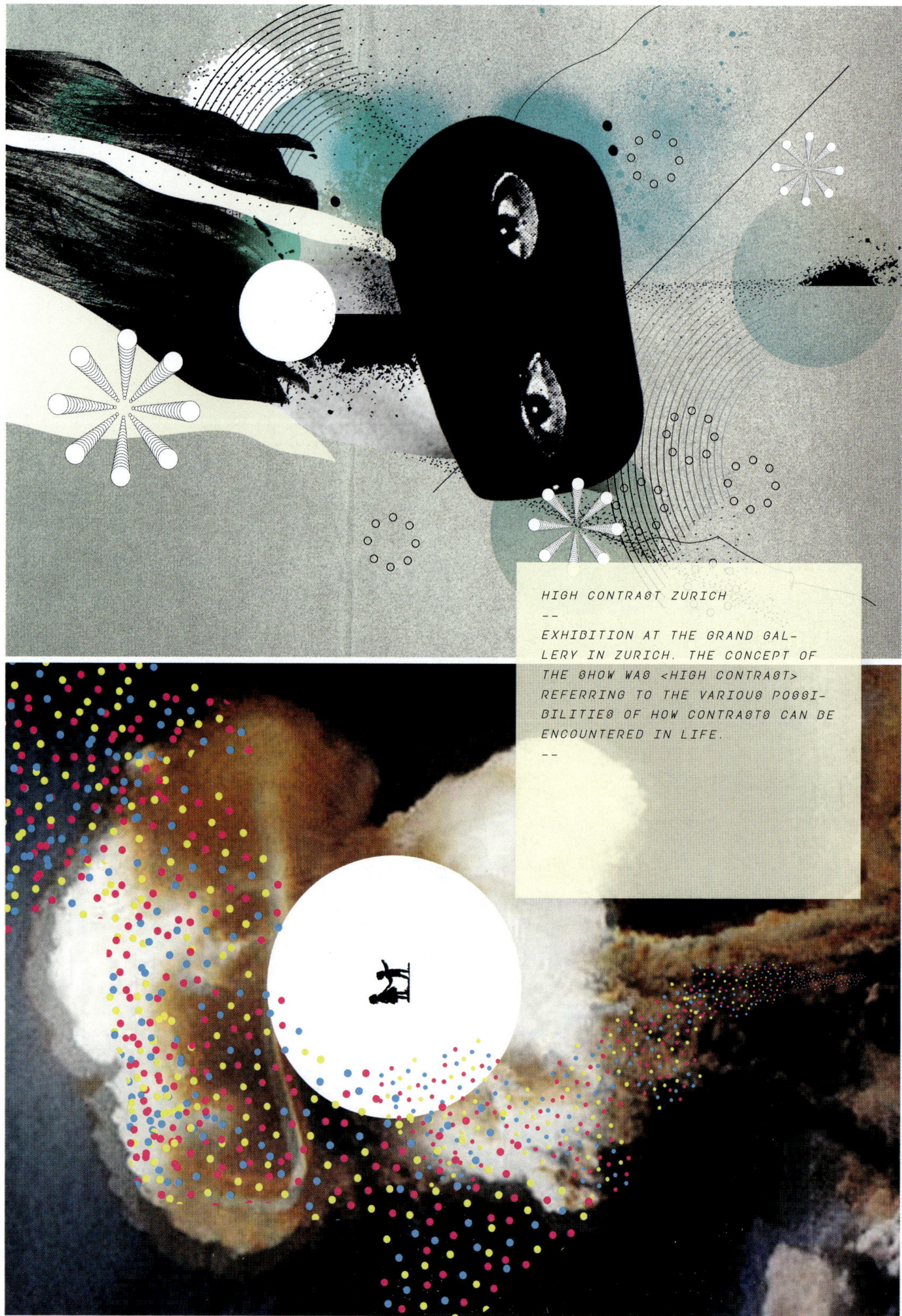

HIGH CONTRAST ZURICH
--
EXHIBITION AT THE GRAND GAL-
LERY IN ZURICH. THE CONCEPT OF
THE SHOW WAS <HIGH CONTRAST>
REFERRING TO THE VARIOUS POSSI-
BILITIES OF HOW CONTRASTS CAN BE
ENCOUNTERED IN LIFE.
--

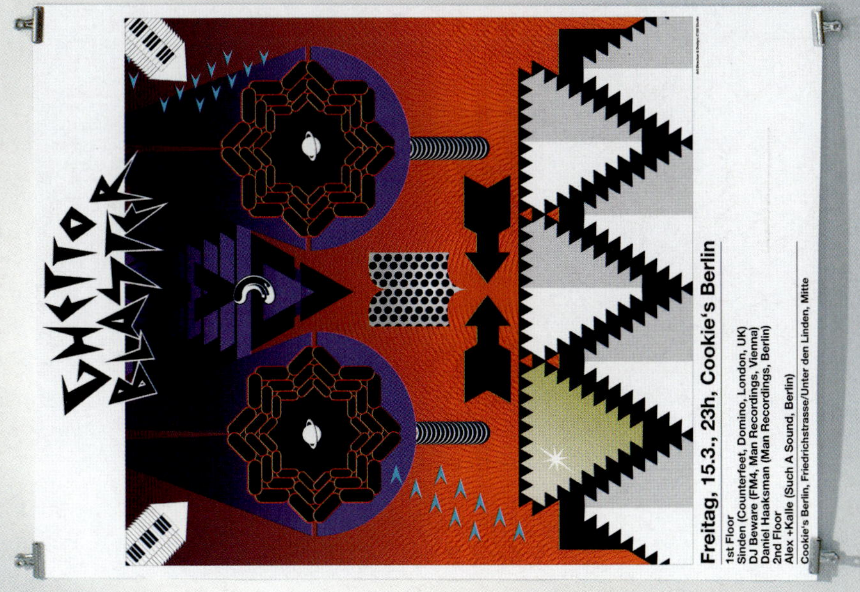

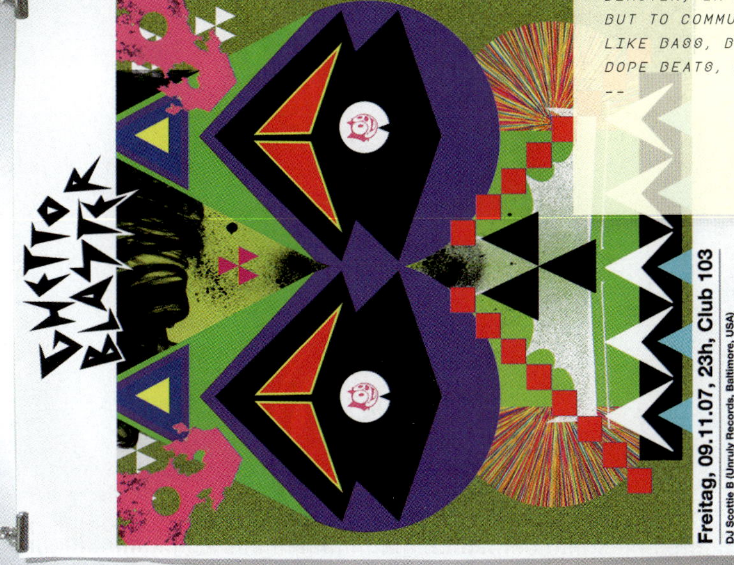

MAN RECORDINGS
--
ART DIRECTION & DESIGN OF A
POSTER FOR A CLUB-NIGHT SERIES
IN BERLIN. THE BRIEF WAS TO VISU-
ALIZE THE EVENT'S NAME, GHETTO-
BLASTER, IN AN UNCLICHÉD STYLE,
BUT TO COMMUNICATE METAPHORS
LIKE BASS, BRASIL, BAILE FUNK,
DOPE BEATS, SNEAKERS, ETC.
--

PURPLE HAZE IS A MULTIDISCIPLINARY
GRAPHIC DESIGN STUDIO BASED IN
MUNICH, GERMANY, WORKING FOR
MISCELLANEOUS PUBLIC AND PRIVATE
CLIENTS ON A VARIETY OF NATIONAL
AND INTERNATIONAL PROJECTS INCLUD-
ING EXPERTISE IN CONCEPTION, ART
DIRECTION, TYPOGRAPHY, DESIGN AND
ILLUSTRATION. IT PRODUCED INTELLI-
GENT AND PROGRESSIVE COMMUNICATION
SOLUTIONS FOR PRINT / PACKAGING,
BRAND APPLICATIONS, PUBLISHING,
EXHIBITIONS AND WEBSITES.

CLEMENS STARTED WITH HIS STUDIES
IN FREE ART AND PAINTING, MOVED
FROM HIS HOME TOWN OF HALLE TO MU-
NICH IN 1998, AND SWITCHED TO THE
ADVERTISING INDUSTRY. AFTER TWO
YEARS OF PRODUCING MULTI-AWARDED
WORKS (E.G. ADC NEW YORK, LONDON
INTERNATIONAL ADVERTISING AWARD,
RED DOT AWARD) HE PHASED DOWN AND
BEGAN TO STUDY GRAPHIC DESIGN.
ALONGSIDE HIS STUDIES HE STARTED
WITH <PURPLE HAZE STUDIO> AS A
FREELANCE UMBRELLA WORKING MAINLY
ON PROJECTS FOR CLUBS AND MUSIC
LABELS, INCLUDING FLYERS, POST-
ERS AND COVER ARTWORKS. AFTER HIS
DIPLOMA IN 2004, CLEMENS CONTIN-
UED WITH HIS STUDIO IN FULL-TIME
OPERATION.

--

WHAT IS GERMAN?

<RAMMSTEIN>, <TOKIO HOTEL> AND
<SCOOTER> ARE TYPICALLY GERMAN.

WHAT IS GERMAN DESIGN?

I THINK GERMAN GRAPHIC DESIGN IS
MOSTLY ACCURATE AND WELL CRAFTED
BUT QUITE UNSPECTACULAR.

PLEASE DESCRIBE YOUR WORKING
PROCESS.

FOR MY PART EVERYTHING IS IN
RELATION, PERSONAL AND COMMER-
CIAL. ONE PART WON'T WORK WITHOUT
THE OTHER. MY ENERGY AND PASSION
EMERGE FROM THE CONTRAST. A VERY
COMMERCIAL PROJECT GIVES GOOD
ENERGY FOR A FREE ONE, AND VICE
VERSA FOR THE FREE ONE.

WHAT DO YOU AIM TO ACHIEVE WITH
YOUR WORK?

IN MY OPINION THERE IS NO GENER-
AL ANSWER TO THAT QUESTION BECAUSE
IT ALWAYS DEPENDS ON THE PROJECT
AND THE CONTEXT THE DESIGN IS FOR.

YOU'VE INVITED A FRIEND TO
GERMANY; NAME ONE PLACE THEY
REALLY MUST VISIT AND A QUINT-
ESSENTIAL EXPERIENCE YOU REC-
OMMEND.

HAVE A NIGHT OUT AT THE
<BERGHAIN/PANORAMA BAR> IN BER-
LIN. A CLUB DEFINITELY WORTH VIS-
ITING. MAYBE THE BEST SOUND SYSTEM
IN GERMANY.

WHAT IS THE MOST IMPORTANT
LESSON YOU HAVE LEARNED IN YOUR
PROFESSION SO FAR?

BELIEVE IN THE PROCESS. BE AU-
THENTIC. BE BRAVE. DO IT WITH PAS-
SION AND ABOVE ALL HAVE FUN.

--

PUR—PLE HAZE STU—DIO

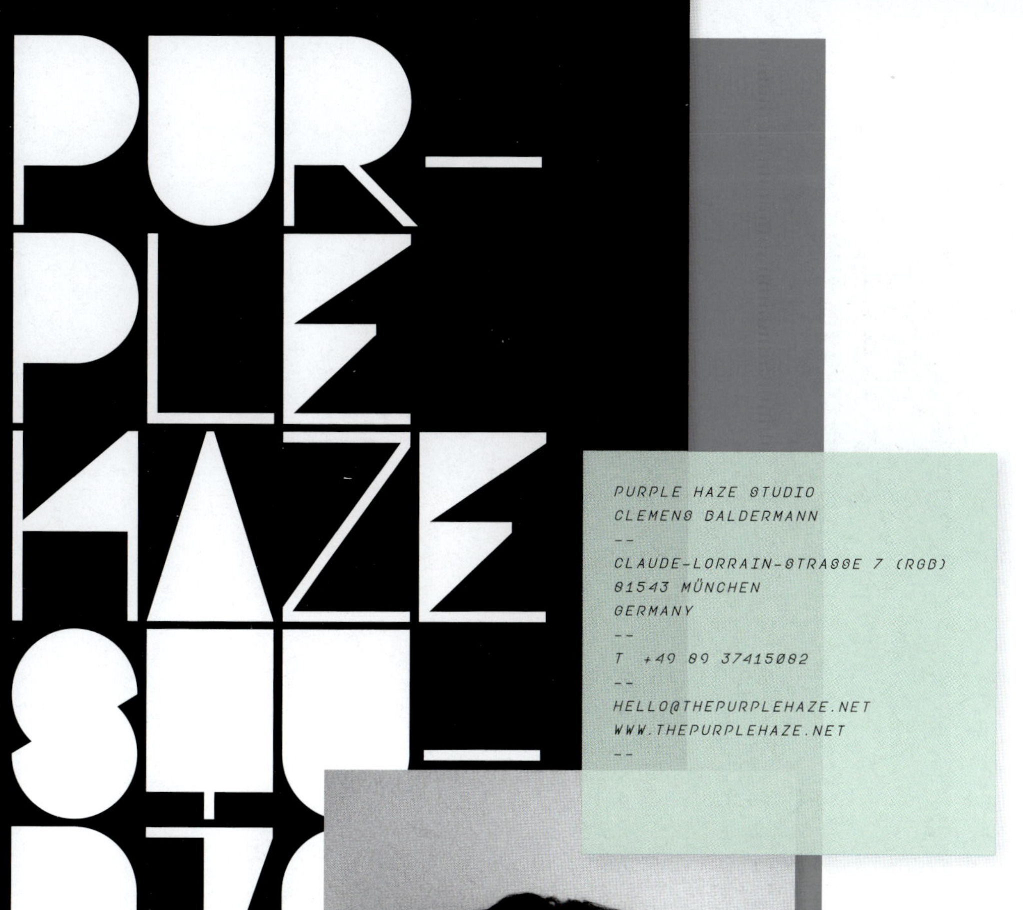

PURPLE HAZE STUDIO
CLEMENS BALDERMANN
--
CLAUDE-LORRAIN-STRASSE 7 (RGB)
81543 MÜNCHEN
GERMANY
--
T +49 89 37415082
--
HELLO@THEPURPLEHAZE.NET
WWW.THEPURPLEHAZE.NET
--

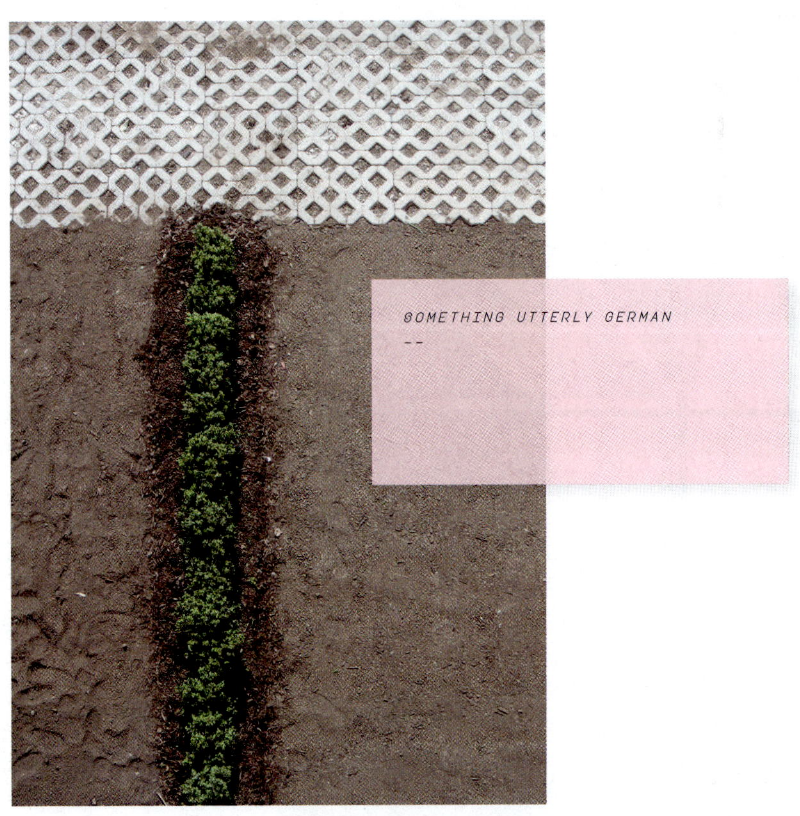
SOMETHING UTTERLY GERMAN
--

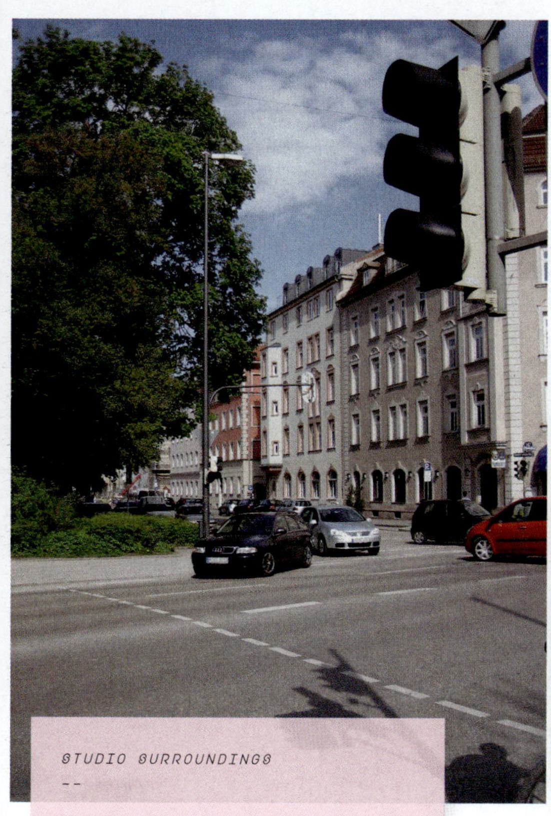

STUDIO SURROUNDINGS
--

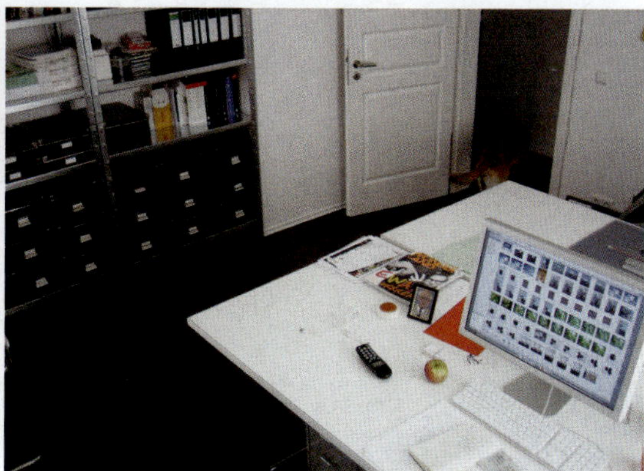

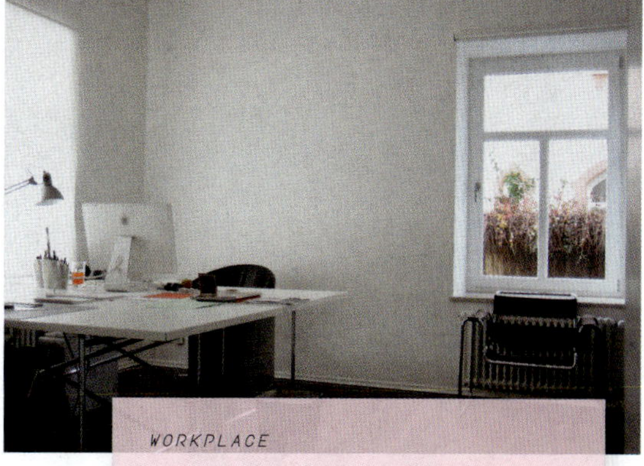

WORKPLACE
--

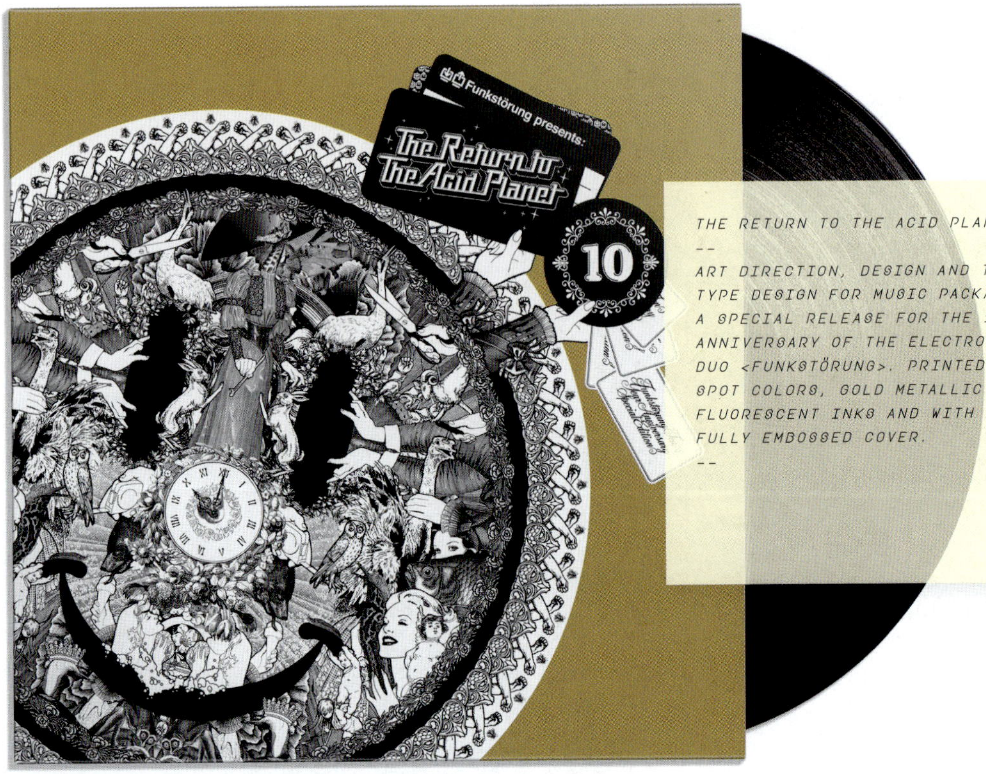

THE RETURN TO THE ACID PLANET
--
ART DIRECTION, DESIGN AND TITLE
TYPE DESIGN FOR MUSIC PACKAGING.
A SPECIAL RELEASE FOR THE 10TH
ANNIVERSARY OF THE ELECTRONICA
DUO <FUNKSTÖRUNG>. PRINTED IN
SPOT COLORS, GOLD METALLIC INK,
FLUORESCENT INKS AND WITH A
FULLY EMBOSSED COVER.
--

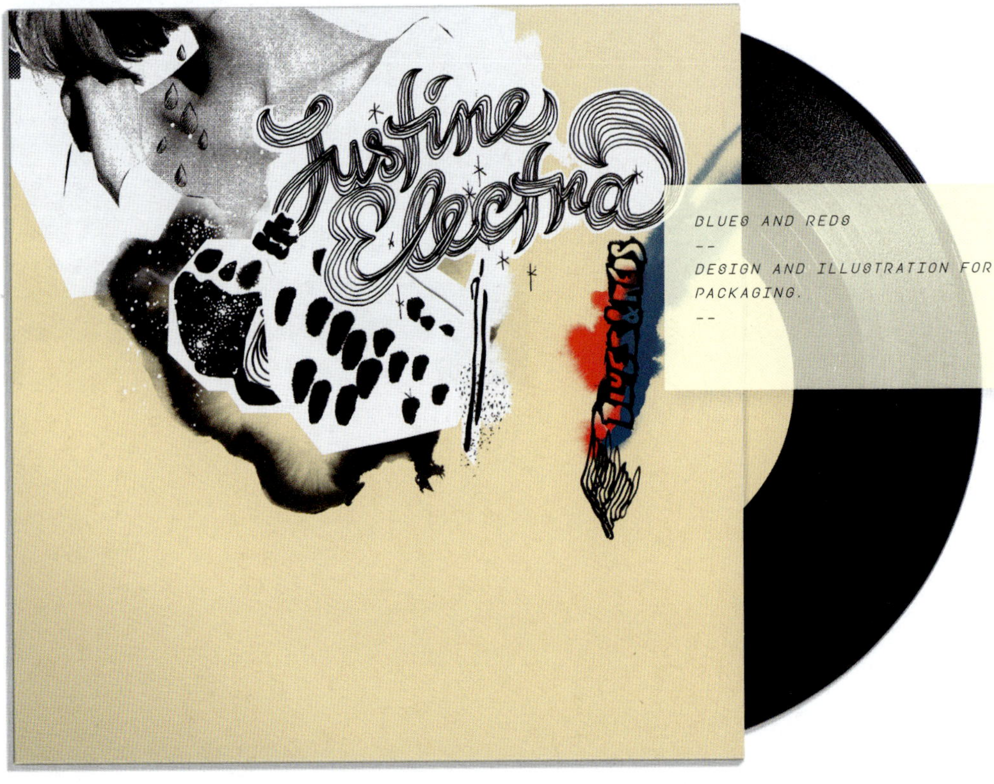

BLUES AND REDS
--
DESIGN AND ILLUSTRATION FOR MUSIC
PACKAGING.
--

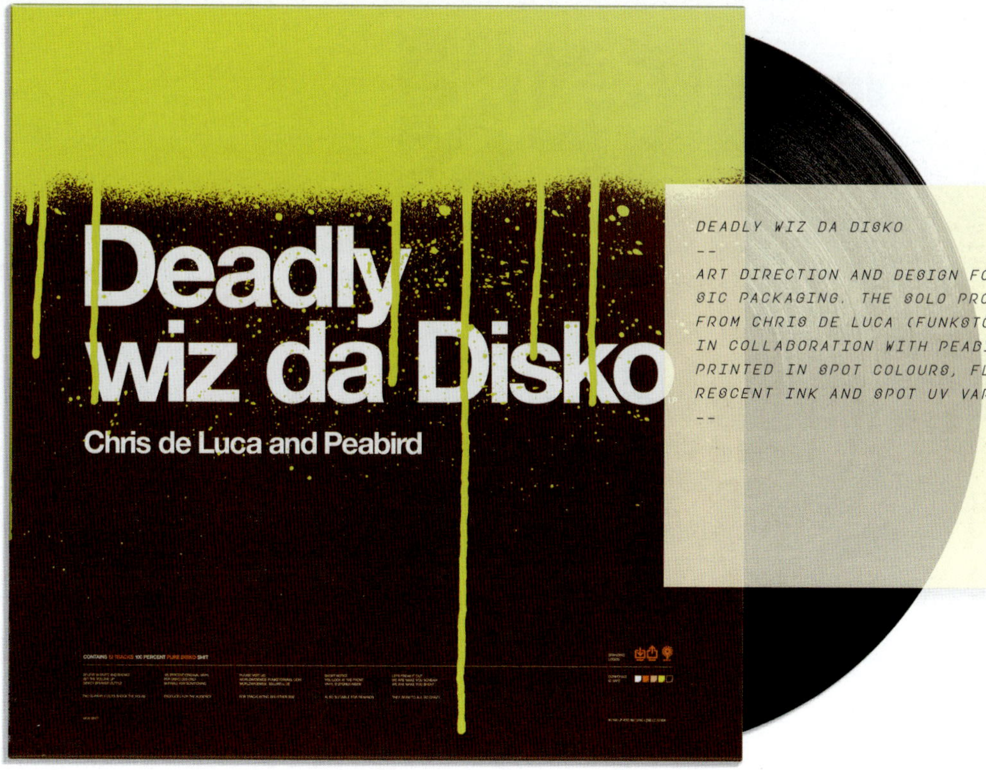

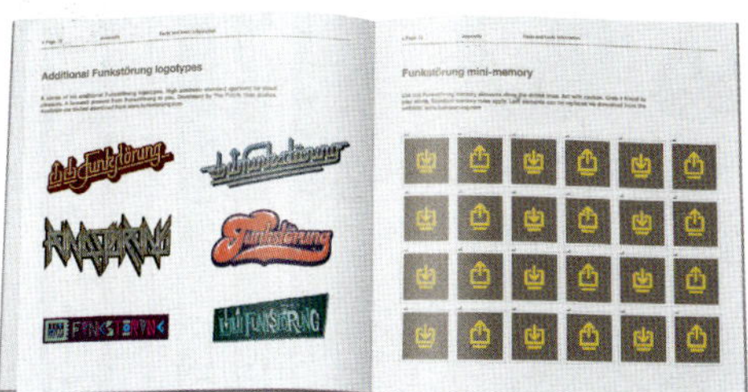

Additional Funkstörung logotypes
Funkstörung mini-memory

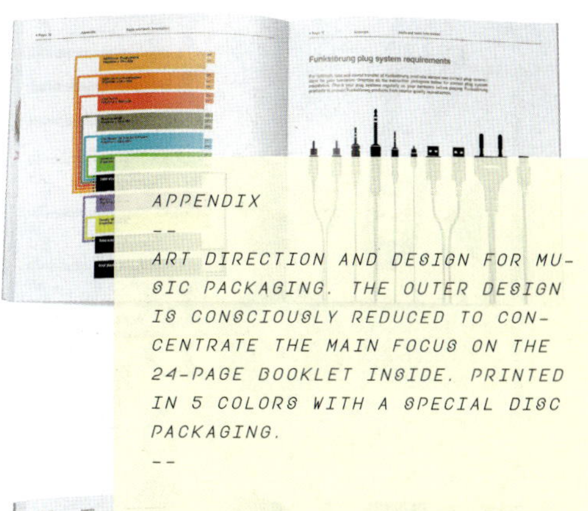

Funkstörung plug system requirements
APPENDIX
--
ART DIRECTION AND DESIGN FOR MU-
SIC PACKAGING. THE OUTER DESIGN
IS CONSCIOUSLY REDUCED TO CON-
CENTRATE THE MAIN FOCUS ON THE
24-PAGE BOOKLET INSIDE. PRINTED
IN 5 COLORS WITH A SPECIAL DISC
PACKAGING.
--

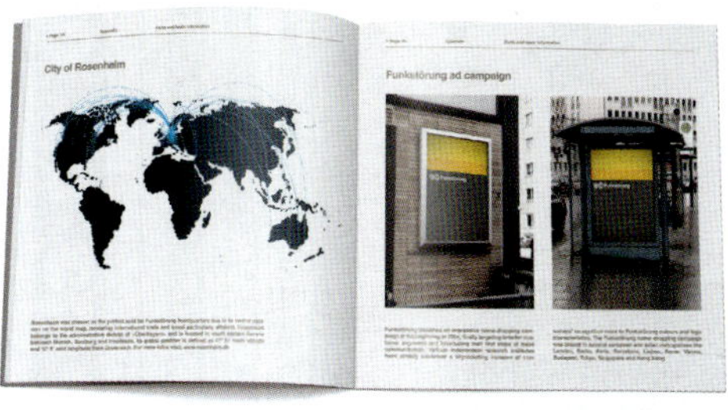

City of Rosenheim
Funkstörung ad campaign

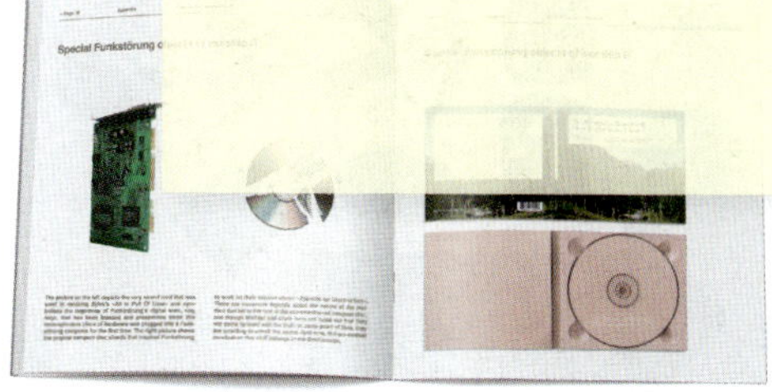

Special Funkstörung

Deadly
wiz da Disko
Chris de Luca and Peabird

DEADLY WIZ DA DISKO
--
ART DIRECTION AND DESIGN FOR MU-
SIC PACKAGING. THE SOLO PROJECT
FROM CHRIS DE LUCA (FUNKSTÖRUNG)
IN COLLABORATION WITH PEABIRD.
PRINTED IN SPOT COLOURS, FLUO-
RESCENT INK AND SPOT UV VARNISH.
--

HIGH CONTRAST
--
POSTER DESIGN FOR A CLUB NIGHT.
--

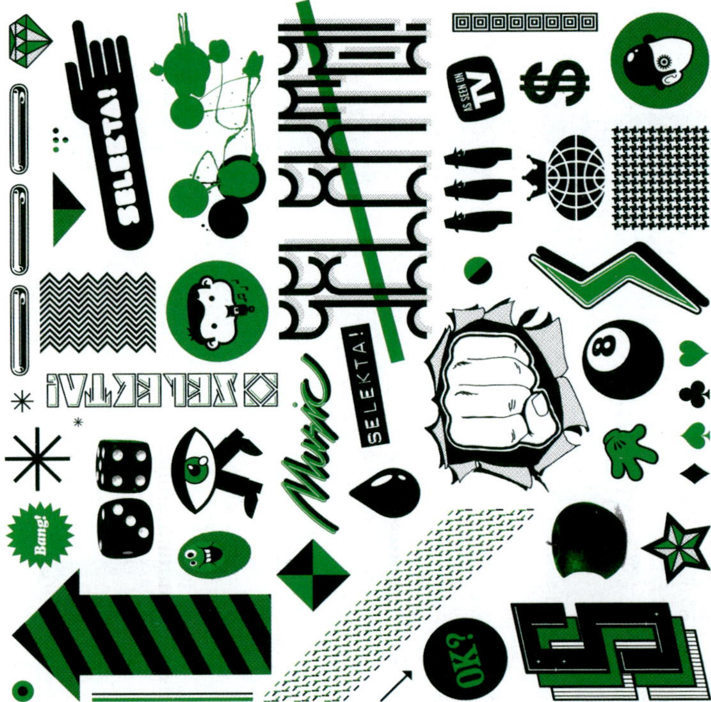
HIGH CONTRAST
»Tough Guys Don't Dance« — Album Release Party!
DO—27.09.
ROTE SONNE
▼ Registratur/Sekretariat
ALIX PEREZ
•Shogun Audio/Bassbin Records/Creative Source — UK
BLACK GAIN LIVE!
•Munich
LA LOAKAII
•Breakbeat-Action — Munich
PEABIRD
•Breakz'R'Uz Records/IK7 Records — Munich
TOBESTAR
•Southern Sessions — Munich
MC SHOOTA
•Shadybrain Records — Munich
▼ Venues
FR/13/04/07/DIE REGISTRATUR
dance different. I♥DB shogun BASSBIN
DIE REGISTRATUR
Blumenstraße 28 | 80331 München | www.dieregistratur.de

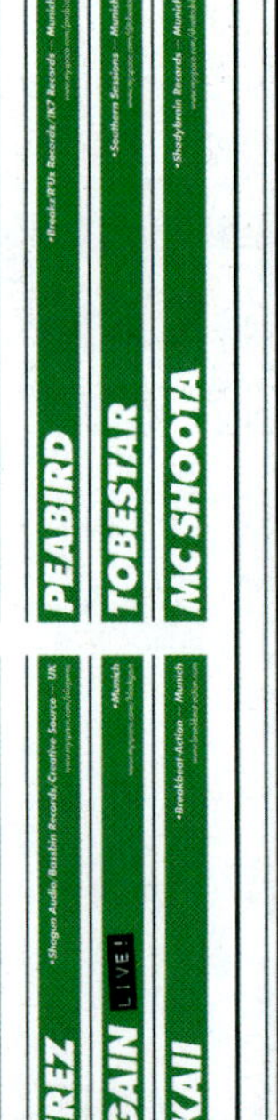

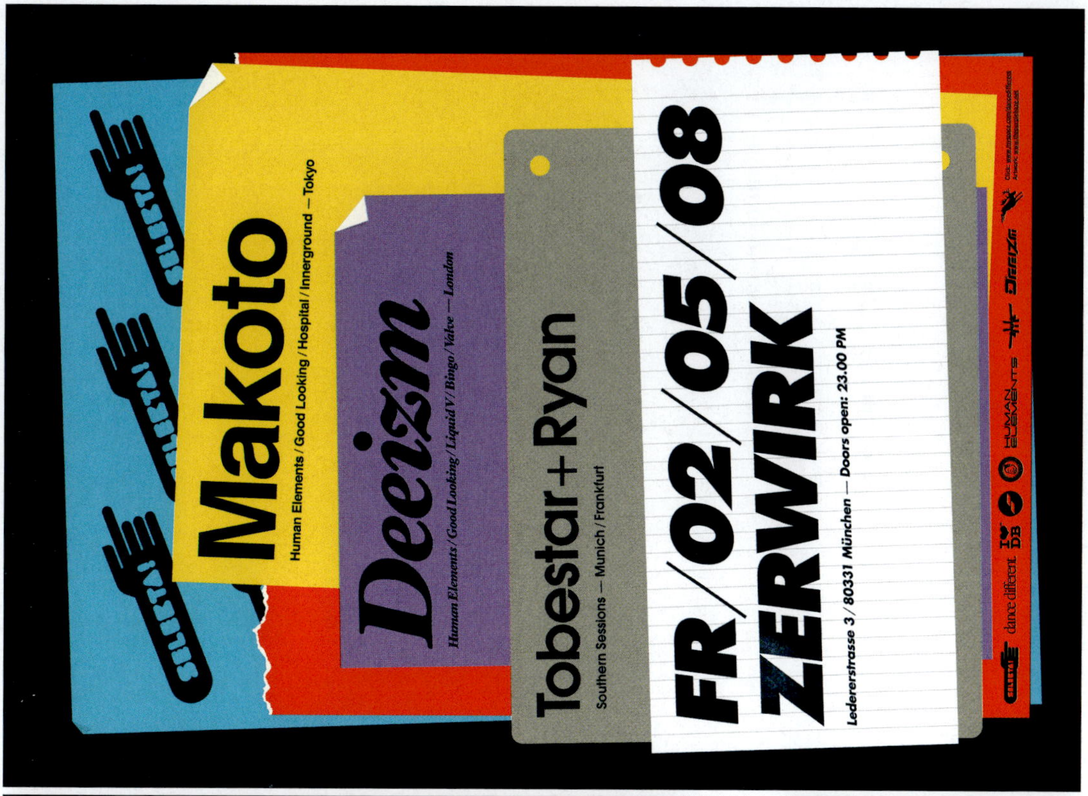

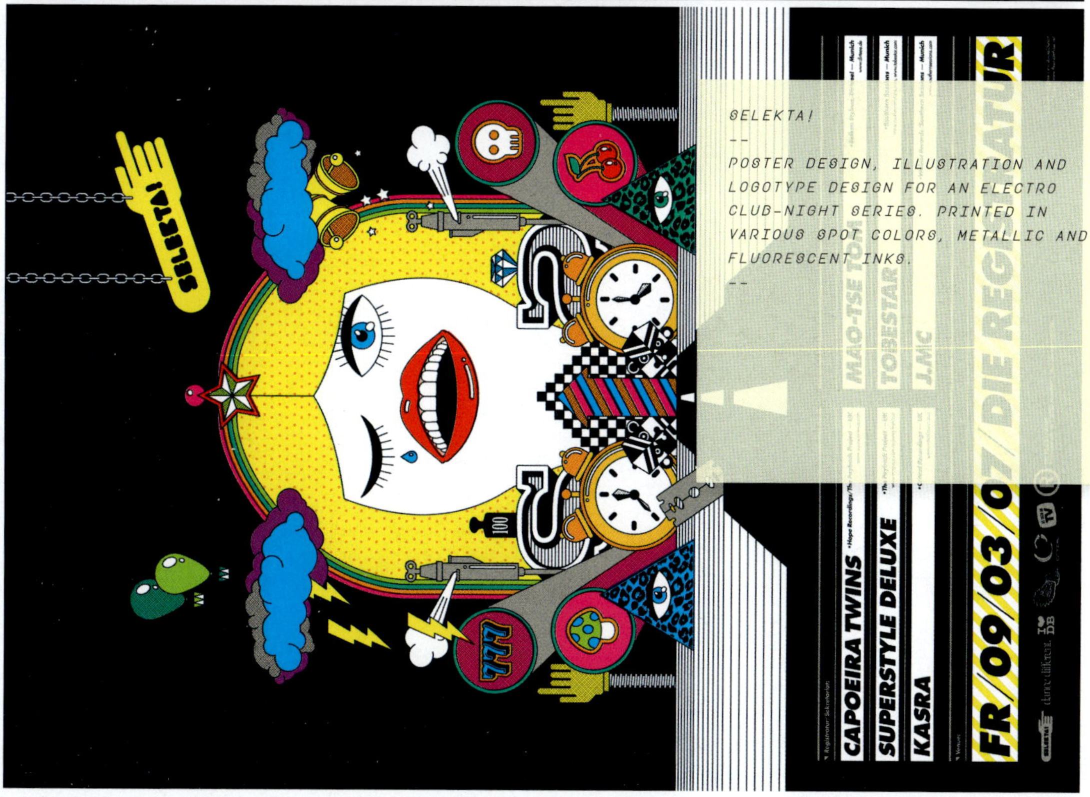

SELEKTA!
--
POSTER DESIGN, ILLUSTRATION AND LOGOTYPE DESIGN FOR AN ELECTRO CLUB-NIGHT SERIES. PRINTED IN VARIOUS SPOT COLORS, METALLIC AND FLUORESCENT INKS.
--

Makoto
Human Elements / Good Looking / Hospital / Innerground — Tokyo

Deeizm
Human Elements / Good Looking / Liquid V / Bingo / Valve — London

Tobestar+Ryan
Southern Sessions — Munich / Frankfurt

FR / 02 / 05 / 08
ZERWIRK
Ledererstrasse 3 / 80331 München — Doors open: 23.00 PM

MAO-TSE TON
TOBESTAR
J.MC
DIE REGELATUR

CAPOEIRA TWINS
SUPERSTYLE DELUXE
KASRA
FR / 09 / 03 / 07

WE, I.E. STEFANO CONZATTI (21
YEARS OLD) AND CHRISTINA HELFEN-
STEIN (24 YEARS OLD), ARE STUDYING
VISUAL COMMUNICATION AT THE MERZ
AKADEMIE IN STUTTGART. WE COL-
LABORATE FREQUENTLY ON A LOT OF
PROJECTS.

--

WHAT IS GERMAN?

ORDER, PUNCTUALITY, RESERVE.

WHAT IS GERMAN DESIGN?

-

DESCRIBE YOUR WORKING PROCESS.

WE WORK QUITE NORMALLY JUST LIKE
A LOT OF OTHER PEOPLE, BUT ULTI-
MATELY BEST UNDER PRESSURE.
- WORKING ON A THING UNTIL SHORTLY
BEFORE IT'S DUE, THEN THROWING
EVERYTHING OVER AND STARTING ALL
OVER AGAIN.

WHAT DO YOU AIM TO ACHIEVE WITH
YOUR WORK?

ATTENTION.

YOU'VE INVITED A FRIEND TO
GERMANY; NAME ONE PLACE THEY
REALLY MUST VISIT AND A QUINT-
ESSENTIAL EXPERIENCE YOU REC-
OMMEND.

-

WHAT IS THE MOST IMPORTANT
LESSON YOU HAVE LEARNED IN YOUR
PROFESSION SO FAR?

TO KEEP STRONG NERVES/NOT TO BE
SPINELESS.

--

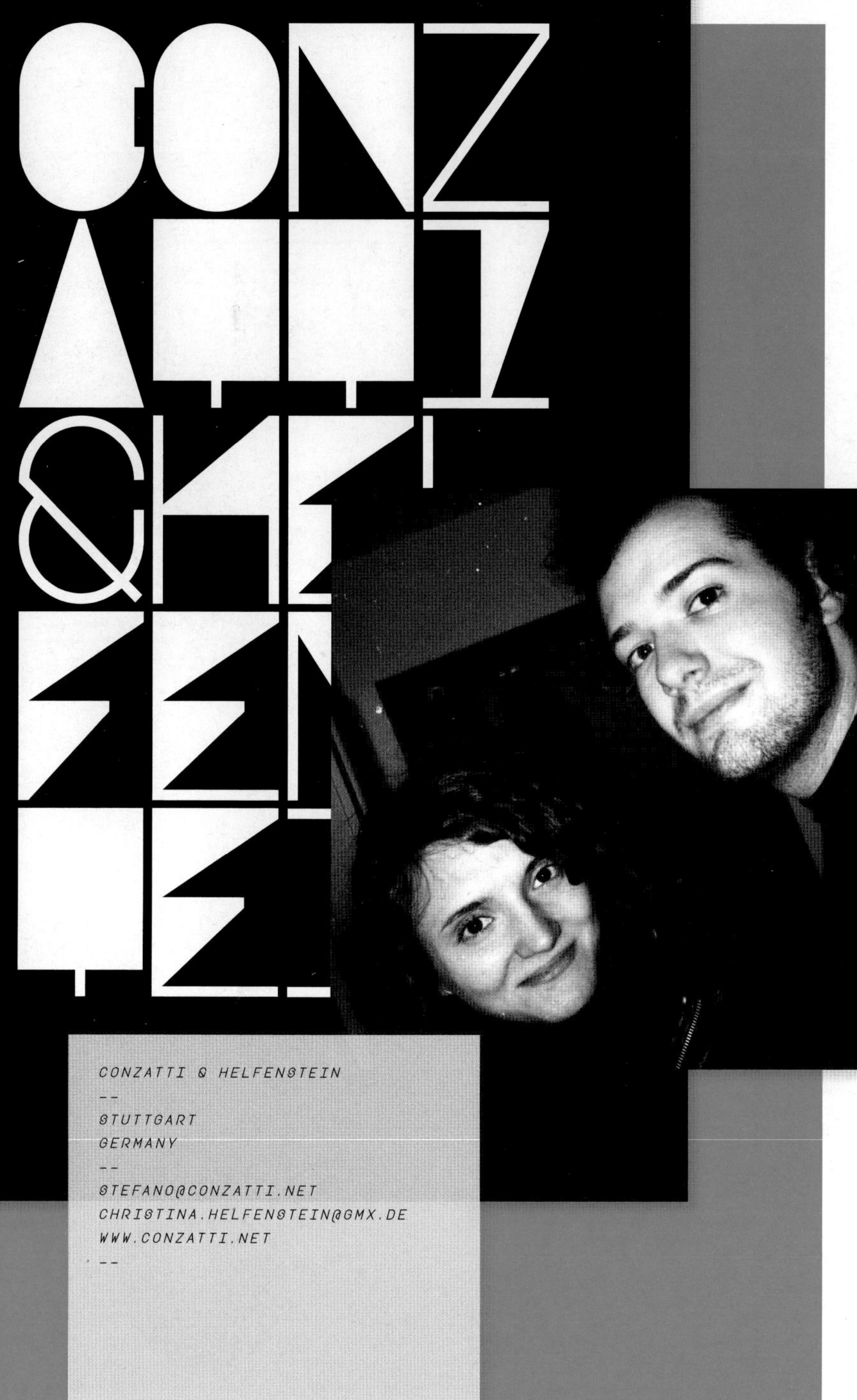

CONZATTI & HELFENSTEIN
--
STUTTGART
GERMANY
--
STEFANO@CONZATTI.NET
CHRISTINA.HELFENSTEIN@GMX.DE
WWW.CONZATTI.NET
--

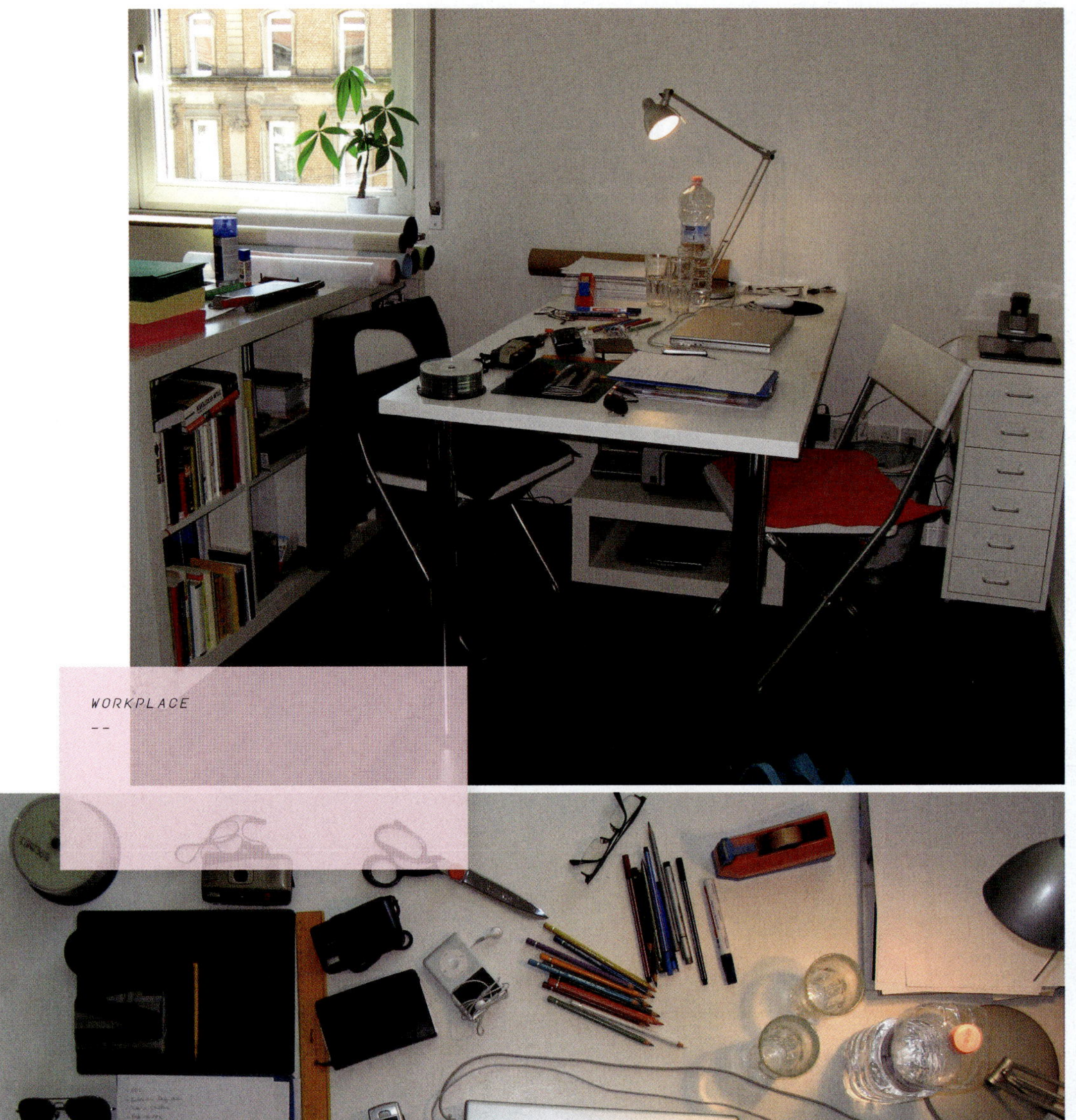

WORKPLACE
--

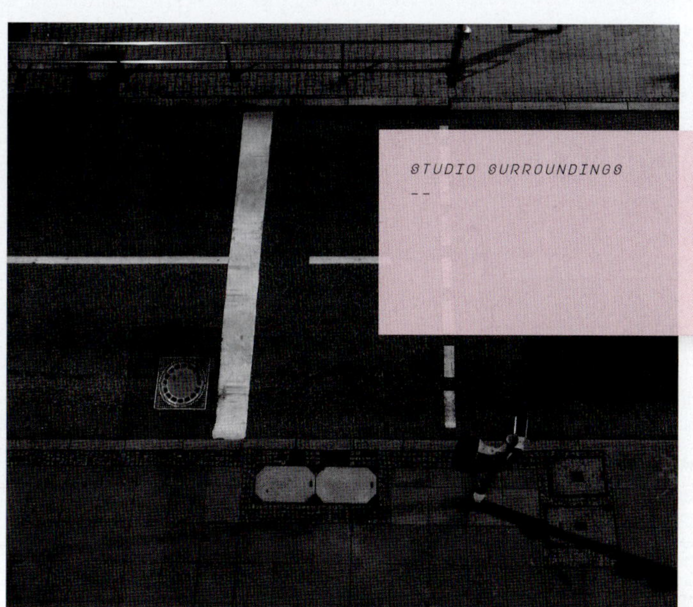

STUDIO SURROUNDINGS
--

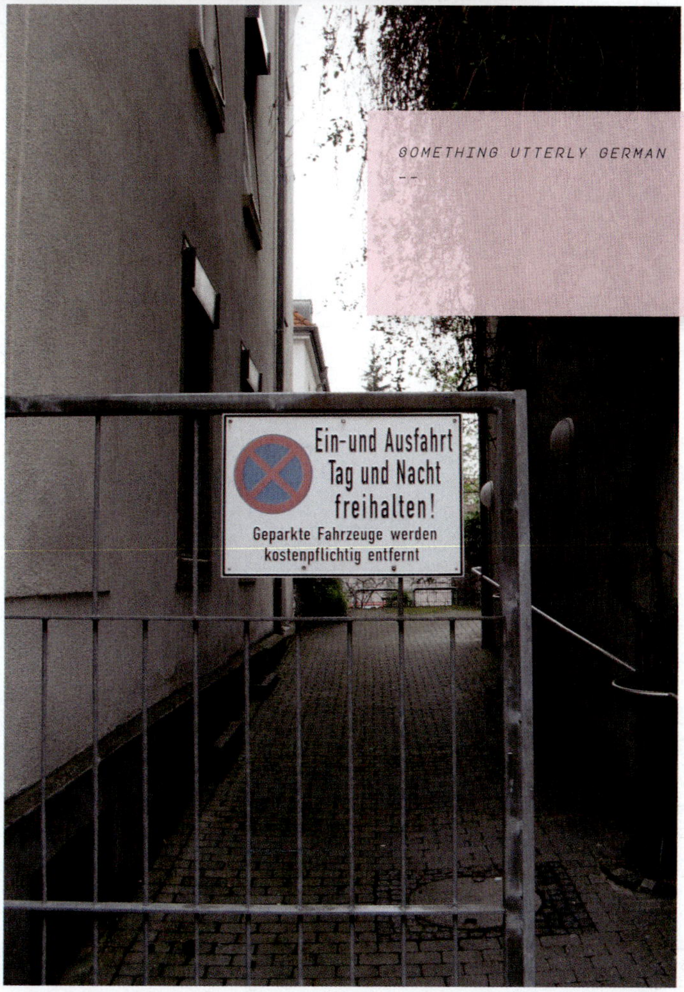

SOMETHING UTTERLY GERMAN
--

Ein-und Ausfahrt
Tag und Nacht
freihalten!
Geparkte Fahrzeuge werden
kostenpflichtig entfernt

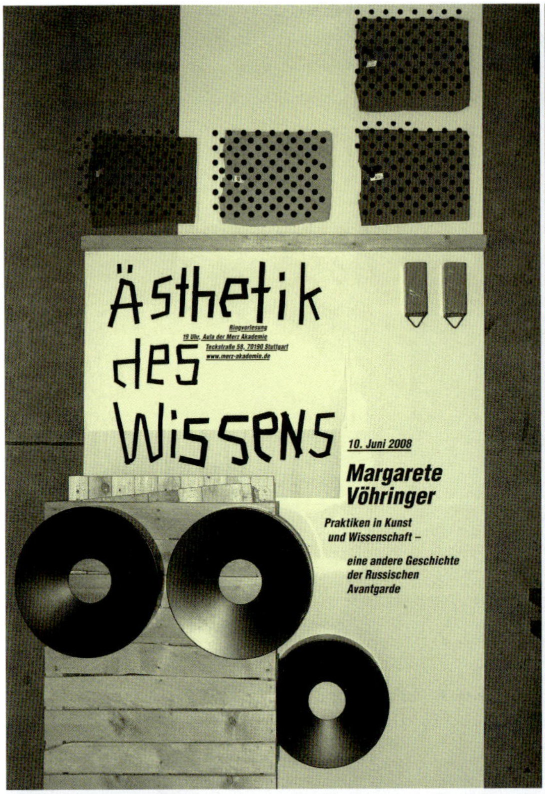

Ästhetik
des
Wissens
10. Juni 2008
Margarete
Vöhringer
Praktiken in Kunst
und Wissenschaft –
eine andere Geschichte
der Russischen
Avantgarde

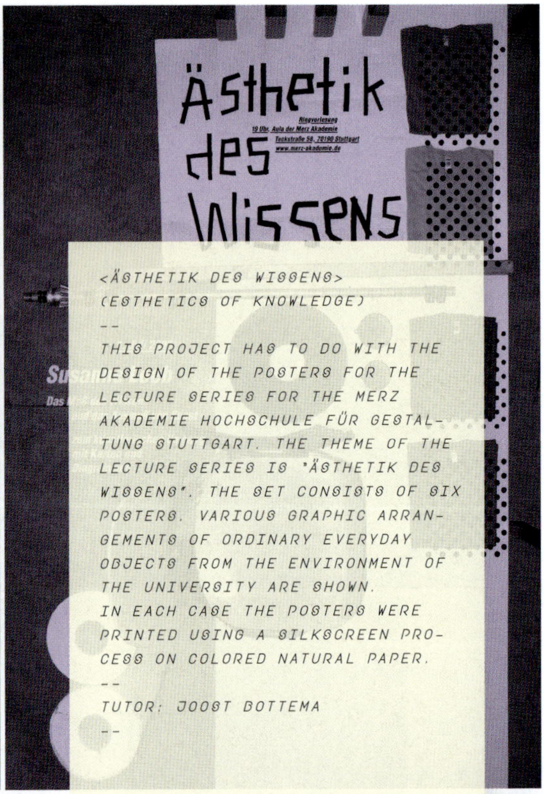

Ästhetik
des
Wissens
<ÄSTHETIK DES WISSENS>
(ESTHETICS OF KNOWLEDGE)
--
THIS PROJECT HAS TO DO WITH THE
DESIGN OF THE POSTERS FOR THE
LECTURE SERIES FOR THE MERZ
AKADEMIE HOCHSCHULE FÜR GESTAL-
TUNG STUTTGART. THE THEME OF THE
LECTURE SERIES IS 'ÄSTHETIK DES
WISSENS". THE SET CONSISTS OF SIX
POSTERS. VARIOUS GRAPHIC ARRAN-
GEMENTS OF ORDINARY EVERYDAY
OBJECTS FROM THE ENVIRONMENT OF
THE UNIVERSITY ARE SHOWN.
IN EACH CASE THE POSTERS WERE
PRINTED USING A SILKSCREEN PRO-
CESS ON COLORED NATURAL PAPER.
--
TUTOR: JOOST BOTTEMA
--

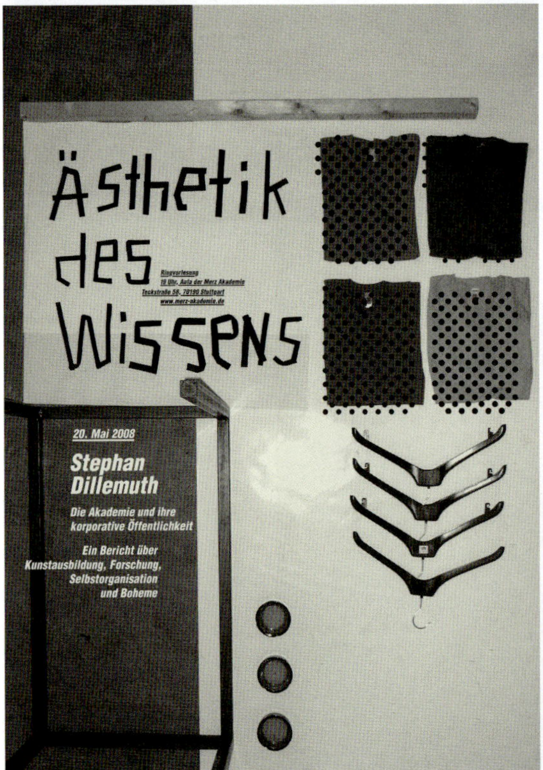

Ästhetik
des
Wissens
20. Mai 2008
Stephan
Dillemuth
Die Akademie und ihre
korporative Öffentlichkeit
Ein Bericht über
Kunstausbildung, Forschung,
Selbstorganisation
und Boheme

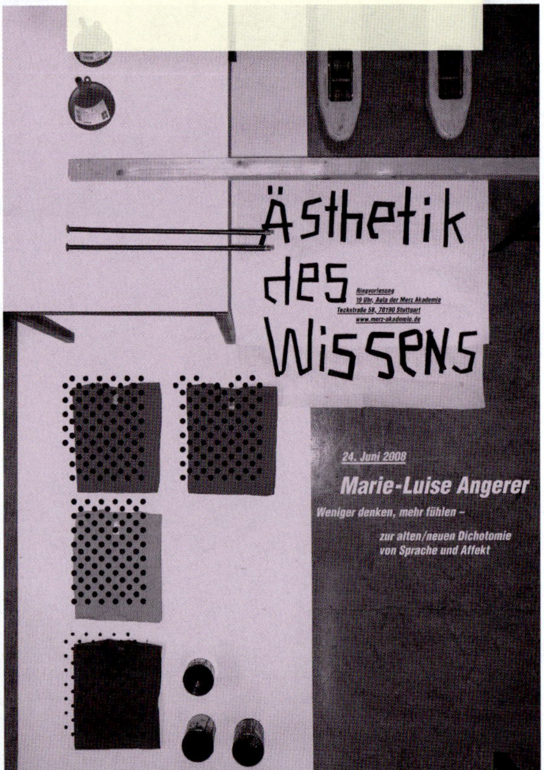

Ästhetik
des
Wissens
24. Juni 2008
Marie-Luise Angerer
Weniger denken, mehr fühlen –
zur alten/neuen Dichotomie
von Sprache und Affekt

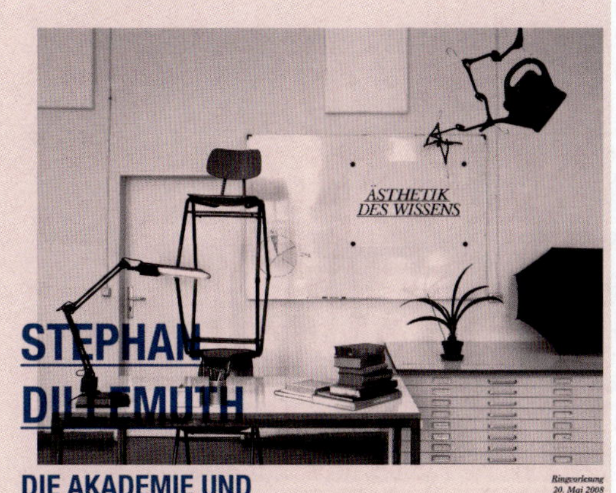

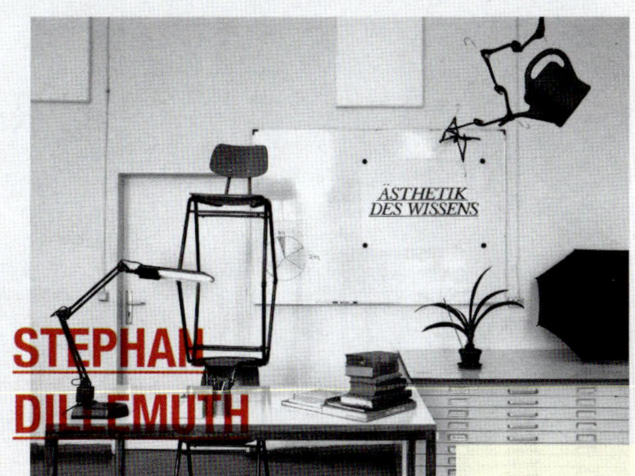

THIS IS THE FORERUNNER OF THE
<ÄSTHETIK DES WISSENS> POSTERS.
AND AS THE DESIGN WAS REJECTED
THERE IS ONLY THIS ONE POSTER.
A SERIES OF SIX POSTERS WAS
PLANNED. AN ABSTRACT CONSTRUC-
TION OF VARIOUS OBJECTS IS SHOWN.
THE POSTERS WERE NOT PRODUCED.
--
TUTOR: JOOST BOTTEMA
--

POLPO SEMPLICE
EINFACHER KRAKE FÜR 6 PERSONEN

Einen großen Topf, für den Sie auch einen schließenden Deckel besitzen, aufsetzen und etwa 7 EL Olivenöl hineingießen. Den Knoblauch, den Chili, die Petersilie und die Zitronenschale darin 1–2 Minuten sanft dünsten, wobei der Knoblauch keine Farbe annehmen darf. Den ganzen Kraken hineinsetzen, den Topf rütteln und den Deckel auflegen. Stellen Sie die Temperatur so ein, dass die Flüssigkeit im Topf nur siedet.
Je nach der Größe des Tieres dauert es 15–20 Minuten, bis es richtig schön zart ist. Es gart im eigenen Saft, der währenddessen reichlich austritt und eine herrlich aromatische Brühe ergibt.
Das Fleisch ist gar, wenn es sich mit einer Gabel mühelos einstechen lässt.
Falls die Garprobe negativ ausfällt, lassen Sie den Topf eben noch ein Weilchen auf dem Herd.
Das ist auch schon das ganze Geheimnis für butterzarten „polpo".

In Italien sieht man es häufig, dass ein Krake einfach so im Topf auf den Tisch kommt. Er wird nur noch in Stücke geschnitten, mit Salz und Pfeffer gewürzt, mit Olivenöl beträufelt und dann mit großen Genuss verputzt. Sie können ihn aber auch vor dem Servieren enthäuten, außerdem die Saugnäpfe entfernen und aus dem Körpersack die Augen, Kauwerkzeuge und Eingeweide herausschneiden.
Das alles ist kein großer Aufwand, und deshalb bereite ich Kraken eigentlich immer auf diese Weise zu.
Wenn Sie jetzt umblättern, finden Sie Vorschläge,
was Sie mit Ihrem Kraken weiter Köstliches anstellen können.

- 7 EL Olivenöl
- 1 Knoblauchknolle, die Zehen zerquetzt, geschält und in dünne Scheiben geschnitten
- 1 frische rote Chilischote, Samen entfernt, in schmale Streifen geschnitten
- 3–4 frische Petersilienstängel, fein gehackt
- dünn abgelöste Schale von 1 unbehandelten Zitrone
- 1 Krake, etwa 1,5 kg
- Meersalz und frisch gemahlener schwarzer Pfeffer

<EINFACHER KRAKE>
(OCTOPUS COOKED SIMPLY)
--
POSTERS RELATING TO A COOKERY BOOK. THE PREDOMINANT IDEA WAS THAT OF AN INFORMATION POSTER WHICH IN THIS CASE SIMULTANEOUSLY WORKS AS A KIND OF RECIPE ON THE KITCHEN WALL.
--

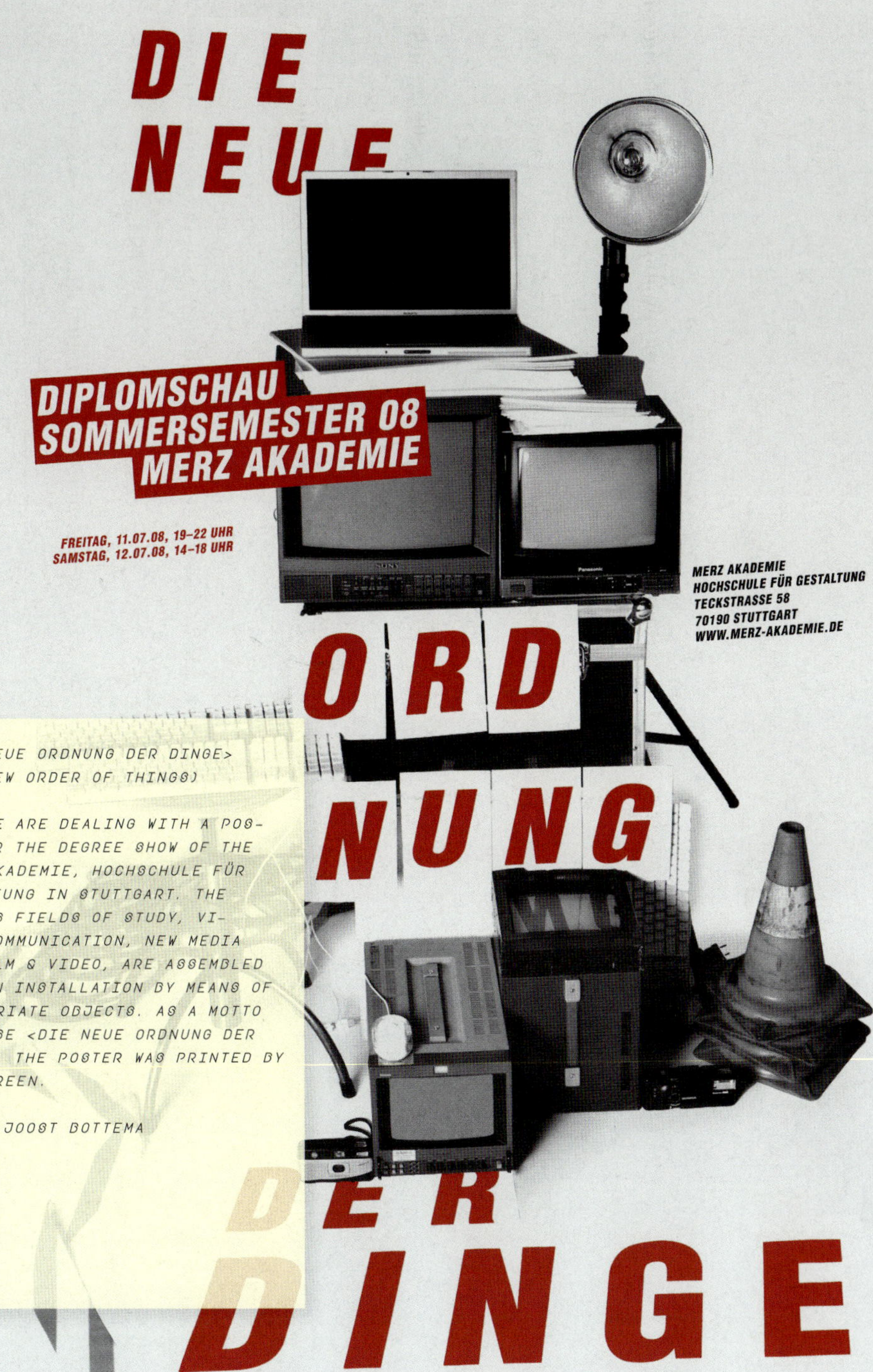

DIE NEUE

DIPLOMSCHAU
SOMMERSEMESTER 08
MERZ AKADEMIE

FREITAG, 11.07.08, 19–22 UHR
SAMSTAG, 12.07.08, 14–18 UHR

MERZ AKADEMIE
HOCHSCHULE FÜR GESTALTUNG
TECKSTRASSE 58
70190 STUTTGART
WWW.MERZ-AKADEMIE.DE

ORD
NUNG
DER
DINGE

<DIE NEUE ORDNUNG DER DINGE>
(THE NEW ORDER OF THINGS)
--
HERE WE ARE DEALING WITH A POS-
TER FOR THE DEGREE SHOW OF THE
MERZ AKADEMIE, HOCHSCHULE FÜR
GESTALTUNG IN STUTTGART. THE
VARIOUS FIELDS OF STUDY, VI-
SUAL COMMUNICATION, NEW MEDIA
AND FILM & VIDEO, ARE ASSEMBLED
INTO AN INSTALLATION BY MEANS OF
APPROPRIATE OBJECTS. AS A MOTTO
WE CHOSE <DIE NEUE ORDNUNG DER
DINGE>. THE POSTER WAS PRINTED BY
SILKSCREEN.
--
TUTOR: JOOST BOTTEMA
--

DIRK WACHOWIAK WAS BORN IN RUIT
(STUTTGART) IN 1974. FROM 1997 TO
2001 HE STUDIED VISUAL COMMUNICA-
TION AT THE HOCHSCHULE FÜR GESTAL-
TUNG IN PFORZHEIM. AFTER GRADUAT-
ING HE WORKED THERE BETWEEN 2001
AND 2003 AS AN ASSISTANT IN THE
VISUAL COMMUNICATION SECTION, AND
A DESIGNER AT THE PLAN B ZENTRALE
DESIGN OFFICE IN STUTTGART. IN
2003, THANKS TO A DAAD (GERMAN
ACADEMIC EXCHANGE SERVICE) BUR-
SARY, HE GOT THE OPPORTUNITY TO
DO A TWO-YEAR MASTER'S COURSE IN
GRAPHIC DESIGN AT YALE UNIVERSITY
SCHOOL OF ART IN NEW HAVEN (USA).
THERE HE CONTINUED THE TYPOGRAPH-
ICAL EXPERIMENTS THAT HAD ALREADY
AROUSED HIS INTEREST IN PFOR-
ZHEIM. SINCE HIS RETURN IN 2005
DIRK WACHOWIAK HAS BEEN WORKING
AS A FREELANCE GRAPHIC DESIGNER IN
STUTTGART, FOR L2M3 KOMMUNIKATION-
SDESIGN AMONG OTHERS. IN PARALLEL
HE CONTINUES TO PRODUCE INDE-
PENDENT FONT DESIGNS AND DESIGN
PROJECTS. IN 2008 HE WAS GIVEN A
TEACHING CONTRACT FOR TYPOGRAPHY
AT THE HOCHSCHULE IN PFORZHEIM.

--

WHAT IS GERMAN?

<DAS ECHTE> [A BRAND OF BEER] BY
SCHWABENBRÄU.

WHAT IS GERMAN DESIGN?

THE PLAYMOBIL TOY SYSTEM BY HANS
BECK.

DESCRIBE YOUR WORKING PROCESS.

THE DEVELOPMENT OF SYSTEMS PLAYS
AN IMPORTANT ROLE IN MY DESIGN
PROCESS. SYSTEMS THAT ARE CON-
CEIVED AS A TOTAL STRUCTURE FROM
THE START, OR SYSTEMS THAT ARE
FIRST PREDEFINED BY PARAMETERS
AND GENERATE DIFFERENT RESULTS IN
THE COURSE OF AN ONGOING PROCESS.

WHAT DO YOU AIM TO ACHIEVE WITH
YOUR WORK?

IN MY PERSONAL WORK IT IS OFTEN
A QUESTION OF CONVENTIONAL AND EX-
PERIMENTAL FONT DESIGNS AND THEIR
APPLICATION. MY INTEREST LIES IN
HOW OTHER DESIGNERS PROCEED WITH
MY TOOLS, AND USING OR EVEN EX-
PANDING THE POTENTIAL INHERENT IN
THE SYSTEMS.

YOU'VE INVITED A FRIEND TO
GERMANY; NAME ONE PLACE THEY
REALLY MUST VISIT AND A QUINT-
ESSENTIAL EXPERIENCE YOU REC-
OMMEND.

GO TO THE KILLESBERG AND TAKE A
LOOK AT THE WEISSENHOF ESTATE.

WHAT IS THE MOST IMPORTANT
LESSON YOU HAVE LEARNED IN YOUR
PROFESSION SO FAR?

TO UNDERSTAND CORRELATIONS BE-
TWEEN DIFFERENT AREAS OF DESIGN
DISCIPLINES (FILM, ARCHITECTURE,
LITERATURE, ART) AND INTEGRATE
THEM INTO MY OWN PROCESS/DESIGN.

--

WA—CHOW—IAK

DIRK WACHOWIAK
--
LERCHENSTRASSE 20
70176 STUTTGART
GERMANY
--
T +49 711 2221953
--
MAIL@DIRKWACHOWIAK.COM
WWW.DIRKWACHOWIAK.COM
--

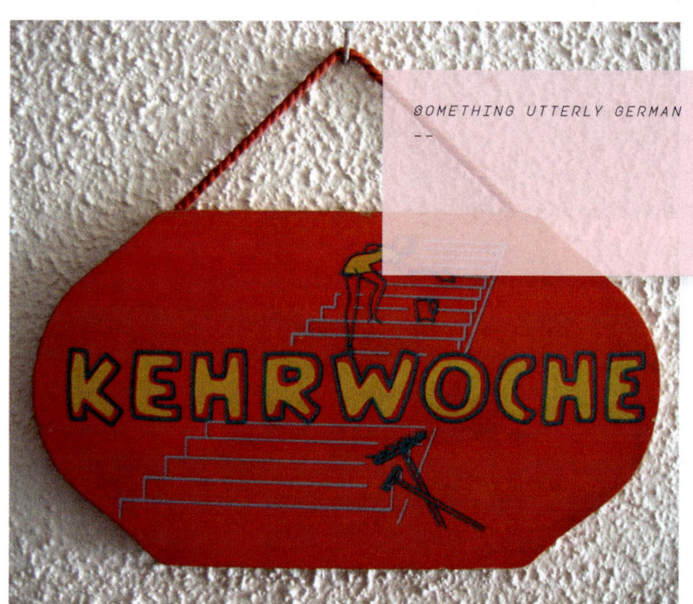

SOMETHING UTTERLY GERMAN
--

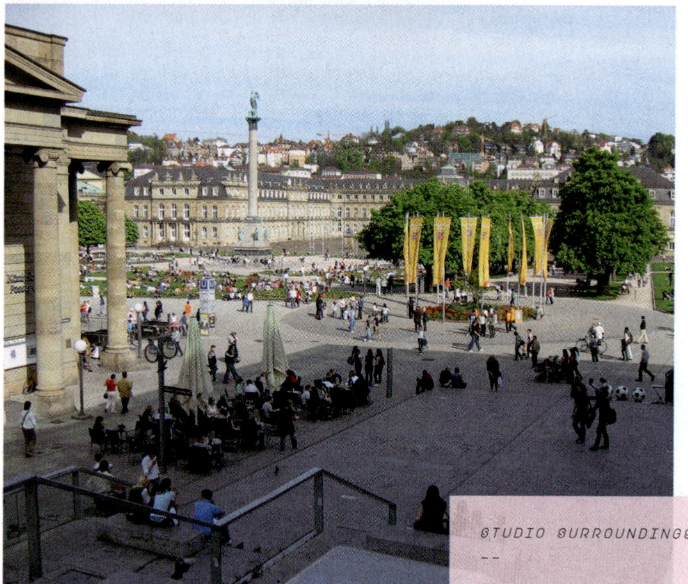

STUDIO SURROUNDINGS
--

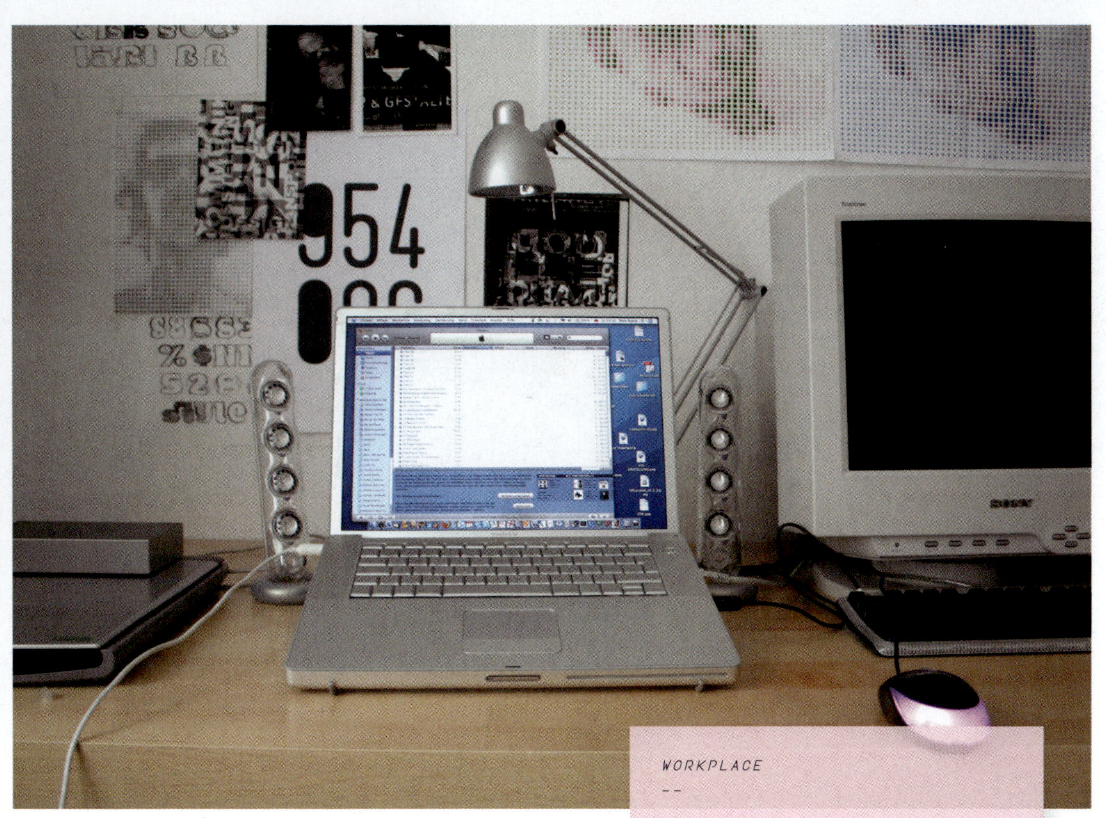

WORKPLACE
--

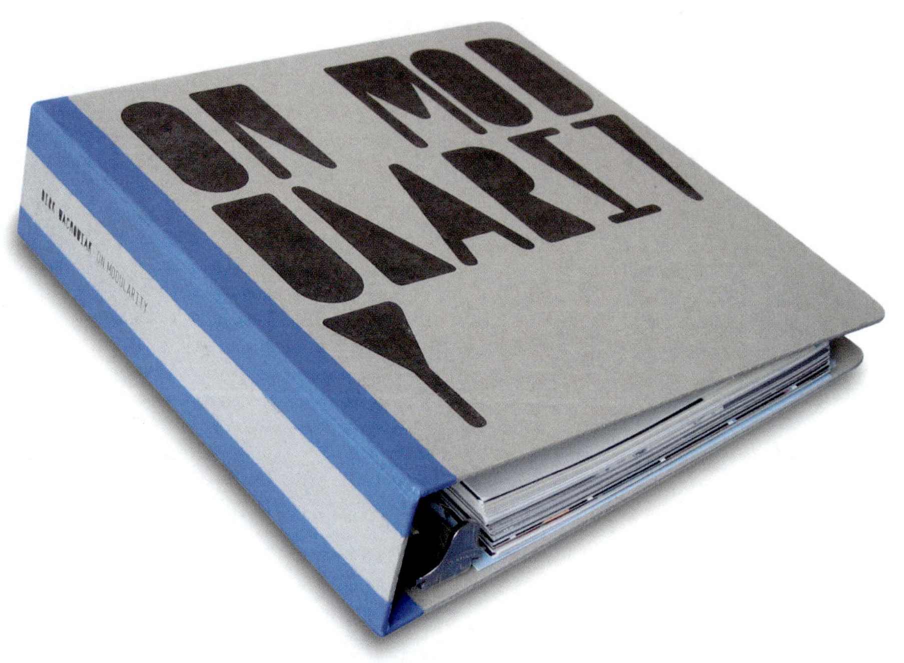

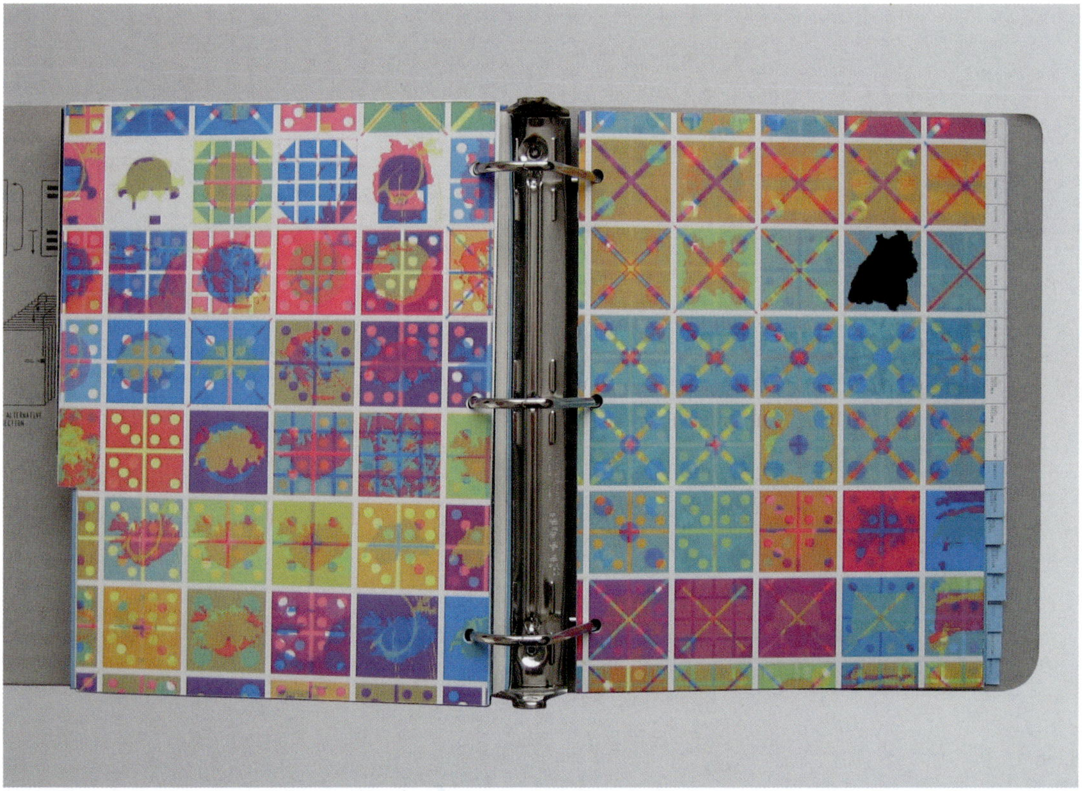

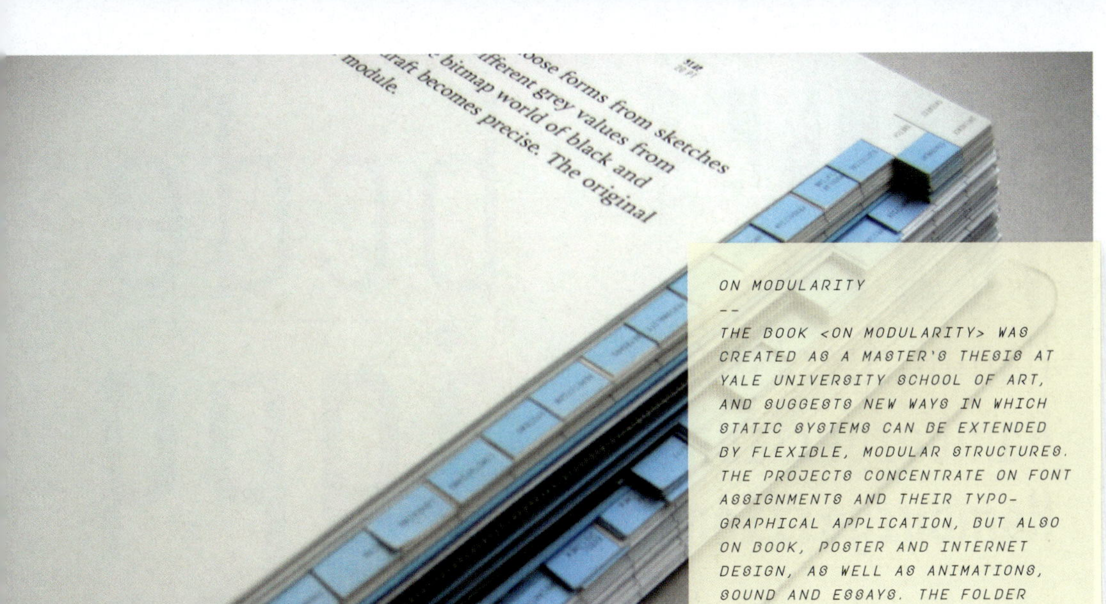
oose forms from sketches
fferent grey values from
e bitmap world of black and
raft becomes precise. The original
module.

ON MODULARITY
--
THE BOOK <ON MODULARITY> WAS
CREATED AS A MASTER'S THESIS AT
YALE UNIVERSITY SCHOOL OF ART,
AND SUGGESTS NEW WAYS IN WHICH
STATIC SYSTEMS CAN BE EXTENDED
BY FLEXIBLE, MODULAR STRUCTURES.
THE PROJECTS CONCENTRATE ON FONT
ASSIGNMENTS AND THEIR TYPO-
GRAPHICAL APPLICATION, BUT ALSO
ON BOOK, POSTER AND INTERNET
DESIGN, AS WELL AS ANIMATIONS,
SOUND AND ESSAYS. THE FOLDER
IS CONCEIVED AS A DESIGN MANU-
AL THAT GIVES READERS GUIDANCE
ON HOW THEY COULD RECREATE THE
PROJECTS SHOWN.
--

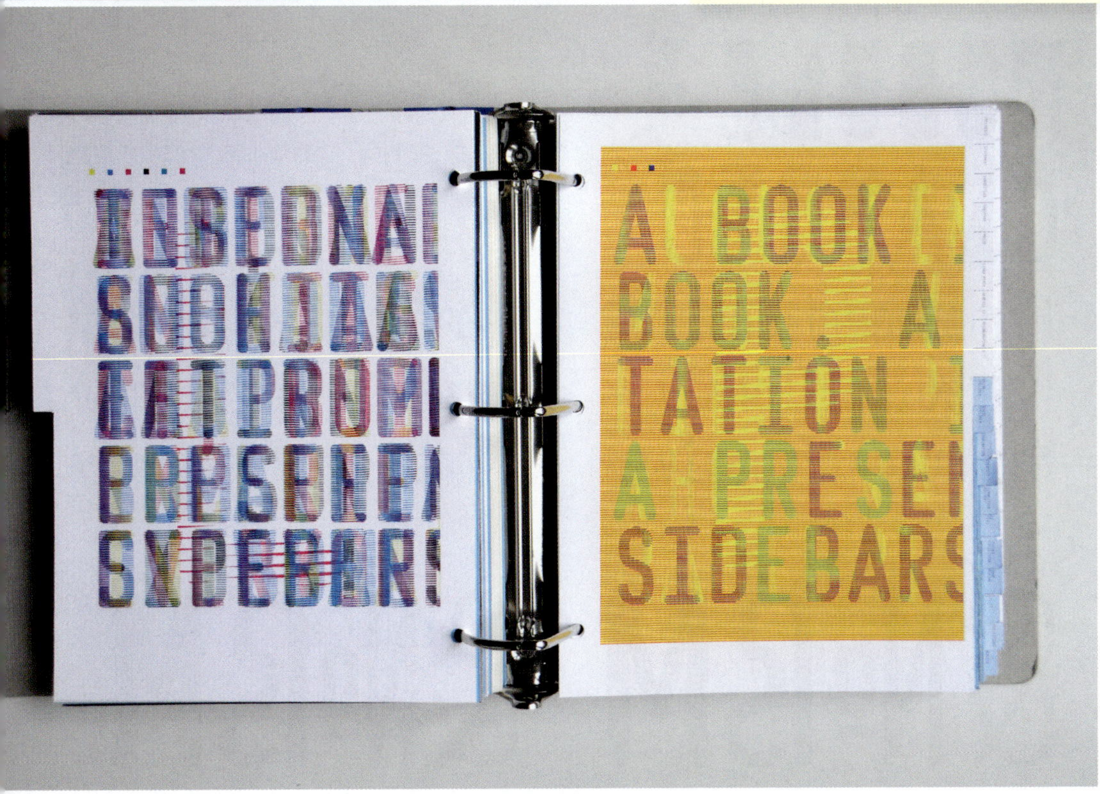

MODULE TEXT

Hamburgerfionsiv
Hamburgerfionsiv
Hamburgerfionsiv

AF Module Text consists of three weights: thin, regular and bold. In contrast to AF Module Classic, this style was designed with cuts between the joints of the round elements and the vertical strokes.

aa nn

Module Classic Module Text Module Classic Module Text

bcde
jgpq
5678

MODULE CLASSIC

Hamburgerfionsiv
Hamburgerfionsiv
Hamburgerfionsiv

AF Module Classic is the successor of AF Module Pressure, as the need for conventional text setting was necessary. The Classic Style offers both a monospaced and a proportional version in three styles: thin, regular and bold.

AF MODULE CLASSIC - MONO

Hamburgerfionsiv
Hamburgerfionsiv
Hamburgerfionsiv

&No₿M   &No₿M

MODULE PRESSURE

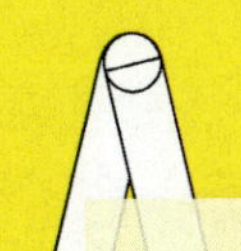

AF Module Pressure was initiated by a project at Yale University School of Art. The idea was to create a corporate font for a self-inking stamp that should incorporate the meaning of the object - accident, randomness and repetition. Different experiments with imprints were conducted. Afterwards the letterforms were transferred into digital styles. In order to combine the different shapes, AF Module Pressure was designed monospaced for exact overprinting. The family increases from the almost abstract style MonoExtraLight to the compact style MonoExtraStrong.

AF MODULE PRESSURE - MONOEXTRASTRONG

TEN

ABCDEFGHIJKLMNOPQRST
UVWXYZabcdefghijklm
opqrstuvwxyz0123456
789?!¡¿&§%‰£€ áâäã
āàżéèêëíìîï-ñóòôöõøçø
¢úùûöüÿłÀÁÀÂÄÆÈÉÊËÑÖÒ
ÓÔÖØÜÚÙŸ¢çÏÍÎÏ

Lorem ipsum dolor sit amet, consectetuer adipiscing elit, sed diam nonummy nibh euismod tincidunt ut laoreet dolore magna aliquam erat volutpat. Ut wisi enim ad minim veniam, quis nostrud exerci tation ullamcorper suscipit lobortis nisl ut aliquip ex ea commodo consequat. Duis autem vel eum iriure dolor in hendrerit in vulputate velit esse molestie consequat, vel illum dolore eu feugiat nulla facilisis at vero et accumsan et iusto odio dignissim qui blandit praesent luptatum zzril delenit augue duis dolore te feugait

APPLICATION

ELEVEN

MODULES

STAPELBERG&FRITZ IS A GRAPHIC DE-
SIGN STUDIO WORKING IN THE FIELDS
OF ART DIRECTION AND DESIGN FOR
CORPORATE AND CULTURAL CLIENTS,
WITH AN EMPHASIS ON CORPORATE AND
EDITORIAL DESIGN. STAPELBERG&FRITZ
WAS FOUNDED IN 2002 BY DANIEL
FRITZ AND MAIK STAPELBERG AND
OPERATES FROM AN OFFICE IN STUT-
TGART, GERMANY.

--

WHAT IS GERMAN?

THE OKTOBERFEST, NEUE NATIONAL-
GALERIE AND THE AUTOBAHN.

WHAT IS GERMAN DESIGN?

OBJECTIVE, CONSTRUCTIVE AND
PROVABLE.

DESCRIBE YOUR WORKING PROCESS.

THINK, DISCUSS, DESIGN.

WHAT DO YOU AIM TO ACHIEVE WITH
YOUR WORK?

GOOD GRAPHIC DESIGN.

YOU'VE INVITED A FRIEND TO
GERMANY; NAME ONE PLACE THEY
REALLY MUST VISIT AND A QUINT-
ESSENTIAL EXPERIENCE YOU REC-
OMMEND.

VISIT THE <WEISSENHOF SIEDLUNG>
IN STUTTGART. THE WEISSENHOF ES-
TATE IS ONE OF THE MOST SIGNIFI-
CANT LANDMARKS LEFT BY THE MOVE-
MENT KNOWN AS <NEUES BAUEN>.

WHAT IS THE MOST IMPORTANT
THING YOU HAVE LEARNED IN YOUR
PROFESSION SO FAR?

ADMINISTRATIVE WORK EATS UP YOUR
TIME.

--

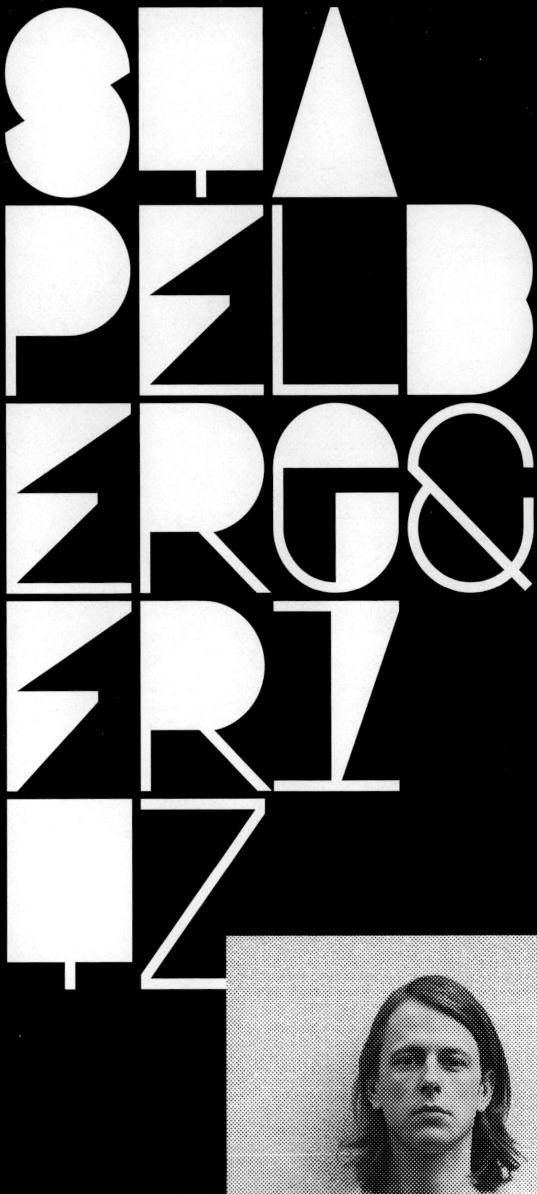

STAPELBERG & FRITZ

STAPELBERG & FRITZ
--
HACKLÄNDERSTRASSE 36
70184 STUTTGART
GERMANY
--
M +49 711 6200451
--
INFO@STAPELBERGUNDFRITZ.COM
WWW.STAPELBERGUNDFRITZ.COM
--

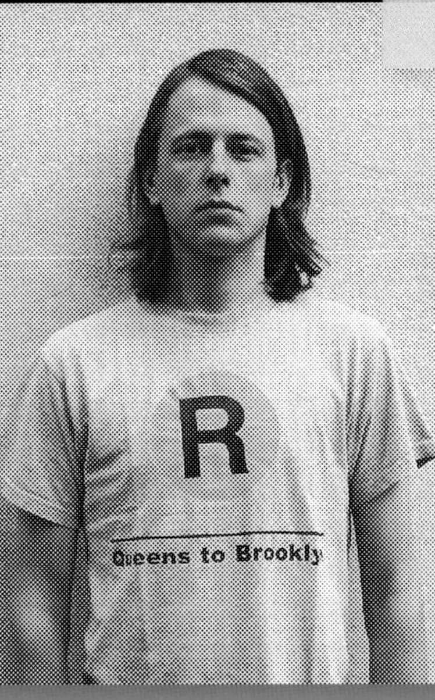

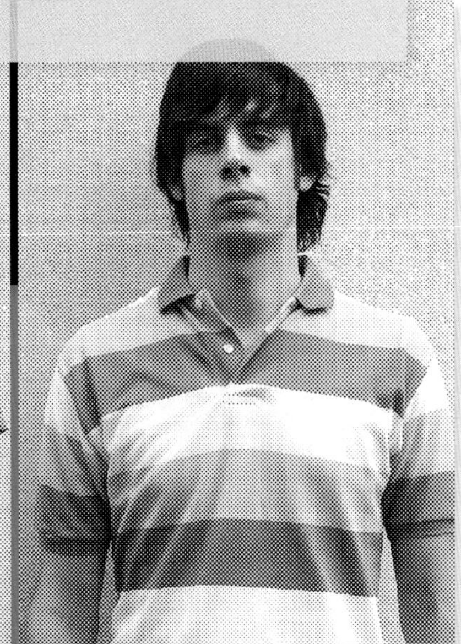

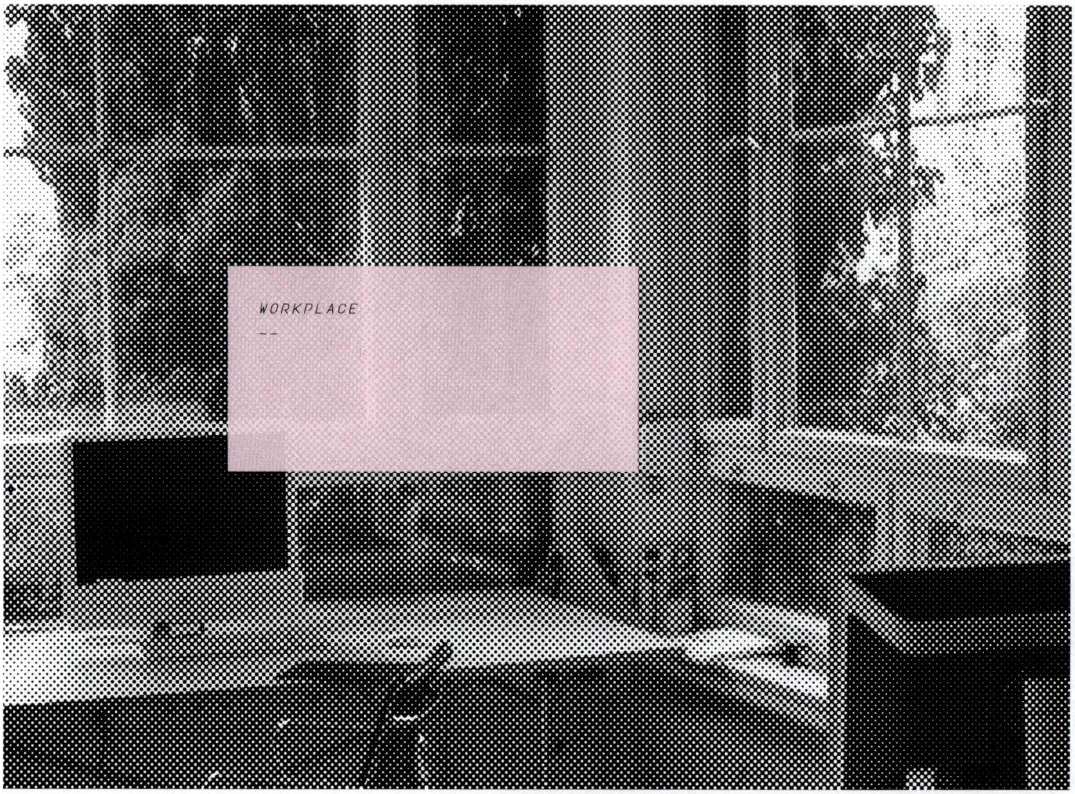

WORKPLACE
--

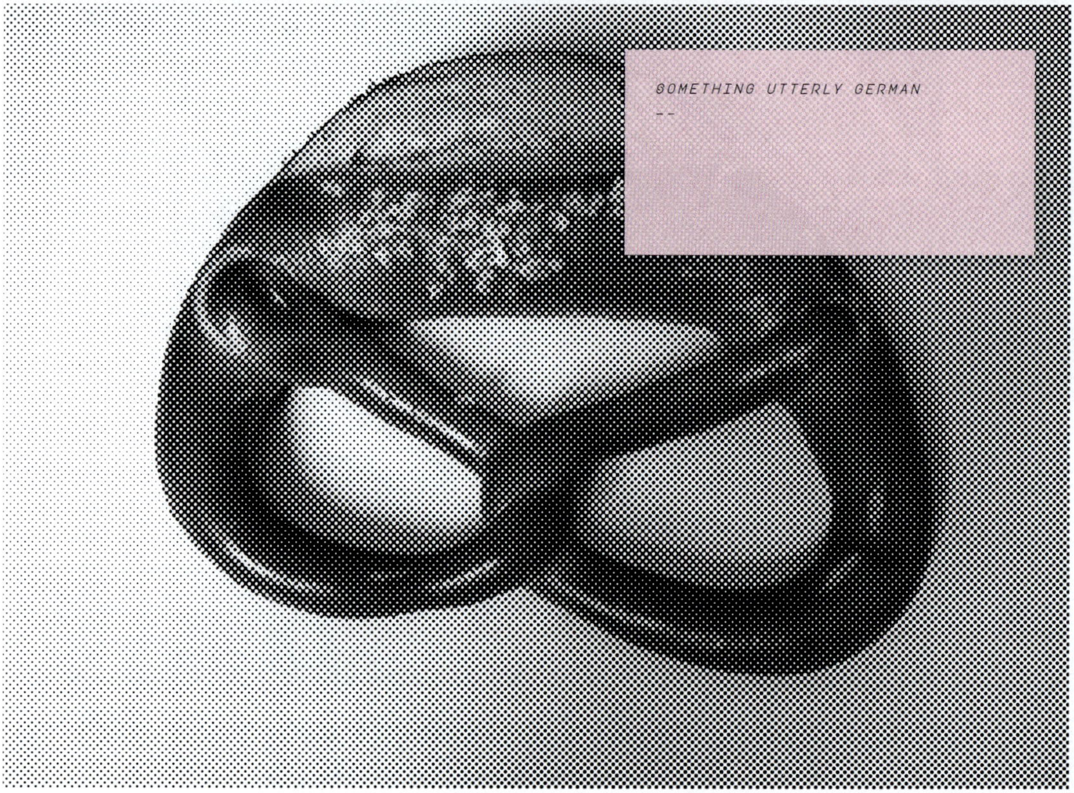

SOMETHING UTTERLY GERMAN
--

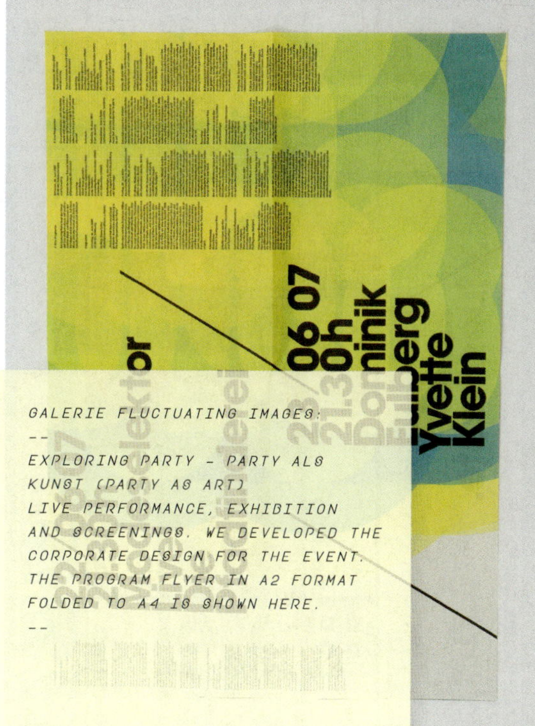
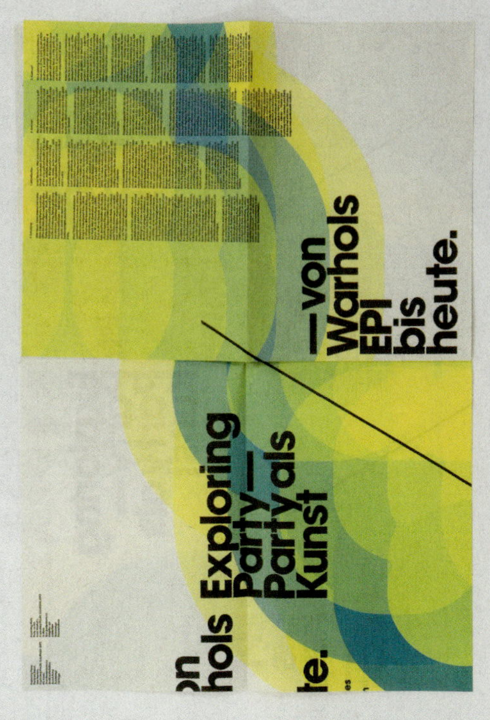

GALERIE FLUCTUATING IMAGES:
--
EXPLORING PARTY - PARTY ALS
KUNST (PARTY AS ART)
LIVE PERFORMANCE, EXHIBITION
AND SCREENINGS. WE DEVELOPED THE
CORPORATE DESIGN FOR THE EVENT.
THE PROGRAM FLYER IN A2 FORMAT
FOLDED TO A4 IS SHOWN HERE.
--

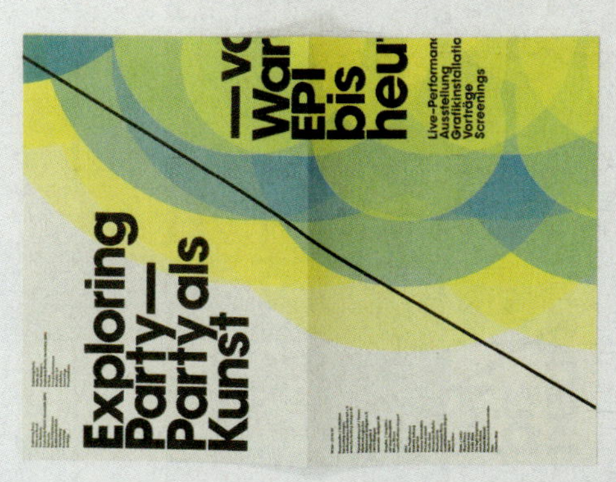
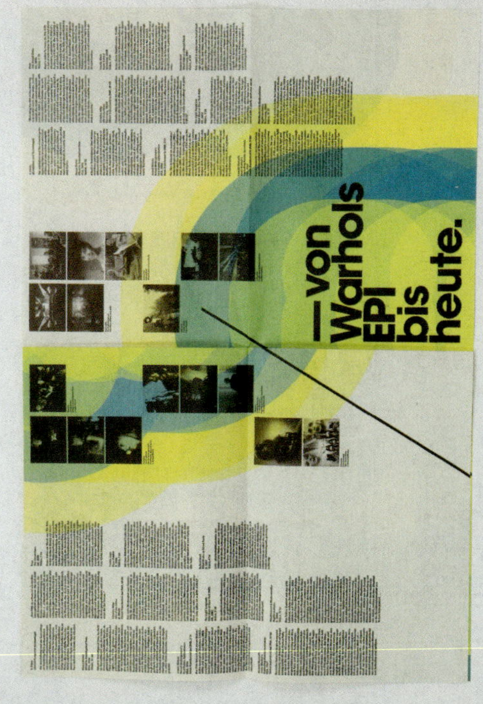

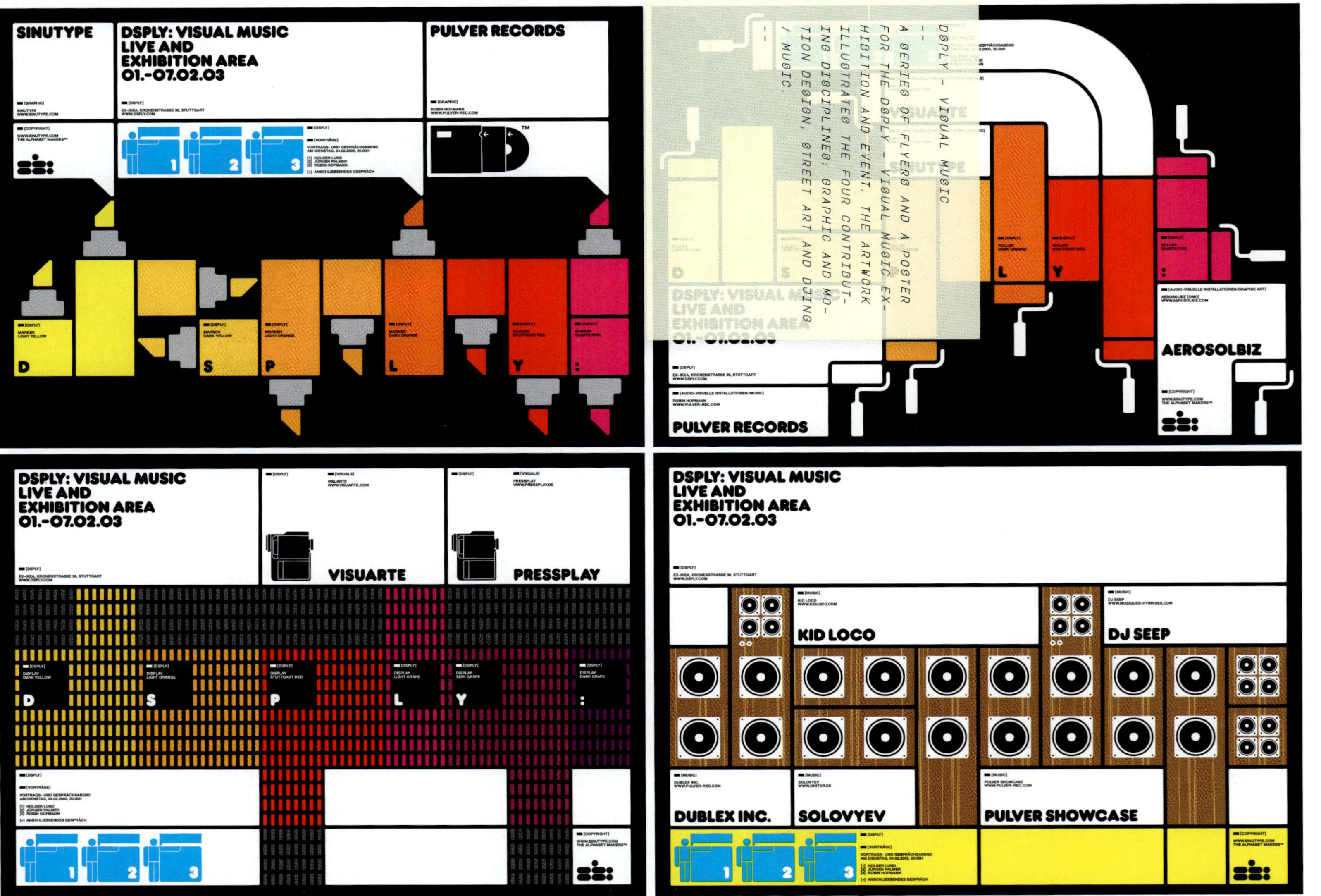

SINUTYPE
DSPLY: VISUAL MUSIC
LIVE AND
EXHIBITION AREA
01.–07.02.03
PULVER RECORDS
[GRAPHIC]
SINUTYPE
WWW.SINUTYPE.COM
[DSPLY]
EX-IKEA, KRONENSTRASSE 36, STUTTGART
WWW.DSPLY.COM
[GRAPHIC]
ROBIN HOFMANN
WWW.PULVER-REC.COM
[COPYRIGHT]
WWW.SINUTYPE.COM
THE ALPHABET MAKERS™
[VORTRÄGE]
VORTRAGS- UND GESPRÄCHSABEND
AM DIENSTAG, 04.02.2003, 20.00H
[1] HOLGER LUND
[2] JÜRGEN PALMER
[3] ROBIN HOFMANN
[+] ANSCHLIESSENDES GESPRÄCH
MARKER LIGHT YELLOW
MARKER DARK YELLOW
MARKER LIGHT ORANGE
MARKER DARK ORANGE
MARKER STUTTGART RED
MARKER GLADYS PINK
D   S   P   L   Y   :

DSPLY – VISUAL MUSIC
--
A SERIES OF FLYERS AND A POSTER
FOR THE DSPLY – VISUAL MUSIC EX-
HIBITION AND EVENT. THE ARTWORK
ILLUSTRATES THE FOUR CONTRIBUT-
ING DISCIPLINES: GRAPHIC AND MO-
TION DESIGN, STREET ART AND DJING
/ MUSIC.
--
DSPLY: VISUAL MUSIC
LIVE AND
EXHIBITION AREA
01.–07.02.03
AEROSOLBIZ
PULVER RECORDS
[DSPLY]
EX-IKEA, KRONENSTRASSE 36, STUTTGART
WWW.DSPLY.COM
[AUDIO-VISUELLE INSTALLATIONEN/MUSIC]
ROBIN HOFMANN
[AUDIO-VISUELLE INSTALLATIONEN/GRAPHIC ART]
AEROSOLBIZ [DMO]
WWW.AEROSOLBIZ.COM
[COPYRIGHT]
WWW.SINUTYPE.COM
THE ALPHABET MAKERS™
ROLLER LIGHT YELLOW
ROLLER DARK ORANGE
ROLLER STUTTGART RED
ROLLER GLADYS PINK
D   S   L   Y   :

DSPLY: VISUAL MUSIC
LIVE AND
EXHIBITION AREA
01.–07.02.03
VISUARTE
PRESSPLAY
[DSPLY]
EX-IKEA, KRONENSTRASSE 36, STUTTGART
WWW.DSPLY.COM
[VISUALS]
VISUARTE
WWW.VISUARTE.COM
[VISUALS]
PRESSPLAY
WWW.PRESSPLAY.DE
[DSPLY]
DISPLAY DARK YELLOW
DISPLAY LIGHT ORANGE
DISPLAY STUTTGART RED
DISPLAY LIGHT GRAPE
DISPLAY SEMI GRAPE
DISPLAY DARK GRAPE
D   S   P   L   Y   :
[VORTRÄGE]
VORTRAGS- UND GESPRÄCHSABEND
AM DIENSTAG, 04.02.2003, 20.00H
[1] HOLGER LUND
[2] JÜRGEN PALMER
[3] ROBIN HOFMANN
[+] ANSCHLIESSENDES GESPRÄCH
[COPYRIGHT]
WWW.SINUTYPE.COM
THE ALPHABET MAKERS™

DSPLY: VISUAL MUSIC
LIVE AND
EXHIBITION AREA
01.–07.02.03
KID LOCO
DJ SEEP
DUBLEX INC.
SOLOVYEV
PULVER SHOWCASE
[DSPLY]
EX-IKEA, KRONENSTRASSE 36, STUTTGART
WWW.DSPLY.COM
[MUSIC]
KID LOCO
WWW.KIDLOCO.COM
[MUSIC]
WWW.MUSIQUES-HYBRIDES.COM
[MUSIC]
DUBLEX INC.
WWW.PULVER-REC.COM
[MUSIC]
SOLOVYEV
WWW.ONITOR.DE
[MUSIC]
PULVER SHOWCASE
WWW.PULVER-REC.COM
[VORTRÄGE]
VORTRAGS- UND GESPRÄCHSABEND
AM DIENSTAG, 04.02.2003, 20.00H
[1] HOLGER LUND
[2] JÜRGEN PALMER
[3] ROBIN HOFMANN
[+] ANSCHLIESSENDES GESPRÄCH
[COPYRIGHT]
WWW.SINUTYPE.COM
THE ALPHABET MAKERS™

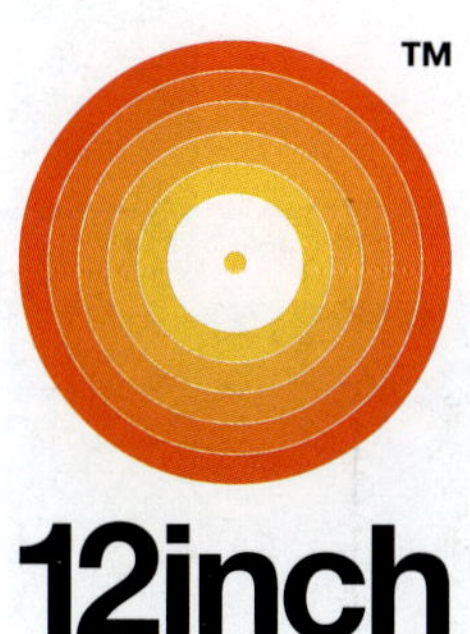

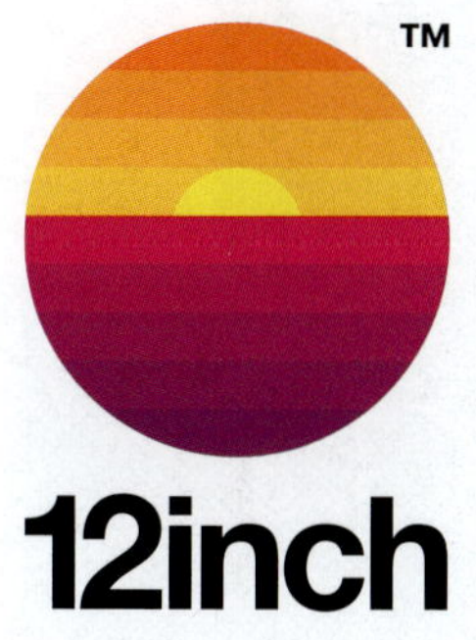

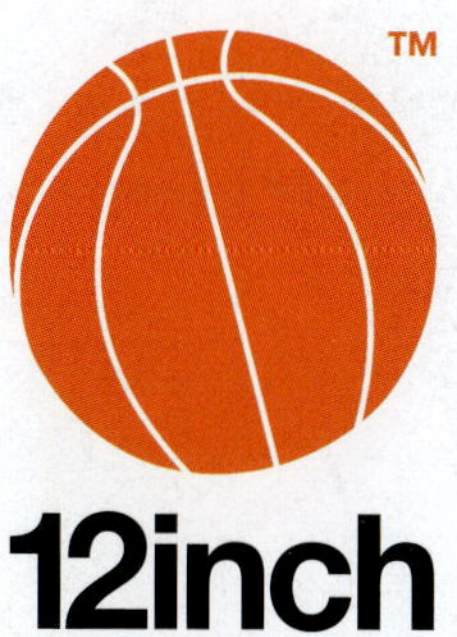

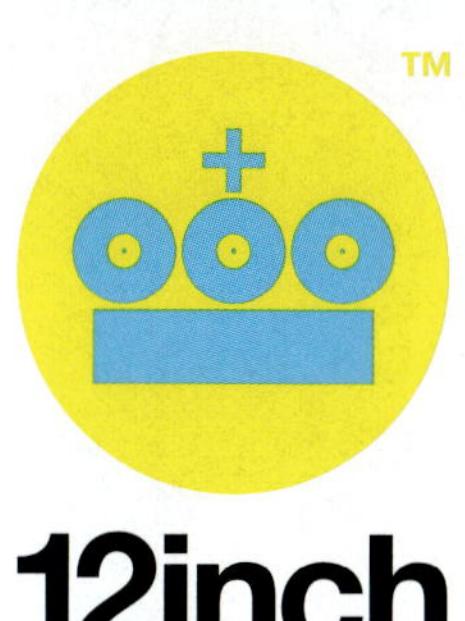

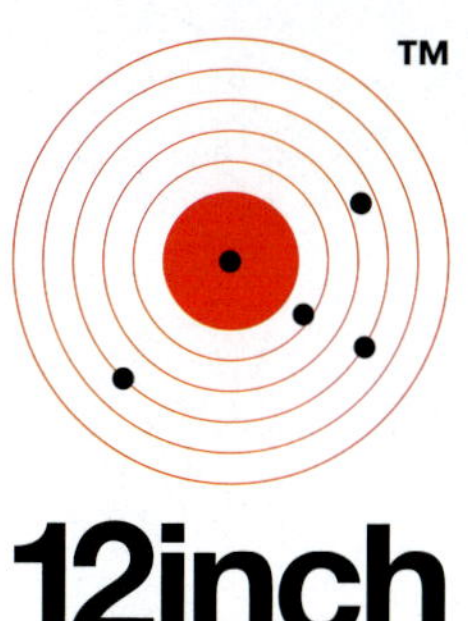

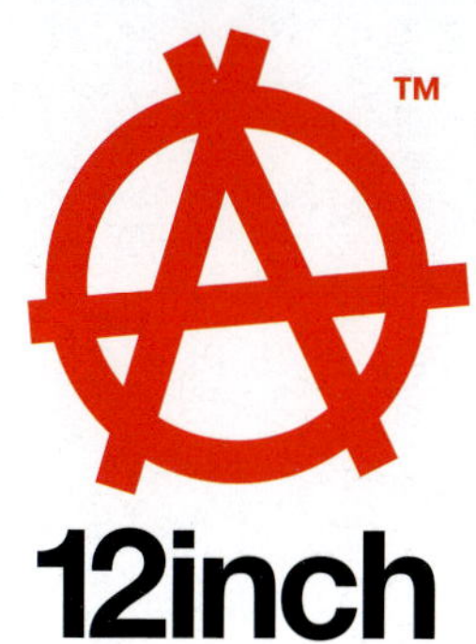

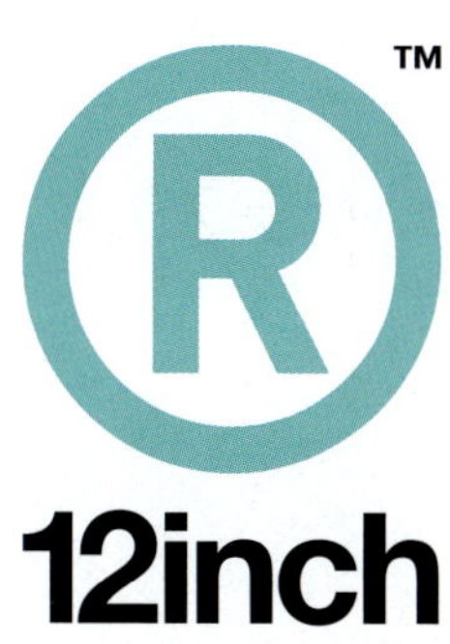

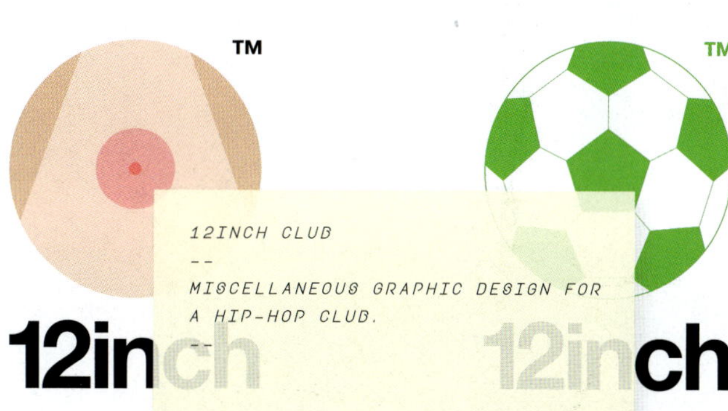

12INCH CLUB
--
MISCELLANEOUS GRAPHIC DESIGN FOR
A HIP-HOP CLUB.
--

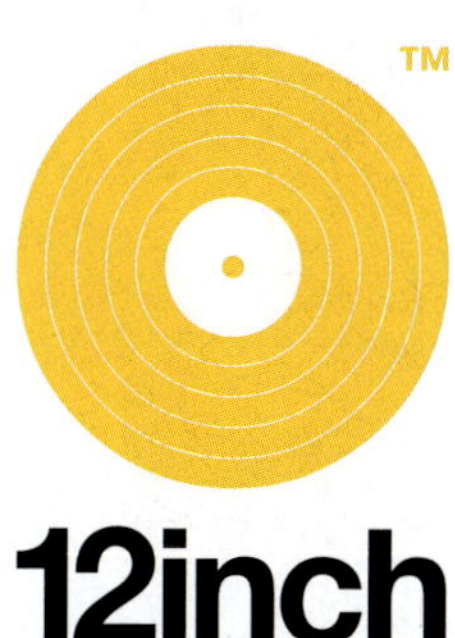

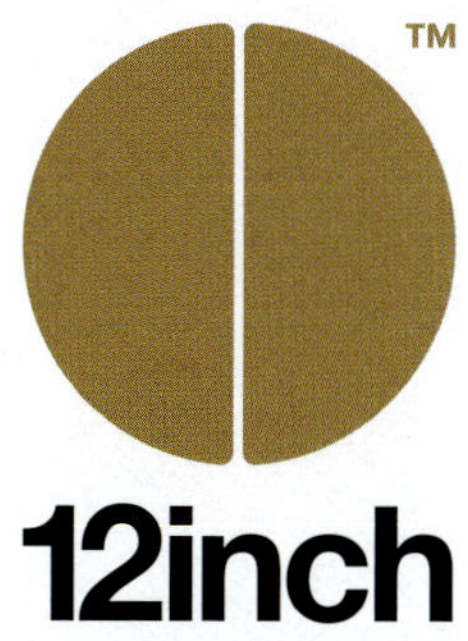

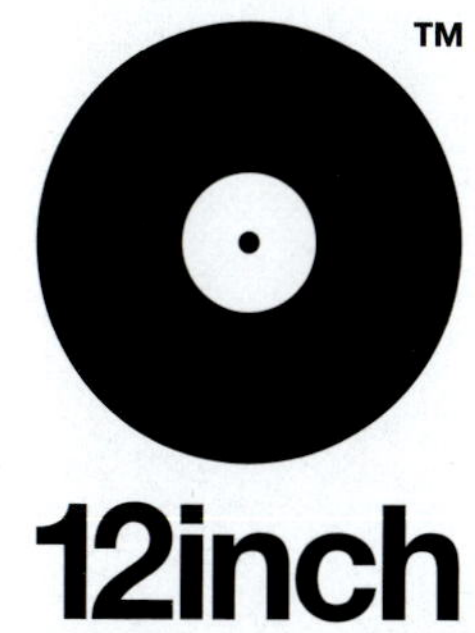

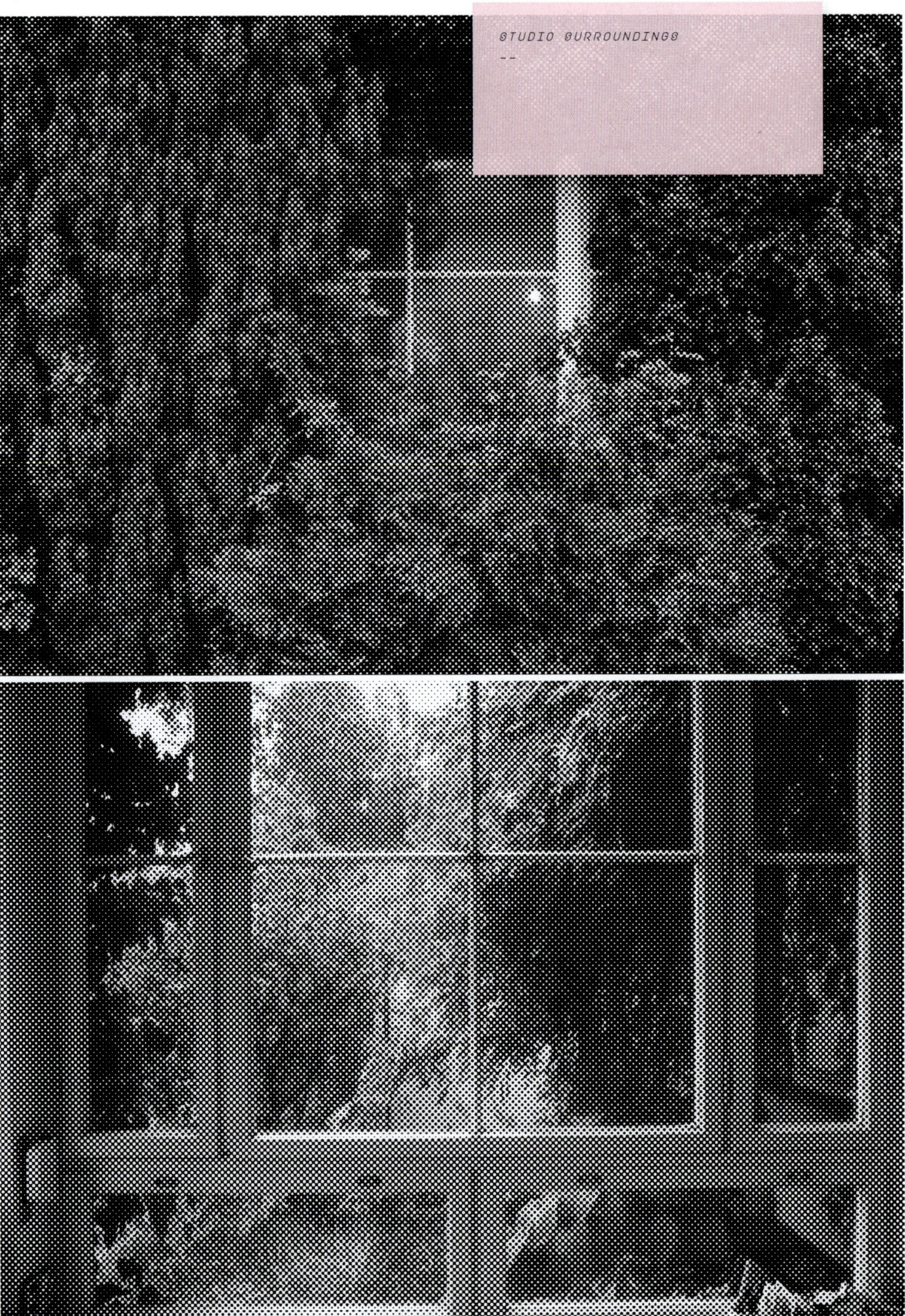

STUDIO SURROUNDINGS
--

GRAFIK FREUNDE STUTTGART
--
POSTER AND FOLDER FOR A GRAPHIC
DESIGN EXHIBITION.
--

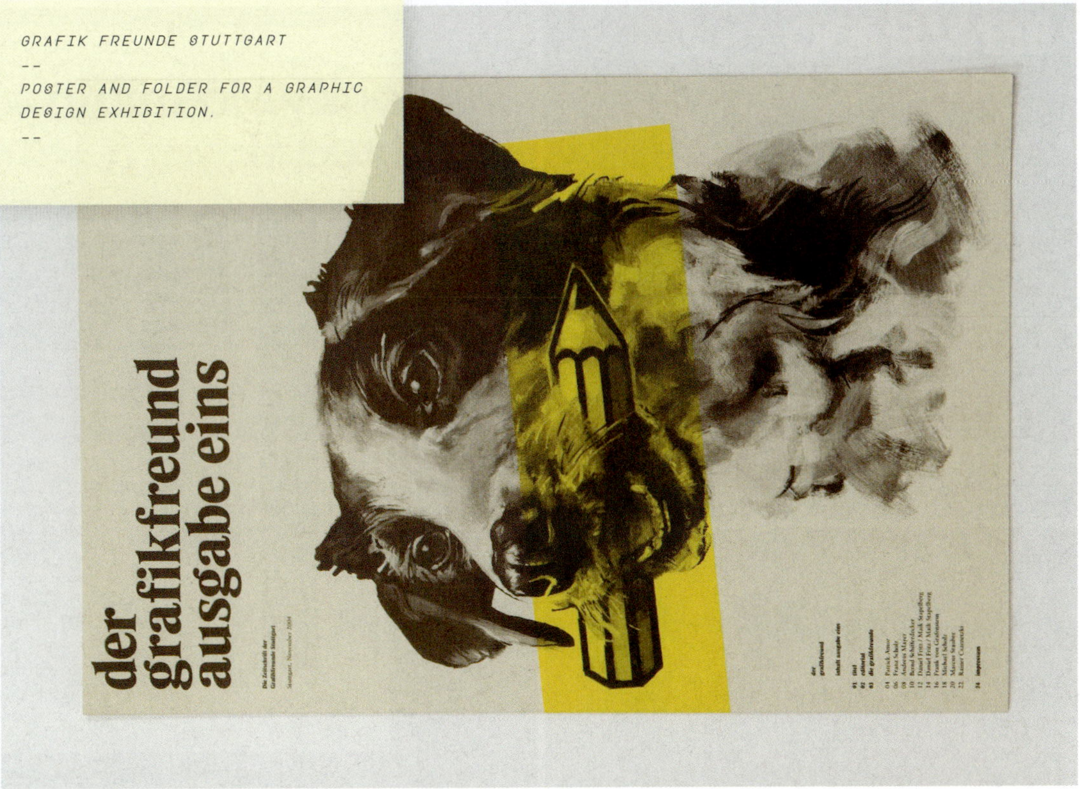

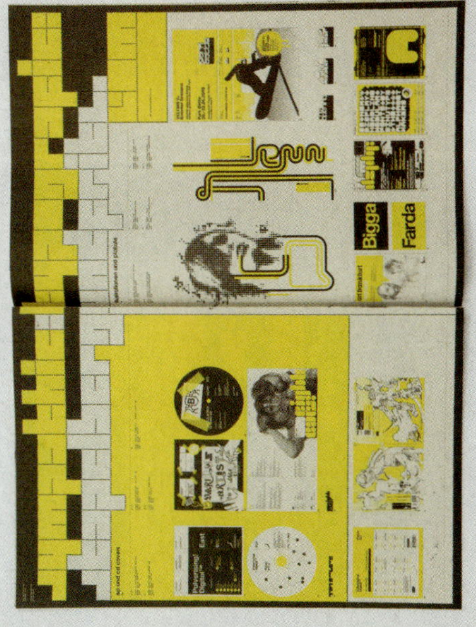

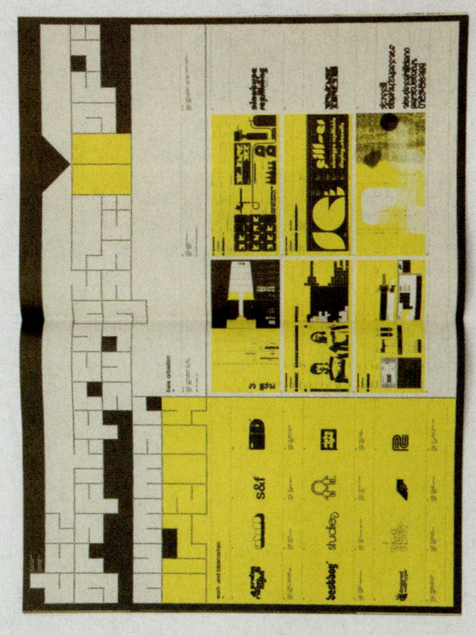

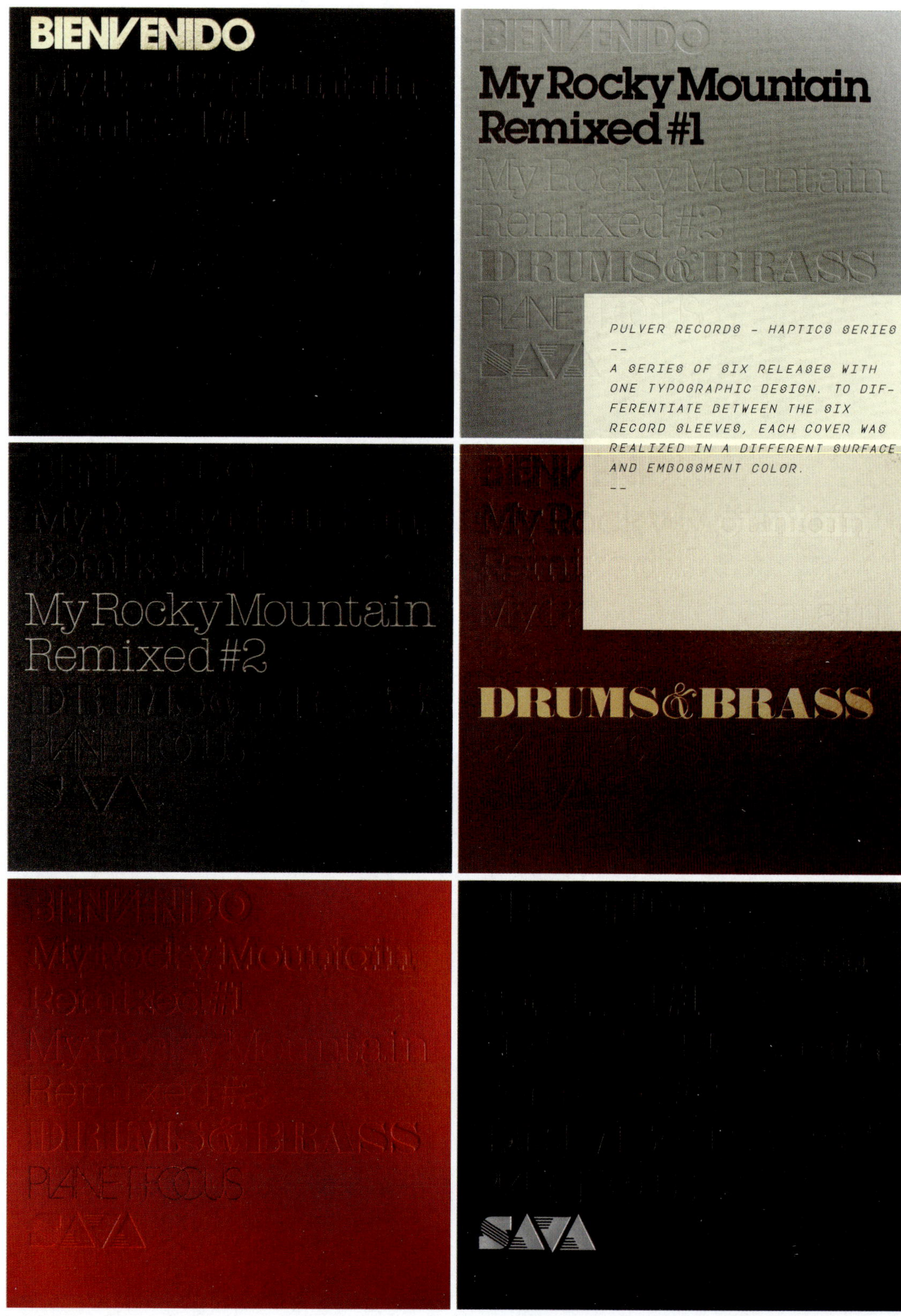
BIENVENIDO
My Rocky Mountain
Remixed #1
My Rocky Mountain
Remixed #2
DRUMS&BRASS
My Rocky Mountain
Remixed #2
DRUMS&BRASS
PULVER RECORDS - HAPTICS SERIES
--
A SERIES OF SIX RELEASES WITH
ONE TYPOGRAPHIC DESIGN. TO DIF-
FERENTIATE BETWEEN THE SIX
RECORD SLEEVES, EACH COVER WAS
REALIZED IN A DIFFERENT SURFACE
AND EMBOSSMENT COLOR.
--
SAVA

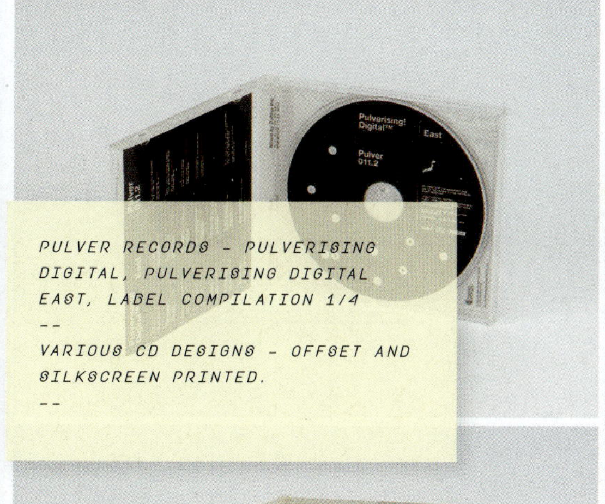

PULVER RECORDS – PULVERISING
DIGITAL, PULVERISING DIGITAL
EAST, LABEL COMPILATION 1/4
--
VARIOUS CD DESIGNS – OFFSET AND
SILKSCREEN PRINTED.
--

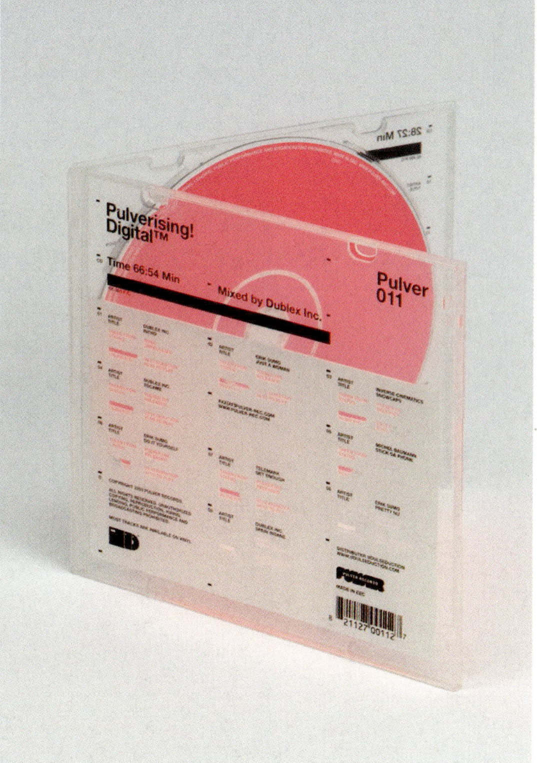

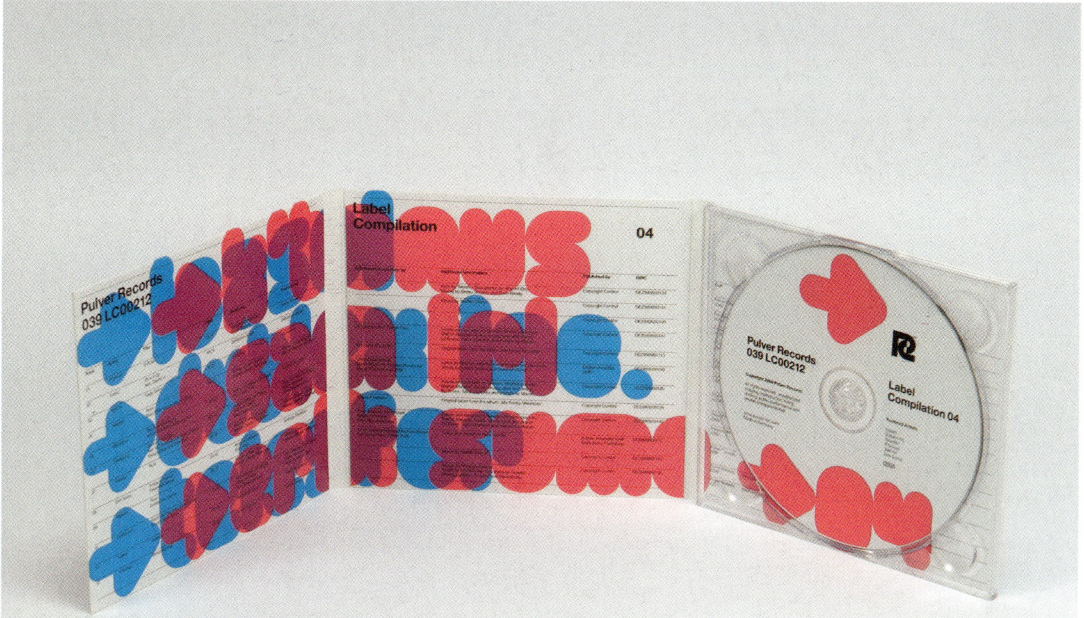

BORN 1979 IN SINGEN AM HOHENTWIEL.
2001 - 2006 VISUAL COMMUNICA-
TION STUDIES AT THE DESIGN FACULTY
IN PFORZHEIM, THE UNIVERSITY OF
GEORGIA (USA) AND THE STAATLI-
CHE AKADEMIE DER BILDENDEN KÜNSTE
IN STUTTGART (TUTOR, ULI CLUSS).
SINCE 2006 FREELANCE DESIGNER IN
STUTTGART AND SCIENTIFIC ASSISTANT
AT THE DESIGN FACULTY IN PFOR-
ZHEIM.

--

WHAT IS GERMAN?

BLACK AND WHITE AND COLORED.

WHAT IS GERMAN DESIGN?

FROM STRAIGHT TO SKEWED TO DIS-
TORTED.

DESCRIBE YOUR WORKING PROCESS.

FINDING, COLLECTING, FILTERING,
SHAPING.

WHAT DO YOU AIM TO ACHIEVE WITH
YOUR WORK?

DEPENDS ON THE PROJECT. GENERAL-
LY TO AWAKEN CURIOSITY AND INTER-
EST SOME WAY OR OTHER.

YOU'VE INVITED A FRIEND TO
GERMANY; NAME ONE PLACE THEY
REALLY MUST VISIT AND A QUINT-
ESSENTIAL EXPERIENCE YOU REC-
OMMEND.

A BEER GARDEN / DRINKING BEER

WHAT IS THE MOST IMPORTANT
LESSON YOU HAVE LEARNED IN YOUR
PROFESSION SO FAR?

TO SWIM AGAINST THE CURRENT NOW
AND THEN.

--

SCH-WARZ

STEFANIE SCHWARZ
--
LERCHENSTRASSE 20
70176 STUTTGART
GERMANY
--
M +49 711 2221953
--
SCHWARZSTEFFI@WEB.DE
WWW.STEFANIESCHWARZ-GRAPHICDESIGN.DE
--

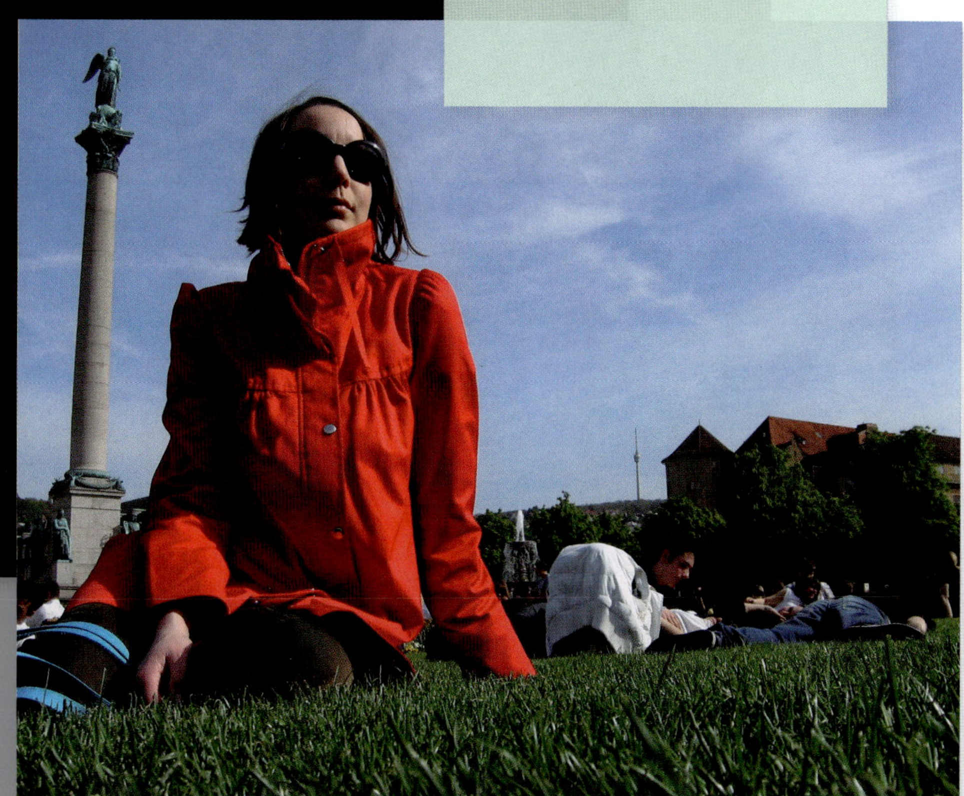

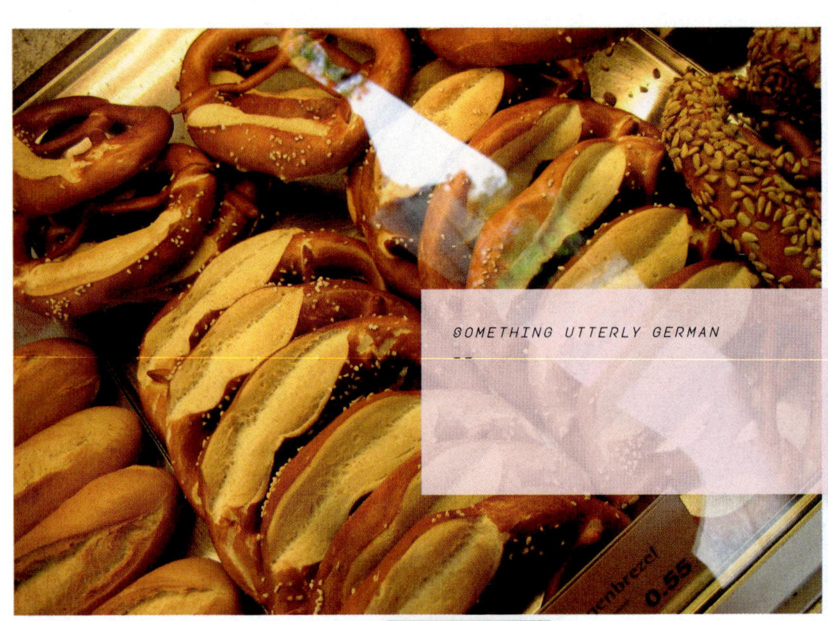
SOMETHING UTTERLY GERMAN

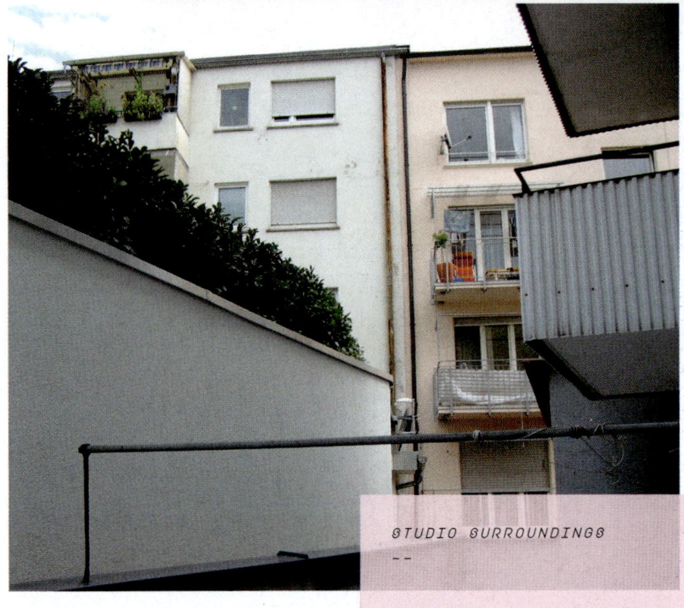
STUDIO SURROUNDINGS

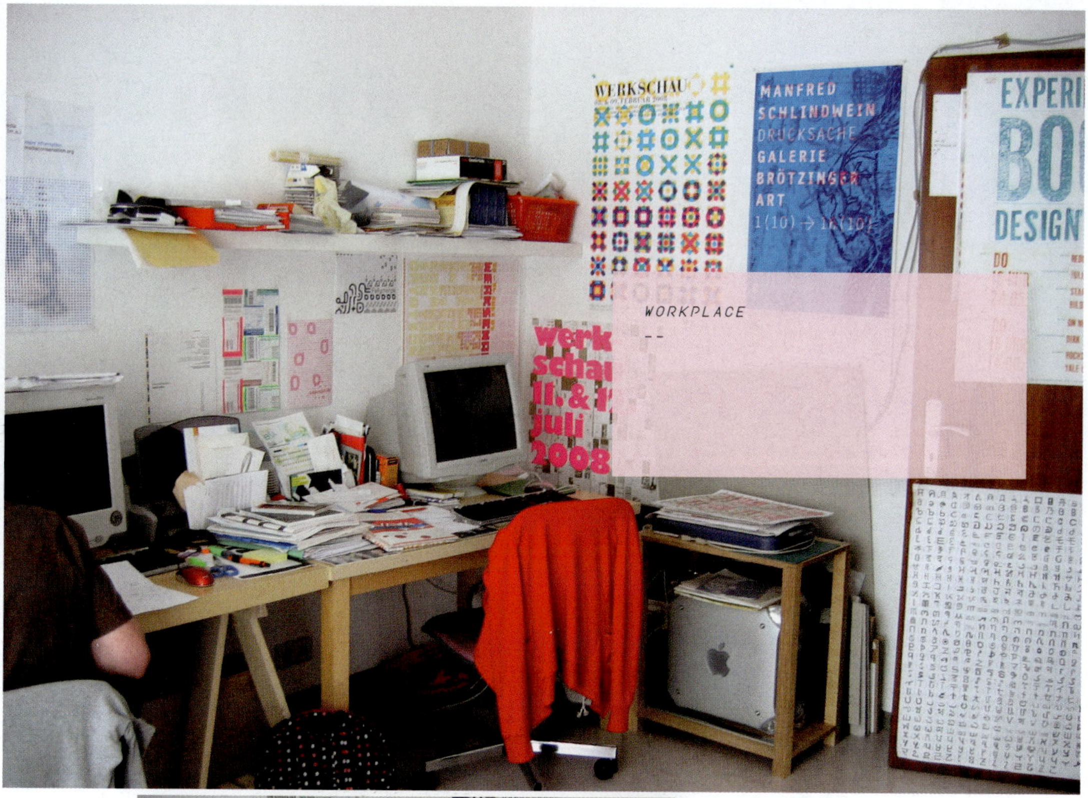

WORKPLACE
--

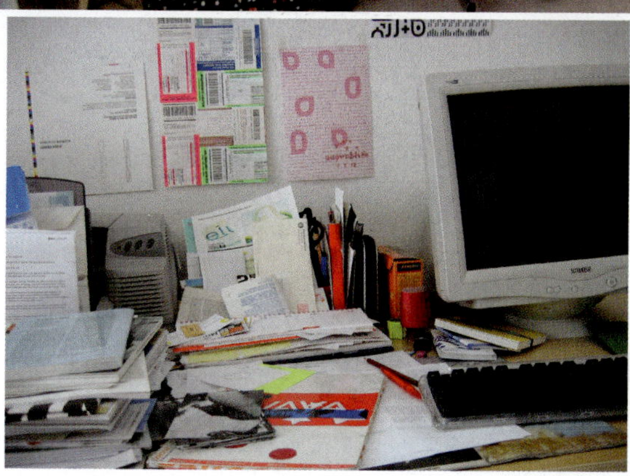

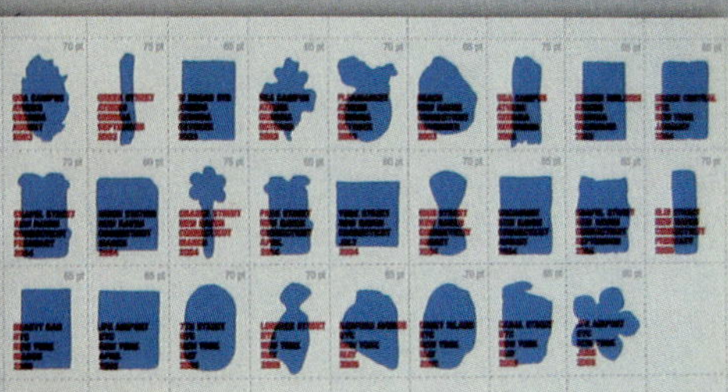

UGA CAMPUS
ATHENS
GEORGIA
AUGUST
2003

UGA CAMPUS
ATHENS
GEORGIA
AUGUST
2003

FLEA MARKET
ATHENS
GEORGIA
OCTOBER
2003

BEACH
NEW HAVEN
CONNECTICUT
NOVEMBER
2003

GRAND CENTRAL
NYC
NEW YORK
JANUARY
2004

ORANGE STREET
NEW HAVEN
CONNECTICUT
MARCH
2004

PARK STREET
NEW HAVEN
CONNECTICUT
APRIL
2004

HIGH STREET
NEW HAVEN
CONNECTICUT
AUGUST
2004

JFK AIRPORT
NYC
NEW YORK
APRIL
2005

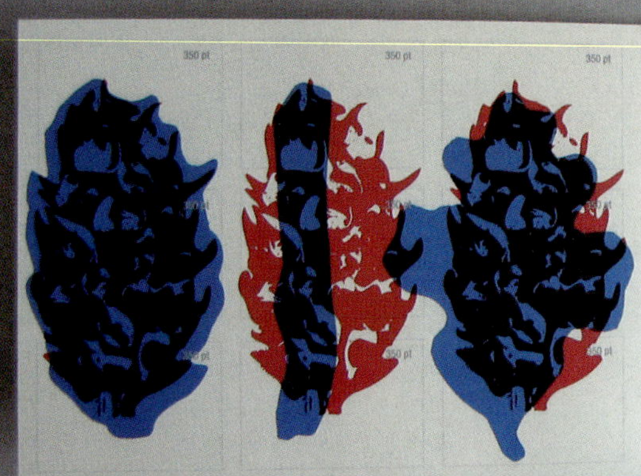

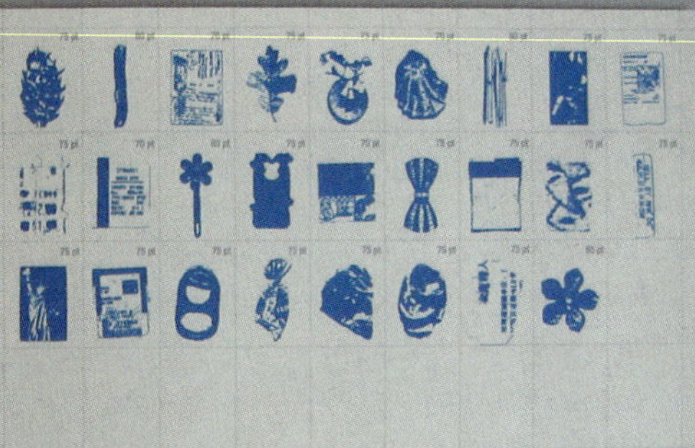

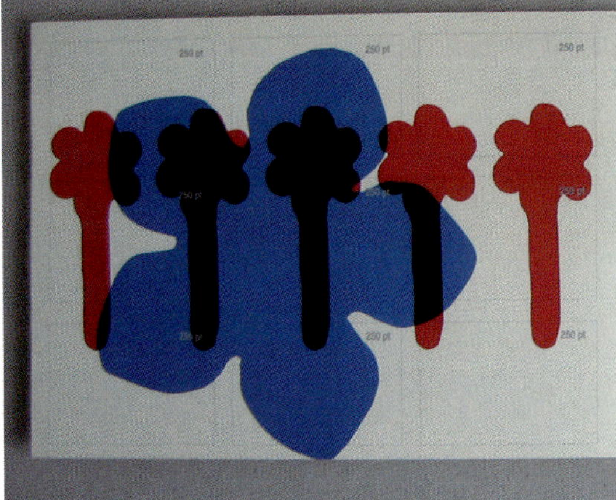

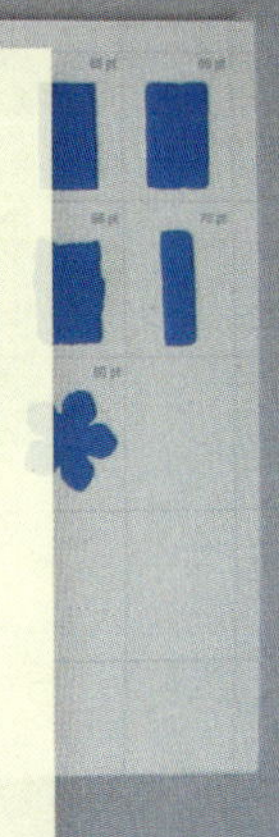

LOST PROPERTY
--
<LOST PROPERTY> IS A FONT CON-
SISTING OF OBJECTS THAT STEFANIE
SCHWARZ FOUND IN THE USA BE-
TWEEN 2003 AND 2005. THE KEY-
BOARD LAYOUT OF THE LOWER CASE
LETTERS SHOWS THE FOUND OBJECTS
IN DETAIL. THE RESPECTIVE UPPER
CASE LETTERS DEPICT THEIR OUT-
LINES. LETTER KEYS PLUS THE ALT
KEY REVEAL THE PLACE AND DATE
THEY WERE FOUND. THE SMALL IM-
AGES THAT WERE CREATED ON TYPING
GAVE STEFANIE SCHWARZ THE IDEA
OF PRESENTING THE FONT TO DESIGN
STAMPS AND A STAMP ALBUM.
--

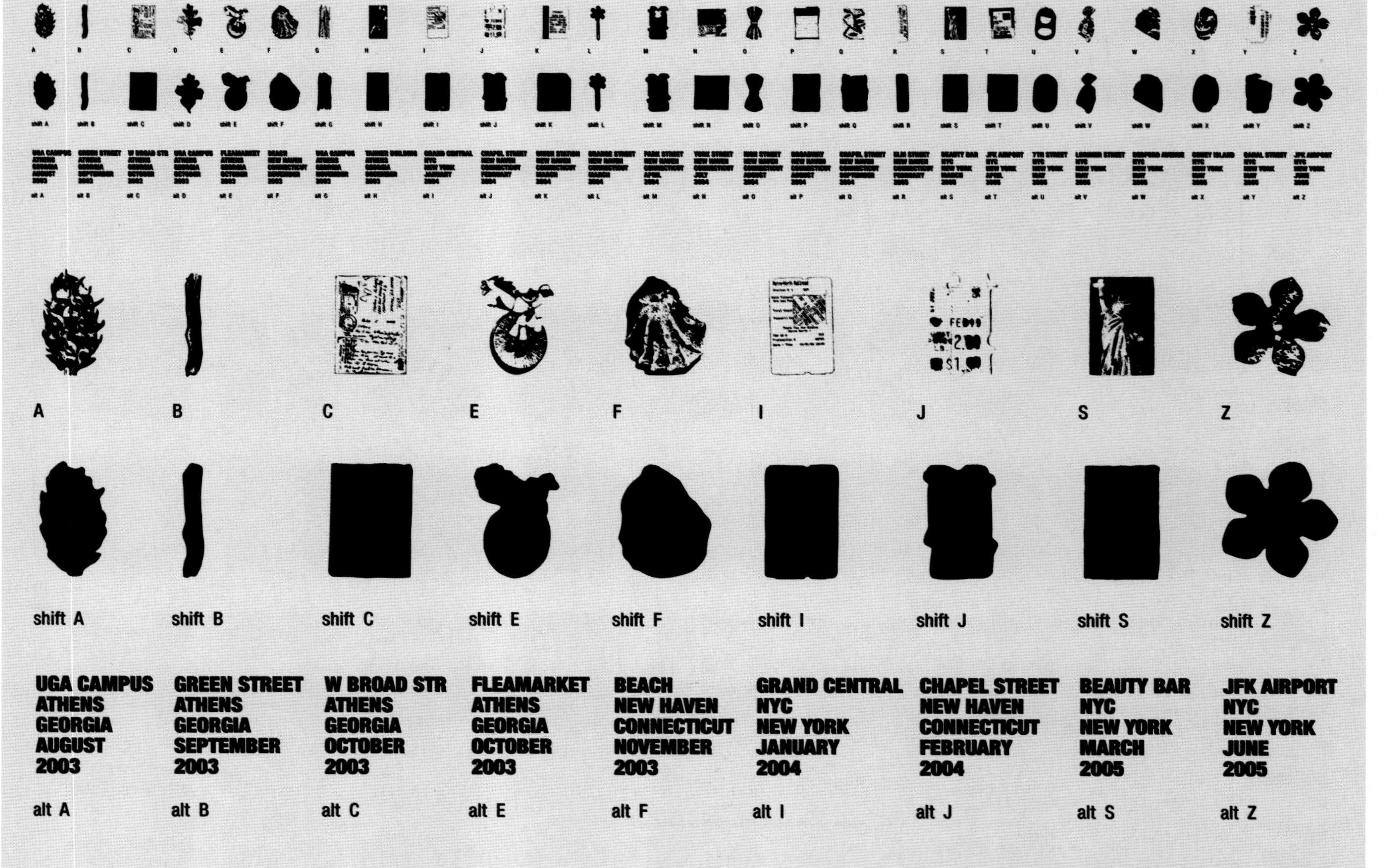

A B C D E F G H I J K L M N O P Q R S T U V W X Y Z
shift A shift B shift C shift D shift E shift F shift G shift H shift I shift J shift K shift L shift M shift N shift O shift P shift Q shift R shift S shift T shift U shift V shift W shift X shift Y shift Z
alt A alt B alt C alt D alt E alt F alt G alt H alt I alt J alt K alt L alt M alt N alt O alt P alt Q alt R alt S alt T alt U alt V alt W alt X alt Y alt Z
A B C E F I J S Z
shift A shift B shift C shift E shift F shift I shift J shift S shift Z
UGA CAMPUS
ATHENS
GEORGIA
AUGUST
2003
GREEN STREET
ATHENS
GEORGIA
SEPTEMBER
2003
W BROAD STR
ATHENS
GEORGIA
OCTOBER
2003
FLEAMARKET
ATHENS
GEORGIA
OCTOBER
2003
BEACH
NEW HAVEN
CONNECTICUT
NOVEMBER
2003
GRAND CENTRAL
NYC
NEW YORK
JANUARY
2004
CHAPEL STREET
NEW HAVEN
CONNECTICUT
FEBRUARY
2004
BEAUTY BAR
NYC
NEW YORK
MARCH
2005
JFK AIRPORT
NYC
NEW YORK
JUNE
2005
alt A alt B alt C alt E alt F alt I alt J alt S alt Z

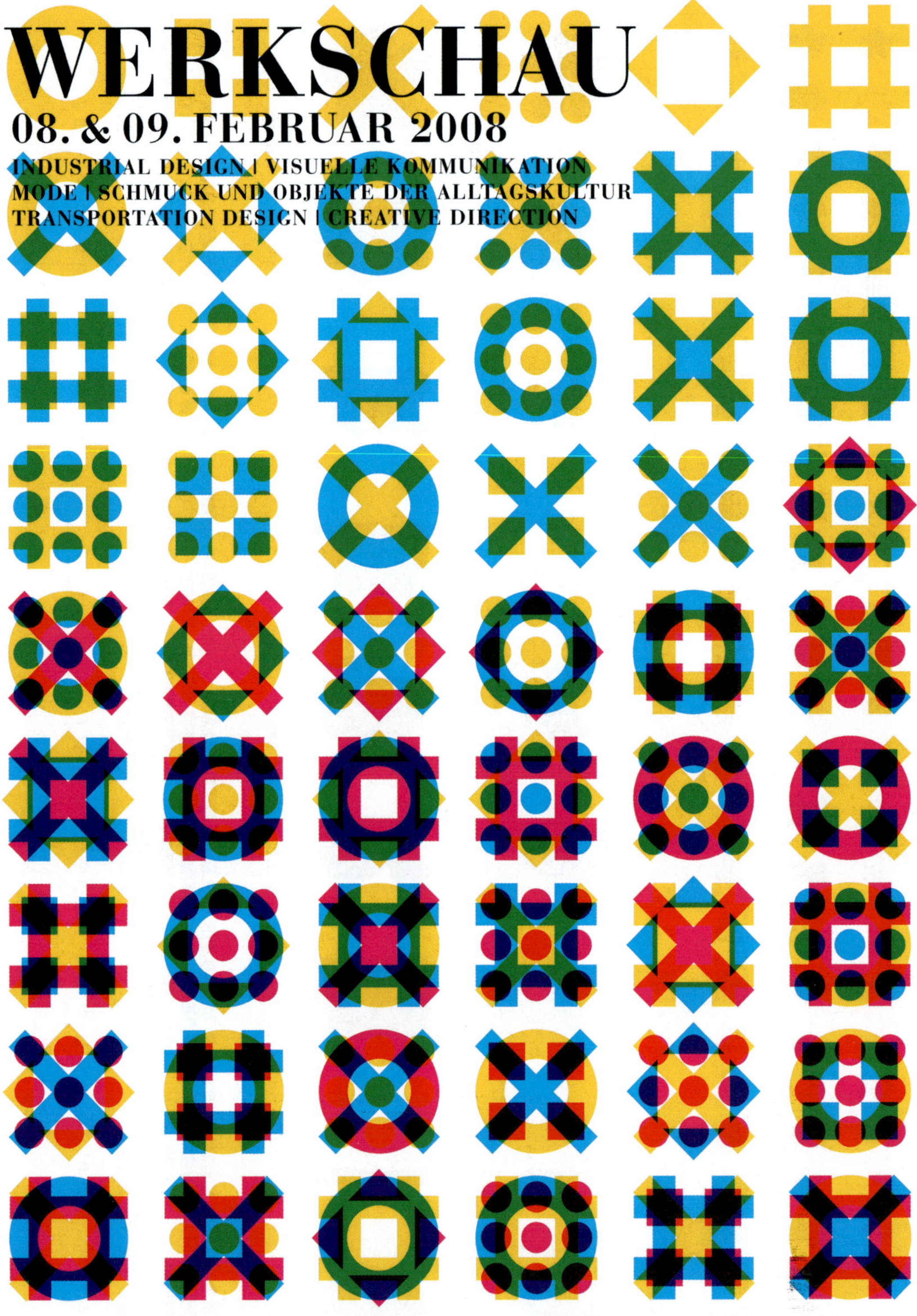

WERKSCHAU
08. & 09. FEBRUAR 2008
INDUSTRIAL DESIGN | VISUELLE KOMMUNIKATION
MODE | SCHMUCK UND OBJEKTE DER ALLTAGSKULTUR
TRANSPORTATION DESIGN | CREATIVE DIRECTION
HOCHSCHULE PFORZHEIM
FAKULTÄT FÜR GESTALTUNG
WERKSCHAU FREITAG / SAMSTAG 10–18 UHR | HOLZGARTENSTRASSE 36 | 75175 PFORZHEIM MODENSCHAU FREITAG
19/21 UHR, SAMSTAG 17/19/21 UHR | INFO KARTENVORVERKAUF: WWW.GESTALTUNG.HS-PFORZHEIM.DE | ABENDKASSE:
FREITAG AB 17 UHR, SAMSTAG AB 15 UHR TRANSPORTATION DESIGN EUTINGER STRASSE 111 | 75175 PFORZHEIM

SOMETHING UTTERLY GERMAN
--

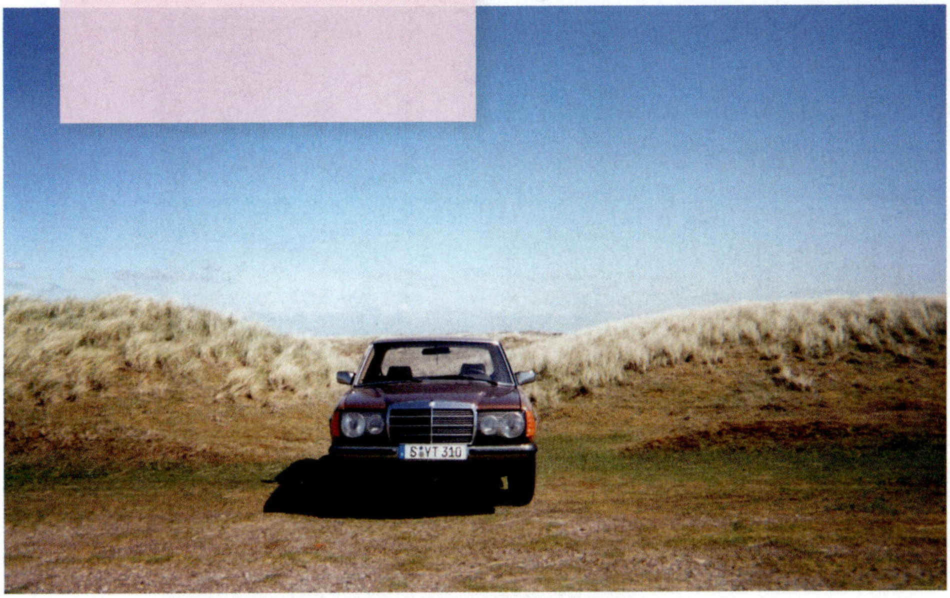

BUERGER

MANUEL <M-BOY> BÜRGER
SHAKE YOUR TREE NETWORK
--
STUTTGART
GERMANY
--
T +49 177 3685537
--
FUNISBACK@MANUELBUERGER.COM
HTTP://WWW.MANUELBUERGER.COM
HTTP://WWW.SHAKEYOURTREE.COM
--

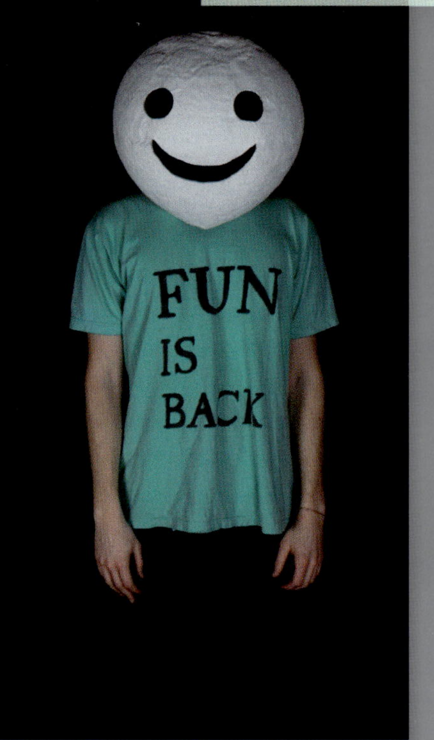

MANUEL BUERGER, WORKING WORLDWIDE
E.G. IN MY SUMMER OFFICE, STUTT-
GART, GERMANY.
MY BASIC APPROACHES:
WORK RATIONALLY, CLEVERLY AND SIM-
PLY. TRY TO DESIGN IN A UNIQUE WAY.
BE CLEAR ABOUT WHAT YOU ARE COM-
MUNICATING. GO WITH THE TREND, BUT
DECONSTRUCT IT AT THE SAME TIME.
HAVE FUN!

--

WHAT IS GERMAN?

ANXIOUSNESS.

WHAT IS GERMAN DESIGN?

LOOKING ALMOST EXCESSIVELY TRA-
DITIONAL, HEAVY ON CONCEPTS.

DESCRIBE YOUR WORKING PROCESS.

IT DEPENDS… OFTEN IT'S JUST
FOOLING AROUND AND DOING THINGS
QUICKLY. OTHERWISE I SPEND WEEKS
ON RESEARCH AND CONCEPTION - IF I
REALLY GET INTO IT. BASICALLY MY
WORKING PROCESS INCLUDES EVERY
EFFORT TO TRY AND GET THE BEST
OUT OF AN IDEA… THE DESIGN PART
DOESN'T HAVE TO BE THE MAIN FOCUS,
THOUGH.

WHAT DO YOU AIM TO ACHIEVE WITH
YOUR WORK?

IT ALSO DEPENDS… SOME WORKS ARE
INTENDED ONLY TO BRING A SMILE TO
YOUR FACE. OTHER WORKS SHOULD MAKE
YOU FEEL INTRIGUED BY A SUBJECT
- PROVIDE SOME DEEPER ACCESS AND
MAKE YOU THINK ABOUT IT. GENERALLY
I'M TRYING TO CONVEY A FEELING
(THE ENTHUSIASM I HAVE FOR SOME-
THING) AND COMMUNICATE VIA THAT.

YOU'VE INVITED A FRIEND TO
GERMANY; NAME ONE PLACE THEY
REALLY MUST VISIT AND A QUINT-
ESSENTIAL EXPERIENCE YOU REC-
OMMEND.

GO TO THE <WILHELMA> ZOO IN
STUTTGART, AFTERWARDS TRY SOME
<KÄSESPÄTZLE> (SWABIAN SPAGHETTI
WITH CHEESE).

WHAT IS THE MOST IMPORTANT
LESSON YOU HAVE LEARNED IN YOUR
PROFESSION SO FAR?

YOU REALLY GET SQUARE EYES FROM
STARING TOO LONG AT YOUR SCREEN…

--

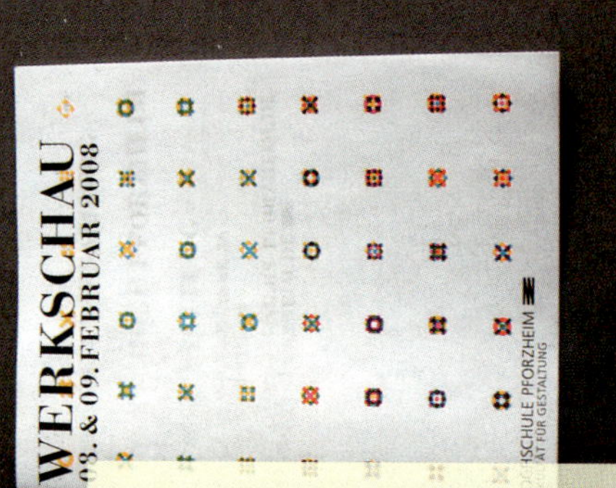

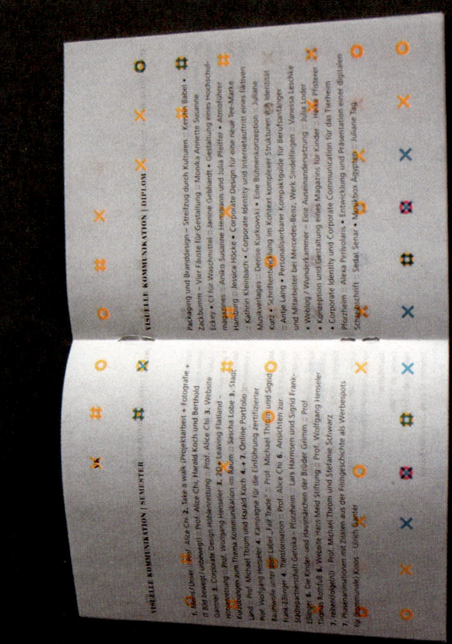

WERKSCHAU (SHOW OF WORK)
--
THE POSTER FOR THE SHOW OF WORK
AT THE DESIGN FACULTY IN PFOR-
ZHEIM REFLECTS THE SCHOOL'S WAY
OF WORKING AND ITS OUTPUT: EX-
PERIMENT, DIVERSITY AND UNIQUE-
NESS. FOR THE INDIVIDUAL COURSES
(VISUAL COMMUNICATION, FASHION,
JEWELRY, TRANSPORTATION DESIGN,
INDUSTRIAL DESIGN, CREATIVE
DIRECTION) SYMBOLS WERE DEVEL-
OPED THAT ARE COMBINED WITH ONE
ANOTHER OVER AND OVER AGAIN,
REPRESENTING AN EXPERIMENTAL,
CROSS-DEPARTMENTAL DESIGN PRO-
CESS IN THE SERIES.
--

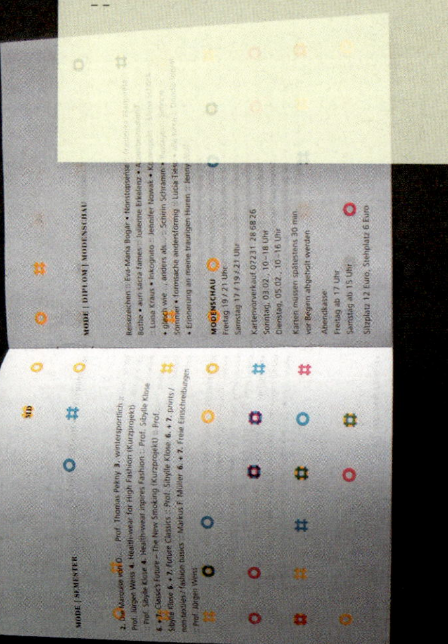

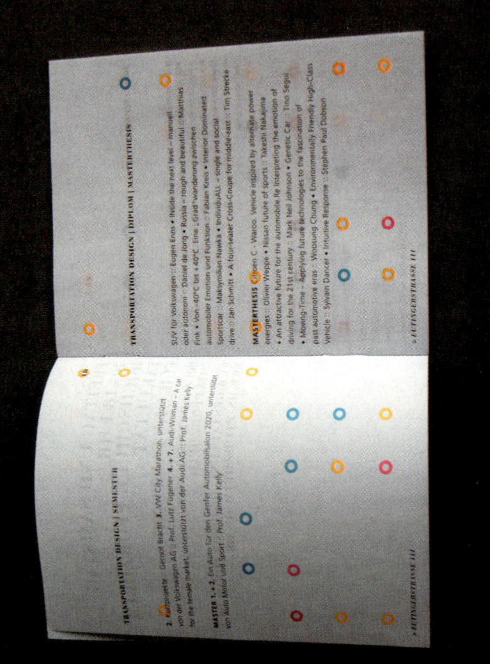

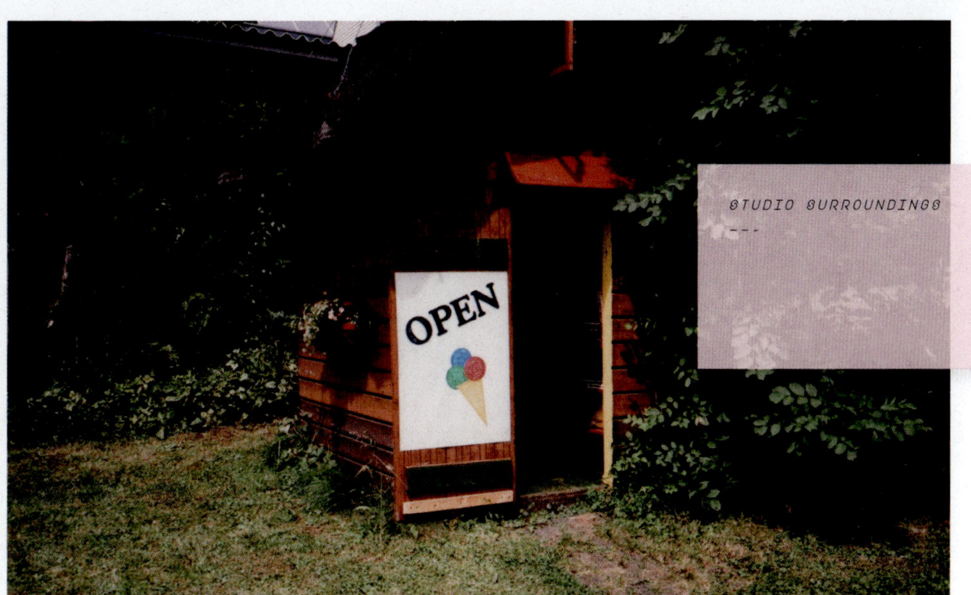
OPEN

STUDIO SURROUNDINGS

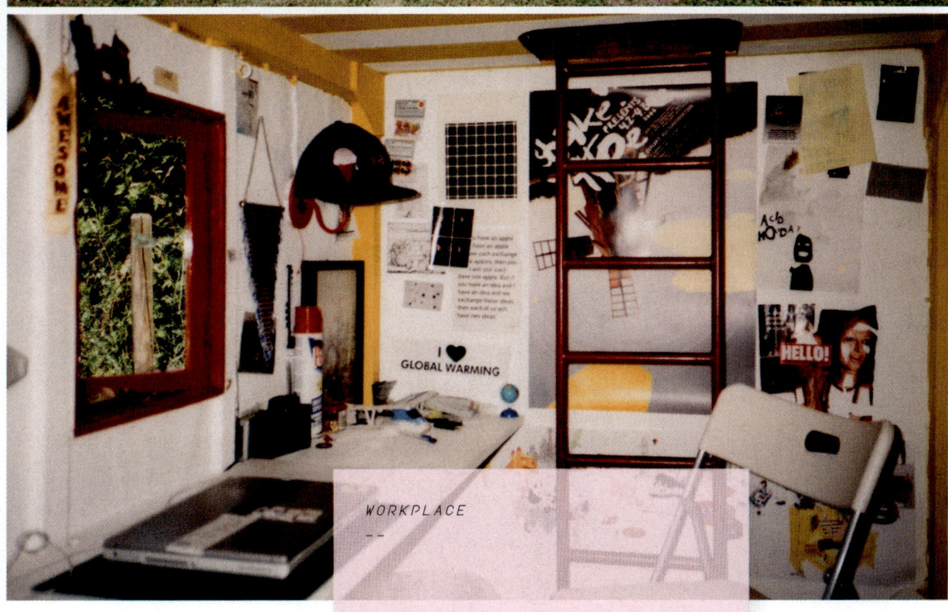
AWESOME
I ♥ GLOBAL WARMING
HELLO!

WORKPLACE
--

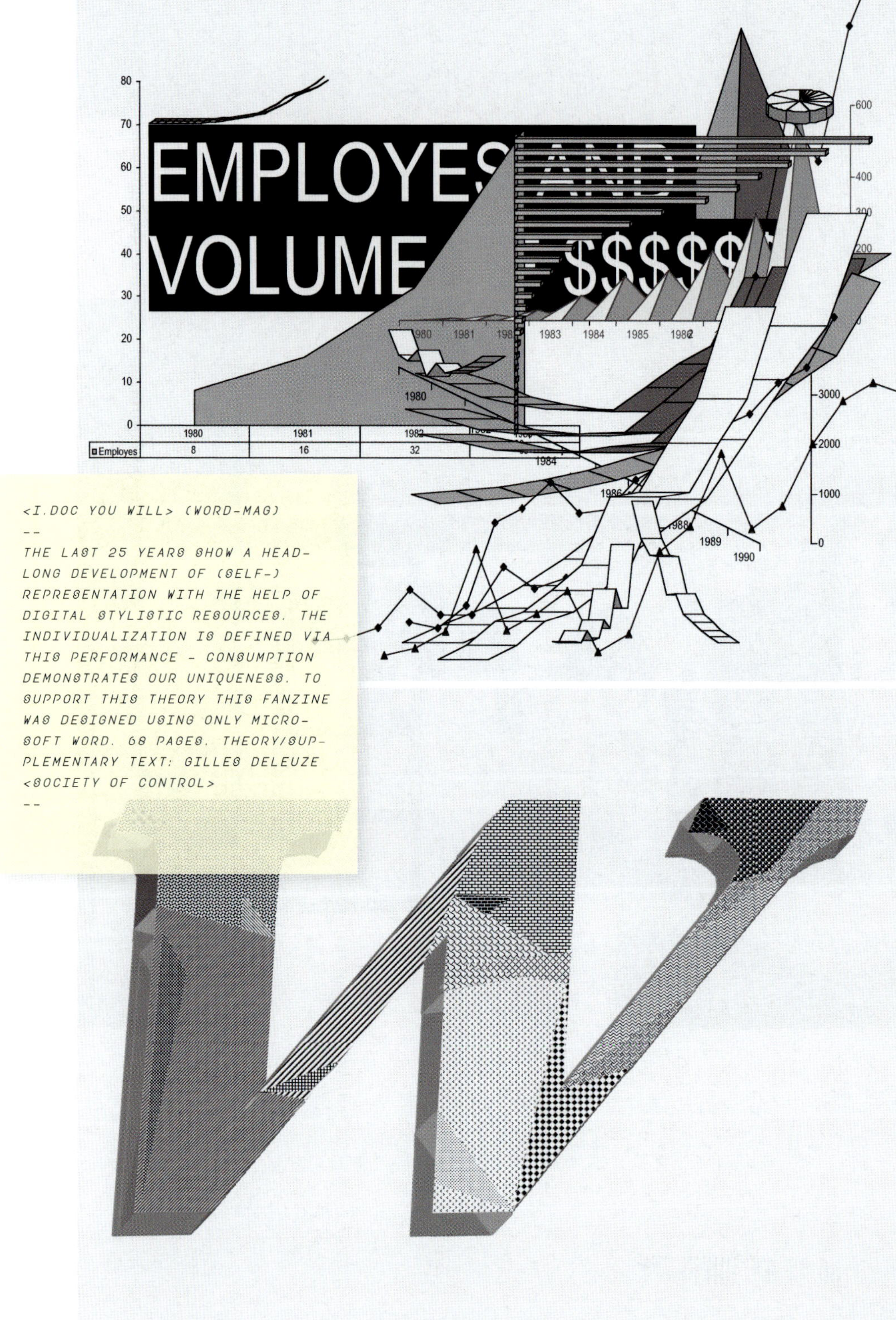
EMPLOYES
VOLUME
AND
$$$$$
80
70
60
50
40
30
20
10
0
600
400
300
200
3000
2000
1000
0
1980
1981
1982
1983
1984
1985
1986
1980
1980
1982
1984
1986
1988
1989
1990
Employes
8
16
32

<I.DOC YOU WILL> (WORD-MAG)
--
THE LAST 25 YEARS SHOW A HEAD-
LONG DEVELOPMENT OF (SELF-)
REPRESENTATION WITH THE HELP OF
DIGITAL STYLISTIC RESOURCES. THE
INDIVIDUALIZATION IS DEFINED VIA
THIS PERFORMANCE - CONSUMPTION
DEMONSTRATES OUR UNIQUENESS. TO
SUPPORT THIS THEORY THIS FANZINE
WAS DESIGNED USING ONLY MICRO-
SOFT WORD. 68 PAGES. THEORY/SUP-
PLEMENTARY TEXT: GILLES DELEUZE
<SOCIETY OF CONTROL>
--

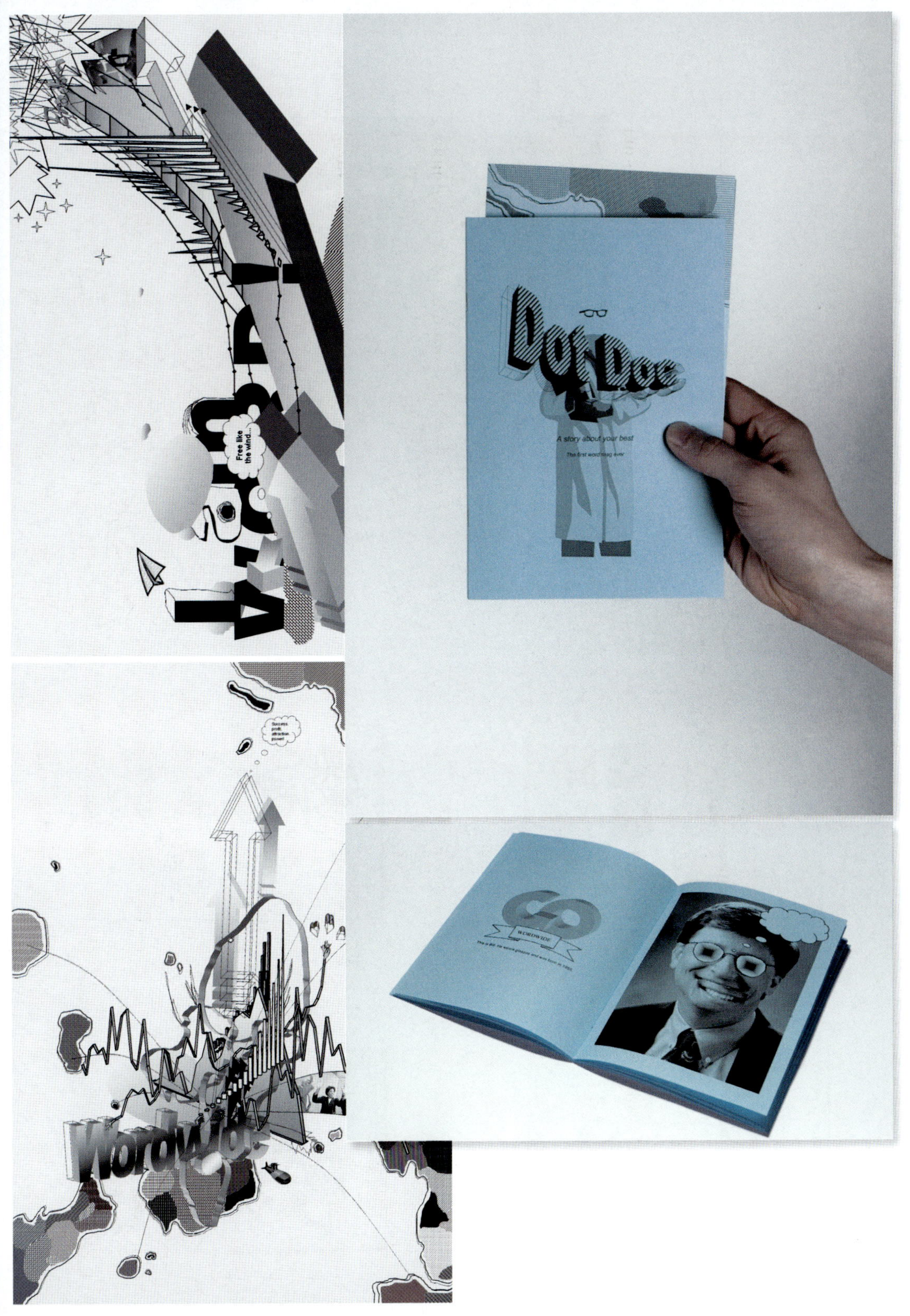
Free like
the wind...
Success
profit
attractive
power!
Worldwide
Doc Doe
A story about your best
The first word mag ever
WORDWIDE

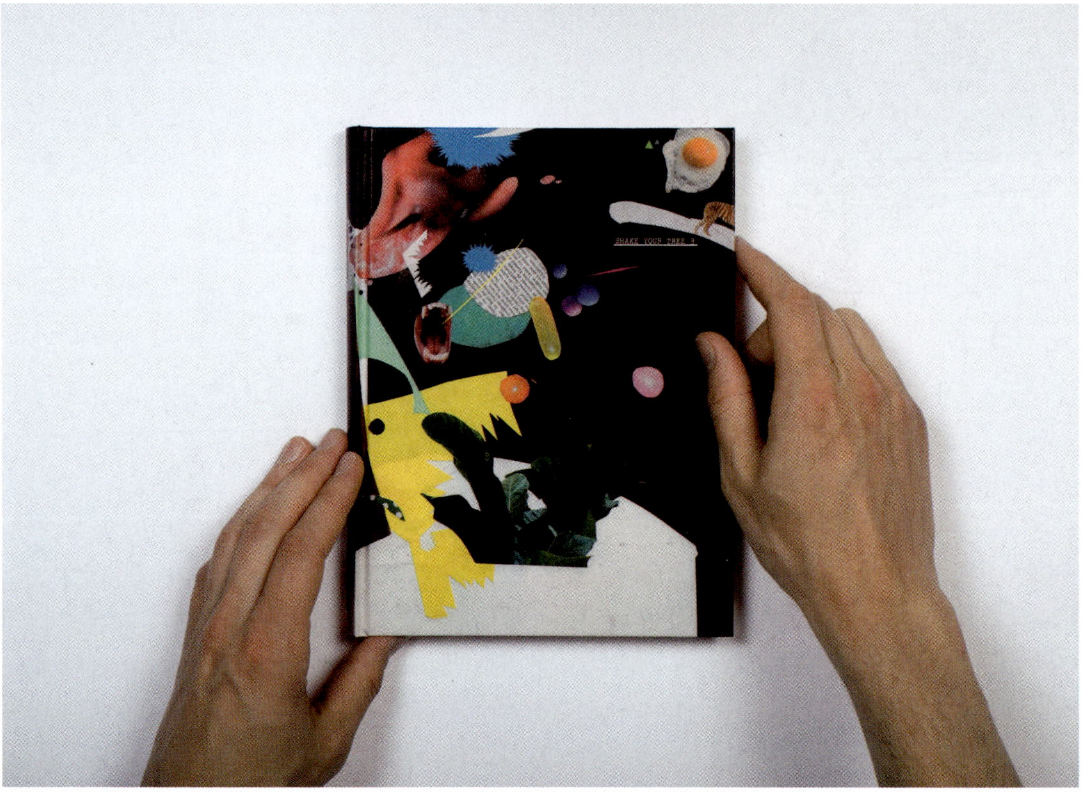

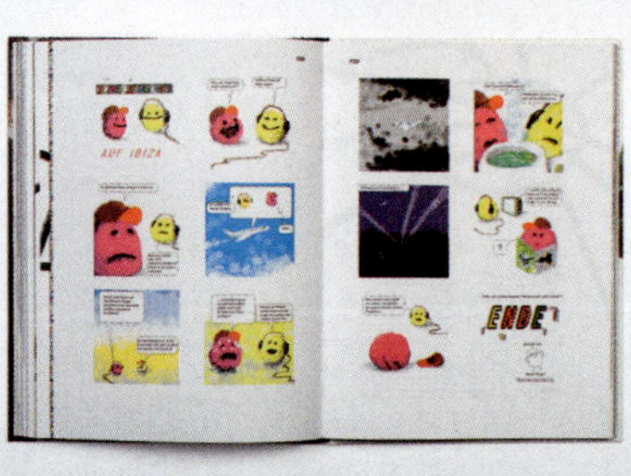
AUF IBIZA
ENDE

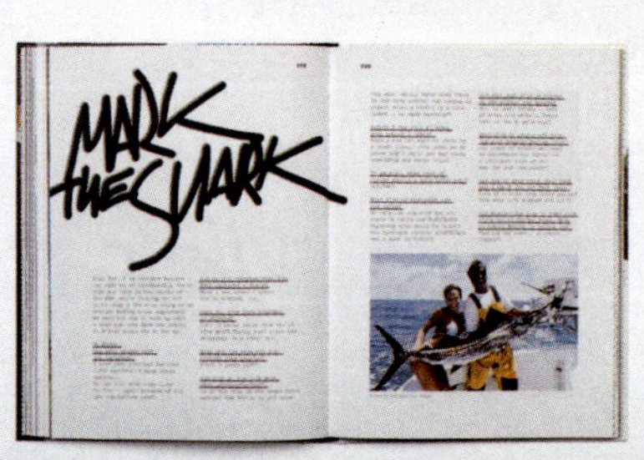
MARK THE SHARK

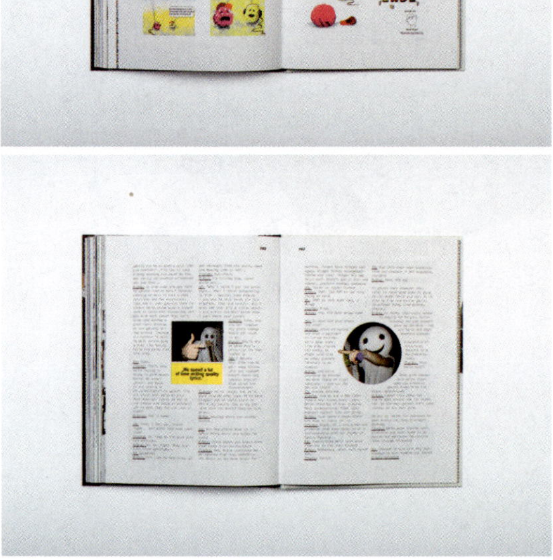

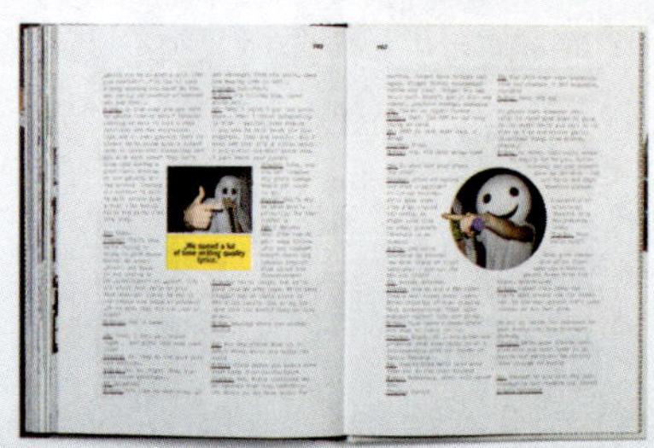

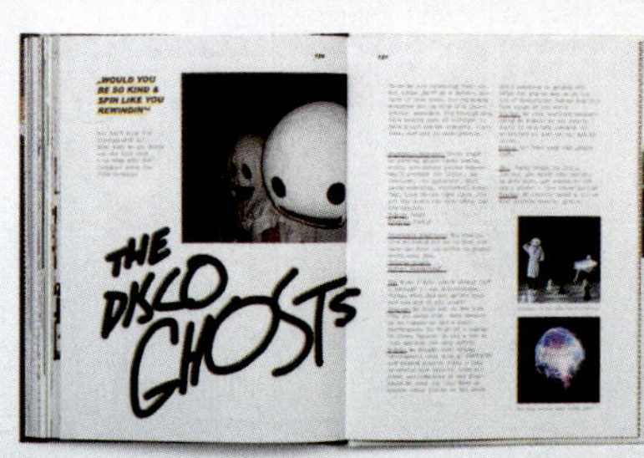
THE DISCO GHOSTS

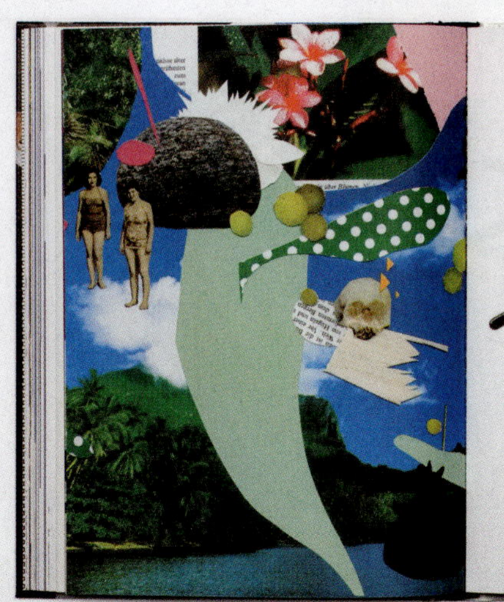

BOOK+FANZINE=SHAKE YOUR TREE #3.
--
THE CURRENT ISSUE OF SHAKE YOUR
TREE, SHAKE YOUR TREE #3, IS
POWERFULLY COLORFUL AND FUNDA-
MENTALLY SURPRISING. ON 200 PAGES
THERE ARE ILLUSTRATIONS, SHORT
STORIES AND HACKNEYED JOKES. THE
DESIGN PLAYS WITH FANZINE STEREO-
TYPES.
--

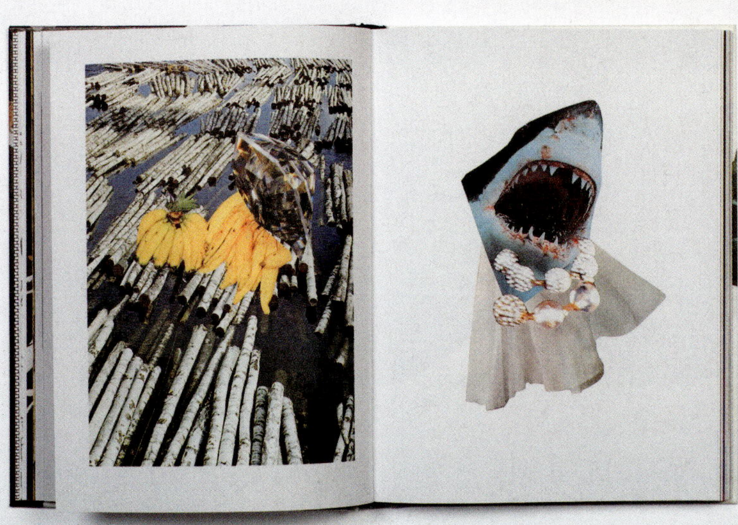

I'M A 26-YEAR-OLD STUDENT OF VISU-
AL COMMUNICATION AT THE UNIVERSITY
OF APPLIED SCIENCE IN PFORZHEIM
(DEPARTMENT OF DESIGN), LIVING IN
KARLSRUHE GERMANY.

IN 2006 I WORKED FOR FINEST /
MAGMA IN KARLSRUHE WITH LARS
HARMSEN AND FLORIAN GÄRTNER. IN
2007 - 2008 I'M GAINING EXPERIENCE
BY WORKING AS A FREELANCER FOR A
COUPLE OF DESIGN AGENCIES ACROSS
THE SOUTH OF GERMANY .

--

WHAT IS GERMAN?

GERMAN IS ACTING UNDER THE CLOAK
OF REASON, MORALITY AND CONVEN-
TION.

WHAT IS GERMAN DESIGN?

FROM A HISTORICAL PERSPECTIVE
GERMAN DESIGN FOR ME IS THE DIS-
PLAYING OF GRANDEUR.

PLEASE DESCRIBE YOUR WORKING
PROCESS.

1. SURVEYING (EMPIRICALLY OR
   BASED ON RESEARCH)
2. EVALUATING AND INTERPRETING
3. VISUALIZING, CONSIDERING AND
   REACTING

WHAT DO YOU AIM TO ACHIEVE WITH
YOUR WORK?

TRANSFORMING <CRAFT> DESIGN
INTO A SET OF INSTRUMENTS FOR THE
SUBTLE SHAPING OF ETHICAL, SOCIAL
AND CORPORATIVE RELEVANCE.

YOU'VE INVITED A FRIEND TO
GERMANY; NAME ONE PLACE THEY
REALLY MUST VISIT AND A QUINT-
ESSENTIAL EXPERIENCE YOU REC-
OMMEND.

GO TO WEEKLY MARKETS AND TRY TO
DO YOUR SHOPPING THERE IN THE COL-
ORS OF THE LOCAL LANGUAGE.

WHAT IS THE MOST IMPORTANT
LESSON YOU HAVE LEARNED IN YOUR
PROFESSION SO FAR?

EVERYTHING THAT I MAKE MANIFEST
WITH GRAPHIC MOLDING IS IN SOME
WAY A CONTENTUAL OFFER OF MEAN-
ING. IT'S IMPORTANT HERE WHETHER
THE MEANING TENDS TO REPRESENT
NONSENSE INSTEAD. WORKING ANALYTI-
CALLY IS EVERYTHING!

--

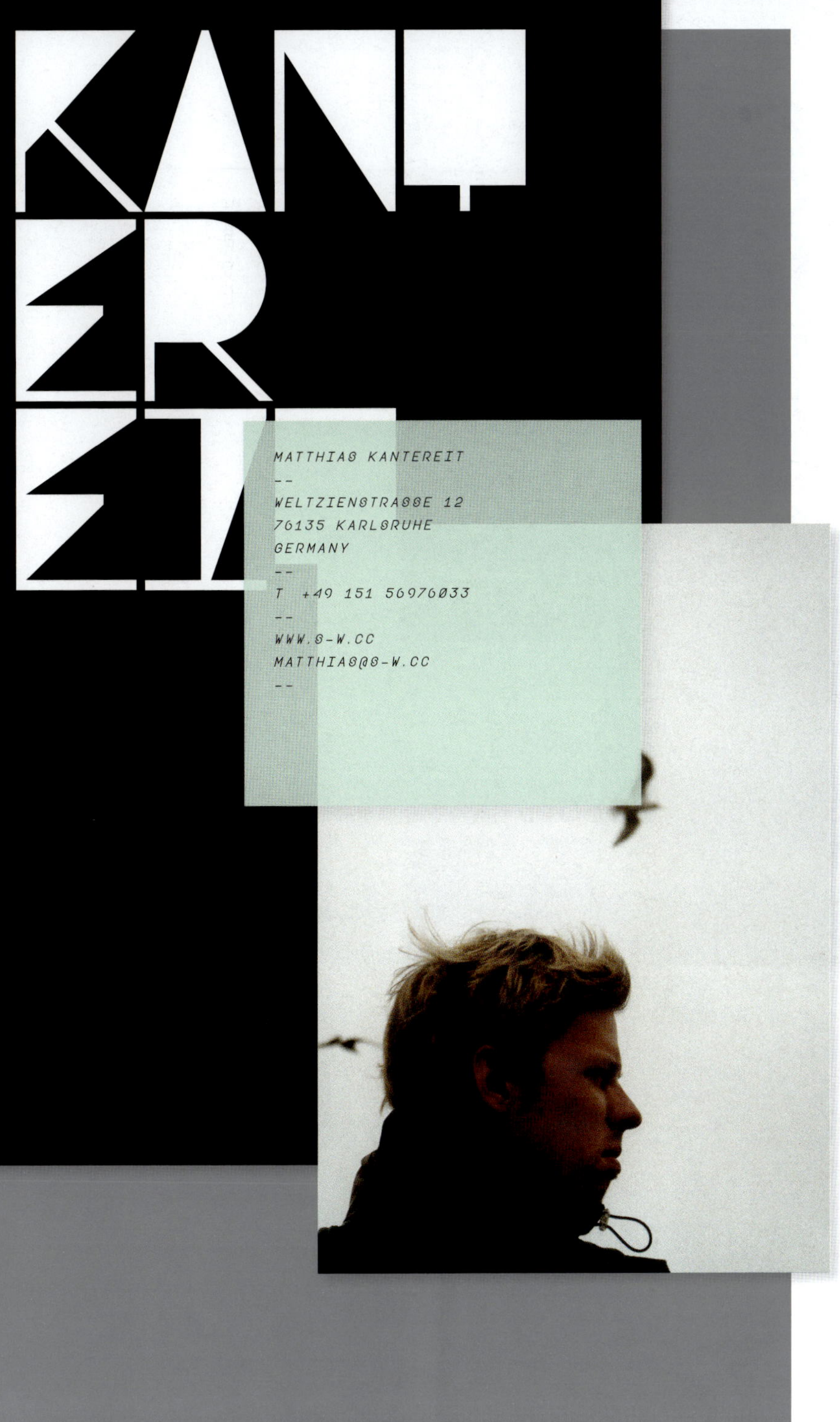

KANTEREIT
MATTHIAS KANTEREIT
--
WELTZIENSTRASSE 12
76135 KARLSRUHE
GERMANY
--
T +49 151 56976033
--
WWW.S-W.CC
MATTHIAS@S-W.CC
--

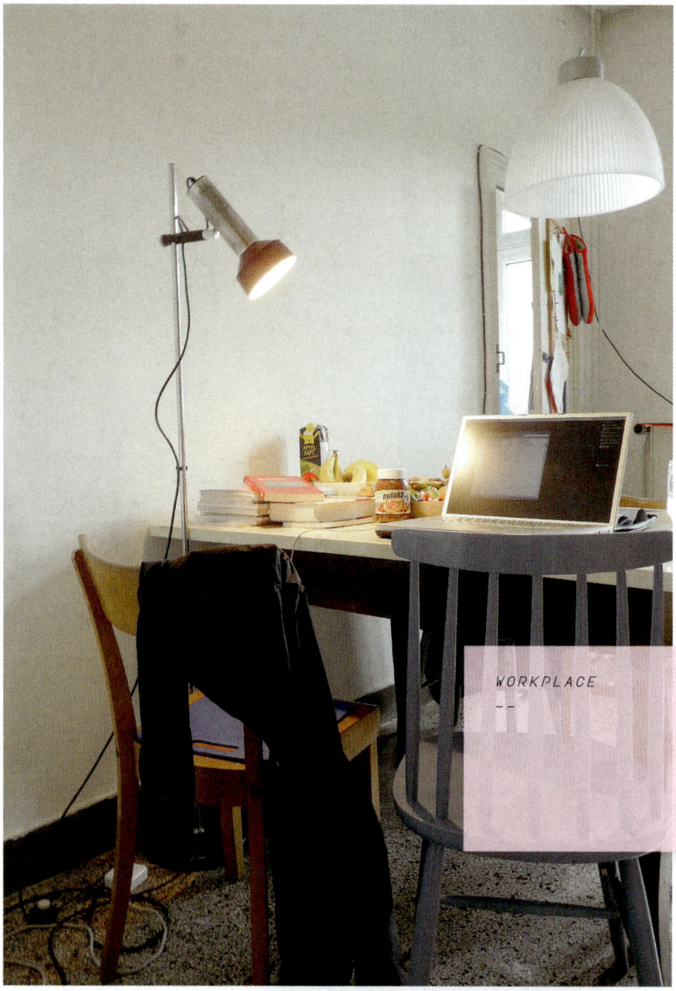

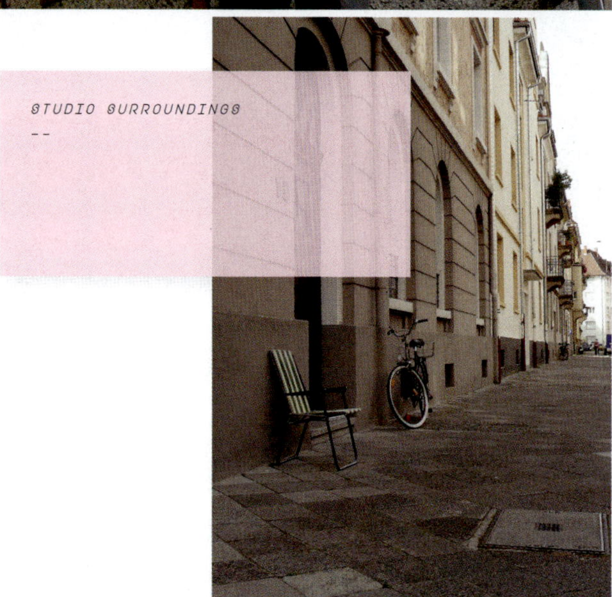
WORKPLACE
--

STUDIO SURROUNDINGS
--

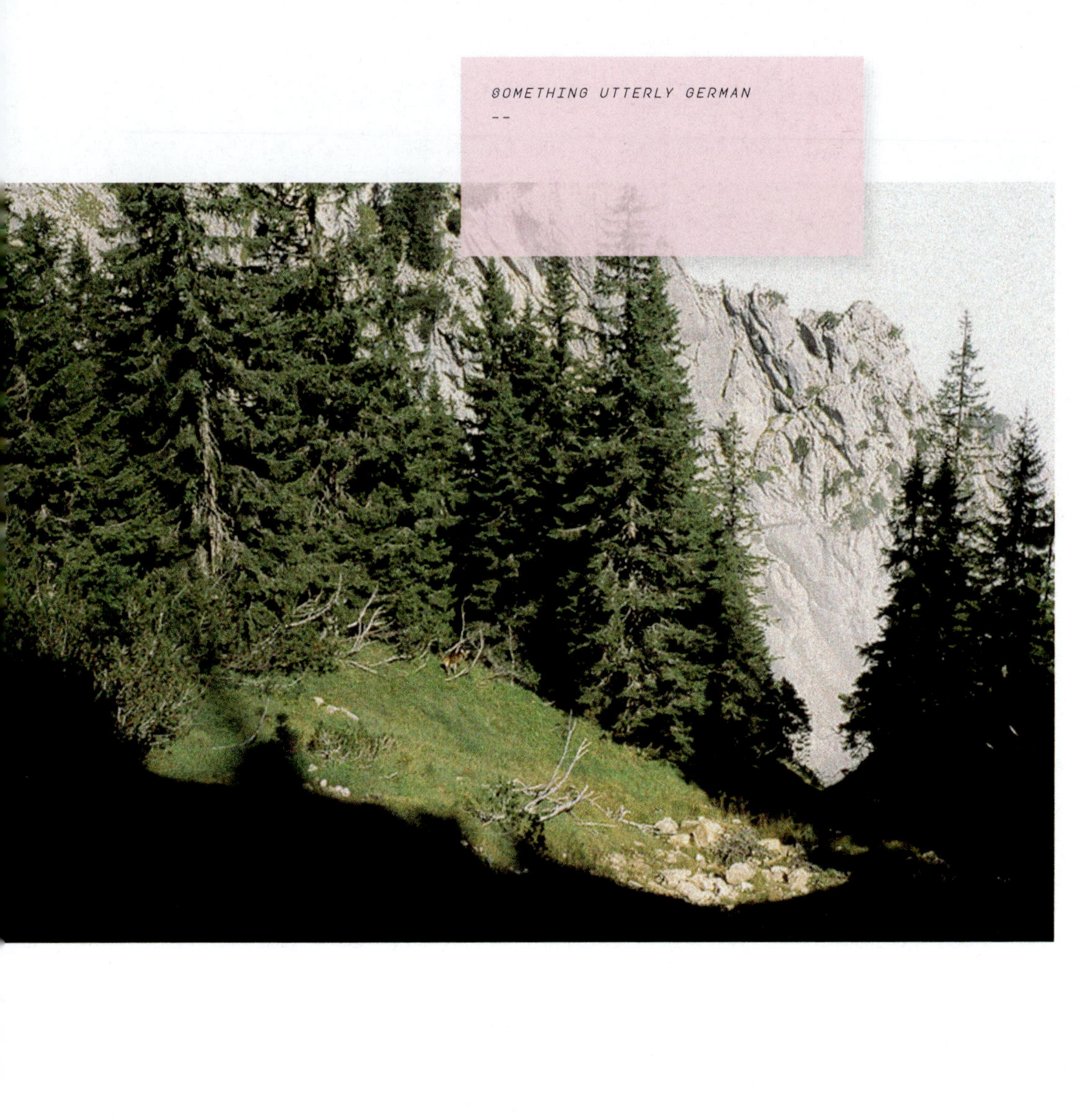

SOMETHING UTTERLY GERMAN
--

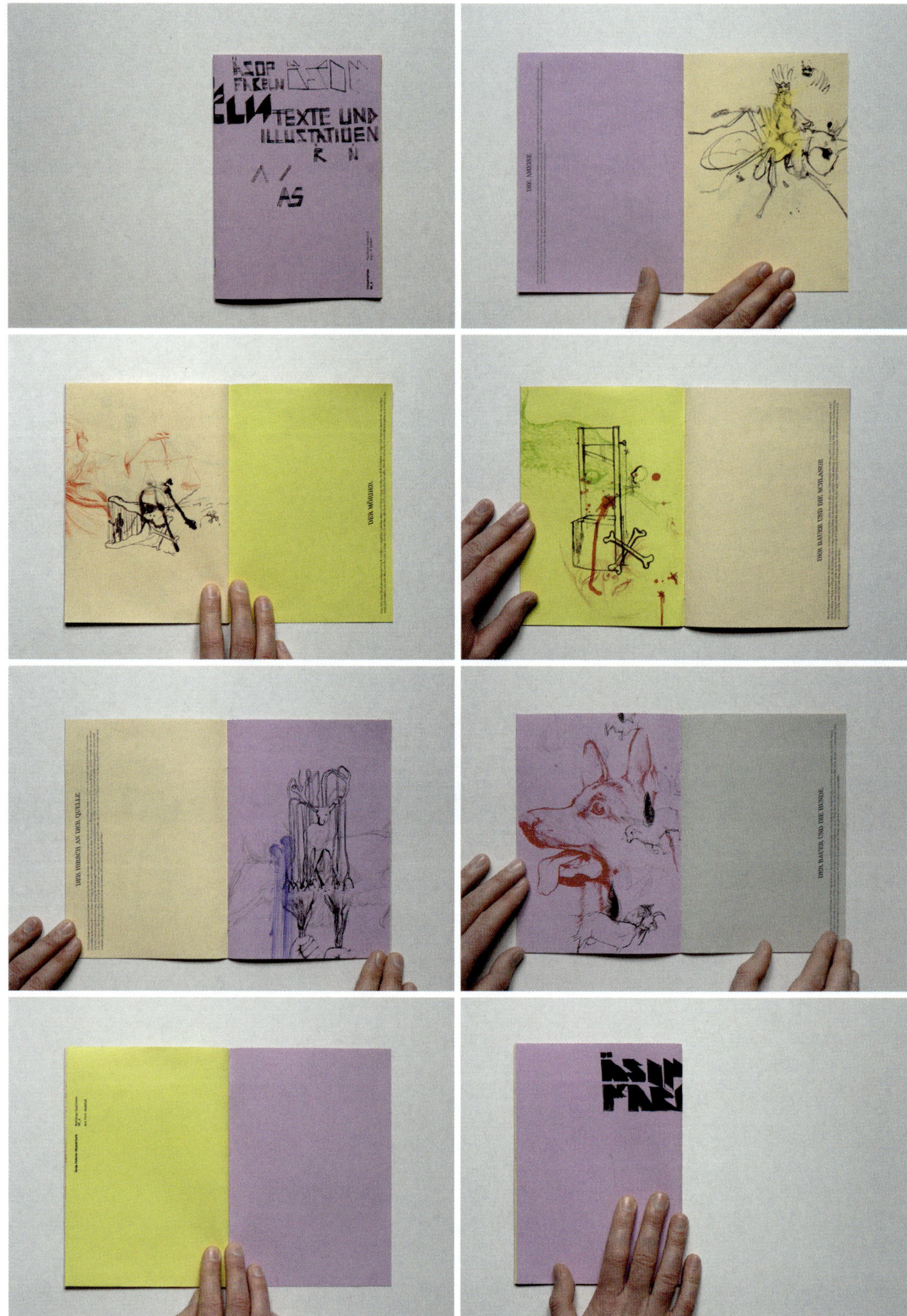

ÄSOP FABELN (AESOP'S FABLES)
--
AN ILLUSTRATED INTERPRETATION
OF THE OLD GREEK FABLES OF AESOP.
THE FABLES DATE FROM AROUND
600 BC.
--

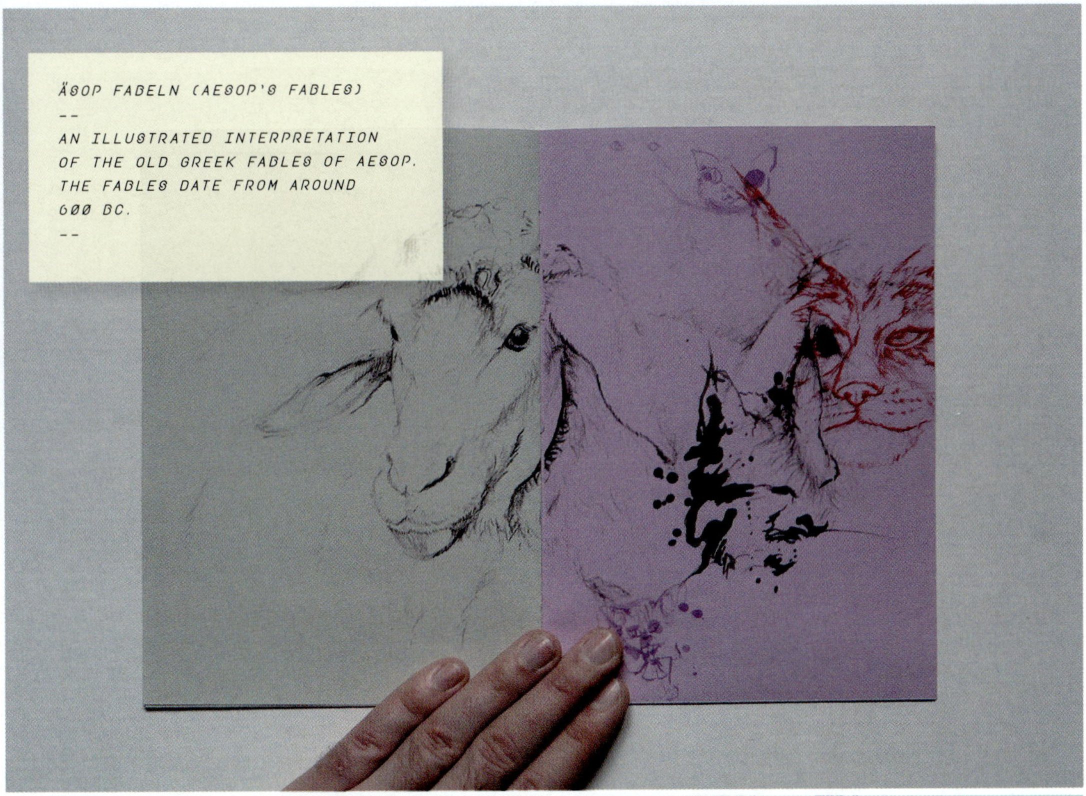

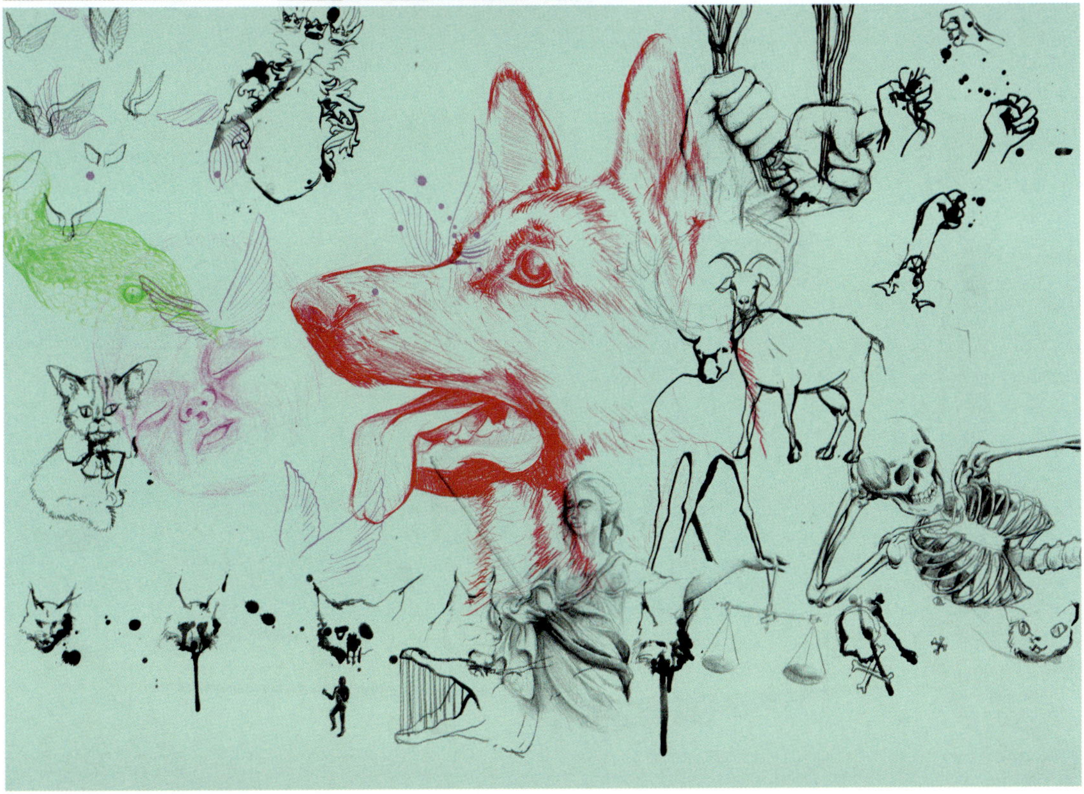

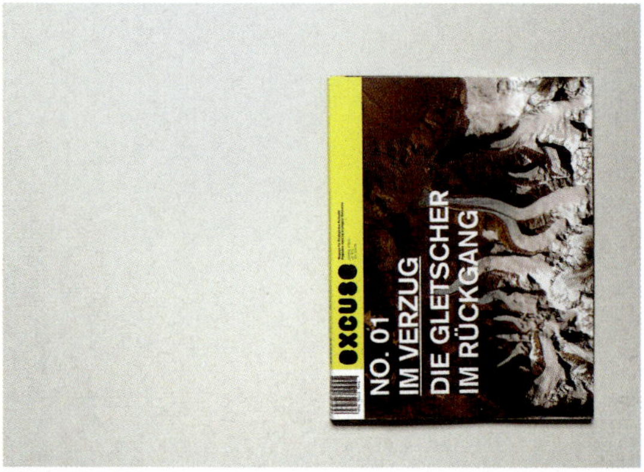

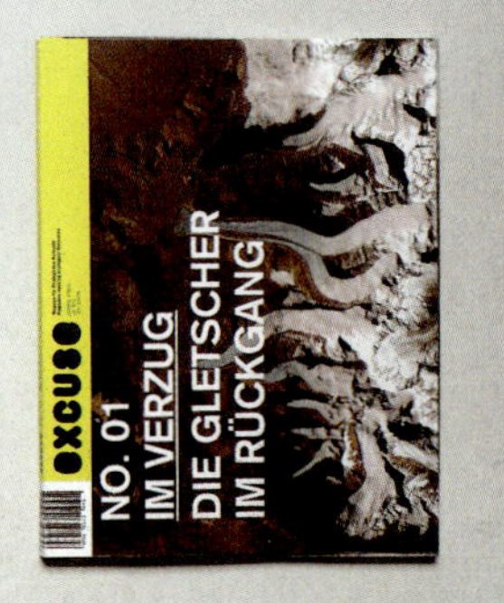

excuse
NO. 01
IM VERZUG
DIE GLETSCHER
IM RÜCKGANG

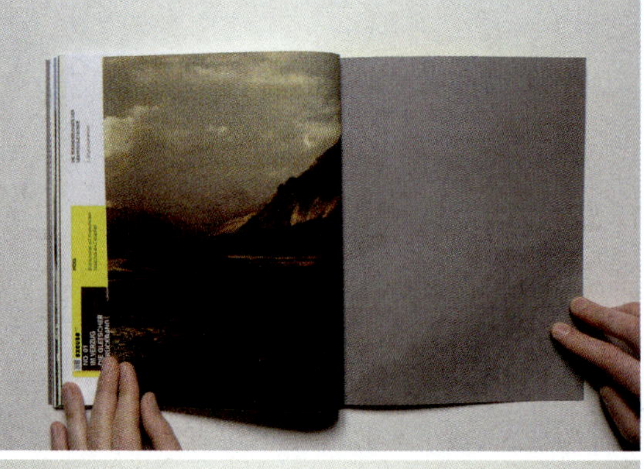

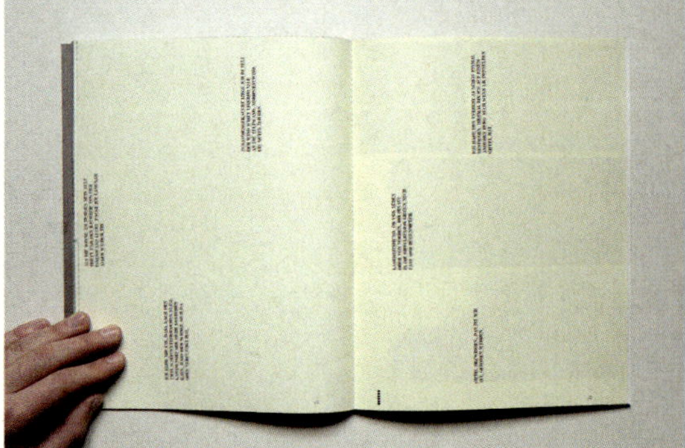

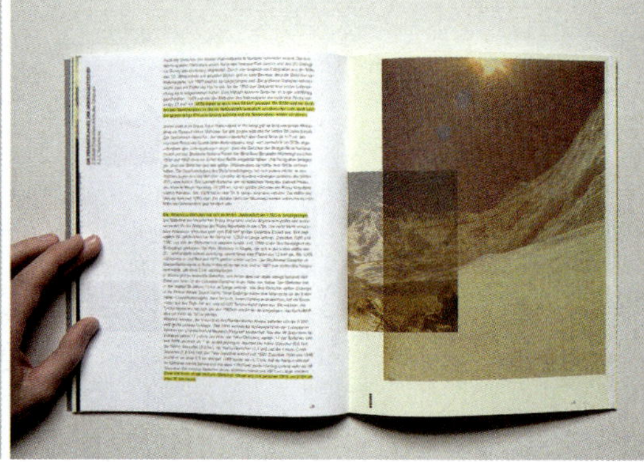

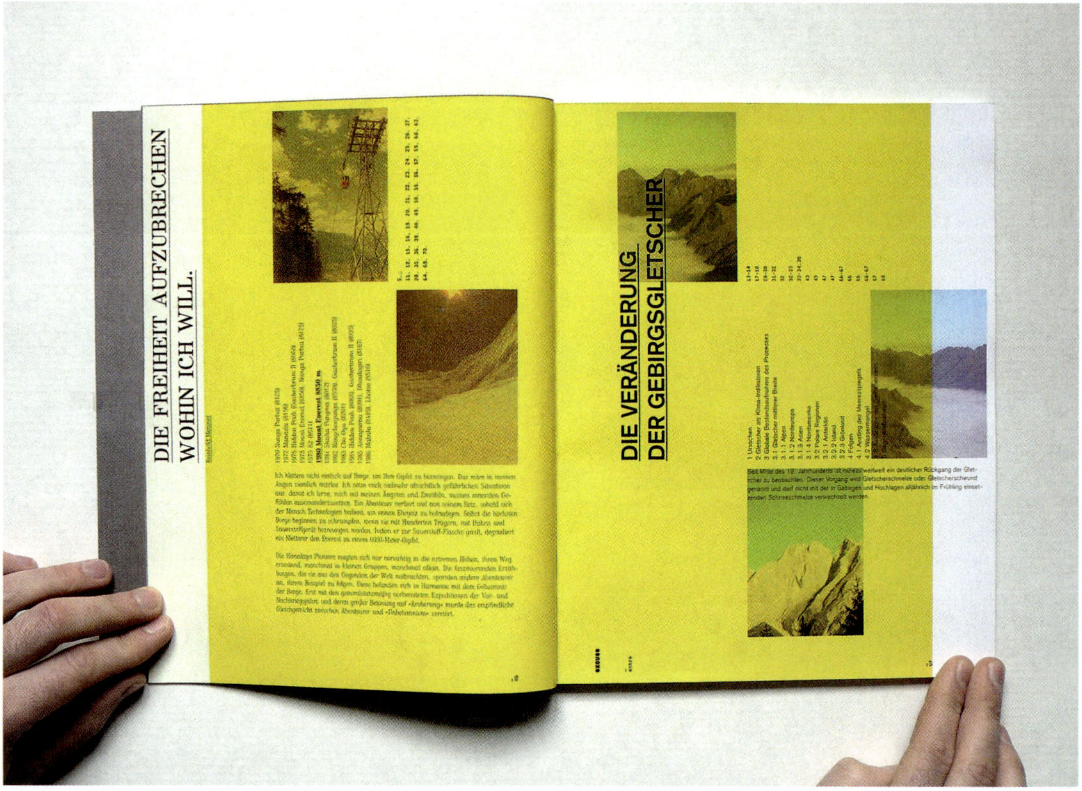

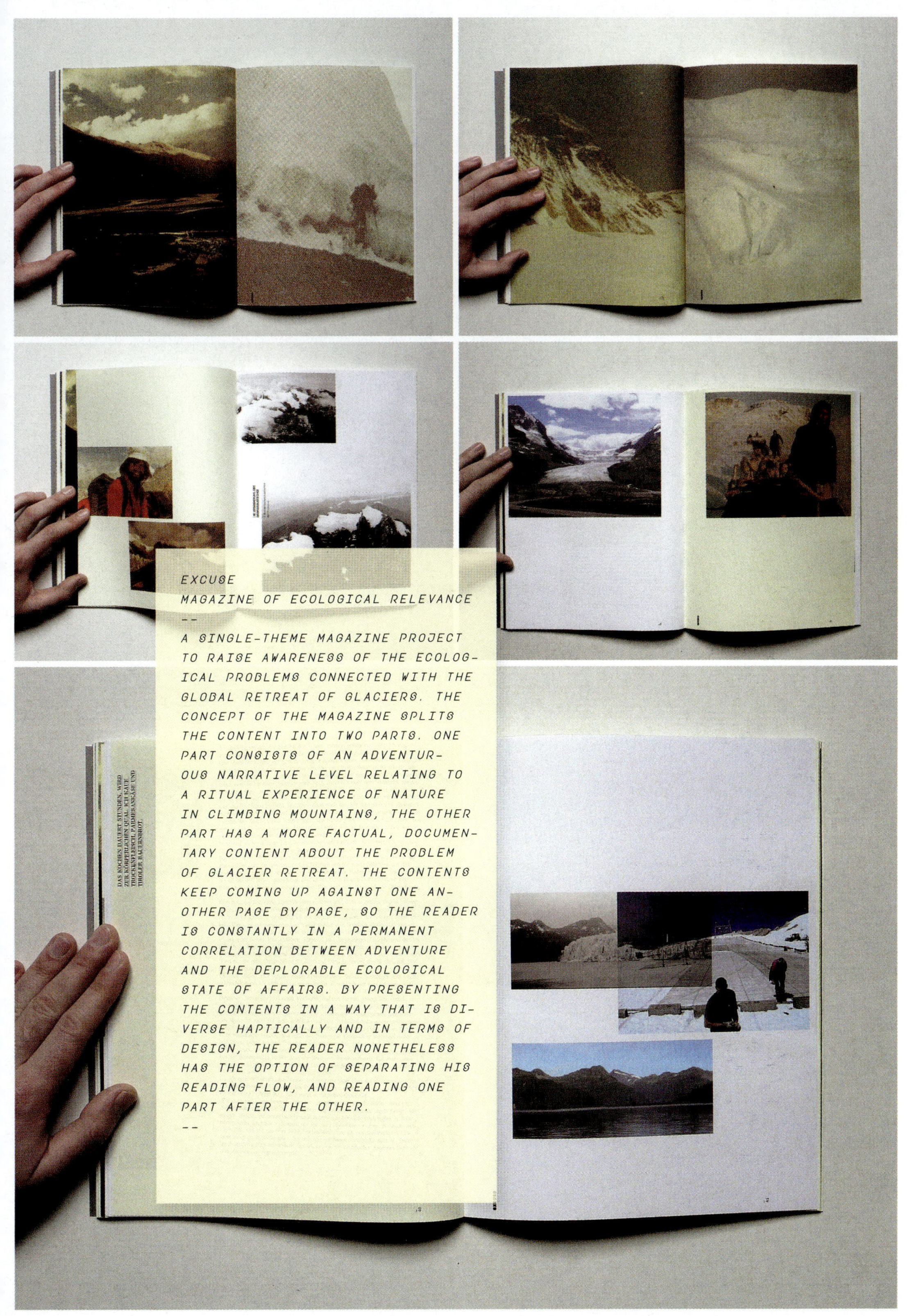
EXCUSE
MAGAZINE OF ECOLOGICAL RELEVANCE
--
A SINGLE-THEME MAGAZINE PROJECT
TO RAISE AWARENESS OF THE ECOLOG-
ICAL PROBLEMS CONNECTED WITH THE
GLOBAL RETREAT OF GLACIERS. THE
CONCEPT OF THE MAGAZINE SPLITS
THE CONTENT INTO TWO PARTS. ONE
PART CONSISTS OF AN ADVENTUR-
OUS NARRATIVE LEVEL RELATING TO
A RITUAL EXPERIENCE OF NATURE
IN CLIMBING MOUNTAINS, THE OTHER
PART HAS A MORE FACTUAL, DOCUMEN-
TARY CONTENT ABOUT THE PROBLEM
OF GLACIER RETREAT. THE CONTENTS
KEEP COMING UP AGAINST ONE AN-
OTHER PAGE BY PAGE, SO THE READER
IS CONSTANTLY IN A PERMANENT
CORRELATION BETWEEN ADVENTURE
AND THE DEPLORABLE ECOLOGICAL
STATE OF AFFAIRS. BY PRESENTING
THE CONTENTS IN A WAY THAT IS DI-
VERSE HAPTICALLY AND IN TERMS OF
DESIGN, THE READER NONETHELESS
HAS THE OPTION OF SEPARATING HIS
READING FLOW, AND READING ONE
PART AFTER THE OTHER.
--

FRÜHTAU
LIFE CULTURE INITIATIVE
--
THIS IS A MAGAZINE PROJECT TO
STRENGTHEN THE COMMUNICATION
NETWORK OF GERMANY'S NATURE-LOV-
ERS (NATURFREUNDE DEUTSCHLANDS).
WITH THIS MINI-MAGAZINE THEY RE-
CEIVE A LEVEL OF PUBLICATION THAT
CAN BE USED TO ATTRACT MEMBERS.
THE LOW-BUDGET MAGAZINE CAN BE
SLIPPED INTO SPECIALIST PUBLICA-
TIONS AND FINDS READERS IN THEIR
PERSONAL FIELD OF INTEREST. THUS
THIS SAMPLE ISSUE IS DEVOTED TO
THE THEME OF ARCHITECTURE AND
THE PHENOMENON OF ORNAMENTATION,
AND AS AN INSERT IN ARCHITEC-
TURE MAGAZINES IT CAN AWAKEN AN
INTEREST IN NATURE AND ECOLOGY
AMONG THE READERS.
--

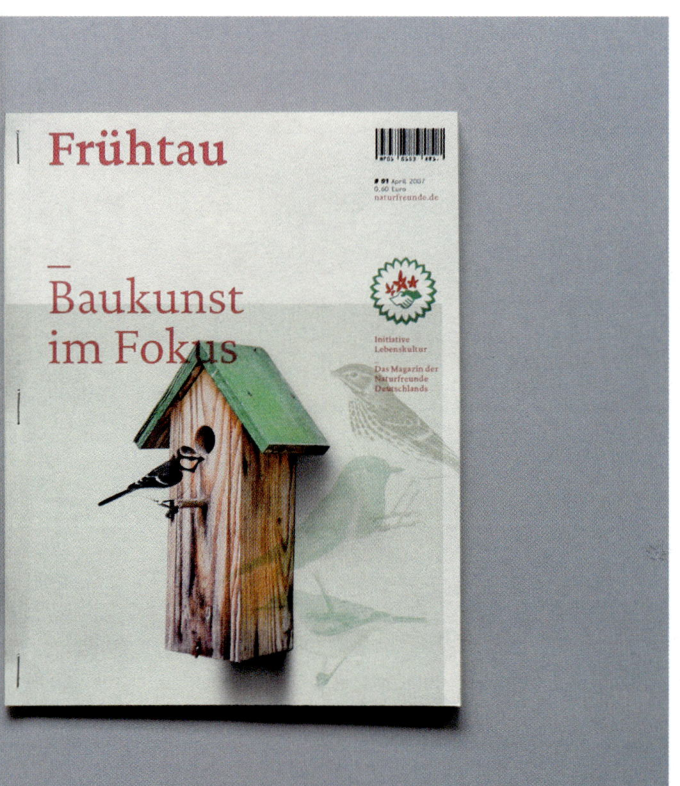

Frühtau
01 April 2007
0,60 Euro
naturfreunde.de
Baukunst
im Fokus
Initiative
Lebenskultur
Das Magazin der
Naturfreunde
Deutschlands

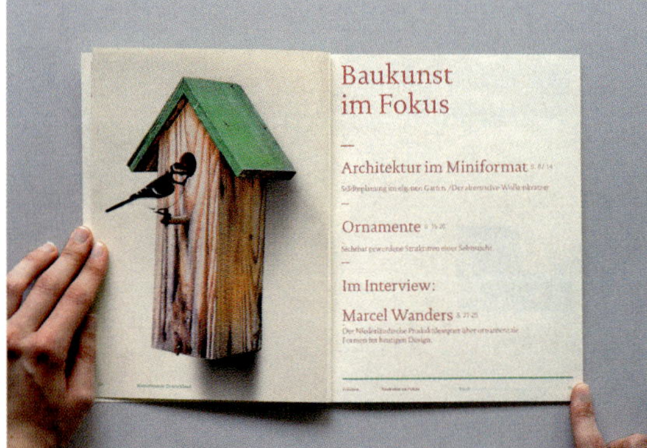

Baukunst
im Fokus
—
Architektur im Miniformat
—
Ornamente
—
Im Interview:
Marcel Wanders

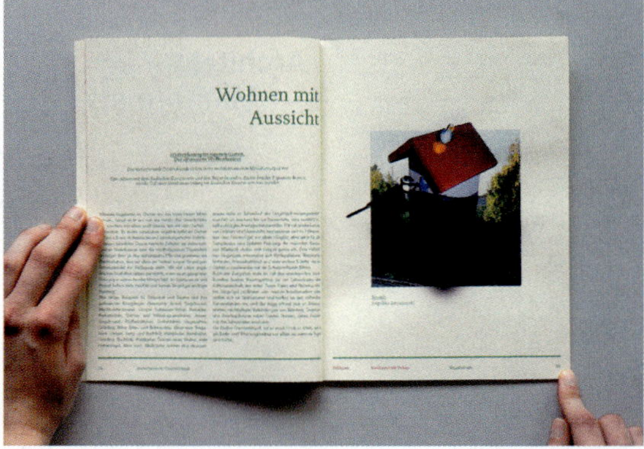

Wohnen mit
Aussicht

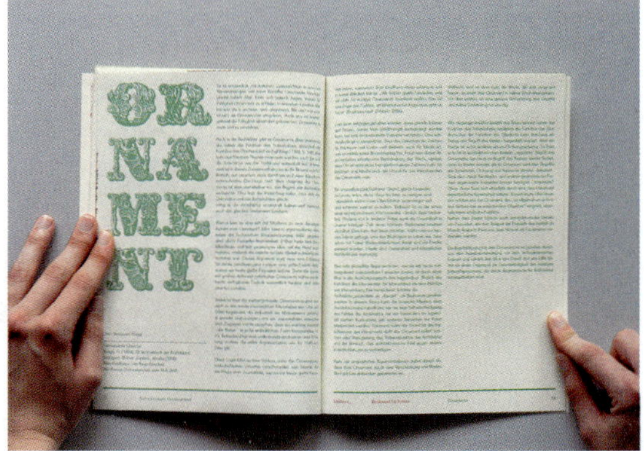

OR
NA
ME
NT

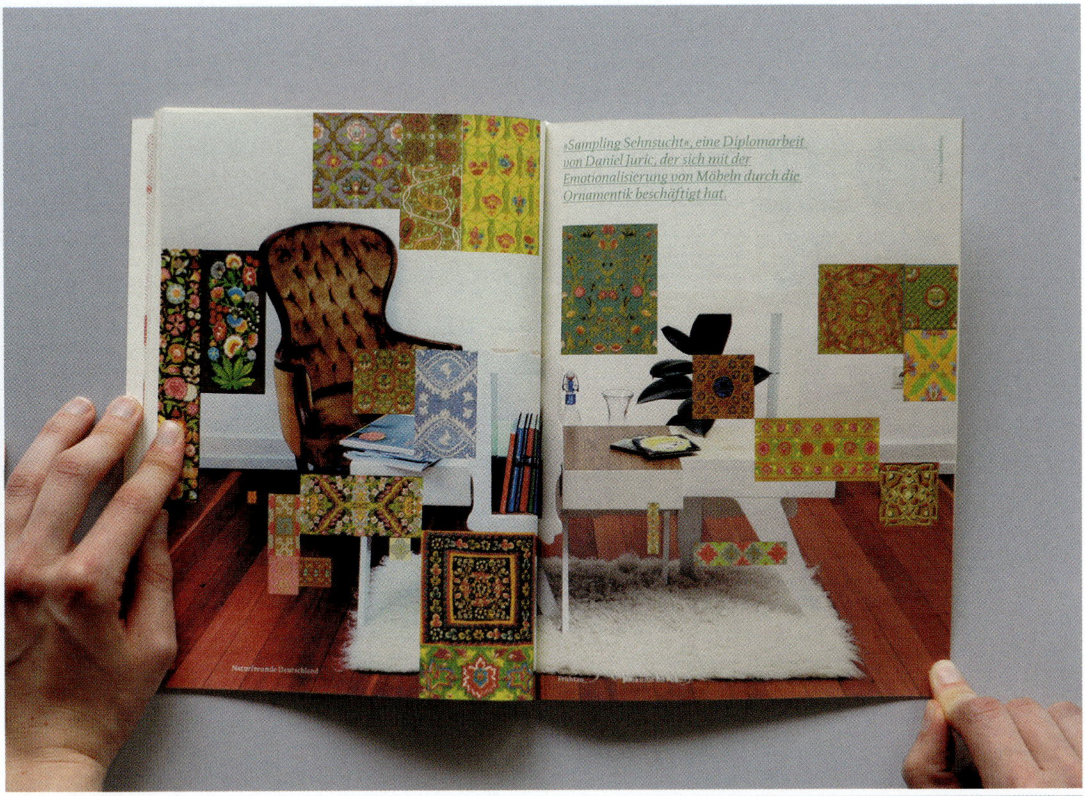

«Sampling Sehnsucht», eine Diplomarbeit
von Daniel Juric, der sich mit der
Emotionalisierung von Möbeln durch die
Ornamentik beschäftigt hat.

Naturfreunde Deutschland

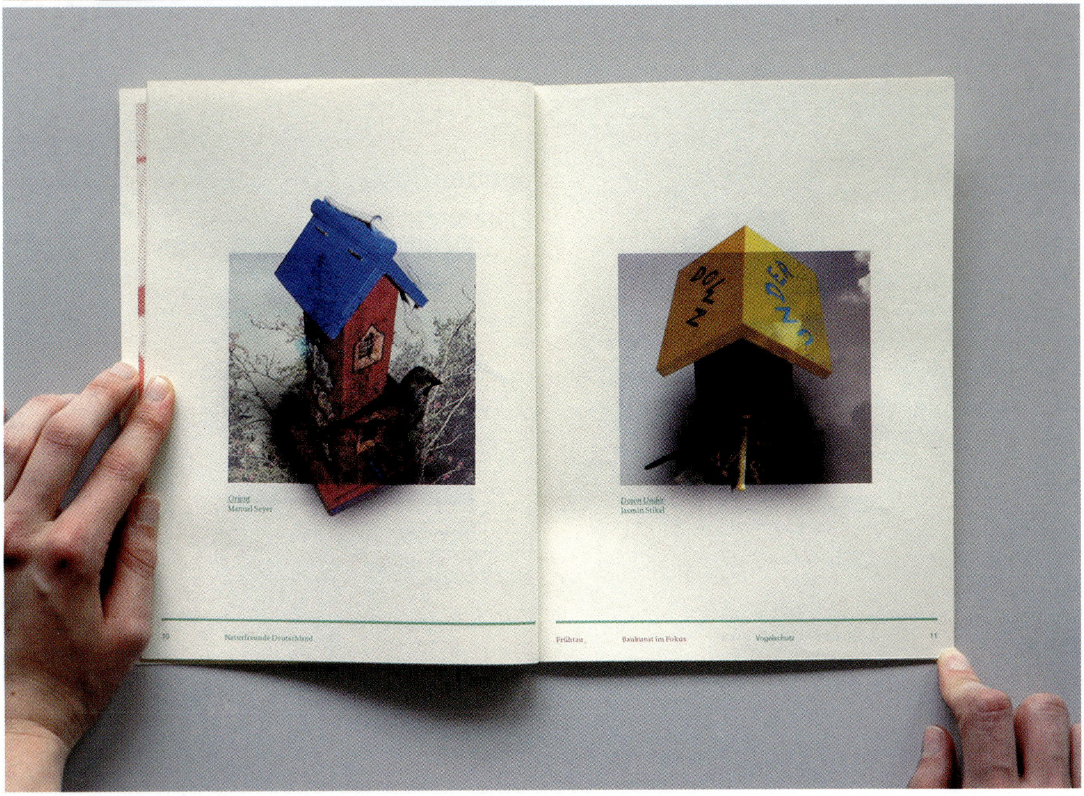

Orient
Manuel Seyer

Down Under
Jasmin Stikel

DOWN
UNDER

10   Naturfreunde Deutschland   Frühtau   Baukunst im Fokus   Vogelschutz   11

BORN IN BRESLAU [WROCLAW], POLAND ON FEBRUARY 1ST, 1978, SEBASTIAN ONUFSZAK IS A GERMAN VISUAL ARTIST FOCUSING ON PRINT, INTERACTIVE MEDIA AND MOTION GRAPHICS. SINCE 2002 HE HAS BEEN WORKING AS AN ART DIRECTOR AND FREELANCER FOR AN INTERNATIONAL RANGE OF HIGH-END CLIENTS INCLUDING MTV, MERCEDES, REDBULL AND SONYERICSSON. AS WELL AS THIS HE IS RENOWNED FOR HIS EXPERIMENTAL LIVE VISUALS WHICH SUPPORTED FUNKSTÖRUNG, MOUSE ON MARS, MICHAEL FAKESCH AND MANY MORE. HIS WORK HAS BEEN FEATURED IN NUMEROUS PUBLICATIONS AND EXHIBITIONS WORLDWIDE. HE IS FOUNDER OF THE WELL-KNOWN ARTISTS' COLLECTIVE <PROPAGANDABÜRO>. CURRENTLY HE IS LIVING IN ROSENHEIM, GERMANY AND WORKING FOR PARASOL ISLAND, AN ANIMATION AND DESIGN STUDIO, AS CREATIVE DIRECTOR.

--

WHAT IS GERMAN DESIGN?

IF YOU LOOK AT THE PAST, THERE GERMAN GRAPHIC DESIGNERS WERE ALWAYS VERY TECHNICAL AND FUNCTIONAL. IN THE FIRST PART OF THE LAST CENTURY ARTWORKS OF THE BAUHAUS WERE BASED ON GEOMETRICAL SHAPES. PROJECTS LIKE THE VISUAL CONCEPT FOR THE OLYMPIC GAMES IN 1972 OR THE CORPORATE IDENTITY FOR BRAUN AND BMW BY OTL AICHER, ONE OF THE MOST FAMOUS GRAPHIC ARTISTS IN GERMANY, WERE ABSOLUTELY MINIMALIST AND REDUCED TO THE POINT. GERMAN DESIGNS ARE STRUCTURED AND WELL THOUGHT-OUT.

DESCRIBE YOUR WORKING PROCESS.

EVERYTHING STARTS OF COURSE WITH A GOOD CONCEPT. WHEN I DON'T HAVE AN IDEA, I TRY TO DERIVE INSPIRATION FROM MY ENVIRONMENT. I READ AN INTERESTING BOOK, VIEW THE LATEST FASHION MAGAZINES OR WALK THROUGH THE CITY WATCHING PEOPLE DOING THEIR THING. A GOOD MANY TIMES IT IS THE DETAILS THAT LEAD TO A BRILLIANT IDEA. ON THE ONE HAND I LOVE TO EXPERIMENT WITH SHAPES, LINES, PLANES AND COLORS USING MY COMPUTER AND CREATING ABSTRACT IDEAS. IT IS MY LITTLE LABORATORY, WHERE I CAN DESIGN WITHOUT ANY GUIDELINES AND WHERE I HAVE THE FREEDOM TO BE ARTISTIC WITHOUT ANY SET OBJECTIVE. ON THE OTHER HAND I START WITH A PARTICULAR IDEA. FOR EXAMPLE I DESIGN WITHOUT ANY EXAMPLES, BUT DURING THE PROCESS I KEEP LOOKING FOR KEY WORDS I MIGHT THEN INTEGRATE IN A GRAPHICAL WAY.

WHAT DO YOU AIM TO ACHIEVE WITH YOUR WORK?

EVERY TIME I START A PROJECT I ATTEMPT TO CREATE SOMETHING NEW, NOT TO STICK TO OLD ATTITUDES. MY FIRST STEP IS TO FIGURE OUT WHAT I COULD OPTIMIZE AND WHICH NEW INSPIRATIONS I COULD INCLUDE. MOST OF THE TIME IT'S REALLY TRICKY BECAUSE YOU ALWAYS TAKE THE EASIEST WAY OF SOLVING A DESIGN CHALLENGE BY USING THE SAME TECHNIQUES OR IDEAS AS IN A PREVIOUS PROJECT. SO WHAT I AIM TO ACHIEVE IS THAT EVERY PROJECT I START SHOULD LOOK DIFFERENT FROM ANY OTHER.

YOU'VE INVITED A FRIEND TO GERMANY; NAME ONE PLACE THEY REALLY MUST VISIT AND A QUINTESSENTIAL EXPERIENCE YOU RECOMMEND.

FIRST OF ALL, TRAVEL TO SOUTHERN GERMANY, MAYBE MUNICH, AND ORDER A GOOD BAVARIAN BEER! SECOND, TRAVEL TO EASTERN GERMANY, PERHAPS BERLIN, AND GO OUT FOR A NIGHT OUT AT ALL THOSE DIFFERENT CLUBS. FINALLY, TRAVEL TO WESTERN GERMANY, PROBABLY COLOGNE, AND WATCH YOUR ASS IF YOU'RE NOT GAY! THESE ARE MY PERSONAL EXPERIENCES.

WHAT IS THE MOST IMPORTANT LESSON YOU HAVE LEARNED IN YOUR PROFESSION SO FAR?

BE PATIENT, BUT NOT LAZY. GET INSPIRED BY OTHERS, BUT DON'T COPY ANYONE. BE A GOOD TEAM-PLAYER, BUT GO YOUR OWN WAY.

--

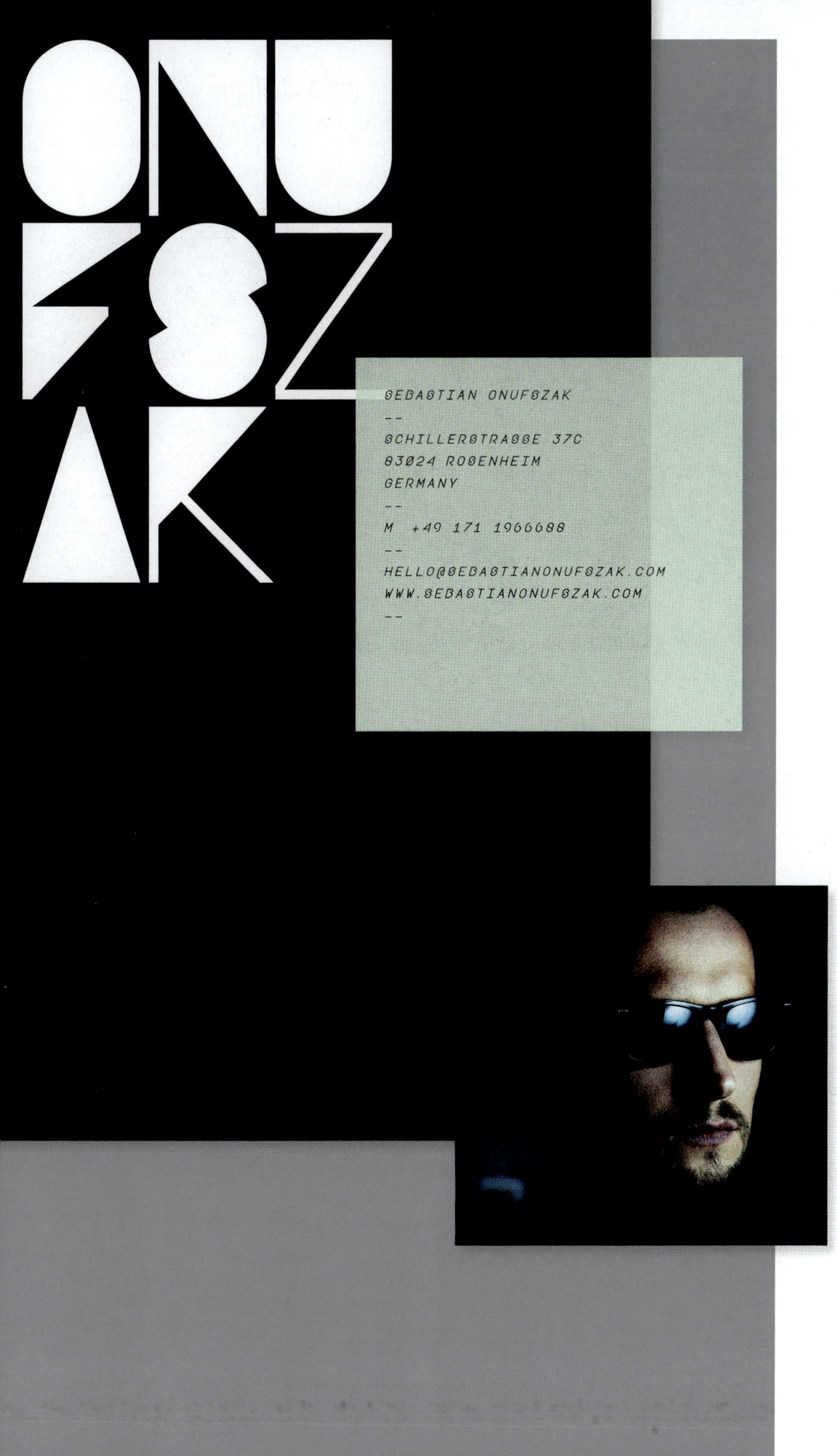

SEBASTIAN ONUFSZAK

--

SCHILLERSTRASSE 37C
83024 ROSENHEIM
GERMANY

--

M +49 171 1966688

--

HELLO@SEBASTIANONUFSZAK.COM
WWW.SEBASTIANONUFSZAK.COM

--

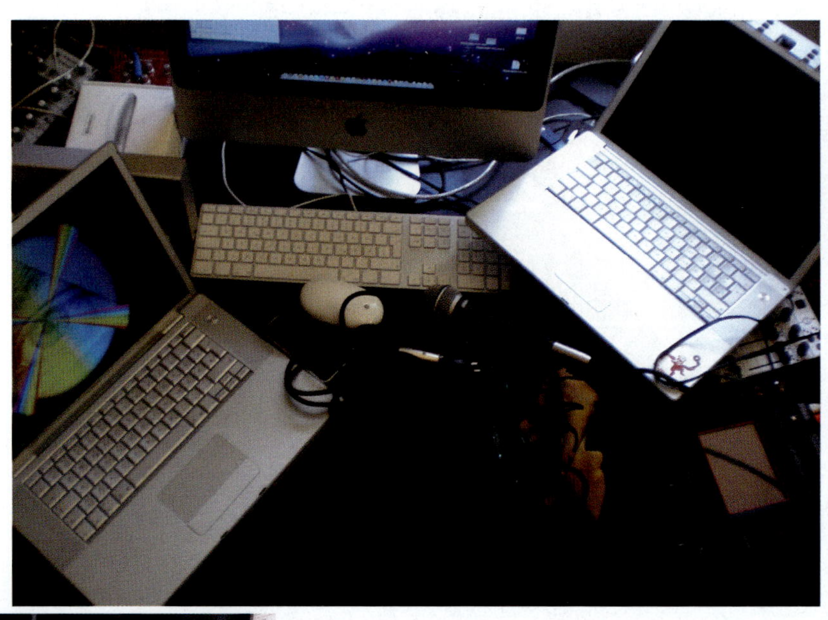

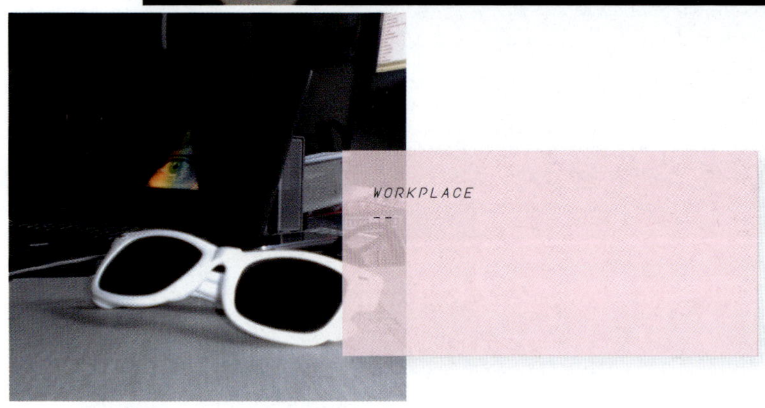
WORKPLACE

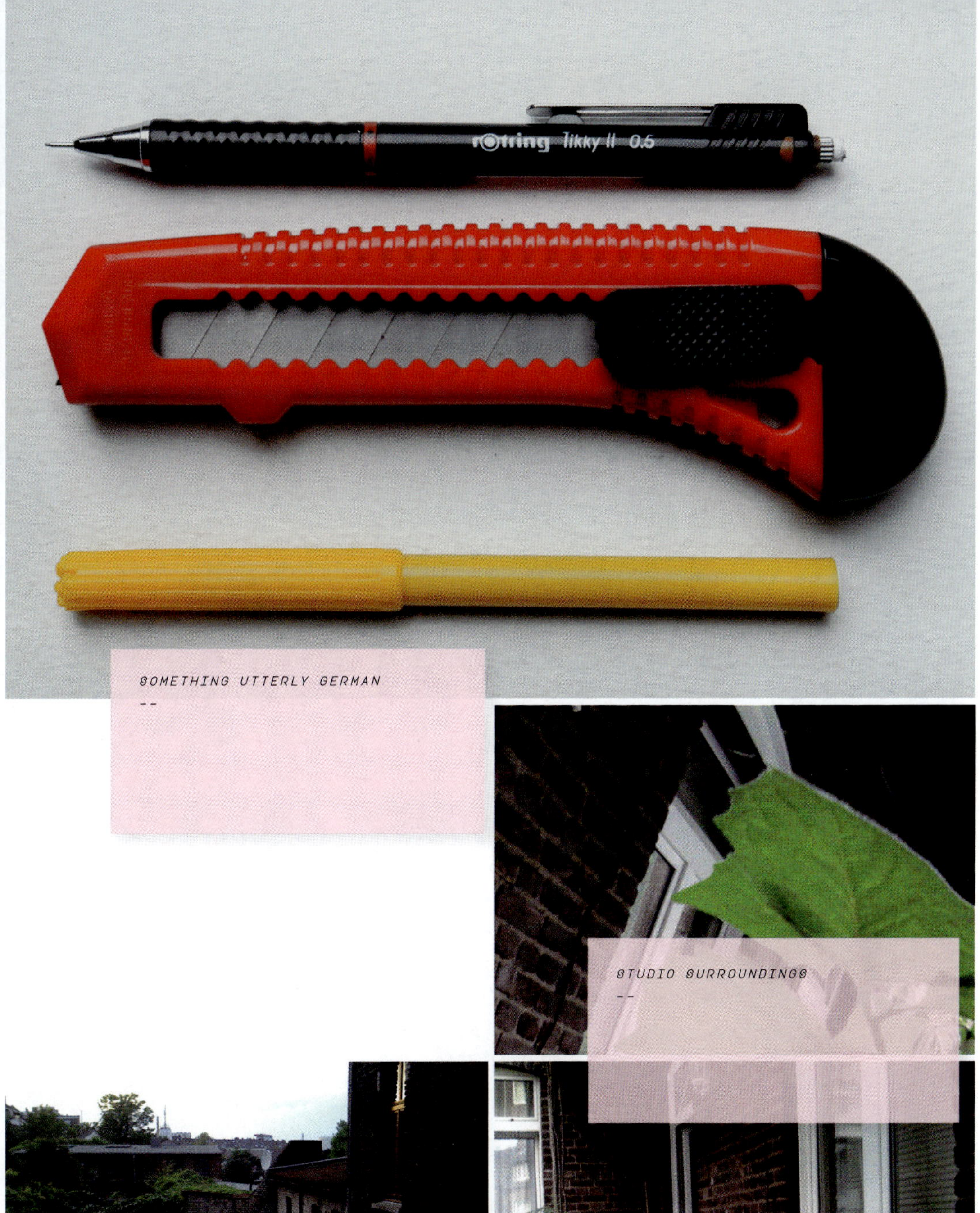

SOMETHING UTTERLY GERMAN
--

STUDIO SURROUNDINGS
--

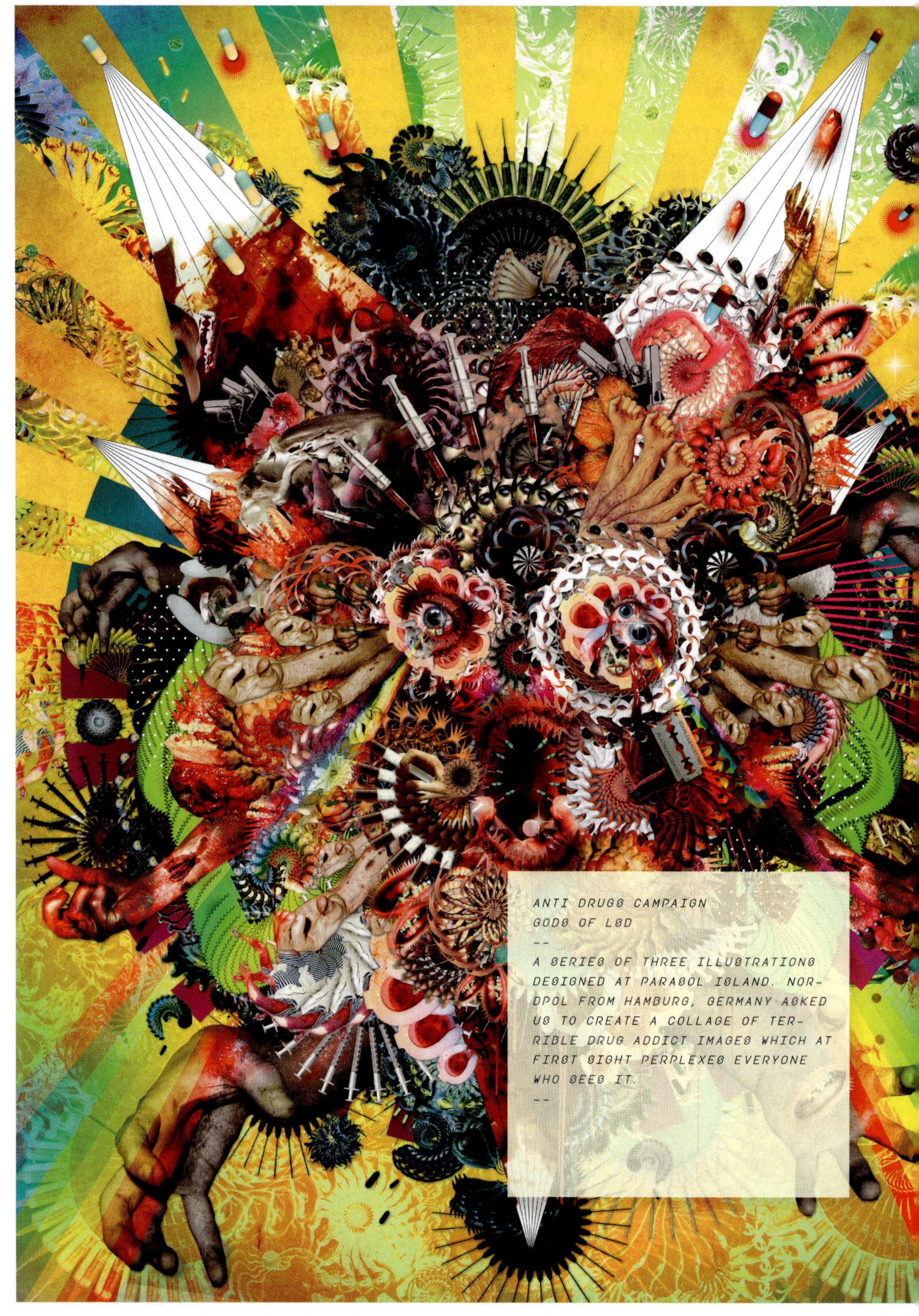

ANTI DRUGS CAMPAIGN
GODS OF LSD
--
A SERIES OF THREE ILLUSTRATIONS
DESIGNED AT PARASOL ISLAND. NOR-
DPOL FROM HAMBURG, GERMANY ASKED
US TO CREATE A COLLAGE OF TER-
RIBLE DRUG ADDICT IMAGES WHICH AT
FIRST SIGHT PERPLEXES EVERYONE
WHO SEES IT.
--

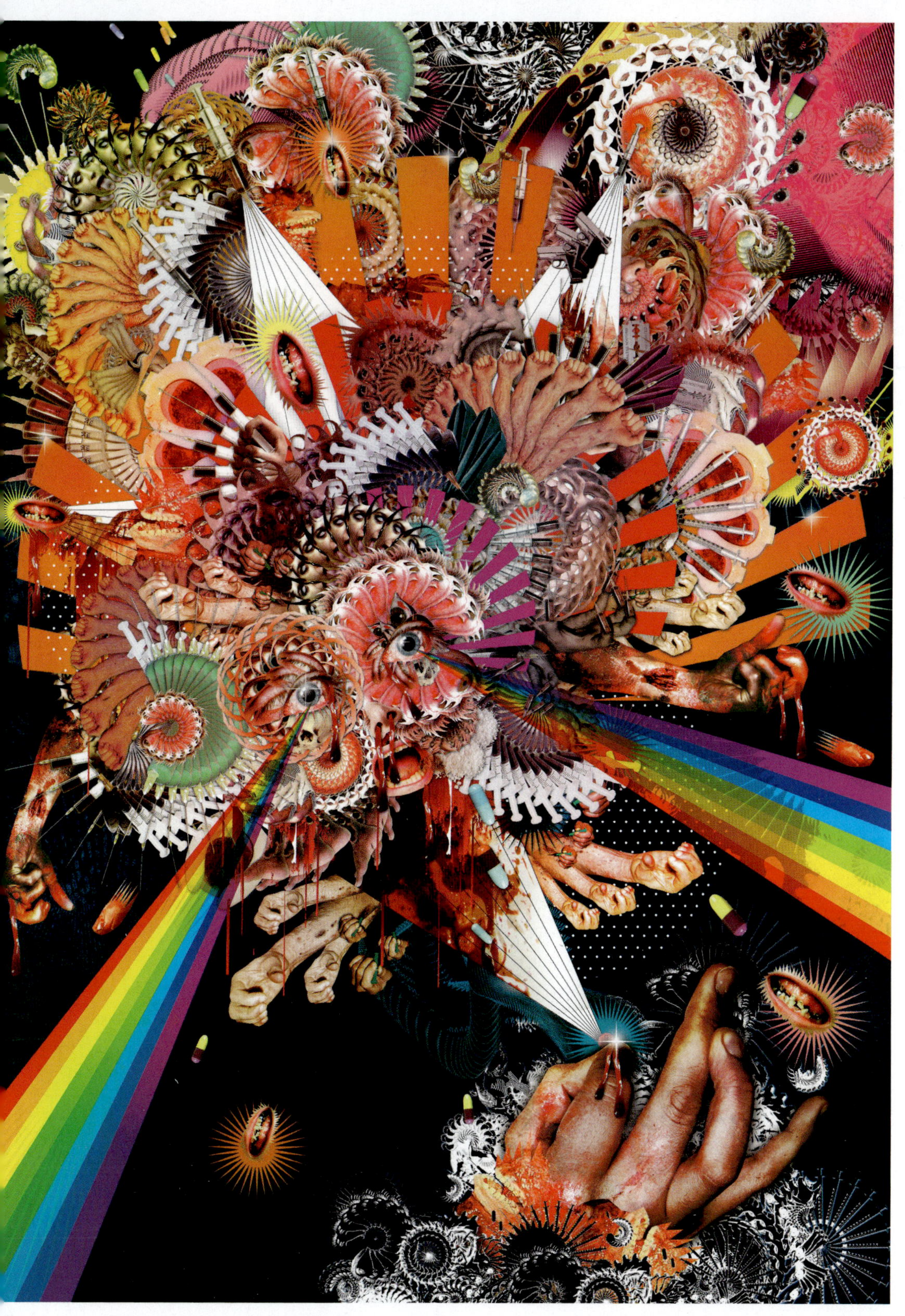

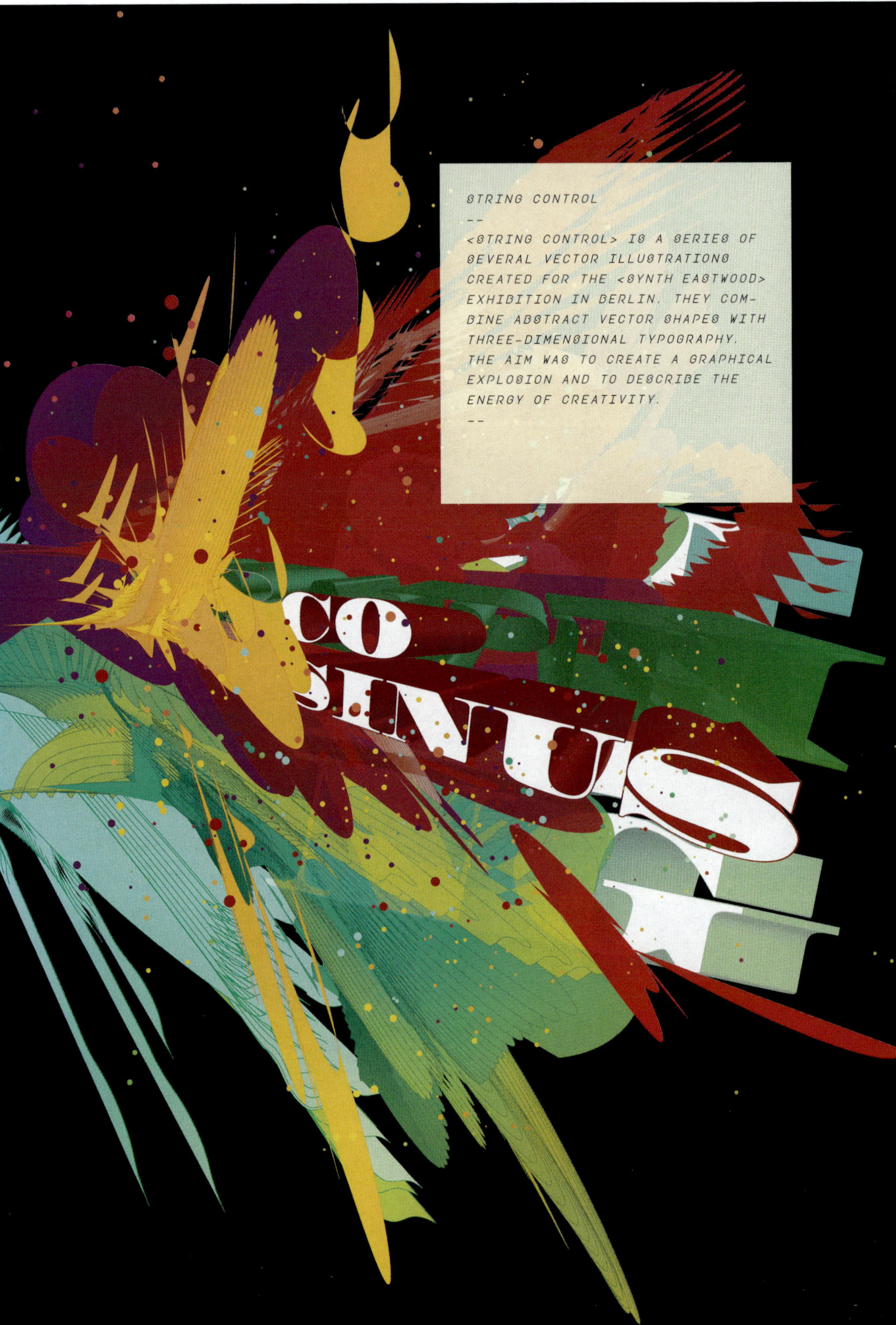

STRING CONTROL
--
<STRING CONTROL> IS A SERIES OF
SEVERAL VECTOR ILLUSTRATIONS
CREATED FOR THE <SYNTH EASTWOOD>
EXHIBITION IN BERLIN. THEY COM-
BINE ABSTRACT VECTOR SHAPES WITH
THREE-DIMENSIONAL TYPOGRAPHY.
THE AIM WAS TO CREATE A GRAPHICAL
EXPLOSION AND TO DESCRIBE THE
ENERGY OF CREATIVITY.
--
CO
SINUS

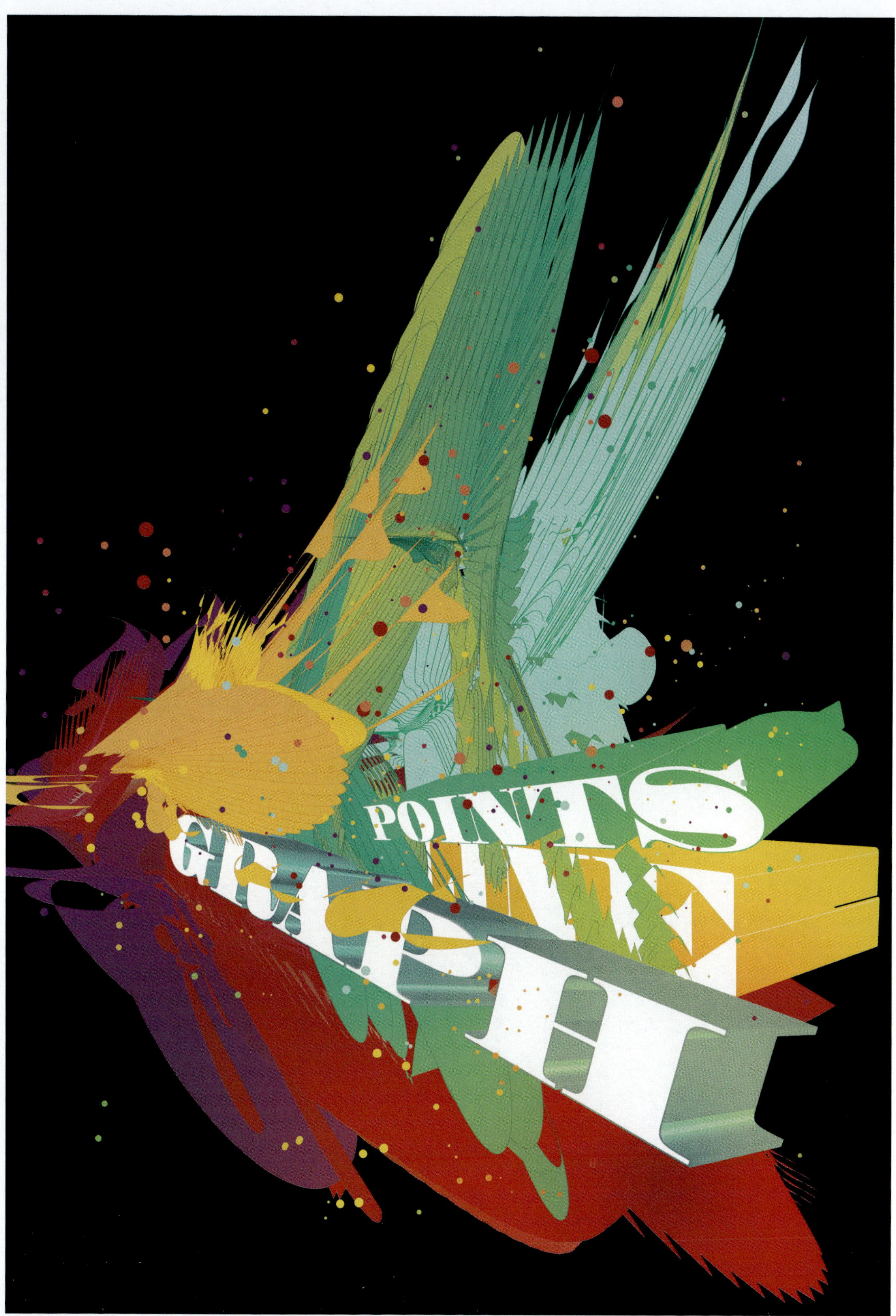

POINTS
GRAPHI

FELIX WEIGAND STUDIED AT THE UDK
(UNIVERSITÄT DER KÜNSTE) BERLIN,
GERRIT RIETVELD AKADEMIE IN AM-
STERDAM AND WERKPLAATS TYPOGRAFIE
IN ARNHEM. SINCE 2005 HE HAS BEEN
WORKING AS A FREELANCE GRAPHIC
DESIGNER IN AMSTERDAM.

--

WHAT IS GERMAN?

HAVING A TOILET ROLL WITH A
HOME-CROCHETED TOILET ROLL COVER
ON THE PARCEL SHELF OF A CAR, BUT
AT THE SAME TIME: DRAGGING A SHIP
OVER A MOUNTAIN IN THE BRAZILIAN
PRIMEVAL FOREST.

WHAT IS GERMAN DESIGN?

THAT'S HARD. FOR ME GERMAN DE-
SIGN IS CURRENTLY CHARACTERIZED BY
THE FACT THAT IT HAS NO CHARACTER
OF ITS OWN.

PLEASE DESCRIBE YOUR WORKING
PROCESS.

I BUSY MYSELF WITH THE MATERIAL
OR THEME ON HAND QUITE A LOT, YOU
COULD SAY I STUDY IT. THE RE-
SULTS OF THAT STUDY ARE MY WORKS.
SOMETIMES YOU FAIL LAMENTABLY IN
STUDYING. BUT FOR ME THAT'S THE
INTERESTING BIT.

WHAT DO YOU AIM TO ACHIEVE WITH
YOUR WORK?

MY GREATEST AIM IS REALLY TO RE-
THINK AND IMPROVE THINGS THAT ARE
REGARDED AS <GIVEN>.

YOU'VE INVITED A FRIEND TO
GERMANY; NAME ONE PLACE THEY
REALLY MUST VISIT AND A QUINT-
ESSENTIAL EXPERIENCE YOU REC-
OMMEND.

1. IN THE SUMMER GO TO HAMBURG
2. AND LOOK AT THE SHIPS ON THE
   ALSTER.

WHAT IS THE MOST IMPORTANT
LESSON YOU HAVE LEARNED IN YOUR
PROFESSION SO FAR?

APFEL + Z

--

WEI—GAND

FELIX WEIGAND
--
EERSTE JAN STEEN STRAAT 90/4
1072 NP AMSTERDAM
THE NETHERLANDS
--
M +31 642801214
--
FELIX@RIVE-GAUCHE.ORG
WWW.FELIXWEIGAND.COM
WWW.SHORTFORMS.ORG
--

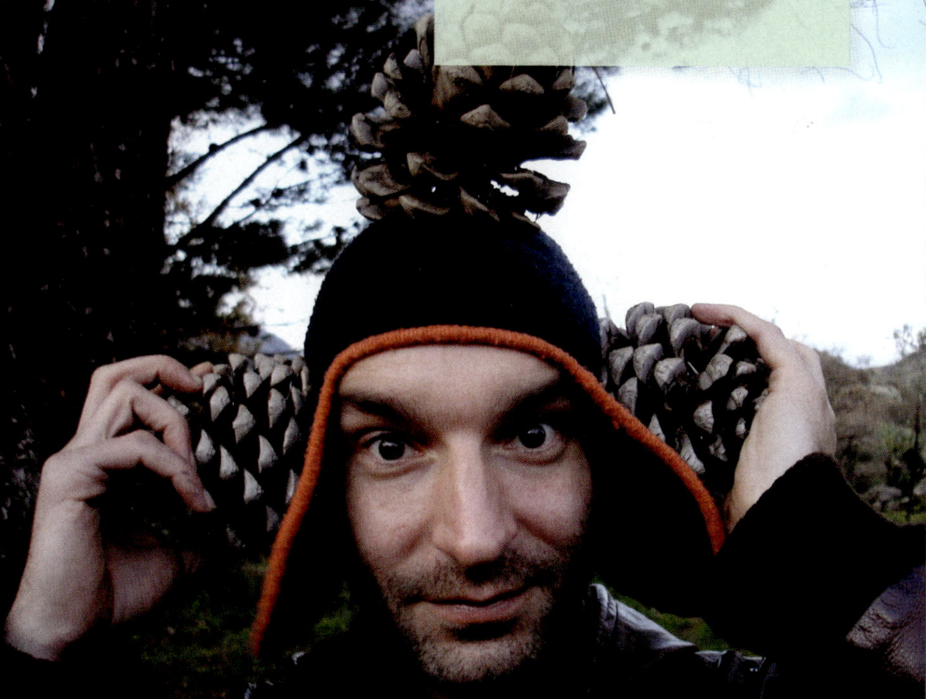

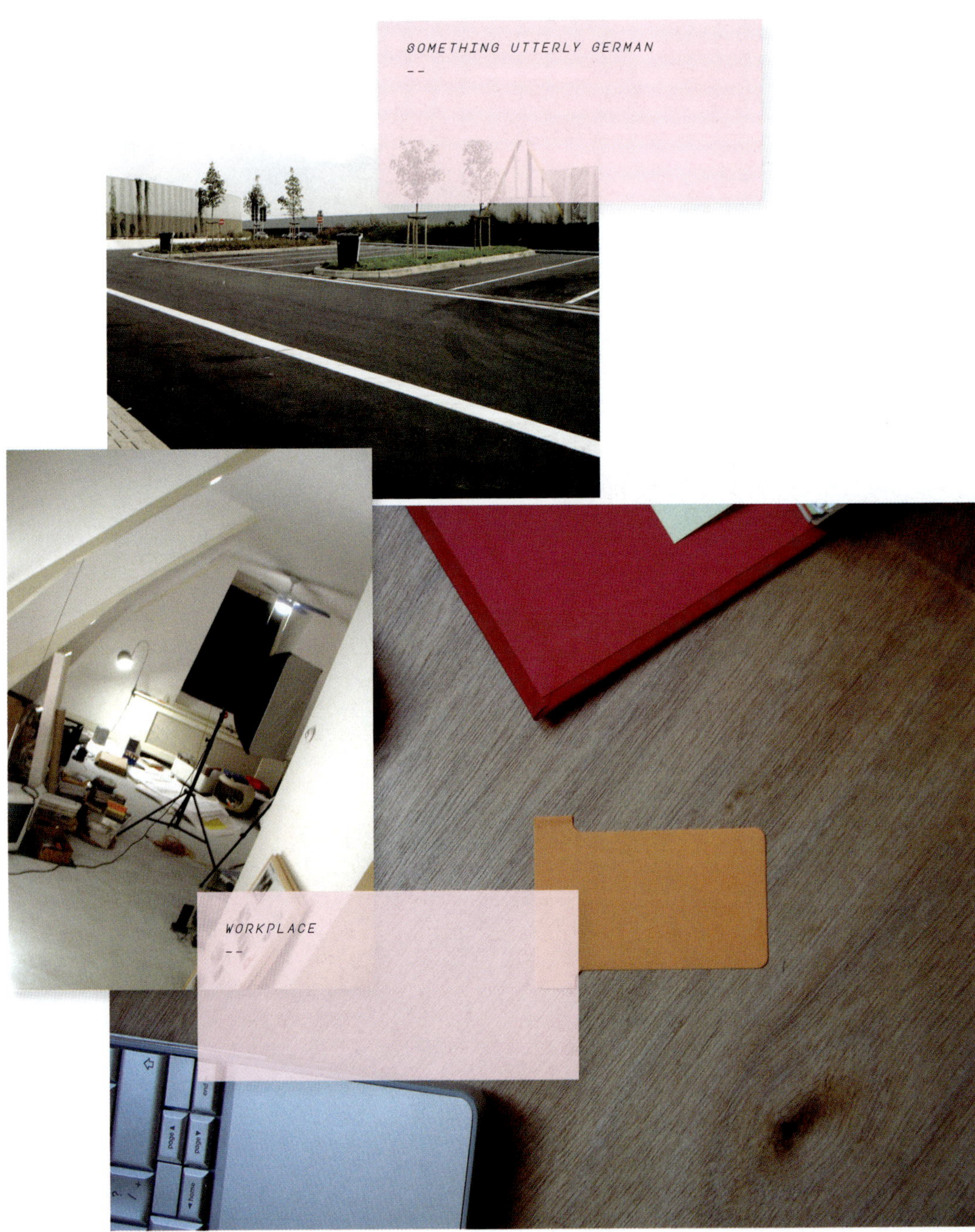
SOMETHING UTTERLY GERMAN
--
WORKPLACE
--

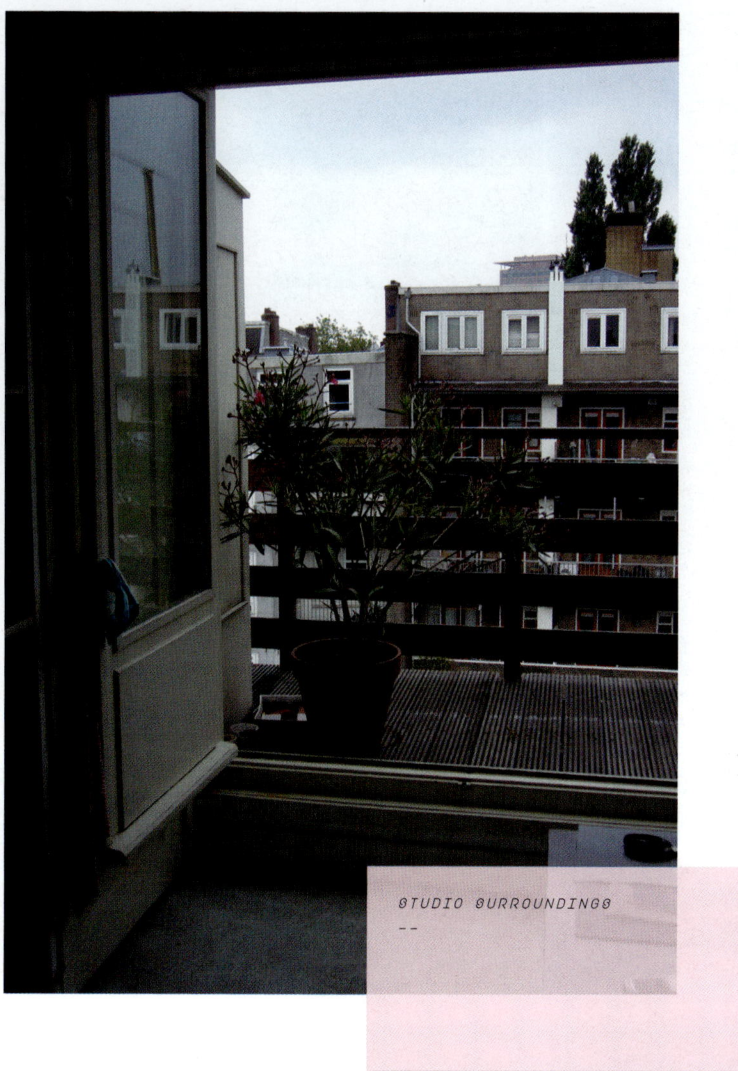
STUDIO SURROUNDINGS
--

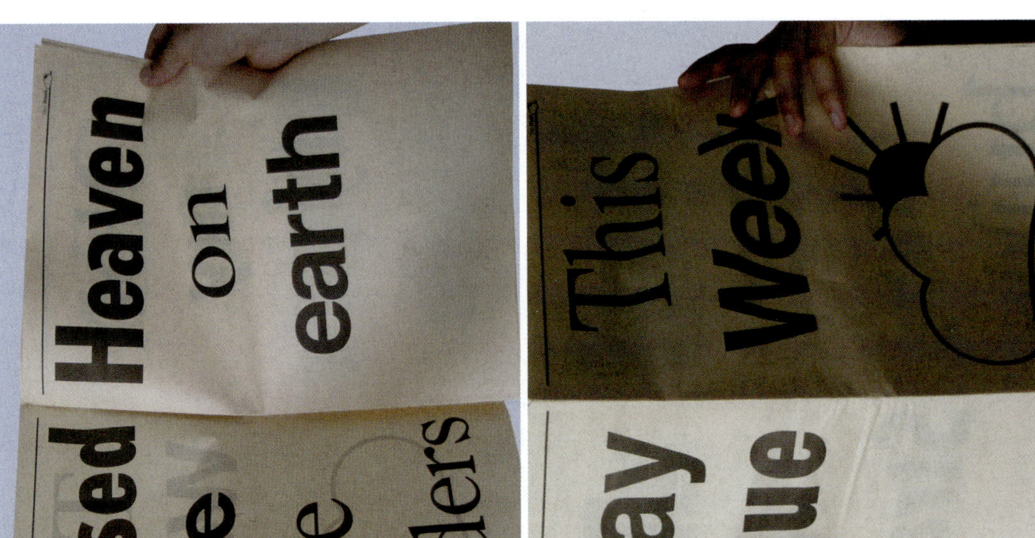

THIS WEEK NEWSPAPER
--
THIS WEEK IS A NEWSPAPER PUBLISHED BY ME, AND ITS CONTENTS CONSIST SOLELY OF NEWSPAPER HEADLINES. ABOVE ALL THIS WEEK NEWSPAPER HAS A FICTIONAL CHARACTER: IT'S FREE AND CONSISTS SOLELY OF NEWSPAPER HEADLINES. IN THE PROCESS ALL HEADLINES ARE FREED OF ANY POLITICAL, GEOGRAPHICAL OR TEMPORAL CONTEXT AND THUS BECOME LANGUAGE CONTAINERS THAT PLAY WITH THE READER'S ASSOCIATIONS. (WWW.SHORTFORMS.ORG)
--

AFTER GRADUATION IN 2004, I CYCLED
AROUND AMSTERDAM, MEETING MY
FAVORITE DESIGNERS AND HAVING A
TALK WITH THEM. THIS RESULTED IN A
FRIENDSHIP WITH ARJAN GROOT AND A
WORK PLACE WITH HIM SITTING RIGHT
NEXT TO ME.

--

WHAT IS GERMAN?

THE GERMAN WAY OF MELANCHOLY
THINKING MIXED WITH THE DUTCH MEN-
TALITY OF LIGHT-HEARTEDNESS HAVE
BLENDED INTO MY PERSONALITY SINCE
I CAME TO THE NETHERLANDS IN 2002.
THIS HAS MADE ME A BETTER PERSON.

WHAT IS GERMAN DESIGN?

DUTCH CLIENTS ARE MUCH MORE
EXPERIMENTAL AND WILLING TO TAKE
A RISK THAN IN GERMANY. IN 2003,
WHEN I WAS DESIGNING A BROCHURE
FOR A SCHOOL IN AMSTERDAM, WE DE-
CIDED TO GO FOR MY RISKY PROPOSAL
OF HIDING THE TEXT IN A JAPANESE
BINDING AND ONLY SHOWING IMAGES.
THE READER HAD TO UNDERSTAND THAT
HE HAD TO RIP THE PAGES OPEN TO
GET TO THE SCHOOL'S VERY VALUABLE
INFORMATION. I FOUND IT AMAZING
THAT THE CLIENT LOVED THAT IDEA OF
SHOWING SOMETHING OTHER THAN YOU
EXPECT. THEY EVEN REPRINTED AFTER
2 YEARS.

PLEASE DESCRIBE YOUR WORKING
PROCESS.

MY WORKING PROCESS IS VERY DIF-
FERENT EACH TIME, BECAUSE I WORK
WITH DIFFERENT COLLABORATORS. WHEN
I WORK WITH ARJAN GROOT, WE BOTH
HAVE DIFFERENT WAYS OF GETTING
TO THE OUTCOME. HE OFTEN STARTS
SKETCHING AND PLAYING ABOUT RIGHT
AWAY WHEREAS I'M STILL SITTING
THERE TRYING TO MAKE A OVERALL
CONCEPT.

WHAT DO YOU AIM TO ACHIEVE WITH
YOUR WORK?

MAKE GREAT GRAPHIC DESIGN AND BE
HAPPY IN LIFE.

YOU'VE INVITED A FRIEND TO
GERMANY; NAME ONE PLACE THEY
REALLY MUST VISIT AND A QUINT-
ESSENTIAL EXPERIENCE YOU REC-
OMMEND.

COME TO AMSTERDAM!
IT'S A GREAT PLACE!!

WHAT IS THE MOST IMPORTANT
LESSON YOU HAVE LEARNED IN YOUR
PROFESSION SO FAR?

<ALWAYS DO YOUR BEST,
NEVER WORRY.> (DAVID KARAM)

--

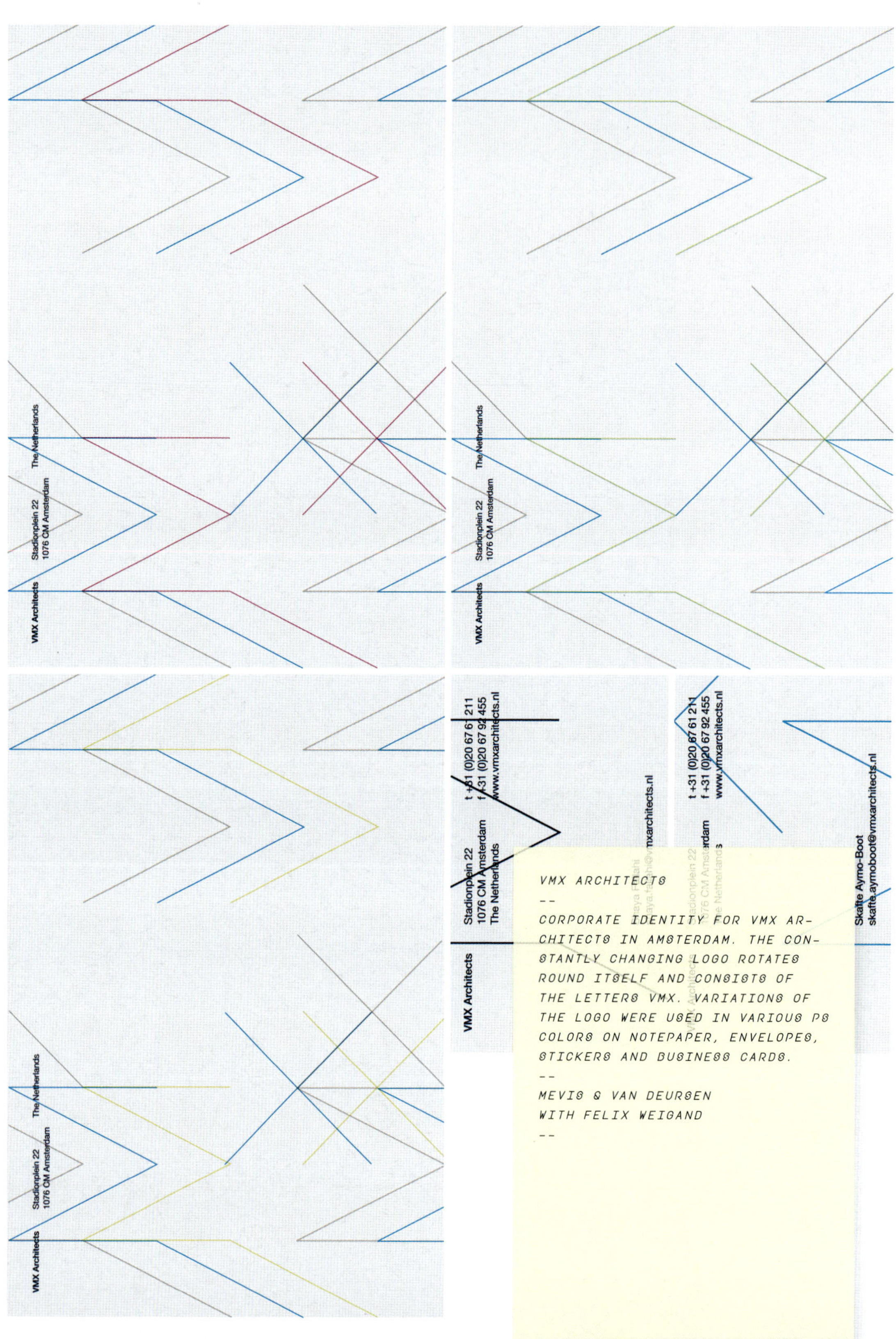

VMX ARCHITECTS
--
CORPORATE IDENTITY FOR VMX AR-
CHITECTS IN AMSTERDAM. THE CON-
STANTLY CHANGING LOGO ROTATES
ROUND ITSELF AND CONSISTS OF
THE LETTERS VMX. VARIATIONS OF
THE LOGO WERE USED IN VARIOUS PS
COLORS ON NOTEPAPER, ENVELOPES,
STICKERS AND BUSINESS CARDS.
--
MEVIS & VAN DEURSEN
WITH FELIX WEIGAND
--

VMX Architects
Stadionplein 22
1076 CM Amsterdam
The Netherlands
t +31 (0)20 67 61 211
f +31 (0)20 67 92 455
www.vmxarchitects.nl
Skafte Aymo-Boot
skafte.aymoboot@vmxarchitects.nl

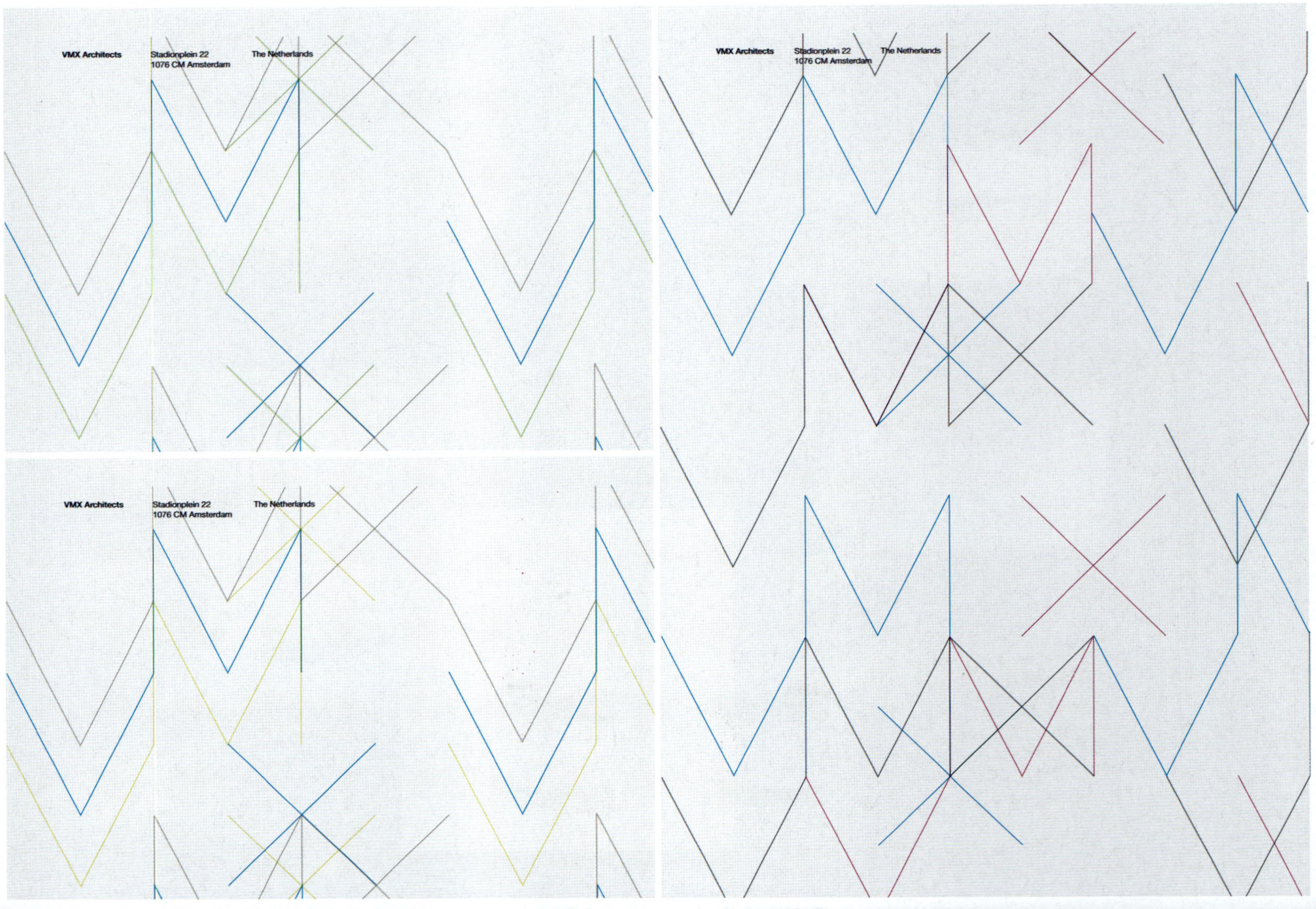

VMX Architects
Stadionplein 22
1076 CM Amsterdam
The Netherlands

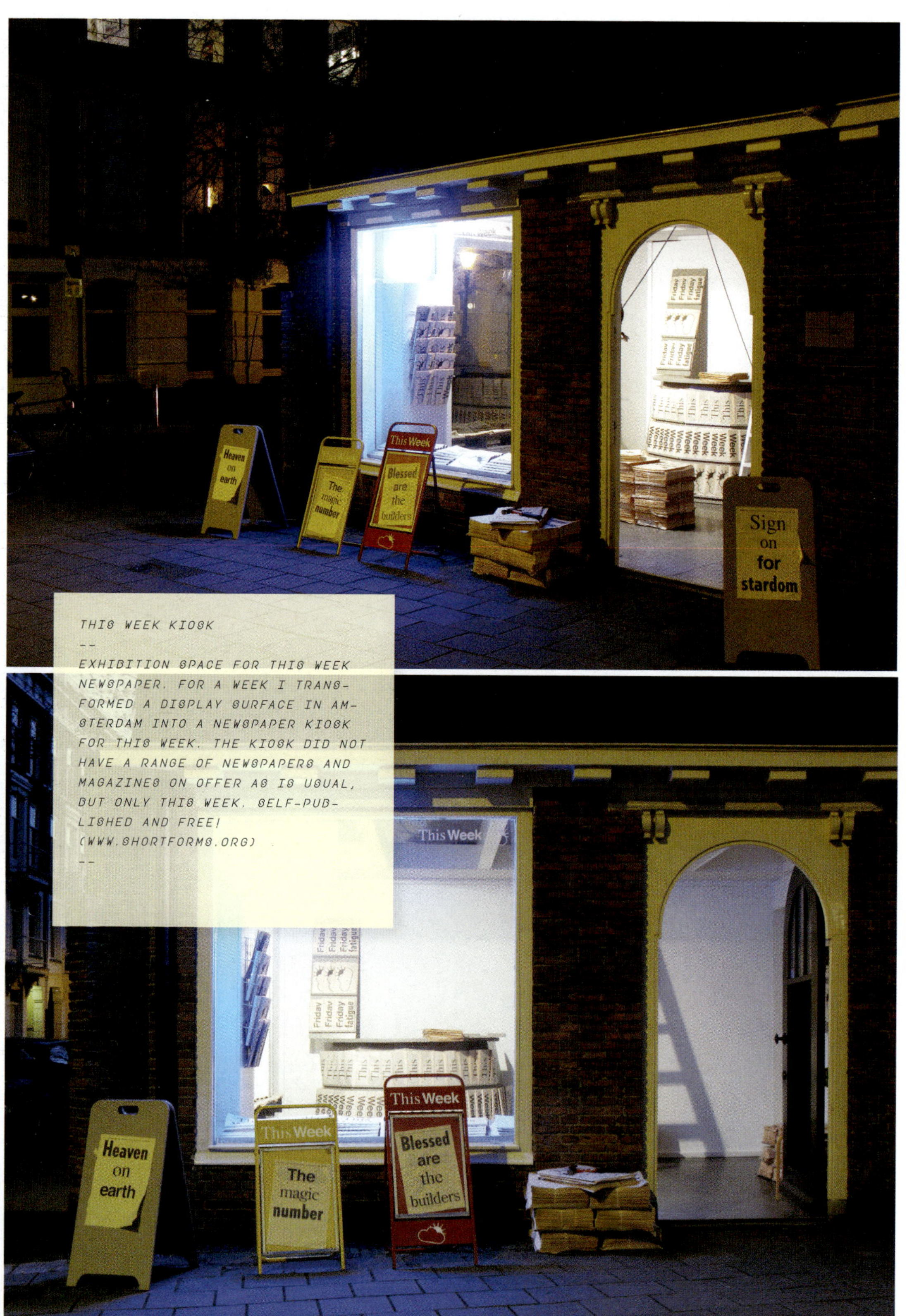

THIS WEEK KIOSK
--
EXHIBITION SPACE FOR THIS WEEK
NEWSPAPER. FOR A WEEK I TRANS-
FORMED A DISPLAY SURFACE IN AM-
STERDAM INTO A NEWSPAPER KIOSK
FOR THIS WEEK. THE KIOSK DID NOT
HAVE A RANGE OF NEWSPAPERS AND
MAGAZINES ON OFFER AS IS USUAL,
BUT ONLY THIS WEEK. SELF-PUB-
LISHED AND FREE!
(WWW.SHORTFORMS.ORG)
--

MÜLLER

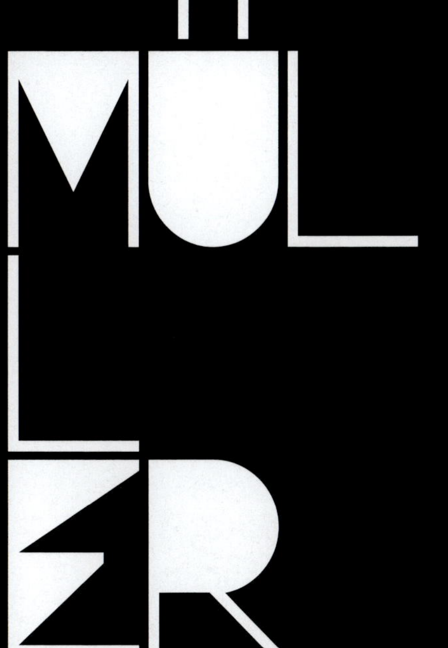

JULIA MÜLLER
--
1092 KØ AMSTERDAM
THE NETHERLANDS
--
T +31 630047753
--
MAILANJULE@GMX.DE
WWW.HELLOJULIA.COM
--

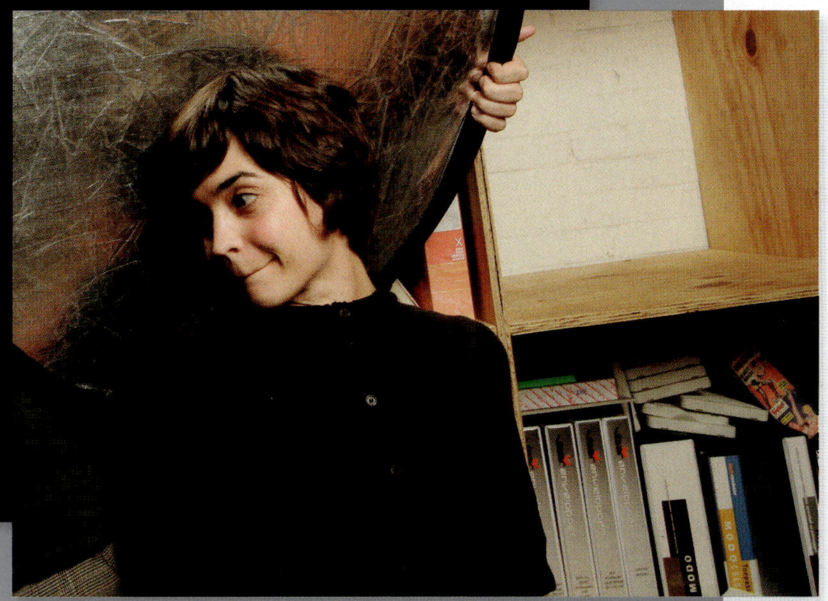

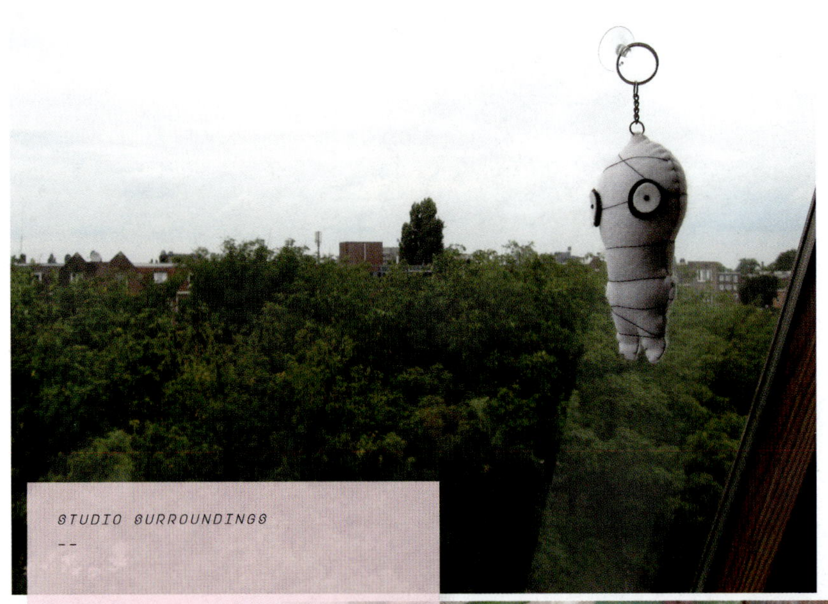

STUDIO SURROUNDINGS
--

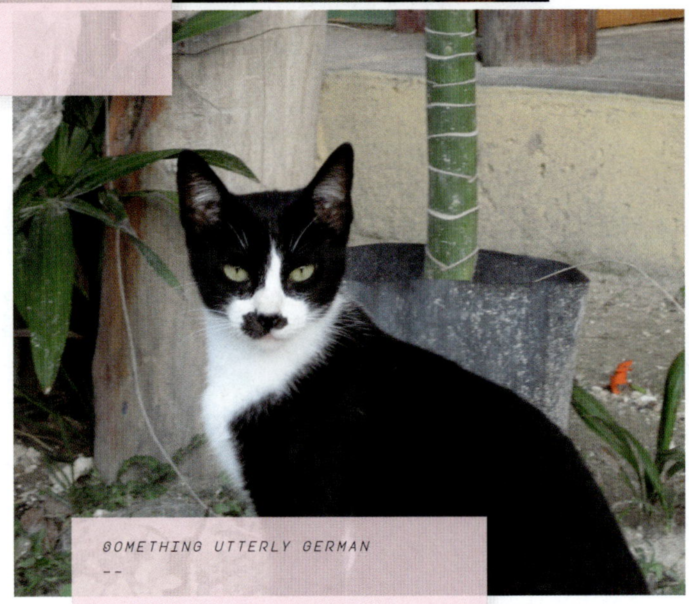

SOMETHING UTTERLY GERMAN
--

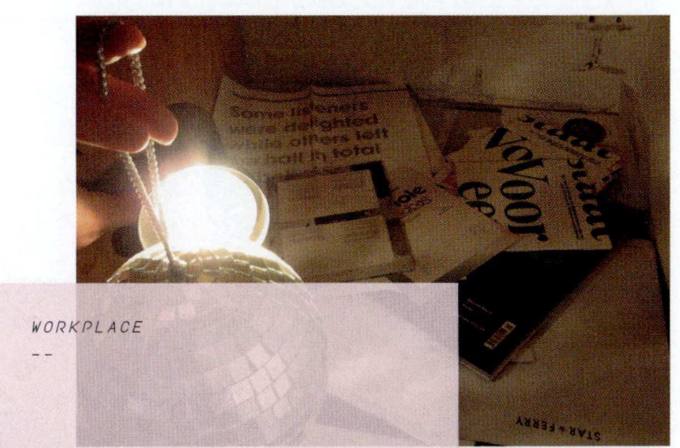

Some listeners
were delighted
while others left
in total
VoVoor
ee
STAR · FERRY

WORKPLACE
--

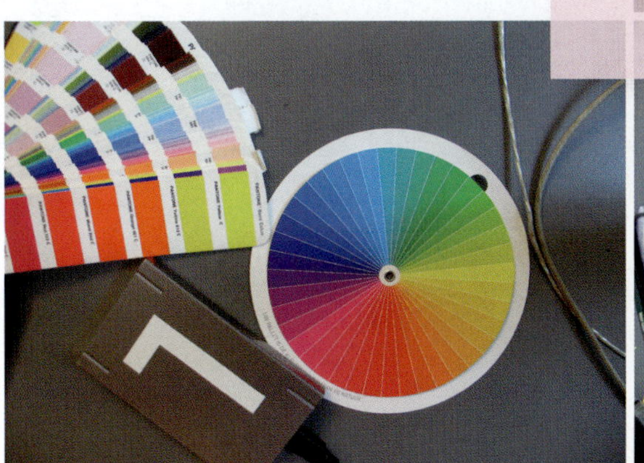

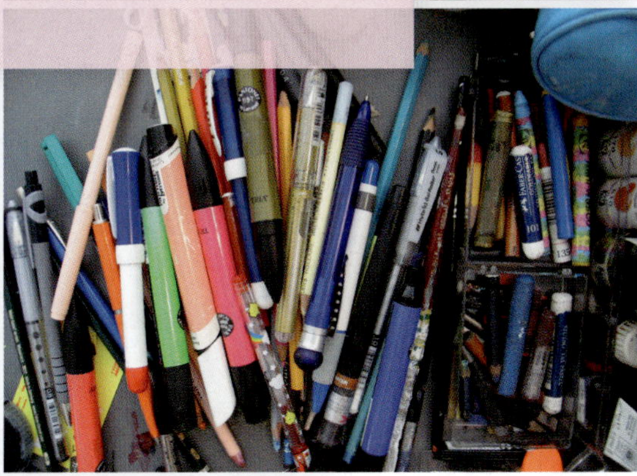

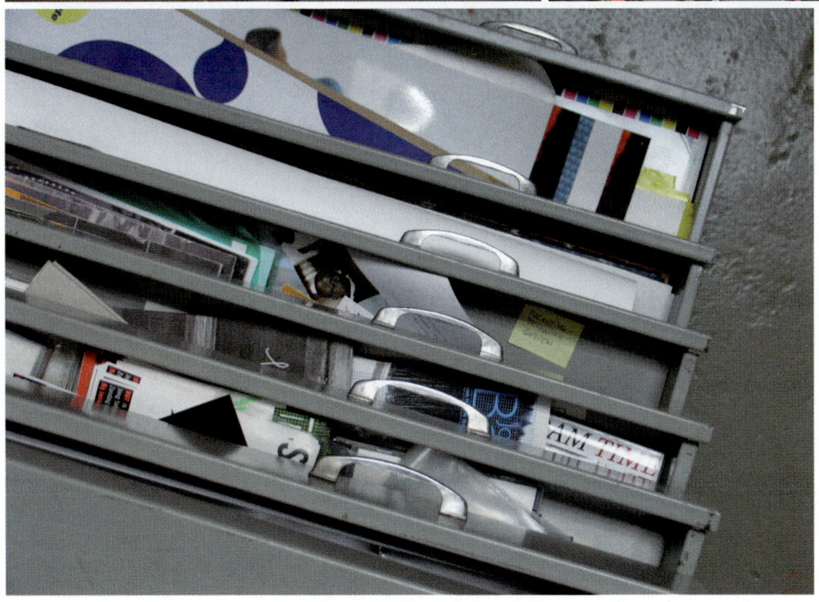

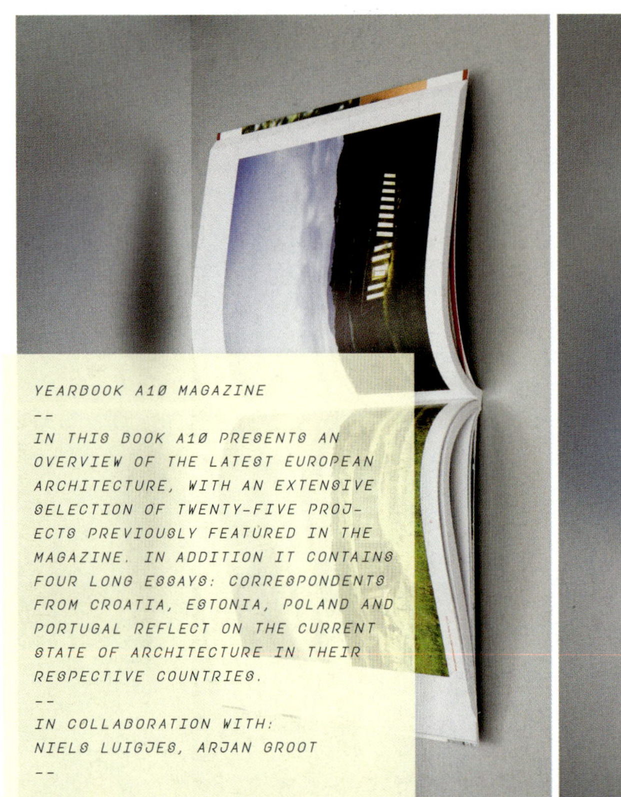

YEARBOOK A10 MAGAZINE
--
IN THIS BOOK A10 PRESENTS AN
OVERVIEW OF THE LATEST EUROPEAN
ARCHITECTURE, WITH AN EXTENSIVE
SELECTION OF TWENTY-FIVE PROJ-
ECTS PREVIOUSLY FEATURED IN THE
MAGAZINE. IN ADDITION IT CONTAINS
FOUR LONG ESSAYS: CORRESPONDENTS
FROM CROATIA, ESTONIA, POLAND AND
PORTUGAL REFLECT ON THE CURRENT
STATE OF ARCHITECTURE IN THEIR
RESPECTIVE COUNTRIES.
--
IN COLLABORATION WITH:
NIELS LUIGJES, ARJAN GROOT
--

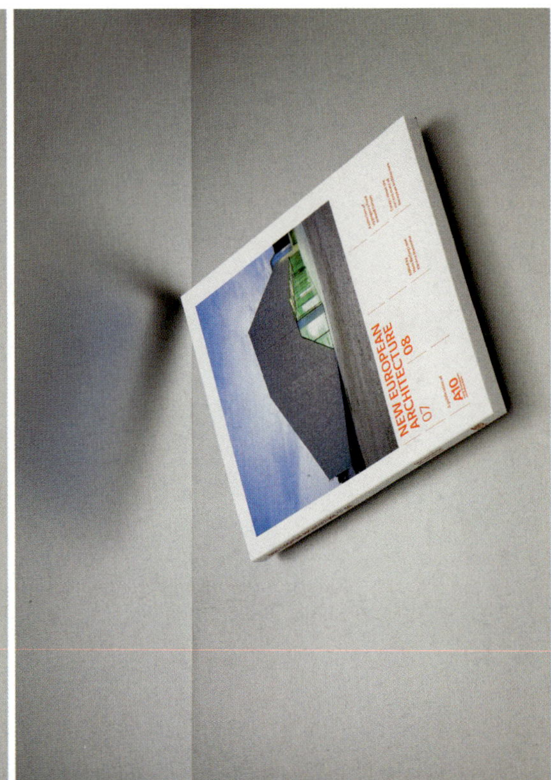

NEW EUROPEAN
ARCHITECTURE 08
07
A10

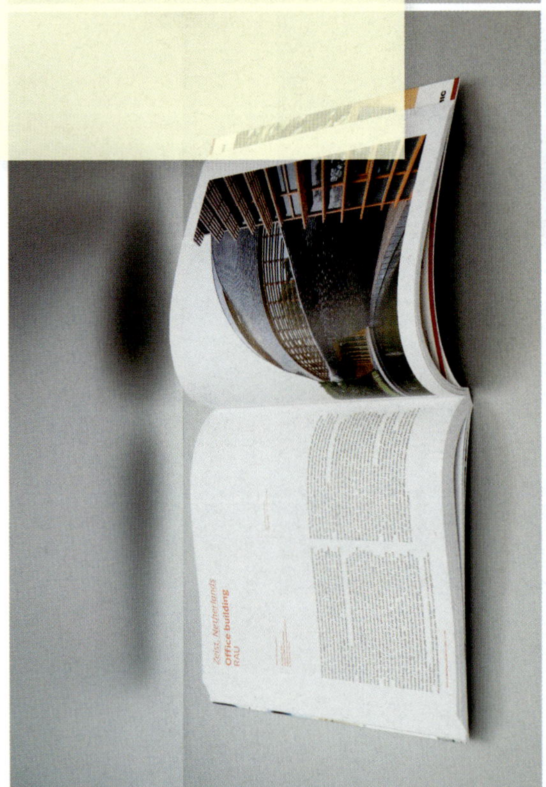

2011, Netherlands
Office building
RAU

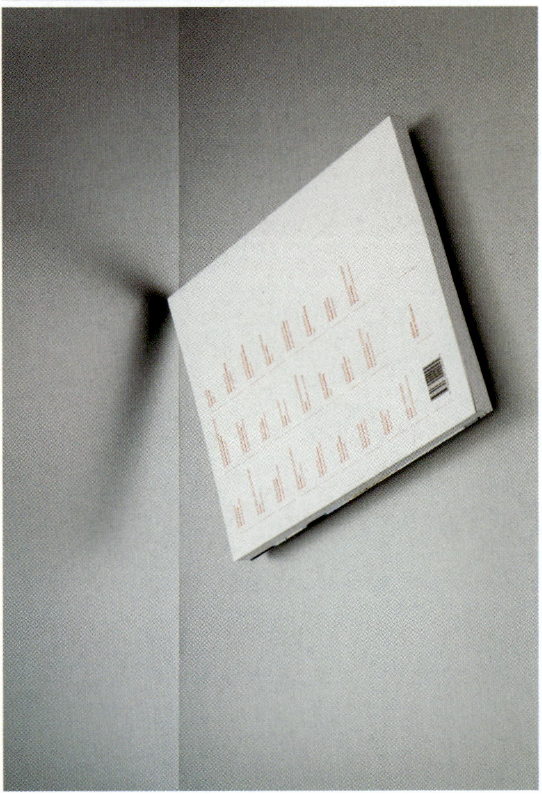

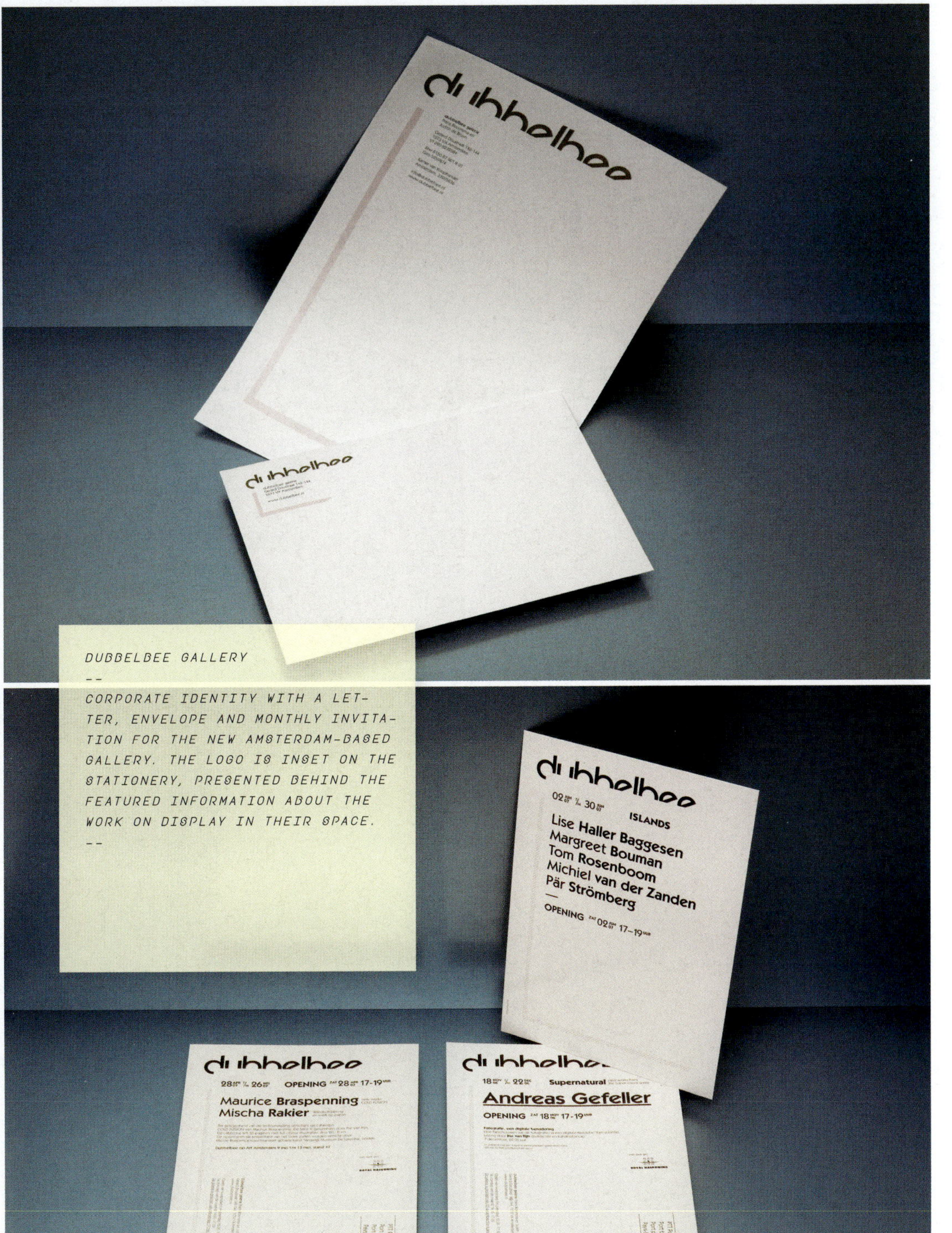

DUBBELBEE GALLERY
--
CORPORATE IDENTITY WITH A LET-
TER, ENVELOPE AND MONTHLY INVITA-
TION FOR THE NEW AMSTERDAM-BASED
GALLERY. THE LOGO IS INSET ON THE
STATIONERY, PRESENTED BEHIND THE
FEATURED INFORMATION ABOUT THE
WORK ON DISPLAY IN THEIR SPACE.
--

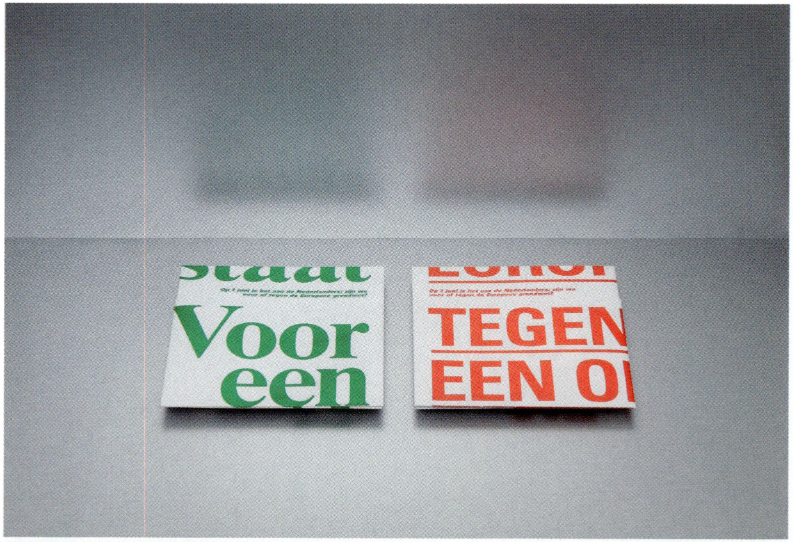

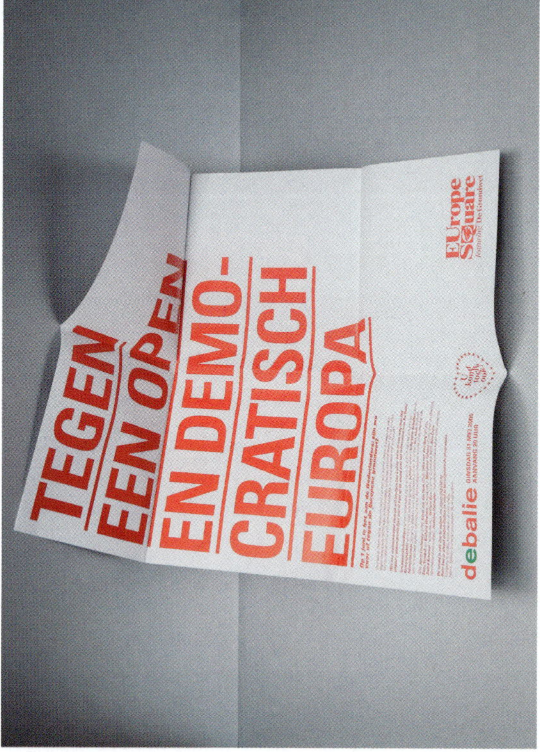

TEGEN
EEN OPEN
EN DEMO-
CRATISCH
EUROPA
EUrope Square
debalie

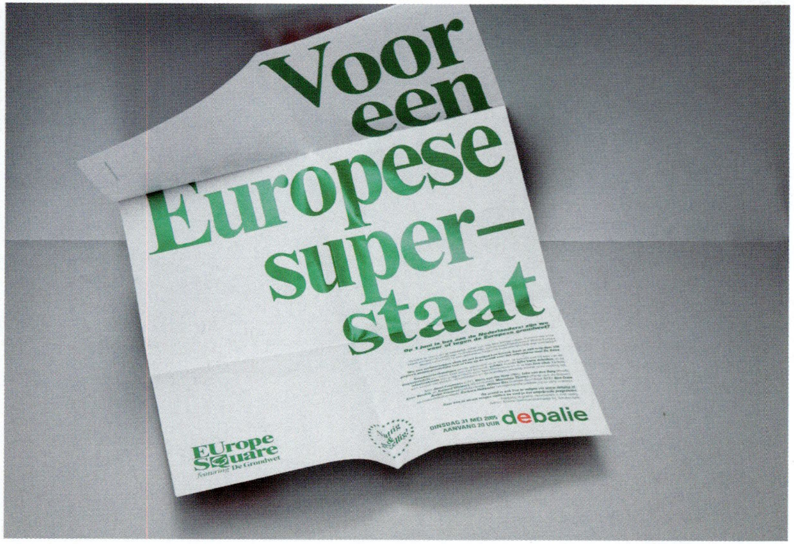

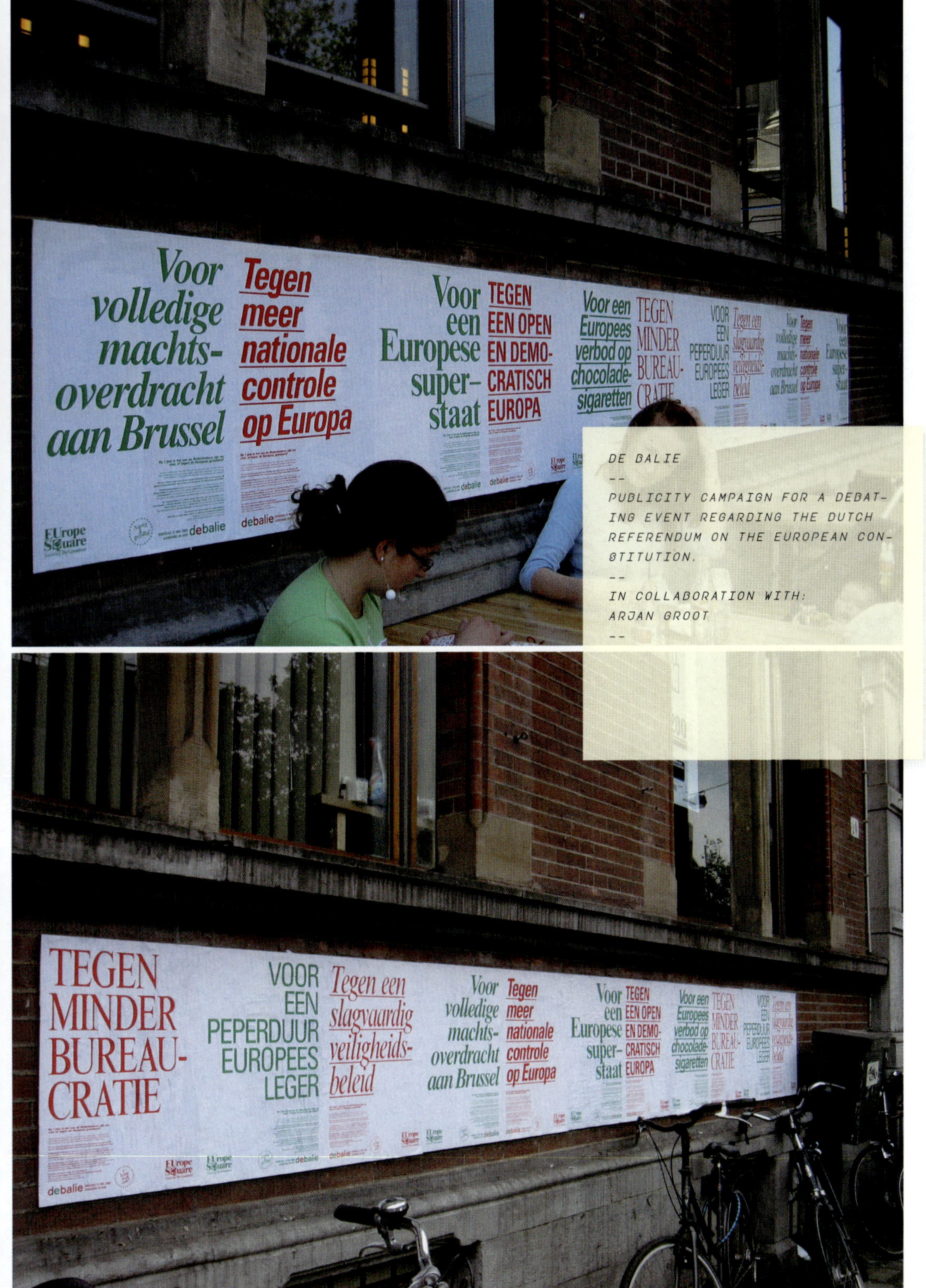

Voor volledige machts-overdracht aan Brussel
Tegen meer nationale controle op Europa
Voor een Europese super-staat
TEGEN EEN OPEN EN DEMO-CRATISCH EUROPA
Voor een Europees verbod op chocolade-sigaretten
TEGEN MINDER BUREAU-CRATIE
VOOR EEN PEPERDUUR EUROPEES LEGER
Tegen een slagvaardig veiligheids-beleid
debalie
EUrope Square
TEGEN MINDER BUREAU-CRATIE
VOOR EEN PEPERDUUR EUROPEES LEGER
Tegen een slagvaardig veiligheids-beleid
Voor volledige machts-overdracht aan Brussel
Tegen meer nationale controle op Europa
Voor een Europese super-staat
TEGEN EEN OPEN EN DEMO-CRATISCH EUROPA
Voor een Europees verbod op chocolade-sigaretten
debalie

DE BALIE
--
PUBLICITY CAMPAIGN FOR A DEBAT-
ING EVENT REGARDING THE DUTCH
REFERENDUM ON THE EUROPEAN CON-
STITUTION.
--
IN COLLABORATION WITH:
ARJAN GROOT
--

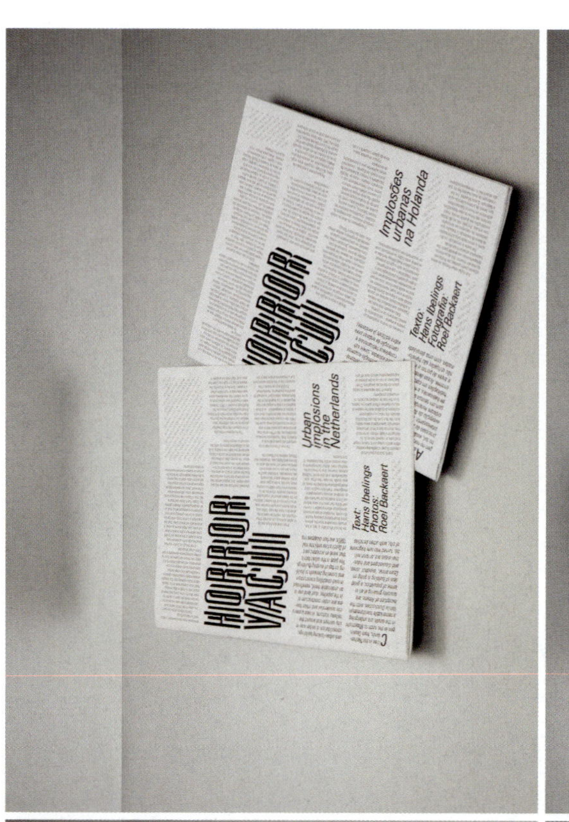

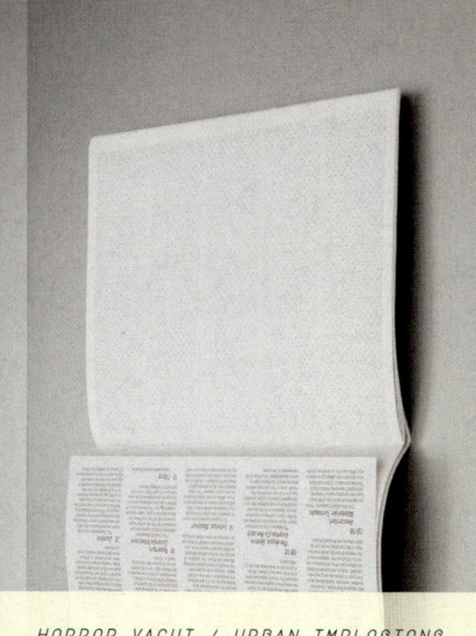

HORROR VACUI / URBAN IMPLOSIONS
--
GRAPHIC DESIGN FOR THE DUTCH EXHIBITION AT THE ARCHITECTURE TRIENNIAL IN LISBON. IN THE LAYOUT OF THE EXHIBITION PANELS AND PUBLICATIONS WE TOOK THE TITLE <HORROR VACUI> (FEAR OF EMPTINESS) QUITE LITERALLY, FILLING EVERY BLANK SPACE WITH TYPOGRAPHY.
--
IN COLLABORATION WITH:
RED, ARJAN GROOT, HANS IBELINGS
--

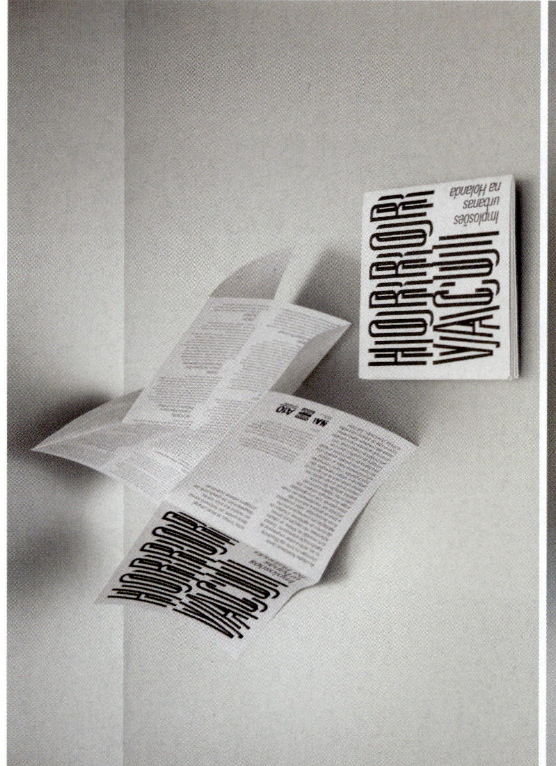

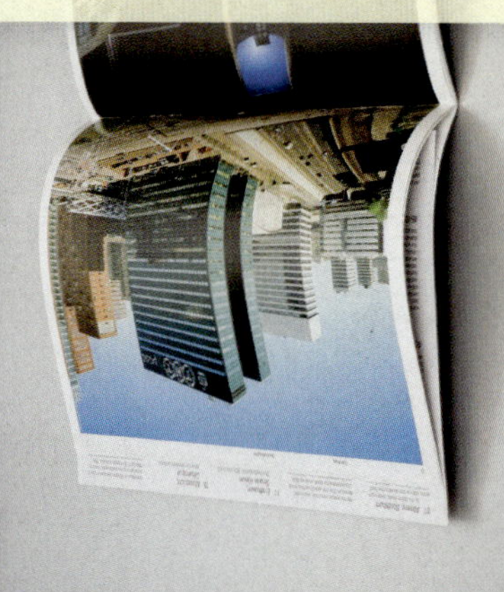

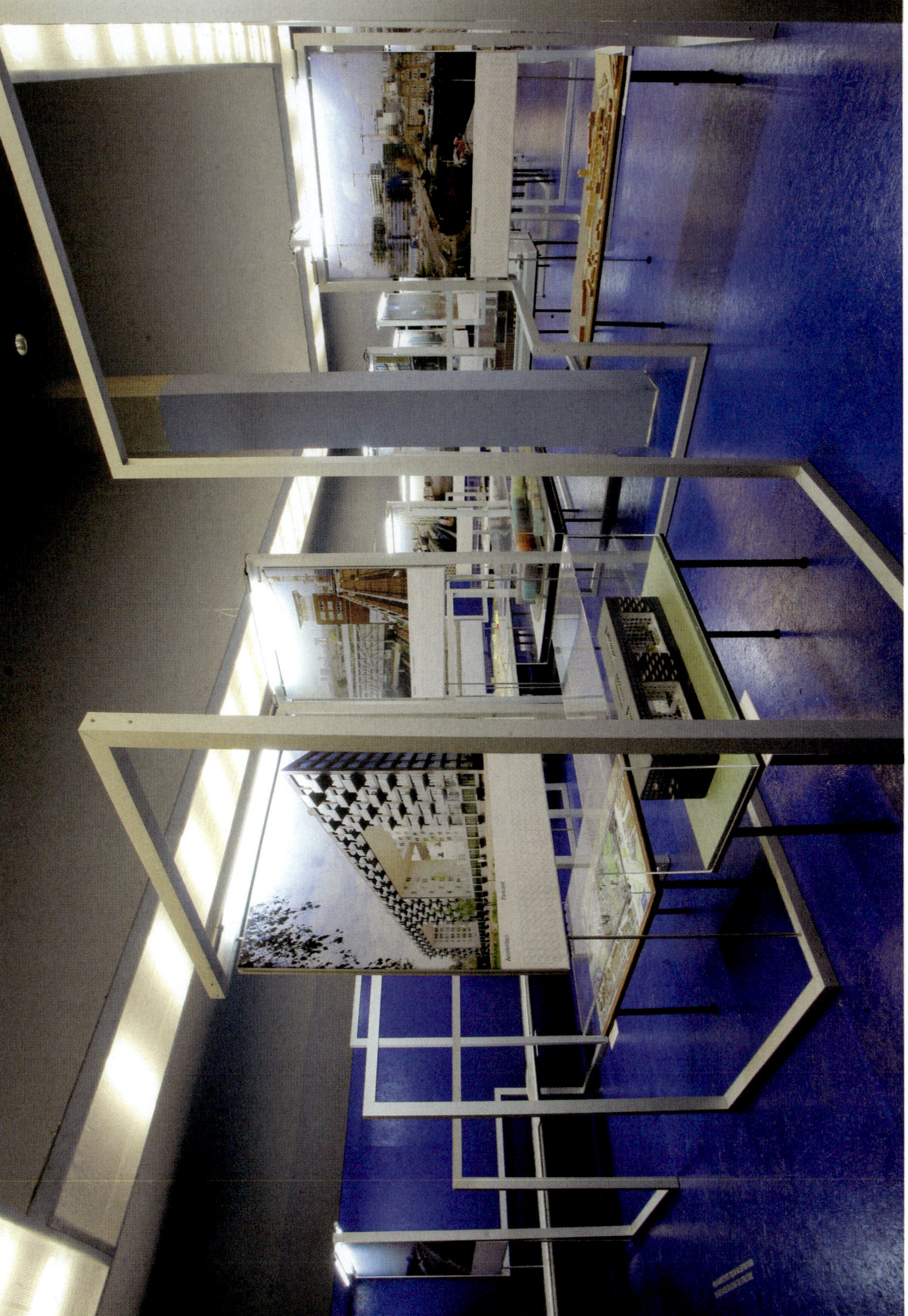

BORN AND RAISED IN LEIPZIG AND SAN
FRANCISCO. HOMETOWN IS ERLANGEN.
STUDYING COMMUNICATION DESIGN AT
HDA IN DARMSTADT. EXCHANGE SE-
MESTERS AT DKDS, COPENHAGEN AND
KABK, THE HAGUE. CURRENTLY DOING
MY MANDATORY INTERNSHIP AT BLEED
DESIGNSTUDIO, OSLO. DIPLOMA IN A
YEAR - HOPEFULLY. THINGS THAT MAKE
MY DAY: HAND-MADE ILLUSTRATIONS
AND GRAFFITI SKETCHES, SARCASM,
LOADS OF MUSIC, FRIENDS AND FAM-
ILY, CHINESE FOOD, VOLCOM, INDIE
MOVIES, SNOWBOARDING, SLEEP DEPRI-
VATION, LOW-FAT MILK, NEON GREEN
AND LIGHT BLUE.

--

WHAT IS GERMAN?

DONER KEBABS AND RATIONAL
THINKING.

WHAT IS GERMAN DESIGN?

A CONGLOMERATE OF SWISS TYPOG-
RAPHY, SCANDINAVIAN ESTHETICS AND
DUTCH STYLING.

PLEASE DESCRIBE YOUR WORKING PROCESS.

HAVING AN IDEA. ENDLESS RESEARCH
FOR ALTERNATIVES, WRITING AND
HAND SKETCHING. FINALLY THROWING
EVERYTHING OUT AND SETTLING FOR A
VARIATION OF THE INITIAL IDEA.

WHAT DO YOU AIM TO ACHIEVE WITH YOUR WORK?

AGITATION, QUESTION MARKS AND
SMILES :D

YOU'VE INVITED A FRIEND TO GERMANY; NAME ONE PLACE THEY REALLY MUST VISIT AND A QUINT-ESSENTIAL EXPERIENCE YOU REC-OMMEND.

NOT TO BERLIN! GO AND SEE THE
BEAUTIFUL NATURE OF THE NEARBY
MECKLENBURGER SEENPLATTE INSTEAD.
THE <BERGKIRCHWEIH> IN ERLANGEN.

WHAT IS THE MOST IMPORTANT LESSON YOU HAVE LEARNED IN YOUR PROFESSION SO FAR?

EVERYTHING'S BEEN DONE BEFORE.
<GETTING INSPIRATION> IS JUST A
PHRASE FOR COPYING OTHER PEOPLE'S
IDEAS.

--

KID YEAH!

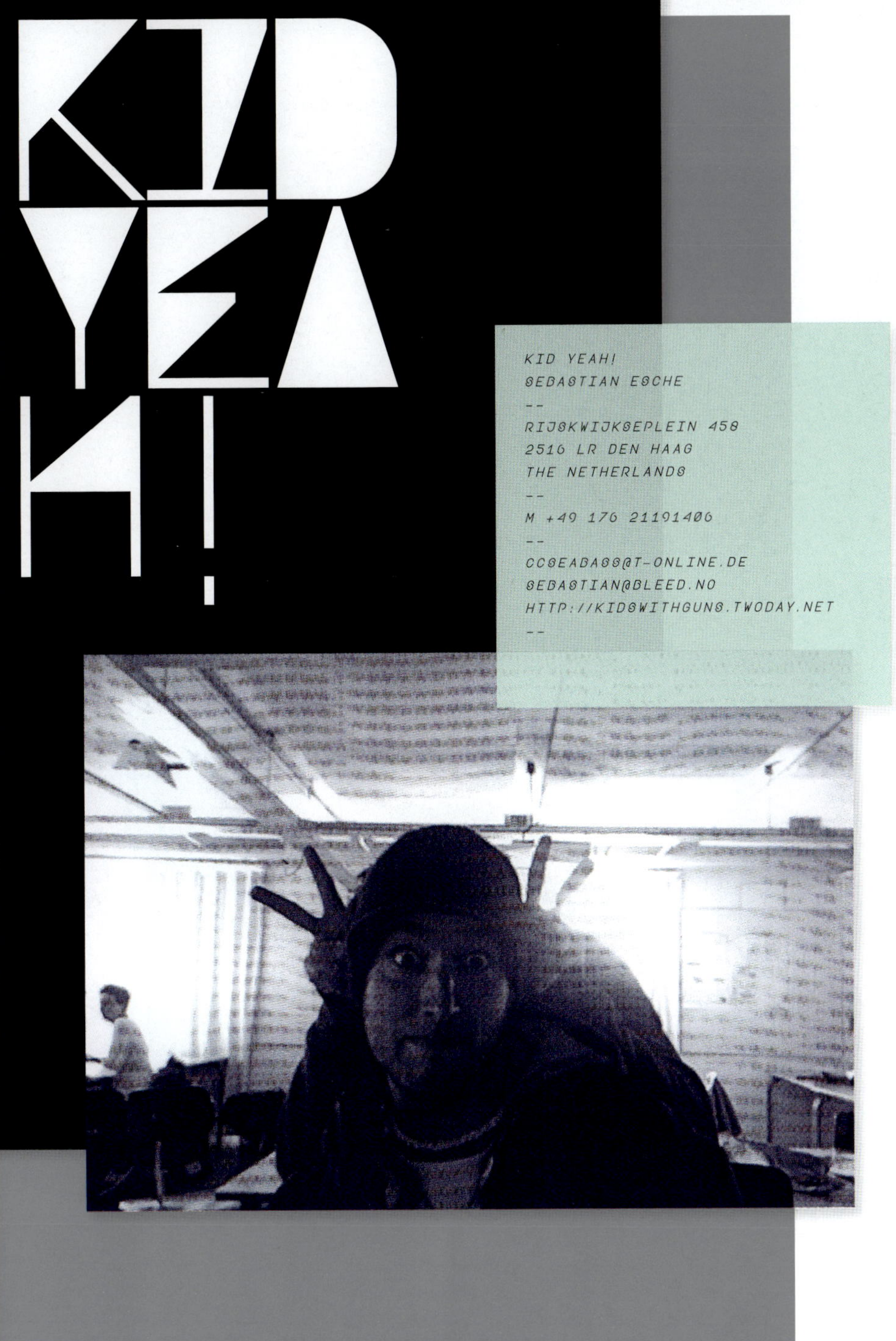

KID YEAH!
SEBASTIAN ESCHE
--
RIJSKWIJKSEPLEIN 458
2516 LR DEN HAAG
THE NETHERLANDS
--
M +49 176 21191406
--
CCSEABASS@T-ONLINE.DE
SEBASTIAN@BLEED.NO
HTTP://KIDSWITHGUNS.TWODAY.NET
--

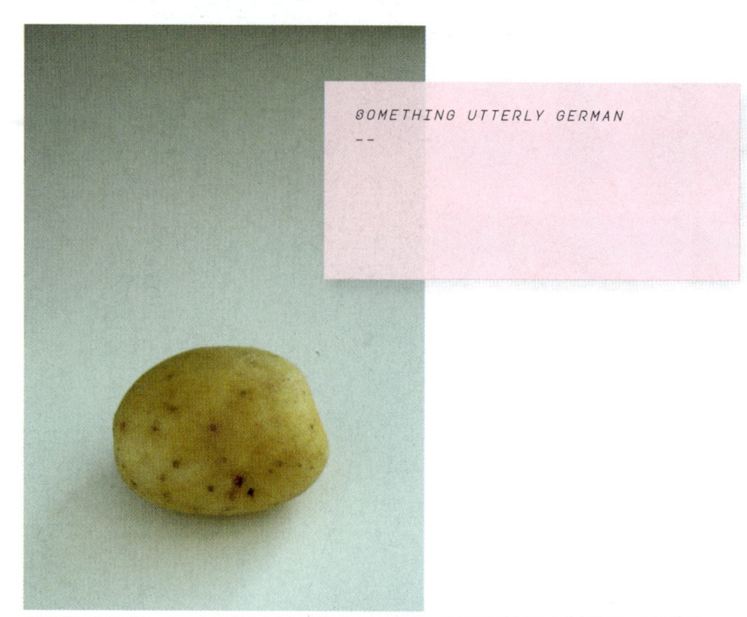

SOMETHING UTTERLY GERMAN
--

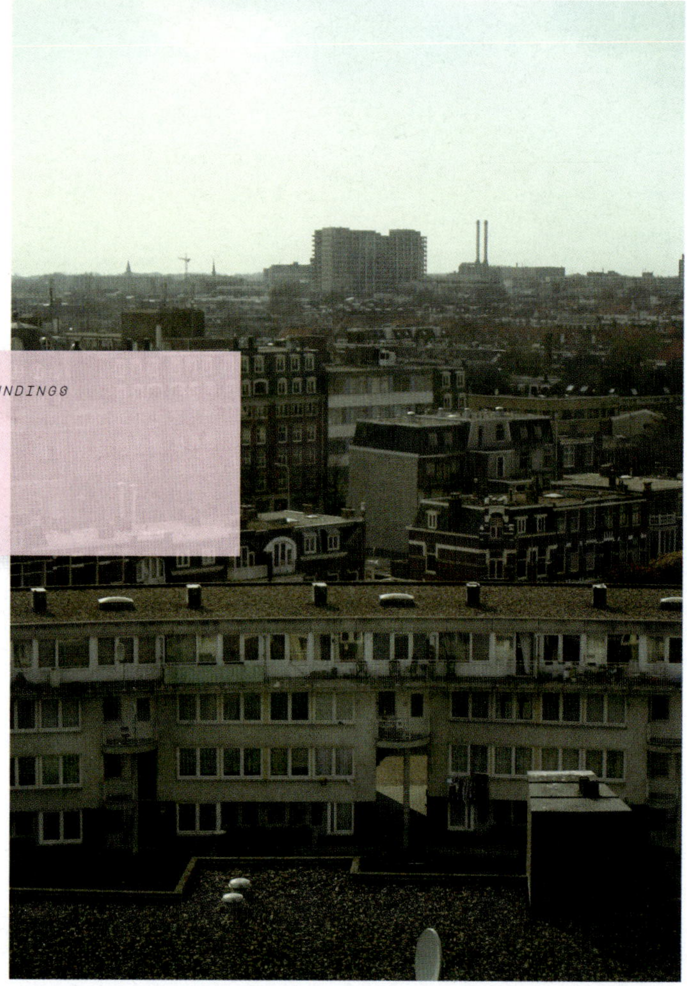

STUDIO SURROUNDINGS
--

WORKPLACE
--

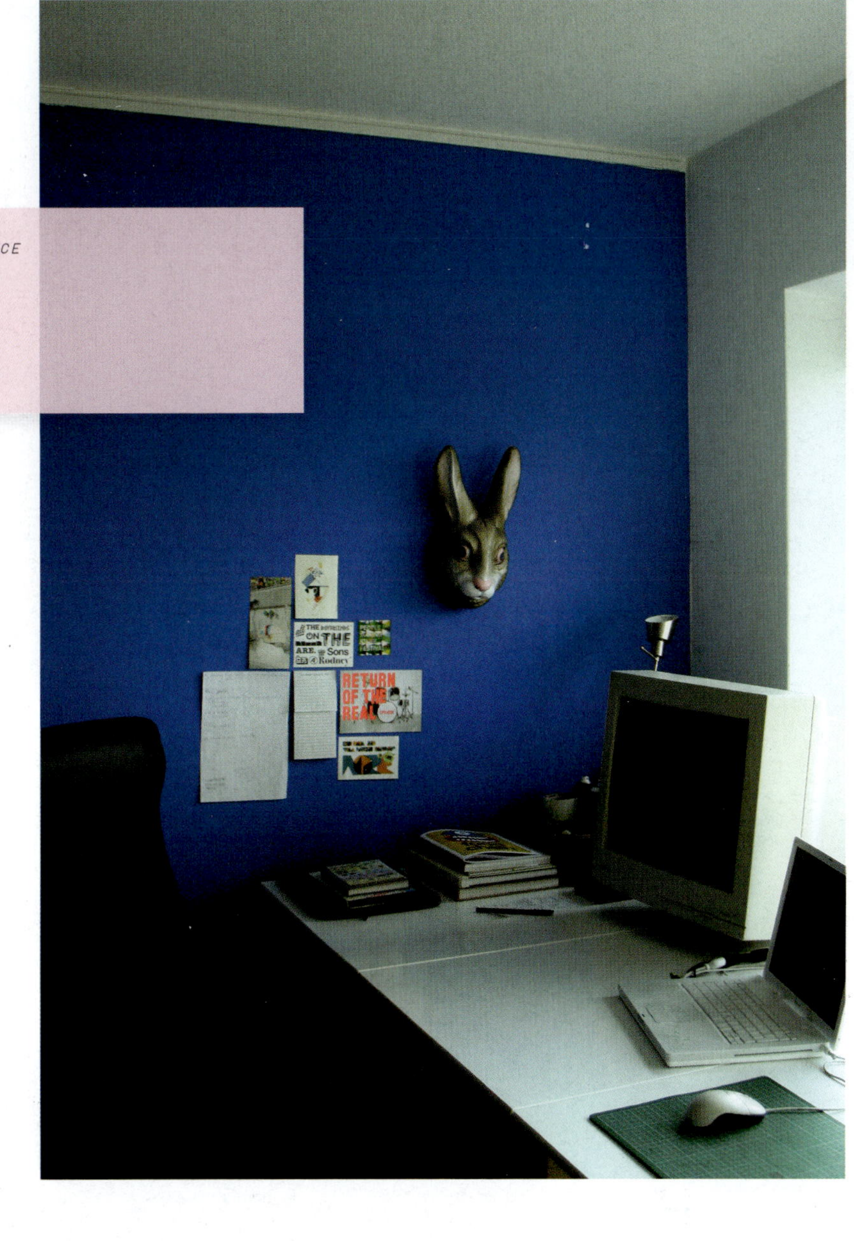

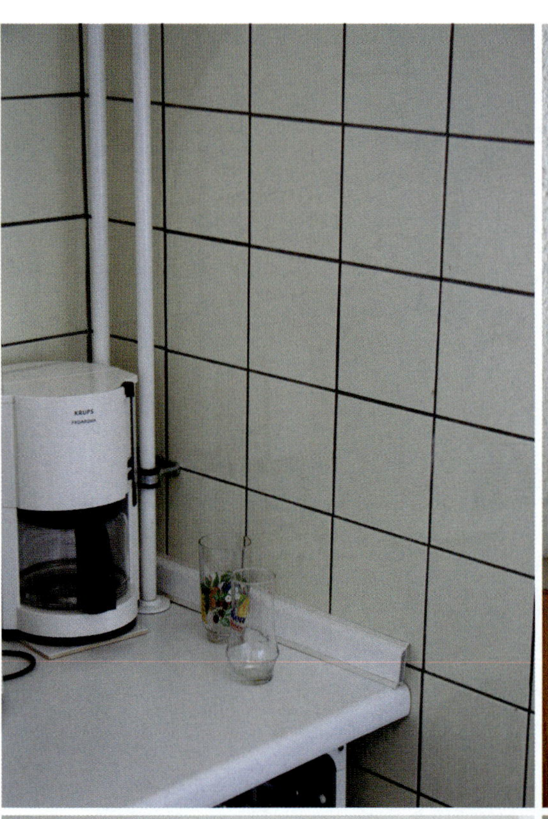

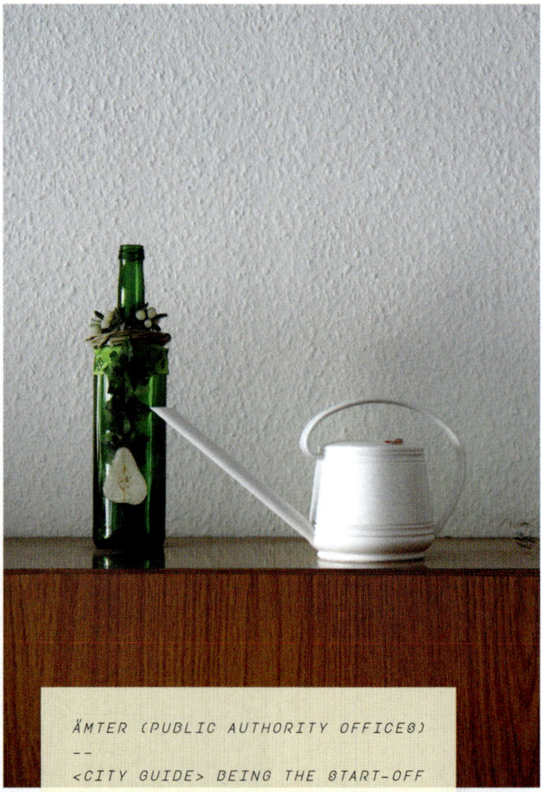

ÄMTER (PUBLIC AUTHORITY OFFICES)
--
<CITY GUIDE> BEING THE START-OFF
TOPIC, OVER SEVERAL DETOURS I
LANDED AT THE CONCEPT OF <WAIT-
ING>. GERMAN PUBLIC AUTHORITIES,
WITH THE REPUTATION OF BEING THE
MOST UNEXCITING PLACES IN THE
WORLD, ARE THE PERFECT ALLEGORY
FOR IDLENESS AND STANDSTILL.
A PHOTO SERIES TO PROVE THAT
POINT.
--

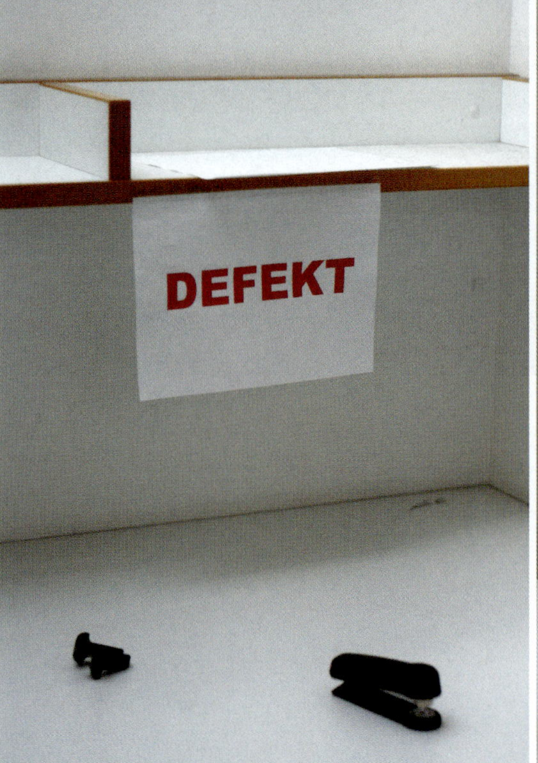

DEFEKT

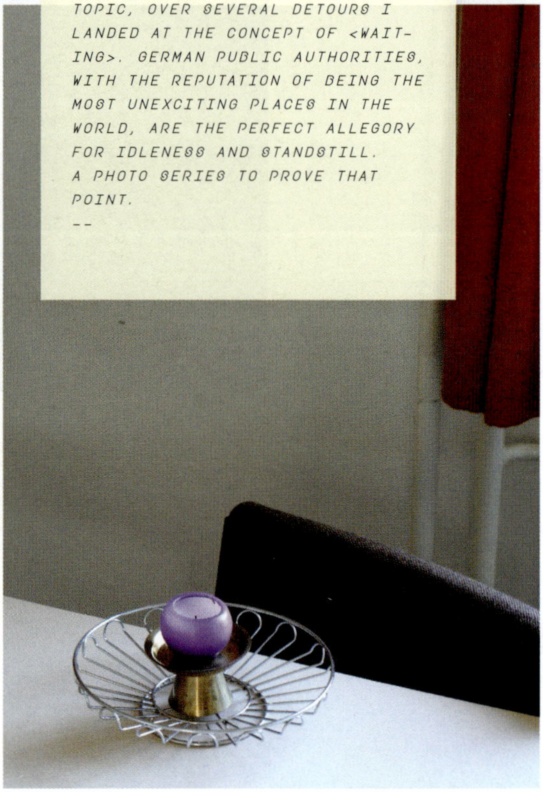

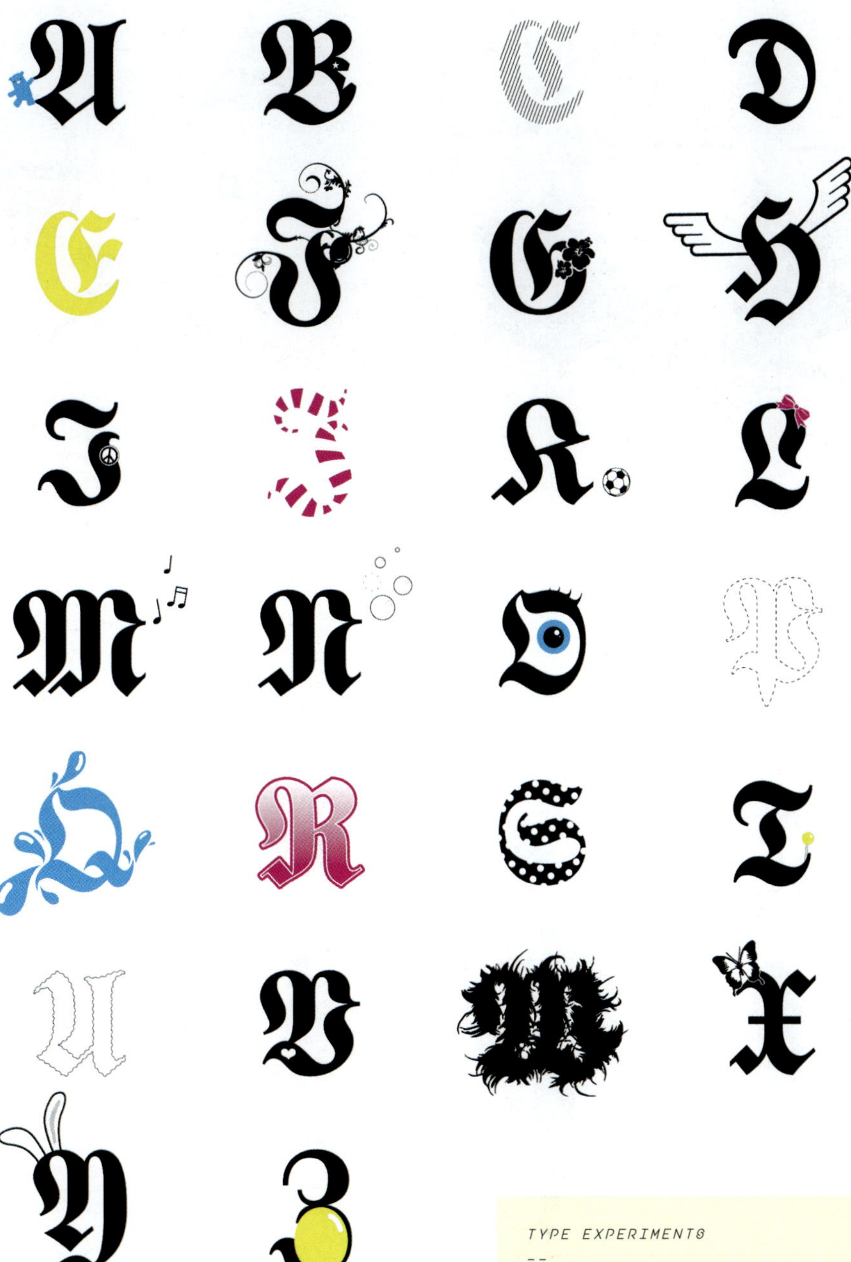

TYPE EXPERIMENTS
--
WITTY & CUTE - MAKING THE WIT-
TENBERG FRAKTUR LOOK MORE <HARM-
LESS>.
--

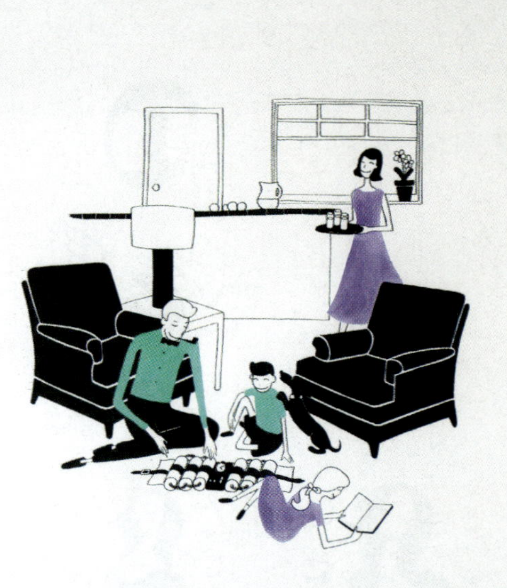

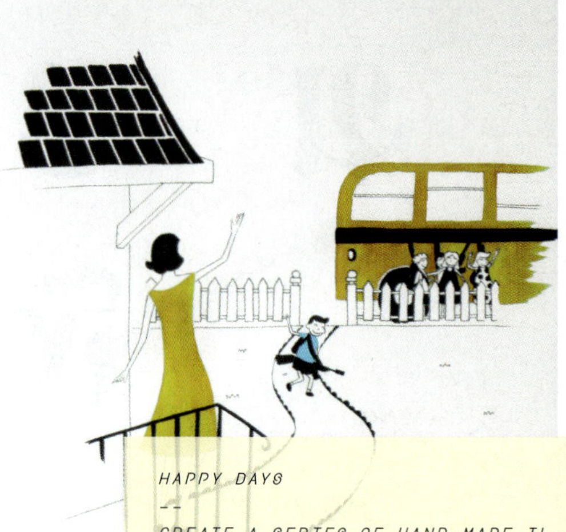

HAPPY DAYS
--
CREATE A SERIES OF HAND-MADE IL-
LUSTRATIONS BASED ON NEWSPAPER
ARTICLES OF YOUR CHOICE. I CHOSE
VERY CONTROVERSIAL TOPICS -
THE HEADLINES: <MY DREAM WAS TO
BE A SUICIDE BOMBER>, <IF ONLY
ALL STUDENTS HAD WEAPONS>, <WE
DON'T HAVE SPACE FOR FOREIGNERS>,
<THE VETERAN SUICIDE EPIDEMIC>.
--

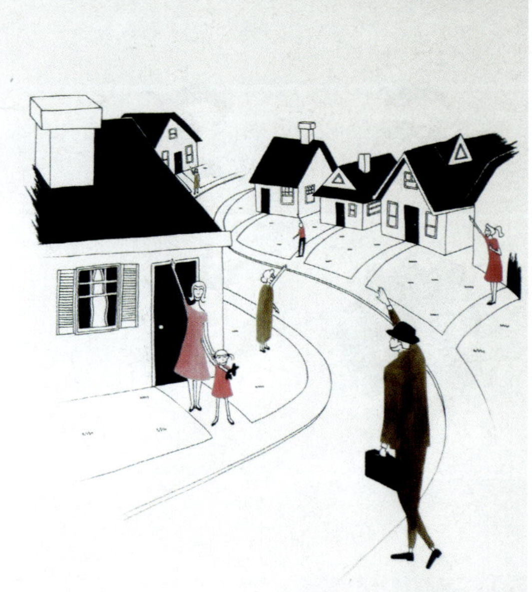

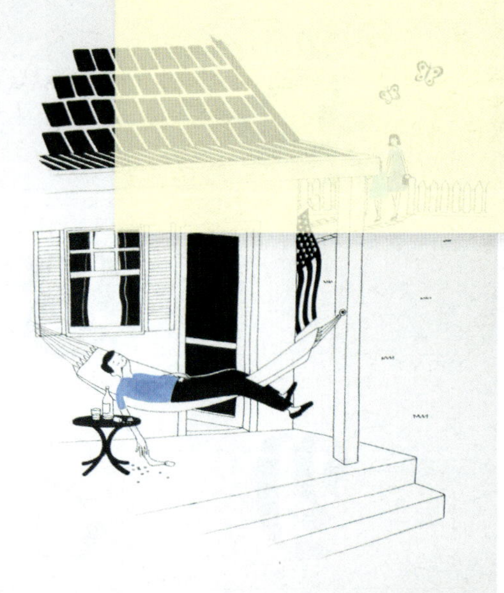

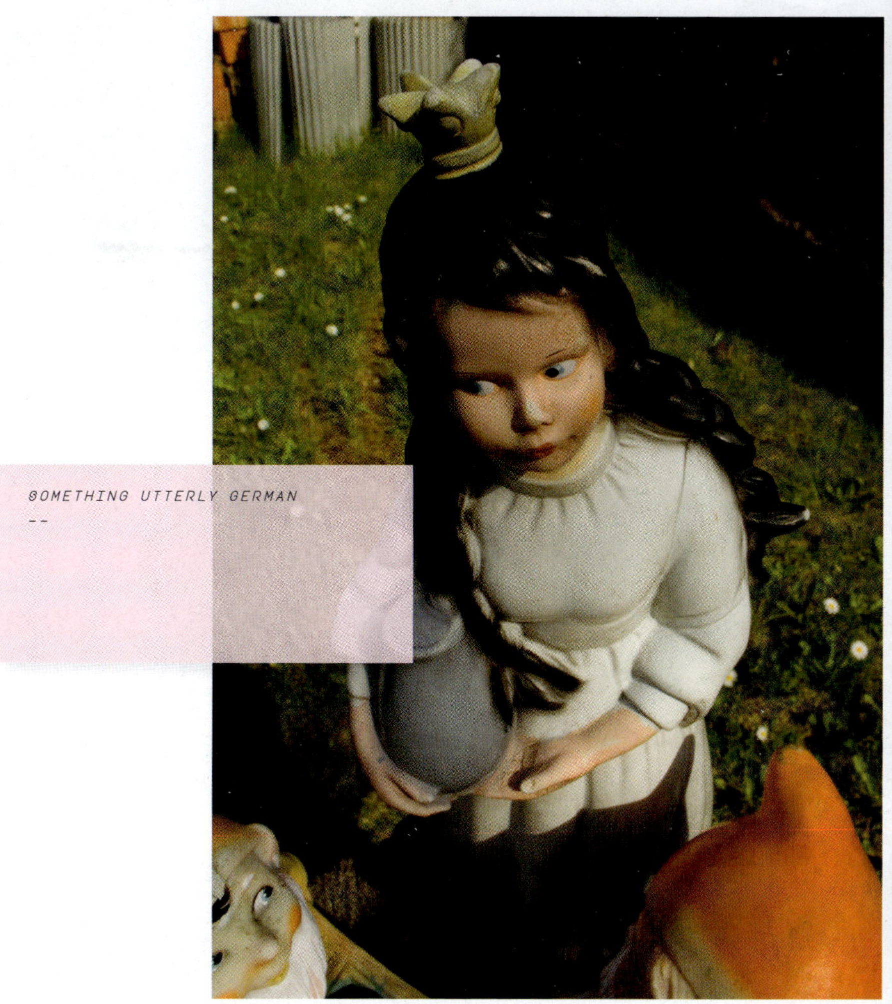

SOMETHING UTTERLY GERMAN
--

SEIBERT

ALTER EGO
MICHAEL SEIBERT
- -
YO@MICHAEL-ALFRED.DE
WWW.MICHAEL-ALFRED.DE
- -

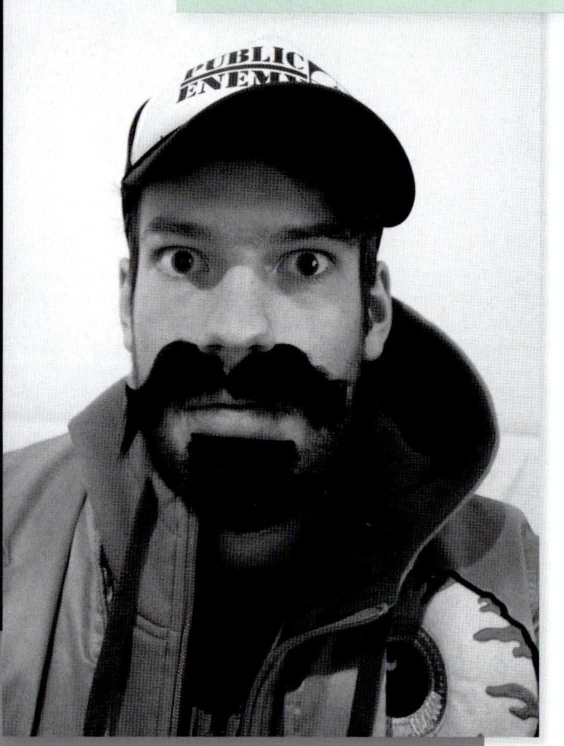

DUMMY TEXTS, FOUND ITEMS, RECORDS,
3-DAY BEARDS, DIGITAL, MOCK-UPS,
KOOL WITH A <K>, FILTER COFFEE,
CARDBOARD BOX, MARCEL REICH-RAN-
ICKI, GOING WALKING AND 36 FELT-
TIP PENS FOR 1 EURO.

--

WHAT IS GERMAN?

LANGUAGE? GERMAN'S A GREAT
LANGUAGE! I LIKE THE WORD <GE-
STALTUNG>, AS WELL AS THE TERM
<VISUELLE KOMMUNIKATION>. DOESN'T
<DESIGN> SOUND FUNNY SOMEHOW? I
FEEL UNCOMFORTABLE AT THE IDEA
I HAVE TO INTRODUCE MYSELF AS A
<DESIGNER>. I STUDY <VISUELLE KOM-
MUNIKATION> OR <KOMMUNIKATIONSGE-
STALTUNG>, NOT SO MUCH <DESIGN>.

WHAT IS GERMAN DESIGN?

FOR MY SWISS FRIENDS AND FEL-
LOW STUDENTS: OBVIOUSLY - BAUHAUS,
TSCHICHOLD, RAMS, BEHRENS, AICHER
- TRADITION, HISTORY OF DESIGN…
  BUT MEANWHILE THERE'S MORE -
  LOTS OF EXCITING OFFICES AND
  DESIGNERS PRODUCING GREAT, IN-
  SPIRING WORK
- INTERNATIONAL, LESS ACADEMIC,
  PLAYFUL
I THINK GERMAN DESIGN IS BOTH OF
THOSE THINGS!

DESCRIBE YOUR WORKING PROCESS.

SWITCH ON, TUNE IN, DO RESEARCH,
OCCASIONALLY FLOUNDER, SOMETIMES
ALSO TACKLE IT HEAD ON, PLAYFUL,
BUT DOING-DOING-DOING SERIOUSLY,
FINALLY POLISHING, SORTING OUT AND
DEFINITELY SWITCHING OFF AGAIN.
FIRST AND FOREMOST A LOT OF LAUGH-
TER, MOTIVATING AND INSPIRING ONE
ANOTHER RECIPROCALLY (RHYTHM).

WHAT DO YOU AIM TO ACHIEVE WITH
YOUR WORK?

I ADMIRE PEOPLE, INCLUDING DE-
SIGNERS, WHO HAPPILY AND WITH LOTS
OF HUMOR TAKE ON RESPONSIBILITY
WITH THEIR WORK IN A SELF-CONFI-
DENT WAY, NOT JUST FOR THEMSELVES.
I'D LIKE TO ACHIEVE THAT TOO.

YOU'VE INVITED A FRIEND TO
GERMANY; NAME ONE PLACE THEY
REALLY MUST VISIT AND A QUINT-
ESSENTIAL EXPERIENCE YOU REC-
OMMEND.

GO TO FRANCONIAN SWITZERLAND
AND MAKE A KNEIPP-CURE (HYDRO-
THERAPY). A PLACE WHERE YOU HAVE
TO TRAMP THROUGH REALLY ICY COLD
WATER WITH YOUR FEET TO GET THERE…
I JUST DON'T UNDERSTAND WHY ONLY
PENSIONERS STILL DO IT? THAT'S RE-
ALLY GENUINE HARDCORE - A TRULY
SACRAMENTAL FEELING WHEN THE OVER-
CHILLED LEGS WARM UP AGAIN AND
LITERALLY BOIL BECAUSE OF SHEER
BLOOD FLOW.

WHAT IS THE MOST IMPORTANT
LESSON YOU HAVE LEARNED IN YOUR
PROFESSION SO FAR?

STUDYING MEANS DISCOVERING AS
YOU STUDY, TRYING OUT, FALLING ON
YOUR FACE, GETTING UP, CONTRADICT-
ING, DISCUSSING, PURSUING GOALS,
AND ALSO UNDERTAKING EXPEDITIONS
INTO THE CREATIVE BLUE… HOPEFULLY
ALWAYS WORKING ON YOURSELF. I BE-
LIEVE CHILDREN WOULD BE THE BEST
STUDENTS!

--

DON'T GET LOCKED IN ANY BUILDING AFTER HOURS. DON'T EVER GET DRUNK IN A CORNFIELD. DON'T SEARCH THE BASEMENT WHEN THE POWERS JUST GONE OFF. DON'T ASSOCIATE YOURSELF WITH YOUNG CHILDREN WHO SPEAK LATIN IN A DEEP VOICE. DON'T WORK THE NIGHT SHIFT. DON'T SHOOT AT RANDOM, AIM FOR THE HEAD. DON'T FEEL SORRY FOR ANYTHING.
ALWAYS RUN OUT THE FRONT DOOR AND NOT UP THE STAIRS.

WEEKEND OF FEAR APRIL 27TH - 29TH MANHATTAN CINEMAS ERLANGEN, GERMANY www.weekend-of-fear.com
11TH INTERNATIONAL FILMFESTIVAL FOR HORROR, THRILLER, SCI-FI AND OBSCURE MOVIES

NEVER WEAR HIGH HEELS WHEN CAMPING. NEVER SPEAK TO CLOWNS IN SEWERS. NEVER LET YOUR PARENTS GET JOBS AS WINTER CARETAKERS AT SECLUDED MOUNTAINTOP HOTELS. NEVER LEAVE THE CUTE KID OR THE TRAINED DOG. NEVER ALLOW YOURSELF TO BE IN BAD PHYSICAL CONDITION. NEVER TAKE SHOWERS IN OUT-OF-THE-WAY MOTELS. NEVER ASSUME IT'S JUST THE WIND.
ALWAYS LISTEN TO THE CRAZY OLD LADY AND THE DRUNK GUY.

WEEKEND OF FEAR APRIL 27TH - 29TH MANHATTAN CINEMAS ERLANGEN, GERMANY www.weekend-of-fear.com
11TH INTERNATIONAL FILMFESTIVAL FOR HORROR, THRILLER, SCI-FI AND OBSCURE MOVIES

WHEN SOMEONE WHO SMILES TOO MUCH OFFERS YOU SOMETHING, SAY NO. WHEN YOU ARE SWIMMING AND SUDDENLY HEAR FAST-PACED CELLO MUSIC, GET OUT OF THE WATER. WHEN THE DOLL WANTS TO WATCH THE NEWS, YOU DO TOO. WHEN YOUR NEW HOUSE TELLS YOU TO GET OUT, DO IT. WHEN YOU GET A LEPRACHAUN TO GRANT YOU THREE WISHES, BE EXTREMELY SPECIFIC. WHEN THE FIRST TEN GUNBLASTS DIDN'T DO ANY GOOD, THE NEXT TEN WON'T WORK EITHER.
ALWAYS HIDE BEHIND METAL DOORS, WOOD WILL BREAK.

WEEKEND OF FEAR APRIL 27TH - 29TH MANHATTAN CINEMAS ERLANGEN, GERMANY www.weekend-of-fear.com
11TH INTERNATIONAL FILMFESTIVAL FOR HORROR, THRILLER, SCI-FI AND OBSCURE MOVIES

HOW TO SURVIVE A HORROR MOVIE
--
CREATE A SERIES OF THREE COM-
PLETELY TYPE-BASED POSTERS FOR
A LOCAL HORROR MOVIE FESTIVAL.
OTHERWISE NO RESTRICTIONS.
--

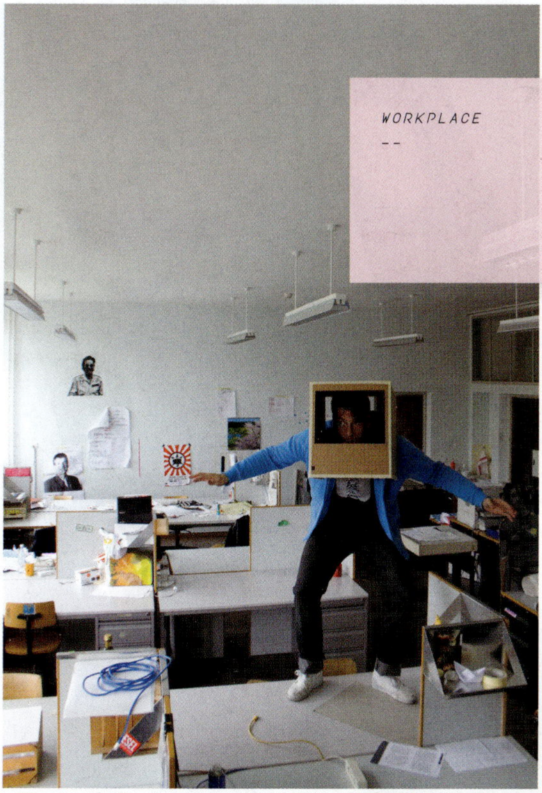

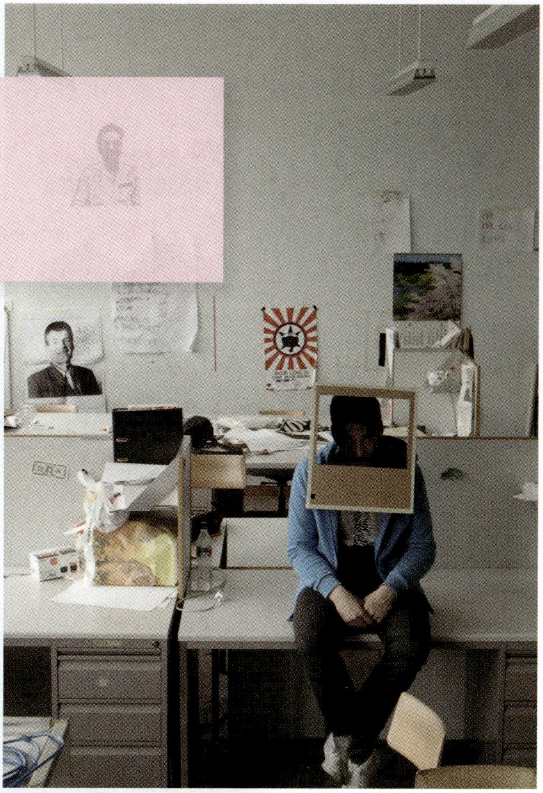

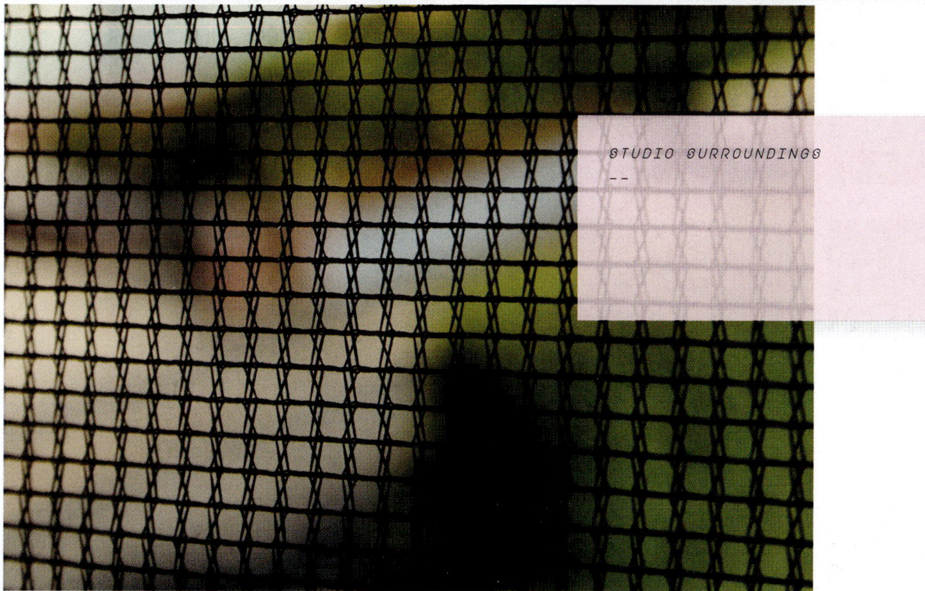

WORKPLACE
--

STUDIO SURROUNDINGS
--

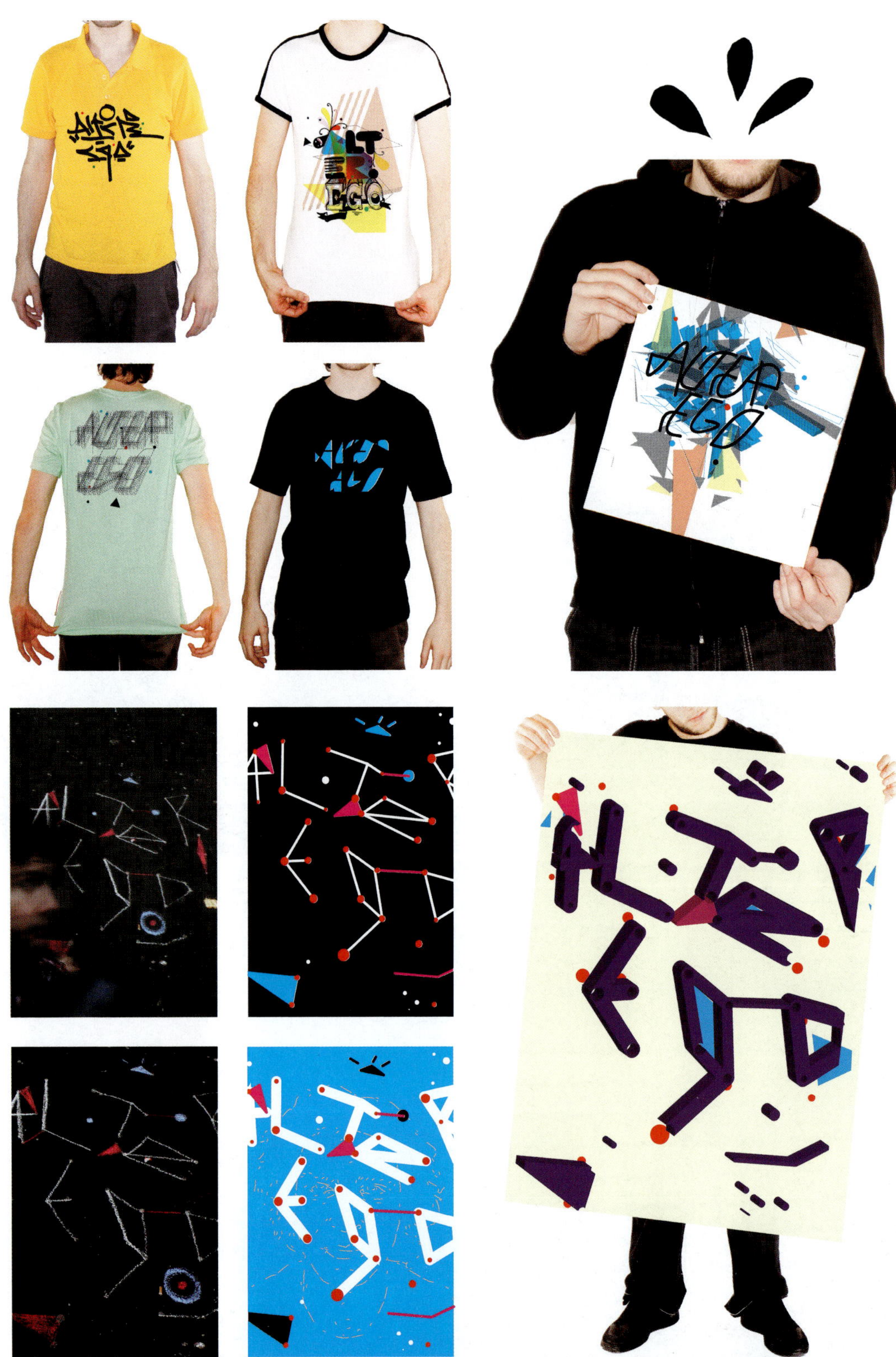

ALTER EGO
(MICHAEL SEIBERT)
--
AT A WORKSHOP ON EXPERIMENTAL
DESIGNING I SPENT THREE DAYS EX-
PLORING THE CONCEPT OF THE ALTER
EGO - MY OTHER SELF SO TO SPEAK,
IN THIS CASE THE CREATIVE OR THE
MORE PLAYFUL ME? FIRST IT WAS A
QUESTION OF APPREHENDING ONE'S
ENVIRONMENT MORE PRECISELY AND
CONSCIOUSLY SO AS TO FORM VARI-
ANTS LATER ON. IF YOU GET INTO
IT, IT'S QUITE INCREDIBLE WHERE
DESIGN AIDS ARE HIDDEN ALL OVER
THE PLACE AND HOW FAR YOU CAN
PUSH VARIATIONS. I CONCENTRATED
ON MATRIX SYSTEMS FOR TYPOGRAPH-
ICAL TRANSPOSITIONS. ENDLESS AND
UNUSED MATRIX SYSTEMS ON CRISP
BREAD, PIECES OF CHEWING GUM
STUCK TO THE FLOOR, IN ARCHITEC-
TURE, ETC.
--

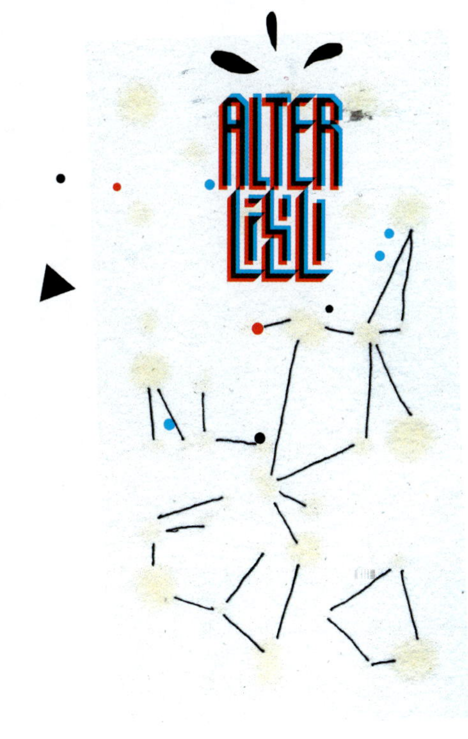

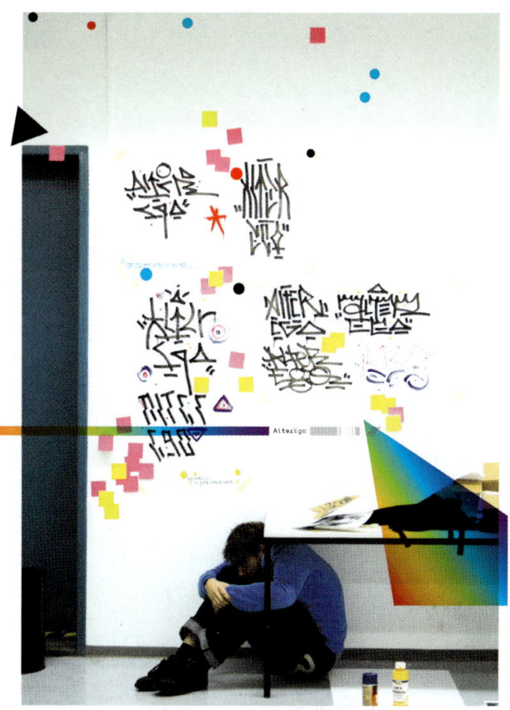

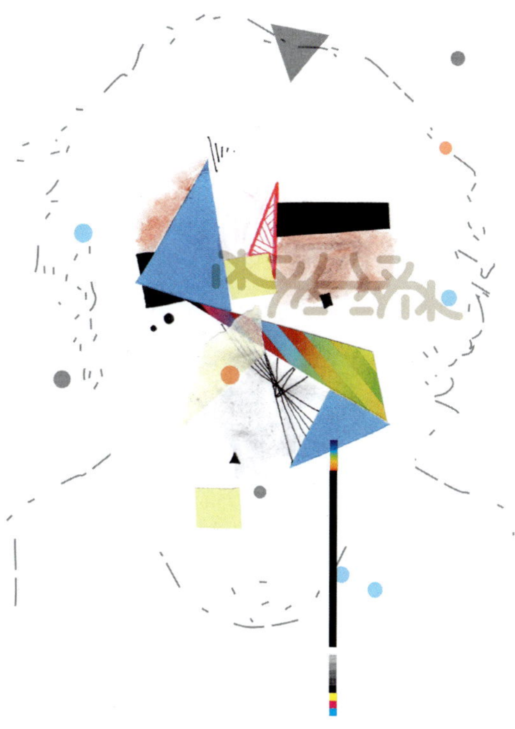

BARBARA HAHN AND CHRISTINE ZIM-
MERMANN WORK IN THE FIELDS OF
COMMUNICATION DESIGN, VISUALIZA-
TION AND DESIGN RESEARCH.

--

WHAT IS GERMAN?

PRETZELS.

WHAT IS GERMAN DESIGN?

CORPORATE A-B-E.

DESCRIBE YOUR WORKING PROCESS.

A CONSTANT OSCILLATION BETWEEN
CREATION AND CONTEXTUALIZATION.

WHAT DO YOU AIM TO ACHIEVE WITH
YOUR WORK?

INTELLIGIBILITY, CLARITY AND IN-
FORMATION.

YOU'VE INVITED A FRIEND TO
GERMANY; NAME ONE PLACE THEY
REALLY MUST VISIT AND A QUINT-
ESSENTIAL EXPERIENCE YOU REC-
OMMEND.

1. STUTTGART TOWN HALL
2. USE A PATERNOSTER LIFT

WHAT IS THE MOST IMPORTANT
LESSON YOU HAVE LEARNED IN YOUR
PROFESSION SO FAR?

STRUCTURED THINKING AND SYSTEM-
ATIC PROCEDURE.

--

VON B UND C

VON B UND C
HAHN UND ZIMMERMANN
--
GUTENBERGSTRASSE 20
3011 BERN
SWITZERLAND
--
T +41 31 3312870
--
MAIL@VON-B-UND-C.NET
WWW.VON-B-UND-C.NET
--

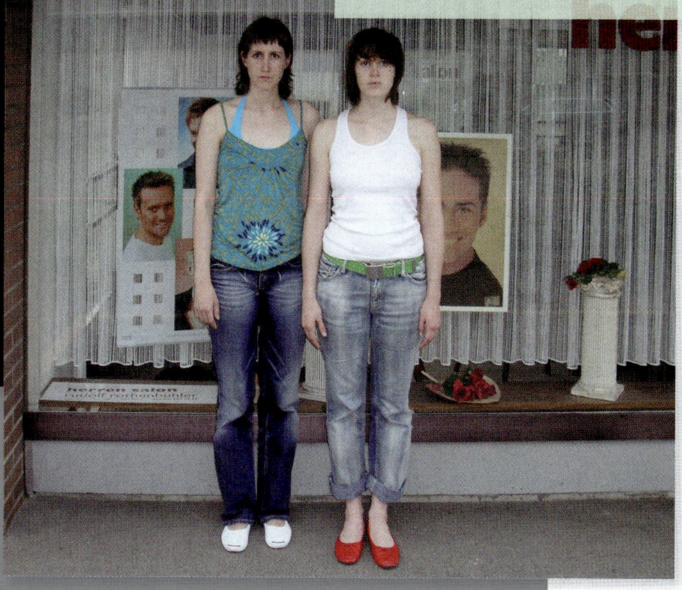

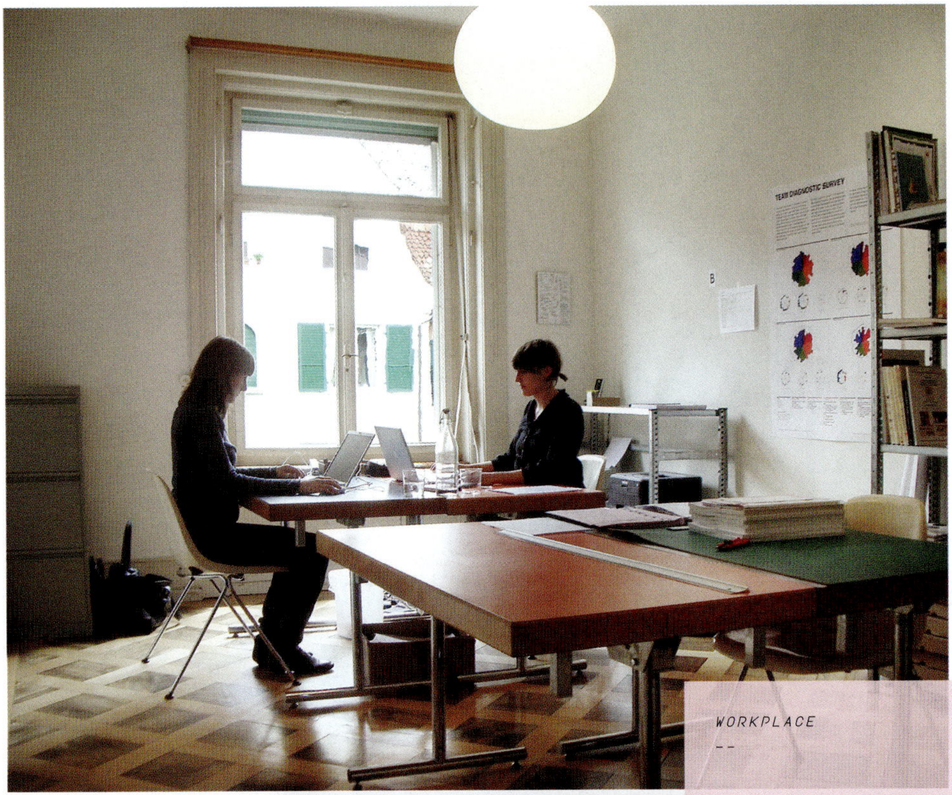

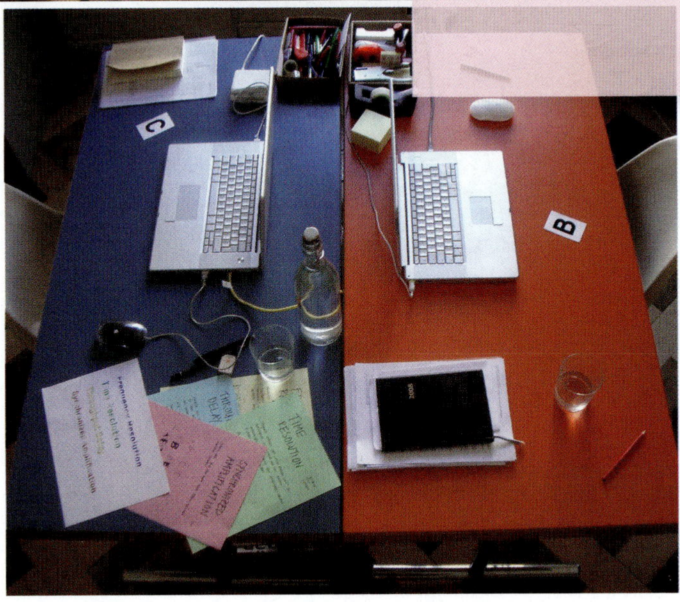

TIME
RESOLUTION

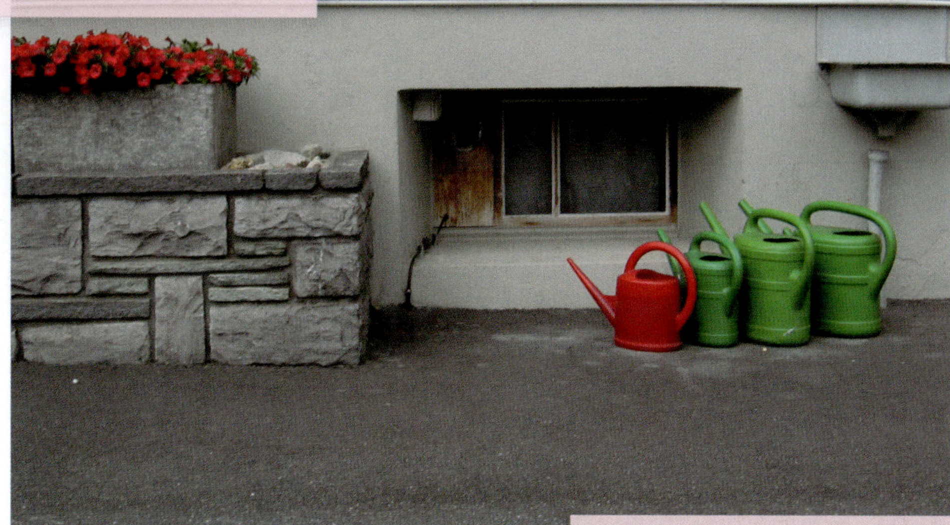
SOMETHING UTTERLY GERMAN
--

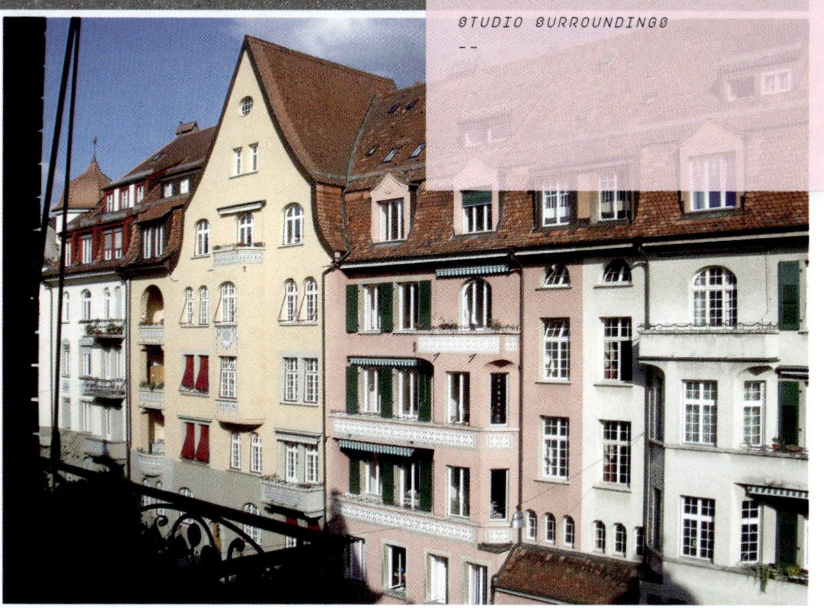
STUDIO SURROUNDINGS
--

Vis. II

Reading behavior of B and C over a period of time, in comparison
between B and C and in relation to individual books

Lektüre / Reading material

Leseverhalten von B und C im Zeitverlauf, im Vergleich zwischen
B und C und in Bezug auf einzelne Bücher

Leseverhalten im Zeitverlauf / Reading behavior over a period of time

VON B UND C - DATENVISUALISIERUNG
JENSEITS VON KUCHEN- UND BALKEN-
DIAGRAMMEN (ABOUT B AND C - DATA
VISUALIZATION BEYOND DIAGRAMS OF
CAKES AND BEAMS)
--
BRIEF: DEVELOPING NEW WAYS AND
POSSIBILITIES OF DATA VISUALIZA-
TION
--
IN THIS WORK NEW WAYS AND POS-
SIBILITIES OF DATA VISUALIZATION
ARE EXPLORED FROM THE VISUAL
COMMUNICATION PERSPECTIVE. THE
WORK COMPRISES NINE INNOVATIVE
VISUALIZATION PROPOSALS AND COM-
PLETE DATA BASES THAT WERE COL-
LECTED DURING THE WORKING PRO-
CESS ITSELF. THE VISUALIZATIONS
DEVELOPED SHOW A BROAD SPECTRUM
OF NEW FORMS OF REPRESENTATION
IN WHICH THE GRAPHIC MEANS TAKE
ACCOUNT OF THE CONTENT DEPICTED,
AND COMMUNICATE ITEMS OF INFOR-
MATION ACCURATELY. THE INFORMA-
TION CONTENT AND THE ESTHETIC
QUALITY OF THE VISUALIZATIONS
ARE GIVEN EQUAL WEIGHT IN THIS
PROCESS.
--

Vis. I

Frequency of the words used in e-mail exchange between B and C
and their mentor Michelle Gubser

wir
und die

der uns
das in es zu vo...
auch für mit ist noch
auf sind Woche dir du einle...
den eine werden nicht
Arbeit sehr am dass wie im
dem Christine Barbara unsere
unserer bei aber um
Grüsse Michelle hat möchten über... wird gut schon
was wenn machen nach nur aus dann Dat... diese sind Th...
als an viel nun sie wann da einen gemacht können...
bis nächste Visualisierungen zum oder so wieder dich di...
des etwas Gefühl gestern heute hier letzten mehr nochmals
jetzt dann müssen treffen unsere unserem wann

Kommunikation / Communication

Häufigkeit der verwendeten Wörter im E-Mail-Austausch zwischen
B und C und ihrer Mentorin Michelle Gubser

ich
ihr
euch. Liebe zu
und von
Michelle
die in mich

Temperatur / Temperature

Vis. III

Individual temperature perception of B and C in comparison to the average daily temperature

Individuelles Temperaturempfinden von B und C im Vergleich zur mittleren Tagestemperatur

Leistung / Performance

Temperatur Vis. IV

Work performance of B and C according to the daily individual self-evaluation

Arbeitsleistung von B und C gemäss täglich vorgenommener individueller Selbsteinschätzung

Besucher / *Visitors*　　　　　　　　　　Vis. V

Besuchshäufigkeit und -dauer verschiedener Besuchergruppen
und Einzelpersonen im Arbeitsraum von B und C

*Visit frequency and duration of various visitor groups and
individual persons in the work room of B and C*

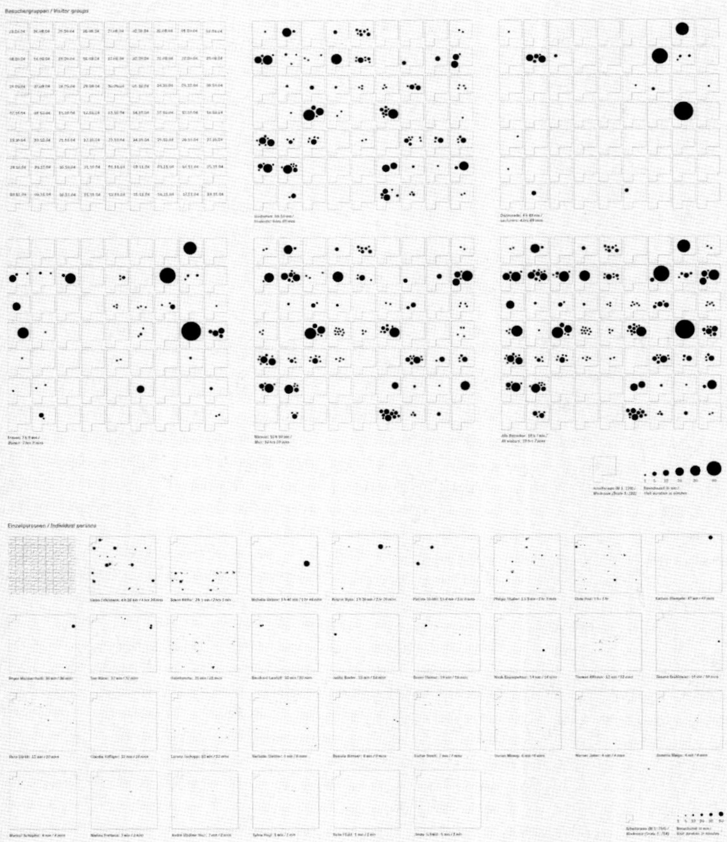

Arbeitsplatz / *Workplace*　　　　　　　　Vis. VI

Vergleich der Arbeitsplätze von B und C und des Gebrauchs einzelner
Arbeitswerkzeuge im Zeitverlauf

*Comparison of the workplaces of B and C and the use of individual tools
over a period of time*

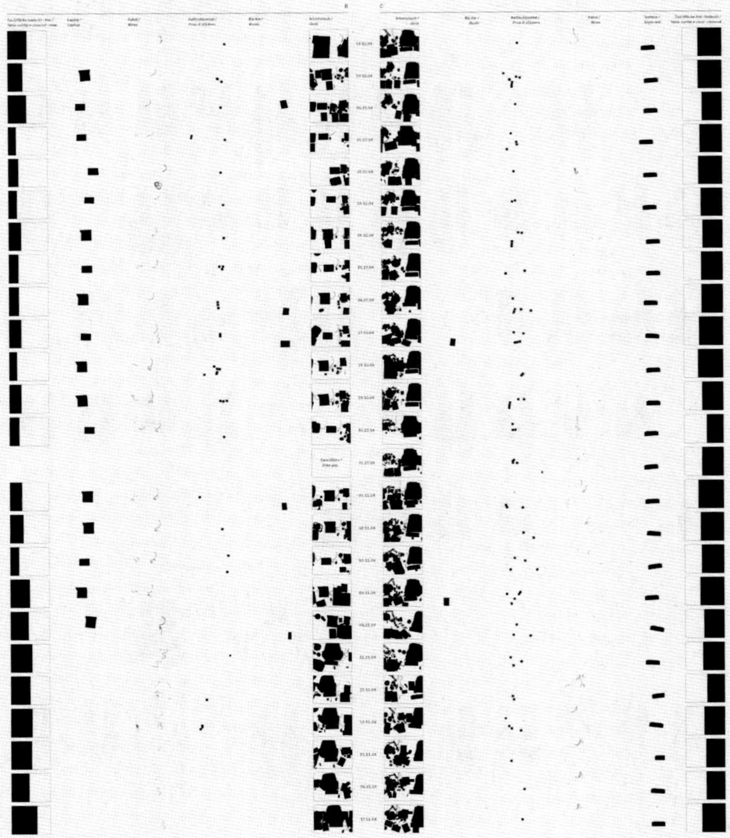

Schritte 1 / *Steps 1*   Vis. VII

Während der Arbeitszeit zu Fuss zurückgelegte Tagesdistanzen
von B und C, anhand eines exemplarischen Weges aufgezeigt

*Daily distances walked during working hours by B and C,
depicted according to an exemplary route*

Schritte 2 / *Steps 2*   Vis. VIII

Während der Arbeitszeit zu Fuss zurückgelegte Tagesdistanzen von B und C,
Fotos von den dabei auf einem exemplarischen Weg erreichten Endpunkten

*Daily distances walked during working hours by B and C, photos of the
final destinations reached by them on an exemplary route*

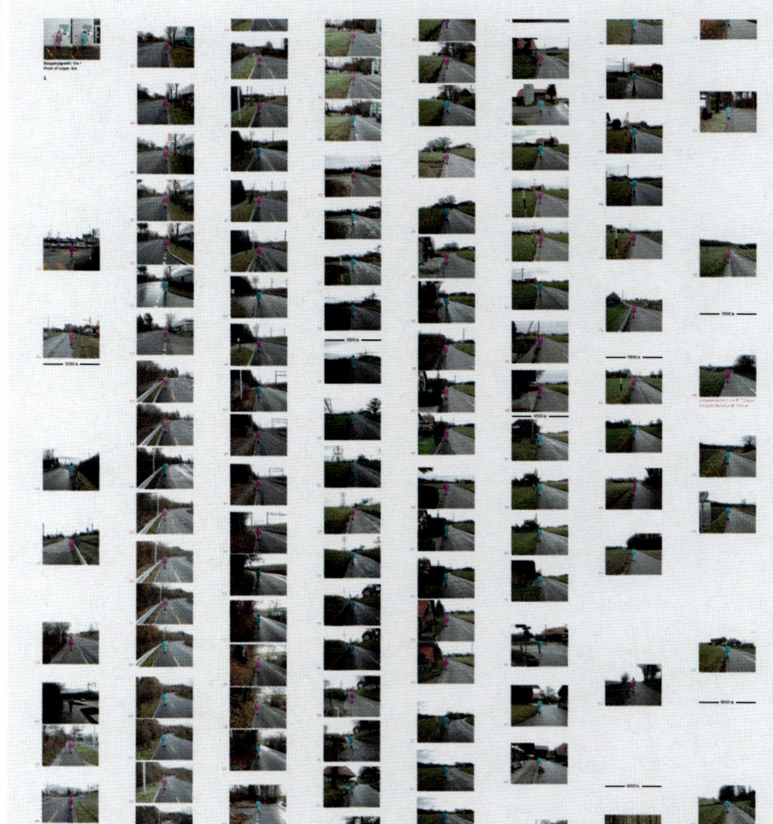

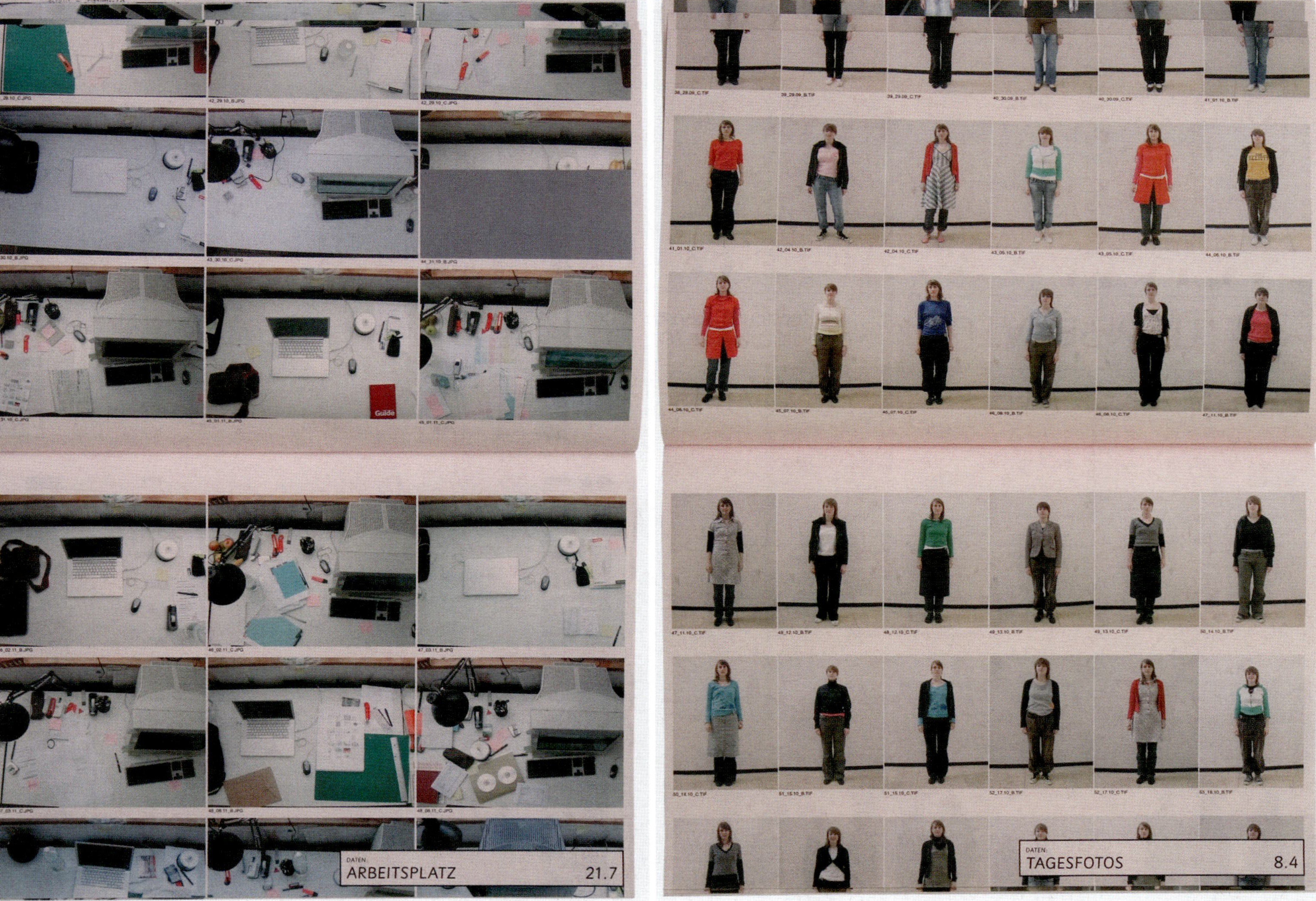
DATEN:
ARBEITSPLATZ
21.7
DATEN:
TAGESFOTOS
8.4

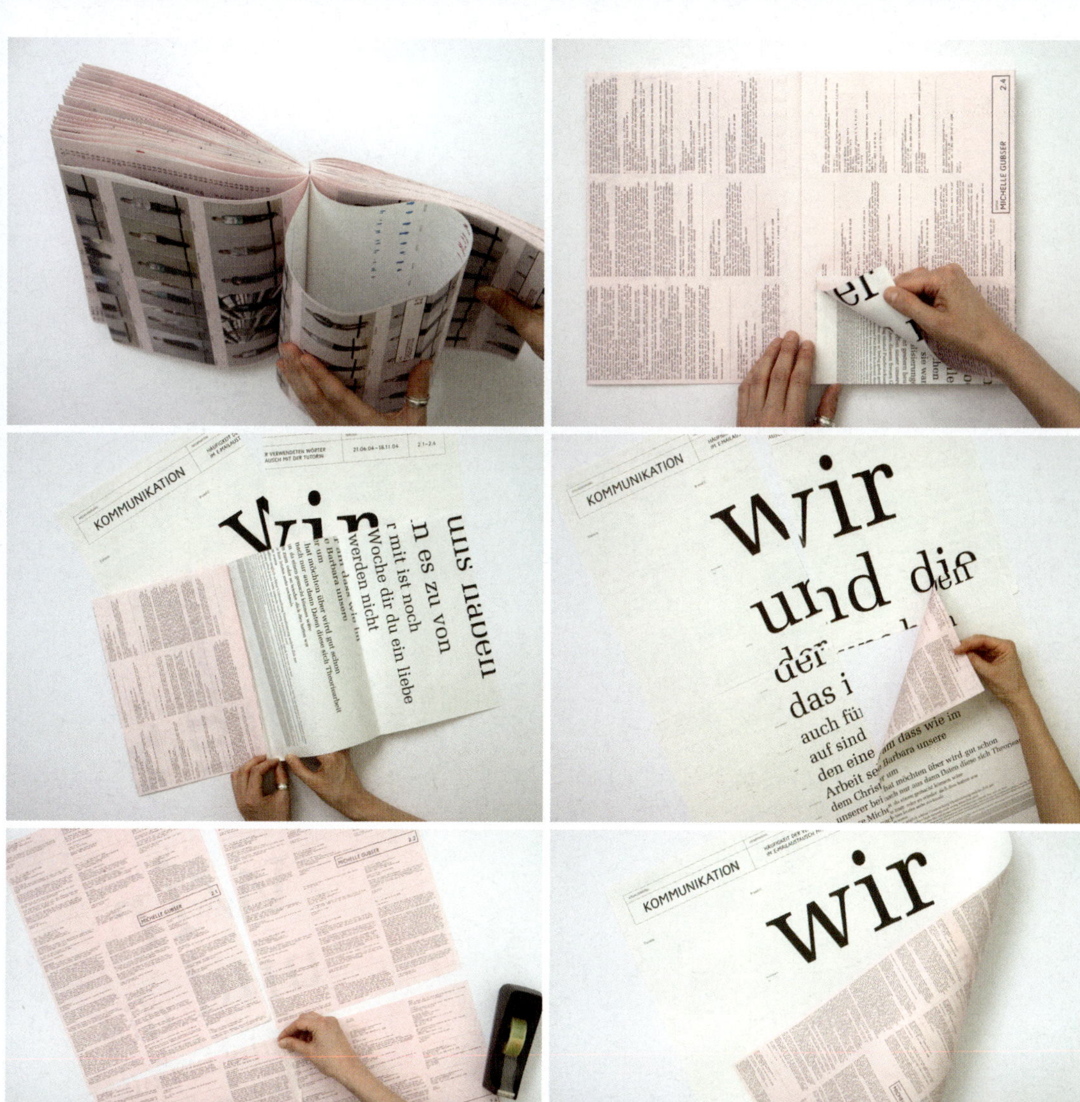

BÜRO INTERNATIONAL LONDON IS A
DESIGN PROJECT BY OLIVER KLIMPEL,
WHICH WORKS IN ASPECTS OF GRAPH-
ICS, ENVIRONMENTAL DESIGN, IDENTI-
TY PROGRAMS AND PRINT. WE APPLY A
CRITICAL AND CONCEPT-DRIVEN DESIGN
APPROACH TO PROJECTS WITH PARTNERS
IN THE CULTURAL AND EDUCATIONAL
SECTOR, AS WELL AS THE COMMERCIAL.

--

WHAT IS GERMAN?

IT'S A METAPHOR, ISN'T IT?

WHAT IS GERMAN DESIGN?

PROTESTANTISM.

DESCRIBE YOUR WORKING PROCESS.

CRITICAL PRACTICE.

WHAT DO YOU AIM TO ACHIEVE WITH
YOUR WORK?

CRITICAL PRACTICE.

YOU'VE INVITED A FRIEND TO
GERMANY; NAME ONE PLACE THEY
REALLY MUST VISIT AND A QUINT-
ESSENTIAL EXPERIENCE YOU REC-
OMMEND.

THE GERMAN FOREST.

WHAT IS THE MOST IMPORTANT
LESSON YOU HAVE LEARNED IN YOUR
PROFESSION SO FAR?

<HOW TO STAY IN BUSINESS AS A
TROUBLE-MAKER> (NORMAN POTTER)

--

BÜRO INTERNATIONAL LONDON
--
11A ILIFFE YARD OFF
CRAMPTON STREET
LONDON SE17 3QA
UK
--
T +44 20 77083708
--
INFO@BUROINTERNATIONAL.CO.UK
WWW.BUROINTERNATIONAL.CO.UK
--

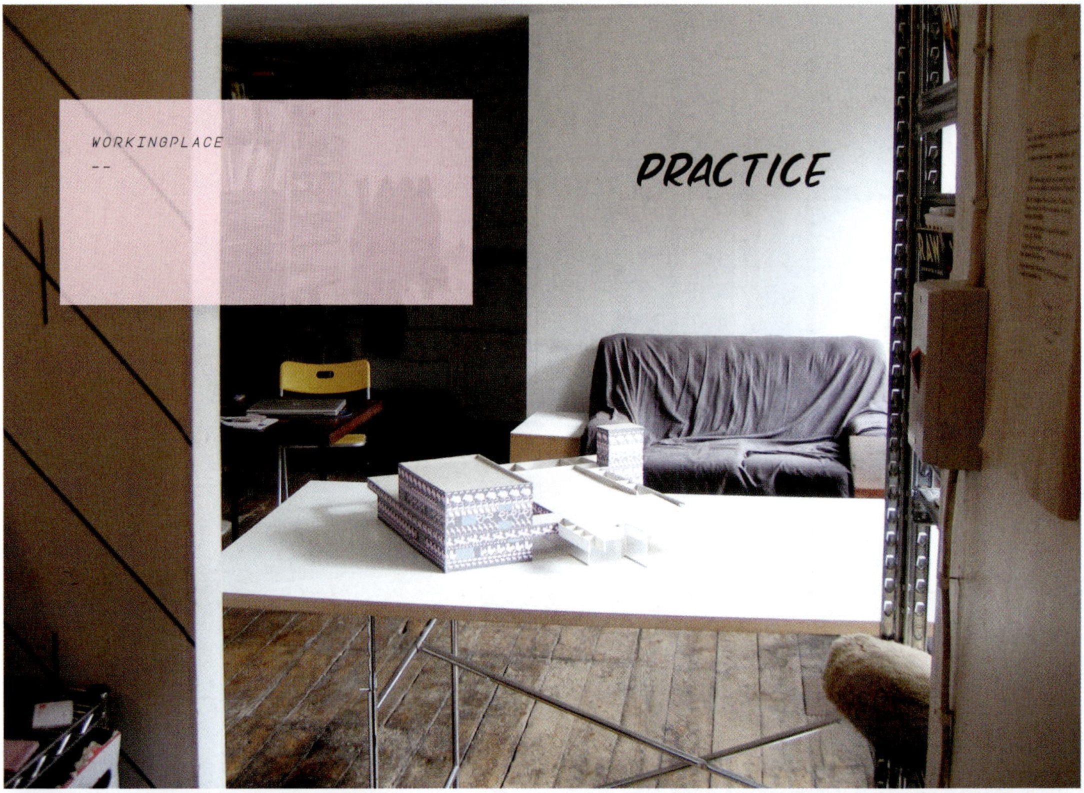

WORKINGPLACE
--
PRACTICE

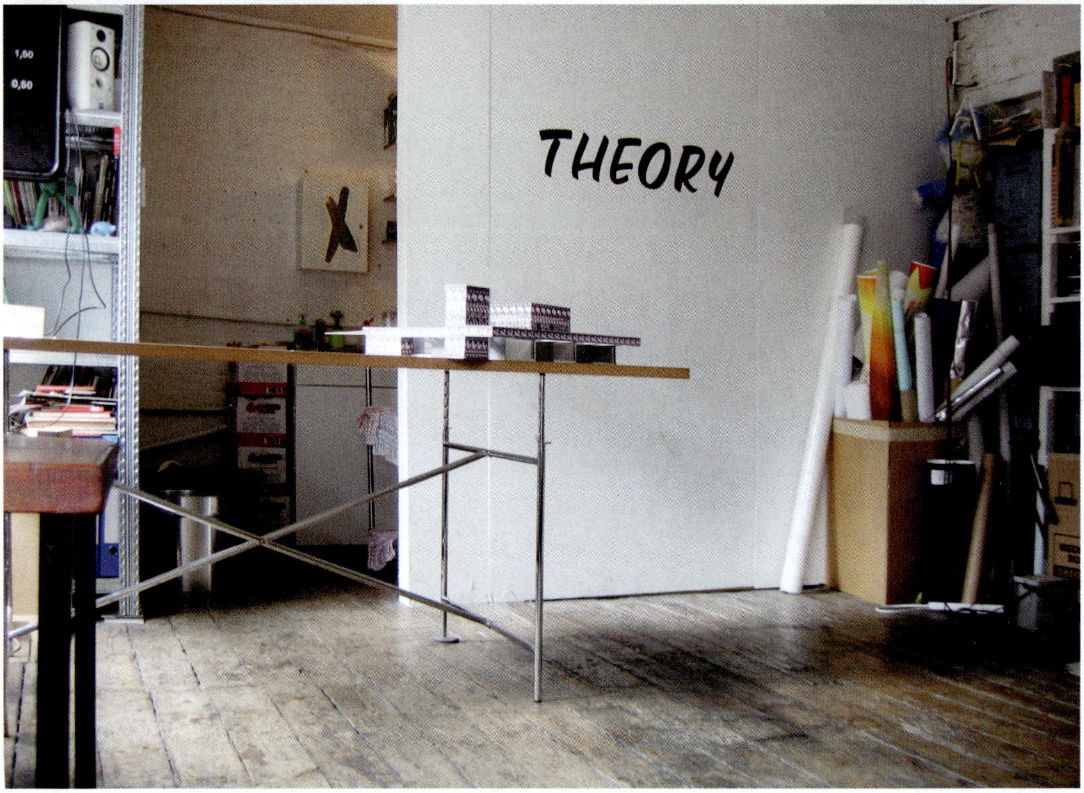

THEORY

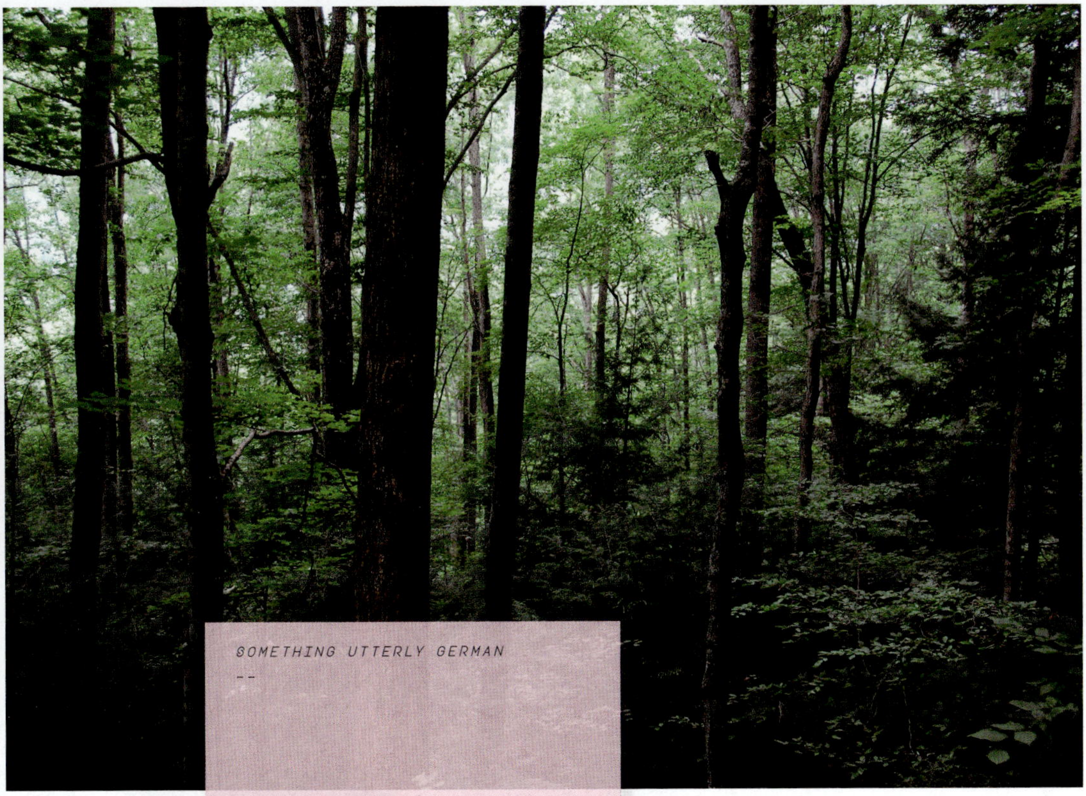

SOMETHING UTTERLY GERMAN
--

Restposten
aus
LONDON

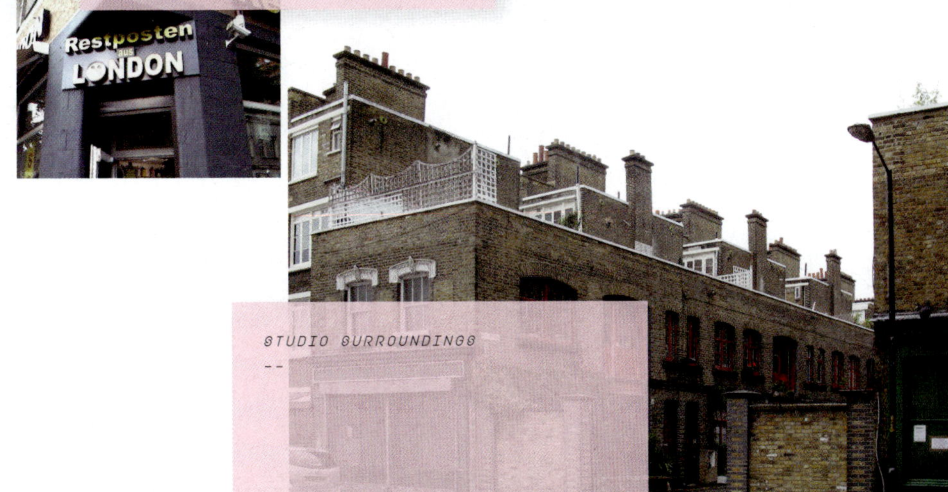
STUDIO SURROUNDINGS
--

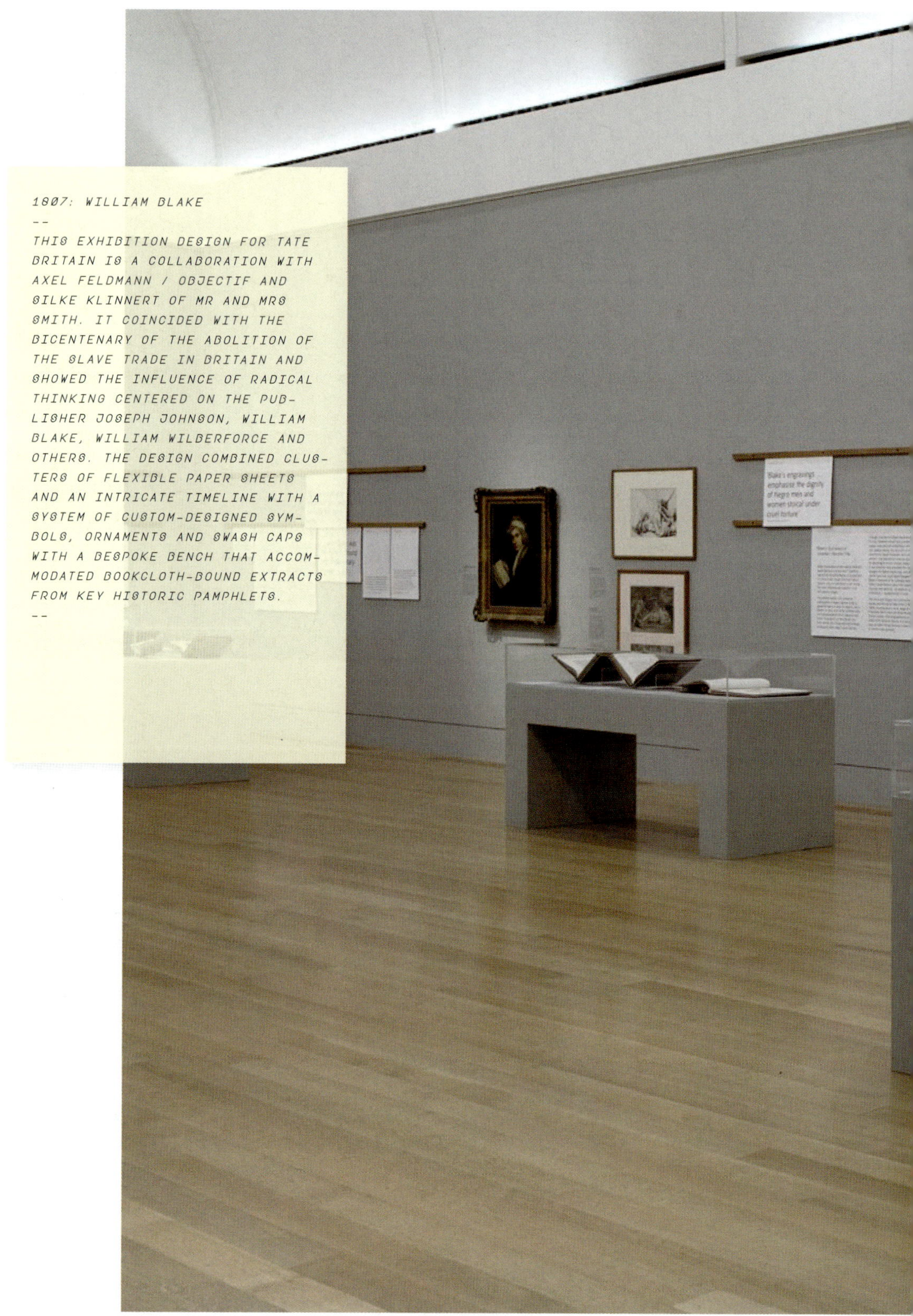
1807: WILLIAM BLAKE
--
THIS EXHIBITION DESIGN FOR TATE
BRITAIN IS A COLLABORATION WITH
AXEL FELDMANN / OBJECTIF AND
SILKE KLINNERT OF MR AND MRS
SMITH. IT COINCIDED WITH THE
BICENTENARY OF THE ABOLITION OF
THE SLAVE TRADE IN BRITAIN AND
SHOWED THE INFLUENCE OF RADICAL
THINKING CENTERED ON THE PUB-
LISHER JOSEPH JOHNSON, WILLIAM
BLAKE, WILLIAM WILBERFORCE AND
OTHERS. THE DESIGN COMBINED CLUS-
TERS OF FLEXIBLE PAPER SHEETS
AND AN INTRICATE TIMELINE WITH A
SYSTEM OF CUSTOM-DESIGNED SYM-
BOLS, ORNAMENTS AND SWASH CAPS
WITH A BESPOKE BENCH THAT ACCOM-
MODATED BOOKCLOTH-BOUND EXTRACTS
FROM KEY HISTORIC PAMPHLETS.
--

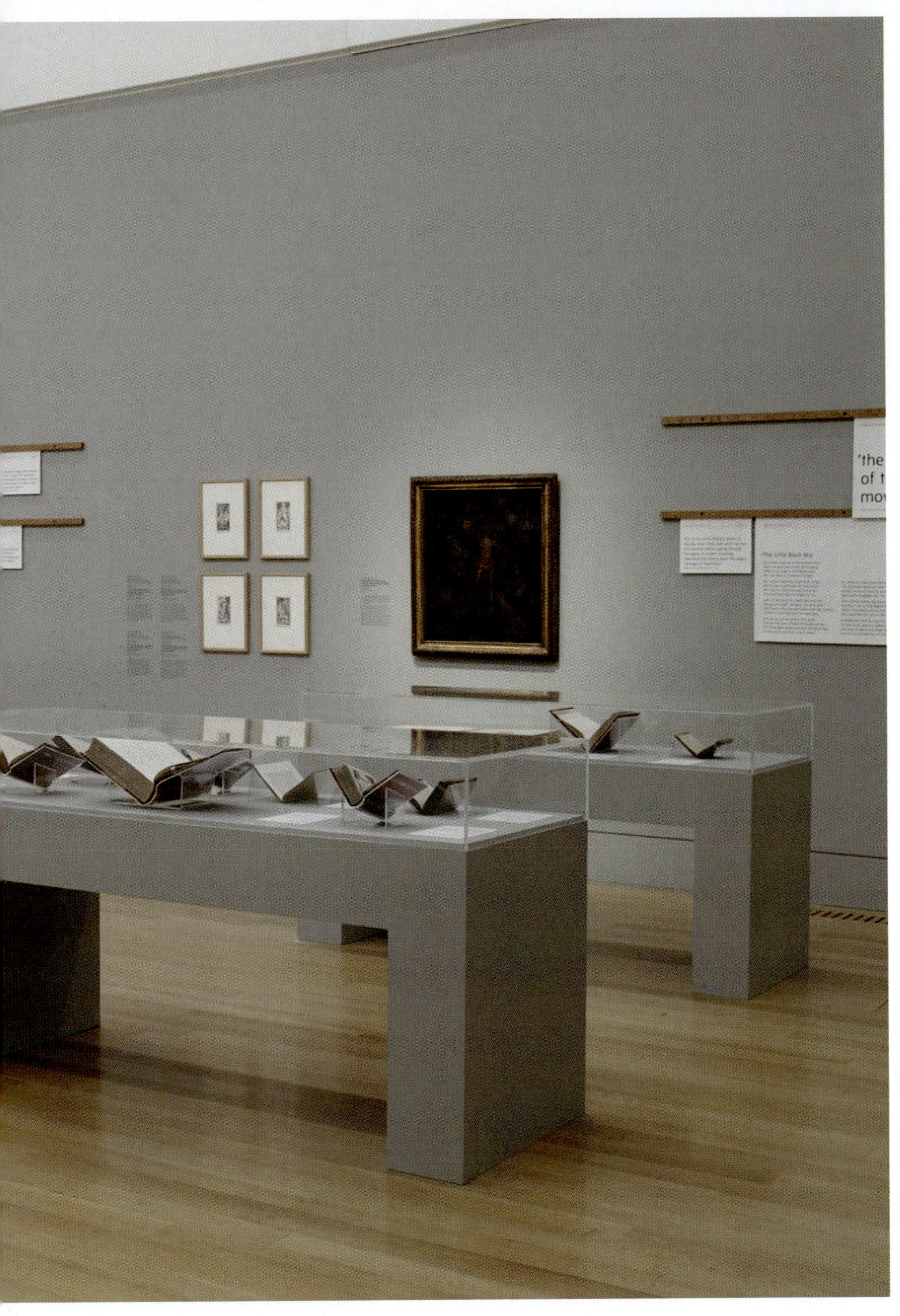

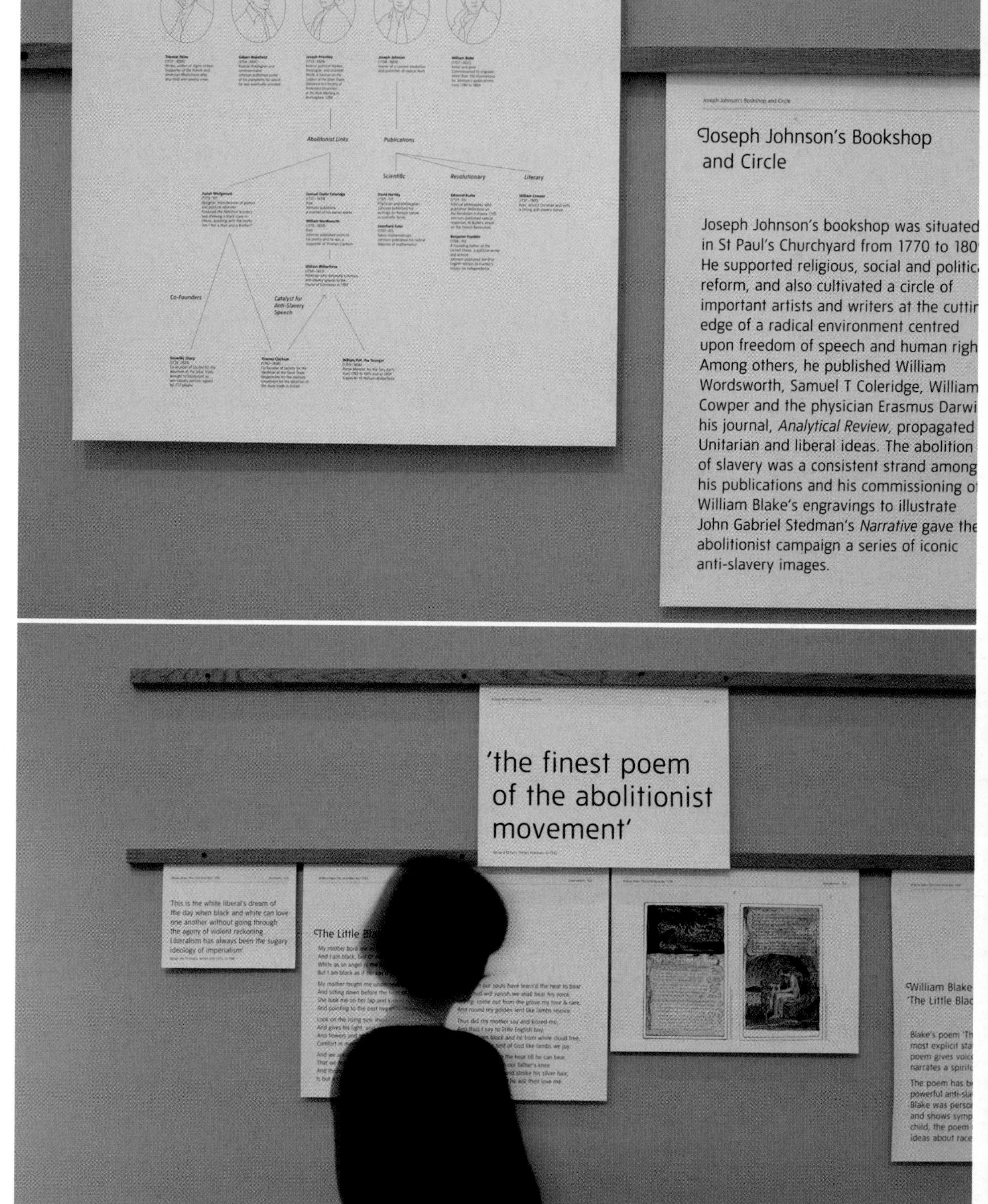
Joseph Johnson's Bookshop and Circle

Joseph Johnson's Bookshop and Circle

Joseph Johnson's bookshop was situated in St Paul's Churchyard from 1770 to 180 He supported religious, social and politic reform, and also cultivated a circle of important artists and writers at the cuttir edge of a radical environment centred upon freedom of speech and human righ Among others, he published William Wordsworth, Samuel T Coleridge, William Cowper and the physician Erasmus Darwi his journal, Analytical Review, propagated Unitarian and liberal ideas. The abolition of slavery was a consistent strand among his publications and his commissioning o William Blake's engravings to illustrate John Gabriel Stedman's Narrative gave the abolitionist campaign a series of iconic anti-slavery images.

Abolitionist Links
Publications
Scientific
Revolutionary
Literary
Co-Founders
Catalyst for Anti-Slavery Speech

'the finest poem of the abolitionist movement'

The Little Bla

This is the white liberal's dream of the day when black and white can love one another without going through the agony of violent reckoning. Liberalism has always been the sugary ideology of imperialism'

William Blake
'The Little Blac

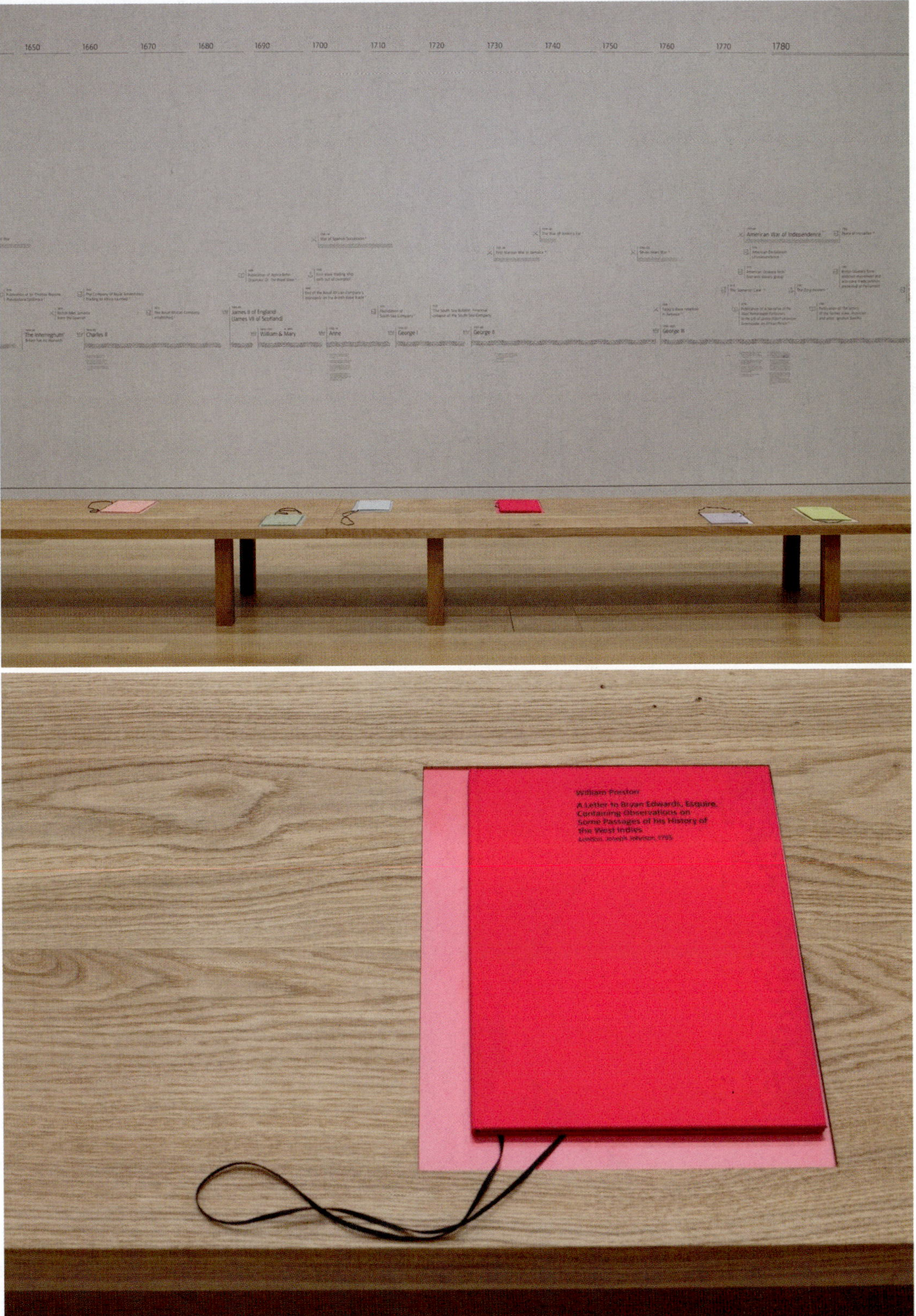

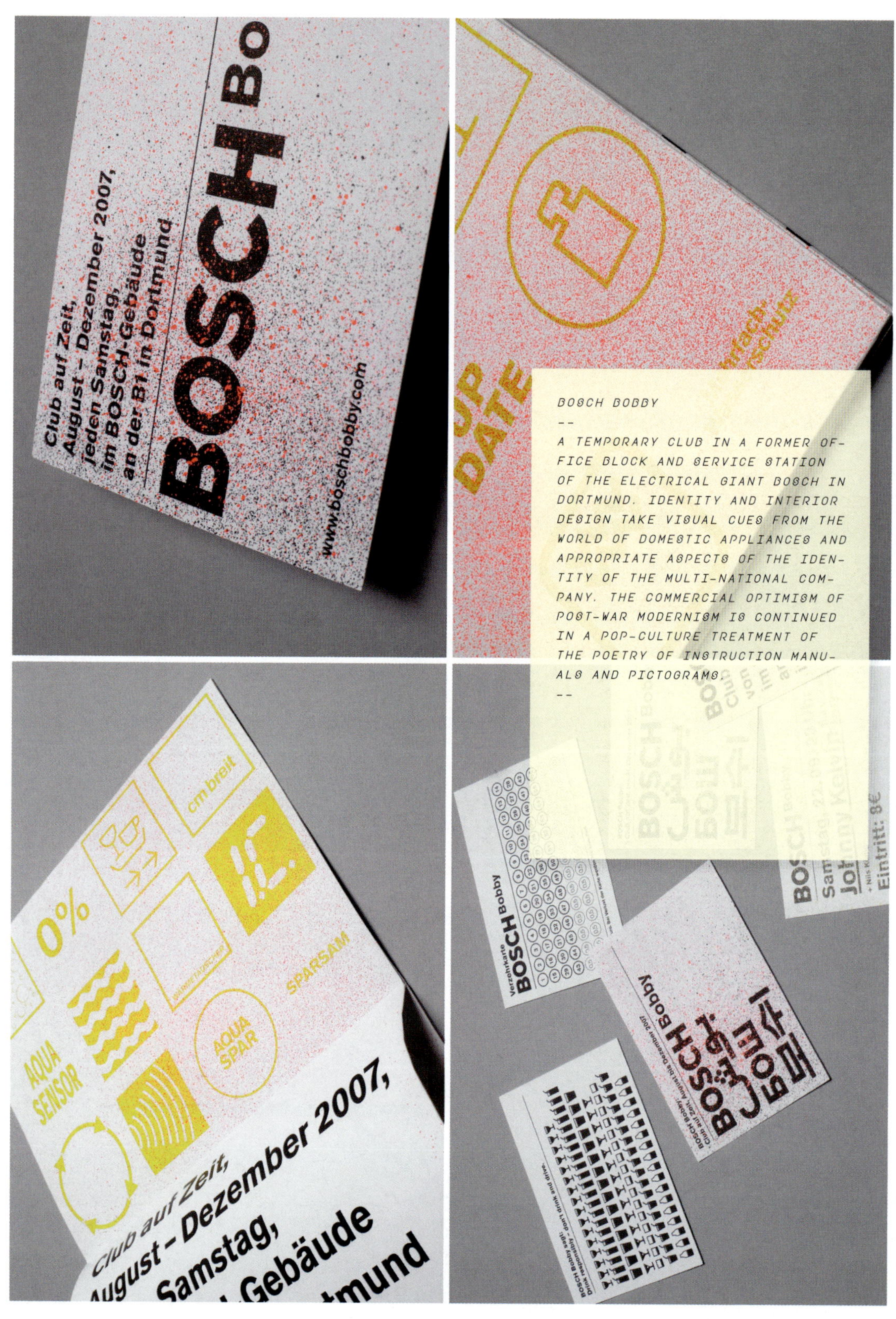

BOSCH BOBBY
--
A TEMPORARY CLUB IN A FORMER OF-
FICE BLOCK AND SERVICE STATION
OF THE ELECTRICAL GIANT BOSCH IN
DORTMUND. IDENTITY AND INTERIOR
DESIGN TAKE VISUAL CUES FROM THE
WORLD OF DOMESTIC APPLIANCES AND
APPROPRIATE ASPECTS OF THE IDEN-
TITY OF THE MULTI-NATIONAL COM-
PANY. THE COMMERCIAL OPTIMISM OF
POST-WAR MODERNISM IS CONTINUED
IN A POP-CULTURE TREATMENT OF
THE POETRY OF INSTRUCTION MANU-
ALS AND PICTOGRAMS.
--

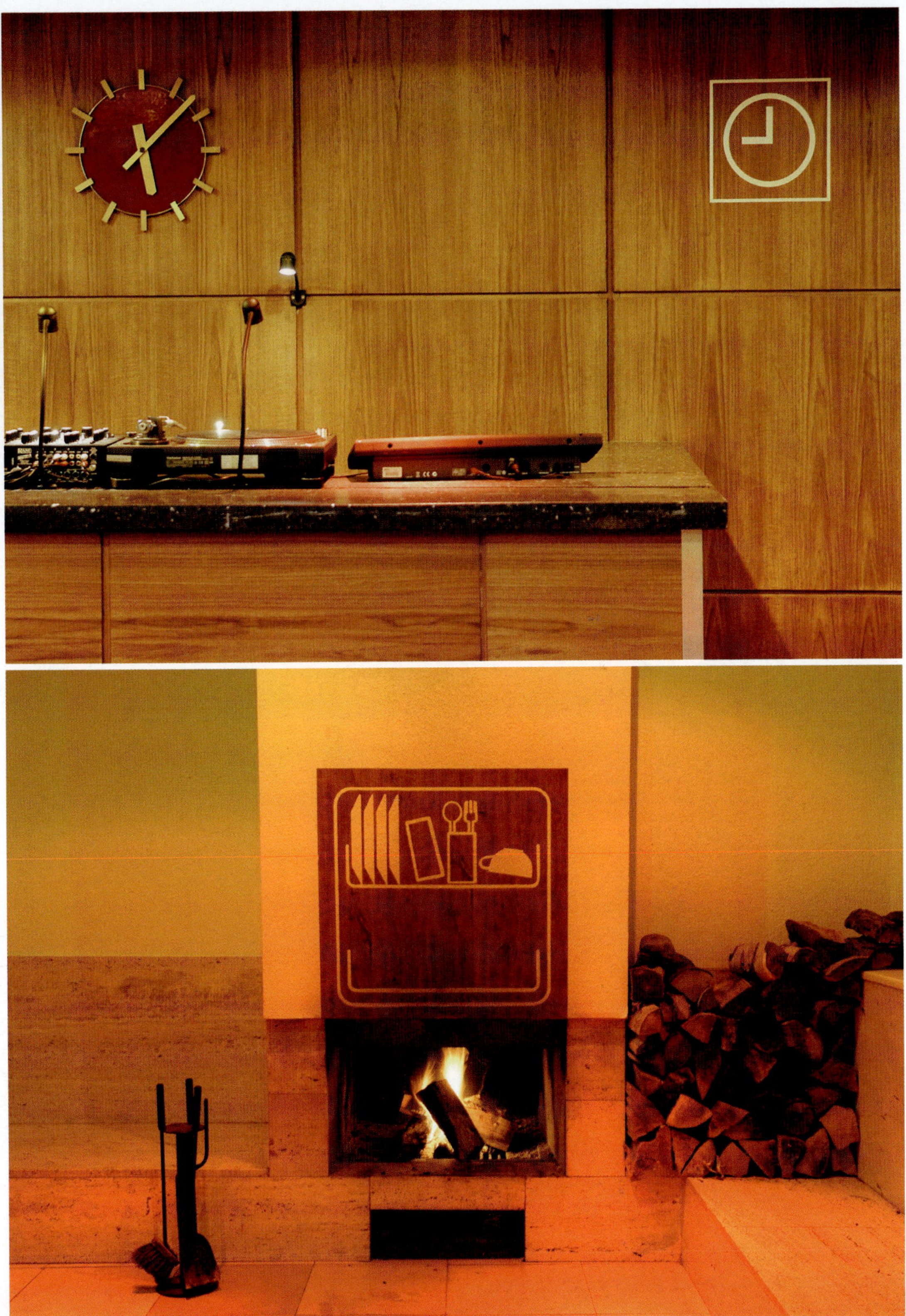

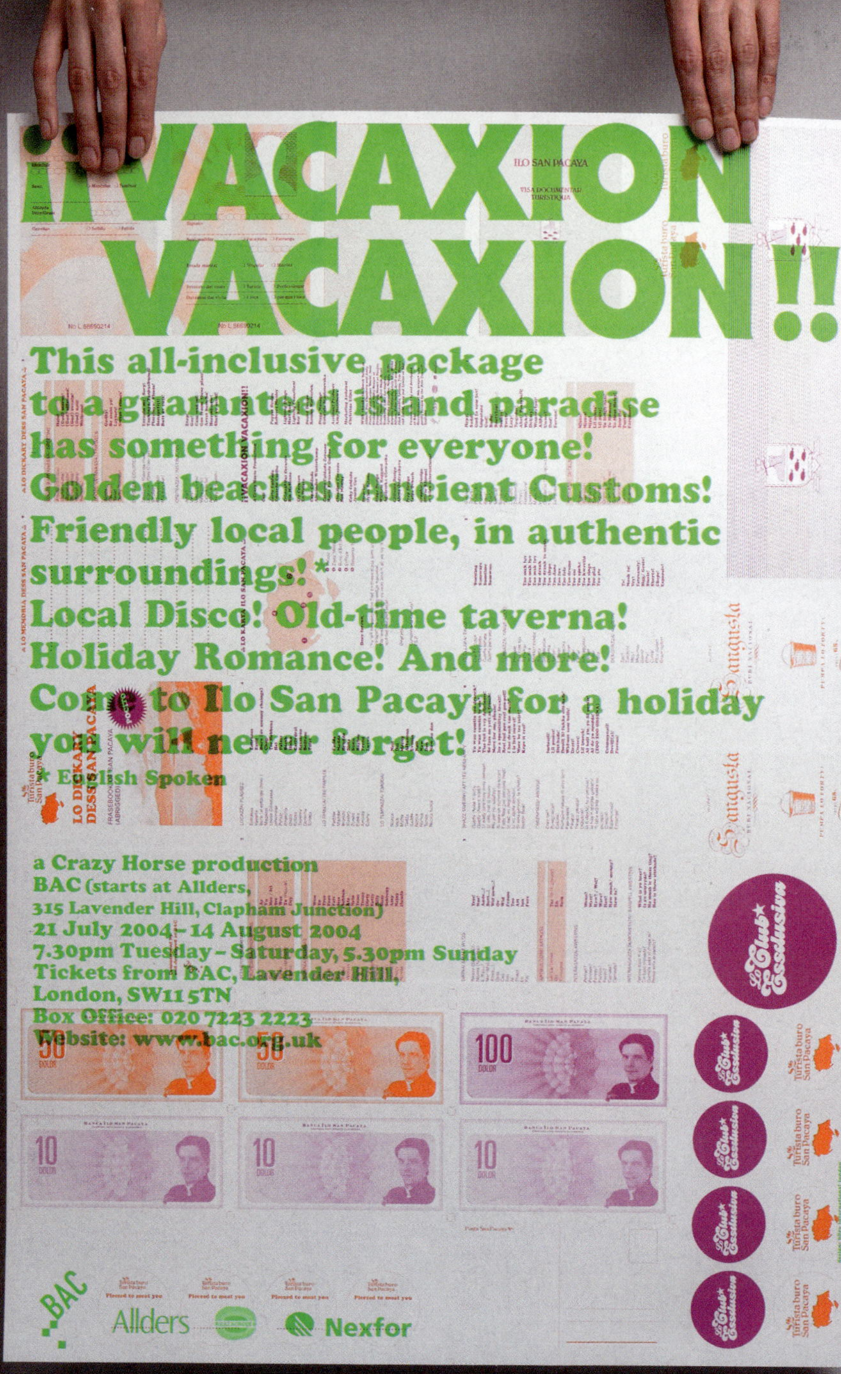

¡¡VACAXION VACAXION VACAXION!!
This all-inclusive package to a guaranteed island paradise has something for everyone!
Golden beaches! Ancient Customs!
Friendly local people, in authentic surroundings!*
Local Disco! Old-time taverna!
Holiday Romance! And more!
Come to Ilo San Pacaya for a holiday you will never forget!
* English Spoken
a Crazy Horse production
BAC (starts at Allders,
315 Lavender Hill, Clapham Junction)
21 July 2004 – 14 August 2004
7.30pm Tuesday – Saturday, 5.30pm Sunday
Tickets from BAC, Lavender Hill,
London, SW11 5TN
Box Office: 020 7223 2223
Website: www.bac.org.uk
BAC
Allders
Nexfor

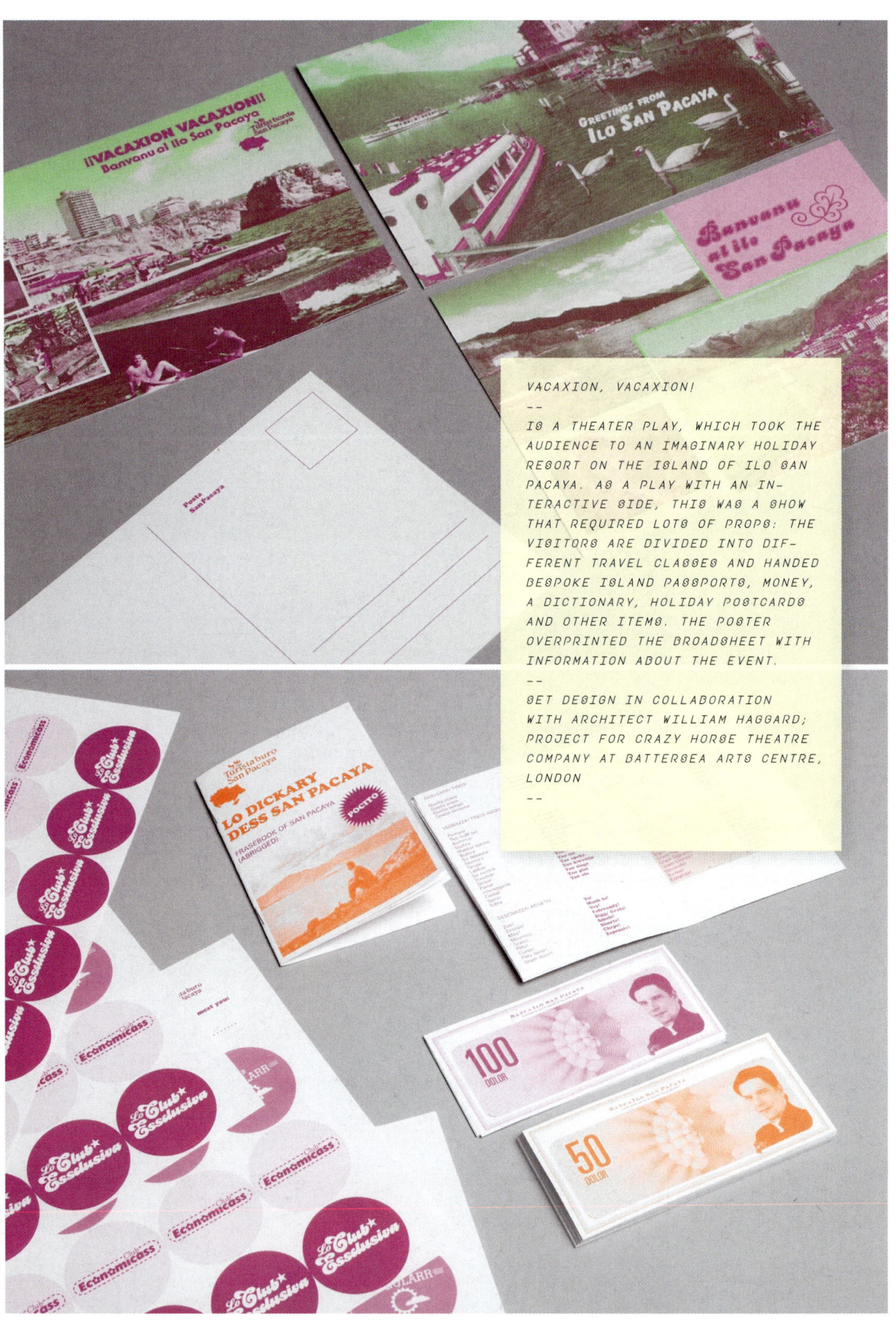

GREETINGS FROM
Ilo San Pacaya

¡¡VACAXION VACAXION!!
Banvanu al Ilo San Pacaya
Turistaburo
San Pacaya

Banvanu
al ilo
San Pacaya

VACAXION, VACAXION!
--
IS A THEATER PLAY, WHICH TOOK THE
AUDIENCE TO AN IMAGINARY HOLIDAY
RESORT ON THE ISLAND OF ILO SAN
PACAYA. AS A PLAY WITH AN IN-
TERACTIVE SIDE, THIS WAS A SHOW
THAT REQUIRED LOTS OF PROPS: THE
VISITORS ARE DIVIDED INTO DIF-
FERENT TRAVEL CLASSES AND HANDED
BESPOKE ISLAND PASSPORTS, MONEY,
A DICTIONARY, HOLIDAY POSTCARDS
AND OTHER ITEMS. THE POSTER
OVERPRINTED THE BROADSHEET WITH
INFORMATION ABOUT THE EVENT.
--
SET DESIGN IN COLLABORATION
WITH ARCHITECT WILLIAM HAGGARD;
PROJECT FOR CRAZY HORSE THEATRE
COMPANY AT BATTERSEA ARTS CENTRE,
LONDON
--

Turistaburo
San Pacaya
LO DICKARY
DESS SAN PACAYA
POCITO
FRASEBOOK OF SAN PACAYA
(ABRIGGED)

Lo Club Esclusiva
Economicass
La buro Pacaya
meat you!

100
DOLOR
50
DOLOR

FL@33 IS A MULTI-LINGUAL AND MULTI-SPECIALTY STUDIO FOR VISUAL COMMUNICATION BASED IN LONDON. ITS FOUNDERS, AGATHE JACQUIL-LAT [FRENCH FROM PARIS; ACADEMY JULIAN/ESAG] AND TOMI VOLLAUSCHEK [AUSTRIAN, ORIGINALLY FROM FRANK-FURT; FH DARMSTADT], MET ON THE ROYAL COLLEGE OF ART'S [RCA] POSTGRADUATE COMMUNICATION ART AND DESIGN COURSE IN 1999 AND SET UP THEIR COMPANY IN LONDON AFTER GRADUATING IN 2001. THE STUDIO WORKS ACROSS ALL MEDIA IN THE AR-EAS OF CONCEPT GENERATION, PRINT, SCREEN-BASED WORK [BROADCAST, MO-TION GRAPHICS, INTERFACE DESIGN, WEBSITES], EXHIBITION DESIGN AND PUBLISHING. FL@33 PROJECTS SUCH AS BZZZPEEK.COM AND STEREOHYPE. COM HAVE BEEN FEATURED ONLINE AND IN NUMEROUS MAGAZINES, NEWSPAPERS AND BOOKS AROUND THE WORLD.

--

WHAT IS GERMAN?

BEING CONSTANTLY VERY CONCERNED ABOUT WHAT THE NEIGHBORS THINK. BEING INSURED AGAINST EVERYTHING. RECYCLING WITH GREAT PASSION. HAVING A VAST NUMBER OF LAWS AND TAX RULES - MORE THAN ANY OTHER EUROPEAN COUNTRY IN FACT.

TRYING TO BE PATRIOTIC WHILE BE-ING HAUNTED BY THE GERMAN PAST AND OVERWHELMED BY GLOBALIZATION. THE MOTHER TONGUE OF SOME OF THE MOST INFLUENTIAL PHILOSOPHERS OF ALL TIME.

EATING A LOT OF BREAD THROUGHOUT THE DAY - EVEN (OR SHOULD I SAY ESPECIALLY) FOR DINNER.

THE ANNUAL BROADCAST OF <DIN-NER FOR ONE> (A RECORDED ENGLISH THEATER PLAY IN B&W) WATCHED BY MILLIONS ON NEW YEAR'S EVE.

WHAT IS GERMAN DESIGN?

WHILE I WAS STUDYING IN GERMANY IN THE MID 90S I WOULD HAVE ASSO-CIATED GERMAN GRAPHIC DESIGN WITH THE BAUHAUS AND THE ULM SCHOOL, PRODUCT DESIGN DEFINITELY WITH BRAUN PRODUCTS AND SIEMENS MEDICAL EQUIPMENT - CONSTANTLY STRIVING FOR THE TIMELESS AS A PROBLEM-SOLVING EXERCISE. NOWADAYS (HAVING LEFT GERMANY ALMOST TEN YEARS AGO) I'M NOT SO SURE ANY MORE. GERMAN CONTEMPORARY DESIGN DOES IN MANY WAYS SEEM TO HAVE LOST ITS NA-TIONAL IDENTITY - AN INTERNATIONAL PHENOMENON OF COURSE RATHER THAN A GERMAN ONE ALONE. A SLIGHTLY MORE EMOTIONAL APPROACH HAS IN MANY CASES FINALLY BEEN EMBRACED IN GERMANY THOUGH, AND MANY OF THE PREVIOUSLY <UNTOUCHABLE> DESIGN RULES SEEM TO HAVE BEEN BENT AND BROKEN. IN THE PROCESS A LOT OF VERY FRESH AND INNOVATIVE WORK HAS BEEN PRODUCED IN THE LAST DECADE - THAT IS OF COURSE IF YOU IGNORE THE OVERWHELMING NUMBER OF GERMAN WEBSITES, BROCHURES AND ANNUAL REPORTS - IDENTICALLY DESIGNED IN GRAY AND BLUE - LOOKING MORE LIKE FINANCIAL OR MEDICAL INSTITUTIONS WHILE ACTUALLY BEING COMMUNICATION DEVICES FOR RETAILERS, CULTURAL INSTITUTIONS AND EVEN DESIGN STU-DIOS…

DESCRIBE YOUR WORKING PROCESS.

FL@33'S WORK PHILOSOPHY IS BASED ON THE <POWER OF 3> THEORY - THE BALANCE OF INTELLECT, SKILL AND EMOTION - A VERY HELPFUL PHILOSO-PHY WE FIRST HEARD ABOUT AT THE RCA. HOWEVER, WE DON'T CONSIDER IT TO BE A STRICT RULE AND DO ENCOUR-AGE SPONTANEOUS VISUAL EXPERIMEN-TATION - WHICH VERY OFTEN HELPS US FIND INTRIGUING STARTING POINTS. IT'S MORE LIKE A GUIDELINE WE SIMPLY TRY TO KEEP IN MIND AND WE DO - AS A RESULT - OFTEN FINE-TUNE CONCEPTS ACCORDINGLY.

WHAT DO YOU AIM TO ACHIEVE WITH YOUR WORK?

FL@33'S MISSION IS TO CREATE A PROFESSIONAL, VIBRANT, FRESH AND ARTISTIC BODY OF WORK WHILE KEEPING A BALANCE BETWEEN COMMIS-SIONED AND SELF-INITIATED PROJECTS AND PUBLICATIONS.

YOU'VE INVITED A FRIEND TO GERMANY; NAME ONE PLACE THEY REALLY MUST VISIT AND A QUINT-ESSENTIAL EXPERIENCE YOU REC-OMMEND.

WE WOULD DEFINITELY HAVE TO VISIT THE AREA I (TOMI) GREW UP IN WHICH IS IN AND AROUND FRANKFURT AND DARMSTADT IN HESSEN, AND GO TO SOME OF THE BEAUTIFUL LAKES THERE.

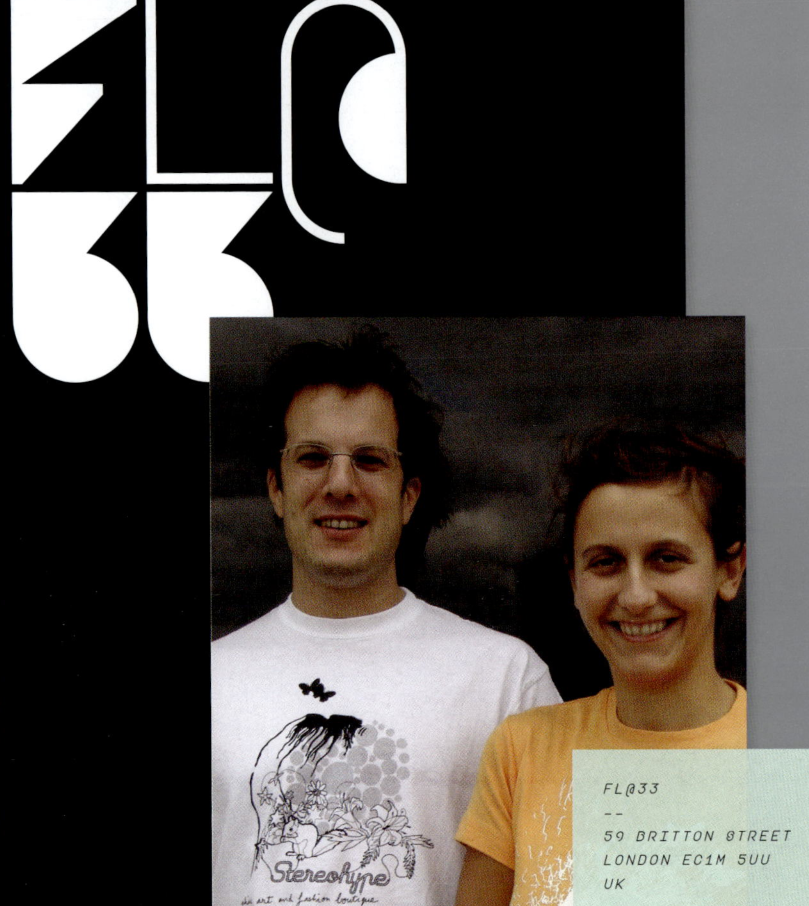

FL@33
--
59 BRITTON STREET
LONDON EC1M 5UU
UK
--
T +44 20 71687990
M +44 7801 950195
--
CONTACT@FLAT33.COM
WWW.FLAT33.COM
--

WHAT IS THE MOST IMPORTANT
LESSON YOU HAVE LEARNED IN YOUR
PROFESSION SO FAR?

NO REST FOR THE WICKED.

--

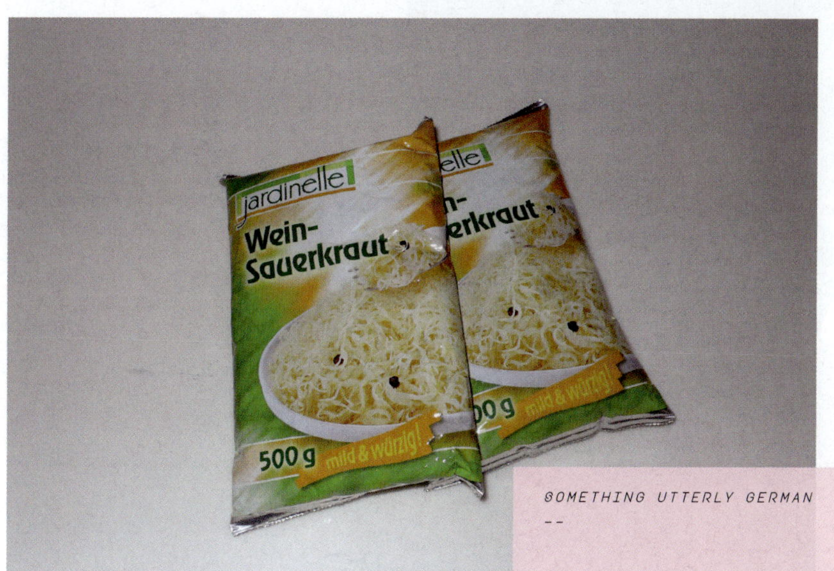

SOMETHING UTTERLY GERMAN
--

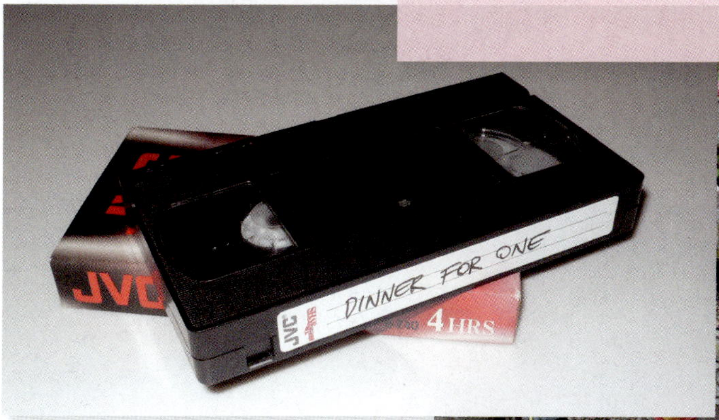

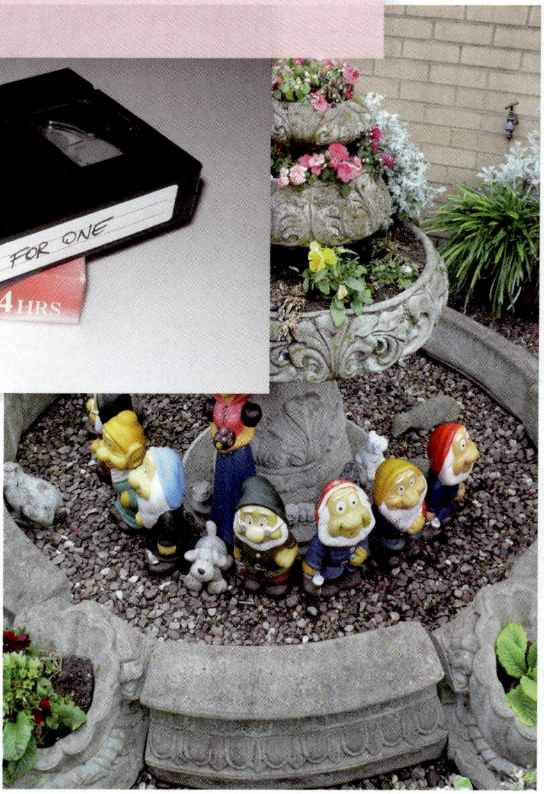

DINNER FOR ONE

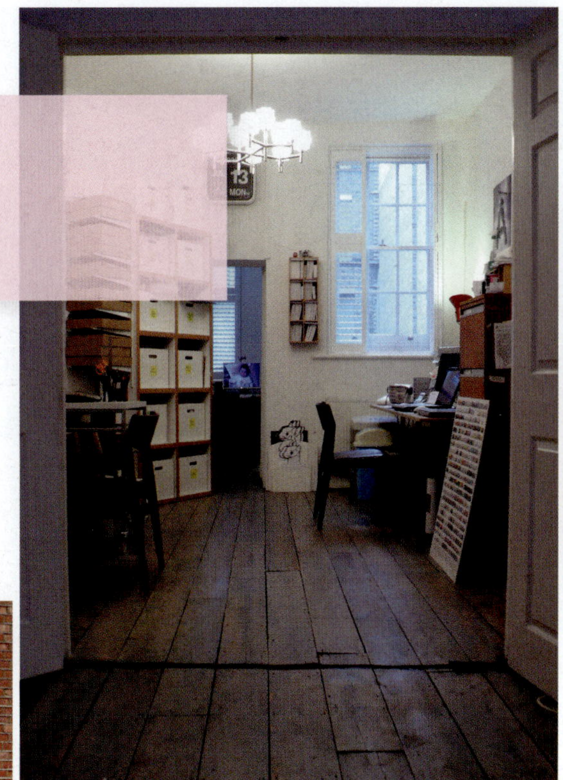

WORKPLACE
--

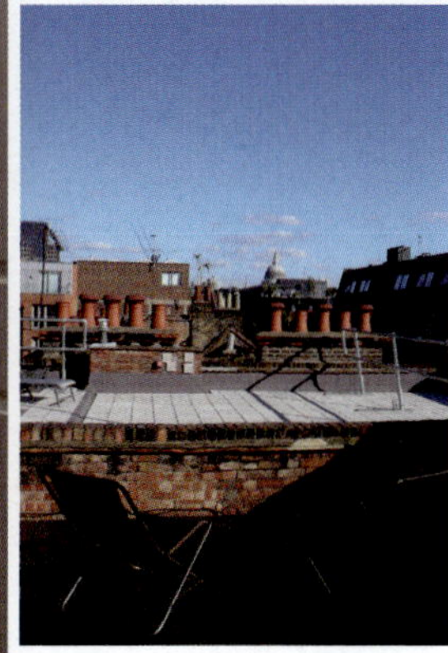

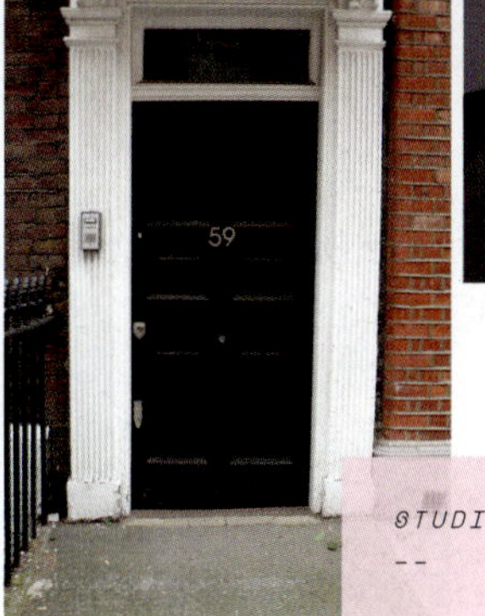

59

STUDIO SURROUNDINGS
--
020 8594 8631

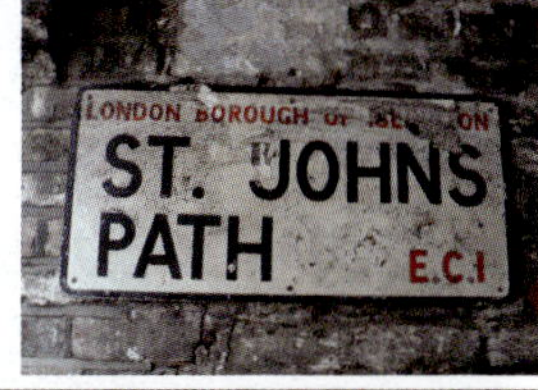

LONDON BOROUGH OF ISLINGTON
ST. JOHNS
PATH   E.C.1

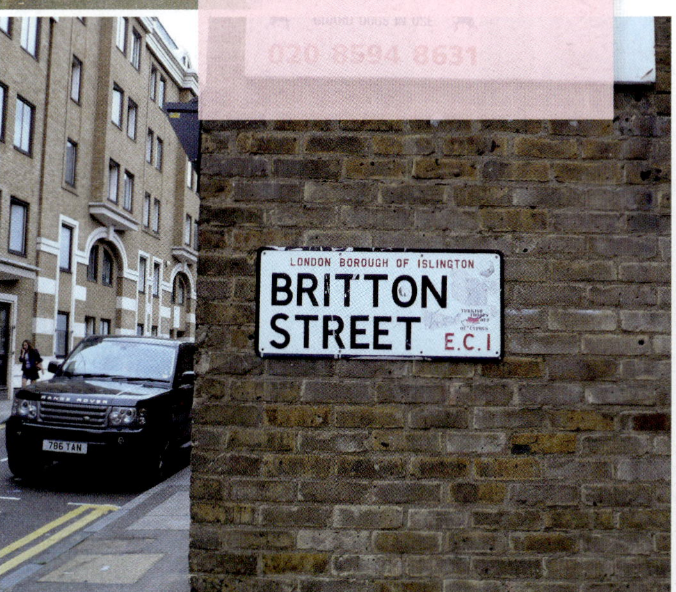

786 TAN
LONDON BOROUGH OF ISLINGTON
BRITTON
STREET
E.C.1

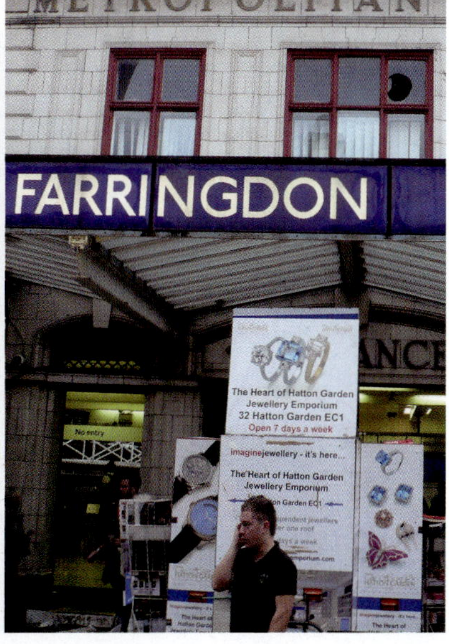

METROPOLITAN
FARRINGDON
No entry
The Heart of Hatton Garden
Jewellery Emporium
32 Hatton Garden EC1
Open 7 days a week
imaginejewellery - it's here...
The Heart of Hatton Garden
Jewellery Emporium

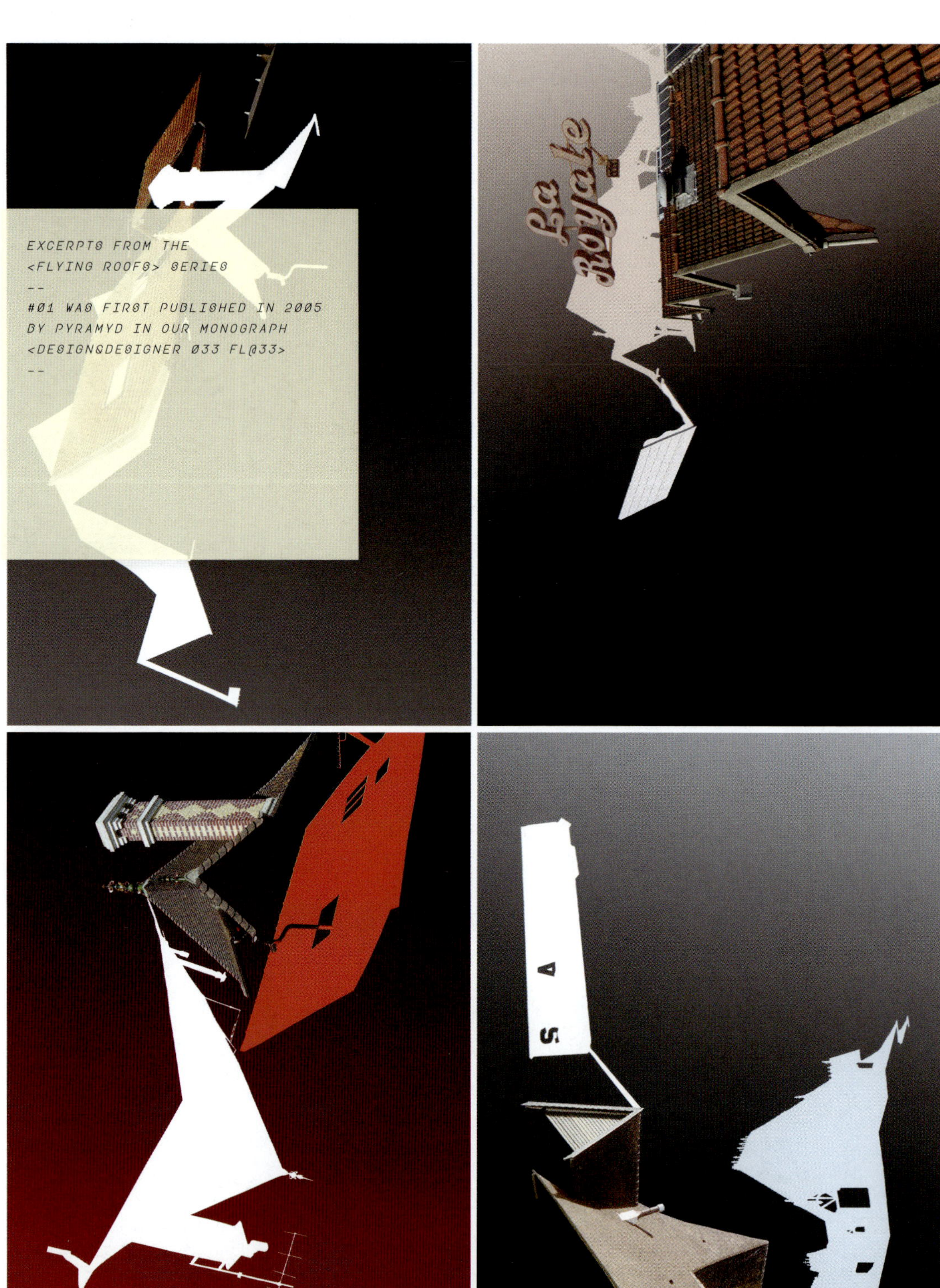

EXCERPTS FROM THE
<FLYING ROOFS> SERIES
--
#01 WAS FIRST PUBLISHED IN 2005
BY PYRAMYD IN OUR MONOGRAPH
<DESIGN&DESIGNER 033 FL@33>
--
La Royale
SA

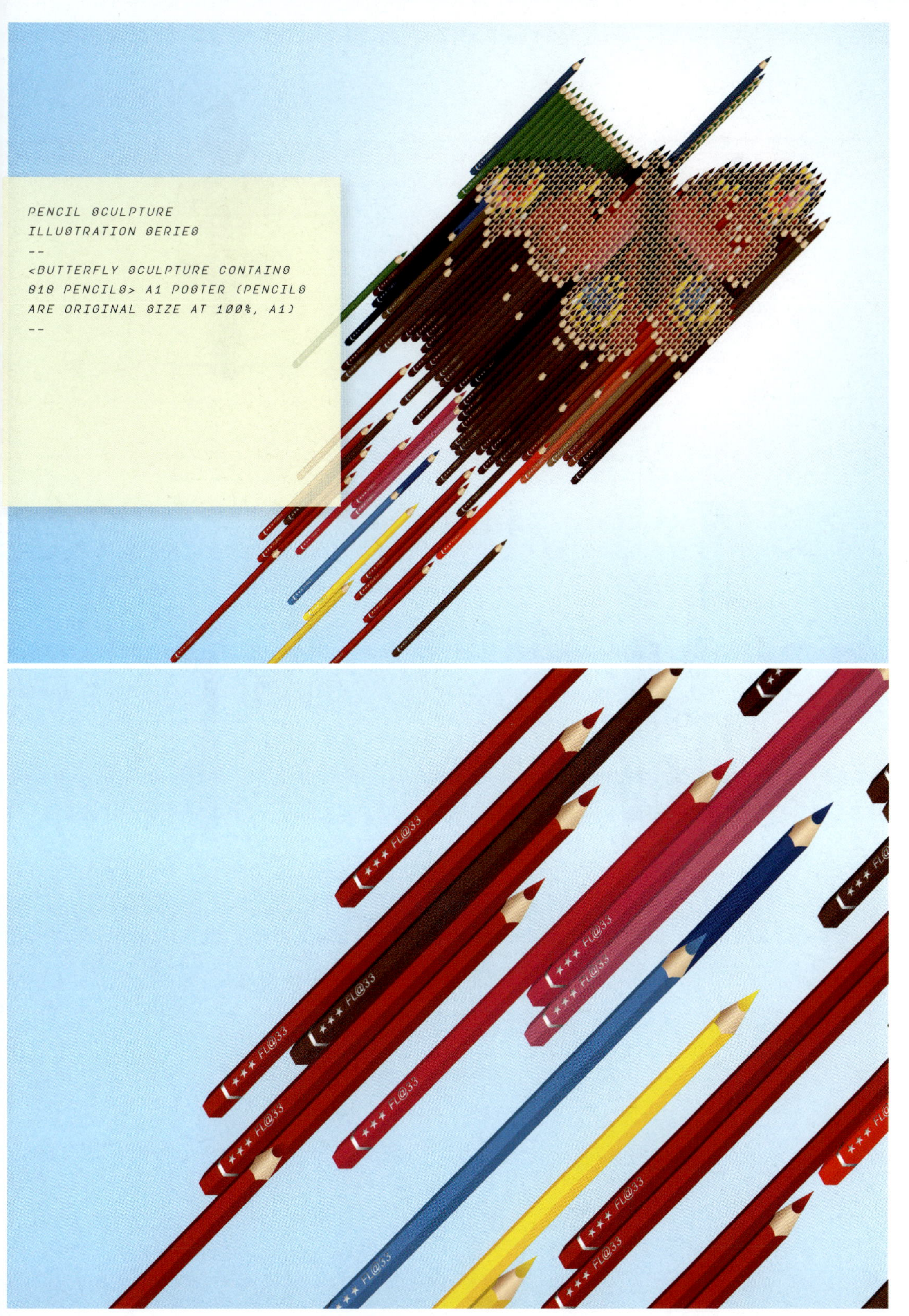

PENCIL SCULPTURE
ILLUSTRATION SERIES
--
<BUTTERFLY SCULPTURE CONTAINS
818 PENCILS> A1 POSTER (PENCILS
ARE ORIGINAL SIZE AT 100%, A1)
--

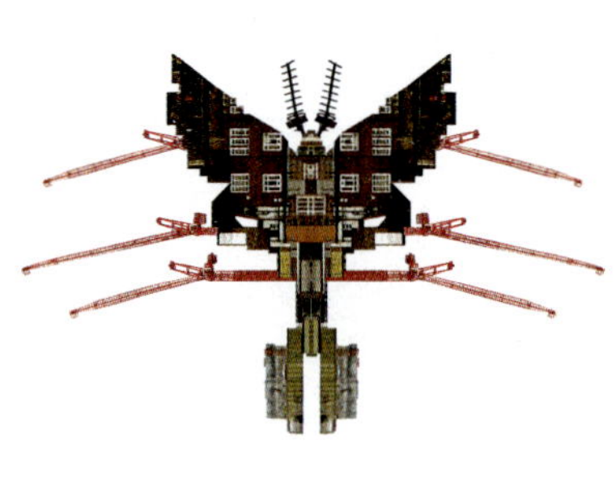

Tolleno Archerontia Atropos Aedificatio

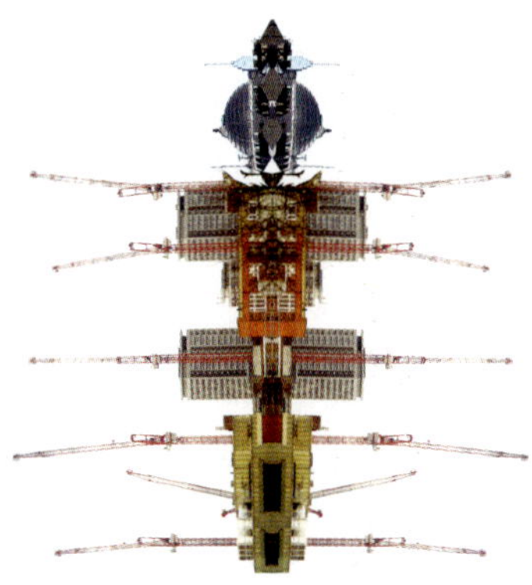

Tolleno Camponotus Herculeanus Aedificatio

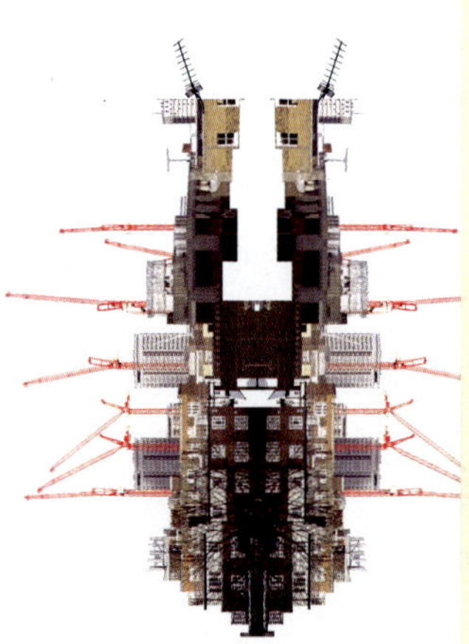

Tolleno Pollyphylla Fullo Aedificatio

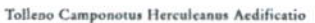

Tolleno Saperda Vittata Aedificatio

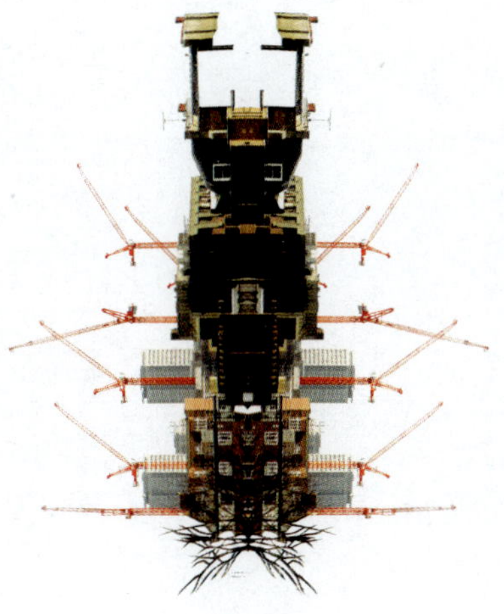

Tolleno Lucanidae Aedificatio

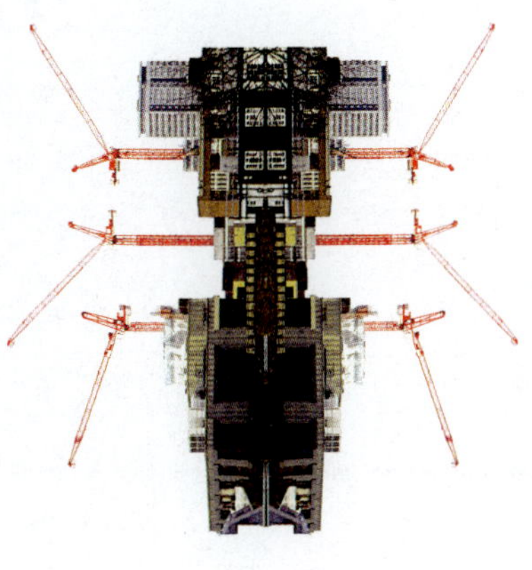

Tolleno Phoenicia Aedificatio

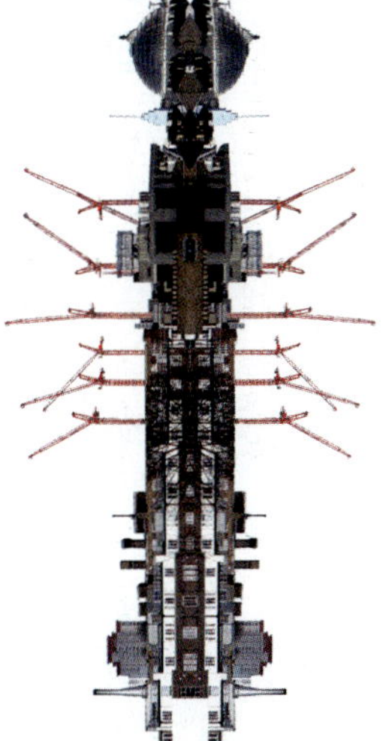

Tolleno Isoptera Aedificatio

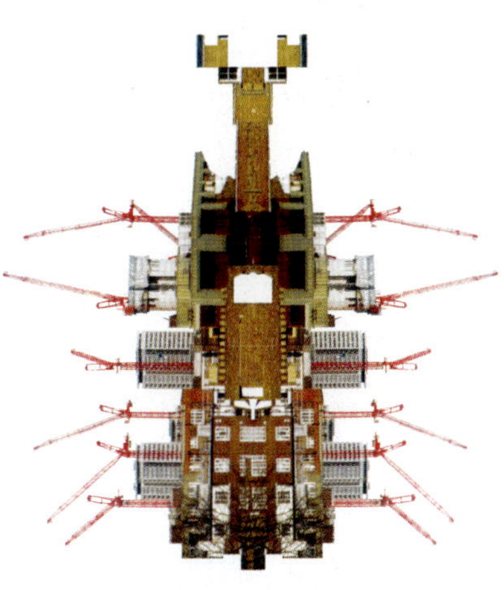

Tolleno Phyllomorpha Laciniata Aedificatio

I'VE BEEN RESIDENT IN LONDON SINCE
LAST YEAR AND AM CURRENTLY WORKING
FOR THE NORTH DESIGN AGENCY WHICH
HAS SPECIALIZED IN CORPORATE IDEN-
TITY PROJECTS.

--

WHAT IS GERMAN?

(DO I HAVE TO ANSWER THAT QUES-
TION? WITH SWEEPING STATEMENTS
ABOUT A WHOLE COUNTRY YOU CAN ONLY
COME UNSTUCK.) APART FROM CLICHÉS
I SIMPLY CAN'T THINK OF ANYTHING
HERE.

WHAT IS GERMAN DESIGN?

PERHAPS GRAPHIC DESIGN FROM
GERMANY DOES NOT IN FACT HAVE SUCH
A STRONG IDENTITY AS TENDS TO BE
ATTRIBUTED TO OTHER COUNTRIES.
WITH TERMS LIKE <LESS EXPERIMEN-
TAL> AND <THOROUGHLY RESPECTABLE>
WE'D BE BACK WITH CLICHÉS AGAIN.

DESCRIBE YOUR WORKING PROCESS.

I SIT DOWN IN FRONT OF THE EMPTY
SCREEN AND THINK: <OH GOODNESS,
I CAN'T DO IT.> A FEW EVASIVE AC-
TIONS (COFFEE, WASHROOM, ITUNES,
BOOKS, BLOGS, BISCUITS) AND ABOR-
TIVE ATTEMPTS LATER, AND IT'S
DONE, AND YOU HAVE SOMETHING YOU
CAN HAPPILY LIVE WITH.

WHAT DO YOU AIM TO ACHIEVE WITH
YOUR WORK?

COMMUNICATING INTELLIGENTLY AND
ELEGANTLY WITHOUT HAVING TO SHOUT.

YOU'VE INVITED A FRIEND TO
GERMANY; NAME ONE PLACE THEY
REALLY MUST VISIT AND A QUINT-
ESSENTIAL EXPERIENCE YOU REC-
OMMEND.

HE SHOULD GO TO THE FISH MARKET
IN HAMBURG ON A SUNDAY MORNING AND
LOOK AT THE PEOPLE.

WHAT IS THE MOST IMPORTANT
LESSON YOU HAVE LEARNED IN YOUR
PROFESSION SO FAR?

IF YOU'RE NOT CONFIDENT ENOUGH
TO CONTRADICT THE CLIENT, IN THE
END BOTH OF YOU ARE DISSATISFIED.

--

GIE— SEL

RASMUS GIESEL
--
FLAT 18 PRINCIPAL SQUARE
16 CHELMER ROAD
LONDON E96AF
UK
--
T +44 7515 661137
--
MAIL@RASMUSIST.NET
WWW.RASMUSIST.NET
--

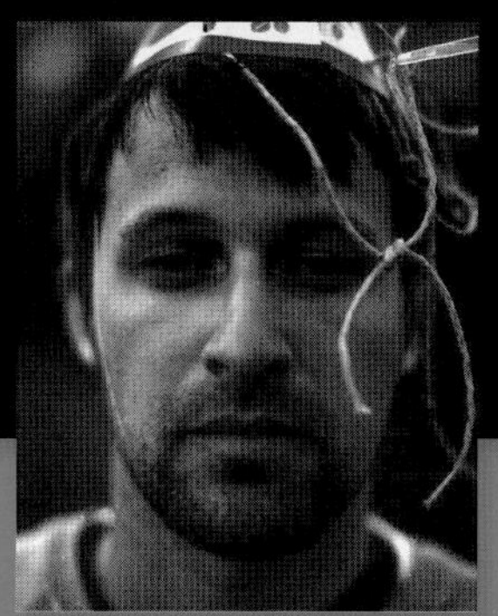

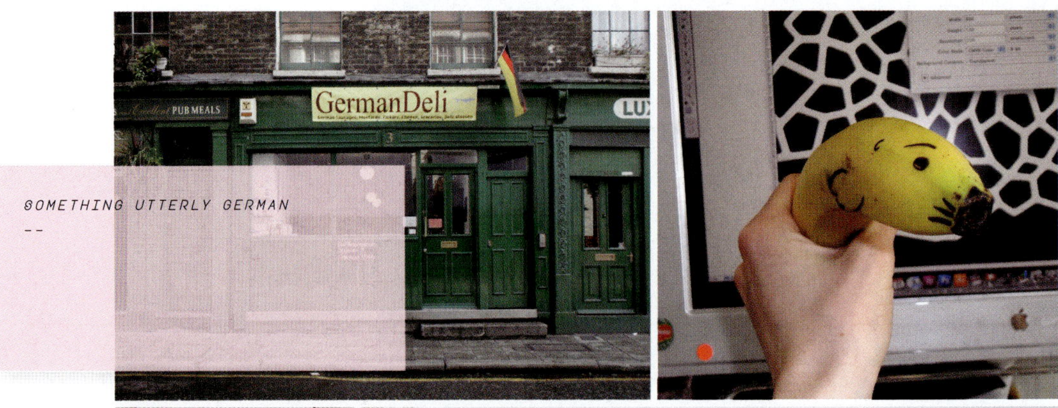

SOMETHING UTTERLY GERMAN
--

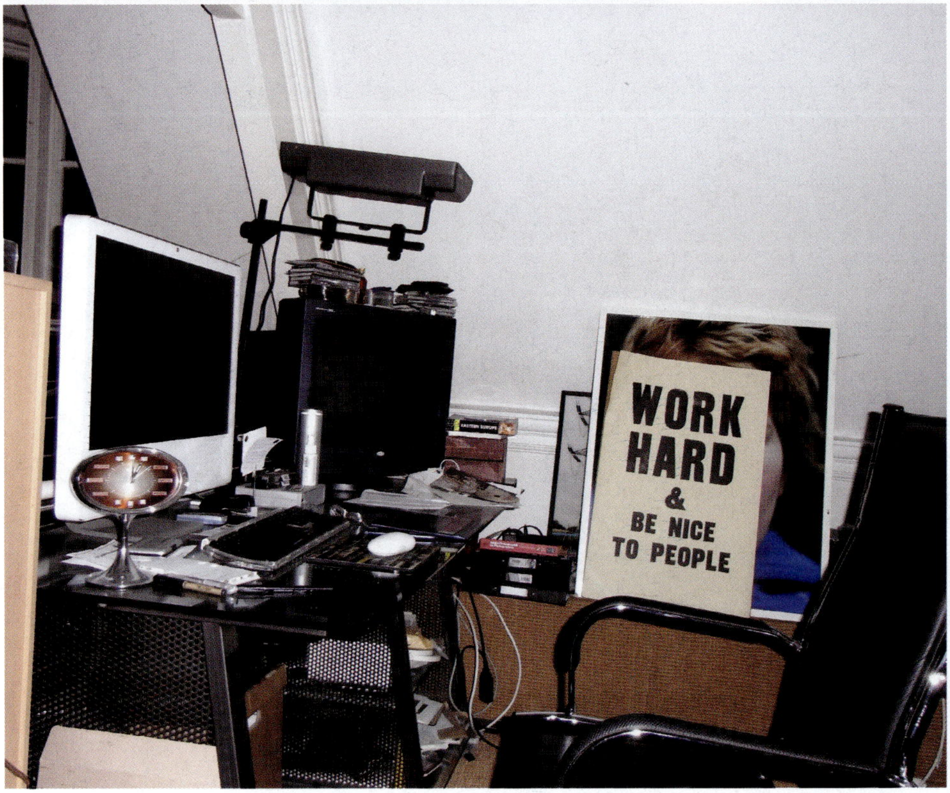

WORKPLACE
--

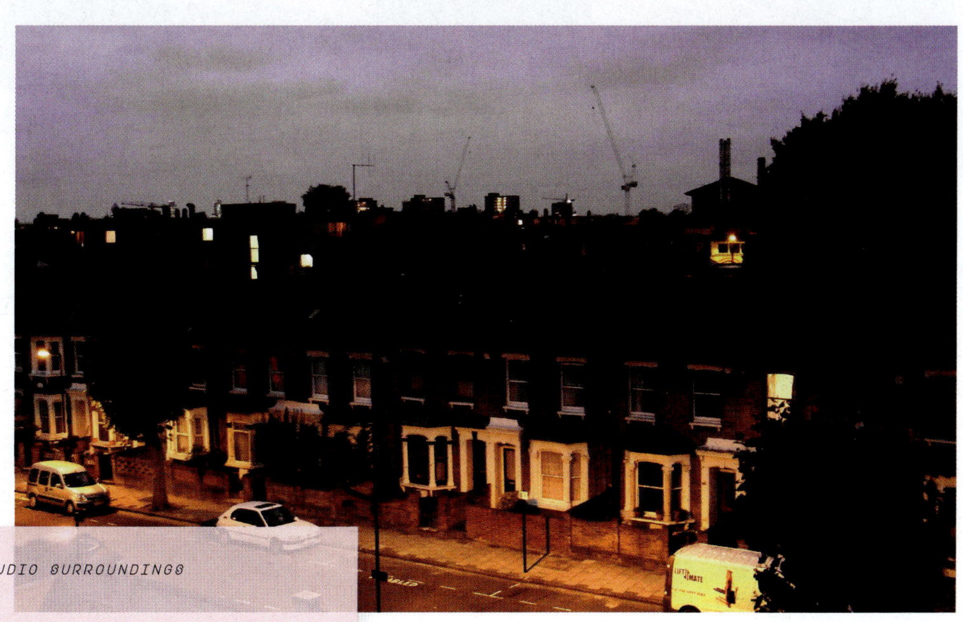

STUDIO SURROUNDINGS
--

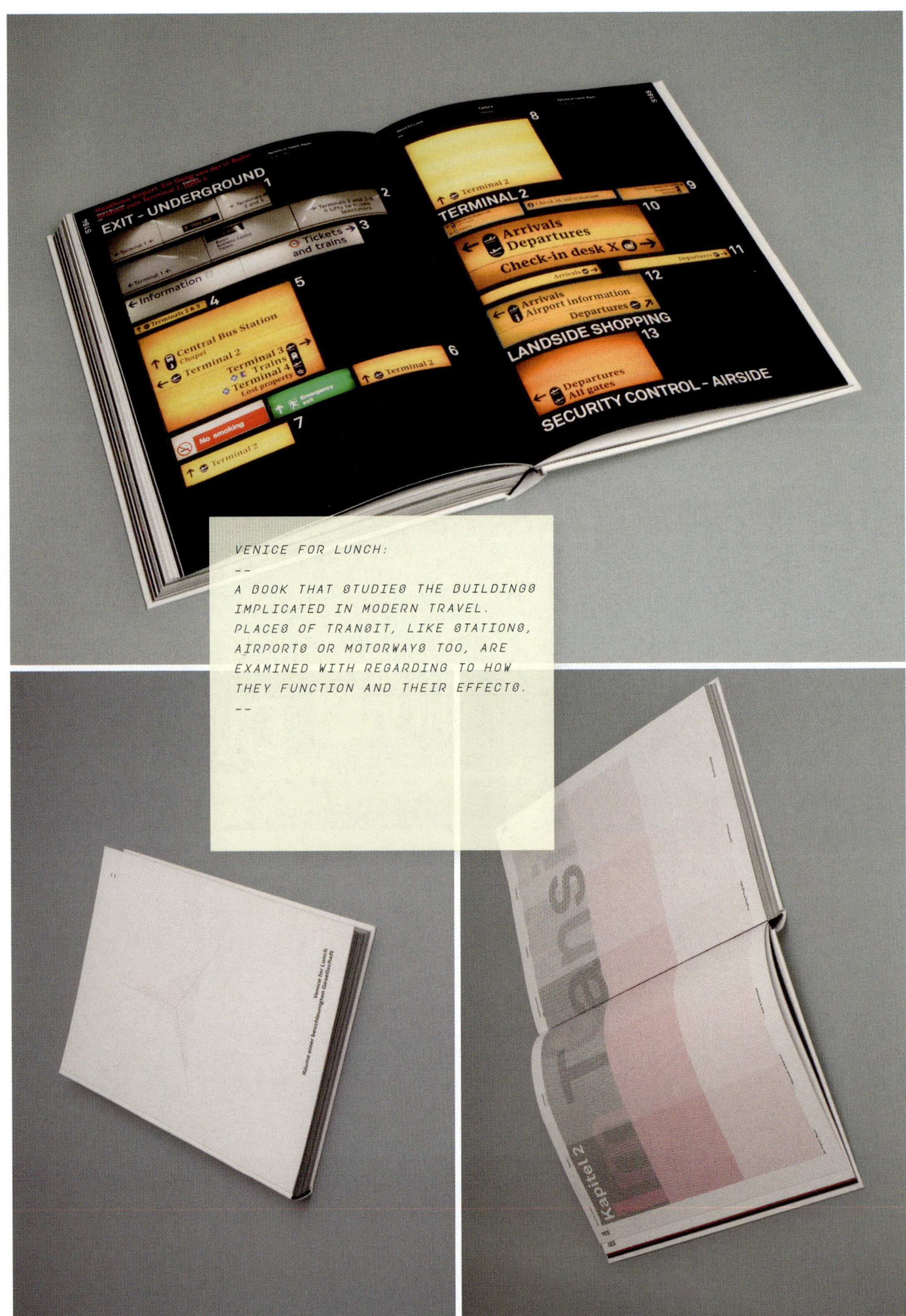

VENICE FOR LUNCH:
--
A BOOK THAT STUDIES THE BUILDINGS
IMPLICATED IN MODERN TRAVEL.
PLACES OF TRANSIT, LIKE STATIONS,
AIRPORTS OR MOTORWAYS TOO, ARE
EXAMINED WITH REGARDING TO HOW
THEY FUNCTION AND THEIR EFFECTS.
--

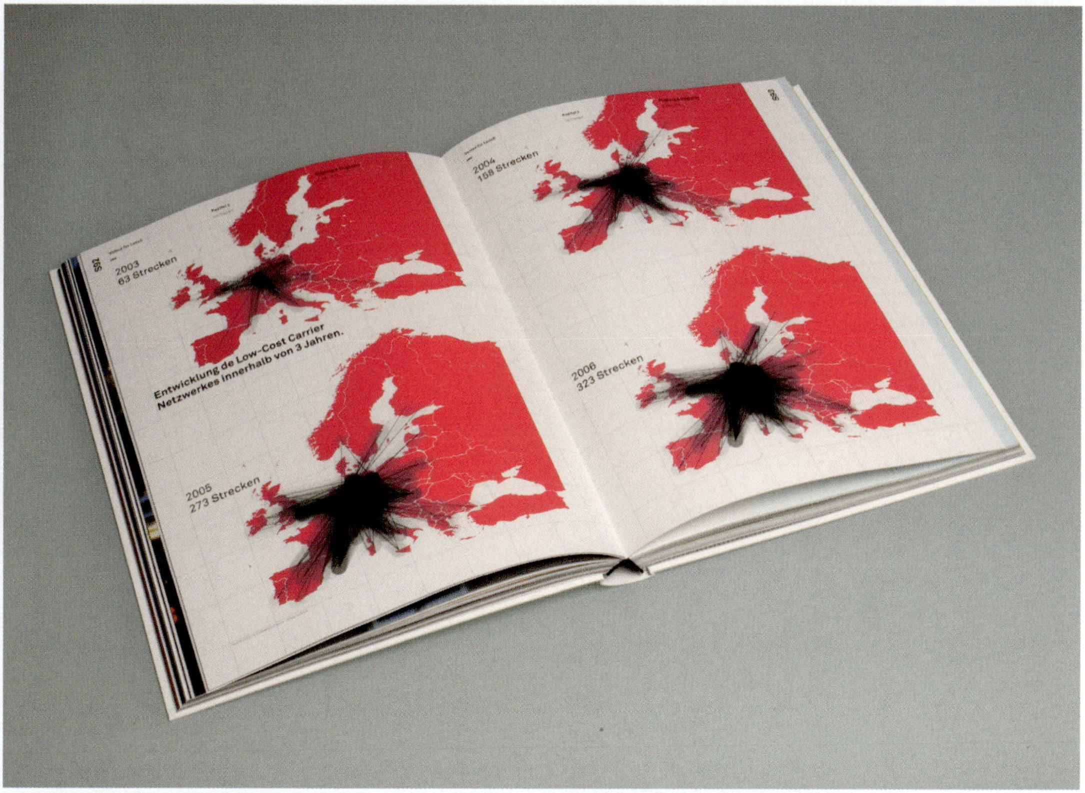

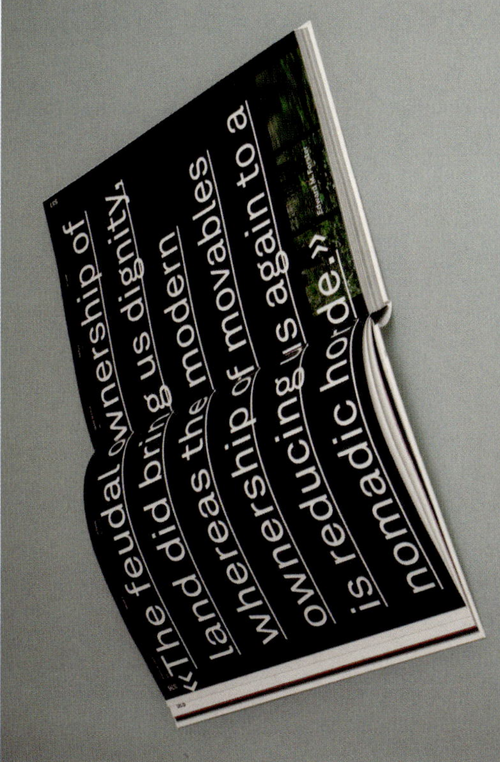

«The feudal ownership of
land did bring us dignity,
whereas the modern
ownership of movables
is reducing us again to a
nomadic horde.»
Edward M. Forster

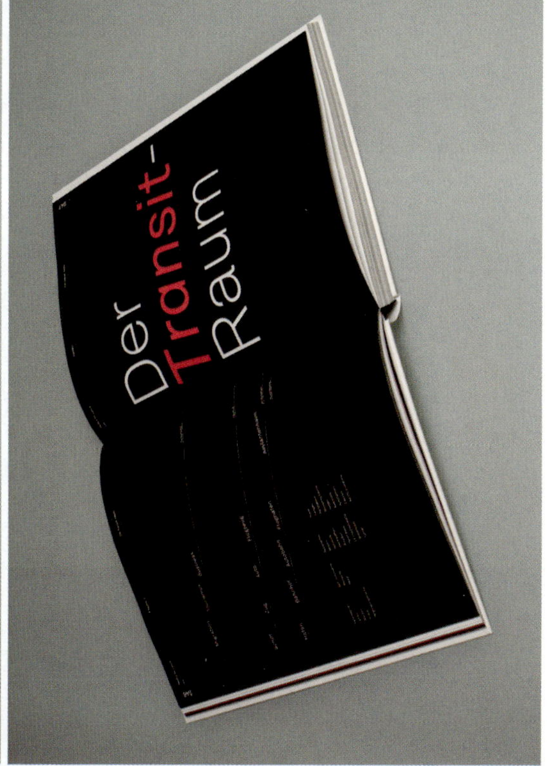

Der
Transit-
Raum

SILJA GOETZ IS A FREELANCE IL-
LUSTRATOR WITH HER HOME IN MADRID/
SPAIN. SHE WAS BORN IN 1974 IN RE-
GENSBURG/ GERMANY, STUDIED COMMU-
NICATION DESIGN IN NUREMBERG, AND
WORKED FOR TWO YEARS AS A GRAPHIC
DESIGNER FOR ALLEGRA MAGAZINE IN
HAMBURG BEFORE DEDICATING HERSELF
ENTIRELY TO ILLUSTRATION.

--

WHAT IS GERMAN?

A CERTAIN HEAVINESS AND RELI-
ABILITY. THINKING PRACTICALLY.

WHAT IS GERMAN DESIGN?

AS I LIVE IN SPAIN I AM NOT SURE
I CAN SAY.

DESCRIBE YOUR WORKING PROCESS.

AFTER GETTING THE BRIEF I USU-
ALLY DO A LITTLE RESEARCH ON THE
INTERNET OR AMONG BOOKS, FOLLOWED
BY A ROUGH SKETCH. ONCE THE IDEA
HAS FORMED, I PROCEED TO DO DE-
TAILED DRAWINGS BY HAND OR TO CUT
OUT FORMS. AFTER EVERYTHING HAS
BEEN SCANNED SEPARATELY I ASSEMBLE
THE PARTS INTO WHAT IS TO BE THE
FINAL RESULT. I CLEAN IT A LITTLE,
CHANGE COLORS, TRY OUT DIFFERENT
COMPOSITIONS AND THEN IT USUALLY
DOESN'T LOOK LIKE THE ORIGINAL
SKETCH ANY MORE.

WHAT DO YOU AIM TO ACHIEVE WITH
YOUR WORK?

TO COMMUNICATE AND GIVE A MOMENT
OF AESTHETIC PLEASURE AT THE SAME
TIME.

YOU'VE INVITED A FRIEND TO
GERMANY; NAME ONE PLACE THEY
REALLY MUST VISIT AND A QUINT-
ESSENTIAL EXPERIENCE YOU REC-
OMMEND.

MY HOME TOWN OF REGENSBURG,
PROUD TO HAVE BEEN RECENTLY ADDED
TO THE UNESCO WORLD HERITAGE LIST.
THERE YOU SHOULD WALK OVER THE OLD
STONE BRIDGE AND THEN FOLLOW THE
SMELL OF THE BEST SAUSAGES IN TOWN
TO THE <HISTORISCHE WURSTKUCHL>.
IT'S ONE OF THE OLDEST RESTAURANTS
IN BAVARIA, IF NOT GERMANY, RIGHT
BESIDE THE DANUBE. VEGETARIANS CAN
OPT FOR THE SECOND DISH: POTATO
SOUP.

WHAT IS THE MOST IMPORTANT
LESSON YOU HAVE LEARNED IN YOUR
PROFESSION SO FAR?

TO GIVE EVERY JOB ALL THE DEDI-
CATION I CAN. AND TO REFUSE AS-
SIGNMENTS THAT DON'T GO WITH MY
STYLE OF ILLUSTRATION.

--

GOETZ

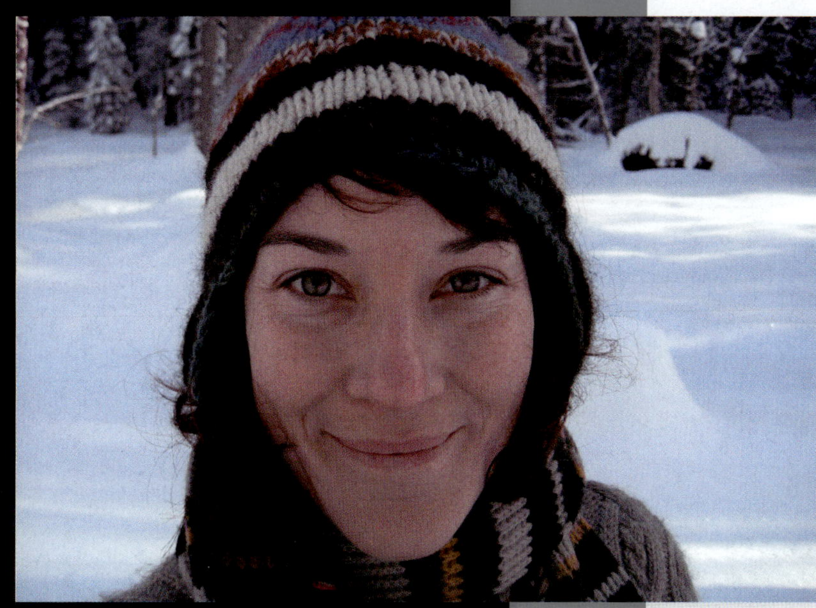

SILJA GOETZ
--
T +34 912924040
M +34 615817660
--
SILJA@SILJAGOETZ.COM
WWW.SILJAGOETZ.COM
--

SOMETHING UTTERLY GERMAN
--

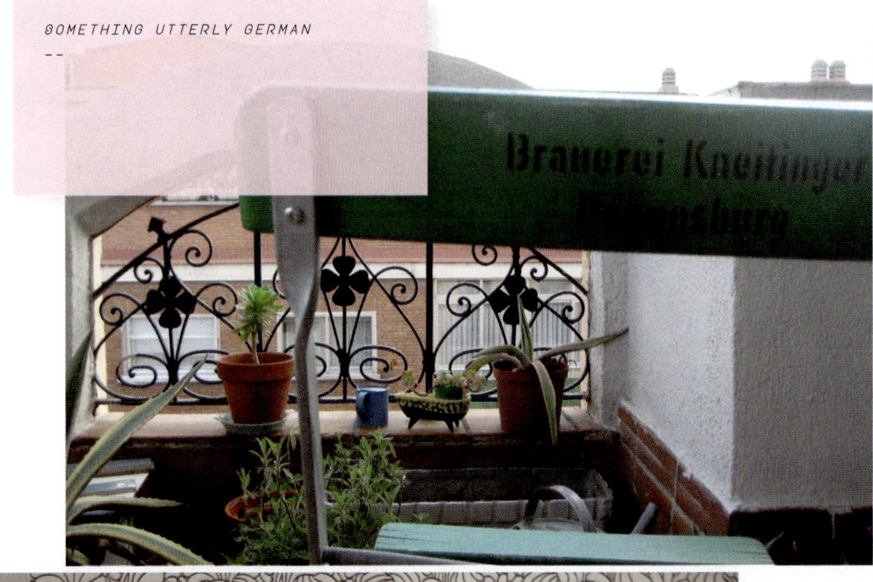
Brauerei Kneitinger
Regensburg

WORKPLACE
--

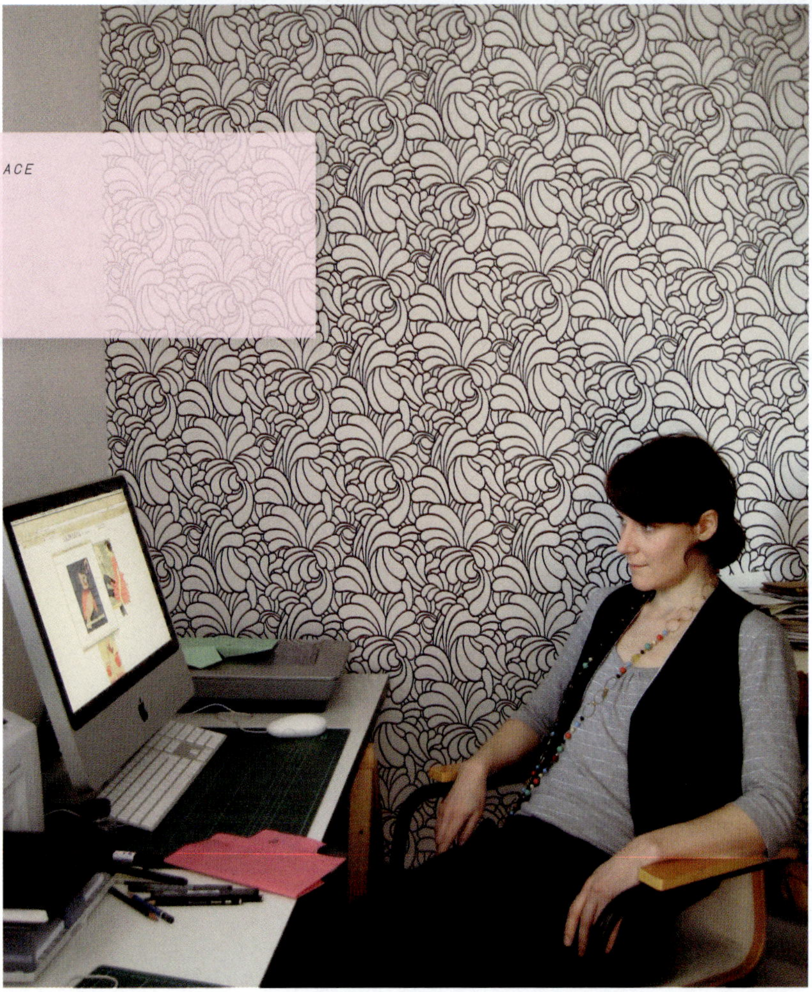

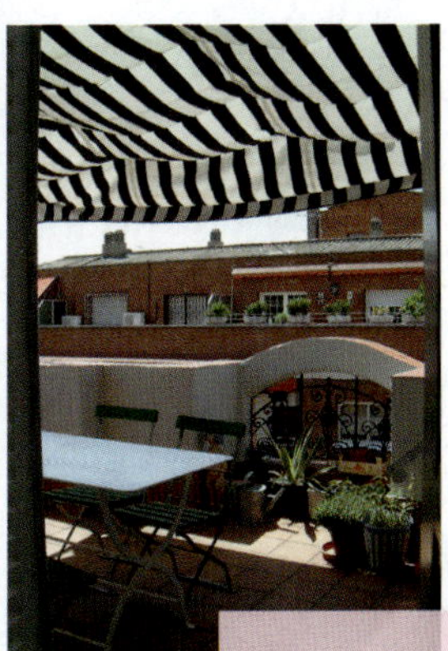

STUDIO SURROUNDINGS
--

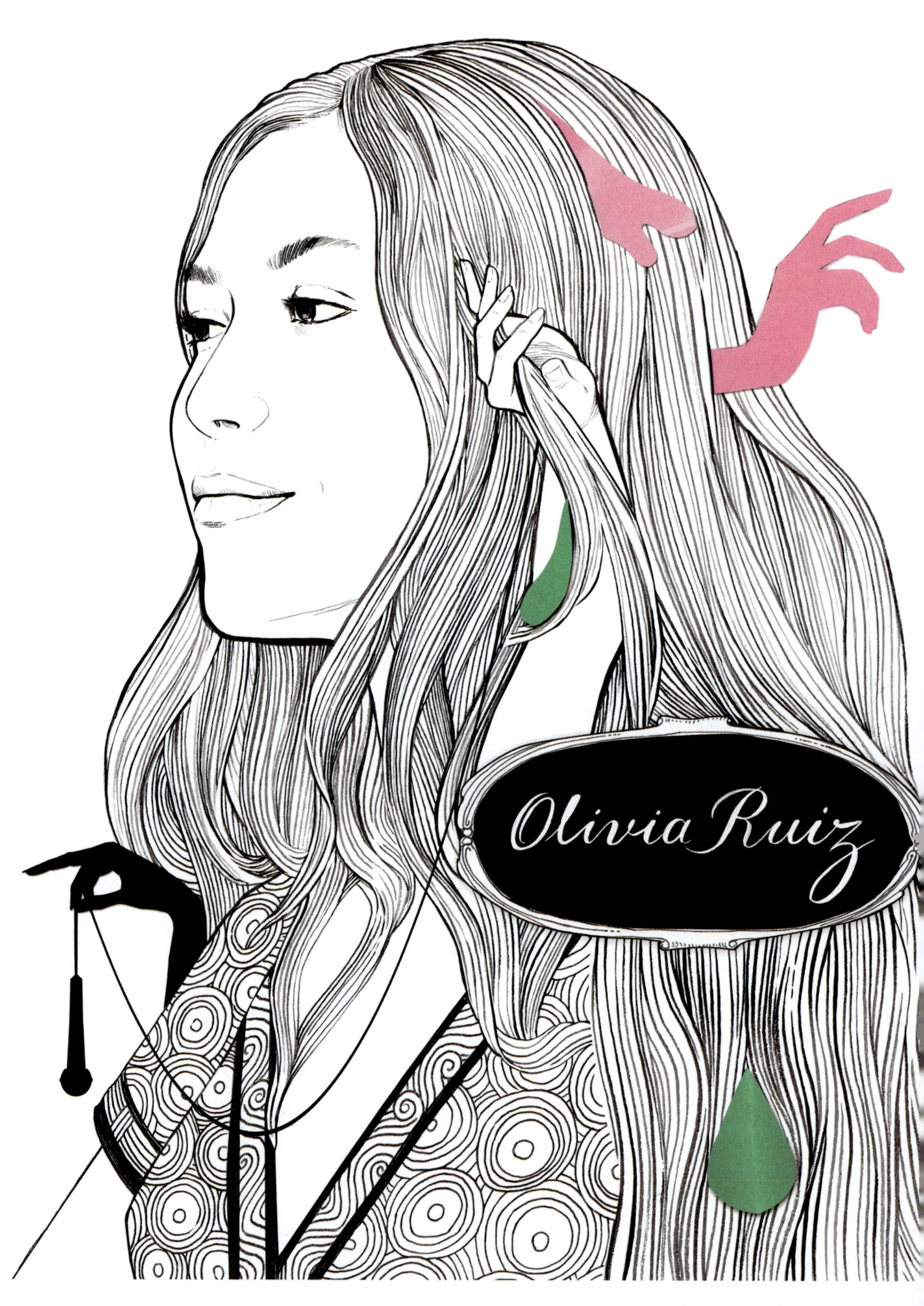

Olivia Ruiz

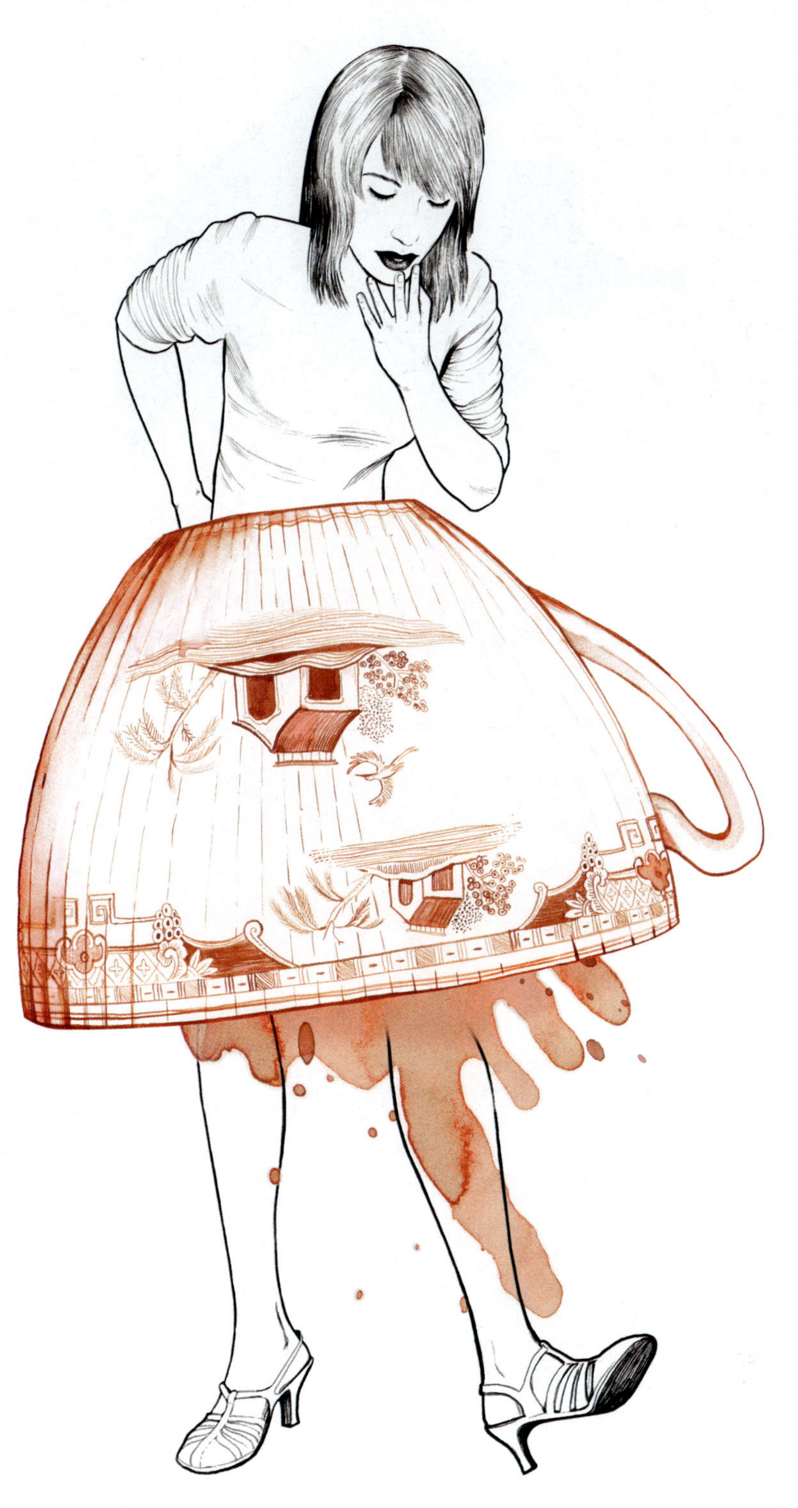

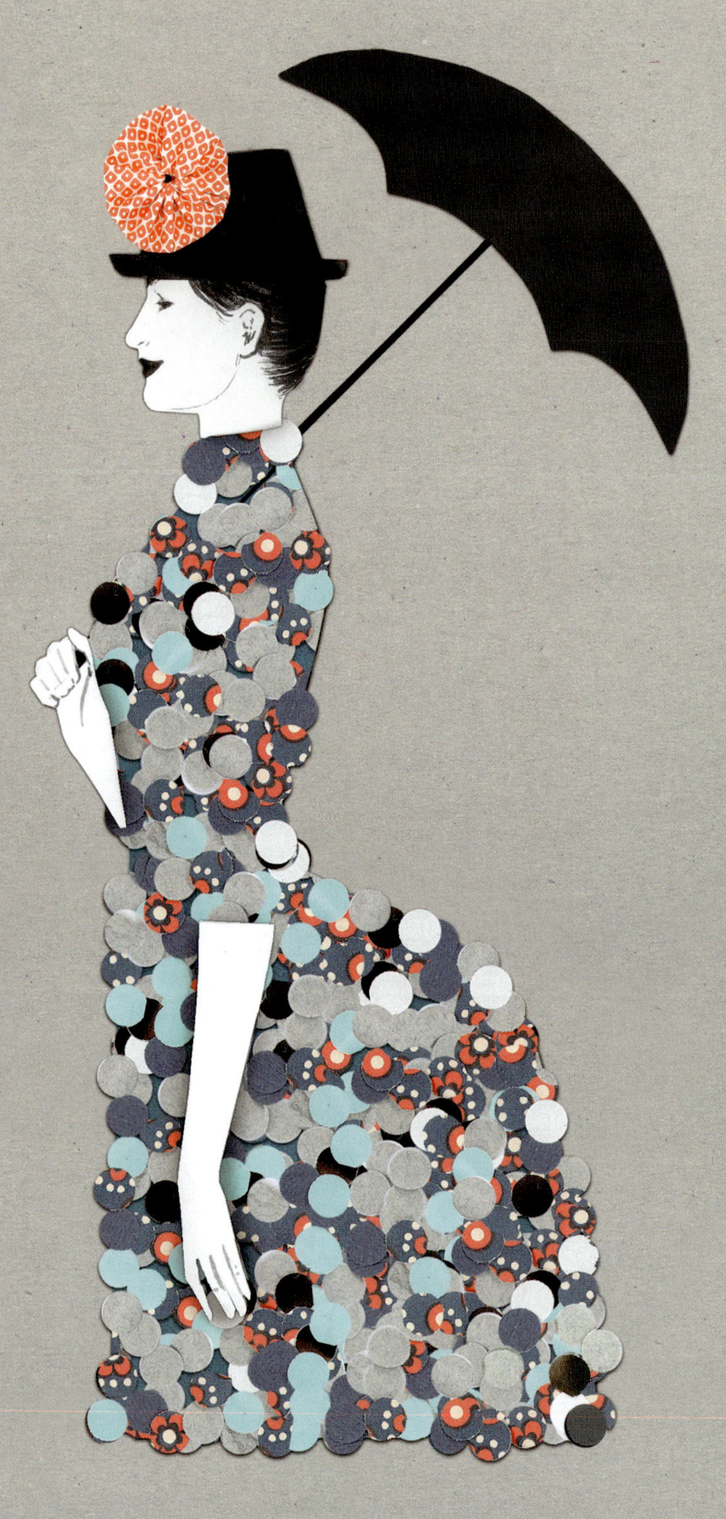

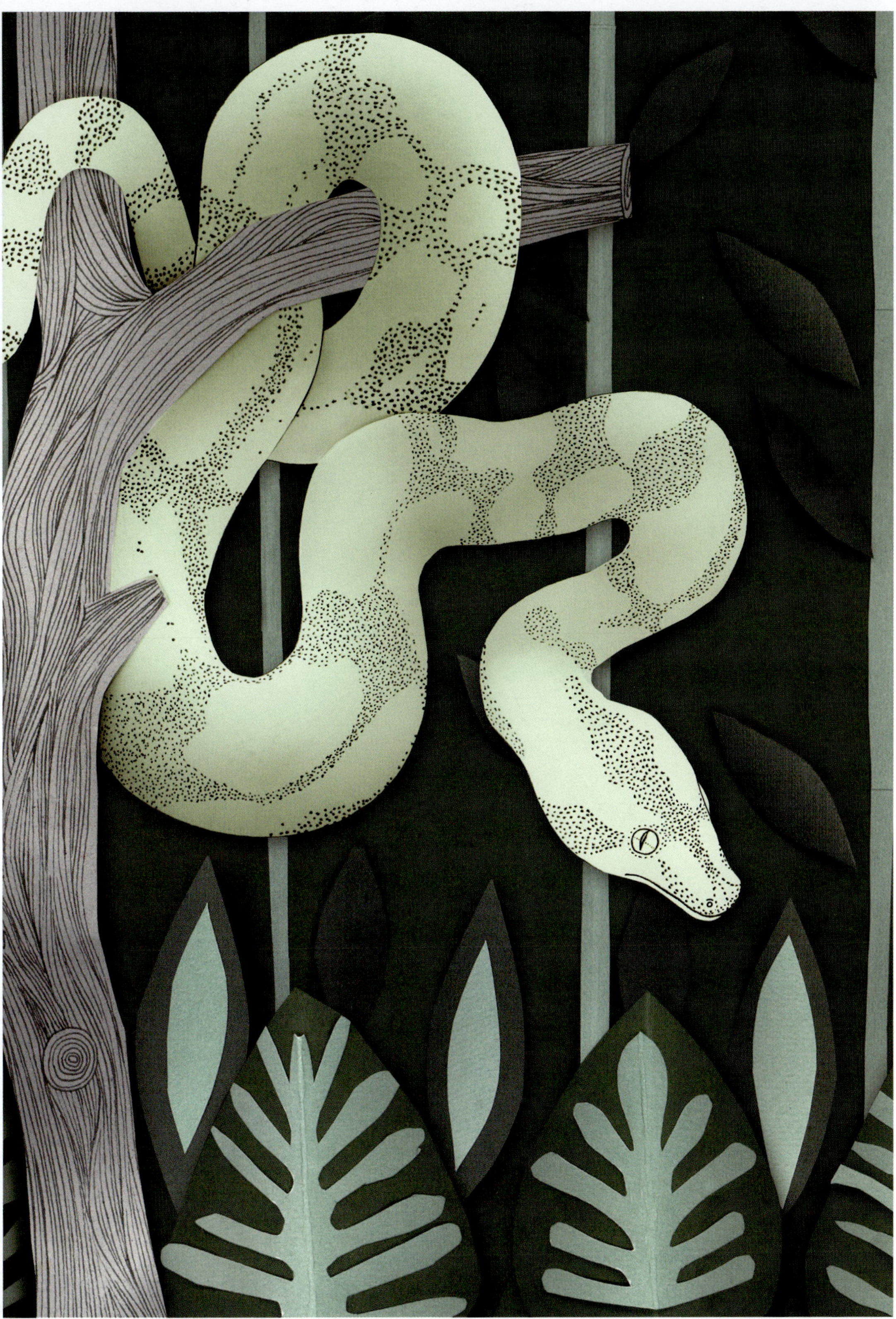

WE, MARTIN LORENZ AND LUPI ASEN-
SIO, RUN A SMALL BUT INTERNATION-
ALLY ACTIVE DESIGN OFFICE CALLED
TWOPOINTS.NET FROM BARCELONA. WE
SPECIALIZE IN THE COORDINATION,
CREATION, DEVELOPMENT AND IMPLE-
MENTATION OF VISUAL IDENTITIES.

TWOPOINTS.NET WAS FOUNDED IN 2000
AS A PLATFORM FOR SELF-INITIATED
PROJECTS AND COLLABORATIONS BE-
TWEEN CREATIVE PROFESSIONALS FROM
DIFFERENT FIELDS AND COUNTRIES. IN
2007, TWOPOINTS.NET BEGAN TO OFFER
DESIGN (WWW.DESIGNBY.TWOPOINTS.
NET) AND DESIGN WORKSHOPS (WWW.
WORKSHOPSBY.TWOPOINTS.NET). AS
WELL AS OUR PROFESSIONAL WORK, WE
TEACH REGULARLY AT VARIOUS DESIGN
SCHOOLS THROUGHOUT EUROPE.

--

WHAT IS GERMAN?

SOMETHING THAT MAY ALSO BE CRE-
ATED BY NON-GERMANS.

WHAT IS GERMAN DESIGN?

THAT'S WHAT WE'RE TRYING TO FIND
OUT WITH THIS BOOK: WHETHER THIS
QUESTION CAN EVEN BE ASKED.

DESCRIBE YOUR WORKING PROCESS.

WE ORGANIZE OUR WORK FLOW IN
A VERY TRADITIONAL WAY. FIRST WE
DEFINE THE PROBLEM AND THEN WE
LOOK FOR ITS SOLUTION. DEFINING
THE PROBLEM CAN BE CONSIDERABLY
MORE COMPLEX THAN SOLVING IT, AND
WE HAVE TO PROCEED CAREFULLY AND
CAUTIOUSLY. HOWEVER, AS SOON AS WE
HAVE REACHED A CONSENSUS WITH OUR
CLIENT REGARDING THE PROBLEM, WE
TAKE THE LIBERTY OF FINDING THE
SOLUTION WITHOUT THE CLIENT. THIS
METHODOLOGY HAS PROVEN TO BE A
VERY EFFECTIVE PROCESS.

WHAT DO YOU AIM TO ACHIEVE WITH YOUR WORK?

WE WANT TO ENJOY OUR LIVES.
IN DOING SO OUR OFFICE SHOULD
NOT ONLY PRODUCE THE FINANCIAL
MEANS THAT ENABLE US TO DO SO,
BUT ALSO BE A KIND OF LABORATORY
OF INVESTIGATION. ULTIMATELY OUR
MOTIVATION IS TO FIND SOLUTIONS
TO PROBLEMS, BUT ALSO CONTRIBUTE
SOMETHING NEW TO THE CULTURE WE
LIVE WITH AND IN.

YOU'VE INVITED A FRIEND TO GERMANY; NAME ONE PLACE THEY REALLY MUST VISIT AND A QUINT-ESSENTIAL EXPERIENCE YOU REC-OMMEND.

HE SHOULD DRINK A BEER ON THE
BANKS OF THE RIVER ELBE IN HAM-
BURG. THERE'S NO BETTER PLACE TO
UNDERSTAND THE CONTEMPORARY GER-
MAN CONCEPT OF BEAUTY.

WHAT IS THE MOST IMPORTANT LESSON YOU HAVE LEARNED IN YOUR PROFESSION SO FAR?

NOT BE FRIGHTENED TO BE OPEN TO
OTHER PEOPLE AND THEIR IDEAS.

--

TWO POINTS. NET

TWOPOINTS.NET
--
VIA LAIETANA 37
4ª PLANTA, DESPACHO 32
08003 BARCELONA
SPAIN
--
T +34 933185372
--
INFO@TWOPOINTS.NET
WWW.TWOPOINTS.NET
--

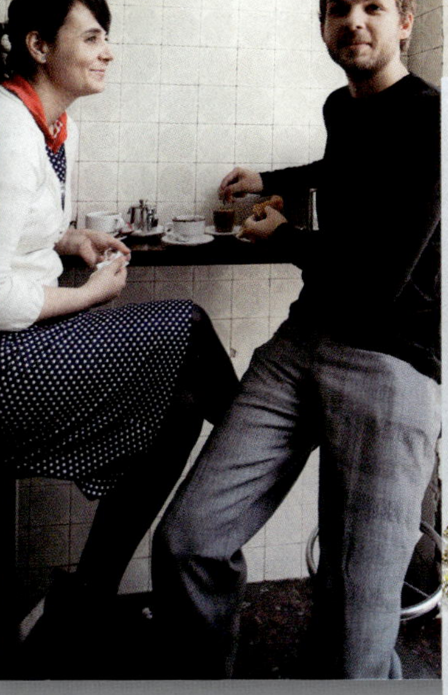

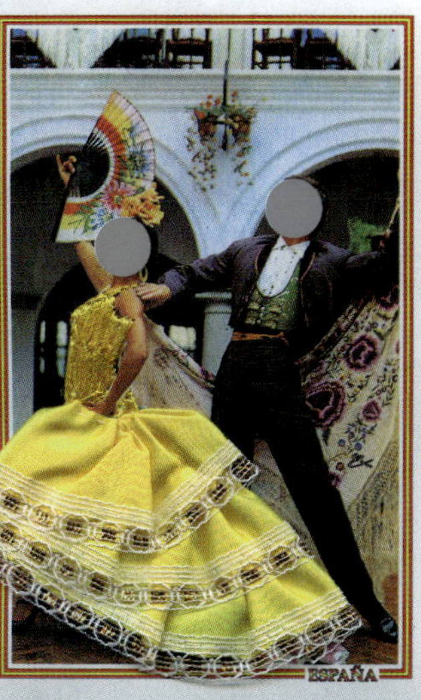

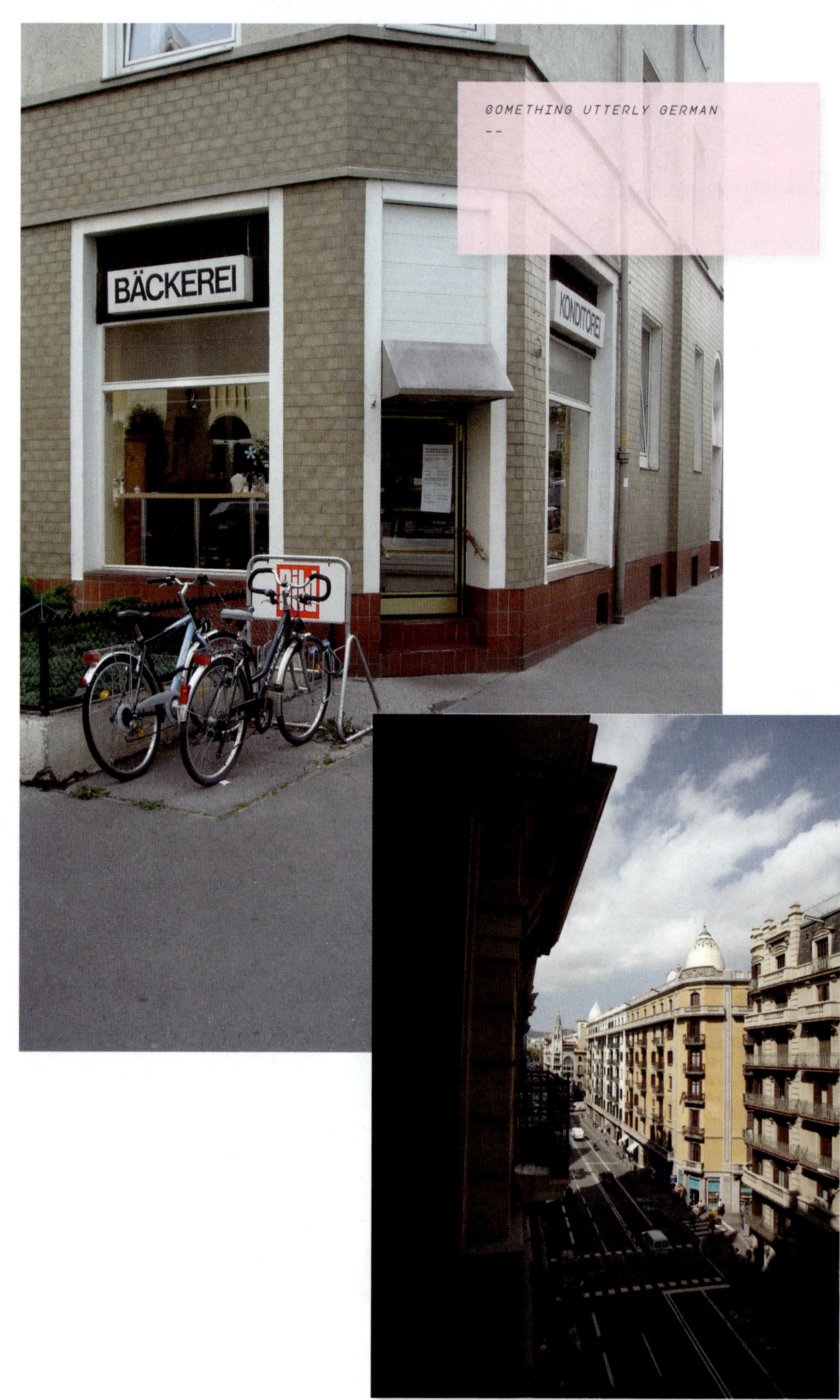

BÄCKEREI
KONDITOREI
SOMETHING UTTERLY GERMAN
--

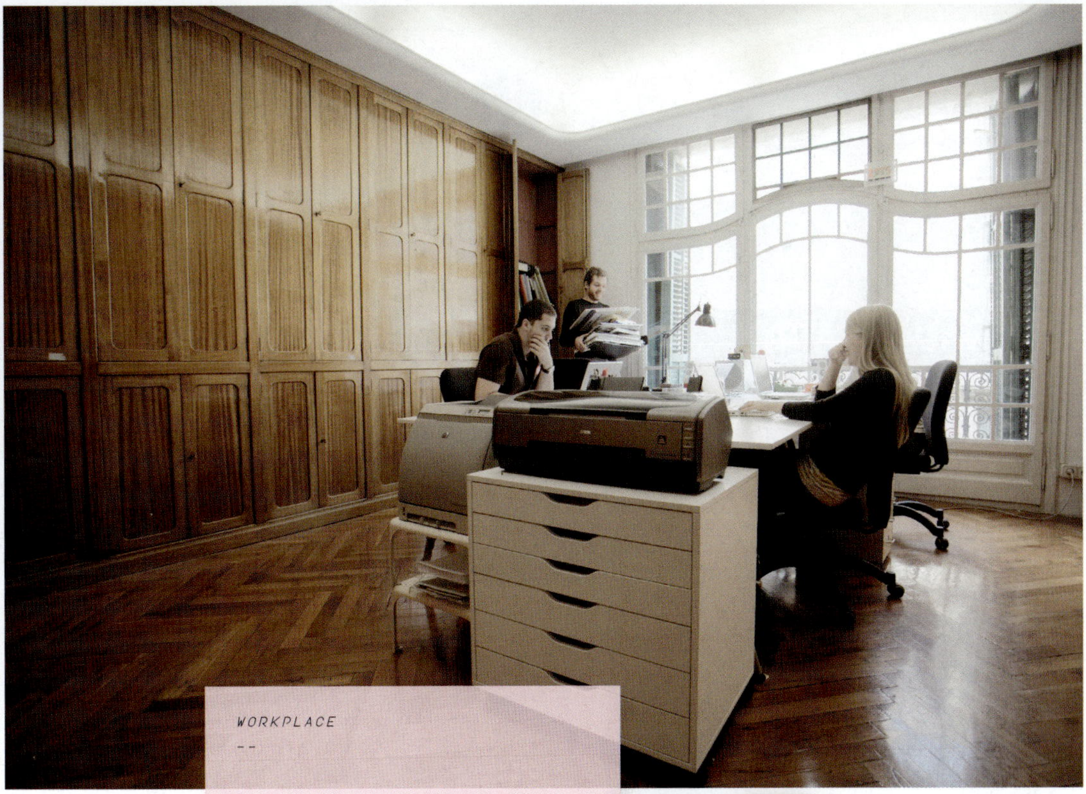

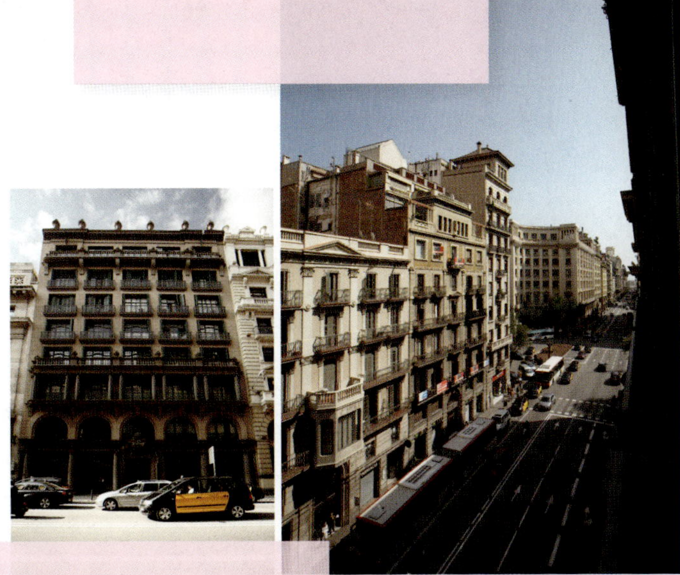

WORKPLACE
--

STUDIO SURROUNDINGS
--

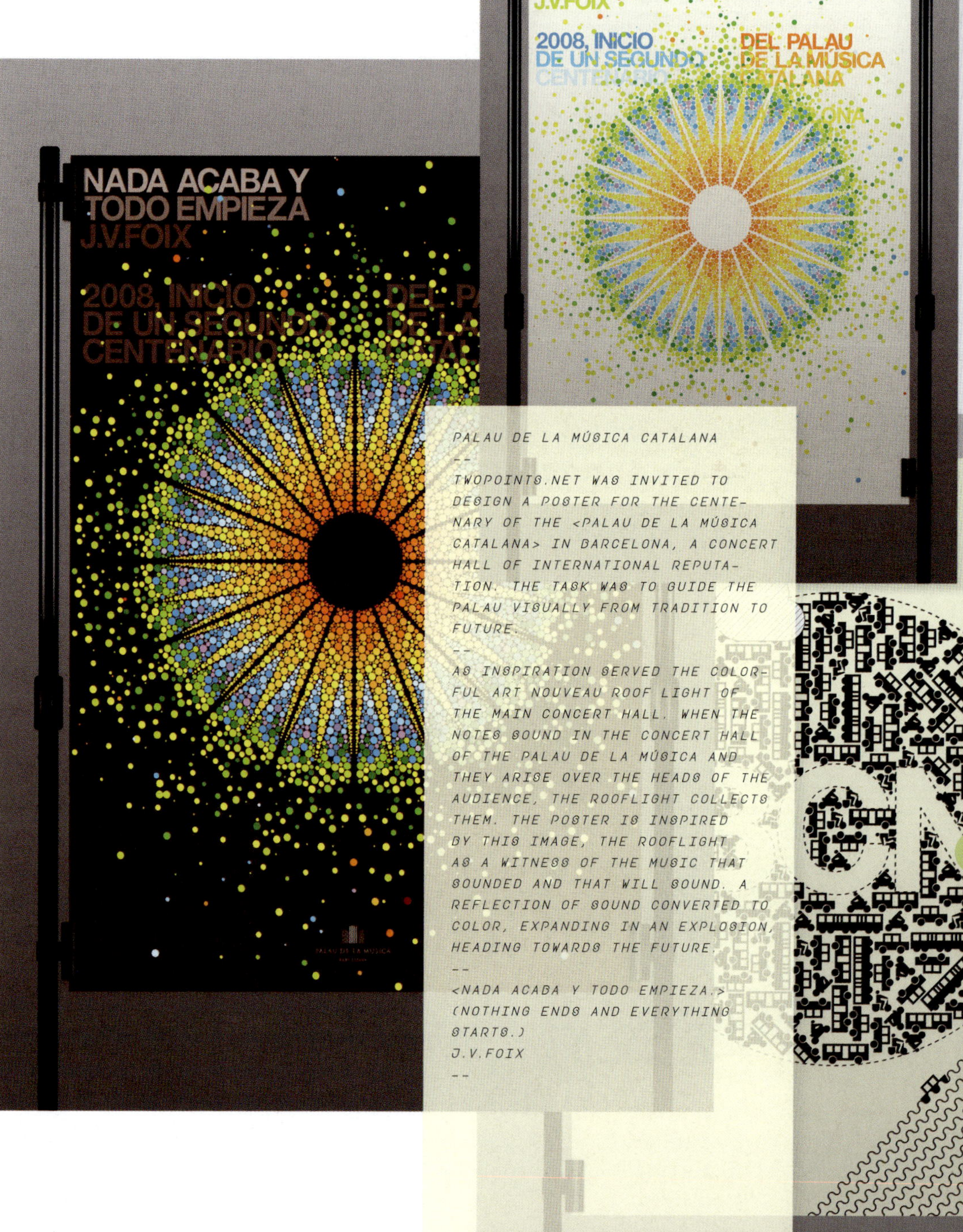
NADA ACABA Y
TODO EMPIEZA
J.V.FOIX

2008, INICIO
DE UN SEGUNDO
CENTENARIO

DEL PALAU
DE LA MÚSICA
CATALANA

PALAU DE LA MÚSICA

PALAU DE LA MÚSICA CATALANA
--
TWOPOINTS.NET WAS INVITED TO
DESIGN A POSTER FOR THE CENTE-
NARY OF THE <PALAU DE LA MÚSICA
CATALANA> IN BARCELONA, A CONCERT
HALL OF INTERNATIONAL REPUTA-
TION. THE TASK WAS TO GUIDE THE
PALAU VISUALLY FROM TRADITION TO
FUTURE.
--
AS INSPIRATION SERVED THE COLOR-
FUL ART NOUVEAU ROOF LIGHT OF
THE MAIN CONCERT HALL. WHEN THE
NOTES SOUND IN THE CONCERT HALL
OF THE PALAU DE LA MÚSICA AND
THEY ARISE OVER THE HEADS OF THE
AUDIENCE, THE ROOFLIGHT COLLECTS
THEM. THE POSTER IS INSPIRED
BY THIS IMAGE, THE ROOFLIGHT
AS A WITNESS OF THE MUSIC THAT
SOUNDED AND THAT WILL SOUND. A
REFLECTION OF SOUND CONVERTED TO
COLOR, EXPANDING IN AN EXPLOSION,
HEADING TOWARDS THE FUTURE.
--
<NADA ACABA Y TODO EMPIEZA.>
(NOTHING ENDS AND EVERYTHING
STARTS.)
J.V.FOIX
--

RUSH HOUR

--

CREATORS MAGAZINE INVITED US
TO DESIGN THREE DOUBLE PAGES ON
BARCELONA BETWEEN 8 AND 9 A.M.
WHILE THIS OF COURSE FORCED US
TO HAVE TO GET UP EARLY, IT GAVE
US THE OPPORTUNITY TO EXPLORE
THE CITY WE LIVE IN.

--

EVEN IF BARCELONA IS NOT VERY
BIG, IT'S AN INCREDIBLY ENERGY-
CHARGED CITY, ESPECIALLY AT RUSH
HOUR. BARCELONA IS CAUGHT BE-
TWEEN THE MEDITERRANEAN AND THE
MOUNTAINS AND CONSEQUENTLY CAN'T
EXPAND ANY FURTHER. THIS LED THE
CITY WHICH WAS BECOMING INCREAS-
INGLY POPULAR TO ENLARGE ITS
SATELLITE TOWNS. NOW EVERY MORN-
ING 332,723 STUDENTS AND WORKERS
HAVE TO SET OUT FOR BARCELONA.
THIS PICTURE FASCINATED US. EVEN
IF WE'VE ALL GOT USED TO IT AND
NO LONGER NOTICE BEING PART OF
THAT MASS MOVEMENT, ONCE YOU'VE
RECOGNIZED IT, IT'S AN ABSURD
SITUATION.

--

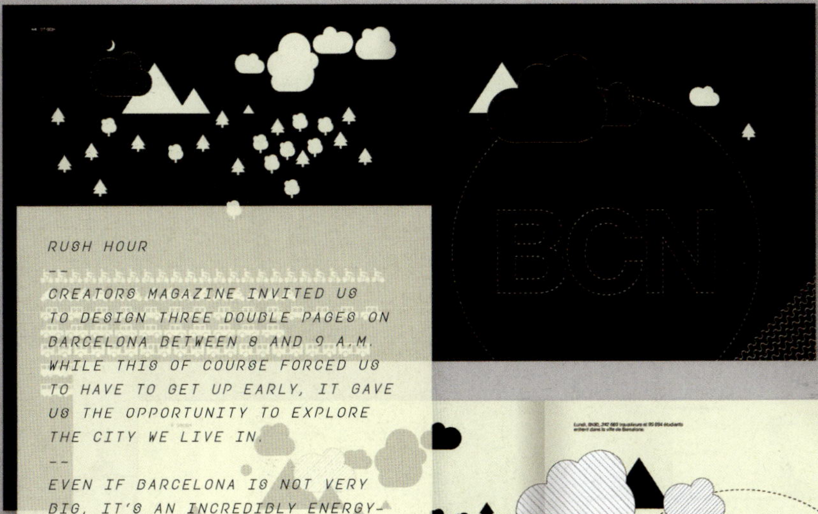

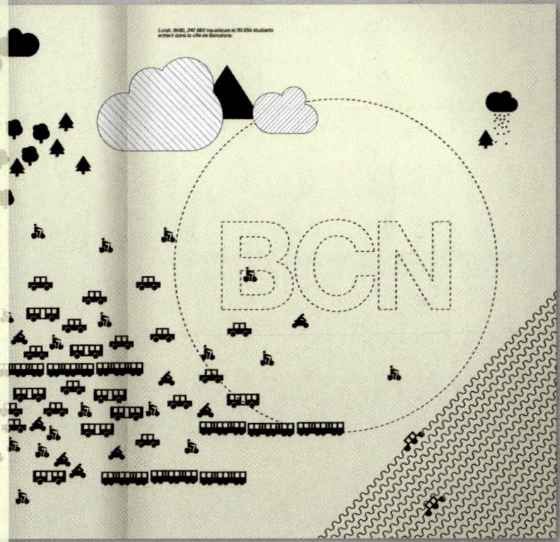

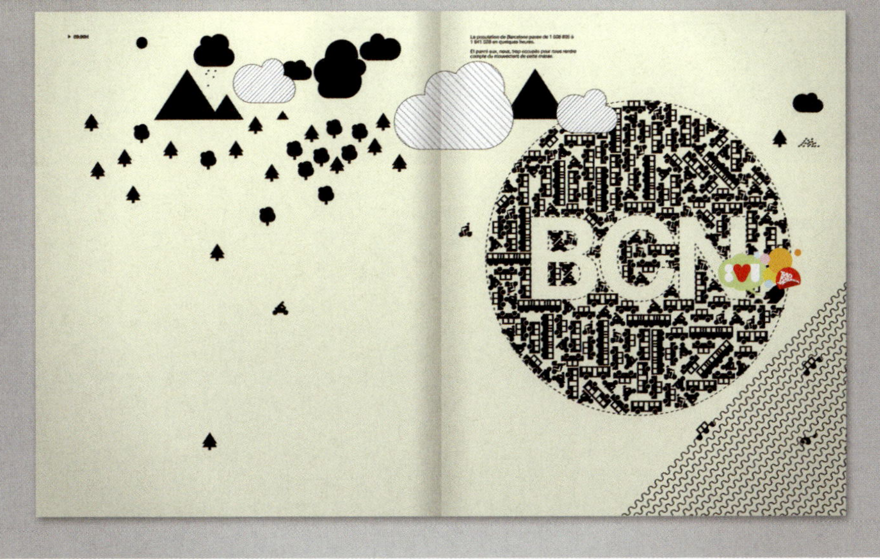

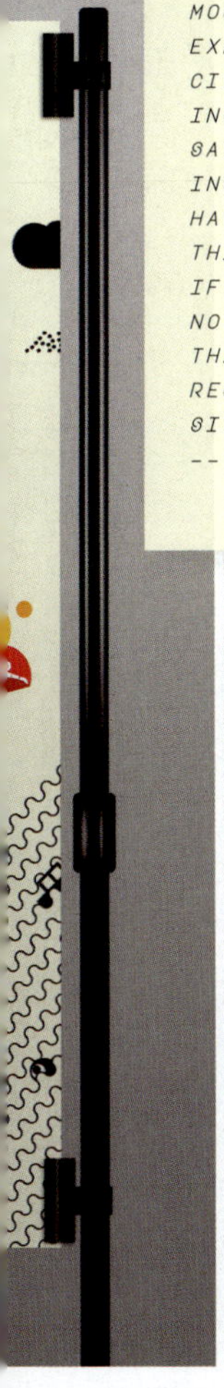

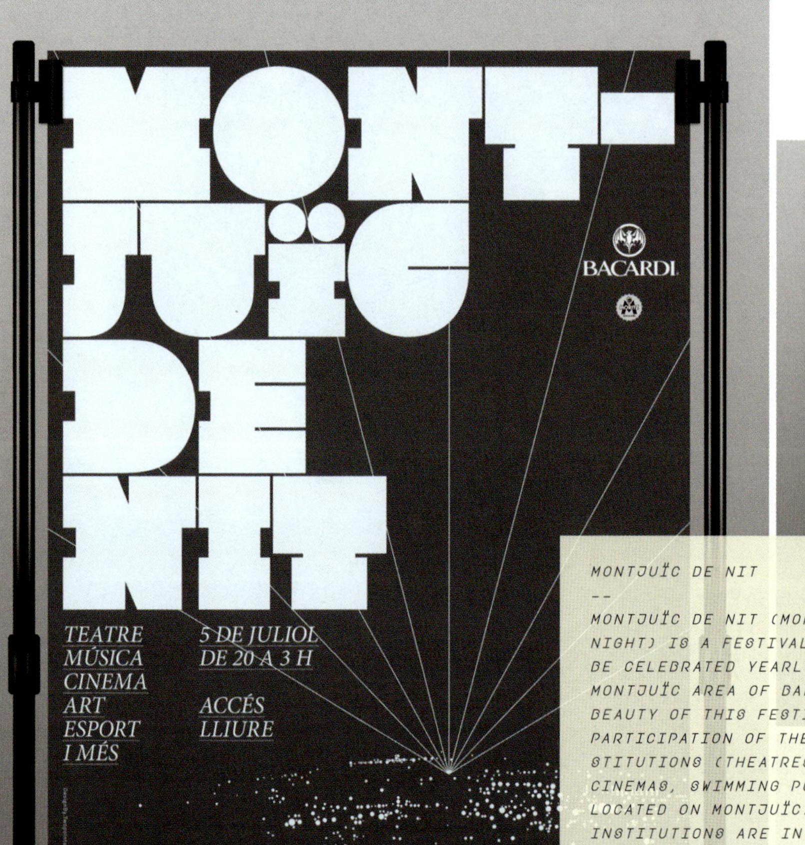

MONT-
JUÏC
DE
NIT
TEATRE
MÚSICA
CINEMA
ART
ESPORT
I MÉS
5 DE JULIOL
DE 20 A 3 H
ACCÉS
LLIURE
BACARDI
Ajuntament de Barcelona
www.bcn.cat/canalcultura
5 DE JULIOL / DE 2
Accés lliure
MONT-
JUÏC
DE
NIT
Ajuntament de Barcelona

MONTJUÏC DE NIT
--
MONTJUÏC DE NIT (MONTJUIC AT
NIGHT) IS A FESTIVAL THAT WILL
BE CELEBRATED YEARLY IN THE
MONTJUÏC AREA OF BARCELONA. THE
BEAUTY OF THIS FESTIVAL IS THE
PARTICIPATION OF THE VARIOUS IN-
STITUTIONS (THEATRES, MUSEUMS,
CINEMAS, SWIMMING POOLS, ETC.)
LOCATED ON MONTJUÏC. ALL OF THESE
INSTITUTIONS ARE INVITED TO OPEN
THEIR DOORS DURING AN ENTIRE
NIGHT DEDICATED TO MONTJUÏC DE
NIT. THE INSTITUT DE CULTURA
SHOWED GREAT FAITH IN US, GIVING
US THE OPPORTUNITY TO DESIGN THE
VISUAL IDENTITY FOR A FESTIVAL
WITHOUT PRECEDENT. THE VISUAL
IDENTITY WE DEVELOPED IS BASED
UPON NIGHT AT MONTJUÏC: ITS MYS-
TERIOUS DARKNESS AND THE MAGIC
OF THE LIGHTS. WE WERE INSPIRED
BY THE SUNSET SKY OF THE CITY. A
SIMPLE, BUT EFFECTIVE COMMUNICA-
TION STRATEGY.
--

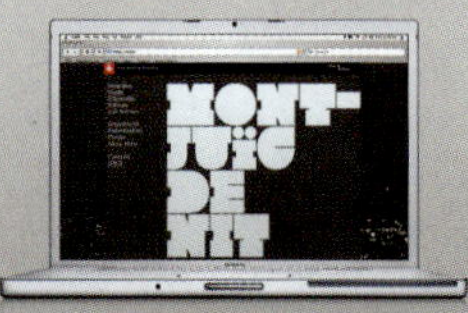

MONT-
JUÏC
DE
NIT

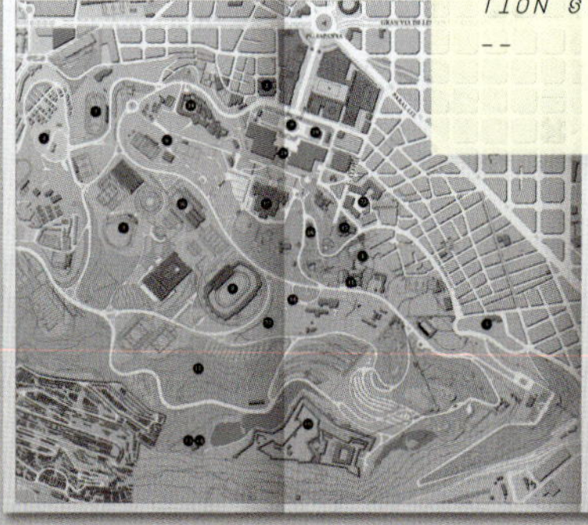

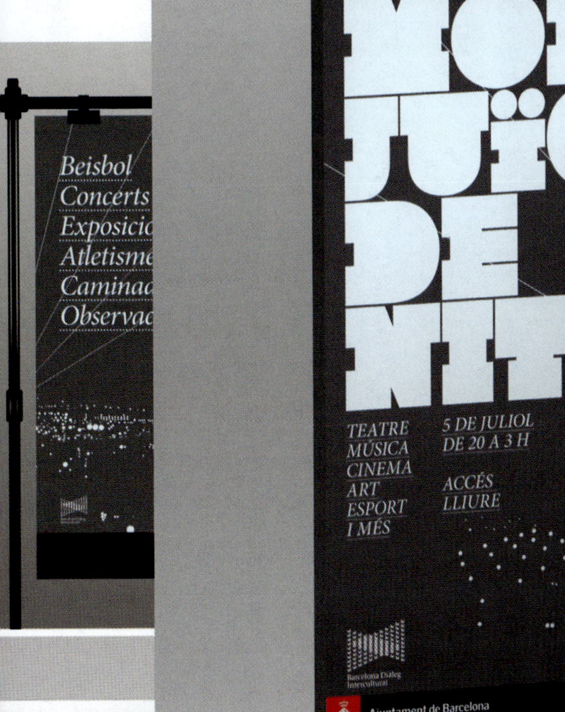

MONT-
JUÏC
DE
NIT
TEATRE
MÚSICA
CINEMA
ART
ESPORT
I MÉS
5 DE JULIOL
DE 20 A 3 H
ACCÉS
LLIURE
Barcelona Diàleg
Intercultural
Institut de cultura
Ajuntament de Barcelona
www.bcn.cat/canalcultura
Beisbol
Concerts
Exposició
Atletisme
Caminada
Observació

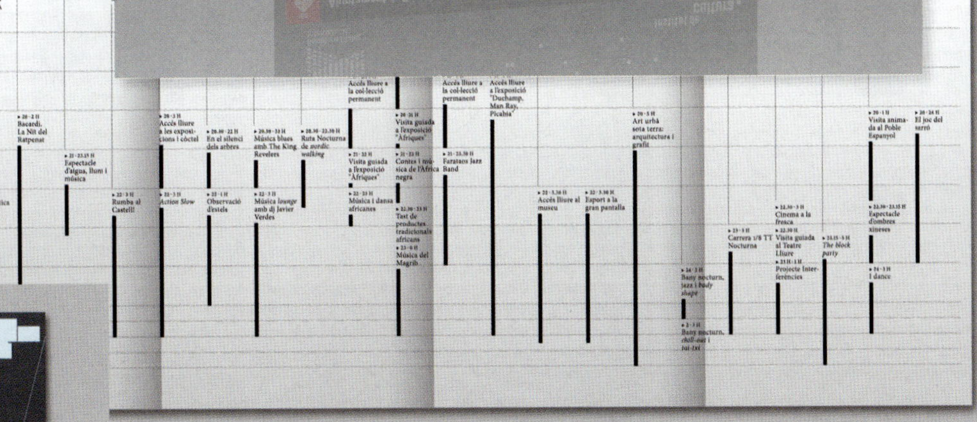

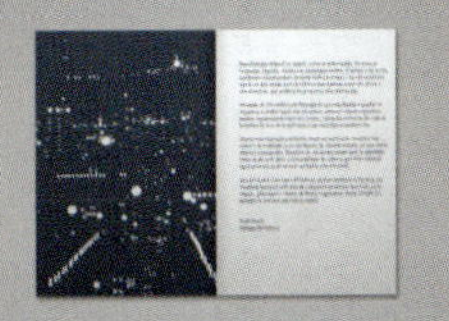

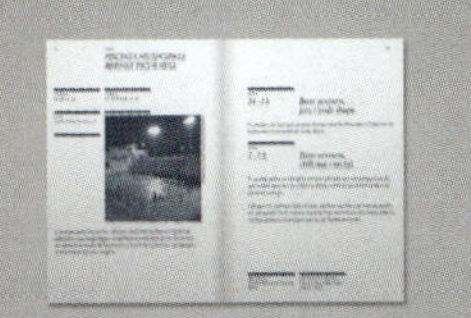

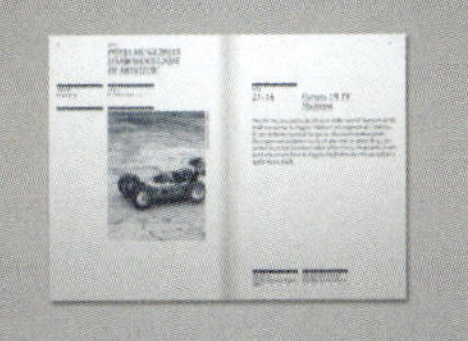

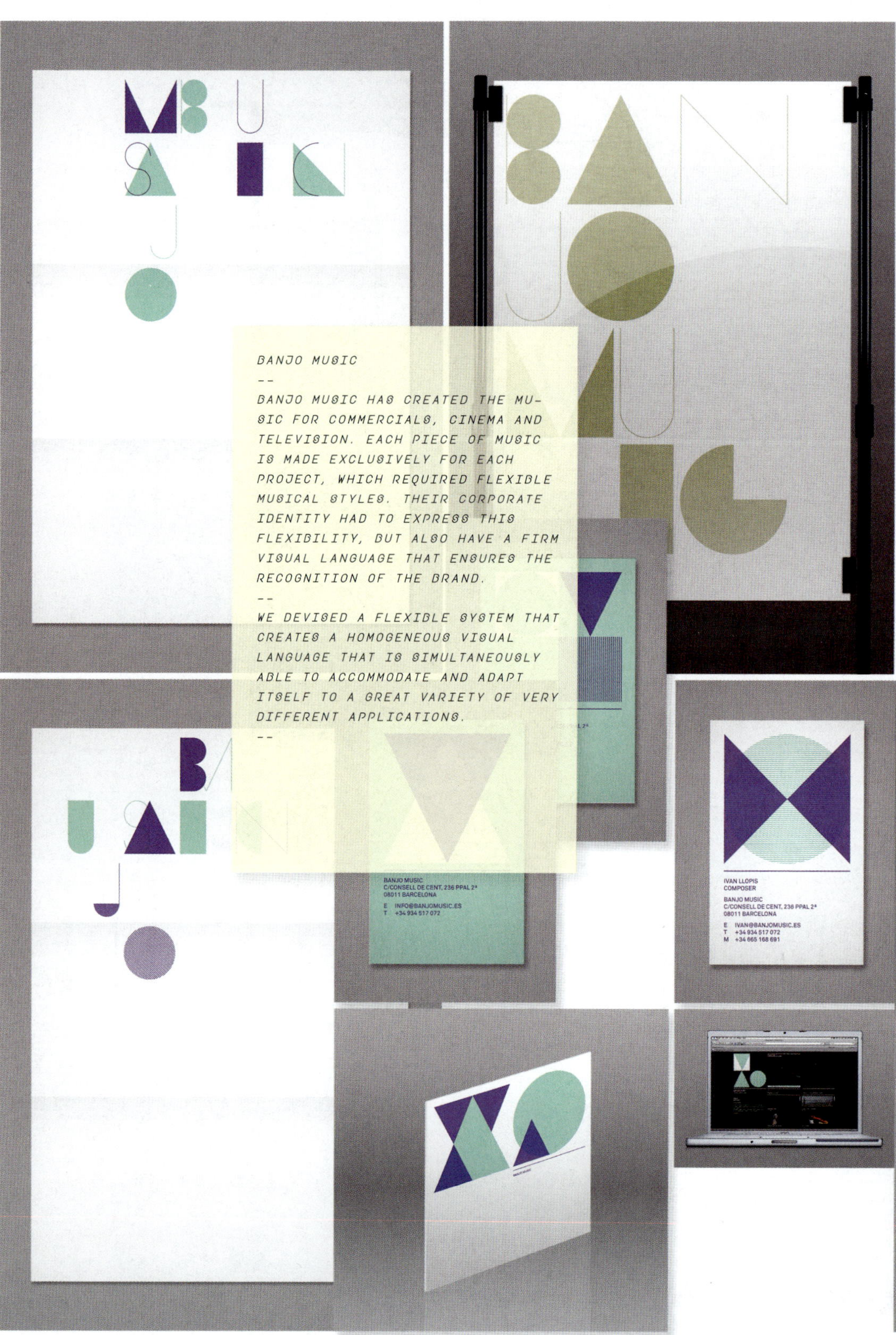

BANJO MUSIC
--
BANJO MUSIC HAS CREATED THE MU-
SIC FOR COMMERCIALS, CINEMA AND
TELEVISION. EACH PIECE OF MUSIC
IS MADE EXCLUSIVELY FOR EACH
PROJECT, WHICH REQUIRED FLEXIBLE
MUSICAL STYLES. THEIR CORPORATE
IDENTITY HAD TO EXPRESS THIS
FLEXIBILITY, BUT ALSO HAVE A FIRM
VISUAL LANGUAGE THAT ENSURES THE
RECOGNITION OF THE BRAND.
--
WE DEVISED A FLEXIBLE SYSTEM THAT
CREATES A HOMOGENEOUS VISUAL
LANGUAGE THAT IS SIMULTANEOUSLY
ABLE TO ACCOMMODATE AND ADAPT
ITSELF TO A GREAT VARIETY OF VERY
DIFFERENT APPLICATIONS.
--
BANJO MUSIC
C/CONSELL DE CENT, 236 PPAL 2ª
08011 BARCELONA
E   INFO@BANJOMUSIC.ES
T   +34 934 517 072
IVAN LLOPIS
COMPOSER
BANJO MUSIC
C/CONSELL DE CENT, 236 PPAL 2ª
08011 BARCELONA
E   IVAN@BANJOMUSIC.ES
T   +34 934 517 072
M   +34 665 168 691

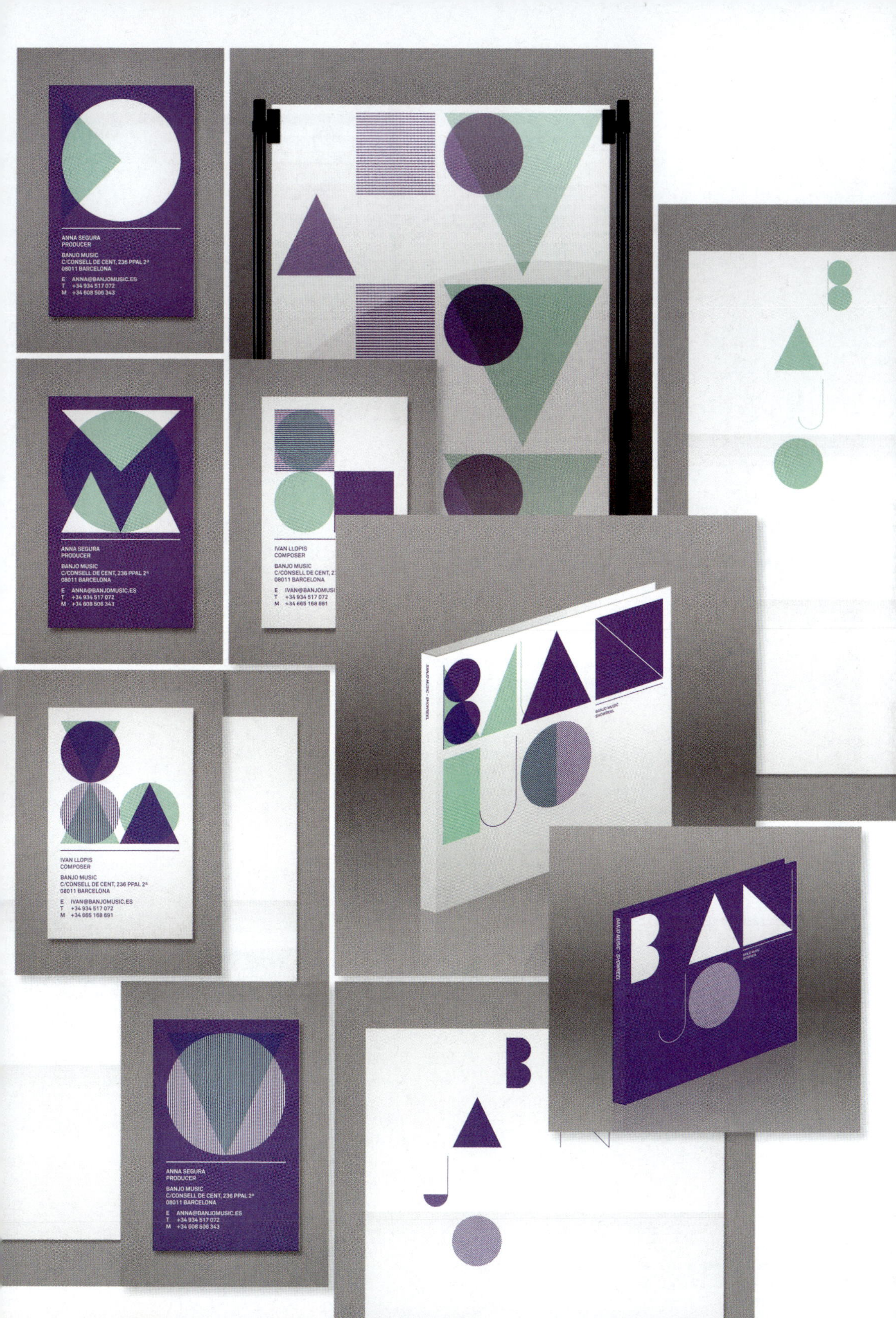
ANNA SEGURA
PRODUCER
BANJO MUSIC
C/CONSELL DE CENT, 236 PPAL 2ª
08011 BARCELONA
E   ANNA@BANJOMUSIC.ES
T   +34 934 517 072
M   +34 608 506 343

ANNA SEGURA
PRODUCER
BANJO MUSIC
C/CONSELL DE CENT, 236 PPAL 2ª
08011 BARCELONA
E   ANNA@BANJOMUSIC.ES
T   +34 934 517 072
M   +34 608 506 343

IVAN LLOPIS
COMPOSER
BANJO MUSIC
C/CONSELL DE CENT, 2
08011 BARCELONA
E   IVAN@BANJOMUSI
T   +34 934 517 072
M   +34 665 168 691

IVAN LLOPIS
COMPOSER
BANJO MUSIC
C/CONSELL DE CENT, 236 PPAL 2ª
08011 BARCELONA
E   IVAN@BANJOMUSIC.ES
T   +34 934 517 072
M   +34 665 168 691

ANNA SEGURA
PRODUCER
BANJO MUSIC
C/CONSELL DE CENT, 236 PPAL 2ª
08011 BARCELONA
E   ANNA@BANJOMUSIC.ES
T   +34 934 517 072
M   +34 608 506 343

BANJO MUSIC SHOWREEL

BANJO MUSIC SHOWREEL

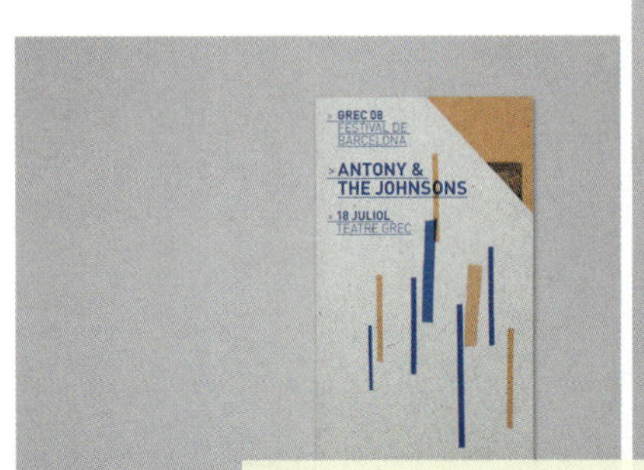

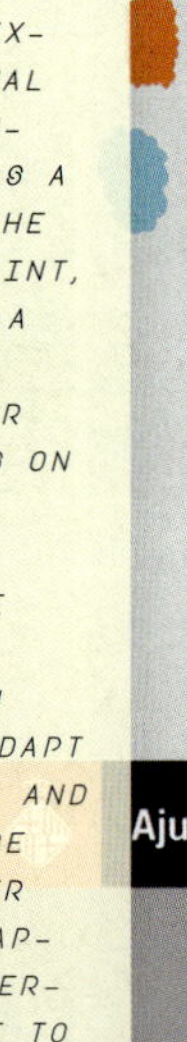

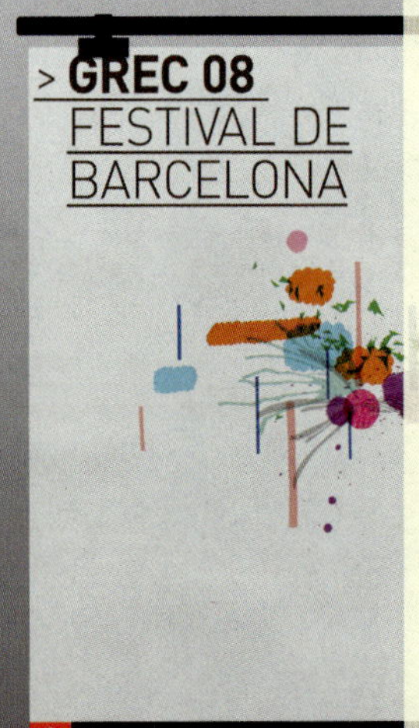

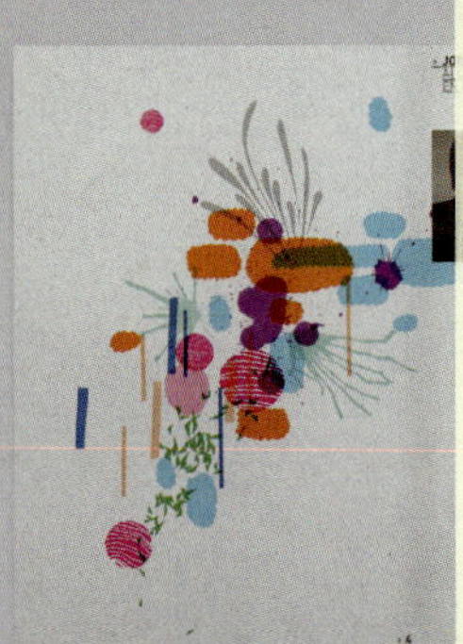

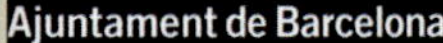

GREC'08
--
GREC IS ONE OF THE MOST SUCCESS-
FUL FESTIVALS FROM BARCELONA. ITS
OFFER IS AS BROAD AS ITS TAR-
GETGROUP. FROM POP CONCERTS AND
OPERA, OVER THEATRE AND BALLET
TO CIRCUS AND PUPPET THEATRE.
THEREFORE IT IS VISITED BY VERY
DIFFERENT PEOPLE.
--
TWOPOINTS.NET DEVELOPED A FLEX-
IBLE, BUT VERY OPERATIVE VISUAL
SYSTEM WHICH IS BASED UPON HU-
MAN AND ARTISTIC EXPRESSION AS A
METAPHOR. THE VISIBILITY OF THE
WORKING MATERIAL AS PAPER, PAINT,
SCISSORS AND MARKERS CREATES A
PROXIMITY THAT CAN BE EXPERI-
ENCED AS WELL IN EVENTS AS FOR
EXAMPLE THEATRE OR DANCE ACTS ON
THE FESTIVAL GREC.
--
EACH OF THE FIVE GENRE BECAME
ITS OWN VISUAL LANGUAGE AND
COLOR CODE. A FLEXIBLE SYSTEM
WAS CREATED THAT IS ABLE TO ADAPT
ITSELF QUICKLY TO EACH FORMAT AND
MEDIA. IT CAN LEAD OR SURPRISE
THE READER. IT HELPS TO DIFFER
BETWEEN DIFFERENT GENRE AND AP-
PLICATIONS. IT REACTS TO DIFFER-
ENT TARGET GROUPS AND IS ABLE TO
COMMUNICATE WITH THEM.
--

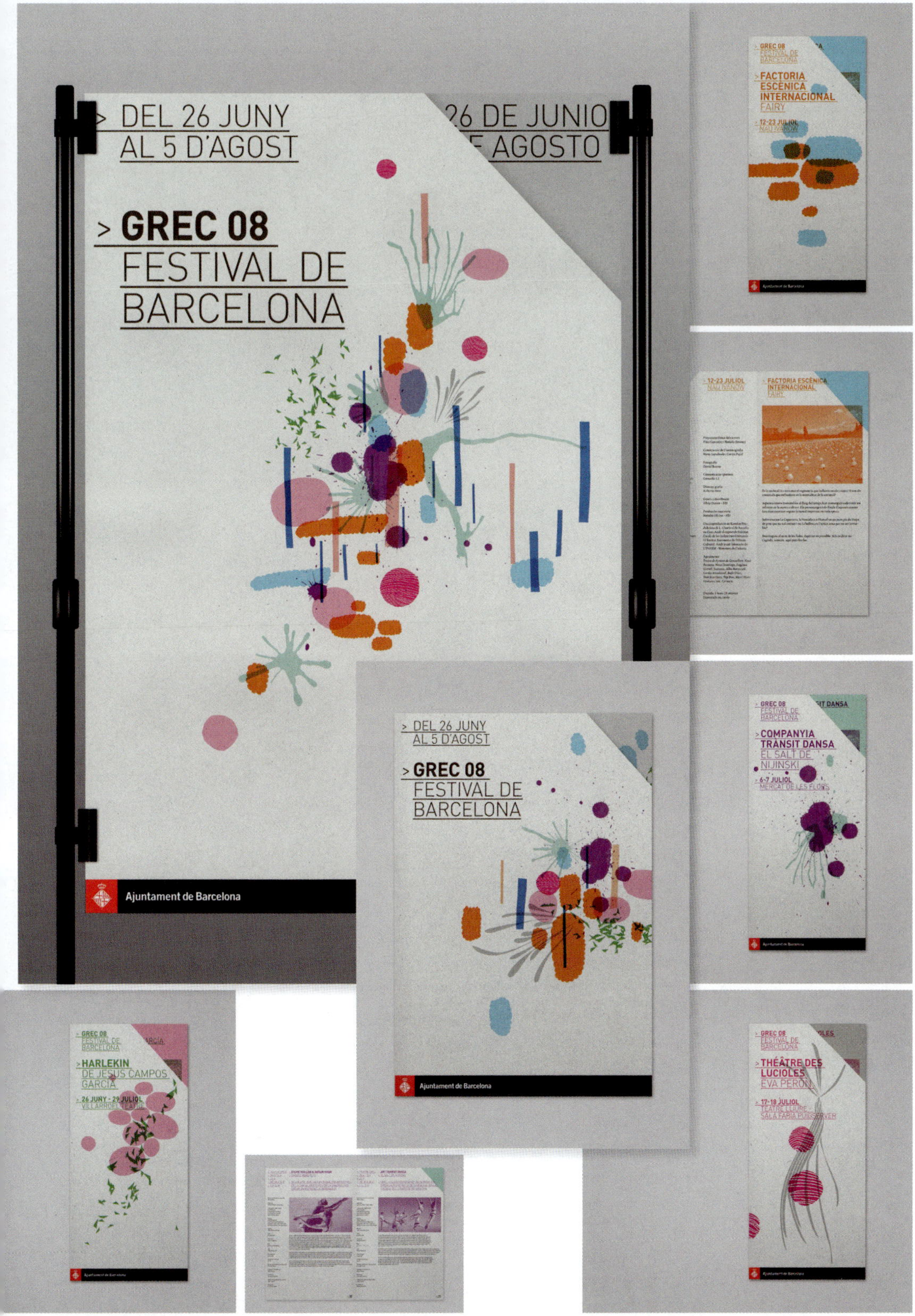

> DEL 26 JUNY
AL 5 D'AGOST
26 DE JUNIO
DE AGOSTO
> GREC 08
FESTIVAL DE
BARCELONA
Ajuntament de Barcelona

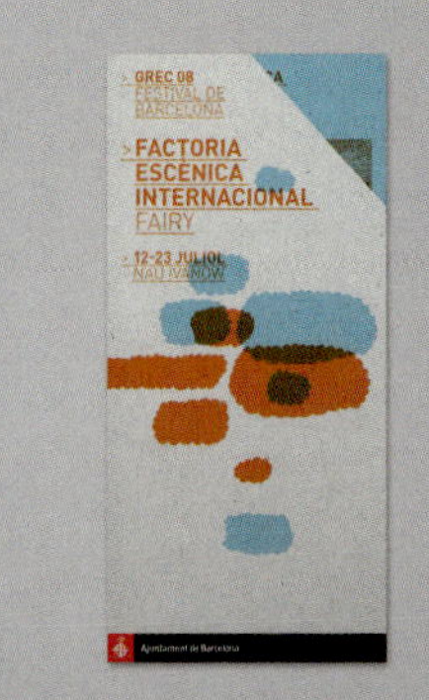
GREC 08
FESTIVAL DE
BARCELONA
> FACTORIA
ESCÈNICA
INTERNACIONAL
FAIRY
> 12-23 JULIOL
NAU IVANOW
Ajuntament de Barcelona

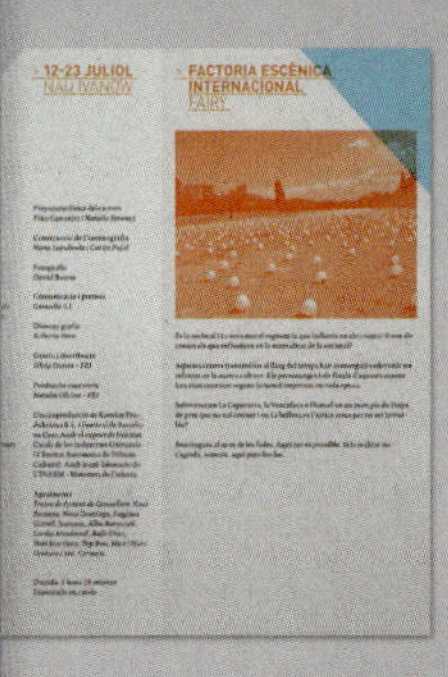
> 12-23 JULIOL
NAU IVANOW
> FACTORIA ESCÈNICA
INTERNACIONAL
FAIRY

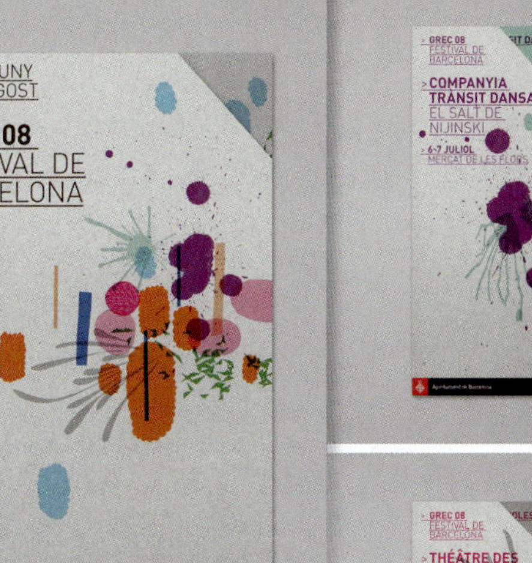
> DEL 26 JUNY
AL 5 D'AGOST
> GREC 08
FESTIVAL DE
BARCELONA
Ajuntament de Barcelona

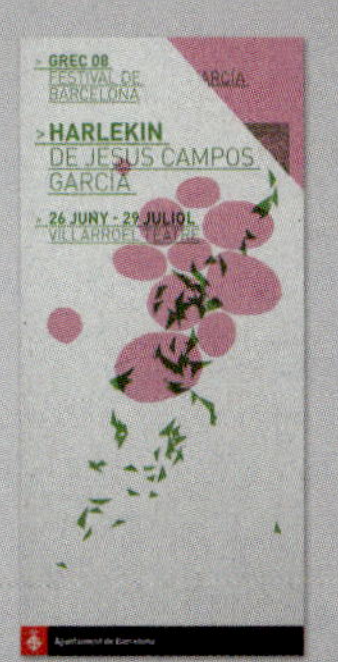
GREC 08
FESTIVAL DE
BARCELONA
> HARLEKIN
DE JESÚS CAMPOS
GARCÍA
> 26 JUNY - 27 JULIOL
VILLARROEL
Ajuntament de Barcelona

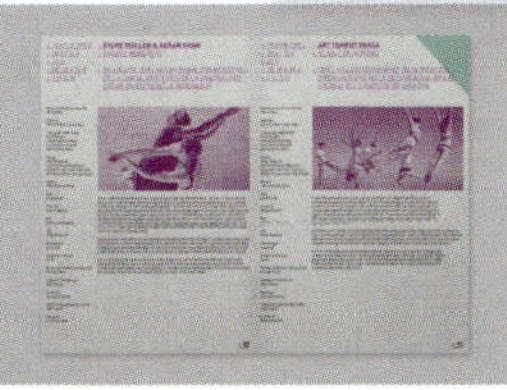

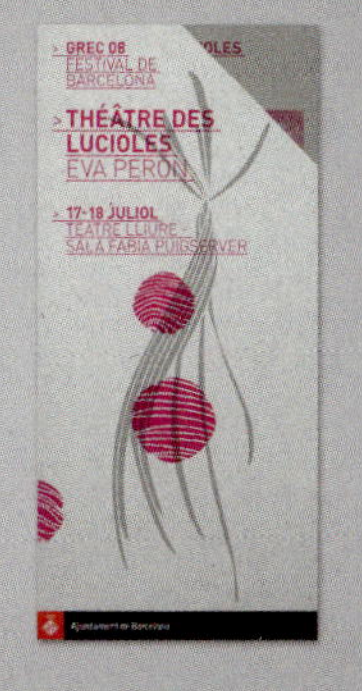
GREC 08
FESTIVAL DE
BARCELONA
> THÉÂTRE DES
LUCIOLES
EVA PERÓN
> 17-18 JULIOL
TEATRE LLIURE
SALA FABIÀ PUIGSERVER
Ajuntament de Barcelona

MARIO WAGNER WAS BORN IN 1974 AND
WORKS AS AN ARTIST AND ILLUSTRA-
TOR IN COLOGNE/GERMANY. HIS UNIQUE
ILLUSTRATIONS AND ARTWORKS ARE
COMMISSIONED BY THE MOST POPULAR
MAGAZINES LIKE PLAYBOY OR THE NEW
YORK TIMES MAGAZINE. WAGNER'S WORK
IS MADE BY ANALOGUE MEANS, HE USES
OLD MAGAZINES, SCISSORS, GLUE AND
ACRYLCOLOR, EVEN FOR HIS ARTWORKS
WHICH ARE ABOUT 6.5 FEET IN SIZE.
HIS WORK HAS ALREADY BEEN SHOWN IN
NUMEROUS GERMAN AND INTERNATIONAL
EXHIBITIONS, INCLUDING THE SCOPE.

PEOPLE ARE THE CENTRAL ELEMENT IN
MARIO WAGNER'S COLLAGES. NARRA-
TIVES DEVELOP, MOODS ARE CONJURED
UP AND RELATIONSHIPS ARE FORMED
BY AND AROUND THE HUMAN BEING.
WAGNER'S REPERTOIRE OFTEN PLAYS ON
FRAGMENTS OF POP CULTURE, TECH-
NOLOGY OR EVERYDAY URBAN LIFE.
THE FIGURES ARE TRIMMED, MASKED
AND DISPLACED IN MORE RECENTLY
BUILT SPACES. MOUNTAINS INTER-
ACT WITH VILLAGES OF BUNGALOWS,
AS DO STAIRWELLS AND FILM CAMERAS
FROM WHICH RAYS OF LIGHT PRO-
TRUDE. PROPORTIONAL CONTRASTS AND
IMPROBABILITIES ARE SPECIFICALLY
RELEVANT WHEN, FOR EXAMPLE, A GAP-
ING RED MOUTH IS DEPICTED FLOATING
NEXT TO A PROPORTIONATELY SMALLER
HEAD. WAGNER'S STRATEGY ALWAYS
ENTAILS THE GENERATION OF INSECU-
RITY IN HIS AUDIENCE, IN ORDER TO
NUDGE THE IMAGINATION INTO ANOTHER
WORLD, INTO AN ARTISTIC PARALLEL
UNIVERSE. THE NARRATIVE ELEMENT
IS ALSO SIGNIFICANT TO A GREAT
EXTENT. SIMILAR TO A PAUSED VIDEO
FILM, ONE ASSUMES THE ABILITY TO
FAST-FORWARD THE IMAGES AND THUS
BE ABLE TO ANTICIPATE MORE OF NAR-
RATIVE. APART FROM THIS ASPECT,
THE IDEA OF AN ANIMATION FILM OF
THE FIGURES AND OTHER CONSTELLA-
TIONS LENDS ITSELF TO A SEQUENTIAL
IMPRESSION.

--

WHAT IS GERMAN?

LIVER SAUSAGE.

WHAT IS GERMAN DESIGN?

FOR ME FIRST AND FOREMOST THE
BAUHAUS, ITS IDEAS AND INFLU-
ENCES ARE STILL DETECTABLE, IT
WAS AND STILL IS OUTSTANDING. IN
GRAPHIC DESIGN AND THE FIELD OF

COLLAGE YOU SIMPLY CAN'T AVOID
KURT SCHWITTERS, HANNAH HÖCH, JOHN
HEARTFIELD AND HEINZ EDELMANN.

PLEASE DESCRIBE YOUR WORKING
PROCESS.

FOR COMMISSIONED WORKS I OFTEN
GET THE FIRST IDEA ON READING
THROUGH THE TEXT THAT'S TO BE IL-
LUSTRATED, AND THEN I ALREADY HAVE
THE SUITABLE IMAGES IN MY HEAD,
ALMOST THE COMPLETE COLLAGE WITH
ALL ITS MOST IMPORTANT ELEMENTS,
COLORS, THE ARRANGEMENT. THEN THE
REAL WORK BEGINS, LOOKING FOR AND
FINDING THE RIGHT PICTURE MATE-
RIAL, FOR THAT I LOOK THROUGH MY
STOCK OF OLD MAGAZINES AND BOOKS.
THEN I CREATE THE FIRST SKETCH ON
THE COMPUTER, COME TO AN AGREE-
MENT WITH THE CLIENT, AND THEN I
AGAIN WORK IN ANALOGUE FORM ON TO
PAPER. IN THE PROCESS THE ILLUS-
TRATION GOES ON EVOLVING, NOT THE
REAL BASIC IDEA, BUT A FEW DETAILS
KEEP BEING ADDED. IN THE CASE OF
SELF-INITIATED WORKS THE SITUA-
TION IS OF COURSE QUITE DIFFERENT,
THERE THE APPROACH IS MUCH MORE
EMOTIONAL AND GRADUALLY RESULTS IN
A TOTAL PICTURE WHICH IS THEN AT
ONE WITH OTHER WORKS.

WHAT DO YOU AIM TO ACHIEVE WITH
YOUR WORK?

THE TOP PRIORITY AND IN MY
EYES ALSO THE ONLY TRUE AIM IS TO
WORK FOR YOURSELF, EXPRESS YOUR-
SELF, VISUALIZE YOUR IDEAS, AND
THEN IDEALLY TO EARN YOUR LIVING
THROUGH IT.

YOU'VE INVITED A FRIEND TO
GERMANY; NAME ONE PLACE THEY
REALLY MUST VISIT AND A QUINT-
ESSENTIAL EXPERIENCE YOU REC-
OMMEND.

GERMANY IS DISTINGUISHED VERY
MUCH BY ITS REGIONAL IDIOSYNCRA-
SIES, CUSTOMS AND TRADITIONS. AS I
LIVE AND WORK IN COLOGNE, I THINK
IT WOULD BE ALMOST NEGLIGENT TO
LEAVE OUT THE COLOGNE CARNIVAL.
OTHERWISE HE SHOULD OF COURSE TAKE
A LOOK AT BERLIN, THE COMPACTNESS
AND DIVERSITY OF HISTORY-IMBUED
BUILDINGS AND SQUARES IS SOME-
THING SPECIAL.

WAGNER

MARIO WAGNER
--
742 UNION STREET
94133 SAN FRANCISCO
CALIFORNIA
US
--
MARIO@REFLEKTORIUM.DE
WWW.MARIO-WAGNER.COM
--

WHAT IS THE MOST IMPORTANT LESSON YOU HAVE LEARNED IN YOUR PROFESSION SO FAR?

THAT YOU HAVE TO WORK HARD ON YOURSELF AND YOUR PROJECTS, HAVE TO KEEP PUSHING YOURSELF EVER FURTHER, TO BELIEVE IN WHAT YOU'RE DOING AND NOT LOSE SIGHT OF THAT OBJECTIVE, EVEN IF THINGS SOME- TIMES AREN'T TURNING OUT THAT WELL.

--

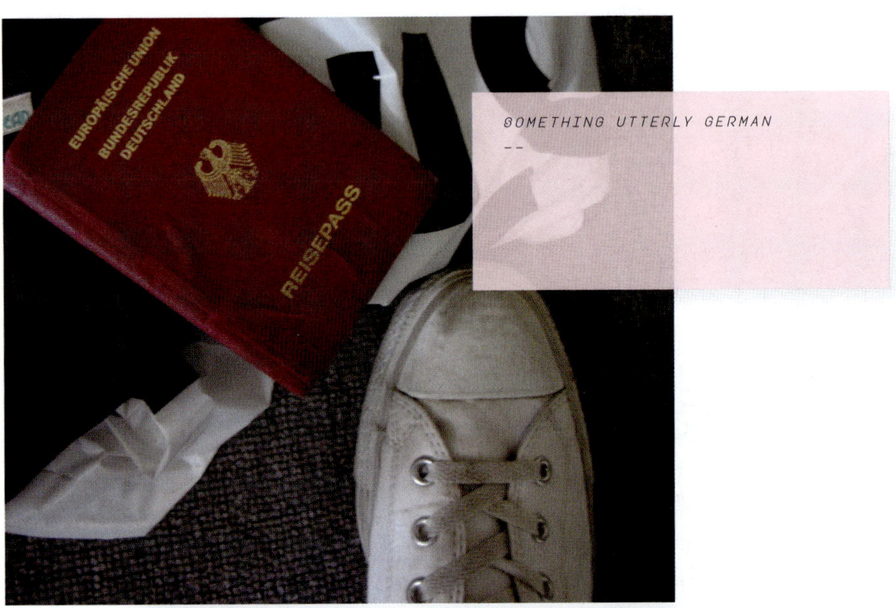
SOMETHING UTTERLY GERMAN
--

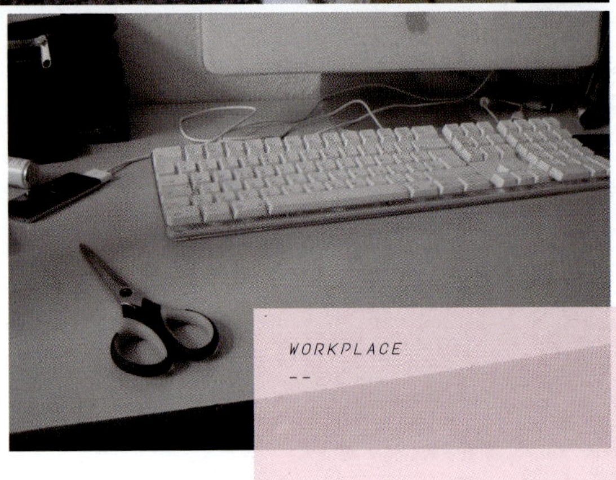
WORKPLACE
--

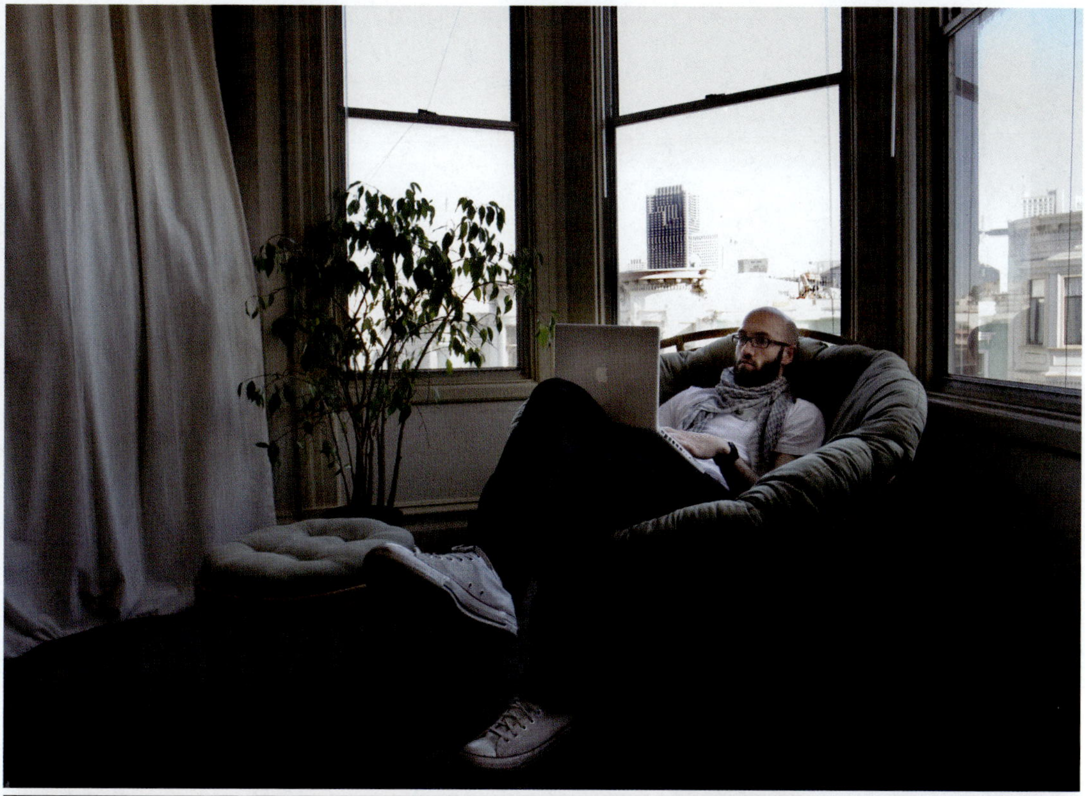

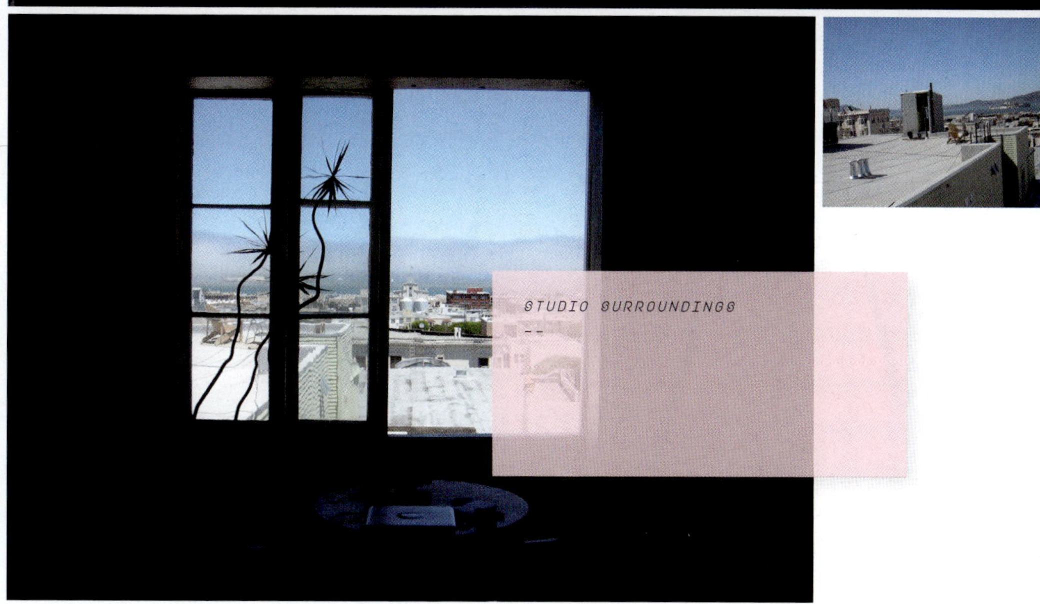
STUDIO SURROUNDINGS

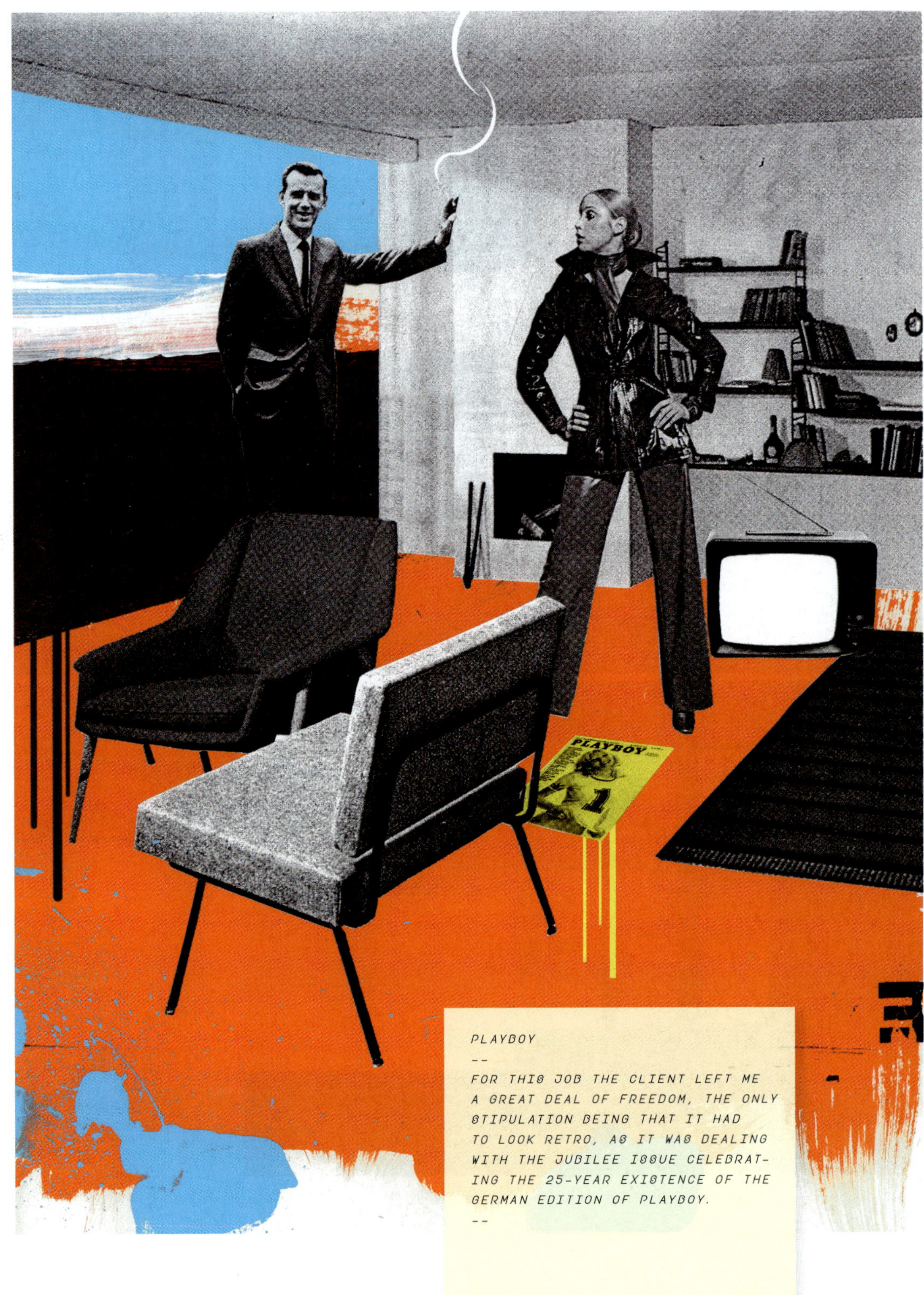

PLAYBOY
--
FOR THIS JOB THE CLIENT LEFT ME
A GREAT DEAL OF FREEDOM, THE ONLY
STIPULATION BEING THAT IT HAD
TO LOOK RETRO, AS IT WAS DEALING
WITH THE JUBILEE ISSUE CELEBRAT-
ING THE 25-YEAR EXISTENCE OF THE
GERMAN EDITION OF PLAYBOY.
--

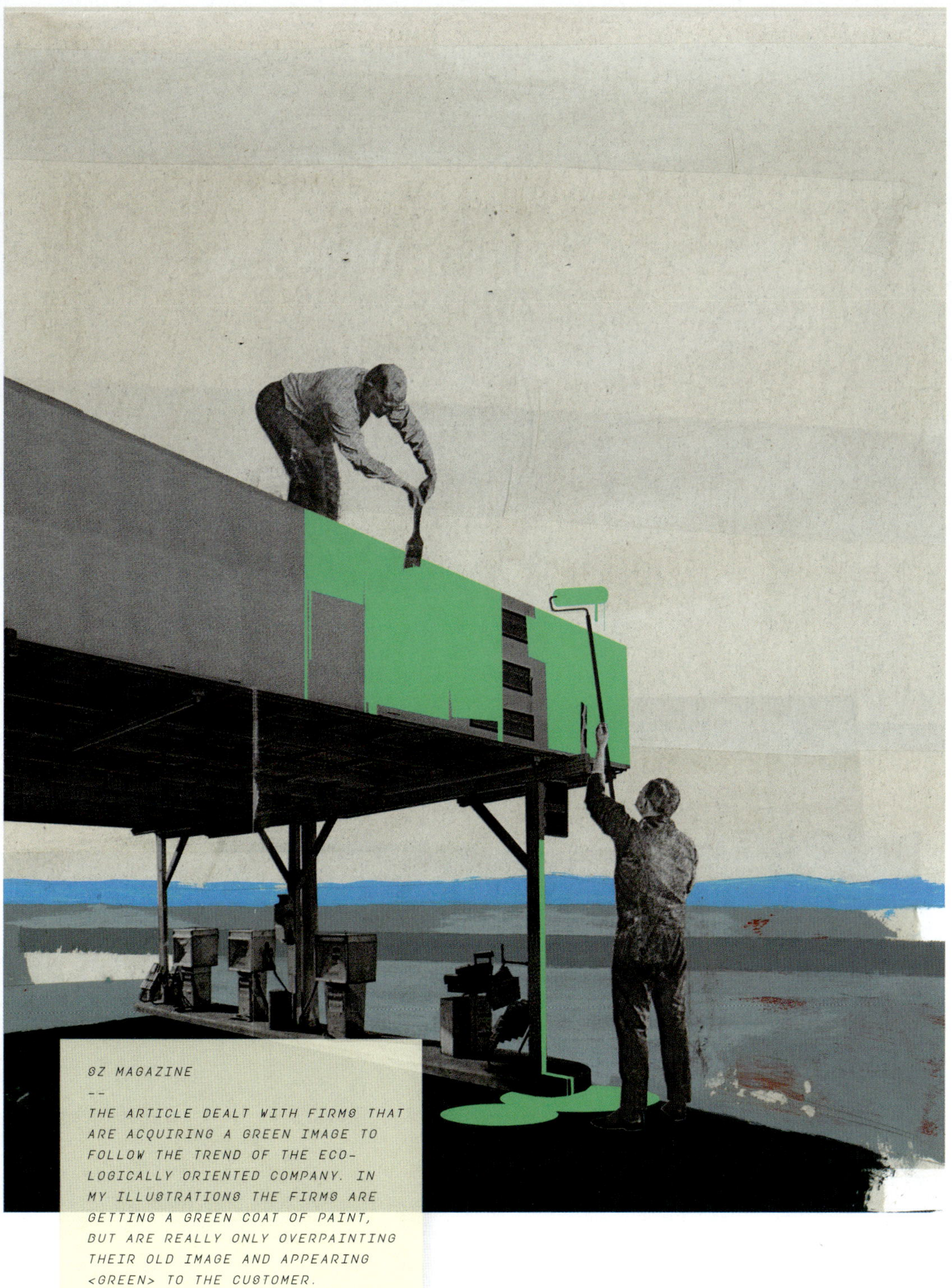

ØZ MAGAZINE
--
THE ARTICLE DEALT WITH FIRMS THAT
ARE ACQUIRING A GREEN IMAGE TO
FOLLOW THE TREND OF THE ECO-
LOGICALLY ORIENTED COMPANY. IN
MY ILLUSTRATIONS THE FIRMS ARE
GETTING A GREEN COAT OF PAINT,
BUT ARE REALLY ONLY OVERPAINTING
THEIR OLD IMAGE AND APPEARING
<GREEN> TO THE CUSTOMER.
--

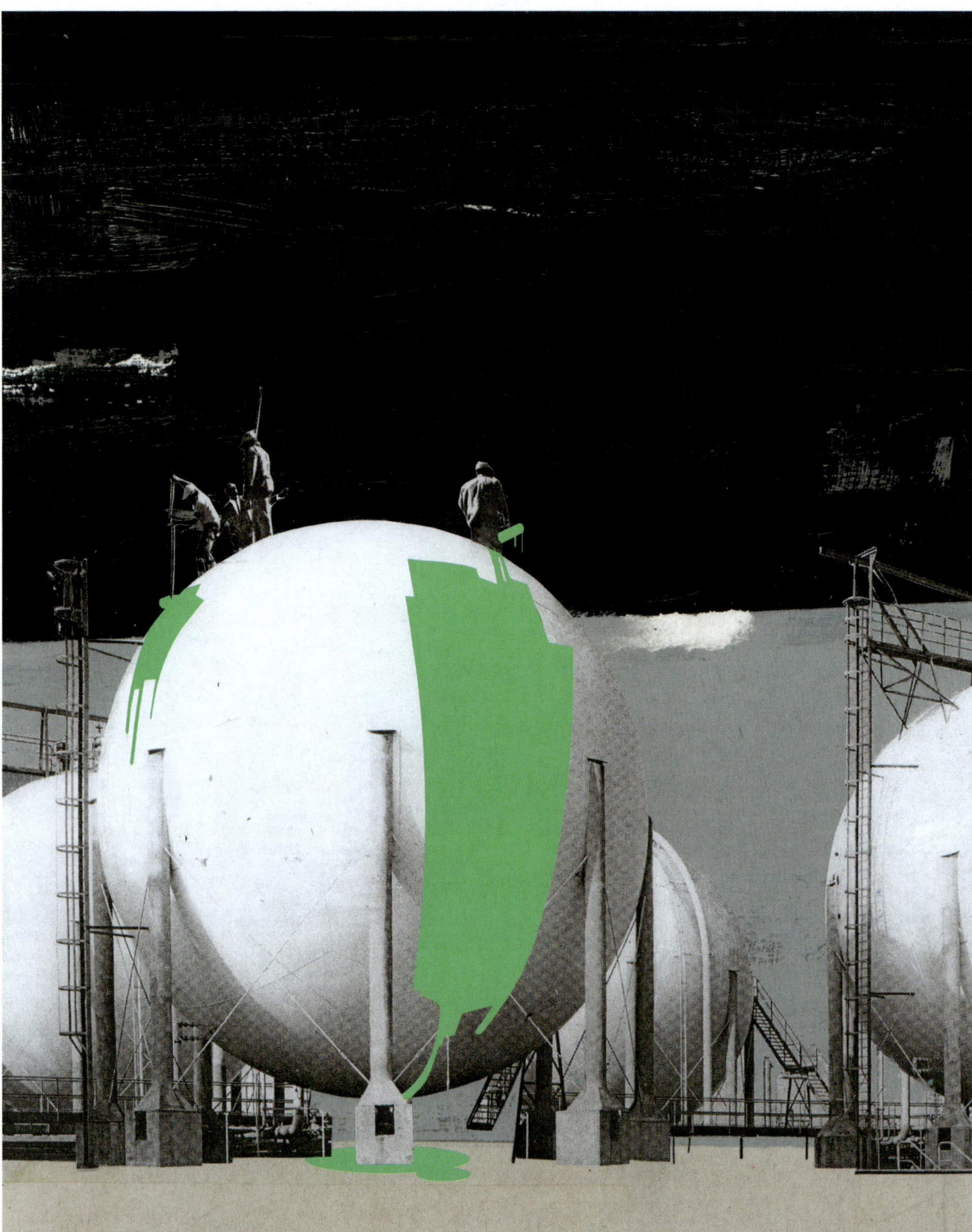

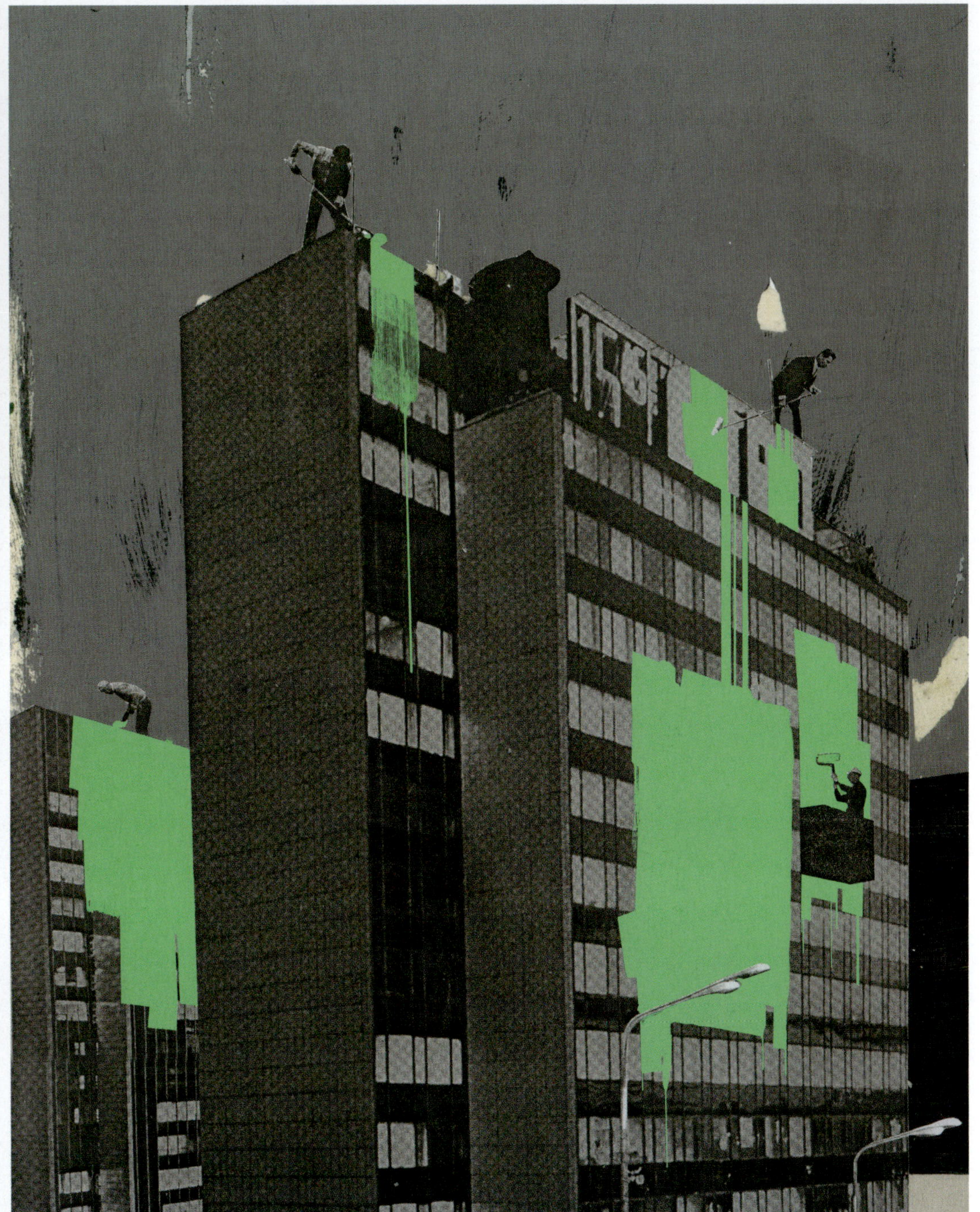

THE RAINBOWMONKEY WAS BORN AND
GREW UP IN AUGSBURG, GERMANY, AND
IS CURRENTLY LIVING AND FREELANC-
ING IN AUCKLAND, NEW ZEALAND.

THE RAINBOWMONKEY REPRESENTS THE
PERSONAL PORTFOLIO OF DESIGNER
MARKUS HOFKO.

--

WHAT IS GERMAN?

SAUSAGE, BALL GAMES, DOGGEDNESS
AND ORDER.

WHAT IS GERMAN DESIGN?

PRECISE, DRY
AND COMICALLY EARNEST.

PLEASE DESCRIBE YOUR WORKING
PROCESS.

A LONG SLAUGHTER OF IDEAS, QUICK
IMPLEMENTATION, LONG PERFECTING
TIME

WHAT DO YOU AIM TO ACHIEVE WITH
YOUR WORK?

LOVE, PEACE, FUN
AND ENTERTAINMENT.

YOU'VE INVITED A FRIEND TO
GERMANY; NAME ONE PLACE THEY
REALLY MUST VISIT AND A QUINT-
ESSENTIAL EXPERIENCE YOU REC-
OMMEND.

1. GO TO THE VEHICLE REGISTRA-
   TION OFFICE AND
2. GET THE ADDRESS FOR YOUR CAR
   CHANGED.

WHAT IS THE MOST IMPORTANT
LESSON YOU HAVE LEARNED IN YOUR
PROFESSION SO FAR?

ABSTRACT EVEN IF YOU COPY. LOOK
AFTER YOUR WEBSITE

--

RAIN BOW MONK EY

RAINBOWMONKEY
MARKUS HOFKO
--
5/283 RICHMOND RD
GREY LYNN
AUCKLAND 1022
NEW ZEALAND
--
T +64 93609685
M +64 211078054
--
WWW.RAINBOWMONKEY.DE
--

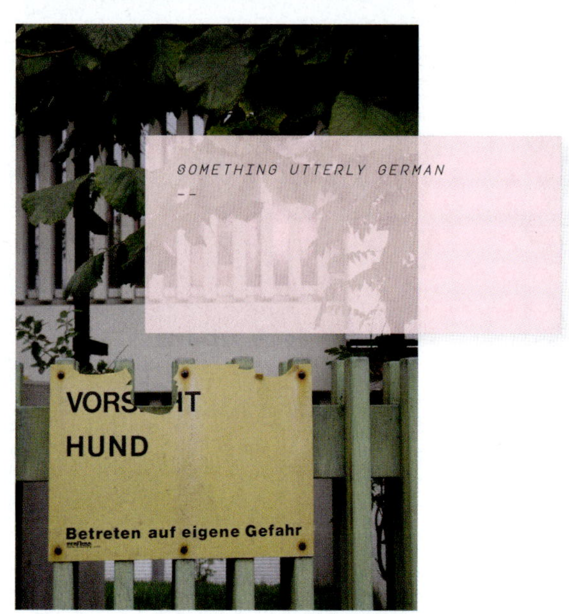
SOMETHING UTTERLY GERMAN
--
VORSICHT
HUND
Betreten auf eigene Gefahr

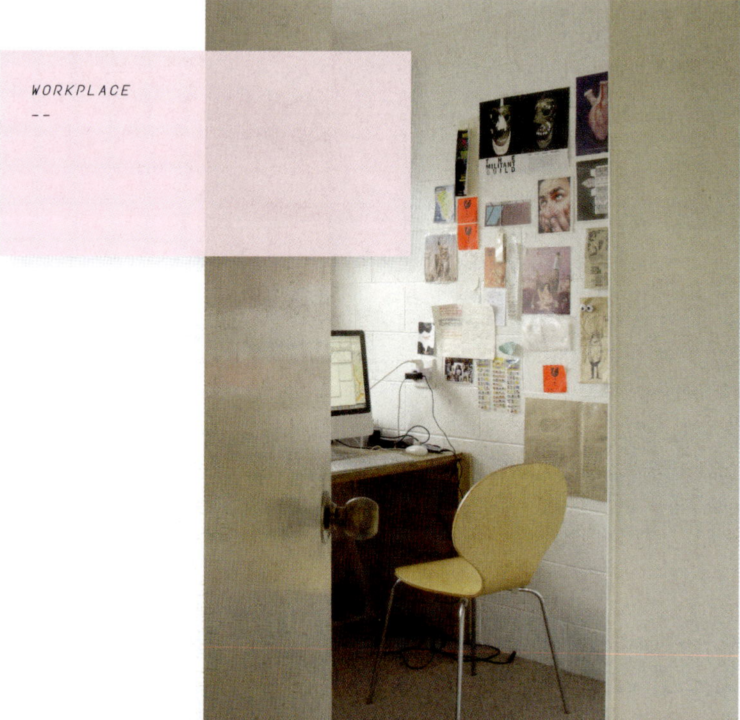
WORKPLACE
--

STUDIO SURROUNDINGS
--

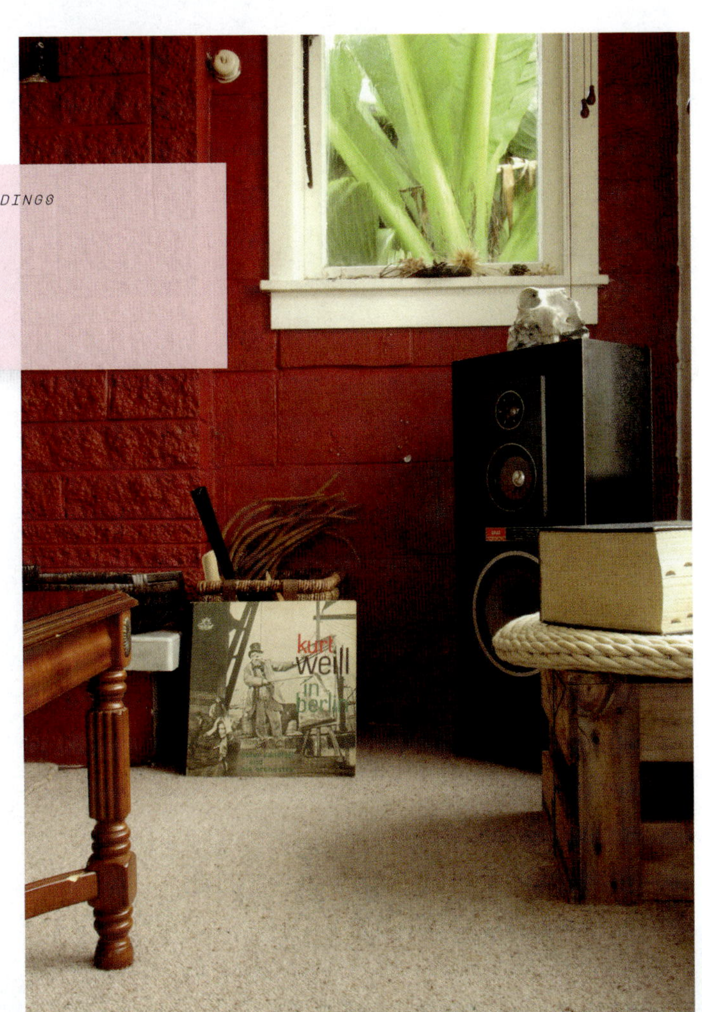
kurt
weill
in berl

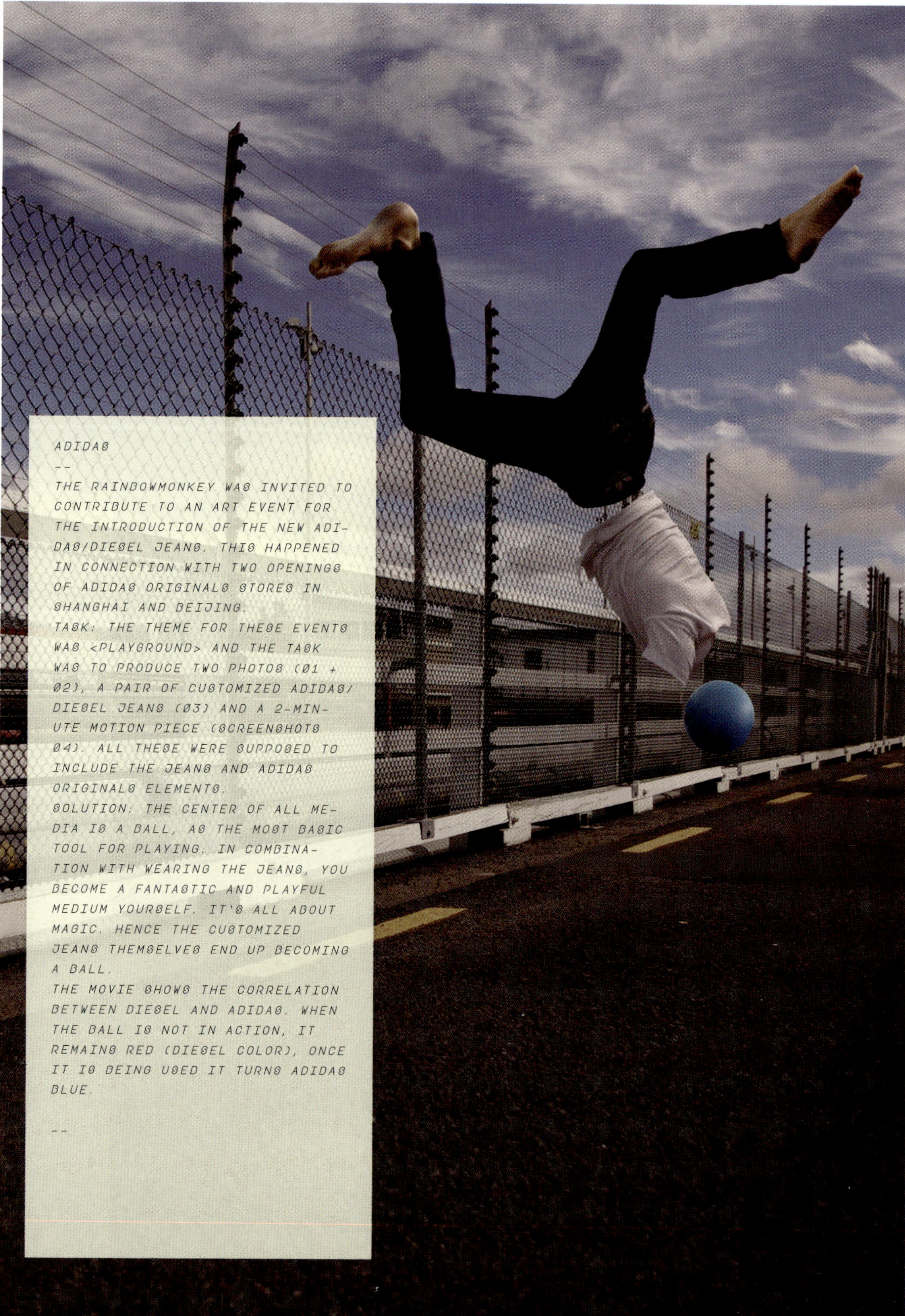

ADIDAS
--
THE RAINBOWMONKEY WAS INVITED TO
CONTRIBUTE TO AN ART EVENT FOR
THE INTRODUCTION OF THE NEW ADI-
DAS/DIESEL JEANS. THIS HAPPENED
IN CONNECTION WITH TWO OPENINGS
OF ADIDAS ORIGINALS STORES IN
SHANGHAI AND BEIJING.
TASK: THE THEME FOR THESE EVENTS
WAS <PLAYGROUND> AND THE TASK
WAS TO PRODUCE TWO PHOTOS (01 +
02), A PAIR OF CUSTOMIZED ADIDAS/
DIESEL JEANS (03) AND A 2-MIN-
UTE MOTION PIECE (SCREENSHOTS
04). ALL THESE WERE SUPPOSED TO
INCLUDE THE JEANS AND ADIDAS
ORIGINALS ELEMENTS.
SOLUTION: THE CENTER OF ALL ME-
DIA IS A BALL, AS THE MOST BASIC
TOOL FOR PLAYING. IN COMBINA-
TION WITH WEARING THE JEANS, YOU
BECOME A FANTASTIC AND PLAYFUL
MEDIUM YOURSELF. IT'S ALL ABOUT
MAGIC. HENCE THE CUSTOMIZED
JEANS THEMSELVES END UP BECOMING
A BALL.
THE MOVIE SHOWS THE CORRELATION
BETWEEN DIESEL AND ADIDAS. WHEN
THE BALL IS NOT IN ACTION, IT
REMAINS RED (DIESEL COLOR), ONCE
IT IS BEING USED IT TURNS ADIDAS
BLUE.

--

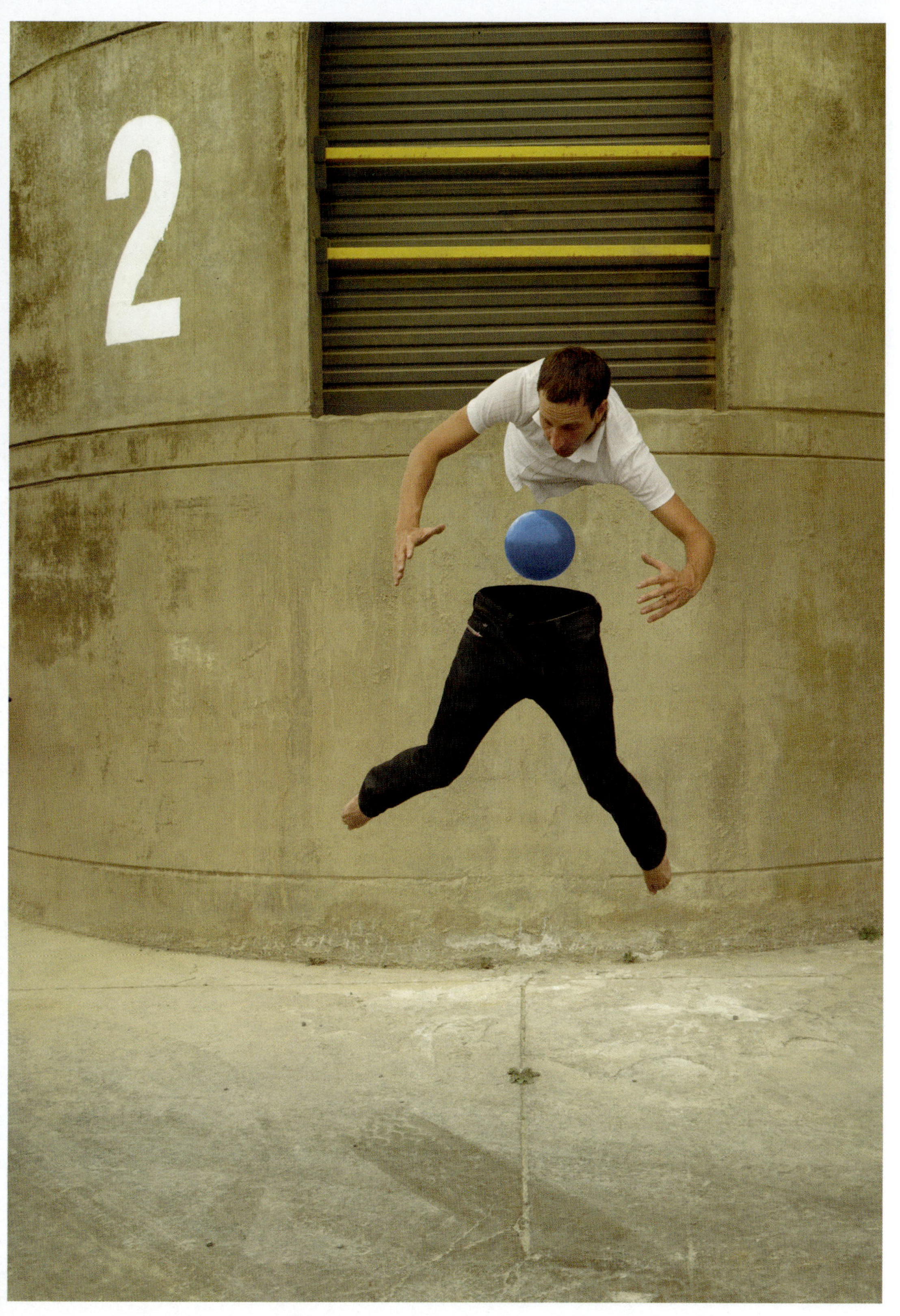

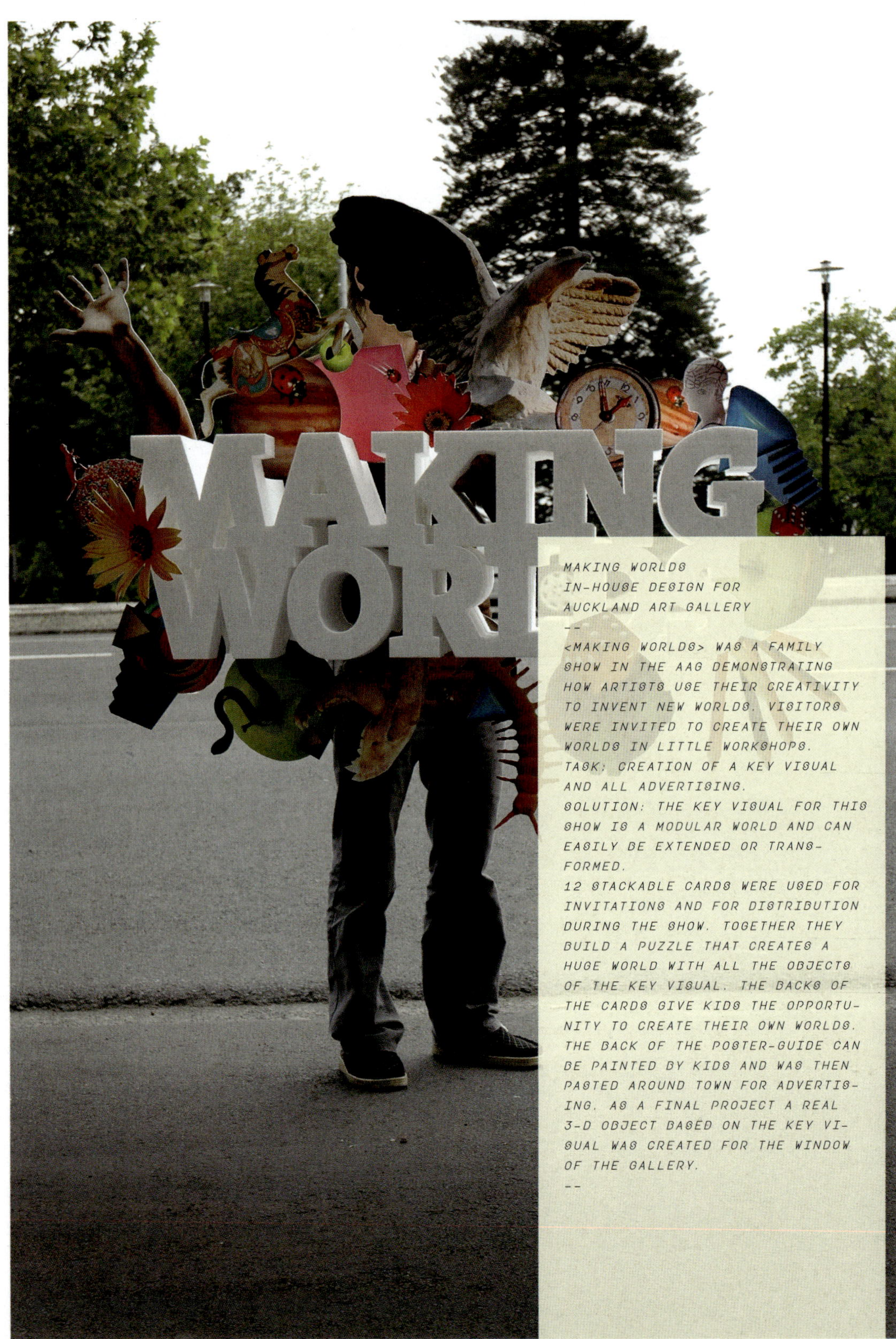
MAKING WORLDS
MAKING WORLDS
IN-HOUSE DESIGN FOR
AUCKLAND ART GALLERY
--
<MAKING WORLDS> WAS A FAMILY
SHOW IN THE AAG DEMONSTRATING
HOW ARTISTS USE THEIR CREATIVITY
TO INVENT NEW WORLDS. VISITORS
WERE INVITED TO CREATE THEIR OWN
WORLDS IN LITTLE WORKSHOPS.
TASK: CREATION OF A KEY VISUAL
AND ALL ADVERTISING.
SOLUTION: THE KEY VISUAL FOR THIS
SHOW IS A MODULAR WORLD AND CAN
EASILY BE EXTENDED OR TRANS-
FORMED.
12 STACKABLE CARDS WERE USED FOR
INVITATIONS AND FOR DISTRIBUTION
DURING THE SHOW. TOGETHER THEY
BUILD A PUZZLE THAT CREATES A
HUGE WORLD WITH ALL THE OBJECTS
OF THE KEY VISUAL. THE BACKS OF
THE CARDS GIVE KIDS THE OPPORTU-
NITY TO CREATE THEIR OWN WORLDS.
THE BACK OF THE POSTER-GUIDE CAN
BE PAINTED BY KIDS AND WAS THEN
PASTED AROUND TOWN FOR ADVERTIS-
ING. AS A FINAL PROJECT A REAL
3-D OBJECT BASED ON THE KEY VI-
SUAL WAS CREATED FOR THE WINDOW
OF THE GALLERY.
--

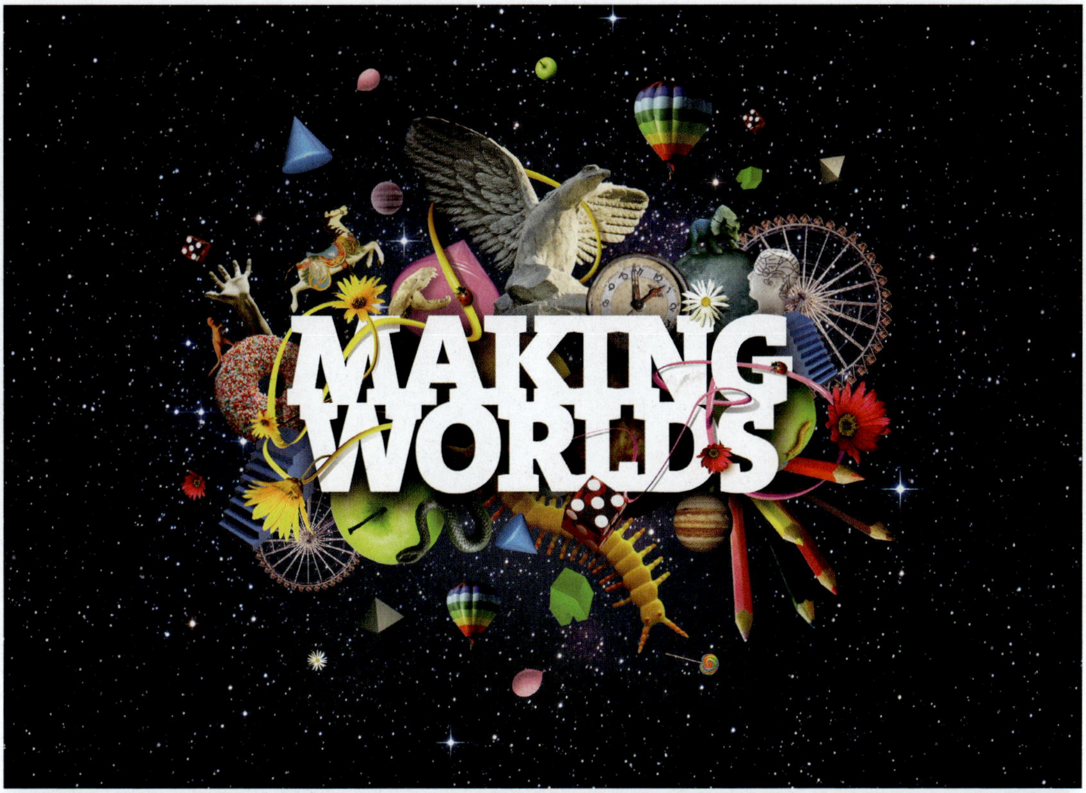

MAKING
WORLDS

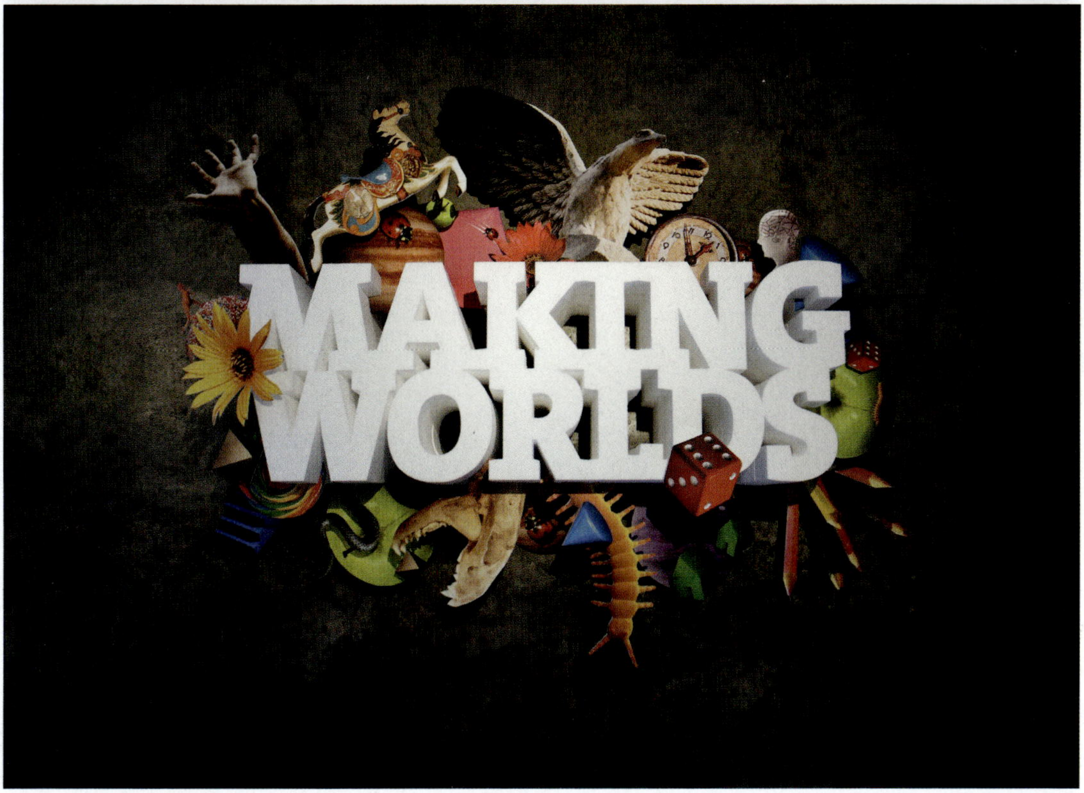

MAKING
WORLDS

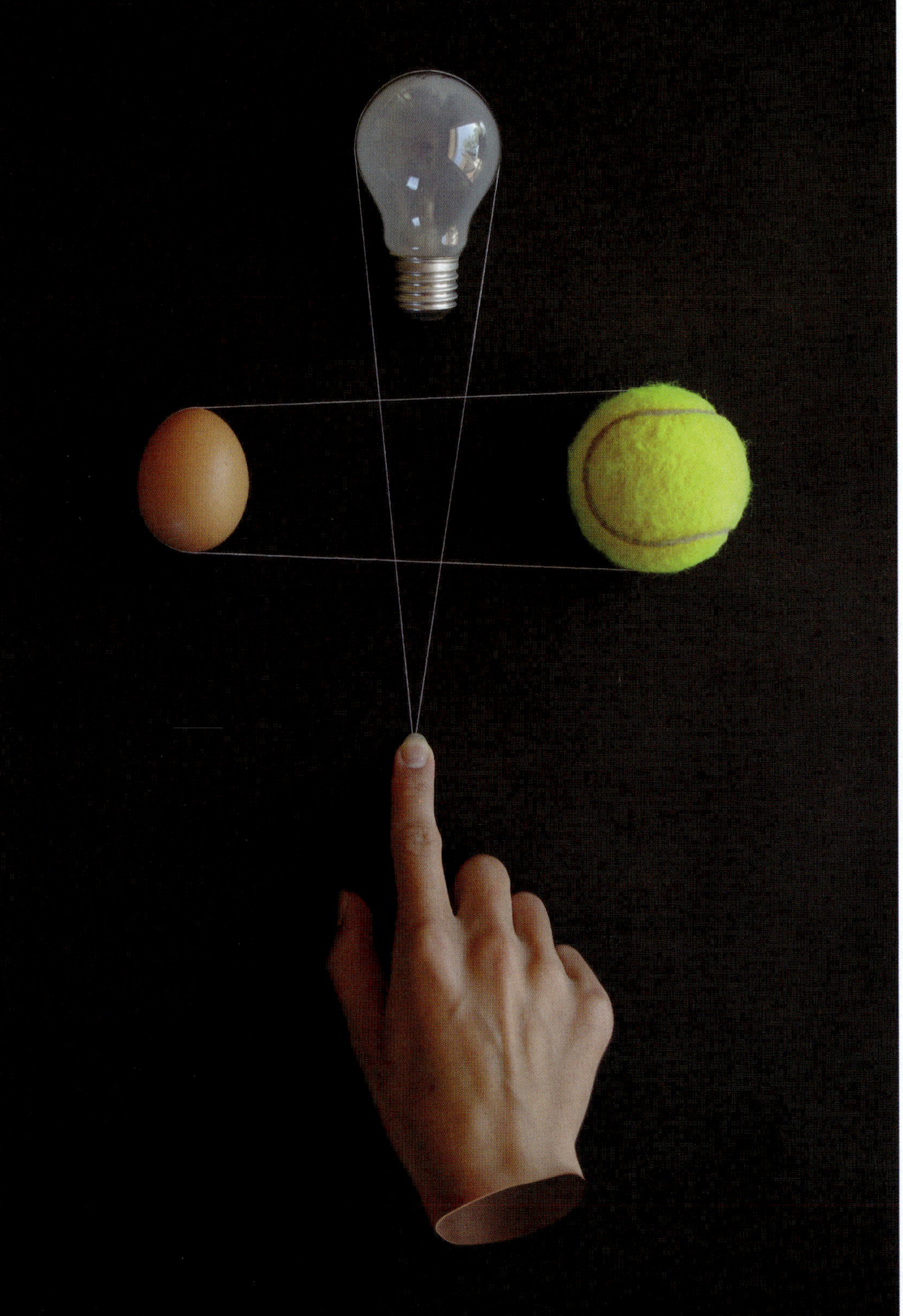

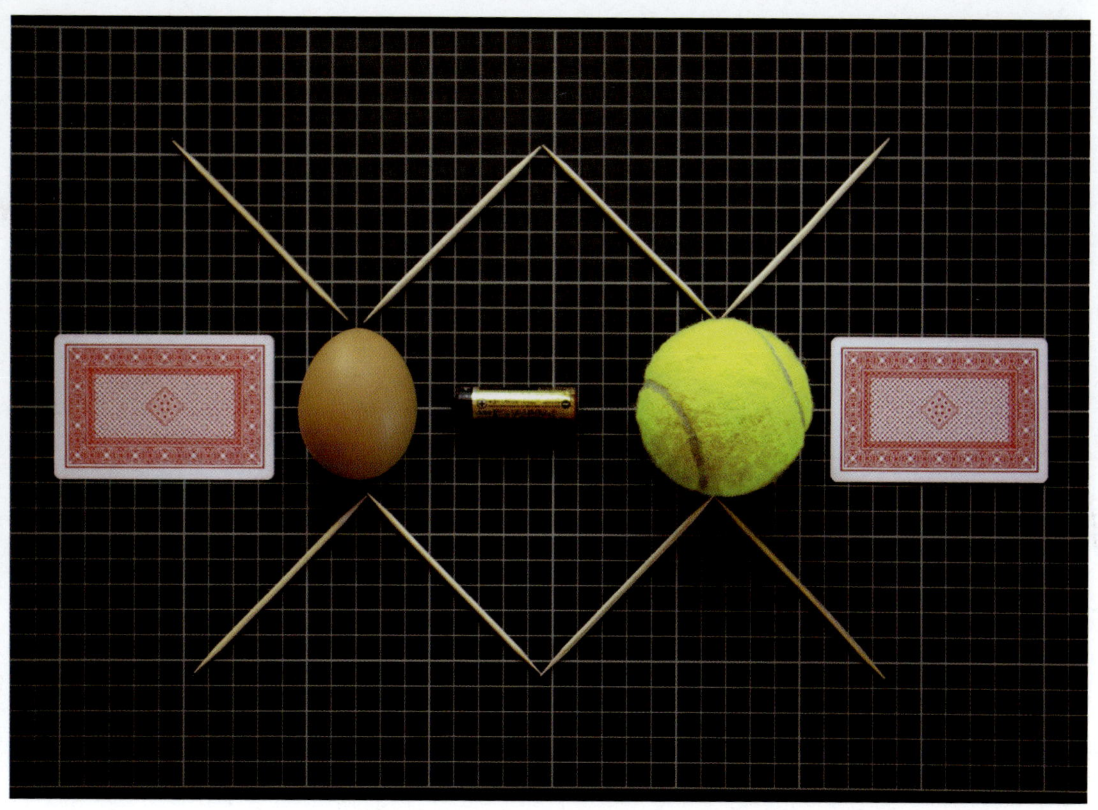

UNIVERSE
IDN MAGAZINE
--
THE HONG KONG-BASED DESIGN MAGA-
ZINE IDN CALLED FOR ENTRIES ON
THE THEME <UNIVERSE>.
TASK: VISUAL INTERPRETATION OF
THE WORD UNIVERSE.
SOLUTION: TRYING TO EXPLAIN THE
UNIVERSE CAN GET VERY COMPLICAT-
ED, SO THE ONLY SOLUTION SEEMED
TO BE TO SHOW HOW IT ACTUALLY
WORKS.
--

WE WOULD LIKE TO TAKE THIS OPPORTUNITY TO EX-
PRESS OUR WARM APPRECIATION TO SANDRA HOFFMANN
WHO WAS ABLE TO RECOMMEND MANY OF HER FORMER
STUDENTS AT THE HOCHSCHULE FÜR GESTALTUNG IN
DARMSTADT FOR THIS BOOK. THE QUALITY OF THE
WORKS ATTESTS NOT ONLY TO THE STUDENTS' TALENT,
BUT ALSO TO THE SUPERB TEACHING THEY RECEIVED.

WE WOULD LIKE TO ALSO THANK ELLA HOWARD AND
KATY SCOTT FOR LENDING THEIR HANDS AND FEET
FOR THE COVER IMAGE, HELGARD LORENZ AND IRENE
HWANG FOR THEIR LINGUISTIC CONSULTATION, AND
LAST BUT NOT LEAST, WE WANT TO EXPRESS OUR
GRATITUDE TO EVERYONE WHO SENT IN WORK FOR OUR
REVIEW, ESPECIALLY TO THOSE DESIGNERS WHO WE
WERE NOT ABLE TO INCLUDE IN THE BOOK DUE TO
SPACE LIMITATIONS.

THANK YOU! ---

PUBLISHED
BY ACTAR BARCELONA / NEW YORK
WWW.ACTAR.COM

EDITED & DESIGNED
BY TWOPOINTS.NET
MARTIN LORENZ, LUPI ASENSIO,
JULIEN ARTS & MELANIE HOMANN

COORDINATED
BY TWOPOINTS.NET
MONICA KRUGER & ÁNGELA MARÍA ECHAVARRÍA SILVA

PHOTOGRAPHY (COVER)
BY STEFAN VORBECK

PRODUCTION MANAGEMENT
BY ACTAR PRO

COPY EDITING & TRANSLATION
BY JUDITH HAYWARD

PRINTED
BY INGOPRINT S.A.

PRINTED AND BOUND IN THE EU

ISBN 978-84-96954-56-4
DL B-21490-2009

DISTRIBUTED
BY ACTAR D
ROCA I BATLLE 2
08023 BARCELONA, SPAIN
T: +34 93 418 7759
F: +34 93 418 6707
OFFICE@ACTAR-D.COM
WWW.ACTAR-D.COM

DISTRIBUTED IN THE UNITED STATES
BY ACTAR D USA
158 LAFAYETTE STREET, 5TH FL.
NEW YORK, NY 10013
T: +1 212 966 2207
F: +1 212 966 2214
OFFICEUSA@ACTAR-D.COM
WWW.ACTAR-D.COM